Ireland

Fionn Davenport

Charlotte Beech, Tom Downs, Des Hannigan, Fran Parnell, Neil Wilson

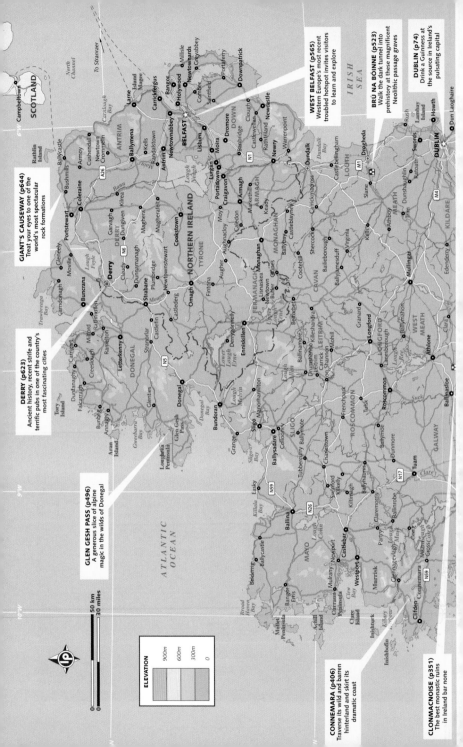

GIANT'S CAUSEWAY (p644)
Treat your eyes to one of the world's most spectacular rock formations

WEST BELFAST (p565)
Western Europe's most recent troubled hotspot invites visitors to learn and explore

BRÚ NA BÓINNE (p523)
Walk the dark tunnel into prehistory at these magnificent Neolithic passage graves

DUBLIN (p74)
Drink a Guinness at the source in Ireland's pulsating capital

DERRY (p623)
Ancient history, recent strife and terrific pubs in one of the country's most fascinating cities

GLEN GESH PASS (p496)
A generous slice of alpine magic in the wilds of Donegal

CONNEMARA (p406)
Traverse its wild and barren hinterland and skirt its dramatic coast

CLONMACNOISE (p351)
The best monastic ruins in Ireland bar none

ELEVATION
900m
600m
300m
0

0   50 km
0   30 miles

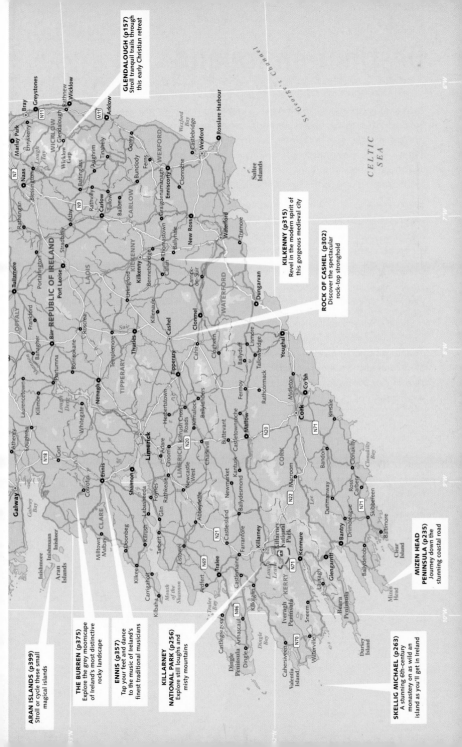

ARAN ISLANDS (p399)
Stroll or cycle these small magical islands

THE BURREN (p375)
Explore the grey moonscape of Ireland's most distinctive rocky landscape

ENNIS (p357)
Tap your feet and dance to the music of Ireland's finest traditional musicians

KILLARNEY NATIONAL PARK (p256)
Explore still loughs and misty mountains

SKELLIG MICHAEL (p263)
A stunning 6th-century monastery on as wild an island as you'll get in Ireland

MIZEN HEAD PENINSULA (p235)
Journey down the stunning coastal road

GLENDALOUGH (p157)
Stroll tranquil trails through this early Christian retreat

KILKENNY (p315)
Revel in the modern spirit of this gorgeous medieval city

ROCK OF CASHEL (p302)
Discover the spectacular rock-top stronghold

Destination Ireland

There's no doubt about it, Ireland gets a pretty big billing for such a tiny country. There are hundreds of songs that sing its praises, intoned in faraway places by Paddies whose ancestors left its starving shores in their ragged millions, never to return or forget. The songs tell of a green landscape brushed with rain, a wild coastline tormented by a windblown sea…it's all enough to keep you sitting safe by the turf fire in the cosy village pub, accompanied by lively conversation and the sound of a fiddle drowning out the gale outside.

Ireland has long since outgrown its forty shades of green and all of the other shamrock-laden clichés that never really did it justice. But the images still endure, inviting you and millions of others to kiss the Blarney Stone, ride a jaunting car around the Killarney lakes, eat an Irish stew and drink that pint of Guinness.

But isn't modern Ireland all about motorways and multiculturalism, commerce and cosmopolitans? Surely there's no time anymore for a slow day, and no room for a history so old that much of it is made up, with myths and little people thrown in to fill the gaps.

Spend a while here and you'll see that everything is possible, for packed into this small country are the compelling contrasts of a nation building its future on the back of its past. Ireland will confound your expectations but it will also exceed them, for tying together all of its contradictions are the people, friendlier and warmer than any clichéd welcome could ever convey. Ireland is a slim volume for sure, but it reads like a blockbuster: turn over the page and see.

Activities

Ireland is justifiably famous for its fishing (p677) – cast a line night or day

Ireland's coast and waterways offer an adrenalin-pumping array of watersports (p681)

OTHER HIGHLIGHTS

- Ride a horse into the sunset on the desolate beaches of Connemara (p410) in County Galway.
- Throw yourself off Mt Leinster (p342) for some exhilarating hang-gliding.
- Go to bird-watchers' heaven at Wexford Wildfowl Reserve (p178).

Cycle through history at the beautiful Muckross Estate (p257) in Killarney National Park, County Kerry

Coasts & Islands

GARETH McCORMACK

Stare out to sea from the dramatic heights of Horn Head (p507), County Donegal

A lighthouse stands sentinel on the Loop Head peninsula (p372), County Clare

RICHARD CUMMINS

OTHER HIGHLIGHTS

- Follow poet WB Yeats and find your muse in the dramatic coastal scenery of County Sligo (p441).
- Slow down and contemplate the stark beauty of the Aran Islands' Inisheer (p405) and Inishmaan (p403).

Play hopscotch on the handiwork of giants at Giant's Causeway (p644), County Antrim

GARETH McCORMACK

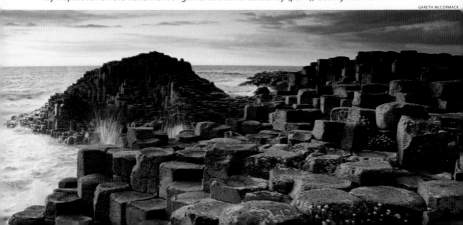

EOIN CLARKE

Thrift speckles the mountainous terrain of Great Blasket Island (p285), County Kerry

RICHARD MILLS

Lose yourself in the windswept coastal landscape of Connemara (p406), County Galway

Take a boat past tiny islands and seal colonies to Garinish (Ilnacullin) Island from Glengarriff (p242), County Cork

RICHARD CUMMINS

Castles & Cloisters

Dublin Castle (p93) is a patchwork of architectural styles

Storm the battlements of Kilkenny Castle (p316), one of Ireland's most impressive fortresses, County Kilkenny

OTHER HIGHLIGHTS

- Sleep in lordly luxury in County Kildare's Kilkea Castle (p337) or County Monaghan's Castle Leslie (p464).
- Visit the stunningly situated monastic ruins at Glendalough (p157), in County Wicklow, and County Roscommon's Cistercian Boyle Abbey (p468), one of Ireland's finest.

Stone carvings adorn the ruins at Jerpoint Abbey (p324), County Kilkenny

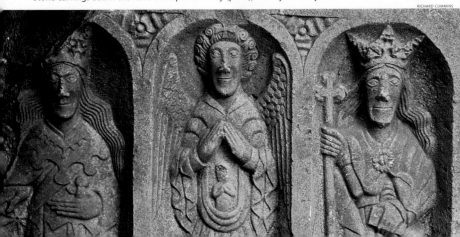

RICHARD CUMMINS

Spend an evening at a medieval banquet in Dunguaire Castle (p417), County Galway

RICHARD CUMMINS

Admire fine 14th- to 17th-century decor at Bunratty Castle (p365), County Clare

Acquire the gift of the gab at Blarney Castle (p217), County Cork

RICHARD CUMMINS

Wilderness Walks

County Donegal's Slieve League (p494), Europe's highest sea cliffs, is not for the faint hearted

OTHER HIGHLIGHTS

- Explore County Tyrone's lonely Sperrin Mountains (p669), dotted with prehistoric tombs.
- Scenic riverside trails wind through Graiguenamanagh (p326) and Inistioge (p325) in County Kilkenny.

Take in ancient sites and the ruins of copper mines in a walk along County Cork's Beara Peninsula (p242)

The Burren Way (p678), one of Ireland's best walks, takes in the dramatic Cliffs of Moher (p375) in County Clare

GARETH McCORMACK

County Down's Mourne Mountains (p611) offer some challenging but rewarding hill walking

DAVID TIPLING

Delight in the colourful wildflowers of the Burren (p375), County Clare

Escape into the sublimely peaceful landscape along the Beara Way (p678) in County Cork

EOIN CLARKE

Towns

DOUG McKINLAY

Traditional Irish music is performed nightly in the pubs of Doolin (p378), County Clare

OTHER HIGHLIGHTS

- Dublin (p74) boasts gorgeous pubs, throbbing clubs and an unparalleled selection of restaurants and cafés.

- For gourmet treats, head to the fish restaurants of Kinsale (p222) in County Cork or the food scene in thriving Enniskillen (p657) in County Fermanagh.

RICHARD CUMMINS

Immerse yourself in the rich culture of Cork city (p205)

Bohemian cafés and lively pubs draw many travellers to atmospheric Galway city (p389)

OLIVER STREWE

Contents

13

Regional Map Contents

The Authors

FIONN DAVENPORT
Coordinating Author, Dublin, Counties Wicklow, Meath & Louth

Fionn ran away from Ireland at every opportunity, but could never stay away long. Paris was a pleasant distraction, New York kept him busy for a few years, but after each and every time he would land at Dublin, jump out of the rain into a taxi, stare at the grey mess of landscape between the airport and the city and ask himself what the hell he was doing. The answer has changed over the years – nowadays it has less to do with better squats and easier dole and more to do with quality of life. The more he writes about it the more he realises that 'knowing' the country isn't the point; it's the 'getting to know' that matters.

The Coordinating Author's Favourite Trip

Luckily, I love my hometown of Dublin (p74) for itself, but also because it's so easy to get out of. Wicklow (p151) is a green lung getaway to the south, where I can hike a bit but mostly potter about the ruins of Glendalough (p157) or sit on the terrace of Powerscourt House (p154). As a kid, my parents used to take me regularly to Tara (p530), whose invisible heritage apparently accounts for my love of history and my propensity for telling stories and making things up. My absolute favourites, though, are a little further afield. In the west, I can't imagine a more beautiful spot than the head of the Killary fjord (p414), and the only place that matches it for me is the tee-box on the 9th hole in Dunfanaghy (p506), County Donegal – my idea of a perfect heaven.

CHARLOTTE BEECH
Counties Mayo, Sligo & Donegal

Charlotte has been nipping across the Irish Sea from her native England ever since she was a girl. As an adult, she thought she had struck gold when offered a job editing guidebooks to Ireland, Dublin and elsewhere in Europe. But reading about the countries she loved proved too much temptation, and Charlotte has since become a freelance travel writer. She has coauthored half a dozen Lonely Planet guidebooks, from Peru to Portugal, but can honestly say that she's covered few places more achingly beautiful than County Donegal on a dew-soaked spring morning.

LONELY PLANET AUTHORS

Why is our travel information the best in the world? It's simple: our authors are independent, dedicated travellers. They don't research using just the Internet or phone, and they don't take freebies in exchange for positive coverage. They travel widely, to all the popular spots and off the beaten track. They personally visit thousands of hotels, restaurants, cafés, bars, galleries, palaces, museums and more – and they take pride in getting all the details right, and telling it how it is. For more, see the authors section on www.lonelyplanet.com.

TOM DOWNS   Counties Kilkenny & Galway

Tom makes regular visits to Ireland to nurse his weakness for Guinness and to tramp through a few bogs. (He says he would live in one, inside a tent, if the situation called for it.) They say it's not wise to mix business and pleasure, but Tom threw all caution to the wind in covering Galway and Kilkenny for this book. He and his family live in Oakland, California.

DES HANNIGAN   Counties Clare, Kerry, Limerick & Tipperary

Des was born in Scotland, but both sides of his family originated in Ireland and he still has family connections there. His previous work in Ireland includes compiling a publishing database of hundreds of archaeological sites, an odyssey that took him into some of the most remote parts of the Atlantic coast, north to south. He did similar work cataloguing notable buildings, churches, museums, art galleries, pubs and clubs in most of Ireland's cities and main towns and has written about Dublin, and about climbing Ireland's mountains for various publications. Des worked on the previous edition of Lonely Planet's *Ireland*. He lives on the Atlantic coast of Cornwall.

FRAN PARNELL   Counties Wexford, Waterford,
Cork, Central South & Central North

Fran has a love of Irish literature developed while studying for a masters degree in Anglo-Saxon, Norse and Celtic. After spending many hours snivelling over a dissertation on Medb, visiting Cruachan Aí, the fabled site of her palace, was one of the highlights of this trip.

NEIL WILSON   Belfast, Counties Down, Armagh,
Derry, Antrim, Fermanagh & Tyrone

Neil's first visit to Northern Ireland was in 1994, during the first flush of post-cease-fire optimism. His interest in the history and politics of the place intensified a few years later when he found out that most of his mum's ancestors were from Ulster. Researching the Northern Ireland chapters for this edition gave him the chance to explore the Causeway Coast, hillwalk in the Mournes and seek out the strange carved stones on Lough Erne's islands, in between crawling round Belfast's bars and restaurants. Neil is a full-time travel writer based in Edinburgh, Scotland, and has written around 40 guidebooks.

Getting Started

Ireland is small, relatively homogenous and fairly manageable, so long as you know what you want and have prepared adequately for it. The weather isn't always cooperative, journey times between destinations aren't always as short as their numerical distances might suggest and budgets need to be pretty elastic to cope with the high price of nearly everything. Keep those points in mind and Ireland is a doddle.

WHEN TO GO

The Irish weather works on the 'all the seasons in a day' principle, which basically means that you can't predict a thing when it comes to the behaviour of the sky. Some basic assumptions, however, can be made.

From June to August, the days are reasonably warm and – most importantly – very long: at the height of summer you won't need to turn on lights until after 10pm. It is also peak tourist season, which means there are far more people pretty much everywhere but the most remote corners of the island, and prices are at their highest. Not surprisingly, most of the yearly festivals occur during these times so as to take advantage of the crowds and the more favourable weather.

See Climate Charts (p683) for more information.

Spring and autumn make good alternatives, although the country's ever-growing popularity as a tourist destination can often blur the lines between mid- and high-season tourism. Still, you have a better chance of some peace and quiet and the weather can be surprisingly better in April and September than in mid-July – again, it's all part of the uncertainty principle. Spring festivities include the ever-popular St Patrick's Festival.

Although temperatures will barely venture below freezing, winter can be brutal, but huge parts of the country – the west and northwest in particular – are at their savage and beautiful best in the cold winter light. Crowds are at their thinnest, but many of the country's tourist attractions and services close down in October and don't reopen until Easter, which paradoxically leaves visitors with a more convincing taste of how Ireland is experienced by most of the Irish: it's cold, grey and dark by 5 o'clock, but there's always a pub to escape into when the rain starts sheeting down.

COSTS

There's no two ways about it: Ireland is an expensive destination by any standards. The country is obsessed with what is termed the 'rip-off culture', which hurts locals as much as visitors. The sting is felt most everywhere, but visitors will feel it most when it comes to bed and board.

DON'T LEAVE HOME WITHOUT...

Ireland won't test your survival skills unless you're the worse for wear in the middle of nowhere, but there are a few essentials you won't want to leave behind:

- Good walking shoes
- Raincoat
- UK/Ireland electrical adapter
- A finely honed sense of humour
- A hollow leg

In Dublin, the bare minimum to survive is about €45 a day: €20 to €25 for a hostel and €15 for sustenance, which leaves enough for a pint. Outside the capital things are a little better, but not much: if you're in a tourist hot zone it'll be reflected in the prices, which are only marginally better than in Dublin. If your purse strings are a little more relaxed, you can get a decent bed for around €80 in the capital, €60 outside of it. For €100 you can sleep pretty luxuriously most anywhere except those *very* special places.

No matter where you are, eating out is expensive. For less than €10, don't expect much more than soup and what comes in between two slices of bread. Very ordinary meals will cost €20 or more; the better restaurants won't blink twice when charging €35 for the fish in a fancy sauce.

Car rental is also costly in Ireland (see p701). Be sure to check your auto insurance policy back home before accepting the exorbitant insurance policies offered at car-rental agencies. If your credit card usually covers car-rental insurance, confirm that the policy applies in Ireland.

TRAVEL LITERATURE

Travel in Ireland seems to inspire writers, and it is equally true that a smartly written travel journal can inspire one to travel well. Hence, the following suggestions.

Silver Linings by Martin Fletcher is a compelling portrait of Northern Ireland at odds with its bruised and tarnished image as a war-scarred region. Northerners on both sides of the divide are friendly, funny and as welcoming as anyone else on the island.

A Place Apart by Dervla Murphy tells of the author's bicycle journey through Northern Ireland in the 1970s. It's a highly readable introduction to such topics as Orangeism, Paisleyism and the problems in South Armagh.

Is Shane McGowan Still Alive? Travels in Irishry is Tim Bradford's epic journey through the myths of modern Ireland. Where have all the legends gone? And where can he get a decent pint of Guinness?

The Truth About the Irish is Terry Eagleton's marvellous and loving poke at the myths peddled about the Irish at home and abroad; more for entertainment than serious information.

The Oxford Illustrated Literary Guide to Great Britain and Ireland traces the movements of famous writers who immortalised various towns and villages in Ireland.

A Literary Guide to Dublin by Vivien Igoe delves into the Irish capital's literary haunts, with pubs and cemeteries naturally using up their share of the word count.

Joyce's Dublin: A Walking Guide to Ulysses by Jack McCarthy caters to Bloomsday junkies wanting a year-round fix. It follows the novel chapter by chapter and has clear maps.

McCarthy's Bar is a colourful account of author Pete McCarthy's attempt to rediscover Ireland by having a pint in every pub that bears his name. His follow-up, *The Road to McCarthy*, is a look at the Irish diaspora.

INTERNET RESOURCES

The Internet has become an indispensable planning tool for travellers. Ireland is well wired, so there's a lot of useful information available online. Here are a few sites to get you started.

Blather (www.blather.net) This wry webzine dishes out healthy portions of irreverent commentary on all things Irish. It's a savvy way to get up to date on current events and attitudes.

TOP TENS

Our Favourite Festivals & Events

You might even plan your trip around one or more of the following events, so mark your calendars.

- Irish National Surfing Championships
  County Donegal; March (p491)

- Puck Fair
  Killorglin, County Kerry; August (p260)

- St Patrick's Festival
  Dublin & Ireland; 17 March (p121)

- Appalachian & Bluegrass Music Festival
  Omagh, County Tyrone; September (p669)

- The Cat Laughs Comedy Festival
  Kilkenny city; late May, early June (p319)

- Ballinasloe Horse Fair
  Ballinasloe, County Galway; October (p418)

- Bloomsday
  Dublin; 16 June (p122)

- Belfast Festival at Queens
  Belfast; October (p571)

- Galway Arts Festival
  Galway city; July (p394)

- Wexford Festival Opera
  Wexford; October (p175)

Must-See Irish Movies

Predeparture planning is always more fun if it includes a few flicks to get you in the mood. The following films are all available on video cassette or DVD. For other information about Irish cinema and television, see p55.

- *Bloody Sunday* (2002)
  Director: Paul Greengrass

- *The Dead* (1987)
  Director: John Huston

- *My Left Foot* (1989)
  Director: Jim Sheridan

- *The Crying Game* (1992)
  Director: Neil Jordan

- *The Quiet Man* (1952)
  Director: John Ford

- *The Field* (1990)
  Director: Jim Sheridan

- *Cal* (1984)
  Director: Pat O'Connor

- *The Snapper* (1993)
  Director: Stephen Frears

- *The Magdalene Sisters* (2002)
  Director: Peter Mullan

- *The Butcher Boy* (1998)
  Director: Neil Jordan

Top Irish Fiction

Getting stuck into some fiction is the best way to gain insight into Irish issues and culture, for there's no greater truth in Ireland than the story that's been made up. Here are the essentials to kick-start a lifelong passion; for more information see p53.

- *Dubliners* (1914)
  James Joyce

- *The Book of Evidence* (1989)
  John Banville

- *The Butcher Boy* (1992)
  Patrick McCabe

- *Paddy Clarke Ha Ha Ha* (1993)
  Roddy Doyle

- *The Third Policeman* (1967)
  Flann O'Brien

- *The Ballroom of Romance & Other Stories*
  (1972) William Trevor

- *Amongst Women* (1990)
  John McGahern

- *Star of the Sea* (2002)
  Joseph O'Connor

- *Rachel's Holiday* (1998)
  Marian Keyes

- *Angela's Ashes* (1996)
  Frank McCourt

Entertainment Ireland (www.entertainmentireland.ie) Countrywide listings for clubs, theatres, festivals, cinemas, museums and much more. It's well worth consulting this site as you plan your next move in Ireland.

Fáilte Ireland (http://ireland.ie) The Republic's tourist board information site has heaps of practical info. It features a huge accommodation database with photos.

Fine Gael (www.ripoff.ie) Not the website of the actual political party, but an anti-government website sponsored by the main opposition party, whose aim is to win favour by appearing alongside the poor consumer; we don't buy it, but it does tell it like it is in relation to prices.

Irish Times (www.ireland.com) The website of Ireland's largest daily newspaper represents a great way to get up to speed on all the latest news before you leave home.

Lonely Planet (www.lonelyplanet.com) Comprehensive travel information and advice.

Northern Ireland Tourism (www.discovernorthernireland.com) Northern Ireland's official tourism information site is particularly strong on activities and accommodation.

Itineraries

CLASSIC ROUTES

INTO THE WEST
One Week/Mayo to West Cork

Begin at the excavated **Céide Fields** (p435) in Mayo. Wind your way round the coast, stopping at some of Ireland's wildest beaches, to the pretty village of **Pollatomish** (p435). Head to the heritage town of **Westport** (p425), with its pubs and restaurants, before heading past **Croagh Patrick** (p428) and through **Leenane** (p414) – situated on Ireland's only fjord – then down to **Connemara National Park** (p414). Take the beautiful coastal route, passing **Kylemore Abbey** (p413) and Clifden's scenic **Sky Road** (p409) through pretty **Roundstone** (p411), or the stunning wilderness of the inland route, passing the **Twelve Bens** (p414) through Maam Cross to **Galway** (p389). Relax in Galway before moving to the fishing villages of **Kinvara** (p417) and **Ballyvaughan** (p382) in the heart of the unique **Burren** (p383) and visiting the ancient **Aillwee Caves** (p383). Enjoy a medieval banquet at **Bunratty Folk Park** (p365) before visiting Limerick's **Hunt Museum** (p292). Explore the **Dingle Peninsula** (p276) before following the **Ring of Kerry** (p259), ending with a trek in **Killarney National Park** (p256). Continue down the **Beara Peninsula** (p242) to the Italianate **Garinish Island** (p243), with its rare and exotic flowers. Follow the coast to **Cork** (p205) through Castletownsend and the fishing village of **Union Hall** (p230).

This tourist trail brings you past some of Ireland's most famous attractions and spectacular countryside. You could manage it in two days but what's the point? You won't be disappointed on this route.

GIANT LOOP

Three Weeks/Starting & Ending in Dublin

Start your loop just north of Dublin at the **Casino at Marino** (p108), not a place to cash your chips but a 19th-century Italianate trompe l'oeil mansion. Continue north to the mind-blowing Neolithic necropolis at **Brú Na Bóinne** (p523), built before the Great Pyramids were even a twinkle in the Pharaoh's eye. Continue north to **Mellifont Abbey** (p546), Ireland's first Cistercian abbey, and on to the pretty village of **Carlingford** (p551) on the lough with its narrow streets and 16th-century buildings. Work your way through the Mourne Mountains – hiking your way to the top of **Slieve Donard** (p613) if you wish – to the **Ards Peninsula** (p599) and **Strangford Lough** (p603). Take a Black Taxi tour in **Belfast** (p554) before moving northwest to the unmissable rock formation and World Heritage site, **Giant's Causeway** (p644), best enjoyed at sunset. Continue around the stunning coastline of north Donegal, stopping at some of Ireland's finest beaches, such as **Killyhoey Beach** (p506), and passing through the beautiful **Glenveagh National Park** (p502). Head south through the monastic ruins of **Glencolumbcille** (p495) and down into lively **Sligo** (p441), where you should climb up to the Stone-Age passage grave, **Carrowkeel** (p448), built on a ley line and with panoramic views of Lough Arrow. For the west coast as far as Cork, follow the Into the West route (opposite). From Cork, head east to **Fota Wildlife Park** (p217) for a picnic and then on to Dungarvan's **King John's Castle** (p198), with its unusual 12th-century shell. Drive around the picturesque **Hook Peninsula** (p182), stopping for ice cream in the seaside town of **Dunmore East** (p195). Spot the unusual varieties of geese in the famous **Wexford Wildfowl Reserve** (p178) before heading up to County Wicklow and **Wicklow Mountains National Park** (p152). Now settle into a well-deserved pint of Guinness at **Mulligan's** (p135), back in Dublin.

A coastal loop to be savoured, giving you a real feel for Ireland's savage and spectacular coastline, as well as the heart of its long history. Four days will see you complete the full circle but little else; best done in a couple of weeks or more.

HEAD TO HEEL   Two Weeks/Derry to Wexford

Begin by walking the city walls of **Derry** (p623) and exploring its fascinating history. Walk around one of Ireland's best museums, the **Ulster American Folk Park** (p669), which reproduces a typical 19th-century Ulster village at the time of mass emigration to America. Just south of here the town of **Omagh** (p668), site of one of the worst single atrocities in the North's history (a car bomb), acts as a stark reminder of the region's tragic political history. From here, head south to **Castle Coole** (p662), a National Trust–restored 18th-century mansion, before spending an afternoon boating or fishing on **Lough Erne** (p662). For more watery pastimes you can't beat **County Cavan** (p456), which has a lake for every day of the year. Hire a boat in **Mountnugent** (p459) and fish on **Lough Sheelin** (p459) before moving on down to **Tullynally Castle's** (p479) Chinese and Tibetan garden in Westmeath. The **Seven Wonders of Fore** (p479), Westmeath's answer to the Seven Wonders of the World, while less awe inspiring, will keep you entertained for an hour or two before a wander around the splendid **Belvedere House** (p478), overlooking Lough Ennell, with its multimedia exhibition. Place a bet at **Kilbeggan Races** (p479) emboldened by a tipple of fine whiskey at **Locke's Distillery** (p478). Take a hike up the beautiful **Slieve Bloom Mountains** (p344) for the best view of the Midlands, before moving south to the delightful village of **Inistioge** (p325) in County Kilkenny, with its quaint village square and rambling estate, Woodstock Park. In County Wexford have a picnic in the **John F Kennedy Park & Arboretum** (p186) before a visit to the tranquil Cistercian **Tintern Abbey** (p182).

From north to south, this route through Ireland covers it all: from Ulster's fine architecture and heritage, through the midlands and its abundance of lakes – a haven for anglers and nature lovers – down to the beautiful countryside of the sunny southeast. You will enjoy this selection of different tastes.

ATLANTIC OCEAN

Derry
Ulster American Folk Park
Omagh
Castle Coole
Lough Erne
Cavan
Lough Sheelin
Mountnugent
Seven Wonders of Fore
Tullynally Castle
Belvedere House
Kilbeggan
Irish Sea
Slieve Bloom Mountains
John F Kennedy Park & Arboretum
Inistioge
Tintern Abbey

ROADS LESS TRAVELLED

NORTH BY NORTHWEST   One Week/Sligo to Donegal

Kick off in **Sligo** (p441), visiting the megalithic cemetery at **Carrowmore** (p446) and **Knocknarea Cairn** (p446), the supposed grave of the legendary Queen Maeve, before heading north to the handsome beach at **Rosses Point** (p446). Visit **Yeats' grave** (p450) in Drumcliff, in the shadow of dominant **Benbulben** (p450). Round the coastline and stop off at another Yeats landmark, **Lissadell House** (p450) before proceeding northward past the wide stretch of **Streedagh Beach** (p451). Cross the border into Donegal, take a peek at the tack in **Bundoran** (p490) and head for **Ballyshannon** (p489), where you can stock up for a beach trip to wonderful **Rossnowlagh** (p489). Follow the coastline west to the ancient monastic settlement at **Glencolumbcille** (p495) before switching back and taking the inland road through the alpine scenery of the **Glen Gesh Pass** (p496), which will lead you to picturesque **Ardara** (p496). Travel inland through the Derryveagh Mountains – stopping for a little fishing in the salmon-rich **River Finn** (p498) – and into **Glenveagh National Park** (p502). Take a day to visit the **Poisoned Glen** (p502) or, if you're up for it, climb **Mount Errigal** (p502) or **Muckish Mountain** (p507) before settling down for a drink and a bit of an Irish sing-along at **Leo's Tavern** (p501) in Crolly, best known as the pub owned by Enya's very musical family. Head east along the stunning coastline, past the pretty village of **Dunfanaghy** (p506) and round to the rugged **Inishowen Peninsula** (p514) before finishing up in the popular seaside resort of **Buncrana** (p519).

A genuine slice of rugged Ireland, its jagged edges left uncaressed by the velvet hand of tourism. This is the Ireland of the scenic postcard before there were postcards.

BEST OF THE ISLANDS   Three Weeks/Tory to West Cork

Ireland's outlying islands are many and varied, and offer the visitor an insight into a traditional lifestyle rarely seen in the Western world. Start at the barren and remote **Tory** (p504), off Bloody Foreland in Donegal, a Gaeltacht (Irish-speaking) area with a school of primitive painters and a wonderful spot for bird-watching. Joined to the mainland by a bridge, **Achill** (p431) in County Mayo, with its deserted Famine village and dramatic cliffs, is Ireland's largest offshore island and is renowned for its water sports. **Inishturk** (p430), just south of Achill, with less than 100 inhabitants, gets very little tourist traffic, despite its sheltered sandy beaches. Off the coast of Galway, the three Aran Islands are probably Ireland's most visited. The largest, **Inishmór** (p400), has some fine archaeo-logical remains, including the magical fort of Dún Aengus. The middle island, **Inishmaan** (p403), favourite of the writer JM Synge, is a pleasure to walk around with its stone walls and tiny fields. The smallest and least visited, **Inisheer** (p405), best accessed from Doolin in County Clare, has some wonderful wild walks. Some of the most special islands to visit are Europe's most westerly **Blasket Islands** (p285), off Kerry, uninhabited since 1953, where you can spot puffins, seals and porpoises. **Skellig Michael** (p263), off Caherciveen in Kerry, a Unesco World Heritage site and home to a 7th-century monastery, is a breathtaking, truly spiritual place and a highlight of any trip to Ireland. Ornithologists and orators alike will enjoy **Clear Island** (p234), also called Cape Clear Island, off the western coast of Cork, famous for its Manx shearwater and its lively Storytelling Festival in September.

If you're one to appreciate the cultural experi-ence and simple pleasures of island life, you won't want to hurry this trail. Take three weeks if you can spare it and experience the unique differences of Ireland's islands properly. Otherwise try to get in at least a day trip.

TAILORED TRIPS

ADRENALINE JUNKIES

Thrill seekers should kick off their action and adventure tour of the west coast of Ireland with a **rock-climbing** (p266) session on the cliffs of the Iveragh Peninsula in County Kerry. The next day, head up the coast to the windy world of Rough Point on the lovely Dingle Peninsula. There, you can take flight with some white-knuckle **kitesurfing** (p281). Stay firmly on the water next and build your biceps even more with some **sea kayaking** (p370) at the small town of Kilrush in County Clare. Cross the wilderness of Connemara by **mountain bike** (p411 and p413) and head for Glassillaun Beach, County Galway. There, go **scuba diving** (p413) in some of the country's clearest waters and see colourful marine life brought north by the Gulf Stream. Down the road in Leenane, scramble down on foot to Killary Harbour to sail its sheltered waters in a **catamaran** (p415). Then test your physical strength and endurance nearby on a **cross-country assault course** (p429) at beautiful Delphi, located next to Ireland's only fjord, before heading north to **surf** (p490) the waves on world-class near-perfect 10ft tubes at Bundoran, County Donegal.

CELTS & CROSSES

Begin at the stunning Neolithic tombs of **Newgrange** (p524) and **Knowth** (p525) in County Meath in the heart of Brú na Bóinne (the Boyne Palace), where the legendary Irish hero Cúchulainn was conceived. Nearby, stand at the top of the celebrated **Hill of Tara** (p530), a site of immense folkloristic significance and seat of the high kings of Ireland until the 11th century. Across the plain is the **Hill of Slane** (p527), where St Patrick lit a fire in 433 to proclaim Christianity throughout the land. Travel west to **Kells** (p537) on the road travelled by Queen Medb herself in the Irish Stone Age epic, the *Táin Bó Cúailnge*, pausing to explore the monastic ruins and high crosses before continuing to County Roscommon. Just outside Tulsk village is **Cruachan Aí** (p467), the most important Celtic site in Europe, with 60 scattered megalithic tombs and burial sites. Head south to **Clonmacnoise Abbey** (p351), the 6th-century monastic site in County Offaly. Continue south through the heart of the country to the impressive monastic site that sits atop the craggy **Rock of Cashel** (p302) in County Tipperary. Turn east and head through County Kilkenny, stopping at the Cistercian **Jerpoint Abbey** (p324) at the pretty village of Thomastown. From here, travel northeast to Wicklow and magnificent **Glendalough** (p157), where the substantial remains of a monastic settlement linger by two lakes – it's as atmospheric a site as you'll ever find.

CHILDREN ON BOARD

For fun historical and zoological, Ireland has a lot to offer. Step back in time with a multimedia tour of medieval Kerry at the **Kerry County Museum** (p271) in Tralee. Recharge your batteries on the Tralee and Dingle light **steam railway** (p271) and chug around Tralee Bay on a trip back in time. About 1km away from here, you can watch wheat being milled at Blennerville in Ireland's largest working **windmill** (p271), built in 1800. Still in County Kerry, you can zip on down the peninsula to

Dingle to see turtles, stingrays and exotic fish up close in the **Dingle Oceanworld** (p277) aquarium. Popular features here are the touch pool, walk-through tunnel, shark tank and Amazon Jungle section complete with piranhas. Pursuing the theme of watery adventures, catch a boat into the bay to see the famously friendly **Fungie the dolphin** (p277) at play; the attention-loving bottlenose shows up most days. The next day make your way to Killarney and take a relaxing tour in the town's beloved horse-drawn **jaunting cars** (p256). From here, head east to the wonderful, fence-free **Fota Wildlife Park** (p217) in Carrigtwohill, East Cork, where you'll see over 90 species of exotic and endangered wildlife like cheetahs, macaques and oryxes.

A TIPPLER'S TOUR

You'll need to know what you're drinking, so take a deep breath and take a tour of the **Old Jameson Distillery** (p104) in Dublin. Head south to Carlow town and get your lips wet at the **Carlow Brewing Company** (p339), a microbrew sensation. Make the short trip down the road to Kilkenny and head straight for the **Smithwick Brewery** (p318); ask nicely and you just might get in. If not, don't despair. Sample the local ale and atmosphere in **O'Riada's** (p322) and hightail it southward to **Midleton** (p220) in County Cork, Irish whiskey's HQ. In Cork city itself, turn a blind eye to the architectural eyesore that is the **Beamish & Crawford Brewery**

(p210) and discover that there is a stout to rival Arthur Guinness' personal best. On the long journey northward, make a pit stop at the **Tullamore Dew Heritage Centre** (p354), where you can sample a snifter of the world-famous whiskey, and a detour to the fabulous **Locke's Distillery** (p478) in Kilbeggan, County Westmeath. The final stop on this epic journey is at Ireland's northeastern tip, in the small town of Bushmills, County Antrim. After a visit to the superb **Bushmills Distillery** (p643), the oldest legal distillery in the world, collapse finally at the **Bushmills Inn** (p643) for a well-deserved rest.

Snapshot

Publicans are unhappy; nurses are angry; politicians are defensive; the opposition is indignant; and Joe and Jane public are fed up. Throughout the country there are rumblings, misgivings and complaints; people are going to the windows, sticking their heads out and yelling 'I'm mad as hell and I'm not going to take it anymore'. Whoa, horsey. What's going on? How can there be so much rot in the state that for the last decade and a half has been the world's favourite poster-child for untrammelled economic development? Isn't Ireland a modern marvel of dynamic entre-preneurialism with a deep heritage and a growing multiculturalism? In a country where everything has been going so right, how can things be so wrong?

Things haven't *really* gone to hell in a hand-basket and Ireland is largely in very good shape. The economy is buoyant and most people are doing just fine. The arrival of immigrants from Europe and all over the world has added a wonderful new dimension to modern Irish culture that has grown in worldliness and self-confidence. There's something so right about a family hailing from Lagos raising kids with strong Dublin accents, or a bunch of Polish workers greeting people in a pub in Cork with a familiar 'howarya lads'. Or the fact that the second-most spoken language in Ireland today is Mandarin Chinese.

But pub conversations aren't as upbeat as some visitors might expect. Part of it is that – contrary to common belief – the Irish aren't natural optimists, but fatalists, only they imbue their fatalism with a bravado and black humour that is often perceived by outsiders as shiny positivity. But it's mostly down to the fact that Ireland's radical economic success has dramatically altered the country's psyche and cultural fabric. Ireland's personality has changed in the last couple of decades, and there's nothing like a bit of change to start an argument.

So, who's arguing? Publicans, for one. Bruised and sore following the smoking ban of 2004, their new crusade is against the liberalisation of the licensing laws, which would see a host of new licenses granted to so-called café-bars – part of Ireland's inevitable march toward European homogeneity. It would be a disaster, they argue (not quite convincingly), for it would make *far* worse one of the country's biggest social ills.

Surprise, surprise, but apparently Ireland has a drinking problem. The nation famed and caricatured throughout the world for its relationship with liquids brewed and distilled has seen its problems get markedly worse in the last decade – a 46% increase in per capita alcohol consumption during the 1990s – forcing the country to finally take a proper look at itself. 'Binge-drinking' is the buzz term used to describe the no-holds-barred boozing that takes place every weekend in every single town in the country. The resultant chaos is obvious and drink-related incidents are a regular and sometimes tragic feature of Irish life. Hospital accident and emergency departments are choked at weekends with drink-related casualties, which puts an enormous strain on a health service that is already in huge trouble.

Which neatly leads us to nurses threatening strikes and the Great Debate about the health service. For all the hoopla about free medical care available to all, generations of mismanagement and neglect have seen waiting lists grow out of control – even for those requiring critical operations – and corridors full of patients on trolleys waiting for beds that just

FAST FACTS

Population: 3.9 million

Unemployment rate: 4.5%

Inflation: 4.3%

Territory size: 70,300 sq km

Annual earnings from tourism: €5 million

Average number of minutes Irish mobile phone users talk per month: 197

Number of visiting tourists per year: 6.3 million (more than there are residents)

Irish adults who have satellite TV: 25%

Biggest no-no: Don't say 'begorrah' – they'll just laugh at you

Second-most spoken language: Mandarin Chinese

aren't available. The government huffs and puffs and talks about committing more money to sorting it out, but in a country with some of the lowest personal taxation rates in Europe it's always going to be an uphill task. Then, in 2004, it was revealed that for generations the state pensions of the elderly in care were being withheld and used to part-pay for their care – a service that they were legally entitled to anyway. That was bad enough, but what really sealed the deal was the admission that successive governments had known about the fraud but had done nothing about it.

The nation was shocked but hardly surprised. It'll end up costing the ordinary taxpayer €1 billion as the government dips into the exchequer to pay the pensioners back, which will undoubtedly infuriate a country already at its wits' end because of a rip-off culture that sees most people pay above the odds for services their European neighbours get for a fraction of the cost. Banks, insurance brokers and phone companies are the big baddies of this scenario, but the culture is endemic and anyone who can overcharge generally does. Visitors can get a taste of this phenomenon easily enough: just check into a hotel or go to a restaurant for a meal. The answer, according to the right-wing Progressive Democrats (the junior partners in a government coalition with Fianna Fáil), is increased competition, and their leader Mary Harney has promised to speed up a mechanism that would allow for insurance and phone monopolies to be smashed. The country is eager for action but it isn't holding its breath.

Where the government is making lots of loud noises is on the continuing problems of Northern Ireland and the sinister activities of the IRA and its political mouthpiece, Sinn Féin. In December 2004 the biggest bank robbery in British history cleared a whopping £26 million, and the fingerprints of the republican movement were all over it. But it got worse. In January 2005 the brutal murder of Robert McCartney by thugs directly connected with the IRA, followed by the high-profile campaign by McCartney's sisters to bring the perpetrators to justice, has exposed the inbuilt hypocrisies in the republican movement for all to see, leaving Sinn Féin with a huge credibility gap that it is struggling to close.

Then on 28 July 2005, an announcement that's been years in the making: the IRA announced an end to the armed struggle and told its volunteers to dump their arms. The war was officially over. In response the British army began dismantling some of its posts and bases. The news was greeted with muted enthusiasm throughout the country; even Loyalists allowed a glimmer of optimism to crack through the wall of pessimism they maintain in face of any announcement by the republican movement.

And, of course, there's Europe's favourite bugbear, illegal immigration. Ireland has its fair share of xenophobic fear-mongers who like to remind the rest of us through the press and the pub that most illegal immigrants are lying spongers not to be trusted. The government doesn't want to appear soft on the issue of illegal immigration, so it talks a tough game, but the truth is that Ireland desperately needs foreign workers – 40,000 of them a year – to make up for acute labour shortages that will just keep on growing. Thankfully, the terrible irony of a country that exported economic migrants throughout its history now getting uppity when others start knocking on its door is not lost on a huge proportion of the Irish population, but even some of them argue that the recent expansion of the EU from 15 to 25 member-states has sufficiently widened the labour pool – which leaves Africans, Asians and others in the same boat as before. It's an argument that won't be resolved any time soon.

'In December 2004 the biggest bank robbery in British history cleared a whopping £26 million, and the fingerprints of the republican movement were all over it'

History

VERY EARLY IRISH & THE CELTS

Our turbulent tale begins about 10,000 years ago, as the last ice caps melted and the rising sea level cut Ireland off from Britain. Hunters and gatherers may first have traversed the narrowing land bridge, but many more crossed the Irish Sea in small hide-covered boats. Farming did not reach Ireland until around 4000 BC. Bronze Age goldworking was of a very high quality in Ireland and stimulated trade with the rest of Europe.

The Celtic warrior tribes who have had such an influence on Irish culture came from central Europe. They had conquered large sections of southern Europe. The Romans called them 'Galli' (Gauls) and the Greeks used the term 'Keltoi', and both societies feared the brutal Celts, who were to plunder Rome in the 4th century AD. They were an imaginative race who put great store in spirituality and the supernatural.

The Celts reached Ireland around 300 BC – they brought the Iron Age with them – and within 200 years they were well ensconced on the island. They established a sophisticated code of law, called the Brehon Law, that remained in use until the early 17th century. Their swirling, mazelike design style, evident on artefacts nearly 2000 years old, is still considered distinctively Irish today. Some excellent ancient Celtic designs survive in the Broighter Collar in the National Museum in Dublin. The Turoe Stone in County Galway is another fine representative of Celtic artwork.

Under the Celts, Ireland was divided into five provinces: Leinster, Meath, Connaught, Ulster and Munster. Meath later merged with Leinster. Within the provinces there were perhaps 100 or more minor kings and chieftains controlling sections of the country, but Tara in County Meath often served as the base for Ireland's most powerful Celtic leaders.

For a concise, 10-minute read on who the Celts were see www.ibiblio .org/gaelic/celts.html.

The Celts controlled the country for 1000 years and left a legacy of language and culture that survives in Ireland, Scotland, Wales and remote parts of Europe.

Christianity, which of course would play a significant part in the island's history, reached Ireland between the 3rd and 5th centuries. Long-forgotten missionaries surely came before St Patrick, but Ireland's patron saint is traditionally credited for proselytising the native Irish (see the boxed text, p34).

While the Dark Ages engulfed much of the rest of Europe, Ireland became known as a land of saints and scholars. During the 7th and 8th centuries, monks in Ireland wrought beautiful objects in semiprecious metals and created illuminated manuscripts including the famous, intricately detailed Book of Kells, which is held in Trinity College, Dublin (p89). Clonmacnoise (p351) in County Offaly and Glendalough (p157) in County Wicklow are outstanding examples of monasteries dating back to those times.

VIKING INVASIONS

At the end of the 8th century, Vikings came sniffing for booty. They first landed their slim, powerful boats at Lambay Island off Dublin in AD 795. They made surprise attacks along the eastern coast and strategic advances

6000–8000 BC	300 BC
After the last Ice Age ends, human beings arrive in Ireland	Celts migrate in huge numbers to Ireland, beginning 1000 years of cultural and political dominance

up rivers to inland terrain, where they set up bases and began plundering the prosperous monasteries. Intertribal squabbles prevented the Irish from establishing a unified defence, and Irish weapons and soldiers proved no match for the superbly armed Norsemen. In many instances, Irish looters joined in the raids for personal profit. In self-defence, the monks built round towers, which served as lookout posts and places of refuge during attacks. Surviving examples of these towers can be seen in monastic sites such as Glendalough (p158).

The Vikings more or less had their way with Ireland, and spread throughout the island during the 9th and 10th centuries. They established a small Viking kingdom called Dubh Linn (Black Pool), which would later become the city of Dublin, and they founded the towns of Wicklow, Waterford and Wexford. In 1014 the Vikings were defeated at Clontarf by Brian Ború, king of Munster, and his forces. Viking domination was broken, but Norsemen stayed in many parts of Ireland, and would soon be joined on the island by another group of former Vikings, the Normans.

The Course of Irish History by TW Moody and FX Martin is a hefty volume by two Trinity College professors who trace much of Ireland's history to its land and its proximity to England.

THE NORMAN CONQUEST

The Normans were originally from Scandinavia, but they had settled large sections of France and, under William the Conqueror, took England in 1066. Their foothold in Ireland came a century later in a deal with Dermot MacMurrough, the king of Leinster, who had been banished by rival kings in 1166. MacMurrough fled to England, where he met Henry II and Richard Fitz-Gilbert de Clare, earl of Pembroke. De Clare, better known as Strongbow, agreed to send an army to Ireland in return for the hand of MacMurrough's daughter and succession to the kingdom of Leinster.

In May 1169, the first Anglo-Norman forces landed in Bannow Bay, County Wexford, and with MacMurrough took Wexford town and Dublin with ease. The following year Strongbow arrived and, after a bloody battle,

ST PATRICK

Ireland's patron saint is remembered all around the world on 17 March, when people of all ethnicities drink Guinness and wear green clothing. But behind the hoopla was a real man with a serious mission. For it was Patrick (389–461) who introduced Christianity to Ireland.

The plain truth of it is he wasn't Irish. The symbol of Irish pride hailed from a part of southeastern Scotland that spoke Welsh at the time of his birth – a time when Britain was under Roman occupation.

Patrick's arrival in Ireland was made possible by Irish raiders who kidnapped him when he was 16, and took him across the channel to work as a slave. He found religion, escaped his captivity and returned to England. But he vowed to make it his life's work to convert the Irish to Christianity. He was ordained, then appointed Bishop of Ireland. Back he went over the channel.

He based himself in Armagh, where St Patrick's Church of Ireland Cathedral (p618) stands on the site of his old church. Patrick quickly converted peasants and noblemen in great numbers. Within 30 years, much of Ireland had been baptised and the country was divided up into Catholic dioceses and parishes. He also established monasteries throughout Ireland, which would be the foundations of Irish scholarship for many centuries.

So next St Paddy's Day, as you're swilling Guinness and chomping down corned beef and cabbage, think of who the man really was. And pinch somebody.

AD 432–61	600–800
St Patrick introduces Christianity to Ireland	Ireland's 'Golden Age': the height of monastic scholarship

took Waterford as well as his new bride. Within 12 months MacMurrough had died, and Strongbow claimed the final part of the bargain – his title as king of Leinster.

Meanwhile, Henry II had taken steps to be recognised by the pope as lord of Ireland, and he watched Strongbow's activities with interest and increasing unease. Strongbow's growing power and his independence of mind were of great concern to the English monarch. In 1171 Henry sent a huge naval force from England, landed at Waterford and declared it a royal city. He assumed a semblance of control, but the Norman lords continued to do pretty much as they pleased. Barons such as de Courcy and de Lacy set up independent power bases.

The Normans, like the Norsemen before them, settled in Ireland and assimilated into the Irish culture. The Normans established beautiful cities, such as Kilkenny, which still retains much of its medieval character today. In 1366, the English Crown attempted to reverse this trend by enacting the Statutes of Kilkenny, which outlawed intermarriage, the Irish language and other Irish customs, but it was too late. By this time the Anglo-Norman barons had established independent power bases. Over the following two centuries English control gradually receded to an area around Dublin known as 'the Pale'.

MONARCHS TAKE CONTROL

In the 16th century Henry VIII, wary of an invasion from the French or Spanish through Ireland, moved to reinforce English authority. He set out to destroy the defiant and influential Anglo-Norman Fitzgeralds, earls of Kildare, who posed a serious threat to his supremacy.

In 1534 Silken Thomas, son of the reigning earl, stormed Dublin and its English garrisons on the false pretext that his father had been executed by Henry in England. Henry retaliated with even greater aggression. The rebellion was squashed, and Thomas and his followers were subsequently executed. In a pattern of retribution that was to be frequently repeated in the following centuries, the Fitzgerald estates were divided among English settlers and an English viceroy was appointed.

Henry then launched an assault on the affluent property of the Catholic Church, with whom he had fallen out over his divorce from Catherine of Aragon. Once his armies had pillaged and plundered the Irish monasteries, Henry ensured that the Irish Parliament declared him king of Ireland in 1541.

Elizabeth I further consolidated English power in Ireland, establishing jurisdiction in Connaught and Munster, despite rebellions by the local ruling families. Ulster remained the last outpost of the Irish chiefs. Hugh O'Neill, earl of Tyrone, led the last serious assault on English power in Ireland for centuries. O'Neill – who supposedly ordered lead from England to reroof his castle, but instead used it for bullets – instigated open conflict with the English, and so began the Nine Years' War (1594–1603). He proved a courageous and crafty foe, and the English forces met with little success against him in the first seven years of fighting.

The Battle of Kinsale, in 1601, spelled the end for O'Neill and for Ulster. Although O'Neill survived the battle, his power was broken and he surrendered to the English Crown. In 1607, O'Neill and 90 other Ulster chiefs

The expression 'beyond the Pale' traces back to when the Pale was the English-controlled part of Ireland. To the British elite, the rest of Ireland was considered uncivilised.

Vikings begin to plunder Irish monasteries; their raping and pillaging urges sated, they establish settlements throughout the country

City of Dublin established

sailed to Europe, leaving Ireland forever. This was known as the Flight of the Earls, and it left Ulster open to English rule.

With the native chiefs gone, Elizabeth and her successor, James I, pursued a policy of colonisation known as the Plantation – an organised, ambitious confiscation of land that sowed the seeds for the division of Ulster that still exists. Huge swathes of land were taken from the Irish and given to English gentlemen 'undertakers', who carved up the land and gave it to Scottish and English settlers. Unlike previous invaders, these new Protestant landowners were not about to assimilate with the impoverished, angry population of Irish and Anglo-Norman Catholics.

THE GROWING RELIGIOUS DIVIDE

For articles tracing the Irish struggle, check out http://larkspirit.com.

The English Civil Wars, which lasted for most of the 1640s, had severe repercussions for Ireland. The native Irish and Anglo-Norman Catholics, allied under the 1641 Confederation of Kilkenny, supported Charles I against the Protestant parliamentarians in the hope of restoring Catholic power in Ireland. Much blood was spilled on Irish soil during the decade-long rebellion.

After Charles' defeat and execution, the victorious Oliver Cromwell, leader of the parliamentarians, decided to 'restore order' in Ireland. He arrived in 1649 and, after a ruthless massacre in Drogheda, rampaged through the country leaving a fearsome trail of death behind him. Word of his barbaric conduct spread quickly and towns often gave up without a fight when his army approached. Many Irish were dispossessed and exiled to the harsh, infertile lands of Connaught. Two million hectares of land were confiscated – more than 25% of the country – and handed over to Cromwell's supporters.

Cromwell: An Honourable Enemy by Tom Reilly advances the unpopular view that perhaps the destruction of Cromwell's campaign is grossly exaggerated. You're no doubt familiar with the common view; here's the contrary position. (Yes, Reilly is Irish.)

In 1689, scarcely more than two decades after Restoration (the re-establishment of the British monarchy after the execution of Charles I), the openly Catholic James II was forced to flee England. He intended to raise an army in Ireland and regain his throne from the Protestant William of Orange, who had been appointed by Parliament. James II arrived at Kinsale in March and headed north to Dublin, where the Irish Parliament recognised him as king and began to organise the return of expropriated land to Catholic landowners. To this end, James' forces began a siege of Derry that would cause mass starvation. The Protestant slogan 'No Surrender!', which acquired mythical status among Irish Protestants over the following centuries, dates from the siege.

The siege lasted from April to July 1690, when William's ships landed with an army of 36,000 men. The Battle of the Boyne was fought between Irish Catholics (led by James II, a Scot) and English Protestants (led by William of Orange, a Dutchman) on 12 July. William's victory was a turning point and is commemorated to this day by Northern Protestants as a pivotal victory over 'popes and popery'.

Oppressive penal laws, known collectively as the 'popery code', were enacted in 1695 to prohibit Catholics from owning land or entering any profession. Irish culture, music and education were banned in the hope that Catholicism would be eradicated. Most Catholics continued to worship at secret locations, but some prosperous Irish converted to Protestantism to preserve their careers and wealth. Land was steadily transferred to Protestant owners, and a significant majority of the Catholic population became tenants living in wretched conditions. By the late 18th century, Catholics owned barely 5% of the land.

THE DAWN OF IRISH NATIONALISM

In the aftermath of the American War of Independence and the French Revolution, a Belfast organisation called the United Irishmen was formed. Its most prominent leader was a young Dublin Protestant, Theobald Wolfe Tone (1763–98). The United Irishmen started out with high ideals of bringing together men of all creeds to reform and reduce Britain's power in Ireland, but their attempts to gain power through straightforward politics proved fruitless.

When war broke out between Britain and France, the United Irishmen found they were no longer tolerated by the establishment. They re-formed themselves as an underground organisation committed to bringing change by any means. Wolfe Tone looked to France for help, and loyalist Protestants prepared for possible conflict by forming the Protestant Orange Society, which later became known as the Orange Order.

In 1796 a French invasion fleet, with thousands of troops and Wolfe Tone aboard, approached Bantry Bay in County Cork. On shore, the local militia were ill-equipped to repel them. However, a strong offshore wind frustrated attempts to land, and the ships and a disappointed Wolfe Tone were forced to return to France.

The government in Ireland began an effective nationwide campaign to hunt out United Irishmen. Floggings and indiscriminate torture sent a wave of panic through the population and sparked the 1798 Rising. Wexford, a county not noted for its rebellious tendencies, experienced the fiercest fighting, with Father John Murphy leading the resistance. After a number of minor victories the rebels were decisively defeated at Vinegar Hill just outside Enniscorthy.

The persistent Wolfe Tone returned later in 1798 with another French fleet, but was defeated at sea. Wolfe Tone was captured and taken to Dublin where he committed suicide in his prison cell. It was the end for the United Irishmen.

The Protestant gentry, alarmed at the level of unrest, now sought the security of British authority, and in 1800 the Act of Union united Ireland politically with Britain. The Irish Parliament voted itself out of existence and around 100 of the Members of Parliament (MPs) moved to the House of Commons in London.

In the meantime, Daniel O'Connell (1775–1847), a Catholic from Kerry, had started on a course that would make him one of Ireland's most significant leaders. In 1823 O'Connell founded the Catholic Association with the aim of achieving political equality for Catholics. The association soon became a vehicle for peaceful mass protest and action. In the 1826 general election it first showed its muscle by backing Protestant candidates who were in favour of Catholic emancipation.

In 1828 O'Connell himself stood for a seat in County Clare even though, being a Catholic, he couldn't take the seat. O'Connell won easily, putting the British Parliament in a quandary. If they didn't allow O'Connell to take his seat, there might be a popular uprising. Many in the House of Commons

For the Cause of Liberty: A Thousand Years of Ireland's Heroes by Terry Golway vividly describes the struggles of Irish Nationalism.

Potatoes from South America are introduced to Ireland, where they eventually become a staple on nearly every table	Trinity College founded in Dublin

favoured emancipation, and the combination of circumstances led them to pass the 1829 Act of Catholic Emancipation, allowing some well-off Catholics voting rights and the right to be elected as MPs.

O'Connell then sought to secure further reforms. He turned his attentions to the repeal of the Act of Union and the re-establishment of an Irish Parliament, which this time would include Catholic MPs. In 1843 the campaign took off, with O'Connell's 'monster meetings' attracting up to half a million supporters and taking place all over Ireland. O'Connell exploited the threat that such gatherings represented to the establishment, but he balked at a genuinely radical confrontation with the British. His bluff was called when a monster meeting at Clontarf was prohibited and he called it off.

The Great Hunger by Cecil Woodham-Smith is the classic study of the Great Famine of 1845–51.

O'Connell was arrested in 1844 and served a short spell in prison. He fell out with the Young Ireland movement (which, having seen pacifism fail, favoured the use of violence) and never again posed a threat to the British. He died in 1847.

PARNELL & THE LAND LEAGUE

In spite of the bitterness aroused by the Great Famine of 1845–51, there was little challenge to Britain's control of Ireland for quite some time. One rebellion was the abortive Fenian (Irish Republican Brotherhood) rising in March 1867.

In 1875 Charles Stewart Parnell (1846–91) was elected to Westminster. The son of a Protestant landowner from County Wicklow, he had much in common with other members of the Anglo-Irish Ascendancy (ruling classes). But Parnell's mother was American and her father had fought the British in the American War of Independence. Parnell's family supported

THE GREAT FAMINE

As a result of the Great Famine of 1845–51, a staggering three million people died or were forced to emigrate from Ireland. This great tragedy is all the more inconceivable given that the scale of suffering was attributable to selfishness as much as natural causes. Potatoes were the staple food of a rapidly growing, desperately poor population, and when a blight hit the crop, prices soared. The repressive penal laws ensured that farmers, already crippled with high rents, could ill afford the little subsistence potatoes provided. Inevitably, most tenants fell into arrears with little or no concession given by mostly indifferent landlords, and were evicted or sent to the dire conditions of the workhouses.

Shamefully, during this time there were abundant harvests of wheat and dairy produce – the country was producing more than enough grain to feed the entire population and it's said that more cattle were sold abroad than there were people on the island. But while millions of its citizens were starving, Ireland was forced to export its food to Britain and overseas.

The Poor Laws in place at the height of the Famine deemed landlords responsible for the maintenance of their poor and encouraged many to 'remove' tenants from their estates by paying their way to America. Many Irish were sent unwittingly to their deaths on board the notorious 'coffin ships'. British Prime Minister Sir Robert Peel made well-intentioned but inadequate gestures at famine relief, and some – but far too few – landlords did their best for their tenants.

Mass emigration continued to reduce the population during the next 100 years and huge numbers of Irish emigrants who found their way abroad, particularly to the USA, carried with them a lasting bitterness.

1649	1690
Cromwell lays waste throughout Ireland after the Irish support Charles I in the English Civil Wars	William of Orange leads his Protestant army to victory over the Catholic forces of James II in the Battle of the Boyne

the principle of Irish independence from Britain. He quickly became noticed in the House of Commons as a passionate, difficult member who asked awkward questions. At 31 he became leader of the new Home Rule Party, which advocated a limited form of autonomy for Ireland.

In 1879 Ireland appeared to be facing another famine as potato crops were failing once again and evictions were becoming widespread. Cheap corn from America had pushed down grain prices and with that the earnings of the tenants who grew grain on their plots. Michael Davitt, a Fenian, began to organise the tenants and found a sympathetic ear in Parnell. Together forming the Land League, Parnell and Davitt initiated widespread agitation for reduced rents and improved working conditions. The conflict heated up and there was violence on both sides. Parnell instigated the strategy of 'boycotting' tenants, agents and landlords who didn't adhere to the Land League's aims: these people were treated like lepers by the local population.

The Land War, as it became known, lasted from 1879 to 1882 and was momentous. For the first time, tenants were defying their landlords en masse. The Land Act of 1881 improved life immeasurably for tenants, creating fair rents and the possibility of tenants owning their land.

A crisis threatened in 1882 when two of the Crown's leading figures in Ireland – the newly appointed Chief Secretary for Ireland Lord Cavendish and his under-secretary Thomas Burke – were murdered by nationalists with links to the Land League. However, reform had been achieved, and Parnell turned his attentions to Home Rule. He had an extraordinary ally in Prime Minister William Gladstone, who was dependent on Parnell for crucial support in Parliament. But Gladstone and Parnell had their Home Rule Bill defeated, partly as a result of defections from Gladstone's own party.

The end was drawing near for Parnell. For 10 years he had been having an affair with Kitty O'Shea, who was married to a member of his own party. When the relationship was exposed in 1890, Parnell refused to resign as party leader and the party split. Parnell married O'Shea, was deposed as leader and the Catholic Church in Ireland quickly turned against him. The 'uncrowned king of Ireland' was no longer welcome. Parnell's health deteriorated rapidly and he died less than a year later.

HOME RULE BECKONS

Gladstone was elected as prime minister for a fourth term in 1892 and this time managed to get his Home Rule for Ireland Bill through the House of Commons, only to see it thrown out by the House of Lords.

By now eastern Ulster was quite prosperous. It had been spared the worst effects of the Famine, and heavy industrialisation meant the Protestant ruling class was doing nicely. While Gladstone had failed for the time being, the Ulster Unionists (the Unionist Party had been formed in 1885) were now acutely aware that Home Rule could resurface and were determined to fight if it became law. The unionists, led by Sir Edward Carson (1854–1935), a Dublin lawyer, formed a Protestant vigilante brigade called the Ulster Volunteer Force (UVF), which held a series of mass paramilitary rallies mustering strong opposition to Home Rule. Carson threatened an armed struggle for a separate Northern Ireland if independence was granted to Ireland. The British began to bend before this Ulster opposition and, in July 1914, Carson

The Irish in America by Michael Coffey takes up the history of the famine where many histories leave off: the turbulent experiences of Irish immigrants in the USA.

In 1870, after the Great Famine and ongoing emigration, more than one-third of all native-born Irish lived outside of Ireland.

The term 'boycott' comes from Charles C Boycott, a County Mayo land agent who was, yes, boycotted by Parnell's Land League in 1880.

THE GAELIC REVIVAL

While Home Rule was being debated and shunted, something of a revolution was taking place in Irish arts, literature and identity. The poet William Butler Yeats and his coterie of literary friends (including Lady Gregory, Douglas Hyde, John Millington Synge and George Russell) championed the Anglo-Irish literary revival, unearthing old Celtic tales and writing with fresh enthusiasm about a romantic Ireland of epic battles and warrior queens. For a country that had suffered centuries of invasion and deprivation, these images presented a much more attractive version of history.

Similarly, Hyde and Eoin MacNeill did much to ensure the survival of the Irish language and the more everyday Irish customs and culture, which they believed to be central to Irish identity. They formed the Gaelic League (Conradh na Gaeilge) in 1893, which, among other things, pushed for the teaching of Irish in schools. Meanwhile, the strongly politicised Gaelic Athletic Association (GAA) promoted Irish sport and culture.

agreed that Home Rule could go through for Ireland, so long as Ulster was kept separate and thus Ireland's partition was established.

In Britain a new Liberal government under Prime Minister Asquith had removed the House of Lords' power to veto bills and began to put another Home Rule for Ireland Bill through Parliament. The bill was passed (but not enacted) in 1912 against strident unionist and Conservative British opposition.

As the UVF grew in strength, a republican group called the Irish Volunteers, led by the academic Eoin MacNeill, was set up in the south to defend Home Rule for the whole of Ireland. They lacked the weapons and organisation of the UVF, however, which succeeded in large-scale gunrunning, and in 1914, with widespread support from the British army, civil war loomed.

A History of Ireland by Mike Cronin summarises all of Ireland's history in less than 300 pages. It's an easy read, but doesn't offer much in the way of analysis.

The Home Rule Act was suspended at the outbreak of WWI in August 1914 and for a time the question of Ulster was left unresolved.

THE EASTER RISING

Many Irishmen with nationalist sympathies went off to the battlefields of Europe believing their sacrifice would compel Britain to follow through on the promise of Home Rule for Ireland. However, a minority of nationalists in Ireland was not so trusting of British resolve. While many Irish Volunteers agreed with John Redmond's wait-and-see approach, a growing radical faction believed a more revolutionary course of action was necessary.

Two small groups – a section of the Irish Volunteers under Pádraig Pearse and the Irish Citizens' Army led by James Connolly – conspired in a rebellion that took the country by surprise. The insurrection was counting on a shipment of arms from Germany, but the arms were intercepted by the British Navy, and Eoin MacNeill, annoyed that the rising had been planned without him, attempted to call the rebellion off. A depleted Volunteer group marched into Dublin on Easter Monday 1916, and took over a number of key positions in the city, claiming the General Post Office on O'Connell St as their headquarters. From its steps, Pearse read out to passers-by a declaration that Ireland was now a republic and that his band was the provisional government. Less than a week of fighting ensued before the rebels surrendered to the superior British forces.

1828   **1845–51**

Daniel O'Connell, a Catholic, wins a seat in Parliament, leading to new laws granting limited voting rights to Catholics | During the Great Famine, caused by blighted potato crops, three million Irish die or are forced to emigrate

The rebels weren't popular and had to be protected from angry Dubliners as they were marched to jail.

Many have speculated that Pearse, realising they didn't stand a chance, had been driven by the need for a blood sacrifice to galvanise the nation. Whether or not he actually believed this, a blood sacrifice was on the way.

The Easter Rising would probably have had little impact on the Irish situation had the British not made martyrs of the rebel leaders. Of the 77 given death sentences, 15 were executed. Pearse was shot three days after the surrender, and nine days later James Connolly was the last to die, shot in a chair because he couldn't stand on a gangrenous ankle. This brought a sea change in public attitudes, and support for the republicans rose dramatically.

Countess Markievicz (1868–1927) was one of those not executed, because she was female, and Eamon de Valera's (1882–1975) death sentence was commuted to life imprisonment because of his US citizenship; he was freed after an amnesty in 1917.

In the 1918 general election, the republicans stood under the banner of Sinn Féin and won a large majority of the Irish seats. Ignoring London's Parliament, where technically they were supposed to sit, the newly elected Sinn Féin deputies – many of them veterans of the 1916 Easter Rising – declared Ireland independent and formed the first Dáil Éireann (Irish assembly or lower house), which sat in Dublin's Mansion House under the leadership of Eamon de Valera. The Irish Volunteers became the Irish Republican Army (IRA) and the Dáil authorised them to wage war on British troops in Ireland.

A lot more blood would soon seep into Irish soil.

The events leading up to the Anglo-Irish War and their effect on ordinary people are movingly and powerfully related in JG Farrell's novel *Troubles*, first published in 1970.

THE ANGLO-IRISH WAR

The day the Dáil convened in Dublin in January 1919, two policemen were shot dead in County Tipperary. Thus began the bitter Anglo-Irish War, which would last 2½ years. The charismatic and ruthless Michael Collins (1890–1922) now came to the fore, masterminding the campaign of violence against the British.

The war quickly became entrenched and bloody. The IRA faced a coalition of the Royal Irish Constabulary, regular British army soldiers and two groups of quasi-military status (the Auxiliaries and the notoriously brutal Black and Tans, who were former British soldiers who wore mixed black and khaki uniforms), who rapidly gained a vicious reputation. The Black and Tans' use of violence and corruption compounded resentment against the British and bolstered fervent support for the nationalist cause. The hunger-strike death of Terence MacSwiney, mayor of Cork, further crystallised Irish opinion. The IRA created 'flying columns', small groups of armed volunteers to ambush British forces, and on home ground they operated successfully. A truce was eventually agreed in July 1921.

To gain some insight into the mind of Michael Collins, read *In His Own Words*, a collection of Collins' writings and speeches.

After months of difficult negotiations in London, the Irish delegation signed the Anglo-Irish Treaty on 6 December 1921. It gave 26 counties of Ireland independence and allowed six largely Protestant Ulster counties the choice of opting out. If they did (a foregone conclusion), a Boundary Commission would decide on the final frontiers between north and south.

The Treaty negotiations had been largely undertaken on the Irish side by Collins and Griffith. Both knew that many Dáil members wouldn't accept

1879–82	1890s
In the Land War, tenant farmers gain fair rents and make it possible for farmers to own their land	Gaelic Revival, championed by poet WB Yeats, helps intensify pride in Irish traditions and culture

the loss of the North, or the fact that the British monarch would still be head of the new Irish Free State and Irish MPs would still have to swear an oath of allegiance to the Crown. Nevertheless, they signed the Treaty without checking with de Valera in Dublin.

Collins regarded the issue of the monarchy and the oath of allegiance as largely symbolic. He also hoped that the six northeastern counties wouldn't be a viable entity and would eventually become part of the Free State. During the Treaty negotiations he was convinced that the Border Commission would decrease the size of that part of Ireland remaining outside the Free State. Knowing the risks of signing the agreement he declared: 'I may have signed my death warrant tonight.'

PARTITION & CIVIL WAR

On 22 June 1921 the Northern Ireland Parliament came into being, with James Craig as the first prime minister. Catholic nationalists elected to the Parliament took up their seats with reluctance and from the start the politics of the North was divided on religious grounds.

Neil Jordan's motion picture *Michael Collins*, starring Liam Neeson as the revolutionary, depicts the Easter Rising, the founding of the Free State and Collins' violent demise.

Meanwhile, the Irish Free State, as southern Ireland was known until 1949, was established and the unpopular treaty was ratified in the Dáil in January 1922. In June the country's first general election resulted in victory for the pro-Treaty forces. Fighting broke out two weeks later. Collins failed to persuade his colleagues to accept the Treaty, and a bitter civil war broke out between comrades who, a year previously, had fought alongside each other. Collins was shot in an ambush in County Cork and Griffith died from pure exhaustion and anxiety. De Valera was briefly imprisoned by the new Free State government, under Prime Minister William Cosgrave, which went so far as to execute 77 of its former comrades. The Civil War then ground to an exhausted halt in 1923.

After boycotting the Dáil for a number of years, de Valera founded a new party, called Fianna Fáil (Warriors of Ireland), which won nearly half the seats in the 1927 election. De Valera and the other new Teachta Dála (TDs; members of the Dáil) entered the Dáil without taking the oath of allegiance to the Crown.

Fianna Fáil won a majority in the 1932 election and remained in power for 16 years. De Valera introduced a new constitution in 1937, doing away with the oath and claiming sovereignty over the six counties of the North. De Valera also refused to pay land annuities, which had been agreed upon in the Anglo-Irish Treaty, to the British government. An economic war with Britain ensued, which severely crippled Irish agriculture and was resolved only shortly before the 1948 general election.

THE REPUBLIC

Fianna Fáil lost the 1948 general election to Fine Gael (the direct descendants of the first Free State government) in coalition with the new republican Clann an Poblachta. The new government declared the Free State to be a republic at last. Ireland left the British Commonwealth in 1949, and in so doing the south cut its final links to the north.

When Sean Lemass came to power in 1959, as successor to de Valera, he sought to stem the continuing emigration by improving the country's economic prospects. By the mid-1960s his policies had reduced emigration

16 June is immortalised in James Joyce's *Ulysses*	Easter Rising gains little support, but subsequent executions of Pádraig Pearse and James Connolly galvanise Irish resistance

to less than half what it had been a decade earlier, and many who had left returned. He also introduced free secondary education.

In 1972 the Republic (along with Northern Ireland) became a member of the European Economic Community (EEC). At first, membership brought a measure of prosperity, but by the early 1980s Ireland was once more in economic difficulties and emigration figures rose again. By the early 1990s the economy began to recover and is now one of the strongest in Europe.

Meanwhile, the Catholic Church's grip on cultural and ethical issues began to loosen. The results of referenda in the 1980s on abortion and divorce left both illegal, but another referendum on divorce in 1995 was narrowly accepted.

Although the president's power is limited, the election of barrister Mary Robinson to the presidency in 1990 saw her modernise the institution and start to wield considerable informal influence over social policies. Her work contributed to a shift away from the traditionally conservative attitudes on issues such as divorce, abortion and gay rights.

Robinson was succeeded as president by Mary McAleese, a Belfast-born Catholic nationalist and Queen's University law lecturer. Although more conservative than Robinson, McAleese was elected on a platform of continuing Robinson's work and has shown a similarly tolerant attitude on social issues. This was illustrated in 1999 by her high-profile visit to Outhouse, a gay, lesbian and transgender community centre in southern Dublin, and the following year by controversially receiving communion at a Church of Ireland service.

Ireland Since the Famine by FSL Lyons is a standard history for all students of modern Ireland.

In 1994 Taoiseach (Prime Minister) Albert Reynolds, who had helped negotiate the first IRA cease-fire with Gerry Adams, was forced to resign. His resignation mainly resulted from the appointment of a president to the High Court – Harry Whelehan, who had been criticised for not tackling sexual scandals involving the Catholic Church more vigorously. Reynolds was succeeded by Fine Gael leader John Bruton, who came to power in coalition with the Labour Party and the Democratic Left. Bruton's government was the first to take office without a general election.

When it did face one in 1997 it was ousted by Fianna Fáil under Bertie Ahern, in partnership with the Progressive Democrats and a number of independents. Mary Harney became Ireland's first female *tánaiste* (deputy prime minister).

Bertie Ahern's government has been closely involved in the peace-making process in Northern Ireland. Among other things the 1998 Good Friday Agreement made provision for a North-South Ministerial Council, of which the Irish government would become a part, to deal with issues affecting the whole island. Another outcome of the search for a settlement in the North has been improved relations between the Republic and Britain, symbolised by the invitation from Bertie Ahern to British Prime Minister Tony Blair to address the Dáil.

THE TROUBLES

For 25 years the story of the Troubles, as the ongoing conflict between northern Catholics and Protestants became euphemistically known, was one of lost opportunities, intransigence on both sides and fleeting moments of hope.

1919–22	1948
Anglo-Irish War leads to partition; Northern Ireland Parliament is established in 1921 and the Irish Free State is founded in 1922	The Irish Free State becomes a Republic

By the 1960s the Northern county of Derry's population was split approximately 60% Catholic to 40% Protestant, yet through rigged electoral districts and restrictive voting rights the city's council always maintained a Protestant majority. What began as a peaceful civil rights movement quickly morphed into a violent struggle. In October 1968 a Catholic march in Derry was violently broken up by the Royal Ulster Constabulary (RUC), signalling the start of the Troubles.

In January 1969 another civil rights movement, called People's Democracy, organised a march from Belfast to Derry. As the marchers neared their destination they were attacked by a Protestant mob. The police first stood to one side and then compounded the problem with a sweep through the predominantly Catholic Bogside district. Further marches, protests and violence followed, and far from keeping the two sides apart, the police were clearly part of the problem. In August British troops went to Derry and then Belfast to maintain law and order. The British army was initially welcomed in some Catholic quarters, but soon it too came to be seen as a tool of the Protestant majority. Overreaction by the army actually fuelled recruitment into the long-dormant IRA. IRA numbers especially increased after Bloody Sunday (30 January 1972), when British troops killed 13 civilians in Derry.

Northern Ireland's Parliament was abolished in 1972, although substantial progress had been made towards civil rights. A new power-sharing arrangement, worked out in the 1973 Sunningdale Agreement, was killed stone dead by the massive and overwhelmingly Protestant Ulster Workers' Strike of 1974.

While continuing to target people in Northern Ireland, the IRA moved its campaign of bombing to mainland Britain. Its activities were increasingly condemned by citizens and parties on all sides of the political spectrum. Meanwhile, loyalist paramilitaries began a sectarian murder campaign against Catholics. Passions reached fever pitch in 1981 when republican prisoners in the North went on a hunger strike, demanding the right to be recognised as political prisoners. Ten of them fasted to death, the best known being an elected MP, Bobby Sands.

The waters were further muddied by an incredible variety of parties splintering into subgroups with different agendas. The IRA had split into 'official' and 'provisional' wings, from which sprang more extreme republican organisations such as the Irish National Liberation Army (INLA). Myriad Protestant, loyalist paramilitary organisations sprang up in opposition to the IRA, and violence was typically met with violence.

GOOD FRIDAY & BEYOND

In the 1990s external circumstances started to alter the picture. Membership of the EU, economic progress in Ireland and the declining importance of the Catholic Church in the South started to reduce differences between the North and South. Also, American interest added an international dimension to the situation.

In December 1993 the Downing Street Declaration was signed by British Prime Minister John Major and the Irish Prime Minister Albert Reynolds. It was a crucial element in the peace process, stating that Britain had no 'selfish, strategic or economic interest in Northern Ireland' and enshrining

Many films depict events related to the Troubles, including *Bloody Sunday* (2002), *The Boxer* (1997; starring Daniel Day-Lewis) and *In the Name of the Father* (1994; also starring Day-Lewis).

1969	1972
The violent conflict between Catholics and Protestants in Northern Ireland, known as the Troubles, begins	On Bloody Sunday, 30 January, 13 civilians are killed by British troops in Derry

the principle of majority consent at the heart of any talks about constitutional change.

Then, on 31 August 1994, the Sinn Féin leader, Gerry Adams, announced a 'cessation of violence' on behalf of the IRA. In October 1994 the Combined Loyalist Military Command also announced a cease-fire. Most British troops were then withdrawn to barracks, and roadblocks were removed. There followed an edgy peace while all the parties restated their agendas.

A major sticking point became the issue of decommissioning (the Unionist requirement that the IRA show good faith in a final peace settlement by surrendering its weapons before talks began). For their part Sinn Féin and the IRA argued that no arms could be given up until British troops withdrew and political prisoners were freed, and that decommissioning should be part of the final settlement. With the peace process stalled, the IRA declared the cease-fire over when it exploded bombs in Canary Wharf in London on 9 February 1996, killing two people and injuring many more.

Encouraged by the rise of Tony Blair in Britain and Bertie Ahern in the Republic of Ireland, who each stated their commitment to resolving the problems in Northern Ireland, the IRA declared another cease-fire from 20 July 1997. Six weeks later Sinn Féin joined the peace talks.

On 10 April 1998 intensive negotiations culminated in the historic Good Friday Agreement. The agreement, which states that the political future of Northern Ireland depends on the consent of the majority of the people of Northern Ireland, was overwhelmingly endorsed by simultaneous referenda held in Northern Ireland and the Republic on 22 May 1998. Just over 71% of people in Northern Ireland voted to accept devolved democracy, while the 94% Yes vote in the Republic accepted the end of Dublin's territorial claim to the North.

> Brendan O'Brien's popular *A Pocket History of the IRA* summarises a lot of complex history in a mere 150 pages, but it's a good introduction.

Under the agreement the new Northern Ireland Assembly was given full legislative and executive authority over agriculture, economic development, education, environment, finance and personnel, and health and social services. It also established the terms of reference for an independent commission on the future of policing, plans for the release of most paramilitary prisoners, the removal of security installations and a major reduction in the RUC.

Unfortunately the year of the peace agreement was also one of violence, with rioting over the Parades Commission ban on the annual Orange Order parade at Drumcree, Portadown. Escalating loyalist violence culminated in a petrol bomb attack that burned to death three young boys on 12 July. Then on 15 August came the single worst atrocity in the entire history of the Troubles: the bombing of Omagh by the Real IRA, a breakaway republican group opposed to the Good Friday Agreement. The 650kg bomb killed 29 people and injured 200. Confused telephone warnings had caused the RUC to evacuate people to the very area where the bomb exploded. Swift action by politicians, including a statement by Gerry Adams condemning the bombing, prevented a loyalist backlash.

Fruitless talks continued until 6 May 1999 when the IRA released a statement saying that it was ready to begin a process that would 'completely and verifiably' put its arms beyond use. At the end of June the arms inspectors reported that they had inspected the arms dumps and concluded that the arms couldn't be used without their detection. But in an October 2000 arms

1990	**Mid-'90s**
Mary Robinson becomes Ireland's first female president	New tech industries set the table for the new prosperity of the 'Celtic Tiger'

inspection the Independent International Decommissioning Commission (IIDC) declared that no progress had been made on actual disarmament.

These ongoing starts and stalls in the peace process clearly demonstrate that the main players remained hostage to the more extreme elements. Sinn Féin, although committed to the peace process, has to keep its supporters on side to prevent any growth in the dissident breakaway republican paramilitary movements. On the Unionist side, the Ulster Unionist Party faces leakage of their support to the Democratic Unionist Party (and their stated opposition to the Good Friday Agreement) unless they maintain a strong anti-IRA stance.

A History of Ulster by Jonathon Bardon is a serious and far-reaching attempt to come to grips with Northern Ireland's saga.

QUESTIONS OF NATIONAL IDENTITY

Ireland is a shining example of how membership in the European Union can benefit a struggling nation, as the country's economic turnaround was aided by EU funding. No-one in the country is lamenting the passing of the massive unemployment of days gone by. At the same time, however, economic prosperity has brought its own challenges. Development has begun to erode the Irish countryside, converting Ireland's cherished greenery into housing tracts and offices for software manufacturers. And suddenly the gap between rich and poor has widened, leading to a rise in mental health issues and an increase in violent crime. Some Dubliners complain that artists and musicians can no longer afford to live in the capital.

Significantly, in the past decade Ireland has transformed from an apparently homogeneous society into a multicultural society. Waves of immigrants from Eastern Europe, Asia and Africa have taken service-industry jobs that the upwardly mobile Irish are less inclined to want. Some new arrivals have found better paying work, and in a few recent instances have even been elected into political offices. The Irish are proving to be predominantly open-minded about such changes, and often celebrate their country's burgeoning diversity. But there is an ongoing, and very thoughtful, debate over issues of national identity, as people grapple with evolving notions of what it means to be Irish.

As a result, public support for EU expansion sometimes wavers, as exemplified by a 2001 vote against the Nice Treaty in a referendum calling for an increased number of member countries in the EU. The treaty eventually passed in a rerun election, but its initial rejection is widely taken as an indication that the Irish view progress and globalisation with a somewhat wary eye.

However, politics in the Republic has been fairly stable of late. In 2002, Taoiseach (prime minister) Bertie Ahern's government was re-elected. It was the first time in over three decades that Irish voters granted a Taoiseach a second term. This despite Ahern's wavering popularity and his controversial split with his wife. In 2004 Ahern took his short turn as president of the Council of the EU (it's a rotating post), during which he came out in favour of EU expansion. His term is up in 2007.

President Mary McAleese was elected to a second seven-year term in 2004. McAleese, a Belfast native who studied at Trinity College in Dublin, is the first Northerner to head the Republic or Ireland. She succeeded Mary Robinson in 1997, so by the time her current term is up in 2011, the Irish presidency will have been held by women for 21 years.

1998	2005
Good Friday agreement is endorsed in the North and the Republic, outlining steps for peace in Northern Ireland	IRA announces an end to its armed campaign in Northern Ireland

The Culture

THE NATIONAL PSYCHE

The friendliness of the Irish is famous the world over. Their welcoming attitude towards strangers, and willingness to help or just to pass the time with conversation, puts anyone who arrives in the country – whether on a business or leisure trip – at ease. The Irish are outward-looking and proud to be a significant member of the European Union.

Almost two centuries of emigration, starting with enforced emigration during the Great Famine in the late 1840s through to the Depression of the 1930s and the recessions of the 1970s and 1980s, have given the Irish a sense that they are truly an international race who can influence world affairs.

Roman Catholicism – the faith on which the Republic's struggle for independence from Protestant Britain was based – is steadily losing its grip on everyday life. Church attendance has been falling steadily, from around 85% in 1990 to less than 50% in 2005, and the Catholic Church has been forced to import priests from abroad. (In 2004, only six priests were ordained in the whole of Ireland.) Nevertheless, the laws and the attitudes of the Irish remain conservative. The repressed attitude towards sex – stemming from the traditional Catholic view that sex is only for procreation – has long gone, but sex is still not something that will be openly discussed or flaunted, especially in rural areas. It was not until a referendum in 1995 that divorce was finally, though narrowly, accepted, and abortion remains illegal except when necessary to save the mother's life. The Irish social conscience remains very strong, and time and time again the Irish prove they give more to charity per capita than any other nation.

The laid-back attitude towards work, however, can be infuriating: hiring equipment, getting repairs to cars or houses, or quickly finding skilled labour can be a bit of a trial with the 'mañana' culture as strong as ever. Alcohol consumption, exacerbated by the new-found wealth of the tiger economy, is also a problem, and only in 2003 did the government start to consider combating the rise in alcoholism through regulation. Drinking is Ireland's single most popular pastime, and it is no accident that the 'Irish bar' is one of the country's most successful exports. Rural Ireland has also caught up with the cities, with drugs more readily available, and drinking an increasing concern among school children.

The most popular names in Ireland are Jack and Sarah.

LIFESTYLE

Large families of up to 13 children, not uncommon in the early 1990s, have now all but disappeared. Two- and three-child families are now the norm and most parents find they both have to work to make ends meet. It is hard to imagine now, with contraceptives widely available, but in the 1980s contraception was still hard to find for unmarried couples outside of Dublin and without a doctor's prescription – a problem which led to a rash of teenage pregnancies.

The attitude towards gay people in Ireland has also changed for the better since the early 1980s, when there was only one gay nightclub in the whole country. Back then it would have been hard to imagine the current climate, with a transvestite presenting a popular primetime TV programme on conservative station RTE.

The bawdy story *Paddy Clarke: Ha Ha Ha* by Roddy Doyle follows the childish adventures of 10-year-old Paddy in the fictitious working-class world of Barrytown in northern Dublin. It won Doyle the Booker Prize in 1993.

The Irish are a pretty homogeneous people and while the traveller (tinker) community would have been the butt of racial intolerance in the past, that minority group has been replaced by others, particularly those with different skin colour. In Dublin and Belfast especially, verbal abuse and even racially motivated attacks have unfortunately become more common. That said, most rural communities have warmly embraced the many nationalities of asylum seekers and refugees who have been dispersed around the country. The sleepy town of Ballaghadereen in County Roscommon, with a population of 1200, is now, somewhat typically, home to 14 different nationalities.

POPULATION

The total population of Ireland is around 5.6 million. This figure is actually lower than 160 years ago. Prior to the 1845–51 Famine the population was around eight million. Death and emigration reduced the population to around five million, and emigration continued at a high level for the next 100 years. Not until the 1960s did this haemorrhaging slow down, but economic difficulties meant that even in the 1980s more than 200,000 people joined the diaspora.

The Republic's population is just more than 3.9 million. Dublin is the largest city and the capital of the Republic, with around 1.1 million people (about 40% of the population) living within commuting distance of the city centre. The Republic's next largest cities are Cork, Galway and Limerick. Ireland's population is predominantly young: 41% is aged under 25 and in fact Ireland has the highest population of 15- to 24-year-olds and second highest of under 15-year-olds in Europe.

Northern Ireland has a population of nearly 1.7 million, and Belfast, the principal city, around 277,000. It has the youngest population in the UK, with 25% aged under 16.

Since the early 1990s there has been less emigration than immigration, which mostly consists of returning Irish but also immigrants from Britain, other EU countries and North America. The country has also admitted a significant number of refugees from Eastern Europe and Africa.

Females outnumber males in Dublin by 20,000.

THE GAELIC HEARTLAND

Were you to limit your travels in Ireland to what was once called the Pale (including Dublin and Counties Wexford and Waterford), or much of the east and south for that matter, you would be forgiven for thinking you were in a monolingual, English-speaking country. That's not the case in the Gaeltacht, a word used collectively to describe the pockets of the Republic where Irish (or Gaelic as it is sometimes called) remains, at least in theory, the first language of communication and commerce among the majority of the population.

Sadly, the Gaeltacht represents only a tiny area of Ireland's linguistic past. If you were to look at a map of Ireland dating from the early 19th century that had been shaded to show the areas in which Irish was spoken as a first language, and then compared it with one marking today's Gaeltacht, you would be shocked to see the extent of decline that the language has suffered over the past 200 years.

The older map would incorporate more than two-thirds of the island, representing some 2.4 million people. On the more recent map there would be just a dozen small smudges in seven counties, mostly along the west coast. Some 90,000 people live in the Gaeltacht today, with the majority of them – just over 70% – being *Gaeilgeoirí* (Irish speakers). But according to the most recent census (2002), only 55.6% of adults there speak Irish on a daily basis.

More than 1.5 million people in the Irish Republic claim to have an ability to speak Irish, but the vast majority say so only because they were required to study it at school for up to 12 years.

These figures (and population counts throughout the book) are based on the last census of 2002.

SPORT

Ireland, by and large, is a nation of sports enthusiasts. Whether it's shouting the team on from the sideline or from a bar stool, the Irish have always taken their sport seriously.

Gaelic Football & Hurling

Ireland has two native games with large, enthusiastic followings – Gaelic football and hurling.

Gaelic football is a fast and exciting spectacle and is hugely popular throughout the country. In recent years, the game has been glamorised by the association of high-profile sponsors and major advertising. The ball is round like a soccer ball and the players can pass it in any direction by kicking or punching it. The goalposts are similar to rugby posts, and a goal, worth three points, is scored by putting the ball below the bar, while a single point is awarded when the ball goes over the bar.

Hurling is a ball-and-stick game something like hockey, but much faster and more physical. Visitors are often taken aback by the crash of players wielding what look like ferocious clubs, but injuries are infrequent. The goalposts and scoring method are the same as Gaelic football, but the leather ball or *sliotar* is the size of a baseball. Players can pick up the ball on their sticks (called a 'hurley', or *camán* in Irish) and run with it for a certain distance. Players can handle the ball briefly and pass it by palming it. Women's hurling is called camogie.

Hurling has an ancient history and is mentioned in many old Irish tales. The mythical Celtic hero Cúchulainn was a legendary exponent of the game. Today hurling is played on a standard field, but in the olden days the game might have been played between two towns or villages, the aim being to get the ball to a certain spot or goal.

Gaelic football and hurling are played nationwide by a network of town and county clubs and under the auspices of the Gaelic Athletic Association (GAA). The most important competitions are played at county level, and the county winners out of each of the sport's four provinces come together in the autumn for the All-Ireland Finals, the climax of Ireland's sporting year. The Gaelic football and hurling finals are both played in September at Dublin's newly revamped world-class stadium, Croke Park (p142). In fact, a match at Croke Park (if you can get your hands on tickets), with the crowd chanting and its electric atmosphere, is a highlight of any trip to the city.

You can find out more about the history and rules of Gaelic sports on the Gaelic Athletic Association website at www.gaa.ie.

Rugby & Football

Rugby and football (soccer) enjoy considerable support all over the country, particularly around Dublin; football is very popular in Northern Ireland.

Ireland's international rugby team consists of players from both Northern Ireland and the Republic and has a tremendous, mostly middle-class, following. The highlights of the rugby year are the international matches played against England, Scotland, Wales, France and Italy in the Six Nations championship between January and March. Home matches are played at Lansdowne Rd Stadium, Dublin. See p142 and www.irishrugby .ie for more details.

Northern Ireland and the Republic of Ireland field separate international football teams. The Republic's team has a good record in competitions, making it to two World Cups, including Japan 2002 when they went on to qualify for the second round. In 2005 they were ranked 15th in the world and, at time writing, stand a good chance of qualifying for the 2006 World Cup in Germany. Although the Northern Ireland team has qualified for three World Cup competitions (1958, 1982 and 1986), they have been less successful in recent years and failed to make it to Germany 2006. International matches are played at the Lansdowne Rd Stadium, Dublin, and Windsor Park, Belfast (see p589).

Many home players from the North and the Republic play professional football in Britain and the most successful have the status of movie stars. Roy Keane plays for Manchester United, Damien Duff for Chelsea, Stephen Carr and Shay Given for Newcastle, and Robbie Keane for Tottenham Hotspur. English clubs Arsenal, Liverpool and Manchester United and Scottish clubs Celtic and Rangers have strong followings in Ireland.

Both the **North** (www.irishfa.com) and the **Republic** (www.fai.ie) have their own professional football league.

Golf

Jim Sheridan's authentic drama *The Boxer* (1998) is a film about a former IRA member's emergence and readjustment from a Belfast prison, to discover everyone, including his girlfriend, has moved on.

Golf is enormously popular in Ireland and there are many fine golf courses. The annual Irish Open takes place in June or July and the Irish Women's Open in September. For details of venues, contact the **Golfing Union of Ireland** (☎ 01-269 4111; www.gui.ie; 81 Eglinton Rd, Donnybrook, Dublin 4). Players to watch out for include Pádraig Harrington, Darren Clarke, Paul McGinley and Graeme McDowell.

Cycling

Cycling is a popular spectator sport and major annual events include the gruelling FBD Insurance Rás (formerly known as the Milk Rás; www.fbdinsuranceras.com), an eight-day stage race held in May which sometimes approaches 1120km (700 miles) in length, and the Tour of Ulster, a three-day stage race held at the end of April. Current top Irish cyclists include Mark Scanlon, David McCann and David O'Loughlin. For more information on events see www.irishcycling.com.

Road Bowling

The object of this sport is to throw a cast-iron ball along a public road (normally one with little traffic) for a designated distance, usually 1km or 2km. The person who does it in the least number of throws is the winner. The main centres are Cork and Armagh and competitions take place throughout the year, attracting considerable crowds. The sport has been taken up in various countries around the world, including the USA, Germany and the Netherlands, and a world championship competition has been set up (see www.irishroadbowling.ie).

Handball

Handball is another Irish sport with ancient origins, and like Gaelic football and hurling is governed by the GAA. It is different from Olympic handball in that it is played by two individuals or two pairs who use their hands to strike a ball against a forecourt wall, rather like squash.

Athletics

Athletics is popular and the Republic has produced a few international stars, particularly in middle- and long-distance events. Cork athlete Sonia O'Sullivan consistently leads in women's long-distance track events worldwide, and Catherina McKiernan is one of the world's top marathon runners. In Ireland, the main athletic meets are held at Morton Stadium, Dublin. The **Dublin Marathon** (www.dublincitymarathon.ie) is run on the last Monday in October, and the **Belfast Marathon** (www.belfastcity marathon.com) on the first Monday in May.

Boxing

Boxing has traditionally had a strong working-class following. Irish boxers have often won Olympic medals or world championships. Barry McGuigan and Steve Collins, both now retired, were world champions in their day; Belfast-born Eamon Magee took the World Boxing Union welterweight title in March 2005, and Irish heavyweight champion Kevin McBride found himself in the right place at the right time in June 2005, when he beat Mike Tyson in the last fight of the former world champion's professional career. The Irishman was not expected to last more than a couple of rounds, but won on a technical knock-out in the sixth.

Greyhound Racing

With fixtures year round, greyhound racing has a strong following in Ireland. There are 20 tracks across the country, administered by the **Irish Greyhound Board** (☎ 061-316 788; www.igb.ie; 104 Henry St, Limerick).

Snooker

Snooker has a cult following in Ireland. Top players include Ken Doherty, who is the only player in the sport ever to have won both the amateur and professional world championships. He is one of the most successful professional players ever, having taken prize money of more than £2 million; he won the world professional championship in 1997 and was runner-up in 1998 and 2003. Up-and-coming young players include Brendan O'Donoghue, Martin McCrudden and Martin O'Donnell. The Irish Masters takes place in Dublin in March.

Horse Racing

Horses have played a big role in Irish life over the centuries and the country has produced a large number of internationally successful racehorses.

A total of 27 racecourses dot the country, including Leopardstown (p142) in County Dublin, Fairyhouse in County Meath, and Punchestown, Naas and the Curragh (p333) in County Kildare. Major annual races include the Irish Grand National (Fairyhouse, April), Irish Derby (the Curragh, June) and Irish Leger (the Curragh, September). For more information on events contact **Horse Racing Ireland** (☎ 045-842800; www.hri.ie; Thoroughbred County House, Kill, Co Kildare).

MEDIA

There are three national newspapers in the Republic – the *Irish Times*, the *Irish Independent* and the *Examiner* – and one national evening paper, the *Evening Herald*. In the north the three main papers are the *Belfast Telegraph*, with the highest circulation, followed by the pro-Unionist *Newsletter* and the equally popular pro-Nationalist *Irish News*.

The West Belfast–based tabloid *Daily Ireland* was launched in February 2005 as a pro-Nationalist and cross-border newspaper, hoping to take sales from the *Irish News*. However, it IS widely regarded as little more than a mouthpiece for Sinn Féin and the IRA.

The Mighty Celt (2005), starring Robert Carlyle (Trainspotting) and Gillian Anderson (X-Files), is set in Belfast and follows its 14-year-old hero as he trains a greyhound for a championship race while his mother copes with the return of her ex-IRA former lover.

The *Irish Times* has long prided itself on being the paper of the liberal intelligentsia with a core readership in Dublin. But its reputation took a dent in 2002 when huge losses were incurred after unbridled expansion into the Internet and a decline in readership in the face of a fierce circulation battle with the *Independent* and Irish editions of the London newspapers.

The *Irish Independent* and its sister Sunday title are owned by one of Ireland's best-known businessmen, Tony O'Reilly, the former boss of Heinz beans and owner of Waterford Glass and Wedgwood China. His papers have always had the upper hand in circulation with a large following in the countryside. And while the *Irish Press*, a paper that had Republican leanings, was around, the paper would have distinguished itself with its anti-Republican stance, a position that is patently continued through the pages of its Sunday edition. Tony O'Reilly has since got special dispensation from the Irish government to accept a knighthood from the UK government and likes to be referred to with his full title as Sir Anthony O'Reilly in his own newspapers. His decision to accept the title from a foreign government brought howls of derision in some quarters, where it was felt to be saying that being Irish was no longer good enough.

Visit www.medialive .ie for everything you wanted to know about Irish media but were afraid to ask.

The real divide in the Irish newspapers, however, is between the UK and Irish newspapers. Every UK tabloid paper now has an Irish edition, leading to accusations by media speculators that Irish culture is being coarsened. The traditions of the UK tabloids, who have built circulation on the back of celebrity buy-ups and salacious stories about sex and crime, have inevitably been exported and are beginning to have an influence on the editorial position of the Irish titles, particularly on Sunday.

The *Daily Mail*, considered one of the most right-wing papers in the UK with its anti-immigration, anti-Europe and anti-women stance, arrived in Ireland in 2002 with a Sunday newspaper, *Ireland on Sunday*, and immediately plunged itself into a bitter war with the *Sunday Independent*.

The Republic has three national TV stations: the relatively conservative public broadcaster RTE, funded by the State, advertising and the licence fee; the newer purely commercial TV3; and the critically acclaimed Irish-language station TG4, which has the most diverse and challenging output.

RELIGION

Racy London-based Edna O'Brien bases her sensationalist 1997 novel *Down by the River* on the controversial true story of a 14-year-old Dublin girl who was raped and went to England for an abortion.

About 90% of residents in the Republic are Roman Catholic, followed by 3% Protestant, 0.1% Jewish and the rest with no religious belief. In the North the breakdown is about 60% Protestant and 40% Catholic. Most Irish Protestants are members of the Church of Ireland, an offshoot of the Church of England, and the Presbyterian and Methodist Churches.

The Catholic Church has always taken a strong conservative line on abortion, contraception, divorce and censorship, and opposed attempts to liberalise the laws on these matters. But the Church has been weakened by drastically declining attendance, the fall in the number of young men and women entering religious life, and by damaging paedophiliac sex scandals. The Church is now treated with a curious mixture of respect and derision by various sections of the community.

Despite its declining power, the Catholic Church still wields considerable influence in the Republic. It retains control of most schools and hospitals (which are funded by the state), and in rural towns and villages large numbers attend Mass every Sunday. Oddly enough, the primates of both the Roman Catholic Church (Archbishop Sean Brady) and the Church of Ireland (Archbishop Robert Eames) sit in Armagh, Northern Ireland, the traditional religious capital of St Patrick. The country's religious history clearly overrides its current divisions.

ARTS
Literature

The Irish have always had a distinctive way of using their adopted tongue which differs from other English speakers, and it's this great oral tradition and love of language that contributes to Ireland's legacy of world-renowned writers and storytellers. If you took all the Irish writers off the university reading lists for English literature, the degree courses could probably be shortened by a year!

The first great work of Irish literature was the Ulaid (Ulster) Cycle, written down from oral tradition between the 8th and 12th centuries. The chief story is the *Táin Bó Cúailnge* (Cattle Raid of Cooley; see the boxed text, p552), about a battle between Queen Maeve of Connaught and Cúchulainn, the principal hero of Irish mythology. Cúchulainn appears in the work of Irish writers right up to the present day, from Samuel Beckett to Frank McCourt.

Some of the more famous names born before 1900 include *Gulliver's Travels* author Jonathan Swift (1667–1745), acclaimed dramatist Oscar Wilde (1854–1900) and, not least, James Joyce (1882–1941).

Patrick McCabe's *The Butcher Boy* is a brilliant, gruesome tragicomedy about an orphaned Monaghan boy's descent into madness, by one of Ireland's most imaginative authors. It has received several awards and was made into a successful film.

THE COUNT O'BLATHER

Half-human bicycles, people born fully-formed at the age of 25, Irish cowboys, a two-dimensional police station, and a novel within a novel where the characters plot to murder their author while he's asleep – these are just a few of the flights of fancy to be enjoyed in the works of Brian O'Nolan (1911–66), one of Ireland's finest comic writers.

Born in Strabane, County Tyrone, but resident for most of his life in Dublin, O'Nolan was a civil servant who wrote satirical columns for the *Irish Times*. Afraid he might lose his job if his hilarious but often irreverent writing was attributed to him, he published under various pseudonyms including Myles na gCopaleen, George Knowall, Brother Barnabus and the Count O'Blather. But he is best known as Flann O'Brien, the name he used on his great comic novels *The Third Policeman* and *At Swim-Two-Birds*.

Fans of Flann can debate for hours which of the two is the finer book. Both are surreal, inventive, hugely original and very, very funny. James Joyce, no less, described *At Swim-Two-Birds* – the convoluted tale of a student novelist writing a novel about a novelist writing a novel – as 'a really funny book', and Dylan Thomas pronounced that 'this is just the book to give your sister … if she's a loud, dirty, boozy girl!'. *The Third Policeman*, which was written around 1940 but not published until after O'Nolan's death, is a darker work exploring the nature of time, death and existence through the story of a murderer's adventures in a very strange police station.

O'Nolan's newspaper work, gathered together in book form as *The Best of Myles*, was filled with brilliantly inventive and amusing word play, including this witty little limerick that has some fun with the spelling and pronunciation of Irish place names:

Said a Sassenach back in Dun Laoghaire
'I pay homage to nationalist thaoghaire,
But wherever I drobh
I found signposts that strobh
To make touring in Ireland so draoghaire.'

The Whitbread Award–winning novel *Dr Copernicus* by *Irish Times* literary editor John Banville is a peculiar but fascinating story set in medieval Europe, centred on the eponymous astronomer and his travails.

Samuel Beckett (1906–89) came from an Anglo-Irish background and studied at Trinity College before moving to Paris where he associated with Joyce. Influenced by the Italian poet Dante and French philosopher Descartes, his work centres on fundamental existential questions about the human condition and the nature of self. He is probably best known for his play *Waiting for Godot* but his unassailable reputation is based on a series of stark novels and plays. A good taster of his work might be *Krapp's Last Tape*, a monologue about an old man listening to a tape-recording of himself as a young, idealistic man talking about his dreams, or the black humoured novel *Molloy*.

Playwright and novelist Brendan Behan (1923–64) led a turbulent life that spawned powerful tragicomic writing. Grappling with alcoholism from an early age, he was expelled from school, and when caught working as a courier for the IRA was sent to reform school in Britain, from where one of his most famous works, *Borstal Boy*, originates. A further incarceration, this time in Mountjoy prison, provided the backdrop for his acclaimed *The Quare Fellow*, a vehicle for Behan's vehement objections to capital punishment. *The Hostage* is one of his most enduring works, a fantastical mixture of slapstick and human anguish. Behan died, a local legend, from alcoholism in Dublin.

CS Lewis (1898–1963), from Belfast, is best known for *The Chronicles of Narnia*, a series of allegorical children's stories. Other Northern writers have, not surprisingly, featured the Troubles in their work.

Ireland has produced its fair share of female writers, and out of the Anglo-Irish Ascendancy (ruling classes), most notably, came literary team EO Somerville (1858–1949) and her cousin Violet Martin (1861–1915), who wrote (under the pseudonym of Martin Ross) and co-penned *The Irish RM*. Molly Keane (1904–96) wrote several books in the 1920s and 1930s under the pseudonym MJ Farrell, then had a literary second life in her 70s when *Good Behaviour* and *Time after Time* came out under her real name.

The Ireland Anthology, edited by the late Seán Dunne, poet and literary editor of the *Examiner*, is a good introduction to Irish literature, though, as with any anthology, some might debate its inclusions and omissions. *The Oxford Companion to Irish Literature*, edited by Robert Welch, is a useful reference.

Ireland can boast four winners of the Nobel Prize for Literature: George Bernard Shaw in 1925, WB Yeats in 1938, Samuel Beckett in 1969 and Seamus Heaney in 1995. The prestigious annual IMPAC awards, administered by Dublin City Public Libraries, accept nominations from public libraries around the world for works of high literary merit and offer a €100,000 award to the winning novelist. Previous winners have included David Malouf (Australian) and Nicola Barker (English).

Circle of Friends by the queen of Irish popular fiction, Maeve Binchy, ably captures the often hilarious peculiarities of the lives of two hapless country girls in the 1940s who come to Dublin in search of romance.

Yeats is Dead, edited by Joseph O'Connor and penned by 15 Irish authors from populist Marian Keyes to heavyweight Anthony Cronin and plenty in between, is a screwball comedic caper about a petty criminal who gets his hands on Joyce's last manuscript.

POETRY

WB Yeats (1865–1939) was both playwright and poet, but it's his poetry that has the greatest appeal. His *Love Poems*, edited by Norman Jeffares, makes a suitable introduction for anyone new to his writing.

Pádraig Pearse (1879–1916) used the Irish language as his medium and was one of the leaders of the 1916 Easter Rising. *Mise Éire* typifies his style and passion.

Patrick Kavanagh (1905–67), one of Ireland's most respected poets, was born in Inniskeen, County Monaghan. *The Great Hunger* and *Tarry Flynn* evoke the atmosphere and often grim reality of life for the poor farming community. You'll find a bronze statue of him in Dublin, sitting beside his beloved Grand Canal (see p117).

Seamus Heaney (born 1939) won the 1995 Nobel Prize for Literature. In 1997 Heaney added the Whitbread Book of the Year to his accolades for *The Spirit Level*. His translation of the 8th-century Anglo-Saxon epic *Beowulf* has been widely praised. Some of his poems reflect the hope, disappointment and disillusionment of the peace process.

Paul Durcan (born 1944) boldly tackles awkward issues such as the oppressive nature of Catholicism and Republican activity in his trade-mark unconventional style.

Cork-born Irish-language poet Louis de Paor has twice won Ireland's prestigious Sean O'Riordan Prize with collections of his poetry. Tom Paulin (born 1949) writes memorable poetry about the North – try *The Strange Museum* – as does Ciaran Carson (born 1948). Many of Paula Meehan's (born 1955) magical, evocative poems speak of cherished relationships.

For a taste of modern Irish poetry try *Contemporary Irish Poetry* edited by Fallon and Mahon. *A Rage for Order*, edited by Frank Ormsby, is a vibrant collection of the poetry of the North.

Cinema & Television

During much of the 20th century Ireland didn't have a particularly active film-making industry, partly because of the small home market, and it was often left to American or British film-makers to represent Ireland to the rest of the world.

This began to change in 1981 following the creation of the Irish Film Board and increased spending on a home-grown film industry, including some attractive tax-incentive packages for foreign film-makers in Ireland. By the mid-1990s the Irish film industry was genuinely booming with big budget American features such as Mel Gibson's *Braveheart* and Stephen Spielberg's *Saving Private Ryan* creating ongoing industry employment and a domestic skills base.

Ireland now has the second highest level of cinema attendance in Europe, and in 2005 became the first country in the world to have all its traditional 35mm film projectors replaced with digital cinema projectors (both in the Republic and in Northern Ireland).

Quite a few Irish actors have achieved extraordinary international success in the last couple of decades. Young Dublin soap actor Colin Farrell shot to stardom in 2001 following his naturalistic portrayal of a pre-Vietnam GI in US boot camp in *Tigerland*, followed up by *Minority Report* in 2003 and *Alexander* in 2004; Jonathan Rhys-Meyers also enjoyed success in glam rock drama *Velvet Goldmine* and *The Age of Innocence*, and Aiden Gillen's versatile talents can be seen in films *The Low Down*, *Mojo*, *Shanghai Knights* and the TV drama *Queer as Folk*. Northern Ireland's James Nesbitt has become almost ubiquitous on British TV after achieving fame in the TV series *Cold Feet* and *Murphy's Law*, and made the transition to the big screen in 2005 with a small part in Woody Allen's *Match Point*.

Liam Neeson (for *Schindler's List*) and Daniel Day-Lewis and Brenda Fricker (for *My Left Foot*) have won Oscars; Belfast-born Kenneth Branagh's career has invited comparisons with Laurence Olivier's; Gabriel Byrne starred in a series of hits *(The Usual Suspects, Man in the Iron Mask)*; and Navan man Pierce Brosnan scored the coveted James Bond role. Other Irish actors who achieved success in the same period include Aidan Quinn *(Legends of the Fall)*, Stephen Rea *(The Crying Game)* and Colm Meaney *(The Commitments)*. They have followed in the footsteps

John McGahern's simple, economical prose *Amongst Women* centres on well drawn, complex yet familiar characters, in this case a west-of-Ireland family in the social aftermath of the War of Independence.

The Pulitzer Prize–winning *Angela's Ashes* by Frank McCourt tells the relentlessly bleak autobiographical story of the author's poverty-stricken Limerick childhood in the Depression of the 1930s, and has been made into a major film by Alan Parker.

John Boorman's film *The General* (1998) about Dublin's most notorious crime boss is both horrific and uneasily funny in its portrayal of the mindless brutality and childlike humour of Martin Cahill.

of the likes of Richard Harris *(The Guns of Navarone, The Field)*, Peter O'Toole *(Lawrence of Arabia)* and Milo O'Shea *(Barbarella)*.

To this crop of acting talent can be added the screenwriter and director Neil Jordan, whose impressive body of work includes *Mona Lisa* (1986), *Interview with the Vampire* (1994), *The Butcher Boy* (1998) and *The Good Thief* (2003). *The Crying Game* (1992), for which Jordan won an Oscar for best screenplay, is perhaps the most intriguing commercial film to feature the IRA. Jordan's powerful *Michael Collins* (1996) stars Liam Neeson and follows the life of Collins from the Easter Rising to the Civil War and his death in 1922 at the hands of his former comrades.

Other important film-makers are producer Noel Pearson and director Jim Sheridan, who worked together on *My Left Foot* (1989) and *The Field* (1990). *My Left Foot* told the true story of Dublin writer Christy Brown, who was crippled with cerebral palsy. Jim Sheridan's *In the Name of the Father* (1993) starred Daniel Day-Lewis as Gerry Conlon and Emma Thompson as his lawyer. It tells the story of the arrest and conviction of the Guildford Four for a pub bombing in England, then of the struggle to clear their names. Jim Sheridan also wrote the screenplay for Mike Newell's *Into the West* (1993), a romantic story of two children and a mythical white horse.

Pat O'Connor's credits as film director include Bernard MacLaverty's *Cal* (1984) and Maeve Binchy's *Circle of Friends* (1994). Dubliner Damien O'Donnell's follow up to *East is East*, was *Heartlands* (2003), the empathetic story of a simple lad who breaks the mould of his northern English small town existence to win back his girlfriend.

Other young directors to watch out for are Kirsten Sheridan (*August Rush*, starring Liv Tyler and Robin Williams, due for release in 2006) and Robert Quinn (*Breakfast on Pluto*, 2005, starring Liam Neeson, Stephen Rea and Brendan Gleeson).

Inevitably, with the arrival of digital TV, terrestrial channels have had to work much harder to maintain audiences. Not that you'd notice though, watching Irish TV. TG4 aside, Irish TV is mainly derivative of British and American programming and reflects commercial rather than critical interests. The current taste for reality TV shows hasn't escaped Irish producers and programmes such as *Treasure Island*, *Who Wants to be a Millionaire* and *Big Brother* have been franchised or reproduced in a thinly veiled guise on Irish channels. The hugely successful, absurd comedy drama series *Father Ted*, featuring the ridiculous exploits of two parish priests, was famously turned down by RTE before being commissioned in Britain.

For a taste of Irish life, tune into the world's longest-running chat show, the *Late Late Show*, now hosted by Pat Kenny and on the go since 1962. It has become more a light-entertainment promotional vehicle than a serious discussion forum in recent years, but still includes plenty of worthwhile material. It is now being challenged by *Tubridy Tonight*, presented by the up-and-coming Ryan Tubridy, which overtook the *Late Late Show* in the ratings in 2005.

Music

Rock band U2 may be Ireland's biggest musical export, but when people talk about Irish music they are generally referring to an older, more intimate style of traditional or folk music. For the visitor, the joy of Irish music lies in its sheer accessibility. The biggest names may play the same major venues as the rock stars, but almost every town and village seems to have a pub renowned for its music where you can show up and find a session in progress, or even join in if you feel so inclined.

Paddy Breathnach's hilarious road movie *I Went Down* (1998) follows the capers of two unlikely petty criminals sent on a mission by a low-rent loan shark.

John Crowley's pacey, well-scripted drama *Intermission* (2003) follows a host of eccentric characters in pursuit of love, starring Colin Farrell, Colm Meaney and Ger Ryan.

The adventure only begins when youngster Tony accidentally bumps off his girlfriend and tries to bury the evidence in Robert Quinn's stylish and accomplished debut thriller *Dead Bodies* (2003).

Until around 1700, the harp was the most important instrument in Irish music. Traditionally, music was performed as a background to dancing, so the 17th-century penal laws did nothing to help by banning all expressions of traditional culture, including dancing. Music was forced underground, which goes some way towards explaining the homely feel of much Irish music today.

In the 1960s, Seán O'Riada (1931–71) of Cork set up Ceoltóirí Chualann, a band featuring a fiddle, flute, accordion, bodhrán and uilleann pipes, and began to perform music to listen to rather than for dancing. When his band performed at the Gaiety Theatre in Dublin, it gave a whole new credibility to traditional music. Members of the band went on to form the Chieftains, who still play an important role in bringing Irish music to an international audience.

With added vocals come bands such as the Dubliners with their notorious drinking songs; the Wolfe Tones, who've been described as 'the rabble end of the rebel song tradition'; and the Fureys. Younger groups such as Clannad, Altan, Dervish and Nomos espouse a quieter, more mystical style of singing, while Kíla stretches the boundaries by combining traditional music with reggae, Eastern and New-Age influences.

Hot Press (www.hotpress .com) is a fortnightly magazine featuring local and international music interviews and listings.

Christy Moore is the most prominent of the contemporary singer-songwriters playing in a broadly traditional idiom. He has been performing since the 1960s, and although a pivotal member of the influential bands Planxty and Moving Hearts, he's probably best known for his solo albums.

The unique Van Morrison, native of Belfast, seems to have been going for ever. In the 1960s he was lead singer with Them, whose anthem 'Gloria' was a Beatles-era classic. Appealing to younger audiences, Paddy Casey has been compared to David Gray for his melodic arrangements and intelligent lyrics. Songwriter Mark Geary, returned from New York, has been wowing audiences with his bittersweet tunes. Dublin-based soul-folk-rockers the Frames have a phenomenally loyal following, as do '60s-American-pop soundalikes the Thrills.

Female singer-songwriters have an equally strong following. The mystical voice of Donegal's Enya, formerly of Clannad, has huge popular appeal internationally. Among the best-known contemporary female singers to look out for are Mary Black, smoky-voiced Mary Coughlan and wild melodion-player Sharon Shannon. Gemma Hayes and Nina

---

TEN BEST IRISH ALBUMS – OUR CHOICE

- *Astral Weeks* (Van Morrison) – one of the seminal records of the 1960s.
- *Music In Mouth* (Bell X1) – acclaimed second album from Ireland's top indie rock band.
- *All That You Can't Leave Behind* (U2) – the album that saw the band back in genuine form after a few overblown albums.
- *24 Star Hotel* (Mundy) – this melodic rocker checks in with some finger-clickingly catchy tunes.
- *Jailbreak* (Thin Lizzy) – famed 1976 album featuring Dublin ditty 'The Boys Are Back in Town'.
- *The Lion and the Cobra* (Sinead O'Connor) – chilling debut with poptastic single 'Mandinka'.
- *The Last Man In Europe* (The Blades) – the first and best album from Dublin's most underrated band.
- *Dance The Devil* (The Frames) – a work of art, no less.
- *Undertones: Greatest Hits* (Undertones) – so many short sharp classics; why not hear them all?
- *Live in Europe* (Rory Gallagher) – rocking 1972 album.

Hynes are two younger, more pop-driven songwriters. And no account of contemporary Irish music would be complete without reference to the popularity of country music singer and boy-next-door Daniel O'Donnell, with huge album sales under his belt.

Ireland's phenomenal success rate in the Eurovision Song Contest is not to be sniffed at either. First in a long line to receive the honour was a fresh-faced, 16-year-old Dana from Derry in 1970 with 'All Kinds of Everything', followed by Johnny Logan (twice, in 1980 and 1987). Ireland won it for three consecutive years from 1992 to 1994, and again in 1996, and came second on four other occasions. Since the turn of the millennium, however, Ireland's Eurovision singers have crashed and burned – in 2005 they did not even qualify for the finals, a cause of much soul-searching in the popular media.

During the 1960s when America and Britain were producing revolutionary acts like the Doors, the Beatles, Led Zeppelin and the Rolling Stones, Ireland had its own genre of popular music – the showband. Dickie Rock, Brendan Boyer and the Big Eight, and the Miami Showband gigged around the country playing covers of Top 40 hits.

It wasn't until the late 1960s and 1970s that Rory Gallagher's band Taste and Phil Lynott's Thin Lizzy put Ireland on the map.

The punk explosion of 1976 saw bands like The Boomtown Rats, fronted by an angry but eloquent Bob Geldof, emerge with hugely successful singles 'Rat Trap' and 'I Don't Like Mondays'.

Foggy Notions is a visually striking, subversive magazine catering to eclectic music tastes.

In Northern Ireland, bands such as the Undertones and Stiff Little Fingers were spearheading the musical anarchy. The Undertones' radio-friendly 'Teenage Kicks' stands out as an all-time classic single of that era.

In 1978 a group of friends from the Dublin suburb of Artane – Bono, The Edge, Adam Clayton and Larry Mullen Jr – formed The Hype, later known as U2. Their debut album *Boy* in 1980 was the first in a series of classic albums that decade. *War*, *The Unforgettable Fire* and *The Joshua Tree* followed as the band went from strength to strength. With Edge's idiosyncratic guitar playing, Clayton's and Mullen's driving rhythm section and Bono's fervent, emotive lyrics and vocal range, U2 were always primed to fill stadiums with their rock anthems. U2's ability to reinvent themselves, from the overblown theatrics of 1993's *Zooropa* to the self-deprecating but no less indulgent *Popmart* tour of 1997, has been a factor in their enduring across-the-board popularity.

In the early 1980s, London-based Irish rabble-rousers Pogue Mahone (the name is phonetically Gaelic for 'kiss my arse') emerged. After a ban by the BBC the more tastefully rechristened Pogues, under the stewardship of singer Shane McGowan, evolved but McGowan's drunken on- and off-stage antics often overshadowed his genuine, empathetic and lucid song-writing talent.

The demise of guitar-based rock music in the early 1990s paved the way for the emergence of boy bands, a formula with which Ireland has had unmitigated success. First off the school bus in 1993 was Boyzone, an innocuous five-piece from Dublin, headed by Ronan Keating. The combination of good-looks and tried and tested hits to cover was a sure-fire winner. Their first 12 singles reached the Top 5 in Britain and, with a solid fan base of adoring prepubescents, they went the way of all boy bands and split up. Boyzone's manager Louis Walsh created a second lucrative prodigy, Westlife, who have topped the Beatles' record with seven consecutive No 1 hits in the UK. Sultry half-Zambian diva Samantha Mumba is also on Walsh's books and has been more critically successful with her singles, Bowie-sampled 'Body II Body' and 'Gotta Tell You'. Easy on the eyes and ears, The Corrs, a sisters and brother act from Dundalk, combine a touch of the traditional with American pop rhythms and harmonies.

The London-based baroque pop act Divine Comedy, fronted by Derry-born composer and lyricist Neil Hannon, blends jazz, classical and pop influences with tongue-in-cheek lyrics. They've had a string of radio-friendly singles such as 'Generation Sex', and the long-awaited 2004 album *Absent Friends* was widely regarded as a return to form for Hannon following a change of musical direction.

One of the biggest hits of recent years was singer-songwriter Damien Rice's debut album *O*, which has sold more than a million copies since its release in 2003 (it received a boost when one of the tracks appeared in the hit movie *Closer*). His moody, melancholic songs and intense, throaty vocals have brought inevitable comparisons with Leonard Cohen and Tom Waits, and a second album is eagerly awaited. The remaining members of Rice's former band Juniper re-grouped as indie rockers Bell X1, and have also gathered a huge following with their first two albums *Neither Am I* and *Music In Mouth* – the latter has been acclaimed as the best album to come out of Ireland in many years.

Other successful debut albums of recent years include *Future Kings of Spain* by the indie rock band of the same name, and the also-eponymous *Hal*, a feast of cheerful and melodic pop that's guaranteed to put a smile on anyone's face.

Architecture

Ireland is packed with prehistoric graves, ruined monasteries, crumbling fortresses and many other solid reminders of its long, often dramatic, history. The principal surviving structures from Stone Age times are the graves and monuments people built for the dead, usually grouped under the heading of megalithic (great stone) tombs. Among the most easily recognisable megalithic tombs are dolmens, massive three-legged structures rather like giant stone stools, most of which are 4000 to 5000 years old. Good examples are the Poulnabrone Dolmen (p383) in the Burren and Browne's Hill Dolmen (p341) near Carlow town.

Passage graves such as Newgrange and Knowth (p525) in Meath are huge mounds with narrow stone-walled passages leading to burial chambers. These chambers are enriched with spiral and chevron symbols and have an opening through which the rising sun penetrates on the winter or summer solstice, thus acting as a giant celestial calendar.

The Irish names for forts – *dun*, *rath*, *caiseal/cashel* and *caher* – have ended up in the names of countless towns and villages. The Irish countryside is peppered with the remains of over 30,000 of them. The earliest known examples date from the Bronze Age, most commonly the ring fort, with circular earth-and-stone banks, topped by a wooden palisade fence to keep out intruders, and surrounded on the outside by a moat-like ditch. Outside Clonakilty in County Cork, the ring fort at Lisnagun (Lios na gCon) has been reconstructed to give some idea of its original appearance (see p228).

Some forts were constructed entirely of stone; the Iron Age fort of Dún Aengus on Inishmór (p401; the largest of the Aran Islands) is a superb example.

After Christianity arrived in Ireland in the 5th century, the first monasteries were built. The early stone churches were often very simple, some roofed with timber, such as the 6th-century Teampall Bheanáin (Church

'The Irish countryside is peppered with the remains of over 30,000 forts'

of St Benen) on Inishmór of the Aran Islands, or built completely of stone, such as the 8th-century Gallarus Oratory (p287) on the Dingle Peninsula. Early hermitages include the small beehive huts and buildings on the summit of Skellig Michael (p263) off County Kerry.

As the monasteries grew in size and stature, so did the architecture. The 12th-century cathedral at Glendalough (p157) and the 10th- to 15th-century cathedral at Clonmacnoise (p351) are good examples, although they're tiny compared with European medieval cathedrals.

Round towers have become symbols of Ireland. These tall, stone, needle-like structures were built largely as lookout posts and refuges in the event of Viking attacks in the late 9th or early 10th centuries. Of the 120 thought to have originally existed, around 20 survive intact; the best examples can be seen at Cashel (p303), Glendalough (p158) and Devenish Island (p663).

With the Normans' arrival in Ireland in 1169, came the Gothic style of architecture, characterised by tall vaulted windows and soaring V-shaped arches. Fine examples of this can be seen in the 1172 Christ Church Cathedral in Dublin (see p98) and the 13th-century St Canice's Cathedral in Kilkenny (see p316).

Authentic, traditional Irish thatched cottages were built of limestone or clay to suit the elements, but weren't durable and have become rare, the tradition dying out around the middle of the 20th century.

In Georgian times, Dublin became one of the architectural glories of Europe, with simple, beautifully built Georgian terraces of red brick, with delicate glass fanlights over large, elegant, curved doorways. From the 1960s Dublin's Georgian heritage suffered badly but you can still see fine examples around Merrion Square (p97).

The marginal note:

The haunting and beautiful novel *The Story of Lucy Gault* by William Trevor, dubbed the Irish Chekhov, tells of a young girl who, believed to be dead, is brought up by a caretaker at the end of the Ascendancy years.

The Anglo-Irish Ascendancy built country houses such as the 1722 Castletown House (p332) near Celbridge, the 1741 Russborough House (p162) near Blessington and Castle Coole (p662), which are all excellent examples of the Palladian style, with their regularity and classical correctness. Prolific German architect Richard Cassels (also known as Richard Castle) came to Ireland in 1728 and designed many landmark buildings including Powerscourt House (p154) in County Wicklow and Leinster House (p95; home to Dáil Éireann, the Irish government) in Dublin.

Ireland has little modern architecture of note. For much of the 20th century the pace of change was slow, and it wasn't until the construction of Dublin's Busáras Station in the 1950s that modernity began to really express itself. It was designed by Michael Scott, who was to have an influence on architects in Ireland for the next two decades. The poorly regulated building boom of the 1960s and 1970s, however, paid little attention to the country's architectural heritage and destroyed more than it created. From that period Paul Koralek's 1967 brutalist-style Berkeley Library in Trinity College, Dublin, has been hailed as Ireland's best example of modern architecture.

Since the 1980s more care has been given to architectural heritage and context, the best example of which has been the redevelopment of Dublin's previously near-derelict Temple Bar area (p92). Ireland's recent boom at the turn of the last century spawned a huge growth of building work around Dublin of mixed quality. Some good examples in the Docklands area include the imposing Financial Services Centre and Custom House Square. The Millennium Wing of the National Gallery (p94) opened the same year and is another terrific example of modern civic architecture with its sculpted Portland stone façade and tall, light-filled atrium. The new James Joyce Bridge over Dublin's River Liffey, built in 2003, was designed by celebrated Spanish architect Santiago Calatrava. Probably the most controversial piece of modern architecture to be unveiled in recent years has been the Monument of Light (p102; rechristened simply The Spire) on Dublin's O'Connell St. At seven times the height of the GPO (120m in total), the brushed steel hollow cone was always going to face opposition, but since its unveiling in spring 2003, the awe-inspiring structure and beautifully reflective surface have won over all but a few hardened cynics.

Visual Arts

Ireland's painting doesn't receive the kind of recognition that its literature and music do. Nevertheless, painting in Ireland has a long tradition dating back to the illuminated manuscripts of the early Christian period, most notably the Book of Kells.

The National Gallery (p94) has an extensive Irish School collection, much of it chronicling the people and pursuits of the Anglo-Irish aristocracy.

Like other European artists of the 18th century, Roderic O'Conor featured portraits and landscapes in his work. His post-impressionist style stood out for its vivid use of colour and sturdy brush strokes. James Malton captured 18th-century Dublin in a series of line drawings and paintings.

In the 19th century there was still no hint of Ireland's political and social problems in the work of its major artists. The most prominent landscape painter was James Arthur O'Connor, while Belfast-born Sir John Lavery became one of London's most celebrated portrait artists.

Just as WB Yeats played a seminal role in the Celtic literary revival, his younger brother, Jack Butler Yeats (1871–1957), inspired an artistic surge of creativity in the early 20th century, taking Celtic mythology and Irish life as his subjects. (Their father, John Butler Yeats, had also been a noted portrait painter.) William John Leech (1881–1961) was fascinated by changing light, an affection reflected in his expressionistic landscapes and flower paintings. Born to English parents in Dublin, Francis Bacon (1909–92) emerged as one of the most powerful figurative artists of the 20th century with his violent depictions of distorted human bodies.

The pioneering work of Irish cubist painter Mainie Jellett (1897–1944) and her friend, modernist stained-glass artist Evie Hone (1894–1955), had an influence on later modernists Barrie Cooke (born 1931) and Camille Souter (born 1929). Together with Louis Le Brocquy (born 1916), Jellett and Hone set up the Irish Exhibition of Living Art in 1943 to foster the work of non-academic artists. Estella Solomons (1882–1968) trained under William Orpen and Walter Osborne in Dublin and was a noted portrait and landscape painter. The rural idyll of the west of Ireland was also a theme of Paul Henry's (1876–1958) landscapes. In the 1950s and 1960s, a school of naïve artists including James Dixon appeared on Tory Island, off Donegal.

Contemporary artists to watch out for include Nick Miller, New York–based Sean Scully and Fionnuala Ní Chíosain.

Experimental photographer Clare Langan's work has gained international recognition with her trademark ethereal images of elemental landscapes.

Murals have been an important way of documenting Ireland's more recent political history. Powerful political murals can be seen in West Belfast (p565) and Derry (see the boxed text, p628).

Reading In the Dark by Seamus Deane is thoughtful prose (the Guardian Fiction Prize winner) and recounts a young boy's struggles to unravel the truth of his own history growing up in the Troubles of Belfast.

Theatre & Dance

Dublin and Belfast are the main centres, but most sizable towns, such as Cork, Derry, Donegal, Limerick and Galway, have their own theatres. Ireland has a theatrical history almost as long as its literary one. Dublin's first theatre was founded in Werburgh St in 1637, although it was closed only four years later by the Puritans. Another theatre, named the Smock Alley Playhouse or Theatre Royal, opened in 1661 and continued to stage plays for more than a century. The literary revival of the late 19th century resulted in the establishment of Dublin's Abbey Theatre (p142), now Ireland's national theatre. Its role is to present works by historical greats such as WB Yeats, George Bernard Shaw (1856–1950), JM Synge (1871–1909) and Sean O'Casey (1880–1964), as well as to promote modern Irish dramatists. Also in Dublin, the Gate Theatre (p142) produces classics and comedies, while the Gaiety and Olympia Theatres (p142) present a range of productions, as does the Grand Opera House (p561) in Belfast. Dublin's Project Arts Centre (p143) offers a more experimental programme.

One of the most outstanding playwrights of the last two decades is Frank McGuinness (born 1956), who has had a prolific output since the 1970s. His plays, such as *The Carthaginians*, explore the consequences of 1972's Bloody Sunday on the people of Derry. Young London-Irish playwright Martin McDonagh (born 1971) uses the darker side of a romantic rural Irish idyll as his inspiration. Among his work, *The Leenane Trilogy* has been performed by Britain's National Theatre and on Broadway, where he has won a number of Tony Awards. *Dancing at Lughnasa* by Brian Friel (born 1929) was a great success on Broadway and in London and has been made into a film.

Other talented young playwrights to watch out for include Dubliner Conor McPherson (whose acclaimed play *The Weir* was commissioned by the Royal Court), who also scripted three Irish films, Donal O'Kelly (*Catalpa*) and Enda Walsh (*Disco Pigs*).

The work of playwright and poet Damian Gorman (born 1962) has received considerable praise. *Broken Nails*, his first play, received four Ulster Theatre awards. Mark O'Rowe (who also wrote the film script *Intermission*) received commendable reviews for his graphically violent and controversial play *Crestfall* in 2003 at the Gate.

The most important form of dance in Ireland is traditional Irish dancing, performed communally at céilidhs, often in an impromptu format and always accompanied by a traditional Irish band. Dances include the hornpipe, jig and reel. Irish dancing has received international attention and success through shows such as *Riverdance* and its offshoots, and while this glamorised style of dance is only loosely based on traditional dancing, it has popularised the real art and given a new lease of life to the moribund Irish dancing schools around the country.

Ireland doesn't have a national dance school, but there are a number of schools and companies around the country teaching and performing ballet and modern dance. The Dance Theatre of Ireland and the Irish Modern Dance Theatre are based in Dublin, while the Firkin Crane Centre in Cork is Ireland's only venue devoted solely to dance.

Double Drink Story by Caitlin Thomas (nee MacNamara), who subjugated her impulse to write under the weight of husband Dylan's celebrity and her own addictions, is an eloquent, self-deprecating account of their debaucherous life, love-hate relationship and the burden of creativity, making a brilliant literary memoir.

Environment

THE LAND

In the literature, songs and paintings of Ireland it is clear that the Irish landscape exerts a powerful sway on Irish souls. The Irish who left, especially, have always spread this notion that the old sod was something worth pining for, and visitors still anticipate experiencing this land's subtle influence on perception and mood. Once you've travelled the country, you can't help but agree that the vibrant greenness of gentle hills, the fearsome violence of jagged coasts and the sombre light of so many cloudy days is an integral part of experiencing Ireland.

The entire island stretches a mere 486km north to south and 275km east to west, so Ireland's impressive topographical variety may come as a surprise. The countryside does indeed have an abundance of the expected

Of the nine counties that originally comprised the province of Ulster, six are now part of Northern Ireland while three are part of the Republic.

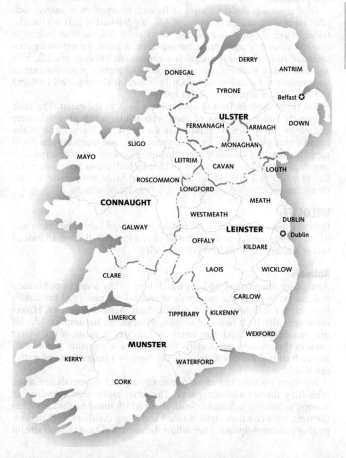

DERRY
ANTRIM
DONEGAL
TYRONE
Belfast ✪
ULSTER
FERMANAGH
ARMAGH
DOWN
SLIGO
MONAGHAN
MAYO
LEITRIM
CAVAN
LOUTH
ROSCOMMON
LONGFORD
CONNAUGHT
MEATH
WESTMEATH
GALWAY
DUBLIN
LEINSTER
✪ Dublin
OFFALY
KILDARE
LAOIS
WICKLOW
CLARE
CARLOW
KILKENNY
LIMERICK
TIPPERARY
WEXFORD
MUNSTER
KERRY
WATERFORD
CORK

greenery. Grass grows nearly everywhere in Ireland, but there are notable exceptions, particularly around the dramatic coasts.

Massive rocky outcrops like the Burren (p375), in County Clare, are for the most part inhospitable to clover, and although even there the green stuff does sprout up in enough patches for sheep and goats to graze on, these vast, otherworldly landscapes are mostly grey and bleak. Nearby, the dramatic Cliffs of Moher (p375) are a sheer drop into the thundering surf below. Similarly, there is no preparing for the extraordinary hexagonal stone columns of the Giant's Causeway (p644) in County Antrim. Sand dunes buffer many of the more gentle stretches of coast.

The boglands, which once covered one-fifth of the island, are more of a whiskey hue than green. Much of the bogs have been dug up for peat, which traditionally was burned for heat, but travellers will likely encounter a bog in County Kildare's Bog of Allen (p332) or along Connemara's bog road (p411). The west coast owes much of its ruggedness to the rock that lies so close to the surface. Much of this rock has been dug up, to create tillable soil, and converted into stone walls that divide tiny paddocks.

An Taisce, the National Trust for Ireland, is a good source of information on all facets of Ireland's environment. See www.antaisce.org.

Smaller islands dot the shores of Ireland, many of them barren rock piles supporting unique ecosystems – Skellig Michael (p263) is a breathtakingly jagged island just off the Kerry coast. The west of Ireland is also the country's most mountainous area. Almost the entire western seaboard from Cork to Donegal is a continuous bulwark of cliffs, hills and mountains, with few safe anchorages. The highest mountains are in the southwest; the tallest mountain in Ireland is Carrantuohil (1041m) in Kerry's MacGillycuddy's Reeks (p258).

But topography in Ireland always leads back to the green. The Irish frequently lament the loss of their woodlands, much of which were cleared by the British to build ships for the Royal Navy. Little of the island's once plentiful oak forest survives today, and much of what you'll see is the result of relatively recent planting. Instead, the countryside is largely comprised of green fields divided by hedgerows and stone walls. Use of this land is divided between cultivated fields and pasture for cattle and sheep.

WILDLIFE

To get information from the Irish Wildlife Trust see www.iwt.ie.

Ireland's flora and fauna is, by and large, shy and subtle, but as in any island environment, travellers who set out on foot will discover an Ireland that is resplendent with interesting species.

Animals

Apart from the fox and badger, which tend to shy away from humans and are rarely seen, the mammals of Ireland are mostly of the ankle-high 'critter' category, such a rabbits, hedgehogs and shrews. Hikers often spot the Irish hare, or at least glimpse the blazing-fast blur of one running away. Red deer roam the hillsides in many of the wilder parts of the country, particularly the Wicklow Mountains, and in Killarney National Park, which holds the country's largest herd of native red deer.

An illustrated pocket guide called The Animals of Ireland by Gordon D'Arcy is a handy, inexpensive introduction.

For most visitors, the most commonly sighted mammals are those inhabiting the sea and waterways. The otter, rarely seen elsewhere in Europe, is thriving in Ireland. Seals, about which many myths are told in the west, are a common sight in rivers and along the shore. Perhaps surprisingly, so are dolphins. They follow the warm waters of the gulf stream towards Ireland, and some colonise the coast of Ireland year round, frequently swimming into the bays and inlets off the western coast.

Many travellers visit Ireland specifically for the birding. Ireland's westerly location on the fringe of Europe makes it an ideal stopover point for birds migrating from North America and the Arctic. In autumn the southern counties become temporary home to the American waders (mainly sandpipers and plovers) and warblers. Migrants from Africa, such as shearwaters, petrels and auks, begin to arrive in spring in the southwestern counties.

The reasonably rare corncrake, which migrates from Africa, can be found in the western counties, in Donegal and around the Shannon Callows, and on islands such as Inishbofin in Galway. In late spring and early summer, the rugged coastlines, particularly cliff areas and islands, become a haven for breeding seabirds, mainly gannet, kittiwake, Manx shearwater, fulmar, cormorant and heron. Puffins, resembling penguins with their tuxedo colour scheme, nest in large colonies on coastal cliffs.

Irish Birds by David Cabot is a pocket guide that describes birds and their habitats and outlines the best places for serious bird-watching.

The lakes and low-lying wetlands attract large numbers of Arctic and northern European waterfowl and waders such as whooper swans, lapwing, barnacle geese, white-fronted geese and golden plover. The important Wexford Wildfowl Reserve (p178) holds half the world's population of Greenland white-fronted geese, and little tern breed on the beach there, protected by the dunes. Also found during the winter are teal, redshank and curlew. The main migration periods are April to May and September to October.

The magnificent peregrine falcon has been making something of a recovery and can be found nesting on cliffs in Wicklow and elsewhere. In 2001, a number of golden eagle chicks from Scotland were released into Glenveagh National Park in Donegal in an effort to reintroduce the species. By 2005, a pair of golden eagles had laid an egg in the park, and although the egg did not hatch (the mother is believed to have been too young) it was a hopeful omen for the species.

Plants

If casually viewing the Irish countryside from the window of a bus or car, most of what you'll see is non-native tree species. Only 1% of the island's native oak forest survives, making Ireland the least wooded country in Europe. However, on closer inspection (and with a good plant guide), you'll discover that the range of surviving plant species is larger here than in many other European countries, thanks in part to the comparatively late arrival of agriculture.

There are remnants of the original oak forest in Killarney National Park and in southern Wicklow near Shillelagh. Far more common are the pine plantations that look so unnatural and regimented in the Irish countryside. Hedgerows, planted to divide fields and delineate land boundaries throughout Ireland, actually host many of the native plant species that once thrived in the oak forests – it's an intriguing example of nature reasserting itself.

The Burren in County Clare was covered in light woodland before the early settlers arrived. Now the area is almost all bare rock, but many of the original plants live on, a remarkable mixture of Mediterranean, alpine and arctic species.

In 1821 the body of an Iron Age man was found in a bog in Galway with his cape, shoes and beard still intact.

The bogs of Ireland are home to a unique flora adapted to wet, acidic, nutrient-poor conditions and whose survival is threatened by the depletion of bogs for energy use. Sphagnum moss is the key bog plant and is joined by plants such as bog rosemary, bog cotton, black-beaked sedge (whose spindly stem grows up to 30cm high) and various types of heather and lichen. Carnivorous plants also thrive, such as the sundew, whose sticky tentacles trap insects, and bladderwort whose tiny explosive bladders trap aquatic animals in bog pools.

NATIONAL PARKS

Ireland has five national parks: the Burren (p375), Connemara (p406), Glenveagh (p502), Killarney (p256) and Wicklow Mountains (p153). These have been developed to protect, preserve and make accessible areas of significant natural heritage. The parks open year round and each has its own information office.

Forests & Forest Parks

Coillte Teoranta (Irish Forestry Board; ☎ 01-661 5666; www.coillte.ie; Leeson Lane, Dublin) administers about 4000 sq km of forested land, which includes designated picnic areas and 12 forest parks. These parks open year round and have a range of wildlife and habitats. Some also have chalets and/or caravan parks, shops, cafés and play areas for children.

National Nature Reserves

For information on parks, gardens, monuments and inland waterways see www.heritageireland.ie.

There are 66 state-owned and 10 privately owned National Nature Reserves (NNRs) in the Republic, represented by Dúchas (the government department in charge of parks, monuments and gardens). In Northern Ireland there are over 40 NNRs, which are leased or owned by the Department of the Environment. These reserves are defined as areas of importance for their special flora, fauna or geology and include the Giant's Causeway (p644) and Glenariff Glen (p651) in Antrim and North Strangford Lough (p603) in County Down. More information is available from the **Environment & Heritage Service** (☎ 028-9054 6533; Commonwealth House, 35 Castle St, Belfast).

ENVIRONMENTAL ISSUES
Urbanisation

Look for *Reading the Irish Landscape* by Frank Mitchell and Michael Ryan to catch up on Ireland's geology, archaeology, urban growth, agriculture and afforestation.

The economic progress seen in Ireland over the past two decades has taken a visible bite out of the island's cherished greenery. Tract homes are popping up around cities and towns throughout the country, bringing with them environmental hazards such as increased waste and sewage. With more people living in these new bedroom communities comes an increase in commute traffic, which of course contributes to air and noise pollution. In general, the Irish have been improving roads and widening them, increasing the amount of leisure-related traffic.

Agriculture

In the past, Ireland experienced limited industrialisation compared to other developed countries, leaving the beautiful Irish countryside mostly untouched. However, in the 1970s, the EU encouraged intensive, specialised farming and the use of pesticides and chemical fertilisers. These caused serious pollution and land degradation in areas such as the Burren in County Clare. More recently, the EU and the Irish government have promoted environmental protection, less-intensive farming methods and the adoption of alternative practices or crops. The result has been a reduction in pollution, though it continues to occur in rivers and lakes.

In the same period the trend towards larger farms led to the destruction of many ring forts and stone walls.

Beaches

Unfortunately a number of Irish beaches suffer from pollution and despite EU directives on waste management, plastic containers and other landfill debris have found their way onto beaches. As part of a scheme to improve the situation, clean beaches are awarded the EU Blue Flag and encouragingly in 2005, 78 beaches in Ireland were awarded a Blue Flag. An Taisce (National Trust for Ireland) keeps a list of these, or you can check them on www.blueflag.org.

Food & Drink

Generations of travellers who visited these shores during bleaker times typically mused that Irish food is great until it's cooked. They advised getting drunk before eating, or complained that a meal was more a flavourless penance rather than a pleasurable repast, and so on. Those days are over.

A culinary renaissance has taken place, and the Irish are now enjoying the fine cuisine that they have long deserved. For the island has always been blessed with a wealth of staples and specialities, with meat, seafood and dairy produce the envy of the world. At the twilight of the 20th century a new wave of cooks began producing what is sometimes promoted as 'New Irish Cuisine'.

In truth, the new cuisine is more a confident return to the traditional practice of combining simple cooking techniques with the finest local ingredients. Many of the new chefs merely strive to offer their patrons the sort of meals that have always been taken for granted on well-run Irish farms. Whatever you want to call it, it has aroused the nation's taste buds.

But gastronomes have more than rediscovered traditions to thank. The Irish diners of today – generally a more affluent and worldly bunch than their forebears – have become more discerning and adventurous. To meet their demands, restaurants are continually springing up on city streets and in old country homes with menus spruced up with all sorts of international ingredients. Ethnic restaurants that once were rare even in Dublin can now be found all over the country.

Of course, you can still find leathery meat, shrivelled fish and overcooked vegetables, if that's what you're looking for. But why punish yourself, when hearty fare that will make your head spin and your palate sing is so readily available?

Visit www.ravensgard.org/prdunham/irishfood.html for a highly readable and complete history of Irish cuisine, with fascinating chapters such as 'The Most Widely Used Cooking Methods in Pre-Potato Ireland' and 'Collecting the Blood for Pudding Making'.

STAPLES & SPECIALITIES
Potatoes

It's a wonder the Irish retain their good humour amid the perpetual potato-baiting they endure. But, despite the stereotyping, and however much we'd like to disprove it, potatoes are still paramount here and you will see lots of them on your travels. The mashed potato dishes colcannon and champ (with cabbage and spring onion respectively) are two of the tastiest potato recipes in the country.

The Potato Year by Lucy Madden and Peter Bland is an intriguing cookbook (if you like spuds) with 365 traditional and novel ways to cook the potato; it has titbits of folklore and local history.

Meat & Seafood

Irish meals are usually meat based, with beef, lamb and pork common options. Seafood, long neglected, is finding a place on the table in Irish homes. It's widely available in restaurants and is often excellent, especially in the west. Oysters, trout and salmon are delicious, particularly if they're direct from the sea or a river rather than a fish farm. The famous Dublin Bay Prawn isn't actually a prawn, but a lobster, sometimes called langoustine. At its best, the Dublin Bay Prawn is superlative, but it is priced accordingly. If you're going to splurge, do so here – but make sure you choose live Dublin Bay Prawns because once these fellas die, they quickly lose their flavour.

More than 100,000 oysters are consumed each year at the Galway International Oyster Festival (p394).

Cheese

One of the most exciting culinary developments in recent decades has been the emergence of local cheese making, and Ireland's farmhouse cheeses have won many awards and plaudits around the world and feature on platters in some of Europe's top restaurants. Specialist producers abound, particularly in Munster (the southern counties), and you should check out notables like Ardrahan, Durrus and Gubbeen from Cork and Tipperary's Cashel Blue.

Bread

The most famous Irish bread, and one of the signature tastes of Ireland, is soda bread. Irish flour is so soft and doesn't take well to yeast as a raising agent, so Irish bakers of the 19th century began to leavened their bread with soda (bicarbonate of soda). Combined with buttermilk, it makes a superbly light-textured and tasty bread.

The Fry

Perhaps the most feared Irish speciality is the traditional fry – the heart attack on a plate that is the second part of so many B&B deals. In spite of the hysterical health fears, the fry is still one of the most common traditional meals in the country. Who can say no to a plate of fried bacon, sausages, black pudding, white pudding, eggs and tomatoes? For the famous Ulster fry, common throughout the North, simply add fadge (potato bread).

DRINKS
Nonalcoholic Drinks
TEA

The Irish drink more tea, per capita, than any other nation in the world and you'll be offered a cup of it as soon as you cross the threshold of any Irish home. It's a leveller and an icebreaker, and an appreciation for 'at least a cup in your hand' is your passport to conviviality here. Preferred blends are very strong, and nothing like the namby-pamby versions that pass for Irish breakfast tea elsewhere.

RED LEMONADE

This product, basically a regular glass of lemonade with colouring, has been produced in Ireland since the end of the 19th century and is still made to virtually the same recipe today. Always more popular in the Republic than the North, it is still a favourite for adults and children alike. It is commonly used as a mixer with brandy and rye whiskeys such as Canadian Club and Southern Comfort.

Alcoholic Drinks

Drinking in Ireland is no mere social activity: it's the foundation on which Irish culture is built. Along with its wonderful drinks, this fact helps to explain why through centuries of poverty and oppression the Irish always retained their reputation for unrivalled hospitality and good humour.

STOUT

Of all Ireland's drinks, the 'black stuff' is the most celebrated. It is simply a way of life in Ireland, as much a part of the culture as the weather, though more fondly regarded. As Irish pubs are the focus of the country's social existence, stout (or 'plain') is the fuel that drives it. Unlike whiskey, stout has always been a sociable drink, to be enjoyed with company in a pub and very rarely drunk at home.

While Guinness has become synonymous with stout the world over, few outside Ireland realise that there are two other major stout producers

The Cork Cook Book edited by Nuala Fenton, Angie Shanahan and Damhnait Sweeney is an excellent selection of favourites from the many restaurants in the culinary capital and from gastrophile West Cork; all proceeds go to the Cork Simon Community, a local charity for the homeless.

Jameson Guide: The Best Places to Eat, Drink & Stay by Georgina Campbell is an annual guide with over 900 recommendations for munching, supping and snoozing on the Emerald Isle.

The Book of Guinness Advertising by Jim Davies. My Goodness! A collection of Guinness' finest posters from the 1920s to the end of the 20th century.

competing for the favour of the Irish drinker: Murphy's and Beamish & Crawford, both based in Cork city in the south of Ireland.

OTHER IRISH BEERS

Guinness Is Guinness: The Colourful Story of a Black and White Brand by Mark Griffiths delves into the origins and eventual worldwide dispersion of the great stout. Guinness devotees will find it colourful and insightful.

Beamish Red Ale This traditional-style red ale, brewed in Cork city by Beamish & Crawford (p210), is sweet and palatable.

Caffrey's Irish Ale One of the most exciting additions to Ireland's beer map, this creamy ale has only been around since 1994. It's a robust cross between a stout and an ale, brewed in County Antrim.

Harp Lager This golden lager is neither here nor there.

Kaliber This nonalcoholic lager was made popular by famous Irish athlete Eamon O'Coughlan. Even in the name of research we couldn't be bothered trying it but it seems to have some credibility among the more clean-living publicans.

McCardles Traditional Ale This wholesome, dark, nutty ale is hard to come by, but worthy of an exploration.

Smithwicks Smithwicks is a lovely, refreshing full 'scoop' with a charming history. It is brewed in Kilkenny (see p318), on the site of the 14th-century St Francis Abbey in what is Ireland's oldest working brewery. John Smithwick set up his brewery in 1710, and the monks brewed ale there since the 14th century. A stronger, drier version is exported worldwide as Kilkenny Irish Beer.

WHISKEY

The Whiskeys of Ireland by Peter Mulryan is an informative tippler's companion, with a comprehensive history of distillation and production and tasting notes to 55 Irish brands.

While whiskey shares only equal billing with stout as the national drink of Ireland, in the home it is paramount. At last call, there were almost 100 different brands of Irish whiskey, with most of them available in the Irish market. Jameson and Bushmills are two great ambassadors but not necessarily Irish whiskey's showcase. A visit to the country reveals a depth of excellence which will make the connoisseur's palate spin, while winning over many new friends to what the Irish call *uisce beatha* (the 'water of life').

IRISH COFFEE

Stories of Irish coffee's origination abound but the most common one credits Joe Sheridan, a barman at Shannon airport, with the creation in the 1940s.

A THIMBLE-FULL OF WHISKEY HISTORY

Nobody really knows whether whiskey was first made in Scotland or Ireland, but for the purpose of this book we'll just go along with the Irish version of the story. Whiskey has been made in Ireland since the 10th century, when monks brought the art of distillation back from their ecclesiastical jaunts to the Middle East. In Arabia, the technique had been used to distil perfume from flowers, but the monks evidently saw a very different use for it. As the legend maintains, they soon developed a method of distilling whiskey from barley. The monks then fiercely protected their secret for several centuries.

Incidentally, Irish monks did have a solid reputation as hard drinkers. Monastic protocol limited monks to a mere gallon (5L) of ale a day. Another rule insisted that they be able to chant the Psalms clearly, so we might reasonably assume the monks managed to build up a sturdy tolerance in order to walk this fine line.

It must be noted that, had the monks not been so secretive, their claim to having invented whiskey might not be disputed today. For the Scots make an equally valid, if much later claim, dating to the 15th century. By the way, Scotch whisky is not only spelled differently, it is distilled twice rather than the three times preferred by the Irish.

Established in 1608, Bushmills in County Antrim is the world's oldest legal distillery (see p643). By the time of Bushmills' official opening, whiskey was already exceedingly popular among the common people of Ireland.

All travellers arriving in Ireland from the USA would stop over in Shannon for an hour or two before heading on to their final destination. Landing in the bracing cold, shivering passengers used to approach Sheridan looking for an alcoholic drink and something that might heat them up. He hit upon the winning blend of Irish whiskey and piping hot coffee, topped with rich cream. It was just the trick then, and still is today.

POITÍN

The making of *poitín* (potch-een), illicit whiskey, has a folkloric respect in Ireland. Those responsible came to be regarded as heroes of the people rather than outlaws of the land as the authorities tried to tar them. In tourist and duty-free shops you'll see a commercial brand of *poitín* which is strictly a gimmick for tourists. Don't bother; it is just an inferior spirit with little to its credit. There are still *poitín* makers plying their trade in the quieter corners of Ireland. It is not uncommon in Donegal, the *poitín* capital, for deals to be sealed or favours repaid with a drop of the 'cratur'. In the quiet, desolate, peaty bogs of Connemara a plume of smoke rising into the sky may not just be a warming fire. Or in West Cork, one of the most fiercely patriotic and traditional pockets of Ireland, a friend of a friend may know something about it.

WHERE TO EAT & DRINK

It's easy to eat well in the cities and you'll be able to find any kind of cuisine your taste buds desire, from Irish seafood to foreign fusion. Along the west coast, you'll be spoilt for choice when it comes to seafood restaurants.

If you ask a local for 'somewhere to eat', you'll probably be directed to his or her favourite pub because, outside the cities, the best place for a feed, particularly lunch, *is* often the pub. Virtually every drinking house will offer the simple fare of soup, potatoes, vegetables, steaks and chicken. Some extend themselves and have separate dining rooms where you can get fresh soda breads, and hearty meals like shepherd's pie, stews and casseroles, and seafood dishes. Normally only pubs with separate dining rooms serve food at night.

For breakfast, you're most likely to be eating at your accommodation, as most lodgings in Ireland offer B&B.

Standard restaurant hours in Ireland are from noon to around 10.30pm with many places closing one day of the week, usually Monday, some on Sunday.

VEGETARIANS & VEGANS

Oh boy, you're a long way from home now. Ireland provides so few vegetarian options that your convictions might be tested. In the cities and bigger towns there will be enough dedicated eateries to keep your spirits up, but once you head out into rural Ireland you enter the vegetarian's wilderness. Take heart, though, as modern restaurants are opening up in old country homes throughout Ireland, and many of them have surprisingly sophisticated menus.

We trust vegans have brought packed lunches; Ireland really won't be your cup of black tea. Save yourself time and heartache and buy the most up-to-date restaurant guide as soon as your plane touches down. And get used to the incredulous question, 'What, you don't eat any dairy produce!?!'

EATING WITH KIDS

You can bring *na páiste* (the children) to just about any Irish eatery, including the pub. However, after 7pm, the kids are banished from most

The Bridgestone Guides by John and Sally McKenna is a well-respected series of Irish food guides written by a husband-and-wife team. Books include the *Vegetarian Guide to Ireland; Food Lover's Guide to Northern Ireland; Traveller's Guide; Shopper's Guide* and the annual *100 Best Restaurants*.

Café Paradiso Cookbook is a creative and modern vegetarian cookbook with ne'er a brown lentil stew in sight; from the eponymous Cork restaurant (p213).

boozers and the smarter restaurants. You will sometimes see children's menus but normally small portions of the adult fare will do. For more information on travelling with children, see p682.

HABITS & CUSTOMS
How the Irish Eat

Visit www.foodisland .com, a site run by Bord Bia, the state food board, for recipes, a short culinary history of Ireland and links to producers of Irish food, from whom you can purchase that prized truckle of farmhouse cheese or whiskey flavoured fruit cake.

The Irish have hefty appetites and eat almost 150% of the recommended daily calorie intake according to the EU. This probably has as much to do with their penchant for snacks as the size of their meals (which *are* big).

When Ireland was predominantly agricultural, breakfast was a leisurely and communal meal shared with family and workers around midmorning, a few hours after rising. As with most of the developed world, it's now a fairly rushed and bleary-eyed affair usually involving toast and cereals. The traditional fry is a weekend indulgence while the contracted version of bacon and eggs is still popular whenever time allows. The day's first cup of tea comes with breakfast and most people will admit to not being themselves until they've had their first cuppa.

Elevenses is the next culinary pit stop and involves tea and snacks to tide appetites over until the next main meal. Afternoon tea takes the same form and serves the same function, breaking up the afternoon.

Lunch was traditionally the biggest meal of the day, which was probably a throwback to farming Ireland, when the workers would return home around 1pm, ravenous after a morning's work. The timing of the main meal today is one of the most visible rural/urban divides. Outside the cities, lunch is still usually the most substantial meal every day of the week, while the workers in urban areas have succumbed to the nine-to-five drudgery and usually eat lunch on the run. However, on weekends, everybody has dinner mid-afternoon, usually around 4pm on Saturday and before 2pm Sunday. They might call it 'lunch' but don't be deceived – it's the most substantial meal of the week.

Festive Food of Ireland by Darina Allen is a smart little cookbook with an emphasis on sturdy Sunday meals and celebration feasts. It's available on both sides of the Atlantic.

'Supper' is increasingly becoming the main meal for urbanites, and it takes place as soon as the last working parent gets home, usually after 6pm. Whatever time it takes place, main meals are still held as precious occasions for catching up on the news and sharing ideas and plans with family, friends and loved ones.

Etiquette

Conviviality is the most important condiment at the Irish table. Meal times are about taking the load off your feet, relaxing and enjoying the company of your fellow diners. There is very little prescribed or restrictive etiquette. In fact, the only behaviour likely to cause offence could be your own haughtiness. The Irish will happily dismiss any faux pas but if they think you have ideas above your station, they're often quick to bring you back down to earth.

EAT YOUR WORDS
Food Glossary

bacon and cabbage – slices of boiled bacon or gammon with boiled cabbage on the side served with boiled potatoes

barm brack – spicy, cakelike bread, traditionally served at Halloween with a ring hidden inside (be careful not to choke on it!)

blaa – soft and floury bread roll

black and white pudding – black pudding is traditionally made from pig's blood, pork skin and seasonings, shaped like a big sausage and cut into discs and fried; white pudding is the same without the blood

boxty – potato pancake, becoming rarer on menus
carrigeen – seaweed dish
champ – Northern Irish dish of potatoes mashed with spring onions (scallions)
coddle – Dublin dish of semi-thick stew made with sausages, bacon, onions and potatoes
colcannon – mashed potato, cabbage and onion fried in butter and milk
crubeens – Cork dish of pigs' trotters
dulse – dried seaweed that's sold salted and ready to eat, mainly in Ballycastle, County Antrim
fadge – Northern Irish potato bread
farl – general name for triangular-shaped baking
Guinness cake – popular fruitcake flavoured with Guinness
Irish stew – quintessential stew of mutton (preferably lamb), potatoes and onions, flavoured with parsley and thyme and simmered slowly
potato bread – thin bread made out of spuds
soda bread – wonderful bread, white or brown, sweet or savoury, made from very soft Irish flour and buttermilk and found throughout the country
yellowman – hard, chewy toffee made in County Antrim

Avoca Café Cookbook by Hugo Smith Ireland contains hearty, wholesome recipes from the family-run Avoca Handweaver restaurants originally based in Wicklow (see p144) and now with seven establishments across the Republic.

Dublin

Delightful, decadent and totally down-to-earth, Dublin is the rarest of beasts: a capital that puts an equal premium on the joys and benefits of heritage and hedonism. History and culture rise up from the foundations, but what'll put a smile on your face is the city's garrulous sociability and irrepressible humour. Dublin's in a great mood these days, and there's plenty to be happy about.

Dublin has never had it so good. The Celtic Tiger may be the most discussed and written-about feline of all, but it has taken the city on one hell of a ride, pausing occasion-ally to take a breath but still going strong. It is a place transformed, virtually unrecognis-able from the grey backwater of only a decade or so ago, a city so devoid of opportunity that the best many of its progeny could do was leave.

Now they just keep coming, from all corners of Ireland, Europe and beyond, adding colour and culture to Dublin's already brilliant personality. It's a proper cosmopolitan metropolis, Dubliners will be proud to tell you, and the evidence is everywhere, from the ethnic shops and restaurants to the swanky cafés and world-class hotels.

But in the end, Dublin's greatest asset is its people, whose infectious charm and sarcastic wit will stick with you long after the museum memories have faded. They take their fun pretty seriously here, but it doesn't take much to get them going. Put a pint in their hand and you've made a friend for life.

HIGHLIGHTS

■ **Educating Rita**
A stroll through the grounds of Trinity College (p89)

■ **Spiritual Scholars**
Books, bibles and other printed wonders from East and West in the Chester Beatty Library (p93)

■ **18th-Century Grazing**
The Georgian architecture surrounding grassy Merrion Square (p97) and St Stephen's Green (p96)

■ **Green Inside & Out**
Celebrations during the four-day St Patrick's Festival (p121)

■ **Mine's a Guinness**
A pint or five in one of Dublin's many pubs and clubs (p135)

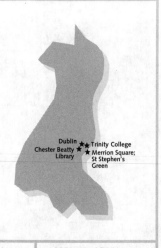

Dublin ★★ Trinity College
Chester Beatty ★ ★ Merrion Square;
Library   St Stephen's
              Green

■ TELEPHONE CODE: 01	■ POPULATION: 1.1 MILLION	■ AREA: 921 SQ KM

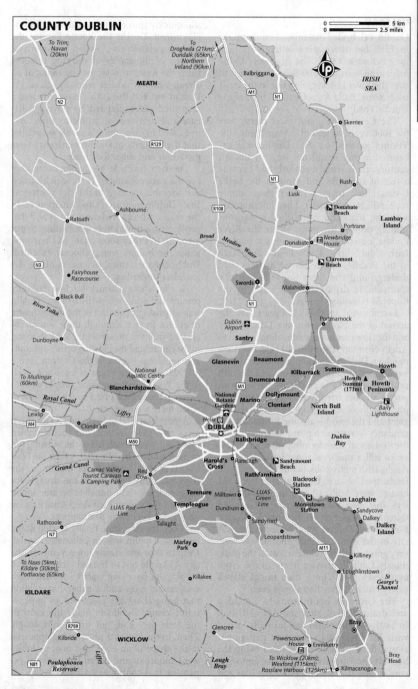

COUNTY DUBLIN

0 _____ 5 km
0 _____ 2.5 miles

To Trim;
Navan
(20km)

To
Drogheda (21km);
Dundalk (65km);
Northern
Ireland (90km)

Balbriggan

MEATH

IRISH
SEA

M1   N1

N2

Skerries

R129

N1

Rush

Lusk

Ashbourne

R108

Donabate
Beach

Ratoath

Portrane

Lambay
Island

Broad   Meadow   Water

Donabate   Newbridge
House

N3

Claremont
Beach

Fairyhouse
Racecourse

Swords

Malahide

Black Bull

River Tolka

N1

Portmarnock

Dunboyne

Dublin
Airport

To Mullingar
(60km)

Santry

Glasnevin   Beaumont

National
Aquatic Centre

Kilbarrack   Sutton

Howth

Drumcondra

Howth
Summit
(171m)

Howth
Peninsula

Blanchardstown

Royal Canal

Dollymount

Leixlip

M1

Marino

Baily
Lighthouse

M4

Liffey

National
Botanic
Gardens

Clontarf

North Bull
Island

Clondalkin

Helix

DUBLIN

Ballsbridge

Dublin
Bay

M50

Grand Canal

Harold's
Cross

Ranelagh   Sandymount
Beach

Camac Valley
Tourist Caravan
& Camping Park

Red
Cow

Rathfarnham

Blackrock
Station

LUAS Red
Line

Terenure   Milltown

Templeogue

Dundrum

LUAS
Green
Line

Monkstown
Station

Dun Laoghaire

Sandycove

Rathcoole

Tallaght

Sandyford

Dalkey

Dalkey
Island

N7

Leopardstown

Marlay
Park

M11

To Naas (5km);
Kildare (30km);
Portlaoise (65km)

Killakee

Killiney

Loughlinstown

KILDARE

St
George's
Channel

WICKLOW

R759

Glencree

Bray

Kilbride

Powerscourt
House   Enniskerry

Bray
Head

N81

Poulaphouca
Reservoir

Lough
Bray

To Wicklow (20km);
Wexford (115km);
Rosslare Harbour (125km)

Kilmacanogue

HISTORY

Dublin celebrated its official millennium in 1988 but there were settlements here long before AD 988. The first early-Celtic habitation – around 500 BC – was at a ford over the River Liffey, giving rise to the city's Irish name, Baile Átha Cliath (Town of the Hurdle Ford).

The Celts went about their merry way for 1000 years or so, but it wasn't until the Vikings showed up that Dublin was urbanised in any significant way. By the 9th century, raids from the north had become a fact of Irish life and some of the fierce Danes chose to stay rather than simply rape, pillage and depart. They intermarried with the Irish and established a vigorous trading port at the point where the River Poddle joined the Liffey in a black pool, in Irish a 'dubh linn'. Today there's little trace of the Poddle, which has been channelled underground and flows under St Patrick's Cathedral to dribble into the Liffey by the Capel St (Grattan) Bridge.

Fast-forward another 1000 years, past the arrival of the Normans in the 12th century and the slow process of subjugating Ireland to Anglo-Norman (then British) rule, a process in which Dublin generally played the role of bandleader. Stop at the beginning of the 18th century, when the squalid city packed with poor Catholics hardly reflected the imperial pretensions of its Anglophile burghers. The great and the good – aka the Protestant Ascendancy – wanted big improvements, and they set about transforming what was in essence still a medieval town into a modern, Anglo-Irish metropolis. Roads were widened, landscaped squares laid out and new town houses built, all in a proto-Palladian style that soon become known as Georgian (after the kings then on the English throne). For a time, Dublin was the second-largest city in the British Empire and all was very, very good – unless you were part of the poor, mostly Catholic masses living in the city's ever-developing slums; then things stayed pretty much as they had always been.

The Georgian boom came to a sudden and dramatic halt after the Act of Union in 1801, when Ireland was formally united with Britain and its separate parliament closed down. Dublin went from being the belle at the Imperial ball to the annoying cousin who just wouldn't take the hint and slid quickly into economic turmoil and social unrest. During the Potato Famine the city's population was swollen by the arrival of tens of thousands of starving refugees from the west, who joined the ranks of an already downtrodden working class. As Dublin entered the 20th century, it was a dispirited place plagued by poverty, disease and more social problems than anyone cared to mention. It's hardly surprising that the majority of Dublin's citizenry were pissed off and eager for change.

The first fusillade of change came during the Easter Rising of 1916, which caused considerable damage to the city centre. At first, Dubliners weren't too enamoured of the rebels, who caused more chaos and disruption than most locals were willing to put up with, but they soon changed their tune when the leaders were callously executed: Dubliners are natural defenders of the defenceless underdog.

As the whole country lurched radically toward full-scale war with Britain, Dublin was surprisingly not part of the main theatre of events. In fact, although there was an increased military presence, the odd shooting in the capital and the blowing up of some notable buildings – such as the Custom House in 1921 – it was business as usual for much of the War of Independence. People went to work and socialised pretty much the same as when there wasn't a war.

A year later, Ireland – minus its northern bit – was independent, but then tumbled into Civil War, which led to the burning out of more notable buildings, this time the Four Courts in 1922. Ironically the war among the Irish was more brutal than the struggle for independence – O'Connell St became sniper row and the violence left deep scars that are only today beginning to disappear.

When the new state finally started doing business, Dublin was an exhausted capital. Despite slow and steady improvements, the city – like the rest of Ireland – continued to be plagued by rising unemployment, high emigration rates and a general stagnation that hung about the place like an impenetrable cloud. Dubliners made the most of the little they had, but times were tough. Then, in the 1960s, a silver lining appeared in the shape of an economic boom: Dublin went suburban and began the outward expansion that continues unabated today.

DUBLIN IN...

Two Days

Kick-start your day with a mean brunch at **Gruel** (p129) on Dame St, a stone's throw from **Trinity College** (p89) where the walking tour includes entry to the **Book of Kells** (p91). Ramble through atmospheric **George's St Arcade** (p144) to **Grafton Street** (p143) to catch the buskers and splurge on Dublin's most exclusive shopping street. Round it off with a cocktail, dinner and outdoor movie on the terrace at **Eden** (p132), one of Dublin's trendiest restaurants in **Temple Bar** (p92), before falling into bed at the fashionable **Clarence Hotel** (p125). The next day marvel at the Oriental art of the **Chester Beatty Library** (p93) before strolling up to the **Guinness Storehouse** (p100) for a tour that ends with a glass of 'plain' in the Gravity Bar with stunning 360-degree views of the city.

Four Days

Follow the two-day itinerary then wander around the historic **Glasnevin Cemetery** (p108) before moseying into the peaceful **National Botanic Gardens** (p107). Back in town, browse the **designer shops** (p144) in Temple Bar and grab a bite in **Diep Noodle Bar** (p134) before taking the **Dublin Literary Pub Crawl** (p120). The following day take the Dublin Area Rapid Transport (DART) along the coast to exclusive suburb **Killiney** (p148) for a stroll on the beach and stop off at the pretty village of **Dalkey** (p147) on the way home. Gather your strength with a fine meal at **Mash** (p134) before a gig at **Vicar Street** (p142).

A boom ain't a miracle, however, and Dublin trudged along for another couple of decades with pretty much the same age-old problems (high unemployment, emigration) and some new ones (drug addiction, gangland criminality) before everything began to change utterly and a terrible beauty known as the Celtic Tiger was born. Fifteen years later, Dublin is a place transformed, a capital in more than name and a city that has finally taken its rightful place as one of the most vibrant in Europe.

ORIENTATION

Greater Dublin sprawls around the arc of Dublin Bay, bounded to the north by the hills at Howth and to the south by the Dalkey headland. Small and compact, the city centre has a clear focus and is a walker's delight. It is split in two by the unremarkable River Liffey, which traditionally marks a psychological and social break between the affluent southside and the poorer northside.

Just south of the river, over O'Connell Bridge, is the Temple Bar area and the expanse of Trinity College. Nassau St, along the southern edge of the campus, and pedestrianised Grafton St are the main shopping streets. At the southern end of Grafton St is St Stephen's Green. About 2km west,

beside the river, is Heuston Station, one of the city's two main train stations.

North of the Liffey are O'Connell St and, just off it, Henry St, the major shopping thoroughfares. Most of the northside's B&Bs are on Gardiner St, which becomes rather run-down as it continues north. At the northern end of O'Connell St is Parnell Sq. The main bus station, Busáras, and the other main train station, Connolly Station, are near the southern end of Gardiner St.

The postcodes for central Dublin are Dublin 1, immediately north of the river and Dublin 2, immediately south. The Dublin 4 postcode, covering the swanky neighbourhoods of Ballsbridge, Donnybrook and Sandymount, is synonymous with affluence and is often used as a descriptive term. A handy tip is to remember that even numbers apply to the southside and odd ones to the north.

See p145 for information on transport to/from the airport and train stations.

Maps

Lonely Planet's *Dublin City Map* has a complete index of all streets and sights, a Dublin Area Rapid Transport (DART) and suburban rail plan and a unique walking tour of the city.

(Continued on page 86)

DUBLIN (pp80-1)

GREATER DUBLIN (£78)

0 — 400 m
0 — 0.2 miles

E **F** **G** **H**

Charleville Ave

Eccles St
Eccles Pl
North Circular Rd
Nelson St
St Joseph's Pde
Lower Dorset St
Berkeley St
Upper Gardiner St
Fitzgibbon La
Fitzgibbon St
Emmet St
North Richmond St
Ballybough Rd
William St
1
St Columba's
Blessington St
Kelly's Row
Belvidere Ct
Belvidere Pl
Great Charles St
Upper Rutland St
North Summer St
North Rutland Pl
Portland Row
North Strand Rd
Blessington La
Lower Wellington St
North Temple St
St Anthony's Pl
Nerney's Ct
63
Mountjoy Square
Mountjoy Sq West
North Mountjoy Sq
Mountjoy Sq East
South Mountjoy Sq
Hutton's La
Summerhill Pde
Summerhill Pl
Buckingham St
Lower Summerhill
Bella St
Seville Pl
2
Lower Wellington St
Frederick St
Hardwicke St
Gardiner Pl
46
Bath La
Grenville St
North Temple La
Gardiner St
Buckingham St Lower
Frankfort Cottages
Coburg Pl
Paradise Pl
14
Dominick St
North Georges St
West Rutland Pl
Gloucester Pl
Gloucester Pl Lower
Railway St
Beaver St
Amiens St
50 **41**
12
31 **22** **32**
Garden of Remembrance
26
53 **56**
North Great
52
North Cumberland St
Britain Pl
Diamond
●16
Lower Sean MacDermot St
Corporation St
Foley St
Connolly Train Station
Upper Dorset St
Granby La
43
Parnell Sq
Gardiner St Lower
Upper Sean MacDermot St
Mabbot La
49
Lower Sheriff St
Granby Row
West Parnell St
58
Parnell St
Cathal Brugha St
Marlborough St
40
Talbot St
Talbot Pl
Lower Dominick St
Granby Pl
7
57
Moore La
15 **44**
61 **48**
Lower Gardiner St
Frenchman's La
45
59
Store St
69
Memorial Rd
Inner Dock
King's Inns La
Dominick Pl
20
5
Henry Pl
13 **1**
O'Connell St
36
42
39
51
St George's Dock
Loftus La
64
Chapel La
67
10
Simpson's La
35
11
North Earl St
12
Henry St
47
27
3
23 **66**
Sackville Pl
Lower Major St
Commons St
6
Mary St
North Prince's St
28
Lower Abbey St
Beresford Pl
19
Custom House Quay
Wolfe Tone St
Jervis St
Jervis La
Upper Liffey St
Middle Abbey St
Harbour
60
Old Abbey St
Eden Quay
George's Quay
3
Capel St
Great Strand St
Lower Ormond Quay
Lotts Rd
4 **21**
O'Connell Bridge
Upper Abbey St
Bachelors Walk
Crampton Quay
Burgh Quay
River Liffey
City Quay
Grattan Bridge
Wellington Quay
Temple Bar
Aston Qu
D'Olier St
Poolbeg St
Tara St Station
Moss St
South Prince's St
South Dowlings Ct
Windmill
Essex Quay
East Essex St
Eustace St
Anglesea
TEMPLE BAR
Fleet St
62
Townsend St
29
Tara St
Luke St
Mark St
Shaw St
Mark's La
East Hanover St
4
Lord Edward St
Dame St
College St
Spring Garden La
Pearse St
68
East Lombard St
Magennis Pl
Lower Sandwith St
Creighton St
Cork Hill
Dublin Castle
TRINITY COLLEGE
Rugby Ground
Westland Row
South Cumberland St
Pearse Station
Ringsend Rd
Great Ship St
Exchequer St
South Great Georges St
South William St
Drury St
Clarendon St
Grafton St
Nassau St
College Park
S Leinster St
Lincoln Pl
College St
Boyne St
5
Golden La
Upper Stephen St
Lower Stephen St
Aungier St
South King St
South Mercer St
Lower Glover's Al
Dawson St
Molesworth St
Kildare St
Duke St
Setanta
South Frederick St
North Merrion Sq
West Merrion Sq
Merrion Square
East Merrion Sq
Lower Mount St
Peter St
Peter Row
York St
GRAFTON ST
St Stephen's Green
North St Stephen's Green
West St Stephen's Green
25
Bishop St
Wexford St
Cuffe St
South St Stephen's Green
East St Stephen's Green
St Stephen's Green
Children's Playground
Huguenot Cemetery
Upper Merrion St
Lower Merrion St
Fitzwilliam La
Hume St
Hume St Pl
Merrion Row
Ely Pl
Upper Pembroke St
Lower Pembroke St
East Merrion Sq
Verschoyle Pl
Upper Mount St
East James's Pl
East Mount St
33
Stephen's La
6
Lower Kevin St
New Bride St
Camden Row
Iveagh Gardens
Harcourt St
Leeson St
Macken Pl
Upper Fitzwilliam St
Lower Fitzwilliam St
East James's St
Herbert

See Trinity College Map (p90)

See Grafton St & St Stephen's Green Map (pp84–5)

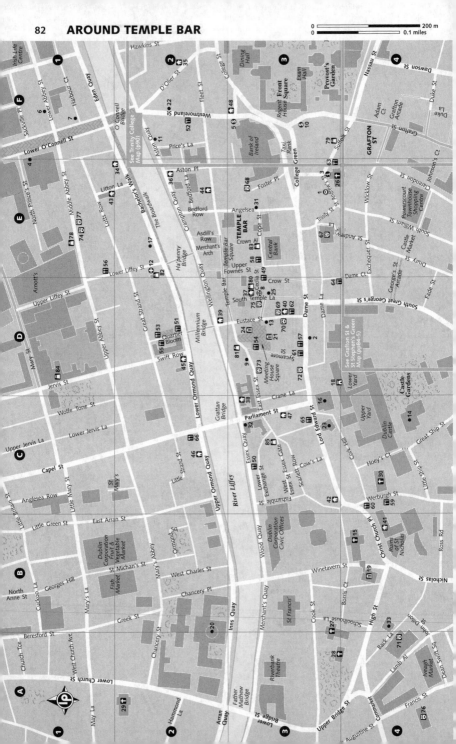

INFORMATION
Alliance Française.....................................1 D1
An Post..2 C2
An Siopa Leabhar..................................3 B4
Candian Embassy....................................4 C4
Cathach Books.......................................5 C1
Central Cyber Café.................................6 C1
Dawson Lounge.......................................7 C2
Dublin Bookshop...................................8 C2
Eason's–Hanna's....................................9 C1
Goethe Institute...................................10 F2
Government Publications
  Bookshop...11 C2
Grafton Medical Centre......................12 C2
Greene's Bookshop.............................13 D1
Heritage Card Service.........................14 E4
Hodges Figgis......................................15 C1
Hughes & Hughes...........................(see 86)
Murder Ink..16 C2
O'Connell's Pharmacy........................17 B2
Stokes Books..18 B1
Waterstone's..19 C1

SIGHTS & ACTIVITIES   (pp88-118)
Dublin Corporation.............................20 F1
Fusiliers' Arch.....................................21 B3
Genealogical Office.........................(see 1)
Government Buildings.........................22 E3
Huguenot Cemetery............................23 D3
Leinster House (Irish Parliament).......24 D2
National Gallery...................................25 E2
National Library...................................26 D2
National Museum.................................27 D2
Natural History Museum.....................28 E2
Newman House......................................29 C4
Newman University Church.................30 B4
Oscar Wilde House...............................31 F2
Oscar Wilde Statue.............................32 F2

Powerscourt Townhouse Shopping
  Centre...33 B1
Royal College of Surgeons.................34 B3
Unitarian Church.................................35 B3

SLEEPING 🏠   (pp121-8)
Avalon House.......................................36 A3
Browne's Townhouse..........................37 C3
Central Hotel..38 A1
Drury Court Hotel...............................39 A2
Grafton Guesthouse............................40 A1
La Stampa...41 C2
Mercer Court..42 A2
Mercer Hotel..43 B2
Merrion..44 E3
Shelbourne..45 D3
Westbury Hotel....................................46 B2

EATING 🍴   (pp128-35)
Aya...47 B1
Ba Mizu..48 B1
Bang...49 D3
Bewley's...(see 52)
Bistro...50 B1
Blazing Salads.....................................51 B1
Café Bardeli...52 B2
Clarendon Café Bar............................53 B2
Cornucopia...54 B1
Dunne & Crescenzi..............................55 D1
El Bahia..56 B1
Ely Wine Bar..57 D4
Fresh..(see 33)
Gotham Café..58 C2
Govinda's...59 A2
Imperial Chinese Restaurant..............60 B1
Jaipur...61 A2
Juice...62 A1
L'Ecrivain...63 F4

L'Gueuleton..64 A1
La Corte...(see 33)
La Maison des Gourmets...............(see 82)
Lemon..65 C1
Lemon..66 B1
Mackerel...(see 52)
Market Bar...67 A1
Peploe's...68 C3
Pizza Milano...69 C2
Rajdoot Tandoori................................70 B2
Restaurant Patrick Guilbaud...........(see 44)
SamSara...(see 73)
Simon's Place......................................71 A1
Thornton's..72 B3
Tiger Becs..73 C2
Wagamama...74 B2
Yamamori...75 A1

ENTERTAINMENT 🎭   (pp138-43)
Gaiety Theatre.....................................76 B2
Rí Rá...77 A1
Village...78 A4
Whelan's...79 A4

SHOPPING 🛍   (pp143-4)
Brown Thomas......................................80 C1
Costume...(see 82)
George St Arcade................................81 A1
Harlequin...82 B1
HMV...83 B2
Jenny Vander.......................................84 B1
Kilkenny Shop......................................85 C1
St Stephen's Green Shopping Centre...86 B2
Tulle...87 A1

TRANSPORT   (pp144-7)
Dan Dooley Car Hire............................88 F1
McDonald Cycles.................................89 A4

(Continued from page 77)

INFORMATION
Bookshops
An Siopa Leabhar (Map p84; ☎ 478 3814; Harcourt St) Stocks books in Irish.

Cathach Books (Map p84; ☎ 671 8676; www.rare books.ie; 10 Duke St) A rich and remarkable collection of second-hand, Irish-interest books, including first editions.

Dublin Bookshop (Map p84; ☎ 677 5568; 36 Grafton St) Excellent local shop with good Irish-interest section.

Dublin Writers Museum (Map pp80–1; ☎ 872 2077; 18 Parnell Sq North)

Eason – Hanna's (Map p84; ☎ 677 1255; 27-29 Nassau St) Academic tomes, bestsellers and stationery.

Eason & Son (Map p82; ☎ 873 3811; 40 O'Connell St) One of the biggest magazine stockists in Ireland.

Government Publications Bookshop (Map p84; ☎ 647 6879; Sun Alliance House, Molesworth St) Official publications and maps.

Greene's Bookshop (Map p84; ☎ 676 2554; www.greenesbookshop.com; 16 Clare St) What all second-hand bookshops should be, packed with dusty tomes.

Hodges Figgis (Map p84; ☎ 677 4754; 56-58 Dawson St) Widest selection of titles in Dublin.

Hughes & Hughes Dublin airport (Map p75; ☎ 814 4034); St Stephen's Green Shopping Centre (Map p84; ☎ 478 3060; St Stephen's Green Shopping Centre) Magazines, bestsellers and new titles.

Irish Museum of Modern Art (IMMA; Map p78; ☎ 612 9900; Royal Hospital, Kilmainham) Contemporary art and Irish-interest books.

Library Book Shop (Map p90; ☎ 608 1171; Trinity College) Irish-interest books, including those on the *Book of Kells*.

Murder Ink (Map p84; ☎ 677 7570; 15 Dawson St) Mystery titles.

National Gallery (Map p84; ☎ 678 5450; Merrion Sq West) Traditional art and Irish interest books.

Sinn Féin Bookshop (Map pp80–1; ☎ 872 7096; 44 Parnell Sq West)

Stokes Books (Map p84; ☎ 671 3584; 19 George's St Arcade) Irish historical books, old and new.

Waterstone's Dawson St (Map p84; ☎ 679 1415; 7 Dawson St); Mary St (Map p82; ☎ 878 1311; Jervis St Centre, Mary St)

Cultural Centres
Alliance Française (Map p84; ☎ 676 1732; 1 Kildare St)

British Council (Map p78; ☎ 676 4088; Newmount House, 22-24 Lower Mount St)

Goethe Institute (Map p84; ☎ 661 1155; 37 Merrion Sq North)

Instituto Cervantes (Map p78; ☎ 668 2024; 58 Northumberland Rd)

Italian Cultural Institute (Map p78; ☎ 676 6662; 11 Fitzwilliam Sq)

Emergency
For national emergency numbers see the inside front cover.

Confidential Line Freefone (☎ 1800 666 111) Garda confidential line to report crime.

Drugs Advisory & Treatment Centre (☎ 677 1122; Trinity Ct, 30-31 Pearse St)

Rape Crisis Centre (☎ 1800 778 888, 661 4911; 70 Lower Leeson St)

Samaritans (☎ 1850 609 090, 872 7700) For people who are depressed or suicidal.

Internet Access
Central Cyber Café (Map p84; ☎ 677 8298; 6 Grafton St)

Global Cyber Café (Map pp80–1; ☎ 878 0295; 8 Lower O'Connell St)

Internet Exchange (Map p82; ☎ 670 3000; 1 Cecilia St; ☿ 24hr)

Internet Resources
www.lunch.ie Take a stranger to lunch in the city and have them return the favour via this unusual meeting-point website.

www.nixers.com A good place to check if you're looking for casual work over the summer.

www.pigsback.com A website that offers all kinds of citywide discounts from cinema tickets to free lunches.

www.visitdublin.com Fáilte Ireland's site with information on accommodation and activities in the city.

Laundry
Laundry facilities can be found quite easily in the city centre with prices starting at about €7.50 a load; ask at your accommodation. Alternatively most hostels, B&Bs and hotels will provide the service. In hostels prices start at about €6 and it's generally self-service.

All-American Laundrette (Map p84; ☎ 677 2779; Wicklow Ct, South Great George's St)

Laundry Shop (Map pp80–1; ☎ 872 3541; 191 Parnell St)

Left Luggage
Left luggage facilities are available at all transport centres, including the airport.

Busáras (Map pp80–1; ☎ 703 2434; per locker €5-10; ☿ 7am-10.30pm) Main bus station north of the Liffey.

Connolly Station (Map pp80–1; ☎ 703 2363; per bag €2.50; ☿ 7am-10pm Mon-Sat, 8am-10pm Sun) The main train station on the northside.

Dublin airport (Map p75; ☎ 814 4633; Greencaps Left Luggage & Porterage, Dublin airport; per bag €4-8; ☼ 6am-11pm)

Heuston Station (Map pp80-1; ☎ 836 6222; per locker for 24hr €1.50-5; ☼ 7am-10pm Mon-Sat, 8am-10pm Sun) Train station on the southside.

Libraries

Dublin Corporation (Map p84; ☎ 661 9000; Cumberland House, Fenian St) For information on public libraries.

ILAC Centre Public Library (Map pp80-1; ☎ 873 4333; ILAC Centre, Henry St) One of the city's largest public libraries.

Media

Besides the national dailies (see p51), there are a number of Dublin-specific publications and media outlets.

NEWSPAPERS & MAGAZINES

Dublin Event Guide (free) Fortnightly coverage of all things entertainment throughout the city.

Evening Press (€1) Evening tabloid with thorough entertainment listings and a terrific flat-finder section.

In Dublin (free) A weekly ad-rag.

RADIO

Newstalk 106 (106 FM) City-specific talk radio and news from 7am to 10pm.

Medical Services

Should you experience an immediate health problem, contact the casualty section of the nearest public hospital; in an emergency call an ambulance (☎ 999). There are no 24-hour pharmacies in Dublin; the latest openings are until 10pm.

Baggot St Hospital (Map p78; ☎ 668 1577; 18 Upper Baggot St) Southside city centre.

City Pharmacy (Map p82; ☎ 670 4523; 14 Dame St)

Doctors on Call (☎ 453 9333) Request a doctor to call out to your accommodation at any time on a 24-hour private service line.

Eastern Regional Health Authority (Map pp80-1; ☎ 679 0700, 1800 520 520; www.erha.ie; Dr Steevens' Hospital, Dublin 8) Central health authority with Choice of Doctor Scheme, which can advise you on a suitable GP from 9am to 5pm Monday to Friday. Information services for those with physical and mental disabilities.

Grafton Medical Centre (Map p84; ☎ 671 2122; www.graftonmedical.ie; 34 Grafton St) One-stop shop with male and female doctors, physiotherapists and a tropical medicine bureau.

Mater Misericordiae Hospital (Map p78; ☎ 830 1122; Eccles St) Northside city centre, off Lower Dorset St.

O'Connell's Pharmacy Grafton St (Map p84; ☎ 679 0467; 21 Grafton St); O'Connell St (Map p82; ☎ 873 0427; 55-56 O'Connell St)

St James's Hospital (Map pp80-1; ☎ 453 7941; James St) Southside.

Well Women Clinic Lower Liffey St (Map p82; ☎ 661 0083; 35 Lower Liffey St); Pembroke Rd (☎ 660 9860; 67 Pembroke Rd) For female health issues. Supplies contraceptives, including the morning-after pill (€52).

Money

There are currency-exchange counters at Dublin airport in the baggage-collection area and on the arrival and departure floors, open 5.30am to 11pm.

There are numerous banks around the city centre with exchange facilities, open during regular bank hours.

American Express (Amex; Map p82; ☎ 605 7709; Dublin Tourism Centre, Andrew's St; ☼ 9am-5pm Mon-Sat)

First Rate (Map p82; ☎ 671 3233; 1 Westmoreland St; ☼ 8am-9pm Mon-Fri, 9am-9pm Sat, 10am-9pm Sun Jun-Sep, 9am-6pm daily Oct-May)

Thomas Cook (Map p82; ☎ 677 1721, 677 1307; 118 Grafton St; ☼ 9am-5.30pm Mon, Tue, Fri & Sat, 10am-5.30pm Wed, 9am-7pm Thu)

Post

An Post Anne St (Map p84; ☎ 677 7127; South Anne St); St Andrew's St (Map p82; ☎ 705 8206; St Andrew's St)

GPO (Map p82; ☎ 705 7000; O'Connell St; ☼ 8am-8pm Mon-Sat) Dublin's famed general post office has a free poste restante service, a philatelic counter and a bank of telephones.

Telephone

Talk Is Cheap (Map pp80-1) Capel St (☎ 872 2235; 87 Capel St); Moore St (☎ 874 6013; 55 Moore St)

Talk Shop Temple Lane (Map p82; ☎ 672 7212; 20 Temple Lane); Upper O'Connell St (Map pp80-1; ☎ 872 0200; 5 Upper O'Connell St) For cheap international phone calls.

Tourist Information

No tourist information offices in Dublin provide any information over the phone – they're exclusively walk-in services.

All telephone bookings and reservations are operated by Gulliver, a computerised information and reservation service that is available at all walk-in offices or from anywhere in the world. It provides up-to-date information on events, attractions and transport, and can also book

AND WHERE ARE YOU ARRIVING FROM...?

In 1998, the trend of emigration was reversed for the first time ever, with more people moving into the country than leaving it. Figures are bolstered by returning emigrants drawn back to the honeypot, but the city has become a destination for refugees, asylum seekers and immigrants – including significant communities from Nigeria, Romania, Bosnia and China – as well as young migrants from all over the EU.

All of a sudden, Dublin wasn't the easygoing, friendly city everyone figured it to be. Verbal abuse, racially motivated attacks and the targeting of non-nationals in crime have become fairly commonplace in Dublin – even a member of the government got in on the disgraceful behaviour, talking about 'kebabs' in reference to a well-publicised case of exploitation involving Turkish workers.

Make no mistake about it though: most Dubs wholeheartedly reject racism and embrace the city's growing multiculturalism, but what is disheartening is that not enough people stand up to the thuggish ignorant few who tarnish their reputation. If you do experience any problems, be sure to report them to the police.

accommodation. In Ireland, call ☎ 1800 668 668; from Britain call ☎ 00800 6686 6866; from the rest of the world call ☎ 353-669 792083.

Dublin Tourism Dublin airport (arrivals hall; ☼ 8am-10pm); Dun Laoghaire (Dun Laoghaire ferryport; ☼ 10am-1pm & 2-6pm Mon-Sat); O'Connell St (Map pp80-1; 14 O'Connell St; ☼ 9am-5pm Mon- Sat); Wilton Tce (Map p78; Wilton Tce; ☼ 9.30am-noon & 12.30-5pm Mon-Fri)

Dublin Tourism Centre (Map p82; ☎ 605 7700; www .visitdublin.com; St Andrew's Church, 2 Suffolk St; ☼ 9am-7pm Mon-Sat, 10.30am-3pm Sun Jul & Aug, 9am-5.30pm Mon-Sat Sep-Jun) Dublin's main tourist office. There is a booking fee of €4.50 for serviced accommodation, €7.50 for self-catering and a 10% deposit that is refunded through your hotel bill.

Fáilte Ireland head office (Map p78; ☎ 1850 230 330; www.ireland.ie; Wilton Tce, Baggot St Bridge; ☼ 9am-5.15pm Mon-Fri)

Travel Agencies

Amex and Thomas Cook both have offices in the centre of Dublin (p87).

USIT (Map p82; ☎ 602 1904; www.usit.ie; 19 Aston Quay; ☼ 9.30am-6.30pm Mon-Wed & Fri, 9.30am-8pm Thu, 9.30am-5pm Sat) Travel agency of the Union of Students in Ireland.

DANGERS & ANNOYANCES

Petty crime of the pickpocketing, bag-snatching and car break-in variety is a low- to midlevel irritant: hired and foreign-registered cars are favoured targets – they seem to have a smash-*my*-window sign splayed across their bonnets. Take sensible precautions; supervised car parks for over-night parking aren't a bad idea. Remember also that insurance policies often don't cover losses from cars.

The area north of Gardiner St, O'Connell St and Mountjoy Sq is not especially salubrious and is afflicted with drug addiction, crime and occasional violence. Phoenix Park is a no-go area after dark; camping there is not just illegal but an invitation to trouble.

The problem of sloppy drunkenness after closing hours is another potential hassle. Where there are pubs and clubs there are revellers the worse for wear looking to get home and/or get laid; sometimes the frustrations of getting neither can result in a trip to the casualty department of the nearest hospital – hospitals are clogged to bursting with drink-related cases throughout the weekend.

SIGHTS
Trinity College & Around

Dublin's oldest and most beautiful university stretches its leafy self across much of the south city centre's most valuable real estate. Just south of it is Grafton St, Dublin's most elegant shopping street, which runs up to the main entrance to St Stephen's Green. Surrounding and beyond Dublin's most popular green lung is the capital's exquisite Georgian heritage, a collection of galleries, museums, private and public buildings as handsome as any you'll see in Europe. Back at Trinity College, take a few steps north-west of the main entrance to find yourself in Temple Bar, where bacchanalia and bohemia scrap it out for supremacy.

TRINITY COLLEGE

On a summer's evening, when the bustling crowds have gone for the day, there's hardly a more delightful place in Dublin than the grounds of Ireland's most prestigious **university** (Map p90; ☎ 677 1724; walking tours ☎ 608 1827; admission incl Book of Kells €9; ☼ tours every 40min 10.15am-3.40pm Mon-Sat, 10.15am-3pm Sun mid-May–Sep), a masterpiece of architecture and landscaping beautifully preserved in Georgian aspic. It is free to wander the gardens on your own between 8am and 10pm. Not only is it Dublin's most attractive bit of historical real estate, but it's also home to one of the world's most famous – and most beautiful – books, the gloriously illuminated *Book of Kells*.

Officially, the university's name is the University of Dublin, but Trinity is its sole college. Its charter was granted by Elizabeth I in 1592 – on grounds confiscated from an Augustinian priory dissolved in 1537 – with the hope that young Dubliners would desist from skipping across to continental Europe for their education and become 'infected with popery'. The 16-hectare site is now in the centre of the city, but when it was founded it was described as 'near Dublin' and was bordered on two sides by the estuary of the Liffey. Nothing now remains of the original Elizabethan college, which was replaced in the Georgian building frenzy of the 18th century. The most significant change, however, is in the makeup of the student population: exclusively Protestant until 1793, today most of its 13,000 students are Catholic, although they were forbidden from attending by their own church until 1970 on pain of excommunication. All of this would surely have horrified Archbishop Ussher, one of the college's founders, whose greatest scientific feat was the precise dating of the act of creation to 4004 BC.

Facing College Green, the **Front Gate** (Regent House entrance) to the college grounds was built between 1752 and 1759 and is guarded by **statues** of the poet **Oliver Goldsmith** (1730–74) and the orator **Edmund Burke** (1729–97). The summer walking tours of the college depart from here.

The open area reached from Regent House is divided into Front Sq, Parliament Sq and Library Sq. The area is dominated by the 30m-high **Campanile**, designed by Edward Lanyon and erected between 1852 and 1853 on what was believed to be the centre of the monastery that preceded the college. To the left of the Campanile is a **statue of George Salmon**, college provost from 1888 to 1904, who fought bitterly to keep women out of the college. He carried out his threat to permit them 'over my dead body' by promptly dropping dead when the worst came to pass.

Clockwise round Front Sq from the Front Gate, the first building is the **chapel** (☎ 608 1260; Front Sq, Trinity College; admission free), built from 1798 to plans made in 1777 by the architect Sir William Chambers (1723–96) and, since 1972, open to all denominations. It's noted for its extremely fine plasterwork by Michael Stapleton, its Ionic columns and its painted, rather than stained-glass, windows. The main window is dedicated to Archbishop Ussher.

Next to the chapel is the **dining hall** (Parliament Sq; ☼ students only), originally designed in 1743 by Richard Cassels (aka Castle), but dismantled 15 years later because of problems caused by inadequate foundations. The replacement was completed in 1761 and may have retained some elements of the original design. It was extensively restored after a fire in 1984.

The 1892 **Graduates' Memorial Building** (Botany Bay; ☼ closed to public) forms the northern side of Library Sq. Behind it are the tennis courts in the open area known as Botany Bay. The popular legend behind this name is that the unruly students housed around the square were suitable candidates for the British penal colony at Botany Bay in Australia.

At the eastern side of Library Sq, the red-brick **Rubrics Building** dates from around 1690, making it the oldest building in the college. It was extensively altered in an 1894 restoration and then underwent major structural modifications in the 1970s.

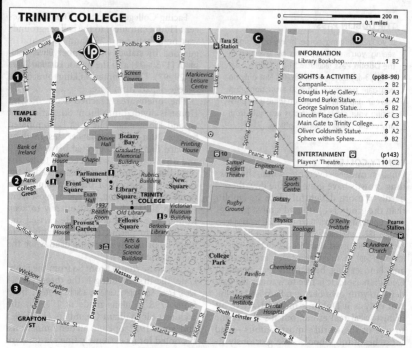

TRINITY COLLEGE

0 ————— 200 m
0 ————— 0.1 miles

INFORMATION
Library Bookshop......................1 B2

SIGHTS & ACTIVITIES   (pp88-98)
Campanile...............................2 B2
Douglas Hyde Gallery...............3 A3
Edmund Burke Statue...............4 A2
George Salmon Statue..............5 B2
Lincoln Place Gate....................6 C3
Main Gate to Trinity College......7 A2
Oliver Goldsmith Statue............8 A2
Sphere within Sphere...............9 B2

ENTERTAINMENT   (p143)
Players' Theatre......................10 C2

To the south of the square is the **Old Library** (☎ 608 2320; Library Sq; admission as part of Book of Kells tour), built in a rather severe style by Thomas Burgh between 1712 and 1732. The Old Library's 65m Long Room contains numerous unique ancient texts, and its biggest attraction is displayed in the Library Colonnades. Despite Ireland's independence, the Library Act of 1801 still entitles Trinity College Library, along with four libraries in Britain, to a free copy of every book published in the UK. Housing this bounty requires nearly another 1km of shelving every year and the collection amounts to around 4½ million books. Of course these cannot all be kept at the college library, so there are now additional library storage facilities dotted around Dublin.

Trinity's greatest treasures are kept in the stunning **Long Room** (☎ 608 2320; East Pavilion, Library Colonnades; adult/child €7.50/free; ⏰ 9.30am-5pm Mon-Sat year round, noon-4.30pm Sun Oct-May, 9.30am-4pm Sun Jun-Sep), which has about 250,000 of the library's oldest volumes, including the superb *Book of Kells* (see the boxed text, opposite). Your entry ticket includes admis-

sion to temporary exhibitions on display in the East Pavilion. Until 1892 the ground floor Colonnades was an open arcade, but it was enclosed at that time to increase the storage area. A previous attempt to increase the room's storage capacity had been made in 1853, when the Long Room ceiling was raised. Other displays include a rare copy of the Proclamation of the Irish Republic, which was read out by Pádraig Pearse at the beginning of the Easter Rising in 1916. Also here is the so-called harp of Brian Ború, which was definitely not in use when the army of this early Irish hero defeated the Danes at the Battle of Clontarf in 1014. It does, however, date from around 1400, making it one of the oldest harps in Ireland.

Continuing clockwise around the Campanile there's the **1937 Reading Room** and the **Exam Hall** (Public Theatre), which dates from 1779 to 1791. Like the chapel it was the work of William Chambers and also has plasterwork by Michael Stapleton. The Exam Hall has an oak chandelier rescued from the Houses of Parliament (now the Bank of Ireland) across College Green and an organ said to have been salvaged from a Spanish ship in 1702, though evidence indicates otherwise.

Behind the Exam Hall is the 1760 **Provost's House**, a very fine Georgian house where the provost (college head) still resides. The house and its adjacent garden are not open to the public.

To one side of the Old Library is Paul Koralek's 1967 **Berkeley Library** (Fellow's Sq; ☿ closed to public). This solid, square brutalist-style building has been hailed as the best example of modern architecture in Ireland, though it has to be admitted the competition isn't great. It's fronted by Arnaldo Pomodoro's 1982 to 1983 sculpture **Sphere within Sphere**.

George Berkeley was born in Kilkenny in 1685, studied at Trinity when he was only 15 years old and went on to a distinguished career in many fields, but particularly in philosophy. His influence spread to the new English colonies in North America where, among other things, he helped to found the University of Pennsylvania. Berkeley in California, and its namesake university, are named after him.

South of the Old Library is the 1978 **Arts & Social Science Building**, which backs on to Nassau St and forms the alternative entrance to the college. Like the Berkeley Library it was designed by Paul Koralek; it also houses the **Douglas Hyde Gallery of Modern Art** (☎ 608 1116; admission free; ☿ 11am-6pm Mon-Wed & Fri, 11am-7pm Thu, 11am-4.45pm Sat).

After the *Book of Kells* the college's other big tourist attraction is the **Dublin Experience** (☎ 608 1688; Arts & Social Science Bldg; adult/student €4.20/3.50, incl Book of Kells €10.50/8.50; ☿ 10am-5pm mid-May–Sep). It's a 45-minute multimedia introduction to the city. Shows take place at the back of the Arts & Social Science Building.

Behind the Rubrics Building, at the eastern end of Library Sq, is New Sq. The highly ornate 1853 to 1857 **Victorian Museum Building** (☎ 608 1477; New Sq; admission free; ☿ by prior arrangement only) has the skeletons of two enormous giant Irish deer just inside the entrance, and the Geological Museum upstairs.

The 1734 **Printing House**, designed by Richard Cassels to resemble a Doric temple and now used for the microelectronics and electrical engineering departments, is on the northern side of New Sq.

At the eastern end of the college grounds are the rugby ground and College Park, where cricket is played. There are a number of science buildings here also. The Lincoln Place Gate at this end is usually open and makes a good entrance or exit from the college, especially if you're on a bicycle.

THE PAGE OF KELLS

Trinity's top show stopper is the world-famous *Book of Kells*, an illuminated manuscript dating from around AD 800, making it one of the oldest books in the world. It was probably produced by monks at St Colmcille's Monastery on the remote island of Iona, off the western coast of Scotland. Repeated looting by marauding Vikings forced the monks to flee to the temporary safety of Kells, County Meath, in Ireland in AD 806, along with their masterpiece. Around 850 years later, the book was brought to the college for safekeeping and has remained here since.

The *Book of Kells* contains the four gospels of the New Testament, written in Latin, as well as prefaces, summaries and other text. If it were merely words, the *Book of Kells* would simply be a very old book – it's the extensive and amazingly complex illustrations (the illuminations) that make it so wonderful. The superbly decorated opening initials are only part of the story, for the book has smaller illustrations between the lines.

And here the problems begin. Of the 680 pages, only two are on display – one showing an illumination, the other showing text – which has led to it being dubbed the *page* of Kells. No getting around that one, though: you can hardly expect the right to thumb through a priceless treasure at random. No, the real problem is its immense popularity, which makes viewing it a rather unsatisfactory pleasure. Punters are herded through the specially constructed viewing room at near lightning pace, making for a there-you-see-it, there-you-don't kind of experience.

To really appreciate the book, you can get your own reproduction copy for a mere €22,000. Failing that, the library bookshop stocks a plethora of souvenirs and other memorabilia, including Otto Simm's excellent *Exploring the Book of Kells* (€10.95), a thorough guide with attractive colour plates, and a popular CD-ROM showing all 800 pages for €29.95.

BANK OF IRELAND

The imposing **Bank of Ireland** (Map p90; ☎ 671 1488; College Green; ☺ 10am-4pm Mon-Wed & Fri, 10am-5pm Thu), directly opposite Trinity College, was originally built in 1729 to house the Irish Parliament. When the Parliament voted itself out of existence by the Act of Union in 1801, it became a building without a role. It was sold in 1803 with instructions that the interior be altered to prevent its being used as a debating chamber in the future. Consequently, the large central House of Commons was remodelled but the smaller chamber of the House of Lords survived. After independence the Irish government chose to make Leinster House the new parliamentary building and ignored the possibility of restoring this fine building to its original use.

Inside, the banking mall occupies what was once the House of Commons, but it offers little indication of its former role. The Irish House of Lords is a much more interesting place, with its Irish-oak woodwork, its late-18th-century Dublin crystal chandelier and tapestries, and 10kg silver-gilt mace.

There are tours of the **House of Lords** (admission free), which also include an informal talk as much about Ireland, and life in general, as the building itself. Tours are on Tuesday at 10.30am, 11.30am and 1.45pm.

TEMPLE BAR

Dublin's top tourist precinct is a maze of cobbled streets sandwiched between Dame St and the Liffey, running from Trinity College to Christ Church Cathedral. In Temple Bar you can browse for vintage clothes, check out the latest art installations, get your nipples pierced and nibble on Mongolian barbecue. In good weather, you can watch outdoor movies in one square or join in a pulsating drum circle in another – it's all part of Dublin's very own Cultural Quarter, now one of Europe's best-known entertainment districts.

Frankly, it's all a little bogus. During the day and on weekday nights Temple Bar does have something of a bohemian bent about it – if you ignore the crappy tourist shops and dreadful restaurants serving bland, overpriced food – but at weekends, when the party really gets going, it all gets very sloppy. The huge, characterless bars crank up the sounds and throw their doors open to the tens of thousands of punters looking to drink and score like the end of the world is nigh. By 3am, the only culture on display is in the pools of vomit and urine that give the whole area the aroma of a sewer – welcome to Temple Barf.

Temple Bar Properties (☎ 677 2255; www.templebar.ie, www.visit-templebar.ie; 12 East Essex St; ☺ 9am-5.30pm Mon-Fri) publishes the Tascq cultural guide to Temple Bar that gives information on attractions and restaurants in the area and is available from its office or in businesses around Temple Bar. It's best to check the websites for details of events and the Diversions festival (see p121).

Meeting House Square is indeed one of the real success stories of Temple Bar. On one side is the excellent **Gallery of Photography** (☎ 671 4653; admission free; ☺ 11am-6pm Mon-Sat), hosting temporary exhibitions of contemporary local and international photographers. Staying with photography, the other side of the square is home to the **National Photographic Archive** (☎ 671 0073; admission free; ☺ 11am-6pm Mon-Sat, 2-6pm Sun), a magnificent resource for anyone interested in a photographic history of Ireland.

At the western end of Temple Bar, in the shadow of Christ Church Cathedral (p98), is **Fishamble Street**, the oldest street in Dublin, dating back to Viking times – not that you'd know that to see it now.

In 1742 Handel conducted the first performance of his *Messiah* in the **Dublin Music Hall**, behind Kinlay House hotel on Lord Edward St. The music hall, which opened in 1741, was designed by Richard Cassels; the only reminder of it today is the entrance and the original door. It is now part of a hotel that bears the composer's name.

On Parliament St, which runs south from the river to the City Hall and Dublin Castle, the **Sunlight Chambers** beside the river has a beautiful frieze around its façade. Sunlight was a brand of soap manufactured by the Lever Brothers, who were responsible for the late-19th-century building. The frieze shows the Lever Brothers' view of the world: men make clothes dirty, women wash them!

Eustace Street is an interesting street. Buildings on it include the 1715 Presbyterian Meeting House, now the **Ark** (☎ 670 7788; 11a Eustace St), a children's cultural centre. The Dublin branch of the Society of United

Irishmen, who sought parliamentary reform and equality for Catholics, was first convened in 1791 in the Eagle Tavern, now the Friends Meeting House. This should not be confused with the other Eagle Tavern, which is on Cork St.

Merchant's Arch leads to the **Ha'penny Bridge**, named after the ha'penny toll once needed to cross. The **Stock Exchange** is on Anglesea St, in a building dating from 1878.

DUBLIN CASTLE

The centre of British power in Ireland and originally built on the orders of King John in 1204, **Dublin Castle** (Map p82; ☎ 677 7129; www.dublincastle.ie; Cork Hill, Dame St; adult/senior & child/student €4.50/2/3.50; ⏲ 10am-4.45pm Mon-Fri, 2-4.45pm Sat & Sun) is more higgledy-piggledy palace than castle. Only the Record Tower, completed in 1258, survives from the original Norman construction. Parts of the castle's foundations remain and a visit to the excavations is the most interesting part of the castle tour. The moats, which are now completely covered by more modern developments, were once filled by the River Poddle. The castle is also home to one of Dublin's best museums, the Chester Beatty Library.

The castle, which tops Cork Hill, behind the City Hall, is still used for government business, and tours (every 20 minutes) are often tailored around meetings and conferences or sometimes cancelled altogether, so it's wise to phone beforehand.

CHESTER BEATTY LIBRARY

Book of Kells, schmells. The world-famous **Chester Beatty Library** (Map p82; ☎ 407 0750; www.cbl.ie; Dublin Castle; admission free; ⏲ 10am-5pm Mon-Fri, 11am-5pm Sat, 1-5pm Sun, tours 1pm Wed, 3pm & 4pm Sun May-Sep, closed Sat-Mon Oct-Apr) houses the collection of mining engineer Sir Alfred Chester Beatty (1875–1968), bequeathed to the Irish State on his death. The breathtaking collection includes over 20,000 manuscripts, rare books, miniature paintings, clay tablets, costumes and other objects spread across two floors. On the ground floor you'll find works of art from the Western, Islamic and east Asian worlds, including perhaps the finest collection of Chinese jade books in the world. Also worth examining are the illuminated European texts.

The 2nd floor is devoted to the major religions of the world – Judaism, Islam, Christianity, Hinduism and Buddhism. The collection of Korans dating from the 9th to the 19th centuries (the library has over 270 of them) are considered by experts to be the best examples of illuminated Islamic texts in the world. And it doesn't stop there. You'll also find some marvellous examples of ancient papyri, including the renowned Egyptian love poems from the 12th century BC, and some of the earliest illuminated gospels in the world, dating to around AD 200. The collection is rounded off with some exquisite scrolls and artwork from China, Japan, Tibet and Southeast Asia.

There's also a full restaurant, gift shop and Oriental roof garden here.

BEDFORD TOWER & GENEALOGICAL OFFICE

Directly across the Upper Yard from the main entrance to the castle are the **Bedford Tower & Genealogical Office** (Map p82). In 1907 the collection known as the Irish Crown Jewels was stolen from the tower and never recovered. The Genealogical Office as an institution dates from 1552. Its present building dates from the 18th century.

The entranceway to the castle yard, beside the Bedford Tower, is topped by a statue of Justice that has always been a subject of mirth. She faces the castle and has her back to the city – seen as a sure indicator of how much justice the average Irish citizen could expect from the British. The scales of justice also had a distinct tendency to fill with rain and tilt in one direction or the other, rather than assuming the approved level position. Eventually a hole was drilled in the bottom of each pan so the rainwater could drain out.

CITY HALL

Fronting Dublin Castle on Lord Edward St, **City Hall** (Map p82; ☎ 672 2204; www.dublincity.ie; Cork Hill; adult/senior & child/student €4/1.50/2; ⏲ 10am-5.15pm Mon-Sat, 2-5pm Sun) was built by Thomas Cooley between 1769 and 1779 as the Royal Exchange and later became the offices of the Dublin Corporation. It stands on the site of the Lucas Coffee House and the Eagle Tavern, in which Dublin's infamous Hell Fire Club was established in 1735. Founded by Richard Parsons, earl of Rosse, it was one of a number of gentlemen's clubs in Dublin where less-than-gentlemanly conduct took place. It gained a reputation for debauchery and black magic, but there's no evidence that such things took place.

'The Story of the Capital' is a multimedia exhibition in the basement tracing the history of Dublin from its earliest beginnings.

The 1781 **Municipal Buildings**, just west of the City Hall, were built by Thomas Ivory (1720–86), who was also responsible for the Genealogical Office in Dublin Castle.

NATIONAL MUSEUM

Designed by Sir Thomas Newenham Deane and completed in 1890, the star attraction of the **National Museum** (Map p84; ☎ 677 7444; www .museum.ie; Kildare St; admission by donation; ☼ 10am-5pm Tue-Sat, 2-5pm Sun) is the Treasury, home to the finest collection of Bronze- and Iron-Age gold artefacts in the world and the world's most complete collection of medieval Celtic metalwork.

The centrepieces of the Treasury's unique collection are Ireland's most famous crafted artefacts, the **Ardagh Chalice** and the **Tara Brooch**. Measuring 17.8cm high and 24.2cm in diameter, the 12th-century Ardagh Chalice is made of gold, silver, bronze, brass, copper and lead. Put simply, this is the finest exemplar of Celtic art ever found. The equally renowned Tara Brooch was crafted around AD 700 primarily in white bronze, but with traces of gold, silver, glass, copper, enamel and wire beading, and was used as a clasp for a cloak.

The Treasury includes many other stunning pieces, many of which are grouped together in 'hoards', after the manner in which they were found, usually by a farmer digging up a field or a bog. Be sure not to miss the Broighter and Mooghaun hoards.

Upstairs, Viking Age Dublin illustrates Dublin's Viking era, with exhibits from the excavations at Wood Quay – the area between Christ Church Cathedral and the river, where Dublin City Council plonked its new headquarters. Other exhibits focus on the 1916 Easter Rising and the independence struggle between 1900 and 1921. Frequent short-term exhibitions are also held.

COLLINS BARRACKS

So much for the austere life of a soldier. This converted barracks, the oldest in Europe, is one of Dublin's most beautiful spaces and a fitting location for the **National Museum of Decorative Arts & History** (Map pp80-1; ☎ 677 7444; Benburb St; admission free; ☼ 10am-5pm Tue-Sat, 2-5pm Sun), a part of the National Museum. The exhibits are good, but the building is stunning: at its heart is the huge central square surrounded by arcaded colonnades and blocks linked by walking bridges. While wandering about the plaza, imagine that it once held up to six regiments in formation. The whole shebang is the work of Thomas Burgh (1670–1730), who also designed the Old Library (p90) in Trinity and St Michan's Church (p105).

Now to the museum, which offers a glimpse at Ireland's social, economic and military history over the last millennium. It's a big ask – too big, say its critics – but well-designed displays, interactive multimedia and a dizzying array of disparate artefacts make for an interesting and valiant effort. We loved the Curator's Choice, which brings together such objects as a 2000-year-old Japanese ceremonial bell (which has little to do with Ireland) and the gloves worn by King William of Orange at the Battle of the Boyne (which has far too much to do with Ireland).

NATIONAL GALLERY

A magnificent Caravaggio and a breathtaking collection of works by Jack B Yeats – William Butler's kid brother – are the main reasons to visit the **National Gallery** (Map p84; ☎ 661 5133; www.nationalgallery.ie; Merrion Sq West; admission free; ☼ 9.30am-5.30pm Mon-Wed, Fri & Sat, to 8.30pm Thu, noon-5.30pm Sun; free tours 3pm Sat, 2pm, 3pm & 4pm Sun), but not the only ones. Its excellent collection is strong in Irish art, but there are also high-quality collections of every major European school of painting.

The gallery has four wings: the original Dargan Wing, the Milltown Rooms, the North Wing and the spectacular new Millennium Wing. On the ground floor of the Dargan Wing (named after railway magnate and art-lover William Dargan, whose statue graces the front lawn) is the imposing Shaw Room (named after writer George Bernard, another great benefactor; his bronze statue keeps Dargan company outside), lined with full-length portraits and illuminated by a series of spectacular Waterford crystal chandeliers. Upstairs, a series of rooms is dedicated to the Italian early and high Renaissance, 16th-century northern Italian art and 17th- and 18th-century Italian art. Fra Angelico, Titian and Tintoretto are among the artists represented, but the highlight is undoubtedly Caravaggio's *The Taking of Christ* (1602), which lay undiscovered for over 60 years in a Jesuit house in Leeson St and was accidentally discovered by chief curator Sergio Benedetti.

The central Milltown Rooms were added between 1899 and 1903 to hold Russborough House's art collection, which was presented to the gallery in 1902. The ground floor displays the gallery's fine Irish collection plus a smaller British collection, with works by Reynolds, Hogarth, Gainsborough, Landseer and Turner. Absolutely unmissable is the **Yeats Collection** at the back of the gallery, displaying more than 30 works by Irish impressionist Jack B Yeats (1871–1957), Ireland's most important 20th-century painter.

Upstairs are works from Germany, the Netherlands and Spain. There are rooms full of works by Rembrandt and his circle, and by the Spanish artists of Seville. The Spanish collection features works by El Greco, Goya and Picasso.

The North Wing was added only between 1964 and 1968, but has already undergone extensive refurbishment. It houses works by British and European artists.

The impressive new Millennium Wing, with its light-filled modern design, can also be entered from Nassau St. It houses a small collection of 20th-century Irish art and high-profile visiting collections (for which there is a charge to visit), an art reference library, a lecture theatre, a good bookshop and Fitzer's Café.

LEINSTER HOUSE

Dublin's grandest Georgian home, built by Richard Cassels between 1745 and 1748 for the very grand James Fitzgerald, earl of Kildare, is now the seat of both houses of the Oireachtas na Éireann (Irish Parliament), the Dáil (Lower House) and Seanad (Upper House). Originally called Kildare House, it was changed to **Leinster House** (Map p84; ☎ 618 3000, for tour information ☎ 618 3271; www.irlgov.ie /oireachtas; Kildare St; admission free; ☒ observation gallery 2.30-8.30pm Tue, 10.30am-8.30pm Wed, 10.30am-5.30pm Thu, Nov-May) following the earl's assuming of the title of duke of Leinster in 1766.

Leinster House's Kildare St frontage was designed by Richard Cassels to look like a town house, whereas the Merrion Sq frontage was made to look like a country house. Hard to imagine it now, but when Cassels built the house it was in the wild expanses south of the Liffey, far from the genteel neighbourhoods of the north city where Dublin's aristocracy lived. Never short of confidence, the earl dismissed his critics by declaring, 'where I go, society will follow'. There's no doubt about it: Jimmy Fitz had a nose for real estate.

The Dublin Society, later named the Royal Dublin Society, bought the building in 1814 but moved out in stages between 1922 and 1925, when the first government of independent Ireland decided to establish Parliament here. The obelisk in front of the building is dedicated to Arthur Griffith, Michael Collins and Kevin O'Higgins, architects of independent Ireland.

The Seanad meets in the north-wing saloon, while the Dáil meets in a less interesting room that was originally a lecture theatre added to the original building in 1897. When Parliament is sitting, visitors are admitted to an observation gallery. You get an entry ticket from the Kildare St entrance on production of some identification. Bags can't be taken in, or notes or photographs taken. Prearranged guided tours are available weekdays when parliament is in session.

NATURAL HISTORY MUSEUM

Very dusty, a little creepy and utterly compelling, the **Natural History Museum** (Map p84; ☎ 677 7444; www.museum.ie; Merrion St; admission free; ☒ 10am-5pm Tue-Sat, 2-5pm Sun) has scarcely changed since 1857 when Scottish explorer Dr David Livingstone delivered the opening lecture. In the face of the city's newer hi-tech museums, its Victorian charm has been beautifully preserved, making the 'dead zoo' one of Dublin's more interesting museums. The huge and well-organised collection numbers about two million, of which about 10,000 are on display. That moth-eaten look often afflicting neglected stuffed-animal collections has been kept at bay, and children are likely to find it fascinating.

On the ground floor, the collection of skeletons, stuffed animals and the like covers the full range of Irish fauna. It includes three skeletons of the Irish giant deer, which became extinct about 10,000 years ago. On the 1st and 2nd floors are fauna from around the world.

GOVERNMENT BUILDINGS

On Upper Merrion St, the domed **Government Buildings** (Map p84; ☎ 662 4888; www.taoiseach.gov.ie; Upper Merrion St; ☺ free tours 10.30am-3.30pm Sat only) were opened for business in 1911. Architecturally, they are a rather heavy-handed Edwardian interpretation of the Georgian style. Each free 40-minute tour takes about 15 people, so you may have to wait a while for a big enough group to assemble. Tours can't be booked in advance, but if you go in on Saturday morning you can put your name down for one later in the day. You get to see the Taoiseach's office, the cabinet room, the ceremonial staircase with a stunning stained-glass window designed by Evie Hone (1894–1955) for the 1939 New York Trade Fair, and innumerable fine examples of modern Irish arts and crafts. Tickets for the tours are available from the National Gallery **ticket office** (☎ 661 5133).

NATIONAL LIBRARY

Flanking the Kildare St entrance to Leinster House is the **National Library** (Map p84; ☎ 603 0200; www.nli.ie; Kildare St; admission free; ☺ 10am-9pm Mon-Wed, 10am-5pm Thu & Fri, 10am-1pm Sat), which was built between 1884 and 1890, at the same time and to a similar design as the National Museum, by Sir Thomas Newenham Deane and his son Sir Thomas Manly Deane. Leinster House, the library and museum were all part of the Royal Dublin Society (formed in 1731), which aimed to improve conditions for poor people and to promote the arts and sciences. The library's extensive collection has many valuable early manuscripts, first editions, maps and other items. The library's reading room featured in James Joyce's *Ulysses*. Temporary displays are often held in the entrance area.

On the 2nd floor is the **Genealogical Office** (Map p84; ☎ 603 0200; National Library, Kildare St; ☺ 10am-4.30pm Mon-Fri, 10am-12.30pm Sat) where you can obtain information on how best to trace your Irish roots. A genealogist can do the trace for you (at a fee dependent on research) or simply point you in the right direction (for free).

ST STEPHEN'S GREEN & AROUND

While enjoying the nine gorgeous, landscaped hectares of Dublin's most popular square, consider that once upon a time **St Stephen's Green** (Map p84; admission free; ☺ dawn-dusk) was an open common used for public whippings, beatings and hangings. Activities in the green have quietened since then and are generally confined to the lunch-time-picnic-and-stroll variety. Still, on a summer's day it is the favourite retreat of office workers, lovers and visitors alike, who come to breath a little fresh air, feed the ducks and cuddle on the grass.

Although a stone wall was erected in the 17th century when Dublin Corporation sold off the surrounding land to property developers, railings and locked gates were only added in 1814 when an annual fee of one guinea was charged to use the green – a great way to keep the poor out. In 1877 Arthur Edward Guinness pushed an act through Parliament opening the green to the public once again. He also paid for the green's lakes and ponds, which were added in 1880.

The fine Georgian buildings around the square date mainly from Dublin's mid- to late-18th-century Georgian prime. At that time the northern side was known as the Beaux Walk and it's still a pretty fancy stretch of real estate; drop in for tea at the imposing 1867 **Shelbourne** hotel and you'll see what we mean. Just beyond the hotel is a small **Huguenot cemetery** dating from 1693, when many French Huguenots fled here from persecution under Louis XIV.

The main entrance to the green is through **Fusiliers' Arch** at the northwestern corner. Modelled on the Arch of Titus in Rome, the arch commemorates the 212 soldiers of the Royal Dublin Fusiliers who died in the Boer War (1899–1902).

Across the road from the western side of the green are the 1863 **Unitarian Church** and the **Royal College of Surgeons** with its fine façade. During the 1916 Easter Rising, the building was occupied by the colourful Countess Markievicz (1868–1927), an Irish nationalist married to a supposed Polish count. The columns still bear bullet marks.

On the southern side of the green is **Newman House** (☎ 716 7422; 85-86 St Stephen's Green; adult/child €5/4; ☺ tours hourly noon & 2-4pm Tue-Fri Jun-Aug only), now part of University College,

Dublin. These buildings have some of the finest plasterwork in the city. The Catholic University of Ireland, predecessor of University College, Dublin, acquired No 85 in 1865, then passed it to the Jesuits. Some of the plasterwork was too detailed for Jesuit tastes, however, so cover-ups were prescribed. On the ceiling of the upstairs saloon, previously naked female figures were clothed in what can best be described as furry swimsuits. One survived the restoration process.

Next to Newman University Church is the **Newman Chapel**, built between 1854 and 1856 with a colourful neo-Byzantine interior that attracted a great deal of criticism at the time. Today it's one of the most fashionable churches in Dublin for weddings.

One of Dublin's most beautiful parks is the landscaped **Iveagh Gardens** (☼ dawn-dusk year round), directly behind Newman House and reached via Clonmel St, just off Harcourt St. The imposing walls give the impression that they are private gardens, but they are one of the nicest places to relax on a summer's day or before a show in the National Concert Hall.

MERRION SQUARE

St Stephen's Green may win the popularity contest, but tranquil **Merrion Square** (Map p84; admission free; ☼ dawn-dusk) is our choice for favourite city park. Surrounding the well-kept lawns and beautifully tended flower beds on three sides are some of Dublin's most exceptional Georgian frontages, with fine doors, peacock fanlights, ornate door knockers and foot scrapers used by gentlemen to scrape mud from their boots before venturing indoors.

Despite the air of affluent calm, life around here hasn't always been just a well-pruned bed of roses. During the Famine, the lawns of the square teemed with destitute rural refugees who lived off the soup kitchen organised here. The British embassy was at 39 Merrion Sq East until 1972, when it was burnt out in protest against the killing of 13 innocent civilians on Bloody Sunday in Derry.

That same side of Merrion Sq once continued into Lower Fitzwilliam St in the longest unbroken series of Georgian houses anywhere in Europe, but in 1961 the Electricity Supply Board (ESB) – in a myopic crime against history and aesthetics – knocked down 26 of the

houses to build an office block that is one of the city's ugliest eyesores.

Just to prove that they are mindful of Dublin's priceless architectural heritage, the ESB had the decency to preserve one fine old Georgian house, **No 29 Lower Fitzwilliam St** (Map pp80-1; ☎ 702 6165; www.esb .ie/education; 29 Lower Fitzwilliam St; adult/child/student €4.50/free/2; ☼ 10am-5pm Tue-Sat, 2-5pm Sun, closed 2 weeks before Christmas) at the southeastern corner of Merrion Sq. It has been restored to give a good impression of genteel home life in Dublin between 1790 and 1820. A short film on its history is followed by a 30-minute guided tour in groups of up to nine.

OSCAR WILDE HOUSE

In 1855 the surgeon Sir William Wilde and the poet Lady 'Speranza' Wilde moved with their one-year-old son Oscar to 1 Merrion Sq North – the first Georgian residence constructed on the square (1762). They stayed here until 1878 and it is likely that Oscar's literary genius was first stimulated by the creative atmosphere of the house, where Lady Wilde hosted the city's most famous (and best frequented) literary salon.

Today it is owned by the American College Dublin, which has converted part of the house into a **museum** (Map p84; ☎ 662 0281; www.amcd.ie/oscarwildehouse/about/html; 1 North Merrion Sq; admission €2.50; ☼ tours 10.15am & 11.15am Mon, Wed & Thu) devoted to Oscar Wilde.

Enthusiasts should check out the **Oscar Wilde statue** at the northwestern corner of the square, as it is adorned with the witty one-liners for which Oscar Wilde became famous.

The Liberties & Kilmainham

At the top of a small hill, just west of Dublin Castle, is the most impressive monument of medieval Dublin, Christ Church Cathedral. It stood firmly inside the city walls unlike that other great place of worship, St Patrick's, which lay to the south and just outside of them. Beneath both of them, to the west, are the Liberties, Dublin's oldest surviving neighbourhood. The western end of the Liberties has a curious aroma in the air: it is the smell of roasting hops, used in the production of Dublin's black gold and, for many visitors, the epitome of all things Irish: Guinness. Further along James St is Kilmainham, home to the old prison that was central to the struggle for Irish independence and an ancient soldiers' hospital, now the country's most important modern art museum.

CHRIST CHURCH CATHEDRAL

The mother of all of Dublin's churches is **Christ Church Cathedral** (Church of the Holy Trinity; Map p82; ☎ 677 8099; www.cccdub.ie; Christ Church Pl; adult/student €5/2.50; ☒ 9.45am-5pm Mon-Fri, 10am-5pm Sat & Sun), just south of the river and west of Temple Bar. It was founded in 1030 on what was then the southern edge of Dublin's Viking settlement. It was later smack in the middle of medieval Dublin: Dublin Castle, the Tholsel (Town Hall; demolished in 1809) and the original Four Courts (demolished in 1796) were all close by. Nearby, on Back Lane, is the only remaining guildhall in Dublin. The 1706 **Tailors Hall** was due for demolition in the 1960s, but survived to become the office of **An Taisce** (National Trust for Ireland).

The original wooden church in this spot wasn't really a keeper, so the Normans rebuilt the lot in stone from 1172, mostly under the impetus of Richard de Clare, earl of Pembroke (better known as Strongbow), the Anglo-Norman noble who invaded Ireland in 1170.

Throughout much of its history Christ Church vied for supremacy with nearby St Patrick's Cathedral but, like its neighbour, it fell on hard times in the 18th and 19th centuries and was virtually derelict by the time restoration took place. Earlier, the nave had been used as a market and the crypt had housed taverns. Today, both Church of Ireland cathedrals are outsiders in a Catholic nation.

From the southeastern entrance to the churchyard you walk past ruins of the chapter house, which dates from 1230. The entrance to the cathedral is at the southwestern corner and as you enter you face the northern wall. This survived the collapse of its southern counterpart but has also suffered from subsiding foundations.

The southern aisle has a monument to the legendary Strongbow. The armoured figure on the tomb is unlikely to be Strongbow (it's more probably the earl of Drogheda), but his internal organs may have been buried here. A popular legend relates that the half-figure beside the tomb is Strongbow's son, who was cut in two by his father when his bravery in battle was suspect.

The southern transept contains the superb baroque tomb of the 19th earl of Kildare (died 1734). His grandson, Lord Edward Fitzgerald, was a member of the United Irishmen and died in the abortive 1798 Rising.

An entrance just by the southern transept descends to the unusually large arched crypt, which dates back to the original Viking church. Curiosities in the crypt include a glass display case housing a mummified cat chasing a mummified mouse that were trapped inside an organ pipe in the 1860s! From the main entrance, a bridge, part of the 1871 to 1878 restoration, leads to Dvblinia.

DVBLINIA

Inside the old Synod Hall attached to Christ Church Cathedral, **Dvblinia** (Map p82; ☎ 679 4611; www.dublinia.ie; adult/child/student €6/3.50/5; ☒ 10am-5pm Apr-Sep, 11am-4pm Mon-Sat & 10am-4.30pm Sun Oct-Mar) is a kitschy and lively attempt to bring medieval Dublin to life. Models, streetscapes and somewhat old-fashioned interactive displays do a fairly decent job of it, at least for kids. The model of a medieval quayside and a cobbler's shop are both excellent, as is the scale model of the medieval city. In 2005 a new exhibition called The Viking World was introduced. Finally, you can climb neighbouring St Michael's Tower for views over the city to the Dublin Hills.

Your ticket gets you into Christ Church Cathedral free (via the link bridge).

ST PATRICK'S CATHEDRAL

It was here – reputedly – that St Paddy himself dunked the Irish heathens into the waters of a well, so the **cathedral** (Map pp80-1; ☎ 475 4817; www.stpatrickscathedral.ie; St Patrick's Close; adult/child/senior & student €4.50/free/3.50; ☒ 9am-6pm Mon-Sat, 9-11am, 12.45-3pm & 4.15-6pm Sun Mar-Oct, 9am-6pm Mon-Fri, to 5pm Sat, 10-11am & 12.45-3pm Sun Nov-Feb) that bears his name stands on one of the earliest Christian sites in the city and a pretty sacred piece of turf. Although there's been a church here since the 5th century, the present building dates from 1190 or 1225 – opinions differ – and even it has been altered several times, most notably in 1864 when the flying buttresses were added, thanks to the neo-Gothic craze that swept the nation. St Patrick's Park, the expanse of green beside the cathedral, was a crowded slum until it was cleared and its residents evicted in the early 20th century.

Like Christ Church Cathedral, the building has suffered a rather dramatic history of storm and fire damage. Oliver Cromwell, during his 1649 visit to Ireland, converted St Patrick's to a stable for his army's horses, an indignity to which he also subjected numerous other Irish churches. Jonathan Swift was the dean of the cathedral from 1713 to 1745, but prior to its restoration it became very neglected.

Entering the cathedral from the south-western porch you come almost immediately, on your right, to the graves of Swift and his longtime companion Esther Johnson, aka Stella. On the wall nearby are Swift's own Latin epitaphs to the two of them, and a bust of him.

The huge, dusty Boyle Monument to the left was erected in 1632 by Richard Boyle, earl of Cork, and is decorated with numerous painted figures of members of his family. The figure in the centre on the bottom level is of the earl's five-year-old son Robert Boyle (1627–91), who grew up to become a noted scientist. His contributions to physics include Boyle's Law, which relates the pressure and volume of gases.

The cathedral's choir school dates back to 1432 and the choir took part in the first performance of Handel's *Messiah* in 1742. You can hear the choir sing at 9.40am and 5.35pm Monday to Friday (no evensong on Wednesday) during the school year. A real treat are the carols performed around Christmas; call ☎ 453 9472 for details of how to obtain a hard-to-get ticket.

To get to the cathedral, take bus No 50, 50A or 56A from Aston Quay or No 54 or 54A from Burgh Quay.

MARSH'S LIBRARY

One of the city's most beautiful open secrets is **Marsh's Library** (Map pp80-1; ☎ 454 3511; www.marshlibrary.ie; St Patrick's Close; adult/child/student €2.50/free/1.50; ☒ 10am-1pm & 2-5pm Mon & Wed-Fri, 10.30am-1pm Sat), just around the corner from St Patrick's Cathedral, a barely visited antique library with a look and atmosphere that has hardly changed a jot since it opened its doors to awkward scholars in 1707. Crammed into its elaborately carved oak bookcases are over 25,000 books dating from the 16th to early 18th centuries, as well as maps, numerous manuscripts and a collection of *incunabula* (books printed before 1500). One of the oldest and finest tomes in the collection is a volume of Cicero's *Letters to His Friends* printed in Milan in 1472.

The building was commissioned by Archbishop Narcissus March (1638–1713) and designed by Sir William Robinson, the creator of the Royal Hospital Kilmainham; today it is one of the only 18th-century buildings in Dublin still used for the purpose for which it was built.

ST WERBURGH'S CHURCH

Of undoubtedly ancient but imprecise origin, **St Werburgh's** (Map p82; ☎ 478 3710; Werburgh St; admission by donation; ☒ 10am-4pm Mon-Fri) has undergone numerous face-lifts: in 1662, 1715 and, with some elegance, in 1759 after a fire in 1754. The church's tall spire was dismantled after Robert Emmet's uprising in 1803 for fear that rebels might use it as a vantage point for snipers. The church is closely linked with the history of uprisings against British rule; interred in the vault is Lord Edward Fitzgerald, a member of the United Irishmen that led the 1798 Rising. In what was a frequent theme of Irish rebellions, compatriots gave him away and he died as a result of the wounds he received during his capture. Ironically, his captor Major Henry Sirr is buried in the adjacent graveyard. In the porch you will notice two fire pumps that date from the time when Dublin's fire department was composed of church volunteers.

You will need to phone or see the caretaker at 8 Castle St to see inside.

ST AUDOEN'S CHURCHES

St Audoen, the 7th-century bishop of Rouen and patron saint of Normandy, must have had a few friends in Dublin to have two churches named after him. Both are just west of Christ Church Cathedral. The more interesting of the two is the smaller **Church of Ireland** (Map p82; ☎ 677 0088; Cornmarket, High St; adult/child/student €2/1/1.25; ⏰ 9.30am-4.45pm Jun-Sep), the only surviving medieval parish church still in use in Dublin. It was built between 1181 and 1212, though recent excavations unearthing a 9th-century burial slab suggest that it was built on top of an even older church. Its tower and door date from the 12th century, and the aisle from the 15th century, but the church today is mainly a 19th-century restoration.

As part of the tour, you can explore the ruins, as well as the present church and the visitor centre in **St Anne's Chapel**, which houses a number of tombstones of leading members of Dublin society from the 16th to the 18th centuries. At the top of the chapel is the tower, which houses the three oldest bells in Ireland, dating from 1423. Although the church's exhibits are hardly spectacular, the building itself is very beautiful and a genuine slice of medieval Dublin.

The church is entered from the north through an arch off High St. Part of the old city wall, this arch was built in 1240 and is the only surviving reminder of the city gates.

Joined onto the older Protestant St Audoen's is the newer and larger **St Audoen's Catholic Church** (Cornmarket, High St; admission free), a large church whose claim to local fame is Father Flash Kavanagh, who used to read Mass at high speed so that his large congregation could head off to more absorbing Sunday pursuits, such as football.

GUINNESS STOREHOUSE & ST JAMES' GATE BREWERY

It should come as no surprise that the number one tourist attraction in Dublin is a multimedia bells-and-whistles homage to Ireland's most famous export and the city's most enduring symbol, Guinness.

The **Guinness Storehouse** (Map pp80–1; ☎ 408 4800; www.guinness-storehouse.com; St James's Gate Brewery; adult/child/student €13.50/3/9; ⏰ 9.30am-5pm), the only part of the massive, 26-hectare brewery open to the public, is a suitable cathedral in which to worship the black gold; shaped like a giant pint of Guinness, it rises seven impressive storeys high around a stunning central atrium. At the top is the head, represented by the Gravity Bar, with a panoramic view of Dublin.

The Gravity Bar is also the best place to get an idea of how big the brewery actually is. From the time Arthur Guinness founded the **St James' Gate Brewery** in 1759, the operation has expanded down to the Liffey and across both sides of the street; at one point, it had its own railroad and there was a giant gate stretching across James' St, hence the brewery's proper name. At its apogee in the 1930s, it employed over 5000 workers, making it the largest employer in the city. Increased automation has reduced the workforce to around 600, but it still produces 2.5 million pints of stout *every day*.

You'll get to drink one of those pints at the end of your tour, but not before you have walked through the extravaganza that is the Guinness floorshow, spread across 1.6 hectares and involving an array of audiovisual, interactive displays that cover pretty much all aspects of the brewery's history and the brewing process. It's slick and sophisticated, but you can't ignore the man behind the curtain: the extensive exhibit on the company's incredibly successful history of advertising is a reminder that for all the talk of mysticism and magic, it's all really about marketing and manipulation.

It's all a moot point, however, when you have that pint in your hand and you're surveying all below you from the vertiginous heights of the Gravity Bar. This is the best pint of Guinness you'll ever drink, the cognoscenti like to claim, but just make sure you've got good friends and conversation to enjoy it with: after all, isn't that the whole point?

Around the corner at **No 1 Thomas St** (⏰ closed to public) a plaque marks the house where Arthur Guinness (1725–1803) lived. In a yard across the road stands **St Patrick's Tower** (⏰ closed to public), Europe's tallest smock windmill (with a revolving top), which was built around 1757.

To get here, take bus No 21A, 78 or 78A from Fleet St.

IRISH MUSEUM OF MODERN ART & ROYAL HOSPITAL KILMAINHAM

Ireland's most important collection of modern and contemporary Irish art is housed in the elegant, airy expanse of the old Royal Hospital at Kilmainham, which in 1991 became the **Irish Museum of Modern Art** (IMMA; Map p78; ☎ 612 9900; www.imma.ie; Military Rd; admission free; ☒ 10am-5.30pm Tue-Sat, noon-5.30pm Sun). Catch bus No 24, 79 or 90 from Aston Quay.

The **Royal Hospital Kilmainham** was designed by William Robinson (also of Marsh's Library, see p99) and was built between 1680 and 1687 as a home for retired soldiers, a role it fulfilled until 1928 after which it languished for nearly 50 years until a 1980s restoration. At the time of its construction, it was one of the finest buildings in Ireland and there were mutterings that it was altogether too good a place for its residents.

There are free guided tours (2.30pm Wednesday, Friday and Sunday) of the museum's exhibits throughout the year, but we strongly recommend the free, seasonal heritage itinerary (Tuesday to Sunday, July to September) of the building itself, which includes the Banqueting Hall and the stunning baroque chapel, which has papier-mâché ceilings and a set of exquisite Queen Anne gates. Tours depart on request, so long as there are enough people to make a small group. Also worth seeing are the fully restored formal gardens. A good café and bookshop are on the grounds.

KILMAINHAM JAIL

If you have *any* desire to understand Irish history – especially the juicy bits about resistance to English rule – then a visit to **Kilmainham Jail** (Map p78; ☎ 453 5984; Inchicore Rd; adult/student & child €5/2; ☒ 9.30am-5pm Apr-Oct, 9.30am-4pm Mon-Sat, 10am-5pm Sun Oct-Mar) is an absolute must. This grey, threatening building, built between 1792 and 1795, has played a role in virtually every act of Ireland's painful path to independence.

The uprisings of 1798, 1803, 1848, 1867 and 1916 ended with the leaders' confinement here. Robert Emmet, Thomas Francis Meagher, Charles Stewart Parnell and the 1916 Easter Rising leaders were all visitors, but it was the executions in 1916 that most deeply etched the jail's name into the Irish consciousness. Of the 15 executions that took place between 3 May and 12 May after

the rising, 14 were conducted here. As a finale, prisoners from the Civil War struggles were held here from 1922. The jail closed in 1924.

An excellent audiovisual introduction to the building is followed by a thought-provoking tour through the eerie prison, the largest unoccupied building of its kind in Europe. Incongruously sitting outside in the yard is the Asgard, the ship that successfully ran the British blockade to deliver arms to nationalist forces in 1914. The tour finishes in the gloomy yard where the 1916 executions took place.

To get here, catch bus No 23, 51, 51A, 78 or 79 from Aston Quay.

WAR MEMORIAL GARDENS

By our reckoning, the most beautiful patch of landscaped greenery in Dublin is the **War Memorial Gardens** (Map p78; ☎ 677 0236; www.heritageireland.ie; South Circular Rd, Islandbridge; admission free; ☒ 8am-twilight Mon-Fri, from 10am Sat & Sun), if only because they're as tranquil a spot as any you'll find in the city. Designed by Sir Edwin Lutyens, they commemorate the 49,400 Irish soldiers who died during WWI – their names are inscribed in the two huge granite bookrooms that stand at one end. A beautiful spot and a bit of history to boot. Take bus No 25, 25A, 26, 68 or 69 from the city centre to get here.

O'Connell Street & Around

After decades of playing second fiddle to Grafton St and the other byways of the southside, the northside's grandest thoroughfare is finally getting its mojo back and can once again declare itself Dublin's finest avenue. Lining and surrounding it are a bunch of fabulous buildings, fascinating museums and a fair few of the city's cultural hotspots too – just a handful of reasons to cross O'Connell Bridge and take on the northside.

O'CONNELL STREET

It's amazing what a few hundred million euros and a new vision will do to a street plagued by years of neglect, a criminally blind development policy and a history as a hothouse of street trouble. It's difficult to fathom why O'Connell St (Map pp80–1), once so proud and elegant, could have been so humbled that the street's top draw was an amusement arcade. One-armed bandits and poker machines on the street that was the main stage for the Easter Rising in 1916? How could it all go so wrong?

A far cry from the 18th-century days of empire, when as Drogheda St (after Viscount Henry Moore, earl of Drogheda) it cut a swathe through a city brimming with Georgian optimism. It became O'Connell St in 1924, but only after spending a few decades as Sackville St – a tribute to a lord lieutenant of Ireland. Whatever its name, it was always an imposing street, at least until the fast-food joints and the crappy shops started invading the retail spaces along it. Thankfully, Dublin Corporation is committed to a thorough reappraisal of the street's appearance: so far, so good, but still far to go.

The first project was the impressive **Spire** (aka the Monument of Light), which graced the spot once occupied by Admiral Nelson (who disappeared in an explosive fashion in 1966). Soaring 120m into the sky, it is, apparently, the world's tallest sculpture – although that hardly impresses the locals who refer to it as the biggest needle around, in reference to the drug blight of the north inner city. Other (ongoing) projects will hopefully make the street a little more user-friendly.

GENERAL POST OFFICE

Talk about going postal. The **GPO building** (Map pp80–1; ☎ 705 7000; www.anpost.ie; O'Connell St; ☷ 8am-8pm Mon-Sat) will forever be linked to the dramatic and tragic events of Easter Week 1916, when Pádraig Pearse, James

Connolly and the other leaders of the rising read their proclamation from the front steps and made the building their headquarters. The building – a neoclassical masterpiece designed by Francis Johnston in 1818 – was burnt out in the subsequent siege, but that wasn't the end of it. There was bitter fighting in and around the building during the Civil War of 1922; you can still see the pockmarks of the struggle in the Doric columns. Since its reopening in 1929 it has lived through quieter times, but its central role in the history of independent Ireland has made it a prime site for everything from official parades to personal protests.

CUSTOM HOUSE

James Gandon (1743–1823) announced his arrival on the Dublin scene with the **Custom House** (Map pp80–1), constructed between 1781 and 1791, in spite of opposition from city merchants and dockers at the original Custom House, upriver in Temple Bar.

In 1921, during the independence struggle, the Custom House was set alight and completely gutted in a fire that burned for five days. The interior was later extensively redesigned, and a further major renovation took place between 1986 and 1988.

The glistening white building stretches for 114m along the Liffey. The best complete view is obtained from across the river, though a close-up inspection of its many fine details is also worthwhile. The building is topped by a copper dome with four clocks. On top stands a 5m-high statue of Hope.

Beneath the dome is the **Custom House Visitor Centre** (☎ 888 2538; Custom House Quay; admission

---

O'CONNELL STREET STATUARY

Although overshadowed by the Spire, O'Connell St is lined with statues of Irish history's good and great. The big daddy of them all is the Liberator himself, **Daniel O'Connell** (Map pp80–1), whose massive bronze bulk soars high above the street at the bridge end. The four winged figures at his feet represent O'Connell's supposed virtues: patriotism, courage, fidelity and eloquence.

O'Connell is rivalled for drama by the spread-armed figure of trade-union leader **Jim Larkin** (1876–1947; Map pp80–1), just outside the GPO; you can almost hear the eloquent tirade.

Looking on with a bemused air from outside Café Kylemore, on the corner of pedestrianised North Earl St, is a small statue of **James Joyce**, who wagsters like to refer to as 'the prick with the stick'. Joyce would have loved the vulgar rhyme.

Further north is the statue of **Father Theobald Mathew** (1790–1856), the 'apostle of temperance' – a hopeless role in Ireland. This quixotic task, however, also resulted in a Liffey bridge bearing his name. The northern end of the street is completed by the imposing statue of **Charles Stewart Parnell** (1846–91), Home Rule advocate and victim of Irish morality.

€1; ☼ 10am-12.30pm Mon-Fri, 2-5.30pm Sat & Sun mid-Mar–Oct, closed Sat Nov–mid-Mar), which features a small museum on Gandon himself as well as the history of the building.

ST MARY'S PRO-CATHEDRAL

Dublin's most important **Catholic church** (Map pp80-1; ☎ 874 5441; Marlborough St; admission free; ☼ 8am-6.30pm) is not quite the showcase you might expect. For one, it's in a cramped street rather than on its intended spot on O'Connell St, where the GPO is now: the city's Protestants had a fit and insisted that it be built on a less conspicuous side street. And less conspicuous it certainly was, unless you were looking for purveyors of the world's oldest profession. Then you were smack in the middle of Monto – as Marlborough St was then known – the busiest red-light district in Europe, thanks to the British army stationed here. After independence and the departure of the British, Monto became plain old Marlborough St and the only enduring evidence is in the writings of James Joyce, who referred to the area where he lost his virginity as 'Nighttown'.

It mightn't be the hotspot it used to be, but at least you won't be distracted in your efforts to admire the six Doric columns of the cathedral, built between 1816 and 1825 and modelled on the Temple of Theseus in Athens. The best time to visit is Sunday at 11am for the Latin Mass sung by the Palestrina Choir, the very one in which Count John McCormack, Ireland's greatest singing export (sorry Bono), began his career in 1904.

Finally, a word about the term 'pro' in the title. It roughly means 'unofficial cathedral,' due to the fact that church leaders saw this building as an interim cathedral that would do until funds were found to build a much grander one. Which has never happened, leaving this most Catholic of cities with two incredible-but-underused Protestant cathedrals and one fairly ordinary Catholic one. Irony one, piety nil.

MUNICIPAL GALLERY OF MODERN ART

The splendid collection of the **Municipal Gallery of Modern Art** (Map pp80-1; ☎ 874 1903; www.hughlane.ie; 22 North Parnell Sq; admission free to permanent collection, Francis Bacon exhibition adult/child €7/3.50, free before noon Tue; ☼ 9.30am- 6pm Tue-Thu, 9.30am-5pm Fri & Sat, 11am-5pm Sun) is top heavy

with French Impressionists and modern Irish artists of the very, very good kind. It is housed in the equally stunning Charlemont House, built by William Chambers in 1763 and home to the collection since 1933.

The gallery was founded in 1908 by Sir Hugh Lane, and his failure to get any funding from an uninterested government was the subject of one of WB Yeats' most vitriolic poems, *September 1913*. Yeats was really annoyed, but we wonder if his ire had anything to do with the fact that the very rich Lane was the nephew of Yeats' own patron, Lady Gregory?

Poor old Lane didn't get to enjoy his wealth for much longer, however, as he was one of the thousands who perished with the sinking of the *Lusitania* by a German U-boat in 1915. There followed a bitter dispute over the Lane Bequest between the gallery and the National Gallery in London. The collection was eventually split in a complicated 1959 settlement that sees some of the paintings move back and forth. The conditions of the exchanges are in the midst of a convoluted negotiation, but for the time being the gallery will hold on to its most prized possession, Renoir's *Les Parapluies*.

The other big highlight is a faithful recreation of Francis Bacon's London studio, complete with all of the painter's personal effects, which opened in 2001. A current expansion – to be completed in March 2006 – will see the addition of a brand-new wing to house, among other arty bits, nine paintings by Irish-born, New York–based Sean Scully, probably the best known Irish artist today.

DUBLIN WRITERS MUSEUM

A collection of memorabilia, ephemera and other stuff that's associated with the rich literary heritage of Dublin makes for a compelling visit for anyone interested in the city's scribblers. Unfortunately, the **museum** (Map pp80-1; ☎ 872 2077; www.writersmuseum .com; 18 North Parnell Sq; adult/child/student €6/3.50/5; ☼ 10am-5pm Mon-Sat, 11am-5pm Sun, till 6pm Mon-Fri Jun-Aug) draws the line in the 1970s, so there's nothing on the new generation of pen merchants. However, if you're interested in the letters, photographs, first editions and other bits and bobs of Beckett, Behan and the like, you won't be disappointed.

The museum also has a bookshop and restaurant, Chapter One (see p134). Admission includes taped guides with readings from relevant texts in English and other languages. If you plan to visit the James Joyce Museum (see p147) and George Bernard Shaw House (see p117) and George Bernard Shaw House (see p117), bear in mind that a combined ticket is cheaper than three separate ones.

While the museum concerns itself primarily with dead authors, next door at No 19, the Irish Writers' Centre provides a meeting and working place for their living successors.

JAMES JOYCE CULTURAL CENTRE

Denis Maginni, the exuberant, flamboyant dance instructor immortalised by James Joyce, taught in this **house** (Map pp80-1; ☎ 878 8547; www.jamesjoyce.ie; 35 North Great George's St; adult/child/student €5/free/3.50; ☒ 9.30am-5pm Mon-Sat, 12.30-5pm Sun). In 1982 Senator David Norris, renowned Joycean scholar and leading gay-rights activist, bought the rundown house and restored it before opening it as a centre for the study of Joyce and his books.

Visitors can see the room where Maginni taught, and a collection of pictures of the 17 different Dublin homes occupied by the nomadic Joyce family and the real individuals fictionalised in the books. Some of the fine plaster ceilings are restored originals, others careful reproductions of Michael Stapleton's designs. For information on James Joyce–related walking tours departing from the centre, see p121.

Smithfield & Phoenix Park

It will be cool, urbane and sophisticated. At its heart will be a handsome, pedestrianised square that plays host to concerts, recitals and other suitably high-minded activities. Surrounding it will be some of the city's most exciting architecture. It will spearhead the northside's cultural renaissance. It's all true, but not just yet. Smithfield is still a work in progress: the sexy new square is there, but much of the construction around it is ongoing. For the time being, you're main reason for visiting is – ironically – to explore the remaining traces of old Dublin. Further west, however, is Dublin's grandest public park, home of the president and the zoo; on the way there is one of the city's best museums.

SMITHFIELD

Earmarked 10 years ago for major residential and cultural development, **Smithfield** (Map pp80-1), bordered to the east by Church St, to the west by Blackhall Pl, to the north by North King St and to the south by Arran Quay, has progressed in fits and starts but has not quite evolved into the cultural quarter promised. At the centre of the development is the old hay, straw, cattle and horse marketplace, Smithfield Market, which has now been replaced by a new open civic space. The flagship of the Historic Area Rejuvenation Project (HARP), whose brief is to restore the northwest inner city, it features a pedestrianised square bordered on one side by 26m-high gas lighting masts, each with a 2m-high flame. The old cobblestones were removed, cleaned up and put back along with new granite slabs that manage to give the whole square a modern feel without sacrificing its traditional beauty.

Bordering the eastern side of the square is the Old Jameson Distillery. In keeping with its traditional past, the old fruit and vegetable market still plies a healthy wholesale trade on the square's western side.

CHIMNEY

As part of the ongoing development of the Smithfield area, a distillery chimney, built by Jameson in 1895, has been converted into Dublin's first and only 360-degree **observation tower** (Map pp80-1; ☎ 817 3820; Smithfield Village; adult/student & child/family €5/3.50/10; ☒ 10am-5pm Mon-Sat, 11am-5.30pm Sun). A glass lift shuttles visitors to the top where, behind the safety of glass, you can see the entire city, the sea and the mountains to the south. On a clear day, it makes for some nice photo opportunities.

OLD JAMESON DISTILLERY

Smithfield's biggest draw is the **Old Jameson Distillery** (Map pp80-1; ☎ 807 2355; www.jameson.ie; Bow St; adult/student €7/6; ☒ tours every 35min 10am-5.30pm), a huge museum devoted to *uisce beatha*, the water of life. To its more serious devotees, that is precisely what whiskey is, although they may be put off by the slickness of the museum, which shepherds visitors through a compulsory tour of the re-created factory and into the ubiquitous gift shop.

On the way, however, there's plenty to discover. Beginning with a short film, the tour runs through the whole process of distilling, from grain to bottle. There are plenty of interesting titbits, such as what makes a single malt, where does whiskey get its colour and bouquet from and what is the difference between Irish whiskey and Scotch (other than the spelling, which prompted one Scot to comment that the Irish thought of everything: they even put an 'e' into whisky).

Then its straight to the bar for a drop of the subject matter; eager drinkers can volunteer for the tasting tour, where you get to sample whiskies from all over the world and learn about the differences between them. Finally, then, to the almighty shop. If you're buying whiskey, go for the stuff you can't buy at home, such as the excellent Red Breast or the superexclusive Midleton, a very limited reserve that is appropriately expensive.

FOUR COURTS

Appellants quake and the accused may shiver, but visitors are only likely to be amazed by James Gandon's imposing **Four Courts** (Map p82; ☎ 872 5555; Inn's Quay; admission free), Ireland's uppermost courts of law. Gandon's Georgian masterpiece is a mammoth structure incorporating a 130m-long façade. The Corinthian-columned central block, connected to flanking wings with enclosed quadrangles, was begun in 1786 and not completed until 1802. The ensemble is topped by a diverse collection of statuary. The original four courts – Exchequer, Common Pleas, King's Bench and Chancery – all branch off the central rotunda.

The Four Courts played a brief role in the 1916 Easter Rising, without suffering damage, but the events of 1922 were not so kind. When anti-Treaty forces seized the building and refused to leave, it was shelled from across the river. As the occupiers retreated, the building was set on fire and many irreplaceable early records were burned. This event sparked off the Civil War. The building wasn't restored until 1932.

Visitors are allowed to wander through, but not to enter courts or other restricted areas. In the lobby of the central rotunda you'll see bewigged barristers conferring, and police officers handcuffed to their charges waiting to enter court.

ST MICHAN'S CHURCH

The macabre remains of the ancient dead are the attraction at **St Michan's Church** (Map p82; ☎ 872 4154; Lower Church St; adult/student €4/3; ⊗ 10am-12.45pm & 2-4.45pm Mon-Fri, 10am-12.45pm Sat), near the Four Courts, founded by the Danes in 1095 and named after one of their saints. The original church has largely disappeared beneath several additions, most dating from the 17th century (except for the battlement tower, which dates from the 15th century). It was considerably restored in the early 19th century and again after the Civil War, during which it had been damaged.

The very unchurch-like interior – it looks a bit like a courtroom – contains an organ from 1724 that Handel may have played for the first performance of his *Messiah*. A skull on the floor on one side of the altar is said to represent Oliver Cromwell. On the opposite side, a penitent's chair was where 'open and notoriously naughty livers' did public penance.

The tours of the subterranean crypt are the big draw, where you'll see bodies between 400 and 800 years old preserved not by mummification, but by the constant dry atmosphere. Tours are organised on an ad hoc basis depending on how many people there are. Catch the No 134 bus from the city centre to get here.

PHOENIX PARK

Take bus No 10 from O'Connell St or 25 and 26 from Middle Abbey St to get to Dublin's beloved playground. Measuring 709 glorious hectares, **Phoenix Park** (Map p78; admission free) is Europe's largest city park and a green lung that is more than double the size of New York's Central Park (a paltry 337 hectares) and all of London's major parks put together. Here you'll find gardens and lakes; pitches for all kinds of *British* sports from soccer to cricket to polo (the dry one, with horses); the second-oldest zoo in Europe; a castle and visitor centre; the headquarters of the Garda Síochána (police); the Ordnance Survey offices; and both the president of Ireland and the US ambassador, who live in two exquisite residences more or less opposite each other. There's even a herd of some 500 fallow deer.

The deer were first introduced by Lord Ormond in 1662, when lands once owned by the Knights of Jerusalem were turned into a royal hunting ground. In 1745 the viceroy Lord Chesterfield threw it open to the public and it has remained so ever since. (The name 'Phoenix' has nothing to do with the mythical bird; it is a corruption of the Irish *fionn uisce*, meaning 'clear water'.)

In 1882 the park played a crucial role in Irish history, when Lord Cavendish, the British chief secretary for Ireland, and his assistant were murdered outside what is now the Irish president's residence by an obscure nationalist group called the Invincibles. Lord Cavendish's home is now called Deerfield and is used as the official residence of the US ambassador.

Near the Parkgate St entrance to the park is the 63m-high **Wellington Monument** obelisk. This took from 1817 to 1861 to build, mainly because the duke of Wellington fell from public favour during its construction. Nearby is the **People's Garden**, dating from 1864, and the bandstand in the Hollow. Behind the zoo, on the edge of the park, the Garda Síochána Headquarters has a small police museum.

In the centre of the park, the **Papal Cross** marks the site where Pope John Paul II preached to 1.25 million people in 1979. The **Phoenix Monument**, erected by Lord Chesterfield in 1747, looks very unphoenix-like and is often referred to as the Eagle Monument. The southern part of the park is a 200-acre (about 81 hectares) stretch known as the Fifteen Acres (don't ask, nobody knows) that is given over to a large number of football pitches – winter Sunday mornings are the time to come and watch. To the west, the rural-looking **Glen Pond** corner of the park is extremely attractive.

Back towards the Parkgate entrance is **Magazine Fort** on Thomas' Hill. Built at snail's pace between 1734 and 1801, the fort has served as an occasional arms depot for the British and, later, the Irish armies. It was a target during the 1916 Easter Rising and again in 1940, when the IRA made off with the entire ammunitions reserve of the Irish army (they retrieved it after a few weeks).

Established in 1830 12-hectare **Dublin Zoo** (☎ 677 1425; www.dublinzoo.ie; Phoenix Park; adult/child/family €13/8.50/36; ⏲ 9.30am-6pm Mon-Sat, 10.30am-6pm Sun Mar-Sep, 9.30am-dusk Mon-Fri, 9.30am-dusk Sat, 10.30am-dusk Sun Oct-Feb) is one of the oldest in the world, but is mainly of interest to children. It used to be a run-down zoo where depressed animals used to depress visitors, but a substantial face-lift, when the African Plains were added, doubled the zoo in size, making it a much more pleasant place for animals to live and for you to stroll around.

The residence of the Irish president, **Áras an Uachtaráin** (Map p78; ☎ 617 1000; Phoenix Park; admission free; ⏲ guided tours hourly 10.30am-4.30pm Sat) was built in 1751 and enlarged in 1782, then again in 1816, this time by noted Irish architect Francis Johnston, who added the Ionic portico. From 1782 to 1922 it was the residence of the British viceroys or lord lieutenants. After independence it became the home of Ireland's governor general until Ireland cut ties with the British Crown and created the office of president in 1937.

Tickets for the tour can be collected from the **Phoenix Park Visitor Centre** (☎ 677 0095; adult/concession/family €2.75/1.25/7; ⏲ 10am-6pm Apr-Sep, 10am-5pm Oct, 10am-5pm Mon-Sat Nov & Dec, 10am-5pm Sat & Sun Jan-Mar), the converted former stables of the papal nunciate, now devoted to the park's history and ecology over the last 3500 years. Next door is the restored four-storey **Ashtown Castle** (admission by guided tour from visitor centre), a 17th-century tower house 'discovered' inside the 18th-century nuncio's mansion when the latter was demolished in 1986 due to dry rot.

Beyond the Royal Canal

These days it makes for a lovely walk, but when Long John Binns put his money into the construction of the Royal Canal from 1790, it was an exercise in misplaced optimism and self-flagellating revenge. The usefulness of such waterways was already on the wane, and he only invested in the project because when he was a board member of the Grand Canal a colleague mocked his day job as a shoemaker. Sure enough, the canal was a massive bust; Binns lost a pile of money and became a figure of fun.

Binns' catastrophe is the stroller's good fortune and the towpath alongside the canal is perfect for a nice walk through the heart of the city. You can join it beside Newcomen Bridge at North Strand Rd, just north of Connolly Station, and follow it to the suburb of Clonsilla and beyond, more than 10km away. The walk is particularly pleas-

---

RULE 42: A STORM IN A STADIUM?

Forty-two may well be the answer to Life, the Universe and Everything – at least in Douglas Adams' world – but in Ireland it's all about sport, nationalism, tribalism and tradition.

The Gaelic Athletic Association's Rule No 42 states that no 'foreign' games should be allowed to be played at any GAA-owned ground, most notably its most glorious cathedral, the superstadium that is Croke Park. By 'foreign', of course, they mean the very British sports of soccer and rugby. Which was OK so long as soccer and rugby could use the smaller Landsdowne Rd stadium, but when it was announced a few years back that it was to be rebuilt, the lads at the IRFU (Irish Rugby Football Union) and FAI (Football Association of Ireland) were in a bit of a pickle: with no alternative stadium in Ireland to stage internationals, they were confronting the possibility of staging home games in…gasp…Britain!

Then the inevitable: what about using Croke Park? Not on your life, barked the GAA; this is holy turf, and there'll be no singing of God Save the Queen on this manicured sod – as would have been the case when the English rugby team came to play. For a couple of years the GAA refused to even debate the issue, and when it was finally discussed in 2004 it was defeated, but by a single vote. For the next year, the debate rumbled on. In favour of change were soccer and rugby fans and all those who felt slightly embarrassed by the GAA's slightly old-fashioned recalcitrance; against it were the old-fashioned recalcitrants of the GAA but also those who felt that the GAA was already at a disadvantage next to soccer and, to a lesser extent, rugby, for these were big-money sports with an international profile. By not allowing any other sports to be played in their wonderful stadium, the GAA was protecting the promise made to every single kid who takes up Gaelic football, hurling or camogie: play well and you too can one day walk out onto Croker's hallowed turf.

When the motion came up for debate again in April 2005, it was clear that the modernisers would have their way. When the motion to end the ban was passed – if only on a temporary basis – it was clear that the GAA had passed a watershed. Congratulated by many on their wisdom and foresight, a gnawing question remains: what if the doubters were right, and by giving the keys of their manor to other sports they were signing their own death warrant? What if even for the GAA 42 was the answer to Life, the Universe and Everything?

---

ant beyond Binns Bridge in Drumcondra. At the top of Blessington St a large pond, used when the canal also supplied drinking water to the city, attracts water birds.

Beyond the Royal Canal lie the suburbs and an authentic slice of north city life. There are also some beautiful gardens, the country's biggest stadium, an historic cemetery and one of the most interesting buildings in all of Dublin.

CROKE PARK & GAELIC ATHLETIC ASSOCIATION MUSEUM

It's a magnificent stadium – if you're impressed by them – that is Ireland's largest and the fourth-largest in Europe, but **Croke Park** (Map p78; ☎ 819 2323; Clonliffe Rd) is about much more than 82,000-plus sporting butts on plastic seats. No, Croker – as it's lovingly known in Dublin – is the fabulous fortress that protects the sanctity and spirit of Gaelic games in Ireland, as well as the administrative HQ of the Gaelic Athletic

Association (GAA), the body that governs them. Sound a little hyperbolic? Well, the GAA considers itself not just the governing body of a bunch of Irish games, but the stout defender of a cultural identity that is ingrained in Ireland's sense of self (see also the boxed text, above). To get an idea of just how important the GAA is in Ireland, a visit to the **museum** (☎ 855 8176; www.gaa.ie; New Stand, Croke Park, Clonliffe Rd; museum only adult/child/student/family €5.50/3.50/4/15, museum & tour adult/child/student/family €9.50/6/7/24; ☒ 9.30am-5pm Mon-Sat & noon-5pm Sun Apr-Oct, 10am-5pm Tue-Sat & noon-4pm Sun Nov-Mar) is a must, though it will help if you're any kind of sporting enthusiast. The twice-daily tours (except match days) of the impressive stadium are excellent.

You can reach the park by taking bus No 3, 11, 11A, 16, 16A or 123 from O'Connell St.

NATIONAL BOTANIC GARDENS

Founded in 1795 the 19.5-hectare **National Botanic Gardens** (Map p75; ☎ 837 7596; Botanic Rd,

Glasnevin; admission free; 9am-6pm Mon-Sat & 11am-6pm Sun Apr-Oct, 10am-4.30pm Mon-Sat & 11am-4.30pm Sun Nov-Mar) are directly north of the centre, flanked to the north by the River Tolka. Take bus No 13, 13A or 19 from O'Connell St, or 34 and 34A from Middle Abbey St.

In the gardens is a series of curvilinear glasshouses dating from 1843 to 1869. The glasshouses were created by Richard Turner, who was also responsible for the glasshouse at Belfast Botanic Gardens and the Palm House in London's Kew Gardens. Within these Victorian masterpieces you will find the latest in botanical technology, including a series of computer-controlled climates reproducing environments of different parts of the world. The gardens also have a palm house. Among the pioneering botanical work conducted here was the first attempt to raise orchids from seed, back in 1844. Pampas grass and the giant lily were first grown in Europe in these gardens.

GLASNEVIN CEMETERY
Bus No 40, 40A or 40B from Parnell St will take you to Ireland's largest and most historically important cemetery, **Prospect Cemetery** (Map p78; ☎ 830 1133; Finglas Rd; admission free; 24hr, tours 2.30pm Wed & Fri), in the northwest suburb of Glasnevin (within walking distance of the National Botanic Gardens). It was established in 1832 as a burial ground for Catholics, who were increasingly prohibited from conducting burials in the city's Protestant cemeteries. Not surprisingly, the cemetery's monuments and memorials have staunchly patriotic overtones, with numerous high crosses, shamrocks, harps and other Irish symbols. The single most imposing memorial is the colossal monument to Cardinal McCabe (1837–1921), archbishop of Dublin and primate of Ireland.

A modern replica of a round tower acts as a handy landmark for locating the tomb of Daniel O'Connell, who died in 1847 and was reinterred here in 1869 when the tower was completed. Charles Stewart Parnell's tomb is topped with a huge granite rock. Other notable people buried here include Sir Roger Casement, who was executed for treason by the British in 1916 and whose remains weren't returned to Ireland until 1964; the republican leader Michael Collins, who died in the Civil War; the docker and trade unionist Jim Larkin, a prime force in the 1913 general strike; and the poet Gerard Manley Hopkins.

There's also a poignant 'class' memorial to the men who have starved themselves to death for the cause of Irish freedom over the century, including 10 men from the 1981 H Block hunger strikes.

The most interesting parts of the cemetery are at the southeastern Prospect Sq end. The watchtowers were once used to keep watch for body snatchers. The cemetery is mentioned in *Ulysses* and there are several clues for Joyce enthusiasts to follow.

CASINO AT MARINO
It's not the roulette-wheel kind of casino, but the original Italian kind, the one that means 'house of pleasure' or 'summer home,' and this particular **casino** (Map p78; ☎ 833 1618; Malahide Rd; adult/concession/family €2.75/1.25/7; by guided tour only, 10am-5pm May & Oct, 10am-6pm Jun-Sep, noon-4pm Sat & Sun Feb-Apr, Nov & Dec, noon-5pm Apr, closed Jan, last tour 45min before closing) is one of the most enchanting constructions in all of Ireland. Get here by bus No 20A, 20B, 27, 27B, 42, 42C or 123 from city centre, or take the DART to Clontarf Rd Station.

It was built in the mid-18th century for the earl of Charlemont, who returned from his grand tour of Europe with more art than he could store in his own home, Marino House – on the same grounds but demolished in the 1920s. He also came home with a big love of the Palladian style, hence the architecture of this wonderful folly.

The building, with its 12 Tuscan columns forming a templelike façade and its huge entrance doorway, creates the expectation that inside it will be a simple single open space. But the interior is an extravagant convoluted maze: flights of fancy include chimneys for the central heating that are disguised as roof urns, downpipes hidden in columns, carved draperies, ornate fireplaces, beautiful parquet floors constructed of rare woods, and a spacious wine cellar. A variety of statuary adorns the outside but it's the amusing fakes that are most enjoyable. The towering front door is a sham and a much smaller panel opens to reveal the secret interior. The windows have blacked-out panels to hide the fact that the interior is a complex of rooms, not a single chamber.

(Continued on page 117)

Previous Page: Green fields around Glencolumbcille (p495), County Donegal
RICHARD CUMMINS

Alfresco dining (p128), Dublin

MARTIN MOOS

Christ Church Cathedral (p98), Dublin
MARTIN MOOS

Phoenix Park (p105), Dublin

OLIVIER CIRENDINI

St Patrick's Cathedral (p99), Dublin

COREY WISE

CORINNE HUMPHREY

Long Room (p90), Trinity College, Dublin

Statues outside the Royal Hospital Kilmainham, home of the Irish Museum of Modern Art (p101), Dublin

MARTIN MOOS

Live Irish music at O'Donoghue's (p137), Dublin

DOUG McKINLAY

St Patrick's Festival (p121), Dublin

Themed headwear, St Patrick's
Festival (p121), Dublin

Ballinasloe Horse Fair (p418), Ballinasloe, County Galway

Traditional Irish music (p56)

ANN CECIL

Local farmer at the Puck Fair Festival (p260), Killorglin, County Kerry

RICHARD CUMMINS

Bloomsday reading (p122), James Joyce Cultural Centre, Dublin

WAYNE WALTON

Hikers on Diamond Hill (p414), Connemara National Park, County Galway

GARETH McCORMACK

Stone walls and traditional farmhouse, Beara Peninsula (p242), County Cork

RICHARD CUMMINS

Currach boat, Achill Island (p431), County Mayo

RICHARD CUMMINS

RICHARD CUMMINS

Staigue Fort (p266), Ring of Kerry, County Kerry

GARETH McCORMACK

Mourne Mountains (p611), County Down

GARETH McCORMACK

Beach at Keem (p433), Achill Island, County Mayo

National Gallery (p94), Dublin

OLIVIER CIRENDINI

The main stairway of the Crawford Municipal Art Gallery (p207), Cork city

RICHARD CUMMINS

Gallery of Photography (p92), Temple Bar, Dublin

DOUG McKINLAY

Titanic display at the Ulster Transport Museum (p592), near Belfast

RICHARD CUMMINS

(Continued from page 108)

Beyond the Grand Canal

The more attractive of Dublin's two canals is the **Grand Canal**, built to connect Dublin with the River Shannon. It makes a graceful 6km loop around the south city centre and has a lovely path running alongside it that is perfect for a pleasant walk or cycle. At its eastern end the canal forms a harbour connected with the Liffey at Ringsend, through locks that were built in 1796. The large Grand Canal Dock, flanked by Hanover and Charlotte Quays, is now used by windsurfers and canoeists and is the site of a major new development, including Dublin's first real skyscraper that will be home to U2's purpose-designed recording studios.

At the northwestern corner of the dock is Misery Hill, once the site for the public execution of criminals. It was once the practice to bring the corpses of those already hung at Gallows Hill, near Upper Baggot St, to this spot, to be strung up for public display for anything from six to 12 months.

The loveliest stretch of the canal is just southwest, between Mount St Bridge and Baggot St. The grassy, tree-lined banks were a favourite haunt of the poet Patrick Kavanagh. The Monaghan-born poet's difficult love affair with the city is echoed in the hauntingly beautiful *On Raglan Road*, later put to music by Van Morrisson. Another Kavanagh poem requested that he be commemorated by 'a canal bank seat for passers-by' and his friends obliged with a seat beside the lock on the southern side of the canal. A little further along on the northern side you can sit down beside Kavanagh himself, cast in bronze, comfortably lounging on a bench and watching his beloved canal.

If you absolutely must know about the construction and operation of Ireland's canals, then catch the DART to Grand Canal Dock for a visit to the **Waterways Visitor Centre** (Map p78; ☎ 677 7510; www.waterwaysireland.org; Grand Canal Quay; adult/child & student €2.50/1.20; ☼ 9.30am-5.30pm Jun-Sep, 12.30-5pm Wed-Sun Oct & May) on the Grand Canal Basin. Otherwise, admiring the 'box on the docks' – as this modern building is nicknamed – is plenty good enough for the average enthusiast of artificial waterways.

Just southeast of the city centre, beyond the canal, is **Ballsbridge** (Map p75), the epitome of posh Dublin and home to most of the embassies and a batch of luxurious B&Bs. The main attractions are the **Royal Dublin Society Showground** and the **Lansdowne Rd rugby stadium** (Map p78), though **Herbert Park** (Map p78) is also a favourite for sport, walking or just sitting around.

ROYAL DUBLIN SOCIETY SHOWGROUND

The **Royal Dublin Society (RDS) Showground** (Map p78; ☎ 668 9878; Merrion Rd, Ballsbridge), about 15 minutes by bus No 7 from Trinity College, is used for various exhibitions throughout the year. The society was founded in 1731 and had its headquarters in a number of well-known Dublin buildings, including Leinster House from 1814 to 1925. The society was involved in the foundation of the National Museum, Library, Gallery and Botanic Gardens. The most important annual event at the showground is the August **Dublin Horse Show** (for tickets ☎ 668 0866), which includes an international showjumping contest. Ask at the tourist office or consult a listings magazine for other events.

GEORGE BERNARD SHAW HOUSE

OK, so it's technically on the city side of the canal, but only just: noted playwright George Bernard Shaw was born and lived until the age of 10 in Dublin in what is now home to a **museum** (☎ 475 0854; 33 Synge St; adult/child/student €6/3.50/5; ☼ 10am-1pm & 2-5pm Mon-Sat, from 11am Sun Easter-Oct) dedicated to him and the times he grew up in. The house re-creates a Victorian household with an audio presentation on Shaw's life. Take bus No 16, 19 or 122 from Trinity College.

Note that it's possible to buy a combination ticket that also gives you access to the Dublin Writers' Museum and James Joyce Museum in Sandycove.

IRISH-JEWISH MUSEUM

Just around the corner from the Shaw House is the **Irish-Jewish Museum** (Map p78; ☎ 453 1797; 4 Walworth Rd; admission free; ☼ 11am-3.30pm Tue, Thu & Sun May-Sep, 10.30am-2.30pm Sun only Oct-Apr). In an old synagogue, it was opened in 1985 by the then Israeli president, Chaim Herzog, who was actually born in Belfast. Dublin's small but culturally important Jewish population is remembered through photographs, paintings, certificates, books and other memorabilia.

ACTIVITIES

Beaches & Swimming

Dublin is hardly the sort of place to work on your suntan, and even a hot Irish summer day is unlikely to raise the water temperature much above freezing. However, there are some pleasant beaches. Many Joyce fans feel compelled to take a dip in **Forty Foot Pool** at Dun Laoghaire (see p147). Sandy beaches to the north of Dublin include **Sutton** (11km), **Portmarnock** (11km), **Malahide** (11km), **Claremount** (14km) and **Donabate** (21km). Although the beach at Sandymount is nothing special, it is only 5km southeast of central Dublin. Take bus No 3 from Fleet St.

The **National Aquatic Centre** (Map p75; ☎ 646 4300; www.nac.ie; Snugborough Rd, Blanchardstown, Dublin 15; adult/child & student €12/10; ☼ 2-10pm Mon-Fri, 9am-8pm Sat & Sun), built to accommodate the Special Olympics World Summer Games in 2003, is the largest indoor water park. Besides its Olympic-size competition pool it has water roller coasters, wave and surf machines, a leisure pool and all types of flumes. It's a great day out for the family but be prepared to join the shivering line of children queuing for slides on weekends. Take bus No 38A from Hawkins St to Snugborough Rd.

There is a dearth of quality pools in the city centre – most are small, crowded and not very hygienic. An excellent exception is the **Markievicz Leisure Centre** (Map pp80-1; ☎ 672 9121; cnr Tara & Townsend Sts; adult/child €5/2.60; ☼ 7am-8.45pm Mon-Fri, 9am-5.45pm Sat, 10am-3.45pm Sun), which has a 25m pool, a workout room and a sauna. For the admission price you can swim pretty much as long as you like; children are only allowed at off-peak times (ie any time except for 7am to 9am, noon to 2pm and 5pm to 7pm Monday to Friday).

Cycling

Dublin is compact and flat, making it a cinch to get around by bike. Rust-red cycle lanes throughout the city make it easier than ever, but traffic congestion, motorised maniacs and roadworks can make for a treacherous obstacle course. Nonetheless, with your wits about you, it's the fastest way to get about the increasingly congested centre.

Bike theft is a major problem, so be sure to park on busier streets, preferably at one of the myriad U-shaped parking bars. Overnight street parking is dodgy; most hostels and hotels offer secure bicycle parking areas.

Irish Cycling Safaris (☎ 260 0749; www.cycling safaris.com; UCD, Belfield; tour €590; ☼ end Apr-early Oct) organises eight highly recommended themed week-long tours of the countryside. Each group cycles at its own pace, with a guide following in a backup vehicle. The price also includes bike hire, and hotel and B&B accommodation.

Recommended bike shops:

Cycle-Logical (Map p82; ☎ 872 4635; 3 Bachelor's Walk) A shop for serious enthusiasts, with top-quality gear and info on cycling events throughout the country. It does not do repairs.

Square Wheel Cycleworks (Map p82; ☎ 679 0838; Temple Lane South) Quick, friendly and excellent for repairs.

HIRE

Bike hire has become increasingly more difficult to find because of crippling insurance costs. Typical hire costs for a mountain bike are between €10 and €25 a day or up to €100 per week. Raleigh Rent-a-Bike agencies can be found through the following businesses:

Cycleways (Map pp80-1; ☎ 873 4748; www.cycle ways.com; 185-186 Parnell St) Dublin's best bike shop, with expert staff who pepper their patter with all the technical lingo. Top-notch rentals.

Eurotrek (☎ 456 8847; www.raleigh.ie)

MacDonalds Cycles (Map p84; ☎ 475 2586; 38 Wexford St) Friendly and helpful, great for the amateur enthusiast.

WALKING TOUR

Dubliners of old would assure their 'bitter halves' that they were 'going to see a man about a dog' before beating a retreat to the nearest watering hole. Visiting barflies need no excuse to enjoy the social and cultural education – ahem – of a tour of Dublin's finest, most charming and hardcore bars.

Start in the excellent **Anseo** (1; p137) on Camden St, which pulls a seriously hip and unpretentious crowd on the strength of its fabulous DJs. Head deep into the city centre and stop at Dublin's smallest pub, the **Dawson Lounge** (2), for an appropriately diminutive tipple before sinking a pint of plain in the snug at South Anne St's **Kehoe's** (3; p136), one of the city centre's most atmospheric bars. Discuss the merits of that unwritten masterpiece with a clutch of frustrated writers and artists in **Grogan's Castle Lounge** (4; p137) on Castle Market, a traditional haunt that admirably refuses to

THE BARFLY TRAIL

Distance of Trail: 2.5km
Duration: one hour to two days!

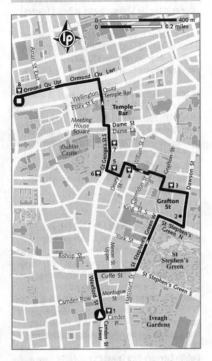

modernise. Just around the corner on Fade St is the music-less **Market Bar** (**5**; p138), favoured by the city's movers and groovers; if it's more conversation you require, cross the street and nip into the **Long Hall** (**6**; p135), where the vicissitudes of life are discussed in a sombre Victorian setting. Shake that booty down the road at the **Globe** (**7**; p138) on South Great George's St. Cross the Liffey and make a beeline for Ormond Quay and **Sin É** (**8**; p138), a small bar with a big reputation for top-class music and a terrific night out. If you've followed the tour correctly, you should not now be referring to this guide. How many fingers?

DUBLIN FOR CHILDREN

Sometimes holidaying with small children requires the organisation of an army boot camp, boundless energy and patience, bot-

tomless pockets and a sense of humour, so it really helps when the facilities and goodwill are there to back up your efforts.

All but a few hotels will provide cots and many have baby-sitting on request (normally €7 to €10 per hour). While waiters may not act like your baby is the first they've ever seen, as in some southern European locations, you'll still find a warm reception for junior travellers in Dublin, at least during the day. Frustratingly, many city-centre restaurants are unwilling to accommodate diners under 12, especially babies, after 6pm. You'll need to check before making a booking. Most restaurants – even exclusive ones – have highchairs and will gladly heat bottles and baby food, but so-called 'kiddie menus' lack imagination and rarely stretch further than the ubiquitous chicken nuggets or sausages with chips. That said, places catering specifically for families who want to eat more nutritious food are cropping up all the time, and pizza chain Milano has resourcefully added free weekend childcare facilities to its Dublin restaurants.

Travellers will find that nappy-changing facilities and city-centre playgrounds are remarkably few and far between. Shopping centres and department stores (or a hotel if you're stuck) are good places to try. There's a reasonably sized playground on Gardiner St and in St Stephen's Green, where you can also feed the ducks, and the **Iveagh Gardens** (Map p84), which doesn't have a playground but has a waterfall and small maze, is a lovely quiet space to relax while your children play.

The **Ark** (Map p82; www.ark.ie; 11a Eustace St) is a children's cultural centre that organises plays, exhibitions and workshops for four to 14 year olds. You really need to book in advance for events.

Lambert Puppet Theatre (☎ 280 0974; www.lambertpuppettheatre.com; Clifton Lane, Monkstown) stages puppet shows for the over-threes in Monkstown, 10km south of Dublin.

The **National Museum** (p94), **Natural History Museum** (p95) and **IMMA** (p101) run fun, educational programmes for children at weekends. The **National Wax Museum** (Map pp80-1; ☎ 873 6340; Granby Row, Parnell Sq; adult/child €7/4; 🕙 10am-5.30pm Mon-Sat, noon-5.30pm Sun) has slightly tired-looking models, but its chamber of horrors and new *Star Wars* exhibit should entertain. Otherwise, a swim or trip to the zoo may well keep little ones happy for at least a few hours.

A nice spot for a picnic is **Newbridge House** with its large **traditional farm** (Map p75; ☎ 843 6534; Donabate; adult/child/family €2.50/1.50/6; ☑ 10am-5pm Tue-Sat, 2-6pm Sun Apr-Sep, 2-5pm Sat & Sun Oct-Mar) northeast of Swords at Donabate, 19km from the centre. It has cows, pigs and chickens, a large parkland and adventure playground. You can get here on the Suburban Rail service (€2.40, 30 minutes), which departs hourly from either Connolly or Pearse Station in the city centre.

The *Irish Times* runs a column on things to do for kids in its Wednesday edition.

If your hotel doesn't have a baby-sitting service, you could try a couple of agencies that provide professional nannies. It's up to you to negotiate a fee with the nanny, but €10 per hour is the average, plus taxi fare if the nanny isn't driving. You'll need to sign a form beforehand that the agency will fax to your hotel.

Recommended agencies:

Belgrave Agency (☎ 280 9341; 55 Mulgrave St, Dun Laoghaire; fee per hr plus 21% VAT €13)

Executive Nannies (☎ 873 1273; 43 Lower Dominick St; fee per hr €20)

TOURS

Dublin is an easy city to see on foot so a guided walking tour is an ideal way to double up on a bit of culture and exercise. For longer tours, or a cushier ride, there are numerous themed city-wide bus tours and several that do day trips further afield.

Bus Tours

City Sightseeing (www.citysightseeing.co.uk; Dublin Tourism, 14 Upper O'Connell St; adult/child/family €14/5/32; ☑ every 8-15min 9am-6pm) Dublin has

recently been added to City Sightseeing's ever-expanding world of open-top, hop-on, hop-off tours. Tours take 1½ hours.

Dublin Bus Tours (☎ 872 0000; www.dublinbus .ie; 59 Upper O'Connell St) Tours can be booked at its office or at the Bus Éireann counter at Dublin Tourism in St Andrew's Church, Suffolk St. They offer a variety of tours, including Dublin City Tour, Ghost Bus Tour, Coast & Castles Tour and South Coast & Gardens Tour. All tours run daily and prices range for €12 to €25.

Grayline Dublin Tour (☎ 872 9010; www.irishcity tours.com; 33 Bachelor's Walk & Dublin Tourism, Suffolk St; adult/child/family €14/12/32; ☑ every 15 mins 9.30am-5pm, to 5.30pm Jul & Aug) Another hop-on-and-off tour (1½ hours) of the city's primary attractions.

Wild Wicklow Tour (☎ 280 1899; www.discover dulin.ie; adult/child €28/25; ☑ 9.10am) Award-winning and lots of fun, this top 8½-hour tour leaves from Dublin Tourism on Suffolk St and does a quick city guide before heading down the coast to Avoca Handweavers, Glendalough and the Sally Gap.

Walking Tours

1916 Easter Rising Walk (☎ 676 2493; www.1916 rising.com; adult/child €10/free; 11.30am & 2.30pm Thu-Sat, 11.30am Tue & Wed, 1pm Sun Mar-Oct) A recommended 1½-hour tour run by graduates of Trinity College taking in parts of Dublin that were directly involved in the Easter Rising. It leaves from International Bar.

Dublin Footsteps Walking Tours (☎ 496 0641; adult €7; ☑ 10.30am Mon, Wed, Fri & Sat Jun-Sep) Departing from the former Bewley's on Grafton St, excellent two-hour tours weaving Georgian, literary and architectural Dublin into a fascinating walk.

Dublin Literary Pub Crawl (☎ 454 0228; www.dublin pubcrawl.com; adult/student €10/8; ☑ 7.30pm daily plus noon Sun Apr-Nov, 7.30pm Thu-Sun only Dec-Mar) An award-winning, 2½-hour walk-and-performance tour led by two actors around pubs with literary connections. There's plenty of drink taken, which makes it all the more popular: get to the Duke pub by 7pm to reserve a spot.

DUBLIN WITH A DIFFERENCE

Check out the antique *incunabula* – so old they're not even called books – at **Marsh's Library** (Map pp80-1; ☎ 454 3511; www.marshlibrary.ie; St Patrick's Close; adult/child/student €2.50/free/1.50; ☑ 10am-1pm & 2-5pm Mon & Wed-Fri, 10.30am-1pm Sat), one of Dublin's least-visited museums. Root for rare original manuscripts or antique maps in cramped **Cathach Books** (☎ 671 8676; www.rarebooks.ie; 10 Duke St). Break out of the book mode with some comedy in the intimate **International Bar** (Map p84; ☎ 677 9250; 23 Wicklow St; admission €8; ☑ 8.30pm) on Wednesday nights. Take a thrill-seeker's safari in a speedboat around Dublin bay and its islands from Malahide to Dalkey with **Sea Safaris** (☎ 806 1626; www.seasafari.ie; Malahide Marina; per hr €25). Don your best Edwardian garb and join in the fun on 16 June as the city celebrates Bloomsday, starting from the **James Joyce Cultural Centre** (Map pp80-1; ☎ 878 8547; 35 North Great George's St).

James Joyce Walking Tour (☎ 878 8547; 35 North Great George's St; adult/student €10/9; ⏱ 2pm Tue, Thu & Sat) Excellent 1¼-hour walking tours of northside attractions associated with James Joyce, departing from James Joyce Cultural Centre.

Water Tours

Viking Splash Tours (Map pp80-1; ☎ 707 6000; www .vikingsplashtours.com; 64-65 Patrick St; adult/child/family from €15.50/8.50/50; ⏱ 10 tours daily 9am-5.30pm Mar-Oct, 10am-4pm Wed-Sun Feb & Tue-Sun Nov) It's hard not to feel a little cheesy with a plastic Viking helmet on your head, but the punters get a real kick out of these amphibious 1¼-hour tours that end up in the Grand Canal Dock.

Musical Walks

Dublin Musical Pub Crawl (☎ 478 0193; www .discoverdublin.com; adult/student €12/10; ⏱ 7.30pm daily Apr-Oct, 7.30pm Thu-Sat Nov-Mar) The story of Irish traditional music and its influence on contemporary styles is explained and demonstrated by two expert musicians in a number of Temple Bar pubs. Tours meet upstairs in the Oliver St John Gogarty (Map p82) and take 2½ hours.

Macabre Tours

Zozimus Ghostly Experience (☎ 661 8646; www .zozimus.com; adult €10; ⏱ 9pm May-Oct, 7pm Nov-Apr) Departing from the gates of Dublin Castle, this is a theatrical and highly entertaining exploration of the ghoulish side of medieval Dublin. You'll need to book in advance.

Carriage Tours

You can pick up a horse and carriage with a driver/commentator at the junction of Grafton St and St Stephen's Green. Half-hour tours cost up to €40 and the carriages can take four or five people. Tours of different lengths can be negotiated with the drivers.

FESTIVALS & EVENTS

It wasn't so long ago that a few trucks dressed up as floats and a flatbed loaded with peat briquettes accompanied by stilt walkers were all you'd expect of Dublin's St Patrick's Day Parade. If you wanted a bit of festive glamour, New York's famous parade was the place to go. But then came the economic boom and the realisation that the event was a tourist bonanza waiting to happen. Now 17 March is St Patrick's *Festival*, a four-day extravaganza of activities from street theatre to fireworks, all fuelled by lots and lots of booze. And therein lies the secret

to Dubliners' love of festive events: sure, *officially* it's all about a celebration of the city's rich cultural heritage, but really it's any old excuse to celebrate and go a little bit mad.

The following list is by no means exhaustive; for more details check out the website run by **Dublin Tourism** (www.visitdublin.com). For information on special events in Ireland as a whole, see p686. For information on Blooms-day, 16 June, see the boxed text, p122.

Jameson International Film Festival (☎ 872 1122; www.dubliniff.com) Local flicks, arty international films and advance releases of mainstream movies make up the menu of the city's film festival, which runs over two weeks in late February.

St Patrick's Festival (☎ 676 3205; www.stpatricks festival.ie) The mother of all festivals: hundreds of thousands gather to 'honour' St Patrick over four days around 17 March on city streets and in venues.

Heineken Green Energy Festival (☎ 1890 925 100; www.mcd.ie) Four-day rock and indie music festival based outside Dublin Castle and adjacent venues in May.

DConvergence Festival (☎ 674 6415; www.sustainable .ie; 15-19 Essex St) Ten-day green festival in late June on sustainable living with a diverse programme of workshops, exhibitions and children's activities in Temple Bar.

Iversions (☎ 677 2255; www.temple-bar.ie) Free outdoor music, children's and film events at weekends from June to September in Temple Bar's Meeting House Sq.

Oxegen (www.mcd.ie) Two-day gig in mid-July at Punches-town Racecourse with heavyweight headline acts.

Liffey Swim (☎ 833 2434) Five hundred lunatics swim 2.5km from Rory O'More Bridge to the Custom House in late July – one can't but admire their steel will.

Dublin Theatre Festival (☎ 677 8439; www.dublin theatrefestival.com) Well-established international theatre festival over a fortnight in late September in most Dublin venues.

Dublin Fringe Festival (☎ 872 9016; www.fringefest .com) Comedy and alternative fringe theatre from late September to early October.

SLEEPING

Where you sleep is a major factor in determining the time you'll have here. Quick-hop visitors will undoubtedly want to stay close to the centre – at the heart of the action. If you're planning to stay a while, you can afford a little more flexibility. Whatever you decide, remember this: public transportation can be slow and unreliable, and virtually nonexistent after midnight. Taxis, the other option for suburb dwellers, can be a nightmare to grab at busy hours and closing time.

BLOOMSDAY

It's 16 June. There's a bunch of weirdos wandering around the city dressed in Edwardian gear talking nonsense in dramatic tones. They're not mad – at least not clinically – they're only Bloomsdayers committed to commemorating James Joyce's epic *Ulysses*, which anyone familiar with the book will tell you (and that doesn't necessarily mean that they've *read* the bloody thing) takes place over the course of one day. What they mightn't be able to tell you is that Leopold Bloom's latter-day odyssey takes place on 16 June 1904 because it was on that day that Joyce first 'stepped out' with Nora Barnacle, the woman he had met six days earlier and with whom he would spend the rest of his life. (When James' father heard about this new love he commented that with a name like that she would surely stick to him.)

Although Ireland treated Joyce like a literary pornographer while he was alive, the country – and especially Dublin – can't get enough of him today. Bloomsday is a slightly gimmicky and touristy phenomenon that appeals almost exclusively to Joyce fanatics and tourists, but it's plenty of fun and a great way to lay the groundwork for actually reading what could be the second-hardest book written in the 20th century (the hardest, of course, being Joyce's follow-up blockbuster *Finnegan's Wake*, the greatest book *never* to be read).

In general, events are designed to follow Bloom's progress around town, and in recent years festivities have expanded to continue over four days around 16 June. On Bloomsday proper you can kick things off with breakfast at the **James Joyce Cultural Centre** (Map pp80–1; ☎ 878 8547; 35 North Great George's St) where the 'inner organs of beast and fowl' come accompanied by celebratory readings.

In the morning, guided tours of Joycean sites usually leave from the GPO, on O'Connell St, and the James Joyce Cultural Centre. Lunch-time activity focuses on **Davy Byrne's** (Map p84; Duke St), Joyce's 'moral pub', where Bloom paused to dine on a glass of Burgundy and a slice of Gorgonzola. Street entertainers are likely to keep you amused as you pass the afternoon on guided walks, topped up with animated readings from *Ulysses* and Joyce's other books at appropriate sites and times: **Ormond Quay Hotel** (Map p82; Ormond Quay) at 4pm and **Harrisons** (Map p82; Westmoreland St) later in the day.

Events also take place in the days leading up to and following Bloomsday. The best source of information about what's on in any particular year is likely to be the **James Joyce Cultural Centre** (www.jamesjoyce.ie) or the free *Dublin Event Guide*, close to the date.

Hardly surprising, but the closer to the centre you stay, the more you'll pay – and in Dublin we're talking as much as the most expensive cities in Europe. With prices, it's not just quality that counts, but position: for instance, a large-roomed comfortable B&B in the northside suburbs may cost as little as €45 per person, while the owners of a small, mediocre guesthouse within walking distance of Stephen's Green won't blink when asking €65 for the box room. A quality guesthouse or midrange hotel can cost anything from €65 to €160, while the city's top accommodations don't get interested for less than €160. At the other end of the scale there's the ubiquitous hostel, the bedrock of cheap accommodations: their standards have uniformly gone up, but so have their prices and a bed will cost anything from €15 to as much as €30.

And then the good news. Many hotels have a weekend or B&B rate that can save you as much as 40% on the rack rate; others offer similar discounts for midweek stays. There are also great savings if you book online (see the boxed text, opposite). These rates are generally available year round, but are tougher to find during the high season. Be sure to book ahead and ask for rates, which are only available on a prebooked basis. If you arrive empty-handed in high season, go to one of the Dublin Tourism offices and ask them to book you a room. For €4 plus a 10% deposit on the cost of the first night, they'll find you somewhere to stay. Sometimes this may require a great deal of phoning, so it can be money well spent.

Trinity College & Around

You can't get more central than the relatively small patch of real estate just south of the Liffey, which has a good mix of options from backpacker hostels to the fanciest hotels. Bear in mind that the location comes with a price.

BUDGET

Barnacles Temple Bar House (Map p82; ☎ 671 6277; www.barnacles.ie; 19 Temple Lane; dm/d from €18/39; 🖳) Bright and spacious, in the heart of Temple Bar, this hostel is immaculately clean, has nicely laid-out en suite dorms and doubles with in-room storage. Because of its location, rooms are quieter to the back. Top facilities, comfy lounge and linen and towels provided.

Ashfield House (Map p82; ☎ 679 7734; www .ashfieldhouse.ie; 19-20 D'Olier St; dm/s/d from €13/50/80; 🖳) A stone's throw from Temple Bar and O'Connell Bridge, this modern hostel in a converted church has a selection of tidy four- and six-bed rooms, one large dorm and 25 en suite private rooms. It's more like a small hotel, but without the price tag; a continental-style breakfast is included – a rare beast indeed for hostels. Maximum stay is six nights.

Avalon House (Map p84; ☎ 475 0001; www.avalon -house.ie; 55 Aungier St; dm/s/d €15/35/64; 🖳) Before there was tourism, this hostel in a gorgeous Victorian building catered to the thin trickle of adventurers who landed in Dublin. They flood in these days – book ahead – but Avalon still takes good care of them, whether they be young backpackers or even families. The lounges are great for hanging out.

Kinlay House (Map p82; ☎ 679 6644; www.kinlay house.ie; 2-12 Lord Edward St; dm/d from €19/34; 🖳) A former boarding house for boys, this busy hostel has some massive, mixed 24-bed

TOP FIVE SLEEPS
- best B&B – Grafton Guesthouse (below)
- best boutique hotel – Number 31 (p124)
- best budget sleep – Isaacs Hostel (p125)
- best luxury hotel – Merrion (p124)
- best sleep with a view – Clarence Hotel (p125)

dorms, as well as smaller rooms. Not for the faint-hearted – the hostel has a reputation for being a bit of a party spot.

MIDRANGE

La Stampa (Map p84; ☎ 677 4444; www.lastampa.ie; 35 Dawson St; r weekday/weekend €160/200; 🖳) These days it's all about boutique chic, and this marvellously atmospheric hotel on trendy Dawson St has got it just right. Up two flights of steep stairs are 22 lovely Asian-influenced white rooms with Oriental rattan furniture, exotic velvet throws, TV, air-conditioning and minibar. It also offers some pretty good deals for dinner in the well-known restaurant downstairs.

Grafton Guesthouse (Map p84; ☎ 679 2041; www .graftonguesthouse.com; 26-27 South Great George's St; s/d from €55/110) This excellent guesthouse is an absolute find and gets the nod in all three key categories: location, price and style. Just next to George's St Arcade, the Grafton offers the traditional friendly welcome of a B&B stay (including a terrific breakfast) coupled with a funky design: check out the psychedelic wallpaper. Hard to beat at this price.

Paramount Hotel (Map p82; ☎ 417 9900; www .paramounthotel.ie; cnr Parliament St & Essex Gate; s/d €160/240) Behind the Victorian façade, the lobby is a faithful re-creation of a 1930s hotel, complete with dark wood floors, deep-red leather Chesterfield couches and heavy velvet drapes. The 70-odd rooms don't quite bring *The Maltese Falcon* to mind, but they're handsomely furnished and very comfortable. Highly recommended.

Central Hotel (Map p84; ☎ 679 7302; www.central hotel.ie; 1-5 Exchequer St; s/d from €100/135) The rooms are a little snug for the grand Edwardian style of the décor, but it's still a classy joint, no more so than in the wonderful 1st-floor Library Bar, all leather armchairs and sofas, and nothing short of

DUBLIN

UNIVERSITY ACCOMMODATION

From mid-June to late September only, you can stay in accommodation provided by the city's universities, but be sure to book well in advance.

Trinity College (Map p90; ☎ 608 1177; www .tcd.ie; Accommodations Office, Trinity College; s/d from €35/70; 🖳) Comfortable rooms of different kinds, from basic to en suite, in one of the most atmospheric settings in Dublin.

Mercer Court (Map p84; ☎ 478 2179; reservations@mercercourt.ie; Lower Mercer St; r from €99; 🖳) Owned and run by the Royal College of Surgeons, the rooms are all modern and up to hotel standard.

---

one of the finest spots for an afternoon drink in the whole city. Location-wise, the name says it all.

Eliza Lodge (Map p82; ☎ 671 8044; www.dublin lodge.com; 23-24 Wellington Quay; s/d/ste from €76/ 130/200) It's priced like a hotel, looks like a hotel, but it's still a guesthouse. Its 18 bedrooms are fabulous: comfortable, spacious and – due to its position right over the Millennium Bridge – have great views of the Liffey. The penthouses even have Jacuzzis.

Morgan Hotel (Map p82; ☎ 679 3939; www.the morgan.com; 10 Fleet St; r from €140; 🖳) Designer cool can often be designer cold and the hyper-trendy Morgan falls on the right side of the line, but only just. The look is all-cream contemporary – nothing too exceptional – but the facilities are all top rate. Aromatherapy treatments and massages are extra, as is breakfast (€18).

Camden Court Hotel (Map p84; ☎ 475 9666; www.camdencourthotel.com; Lower Camden St; s/d from €100/125; 🐾 🖳 🅿) The rooms are big and bland, the amenities – including a 16m pool and a well-equipped health club – are geared towards business travellers, who are very enthusiastic about this hotel only 500m from St Stephen's Green.

Aston Hotel (Map p82; ☎ 677 9300; www.aston -hotel.com; 7-9 Aston Quay; s/d incl buffet breakfast from €100/114; 🐾) The Aston, just off O'Connell Bridge, is a small, friendly hotel with spacious, inoffensively decorated rooms all equipped with cable TV and en suite.

Mercer Hotel (Map p84; ☎ 478 2179; www .mercerhotel.ie; Lower Mercer St; s/d from €89/150) A fairly plain frontage hides a pretty decent

hotel, with largish rooms dressed in antiques giving the whole place an elegant, classical look. There is a dizzying array of room deals available; the off-peak rates are sensational.

Drury Court Hotel (Map p84; ☎ 475 1988; www .drurycourthotel.com; 28-30 Lower Stephen's St; s/d €70/100; 🖳) Centrally located with rooms primarily aimed at the business traveller, the Drury Court is a good choice if you're not looking to be inspired by your surroundings, but still fancy a good night's kip in comfort.

TOP END

Merrion (Map p84; ☎ 603 0600; www.merrionhotel .com; Upper Merrion St; s/d €300/325; 🅿 🖳) A leading contender for top dog in Dublin, the resplendent five-star Merrion occupies five beautifully restored Georgian town houses – one of which was the birthplace of Napoleon's nemesis at Waterloo, Arthur Wellesely, the duke of Wellington. Its sophisticated comforts – the finest linen, Carrara marble in the bathrooms and fancy plasterwork all around – are best appreciated in the old house rather than the new wing out the back. Even if you don't stay, come for the superb afternoon tea (€29),

---

SOMETHING SPECIAL

Number 31 (Map p78; ☎ 676 5011; www .number31.ie; 31 Leeson Close; s/d/t from €105/150/210) Number 31 could be a set from the Zeitgeist film *The Ice Storm*. The coach house and former home of modernist architect Sam Stephenson (of Central Bank fame) still feels like a real 1960s home, intact with its sunken sitting room, leather sofas, mirrored bar, Perspex lamps and floor-to-ceiling windows. A hidden oasis of calm, a five-minute walk from St Stephen's Green, this is one of our favourite places to stay in Dublin. Its 21 bedrooms are split between the retro coach house with its chichi rooms, and the more gracious Georgian house through the garden, where rooms are individually furnished with tasteful French antiques and big comfortable beds. Gourmet breakfasts with kippers, homemade breads and granola are served in the conservatory. Children under 10 are not permitted.

---

with endless cups of tea served out of silver pots near a raging fire.

Shelbourne (Map p84; ☎ 676 6471; www.shelbourne.ie; 27 St Stephen's Green North) The best address in town is still Dublin's famous Shelbourne, where old-world grandeur and service combine to make for a memorable stay. At the time of writing, the hotel was closed until September 2006 for a major renovation.

Westbury Hotel (Map p84; ☎ 679 1122; www.jurysdoyle.com; Grafton St; s/d/ste from €200/240/750; 🖳 P) Visiting celebs looking for some quiet time have long favoured the Westbury's elegant suites, where they can watch TV from the Jacuzzi before retiring to a four-poster bed. Mere mortals tend to make do with the standard rooms, which are comfortable enough but lack the sophisticated grandeur promised by the luxurious public spaces.

Westin Dublin (Map p82; ☎ 645 1000; www.westin.com; Westmoreland St; r from €340; 🖳 P) The Westin began life as an Allied Irish Bank and now uses the old bank vaults and marble counters in its basement Mint Bar. Its rooms exude a classical American grandeur with an understated style that includes separate shower and bath, laptop-size safe and Westin's trademark Heavenly Bed with 10 luxurious layers to envelop you. Ask to take a look at the beautiful banqueting hall, in the former banking area, with its exquisite ceiling and gold-leaf plasterwork. Breakfast will set you back €25.

Browne's Townhouse (Map p84; ☎ 638 3939; www.brownesdublin.com; 22 St Stephen's Green North; s/d from €175/220; 🖳) An exquisite Georgian building in a perfect location; above the reputable restaurant are 11 superb, individually styled bedrooms, each the height of comfort and elegance. It's a little bit of 18th-century elegance updated to suit the needs of the 21st.

Clarence Hotel (Map p82; ☎ 407 0800; www.clarence.ie; 6-8 Wellington Quay; r €330-350, ste €640-2100; 🖳) Dublin's coolest hotel is virtually synonymous with its rock-star owners, Bono and The Edge, so it's hardly surprising that it is well used to dealing with celebrity heavyweights. The 50-odd rooms aren't short on style but they lack that grandeur you should expect from a top hotel. It's one of the hottest beds in town for sure, but what you're really paying for is the hype.

SOMETHING SPECIAL

Irish Landmark Trust (Map p82; ☎ 670 4733; www.irishlandmark.com; 25 Eustace St; 2/3 nights from €620/791) This fabulous heritage 18th-century house has been gloriously restored to the highest standard by the Irish Landmark Trust charity. You can have this unique house, which sleeps up to seven in its double, twin and triple bedrooms, for two or more nights all to yourself – single nights, alas, are not available. Furnished with tasteful antiques, authentic furniture and fittings (including a grand piano in the drawing room), this kind of period rental accommodation is unique and utterly special.

The Liberties & Kilmainham

There isn't much on offer in this part of town, but one exception has a terrific view.

Jurys Inn Christchurch (Map p82; ☎ 454 0000; www.jurysinns.com; Christchurch Pl; r from €108) This large hotel with limited services, opposite Christ Church Cathedral in a great location, has clean but anodyne rooms sleeping up to three. Ask for a room with a church view.

O'Connell Street & Around

There are a few elegant hotels around O'Connell St, but the real draw round these parts is just to the east on Gardiner St, Dublin's B&B row. Caveat emptor, however: there are some bad B&Bs on the street as well as some excellent choices; here we only include ones we feel are the latter. The further north you go the dodgier the neighbourhood gets – that heady inner-city mix of drugs and crime – so stay alert, especially on Upper Gardiner St past Mountjoy Sq.

BUDGET

Isaacs Hostel (Map pp80-1; ☎ 855 6215; www.isaacs.ie; 2-5 Frenchman's Lane; dm/d from €12/58; 🖳) Located in a 200-year-old wine vault, this popular, grungy hostel with loads of character is the cheapest bed in town – without sacrificing the basics of health and hygiene. The lounge area is where it all happens, from summer BBQs to live music, and the easygoing staff are on-hand 24/7 for advice and help. Global nomads will feel right at home.

Abbey Court Hostel (Map p82; ☎ 878 0700; www.abbey-court.com; 29 Bachelor's Walk; dm/d €21/88; 🖳)

Spread over two buildings on the Liffey quays, this large, well-run hostel has 33 clean dorms with good storage. En suite doubles are in the newer building where a light breakfast is also provided in the adjacent café, Juice.

Litton Lane Hostel (Map p82; ☎ 872 8389; litton@indigo.ie; 2-4 Litton Lane; dm/d from €15/70) True to its dog-eared recording studio origins (once patronised by Van Morrison), this friendly hostel could do with a lick of paint but retains a certain grungy charm. Dorms are mixed, as are the showers, which all kind of lends new meaning to their motto, 'don't sleep around; sleep with us.'

Marlborough Hostel (Map pp80-1; ☎ 874 7629; www.marlboroughhostel.com; 81-82 Marlborough St; dm/d from €11/51; 🖳) Next to the Pro-Cathedral, this well-located hostel has 76 beds and adequate facilities. High Georgian ceilings make up for small rooms, and the slightly jaded showers, in the basement, are a bit of a trek from the dorms.

MIDRANGE

Anchor Guesthouse (Map pp80-1; ☎ 878 6913; www.anchorguesthouse.com; 49 Lower Gardiner St; s/d from €55/75) Most B&Bs round these parts offer pretty much the same stuff: TVs, tea- and coffee-making facilities, a half-decent shower and clean linen. The Anchor does all of that, but it just has an elegance you won't find in many of the other B&Bs along this stretch. This lovely Georgian guesthouse, with its delicious wholesome breakfasts, comes highly recommended by readers. They're dead right.

Lynham's Hotel (Map pp80-1; ☎ 888 0886; www.lynams-hotel.com; 63-64 O'Connell St; s/d/tr from €85/130/170) A midrange hotel smack in the middle of O'Connell St is almost too good to be true. Now that Dublin's premier street is halfway back to its glorious best, Lynham's becomes a rare gem indeed – a smart, friendly hotel with 42 pleasant rooms decorated in country pine furniture. Room No 41 is a lovely dormer triple with an additional camp bed, handy for groups who want to share. Ask for discounts midweek.

Castle Hotel (Map pp80-1; ☎ 874 6949; www.castle-hotel.ie; 3-4 Great Denmark St; s/d/tr from €75/115/145) In business since 1809, the Castle may be slightly rough around the edges but it's one of the most pleasant hotels this side of the Liffey. The fabulous palazzo-style grand staircase leads to the 50-odd bed-

rooms, whose furnishings are traditional and a tad antiquated but perfectly good throughout – check out the original Georgian cornicing around the high ceilings.

Walton's Hotel (Map pp80-1; ☎ 878 3131; www.waltons-hotel.ie; 2-5 North Frederick St; s/d/tr €80/120/160) Better known for their legendary musical instrument shop next door, the Walton family opened this friendly hotel in an effort to preserve the traditional Georgian heritage of the building. With the help of the Castle Hotel they have done just that; the 43 rooms are clean and spacious – an excellent choice with a superb location overlooking Findlater's Church and the Rotunda Hospital. Children under 12 stay for free.

Charles Stewart (Map pp80-1; ☎ 878 0350; www.charlesstewart.ie; 5-6 Parnell Sq; s/d from €35/70) Clean and unfussy, the Charles Stewart's rooms are perfect if you're looking for somewhere functional rather than stylish; rooms in the extension to the rear are bigger and quieter. Poet Oliver St John Gogarty was born here.

Old Dubliner (Map pp80-1; ☎ 855 5666; www.olddubliner.ie; 62 Amiens St; s/d from €70/90; Ⓟ) A long-established elegant guesthouse, virtually opposite Connolly Station, that has 14 very well appointed rooms. Ask for midweek discounts.

Browns Hotel (Map pp80-1; ☎ 855 0034; www.brownshotelireland.com; 80-90 Lower Gardiner St; s/d €85/109) The 22 rooms fill up pretty quickly at this small hotel, whose popularity is cemented by the neat and tidy rooms replete with modern furnishings. Book early.

Celtic Lodge (Map pp80-1; ☎ 677 9955; www.celticlodge.ie; 81-82 Talbot St; s/d €65/70) A fairly tidy and basic guesthouse situated above a pub with 29 simply furnished rooms. Because of the live music in the pub below, you may want to ask for a room at the back if you'd rather not join in the sing-along from your bed.

Lyndon House (Map pp80-1; ☎ 878 6950; 26 Gardiner Pl; s/d from €50/85) There are seven simple en suite rooms and two small standard rooms in this modestly furnished but very friendly Georgian house.

TOP END

Gresham Hotel (Map pp80-1; ☎ 874 6881; www.gresham-hotels.com; Upper O'Connell St; r €100-310, ste €250-2000; 🖳) Well-heeled Americans and elderly groups on shopping breaks to the capital swear by this landmark hotel, the fanciest on O'Connell St. In an effort to attract a new generation of the platinum-card set, the owners have undertaken a substantial refurbishment of the whole property – so far, so very good. The understated grandeur of the public spaces promises much; the refurbished rooms will not disappoint.

Smithfield & Phoenix Park

It's still an area in development, but Smithfield – especially along the quays – is a good spot to stay as it's close to all the action.

MIDRANGE

Ormond Quay Hotel (Map p82; ☎ 872 1811; www .ormondquayhotel.ie; 7-11 Upper Ormond Quay; s/d €69/110) Dublin's most openly gay-friendly hotel has a terrific location on the river; a plaque outside notes its role in the Sirens episode of *Ulysses*. The hotel closed for renovations in the summer of 2005, but should be back in business at the same time in 2006.

TOP END

Morrison Hotel (Map p82; ☎ 887 2400; www.morrison hotel.ie; Lower Ormond Quay; r €285-580, ste €1400; 💻) It's named after a Doors album, but there's no hint of '70s slacker cool about this place. Hong Kong–Irish fashion designer John Rocha was given a virtual free hand in the design, and what he came up with was New York minimalist chic – plenty of straight lines, dark wood and lots of white leather. The loosely Oriental-style rooms are bright, if a little compact, and feature Egyptian cotton linen, CD players, modem facilities and pieces of Rocha's own line of crystal.

Beyond the Royal Canal

The Royal Canal winds its way through the leafy suburb of Drumcondra, about 3km east of Upper O'Connell St along Dorset St. There are B&Bs aplenty here, with most of the houses being late-Victorian or Edwardian beauties that are generally extremely well kept and comfortable. As they're on the airport road, they tend to be full virtually throughout the year, so advance booking is recommended. Bus No 3, 11, 11A, 16 or 36A from Trinity College and O'Connell St all stop along the Drumcondra Rd.

MIDRANGE

House (☎ 837 5030; www.griffithhouse.com; 125 Griffith Ave; s/d €40/70) This elegant house, on a beautiful, tree-lined avenue, has four double rooms, three of them with en suite. Each room is tastefully appointed, with large, comfortable beds and nice furniture.

St Andrew's Guesthouse (☎ 837 4684; 1-3 Lambay Rd; s/d from €45/85) This place has 16 comfortable en suite rooms, with elegant period-style beds. It's located off the Drumcondra Rd, down Griffith Ave and the third turn to the left. Bus No 11A or 11B stops along the adjacent Home Farm Rd.

Tinode House (☎ 837 2277; www.tinodehouse.com; 170 Upper Drumcondra Rd; s/d €55/65) This comfortable Edwardian town house has four elegant bedrooms, all with bathrooms. A familial welcome and excellent breakfast are part of the package.

Beyond the Grand Canal

The south city suburb of Ballsbridge is full of quality hotels and guesthouses that generally offer more for your euro than the city centre. Buses No 5, 7, 7A, 8, 18 or 45 will get you there in about 10 minutes, or it's a 30-minute walk. Also worth checking out is the increasingly gentrified suburb of Ranelagh, immediately accessible from the city centre via the Luas, the light-rail system.

MIDRANGE

Pembroke Townhouse (Map p78; ☎ 660 0277; www .pembroketownhouse.ie; 90 Pembroke Rd, Ballsbridge; s €90-165, d €100-210; P) This superluxurious town house is a perfect example of what happens when traditional and modern combine to great effect. A classical Georgian house has been transformed into a superb boutique hotel, with each room carefully crafted and appointed to reflect the best of contemporary design and style, right down to the modern art on the walls and the handy lift to the upper floors. May we borrow your designer?

Schoolhouse Hotel (Map p78; ☎ 667 5014; www .schoolhousehotel.com; 2-8 Northumberland Rd, Ballsbridge; s/d from €169/199; P) A real beauty: a converted Victorian schoolhouse that is now a superb boutique hotel with 31 exquisite rooms, each named after an Irish writer, and stocked with luxury toiletries and all sorts of modern amenities. A place (ahem) ahead of its class.

Ariel House (Map p78; ☎ 668 5512; www.ariel -house.net; 52 Lansdowne Rd, Ballsbridge; r from €99; (P)) Treading the fine line between boutique hotel and luxury B&B, the 28 en suite rooms in this highly rated Victorian-era property are all individually decorated in period furniture, which lends the place an air of genuine luxury. A far better choice than most hotels.

Waterloo House (Map p78; ☎ 660 1888; www .waterloohouse.ie; 8-10 Waterloo Rd, Ballsbridge; s/d €65/118; (P)) A short walk from St Stephen's Green, off Baggot St, this lovely guesthouse is spread over two ivy-clad Georgian houses. Rooms are tastefully decorated with high quality furnishings in authentic Farrow & Ball Georgian colours and all have cable TV and kettles. Home-cooked breakfast is served in the conservatory or garden on sunny days.

Sandford Townhouse (Map p78; ☎ 412 6880; 52 Sandford Rd, Ranelagh; s/d €50/70; (P)) An elegant Victorian home with three large and comfortable rooms, the town house is within a short walking distance of the Luas, making it a convenient hop to and from the city centre.

TOP END

Four Seasons (Map p78; ☎ 665 4000; www.four seasons.com; Simmonscourt Rd, Ballsbridge; r from €275; (P) (💻)) The muscular, no-holds-barred style of American corporate inn-keeping is in full force at this huge hotel that has sought to raise the hospitality bar. Its over-the-top look – lots of marble effect, fancy chandeliers and carefully pruned floral arrangements – has its critics, who think it garish, but there's no denying the sheer quality of the place. For many, this is the best hotel in town. We're suckers for a slightly more demure luxury, so we'll stick it in the Top Three. It is in the grounds of the Royal Dublin Society Showground.

Berkeley Court (Map p78; ☎ 660 1711; www .jurysdoyle.com; Lansdowne Rd, Ballsbridge; s/d from €250/330; (P) (💻)) This upmarket hotel, southeast of the city centre, caters mainly to business travellers. While its décor is firmly traditional, rooms are kitted-out to the highest standard and offer every modern amenity. Check the website for special offers because, at the time of writing, rooms were selling for less than half the quoted rate.

EATING

A couple of decades ago, eating out was the sole preserve of the idle rich, the business lunch and the very special occasion. Which was kind of handy, as there were literally only a handful of decent restaurants to choose from. These days, Dublin has more restaurants than it knows what to do with and a population that has made fashion out of food to the point that, for many, you aren't what you eat but *where* you eat.

Quantity may not be a problem, but invariably quality is. Generally, standards are pretty good throughout – a demanding populace and stiff competition ensure that crimes against the palate are kept to a minimum – but considering what most places are charging, the selection of eateries that really stand out gets pretty thin indeed. Eating out ain't cheap and comparisons with other European capitals leave Dublin a little shy.

But here's the good news: Dublin's dining scene is so diverse that it's virtually impossible for you not to find something to your taste. Most of the dining options are concentrated on the south side of the Liffey, but the number of quality restaurants and cafés on the northside is steadily growing. The area around Parnell St, in particular, is worth checking out for the spate of new exotic restaurants – a reflection of the increasingly diverse ethnic communities that have settled in the area.

Temple Bar is chock full of eateries, and while a handful are pretty good, most offer mundane, overpriced belly-fill rather than anything you'd want to ask the chef how to make. There are plenty of excellent choices in the area outside Temple Bar. A little further afield, the near suburb of Ranelagh – easily reached by Luas – has a growing reputation for fine dining. Finally, note that getting a table on a busy night can

TOP FIVE BITES

- best budget eats – Gruel (opposite)
- best brunch – Odessa (p130)
- best ethnic – Monty's of Kathmandu (p130)
- best lunch – L'Gueuleton (p130)
- best splurge – Bang (p132)

be a nightmare, so be sure to book early. Unless otherwise mentioned, all the places below accept reservations.

Trinity College & Around

If you spent your whole time in this area you would still eat pretty well; the south city centre is the hub (with some notable exceptions) of the best the city has to offer.

BUDGET

Dunne & Crescenzi (Map p84; ☎ 677 3815; 14 South Frederick St; mains €5-9; ☺ 9am-7pm Mon & Tue, to 10pm Wed-Sat) This exceptional Italian eatery delights its regulars with a basic menu of rustic pleasures: *panini* (Italian sandwiches), a single pasta dish and a superb plate of mixed antipastos drizzled in olive oil. The shelves are stacked with wine, the coffee is perfect and the desserts are sinfully good.

Queen of Tarts (Map p82; ☎ 670 7499; Lord Edward St; goods from €3.50; ☺ 7am-6pm) Pocket-sized Queen of Tarts is the mother of all bakery-cafés with its mouthwatering array of savoury tarts and filled focaccias, fruit crumbles and wicked pastries. It's perfect for breakfast or lunch – if it's full you can take away to the quiet Chester Beatty garden across the road.

Simon's Place (Map p84; ☎ 679 7821; George's St Arcade, South Great George's St; mains from €4.50) Simon has been serving his unchanged menu of doorstep sandwiches and wholesome vegetarian soups to an adoring public for years. It's also a good place to mull over a coffee and watch life go by in the old-fashioned arcade.

Listons (Map p78; ☎ 405 4779; 25 Camden St; lunch €3-8) Lunch-time queues out the door testify that Listons is undoubtedly the best deli in Dublin. Its sandwiches with fresh, delicious fillings, roasted vegetable quiches, rosemary potato cakes and sublime salads will have you coming back again and again. The only problem is there's too much to choose from. On fine days it's great to retreat to the solitude of the nearby Iveagh Gardens with your gourmet picnic.

La Corte (Map p84; ☎ 633 4477; Powerscourt Townhouse Shopping Centre, South William St; mains €8-10; ☺ 10am-6pm) Another terrific Italian eatery, stretched across the top-floor balcony of the Powerscourt Townhouse: lovely position, super food. From *panini* to the daily

special (pasta or risotto), you won't go wrong.

Nude (Map p82; ☎ 675 5577; 21 Suffolk St; wraps from €5) This ultracool place, owned by Bono's brother Norman, has been a huge hit since it opened, serving tasty wraps with all kinds of Asian fillings. You can eat in or take away, but be sure to try one of the freshly squeezed fruit juices.

Bar Italia (Map p82; ☎ 679 5128; 4 Essex Quay; lunch €6-9; ☺ 8am-6pm Mon-Fri, 9am-6pm Sat, noon-6pm Sun) One of a new generation of eateries to show the more established Italian restaurants how the Old Country *really* eats, Bar Italia is a favourite with the lunch-time crowd, who come for the ever-changing pasta dishes, homemade risottos and sensational *panini* with Italian fillings.

Lemon (Map p84; ☎ 672 9044; 66 South William St; pancakes from €3.75) Dublin's first and best pancake joint is staffed by a terrific bunch who like their music loud and their pancakes good: proper, paper-thin, sweet and savoury crêpes, smothered, stuffed and sprinkled with a variety of toppings, fillings and sauces. It's so popular that in the summer of 2005 a second branch opened on nearby Dawson St.

Market Bar (Map p136; ☎ 677 4835; Fade St; mains €6-10) This one-time sausage factory, now fashionable watering hole, also has a super kitchen knocking out Spanish tapas and other Iberian-influenced bites. Proof that the carvery lunch isn't the height of pub dining.

Ba Mizu (Map p84; ☎ 674 6712, ground fl Powerscourt Townhouse Shopping Centre; mains €7-14) The laidback atmosphere of this new bar, with its vaulted stone ceiling and leather sofas, is conducive to a leisurely lunch of better-than-average bar food. The all-day menu is loosely Irish, with favourites such as beef in Guinness stew and mimosa chicken with champ, but it also has good vegetarian pastas or dishes like *spanakopita* (spinach pancake) with mint and cucumber.

MIDRANGE

L'Gueuleton (Map p84; ☎ 675 3708; 1 Fade St; mains €11-23; ☑ noon-3pm, 6-11.30pm Mon-Sat) Dubliners have a devil of a time pronouncing the name (which means 'the gluttonous feast' in French) and have had their patience tested with the no-reservations-get-in-line-and-wait policy, but they just can't get enough of this restaurant's take on French rustic cuisine that makes twisted tongues and sore feet a small price to pay. The steak is sensational, but the Toulouse sausages with *choucroute* (sauerkraut) and Lyonnaise potatoes is a timely reminder that when it comes to the pleasures of the palate, the French really know what they're doing.

Café Bardeli (Map p84; ☎ 672 7720; www.cafe bardeli.ie; Bewley's Bldg, Grafton St; mains €9-13; ☑ 7am-11pm) Dublin's most famous café closed its doors in 2004 to muted shock and not a little dismay; a few months later, it reopened as a wonderful hybrid, with three separate eateries in one stunning building, the largest of which is the brand new, high profile branch of the super-successful Café Bardeli chain, whose first restaurant is still doing a roaring trade on South Great George's St (☎ 677 1646; 12-13 South Great George's St) with the same menu of thin-crust pizzas (with imaginative toppings) and a selection of homemade pastas that mixes old faves like spag bol with newer creations like tagliatelle with haddock and peas that are also sold by the family-size bowl. Good, fresh food at prices that won't break the bank in a buzzing atmosphere. No reservations allowed, so prepare to wait on a busy night.

Odessa (Map p82; ☎ 670 7634; 13 Dame Ct; mains €13-20) Just off Exchequer St, Odessa's loungy atmosphere with comfy sofas and retro standard lamps attract the city's hipsters who flock in for its homemade burgers, steaks or daily fish specials. You may not escape the sofa after a few of Odessa's renowned cocktails quaffed to a game of backgammon. Weekend brunch is *extremely* popular: you were warned.

Monty's of Kathmandu (Map p82; ☎ 670 4911; 28 Eustace St; mains €13-21; ☑ 12.30-2.30pm & 6-11.30pm Mon-Sat, 6-11pm Sun) Award-winning Monty's trade is built on people who keep returning for typical Nepalese dishes such as *gorkhali* (chicken cooked in chilli, yoghurt and ginger) or *kachela* (raw marinated meat). The Shiva beer complements these hearty, spicy dishes. Ethnic food doesn't get much better than this.

La Maison des Gourmets (Map p84; ☎ 672 7258; 15 Castle Market; mains €5-15) The city's Francophiles all seem to amass at this tiny French café above a bakery – and for good reason. The menu is small but its *tartines* (open sandwiches) with daily toppings such as roast aubergine and pesto, salad specials or plates of charcuterie are divine. It also has

---

VEGGIE BUDGET BITES

Blazing Salads (Map p84; ☎ 671 9552; 42 Drury St; mains €2.50-7) Organic breads (many special diet), Californian-style salads, smoothies and pizza slices can all be taken away from this delicious vegetarian deli.

Cornucopia (Map p84; ☎ 677 7583; 19 Wicklow St; mains from €6) For those escaping the Irish cholesterol habit, Cornucopia is a popular wholefood café turning out healthy goodies. There's even a hot vegetarian breakfast as an alternative to muesli.

Fresh (Map p84; ☎ 671 9552; top fl Powerscourt Townhouse Shopping Centre; lunch €5-9) This long-standing vegetarian restaurant serves a variety of salads and filling hot daily specials. Many dishes are dairy-and gluten-free without compromising on taste. The baked potato topped with organic cheese (€5.50) comes with two salads and is a hearty meal in itself.

Govinda's (Map p84; ☎ 475 0309; 4 Aungier St; mains €5-10) Authentic beans-and-pulses vegetarian place run by the Hare Krishna. Its cheap, wholesome mix of salads and Indian-influenced hot daily specials are filling and tasty.

a fine range of pastries, baked goodies and herbal teas. You can get a traditional country breakfast of meats, cheeses and warm crusty bread for €9.50.

Ar Vicoletto (Map p82; ☎ 670 8662; 5 Crow St; mains €12-25) When it's good, it's very, very good, with superb Italian dishes washed down with splendid local reds and enjoyed in a convivial atmosphere. But it can be a little inconsistent and sometimes quite disappointing. Still, it's worth the risk.

Jaipur (Map p84; ☎ 677 0999; 41 South Great George's St; mains €17-20) Critics rave about the subtle and varied flavours produced by Jaipur's kitchen, which is down to its refusal to skimp on even the smallest dash of spice. What you get here is as close to the real deal as you'd get anywhere outside of Delhi.

Village (Map p136; ☎ 475 8555; 26 Wexford St; mains €10-15; ☼ noon-8.30pm Mon-Fri & Sun) Forget plain old pub grub: even an accomplished chef would be proud of the menu at one of Dublin's most popular pub venues. How about pan-fried piri-piri perch with vegetable ratatouille (€13.95)? A great choice for lunch or early dinner.

Avoca Handweavers (Map p82; ☎ 677 4215; 11-13 Suffolk St; mains €8-15) This airy 1st-floor café was one of Dublin's best-kept secrets (because of an absence of any obvious signs) until discovered by the Ladies Who Lunch. If you can battle your way past the designer shopping bags to a table, you'll relish the simply delicious, rustic delights of organic shepherd's pie, roast lamb with couscous, or sumptuous salads from the Avoca kitchen. There's also a take-away salad bar and hot counter in the basement. For more information on the handicrafts, see p144.

Imperial Chinese Restaurant (Map p84; ☎ 677 2580; 12a Wicklow St; dim sum dish €4, mains €10-17) This long-established place is a favourite with the Chinese community and is noted for its lunch-time dim sum. These Chinese snacks are popular on Sunday, when the Imperial serves *yum cha* brunch and 'drink tea', the traditional accompaniment to dim sum.

Aya (Map p84; ☎ 677 1544; Clarendon St; mains €12-25) Attached to the Brown Thomas department store, Aya is the best Japanese restaurant in town. There's a revolving sushi bar where you can eat your fill for €25 every night, except Thursday and Saturday, between 5pm and 9pm (maximum 55 minutes) or else go á la carte from the great menu.

Clarendon Café Bar (Map p84; ☎ 679 2909; Clarendon St; mains €10-16; ☼ noon-8pm Mon-Sat, to 6pm Sun) Spread across three stylishly designed floors, the Stokes brothers (of Bang fame; see p132) have given pub food a go and come up trumps. The only difference between here and a proper restaurant is that the waitstaff won't flinch when you order lager to go with your meal.

Hô Sen (Map p82; ☎ 671 8181; 6 Cope St; mains €15-17; ☼ dinner only) Dublin's only genuine Vietnamese restaurant is spreading the gospel of Southeast Asia's healthiest and lightest cuisine to a growing number of willing converts, who ensure that this place is packed almost every night. It helps that the staff are almost impossibly friendly.

El Bahia (Map p84; ☎ 677 0213; 1st fl, 37 Wicklow St; mains €10-19) Dark and sultry, the intimate atmosphere at El Bahia, reputedly Ireland's only Moroccan restaurant, is like that of a desert harem. The food is equally exotic with a range of daily *tagines* (stews), couscous and *bastilles* (pastry stuffed with chicken or fish) to tempt you. The sweet Moroccan coffee brewed with five warming spices is delicious.

Ely Wine Bar (Map p84; ☎ 676 8986; 22 Ely Pl; mains €11-18) All dishes – homemade burgers, bangers and mash, and pasta dishes – at this intimate basement restaurant are prepared with organic and free-range produce from the owner's organic family farm in County Clare, so you can rest assured of the quality. There's a large wine list to choose from, with over 70 sold by the glass. Its friendly, relaxed atmosphere makes it popular with women and lone diners.

Peploe's (Map p84; ☎ 676 3144; 16 St Stephen's Green North; mains €9-19; ☼ noon-11pm Mon-Sat) Lots of air-kissing and comparing of shopping-bag contents take place at this sophisticated and sumptuous wine-bar at one of the fanciest addresses in town. A highly ambitious menu complements the superb wine list.

Tiger Becs (Map p84; ☎ 677 8677; 36 Dawson St; mains €9-25) Below Oriental superpub SamSara, Tiger Becs is a long, cavernous eating hall serving good Thai nosh to Dublin's fine young things. The starter crispy aromatic duck is delicious and a meal in itself. A loud, buzzing place with plenty of atmosphere; a great place to kick off the party.

Wagamama (Map p84; ☎ 478 2152; South King St; mains €11-18) Production line rice-and-noodles dishes served pronto at canteen-style tables mightn't seem like the most inviting way to dine, but boy this food is good and the basement it's served in is surprisingly light and airy – for a place with absolutely no natural light.

Bistro (Map p84; ☎ 671 5430; 4-5 Castle Market; mains €10-19) The real draw at this place is its outdoor seating in summer, on a lively pedestrianised strip behind the George's St Arcade. Its fish, pasta and pizza specials are sinfully rich but very tasty.

Juice (Map p84; ☎ 475 7856; 73 South Great George's St; mains €8-16) A creative vegetarian restaurant, Juice puts an imaginative, California-type spin on all kinds of dishes. The real treat is the selection of fruit smoothies, a delicious and healthy alternative to soft drinks.

Yamamori (Map p84; ☎ 475 5001; 71 South Great George's St; mains €9-24) This popular Asian restaurant, with its long communal tables, serves filling noodle- and rice-based staples. Children are welcome and well catered for and service is smart, which is handy for a pre-cinema bite.

Gotham Café (Map p84; ☎ 679 5266; 8 South Anne St; mains €7.50-14) It's not easy to get a table at child-friendly Gotham at peak times; its massive selection of pizzas with unusual toppings is just too popular.

Pizza Milano (Map p84; ☎ 670 7744; 38 Dawson St; main €7-15) Pizzas are pretty good in this large but stylish pizza emporium, but what we really like are the on-site free child-minders, who entertain your little ones while you eat, on Sunday between noon and 4.30pm.

Rajdoot Tandoori (Map p84; ☎ 679 4274; 26-28 Clarendon St; mains €11-19) Visitors to India may remember Rajdoot as a popular brand of Indian motorcycle. In Dublin, however, the name is a byword for Indian cuisine at its very best, particularly the more aromatic flavours of North India.

TOP END

Bang (Map p84; ☎ 676 0898; 11 Merrion Row; mains €13-24; ⏰ closed Sun) The hip and handsome Stoke twins have brought a touch of Danish to Dublin in appropriately stylish surrounds – and created a favourite with the 30-somethings who have a little cash to burn. The modern European grub – carefully created by chef Lorcan Cribbin (ex-Ivy in London, don't you know) – is sharp, tasty and very much in demand: Thai

baked sea bass, medallions of beef and melt-in-your-mouth roast scallops are just a random selection. Reservations are a must, even for lunch.

Restaurant Patrick Guilbaud (Map p84; ☎ 676 4192; 21 Upper Merrion St; 2-/3-course set lunch €33/45, dinner mains about €35; ⏰ 12.30-2.30pm & 7.30-10.30pm Tue-Sat) With two Michelin stars on its résumé, this elegant restaurant is one of the best in Ireland, and head chef Guillaume Lebrun does his best to ensure that it stays that way. Next door to the Merrion Hotel, Guilbaud's French *haute cuisine* is beautifully executed and served in delectable surroundings. The lunch menu is a steal, at least in this stratosphere.

Eden (Map p82; ☎ 670 5372; Meeting House Sq; mains €15-25; ⏰ noon-2.30pm & 6-10.30pm Mon-Fri, noon-3pm & 6-11pm Sat & Sun) Eden is the epitome of Temple Bar chic with its trendy waitstaff, minimalist surroundings, high ceiling, hanging plants and terrace onto Meeting House Sq. But the food is the real star: Eleanor Walsh's unfussy modern Irish cuisine uses organic seasonal produce, complemented by a carefully chosen wine list. Seating on the gas-heated terrace is at a premium on summer evenings, when classic films are projected onto the nearby Gallery of Photography.

L'Ecrivain (Map p84; ☎ 661 1919; www.lecrivain. com; 109 Lower Baggot St; mains €22-45; ⏰ closed Sat lunch & Sun) A firm favourite with many a gourmet foodie, L'Ecrivain trundles along with just one Michelin star to its name, but the plaudits just keep coming. Plenty of Irish ingredients – local salmon, Dublin Bay prawns, Guinness and the like – are given the classic French treatment and the result is divine dining.

Mackerel (Map p84; ☎ 672 7719; www.mackerel.ie; Bewley's Building, 34 Grafton St; mains €20-30; ⏰ noon-11pm) Part of the Bewley's Building revamp that saw the arrival of Café Bardeli, the very elegant and balconied James Joyce Room has been converted into a wonderful new fish restaurant that manages to go upscale without getting up its own...nose. The mouth-watering starters – we're addicted to the ceviche – is merely the warm-up for the main show, a constantly changing list of sublime whole fish done in a variety of ways.

Tea Rooms (Map p82; ☎ 407 0813; Clarence Hotel, 6-8 Wellington Quay; 2-course lunch €24, 2-/3-course dinner €42/53; ⏰ 12.30-2.30pm Mon-Fri, 6.30-10.30pm

Mon-Sat, 12.30-3pm & 6.30-9.30pm Sun) Anthony Ely's ambitious menu in the Clarence Hotel's Tea Rooms features classic French cuisine – based equally on fish as meat – with an Irish twist. This is *haute cuisine* stripped of pretension, leaving solid, well-prepared seasonal food that is beautifully presented.

Thornton's (Map p84; ☎ 478 7000; Fitzwilliam Hotel; midweek 3-course lunch/dinner €40/65; mains €50) Kevin Thornton is probably the only chef in Dublin able to challenge Guilbaud's top-dog slot with two Michelin stars apiece, and he does so with a mouthwatering interpretation of new French cuisine. The service is faultless, if a little too formal in this *uber*trendy room overlooking St Stephen's Green. Want to watch a grown-up squirm? Ask for ketchup.

Mermaid Café (Map p82; ☎ 670 8236; 22 Dame St; mains €18-31; ⏰ 12.30-2.30pm & 6-11pm Mon-Sat, 12.30-3pm & 6-9pm Sun) The Mermaid is an American-style bistro with natural wood furniture and abstract canvasses on its panelled walls. It caters mainly to a hip gourmand crowd who appreciate inventive ingredient-led, organic food such as monkfish with buttered red chard or braised lamb shank with apricot couscous. Its informal atmosphere, pure food and friendly staff make it difficult to get a table without notice.

The Liberties & Kilmainham

Fast-food outlets and greasy-spoon diners still dominate the food map in this part of the city, but there's one spot that rises out of the boiling oil and batter-in-a-bucket and takes its place among the legends.

BUDGET

Leo Burdock's (Map p82; ☎ 454 0306; 2 Werburgh St; cod 'n' chips €7) You will often hear that you haven't eaten in Dublin until you've queued in the cold for a cod 'n' chips wrapped in paper from the city's most famous chipper. Total codswallop, of course, but there's something about sitting on the street, balancing the bag on your lap and trying to eat the chips quickly before they go cold and horrible that smacks of Dublin in a bygone age. It's nice to revisit the past, especially if you don't have to get stuck there.

MIDRANGE

Lord Edward (Map p82; ☎ 454 2420; 23 Christchurch Pl; mains €16-18; ⏰ noon-3pm & 6-10.30pm Mon-Fri, dinner only Sat) This well-established and respected seafood restaurant (above the eponymous pub) has pointedly avoided the modern make-over and has continued to rely on the outstanding quality of its catch to do the talking. If you're looking for a seafood feast in Dublin, this is the place to go.

O'Connell Street & Around

The capital's premier street is still playing catch-up to the southside, but it's getting closer. Ignore the unfortunate plethora of fast-food joints that still plague O'Connell St itself, and seek out our selection of quality eateries that more than make the grade.

BUDGET

Enoteca delle Langhe & Caffé Cagliostro (Map p82; ☎ 888 0834; Quartier Bloom; salads & sandwiches €5-8, mains €8-9; ⏰ 12.30pm-midnight Mon-Sat, from 5pm Sun) Dublin's very own Little Italy (emphasis on 'little') is a brand new development just off the Millennium Bridge. A superb wine bar and shop (the Enoteca) sits on one side and the excellent café on the other – both are owned by an Irish builder with a genuine love for all things Italian – and in the middle is an alfresco dining area that is very, very popular at the first hint of good weather. Typical Italian salads, mixed meat and cheese plates and a selection of pasta dishes are about as far as the menu goes, but the coffees are sensational, the wine exquisite and the atmosphere second to none.

Soup Dragon (Map p82; ☎ 872 3277; 168 Capel St; soups €4.50-9.50; ⏰ 8am-5.30pm Mon-Fri, 11am-5pm Sat) Eat in or take away one of 12 tasty varieties of homemade soups, including shepherd's pie or spicy vegetable gumbo. Bowls come in three different sizes, and prices include fresh bread and a piece of fruit. Kick start your day (or afternoon) with a healthy all-day breakfast selection: fresh smoothies (€3.75), generous bowls of yoghurt, fruit and muesli (€4) or poached egg in a bagel (€3.20).

Cobalt Café & Gallery (Map pp80-1; ☎ 873 0313; 16 North Great George's St; mains €4-7; ⏰ 10am-4.30pm Mon-Fri) This gorgeous, elegant café in a bright and airy Georgian drawing room is a must if you're in the hood. Almost opposite the James Joyce Cultural Centre, the menu is simple but you'll be welcomed with hearty soups by a roaring fire in winter, or fresh sandwiches in the garden on warmer days.

Epicurean Food Hall (Map p82; Lower Liffey St; lunch €3-12; 9.30am-5.30pm Mon-Sat) You'll be spoilt for choice in this arcade that has almost every imaginable type of food stall to tempt the appetite. The quality varies, but good choices include Itsabagel, Taco Taco and Istanbul House.

MIDRANGE

Ailang (Map pp80-1; ☎ 874 6766; 102 Parnell St; mains €7-15; noon-2.30pm Mon-Fri, 5.30-11.30pm Mon-Thu, 5.30pm-midnight Fri, 12.30pm-midnight Sat & Sun) With elements of Chinese, Japanese and Thai cuisine, this Korean restaurant on diverse Parnell St has plenty to whet appetites. Tasty dishes such as *padun* (a seafood pancake), cod and tofu hotpot or barbecued meats brought to your table DIY-style, with gas burner, skillet and spicy marinade, make the food a talking piece. Although the bright and shiny décor may not be conducive to romantic first dates, the atmosphere at Ailang is strangely inviting. Steer clear of the dull wine list in favour of Ailang's own Hite beer.

Bar Italia (Map p82; ☎ 874 1000; 28 Lower Ormond Quay, Quartier Bloom; mains €9-15; 10.30am-11pm Mon-Sat, 1-9pm Sun) The slightly fancier, younger brother of the immensely successful café just across the Liffey (see p129) is bigger and just as good; it's as if they were using the same kitchen.

101 Talbot (Map pp80-1; ☎ 874 5011; 100-102 Talbot St; mains €12-19; 5-11pm Tue-Sat) This is a funky little restaurant with brightly painted walls, wooden floorboards and check tablecloths. The eclectic menu, which changes daily, is loosely based on Mediterranean and Middle Eastern cuisine with, as you'd expect, plenty of vegetarian dishes. The homemade pork, sage and apricot sausage with red onion relish starter (€5.50) is a particular favourite.

TOP END

Chapter One (Map pp80-1; ☎ 873 2266; 18-19 North Parnell Sq; mains €23-30; lunch Tue-Fri, dinner Tue-Sat) Savour classic French cuisine such as foie gras, duck *confit* or rabbit cassoulet, to the tinkle of the grand piano, in the lovely vaulted basement of the Dublin Writers Museum. This place is one of the city's top 10 restaurants. Try to arrive before 7pm for the three-course Pre-Theatre Special (€34).

Beyond the Grand Canal

The fancy suburbs of the south city centre have long been home to a handful of terrific restaurants, but the leading light these days is Ranelagh, which has undergone a mini-revolution in recent years. Located only 10 minutes or so away from town by Luas, it is a convenient destination when town is packed to overflowing.

MIDRANGE

Diep Noodle Bar (Map p78; ☎ 497 6550; 19 Ranelagh Rd; mains €9-17; 2.30-11.30pm) Thai and Vietnamese noodle dishes dominate the menu at this supercool joint that has really put Ranelagh on the dining map. Dishes like seafood rice noodles and red snapper vermicelli have them coming in droves and make sure that it's packed at weekends. Come early or late, though, and you'll get a table.

Café Bardeli (Map p84; ☎ 496 1886; 62 Ranelagh Rd; mains €9-13; 12.30-11pm Mon-Sat, to 10pm Sun) If it ain't broke, do it again: CBD hit Ranelagh in 2004 with the same no-fuss menu that made its big sister such a roaring success on South Great George's St (see p129) and just hasn't looked back.

Mint (Map p78; ☎ 497 8655; 47 Ranelagh Rd; mains around €15; noon-3pm & 6-10pm Tue-Sun) Cool to near freezing point, Mint takes the dining high ground and refuses to compromise in the face of populist, local competition: each dish – of the contemporary European cuisine kind – is like a little work of art, and what it lacks in size it more than makes up for in density. It mightn't seem like a lot, but you'll know you've eaten a proper meal when you're done.

Langkawi (Map p78; ☎ 668 2760; 46 Upper Baggot St; set lunch €15, mains €15-35) This upmarket Pacific Rim restaurant has a loyal clientele who return for its good food and relaxed atmosphere. *Nasi goreng* (spicy rice dish with prawn and satay chicken) is a popular choice.

Mash (Map p78; ☎ 497 9463; Castlewood Ave, Rathmines; mains €6-20) This tiny eclectic place, opposite the Swan Centre, run by possibly the friendliest duo in Ireland, Bobby and Jerome, serves fresh, homemade dishes in a cosy atmosphere. The small menu consists of daily specials such as Thai chicken curry, roast red snapper, organic steaks or the popular range of mash potato cakes, all made with TLC and served with a smile.

Get there while the prices are still reasonable and you can get a table. Come back once and they'll remember your name.

French Paradox (Map p78; ☎ 660 4068; 53 Shelbourne Rd; mains €9-16; ☒ closed Sun) This bright and airy wine bar, over an excellent wine shop of the same name, serves fine authentic French dishes such as cassoulet, a variety of foie gras, cheese and charcuterie plates, and large green salads. All are there to complement the main attraction: a dazzling array of fine wines, mostly French unsurprisingly, sold by the bottle, glass or even 6.25cL taste! A little slice of Paris in Dublin 4.

DRINKING

When they talk of Dublin being a great party town, what they're really saying is that it's a great drinking town. Which it most certainly is, and there's a pretty good chance that it's one of the main reasons you came in the first place. The pub remains the alpha and omega of all social life; a meeting point for friends and strangers alike, and where Dubliners are at their friendly and convivial best (and, it must be said, sometimes their drunken and belligerent worst!).

There are pubs for every taste and sensibility, although the traditional haunt populated by flat-capped pensioners bursting with insightful anecdotes is disappearing under a modern wave of designer bars and themed locales that wouldn't seem out of place in any other city in the world. All the while, of course, the Irish pub theme is being exported throughout the world like a McPub; if the trend continues Dublin may be the last place to come to if you're looking for a spit-and-sawdust boozer.

Dublin's infamous party zone is Temple Bar, where giant bars pump out booze and chart music to a thirsty, animated throng of revellers – Ireland's own 'Ibiza in the rain.' It's not so bad for a midweek drink, but come the weekend it's strictly for tourists and visitors with T-shirts advertising themselves as part of a hen or stag group. More discerning party animals favour the strip of supersized bars on Dawson St and – more recently – the bars along Wexford and Camden Sts, southwest of St Stephen's Green. But don't worry: you can't go too far in the city centre without finding a pub with a bit of life in it.

Last orders are at 11.30pm Monday to Thursday, 12.30am Friday and Saturday and 11pm on Sunday, with 30 minutes' drinking up time each night. However, many central pubs have licenses to serve until 1.30am, 2.30am and – for those with a superspecial 'theatre license' – until 3am.

Traditional Pubs

Dublin is full of old-style, traditional establishments. Here are some of the best.

Flowing Tide (Map p136; ☎ 874 0842; 9 Lower Abbey St) Directly opposite the Abbey Theatre, this place attracts a great mix of theatre-goers and northside locals. It's loud, full of chat and a great place to drink.

Patrick Conway's (Map p136; ☎ 873 2687; 70 Parnell St) Although slightly out of the way, this place is a true gem of a pub. It has been operating since 1745, and no doubt new fathers have been stopping in here for a celebratory pint since the day the Rotunda Maternity Hospital opened across the road in 1757.

Palace Bar (Map p136; ☎ 677 9290; 21 Fleet St) With its mirrors and wooden niches, Palace Bar is often said to be the perfect example of an old Dublin pub. It's within Temple Bar and is popular with journalists from the nearby *Irish Times*.

John Mulligan's (Map p136; ☎ 677 5582; 8 Poolbeg St) Just off Fleet St, outside the eastern boundary of Temple Bar, John Mulligan's is another pub that has scarcely changed over the years. It featured as the local in the film *My Left Foot* and is also popular with journalists from the nearby newspaper offices. Mulligan's was established in 1782 and has long been reputed to have the best Guinness in Ireland, as well as a wonderfully varied collection of regulars.

Stag's Head (Map p136; ☎ 679 3701; 1 Dame Ct) At the intersection of Dame Ct and Dame Lane, just off Dame St, the Stag's Head was built in 1770 and remodelled in 1895. It's sufficiently picturesque to have featured in a postage stamp series of Irish pubs.

Long Hall (Map p136; ☎ 475 1590; 51 South Great George's St) Luxuriating in full Victorian splendour, this is one of the city's most beautiful and best-loved pubs. Check out the ornate carvings in the woodwork behind the bar and the elegant chandeliers. The bartenders are experts at their craft, an increasingly rare sight in Dublin these days.

Kehoe's (Map p136; ☎ 677 8312; 9 South Anne St) This is one of the most atmospheric pubs in the city centre and a real favourite with all kinds of Dubliners. It has a beautiful Victorian bar, a wonderful snug and plenty of other little nooks and crannies. Upstairs drinks are served in what was once the publican's living room. And it looks it!

Neary's (Map p136; ☎ 677 8596; 1 Chatham St) A showy Victorian-era pub with a fine front-

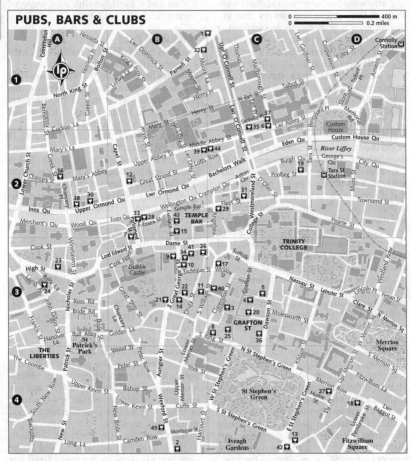

PUBS, BARS & CLUBS

0 — 400 m
0 — 0.2 miles

age, Neary's is popular with actors from the nearby Gaiety Theatre. The upstairs bar is one of the only spots in the city centre where you stand a chance of getting a seat on a Friday or Saturday night.

Grogan's Castle Lounge (Map p136; ☎ 677 9320; 15 South William St) A city-centre institution, Grogan's has long been a favourite haunt of Dublin's writers and painters, as well as others from the bohemian, alternative set. An odd quirk of the pub is that drinks are marginally cheaper in the stone-floor bar than the carpeted lounge, even though they are served by the same bar!

James Toner's (Map p136; ☎ 676 3090; 139 Lower Baggot St) With its stone floor, Toner's is almost a country pub in the heart of the city, and the shelves and drawers are reminders that it once doubled as a grocery store. Not that its suit-wearing business crowd would ever have shopped here…

Hartigan's (Map p136; ☎ 676 2280; 100 Lower Leeson St) This is about as spartan a bar as you'll find in the city and is the daytime home to some serious drinkers, who appreciate the quiet, no-frills surroundings. In the evening it's popular with students from the medical faculty of University College Dublin.

Sackville Lounge (Map p136; Sackville Pl) Just off O'Connell St, this tiny wood-panelled bar dating from the 1880s claims to be one of Dublin's smallest. Full of local traders and actors from the nearby Abbey and Peacock Theatres, its relaxed, down-at-heel atmosphere makes it a great place for a drink and a chinwag.

Live Music Pubs

The following places are excellent venues for catching some traditional Irish and contemporary music.

Sean O'Casey's (Map p136; ☎ 874 8675; 105 Marlborough St) This place has a weekly menu of live rock and some Irish traditional music sessions.

Hughes' Bar (Map p136; ☎ 872 6540; 19 Chancery St) This pub is directly behind the Four Courts and has nightly, if impromptu, sessions which often result in a closed door – that is, they go on long past official closing time. The pub is also a popular lunch-time spot with barristers working nearby.

Cobblestone (Map pp80-1; ☎ 872 1799; North King St) This pub is on the main square in Smithfield, an old northside marketplace. There's

a great atmosphere in the cosy upstairs bar where nightly music sessions, both traditional and up-and-coming folk and singer-songwriter acts, are superb.

Oliver St John Gogarty (Map p136; ☎ 671 1822; 58-59 Fleet St) There's live traditional music nightly at this busy Temple Bar pub, catering to a mostly tourist crowd.

International Bar (Map p136; ☎ 677 9250; 23 Wicklow St) The International has live jazz and blues most nights.

Bruxelles (Map p136; ☎ 677 5362; 7-8 Harry St) This place has weekly live rock music, perhaps the only link the now-trendy pub has to its heavy metal past.

O'Donoghue's (Map p136; ☎ 661 4303; 15 Merrion Row) This, the most famous traditional music bar in Dublin, is where world-famous folk group the Dubliners started off in the 1960s. On summer evenings a young, international crowd spills out into the courtyard beside the pub.

Mother Redcaps (Map p136; ☎ 453 8306; Back Lane, Christchurch) A legendary, spit-on-the-floor, no-frills folk-music venue, which reopened after a few year's respite, above a pub of the same name.

Trendy Bars

These modern bars are Dublin's current hot spots.

Anseo (Map p136; ☎ 475 1321; 28 Camden St) Unpretentious, unaffected and incredibly popular, this cosy alternative bar is a favourite with those who live by the credo that to try too hard is far worse than not trying at all. Wearing cool like a loose garment, the punters thrive on the mix of chat and terrific music.

Dice Bar (Map pp80-1; ☎ 674 6710; 79 Queen St) Coowned by singer Huey from band Fun Lovin' Criminals, the Dice Bar looks like something you'd find on New York's Lower

East Side. Its black-and-red painted interior, dripping candles and stressed seating, combined with rocking DJs most nights, make it a magnet for Dublin's beatnik crowds.

Forum Bar (Map pp80–1; ☎ 878 7084; 144 Parnell St) A welcome addition to the scene, this bar is the first run by and catering (though not exclusively) to Dublin's thriving Black community – and not before time. The place heaves from Thursday to Saturday night, with young scenesters and bar staff getting on down to the DJ's hip-hop beats.

No 4 Dame Lane (Map p136; ☎ 679 0291; 4 Dame Lane) A pretty stylish bar across two floors that is popular with clubby kids and professionals alike; they come for the modern ambience and the DJ-led entertainment – mellow midweek but loud and dancy weekends.

Market Bar (Map p136; ☎ 677 4835; Fade St) This fashionable watering hole is run by the same guys as the Globe around the corner. Little would you know this beautiful airy Victorian space was a sausage factory in a former life.

Globe (Map p136; ☎ 671 1220; 11 South Great George's St) One of Dublin's first proper café-bars, the Globe, with its wooden floors and plain brick walls, is as much a daytime haunt for a good latte as a supercool watering hole by night. Nightly DJs, a relaxed atmosphere and friendly staff keep the place buzzing with a mix of hip young locals and clued-in visitors.

Hogan's (Map p136; ☎ 677 5904; 35 South Great George's St) Hogan's is a gigantic boozer that is spread across two floors. A popular hangout for young professionals, it gets very full at the weekend with folks eager to take advantage of its late licence.

Octagon Bar (Map p136; ☎ 670 9000; Clarence Hotel, 6-8 Wellington Quay) Temple Bar's most chic watering hole is where you'll find Dublin's celebrities and their hangers-on. Drinks are more expensive than elsewhere – a flute of bilini will set you back €13 – but judging by the clientele that have passed the bouncer's strict entry test this is hardly a concern.

Porterhouse (Map p136; ☎ 679 8847; 16-18 Parliament St) Dublin's first microbrewery is our favourite Temple Bar watering hole. Especially popular with foreign residents and visitors, the Porterhouse sells only its own stouts and beers – and they're all excellent.

SamSara (Map p136; ☎ 671 7723; 35-36 Dawson St) This huge Middle Eastern–themed drinking emporium packs young office types and pre-clubbers in at weekends when the bar runs late.

Sin É (Map p136; ☎ 878 7009; 14-15 Upper Ormond Quay) This excellent quayside bar is proof that the most important quality for any pub is ambience. There's no real décor to speak of, but this place buzzes almost nightly with a terrific mix of students, professionals, the hip and the uncool. It helps that the DJs are all uniformly excellent.

Traffic (Map p136; ☎ 873 4800; www.traffic54.net; 54 Middle Abbey St) Clubbers and other creatures of the night have made this ultramodern bar their home away from the dancefloor (which for many is in the basement; see opposite); with nightly DJs, Traffic is a must if you're into good contemporary dance music.

Village (Map p136; ☎ 475 8555; www.thevillage venue.com; 26 Wexford St) Packed to overflowing every weekend, this large modern bar is where the lovely lads and gorgeous gals show off their plumage in a fun-time courting ritual that has the rest of them queuing up at the door to join in. There are excellent DJs nightly; the nightclub bit of the venue (see p140) opens Thursday through Saturday.

ENTERTAINMENT

Dublin's status as an entertainment capital has been hyped out of all reality by tourist authorities and other interested parties. Fact is – for its diminutive size – it's *pretty* good, with a range of options to satisfy nearly all desires, from theatre to dog racing and most distractions in between.

For entertainment information, pick up a copy of the *Event Guide*, a bimonthly freebie available at many locations, including bars, cafés and hostels; the weekly music review *Hot Press*; or the fortnightly freebie *In Dublin*. Friday's *Irish Times* has a pull-out entertainment section called the *Ticket*, which has comprehensive listings of clubs and gigs.

Cinemas

Ireland boasts the highest attendances in Europe of young cinema-goers. Consequently it's best to book in advance by credit card, or be prepared to queue for up to half an hour for tickets at night-time screenings. Dublin's cinemas are more heavily concentrated on the northern side of the Liffey. Admission prices are generally €6 for afternoon shows, rising to around €8 in the evening.

Irish Film Institute (Map p82; ☎ 679 5744; 6 Eustace St) The multiscreen cinema shows classics and art-house films. The complex also has a bar, a café and a bookshop. Weekly (€1.30) or annual (€14, €10 with concession) membership is required for some uncertified films, which can only be screened as part of a 'club.'

Savoy (Map pp80-1; ☎ 874 6000; Upper O'Connell St) A traditional four-screen first-run cinema, Savoy has late-night shows on weekends.

Screen (Map pp80-1; ☎ 671 4988; 2 Townsend St) Between Trinity College and O'Connell Bridge, the Screen shows new independent and smaller commercial films on its three screens.

UGC Multiplex (Map pp80-1; ☎ 872 8400; Parnell Centre, Parnell St) This seven-screen cinema has replaced many smaller cinemas and shows only commercial releases.

Nightclubs

A decade-long rollercoaster ride has left Dublin's club-land a little dizzy. From crap to brilliant and then to…well, less than brilliant, clubs have had a rude awakening in the last few years. These days, clubs have to tackle restrictive opening hours, late-night bars offering a free version of the same and the continuing squeeze of the musical mainstream: Dublin's population may be increasingly multicultural, but they're a largely conservative bunch whose tastes range from charty stuff to a bit of alternative rock, and from R&B to commercially flavoured dance music. Still, the reputation as a party town persists, which is down to the punters themselves, for Dubliners really know how to have a good time.

The seemingly endless list of 'what's on' is constantly changing, so check out the listings in the *Event Guide* and *In Dublin*; the listings here are by no means exhaustive. Most clubs open just after pubs close (11.30pm to midnight) and close at 2.30am or 3am. Admission to most costs between €5 and €8 Sunday to Thursday, rising to as much as €15 or €20 on Friday and Saturday. For gay and lesbian clubs, see the boxed text, p141.

Hub (Map p136; ☎ 670 7655; 11 Eustace St; admission €7-15) Located beneath a pretty cheesy bar,

it's small, sweaty and hip, with a good mix of dance music and live rock.

PoD (Map p78; ☎ 478 0025; www.pod.ie; 35 Harcourt St; admission €5-20; ☉ Mon-Sat) Once the city's only real nightclub, this metal-Gothic cathedral of dance has recently been remodelled and relaunched as…more of the same. House and techno rule the DJ box here.

Red Box (Map p78; ☎ 478 0225; 35 Harcourt St; admission €5-20; ☉ Mon-Sat) The favoured venue for big-name DJs, the Red Box' huge dancefloor has borne the brunt of many a top-class night over the years, and there's no sign of it wearing thin. In recent times it has also hosted plenty of live acts.

Rí Rá (Map p136; ☎ 677 4835; Dame Ct; admission €5-11; ☉ Mon-Sat) This is one of the friendlier clubs in the city centre and is full nearly every night with a diverse crowd who come for the funky freestyle of the basement dancefloor, and the laid-back grooves and movies upstairs in the bar. Refreshingly the bouncers here are friendly, funny and very fair. Monday's '80s club Strictly Handbag is now in its 10th year.

Spirit (Map p136; ☎ 877 9999; 57 Middle Abbey St; admission €5-20; ☉ Thu-Sat) A veritable temple to hardcore clubbing and the New Age mantra of mind-body-spirit, this three-floor club features fairly commercial house on one floor, soul and funk in the middle (complete with sound-proofed cinema) and downstairs – wait for it – a classical cellist plays in the chill-out area, complete with on-site massage therapists, tarot readers and body painters. Sounds great, but there's a edginess to the place that belies its touchy-feely promos.

Spy (Map p136; ☎ 679 0014; 59 South William St) In a beautiful Georgian building in the Powerscourt Townhouse Shopping Centre, Spy attracts the city's fine young things in search of a good time. But there's a distinction: easy-access clubs in the small vaulted basement are strictly for dancing and drinking, while upstairs an exclusive door policy ensures that only those with the right look or the right shade of platinum on their credit card get in.

Temple Bar Music Centre (Map p136; ☎ 670 9202; Curved St) There's something going on every night at the no-frills, factorylike TBMC to suit lovers of indie, garage and funk sounds.

Traffic (Map p136; ☎ 873 4800; www.traffic54.net; 54 Middle Abbey St; admission €7-8 ☉ Thu-Sat) Three nights of clubalicious treats, from the sexy house of Eye Candy on Thursday to the eclectic dancefloor party led by DJ Arveene on Saturday's superpopular Nylon. This is one of the best clubs in the city and – alas – one of the few places that keeps the underground alive.

Village (Map p136; ☎ 475 8555; 26 Wexford St; www.thevillagevenue.com; admission €8-10; ۞ Thu-Sat) When the live music ends, the club kicks off and takes 600-odd groovers through a consistent mix of new and old tunes, dancefloor classics and whatever else will shake that booty; a great venue, an eager crowd and an overall top night out.

Live Music

Bookings can be made either directly at the venues or through **HMV** (Map p84; ☎ 679 5334; 65 Grafton St) or **Ticketmaster** (☎ 0818 719 300, 456 9569; www.ticketmaster.ie), but they charge between 9% and 12.5% service charge *per ticket*, not per booking, on credit card bookings.

CLASSICAL MUSIC & OPERA VENUES

Classical music concerts and opera take place in a number of city-centre venues. There are also occasional performances in churches: check the press for details.

Bank of Ireland Arts Centre (Map p82; ☎ 671 1488; Foster Pl) The arts centre hosts a free, regular midweek lunch-time recital beginning at 1.15pm, as well as an occasional evening programme of concerts. Call for details.

Gaiety Theatre (Map p84; ☎ 677 1717; www.gaietytheatre.com; South King St) This popular Dublin theatre hosts, among other things, a programme of classical concerts and opera.

Helix (Map p75; ☎ 700 7000; www.thehelix.ie; Collins Ave, Glasnevin) Based in Dublin City University, the Helix hosts, among other things, an impressive array of international operatic and classical recitals and performances. To get here, take bus No 11, 13, 13A or 19A from O'Connell St.

Municipal Gallery of Modern Art (Map pp80-1; ☎ 874 1903; www.hughlane.ie; Charlemont House, Parnell Sq) From September to June the art gallery hosts up to 30 concerts of contemporary classical music at noon on Sunday.

National Concert Hall (Map p78; ☎ 417 0000; www.nch.ie; Earlsfort Tce) Ireland's premier orchestral hall hosts a variety of concerts year round, including a series of lunchtime concerts from 1.05pm to 2pm on Tuesday, June to August.

Royal Dublin Showground Concert Hall (Map p78; ☎ 668 0866; www.rds.ie; Ballsbridge) The huge hall of the RDS Showground hosts a rich programme of classical music and opera throughout the year.

ROCK & POP VENUES

Ambassador Theatre (Map pp80-1; ☎ 1890 925 100; O'Connell St) The Ambassador started life as a theatre and then became a cinema. Not much has changed inside, making it a cool retro place to see visiting and local rock acts perform.

Crawdaddy (Map p78; ☎ 478 0225; www.pod.ie; 35A Harcourt St) Named after the London club where the Stones launched their professional careers in 1963, Crawdaddy is an intimate bar-venue that specialises in putting on rootsy performers – from African drum bands to avant-garde jazz artists and flamenco guitarists. It is attached to the nightclub PoD (p139).

Gaiety Theatre (Map p84; ☎ 677 1717; www.gaietytheatre.com; South King St; ۞ to 4am) This old Victorian theatre is an atmospheric place to come and listen to late-night jazz, rock or blues on weekends.

Isaac Butt (Map pp80-1; ☎ 855 5884; Store St) Local garage, rock, metal and indie bands sweat it out most nights in this grungy venue opposite Busáras.

Olympia Theatre (Map p82; ☎ 677 7744; Dame St) This pleasantly tatty place features everything from disco to country on Friday night. Midnight at the Olympia runs from midnight to 2am on Friday.

Point Depot (Map p78; ☎ 836 3633; East Link Bridge, North Wall Quay) This is the premier indoor venue for all rock and pop acts playing in Dublin. Artists such as Diana Ross, Prince and Jamiroquai have all played here. Originally constructed as a rail terminus in 1878, it has a capacity of around 6000.

Red Box (Map p78; ☎ 478 0166; Harcourt St) In the old Harcourt St station, this is one of the best venues for dance gigs, with top European dance bands and DJs strutting their stuff to a largely young crowd. Queues go all the way around the corner from about 10pm on Friday and Saturday nights.

Sugar Club (Map p78; ☎ 678 7188; 8 Lower Leeson St) There's live jazz, cabaret and soul music

GAY & LESBIAN DUBLIN

Dublin's not a bad place to be gay. Most people wouldn't bat an eyelid at public displays of affection between same-sex couples, or cross-dressing in the city centre, but discretion is advised in the suburbs.

Gay & Lesbian Services

Frankies Guesthouse (Map p84; ☎ 478 3087; www.frankiesguesthouse.com; 8 Camden Pl; s €60-75, d €78-95) Although most of the city's hotels wouldn't think twice about checking in same-sex couples, the same cannot be said of many of the city's B&Bs. One central option is this comfortable, exclusively gay and lesbian B&B with pleasant rooms equipped with TV and tea and coffee facilities.

Gay & Lesbian Garda Liaison Officer (☎ 666 9000) If you do encounter any sort of trouble or harassment on the streets, don't hesitate to call.

Gay Community News (www.gcn.ie) A useful nationwide news- and issues-based monthly paper, plus the new glossy *Q-Life* and *Free!* are entertainment guides that can be found in Temple Bar businesses and the Irish Film Institute on Eustace St.

Gay Switchboard Dublin (☎ 872 1055; www.gayswitchboard.ie) A friendly and useful voluntary service that provides information from where to find accommodation to legal issues.

Outhouse (Map pp80-1; ☎ 873 4932; www.outhouse.ie; 105 Capel St) Top gay, lesbian and bisexual resource centre. Great stop-off point to see what's on, check noticeboards and meet people. It publishes the free *Ireland's Pink Pages*, a directory of gay-centric services, which is also accessible on the website. If you do encounter any sort of trouble or harassment on the streets, don't hesitate to call the Outhouse.

Sexual Assault Unit (☎ 666 6000) Call or visit the Pearse St Garda station.

Gay & Lesbian Nightspots

There are plenty of clubs that run gay and lesbian nights. The scene is constantly changing, however, and while the nights listed are pretty regular and steady, we recommend that you call ahead to confirm that they're still on. Check www.gay-ireland.com for other entertainment venues.

George (Map p136; ☎ 478 2983; 89 South Great George's St) One of the longest established and biggest gay bars/clubs in town and a good spot for cruising. Bingo on Sunday night is a mecca for divas who flock to see gorgeous drag queen Miss Shirley Temple Bar grab those rattling balls.

Out on the Liffey (Map p136; ☎ 872 2480; 27 Upper Ormond Quay) A 'harder' rough and ready pub, popular with the biker or butch set of both sexes.

Front Lounge (Map p136; ☎ 670 4112; 33 Parliament St) A lavish lounge attracting a mixed upmarket clientele. Drag queen Panti runs the cabaret and karaoke night, Casting Couch, on Tuesday.

Gubu (Map p136; ☎ 874 0483; 7-8 Capel St) One of the newer, trendier gay- and lesbian-friendly bars on the northside which shows movies and hosts comedy nights midweek.

PoD (Place of Dance; Map p78; ☎ 478 0166; 35 Harcourt St) Friday night's HAM, aka Homo Action Movies, is one of Dublin's most enduring gay and lesbian nights. The soundtrack is thumping house, uplifting and progressive.

Molloy's (Map p136; ☎ 677 3207; 13 High St) Near Christ Church Cathedral, this bar has a lesbian-only night on Saturday called Stonewallz.

Rí Rá (Map p136; ☎ 677 4835; Dame Ct) Strictly Handbag is a long-running Monday night at one of Dublin's friendlier clubs. It's not exclusively gay, but it is popular with the gay community.

Spy (Map p136; ☎ 677 0014; Powerscourt Townhouse Shopping Centre, South William St) This is one the hardest places to get in to unless you're dripping with glamour, but Sunday night's Hilton Edwards club (named after the gay cofounder of the Gate Theatre) requests only that you're gay and reasonably well dressed. It's cool, chic and, at the time of writing, the hottest ticket in town.

Gay & Lesbian Festivals

Some annual events include:

Pride (www.dublinpride.org), a week-long festival of theatre, performance, music, readings and – inevitably – a high-energy, colourful parade through the city centre for the city's queers, dykes, bis and fetishists.

Lesbian & Gay Film Festival (☎ 670 6377; www.irishculture.net/filmfestival), an international film and documentary festival held in the Irish Film Institute in August.

at weekends in this comfortable new theatre-style venue on the corner of St Stephen's Green.

Temple Bar Music Centre (Map p82; ☎ 670 0533; Curved St) The centre hosts all kinds of gigs from Irish traditional to drum-and-bass for a non–image conscious crowd.

Vicar Street (Map pp80-1; ☎ 454 5533; www.vicarstreet.com; 58-59 Thomas St) Smaller performances take place at this intimate venue, near Christ Church Cathedral. It has a capacity of 1000 between its table-serviced group seating downstairs and theatre-style balcony. It has a varied programme of performers, with a strong emphasis on folk and jazz.

Village (Map p84; ☎ 475 8555; www.thevillagevenue.com; 26 Wexford St) An attractive midsize venue that is a popular stop for acts on the way up and down, the Village has gigs virtually every night of the week, featuring a diverse range of rock bands and solo performers. It is also a good showcase for local singer-songwriters.

Whelan's (Map p84; ☎ 478 0766; 25 Wexford St; www.whelanslive.com) Whelan's is such an institution with Irish singer-songwriters and other lo-fi performers that the press often refer to them as the 'Whelan's clique,' including the likes of Glen Hansard & The Frames, Paddy Casey, Mark Geary, Damien Rice and Mundy.

Sport

Croke Park Stadium (Map p78; ☎ 836 3222; www.gaa.ie; Clonliffe Rd) Hurling and Gaelic football games are held from February to November here, north of the Royal Canal in Drumcondra. Catch bus No 19 or 19A to get here. For more on the stadium, see the boxed text, p107.

Harold's Cross Park (Map p78; ☎ 497 1081; 151 Harold's Cross Rd; adult/child €7/2; ⏰ 6.30-10.30pm Mon, Tue & Fri) Greyhound racing takes place near Rathmines in this newly revamped venue. Take bus No 16 or 16A from the city centre.

Lansdowne Rd Stadium (Map p78; ☎ 647 3800; Ballsbridge) Catch the DART to Landsdowne Rd to see the rugby and international football matches that take place here, near Ballsbridge. The rugby season is from September to April and the football season from August to May.

Leopardstown Race Course (Map p75; ☎ 289 3607; Foxrock) The Irish love of horse racing

can be observed about 10km south of the city centre in Foxrock. Special buses depart the city centre on race days; call the race course for details.

Shelbourne Park Greyhound Stadium (Map p78; ☎ 668 3502, on race nights ☎ 202 6601; Bridge Town Rd, Ringsend; adult/child €8/4; ⏰ 6.30-10.30pm Wed, Thu & Sat) A top-class dog track with terrific vantage points from the glassed-in restaurant, where you can eat, bet and watch without leaving your seat. Take bus No 3 from D'Olier St.

Theatre

Dublin's theatre scene is small but busy. Bookings can usually be made by quoting a credit card number over the phone, and the tickets can then be collected just before the performance.

Abbey Theatre (Map pp80-1; ☎ 878 7222; www.abbeytheatre.ie; Lower Abbey St) The famous Abbey Theatre, near the river, is Ireland's national theatre. It puts on new Irish works, as well as revivals of classic Irish works by writers such as WB Yeats, JM Synge, Sean O'Casey, Brendan Behan and Samuel Beckett. Tickets for evening performances cost up to €25, except on Monday when they are cheaper. The smaller and less expensive Peacock Theatre (Map pp80–1; ☎ 878 7222) is part of the same complex.

Andrew's Lane Theatre (Map p82; ☎ 679 5720; 9-17 St Andrew's Lane) This is a well-established fringe theatre.

Ark (Map p82; ☎ 670 7788; 11a Eustace St) A 150-seater venue that stages shows for kids aged between five and 13.

Gaiety Theatre (Map p84; ☎ 677 1717; www.gaietytheatre.com; South King St) Opened in 1871 the theatre is used for modern plays, TV shows, musical comedies and revues.

Gate Theatre (Map pp80-1; ☎ 874 4045; www.gatetheatre.ie; 1 Cavendish Row) Also to the north of the Liffey the Gate Theatre specialises in international classics and older Irish works with a touch of comedy by playwrights such as Oscar Wilde, George Bernard Shaw and Oliver Goldsmith, although newer plays are sometimes staged too. Prices vary according to what's on, but they're usually around €20.

Helix (Map p75; ☎ 700 7000; www.thehelix.ie; Collins Ave, Glasnevin) The Helix, Dublin City University's new theatre venue, has already established its reputation as a serious theatre with its mix of both accessible and more challenging productions. To get here, take bus No 11, 13, 13A or 19A from O'Connell St.

International Bar (Map p84; ☎ 677 9250; 23 Wicklow St) This is one of several pubs that host theatrical performances.

Olympia Theatre (Map p82; ☎ 677 7744; 72 Dame St) This theatre specialises in light plays and, at Christmas time, pantomime.

Players' Theatre (Map p90; ☎ 677 2941, ext 1239; Regent House, Trinity College) The Trinity College Players' Theatre hosts student productions throughout the academic year, as well as the most prestigious plays from the Dublin Theatre Festival in October.

Project Arts Centre (Map p82; ☎ 1850 260 027; www .project.ie; 39 East Essex St) The centre puts on excellent productions of experimental plays by up-and-coming Irish and foreign writers.

Tivoli Theatre (Map p82; ☎ 454 4472; 135-136 Francis St) Experimental and less-commercial performances take place here.

SHOPPING

If it's made in Ireland, you can buy it in Dublin. In fact, if it's made at all you can probably buy it here. The last decade has seen the arrival (invasion?) of virtually every English high-street chain store and a few European ones, with more on the way every day. Home-grown shops have had their mettle sorely tested: those that could compete have adapted to increasingly competitive markets while those that couldn't simply closed their doors. A case in point is Grafton St, Dublin's premier shopping street, where you can count the Irish-owned shops on one hand. No matter, say the shopaholics, for there's never been a better time to go on a spree. The recent opening of Europe's largest shopping mall in a south Dublin suburb seems to say so.

Besides Grafton St (and south Dublin's new temple of trade), the best places to shop are on and around Henry St, off O'Connell St, where you'll find mostly midrange chain stores; in the warren of streets between Grafton St and South Great George's St, home to a plethora of Irish-owned fashion outlets, jewellers and second-hand stores; and, for Irish antiques, on Francis St in the Liberties.

Citizens of non-EU countries can reclaim the VAT (value-added tax) paid on purchases made at stores displaying a cashback sticker; ask for details. For information on bookshops, see p86.

Most department stores and shopping centres are open from 9am to 6pm Monday to Saturday (open to 8pm Thursday) and noon to 6pm Sunday.

Department Stores & Shopping Centres

Arnott's (Map p82; ☎ 805 0400; 12 Henry St) Occupying a huge block with entrances on Henry, Liffey and Abbey Sts, this formerly mediocre department store has been completely overhauled and is now probably Dublin's best. It stocks virtually everything you could possibly want to buy, from garden furniture to high fashion, and everything is relatively affordable.

Brown Thomas (Map p84; ☎ 605 6666; 92 Grafton St) This is Dublin's most expensive department store, suitably stocked to cater for the city's more moneyed shoppers. You'll find every top label represented here.

Clery's & Co (Map pp80-1; ☎ 878 6000; O'Connell St) This graceful shop is a Dublin classic. Recently restored to its elegant best, it caters to the more conservative Dublin shopper.

Dundrum Town Centre (Map p75; ☎ 299 1700; Sandyford Rd, Dundrum; ☺ 9am-9pm Mon-Fri, 8.30am-7pm Sat, 10am-7pm Sun) Modern Ireland has its newest, grandest cathedral: a huge shopping and entertainment complex rumoured to be the largest in Europe. Over 100 retail outlets and counting; the end of 2005 will have seen the arrival of English top dog Harvey Nichols to these desperate shores. Take the Luas to Ballaly or bus No 17, 44C, 48A or 75 from the city centre.

ILAC Centre (Map pp80-1; ☎ 704 1460) The ILAC Centre, off Henry St near O'Connell St, is a little dilapidated but has some interesting outlets with goods at affordable prices.

Jervis St Centre (Map p82; ☎ 878 1323; Jervis St) Just north of the Capel St Bridge, this is an ultramodern mall with dozens of outlets.

Powerscourt Townhouse Shopping Centre (Map p84; ☎ 679 4144; 59 South William St) The wonderful Powerscourt Townhouse Shopping Centre, just to the west of Grafton St, is a big, modern shopping centre in a fine old building. There are some decent restaurants on all its floors and the Irish Design Centre sells the work of up-and-coming Irish fashion designers.

St Stephen's Green Shopping Centre (Map p84; ☎ 478 0888; St Stephen's Green) Inside this flash

---

DUBLIN MARKETS

George's St Arcade (Map p84; btwn South Great George's & Drury Sts) This excellent covered market has some great second-hand clothes shops, and stalls selling Mediterranean food, jewellery and records.

Meeting House Square Market (Map p82; Meeting House Sq) This open-air food market in Temple Bar takes place every Saturday, but get here early for best pickings and to avoid the huge crowds. With a multitude of stalls selling top organic produce from around the country, you can also buy diverse snacks such as sushi, waffles, tapas, oysters and handmade cheeses.

Blackberry Fair (Map p78; Lower Rathmines Rd) You'll have to rummage through a lot of junk to find a gem in this charmingly run-down weekend market that stocks furniture, records and a few clothes stalls. It's cheap though.

Blackrock Market (Map p75; Main St, Blackrock; 11am-5.30pm Sat & Sun) The long-running Blackrock Market, in an old merchant house and yard in this seaside village, has all manner of stalls selling everything from New Age crystals to futons.

---

shopping centre you'll discover a diverse mixture of chain stores and individual shops.

Designer Clothes

Temple Bar and the area around Grafton St are the best places for all kinds of designer gear, both new and second-hand.

Costume (Map p84; 679 5200; 10 Castle Market) This chic upmarket shop sells a range of women's European designer labels that include Temperley and emerging Irish designers Leigh Lee and Helen James.

Smock (Map p82; 613 9000; Smock Alley Ct, West Essex St) This little designer shop sells quirky international womenswear from investment labels Easton Pearson, Veronique Branquinho and AF Vandevorst and a small range of interesting jewellery.

Tulle (Map p84; 679 9115; 29 George's St Arcade) International designers with attitude Matthew Williamson, Stella Forest and Wheels & Dollbaby are stocked in this small outlet for young women.

Second-hand Shops

Eager Beaver (Map p82; 677 3342; 17 Crown Alley) Need a black suit for a wedding? A cricket jumper? A Victorian shirt? Don't want to spend a fortune? Then this is your place – it's a clothes hunter's paradise.

Harlequin (Map p84; 671 0202; 13 Castle Market) This is a wonderful store with a great selection of second-hand jeans, shirts and suits.

Jenny Vander (Map p84; 677 0406; 50 Drury St) A visit to Jenny Vander is like walking into an exotic 1940s boudoir: the selection of antique clothing, hats and jewellery is

pretty wild. You won't find many bargains here though.

Irish Crafts & Souvenirs

Avoca Handweavers (Map p82; 677 4215; 11-13 Suffolk St) Contemporary craft shop Avoca, with another branch in County Wicklow, is a treasure-trove of interesting Irish and foreign products. The colourful shop is choc-a-bloc with woollen knits, ceramics, hand-crafted gadgets and a wonderful toy selection – and not a tweed cap in sight.

Claddagh Records (Map p82; 677 0262; 2 Cecilia St) This shop sells a wide range of Irish traditional and folk music.

DesignYard (Map p82; 677 8453; 12 East Essex St) This modern warehouse space showcases some beautiful contemporary work by Irish and European jewellers, potters and craftspeople.

Dublin Woollen Company (Map p82; 677 5014; 41 Lower Ormond Quay) Near the Ha'penny Bridge, this is one of the major wool outlets in Dublin. It has a large collection of sweaters, cardigans, scarves, rugs, shawls and other woollen goods and runs a tax-free shopping scheme.

Kilkenny Shop (Map p84; 677 7066; 6 Nassau St) This shop has a wonderful selection of finely made Irish crafts, featuring clothing, glassware, pottery, jewellery, crystal and silver from some of Ireland's best designers.

GETTING THERE & AWAY
Air

Dublin airport (Map p75; 814 1111; www.dublin airport.com), 13km north of the centre, is Ireland's major international gateway airport, with direct flights from Europe, North America and Asia. For information on who flies in and out of here, see p695. It has a **left-luggage office** (☎ 814 4633; per item daily €6; ✆ 6am-11pm).

Boat

Dublin has two ferry ports: the **Dun Laoghaire ferry terminal** (☎ 280 1905; Dun Laoghaire), 13km southeast of the city, serves Holyhead in Wales and can be reached by DART to Dun Laoghaire, or bus No 7, 7A or 8 from Burgh Quay or 46A from Trinity College; and the **Dublin Port terminal** (☎ 855 2222; Alexandra Rd), 3km northeast of the city centre, which serves Holyhead, Mostyn and Liverpool. Buses from Busáras are timed to coincide with arrivals and departures: for the 9.45am ferry departure from Dublin, buses leave Busáras at 8.30am. For the 9.45pm departure, buses depart from Busáras at 8.30pm. For the 1am sailing to Liverpool, the bus departs from Busáras at 11.45pm. All buses cost €2.

You can take advantage of bus/train and ferry combinations in the UK. See the boxed text, p699 for more information.

Bus

Busáras (Map pp80-1; ☎ 836 6111; www.buseireann .ie; Store St) is just north of the river behind Custom House; it has a left-luggage facility charging €2.50 per item.

For information on fares, frequencies and durations to various destinations in the Republic and Northern Ireland, see p700.

Car & Motorcycle

HIRE

A number of hire companies have desks at the airport, and other operators are based close to the airport and deliver cars for airport collection. Listed are some of the main hire companies in Dublin:

Avis (www.avis.com) city (Map pp80-1; ☎ 605 7500; 1 East Hanover St); Dublin airport (☎ 844 5204)

Budget (www.budgetcarrental.ie) city (☎ 837 9802; 151 Lower Drumcondra Rd); Dublin airport (☎ 844 5150)

Dan Dooley Car Hire(www.dan-dooley.ie) city (Map p84; ☎ 677 2723; 42-43 Westland Row); Dublin aiport (☎ 844 5156)

Europcar (www.europcar.com) city (Map pp80-1; ☎ 614 2800; Baggot St Bridge); Dublin airport (☎ 844 4199)

Hertz (www.hertz.com) city (Map p78; ☎ 660 2255; 149 Upper Leeson St); Dublin airport (☎ 844 5466)

Sixt Rent-a-Car (www.icr.ie) city (☎ 862 2715; Old Airport Rd, Santry); Dublin airport (☎ 844 4199)

Thrifty (www.thrifty.ie) city (☎ 1800 515 800; 125 Herberton Bridge, South Circular Rd); Dublin airport (☎ 840 0800)

Train

For general train information contact **Iarnród Éireann Travel Centre** (Map p82; ☎ 836 6222; www.irishrail.ie; 35 Lower Abbey St; ✆ 9am-5pm Mon-Fri, 9am-1pm Sat). **Connolly Station** (Map pp80-1; ☎ 836 3333), just north of the Liffey and the city centre, is the station for Belfast, Derry, Sligo and other northern destinations. **Heuston Station** (Map pp80-1; ☎ 836 5421), just south of the Liffey and well west of the centre, is the station for Cork, Galway, Killarney, Limerick, Wexford, Waterford and other destinations west, south and southwest of Dublin. See p704 for more information.

GETTING AROUND
To/From the Airport

There is no train service to/from the airport, but there are bus and taxi options.

BUS

Aircoach (☎ 844 7118; www.aircoach.ie; one way/ return €7/12) Private coach service with two routes from the airport to 18 destinations throughout the city, including the main streets of city centre. Coaches run every 10 to 15 minutes between 6am and midnight, then hourly from midnight until 6am.

Airlink Express Coach (☎ 872 0000, 873 4222; www.dublinbus.ie; adult/child €5/2) Bus 747 runs every 10 to 20 minutes from 5.45am to 11.30pm between the airport, central bus station (Busáras) and Dublin Bus office on Upper O'Connell St; bus 748 runs every 15 to 30 minutes from 6.50am to 22.05pm between the airport and Heuston and Connolly Stations.

Dublin Bus (☎ 872 0000; www.dublinbus.ie; 59 Upper O'Connell St; adult/child €2/0.75) A number of buses serve the airport from various points in Dublin, including buses 16A (Rathfarnham), 746 (Dun Laoghaire) and 230 (Portmarnock); all cross the city centre on their way to the airport.

TAXI

There is a taxi rank directly outside the arrivals concourse. A taxi should cost about €20 from the airport to the city centre, including a supplementary charge of €2.50 (not applied going to the airport). Make sure the meter is switched on.

DUBLIN

Car & Motorcycle

Traffic in Dublin is a nightmare and parking is an expensive headache. There are no free spots to park anywhere in the city centre during business hours (7am to 7pm Monday to Saturday), but there are plenty of parking meters, 'pay and display' spots (€2.50 to €4.80 per hour) and over a dozen sheltered and supervised car parks (around €5 per hour).

Clamping of illegally parked cars is thoroughly enforced, with a €80 charge for removal. Parking is free after 7pm Monday to Saturday and all day Sunday in all metered spots and on single yellow lines.

Car theft and break-ins are a problem, and the police advise visitors to park in a supervised car park. Cars with foreign number plates are prime targets; never leave your valuables behind. When you're booking accommodation check on parking facilities.

Public Transport

BUS

The office of **Dublin Bus** (Map pp80-1; ☎ 872 0000; www.dublinbus.ie; 59 Upper O'Connell St; ☒ 9am-5.30pm Mon-Fri, 9am-2pm Sat) has free single-route timetables of all its services.

Buses run from around 6am (some start at 5.30am) to 11.30pm. Fares are calculated according to stages: one to three stages €0.90, four to seven stages €1.30, eight to 13 stages €1.50, 14 to 23 stages €1.75, more than 23 stages €1.85 (inside Citizone), €2.10 (outside Citizone).

The city centre (Citizone) is within a 13-stage radius. You must tender exact change for tickets when boarding buses; anything more and you will be given a receipt for reimbursement, only possible at the Dublin Bus main office.

Some fare-saver passes:

Adult (Bus & Rail) Short Hop (€8.20) Valid for unlimited one-day travel on Dublin Bus, DART and suburban rail travel, but not Nitelink or Airlink.

Bus/Luas Pass (adult/child €6/3) One day unlimited travel on both bus and Luas.

Family Bus & Rail Short Hop (€12.50) Valid for travel for one day for a family of two adults and two children aged under 16 on all bus and rail services except for Nitelink, Airlink, ferry services and tours.

Rambler Pass (1/2/5/7 days €5/10/15.50/19) Valid for unlimited travel on all Dublin Bus and Airlink services, but not Nitelink.

LUAS

The brand-new **Luas** (www.luas.ie; 5.30am-12.30am Mon-Fri, from 6.30am Sat, 7am-11.30pm Sun) light-rail system has two lines: the green line (trains every five to 15 minutes), which connects St Stephen's Green with Sandyford in south Dublin via Ranelagh and Dundrum; and the red line (trains every 20 minutes), which runs from Lower Abbey St to Tallaght via the north quays and Heuston Station. There are ticket machines at every stop or you can buy tickets from newsagencies throughout the city centre; a typical short-hop fare is €1.30.

NITELINK

These late-night buses run from the College St, Westmoreland St and D'Olier St triangle, covering most of Dublin's suburbs. Buses leave at 12.30am and 2am Monday to Wednesday, and every 20 minutes between 12.30am and 3.30am Thursday to Saturday. Tickets start at €4.

TRAIN

The **Dublin Area Rapid Transport** (DART; ☎ 836 6222; www.irishrail.ie) provides quick train access to the coast as far north as Howth (about 30 minutes) and as far south as Greystones in County Wicklow. Pearse Station is convenient for central Dublin south of the Liffey, and Connolly Station for north of the Liffey. There are services every 10 to 20 minutes, sometimes even more frequently, from around 6.30am to midnight Monday to Saturday. Services are less frequent on Sunday. Dublin to Dun Laoghaire takes about 15 to 20 minutes. A one-way DART ticket from Dublin to Dun Laoghaire or Howth costs €1.90; to Bray it's €2.20.

There are also suburban rail services north as far as Dundalk, inland to Mullingar and south past Bray to Arklow.

Some DART passes:

Adult Weekly Inner Rail Pass (€21.60) Valid on all DART and suburban train services between Bray to the south and Rush and Lusk to the north.

All Day Ticket (adult/child €6.80/5) One-day unlimited travel on DART and suburban rail services.

Taxi

All taxi fares begin with a flagfall fare of €3.40 (€3.70 between 10pm and 8am), followed by €0.15 per unit (one-sixth of a kilometre or 30 seconds) thereafter from 8am to 10pm, or €0.20 per unit from 10pm to 8am and bank holidays. In addition there are a number of extra charges – €0.50 for each extra passenger, €0.50 for each piece of luggage and €1.50 for telephone bookings.

Taxis can be hailed on the street and found at taxi ranks around the city, including O'Connell St, College Green in front of Trinity College and St Stephen's Green at the end of Grafton St. There are numerous taxi companies that will dispatch taxis by radio. Some options:

City Cabs (☎ 872 2688)
National Radio Cabs (☎ 677 2222)

Phone the **Garda Carriage Office** (☎ 475 5888) if you have any complaints about taxis or queries regarding lost property.

AROUND DUBLIN

At the first sight of the sun – or any kind of tolerable weather – Dubliners like to get out of the city, and for many their destination is one of the small seaside villages that surround the capital. To the north are the lovely villages of Howth and Malahide, slowly and reluctantly being sucked into the Dublin conglomeration; while to the south is Dalkey, which has long since given up the fight but has managed to retain that village vibe.

DALKEY

About 1km south of Sandycove is Dalkey (Deilginis), which has the remains of a number of old castles. On Castle St, the main street, two 16th-century castles face each other: **Archibold's Castle** and **Goat Castle**. Next to the latter is the ancient **St Begnet's Church**, dating from the 9th century. **Bulloch Castle**, overlooking Bullock Harbour, north of town, was built by the monks of St Mary's Abbey in Dublin in the 12th century.

Goat Castle and St Begnet's Church have recently been converted into the **Dalkey Castle & Heritage Centre** (☎ 285 8366; Castle St; adult/child/student €4/2.50/3.50; ⏰ 9.30am-5pm Mon-Fri May-Oct, 11am-5pm Sat & Sun). Models, displays and exhibitions form a pretty interesting history of Dalkey and give an insight into the area during medieval times.

Dalkey has several holy wells, including **St Begnet's Holy Well** next to the ruins of another church dedicated to St Begnet on the 9-hectare **Dalkey Island**, a few hundred metres offshore from Coliemore Harbour. Reputed to cure rheumatism, the well is a popular destination for tourists and the faithful alike. To get here, you can hire a boat with a small outboard engine in Coliemore Harbour. To get one, simply show up (you can't book them in advance); they cost around €25 per hour.

To the south there are good views from the small park at Sorrento Point and from Killiney Hill. Dalkey Quarry is a popular site for rock climbers, and originally provided most of the granite for the gigantic piers at Dun Laoghaire Harbour. A number of rocky swimming pools are found along the Dalkey coast.

About 1km north of Dalkey is **Sandycove**, with a pretty little beach and the **Martello tower** – built by British forces to keep an eye out for a Napoleonic invasion – now housing the **James Joyce Museum** (☎ 280 9265; Sandycove; adult/child/student €6.50/4/5.50; ⏰ 10am-1pm & 2-5pm Mon-Sat, 2-6pm Sun Apr-Oct, by arrangement only Nov-Mar). This is where the action begins in James Joyce's epic novel *Ulysses*. The museum was opened in 1962 by Sylvia Beach, the Paris-based publisher who first dared to put *Ulysses* into print, and has photographs, letters, documents, various editions of Joyce's work and two death masks of Joyce on display.

Below the Martello tower is the **Forty Foot Pool**, an open-air sea-water bathing pool that took its name from the army regiment, the Fortieth Foot, that was stationed at the tower until the regiment was disbanded in 1904. At the close of the 1st chapter of *Ulysses*, Buck Mulligan heads off to the Forty Foot Pool for a morning swim. A morning wake-up here is still a local tradition, winter or summer. In fact, a winter dip isn't much braver than a summer one since the water temperature varies by only about 5°C. Basically, it's always bloody cold.

Pressure from female bathers eventually opened this public stretch of water, originally nudist and for men only, to both sexes despite strong opposition from the 'forty foot gentlemen.' They eventually compromised with the ruling that a 'Togs Must Be Worn' sign would now apply after 9am. Prior to that time nudity prevails and swimmers are still predominantly male.

About 2.5km further south from Dalkey is the affluent seaside suburb of **Killiney** with its wonderful curving sandy beach. It's home to some of Ireland's wealthiest businesspeople and a handful of celebrities – Bono, Enya and film-maker Neil Jordan included. Though rarely on the market, a five-bedroom house on the ultradesirable Sorrento Tce overlooking Killiney Bay sells for about €5 million.

Eating

Caviston's Seafood Restaurant (☎ 280 9245; Glasthule Rd, Sandycove; mains €14-23) OK, so it's not strictly Dalkey but self-respecting crustacean lovers should make the 1km trip to Caviston's for a meal to remember. Local fish and seafood are cooked simply with imaginative ingredients that enhance rather than overpower their flavour.

Nosh (☎ 284 0666; www.nosh.ie; 111 Coliemore Rd; mains €9.50-13; ☾ closed Mon) A newish restaurant with an exceptional menu at lunch and dinner featuring a wide range of international dishes.

Queen's (☎ 285 4569; 12 Castle St; lunch €8-10) A Dalkey institution offering a great pub lunch of meat and fish dishes.

Jaipur (☎ 285 0552; 23 Castle St; mains €17-20) The Dalkey branch of this excellent city-centre Indian restaurant does more of the same here.

Getting There & Away

Dalkey is on the DART suburban train line, or, for a slower journey, you can catch bus No 8 from Burgh Quay in Dublin. Both cost €1.70.

HOWTH

The bulbous Howth Peninsula forms the northern end of Dublin Bay. Howth (Binn Éadair) town is only 15km from central Dublin and is easily reached by DART or by simply following the Clontarf Rd out around the northern bay shoreline. En route you pass Clontarf, site of the pivotal clash between Celtic and Viking forces at the Battle of Clontarf in 1014. Further along is North Bull Island, a wildlife sanctuary where many migratory birds pause in winter.

Howth is a popular excursion from Dublin and has developed as a residential suburb. It is a pretty little town built on steep streets running down to the waterfront.

Although the harbour's role as a shipping port has long gone, Howth is now a major fishing centre and yachting harbour.

History

Howth's name (which rhymes with 'both') has Viking origins and comes from the Danish word 'hoved' (head). Howth Harbour was built from 1807 and was at that time the main Dublin harbour for the packet boats from England. Howth Rd was built to ensure rapid transfer of incoming mail and dispatches from the harbour to the city. The replacement of sailing packets with steam packets in 1818 reduced the transit time from Holyhead to seven hours, but Howth's period of importance was short because by 1813 the harbour was already showing signs of silting up. It was superseded by Dun Laoghaire in 1833. The most famous arrival to Howth was King George IV, who visited Ireland in 1821 and is chiefly remembered because he staggered off the boat in a highly inebriated state. He did manage to leave his footprint at the point where he stepped ashore on the West Pier.

In 1914 Robert Erskine Childers' yacht, *Asgard*, brought a cargo of 900 rifles into the port to arm the nationalists. During the Civil War, Childers was court-martialled by his former comrades and executed by firing squad for illegal possession of a revolver. The *Asgard* is now on display at Kilmainham Jail in Dublin.

Sights

AROUND THE PENINSULA

Most of the town backs onto the extensive grounds of **Howth Castle**, built in 1564 but much changed over the years, most recently in 1910 when Sir Edwin Lutyens gave it a modernist make-over. Today the castle is divided into four separate – very posh and private – residences. The original estate was acquired in 1177 by the Norman noble Sir Almeric Tristram, who changed his surname to St Lawrence after winning a battle at the behest (or so he believed) of his favourite saint. The family has owned the land ever since, though the unbroken chain of male succession came to an end in 1909. Also on the grounds are the ruins of the 16th-century **Corr Castle** and an ancient dolmen (a Neolithic grave memorial built of vertical stones and topped by a table stone) known as **Aideen's Grave**. Legend has it that Aideen died of a broken heart after her husband was killed at the Battle of Gavra near Tara in AD 184, but the legend is rubbish because the dolmen is at least 300 years older than that.

The **castle gardens** (admission free; ☺ always open) are worth visiting, however, as they're noted for their rhododendrons, which bloom in May and June, for their azaleas and for a long, 10m-high beech hedge planted in 1710.

Also within the grounds are the ruins of **St Mary's Abbey** (Abbey St, Howth Castle; admission free), originally founded in 1042 by the Viking King Sitric, who also founded the original church on the site of Christ Church Cathedral. The abbey was amalgamated with the monastery on Ireland's Eye in 1235. Some parts of the ruins date from that time, but most are from the 15th and 16th centuries. The tomb of Christopher St Lawrence (Lord Howth), in the southeastern corner, dates from around 1470. See the caretaker or read instructions on the gate for opening times.

A more recent addition is the rather ramshackle **National Transport Museum** (☎ 832 0427; Howth Castle; adult/student & child €3/1.50; ☺ 10am-5pm Mon-Fri, 2-5pm Sat & Sun Easter-Aug, 2-5pm Sat & Sun rest of year), which has a range of exhibits including double-decker buses, a bakery van, fire engines and trams – most notably a Hill of Howth electric that operated from 1901 to 1959. To reach the museum go through the castle gates and turn right just before the castle.

The allure of history and public transportation aside, most visitors set foot in the demesne armed with golf clubs, as here you'll find **Deer Park Golf Course** (☎ 832 2624; Howth Castle; 18-holes Mon-Fri €16.50, Sat & Sun €24, club rental €7; ☺ 8am-dusk Mon-Fri, 6.30am-dusk Sat & Sun), a public facility attached to a hotel. An 18-hole course, two nine-hole courses and a Par-3 course, all with splendid views of Dublin Bay and the surrounding countryside – once described by HG Wells as the best view west of Naples – are the big draw.

Howth is essentially a very large hill surrounded by cliffs, and the **Summit** (171m) has excellent views across Dublin Bay right down to Wicklow. From the Summit you can walk to the top of the Ben of Howth, which has a cairn said to mark a 2000-year-old Celtic

royal grave. The **1814 Baily Lighthouse** at the southeastern corner is on the site of an old stone fort and can be reached by a dramatic cliff-top walk. There was an earlier hill-top beacon here in 1670.

IRELAND'S EYE

A short distance offshore from Howth is **Ireland's Eye**, a rocky sea-bird sanctuary with the ruins of a 6th-century monastery. There's a Martello tower at the northwestern end of the island, where boats from Howth land, while the eastern end plummets into the sea in a spectacularly sheer rock face. As well as the sea birds overhead, you can see young birds on the ground during the nesting season. Seals can also be spotted around the island.

Doyle & Sons (☎ 831 4200; return €10) takes boats out to the island from the East Pier of Howth Harbour during the summer, usually on weekend afternoons. Don't wear shorts if you're planning to visit the monastery ruins because they're surrounded by a thicket of stinging nettles. And bring your rubbish back with you – far too many island visitors don't.

Further north from Ireland's Eye is **Lambay Island**, an important sea-bird sanctuary that cannot be visited.

Sleeping & Eating

All of the B&Bs listed here are on Howth Hill, above the town. You can walk, but they are all served by bus No 31A from the port. The fare is €0.70.

Inisradharc (☎ 832 2306; Balkill Rd; s/d from €54/76) Inisradharc means 'island view' and that's just what you get from the three lovely en suite rooms in this modernist 1950s B&B.

Highfield (☎ 832 3936; highfieldhowth@eircom.net; Thormanby Rd; s/d €40/64) This is a fine Victorian house set back from the road. Its three rooms are beautifully decorated with a mix of antiques and modern comforts.

King Sitric (☎ 832 5235; www.kingsitric.ie; East Pier; mains €35-45, 5-course dinner €52; ☺ lunch & dinner Mon-Fri, dinner only Sat) Howth's most famous restaurant, always praised for the superb seafood and prize-winning wine list, has added eight marvellous rooms (€138 to €200) to its premises right on the port. Each is named after a lighthouse and is extremely well decorated with wonderful views of the port.

Aqua (☎ 832 0690; West Pier; mains €24-32) A modern place with a minimalist interior, Aqua serves variations on traditional seafood dishes. Meat dishes are also good.

Abbey Tavern (☎ 839 0307; Abbey St; mains €22-26, 3-course dinner €35) Abbey serves better-than-average pub grub, with the emphasis on seafood and meat in this atmospheric 16th-century tavern. There's a bar menu all day.

If you want to buy food and prepare it yourself, Howth has fine seafood that you can buy fresh from the string of seafood shops on West Pier.

Getting There & Away

The easiest and quickest way to get to Howth from Dublin is on the DART, which whisks you there in just over 20 minutes for a fare of €1.70. For the same fare, bus No 31 and 31A from Lower Abbey St in the city centre run as far as the Summit, 5km to the southeast of Howth.

MALAHIDE

Once a small village with its own harbour, a long way from the urban jungle of Dublin, the only thing protecting Malahide (Mullach Ide) from the northwards expansion of Dublin's suburbs is Malahide Demesne, 101 well-tended hectares of parkland dominated by a castle once owned by the powerful Talbot family. The handsome village remains relatively intact, but the once quiet marina has been massively developed and is now a bustling centre with a pleasant promenade and plenty of restaurants and shops.

Sights

MALAHIDE CASTLE

Despite the vicissitudes of Irish history, the Talbot family managed to keep **Malahide Castle** (☎ 846 2184; www.malahidecastle.com; Malahide; adult/child/student/family €6.50/4/5.50/18, incl Fry Model Railway €11/6.50/9/30; ☉ 10am-5pm Mon-Sat, 11am-6pm Sun Apr-Oct, 11am-5pm Sat & Sun Nov-Mar) under

its control from 1185 to 1976, apart from when Cromwell was around (1649–60). It's now owned by Dublin County Council. The castle is the usual hotchpotch of additions and renovations; the oldest part is a three-storey, 12th-century tower house. The façade is flanked by circular towers that were tacked on in 1765.

The castle is packed with furniture and paintings. Highlights are a 16th-century oak room with decorative carvings, and the medieval Great Hall with family portraits, a minstrel's gallery and a painting of the Battle of the Boyne. Puck, the Talbot family ghost, is said to have last appeared in 1975.

The **parkland** (admission free; ☉ 10am-9pm Apr-Oct, 10am-5pm Nov-Mar) around the castle is a good place for a picnic.

FRY MODEL RAILWAY

Ireland's biggest **model railway** (☎ 846 3779; Malahide Castle; adult/child/student/family €6.50/4/5.50/18; ☉ 10am-1pm & 2-5pm Mon-Sat, 2-6pm Sun Apr-Sep, 2-5pm Sat, Sun & holidays only rest of year) at 240 sq metres, this model authentically displays much of Ireland's rail and public transport system, including the DART line and Irish Sea ferry services, in O-gauge (32mm track width). A separate room features model trains and other memorabilia. Unfortunately the operators suffer from the over-seriousness of some grown men with complicated toys; rather than let you simply look and admire, they herd you into the control room in groups for demonstrations.

Getting There & Away

Malahide is 13km north of Dublin. Bus No 42 (€1.70) from Talbot St takes around 45 minutes. The DART now stops in Malahide (€2.50), but be sure to get on the right train (it's marked at the front of the train) as the line splits at Howth Junction.

County Wicklow

COUNTY WICKLOW

Wild and mountainous Wicklow (Cill Mhantáin) may only be a short drive south of Dublin's city centre, but it's a world away from the capital's urban jungle. It's nicknamed the 'Garden of Ireland', but that barely does justice to a county with some of richest and most varied greenery in Ireland.

Wicklow's most imposing natural feature is its mountains, a gorse-and-bracken spine that cuts through the county from north to south. Here, geology and history have combined to conjure up one of the country's most beautiful landscapes, home to rugged mountaintops, deep wooded valleys, cascading waterfalls, still lakes, magnificent country homes and some of the best-preserved early Christian remains in Ireland.

Wicklow is a walker's paradise, not least along the 132km-long Wicklow Way, Ireland's most popular trail and the best way to explore the county. From Marlay Park in south Dublin, the Way runs along disused military supply lines, old bog roads and nature trails over the eastern flanks of the mountains down to Clonegal, County Carlow.

Away from the mountains, Wicklow offers plenty for those inclined toward gentler pursuits. The county is renowned for its beautiful gardens, which are best explored during the Wicklow Gardens Festival from May to August, when many gardens that are not usually open to the public welcome visitors. Most of Wicklow's main towns lie on the coast, where you'll also find some fine beaches.

HIGHLIGHTS

- **Monastic Magic**
  Evocative ruins and marvellous slopes and forests of gorgeous Glendalough (p157), one of the most important monastic sites in Ireland

- **Contemplate the Navel**
  Craft a spiritual journey in the footsteps of St Kevin at Glendalough Cillíns (p161)

- **The Hills Are Alive**
  Ireland's most popular hiking trail, the Wicklow Way (p680)

- **The Art Is Hot**
  Art and atmosphere of magnificent Russborough House (p162)

- **The Glory of the Garden**
  Gorgeous Italianate gardens and the impressive waterfall at Powerscourt Estate (p154)

★ Russborough House
★ Powerscourt Estate
★ Glendalough
★ The Wicklow Way

- POPULATION: 114,676
- AREA: 2025 SQ KM

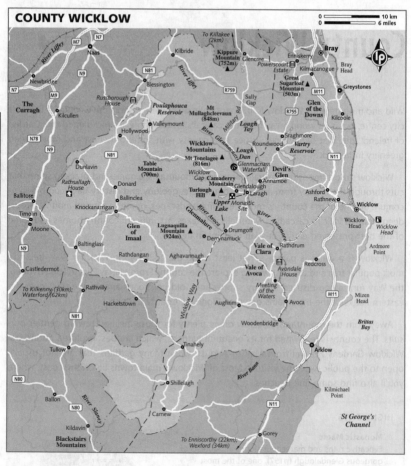

National Parks

Wicklow Mountains National Park covers more than 20,000 hectares of mountainous blanket bogs and woodland. Eventually, virtually all of the higher ground stretching the length of the mountains will fall under the protection of the national park, which will cover over 30,000 hectares.

Within the boundaries of the protected area are two nature reserves, owned and managed by Dúchas, and legally protected by the Wildlife Act. The larger reserve, west of the Glendalough Visitor Centre, conserves the extensive heath and bog of the Glendalough Valley plus the Upper Lake and valley slopes on either side. The second, Glendalough Wood Nature Reserve,

conserves oak woods stretching from the Upper Lake as far as the Rathdrum road to the east.

Most of Ireland's native mammal species can be found within the confines of the park. Large herds of deer roam on the open hill areas, though these were introduced in the 20th century after the native red deer population became extinct during the first half of the 18th century. The uplands are the preserve of foxes, badgers and hares. Red squirrels are usually found in the pine woodlands – look out for them around the Upper Lake.

The bird population of the park is plentiful. Birds of prey abound, the most common being peregrine falcons, marlins, kestrels, hawks and sparrowhawks. Hen harriers are a rarer sight, though they too live in the park. Moorland birds found in the area include meadow pipits and skylarks. Less common birds such as whinchats, ring ouzels and dippers can be spotted, as can red grouse, whose numbers are quickly disappearing in other parts of Ireland. For information, call in or contact the **National Park Information Point** (☎ 0404-45425; Upper Lake, Glendalough; ☺ 10am-6pm May-Sep, 10am-dusk Sat & Sun Oct-Apr), off the Green Rd that runs by the Upper Lake, about 2km from the Glendalough Visitor Centre. There's usually someone on hand to help, but if you find it closed the staff may be out running guided walks. *Exploring the Glendalough Valley* (Dúchas, €1.60) is a good booklet on the trails in the area.

Getting There & Away

Wicklow is a cinch to get to from Dublin. The main routes through the county are the N11 (M11), which runs north–south from Dublin all the way through to Wexford, taking in all of the coastal towns; and the N81, which runs down the western spine of the county through Blessington and into County Carlow. The Dublin Area Rapid Transport (DART) line runs southward from Dublin as far as Bray, and there are regular train and bus connections from the capital to Wicklow town and Arklow.

For Glendalough, **St Kevin's Bus** (☎ 01-281 8119; www.glendaloughbus.com) runs twice daily from Dublin and Bray, also stopping in Roundwood. For the western parts of the county, Dublin Bus No 65 runs regularly as far as Blessington. For more details, see under each relevant section.

WICKLOW MOUNTAINS

No sooner do you leave Dublin and cross into Wicklow than the landscape changes – dramatically. From Killakee, still in Dublin, the Military Rd begins a 30km southward journey across vast sweeps of gorse-, bracken- and heather-clad moors, bogs, and mountains dotted with small corrie lakes.

The numbers and statistics aren't all that impressive. The highest peak in the range, Lugnaquilla (924m) is really more of a very large hill, but that hardly matters here.

TOP FIVE EATS

- Roundwood Inn (p156)
- Rathsallagh House (p163)
- Tinakilly Country House (p168)
- Grangecon Café (p162)
- Johnny Fox (p155)

This vast granite intrusion, a welling-up of hot igneous rock that solidified some 400 million years ago, was shaped during the Ice Ages into the schist-capped mountains visible today. The peaks are marvellously desolate and as raw as only nature can be. Between the mountains are a number of deep glacial valleys, most notably Glenmacnass, Glenmalure and Glendalough, while corrie lakes such as Lough Bray Upper and Lower – gouged out by ice at the head of the glaciers – complete the wild topography.

Beginning on Dublin's southern fringes, the narrow Military Rd winds its way through the remotest parts of the mountains, offering some extraordinary views of the surrounding countryside. The best place to join it is at Glencree (from Enniskerry). It then runs south through the Sally Gap, Glenmacnass, Laragh, Glendalough and on to Glenmalure and Aghavannagh.

On the trip south you can divert east at the Sally Gap to look at Loughs Tay and Dan. Further south you pass the great waterfall at Glenmacnass before dropping down into Laragh, with the magnificent monastic ruins of Glendalough nearby. Continue south through the valley of Glenmalure and, if you're fit enough, climb Lugnaquilla.

ENNISKERRY & POWERSCOURT ESTATE

☎ 01 / pop 2804

On a summer's day there are few lovelier spots than the village of Enniskerry, replete with art galleries and the kind of all-organic gourmet cafés that would have you arrested if you admitted to eating battery eggs. It's all a far cry from the village's origins, when Richard Wingfield, earl of nearby Powerscourt, commissioned a row of terraced cottages for his labourers in 1760. These days, you'd want to have laboured pretty successfully to get your hands on one of them.

Powerscourt Estate & Waterfall

The village is lovely, but the main reason for its popularity is the magnificent 64-sq-km **Powerscourt Estate** (☎ 204 6000; www.powers court.ie; house & gardens adult/child/student €9/3.50/5.50, house only €2.50/1.60/2.20; ☉ 9.30am-5.30pm Feb-Oct, 9.30am-4.30pm Nov-Jan) that gives contemporary observers a true insight into the style of the 18th-century super-rich. The main entrance is 500m south of the village square.

The estate has existed more or less since 1300 when the LePoer (later anglicised to Power) family built themselves a castle here. The property changed Anglo-Norman hands a few times before coming into the possession of Richard Wingfield, newly appointed Marshall of Ireland, in 1603 – his descendants were to live here for the next 350 years. In 1731 the Georgian wunderkind Richard Cassels (or Castle) was given the job of building a Palladian-style mansion around the core of the old castle. He finished the job in 1743, but an extra storey was added in 1787 and other alterations were made in the 19th century. The Wingfields left during the 1950s, after which the house had a massive restoration. Then, on the eve of its opening to the public in 1974, a massive fire gutted the whole building. The estate was eventually bought by the Slazenger sporting goods family who have overseen a second restoration, as well as the addition of two golf courses, a café, a huge garden centre and a bunch of cutesy little retail outlets as well as a small exhibition on the house's history. Basically, it's all intended to draw in the punters and wring as many euros out of their pockets in order to finish the huge restoration job and make the estate a kind of profitable wonderland.

If you can deal with the crowds (summer weekends are the worst) or, better still, avoid the worst of them and visit mid-week, you're in for a real treat, for easily the biggest drawcards of the whole pile are the simply magnificent 20-hectare formal gardens and the breathtaking views that accompany them.

Originally laid out in the 1740s, they were redesigned in the 19th century by Daniel Robinson, who had as much a fondness for the booze as he did for horticultural pursuits. Perhaps this influenced his largely informal style, which resulted in a magnificent blend of landscaped gardens, sweeping terraces, statuary, ornamental lakes, secret hollows, rambling walks and walled enclosures replete with over 200 types of trees and shrubs, all beneath the stunning natural backdrop of the Great Sugarloaf Mountain to the southeast. Tickets come with a map laying out 40-minute and hour-long tours of the gardens. Don't miss the exquisite Japanese Gardens or the Pepperpot Tower, modelled on a three-inch actual pepperpot owned by Lady Wingfield. Our own favourite, however, is the animal cemetery, final resting place of the Wingfield pets and even some of their favourite milking cows. Some of the epitaphs are astonishingly personal.

A 7km walk to a separate part of the estate takes you to the 130m **Powerscourt Waterfall** (☎ 204 6000; adult/child/student €4/3/3.50; ☉ 9.30am-7pm, to dusk Oct-Jan). It's the highest waterfall in Britain and Ireland, and is most impressive after heavy rain. You can also get to the falls by road, following the signs from the estate. A nature trail has been laid out around the base of the waterfall, taking you past giant redwoods, ancient oaks, beech, birch and rowan trees. There are plenty of birds in the vicinity, including the chaffinch, cuckoo, chiffchaff, raven and willow warbler.

Sleeping

Summerhill House Hotel (☎ 286 7928; www.summer hillhousehotel.com; s/d from €75/100; P) A truly superb country mansion about 700m south of town just off the N11 is the best place around to lay your head, on soft cotton pillows surrounded by delicate antiques and pastoral views in oils. Everything about the place – including the top-notch breakfast (included in the price) – is memorable.

Coolakay House (☎ 286 2423; www.coolakay house.com; Waterfall Rd, Coolakay; s/d €40/75; mains around €9; P) A modern working farm about 3km south of Enniskerry (it is signposted along the road), this is a great option for walkers along the Wicklow Way. The four bedrooms are all very comfortable and have terrific views, but the real draw is the restaurant, which does a roaring trade in snacks and full meals.

Corner House (☎ 286 0149; Main St; s/d €35/70; P) This 200-year-old place in Enniskerry has three large doubles, and although none has an en suite (there are two shared bathrooms), each room has its own shower.

The nearest youth hostel is in Glencree, 10km west of here.

Eating

Powerscourt Terrace Café (☎ 204 6070; Powerscourt House; mains €8-13; ◷ 10am-5pm) The folks at Avoca Handweavers (see p165) have applied all their know-how and turned what could have easily been just another run-of-the-mill tourist attraction café into something of a gourmet experience. A slice of quiche on the terrace, overlooking the gardens in the shadow of the Great Sugarloaf? Yes please.

Emilia's Ristorante (☎ 276 1834; the Square; mains €13-21; ◷ 5-10.45pm Mon-Sat, noon-9.30pm Sun) A lovely 1st-floor restaurant to satisfy even the most ardent craving for thin-crust pizzas, Emilia's does everything else just right too, from the organic soups to the perfect steaks down to the gorgeous meringue desserts.

Poppies Country Cooking (☎ 282 8869; the Square; mains around €8; ◷ 8.30am-6pm) If the service wasn't so slow and the organisation so frustratingly haphazard, this pokey little café on the main square would be one of the best spots in Wicklow. The food – when you finally get a chance to eat it – is sensational: wholesome salads, filling sandwiches on doorstep-cut bread and award-winning ice-cream will leave you plenty satisfied.

Johnnie Fox (☎ 295 5647; Glencullen; Hungry Fisherman's seafood platter €28; ◷ noon-10pm) Busloads of tourists fill the place nightly throughout the summer, mostly for the knees-up, faux-Irish floorshow of music and dancing, but there's nothing contrived about the seafood, which is so damn good we'd happily sit through yet another chorus of *Danny Boy* and even consider joining in the jig. The pub is 3km northwest of Enniskerry in Glencullen.

Tours

All tours that take in Powerscourt start in Dublin.

Bus Éireann (☎ 836 6111; www.buseireann.ie; Busáras; adult/child/student €27/18/25.20; ◷ 10.30am mid-Mar–Oct) A whole day tour that takes in Powerscourt and Glendalough (all admissions included).

Dublin Bus Tours (☎ 872 0000; www.dublinbus.ie; 59 Upper O'Connell St; adult/child €22/10; ◷ 11am & 2pm) A visit to Powerscourt is included in this four-hour South Coast & Gardens tour, which takes in the stretch of coastline between Dun Laoghaire and Killiney before turning inland into Wicklow and on to Enniskerry. Admission is included.

Grayline Tours (☎ 872 9010; www.irishcitytours .com; Gresham Hotel, O'Connell St; adult/child €20/10; ◷ 10.15am) A similar coast and gardens tour takes in Dun Laoghaire and Dalkey before dropping you off at Powerscourt for a visit and a coffee (admission, but not coffee, included).

Getting There & Away

Enniskerry is 18km south of Dublin, just 3km west of the M11 along the R117. **Dublin Bus** (☎ 872 0000, 873 4222) No 44 (€1.85, every 20 minutes) takes about 1¼ hours to get to Enniskerry from Hawkins St in Dublin. Alternatively, you can take the DART train to Bray (€2.20) and catch bus No 185 (€1.35, hourly) from the station, which takes an extra 40 minutes.

Getting to Powerscourt House under your own steam is not a problem (it's 500m from the town), but getting to the waterfall is tricky. **Alpine Coaches** (☎ 286 2547) runs a shuttle service between the DART station in Bray, the waterfall (€5 return) and the house (€4). Shuttles leave Bray at 11.05am, (11.30am July and August), 12.30pm, 1.30pm (and 3.30pm September to June) Monday to Saturday, and 11am, noon and 1pm Sunday. The last departure from Powerscourt House is at 5.30pm.

GLENCREE

☎ 01

Just south of the County Dublin border and 10km west of Enniskerry is Glencree, a leafy hamlet set into the side of the valley of the same name, which opens east to give a magnificent view down to Great Sugarloaf Mountain and the sea.

The valley floor is home to the Glencree Oak Project, an ambitious plan to reforest part of Glencree with the native oak vegetation, mostly broadleaf trees, that once covered most of the country but now covers only 1% of Ireland's landmass.

The village, such as it is, has a tiny shop and a hostel but no pub. There's a poignant **German cemetery** dedicated to 134 servicemen who died in Ireland during WWI and WWII. Just south of the village, the former military barracks are now a retreat house and reconciliation centre for people of different religions from the Republic and the North.

Sleeping

Knockree Hostel (☎ 286 4036, for bookings ☎ 830 4555; www.irelandyha.org; Knockree, Enniskerry; dm €12; ◷ 8-10am & 5-10pm; **P**) A gorgeous 18th-century farmhouse with wonderful views over Glencree is the perfect setting for this 58-bed hostel, which is also conveniently on the Wicklow Way. Although it's very comfortable (sheets cost €2 to rent) the conditions are a little spartan, which suits the overall lost-in-the-mountains tone of the place.

SALLY GAP

One of the two main east–west passes across the Wicklow Mountains, the Sally Gap, is surrounded by some spectacular countryside. From the turn-off on the lower road (R755) between Roundwood and Kilmacanogue near Bray, the narrow road (R759) passes above the dark and dramatic Lough Tay, whose scree slopes slide into **Luggala** (Fancy Mountain), the almost fairytale estate owned by one Garech de Brún, member of the Guinness family and founder of Claddagh Records, a leading producer of Irish traditional and folk music. The small River Cloghoge links Lough Tay with Lough Dan just to the south. It then heads up to the Sally Gap crossroads, where it cuts across the Military Rd and heads northwest for Kilbride and the N81, following the young River Liffey, still only a stream.

ROUNDWOOD

☎ 01 / pop 440

A popular stop for tired walkers along the Wicklow Way, Roundwood is a pleasant if unremarkable village that has the largely irrelevant honour of being Ireland's highest, at 238m above sea level. The long main street leads south to Glendalough and southern Wicklow. Turn-offs lead to Ashford to the east and the southern shore of Lough Dan to the west. Unfortunately, almost all Lough Dan's southern shoreline is private property and you can't get to the lake on this side.

The town has shops and a post office, but not a bank or an ATM; Glendalough doesn't have one either. The nearest ATM is at the petrol station in Kilmacanogue, at the junction of the M11 and the R755.

Sleeping & Eating

Ballinacor House (☎ 281 8168; ballinacor@eircom.net; s/d €28/60; ♥ May-Sep) Highly recommended is this super-comfortable house about 2km south of town on the road to Laragh, which is popular with walkers and has some commanding views over the lovely countryside.

The owners are friendly and have been known to give lifts into Laragh to guests.

Tochar House (☎ 281 8247; dm/s/d €20/35/70) In the middle of Main St, the house has newly renovated rooms where a liberal use of pine wood lends plenty of light. The dorm – which is extremely popular with walkers and cyclists – has a bathroom, shower, and tea and coffee facilities, but is not available to single travellers, only to groups of two or more. It is directly behind the pub, so there's plenty of noise at weekends.

Roundwood Inn (☎ 281 8107; Main St; mains around €16, bar food €8-12; ♥ bar noon-9pm, restaurant 7.30-9.30pm Fri & Sat, 1-3pm Sun) This 17th-century German-owned house has a gorgeous bar with a snug and open fire, in front of which you can sample bar food with a difference: on the menu are dishes like Hungarian goulash and Irish stew with a German twist. The more-formal restaurant is the best in town, and has earned deserved praise for its hearty, delicious cuisine. The menu favours meat dishes, including season game, Wicklow rack of lamb, and a particularly good roast suckling pig. Reservations are required.

Roundwood Caravan & Camping Park (☎ 281 8163; www.dublinwicklowcamping.com; camp sites €6; ♥ Apr-Sep) Top-notch facilities, including a kitchen, dining area and TV lounge, make this one of the best camp sites in all of Wicklow. It is about 500m south of the village and is served by the daily St Kevin's Bus service between Dublin and Glendalough.

Getting There & Away

St Kevin's Bus (☎ 281 8119; www.glendaloughbus.com) passes through Roundwood on its twice-daily jaunt between Dublin and Glendalough (one way/return €7/12, 1¼ hours).

GLENMACNASS

Desolate and utterly deserted, the Glenmacnass Valley – a stretch of wild bogland between the Sally Gap crossroads and Laragh – is one of the most beautiful parts of the mountains, although the sense of isolation is quite dramatic.

The highest mountain to the west is Mt Mullaghcleevaun (848m), and River Glenmacnass flows south and tumbles over the edge of the mountain plateau in a great foaming cascade. There's a car park near the top of the waterfall. Be careful when walking on rocks near **Glenmacnass Water-**

fall as a few people have slipped to their deaths. There are fine walks up Mt Mullaghcleevaun or in the hills to the east of the car park.

WICKLOW GAP

Between Mt Tonelagee (816m) to the north and Table Mountain (700m) to the southwest, the Wicklow Gap is the second major pass over the mountains. The eastern end of the road begins just to the north of Glendalough and climbs through some lovely scenery northwestwards up along the Glendassan Valley. It passes the remains of some old lead and zinc workings before meeting a side road that leads south and up Turlough Hill, the location of Ireland's only pumped storage power station. You can walk up the hill for a look over the Upper Lake.

GLENDALOUGH

☎ 0404 / pop 280

Glendalough (Gleann dá Loch, 'Valley of the Two Lakes') is truly one of the most beautiful places in Ireland and a highlight of any trip to the island. The substantial remains of this important monastic settlement are certainly impressive, but the real draw is the splendid setting, two dark and mysterious lakes tucked into a deep valley covered in forest. It is, despite its immense popularity, a deeply tranquil and spiritual place, and you will have little difficulty in understanding why those solitude-seeking monks came here in the first place.

History

In AD 498 a young monk named Kevin arrived in the valley and decided that it would be a good spot for a bit of silent meditation, so he set up house in what had been a Bronze Age tomb on the southern side of the Upper Lake. For the next seven years he slept on stones, wore animal skins, maintained a near-starvation diet and – according to the legend – made friends with the birds and animals. Word eventually spread of Kevin's natural lifestyle, and he began attracting disciples who were seemingly unaware of the irony that they were flocking to hang out with a hermit who wanted to live as far away from other people as possible.

Kevin's preferred isolation notwithstanding, a settlement quickly grew and by the 9th century Glendalough rivalled Clonmac-

noise (see p351) as Ireland's premier monastic city: thousands of students studied and lived in a thriving community that was spread over a considerable area. Inevitably, Glendalough's success made it a key target of Viking raiders, who sacked the monastery at least four times between AD 775 and 1071. The final blow came in 1398, when English forces from Dublin almost completely destroyed it. Efforts were made to rebuild and some life lingered on here as late as the 17th century, when, under renewed repression, the monastery finally died.

Orientation & Information

At the valley entrance, before the Glendalough Hotel, is **Glendalough Visitor Centre** (☎ 45325; adult/child & student €2.75/1.25; ☼ 9.30am-6pm mid-Mar–Oct, 9.30am-5pm Nov–mid-Mar). It has a high-quality 20-minute audiovisual presentation called 'Ireland of the Monasteries', which does exactly what it says on the tin.

Coming from Laragh you first see the visitor centre, then the Glendalough Hotel, which is beside the entrance to the main group of ruins and the round tower. The Lower Lake is a small dark lake to the west, while further west up the valley is the much bigger and more impressive Upper Lake, with a large car park and more ruins nearby. Be sure to visit the Upper Lake and take one of the surrounding walks.

A model in the visitor centre should help you fix where everything is in relation to everything else.

Sights
UPPER LAKE

The original site of St Kevin's settlement, **Teampall na Skellig**, is at the base of the cliffs towering over the southern side of Upper Lake and accessible only by boat; unfortunately, there's no boat service to the site and you'll have to settle for looking at it across the lake. The terraced shelf has the reconstructed ruins of a church and early graveyard. Rough wattle huts once stood on the raised ground nearby. Scattered around are some early grave slabs and simple stone crosses.

Just east of here and 10m above the lake waters is the 2m-deep artificial cave called **St Kevin's Bed**, said to be where Kevin lived. The earliest human habitation of the cave was long before St Kevin's era – there's evidence that people lived in the valley for thousands of years before the monks arrived. In the green area just south of the car park is a large circular wall thought to be the remains of an early Christian *caher* or **stone fort**.

Follow the lakeshore path southwest of the car park until you come to the considerable remains of **Reefert Church** above the tiny River Poulanass. It's a small, plain, 11th-century Romanesque nave-and-chancel church with some reassembled arches and walls. Traditionally, Reefert (literally 'Royal Burial Place') was the burial site of the chiefs of the local O'Toole family. The surrounding graveyard contains a number of rough stone crosses and slabs, most made of shiny mica schist.

Climb the steps at the back of the churchyard and follow the path to the west and you'll find, at the top of a rise overlooking the lake, the scant remains of **St Kevin's Cell**, a small beehive hut.

LOWER LAKE

While the Upper Lake has the best scenery, the most fascinating buildings lie in the lower part of the valley east of the Lower Lake.

Just round the bend from the Glendalough Hotel is the stone arch of the **monastery gatehouse**, the only surviving example of a monastic entranceway in the country. Just inside the entrance is a large slab with an incised cross.

Beyond that lies a **graveyard**, which is still in use. The 10th-century **round tower** is 33m tall and 16m in circumference at the base. The upper storeys and conical roof were reconstructed in 1876. Near the tower, to the southeast, is the **Cathedral of St Peter and St Paul** with a 10th-century nave. The chancel and sacristy date from the 12th century.

At the centre of the graveyard to the south of the round tower is the **Priest's House**. This odd building dates from 1170 but has been heavily reconstructed. It may have been the location of shrines of St Kevin. Later, during penal times, it became a burial site for local priests – hence the name. The 10th-century **St Mary's Church**, 140m southwest of the round tower, probably originally stood outside the walls of the monastery and belonged to local nuns. It has a lovely western doorway. A little to the east are the scant

remains of **St Kieran's Church**, the smallest at Glendalough.

Glendalough's trademark is **St Kevin's Kitchen** or Church at the southern edge of the enclosure. This church, with a miniature round tower–like belfry, protruding sacristy and steep stone roof, is a masterpiece. How it came to be known as a kitchen is a mystery as there's no indication that it was anything other than a church. The oldest parts of the building date from the 11th century – the structure has been remodelled since but it's still a classic early Irish church.

At the junction with Green Rd as you cross the river just south of these two churches is the **Deer Stone** in the middle of a group of rocks. Legend claims that, when St Kevin needed milk for two orphaned babies, a doe stood here waiting to be milked. The stone is actually a *bullaun* (a stone used as a mortar for grinding medicines or food). Many such stones are thought to be prehistoric and they were widely regarded as having supernatural properties: women who bathed their faces with water from the hollow were supposed to keep their looks forever. The early churchmen brought the stones into their monasteries, perhaps hoping to inherit some of their powers.

The road east leads to **St Saviour's Church**, with its detailed Romanesque carvings To the west, a nice woodland trail leads up the valley past the Lower Lake to the Upper Lake.

Activities

The Glendalough Valley is all about walking and clambering. There are nine marked ways in the valley, the longest of which is about 10km, or about four hours walking. Before you set off, drop by the **National Park Information Point** (☎ 45425; ☼ 10am-6pm daily May-Sep, 10am-dusk Sat & Sun Oct-Apr) and pick up the relevant leaflet and trail map (all around €0.50) or, if you're solo, arrange for walking partners. It also has a number of excellent guides for sale – you won't go far wrong with David Herman's *Hillwalker's Wicklow* (€5.70) or Joss Lynam's *Easy Walks Near Dublin* (€9.99). A word of warning: don't be fooled by the relative gentleness of the surrounding countryside or the fact that the Wicklow Mountains are really no taller than big hills. The weather can be merciless, so make sure to take the usual precautions, have the right equipment and tell someone

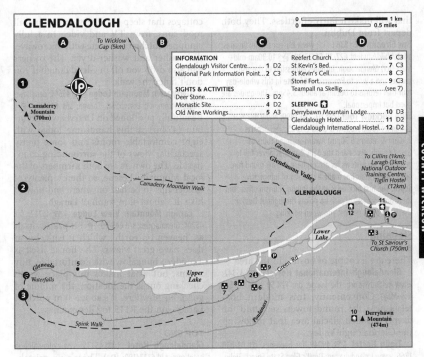

GLENDALOUGH

To Wicklow Gap (5km)

Camaderry Mountain (700m)

Glendassan

Glendassan Valley

Camaderry Mountain Walk

GLENDALOUGH

To Cillins (1km); Laragh (3km); National Outdoor Training Centre; Tiglin Hostel (12km)

Lower Lake

To St Saviour's Church (750m)

Glenealo Waterfalls

Upper Lake

Green Rd

Poulanass

Spink Walk

Derrybawn Mountain (474m)

INFORMATION
Glendalough Visitor Centre.......... 1 D2
National Park Information Point... 2 C3

SIGHTS & ACTIVITIES
Deer Stone................................ 3 D2
Monastic Site............................ 4 D2
Old Mine Workings..................... 5 A3

Reefert Church............................ 6 C3
St Kevin's Bed............................ 7 C3
St Kevin's Cell............................ 8 C3
Stone Fort................................. 9 C3
Teampall na Skellig......................(see 7)

SLEEPING
Derrybawn Mountain Lodge.......... 10 D3
Glendalough Hotel...................... 11 D2
Glendalough International Hostel... 12 D2

COUNTY WICKLOW

where you're going and when you should be back. For Mountain Rescue call ☎ 999.

The easiest and most popular walk is the gentle hike along the northern shore of the Upper Lake to the lead and zinc **mine workings**, which date from 1800. The better route is along the lakeshore rather than on the road (which runs 30m in from the shore), a distance of about 2.5km, one way, from the Glendalough Visitor Centre. Continue on up the head of the valley if you wish.

Alternatively, you can walk up the **Spink** (from the Irish for 'pointed hill', 380m), the steep ridge with vertical cliffs running along the southern flanks of the Upper Lake. You can go part of the way and turn back, or complete a circuit of the Upper Lake by following the top of the cliff, eventually coming down by the mine workings and going back along the northern shore. The circuit is about 6km long and takes about three hours.

The third option is a hike up **Camaderry Mountain** (700m), hidden behind the hills that flank the northern side of the valley. The walk starts on the road just 50m back

towards Glendalough from the entrance to the Upper Lake car park. Head straight up the steep hill to the north and you come out on open mountains with sweeping views in all directions. You can then continue up Camaderry to the northwest or just follow the ridge west looking over the Upper Lake. To the top of Camaderry and back is about 7.5km and takes about four hours.

The **National Outdoor Training Centre** (☎ 40169; www.tiglin.com; Tiglin, Ashford; weekend courses €200-275; ⌚ 9am-5pm Mon-Fri, 9am-1pm Sat), directly across from the Tiglin Hostel runs courses in outdoor pursuits like hill walking, mountaineering, rock climbing, canoeing and kayaking. Most courses are held during a weekend and all prices include accommodation, food, gear rental, in-course transportation and training. It's a terrific place, run by enthusiastic and knowledgeable instructors who are all experts in their chosen field.

Tours

If you don't fancy doing Glendalough on your own steam, there are a couple of tours that will make it fairly effortless. They both depart from Dublin.

Bus Éireann (☎ 836 6111; www.buseireann.ie; Busáras; adult/child/student €27/17.55/25.20; ⏰ 10.30am mid-Mar–Oct) Glendalough, includes admission to the visitor centre, and a visit to Powerscourt Estate in this whole-day tour that returns to Dublin at about 5.45pm. The guides are good but impersonal.

Wild Wicklow Tour (☎ 01-280 1899; www.discover dublin.ie; adult/student & child €28/25; ⏰ departs 9.10am & returns 5.30pm) Award-winning tours of Glendalough, Avoca and the Sally Gap that never fail to generate rave reviews for atmosphere and all-round fun, but so much craic has made a casualty of informative depth. The first pick-up is at the Dublin Tourism office, but there are a variety of pick-up points throughout Dublin; check the point nearest you when booking.

Sleeping
BUDGET
There are a couple of hostels in the area.

Glendalough International Hostel (☎ 45342; www.irelandyha.org; the Lodge; dm €24.50 Jun-Oct, €20 Nov-May) Conveniently, this modern hostel is near the round tower, set amid the deeply wooded glacial area that makes up the Glendalough Valley.

Tiglin Hostel (☎ 49049, for bookings ☎ 01-830 1766; www.irelandyha.org; Devil's Glen State Forest, Tiglin, Ashford; dm €15; ⏰ 7-10am & 5-11pm) About 10km northeast of Laragh via Annamoe, this 50-bed An Óige hostel was built in 1870. It was originally a farmhouse frequented by the playwright JM Synge. You can book only through the An Óige head office in Dublin.

MIDRANGE
Most B&Bs are in or around Laragh, a village 3km east of Glendalough, or on the way there from Glendalough.

Glendalough River House (☎ 45577; www.glenda loughriverhouse.com; Laragh; s/d €60/80; Ⓟ) This 200-year-old restored farmhouse on the river at the beginning of the Green pedestrian path to Glendalough from Laragh is an absolute delight. The bedrooms are large and well-appointed, while the breakfast will load you up with all the energy you'll need for a hike in the surrounding hills.

Glendale (☎ 45410; www.glendale-glendalough .com; Laragh East; s/d €50/66, cottage per week €250-600; Ⓟ) This is an immaculately modern and tidy B&B with large, comfortable rooms. Also available are five modern self-catering

cottages that sleep six. Every cottage has all mod cons, from TV and video to a fully equipped kitchen complete with microwave, dishwasher and washer-dryer. The owners will also drop you off in Glendalough if you don't fancy the walk.

Derrybawn Mountain Lodge (☎ 45644; derrybawn lodge@eircom.net; Derrybawn, Laragh; s/d €40/80; Ⓟ) Beautifully positioned on Derrybawn Mountain (474m) is this handsome lodge with eight comfortable rooms and some pretty spectacular views of the surrounding countryside. The owners are both members of the local Mountain Rescue, so there's plenty of insider tips to be had on where and how to hike. It's about 4km south of Laragh.

Laragh Mountain View Lodge (☎ 45282; fax 45204; Glenmacnass; s/d €45/70; Ⓟ) It praises itself as 'heaven on earth', which it isn't, but it does have great views. The house itself is a modern bungalow with comfortable, tidy rooms, but what makes this place worth checking out is the location: the middle of gorgeous nowhere. It's about 3km north of Laragh, on the R115 to Glenmacnass.

TOP END
Glendalough Hotel (☎ 45135; www.glendalough hotel.com; s/d €117/190; Ⓟ) There's no mistaking Glendalough's best hotel, conveniently located next door to the visitor centre. There is no shortage of takers for its 44 fairly luxurious bedrooms.

Eating
Laragh's the place for a bit of grub, as there's only one sit-down spot in Glendalough.

Wicklow Heather Restaurant (☎ 45157; Main St, Laragh; mains €12-15; ⏰ noon-8.30pm) This is the best place for anything substantial. The trout (farmed locally) is excellent. During summer, villagers put out signs and serve tea and scones on the village green.

Glendalough Hotel (☎ 45135; 3-course lunch €19, bar mains around €9; ⏰ noon-6pm) The hotel's enormous restaurant serves a very good lunch of unsurprising dishes usually involving some chicken, beef and fish. The bar menu – burgers, sandwiches, sausages and the like – is also quite filling.

Getting There & Away
St Kevin's Bus (☎ 281 8119; www.glendaloughbus .com) departs from outside the Mansion House on Dawson St in Dublin at 11.30am

SOMETHING SPECIAL

Glendalough Cillíns (☎ 45140, for bookings ☎ 45777; St Kevin's Parish Church, Glendalough; r €40) In an effort to re-create something of the contemplative spirit of Kevin's early years in the valley, St Kevin's Parish Church rents out six hermitages, or cillíns, to folks looking to take time out from the bustle of daily life and reflect on more spiritual matters. In keeping with more modern needs, however, there are a few more facilities than were present in Kevin's cave. Each hermitage is a bungalow consisting of a bedroom, a bathroom, a small kitchen area and an open fire supplemented by a storage heating facility. The whole venture is managed by the local parish, and while there is a strong spiritual emphasis here, it is not necessarily a Catholic one. Visitors of all denominations and creeds are welcome, so long as their intentions are reflective and meditative; backpackers looking for a cheap place to bed down are not. The hermitages are in a field next to St Kevin's Parish Church, about 1km east of Glendalough on the R756 to Laragh.

and 6pm Monday to Saturday, and 11.30am and 7pm Sunday (one way/return €10/16, 1½ hours). It also stops at the Town Hall in Bray. Departures from Glendalough are at 7.15am and 4.30pm Monday to Saturday. During the week in July and August the later bus runs at 5.30pm, and there is an additional service at 9.45am.

GLENMALURE

As you go deeper into the mountains southwest of Glendalough near the southern end of the Military Rd, everything gets that little bit wilder and more remote. Beneath the western slopes of Wicklow's highest peak, Lugnaquilla (924m), is Glenmalure, a dark and sombre blind valley flanked by classic scree slopes of loose boulders. After coming over the mountains into Glenmalure you turn northwest at the Drumgoff bridge. From there it's about 6km up the road beside the River Avonbeg to a car park where trails lead off in various directions.

Glenmalure figures prominently in the national tale of resistance against the British. The valley was a clan stronghold, and in 1580 the redoubtable chieftain Fiach MacHugh O'Byrne (1544–97) and his band of merry men actually managed to defeat an army of 1000 English soldiers; the battle cost the lives of 800 men and drove Queen Elizabeth into an apoplectic rage. In 1597 the English avenged the disaster when they captured O'Byrne and impaled his head on the gates of Dublin Castle.

Sights & Activities

Near Drumgoff is Dwyer's or **Cullen's Rock**, which commemorates both the Glenmalure battle and Michael Dwyer, a 1798 Rising

rebel who holed up here. Men were hanged from the rock during the Rising.

You can walk up Lugnaquilla Mountain or head up the blind Fraughan Rock Glen east of the car park. Alternatively, you can go straight up Glenmalure Valley passing the small, seasonal An Óige Glenmalure Hostel, after which the trail divides – heading northeast, the trail takes you over the hills to Glendalough, while going northwest brings you into the Glen of Imaal (p163).

The head of Glenmalure and parts of the neighbouring Glen of Imaal are off-limits – it's military land, well posted with warning signs.

Sleeping

Glenmalure Hostel (☎ 01-830 4555; www.irelandyha .org; Greenane; dm €15; ☒ Jun-Aug, Fri & Sat only Sep-May) No phone, no electricity (lighting is by gas), just a rustic two-storey cottage with 19 beds and running water, this place has a couple of heavyweight literary links: it was once owned by WB Yeats' femme fatale, Maud Gonne, and was also the setting for JM Synge's play, Shadow of a Gunman. It's an isolated place, but it is beautifully situated beneath Lugnaquilla.

Glenmalure Log Cabin (☎ 01-269 6979; www.glen malure.com; 11 Glenmalure Pines, Greenane; 3 nights €350-500, 7 nights €500-800) In the heart of Glenmalure, this modern, Scandinavian-style lodge has two en-suite rooms, a fully equipped kitchen, a living room kitted out with all kinds of electronic amusements, including your very own DVD library. Hopefully, though, you'll spend much of your time here enjoying the panorama from the sun deck. There's a three-night minimum stay, except for July and August when it's seven days.

Otherwise, **Birchdale House** (☎ 46061; tmoy lan@wicklowcoco.ie; Greenane; s/d €30/60) and **Woodside** (☎ 43605; www.woodsideglenmalure.com; Greenane; s/d €40/70) are two comfortable, modern homes in Greenane, toward the southern end of the valley.

WESTERN WICKLOW

As you go west through the county, the landscape gets less rugged and more rural, especially toward the borders of Kildare and Carlow. The wild terrain gives way to rich pastures: east of Blessington the countryside is dotted with private stud farms where some of the world's most expensive horses are trained in jealously guarded secrecy.

The main attraction in this part of Wicklow is the magnificent Palladian pile at Russborough House, just outside of Blessington, but if it's more wild scenery you're after, you'll find it around Kilbride and the upper reaches of the River Liffey, as well as further south in the Glen of Imaal.

BLESSINGTON

☎ 045 / pop 3147

There's little to see in Blessington; it is basically made up of a long row of pubs, shops and 17th- and 18th-century town houses. It's the main town in the area, and as such makes a decent exploring base. Just outside of Blessington is the Poulaphouca Reservoir, created in 1940 to drive the turbines of the local power station to the east of town and to supply Dublin with water.

The **tourist office** (☎ 865 850; Blessington Craft Centre, Main St; ☼ 10am-5pm Mon-Fri) is across the road from the Downshire House Hotel.

Activities

Rathsallagh Golf Club (☎ 403 316; green fees hotel guest/visitor €55/65; ☼ for nonhotel guests Mon-Thu only) is known – somewhat optimistically – as 'Augusta without the Azelias,' but it is still one of the best parkland courses in Ireland, stretching over 6.5km amid mature trees, small lakes and shallow streams.

Sleeping & Eating

Haylands House (☎ 865 183; haylands@eircom.net; Dublin Rd; s/d €42/60; ℗) We highly recommend this comfortable B&B for its lovely rooms (all with en suite), warm welcome and excellent breakfast. It's only 500m out of town on the main Dublin road. As it's popular, book early if you can.

Downshire House Hotel (☎ 865 199; www.downshirehouse.com; Main St; s/d €69/120; ℗) Blessington's most prominent landmark is this family-run hotel with an old-fashioned atmosphere; the rooms, however, have all been given a modern makeover and are perfectly comfortable, even though the furnishings are basic enough.

Grangecon Cafe (☎ 857 892; Tullow Rd; mains €8-13; ☼ 10am-5pm Tue-Sat) Salads, home-baked dishes and a full menu of Irish cheeses are the staples at this tiny, terrific café in a converted schoolhouse. Everything here – from the pasta to the delicious apple juice – has a wholesome flavour and many of the ingredients are organic. A short but solid menu will leave you nothing short of satisfied and encouraged about the future of Irish dining.

Getting There & Away

Blessington is 35km southwest of Dublin on the N81. There are regular daily services by **Dublin Bus** (☎ 01-872 0000, 873 4222) No 65 from Eden Quay in Dublin (€3.40, 1½ hours, every 1½ hours). **Bus Éireann** (☎ 01-836 6111) express bus No 005 to and from Waterford stops in Blessington two or three times daily; from Dublin it's pick-up only, from Waterford drop-off only.

RUSSBOROUGH HOUSE

Magnificent **Russborough House** (☎ 045-865 239; Blessington; adult/child/student €6/3/4.50; ☼ 10am-5pm Mon-Sat May-Sep, 10.30am-5.30pm Sun & bank holidays Apr & Oct, closed rest of year) is one of Ireland's finest stately homes, a Palladian pleasure palace built for Joseph Leeson (1705–83), later the first earl of Milltown and, later still, Lord Russborough. It was built between 1741 and 1751 to the design of Richard Cassels, who was at the height of his fame as an architect. Poor old Richard didn't live to see it finished, but the job was well executed by Francis Bindon. Now, let's get down to the juicy bits.

The house has always attracted unwelcome attention, beginning in 1798 when Irish forces took hold of the place during the Rising; they were soon turfed out by the British Army who got so used to the

COUNTY WICKLOW

SOMETHING SPECIAL

Rathsallagh House & Country Club (☎ 403 112; www.rathsallaghhousehotel.com; Dunlavin; s/d from €175/250, 5-course meal €65) About 20km south of Blessington, this fabulous country manor, converted from Queen Anne stables in 1798, is more than just a fancy hotel. Luxury is par for the course here – from the splendidly appointed rooms to the exquisite country-house dining (the food here is some of the best you'll eat anywhere in Ireland) and the marvellous golf course that surrounds the estate. Even the breakfast is extraordinary: it has won the National Breakfast Award three times. (Is there anything Irish tourism doesn't have an award for?)

comforts of the place that they didn't leave until 1801, and then only after a raging Lord Russborough challenged their commander, Lord Tyrawley, to a duel 'with blunderbusses and slugs in a sawpit'. Miaow.

The house remained in the Leeson family until 1931. In 1952 it was sold to Sir Alfred Beit, the eponymous nephew of the co-founder of the de Beers diamond-mining company. Uncle Alfred was an obsessive art collector, and when he died his impressive haul – which includes works by Velázquez, Vermeer, Goya and Rubens – was passed on to his nephew, who brought it to Russborough House. The collection was to attract the interest of more than just art lovers.

In 1974 the IRA decided to get into the art business by robbing 16 of the paintings. They were eventually all recovered, but 10 years later the notorious Dublin criminal Martin Cahill – aka the General – masterminded another robbery, but this time for Loyalist paramilitaries. This time, however, only some of the works were recovered and of those several were damaged beyond repair – a good thief does not a gentle curator make. In 1988 Beit got the picture and decided to hand over the most valuable of the paintings to the National Gallery; in return for the gift, the gallery agreed to lend other paintings to the collection as temporary exhibits. The sorry story didn't conclude there. In 2001 a pair of thieves took the direct approach and drove a jeep through the front doors, making off with two paintings worth

nearly €4 million, including a Gainsborough that had been stolen – and recovered – twice before. And then, to add abuse to the insult already added to injury, the house was broken into again in 2002, with the thieves taking five more paintings, including two by Rubens. Incredibly, however, both hauls were quickly recovered.

The admission price includes a 45-minute tour of the house and all the important paintings, which, given the history, is a monumental exercise in staying positive. Whatever you do, make no sudden moves. You can take an additional 30-minute **tour** (adult/child €3.50/free; ☼ 2.15pm Mon-Sat, hourly on Sun) of the bedrooms upstairs, which contain more silver and furniture.

GLEN OF IMAAL

About 7km southeast of Donard, the lovely Glen of Imaal is about the only scenery of consequence on the western flanks of the Wicklow Mountains. It's named after Mal, brother of the 2nd-century king of Ireland, Cathal Mór. Unfortunately, the glen's northeastern slopes are mostly cordoned off as an army firing range and for manoeuvres. Look out for red danger signs.

The area's most famous son was Michael Dwyer, who led rebel forces during the 1798 Rising and held out for five years in the local hills and glens. On the southeastern side of the glen at Derrynamuck is a small whitewashed, thatched cottage where Dwyer and three friends were surrounded by 100 English soldiers. One of his companions, Samuel McAllister, ran out the front, drawing fire and meeting his death, while Dwyer escaped into the night. He was eventually deported in 1803 and jailed on Norfolk Island, off the eastern coast of Australia, but became chief constable of Liverpool, near Sydney, before he died in 1825. The cottage is now a small **folk museum** (☎ 0404-45325; Derrynamuck; admission free; ☼ 2-6pm mid-Jun–Sep) located on the Knockanarrigan–Rathdangan road.

THE COAST

Mountains and other inland marvels dominate Wicklow's impressive scenery, but the coastline has some very pretty spots inbetween the largely unassuming towns and small coastal resorts. Most attractive of all are the fine beaches of Brittas Bay, a wide lazy arc of coastline between Wicklow and Arklow. Running alongside it is the N11 (M11) from Dublin to Wexford, a busy road that cuts through a great glacial rift, the **Glen of the Downs**, carved out of an Ice Age lake by floodwaters. There's a forest walk up to a ruined teahouse on top of the ridge to the east. If you're looking for quieter and more scenic coastal byways, we recommend the coastal route through Greystones, Kilcoole and then along country lanes to Rathnew.

BRAY
☎ 01 / pop 26,215

You'd be hard pressed to find traces of the glorious seaside resort once described as the 'Irish Brighton,' but the sleepy dormitory town of Bray is a fairly pleasant spot, and you could do far worse than spend an afternoon strolling up and down the promenade or messing about on the beach. It's proximity to Dublin on the DART line means that there's no reason to overnight here, but you'll have to resist the late-night temptations of one of our favourite bars in Ireland. There's also a great scenic walk from here south to Greystones.

Information
The **tourist office** (☎ 286 7128, 286 6796; ☻ 9.30am-1pm & 2-5pm Mon-Sat Jun-Sep, 2-4.30pm Oct-May) is in the courthouse (built in 1841) beside the Royal Hotel at the bottom of Main St.

Sights
Top of the pretty small heap is the **heritage centre** (☎ 286 7128; Old Courthouse; adult/student €3.50/1.50; ☻ 9am-5pm Mon-Fri, 10am-3pm Sat) above the tourist office, where you can explore Bray's 1000-year history and examine the lengths to which engineer William Dargan (1799–1867) went to bring the railroad to Bray. Your kids will hate you for it.

You can make it up to them at the **National Sealife Centre** (☎ 286 6939; www.sealifeeurope.com; Strand Rd; adult/child €9.75/6.50; ☻ 11am-5pm Mon-Sat, 10am-5pm Sun). The British-run aquarium has a fairly big selection of tanks stocked with 70 different sea and freshwater species.

About 3km south of Bray on the Greystones road are **Killruddery House & Gardens** (☎ 286 3405; www.killruddery.com; Killruddery; house

& gardens adult/child €8/3, gardens only €5/2; ☻ 1-5pm May, Jun & Sep). A stunning mansion in the Elizabethan-Revival style, Killruddery has been home to the Brabazon family (earls of Meath) since 1618 and has one of the oldest gardens in Ireland. The house, designed by trendy 19th-century architects Richard Morrison and his son William in 1820, was *reduced* to its present-day huge proportions by the 14th earl in 1953; he obviously was looking for something a little more bijou. The house is impressive, but the prize-winner here is the magnificent orangery, built in 1852 and chock full of statuary and plant life. If you like fancy glasshouses, this is the one for you.

Activities
One of the most beautiful **coastal walks** in Wicklow stretches from the southern end of Bray's promenade over Bray Head and down to the tiny commuter town of Greystones, 7km further south. The path is pretty smooth and easy to follow, but you can make a detour and clamber up **Bray Head** (240m) through the pine trees all the way to the large cross, erected in 1950. The head is full of old smuggling caves and railway tunnels, including one that's 1.5km long. From the top, there are fine views of the Great Sugarloaf Mountain. Back on the coastal path, you approach Greystones via a narrow footbridge over the railway, after which the path narrows until you hit the lovely harbour in Greystones. Here you should relax in **Byrne's** (Greystones Pier), better known as Dan's, which serves a gorgeous pint.

Eating
There are a couple of half-decent spots for a bite of lunch in Bray; one in particular has a lovely seafront setting.

Betelnut Café (☎ 272 4030; Mermaid Art Centre, Main St; snacks €3-7; ☻ 8am-6pm Mon-Fri, 10am-6pm Sat, noon-6pm Sun, late on show nights) A decent café in an arts centre? Rather than reflect on Bray's lack of choice, this is a really good spot for a lunchtime nibble or a pre-theatre bite; sandwiches and salads are freshly prepared and the coffee done just right.

Barracuda (☎ 276 5686; Strand Rd; mains €16-25; ☻ noon-9pm) When you've had your fill of live sea creatures in the National Sealife Centre, head upstairs to this minimalist, metal-and-mirrors restaurant and see what happens to Nemo when a really good chef gets his hands on him…or not. For your newly found love of the sea and all its lovely inhabitants, there's always a good steak.

Drinking & Entertainment

Harbour Bar (☎ 286 2274; Seapoint Rd) A strong contender for Ireland's best pub, here you can enjoy an excellent pint of Guinness in a quiet atmosphere of conviviality. There is a separate lounge with velvet curtains, assorted paintings and cosy couches. Sundays see the gay and lesbian community chill to some terrific DJs.

Clancy's Bar (☎ 286 3191; Quinnsboro Rd) A real spit-and-sawdust kind of place with a clientele as old as the wood in the bar; it's perfect for a quiet pint and a chat.

Porter House (☎ 286 0668; Strand Rd) The Bray branch of one of Temple Bar's most popular pubs, this equally popular watering hole does a roaring trade in beers from around the world as well as its own selection of intoxicating brews – literally. It's all a little too cheesy for our tastes.

Mermaid Art Centre (☎ 272 4030; Main St; admission free; 🕑 10am-6pm Mon-Sat) An art gallery, theatre and cinema. The theatre puts on excellent gigs and modern, experimental-style plays, while the cinema shows art-house movies almost exclusively. Call to check prices. The art gallery has constantly changing exhibitions featuring the latest Irish and European works.

Getting There & Away

BUS

Dublin Bus (☎ 872 0000) No 45 (from Hawkins St) and No 84 (from Burgh Quay) serve Bray (one way €2.30, one hour).

St Kevin's Bus (☎ 281 8119; www.glendalough bus.com) departs from Bray Town Hall (€2, 50 minutes) at 8am and 5pm Monday to Friday, 10.30am and 5pm Saturday, 10.30am and 6.30pm Sunday. From Dublin, buses depart from in front of the Mansion House on Dawson St.

TRAIN

Bray train station (☎ 236 3333) is 500m east of Main St just before the seafront. The DART (one way €2.80, 30 minutes) runs into Dublin and further north to Howth every five minutes at peak times and every 20 or 30 minutes at quiet times.

The station is also on the main line from Dublin to Wexford and Rosslare Harbour, with up to five trains daily in each direction Monday to Saturday, four on Sunday.

KILMACANOGUE & THE GREAT SUGARLOAF

☎ 01 / pop 834

At 503m, it's not even Wicklow's highest mountain, but the Great Sugarloaf is one of the most distinctive peaks in Ireland, its conical tip visible for many miles around. The mountain towers over the small village of Kilmacanogue, on the N11 about 4km south of Bray, which would barely merit a passing nod were it not for the presence of the mother of all Irish craft shops just across the road from the village.

Avoca Handweavers (☎ 286 7466; www.avoca.ie; Main St) is one hell of an operation, with seven branches nationwide and an even more widespread reputation for adding elegance and style to traditional rural handicrafts. Operational HQ is in a 19th-century arboretum, and its showroom will leave you in no doubt as to the company's incredible success.

Shopping for pashmenas and placemats can put a fierce hunger on you, and there's no better place to satisfy it than at the shop's splendid **restaurant** (mains €11-16; 🕑 9.30am-5.30pm), which puts a premium on sourcing the very best ingredients for its dishes. It is best known for its beef-and-Guinness casserole, but vegetarians are very well catered for as well. Many of the recipes are available in the two volumes of the *Avoca Cookbook*, both on sale for €24.99.

Climbing the Great Sugarloaf

Before you attack the 7km, moderately difficult walk to the summit, we recommend that you get the *Wicklow Trail Sheet No 4* (€1.50) from the tourist office in Bray.

Start your walk by taking the small road opposite **St Mochonog's Church** (named after the missionary who administered the last rites to St Kevin). Ignore the left turn and continue round the bend until you get to a small bridge on your right. To your right, you'll see the expanse of the **Rocky Valley** below, a defile eroded by water escaping from a glacial lake that developed during the last Ice Age about 10,000 years ago. Continue on the path until you reach a fork: the lower road to the right continues round the mountain, while the left turn will take you up to the summit. As you reach the top, the track starts to drop; turn left and scramble up the rocky gully to the top. Return by the same path and continue southwards until you reach a large grassy area. Cross it, keeping to your left until you reach a gate. With the fence on your right, go downhill until you reach a path of grass and stones. This path takes you around the southern side of the mountain, where you will eventually pass a small wood on your right. Immediately afterwards you will see, on your left, a sports pitch known as the Quill. Beyond it is Kilmacanogue.

Getting There & Away

Bus Éireann (☎ 836 6111) bus No 133 from Dublin to Wicklow town and Arklow stops in Kilmacanogue (one way/return €3.20/5.10, 30 minutes, 10 daily).

GREYSTONES TO WICKLOW

The resort of Greystones, 8km south of Bray, was once a charming fishing village, and the seafront around the little harbour is idyllic. In summer, the bay is dotted with dinghies and windsurfers. Sadly, the surrounding countryside is vanishing beneath housing developments.

The **Hungry Monk** (☎ 287 5759; Church Rd; mains €13-20; 7-11pm Wed-Sat, 12.30-9pm Sun) is an excellent 1st-floor restaurant on Greystones' main street. The blackboard specials are the real treat, with dishes like suckling pig with a prune and apricot stuffing to complement the fixed menu's classic choices – fresh seafood, Wicklow rack of lamb, bangers 'n' mash and so forth – this is one of the better places to get a bite along the whole of the Wicklow coast.

Mt Usher Gardens

Horticulturalists from around the world can be found salivating and muttering in approval as they walk around the 8-hectare **Mt Usher Gardens** (☎ 0404-40116; www.mount-usher-gardens.com; adult/student & child €6.50/5.50; 10.30am-6pm Mar-Oct), just outside the unremarkable town of Ashford, about 10km south of Greystones on the N11. OK, not really, but the gardens are pretty special, with trees, shrubs and herbaceous plants from around the world laid out in Robinsonian style – ie according to the naturalist principles of famous Irish gardener William Robinson (d 1890) – rather than the formalist style of preceding gardens.

SLEEPING

Hunter's Hotel (☎ 40106; www.hunters.ie; Newrath Bridge, Rathnew; s/d from €90/180; P) This exquisite property just outside Rathnew on the R761 is an absolute find, with 16 stunning rooms, each decorated with unerringly good taste. The house, one of Ireland's oldest coaching inns, is surrounded by an award-winning garden that is part of the Wicklow Gardens Festival (see boxed text, opposite).

GETTING THERE & AWAY

Bus Éireann (☎ 836 6111) bus No 133 from Dublin to Wicklow Town and Arklow stops outside Ashford House (one way/return €5.20/7.50, one hour, 10 daily).

WICKLOW TOWN

☎ 0404 / pop 7031

Bustling Wicklow town has a fine harbour and a commanding position on the crescent curve of the wide bay, which stretches north for about 12km and includes a long pebble beach that makes for a fine walk. Besides one top-notch attraction, there's not much to keep the visitor but it does make for a decent exploring base. The **tourist office** (☎ 69117; www.wicklow.ie; Fitzwilliam Sq; 9.30am-6pm Jun-Sep, 9am-1pm & 2-5pm Oct-May, closed Sun) is in the heart of town.

Sights

WICKLOW'S HISTORIC GAOL

Wicklow's infamous **gaol** (☎ 61599; www.wicklowshistoricgaol.com; Kilmantin Hill; adult/child/student incl tour €6.80/3.95/4.90; 10am-6pm, last admission 5pm), opened in 1702 to deal with prisoners sentenced under the repressive Penal Laws, was renowned throughout Ireland for the brutality of its keepers and the harsh conditions suffered by its inmates. The smells, vicious beatings, shocking food and disease-ridden air have long since gone, but adults and children alike can experience a sanitised version of what the prison was like – and stimulate the secret sadist buried deep within – in the highly entertaining tour of the prison, now one of Wicklow's most popular tourist attractions. Actors play the roles of the various gaolers and prisoners, adding to the sense of drama already heightened by the various exhibits on show, including a

---

WICKLOW GARDENS FESTIVAL

Over 40 private and public gardens participate in the yearly **Wicklow Gardens Festival** (☎ 20070; www.wicklow.ie), which runs from the beginning of May roughly through the middle of August. The obvious advantage for green thumbs and other garden enthusiasts is access to beautiful gardens that would ordinarily be closed to the public. Some of the larger gardens are open throughout the festival, while other smaller ones only open at specific times; call or check the website for details of entrants, openings and special events, including all manner of horticultural courses.

---

life-size treadmill that prisoners would have to turn for hours on end as punishment, and the gruesome dungeon.

On the 2nd floor is a model of the HMS *Hercules*, a convict ship that was used to transport convicts to New South Wales under the captaincy of the psychotic Luckyn Betts: six months under his iron rule and most began to see death as a form of mercy. The top floor is devoted to the stories of the prisoners once they arrived in Australia. Tours are every 10 minutes except between 1pm and 2pm.

OTHER SIGHTS

The few remaining fragments of the **Black Castle** are on the shore at the southern end of town, with pleasant views up and down the coast. The castle was built in 1169 by the Fitzgeralds from Wales after they were granted land in the area by the Anglo-Norman conqueror, Strongbow. It used to be linked to the mainland by a drawbridge, and rumour has it that an escape tunnel ran from the sea cave underneath up into the town. At low tide you can swim or snorkel into the cave.

The walk south of town along the cliffs to **Wicklow Head** offers great views of the Wicklow Mountains. A string of **beaches** – Silver Strand, Brittas Bay and Maheramore – start 16km south of Wicklow; with high dunes, safe bathing and powdery sand, the beaches attract droves of Dubliners in good weather.

Special Events

The long-established **Wicklow Regatta Festival** (☎ 68354) is held every year for 10 days over July and August. The extensive programme of events and activities includes swimming, rowing, sailing and raft races, singing competitions, concerts and a Festival Queen Ball.

Sleeping & Eating

Town lodgings aren't anything special, but there are a couple of places within a few kilometres of Wicklow that are pretty special. If you're looking for something central for a night's stay, there's a clutch of B&Bs in and around Dunbur Hill and a few more uphill along St Patrick's Rd.

Grand Hotel (☎ 67337; www.grandhotel.ie; Abbey St; s/d from €85/125; ℗) Wicklow town's best accommodation is this mock-Tudor hotel that is quite a bit short of 'grand', but it's a handsome, comfortable place nonetheless. The rooms are immaculate and the smallish size of the place assures a personalised, friendly service.

Wicklow Bay Hostel (☎ 69213, 61174; www.wicklowbayhostel.com; Marine House; dm €15; ℗) A large, bright-yellow hostel overlooking the harbour that is a long-standing favourite with backpackers, who appreciate the spotless dorms, friendly buzz and two enormous kitchens.

Bakery Restaurant (☎ 66770; Church St; mains €18-32; ⌚ 6-10pm Mon-Sat, 11.30am-3.30pm & 6-10pm Sun) A mouthwatering menu that changes monthly offers all kinds of good dishes – from rich game meats to interesting vegetarian options. This is perhaps the best restaurant in town.

Getting There & Away

Bus Éireann (☎ 836 6111) bus No 133 serves Wicklow town from Dublin (€7, 1½ hours, 10 daily); Wicklow town is also served by express bus No 2 running between Dublin (one hour, 12 daily) and Rosslare Harbour.

Iarnród Éireann (Irish Rail; ☎ 01-836 6222) serves Wicklow town from Dublin on the main Dublin to Rosslare Harbour line (one way/return €12.50/15.50, one hour, five daily). The station is a 10-minute walk north of the town centre.

Getting Around

Wicklow Cabs (☎ 66888; Main St) usually sends a few cabs to meet the evening trains from Dublin. The fare to anywhere in town should be no more than €5.

COUNTY WICKLOW

SOUTHERN WICKLOW

RATHDRUM

☎ 0404 / pop 2123

The quiet village of Rathdrum at the foot of the Vale of Clara comprises little more than a few old houses and shops, but in the late 19th century it had a healthy flannel industry and a poorhouse. It's not what's in the town that's of interest to visitors, however, but what's just outside it.

The small **tourist office** (☎ 46262; 29 Main St; ☹ 9am-5.30pm Mon-Fri) has leaflets and information on the town and surrounding area, including the Wicklow Way.

Avondale House

Woe be to the man by whom the scandal cometh…It would be better for him that a millstone were tied about his neck and that he were cast into the depth of the sea rather than he should scandalise one of these, my least little ones.

James Joyce, A Portrait of the Artist as a Young Man

Joyce's fictional dinner-table argument wasn't about a murderer or any such criminal, but about Charles Stewart Parnell (1846–91), the 'uncrowned king of Ireland' and unquestionably one of the key figures in the Irish independence movement. This marvellous 209-hectare estate, dominated by the fine Palladian **mansion** (☎ 46111; adult/student & child €5/4.50; ☹ 11am-6pm May-Aug, Tue-Sun Mar, Apr, Sep & Oct, by appointment only rest of year), designed by James Wyatt in 1779, was his birthplace and Irish headquarters. Of the house's many highlights, the most impressive are the stunning vermilion-coloured library (Parnell's favourite room) and beautiful dining room.

From 1880 to 1890, Avondale was synonymous with the fight for Home Rule, which was brilliantly led by Parnell until 1890 when a member of his own Irish Parliamentary Party, Captain William O'Shea, sued his wife Kitty for divorce and named Parnell as co-respondent. Parnell's affair with Kitty scandalised this 'priest-ridden' nation, and the ultraconservative clergy declared that Parnell was 'unfit to lead' – despite the fact that as soon as the divorce was granted the two lovers were quickly

married. Parnell resigned as leader of the party and withdrew in despair to Avondale, where he died the following year.

Surrounding the house are 200 hectares of forest and parkland, where the first silvicultural experiments by the Irish Forestry Service (Coillte) were conceived, after the purchase of the house by the state in 1904. These plots, about half a hectare in size, are still visible today, flanking what many consider to be the best of Avondale's many walking trails, the Great Ride. You can visit the park during daylight hours year round.

Sleeping

Old Presbytery Hostel (☎ 46930; www.hostels-ireland.com; the Fairgreen, Rathdrum; dm/d €15/40; ℗) A modern, centrally located IHH hostel that looks more like campus accommodation. There is a mix of large, comfy dorms and well-appointed en-suite doubles as well as family rooms. A laundry and TV room round off the facilities. You can also camp in the grounds.

Getting There & Away

Bus Éireann (☎ 836 6111) bus No 133 serves Rathdrum from Dublin (one way/return €8/10.20, 1¾ hours, 10 daily) on its way to Arklow.

Iarnród Éireann (☎ 01-836 6222) serves Rathdrum from Dublin on the main Dublin

---

SOMETHING SPECIAL

BrookLodge & Wells Spa (☎ 0402-36444; www.brooklodge.com; Macreddin; r/ste from €240/310; P) The favourite chill-out spot for Dublin's high-flyers is this luxurious country house about 3km west of Rathdrum in the village Macreddin. The 39 standard rooms set a pretty high tone, with four-poster and sleigh beds dressed in crisp Frette linen, but the suites sing an altogether more harmonious tune, each a minimalist marvel that wouldn't seem out of place in a New York boutique hotel – massive beds, flat-screen plasma TVs, top-of-the-range sound system and every other possible style sundry. The accommodation is pure luxury, but it's the outstanding spa that keeps them coming back for more. Mud and flotation chambers, Finnish and aroma baths, Hammam massages and a full-range of Decleor and Carita treatments make this one of the top spas in the country. Your credit card will never have nestled in softer hands.

---

to Rosslare Harbour line (one way/return €13.50/16.50, 1¼ hours, five daily).

VALE OF AVOCA

In summer, tour buses and other interested parties clog the road through the scenic Vale of Avoca on their way to the renowned mills in the eponymous village. On their way, tourists ooh and aah at the gorgeous scenery of the darkly wooded valley that begins where the Rivers Avonbeg and Avonmore come together to form the River Avoca – a lovely spot suitably named the **Meeting of the Waters**, made famous by Thomas Moore's 1808 poem of the same name.

The Meeting of the Waters is marked by a pub called the **Meetings** (☎ 0402-35226; www .themeetingsavoca.com; s/d €40/65, mains €10-15; ☽ noon-9pm), which serves food and has music on weekends year round. There are *céilidhs* (traditional music and dancing sessions) between 4pm and 6pm Sunday, April to October. There's also a guesthouse attached (known as Robin's Nest) with decent, clean rooms. Buses to Avoca from Dublin stop at the Meetings, or you can walk from Avoca, 3km south of here.

Avoca

☎ 0402 / pop 564

The tiny village of Avoca (Abhóca) still trades on its setting for the now-defunct BBC TV series *Ballykissangel*, but the main reason to visit is to amble about – and hopefully spend loads of money in – the superstar of all Irish cottage industries, **Avoca Handweavers** (☎ 35105; www.avoca.ie; Old Mill, Main St; ☽ 9.30am-6pm), housed in Ireland's oldest working mill.

It's been turning out linens, wools and other fabrics since 1723, and all of Avoca's much-admired line is produced here. You

are free to wander in and out of the weaving sheds.

Just in case you might want some local info, the **tourist office** (☎ 35022; Old Courthouse; ☽ 10am-5pm Mon-Sat) is in the library.

Sleeping

Sheepwalk House & Cottages (☎ 35189; www .sheepwalk.com; Arklow Rd; s/d €55/100, cottages per week €425-700) Built in 1727 for the earl of Wicklow, this is our favourite place to stay in Avoca (although it's 2km out of town). The main house is splendid, with beautifully appointed rooms, while the converted outbuildings – complete with beamed ceilings, fireplaces and flagstone floors – are a wonderful option for groups of four or six.

Koliba (☎/fax 32737; www.koliba.com; Beech Rd; s/d €50/80; ☽ Apr-Oct) A thoroughly modern bungalow with comfortable, well-appointed rooms (all with en suite), it's 3km out of Avoca on the Arklow road.

River Valley Park (☎ 41647; fax 41677; camp sites €13) This well-equipped camp site is about 1km south of the village of Redcross, 7km northeast of Avoca on the R754 country road.

Getting There & Away

Bus Éireann (☎ 836 6111) bus No 133 from Dublin serves Avoca via Bray, Wicklow and Rathdrum on its way to Arklow (one way/ return €8.40/11.30, two hours, 10 daily).

ARKLOW

☎ 0402 / pop 9955

Wicklow's biggest and busiest town is a thriving commercial centre built around what was once an important local port, which won't inspire you to change route and come here, but chances are if you're in this part of the county you'll probably end up here anyway. There's a local belief that the town is included in Ptolemy's 2nd-century map of Europe, but what is absolutely verifiable is that Sir Francis Chichester's prize-winning transatlantic yacht *Gypsy Moth III* (now in Greenwich, England) was built here.

The town's seafaring past is explored in the small **maritime museum** (☎ 32868; St Mary's Rd; €3.50; ⏱ 10am-1pm & 2-5pm Mon-Sat May-Sep), which features a model of the *Titanic*, some salvaged items from the *Lusitania* and an extraordinary model of a ship made from 10,000 matchsticks.

For all other info, there's the **tourist office** (☎ 32484; www.arklow.ie; ⏱ 9.30am-1pm Mon-Sat, Jun-Sep) in the Coach House.

There is a white, sandy beach, but it lies between the docks and a gravel plant; you're better off heading 10km north to **Brittas Bay** or 7km south to the more sheltered **Clogga Beach**.

Sleeping & Eating

Plattenstown House (☎ /fax 37822; Coolgreany Rd; s/d €40/65; ℗) A gorgeous traditional farmhouse set in 50 acres of land about 5km south of town. Family antiques throughout this elegant 19th-century home, great views of the lovingly tended gardens and comfortable, well-appointed rooms make this place a terrific choice in the area.

Otherwise, there's a fairly broad choice of decent B&Bs, each offering comfortable rooms and a well-cooked breakfast. Try **Valentia House** (☎ 39200; www.geocities.com /valentiahouse; Coolgreany Rd; s/d €42/70; ℗) or **Pinebrook** (☎ 31527; www.pinebrook.net; Ticknock Close, Briggs La; s/d €37/60; ℗).

Kitty's of Arklow (☎ 31669; Main St; lunch mains €8.50-15, dinner mains €23-26; ⏱ noon-5pm & 6-10.30pm) An Arklow institution, Kitty's serves a great version of the usual bar food choices during the day – from beef burgers to fillets of plaice – while the evening menu tackles some exciting seafood dishes and an impressive range of meat dishes. It's not new cuisine, but it's a fine take on the classics.

Getting There & Away

Bus Éireann (☎ 836 6111) bus No 133 from Dublin serves Avoca via Bray, Wicklow and Rathdrum on its way to Arklow (one way/ return €9.50/12.20, 2¼ hours, 10 daily); Arklow is also served by express bus No 2 between Dublin and Rosslare Harbour (1½ hours, 12 daily). All buses stop outside the Chocolate Shop.

Iarnród Éireann (☎ 01-836 6222) serves Arklow from Dublin (one way/return €12.50/ 15.50, 1¼ hours, five daily) on the Arrow suburban line as well as by Intercity train to Rosslare Harbour – the price is the same no matter which train you take.

Counties Wexford & Waterford

Ireland's warmest, driest counties contain some stunning little places between them: the trick is to pick out those golden nuggets. Beach babies have a wealth of choice, from long kilometres of honeyed sand at Curracloe Beach to cheap 'n' cheerful seaside resorts like Tramore. Lovers of tougher seascapes can worship rugged Helvick Head or the fantastic fossil-filled rocks and blowholes of Hook Head, tipped by Europe's oldest lighthouse.

Let no-one doubt the cultural southeast: the unspoilt Ring Peninsula is home to a thriving Gaeltacht (Irish speaking) community; and Wexford town has its world-famous opera festival. Gastronomically, there's some unbeatable seafood about: try the tiny, thatched fishing villages of Kilmore Quay or Carne for top-quality lobster, chowder and fish.

Attracted by easily navigable rivers, deep sheltered harbours and rich soil, the southeast corner of Ireland was usually the first stop for foreign invaders: Waterford and Wexford are the birthplaces of Viking and Norman history. Ferns, Lismore and Johnstown castle, once impregnable, are now home to the magnificent ruins of these faded empires. The fire of Cromwell's rage was also felt in the major towns of the region, long known for its rebellious streak.

The interior is made up of peaceful river valleys and lush rolling farmland, reaching a crescendo at Mt Leinster in Wexford and the Comeragh Mountains in Waterford, both ideal for uphill walking and climbing.

COUNTIES WEXFORD & WATERFORD

HIGHLIGHTS

- **Get Pedalling**
  The beautiful Hook Peninsula (p182) explored by bicycle

- **Vive la Révolution!**
  The history of Wexford's insubordination at the National 1798 Rebellion Centre (p186) in Enniscorthy

- **Sandy Strands**
  The surf in Tramore (p197) or the sand and sun on secluded beaches such as Curracloe (p178)

- **Sail into History**
  The Dunbrody Heritage Ship (p185) in New Ross provides an emigrant's view of the world

- **No 1 Hideaway**
  A spa with a view of the unspoilt Nire Valley from secluded Hanora's Cottage (p201)

- POPULATION: 218,142
- AREA: 4224 SQ KM

COUNTY WEXFORD

Invaders and privateers have always had a magnetic attraction to County Wexford, lured by its sexily navigable rivers and fertile land…oh baby. The Vikings founded Ireland's first major towns on the wide, easy-flowing River Slaney, which cuts a swathe through the middle of the county. These days, the hordes descend on Wexford's fine beaches to build more innocent sandcastles.

Wexford town is pleasant enough but only retains a few traces of its Viking past. To feast on big dollops of history, visit Enniscorthy's National 1798 Rebellion Centre and the site of the insurgents'

last stand, Vinegar Hill, or put yourself into the shoes of Famine emigrants by boarding the Dunbrody Heritage Ship at New Ross.

Offshore, over 1000 wrecks litter the sea from Hook Head to Arklow: pretty Kilmore Quay makes an excellent diving base. Further west, lonely Hook Peninsula, home to Europe's oldest lighthouse, has mini surprises everywhere: cycling is the best way to slowly unwrap this landscape. Walkers should try the 221km Wexford Coastal Walk (Slí Charman), or pop up Mt Leinster (796m) for stunning views of four counties from its summit.

Keep your ears open for remnants of a dialect called Yola, sometimes called 'Forth

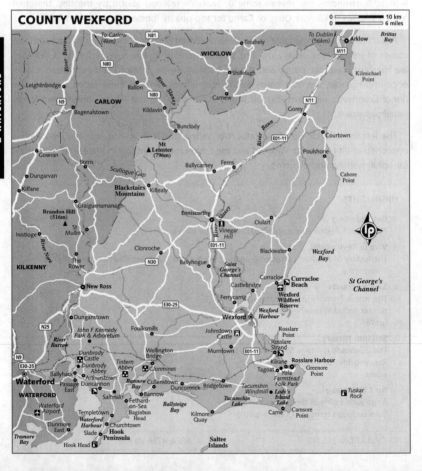

COUNTY WEXFORD

and Bargy', which still survives in south-eastern County Wexford. Yola stands for 'ye olde language' and is a mixture of old French, English, Irish, Welsh and Flemish. Examples of the language would be *kyne* (cow), *hime* (home), *hachee* (bad-tempered) and *stouk* (a truculent woman).

WEXFORD TOWN
☎ 053 / pop 9449

Defiant West Gate and the narrow, mean-dering lanes off Main St are a few reminders that Wexford (Loch Garman) has a glorious Viking and Norman past. It was once a thriving port but the estuary has gradually filled with silt and mud and has become almost unusable. Now most commercial sea traffic goes through Waterford and all passenger traffic through Rosslare Harbour, 20km southeast.

The liveliest, busiest and best time to visit is during Wexford's world-famous opera festival, in late October (see p175).

History
The Vikings named it Waesfjord (meaning 'harbour of mud flats') and its handy location near the mouth of the Slaney encouraged landings as early as AD 850. The Normans captured the town in 1169; traces of their fort can still be seen in the grounds of the Irish National Heritage Park.

Cromwell included Wexford in his Irish tour from 1649 to 1650. Around 1500 of the town's 2000 inhabitants were put to the sword, including all the Franciscan friars – the standard treatment for towns that refused to capitulate. Not surprisingly, after the massacre at Wexford surrender became a popular option. During the 1798 Rising, rebels made a determined, bloody stand in Wexford town before they were defeated.

Orientation
From Wexford Bridge at the northern end of the town, the quays lead southeast along the waterfront, with the tourist office in the small kink called The Crescent.

The Crescent is also home to a wind-swept statue of Commodore John Barry (1745–1803), who emigrated from Wexford to America and founded the US navy.

North and South Main St, a block inland, are where you'll find most of the shops.

Information
BOOKSHOPS
Readers' Paradise (☎ 71886; 3 Selskar St; ◷ 9am-5.30pm Mon-Sat) A good spot for Irish-interest second-hand paperbacks.

Wexford Book Centre (☎ 23543; 5 South Main St; ◷ 9am-5.30pm Mon-Sat) Has books on Irish topics plus a limited selection of foreign newspapers and magazines.

INTERNET ACCESS
IO Internet Café (☎ 23729; www.iocafe.com; 5 The Cornmarket; per hr €6; ◷ 11am-6pm Mon-Thu, 11am-7.30pm Fri, 10am-6pm Sat, 1-6pm Sun)

Megabytes (☎ 23262; FDYS, Francis St; per hr €3; ◷ 9am-9.30pm Mon-Thu, 9am-5pm Fri, noon-4pm Sat) Really a youth club, but they're happy for you to go online. Minimum charge is €1.50.

LAUNDRY
My Beautiful Laundrette (☎ /fax 24317; St Peters Sq; ◷ 9.30am-6pm Mon-Sat) Self-service small/large wash €5.50/7, wash & dry €9.20/11.25.

LEFT LUGGAGE
O'Hanrahan Station (☎ 22522; Redmond Pl) Has left-luggage facilities for €2.50 per item per day.

MEDICAL SERVICES
Wexford General Hospital (☎ 42233) On the N25, 2.5km west of the centre.

MONEY
There is an AIB and National Irish Bank on North Main St near Common Quay St, and a Bank of Ireland on the corner of Common Quay St and Custom House Quay.

POST
Main post office (☎ 45314; Anne St)
Sub post office (☎ 45314; 1a Redmond Sq) Inside Railway News.

TOILETS
There are public toilets near the tourist office and near St Iberius' Church.

TOURIST INFORMATION
Tourist office (☎ 23111; Chamber of Commerce, Crescent Quay; ◷ 9am-1pm & 2-5pm Mon-Fri Nov-Mar, 9am-1pm & 2-6pm Mon-Sat Apr-Oct)

Sights
BULL RING
Originally a beach where provisions were boated into the city, the Bull Ring became

a centre for bull-baiting in medieval times: the town's butchers gained their guild charter by providing a bull each year for the sport. The **Lone Pikeman statue** commemorates the participants in the 1798 Rising, who used the place as an open-air armaments factory.

There's usually a Friday **market** beside the Bull Ring from 9am.

Westgate

The only survivor of the six original town gates is the 14th-century **West Gate** (not to be confused with Westgate, the area around it), at the northern end of town. It was originally a tollgate, and the recesses used by the toll collectors are still intact, as is the lockup used to incarcerate 'runagates' –

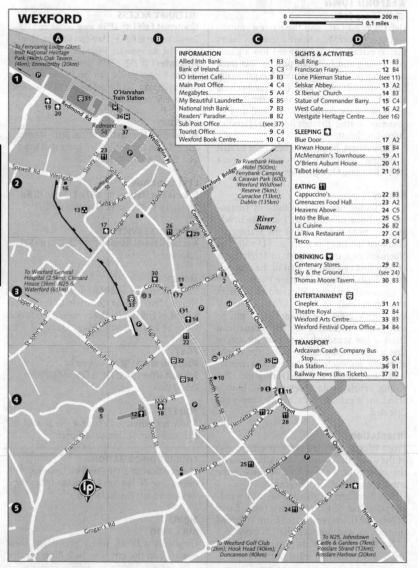

WEXFORD

0 _____ 200 m
0 _____ 0.1 miles

INFORMATION	
Allied Irish Bank	1 B3
Bank of Ireland	2 C3
IO Internet Café	3 B3
Main Post Office	4 C4
Megabytes	5 A4
My Beautiful Laundrette	6 B5
National Irish Bank	7 B3
Readers' Paradise	8 B2
Sub Post Office	(see 37)
Tourist Office	9 C4
Wexford Book Centre	10 C4

SIGHTS & ACTIVITIES	
Bull Ring	11 B3
Franciscan Friary	12 B4
Lone Pikeman Statue	(see 11)
Selskar Abbey	13 A2
St Iberius' Church	14 B3
Statue of Commander Barry	15 C4
West Gate	16 A2
Westgate Heritage Centre	(see 16)

SLEEPING	
Blue Door	17 A2
Kirwan House	18 B4
McMenamin's Townhouse	19 A1
O'Briens Auburn House	20 A1
Talbot Hotel	21 D5

EATING	
Cappuccino's	22 B3
Greenacres Food Hall	23 A2
Heavens Above	24 C5
Into the Blue	25 C5
La Cuisine	26 B2
La Riva Restaurant	27 C4
Tesco	28 C4

DRINKING	
Centenary Stores	29 B2
Sky & the Ground	(see 24)
Thomas Moore Tavern	30 B3

ENTERTAINMENT	
Cineplex	31 A1
Theatre Royal	32 B4
Wexford Arts Centre	33 B3
Wexford Festival Opera Office	34 B4

TRANSPORT	
Ardcavan Coach Company Bus Stop	35 C4
Bus Station	36 B1
Railway News (Bus Tickets)	37 B2

To Ferrycarrig Lodge (2km);
Irish National Heritage
Park (4km); Oak Tavern
(4km); Enniscorthy (20km)

O'Hanrahan
Train Station

Redmond Rd

Redmond Sq

Wellington Pl

Wexford Bridge

To Riverbank House
Hotel (500m);
Ferrybank Camping
& Caravan Park (600);
Wexford Wildfowl
Reserve (5km);
Curracloe (13km);
Dublin (135km)

*River
Slaney*

Spawell Rd

Westgate

Slaney St

Skeffington St

Selskar St

Selskar Ave

Monck St

Charlotte St

Commercial Quay

To Wexford General
Hospital (2.5km); Clonard
House (3km); N25 &
Waterford (61km)

Upper John St

George St

Cornmarket

Common Quay St

Custom House Quay

St John's Rd

John's Gate St

High St

Lower John St

Rowe St

Anne St

North Main St

Mary St

School St

Francis St

Henrietta St

Harper's La

Allen St

Peter's St

Oyster La

South Main St

King St Lower

King St Upper

Bride St

The Crescent

Paul Quay

Trinity St

Grogan's Rd

To Wexford Golf Club
(2km); Hook Head (40km);
Duncannon (40km)

To N25, Johnstown
Castle & Gardens (7km);
Rosslare Strand (12km);
Rosslare Harbour (20km)

VIKING RIVER PATHS

Although little remains of Viking Wexford, the *keysers* (meaning 'roads to the quays') still exist. These tiny arteries, just one packhorse wide, fall at right angles to the river and were of vast importance. The lifeblood of the city ran through them: honey, wheat and malt were taken from Wexford's wharves to the waterside, and whale oil, wool and fish came from the harbour into town.

The main road was Keysers Lane, which led from Keysergate in the old city walls to the Viking ship pool (now the semicircular Crescent). The gradual silting up of the harbour left the *keysers* as an interesting historical footnote...and a modern traffic nightmare.

those who tried to avoid paying. Some stretches of the town wall are also in good nick, including a particularly intact section near Cornmarket.

Beside the gate is the **Westgate Heritage Centre** (☎ 46506; Westgate; ⊙ 10am-6pm Mon-Sat Apr-Dec, 10am-5pm Mon-Sat Feb & Mar), where there's a 25-minute audiovisual display (€3) telling the history of Wexford.

Selskar Abbey

After Henry II murdered his friend Thomas á Becket, he did penance for the bloody deed at **Selskar Abbey** (⊙ Feb-Dec), founded by Alexander de la Roche in 1190. Strongbow's sister Bascilla is supposed to have married one of Henry II's lieutenants in the abbey. Its present ruinous state is a result of Cromwell's visit in 1649.

If the ruins are locked, ask the Westgate Heritage Centre for the key.

St Iberius' Church

South of the Bull Ring, **St Iberius' Church** (☎ 22936; North Main St; ⊙ 10am-4.30pm Mon-Sat) was built in 1760 on the site of several previous churches (including one reputed to have been founded before St Patrick came to Ireland). The Renaissance-style frontage is worth a look, but the real treat is the Georgian interior with its finely crafted altar rails and set of 18th-century monuments in the gallery. Phone ahead to organise a guided tour (donations of €2 appreciated).

Franciscan Friary

In 1649 Cromwell's forces made a bonfire of the original 13th-century friary, so most of the present building is from the 19th-century. Only two original walls remain. Some parts, such as the tabernacle, are very modern, creating an architectural incongruity that's quite appealing. The **friary** (☎ 22758; cnr Francis & School Sts; ⊙ 10am-5pm) houses a relic and wax effigy of St Adjutor, a boy martyr slain by his own father in ancient Rome.

Activities

Wexford Golf Club (☎ 42238; Mulgannon; 18 holes weekdays/weekends €32/38; ⊙ 8am-dusk Mon-Sat, members only Sun) is well signposted off the R733, about 2km southwest of town. Even hackers will appreciate the views of Wexford and the harbour.

Tours

Guided one-hour **walking tours** (☎ 52900; adult/concession/family €4/3.50/10; ⊙ 10.30am & 2.30pm Mon-Sat) leave year-round from outside the Westgate Heritage Centre.

Festivals & Events

The **Wexford Festival Opera** (☎ 22400, box office ☎ 22144; www.wexfordopera.com; Theatre Royal, 27 High St), an 18-day extravaganza held in October, began in 1951 and has grown to be the country's premier opera event. Rarely performed operas and shows are performed to packed audiences, and fringe street theatre, poetry readings and exhibitions give the town a fiesta atmosphere. Many local bars even run their own an amateur song competition.

Booking is essential and should be done at least three months in advance; the programme usually comes out in June.

Sleeping

Accommodation for October, when the Wexford Festival Opera takes place, is often booked out months in advance.

BUDGET

Kirwan House (☎ 21208; kirwanhostel@eircom.net; 3 Mary St; dm/q/tr per person €14/14/18) This strange hostel is in an exceptionally narrow building. Dorms are on the small side but have their own bathrooms, and a garden adds extra tranquillity (and many cigarette butts) to the old Georgian building. The hostel was completely redecorated in 2005, and blasting new showers were added.

Ferrybank Camping & Caravan Park (☎ 43274; www.wexfordcorp.ie; Ferrybank; camp sites €12; ⊗ May–mid-Sep) Right across the river from the centre, you get fantastic panoramic views of the town from your tent. Luxurious Ferrybank, the only council-run camping ground in the country approved by the Irish Tourist Board, has a heated pool next door (adult/child per hour €3.50/1.80), laundry facilities and children's play area.

MIDRANGE
Decent midrange accommodation is fairly sparse in the city centre.

McMenamin's Townhouse (☎ /fax 46442; www.wexford-bedandbreakfast.com; 3 Auburn Tce, Redmond Rd; s/d €50/90; P) This wonderful award-winning seven-bedroom B&B has large en-suite rooms furnished with Victorian antiques (including canopied beds). You get well looked after, with a warm welcome and fantastic breakfasts featuring all kinds of homemade breads, jams and yoghurts, and escape-the-full-Irish items like pancakes or kidneys with sherry. It's central, and particularly handy for the train station and buses.

Clonard House (☎ /fax 43141; www.clonardhouse.com; Clonard Great; s/d €45/80; ⊗ mid-Apr–Oct; P) A diamond find, this is like stepping into a stately home, but then being allowed to stay – and for a very reasonable price. The 1780s farmhouse has grand Georgian reception rooms where you can down Irish coffee and meet other guests. The nine bedrooms are equally spacious; some have four-poster beds and all of them overlook gardens, farmyard or rolling countryside. Clonard House is 3km west of town off the N25 to Waterford.

Blue Door (☎ 21047; bluedoor@indigo.ie; 18 Lower George St; s/d €45/70) The breakfasts are a plus at this 200-year-old town house, with smoked salmon and vegetarian alternatives. It's central but on a peaceful street, and floor-to-ceiling windows make the bedrooms bright and airy.

Ferrycarrig Lodge (☎ 42605; www.wexford-accommodation.com; Ferrycarrig Rd; s/d €60/80; ⊗ closed Jan; P) On the banks of the Slaney 2km north of town and a 10-minute walk from the National Irish Heritage Park, Ferrycarrig has a great little pub attached. There are four en-suite rooms, which are simply and effectively decorated; a couple have balconies.

O'Briens Auburn House (☎ 23605; www.obriensauburnhouse.com; 2 Auburn Tce, Redmond Rd; s/d €65/90; P) Next door to McMenamin's, this too is a lovely late-Victorian town house, sensitively decorated with period colours and furniture.

TOP END
Talbot Hotel (☎ 22566; www.talbothotel.ie; Trinity St; s/d €105/170; P) This huge 132-room hotel on the quayside has big, stylish modern bedrooms, many with river views. A classy new bar and grill has just opened, with vaulted ceilings and lots of fancy woodwork, and there's a top restaurant and leisure centre on the premises too.

Riverbank House Hotel (☎ 23611; www.riverbankhousehotel.com; Wexford Estuary; s/d €105/160; P) Located over the bridge from the town centre, the Riverbank is a more old-fashioned establishment with pleasant Victorian décor. Make sure you get a room with a panoramic view of Wexford and the river.

Eating
La Riva Restaurant (☎ 24330; warrengillen@dol.ie; The Crescent; mains €18-23; ⊗ 6-11pm Mon-Sat) This 1st-floor bistro (entrance on Henrietta St) is casual about everything except the food: its modern Irish/Mediterranean menu is prepared with organic, locally sourced ingredients and presented beautifully. Admire the fancy flashes of sauce and the glittering views of the night-time quay.

Heavens Above (☎ 21273; 112-113 South Main St; mains €10-17; ⊗ 5-10pm Mon-Sat, 4-9pm Sun) Several floors above the attached Sky & the Ground pub, this dark-wood-and-candles restaurant casts a hypnotic spell. The atmosphere is just right for those wanting an eat-out treat without too much formality, and the massive portions of food are good value and tasty. Veggies should be pleasantly surprised by the number of options.

Into the Blue (☎ 22011; 80 South Main St; lunch €4-9, set dinner menu €24-28; ⊗ 8.30am-5.30pm Mon-Sat, 6-9.30pm Wed-Sat) An upmarket deli recommended by locals, this is a café during the day, with breakfasts, sandwiches and cracking homemade soup, and a restaurant in the evening. On Friday nights the chef prepares a menu of excellent authentic curries.

Oak Tavern (☎ 20922; Enniscorthy Rd; mains €10-15; ⊗ noon-11pm) Near the gates to the Irish National Heritage Park (4km outside Wexford), this family-run tavern on the banks of the Slaney is renowned for its surf 'n' turf, salmon and steak. The big open fire is perfect in winter.

La Cuisine (☎ 24986; 80 North Main St; sandwiches €3-6; 🕑 9am-6pm Mon-Sat) Expect a dinnertime queue at this popular deli and health-food shop, which has an equally busy café at the back.

Cappuccino's (☎ 23669; 25 North Main St; breakfast €4-7.50; 🕑 8am-6pm Mon-Sat, 10am-6.30pm Sun) From heart-stopper to healthy, from full Irish to bagel with cream cheese, this upstairs-downstairs eatery is perfect for breakfast. It's a particular favourite with groups of teens and families.

For all those self-caterers, there's a late-opening **Tesco's** (The Crescent; 🕑 8am-10pm Mon-Sat, 10am-8pm Sun), or you could put together a gourmet picnic at **Greenacres Food Hall** (☎ 22975; 3 Selskar St; 🕑 9.30am-6pm Mon-Sat), which has a great selection of cheese, meats, olives and wine.

Drinking

Sky & the Ground (☎ 21273; 112-113 South Main St) This top-quality watering hole is one of the most renowned pubs in town. Cheerful, dark and warm, it's decorated with old enamel signage and serves a mean lunch. It offers the same food as the Heavens Above restaurant but at half the price (anyone for wild venison?). It's also the best place for music, with trad or blues sessions every night except Saturday.

Thomas Moore Tavern (☎ 24348; Cornmarket) This old man's pub is the one for a quiet drink and a good chat. The Wexford Film Society meets here every Tuesday night to quaff ale and dissect the just-watched movie.

Centenary Stores (☎ 24424; thecstores@eircom.net; Charlotte St) One of Wexford's livelier, spots this is frequented by the younger crowd. A former warehouse, it has DJs until 2am between Thursday and Sunday. More civilised are the trad music sessions from 1pm on a Sunday afternoon – soothe your hangover away with a hair of the dog and some diddly-dee tunes.

Entertainment

THEATRE & CINEMA

Theatre Royal (☎ 22144; 27 High St) The Royal stages drama and opera by local and touring companies. At the time of writing, plans were afoot to completely transform the theatre, by adding 200 extra seats, an additional smaller theatre and an art gallery. The swish new complex should be completed by 2008.

Wexford Arts Centre (☎ 23764; www.wexfordartscentre.ie; Cornmarket) In the 18th-century Market House and Assembly Room, this centre caters for exhibitions, theatre, dance and music, and screens arts films at 8pm on a Tuesday (€7).

Cineplex (☎ 22321; the Square, Redmond Sq; adult/child €7/4) This multiscreen cinema is near the train station.

Getting There & Away

The N25 leads southeast from the quays and Trinity St to Rosslare Harbour. For Duncannon or Hook Head, turn west either at The Crescent along Harpers Lane or from Paul Quay along King St. For bus and train information to/from Wexford phone ☎ 33114 or ☎ 33162.

BUS

Bus Éireann (☎ 22522) buses leave from O'Hanrahan train station on Redmond Place and travel to Rosslare Harbour (€4, 30 minutes, every 45 minutes Monday to Saturday, 11 Sunday), Dublin (€12, 2¼ hours, 12 daily Monday to Saturday, nine Sunday), Killarney (€23, 5½ hours, four daily Monday to Saturday, two Sunday), Waterford (€11.50, one hour, eight daily Monday to Saturday, three Sunday), Enniscorthy (€5.10, 25 minutes, 10 daily Monday to Saturday, nine Sunday) and Cork (€18, 3½ hours, six daily Monday to Saturday, three Sunday). Tickets are available from **Railway News** (☎ 23939; 1a Redmond Sq; 🕑 6.30am-10.30pm), the newsagency across from the station on the corner.

Ardcavan Coach Company (☎ 22561) runs one service Monday to Saturday to/from Dublin (€12, 2¼ hours); buses leave Dublin at 6pm, and leave The Crescent, Wexford at 8am.

TRAIN

O'Hanrahan Station (☎ 22522; Redmond Sq) is at the northern end of town. Wexford is on the Dublin (€18.50, three hours) to Rosslare Europort (€4, 30 minutes) line (via Enniscorthy and Wicklow) and is serviced by three trains daily in each direction.

Getting Around

Parking discs (per hour €1.20) for street parking can be bought at most newsagencies.

For a 24-hour taxi service, call **Wexford Cabs** (☎ 23123; 3 Charlotte St) or **AA Cabs** (☎ 40222). Most fares around the centre are €4.

AROUND WEXFORD TOWN
Irish National Heritage Park

The excellent **Irish National Heritage Park** (☎ 053-20733; Ferrycarrig; adult/child under 13/child 13-18/family €7.50/3.50/4/19; ⏰ 9.30am-6.30pm, last admission 5pm) makes a brave and extremely successful attempt to squash 9000 years of Irish history (up to the Normans) into one outdoor theme park.

Take a deep breath and plunge in, past a re-created Neolithic farmstead, stone circle, ring fort, monastery, *crannóg* (lake settlement), Viking shipyard, Norman castle and more. Sound effects and smoking fires add to the realism; or you can tag onto one of the frequent 1½-hour guided tours, where knowledgeable costumed actors really bring the place to life.

The park is about 3.5km northwest of Wexford town on the N11. A taxi from Wexford should cost about €7.

Johnstown Castle & Gardens

Parading peacocks guard this splendid 19th-century castellated house, the former home of the once-mighty Fitzgerald and Esmonde families.

The castle overlooks a small lake and is surrounded by 20 hectares of thickly wooded **gardens** (adult/child/car & passengers €2/0.50/5; ⏰ 9am-5.30pm), which are open to the public. However, the buildings house an agricultural research centre and the Irish Environmental Protection Agency. The only indoor bit you can visit is the **Irish Agricultural Museum** (☎ 053-42888; adult/child €5/3; ⏰ 9am-12.30pm & 1.30-5pm Mon-Fri, 2-5pm Sat & Sun, closed Sat & Sun Nov-Mar), in the stables, with collections of farm machinery and Irish country furniture, a horse-drawn caravan and a small Famine exhibition.

The castle is 7km southwest of Wexford town on the way to Murntown.

Wexford Wildfowl Reserve

Welcome to bird heaven. The superbly named Sloblands (from Irish *slab*, meaning 'mud, mire or a soft-fleshed person'!) is a swathe of low-lying land reclaimed from the sea. It's home to half the world's population of Greenland white-fronted geese – some 10,000 birds in total.

Wexford Wildfowl Reserve (☎ 053-23129; North Slob; admission free, guided tours on request; ⏰ 9am-6pm mid-Apr–Sep, 10am-5pm Oct–mid-Apr), comprising a visitor centre, observation tower and assorted hides, was set up to protect the birds' feeding grounds. Winter is a good time to spot the brent goose from Arctic Canada, and throughout the year you'll see numerous species of wader and wildfowl.

The reserve is on the Wexford to Dublin road; head north for 3.5km, before taking the signposted right turn by the Mazda garage. The visitor centre is another 2km along the lane.

Curracloe Beach

Over 11km long, Curracloe is one of a string of magnificent beaches that line the coast north of Wexford town. The high-octane, opening Normandy landing scenes of *Saving Private Ryan* (1997) were filmed here. It's 13km northeast of Wexford off the Dublin road. If you're discreet you can pitch a tent in the sheltered dunes.

Curracloe House Equestrian Centre (☎ 053-37582; Curracloe) offers beach rides lasting one to 1½ hours for €27/22 per adult/child.

Hotel Curracloe (☎ 053-37308; www.hotelcurracloe.com; s/d €45/80) is a small, family-run hotel with a staid, but snug, interior and great traditional sessions on Friday, Saturday and Sunday nights. It's about a 20-minute walk from the beach.

ROSSLARE STRAND
☎ 053

If you don't like crowds or children, avoid Rosslare Strand in the height of summer. The beaches are long and golden and the long shallow bay is perfect for windsurfing.

TOP BLUE-FLAG WEXFORD BEACHES

■ Curracloe (right) – eleven sandy kilometres of film set

■ Duncannon (p183) – gradually sloping beach ideal for paddlers

■ Rosslare (right) – sand-and-stone strand, just outside Wexford town

---

Boards, wetsuits and tuition, as well as canoe and dinghy rental and sailing lessons, are available from the **Rosslare Watersports Centre** (☎ 32566; ☺ 10am-6pm Jul & Aug). **Rosslare Golf Links** (☎ 32203; green fee weekdays/weekends €40/60) runs along the beach road. There are gentle walks north to Rosslare Point.

Sleeping & Eating

Burrow Holiday Park (☎ 32190; burrowpk@iol.ie; camp sites €20) Just south of the village, this popular park has excellent facilities, particularly for children: there's a games room, tennis courts, crazy golf and an adventure playground. The fee takes no account of tent size or number of people.

Lyngfields B&B (☎ 32593; Tagoat; s/d €40/66; **P**) Simple but very comfortable en-suite rooms make this roomy modern bungalow a good bet. Watch out for the signpost about 3km from Rosslare on the road to Tagoat.

Kelly's Resort Hotel (☎ 32114; www.kellys.ie; s/d incl meals €138/256; **P**) Kelly's is a Wexford institution and a massive hit with families. Everything, but everything, is on offer: tennis, golf, crazy golf, snooker, table tennis, badminton, yoga, croquet…and the SeaSpa (seaspa@kellys.ie), where you can pamper yourself silly with a range of treatments too large to mention here! There's a good restaurant, and a café for snacks. Most accommodation is sold as packages: for example, a double room over a Bank Holiday weekend (Friday, Saturday and Sunday night, including all meals) costs €880.

Rosslare Strand's eating options are few: try Le Colosseo (%73975; fax 73061; Strand Rd; mains €16-24; h10am-10pm daily Jun-Aug, 5-9.30pm Tue-Sat, 12.30-3.30pm Sun Sep-May), this meaty-and-fishy Italian restaurant is one of Rosslare Strand's few eating options.

Getting There & Away

The 9.30am Wexford bus from Rosslare Harbour (€7, 10 minutes, Monday to Saturday) and the 6pm Rosslare Harbour bus from Wexford (€5, 20 minutes, Monday to Saturday) stop at Rosslare Strand.

On the main Dublin–Wexford–Rosslare Europort line, three trains per day in each direction call at Rosslare Strand (from Dublin €23.50, three hours; from Wexford €9.50, 20 minutes; from Rosslare Europort

€9.50, five minutes). Trains to Waterford (€18, 1¼ hours) leave twice daily.

ROSSLARE HARBOUR
☎ 053 / pop 900

Rosslare (Ros Láir) Harbour is a busy port with connections to Wales and France. It's not particularly pretty or pedestrian-friendly and you might prefer to head straight on to Wexford. If you do need to stay, there's plenty of accommodation in what is really a large village.

Orientation & Information

The ferry port is the main focus of the town, where you will also find Rosslare Europort train station. A road leading uphill from the harbour becomes the N25 and takes you to the B&Bs and hotels. Further along this road is Kilrane where there are a few more B&Bs and a pub. There's a **Bank of Ireland** (St Martin's Rd) with an ATM and bureau de change, just off the N25.

Yola Farmstead Folk Park

This slightly twee but interesting-all-the-same **folk park** (☎ 32610; Tagoat; adult/child/family €6/4.50/15; ☺ 10am-6pm May-Oct, 10am-4.30pm Mon-Fri Apr & Nov) is a good place to come with the little 'uns. It's basically a reconstructed 18th-century village with thatched cottages, a working windmill and a tiny church, all intended to give visitors an impression of what life was like in rural Ireland (minus the hopeless poverty and the smells). There are hens, sheep, deer, rabbits, pigs and exotic birds for small kids to marvel at, and a genealogy centre where bigger visitors can trace their roots. The park is just outside Tagoat, on the N25.

Sleeping & Eating

If you're waiting for a ferry, or have just arrived and are too tired to go any further, there are plenty of B&Bs on St Martin's Rd.

St Martin's B&B (☎ /fax 33133; www.saintmartins rosslare.com; St Martin's Rd; s/d €50/79; **P**) The beautifully decorated rooms in this purpose-built, homey B&B are better than most of the local hotels. Room No 7 is perhaps the best: it has its own four-poster bed. John, the owner, is tremendously helpful, and early breakfasts are available for ferry-catchers.

Harbour View Hotel (☎ 61450; www.harbourview hotel.ie; s/d €90/150) This place, overlooking the Europort, has gone through a huge modernisation programme recently, leaving it with 24 fresh and cheerful rooms. Its Seasons Restaurant (mains €12-22; h5.30-9.30pm) is the best place to eat in town, and has a particularly large Chinese menu of curry, noodle and seafood dishes.

Getting There & Away

BOAT
Stena Line (☎ 33115; www.stenaline.com) sails between Rosslare Harbour and Fishguard in Wales (adult €33, motorbike and driver €109, car and driver €270, 1¾ hours, two to three sailings per day May to September). Check-in is about one hour before sailing. Stena also runs its Superferry (adult €33, motorbike and driver €78, car and driver €250, 3½ hours, two sailings per day) year round.

Irish Ferries (☎ 33158; www.irishferries.com) sails to Pembroke in Wales (foot passenger €33, motorbike and driver €78, car and driver €250, 3¾ hours, two daily). It also sails to Cherbourg in France, and from April to September there are sailings to Roscoff in France (foot passenger €120, motorbike and driver €180, car and two adults €550, 16 to 24 hours, three to six a week).

For more information see p697.

BUS
Buses and trains depart from the Rosslare Europort station, which you'll find at the ferry terminal.

Bus Éireann (☎ 01-836 6111) has services to lots of Irish towns and cities, including Dublin (€15, three hours, 13 daily Monday to Saturday, 11 Sunday), Wexford (€12, 30 minutes, 13 daily Monday to Saturday, 11 Sunday) and Cork (€19.50, four hours, five daily Monday to Saturday, three Sunday) via Waterford (€13.50, 1½ hours).

CAR
Budget (☎ 33318), **Hertz** (☎ 23511) and **Europcar Murrays** (☎ 33634) share a desk in the ferry terminal.

TRAIN
Three trains daily in each direction operate on the Rosslare Europort–Rosslare Strand–Wexford–Dublin route (to Rosslare Strand €4.50, five minutes; to Wexford €4.50, 25 minutes; to Dublin €18.50, three hours).

Trains on the Rosslare Europort–Limerick route stop in Waterford (€9, 1¼ hours, two daily Monday to Saturday). For more information call ☎ 33114.

SOUTH OF ROSSLARE HARBOUR
Thank God for government cutbacks. About 9km south of Rosslare Harbour is Carnsore Point, where Ireland's first four nuclear power stations were to be built had cost (and huge protests) not killed the plan off. It's now home to the east coast's first wind farm.

The village of **Carne** has a few pretty, whitewashed, thatched cottages and a fine beach. Locals and visitors alike pack the **Lobster Pot** (☎ 053-31110; Carne; mains €18-27; restaurant ⓨ 6-9pm Tue-Sat, 12.30-7.30pm Sun, from noon Tue-Sat Jun-Aug) in summer, but it's worth the squeeze to get at the super-fresh seafood in this gorgeous pub/restaurant. The chowder is one of the best on this planet.

Heading back up the road takes you past Lady's Island Lake containing **Our Lady's Island**, site of an early Augustinian priory and still a centre of devotion: the most fervent pilgrims crawl round the island on their knees. Look out for the tilting Norman tower, which leans more than the Leaning Tower of Pisa!

There's no public transport to this area.

KILMORE QUAY
☎ 053 / pop 407
Straight out of a postcard, peaceful Kilmore Quay is a small, working fishing village noted for its quaint thatched cottages, lobsters and great restaurants. The harbour is the jumping-off point for the Saltee Islands (see opposite), Ireland's largest bird sanctuary, which are clearly visible out to sea.

Mussel in on the nine-day **Seafood Festival** (☎ 29918) in the second week of July, which involves tastings, music and dancing, and ends with a 'Blessing of the Boats' by local priest Father Jim.

Sights & Activities
In the harbour aboard a lightship, with its original furniture and fittings, the **Guillemot Maritime Museum** (☎ 21572; adult/child €4/2; ⓨ noon-5.30pm daily Jun-Aug, noon-5.30pm Sat & Sun May & Sep) explains the history of the town's lifeboat.

Wrecks like the SS *Lennox* and extraordinary marine life should keep divers off the streets. Contact **Pier House Dive Centre** (☎ 29703; scubabreaks@eircom.net; Pier House) to hire gear, arrange a dive (€50) or refill air tanks (€5).

Friendly Mick O'Meara at **Sea Paddling** (☎ 087-268 6529; www.seapaddling.com) can arrange kayaking trips (full day €75) to the Saltee Islands for seasoned paddlers; you'll need to book ahead.

Sea anglers should contact **John Devereaux** (☎ 053-29637, 087-292 6469) to charter a boat.

To the northwest, a sandy beach stretches towards Cullenstown. There are some signposted **walking trails** behind the peaceful dunes, circled by serenading skylarks.

Sleeping & Eating

Sadly, Kilmore's hostel has closed down.

Pier House Dive Centre (☎/fax 29703; scuba breaks@eircom.net; dm €15) Offers budget accommodation, but it's very basic and often full of divers on package holidays.

Haven (☎ 29979; s/d €35/70; **P**) The lady who runs this B&B is a sweetie. Her five rooms (four en suite) are simple patchwork-bedspread affairs, but several have breathtaking sea views. Off Main St near Quay house, Haven is definitely the best value of Kilmore's accommodation options.

Quay House (☎ 29988; www.kilmorequay.net; s/d €80/100; **P** 🖳) Just next door is this roomy whitewashed guesthouse, once the village post office. It's all country-pine floors and bedroom furniture, with amiable if slightly impersonal service. The guest lounge is a great place to meet fellow visitors.

Mill Road Farm (☎ 29633; info@millroadfarm.com; R739; s/d €38/62; 🕑 closed end Dec; **P**) About 2km outside Kilmore Quay on the road to Kilmore, this modern working farm has four simple, ample-sized en-suite rooms and breakfasts featuring homemade goodies.

Silver Fox Restaurant (☎ 29888; fax 48967; starters €5-9, mains €15-28; 🕑 5-9.30pm Thu-Sat, 12.30-3.30pm & 5-9.30pm Sun) Book in advance because chef-owner Nicky Cullen's exceptional restaurant attracts big crowds. It's famed for its seafood – crab, black sole, salmon, scampi and monkfish are all cooked to perfection – but you won't be disappointed by the land-lubber or veggie options.

Wooden House Restaurant & Bar (☎ 29804; mains €12-16) Traditional music and a great pint of stout add to the atmosphere at this pub-restaurant.

Getting There & Away

Public transport is limited. Viking Buses travel between Kilmore Quay and Wexford three times per day on Monday, Tuesday, Thursday and Friday. For times, ask at the post office. **Bus Éireann** (☎ 01-836 6111) No 383 runs to/from Wexford on Wednesday and Saturday (€3, 45 minutes, two services in each direction daily).

SALTEE ISLANDS

Once the haunt of privateers, smugglers and 'dyvars pyrates', the Saltees now have a peaceful existence as one of Europe's most important bird sanctuaries. Over 375 recorded species make their home here, 4km offshore from Kilmore Quay, principally the gannet, guillemot, cormorant, kittiwake, puffin and the Manx shearwater. The best time to visit is the spring and early-summer nesting season. The birds leave once the chicks can fly, and by early August it's eerily quiet.

The two islands feature some of the oldest rocks in Europe, dating back 2000 million years or more, and were inhabited as long ago as 3500 to 2000 BC. From the 13th century until the dissolution of the monasteries in 1538, they were the property of Tintern Abbey, after which various owners were granted the land.

Two of the Wexford rebel leaders, Bagenal Harvey and Dr John Colclough, hid here after the failed 1798 Rising. The men were betrayed by a paid informer, tracked down in a six-hour manhunt, brought to Wexford, hanged, and their heads stuck on spikes.

To book a crossing to the Saltees try local boatmen such as **Declan Bates** (☎ 053-29684, 087-252 9736) or **Dick Hayes** (☎ 053-29704, 087-254 9111).

Boats travel from Kilmore Quay harbour roughly every hour in summer, between about 10.30am and 3pm. Actually docking on the islands depends on the wind direction: the operators will know the night before whether a landing is possible or not. It's a 30-minute crossing and the return fare is €20 per person (half price for children) if the boat is full, €80 if you're the only one on the boat.

For more on the islands read *Saltees: Islands of Birds and Legends* by Richard Roche and Oscar Merne (O'Brien Press).

COUNTIES WEXFORD & WATERFORD

PRINCE OF THE SALTEES

The Saltees were bought in 1943 by Michael Neale, who immediately proclaimed himself 'Prince of the Saltees'. Something of a strange one, he erected a throne and obelisk in his own honour on the Great Saltee, and had a full-blown coronation ceremony there in 1956. Although the College of Arms in London refuted Neale's claim to blue blood, he won a small victory when Wexford County Council began addressing letters to 'Prince Michael Neale'.

The prince broadcast his intentions of turning Great Saltee into a second Monte Carlo (once WWIII was over), but his immediate concern was a war right on his doorstep. In an escalation of hostilities, Neale released two ferrets, then a dozen foxes, then 46 cats onto the island to kill the rabbits that he hated so.

Prince Michael died in 1998, but before his death decreed 'All people, young and old, are welcome to come, see and enjoy the Islands, and leave them as they found them for the unborn generations to come, see and enjoy'.

HOOK PENINSULA & AROUND

☎ 051

The long, tapering finger of the Hook Peninsula is an undiscovered joy. There are no blockbustingly major visitor attractions, but around every other bend is a quiet beach, a crumbling fortress, a stately abbey or a mouthwatering seafood restaurant. In good weather, it's a fine journey out to the lighthouse at the tip of Hook Head, then back along the western side to Duncannon.

Cromwell's statement that Waterford town would fall 'by Hook or by Crooke' referred to the two possible landing points from which to take the area: here or at Crooke in County Waterford.

Duncormick to Wellington Bridge

Signposted as the Bannow Drive, this part of the county just east of the Hook Peninsula is littered with Norman ruins. **Baginbun Head**, south of Bannow Bay, was where the Normans' first landed (1169) for their conquest of Ireland. At **Bannow Bay** are the overgrown earthen ramparts built by the Normans when they first arrived. The stone **Martello tower** dates back to the early 19th century. The estuary here is a wildfowl sanctuary, rich in birdlife such as brent geese, redshank, wigeon and teal. It's also a top cultivation site for Irish oysters.

Look out for the ruins of a medieval village called **Clonmines**, which fell into decline when its estuary silted up. The ruins are on private land and access is prohibited, but you get a good view of them just south of the bridge as you come east into town.

The redbrick chimney in a paddock by the roadside on the north side of the bridge is an old **silver mine**. It was in operation from the 16th to the 19th century and supplied the Irish mint.

Tintern Abbey

On the way from Wellington Bridge out to Hook is a 12th-century Cistercian abbey in a lovely rural setting. **Tintern Abbey** (☎ 562 650; Saltmills; adult/child incl guided tour €2/1; ☼ 10am-6pm mid-Jun–Sep) was founded by William Marshall, earl of Pembroke, after he nearly perished at sea and swore to found a church if he ever made it back to dry land. The abbey was named after another abbey in Wales where its first monks came from. Make time for the **Tintern Trails**, 3km of woodland walks around the abbey estate, which is home to the whiskered bat, Ireland's rarest.

To get there, follow the signed left turn off the R734 at Saltmills.

Fethard-on-Sea

pop 863

Continuing southwards towards the Head, Fethard-on-Sea is the largest village in the area and home to the scant ruins of a 9th-century church and a 15th-century castle (too unstable to walk inside), which once belonged to the bishop of Ferns. There's a small but helpful **tourist office** (☎ /fax 397 502; www.thehook-wexford.com; Main St; ☼ 9.30am-5.30pm Mon-Fri) next door to the castle.

SLEEPING & EATING

Hotel Naomh Seosamh (☎ 397 129; Main St; s/d €30/60; **P**) Sitting right in the middle of Main St is this small-town hotel. It's under new management, and the new broom sure is sweeping clean: its rather old-fashioned rooms are to be completely revamped, and at the time of writing work was about to start on 30 brand-new bedrooms, to be built by summer 2006.

Ocean Island Camping & Caravan Park (☎ /fax 397 148; camp sites €18) This quiet little site about 1km north of town has a shop, a playground and a games room.

Village Kitchen (☎ 397 460; snacks €3.50-9; 🕑 11am-8pm Tue-Sun May-Oct, 11am-8pm Thu-Sat Nov-Apr) This is a pleasant coffee shop selling sandwiches and kids' favourites like burgers, chips and sausage-and-bacon baps.

Hook Head

The journey from Fethard out to **Hook Head** is a dream, with few houses interrupting the flat, open land. On a clear day you can see to the Blackstairs Mountains to the north. About 2km from the head, turning left at a T-junction brings you down to the village of **Slade**, where a ruined castle dominates the harbour.

Further south, dramatic Hook Head is crowned by Europe's, and possibly the world's, oldest working **lighthouse** (☎ 397 055; guided tours adult/child €5.50/3; 🕑 9am-5.30pm daily Mar-Oct, 9am-5.30pm Sat & Sun Nov-Feb), manned until 1996. In bad weather, sea spray often reaches the top of the 36m tower. It's said that monks lit a beacon on the Head from the 5th century and that the first Viking invaders were so happy to have a guiding light that they left the monks alone. In the 13th century a more-solid beacon was erected by Raymond le Gros, a structure that has remained almost unchanged for 800 years. Access to the lighthouse is by tour only: half-hourly in summer, hourly on winter weekends.

There are brilliant, blustery **walks** on both sides of the head, a haunting place in the evening. Be careful of the freak waves and numerous blowholes on the western side of the peninsula. The rocks around the lighthouse are Carboniferous limestone, rich in **fossils**. If you search carefully, you may find 350-million-year-old shells and tiny disc-like pieces of crinoids, a type of starfish. Hook Head is also a good vantage point for **bird-watching**: over 200 species have been recorded passing through. You might even get lucky and see dolphins or **whales**, particularly between November and February.

Coming back up the other side of the peninsula, about 5km from the lighthouse, is the enormous **Loftus Hall**, a privately owned, English-style mansion which looks desperately out of place here. The entire Hook Peninsula once formed part of the Loftus Estate.

Duncannon & Around

Driving from Hook Head towards Duncannon, you'll come across the ruins of a fortified **medieval church** on the left of the road opposite the Templar's Inn. In 1172, Henry II granted huge chunks of land hereabouts to the Knights Templar: they made nearby Templetown their HQ and built various churches, including this fairly intact 13th-century example.

There's something fantastically pleasing about the small holiday resort of Duncannon: the sandy Blue Flag beach, fine views of Waterford Harbour, pleasant eating-and-drinking options, and laid-back air all work a calming alchemy on your brain. In August, sand-sculptors transform the beach into a dream-like artwork at the **Duncannon International Sand Festival** (☎ 087-205 8491; ammonite@ireland.com).

To the west of the village is star-shaped **Duncannon Fort** (☎ 389 454; duncannonfort@hotmail .com; adult/child €4/2; 🕑 10am-5.30pm Jun–mid-Sep), used as a set for *The Count of Monte Cristo* starring Richard Harris and Guy Pearce. It was built in 1586 to stave off a feared attack by the Spanish Armada, and was later used by the Irish army as a WWI training base. There's a small maritime museum and a café.

About 4km northwest of Duncannon is pretty **Ballyhack**, from where a ferry sails year round to Passage East in County Waterford (see the boxed text, p196). It's dominated by 15th-century **Ballyhack Castle** (☎ 389 468; adult/child €1.50/75¢; 🕑 10am-6pm mid-Jun–mid-Sep), a Knights Hospitallers tower house, containing a small exhibition on the Crusades.

SLEEPING & EATING
Dunbrody Country House Hotel & Restaurant (☎ 389 600; www.dunbrodyhouse.com; Duncannon Hill, Arthurstown; s/d from €148/245, restaurant mains €19-27) This luxurious 1830s country manor has period-decorated rooms and some stunning grounds. Beds are encased in dazzling white linen, and fresh fruit and fluffy bathrobes

COUNTIES WEXFORD & WATERFORD

are provided. To further nourish body and soul, there's a spa and a superb gourmet restaurant, which has had hat-fulls of rave reviews. Learn some of their secrets by enlisting with the Dunbrody Cookery School.

Glendine House (☎ 389 258; www.glendine house.com; Duncannon Hill; s/d €65/100) Antique-decorated bedrooms with positively regal beds grace this gorgeous guesthouse. Bay windows overlook the sumptuous garden, where horses and deer graze and rabbits scamper. The staff are treasures, and there's Guinness bread for breakfast!

Sqigl Restaurant & Roches Bar (☎ 389 188; sqigl restaurant@eircom.net; Quay Rd, Duncannon; mains €10-18; bar food ☯ 12.30-5pm daily, restaurant ☯ 7-10.30pm Tue-Sat Apr-Sep, Wed-Sat Oct-Mar) Local produce – mostly seafood and lamb – is the mainstay of this fabulous barnyard restaurant (pronounced 'squiggle'). The pub next door (don't trip over the cannon) also serves some top-notch pub grub.

Templar's Inn (☎ 397 162; Templetown; dishes €4-15; ☯ 12.30-9pm daily Easter-Oct, noon-3pm & 5-8pm Mon-Sat, 12.30-9pm Sun Nov-Easter) This much-loved pub specialises in seafood and gets very crowded at lunchtimes. Outdoor seats look over green fields, a fortified medieval church and the swirling sea.

Dunbrody Abbey

Dunbrody Abbey is a beautiful 12th-century ruin on the western side of Hook Head, near the village of Campile (about 9km north of Duncannon). The **Dunbrody Abbey Visitor Centre** (☎ 388 603; www.dunbrodyabbey.com; adult/child €2/1; ☯ 10am-6pm Jul & Aug, 11am-5pm May, Jun & early Sep), as well as allowing entry to the abbey, contains the ruins of Dunbrody Castle, a small museum with a huge doll's house, a craft shop, pitch and putt, and an intricate yew-hedge **maze** (adult/child €4/2). Don't expect to get lost, though – it's still growing!

Scuba Diving

Hook Head is a favourite with divers. The best sites are out from the inlet under the lighthouse or from the rocks at the south-western corner of the head. Underwater scenery is pleasant, with lots of caves, crevasses and gullies, and it's a maximum of 15m deep. If it's too rough, try Church-town, about 1km back from the point just before the road goes inland by the ruined

church. Follow the path west to some gullies and coves. Otherwise, try the rocks south of Slade Harbour, a popular area.

The Pier House Dive Centre (see p181) in Kilmore Quay runs diving trips.

Getting There & Away
BUS
Bus services are virtually nonexistent to this part of Wexford. If you do catch one, you may end up stuck somewhere for a couple of days.

On Monday, Wednesday, Thursday and Saturday, **Bus Éireann** (☎ 01-836 6111) No 370 between Waterford and Wexford stops in Wellington Bridge. The trip takes about 40 minutes and you need to ask the bus driver for the price.

On Mondays and Thursdays, a Bus Éireann Waterford–New Ross–Wexford service runs in each direction, leaving Waterford at 9.45am, and returning from Wexford at 2.50pm, calling at Fethard-on-Sea (€9, one hour), Templetown (€8.20, 1¼ hours), Duncannon (€8.20, 1½ hours) and Campile (€8.20, 1¾ hours).

One service per day runs from Monday to Saturday between Waterford and Duncannon.

One **RTI bus** (☎ 087-251 9614) runs on Saturday between Fethard-on-Sea, Duncannon, Arthurstown, Campile, New Ross and Waterford, leaving Fethard at 10am and returning from Waterford at 4pm. Another **RTI bus** (☎ 389 418) runs on Tuesday and Thursday between Fethard and New Ross, leaving Fethard at 9.35am and New Ross at 12.45pm. Return to New Ross/Waterford costs €5/8.

FERRY
If you're travelling on to Waterford, it's well worth taking the Ballyhack to Passage East ferry, which saves you a long drive northwards via New Ross. For details see the boxed text on p196.

NEW ROSS
☎ 051 / pop 4810
The big attraction at New Ross (Rhos Mhic Triúin), 34km west of Wexford town, is the unique opportunity to board a 19th-century Famine ship. The town, which developed as a 12th-century Norman port on the River Barrow, also advertises itself as

the 'Norman gateway to the Barrow Valley', although you'd have to squint to find any traces of its Norman past. It's not especially pretty, with large oil-storage tanks and looming old warehouses, but the eastern bank has some intriguing steep, narrow streets and St Mary's Church.

New Ross was the scene of fierce fighting during the 1798 Rising when a group of rebels tried to take the town. They were repelled by the defending garrison, leaving 3000 people dead and much of the place in ruins.

The **tourist office** (☎ 421 857; The Quay; ⓨ 9am-6pm Apr-Sep, 10am-5pm Oct-Mar) is inside the Dunbrody Visitor Centre, where there's also a small café. Surf the net at **Ross Net** (92 Mary St; per hr €5; ⓨ 11am-10pm).

Sights & Activities

Clutching an 1840s ticket, you can board the **Dunbrody Heritage Ship** (☎ 425 239; www .dunbrody.com; adult/child €6.50/4; ⓨ 9am-6pm Apr-Sep, 10am-5pm Oct-Mar), a full-scale reconstruction of an 1845 sailing ship, and learn about the poor souls forced to emigrate to the US during the Famine. Their sorrowful, sometimes inspiring stories are brought to life by actors. The quayside visitor centre has a short film detailing the history of the original three-masted barque and the construction of the new one. There's also a database of Irish emigration to America from 1820 to 1920, containing over two million records.

A great idea for a drowsy day is to book a two- to three-hour cruise on the **Galley River Cruising Restaurant** (☎ 421 723; www.river cruises.ie; North Quay; cruise €25, cruise & dinner €40; ⓨ Easter-Oct). The boat drifts slowly up the River Barrow, through rolling fields and peaceful farmlands, while you just enjoy the ride (€10 to €15), or enhance it by tucking into a quality meal and some good wine.

The roofless ruin on Church Lane is **St Mary's Abbey**, one of the largest medieval churches in Ireland. It was founded by Isabella of Leinster and her husband, William, in the 13th century. The church key is available from the caretaker at 10 Church Lane.

Sleeping & Eating

MacMurrough Farm Hostel (☎ 421 383; www.mac murrough.com; MacMurrough; dm €13-15, d €30; ⓟ) Brian, Jenny and the family dog give every

visitor a warm reception at this wonderfully peaceful hostel. It's so snug, you'd never guess it used to be a hen house! There's equally quaint two-person self-catering accommodation (€350 per week) in the old stables. The hostel is 5km northeast of town: phone first for directions.

Riversdale House (☎ 422 515; www.riversdale house.com; Lower William St; s/d €45/70; ⓨ Feb-Nov; ⓟ) This is the only town-centre B&B, so it's good news that it's such a welcoming place to stay. The mellow orange rooms are spotless, and look out onto tranquil gardens, and you can relax in the pleasant conservatory. Ann, the owner, is a cheery, energetic type who makes guests feel right at home.

Brandon House Hotel (☎ 421 703; www.brandon househotel.ie; Rosslare Rd; s/d €110/170; ⓟ ▣ ▢) The Brandon, 2km south of New Ross, is an upscale hotel: open log fires in the lobby, quality art on the walls, extensive gardens, and rooms big enough for a small family. There's also a deluxe health and leisure club, featuring the full Jacuzzi-pool-gym-sauna-spa complement.

Upper Deck Café (☎ /fax 425 391; 8 Mary St; sandwiches €4-7, mains €6-10; ⓨ 9am-5.30pm Mon-Sat) This café tries hard despite the lack of competition: it's cosy, modern, and offers a decent array of comforting grub. Grab a quick sandwich, or make a meal of it with a hot-counter special: chicken and broccoli bake, steaks, lasagnes and grills.

Getting There & Away

Bus Éireann (☎ 051-879 000) buses depart from Ryan Brothers on the quay and travel to Waterford (€5.50, 20 minutes, nine daily Monday to Saturday, seven Sunday), Dublin (€10.50, three hours, four daily), Rosslare Harbour (€10.80, one hour, four daily Monday to Saturday, three Sunday) and Wexford (€8.50, 40 minutes, six daily Monday to Saturday, two Sunday).

AROUND NEW ROSS

About 5km south of New Ross, **Dunganstown** was the birthplace of Patrick Kennedy, grandfather of John F Kennedy, who left Ireland for the USA in 1858. JFK visited the town during his presidency. The original Kennedy house no longer exists, but a small plaque marks the spot where it stood. Nearby is the **Kennedy Visitor Centre** (☎ 051-388264; www.kennedyhomestead.com; Dunganstown;

adult/child €4/2.50; ⏲ 10am-5pm Jul & Aug, 11.30am-4.30pm Mon-Fri May, Jun & Sep), which celebrates five generations of the Irish-American dynasty – no mention of Grandad Kennedy's bootlegging career or JFK's penchant for ladies that he wasn't married to.

Containing an awesome 4500 species of trees and shrubs, all thriving in 252 hectares of woodlands and gardens, the **John F Kennedy Arboretum** (☎ 051-388 171; jfkarboretum@opw.ie; New Ross; adult/child €2.75/1.25; ⏲ 10am-6.30pm Apr & Sep, 10am-5pm Oct-Mar) is one for a sunny day. The park, 2km south of the Kennedy Visitor Centre, was funded by prominent Irish-Americans as a memorial to JFK, and was opened by Eamon de Valera in 1968. There's a small visitor centre, tearooms and a picnic area.

Slieve Coillte, opposite the park entrance, has a viewing point at the top from where you can see the whole of the arboretum and six counties on a clear day.

ENNISCORTHY
☎ 054 / pop 3764

An attractive market town, Enniscorthy (Inis Coirthaidh) has lots of steep little lanes, running from Pugin's cathedral past the mighty castle and down across the meandering River Slaney.

For the Irish, Enniscorthy is forever linked to some of the fiercest fighting of the 1798 Rising, when rebels captured the town and set up camp nearby at Vinegar Hill. A visitor centre tells the bloody story brilliantly.

Information

The local **tourist office** (☎ 37596; Mill Park Rd; ⏲ 9.30am-5pm Mon-Fri, 11am-5pm Sat & Sun Easter-Sep, 9.30am-4pm Mon-Fri Oct-Easter) is inside the 1798 Visitor Centre. Grab a free *Enniscorthy Town Trail* map.

One-hour **guided walks** (€5), in English or French, of the town can be booked for a minimum of five people at **Castle Hill Crafts & Tours** (☎ 36800; fax 35910; Castle Hill), run by the knowledgeable Maura.

At the bottom of Castle Hill, on Abbey Sq, there's a Bank of Ireland and the main post office.

Sights
NATIONAL 1798 REBELLION CENTRE
Heralded as Ireland's best museum, the interpretative **National 1798 Rebellion Centre**

(☎ 37596; 98com@iol.ie; Mill Park Rd; adult/child €6/3.50; ⏲ 9.30am-5pm Mon-Fri, 11am-5pm Sat & Sun Easter-Sep, 9.30am-4pm Mon-Fri Oct-Easter) is well worth the admission cost. It explores 18th-century revolutionary ideals, and commemorates Wexford's abortive uprising against British rule in Ireland. Rich interactive displays and audiovisuals highlight the circumstances and events surrounding the rebellion, as well as the fate of the rebels, most of whom were butchered with impunity by Crown forces.

From Abbey Sq walk along Mill Park Rd, then take the first right after the school.

ENNISCORTHY CASTLE & WEXFORD COUNTY MUSEUM
The Normans left Enniscorthy a strong, stout, four-towered **castle** (☎ 35926; Castle St; adult/child €4.50/1; ⏲ 10am-1pm & 2-6pm Mon-Sat, 2-5.30pm Sun Jun-Sep, 2-5.30pm daily Oct-Nov & Feb-May, 2-5.30pm Sun Dec & Jan). Queen Elizabeth I awarded its lease to the poet Edmund Spenser for the flattering things he said about her in his epic *The Faerie Queene*. Rather ungratefully, he sold it on to a local landlord.

Like everything else in these parts, the castle was attacked by Cromwell in 1649. During the 1798 Rising rebels took control of the town and used the building as a prison.

Inside the castle is the Wexford County Museum, a rare specimen itself: information comes at you, not on interactive computer screens, but on charming hand-written labels, yellowed with age. The ground floor contains a jaunting car and brougham carriage; the 1st floor covers the 1916 Easter Rising and the 1798 Rebellion; and a delightfully dusty display of battered ships' figureheads, ancient bicycles and rusty farm implements greets you at the top. You can also visit the dungeon, a horrid cramped cell with Elizabethan graffiti scratched into the wall.

ST AIDAN'S CATHEDRAL
Lovingly restored to its original glory (check out the star-spangled roof), this impressive Roman Catholic cathedral (1846) was designed by Augustus Pugin, who had a passion for late-13th- and early-14th-century Gothic architecture. The son of a French immigrant, he was also respon-

sible for designing the Houses of Parliament in London.

VINEGAR HILL

Every Irish schoolchild knows the name of Vinegar Hill, associated with bravery, butchery, and one of the most bloodthirsty battles of the 1798 Rebellion.

After capturing Enniscorthy, a group of rebels set up camp around the 17th-century windmill on Vinegar Hill. A month later, on the morning of 21 June, English troops attacked and eventually forced the rebels to retreat. Hundreds of camp followers – women and children – were massacred in the 'follow-up' operation. The insurgents' defeat was a turning point in the rebellion.

At the top of the hill there's a memorial to the uprising, and panoramic views of the Slaney and surrounding countryside. To get there, follow the sign from Templeshannon on the eastern side of the river that says 'Vinegar Hill 2km' – *not* the sign that mentions the golf course and Country House as well. It should take you about 30 minutes to walk there.

Activities

Enniscorthy Golf Club (☎ 37600; New Ross Rd; green fee weekday/weekend €25/35), with an 18-hole course, is 2.5km southwest of town.

There's plenty of good **fishing** in the Slaney.

Festivals & Events

Enniscorthy holds its **Strawberry Fair** in late June/early July, when pubs extend their hours, and strawberries and cream are laid on heavily. For exact dates and details phone ☎ 21688.

The **Blackstair Blues Festival** (☎ 35364), over a weekend in mid-September, attracts international artists and appreciators.

Sleeping

Old Bridge House (☎ 34222; obhouse@indigo.ie; Slaney Pl; s/d €35/60) This individualistic B&B is the perfect antidote to big-hotel blandness. It's a homy house overlooking the river, where Indian wall hangings nestle alongside WWI rifles. In summer, visitors can relax on the small sundeck.

Treacy's Hotel (☎ 37798; www.treacyshotel.com; Templeshannon; s/d €80/140) Just over Enniscorthy Bridge, the 60 rooms at Treacy's are a little

overpriced, but service is good. It's geared to overseas tourists, with laid-on entertainments like Irish-dancing displays. Guests can use the leisure centre opposite for free, with its pool, sauna and gym. The hotel's Thai restaurant is popular with locals.

Murphy Floods Hotel (☎ 39252; fax 39255; 27 Main St; s/d €50/90; **P**) Conveniently close to Market Sq, two-star Murphy Floods is something of an Enniscorthy institution. Rooms are cheerful, rates include breakfast, and prices drop slightly during the week.

PJ Murphy's (☎ 33522; 9 Main St; s/d from €30/50; **P**) This funny little place makes no concessions to the 21st century. Mrs Murphy's B&B rooms are located above a pub, so a malty, beery scent wafts occasionally up the stairs. The place is comfortable enough for the price, though, and there's a (microscopic) car park out back.

Eating

Galo Chargrill Restaurant (☎ 38077; 19 Main St; mains €10-16; ☽ noon-3pm & 5.30-10pm Tue-Sun) Great smells emanate from this Portuguese place. It specialises in grilled meat and fish, but you can also get pasta and vegetarian dishes. Bookings are advisable on Friday and Saturday nights.

De Olde Bridge (☎ 38624; 2 Templeshannon; snacks €2.50-4, meals €4-10; ☽ 8am-4pm Mon-Sat, 9am-4pm Sun) This is the place to go for cheap, old-fashioned meals, like stuffed turkey, lamb cutlets or a full Irish breakfast.

A good **farmers' market** (☎ 087-411 4481; Abbey Sq; ☽ 9am-2pm Sat) sells local and organic veg, bacon, cheese, bread, fish and fruit.

There are three recommended cafés on Rafter St: **Toffee & Thyme** (☎ 37144; meals €4.50-8; ☽ 8.30am-6pm Mon-Sat), **Baked Potato** (☎ 34085; meals €4-8; ☽ 8am-6pm Mon-Sat) and **Cozy Kitchen** (☎ 36488; meals €5-6.50; ☽ 9am-6pm Mon-Sat), selling a combination of spuds, salads, soups, homemade bread and cakes.

Drinking & Entertainment

There are plenty of pubs in Enniscorthy. Most of those directed at a younger crowd are on the eastern side of the river, especially along Templeshannon.

Antique Tavern (☎ 33428; 14 Slaney St) This tiny, half-timbered tavern down by the river is closed to 'footpads, thimblemen or three-card tricksters'.

White House (☎ 33096; Templeshannon) The

small, inviting White House has live music every weekend during summer (Sundays only the rest of the year).

Slaney Plaza Cinema (☎ 37060; www.slaneyplaza .net; Templeshannon) Mainstream and art-house films cost €4/7 for matinée/evening shows.

Shopping

The Enniscorthy area has been recognised as a centre of pottery since the 17th century. The tourist office has a free pottery-trail guide. One of the oldest, dating back to the 1650s, is **Carley's Bridge Potteries** (☎ 33512; fax 34360; � 9am-5.30pm Mon-Fri, 11am-4.30pm Sat, 2-4.30pm Sun), on the road to New Ross.

Getting There & Away
BUS

Bus Éireann (☎ 01-836 6111) stops on Templeshannon Quay on the eastern bank of the river, outside the **Bus Stop Shop** (☎ 33291; � 9am-10pm) where you can buy tickets. There are 11 buses daily Monday to Saturday (10 Sunday) to Dublin (€10.50, two hours), Wexford (€5.10, one hour) and Rosslare Harbour (€8.20, one hour).

TRAIN

The **train station** (☎ 33488) is on the eastern bank of the river. The one line serves Dublin (€18.50, 2¼ hours), Wexford (€5.50, 30 minutes) and Rosslare Europort (€6.50, one hour) three times daily.

FERNS
☎ 054 / pop 1230

Pay a visit to this sleepy village to ruminate on the crumbling of empires. Ferns was the powerhouse of the kings of Leinster, in particular Dermot MacMurrough (1110–71), whose name is forever associated with bringing the Normans to Ireland (see p34). The Normans left behind a doughty castle, later smashed to pieces by Cromwell, and the remains of a cathedral.

As you only need an hour or so to take in the sights, you're better off using bigger Enniscorthy, about 12km southwest, as a base.

Sights

The most impressive sight is **Ferns Castle** (adult/child €1.50/75¢; � 10am-6pm mid-Jun–mid-Sep, last admission 45 mins before closing), built around 1220 at the northwestern end of the vil-

lage. A couple of walls and part of the moat survive, and you can climb to the top of the one complete tower. Parliamentarians destroyed the castle and put most of the local population to death in 1649. The ruins are thought to stand on the site of Dermot MacMurrough's old fortress.

At the eastern end of the main street is **St Edan's Cathedral**, built in early Gothic style in 1817. Its **graveyard** contains a ruined high cross, said to mark the resting place of Dermot MacMurrough.

Behind the cathedral are two shells of buildings: **Ferns Cathedral**, built by Normans in the 13th century; and behind that, the remains of **St Mary's Abbey**. It was founded by Dermot MacMurrough in 1158 and has an unusual square-based round tower. Down the main road is **St Peter's Church**, built from stones taken magpie-like from Ferns Cathedral and St Mary's Abbey.

Getting There & Away

Ferns is on the **Bus Éireann** (☎ 01-836 6111) Dublin to Rosslare Harbour route via Wexford and Enniscorthy, with 11 buses Monday to Saturday, 10 Sunday. Buses from Dublin to Waterford also stop in Ferns three times per day (€10.50, three hours).

MT LEINSTER

The highest peak in the Blackstairs is Mt Leinster (796m), which has magnificent views of counties Waterford, Carlow, Kilkenny and Wicklow from the top.

If you're walking, Bunclody (16km northwest of Ferns) is a good place to start from. Drivers should follow the South Leinster Scenic Drive signs, which appear around Borris. The last few kilometres are on narrow, exposed roads with steep fall-offs, so drive slowly and watch out for sheep.

Mt Leinster is home to some of Ireland's best hang-gliding: contact the **Irish Hang Gliding & Paragliding Association** (http://ihpa.ie) for up-to-date information.

For guided walks in the Blackstairs Mountains, contact **Brian Gilsenan** (☎ 054-77828).

COUNTY WATERFORD

It feels as though the Celtic Tiger wandered off for a snooze before it reached County Waterford, but that's all to the good. The

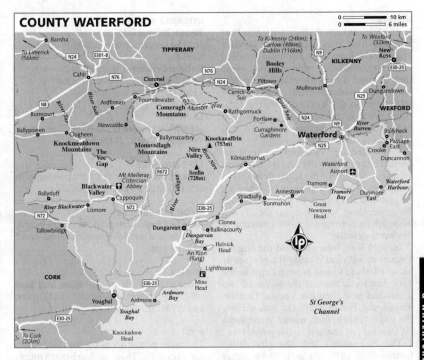

COUNTY WATERFORD

county's charms haven't been overhyped by aggressive marketing: they're just left for you to discover at your own pace.

Waterford's attractive sandy coastline has seaside resorts to suit everyone, with the candy-floss-and-chips town of Tramore, genteel Dunmore East, and historic Ardmore's golden beaches and cliff-top walks. Jutting out to sea, Helvick Head hides unspoilt An Rinn, a Gaeltacht (Irish-speaking) area with its own road signs, heritage and culture.

Long maligned Waterford town has been rejuvenated in the last few years and now contains one of Ireland's flashiest attractions: half theme-park, half museum.

The Nire Valley, nestling between the Comeragh and Monavullagh Mountains, feels like a lost world. Its easy air, friendly folk and beautiful rolling hills are worth exploring: walks are enlivened by countless barrows and standing stones, and a Bronze Age stone circle.

The tranquil River Blackwater runs through the county, gathering up the little towns of Cappoquin and lovely Lismore

on its banks. The latter is home to a pre-Raphaelite window by Edward Burne-Jones (the only one in Ireland) and more history than a person knows what to do with.

WATERFORD TOWN

☎ 051 / pop 44,594

Ireland's oldest city, Waterford (Port Láirge), is first and foremost a busy commercial port. Some parts of the city still feel almost medieval, though, with narrow alleyways leading off many of the larger streets. Reginald's Tower marks the city's Viking heart and there are some attractive Georgian homes and warehouses. Ireland's flashiest museum, on the quays, uses state-of-the-art computer wizardry to get Waterford's history across; continue the sensory stimulation with a tour round the Waterford Crystal factory.

Although that seedy port-town feel is still evident in places, the city has received a facelift in recent years. Pedestrianised streets and public artworks have improved the centre, and it's now a more attractive place to stroll around.

History

In the 8th century Vikings settled at Port Láirge, which they renamed Vadrafjord and quickly turned into a booming trading post. To consolidate their presence there, they adopted a ferocity which made Waterford the most powerful – and feared – settlement in the country. All the local tribes paid a tribute known as *Airgead Sróine* (nose money): any defaulters had their noses cut off!

Acknowledging Waterford's strategic importance, the newly arrived Anglo-Normans attacked the town in 1170, defeating a combined Irish-Viking army and hurling 70 prominent citizens to their deaths off Baginbun Head. Later that year the city was besieged by Strongbow, who overcame a desperate defence.

In 1210 King John extended the original Viking city walls and Waterford subsequently became Ireland's most powerful city. In the 15th century it resisted the forces of two pretenders to the English Crown, Lambert Simnel and Perkin Warbeck, thus earning the motto *Urbs intacta manet Waterfordia* (Waterford city remains unconquered).

The luck didn't last: the city defied Cromwell in 1649, but in 1650 his forces returned and Waterford surrendered. Although the town escaped the customary slaughter, Waterford's Catholics were either exiled to the west or shipped as slaves to the Caribbean, and the population declined.

Orientation

Waterford lies on the tidal reach of the River Suir, 16km from the coast. The main shopping street runs directly south from the Suir, beginning as Barronstrand St and changing names to become Michael St and John St before it intersects with Parnell St. This runs northeast back up to the river, becoming The Mall on the way. Most of the sights and shopping areas lie within this triangle.

Information

BOOKSHOPS

Gladstone's Book Shop (12 Gladstone St) Second-hand paperbacks.

Waterford Book Centre (☎ 873 823; 25 Barronstrand St; ⏰ 9am-6pm Mon-Thu & Sat, 9am-9pm Fri, 2-6pm Sun) An excellent store with three floors of books (including some foreign papers and magazines) and records; there's also a café.

INTERNET ACCESS

Voyager Internet Café (☎ 843 843; www.voyager .ie; 85 The Quay; per 30/60min €3.60/6; ⏰ 10am-9pm Mon-Sat)

Waterford e-Centre (☎ 878 448; 10 O'Connell St; per 30/60min €3.20/5; ⏰ 9.30am-9pm Mon-Thu, 9.30am-8pm Fri & Sat, 11am-6pm Sun)

LAUNDRY

Snow White Laundrette (☎ 858 905; Mayor's Walk; ⏰ 9.30am-1.30pm & 2.30-6pm Mon-Sat)

LEFT LUGGAGE

Plunkett train station (☎ 873 401) Leave luggage for €2.50 per item per 24 hours.

MEDICAL SERVICES

Waterford Regional Hospital (☎ 873 321; Dunmore Rd) A little out of town. Follow the quays east and watch out for the signs.

MONEY

There's a branch of the **Allied Irish Bank** (☎ 874 824; Meagher Quay) by the clock tower, and ATMs throughout the town.

POST

The main post office is on Parade Quay in the city centre. There are two branch offices on O'Connell St and High St, open weekdays only (half-day Thursday).

TOILETS

You'll find public toilets on Merchant's Quay near the bus station, and others further down near the clock tower.

TOURIST INFORMATION

Waterford city tourist office (☎ 875 788; www .southeastireland.com; Merchants Quay; ⏰ 9am-6pm Mon-Fri, 10am-6pm Sat May-Sep, 9am-5pm Mon-Sat Oct-Apr) Friendly central office, based in the Granary.

Waterford Crystal tourist office (☎ 332 585; www .southeastireland.com; Cork Rd; ⏰ 8.30am-6pm Mar-Oct, 9am-5pm Nov-Feb) If the central office is closed, this one has longer opening hours.

Sights & Activities

WATERFORD MUSEUM OF TREASURES

Ireland's most hi-tech attraction has to be the **Waterford Museum of Treasures** (☎ 304 500; www.waterfordtreasures.com; Hanover St; adult/child €6/3.20; ⏰ 9am-6pm Mon-Sat, 11am-6pm Sun Apr-Sep, 10am-5pm Mon-Sat, 11am-5pm Sun Oct-Mar), a dazzling, intriguing, provoking and at times

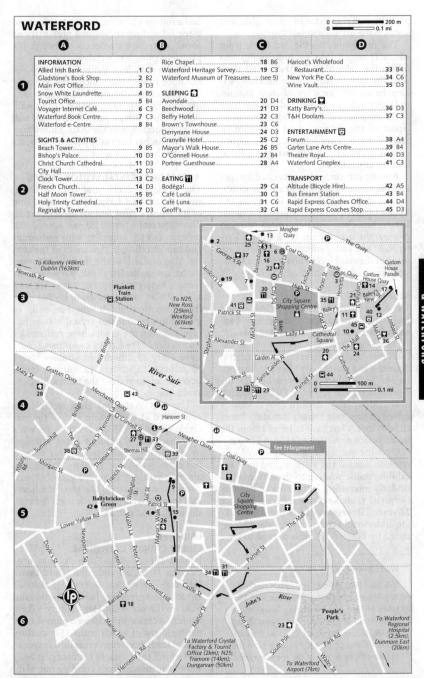

WATERFORD

0 — 200 m
0 — 0.1 mi

INFORMATION
Allied Irish Bank................................1 C3
Gladstone's Book Shop.....................2 B2
Main Post Office..............................3 D3
Snow White Laundrette.....................4 B5
Tourist Office..................................5 B4
Voyager Internet Café.......................6 C3
Waterford Book Centre......................7 C3
Waterford e-Centre..........................8 B4

SIGHTS & ACTIVITIES
Beach Tower....................................9 B5
Bishop's Palace..............................10 D3
Christ Church Cathedral...................11 D3
City Hall.......................................12 D3
Clock Tower...................................13 C2
French Church................................14 D3
Half Moon Tower............................15 B5
Holy Trinity Cathedral.....................16 C3
Reginald's Tower.............................17 D3

Rice Chapel...................................18 B6
Waterford Heritage Survey...............19 C3
Waterford Museum of Treasures.....(see 5)

SLEEPING 🏠
Avondale......................................20 D4
Beechwood...................................21 D3
Belfry Hotel..................................22 C3
Brown's Townhouse........................23 C6
Derrynane House............................24 D3
Granville Hotel..............................25 C2
Mayor's Walk House.......................26 B5
O'Connell House............................27 B4
Portree Guesthouse.......................28 A4

EATING 🍴
Bodéga!.......................................29 C4
Café Lucia....................................30 C3
Café Luna.....................................31 C6
Geoff's..32 C4

Haricot's Wholefood
   Restaurant.................................33 B4
New York Pie Co............................34 C6
Wine Vault...................................35 D3

DRINKING 🍷
Katty Barry's.................................36 D3
T&H Doolans.................................37 C3

ENTERTAINMENT 🎭
Forum..38 A4
Garter Lane Arts Centre..................39 D3
Theatre Royal...............................40 D3
Waterford Cineplex........................41 C3

TRANSPORT
Altitude (Bicycle Hire).....................42 A5
Bus Éireann Station........................43 B4
Rapid Express Coaches Office...........44 D4
Rapid Express Coaches Stop.............45 D3

To Kilkenny (48km);
Dublin (163km)
Newrath Rd

Plunkett Train Station

To N25, New Ross (25km); Wexford (61km)

Dock Rd

Rice Bridge

River Suir

Grattan Quay

Mary St

Merchants Quay

Hanover St

Meagher Quay

Coal Quay

See Enlargement

City Square Shopping Centre

The Mall

Parnell St

John's River

People's Park

Castle St

Manor St

John St

South Pde

Park Rd

Water St

Convent Hill

Barrack St

Manor Hill

Hennessy's Rd

To Waterford Crystal Factory & Tourist Office (2km); N25; Tramore (14km); Dungarvan (50km)

To Waterford Airport (7km)

To Waterford Regional Hospital (2.5km); Dunmore East (20km)

Ballybricken Green

Meagher Quay

George's St

Jenkin's La

Patrick St

Alexander St

New St

John's La

City Square Shopping Centre

Custom House Parade

Lombard St

The Mall

Cathedral Square

Garden Al

Spring Garden Al

Catherine St

Parnell St

100 m
0.1 mi

plain bewildering maze of metal, glass and state-of-the-art audiovisual displays.

The fun begins on the 3rd floor, from where (plugged into an audioguide) you follow the exhibitions as they wend their way through history. Disembodied Viking heads tell the story of their journey to Waterford; you can attend the marriage of Strongbow and Aiofe (strangely reminiscent of the Princess Leia hologram in *Star Wars*); or have a laugh at the silhouette show, which actually makes medieval statutes entertaining.

Among the computer-generated images and the smoke-and-mirrors are real exhibits, but they can feel a little lost under the weight of 21st-century technology! Golden Viking brooches, jewel-encrusted Norman crosses, the magnificent 1372 Great Charter Roll, and 18th-century church silver are some of the solid bits of booty from a thousand years of urban history.

REGINALD'S TOWER

The oldest complete building in Ireland and the first to use mortar, 12th-century **Reginald's Tower** (☎ 873 501; The Quay; adult/child €2/1; ⏰ 10am-5.15pm Easter-Oct, 10am-4.15pm Wed-Sun Nov-Easter) is an outstanding example of medieval defences, and was the city's key fortification. Its 3m- to 4m-thick walls were built by the Normans on the site of a Viking wooden tower. Many of Waterford's royal visitors stayed in this 'safe house', including James II, who took a last look at Ireland from the tower before departing to exile in France.

Over the years, the building served as a mint, an arsenal and a prison, and there are exhibits inside relating to these roles. Particularly interesting is the story of bad boy Germyn Lynch, Keeper of the Irish Mint for 22 years. He was sacked five times for making underweight coins, but was always reinstated by Edward IV, who seemed to have

had a soft spot for him! On the top floor are three interesting audiovisual presentations about Waterford's defences, although it's probably enough to watch just one.

On the outside of the building, look for the door into space, which once led onto the city ramparts; and Cromwell's calling card, a cannonball lodged in the wall. Behind the tower, a section of the **old wall** is incorporated into the Axis Mundi bar. The two arches were sally ports, to let boats 'sally forth' into the inlet.

WATERFORD CRYSTAL VISITOR CENTRE

The pride of every middle-class living room, Waterford Crystal has become one of the world's most famous luxury brands. The **visitor centre** (☎ 332 500; www.waterfordvisitor centre.com; Cork Rd), complete with restaurant and tourist office, is 2km south of the centre. You can lurk in the **shop** (⏰ 8.30am-6pm Mar-Oct, 9am-5pm Nov-Feb) at will, but we recommend a **factory tour** (adult/child €8/free; ⏰ 8.30am-4.15pm Mar-Oct, 9am-3.15pm Mon-Fri Nov-Feb). The transformation of glowing-hot balls of glass into diamond-cut crystal is near miraculous, and the guides have real insider knowledge of the factory's workings. Tours leave every 15 minutes in summer (every 45 minutes in winter). In summer buy a ticket in advance from the tourist office to avoid queues.

The first Waterford glass factory was established at the western end of the riverside quays in 1783, but closed 68 years later because of punitive taxes imposed by the British. The business was revived last century and now employs 700 people, among them highly skilled glass blowers, cutters and engravers. The glass is a heavy lead (over 30%) crystal made from red lead, silica sand and potash.

Churches

CHRIST CHURCH CATHEDRAL

Behind City Hall is Europe's only neo-classical Georgian cathedral, **Christ Church Cathedral** (☎ 858 958; Cathedral Sq; adult/child €3/1.50), designed by John Roberts and built on the site of an 11th-century Viking church. Admission includes a guided tour, the highlight of which is the 15th-century **tomb of James Rice**, seven times lord mayor of Waterford: the statue of his decaying body shows worms and frogs crawling out of it.

COUNTIES WEXFORD & WATERFORD

WATERFORD CITY PASS

This pass (€10.25) gets you into Waterford's 'Big Three' attractions: the Waterford Museum of Treasures, Reginald's Tower and a guided tour of the Waterford Crystal Visitor Centre, saving you a nifty €5.75 on the individual admission prices. Pick it up from the tourist offices or any of the three centres.

Fantastic acoustics mean that the building is a prime **concert venue**, and not just for churchy music. Traditional fiddlers, a baroque orchestra and a uilleann piper were just some of the performers at the time of writing. Pick up a programme from the cathedral's information desk.

HOLY TRINITY CATHEDRAL

The sumptuous interior of the Catholic **Holy Trinity Cathedral** (Barronstrand St) boasts a carved-oak Baroque pulpit, painted pillars with Corinthian capitals and 10 Waterford Crystal chandeliers. It was built between 1792 and 1796 by John Roberts, who (equitably) also designed the Protestant Christ Church Cathedral.

FRENCH CHURCH

Sitting on Greyfriars St you'll find the elegant ruins of a French Church given to Franciscan monks in 1240 by Hugh Purcell. In exchange he asked them to pray for him once a day. The church became a hospital after the dissolution of the monasteries, and was then occupied by French Huguenot refugees between 1693 and 1815. Ask the staff at Reginald's Tower to let you in.

RICE CHAPEL

Edmund Ignatius Rice, founder of the Christian Brothers, established his first school at Mt Sion on Barrack St, where the Rice Chapel is a delightful combination of red brick and stained glass. Rice's tomb takes pride of place, awaiting the likely canonisation of its occupant.

Other Buildings

The Mall, a wide 18th-century street built on reclaimed land, was once a tidal inlet. From the river end, its stateliest buildings are **City Hall**, built in 1788 by local architect John Roberts; the **Theatre Royal**, also designed by Roberts and arguably Ireland's most intact 18th-century theatre; and the austere **Bishop's Palace** (1741), a Richard Cassels creation, now the city engineering offices.

Crumbling fragments of the old city wall include **Half Moon Tower** near Patrick St, and **Beach Tower** at the top of Jenkin's Lane.

Genealogical Centre

If you have ancestors from the county, **Waterford Heritage Survey** (☎ 876 123; Jenkin's La;

(✆ 9am-1pm & 2-5pm Mon-Thu, 9am-2pm Fri) may have the details you need to complete the family tree.

Tours

A must-do for any visitor to Waterford is Jack Burtchaell's **guided walking tour** (☎ 873 711, 851 043; €5; ✆ 11.45am & 1.45pm Easter-Sep). Jack is blessed with the 'gift of the gab', and brings every nook and cranny of this tiny city alive, effortlessly squeezing 1000 years of history into one wonderful hour. Be warned, audience participation is expected! Tours leave from outside the Waterford Museum of Treasures, picking up walkers from the Granville Hotel en route.

Festivals & Events

Waterford's **International Light Opera Festival** takes place in September and October. It's cheaper and more easily accessible than the more famous Wexford Festival Opera but booking is still advisable. For more details contact the **Theatre Royal** (☎ 874 402; The Mall).

Sleeping

The frequency of buses to Tramore means you can stay there and commute into town. Waterford is disappointingly lacking in good, central B&Bs, and since the closure of Waterford's hostel, Tramore's certainly the better option for budget accommodation.

MIDRANGE

Brown's Townhouse (☎ 870 594; www.brownstownhouse.com; 29 South Pde; d €100; ✆ closed Jan; 🖳) This lovely Victorian town house, near the People's Park, has snug beds in comfy rooms. There's broadband Internet connection, and breakfasts are the most thoughtful in town: guests sit sociably round one table, and can choose alternatives like pancakes instead of a full-on Irish fry.

Portree Guesthouse (☎ 874 574; Mary St; s/d/tr €45/70/105; 🅿) You might not guess from the drab grey exterior, but the Portree hides fine Georgian innards and a smashing B&B. It's on a quiet street, which is a huge bonus in noisy Waterford.

Beechwood (☎ 876 677; marybryan05@yahoo.co.uk; 7 Cathedral Sq; s/d €40/55) Welcome to Mrs Ryan's house, where you'll soon feel like one of the family. This cosy little B&B is a real home-away-from-home, on peaceful Cathedral Sq.

THREE THINGS YOU DIDN'T KNOW ABOUT WATERFORD

- Ireland's first frog was released here.

- A *shellicky boo-ky* is a Waterford garden snail.

- To save on grave diggers and gallows, prisoners of the 1798 Rebellion were hung from a lifting bridge, then cut down into the river once they were dead!

Avondale (☎ 852 267; www.staywithus.net; 2 Parnell St; d €80) Red-carpeted Avondale has a homy feel, with pleasant no-smoking rooms in a central location. The road's noisy, though: if it's likely to bother you, ask for a room at the back.

Mayor's Walk House (☎ 855 427; mayorswalk bandb@eircom.net; 12 Mayor's Walk; s/d €26/46) This is a respectable B&B in a tall, thin building. The landing bathrooms are shared, but the large (if dated) rooms have their own washbasins.

TOP END

Granville Hotel (☎ 305 555; www.granville-hotel.ie; Meagher Quay; s/d €130/190; P) In a floodlit 18th-century building overlooking the river is the Granville, one of Ireland's oldest hotels. Public rooms and bedrooms maintain a touch of Georgian elegance. The hotel's had its share of famous guests: Charles Stuart Parnell gave one of his last speeches from a 1st-floor window.

Belfry Hotel (☎ 844 800; www.belfryhotel.ie; Conduit La; s/d €100/150) Waterford's new city-centre hotel has standard, modern card-key rooms, which are devoid of personality but clean as whistles. If you're looking for simple and anonymous, you've found it.

Eating

BUDGET & MIDRANGE

Geoff's (☎ 874 787; 9 John St; mains €4-8; food served noon-8.30pm Mon-Sat) A busy and much respected pub, Geoff's serves *panini* (type of Italian sandwich), sandwiches and Mexican-influenced meals. It's all well-priced, well-tasty stuff, which explains the well-eager crowds.

Haricot's Wholefood Restaurant (☎ 841 299; 11 O'Connell St; mains €8-10; 9am-8pm Mon-Sat) The staff here are so smiley and considerate,

it makes you wonder what's in the water! Decent portions of organic and whole-foods (with a couple of veggie choices) are served up: try the Irish stew. Bookshelves, beaten-up wooden tables and a mellow atmosphere encourage you to lounge and linger.

Café Lucia (☎ 854 023; 2 Arundel La; mains €6-9.50; 9.30am-5pm Mon-Sat) Funky, high-backed seats in a patchwork of colours set the tone for this young, cheerful place. There are impressive breakfast menus (including home-made muesli), and hot lunchtime specials like Thai fishcakes.

New York Pie Co (☎ 304 204; 17 John St; mains €3-6; 5pm-3am Wed-Fri & Sun, 2pm-4am Sat) The weekend after-pub crowds pour themselves in here for hotdogs and a huge selection of pies, including such oddities as Thai chicken curry, pepper steak, and sausage-beans-and-cheese pies.

Café Luna (☎ 843 439; 53 John St; mains €5-10; 8.30am-midnight Mon-Wed, 8.30-3.30am Thu-Sun) Service is rather dour, but when you look at the opening times, perhaps it's understandable. It's popular with students, drawn by wholesome homemade soup and bread…or maybe for the late bar, who knows?

TOP END

Bodéga! (☎ 844 177; 54 John St; mains €10-18; noon-2.30pm & 6.30-10pm Mon-Sat) This is the best restaurant in Waterford. The décor is all Spanish cantina, but the food is pure country French. Half the Cronan family seem to be on hand at any one time to serve up wonderful dishes like *escargot* in puff pastry and fish pie with salad. There's an ever-changing menu, altered according to what's freshest, and the wine bar stays open until around 2am. Locals love to gather here for a late-night chat.

Wine Vault (☎ 853 444; www.waterfordwinevault .com; High St; mains €14-20; 12.30-2.30pm & 5.30-10.30pm Mon-Sat) A choice of 350 different wine labels, a beautiful setting in the cellar of an Elizabethan town house, and a quality menu including roast rack of lamb with bacon-wrapped green beans and crispy potato cake: what is there to not like?

Drinking

Waterford's nightlife relies heavily on the presence of students attending the local technical college.

T&H Doolans (☎ 841 504; 32 George's St) The venerable T&H Doolans incorporates a remnant of the 1000-year-old city wall. Sinead O'Connor played here before she hit the big time and there is still live music most nights.

Katty Barry's (☎ 855 095; Mall La) This small, dark and friendly place is rumoured to serve the best Guinness in the area.

Entertainment

Most clubs stay open till around 4am and are concentrated around the intersection of Parnell St, John St and John's Lane.

THEATRE & CINEMAS

Garter Lane Arts Centre (☎ 855 038; boxoffice@ garterlane.ie; 22a O'Connell St) This is a much-complimented theatre, in an 18th-century building. It stages arts films, exhibitions, music, poetry readings and plays.

Forum (☎ 871 111; www.forumwaterford.com; The Glen) The mighty Forum contains four venues, including the Gallery Theatre, which host everything from gay club nights to big comedy names. Buy tickets from the Forum here. It is attached to the Forum building.

Waterford Cineplex (☎ 843 399; Patrick St) This five-screen complex shows mainstream films for €7/4 per adult/child.

Getting There & Away

AIR

Waterford Airport (☎ 875 589; www.flywaterford.com; ⏰ 8am-8.30pm Mon-Sat, 9am-8.30pm Sun) is 7km south of the city at Killowen. **AerArann** (in the UK ☎ 0800 587 23 24, in the Republic ☎ 1890 46 27 26; www.aerarann.com) has a daily flight to London's Luton airport, and flights on Tuesday, Thursday and Sunday to Manchester airport. Prices to both cost from €80 one way, including taxes.

BUS

The **Bus Éireann** (☎ 879 000) station is on the waterfront at Merchant's Quay. There are plenty of buses daily to Dublin (€10.50, three hours), Cork (€15.50, 2¼ hours), Wexford (€11.50, 1½ hours), Killarney (€19.50, 4¼ hours) and Dungarvan (€9, 50 minutes).

Rapid Express Coaches (☎ 872 149; Olympia Court, Parnell St; ⏰ 9am-5.30pm Mon-Fri) runs a service between Waterford and Dublin (€10, three hours, 10 daily Monday to Saturday, nine Sunday) via Dungarvan and Carlow. The bus continues through Dublin to the airport (€14, four hours).

Suirway (office ☎ 382 209, 24hr timetable ☎ 382 422; www.suirway.com) buses depart to Dunmore East (€3, 30 minutes, three to four daily Monday to Saturday) and Passage East (€2.80, 30 minutes, three daily Monday to Saturday) from next to the Bus Éireann station. Look for the red-and-white buses.

TRAIN

Plunkett train station (☎ 873 401) is on the northern side of the river. Trains run to Dublin (€28, three hours, four or five daily), Kilkenny (€12.50, 45 minutes, four or five daily) and Limerick (€21.50, three hours, three daily Monday to Saturday). You can leave luggage at the station for €2.50 per item per 24 hours.

Getting Around

There is no bus service to the airport. A **taxi** (☎ 877 773) will cost around €17.

Disc parking (per hour €1.20) is in operation in the centre and there are paid car parks along the quays and at The Glen, just west of the centre.

There are taxi ranks at Plunkett train station and at the top of Barronstrand St.

Altitude (☎ 870 356; altitude@indigo.ie; 22 Ballybricken; ⏰ 9.30am-6pm Mon-Sat) hires bicycles between April and September for €15 per day.

DUNMORE EAST

☎ 051 / pop 1750

Strung out along a coastline of red sandstone cliffs and discreet coves, Dunmore East (Dún Mór) is a really special spot. The views across to Hook Head lighthouse in County Wexford are magnificent; the main

---

TOP THREE BLUE-FLAG WATERFORD BEACHES

- Counsellor's Beach (above) – just one of several sandy beaches at Dunmore East
- Clonea Strand (p198) – near Dungarvan, this popular place has lifeguards in July and August
- Bonmahon (p197) – rare species of plants grow among the dunes at Bonmahon, between Tramore and Dungarvan

street is lined with thatched cottages; and the working harbour is overlooked by an unusual **Doric lighthouse** (1823) and cliffs full of screaming kittiwakes.

Dunmore's most popular beaches are the south-facing Blue Flag **Counsellor's Beach**, among the cliffs, and **Ladies Cove** in the village. They can get busy with day-trippers from Waterford, 20km away.

In the 19th century, the town was a station for the steam packets that carried mail between England and the south of Ireland.

Activities

Dunmore East Adventure Centre (☎ 383 783; www .dunmoreadventure.com) hires out equipment to use for windsurfing, canoeing, surfing and snorkelling, and can also do archery and rock-climbing courses. Two-hour tasters to week-long activity packages are available in most of these sports.

If you fancy a bit of shark fishing or exploring old wrecks off the coast contact **Dunmore East Angling Charters** (☎ 087 268 2794; workboat@oceanfree.net).

Sleeping

Beach Guesthouse (☎ 383 316; beachouse@eircom.net; 1 Lower Dunmore; s/d €60/80; P &) Down by Ladies Cove, this brand-new upmarket guesthouse has speckless pine-floored rooms, five with fantastic vistas of Hook Head. Private balconies or bay windows add to the viewing pleasure.

Creaden View (☎ 383 339; creadenvw@eircom.net; Harbour Rd; s/d €45/66) This pleasant, warm-atmosphered B&B is excellent value. Rooms are on the smallish side, but are tastefully decorated, and three of the six have sea views: the one from room No 2 is the best of them.

Church Villa (☎ 383 390; churchvilla@eircom.net; s €38-45, d €56-66) This house (near the Ship) has been torn down and put together again to create pleasantly frilly accommodation with private bathrooms. Bedrooms at the front have lovely views. Breakfast is served in a sunny conservatory dining room by tremendously helpful hosts.

Eating & Drinking

Bay Café (☎ 383 900; Harbour Rd; mains €3-6; 8am-6pm) A standard café made special by its harbour views.

Ship (☎ 383 141, 383 144; Harbour Rd; mains €18-22; 1-3.30pm & 6.30-10pm Jul & Aug, 6.30-10pm Mon-Sat, 1-3.30pm Sun May, Jun & Sep, 6.30-10pm Wed-Sat, 1-5pm Sun Oct-Apr) This bar/restaurant serves up the best seafood for miles.

Strand Inn (☎ 383 174; www.thestrandinn.com; Ladies Cove; mains €20-25; 7-10pm Mon-Sat, 12.30-2.15pm Sun, closed Jan) Overlooking Ladies Cove, this inn also has a recommended fish restaurant with catch-of-the-day specials. Non-piscivorous people can tuck into steak, lamb or veggie alternatives. During peak-tourist season, it opens for lunch and dinner every day.

Getting There & Away

Suirway (24hr timetable ☎ 382 422, office ☎ 382 209) runs buses here from Waterford; see p195 for details.

TRAMORE

☎ 051 / pop 7138

Amusement arcades, sandcastles and candy floss – hurray, hurray, hurray! Tramore's fairground and fast-food outlets along the seafront are terrifically tacky, and the town itself, stacked up on a steep hill-

---

A SNEAKY SHORTCUT: PASSAGE EAST TO BALLYHACK

If you're travelling between Counties Waterford and Wexford, cut out a long drive around the edges of Waterford Harbour by taking a **car ferry** (☎ 051-382 480; www.passageferry.com) straight across it.

The boat runs between Passage East, about 11km east of Waterford town, to Ballyhack in Wexford. Both are pretty little places, with thatched cottages and neat harbours, and the five-minute crossing is a short burst of pleasure.

There's a continuous service throughout the day. Return tickets (pedestrian/cyclist/car €2/3/10) are valid for an unlimited time. The ferry operates from 7am to 10pm Monday to Saturday and 9.30am to 10pm Sunday from April to September, 7am to 8pm Monday to Saturday and 9.30am to 8pm Sunday October to March.

Suirway (☎ 051-382 422) runs buses to Passage East from Waterford.

side, is sober and sweet: it makes a perfect combination.

Tramore (meaning 'big beach' in Irish) is the busiest of County Waterford's seaside resorts, with a delightful 5km beach and 30m-high sand dunes at its eastern end. It's also a premier surfing spot.

The **tourist office** (☎ 381 572; www.tramore.net; Railway Sq; ⏰ 10am-6pm Mon-Sat Jun-Aug) is in the old train station. It has a brochure detailing walks in and around town, and another called the *Dolmen Drive*, outlining a 35km route that takes in **megalithic tombs** and **standing stones** in the area.

Sights

Standing on the shore, the bay is hemmed in by **Great Newtown Head** to the southwest and **Brownstown Head** to the northeast. Their 20m-high concrete pillars were erected by Lloyds of London in 1816 after a shipping tragedy: 363 lives were lost when the *Seahorse* mistook Tramore Bay for Waterford Harbour and was wrecked.

The **Metal Man**, a huge 18th-century sailor made from iron, stands on the central pillar at Great Newton Head. In white breeches and blue jacket, he points dramatically seawards as a warning to approaching ships.

Activities

One of Tramore's biggest attractions is **Splashworld** (☎ 390 176; www.splashworld.ie; Railway Sq; adult/child €9/7; ⏰ 10am-6pm) waterpark, with slides, wave machines, pirate ships and the like, and 'tropical temperatures all year round'. Opening hours are reduced from November to February.

The excellent nonprofit-making **T-Bay** (☎ 391 297; www.surftbay.com; The Beach; ⏰ 9am-8pm May-Aug, 10am-5.30pm Sep-Apr) is not only Ireland's biggest surf school, but runs eco-friendly wildlife and whale-watching tours for kids. Surfing lessons cost from €25 to €45, depending on whether you have group or private lessons; or you could just hire the equipment (€15) and hit the waves.

For a quieter stretch of shoreline, head 14km west to the Blue Flag beach of **Bonmahon**, backed by sand dunes where rare plants grow.

Tramore is a good base for year-round sea kayaking: contact **Sea Paddling** (☎ 358 995; www.seapaddling.com), which runs one-day beginners' courses for €85.

The first horse-race meeting of the year is always held at **Tramore Racecourse** (☎ 390 944; www.tramore-racecourse.com; Graun Hill) on 1 January.

Sleeping

Coast Townhouse (☎ 393 646; www.coast.ie; Upper Branch Rd; d/ste €100/160) Sexy, sleek and utterly luxurious, you'll want to whisk your lover away to one of these rooms and not come out! Super-size beds, sensuous silk, glass-walled bathrooms, and soft lighting give Coast an unbelievably romantic appeal. There's not a fry in sight for breakfast; feast instead on brioche, smoked salmon and passionfruit smoothies.

Beach Haven House B&B & Hostel (☎ 390 208; www.beachhavenhouse.com; Waterford Rd; B&B s/d €50/60, hostel dm/d €15/40; **P**) The delightful B&B has eight light, modern cream-coloured rooms, with wafting white embroidered curtains and seashell decorations – ask for one at the top of the house, with sea views. The cosy lounge contains lots of games for the kids. The hostel is equally well run: dorms are clean and ship-shape, and there's a snug sitting room with a real fire. You can also camp (per tent €5) in the small strip of garden to the side.

Cliff House (☎ 381 497; www.cliffhouse.ie; 14 Cliff Rd; s/d €55/75; **P**) There are stunning cliff-top views from this spotless modern B&B. Two rooms have their own balconies on the seaward side; if you don't get one, you can still marvel out of the window of the guest conservatory. A thoughtful breakfast selection includes maple-syrup pancakes and black pudding with apple sauce. It's a long walk to the centre of town, but there's a shortcut along the cliffside Doneraile Walk.

Newtown Caravan & Camping Park (☎ 381 979; www.newtowncove.com; Dungarvan Coast Rd; camp sites €19.50; ⏰ Easter-Sep) About 2km outside of town, this family-run affair is the best local camp site.

Eating

Tramore possibly has more fast food per square foot than anywhere on the planet, but there are some great gourmet options for those who don't like candyfloss and chips.

Coast Restaurant (☎ 393 646; www.coast.ie; Upper Branch Rd; mains €19-26; ⏰ 6.30-10pm Tue-Sat, 1-3pm Sun year-round, plus 6.30-10pm Sun in Jul & Aug) For example, at this avant-garde, sea-view restaurant, decked out with stylish satin, mirrors and contemporary works of art, the food is tremendous, taking old staples and giving them it-shouldn't-work-but-it-does twists: how about fish and chips with minted pea purée?! Save room for the perfect desserts.

Esquire (☎ 381 324; Little Market St; mains €15-22; bar food ☺ noon-7pm, restaurant ☺ noon-4pm & 6-9pm) For the freshest seafood in town, try this relaxed pub/restaurant, which serves locally caught fish (hake with lemon butter, nut-roasted salmon with oyster sauce, crab claws and mussels) in slurpcious portions. It also does traditional meaty dishes like duck, lamb and veal, and one veggie option.

Getting There & Away

Bus Éireann (☎ 879 000) runs 28 buses daily Monday to Saturday (18 Sunday) from Waterford to Tramore (€2.40, 30 minutes). Rapid Express buses also serve Tramore from Waterford. The bus stop is outside the tourist office near Splashworld.

DUNGARVAN

☎ 058 / pop 7220

Nestled among a patchwork of pine-covered hills, Dungarvan (Dún Garbhán) is a lively market town with a picturesque waterfront. It sits on the wide bay where the River Colligan meets the sea, overlooked by the ruins of King John's Castle and an Augustinian abbey.

St Garvan founded a monastery here in the 7th century, but most of the centre dates from the early 19th century when the duke of Devonshire rebuilt the streets around Grattan Sq. Modern Dungarvan is the administrative centre of Waterford.

Dungarvan has some great restaurants and makes a convenient base for exploring western County Waterford, the Ring Peninsula and the mountainous north.

Orientation & Information

Dungarvan's main shopping area is Grattan Sq on the southern side of the river. Main St (also called O'Connell St) runs along one side of it. Parnell St, which comes off the square towards the harbour, is also called Lower Main St.

The **tourist office** (☎ 41741; info@dungarvan tourism.com; TF Meagher St; ☺ 9.30am-5pm Mon-Fri year round, plus 10am-5pm Sat May-Sep) is next to the post office.

Most of the banks are on Grattan Sq. Up to one hour's free Internet access is available at the **library** (☎ 41231; The Quay).

Sights

Dungarvan's colourful 18th-century **Davitt Quay** is the best bit of town; grab a pint and watch the boats sail in.

A major renovation project has restored the walls of **King John's Castle** (☎ 48144; adult/child €2/1; ☺ tours 10.30am, 11.30am, 12.30pm, 2pm, 3pm, 4pm & 5pm Jun-Sep), a Norman castle that once defended the river: admission is by one-hour guided tour only. The former British Army barracks building nearby has been turned into a visitor centre with various exhibits concerning the castle and the barracks itself.

Dungarvan Museum (☎ 45960; www.dungarvan museum.org; St Augustine St; admission free; ☺ 10am-1pm & 2-4pm Mon-Fri) is small but nicely presented and worth a visit. It covers the town's maritime history (with relics from shipwrecks), Famine history, local personalities and various other titbits, all displayed in the former town hall.

The solitary **Augustinian Abbey** on the other side of the bridge overlooks Dungarvan Harbour. It dates mainly from the 19th century but incorporates features from the original 13th-century building, including a well-preserved tower and nave. The original abbey was destroyed during the Cromwellian occupation of the town.

The **Old Market House Arts Centre** (☎ 48944; Lower Main St; admission free; ☺ 11am-5pm Tue-Sat) hosts regular exhibitions.

Activities

Near Dungarvan, back towards Tramore is **Clonea Strand**, a beautiful patch of pristine beach.

Festivals & Events

Over the early May bank-holiday weekend, 17 Dungarvan pubs and two hotels play host to the **Féile na nDéise**, a lively traditional music and dance festival that attracts around 200 musicians. For more information phone ☎ 42998.

Sleeping

Tannery Townhouse (☎ 45420; www.tannery.ie; Church St; s/d €65/100; ☺ mid-Jan–Dec; **P** ▫) The Tannery Restaurant has branched out, applying all its taste and talent to this brand-new boutique guesthouse. Velvety rooms are fresh and tactile, and come fitted with plasma tellies. Personalised continental breakfasts are served in the morning. Reception is at the restaurant.

Mountain View House (☎ /fax 42588; www .mountainviewhse.com; O'Connell St; r from €85; **P** 🖳) With great high-ceilinged rooms decorated in Eastery colours, this old Georgian house, set in walled grounds, is a grand place to stay. There's a split-level landing, where you can sit in comfort to admire the mountain views. Internet use costs €5 per 30 minutes. Walk for about five minutes down O'Connell St from Gratton Sq, then turn left before the technical college.

Moorings (☎ 41461; Davitt's Quay; s/d €35/70) Consider one of the spacious, airy rooms above this fine pub: ask for one of the two on the front and you're guaranteed the most excellent views of the harbour and mountains in Dungarvan.

Casey's Townhouse (☎ 44912; mauriceandmarie@ eircom.net; 8 Emmet Tce; s/d €40/60) There's a real sense of house-proudness at this pleasant family-run B&B. Breakfasts are huge and delicious, with a scrambled-egg-and-smoked-salmon escape from the Irish fry-up.

Dungarvan Holiday Hostel (☎ 44340; info@ dungarvanhostel.com; Youghal Rd; dm €18-22, d €52; ☯ Easter-Oct; **P**) Located in a former friary opposite the garda station on the N25, this place is not in an attractive part of town but it's only a three-minute walk to the centre.

Eating

Tannery Restaurant (☎ 45420; www.tannery.ie; 10 Quay St; mains €18-26; ☯ noon-2.30pm & 6-10pm Tue-Sat, noon-2.30pm Sun year round, plus 6-10pm Sun Jun-Aug) An old leather tannery has been miraculously transformed into one of Ireland's most innovative restaurants. Top chef Paul Flynn creates seasonally changing dishes (described as 'contemporary Irish with a continental twist'), like baked monkfish with fennel and lime butter, or honey-roast quail with cottechino sausage. Everything is served so beautifully, it's almost – almost – a shame to eat it.

Mill Restaurant (☎ 45488; Davitt's Quay; mains €16-25; ☯ 5-9.45pm Mon-Sat, 3-9.45pm Sun) From the moment you walk in the door, you feel at ease: staff are particularly patient with kids, the place is smart but relaxed, and it's clear

that everyone's having a good time. Seafood and steak are the specialities, but there's a hotchpotch of dishes from around the world, including Cajun and Louisiana cuisine.

Interlude (☎ 45898; Castle House, Davitt's Quay; lunch €3.50-8; ☯ 10.30am-5.30pm Tue-Sun, 7-9pm Thu-Sat) For a cheap lunch, look no further than this funky caf, full of weird knobbly furniture and Australians. Jazz/funk music gives the place an upbeat vibe, and there's a wide range of snackettes: chowder, salads, pancakes, nachos, baked spuds and buns.

Entertainment

Moorings (☎ 41461; Davitt's Quay; s/d €35/70) Enjoy this laid-back quayside bar with a heated beer garden, palm trees and summer music sessions on Tuesdays or Wednesdays. The intimate and fresh-as-you-like **seafood restaurant** (mains €16-23; ☯ 6-9.15pm daily Easter-Oct, 6-9.15pm Thu-Sun Nov-Easter) is also worth a visit.

Getting There & Away

Bus Éireann (☎ 051-873 401) buses pick up and drop off on Davitt's Quay on the way to and from Dublin (€13.50, 3½ hours, five daily Monday to Saturday, four Sunday), Waterford (€9, one hour, five daily Monday to Saturday, four Sunday) and Cork (€13.50, 1¾ hours, 10 daily Monday to Saturday, six Sunday).

RING PENINSULA

☎ 058 / pop 332

Rugged and unspoiled, An Rinn (meaning 'the headland') is one of the most famous Gaeltacht areas in Ireland. The drive along Helvick Head (where all the road signs are in Irish) looks onto spectacular views of sparkling sea, green hills and mountains, and picturesque Dungarvan Bay.

At the small working harbour in Helvick Head is a **monument** to the crew of *Erin's Hope* who died when it sank near here in 1867. Nearby is an interesting house, sitting on rocks right over the water, that was once a monastery. You can look down on its roof from high spots in the town.

Coláiste na Rinne (☎ /fax 46128; www.anrinn.com), the prestigious 100-year-old Irish language college just off the Helvick Head road, runs summer language courses for 10- to 19-year-olds.

Ex–Waterford Crystal worker Eamonn Terry returned home to set up his own workshop, **Criostal na Rinne** (☎ 42127; ☷ 9am-6pm Mon-Fri), where you can buy glassy items or have them inscribed.

Sleeping & Eating

Ceol na Mara B&B (☎ 46425; deshearns@hotmail.com; An Rinn; s/d €38/60; ☷ Easter-Oct; ⓟ) Sitting high above the town, this pleasant B&B in a big old 19th-century house also hires beds without the breakfast (€25 per person). Its former hostel section has been turned into an attached self-catering apartment, available for €50 per night.

Helvick View (☎ 46297; Helvick Head Rd; s/d €25/50) This B&B offers basic accommodation and stunning views of Dungarvan Bay and the surrounding countryside.

Eateries are few and far between; if you're heading to the peninsula on a day trip, it's a good idea to bring your own picnic. For self-caterers, there's a small grocery shop near the post office (on the Helvick Head road).

Getting There & Around

The limited **Bus Éireann** (☎ 051-873 401) service runs from Waterford (€10) at 1.45pm on Saturday year round, with an additional two buses per day Monday to Friday (at 7.30am and 1.45pm) during July and August.

Pubs, accommodation and shops are scattered up and down the peninsula; you really need a car or bicycle to get around in the evenings.

ARDMORE

☎ 024 / pop 459

This pretty, petite and popular seaside resort has a long golden beach, wonderful cliff walks and a finely preserved 12th-century **round tower** looking benignly over all. It's claimed locally that St Declan set up shop here between AD 350 and 420, well before St Patrick arrived from Britain to convert the heathens.

Sights

ST DECLAN'S CHURCH & ORATORY

In a striking position on a hill above the town, the ruins of St Declan's Church and a slender, cone-roofed 29m-high **round tower** stand on the site of St Declan's original monastery. The 12th-century tower is one of the best in Ireland.

Weathered 9th-century carvings set in unusual arched panels (on the outer west-

ern gable wall of the 13th-century church) show the Archangel Michael weighing souls, the adoration of the Magi, Adam and Eve, and a clear depiction of the judgement of Solomon. Inside the church are two ogham stones (the earliest form of writing in Ireland), one with the longest ogham inscription in Ireland.

Local lore tells that St Declan is buried in the 8th-century Oratory (Beannachán), the smaller building within the compound. Over the centuries, worshippers have removed earth from the gravesite to ward off disease, leaving a depression in the floor.

The site was leased to Sir Walter Raleigh in 1591 after the dissolution of the monasteries. In 1642, the building was occupied by Royalist troops, 117 of whom were hanged here.

ST DECLAN'S WELL

Pilgrims once washed in St Declan's Well, overlooking the sea to the south of town next to the ruins of Dysert Church. A 5km blast-away-the-cobwebs **cliff walk** leads from the well; pick up a free map from the tourist office. On the way you'll pass the wreck of a crane ship that was blown ashore in 1987 on its way from Liverpool to Malta.

At the southern end of the beach is **St Declan's Stone**, different geologically to other rocks in the area, and said to have miraculously floated across the sea from Wales (or perhaps been brought by glacier from the Comeragh Mountains). Crawling under it on St Declan's Day (24 July) is said to be a cure for rheumatism.

Activities

The 94km **St Declan's Way** walk mostly traces an old pilgrimage route from Ardmore to the Rock of Cashel (County Tipperary). A map guide (€6), which also shows circular walks taking in parts of it, is available from the tourist office.

Sleeping & Eating

Cush (☎ 94474; mttroy@eircom.net; Dungarvan Rd, Duffcarrick; s/d €30/60) There are fine bay views and lots of peace and quiet at this elevated B&B, a modern dormer bungalow 2km from Ardmore.

White Horses Restaurant (☎ 94040; Main St; lunch mains €8-13, dinner mains €13-24; ☷ 11am-4pm & 6-11pm Tue-Sun May-Sep, 6-10pm Fri, 11am-4pm & 6-11pm Sat, noon-4pm Sun Oct-Apr) This smashing bistro serves nourishing standards, like fresh seafood chowder, or fried brie with tomato chutney, on plates handmade in the village. Staff are great, and will serve kids half portions from the adult menu if they fancy something more adventurous than burgers.

Paddy Mac's (☎ 94166; Main St; bar food €5-9) There's music every weekend in summer and a good pub carvery brings regular crowds to this local favourite. It makes a mean sandwich too.

Getting There & Away

There are three buses daily Monday to Saturday (one Sunday) from Cork (€11.10, 1¾ hours) to Ardmore. There are two daily to Waterford (€12, two hours) via Dungarvan in July and August (otherwise it's only a Friday and Saturday service). Buses stop outside O'Reilly's pub on Main St.

NORTHERN COUNTY WATERFORD

Some of the most scenic parts of County Waterford are in the north around Ballymacarbry and in the Nire Valley, which runs between the Comeragh and Monavullagh Mountains. While not as rugged as the west of Ireland, with which it shares the same 370-million-year-old red sandstone, this mountain scenery has a stark beauty of its own and doesn't attract much tourist traffic. Beware of stock and slow-moving tractors when driving in the area.

Sights

Lord and Lady Waterford dwell in the fine Georgian house set in **Curraghmore Gardens** (☎ 051-387 102; fax 051-387 481; Portlaw; admission by guided tour €4; 🕙 2-5pm Thu Easter–mid-Oct), 14km northwest of Waterford town near Portlaw; the estate has belonged to the family since the 12th century. At certain times of year, the **house** (admission €10; 🕙 9am-1pm Mon-Fri Jan, May & Jun), containing some superior plasterwork, is open to visitors; phone first to check.

Activities

It's a superb area for walkers, with rolling hills stuffed full of megalithic remains. Stop for a pint in **Melody's Nire View Pub** (☎ 052-36169; Ballymacarbry) where the genial folk can advise you on local walks.

Otherwise make sure you're around for the **Comeragh Mountain Walking Festival** (☎ 052-

36239), which takes place on the second weekend in October, with guided walks for all and traditional music in the pubs.

The **East Munster Way** walking trail covers some 70km between Carrick-on-Suir in County Tipperary and the northern slopes of the Knockmealdown Mountains. Access is at Fourmilewater, a few kilometres northwest of Ballymacarbry. For more details see p679.

From March to September, the Rivers Nire and Suir are great for **fishing**. Permits can be arranged through Hanora's Cottage (see boxed text, below).

Sleeping

Powers the Pot (☎ 052-23085; www.powersthepot.net; Harney's Cross; camp sites €12.50; 🕙 May-Sep) An intimate little camping ground, Powers the Pot has a smashing on-site pub with open peat fire, homemade soda bread and filling bar meals. It's signposted off the road between Rathgormuck and Clonmel, about 5km east of Clonmel.

Getting There & Away

There's a Tuesday-only bus from Dungarvan at 9am, and a Friday-only bus from Clonmel at 1.20pm and 5.35pm.

CAPPOQUIN

☎ 058 / pop 756

The small market town of Cappoquin is often overlooked by the rounded, heathery

---

SOMETHING SPECIAL

Hanora's Cottage (☎ 052-36134; www.hanorascottage.com; Nire Valley, Ballymacarbry; s €100-150, d €150-250) Put simply, this is one of the best B&Bs in the country. The spacious rooms at this 19th-century ancestral home have been beautifully decorated and all have hot tubs. There's also a larger spa in the conservatory, where visitors can relax and gaze at the surrounding mountains. There's an excellent gourmet restaurant (mains €23-29; 7-9pm Monday to Saturday), and unbeatable packed lunches made with Hanora's famous brown bread. The cottage is for adults only. Take the road east out of Ballymacarbry (opposite Melody's Pub), signposted to Nire Church; the Cottage is about 5km further on.

COUNTIES WEXFORD & WATERFORD

Knockmealdown Mountains. To the west lies the picturesque Blackwater Valley, where traces of the earliest Irish peoples have been discovered.

There's excellent coarse and game fishing locally, with salmon-fishing permits available from **Titelines** (☎ 54152) tackle shop in the main street.

Glenshelane Park, just outside the town, offers forest walks and picnic spots.

Mt Melleray Cistercian Abbey (☎ 54404; ☼ year round) is a fully functioning monastery, just over 6km north of town (signposted). The abbey was founded in 1832 by 64 Irish monks who were expelled from a monastery near Melleray in Brittany, France. The monastery opens to visitors seeking quiet reflection and to those who wish to see something of the daily routine. Although no admission is charged, a donation is appreciated, and it's best to contact the abbey first before visiting.

Cappoquin House & Gardens (☎ 54004; adult/child €10/free; ☼ 9am-1pm Mon-Sat May-Jul) is a Georgian mansion (built 1779) and gardens overlooking the River Blackwater. It's the private residence of the Keane family who've lived here for 200 years. The entrance to the house is in the centre of Cappoquin; take the road to the monastery and look for a set of huge black iron gates just a few metres up on your left.

Barron's Bakery (☎ 54045; the Square) sells warm bread and buns, and also has its own coffee shop. It is the only bakery in Ireland to have retained its original brick ovens.

Getting There & Away

A bus leaves Dungarvan for Cappoquin (€4, 20 minutes) at 9.50pm Monday to Saturday and returns to Dungarvan at 7am. There are two buses per week from Waterford (€11.50, 1¼ hours) via Dungarvan leaving at 8.30am Friday and 5pm Sunday (returning Friday only, 5.50pm from Cappoquin). There's also one bus a week leaving Cork (€11.50, 1¼ hours) at 4.30pm on Friday. Buses stop outside Morrissey's pub. For details contact **Waterford bus station** (☎ 051-879 000).

LISMORE

☎ 058 / pop 788

$P_1V_1 = P_2V_2$. If this elegant little equation sends thrills down your spine, you'll love Lismore for its associations with the 'father of modern chemistry', Robert Boyle. Even if you couldn't give a fig about Boyle's Law, there are plenty of low-key amusements here.

Lismore is perfectly situated on the River Blackwater and dominated by a spectacular castle. Its cathedral contains a window by Edward Burne-Jones, and Fred Astaire lounged around the town's streets and pubs when he wasn't tap dancing. There's a real sense of civic pride, with well-kept buildings and bits of greenery everywhere: picnic in the **Millennium Gardens**, or take a riverbank stroll down **Lady Louisa's Walk**.

Although most of its buildings date from the early 19th century, Lismore was the location of a great monastic university first founded by St Cartach, or Carthage, in the 7th century. Things went downhill during the 10th century, when it was repeatedly attacked by Vikings.

Information

The helpful **tourist office** (☎ 54975; lismore heritage@eircom.net; Old Courthouse, Main St; ☼ 9.30am-5.30pm Mon-Fri, 10am-5.30pm Sat, noon-5.30pm Sun May-Oct, 9.30am-5.30pm Mon-Fri Nov-Apr) is inside the Lismore Heritage Centre. Guided tours of town take place at 11am and 3pm daily in July and August. Alternatively, you can buy the informative *A Walking Tour of Lismore* (€3), which describes all the local sights.

Sights

ST CARTHAGE'S CATHEDRAL

'One of the neatest and prettiest edifices I have seen', commented William Thackeray in 1842 about this striking cathedral (1633). And that was before an achingly beautiful pre-Raphaelite **stained-glass window**, designed by Edward Burne-Jones, was added – the only one of its kind in Ireland. Justice (a man with sword and scales) and Humility (a woman holding a lamb) stand against a background of flowers, honouring the virtues of kind-hearted Francis Currey, who helped to relieve the suffering of the poor during the Famine.

The cathedral also contains some noteworthy **tombs**, including the elaborately carved MacGrath family crypt dating from 1557. A good tour leaflet (€2), aimed at kids but fun for all, leads you round the

COUNTIES WEXFORD & WATERFORD

building's oddities and wonders, including the fossils in the pulpit!

LISMORE CASTLE GARDENS

From the Cappoquin road there are stunning glimpses of **Lismore Castle** (closed to day-trippers but rentable for functions), overlooking the river. You can visit the three hectares of **gardens** (☎ 54424; www.lismore castle.com; adult/child €5/2.50; ☺ 11am-4.45pm Jun-Aug, 1.45-4.45pm Easter-May & Sep), thought to be the oldest in Ireland, with sections dating back to Jacobean times. There are brilliant herbaceous borders, magnolias and camellias, and a splendid yew walk where Edmund Spenser is said to have written *The Faerie Queen.*

The original castle was erected by Prince John, Lord of Ireland, in 1185. After a stint as the local bishop's residence, it was presented to Sir Walter Raleigh in 1589 along with 200 sq km of the surrounding countryside. He later sold it to the earl of Cork, Richard Boyle, whose son Robert Boyle (1627–91) was born here.

Most of the current castle was constructed in the early 19th century. During its rebuilding, the 15th-century *Book of Lismore* and the Lismore Crozier (both in the National Museum in Dublin) were discovered. The book not only documents Irish saints' lives, but also holds an account of Marco Polo's voyages. A more recent castle occupant was Adele Astaire, sister of the famous Fred.

LISMORE HERITAGE CENTRE

In the old courthouse is the **Lismore Heritage Centre** (☎ 54975; fax 53009; Main St; adult/child €4/3.50; ☺ 9.30am-5.30pm Mon-Fri, 10am-5.30pm Sat, noon-5.30pm Sun May-Oct, 9.30am-5.30pm Mon-Fri Nov-Apr). A half-hourly audiovisual presentation takes you from the arrival of St

Carthagein AD 636 to the present day, telling the story of the *Book of Lismore* on the way. There's also a funny nine-minute cartoon about scientist, theologian, philosopher and medic Robert Boyle, aimed at schoolkids but worth watching.

Sleeping & Eating

Ballyrafter House Hotel (☎ 54002; fax 53050; s/d €95/170, lunch menu €28, dinner menu €44; ☺ Mar-Oct; P) Log fires and home cooking make this country-house hotel a cosy place to stay. The simple bedrooms overlook stately gardens complete with peacocks. There are good views of the castle from the restaurant, where you can sample local salmon, honey and cheeses.

Beechcroft (☎ 54273; beechcroftbandb@eircom.net; Deerpark Rd; s/d €40/60; ☺ Easter-Sep) The lovely garden is the selling point of this comfortable spot. It's in a high part of town and there are pleasant views of the surrounding countryside.

Café Molise (☎ 53778; East Main St; lunch mains €4-8, dinner mains €13-24; ☺ 9am-5pm daily, 6.30-9.30pm Thu-Sun) Snack on gourmet sandwiches at this pleasant coffee shop. Evening meals are the real Italian deal, with dishes based around porcini (mushroom) sausage, pasta, *bresaola* (dried beef) and Parma ham.

Getting There & Away

One bus leaves daily Monday to Saturday from Dungarvan for Lismore (€5.10, 25 minutes) via Cappoquin at 9.50pm, and returns to Dungarvan at 6.45am. There are two buses per week from Waterford (€12, 1¼ hours) via Dungarvan leaving at 8.30am Friday and 5pm Sunday (returning Friday only at 5.40pm from Lismore). Buses stop outside O'Dowd's pub on West St. For details contact **Waterford bus station** (☎ 051-873 401).

County Cork

If you took the country, crumpled it up and threw it somewhere out into the Atlantic, but kept hold of County Cork (Corcaigh), you'd still have a microcosm of Ireland clutched in your godlike hands.

Lower one giant eye to the capital, Cork, and see a sizzling city that easily rivals Dublin in the quality of its live music, modern galleries, delectable restaurants and quirky, packed-out pubs. Fresh-faced and full of beans after its stint as European Capital of Culture, it's a city brimful of confidence and charm.

Trace a fingertip lightly along the southern edge, and you're stroking the country's most beautiful whorling inlets and jagged outcrops. Colourful fishing villages, seaside resorts and medieval castles stud the coastline, all warmed by the clear waters of the Gulf Stream.

Follow the trail of music, food festivals and sailing regattas further west, and you'll be led inexorably to Cork's captivating peninsulas. Sliding through gorse, heather and mountainous scenery to the tips, you'll uncover surprises like the perfect beach at Barleycove, the unique Signal Centre on Mizen Head, and seductive Beara's wobbling cable car, where sheep take priority!

So set Cork down, remember that you aren't several miles tall, and step into this most varied, vibrant and valuable of counties.

HIGHLIGHTS

■ **City Spectacular**
Confident Cork city, still buzzing after its blast as European Capital of Culture 2005, with its great selection of restaurants (p212), pubs (p214), music (p215) and theatres (p214)

■ **I Want to Be Alone...**
Journey down the stunning coastal road to the Mizen Head Peninsula (p235)

■ **Taste of the Sea**
Some of the best seafood in existence along Cork's southern coast, from Kinsale (p222) to Baltimore (p232)

■ **Animal Magic**
Coming face-to-face with penguins, giraffes and kangaroos at the fence-free Fota Wildlife Park (p217)

■ **Dangle by a Thread**
The rickety terror and wriggling delight of Ireland's only cable car, at Dursey Island (p246)

■ POPULATION: 447,829   ■ AREA: 7508 SQ KM

CORK CITY

☎ 021 / pop 123,062

Cork buzzes with the energy and promise of a city on the rise. A university and a burgeoning arts and music scene give this once hard-nosed commercial port a cosmopolitan edge, and its upbeat renaissance won it a stint as European Capital of Culture for 2005. Cork rivals Dublin in the quality, if not the quantity, of its restaurants, pubs and clubs. It has enough cultural venues for several days of satisfactory browsing.

The River Lee flows around the centre, an almost-island packed with grand Georgian parades, cramped 17th-century alleys, and modern masterpieces like the opera house. To meet the profile of European culture capital, there's been a flurry of urban renewal; the city's main drag, St Patrick's St, has been spruced up, with new pedestrian areas and street furniture. A spanking-new art space, the Lewis Gluckman Gallery, has also mushroomed up at the university.

The city's population has a strong element of mainland Europeans and is growing fast as service industries seek people with language skills. General regeneration is also attracting all kinds of new business interests.

Like all riverside settlements, Cork suffers from traffic congestion, as a handful of bridges struggle to channel heavy flows from side to side of the River Lee.

HISTORY

Cork has had a long, distinguished and often bruising history, inextricably linked with Ireland's struggle for nationhood.

The city's recorded history dates from the 7th century, when St Finbarre founded a monastery here. By the 12th century the settlement had become the chief city of the Kingdom of South Munster, having survived raids and some sporadic settlement by Norsemen. Irish rule was short-lived, however, and by 1185 Cork was under the English Crown. Thereafter it changed hands regularly during the relentless struggle between Irish and Crown forces. It survived Cromwellian assault only to fall to that merciless champion of Protestantism and commerce, William of Orange.

During the 18th century Cork prospered, but a century later famine devastated both county and city, and robbed Cork of its people, either by death or emigration.

Cork's deep-seated Irishness ensured that the city played a key role in Ireland's struggle for independence. Thomas MacCurtain, a mayor of the city, was killed by the Black and Tans in 1920. His successor, Terence MacSwiney, died in London's Brixton prison after a 75-day hunger strike. The British were at their most brutally repressive in Cork and, among general atrocities, much of the city centre, including St Patrick's St, the City Hall and the Public Library, was burned down. Ever-turbulent, Cork was also a regional focus of Ireland's self-destructive Civil War.

ORIENTATION

The city centre is located, island-like, between two channels of the River Lee. The graceful curve of St Patrick's St runs from St Patrick's Bridge on the North Channel of the Lee, through the heart of the city's main shopping and commercial area, to the Georgian Grand Parade that runs down to the river's South Channel. North and south of St Patrick's St lie the city's most entertaining quarters; webs of narrow streets crammed with pubs, cafés, restaurants and all kinds of shops.

Across St Patrick's Bridge is an equally bustling area, focused around MacCurtain St, with its own rewarding spread of pubs, restaurants and shops. East of MacCurtain St you'll find Kent Train Station, budget B&Bs and the road to Youghal, Waterford and Rosslare. West is the distinctive Shandon area which has a real village-like atmosphere, especially in the narrow lanes around its hilltop churches.

From midway down Grand Parade, Washington St (which becomes Lancaster Quay and Western Rd) leads southwest to the university, Killarney and West Cork.

INFORMATION
Bookshops

Connolly's Bookshop (☎ 427 5366; Rory Gallagher Pl, Paul St) Great chat and masses of second-hand books.

Liam Ruiséal Teo (☎ 427 0981; 49-50 Oliver Plunkett St) New books, including plenty on Cork.

Mainly Murder (☎ 427 2413; 2a Paul St) Crime novels galore.

Shelf (☎ 431 2264; 12 George's Quay; ⏰ 9am-5.45pm Mon-Sat) A little shop with a pleasant jumble of second-hand stock.

COUNTY CORK

COUNTY CORK

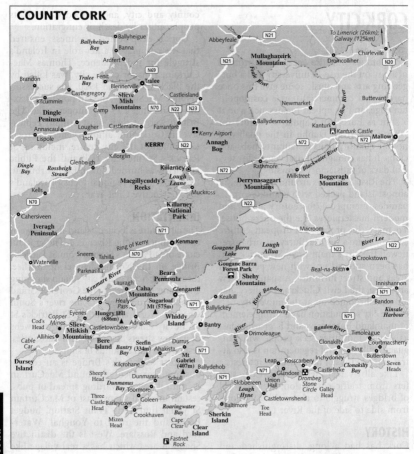

Vibes & Scribes (☎ 450 5370; 3 Bridge St; 🕒 10am-6.30pm Mon-Sat, 12.30-6.30pm Sun) Four fantastic floors of new and second-hand books, records, CDs and DVDs.
Waterstone's (☎ 427 6522; 69 St Patrick's St; 🕒 9am-7pm Mon-Thu & Sat, 9am-8pm Fri, noon-6pm Sun) This branch has the best travel section in the southwest. Entrances on St Patrick's and Paul Sts.

Emergency
City General Hospital (☎ 431 1656; 6 Infirmary Rd) About 1km southeast of the centre, via Anglesea St, just south of the river.

Internet Access
Cork City Library (☎ 427 7110; www.corkcitylibrary.ie; 57-61 Grand Pde; per 30 min €1; 🕒 10am-5.30pm Mon-Sat)

Net House (☎ 422 2174; www.nethousecaffs.com; 128 Oliver Plunkett St; per hr €5; 🕒 24 hr) Deals like free coffee sweeten the spending.
Webworkhouse.com (☎ 427 3090; www.webwork house.com; 8a Winthrop St; per hr €1.25-5; 🕒 24hr) Prices vary according to the time of day. You can also make low-cost international phone calls.

Laundry
Clifton Laundrette (Western Rd; 🕒 9am-9pm Mon-Fri, 9am-6pm Sat; per 0.5kg €1) Opposite the gates of University College Cork (UCC).

Left Luggage
You can't leave luggage at Kent station.
Cork Bus Station (☎ 450 8188; cnr Merchant's Quay & Parnell Pl; per item for 24hr €2.60; 🕒 8am-7pm Mon-Sat)

Libraries

Cork City Library (☎ 427 7110; www.corkcitylibrary.ie; 57-61 Grand Pde; ⏱ 10am-5.30pm Mon-Sat)

Money

The Bank of Ireland and Allied Irish Bank, both on St Patrick's St, have ATMs and currency-exchange facilities. There are bureaux de change in the Cork tourist office and in Cork bus station.

Post

Main post office (☎ 485 1032; Oliver Plunkett St; ⏱ 9am-5.30pm) There are sub-post offices on Mac-Curtain St (in the Spar shop) and on Grand Pde, which close for lunch between 1pm and 2pm and at 1pm on Saturdays.

Tourist Information

Cork Tourist Office (☎ 425 5100; www.corkkerry.ie; Grand Pde; ⏱ 9am-6pm Mon-Sat, 10am-5pm Sun Jul & Aug, 9.15am-5pm Mon-Fri, 9.30am-4.30pm Sat Sep-Jun) An extensive souvenir shop with attached information desk that has plenty of free and pay-for brochures and books about the city and county. Budget Car and Stena Line Ferries have desks here.

DANGERS & ANNOYANCES

Cork cherishes its reputation as being a friendlier and less hard-skinned place than Dublin, but late at night and in the early hours there can be some ugly scenes around central pubs and clubs. At these times it's best not to linger at such places as the Fountain in Grand Parade.

SIGHTS
Cork City Gaol

Castle-like **Cork City Gaol** (☎ 430 5022; www.cork citygaol.com; Convent Ave; adult/child €6/3.50; ⏱ 9.30am-6pm Mar-Oct, 10am-5pm Nov-Feb, last admission 1hr before closing) may be too grim a spectacle for faint-hearted souls, but it's certainly a highly unusual and worthwhile tourist attraction. A 35-minute audio-tour guides you around the restored cells, which feature lifelike models of suffering prisoners and sadistic-looking guards. It's actually very moving, bringing home the harshness of the 19th-century penal system; many of the inmates were sentenced to hard labour for stealing trifles like loaves of bread.

Upstairs is the **National Radio Museum** (adult/child €6/3.50) where, alongside collections of beautiful old radios, you can hear the story of Guglielmo Marconi's conquest of the airwaves.

Drive or walk from the city centre, or take bus No 8 from the bus station to the stop outside UCC, then walk north across Fitzgerald Park and over Daly Bridge, up Sunday's Well Rd, then left along Convent Ave.

Crawford Municipal Art Gallery

Cork's public **gallery** (☎ 490 7855; www.crawford artgallery.ie; Emmet Pl; admission free; ⏱ 10am-5pm Mon-Sat, last admission 15 min before closing) houses a small but excellent permanent collection, featuring works by Irish artists such as Jack Yeats and Seán Keating. Look out for Keating's *Men of the South* (1921), a fine piece of historical romanticism depicting members of the North Cork Batallion of the IRA.

COUNTY CORK

CORK

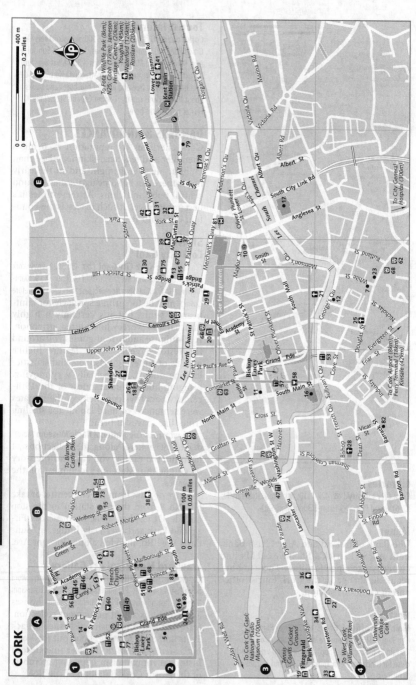

COUNTY CORK

The marvellous Sculpture Galleries contain snow-white plaster casts of Roman and Greek statues, given to King George IV by the pope in 1822. Unfortunately, George didn't like the present, and stuck the sculptures in the cellar until someone suggested that Cork might appreciate them. *Venus de Milo* and *Laocoön and His Sons* rub shoulders with later works – check out handsome Michael Collins as he casts an appreciative eye over *Susannah at the Bath* and *Venus Italica*. The downstairs exhibition hall hosts some superior displays, which change roughly every two months, and there's a stylish café (see p212).

St Finbarre's Cathedral

Spiky spires, girning gargoyles and rich sculpture make up the exterior of Cork's imposing Protestant **cathedral** (☎ 496 3387; cathedral@cork .anglican.org; Bishop St; adult/child €3/1.50; ☒ 9.30am-5.30pm Mon-Sat Apr-Sep, 10am-12.45pm & 2-5pm Mon-Sat Oct-Mar), an attention-grabbing mixture of French Gothic and medieval whimsy. Local legend says that the glitzy Golden Angel on the eastern side will blow its horn when the Apocalypse is due to start…

All the grandeur continues inside, with marble floor mosaics, a colourful chancel ceiling, a huge pulpit and Bishop's Throne, and restored stained glass. Quirky items on display include a cannonball that was blasted into an earlier medieval spire during the Siege of Cork (1690).

Most of the ostentation is the result of a competition, held in 1863, to choose an architect for the building. William Burges was the hands-down winner and once victory was assured he promptly redrew all his plans – with an extra choir bay, taller towers, finer stone – and his £15,000 budget went out of the window. Luckily, the bishop understood such perfectionism and spent the rest of his life fundraising! When Burges died in 1881, the interior was still unfinished.

The cathedral is perched at an aloof distance south of the centre, on the spot where Cork's patron saint, St Finbarre, founded his monastery in the 7th century.

Lewis Glucksman Gallery

Ireland's newest **art gallery** (☎ 490 1844; www .glucksman.org; University College Cork; ☒ 10am-5pm Tue, Wed, Fri & Sat, 10am-9pm Thu, noon-5pm Sun) is a startling limestone, steel and timber construction, and a visible symbol of Corkonian optimism. Opened in 2004 to great excitement, the €12-million building has three huge display areas, which host ever-changing exhibitions and installations. Its situation in the grounds of UCC means that it's always buzzing with people coming to attend lectures, view the artwork, or nibble hummus and olives in the basement café.

Cork Public Museum

Located in a pleasant Georgian house in Fitzgerald Park, this **museum** (☎ 427 0679; www.corkcitycouncil.ie/amenities; Fitzgerald Park; admission free; ⊗ 11am-1pm & 2.15-5pm Mon-Fri, 3-5pm Sun) has a fine collection of artefacts that reflect Cork's history from the early Stone Age onwards. The newly opened extension contains contemporary exhibitions.

Take bus No 8 to the main gates of UCC and follow the brown signs.

Beamish & Crawford Brewery

This famous **brewery** (☎ 491 1100; www.beamish .ie; South Main St; guided tour adult/concession €7/5; ⊗ 10.30am & noon Tue & Thu May-Sep, 11am Thu Oct-Apr) is the most ancient porter brewery in Ireland. It runs enjoyable tours that end with a tasting. It is fronted by the Counting House, a building that takes first prize for eye-blinding architectural awfulness (mock Tudor, crow-stepped gables, classical pediment *and* pebbledash).

Shandon

Throw a few galleries, antique shops and cafés among the little lanes and squares (and wash away the graffiti) and **Shandon** could easily emerge as Cork's 'Latin' quarter. Perched on a hillside overlooking the city centre, it's worth climbing up here for the views alone.

Shandon is dominated by the 'Four-Faced Liar', also known as **St Anne's Church** (☎ 4505906; www.stanneshandon.ie; John Redmond St; ⊗ 9.30am-4.30pm Mon-Sat). Wannabe campanologists can play tunes on the **bells** (adult/child €6/3.90) at the top of the 18th-century Italianate tower. The church also contains a small collection of 17th-century Bibles and letters written by the poet John Donne.

Cork had the largest butter market in the world during the 1860s, exporting Irish butter as far as India, South America and Australia. Trace history at the **Cork Butter Museum** (☎ 430 0600; www.corkbutter.museum; O'Connell Sq; adult/child €3/2.50; ⊗ 10am-5pm Mar-Oct, by arrangement Nov-Feb) with a 25-minute

video, butter-making artefacts and history panels. Next door, in the old Cork Butter Exchange, is **Shandon Craft Centre** (O'Connell Sq), containing a few souvenir shops and the pleasant courtyard **Butter Market Café** (☎ 430 2303; ⊗ 7.30am-2.30pm Mon-Sat), where you can treat yourself to a cup of tea after the climb from the city centre.

Other Monuments

One of Cork's most famous figures was Father Theobald Mathew, the 'Apostle of Temperance', who went on an effective, but short-lived, crusade against alcohol in the 1830s and 1840s – during which a quarter of a million people took the 'pledge', and whiskey production halved. The **Holy Trinity Church** (Fr Mathew Quay) was designed by the Pain brothers in 1834 in his honour, and the, erm, Father Mathew Bingo Hall round the corner also celebrates his memory. Theobald Mathew's **statue** stands on St Patrick's St.

The medieval **Red Abbey Tower** (Red Abbey St) is the oldest building in Cork and all that's left of a 14th-century Augustinian priory. Its location is fairly anonymous, but it helps to create a stirring sense of antiquity.

On Grand Parade, near the tourist office, is the ornate **Nationalist Monument**, erected in memory of the Irish patriots who died during the 1798 and 1867 Risings.

TOURS

Arrange Unlimited (☎ 429 3873; arrange@iol.ie) can organise walking tours on request all year round.

The open-topped **Cork City Tour** (☎ 430 9090; adult/child €12/4) bus has a hop-on-hop-off tour leaving from outside the tourist office (every 45 minutes between 9.30am and 5pm April to September). Buy tickets at the tourist office or on the bus.

Bus Éireann (☎ 450 8188; www.buseireann.ie) operates a three-hour, open-top bus tour of Cork and Blarney Castle from Easter to September (adult/child €10/6) departing from the bus station at 10.30am daily.

FESTIVALS & EVENTS

The **Cork International Jazz Festival** and the **International Film Festival** both take place in October, but tickets sell out quickly. Programmes are available from **Cork Opera House** (☎ 427 0022; www.corkoperahouse.ie; Emmet Pl).

COUNTY CORK

The **International Choral Festival** (www.cork choral.ie) runs from late April to early May in the City Hall and other venues.

The **Eigse Literary Festival** takes the form of writing workshops, readings, seminars and exhibitions during February. It attracts around 50 local and overseas writers. For details contact **Munster Literature Centre** (Tigh Litríochta; ☎ 431 2955; www.munsterlit.ie; 84 Douglas St).

SLEEPING
Budget

Sheila's Hostel (☎ 450 5562; www.sheilashostel.ie; Belgrave Pl, Wellington Rd; 8-bed dm €14, 4-bed dm 15.50-16.50, d €50; 🖳) This hugely popular place heaves with young travellers. It's just undergone a big refurbishment – new rooms have popped up and a sauna (€2 per 40 minutes) has appeared. A couple of parts, including the pool room, were still waiting for a lick of paint at the time of writing. The hostel is handy for MacCurtain St, and you can arrange bicycle and car hire. Internet access is €2.50 per hour.

Brú Bar & Hostel (☎ 455 9667; www.bruhostel .com; 57 MacCurtain St; 6-/4-bed dm €16.50/21, d €50; P 🖳 &) This brand-new buzzing hostel is right on MacCurtain St and has its own broadband Internet café and flash little bar. The (en-suite) dorms are on the small side, but the brushed-steel kitchens are spacious, and the black, white and silver colour scheme keeps things looking smart. Readers have written in to praise the helpful Kiwi managers. Internet access is €3 per hour, and breakfast is included in room price.

Kinlay House Shandon (☎ 450 8966; kinlay.cork@ usit.ie; Bob & Joan's Walk; dm €14-16, s/d €30/44, r with-bathroom €50; 🖳 &) This excellent hostel has smart décor, a fun but sensible atmosphere and a sense of security. It's quieter than other Cork hostels. Internet access is €4 per hour, and breakfast is included in room price.

Cork International Hostel (☎ 454 3289; corkyh@ gofree.indigo.ie; 1 & 2 Redclyffe, Western Rd; 6-/4-bed dm €17/19, d €42; P 🖳) Near the university, this busy An Óige hostel has cheerful staff who do a great job coping with the busy flow of traffic. The drawback is the dull 2km walk (or No 8 bus ride) to the centre, along a busy road. Internet access costs €2 per 40 minutes and breakfast is €6.50.

Close to the train station in Glanmire Rd are a handful of basic but clean B&Bs, including **Tara House** (☎ 450 0294; 52 Lower Glanmire Rd; s/d €40/60) and neighbouring **Oaklands** (☎ 450 0578; s/d €40/64).

Midrange

Some B&B prices in the city centre have risen alarmingly and hotels have responded with price cuts that offer bigger rooms and better facilities. Lower Glanmire Rd, near the train station, has the cheapest places. Western Rd has a big choice of pricier options.

Garnish House (☎ 427 5111; www.garnish.ie; Western Rd; s €55-75, d 80-120; P) An outstanding place to stay. Welcomed in with tea and treats, every attention is lavished upon you until you depart. Rooms are comfy, with charming touches, and the breakfast choice alone would make it worth staying, from waffles and Blarney ham to porridge with cream, honey and Bailey's! Why aren't all B&Bs like this one?

Crawford House (☎ 427 9000; crawford@indigo.ie; Western Rd; s/d €65/90; P) Another top-notch B&B, Crawford House has spacious rooms, gracious furnishings, and some bodacious Jacuzzis to splash around in. The standard is that of a contemporary hotel, but without the formal atmosphere.

Acorn House (☎ /fax 450 2474; www.acornhouse -cork.com; 14 St Patrick's Hill; s/d €65/110) A handsome, high-ceilinged, part-Georgian terrace house, this listed building has attractive rooms painted in mellow yellows and soothing greens. Antiques like washstands and ewers give a historical and personal touch, and the house has the added advantage of being on a quiet street, handy for the city centre.

Victoria Hotel (☎ 427 8788; www.thevictoriahotel .com; Patrick St; r incl breakfast €100-140) You can't get more central than this old established hotel, where Charles Stuart Parnell and James Joyce once stayed. At the time of writing, general refurbishments were taking place, including the reopening of the St Patrick's St entrance. The rooms don't have grand views, but they're staidly decorated and a decent size.

Auburn House (☎ 450 8555; www.auburnguest house.com; 3 Garfield Tce, Wellington Rd; s/d €40/66, with bathroom €50/74; **P**) There's a friendly welcome at this neat B&B, which has smallish but impeccably kept rooms brightened by flowery window boxes. Veggies who are sick of being fobbed off with grilled tomatoes and scrambled eggs will relish the meat-free sausages for breakfast. The area itself has a village-like quality, strange considering it's so close to the city.

Emerson House (☎ 450 3647; emersonhouse@eircom .net; 2 Clarence Tce, North Summer Hill; s/d €40/80; **P**) Tucked away on a quiet terrace near the top of busy Summer Hill is this exclusively gay and lesbian B&B, with a relaxing mood and elegant, comfy surroundings.

Top End

Imperial Hotel (☎ 427 4040; www.imperialhotelcork .ie; South Mall; s/d standard €130/145, executive €180/195; **P** &) A very tricky balancing act has successfully taken place in the 190-year-old Imperial; large-scale refurbishments have added contemporary touches to the hotel without it losing any sense of period superiority. Executive rooms are much the same as standard, but have DVD players and modems. These days no top hotel would be complete without a sauna – luckily one opened here in spring 2005!

Gresham Metropole (☎ 450 8122; www.gresham -hotels.com; MacCurtain St; s/d €110/140; **P**) This long-established hotel has been completely overhauled over the last couple of years, and is now luxury itself. You can pad soundlessly around on plush carpets and feel comfortably corporate in the lavish rooms, 20m swimming pool, health club and elegant bars and restaurant.

Isaac's Hotel (☎ 450 0011; www.isaacs.ie; 48 Mac-Curtain St; s/d up to €125/200; **P**) Rooms have pleasant furnishings and wooden floors at this old hotel on the north side of the river. The hotel's Greene's Restaurant does

a three-course early-bird menu (€20) from 6pm to 7pm, against an outside backdrop of a floodlit rocky waterfall. It's very impressive for a city venue.

EATING
Budget

Quay Co-op (☎ 431 7026; www.quaycoop.com; 24 Sullivan's Quay; mains €7-10; ☾ 9am-9pm Mon-Sat) Flying a cheerful flag for alternative Cork, this favourite offers a great range of self-service veggie options, including big breakfasts, rib-sticking soups, casseroles, lasagnes and pizzas. It's all organic food and caters for gluten-free, dairy-free and wheat-free needs, as well as being amazingly child-friendly. You can track down most of Cork's alternative and minority organisations and events on the noticeboard downstairs. Next door is the **Quay Co-op Organic & Wholefood Shop** (☎ 431 7753; ☾ 9am-6.15pm Mon-Sat), excellent for self-caterers.

Amicus Café & Restaurant (☎ 427 6455; 14a French Church St; lunch mains €6-8.50; ☾ 10am til late) The best thing about this place are the outdoor tables, on a pedestrianised street in the Huguenot quarter – people-watching and listening to nearby buskers feels very continental. The catch-all 'New World' menu covers just about everything you might fancy, and the portions are big enough to keep you going for days. Sunday brunch is a particularly satisfying experience.

Crawford Gallery Café (☎ 427 4415; Emmet Pl; lunch mains €5-9; ☾ 10am-5pm Mon-Sat) Elegant, minimalist surroundings and simply exquisite food complement gallery grazing at the Crawford. It's also a quality place for a spot of eavesdropping. There's a set lunch for €18.

Clancy's (☎ 427 6097; www.clancys-bar.com; 15-16 Princes St; bar meals €5-11.50, restaurant mains €8-16; bar ☾ 8am-10pm Mon-Fri, 10am-10pm Sat, noon-4.30pm Sun, restaurant ☾ 5.30pm-10pm) You can eat all day in this huge, cheerful pub, which prides itself on its steaks (although it concedes a dish or two to 'herbivorous' types). Coffees and teas come with a free refill.

O'Brien's Irish Sandwich Bar (☎ 427 9522; 58 Oliver Plunkett St & Grand Pde; sandwiches €3-6; ☾ 8am-5.30pm Mon-Sat) This handy budget chain has two outlets right in the heart of the city centre, with the usual good selection of sandwich fillings. They get packed out at lunch-time.

Cork picnickers are a fortunate bunch, with the wonderful **English Market** (9am-5.30pm Mon-Sat) and all its wares just off the western end of St Patrick's St. There's great local and imported produce here, such as cheeses, pâté, terrines, smoked fish, bread, olives and wine. If you have cooking facilities, the knowledgeable fresh-fish sellers will tell you exactly what to buy and how to cook it. Take your lunch items to Bishop Lucey Park, a very popular local alfresco eating spot.

Midrange

Farmgate Café (427 8134; English Market; mains €8.50-10; 8.30am-5pm Mon-Sat) An unmissable Cork experience at the heart of the colourful English Market, the Farmgate, like its sister restaurant at Midleton (see p220), has mastered the magic art of producing delicious food without fuss or bowing to fleeting fashion. Some featured fare includes filling breakfasts, morning and afternoon tea and coffee (with several refills), bouncingly fresh lunch-time salads, Irish lamb and shepherd's pie, all drawing a regular Cork clientele to the Farmgate's balcony. If you're lucky you may catch the eloquent pianist Donal Casey at the corner piano.

Café Mexicana (427 6433; 1 Carey's Lane; mains €13.50-17; noon-10pm) Authentic surroundings and great food make this café an enduring favourite. It manages to be vividly turquoise yet really cosy, and is touching in its detail (check out the hand-painted table mats). A cool cross of cultures mixes Mexican and Spanish staples with subtle French and Italian influences. There's a rising scale of nachos – try the 'Dynamite' option if you like it hot. Although the café's nominally open all day, it sometimes stops serving after 3pm if it's quiet.

Boqueria (455 9049; www.boqueriasixbridgest .com; 6 Bridge St; breakfast €2.50-4.50, tapas €2.70-16.50; breakfast 8am-11am, tapas noon-late) This new tapas bar is a shining addition to Cork's wonderful eateries. In addition to the usual olive-garlic-peppers-anchovy, the chefs here use local creations like sourdough, Ballycotton mussels, Gubbeen cheese and West Cork saucisson to create tasty Irishified tapas. It's a small, dusky, intimate spot, favoured by couples in the evenings, and at lunch-times by friends seeking a civilised glass of wine.

Triskelcafébar (422 2444; www.triskelart.com; breakfast €0.50-4.50, lunch mains €4-7.50; 8am-6pm Mon-Fri, 11am-5pm Sat, eves on performance nights) Attached to the Triskel Arts Centre, this dinky café is often quiet during the day, when you can scoff veggie lasagne, salads, toasted *panini* and the finest carrot cake known to mankind in peace. Wine is by the glass, or go for a healthy smoothie or fresh juice.

Isaac's Restaurant (450 3805; 48a MacCurtain St; lunch €9.65, dinner €7.50-15; 12.30-2.30pm & 6.30-10.30pm Mon-Sat, to 9pm Sun) Housed in a converted 18th-century warehouse, Isaac's captures a nostalgic southern-European atmosphere to go with its lively menu. The tapas plate adds to the tone and there's excellent vegetarian choices amid the inventive meat and fish dishes.

Scoozi's (427 5077; www.scoozis.com; 3-4 Winthrop Ave; mains €10-12; 9am-11pm Mon-Sat, noon-10pm Sun) There's lots of exposed brickwork and burnished wood inside this hugely popular break-time café-restaurant, tucked down a little lane between Winthrop and Caroline Sts. Snug alcoves add intimacy as the fast and friendly young staff dish up breakfasts, pizzas, pastas, grills and salads and a fair selection of French and New World wines. It's a great place to take children; highchairs abound, and we saw a waiter pausing to play peek-a-boo!

Top End

Café Paradiso (427 7939; 16 Lancaster Quay; mains €11-22; 12.30-3pm & 6.30-10.30pm Tue-Sat) The top-class vegetarian dishes here will seduce even the most committed carnivore. It's small and lively, the charming staff promote happy interaction and there's a Mediterranean ambience. Creativity maintains the standard of dishes, desserts are divine and the wine list is terrific – reflecting a passion for the vine rather than just passing fancy.

Ivory Tower (427 4665; The Exchange Bldgs, 35 Princes St; mains €20-50, 5-course menu €60; 6.30-10pm Wed-Sat) Chef Seamus O'Connell's 'culinary missions' to Japan have influenced the menu at this place and his speciality is blackened shark with banana ketchup. The best way to experience O'Connell's unusual combinations is through the tasting menu (Wednesdays and Thursdays; €75), where you get to nibble eight or nine courses of eclectic, exquisite dishes.

COUNTY CORK

A DRISHEEN DARE

If you're feeling brave, you could try some traditional Cork *drisheen* at the English Market – intestines stuffed with sheep or pigs' blood and bitter tansey, boiled in milk.

Star Anise (☎ 455 1635; 4 Bridge St; lunch €8.40-9.50, dinner €18-22; 🕙 noon-3pm Tue-Fri, 6-11pm Tue-Sat) Ultra-cool orange and blond wood surrounds make this small restaurant a cosmopolitan Cork experience. The appealing international menu, with its strong Mediterranean influences, makes the beachy atmosphere here even more persuasive. From juice bar to pan-fried chicken schnitzel, and pastas to seafood chowder, the choice is delectable.

Table 8 (☎ 427 0725; 8/9 Carey's Lane; mains €12-20; 🕙 noon-3pm Mon-Fri, noon-4pm Sat, 5.30pm-late daily) A rather elegant option, Table 8 advertises its 'Modern Irish Cuisine', but what you really want to eat here are the fine fresh fish dishes. Particularly tasty are the haddock pies, and skate with tantalisingly spicy ginger, chilli, garlic and lime.

DRINKING

Cork's pub life is cracking, and the choice of pubs rivals that of Dublin's in quality. Two stouts, Murphy's and Beamish (the cheaper of the two), are brewed locally – drink Guinness at your peril!

An Spailpín Fánac (☎ 427 7949; South Main St) 'The Wandering Labourer' really hangs on to its character, with exposed brickwork, stone-flagged floors, snug corners and open fires. There are good trad sessions every night except Saturday. It gets very busy and there's a fair request not to stand drinking at the fairly cramped bar after 8.30pm.

Sin É (☎ 450 2266; Coburg St) This great old pub over the north river is dark, comfy and very cosy. There's music on Tuesday at 9.30pm, and on Friday and Sunday evenings from 6.30pm (sometimes other nights too), much of it traditional but with the odd surprise. The pub also doubles as a barber's shop – sup a pint and get your hair chopped in the padded seat upstairs.

Mutton Lane Inn (☎ 427 3471; Mutton Lane) Tucked down the tiniest of laneways off St Patrick's St, this wood-smelling pub is lit by candles and fairy lights, and is one of the most intimate of Cork's drinking holes. It is minute and much-admired – try to get in early to bag the snug.

Long Valley (☎ 427 2144; Winthrop St) A Cork institution that dates from the mid-19th century and is still going strong, the Long Valley has a landscape that fits its name. It does great sandwiches that go very well with your pint. The main bar is almost always busy, but the upstairs Hayloft is usually quieter.

ENTERTAINMENT

For information about what's on in Cork city pick up a copy of *WhazOn?*, available from the tourist office, newsagencies, some clothes and record shops, hostels and a few B&Bs.

Theatre

Cork's cultural life is as fine as any in Ireland and attracts internationally renowned performers.

Cork Opera House (☎ 427 0022; www.corkoperahouse.ie; Emmet Pl; box office 🕙 9am-8.30pm, to 5.30pm non-performance nights) This leading venue has been entertaining the city for 150 years, with everything from opera and ballet to stand-up and puppet shows. Performances are as varied as *Swan Lake*, *La Traviata*, *Blood Brothers* and the *Vagina Monologues*; ticket prices vary enormously.

Everyman Palace Theatre (☎ 450 1673; www.everymanpalace.com; 15 MacCurtain St; box office 🕙 10am-7.30pm Mon-Sat, to 6pm non-performance nights) Musical and dramatic stage productions are the main bill of fare here, but there's also the occasional high-quality opera, rock band, storyteller or comedian. Tickets are €23 upwards.

UCC Granary Theatre (☎ 490 4272, box office ☎ 490 4275; www.granary.ie; Dyke Pde) Contemporary and experimental works (eg a 100-person choir headbanging to Beethoven's Ninth Symphony!) are staged at the Granary by the university drama group and by visiting companies. Look out for any related workshops, symposiums and installations. Tickets cost around €12.

Cork Arts Theatre (☎ 450 8398; Knapps Sq) Under demolition at the time of writing, this excellent experimental theatre should be rebuilt on the same spot by 2007.

Cinemas

Cork has a number of cinemas that screen both specialist films and the stuff for mass consumption.

Capitol Cineplex (☎ 427 8777; Grand Pde; films €7) Serves up standard Hollywood fare.

Gate Multiplex (☎ 427 9595; North Main St; films €7.50) Puts on mainstream films over several screens.

Kino (☎ 427 1571; www.kinocinema.net; Washington St West; films €7.50, matinee €5) Shows art-house flicks.

Queerscreen (☎ 427 8470; john@gayprojectcork.com; 8 South Main St; films €6; ⌚ 7pm Thu) Has weekly screenings of new and classic films with a gay interest.

Live Music

Cork overflows with tunes. As well as the session pubs mentioned earlier (opposite), the following places are either dedicated music venues or bars known particularly for their live events. These are just the tip of the iceberg – refer to *WhazOn?* and ask around for more.

An Cruiscín Lán (☎ 484 0941; www.cruiscin.com; Douglas St) Trad bands and world, blues and pop musicians all play at this acclaimed bar. Tickets are sold at An Cruiscín Lán, in the off-licence next-door, or at Plugd Records (right).

Fred Zeppelins (☎ 427 3500; 8 Parliament St) There's hard-edged action at this rock bar on the south side, with a good mix of weekend DJs and live gigs. Happy hours are 4pm to 8pm Monday to Thursday, when all pints are €3.

Savoy (☎ 425 1419; www.savoycork.com; St Patrick's St) Tribute acts, singer-songwriters and rock bands strut the stage at the Savoy, one of Cork's newest venues, right on the bend in St Patrick's St. You can buy tickets online, at the venue or at Fred Zeppelins or Plugd Records (right).

Half Moon Theatre (☎ 427 0022) This is one of Cork's best places for live acts and top DJs. The Half Moon (behind Cork Opera House) has featured acts such as Ruby Horse and Jerry Dammers. Saturday night's Planet Funk piles on some great raw talent.

Nightclubs

Cork's club life really does rival Dublin's. With a vibrant university population to fuel the beat, Cork rocks just about every night of the week. Entry ranges from free to €15 and most of these places open until 2am on Friday and Saturday.

Bodega (☎ 427 2878; bodega@indigo.ie; 46-49 Cornmarket St) This is a big bouncing pub-café-club, packed into the old Cork workhouse. There's a big food choice (€8 to €15) in the Café Bar Deli, and full-on music in the huge front bar, or in the White and Green Rooms. Punters are entertained in a myriad of quirky ways – past extravaganzas have included céilidhs, open-mic nights, Playstation tournaments and duelling DJs.

Scott's (☎ 422 2779; Caroline St) This deluxe venue has a fine restaurant downstairs and an upstairs club that features mainstream disco music for the over-20s smart crowd.

Rhino Rooms (☎ 427 7682; 1 Castle St) DJs and live bands add to the cool trappings of this indie nightclub, especially popular with students.

SHOPPING

As well as the full range of national and international stores, there are some excellent specialist outlets in Cork. The little streets north of St Patrick's St are the most interesting.

Ó Conaill (☎ 437 3407; 16b French Church St) Do not leave Cork without sampling the delights of this local chocolatier. Wafer-thin slivers of white, milk or dark chocolate are flavoured with exotic flourishes such as coffee beans or chilli, and you can sup rich hot chocolate (from €2.95) at a tiny counter at the back of the shop.

Living Tradition (☎ 450 2564; 40 MacCurtain St; ⌚ 10am-6pm Mon-Sat) If you like traditional music, this is the best shop for tapes, CDs and publications.

Plugd Records (☎ 427 6300; 4 Washington St) A terrific music shop that stocks everything from techno to nu jazz beats. You can also buy tickets for various gigs and pick up the very latest info on the club scene.

Union Chandlery (☎ 455 4334; 4-5 Penrose's Quay) The Chandlery sells camping and trekking gear, wetsuits, sailing equipment and guides, and there's an information board on sporting activities around County Cork.

GETTING THERE & AWAY
Air

Cork airport (☎ 431 3131; www.cork-airport.com) is 8km south of the city on the N27. Airlines servicing the airport are Aer Arann, Aer Lingus, Air Malta, Air Wales, bmi British Midland, bmibaby, British Airways, Czech

COUNTY CORK

Air, EasyJet, Malev and Ryanair (see p695 for contact details). There are direct flights to Amsterdam, Budapest, Belfast, Birmingham, Bristol, Cardiff, Dublin, Durham, Edinburgh, Faro, Leeds, Liverpool, London, Malta, Manchester, Munich, Nice, Nottingham, Paris, Plymouth, Prague and Southampton. Other overseas flights go via Dublin.

Boat

Regular ferries link Cork with France and the UK.

Brittany Ferries (☎ 427 7801; 42 Grand Pde) sails to Roscoff (France) at 5.30pm every Saturday from mid-March to October; the crossing takes 14 hours and you have to pre-book accommodation (reclining seat/2-/4-berth cabin €7/120/144), not included in these sample high-season one-way fares:

Car & 2 passengers €433
Motorbike & driver €124
Foot passenger €76

Swansea Cork Ferries (☎ 427 1166; www.swanseacork ferries.com; 52 South Mall & ferry terminal) has a service that runs four times per week from mid-March to June and September to December, plus six times per week in July and August. The crossing between Cork and Swansea takes around 10 hours. For more details see p697. Sample high-season one-way fares are:

Car & driver €225
Car, driver & up to 5 adults €259
Motorbike & driver €89
Foot passenger €45
Bicycle €11 (year round)

Bus

Bus Éireann (☎ 450 8188) operates from the bus station on the corner of Merchant's Quay and Parnell Place. You can get to most places from Cork, including Dublin (€16, 4¼ hours, six daily), Killarney (€14, two hours, 12 daily), Waterford (€15, 2¼ hours, 13 daily) and Kilkenny (€17, three hours, four daily).

Car

Budget (tourist office ☎ 427 4755; airport ☎ 431 4000; www.budget.ie) and **Thrifty** (tourist office ☎ 427 3257, airport ☎ 434 8488; www.thrifty.ie) have desks at the tourist information office, as well as at the airport. **Avis** (☎ 1890 40 50 60; www.avis .ie) is on Alfred St at the east end of Mac-Curtain St.

Train

Kent Train Station (☎ 450 4777) is north of the River Lee on Lower Glanmire Rd. There's a direct train connection to Dublin (€52.50, three hours, nine daily) and Limerick (€21, 1½ hours, eight daily). There's a service to Tralee (€27.50, 2¼ hours) via Killarney (€21, 1½ hours) five times a day. The train journey to Waterford is long and circuitous: better to take the bus.

An hourly service to Cobh (€4.90 return, 24 minutes) stops at Fota (€3.60 return, 14 minutes), enabling you to take in Fota Wildlife Park and Cobh Heritage Centre on a round trip.

GETTING AROUND
To/From the Airport

The airport is 8km south of the city centre on the South City Link Rd. It takes about 20 minutes to get there by car. Taxis cost around €15. Bus Éireann No 226 runs between the airport and the bus station on Parnell Place, and into the city centre (€3.70, 25 minutes).

To/From the Ferry Terminal

The ferry terminal is at Ringaskiddy, which is about 15 minutes by car southeast from the city centre along the N28. Taxis cost around €25. Bus Éireann runs a fairly frequent daily service to the terminal to link up with sailings (€5.50/3.50 per adult/child, 45 minutes).

Bus

Most places are within easy walking distance of the centre. If you're staying a long time, consider getting a weekly ticket.

Car

Streetside parking requires scratchcard parking discs (€1.80 for two hours) obtained from the tourist office and some newsagencies. Be warned, clamping of vehicles is sharpish once you're over time and the cost of retrieving your vehicle is hefty. There are 10 or so signposted public car parks dotted round the central area, with charges of about €2 for one to four hours, €5 overnight.

Cork is currently building up a Park & Ride system (€5 for return bus fare into centre, 7.30am to 7.30pm Monday to Saturday) to cut down on city-centre congestion. So far, there's only one car park on the southern approach from Kinsale, but another three car parks are to be built by 2007.

Taxi

Try **Shandon Cabs** (☎ 450 2255) or the **Cork Taxi Co-op** (☎ 427 2222).

Bicycle

For bicycle hire try **Rothar Cycles** (☎ 431 3133; 55 Barrack St; per day/week €20/80). Rothar's offers a one-way pick-up service from other towns for €30 (€100 refundable deposit).

From mid-April to mid-September you can join a weekly sociable cycle trip from Cork into the surrounding countryside. Cyclists meet outside the opera house at 6.50pm on Thursdays, and there's a get-together in a local café afterwards. Contact Rothar Cycles for details.

AROUND CORK CITY

BLARNEY CASTLE

One of the most popular tourist stops in Ireland is **Blarney Castle** (☎ 021-438 5252; Blarney; adult/child €7/2.50; ☽ 9am-6.30pm Mon-Sat, 9.30am-5.30pm Sun May & Sep, 9am-7pm Mon-Sat, 9.30am-5.30pm Sun Jun-Aug, 9am-6pm or sundown Mon-Sat, 9.30am-5pm or sundown Sun Oct-Apr, last admission 30 min before closing). Crowds flock here to kiss the **Blarney Stone**, said to grant the gift of the gab.

The way is not easy for those seeking eloquence. The stone is perched right at the top of the 15th-century castle, reached by a steep climb up slippery spiral staircases. On the battlements, you bend backwards over a long, long drop (with safety grill and attendant to prevent messy accidents) to kiss the Blarney Stone; as your shirt rides up around your neck, coachloads of onlookers stare up your nose. Once you're upright, don't forget to admire the stunning views before you descend. You'll also have to pay extra for a photo.

The custom of kissing the stone is a relatively modern one, but Blarney's association with smooth talking goes back a long time. Queen Elizabeth I is said to have invented the term 'to talk blarney' out of exasperation with Lord Blarney's ability to talk endlessly without ever actually agreeing to her demands.

A SNEAKY SHORTCUT: PASSAGE WEST

If you're travelling between east and west Cork, avoid Cork city centre by using the **Ferry Link** (☎ 021-481 1223; pedestrian/car €0.80/3.50; ☽ 7am-12.15am). The crossing connects Passage West and Glenbrook with Carrigaloe, and only takes five minutes. Bikes are free.

Be warned: quiet Blarney moments don't exist in the race for the stone. If it all gets too much, vanish into the **Rock Close**, part of the wonderful castle gardens, which includes a fairy glade, a witch's kitchen and a set of wishing steps.

Blarney is 8km northwest of Cork and buses run there regularly from Cork bus station (€2.70, 30 minutes).

FOTA
Fota Wildlife Park

Fota Wildlife Park (☎ 021-481 2678; Carrigtwohill; adult/child €10.50/6.50; ☽ 10am-5pm Mon-Sat, 11am-5pm Sun mid-Mar-Oct, 10am-3pm Mon-Sat, 11am-3pm Sun Nov–mid-Mar) is a great place, where animals roam without a cage or fence in sight. Kangaroos bound past, monkeys and gibbons leap and scream on water-bound islands, and capybaras root about in the bushes. Other beasts include graceful giraffes, ostriches, penguins, flamingos, and the scimitar-horned oryx, believed to be extinct in the wild.

A wildlife tour train runs a circuit round the park every 15 minutes (one way/round trip €0.80/1.60) in high season, otherwise it's a 2km walk on a circular trail.

Fota House

From the wildlife park, you can take a stroll down to the Regency-style **Fota House** (☎ 021-481 5543; Carrigtwohill; adult/child €5/2; ☽ 10am-5pm Mon-Sat, 11am-5pm Sun Apr-Oct, 11am-4pm daily Nov-Mar, last admission 30 min before closing). The interior contains a fine kitchen and plasterwork ceilings. The lack of 18th- and 19th-century furnishings is compensated by touch-screen stories which bring the rooms to life.

Attached to the house is the 150-year-old **arboretum** (free), which has some beautiful trees including giant redwoods, Chilean flame trees and the Chinese ghost tree. In spring, the magnolia walk is lovely.

Getting There & Around

Fota is 10km east of Cork. The hourly Cork to Fota train (€3.60 return, 14 minutes) goes on to Cobh.

There's a large car park (€2) shared by the park and the house. Pay at the barrier on the way out.

COBH

☎ 021 / pop 6767

In the wake of the Famine, around 2.5 million people emigrated from the port of Cobh (pronounced cove); go on a grey day, and the sense of loss is still almost palpable. When the sun shines and the crowds flock in, though, you'll see another side to this hilly little town. The spectacular cathedral looks down over brightly coloured houses, the wide seaside promenade and the glittering estuary, and Cobh seems to shake off its sad past.

Cobh has become a popular stopover for visiting cruise liners whose clientele are whisked off in coaches to tourist hot spots.

History

Cobh was for many years the port of Cork and has always had a strong connection with Atlantic crossings. In 1838 the *Sirius*, the first steamship to cross the Atlantic, sailed from Cobh. The *Titanic* made its last stop here before its fateful journey in 1912, and when the *Lusitania* was torpedoed off the coast of Kinsale in 1915, it was here that many of the survivors were brought and the dead buried. Cobh was also the last glimpse of Ireland for the millions of people who emigrated from here during the Famine.

In 1849 Cobh was renamed Queenstown after Queen Victoria paid a visit. The name lasted until Irish independence in 1921 when, not surprisingly, the local council reverted to the Irish Cobh.

The world's first yacht club, the Royal Cork Yacht Club, was founded here in 1720, but now operates from Crosshaven on the other side of Cork Harbour.

Orientation

Cobh is on Great Island, which fills much of Cork Harbour, and is joined to the mainland by a causeway. It faces Haulbowline Island (once the base of the Irish Naval Service) and the greener Spike Island (which houses a prison). The waterfront area comprises the broad Westbourne Place and West Beach, from where steep streets climb inland. There's a delightful waterside park with seating, a bandstand and a children's play area next to the tourist office.

Information

The old yacht club now contains a small **tourist office** (☎ 481 3301; ◷ 9.30am-5.30pm Mon-Fri, 1-5pm Sat & Sun Mar-Sep) and arts centre. At the time of writing there was some uncertainty about staffing levels and whether or not these hours would be strictly maintained.

Sights

COBH, THE QUEENSTOWN STORY

Part of Cobh train station has been cleverly converted into a **heritage centre** (☎ 481 3591; www.cobhheritage.com; Old Railway Station; adult/child €6/3; ◷ 10am-6pm, last admission 5pm May-Oct, 10am-5pm, last admission 4pm Nov-Apr;). It contains an impressive series of exhibitions about Ireland's mass emigrations in the wake of the Famine – 2.5 million people left from Cobh alone. There's also some shocking stuff on the fate of convicts, like the insurgents from the 1798 Rebellion, who were shipped to Australia in transport 'so airless that candles could not burn'. The era of the great liners is covered, including the tragedies of the *Titanic* and *Lusitania*, both intimately connected to Cobh. The Queenstown Story is fascinating, and the place is a cut above many other 'interpretive centres'.

For people trying to trace ancestors there's a genealogy centre attached, and for those more interested in a bun and a cup of tea, there's an adjoining café (see opposite).

ST COLMAN'S CATHEDRAL

Standing dramatically above Cobh on a hillside terrace, the massive French Gothic **St Colman's** (☎ 481 3222; Cathedral Pl; admission by donation) is out of all proportion to the unassuming town. Its most exceptional feature is the 47-bell carillon, the largest in Ireland, with a range of around four octaves. The biggest bell weighs a stonking 3440kg – about as much as a full-grown elephant! You can hear carillon recitals at 4.30pm on Sundays between May and September.

The cathedral, designed by Pugin, was begun in 1868 but not completed until 1915. Much of the funding was raised by nostalgic Irish communities in Australia and the USA.

COUNTY CORK

COBH MUSEUM

A small history **museum** (☎ 481 4240; www
.cobhmuseum.com; High Rd; adult/child €1.50/0.75;
☯ 11am-1pm & 2-5.30pm Mon-Sat, 3-6pm Sun Easter-
Oct) is housed in the 19th-century Scottish
Presbyterian church overlooking the train
station. There are model ships, paintings,
photographs and some artefacts from 18th-
and 19th-century Cobh.

Tours

June to September, **Marine Transport Services**
(☎ 481 1485; www.mts.ie) organises one-hour
harbour tours (€5.50/3.50 per adult/child)
three times per day.

Michael Martin's 1¼-hour guided walk,
Titanic Trail (☎ 481 5211, 087 276 7218; www.titanic
-trail.com; adult/child €7.50/3.80; ☯ 11am May & Sep,
11am, 2pm & 4pm Jun-Aug), leaves from the Commodore Hotel on Westbourne Pl. You get a
free sampling of stout at the end. He's also
devised a ghoulish 45-minute **Ghost Walk**
(€11.50); contact him for further details.

Sleeping

Knockeven House (☎ 481 1778; www.knockeven
house.com; Rushbrooke; s/d €65/100; **P**) Knockeven
is a splendid but relaxed Victorian house,
1.5km north of Cobh. Huge bedrooms are
done out with period furniture, and overlook a magnificent garden full of magnolias

and camellias. Breakfasts are great too –
homemade breads and fresh fruit – served
in the sumptuous dining room.

Water's Edge Hotel (☎ 481 5566; www.waters
edgehotel.ie; s/d €85/150; **P** **&**) Loads of eye-
catching colours and an almost cruise-liner
feel along the verandas add to the appeal
of this smart family-run hotel that stands
right where its name implies. There's also a
restaurant, Jacob's Ladder (see p220).

Commodore Hotel (☎ 481 1277; commodorehotel@
eircom.net; Westbourne Pl; s/d €70/120, with sea view
€76/132) Rates drop by up to 20% in the off-
season at this classic seaside hotel, which has
all the mod cons but retains a pleasant retro
appeal.

Westbourne House (☎ 481 1391; 12 Westbourne Pl;
s/d €20/40) The friendly owner of this sunny
and historical house (an old shipping
agent's) provides good value beyond the
reasonable price. Don't expect lavishness,
but the rooms are big and the many yachting pictures go with the harbour views.

Eating & Drinking

Queenstown Restaurant (☎ 481 3591; lunch €3.50-6;
☯ 10am-4.45pm) Coffee, tea and tasty lunches,
including salads and lasagne, are served up in
Cobh's old train station. You can eat on the
platform in far better surroundings and with
tastier food than in most real railway cafés.

LUSITANIA

On 7 May 1915, the Cunard liner RMS *Lusitania*, on its way from New York to Liverpool, was
torpedoed by a German U-boat about 19km south of the Old Head of Kinsale. It sank within 18
minutes with the loss of 1198 souls. As soon as the ship's distress call was received, boats were
mobilised from Cork's southern coastline; most belonged to local fishermen, who risked their
own lives to bring survivors and the dead into Cobh and Kinsale.

On the back of the tragedy the British sought to portray the German Navy as 'slaughterers
of innocents'. German propaganda, in the form of the Goetz Medallion, showed the grim reaper
selling liner tickets on one side and an armed, sinking ship on the other. It was intended to
satirise the British government's irresponsibility in loading a passenger ship with weapons, then
letting it sail unescorted through U-boat–infested waters, but it backfired and was seized on as
a sick celebration of an atrocity.

Although the British denied it at the time, it's now widely accepted that the *Lusitania* was
carrying arms. A second, larger explosion occurred after the torpedo had struck, contributing to
the incredible speed with which the ship sank. The most likely explanation is that the ship was
transporting US-manufactured munitions in the forward hold.

Amongst the dead were 120 Americans, which placed a strain on US–German relations and
pushed the US closer to the Allies' cause. The tragedy is thought to have influenced the United
States' decision to join the war two years later.

Victims of the disaster are buried in mass graves in the Old Church Cemetery in Cobh, and
in St Multose Church, Kinsale.

Jacob's Ladder (☎ 481 5566; www.watersedgehotel .ie; lunch mains €5-12.50, dinner mains €18-26; ☿ 11.30am-9pm) This bright and upbeat restaurant at the Water's Edge Hotel has a great view over the harbour. It is fairly pricey but has a wide range of meat, poultry and excellent fish dishes, all done with some creativity.

Mansworths Bar (☎ 481 1965; 4 Midleton St, Top o' the Hill) This characterful old pub is a local favourite and pulls one of the best pints of stout you're likely to get. There's music most weekends; otherwise the feast of Cobh maritime photos and artefacts will keep you entertained.

Getting There & Away
Cobh is 24km southeast of Cork, off the main N25 Cork to Rosslare road. Hourly trains connect Cobh with Cork (€4.90 return, 25 minutes).

Getting Around
All of Cobh's sites are within easy walking distance. If you need a cab try the **Cobh Taxi Association** (☎ 086 815 8631).

MIDLETON & AROUND
☎ 021 / pop 3798

Information
There's a **tourist office** (☎ 461 3702; ☿ 9.15am-1pm & 2-5pm Mon-Fri May-Sep) by the entrance gate to the distillery.

Sights
The big attraction in town is the former Jameson **Old Midleton Distillery** (☎ 461 3594; www .whiskeytours.ie; adult/concession €8.50/3.95; ☿ 9am-6pm), where coachloads pour in to tour the restored 200-year-old building and purchase bottles from the vast gift shop.

One-hour **guided tours** (☿ 10am-5pm Mar-Oct, at 11.30am, 2.30pm & 4pm Nov-Feb) start with a film show and continue with a walk that reveals the whole whiskey-making process, including a gleaming glimpse of the world's largest pot still, and a working waterwheel. The tour ends in the bar, where everyone gets a free snifter, and luckier volunteers get to taste-test assorted Irish whiskeys, Scotch and bourbon.

Sleeping & Eating
Farmgate Restaurant (☎ 463 2771; The Coolbawn; ☿ coffee & snacks 10am-5pm Mon-Sat, lunch noon-4pm, dinner 6.30-9.45pm Thu-Sat) This sister estab-lishment to Cork's Farmgate Café and it has the same superb blend of traditional and modern Irish in its approach to food and to cooking. In the front is a shop selling local produce, including organic fruit and vegetables, cheeses and preserves. Behind is the café-restaurant, where you'll eat as well as anywhere in Ireland.

Ballymaloe House (☎ 465 2531; www.ballymaloe .ie; Shanagarry; s/d from €135/242; ℗ ☂) This guesthouse, restaurant and cookery school is of the highest standard. Rooms are elegant and superbly furnished, and guests can enjoy the garden and woodland walks. The restaurant serves Modern Irish cuisine at its best, with a five-course set menu for around €60 per person. The cookery school (www.cookingisfun.ie) offers tuition from half-day courses in a variety of styles (€95 plus) to 12-week certificate courses (around €8000). It's about 12km southeast of Midleton on the R629 between Shanagarry and Cloyne.

Getting There & Away
Midleton is about 20km east of Cork. There are 18 buses that run from Monday to Saturday (13 Sunday) from Cork bus station (€5.10, 25 minutes).

YOUGHAL
☎ 024 / pop 6203

The ancient walled sea port of Youghal (Eochaill; pronounced yawl), at the mouth of the River Blackwater, has history coming out of its ears and really makes the best of it.

The town was granted to Sir Walter Raleigh during the Elizabethan Plantation of Munster, and he spent brief spells living in Youghal, in his house Myrtle Grove. Local tradition claims that he smoked the first cigarette there, and planted the first potatoes in his garden, but historians (the spoilsports) tend to disagree.

With the opening of a bypass in 2003, the once traffic-logged Main St has regained *some* semblance of calm. Youghal is a good base for exploring the surrounding area and there are a couple of beaches nearby.

Orientation & Information
The Clock Gate, which is found at the southern end of North Main St, is Youghal's major landmark.

Youghal Visitor Centre (☎ 20170; tourism@ youghalchamber.net; Market Sq; 🕑 9am-5.30pm Mon-Fri, 9.30am-5pm Sat & Sun May-Sep, 9am-5pm Mon-Fri Oct-Apr), in an attractive old market house on the waterfront, also contains a small **heritage centre** (adult/child €3/free) that gives a very good overview of the town. Pick up the free leaflet, *Youghal Town Trail*, or the excellent booklet *Youghal: Historic Walled Port* (€3.50) to learn more.

Guided tours (adult/child €5/free), lasting 1½ hours, leave the visitor centre at 10.30am Monday to Friday during July and August (on request at other times).

Sights & Activities

Youghal has not one but two Blue Flag **beaches**, ideal for sandcastles and swimming. Claycastle and Front Strand are both within walking distance of Youghal, off the N25; Claycastle has wheelchair access and summer lifeguards.

Heading from south to north, some of the town's sights are detailed here.

Fox's Lane Folk Museum (☎ 20170, 291 145; North Cross Lane; adult/child €4/2; 🕑 10am-1pm & 2-5.30pm Tue-Sat Jul & Aug), tucked down an alley (signposted from the visitor centre), is a dinky place containing over 600 hand-labelled household items dating from 1850 to 1950, and a Victorian kitchen.

The curious **Clock Gate** was built in 1777, and was used as a combination clock tower and jail: several prisoners taken in the 1798 Rebellion were hung from its windows.

The beautifully proportioned brick **Red House**, on North Main St, was designed in 1706 by the Dutch architect Leuventhen, and features some Dutch Renaissance details. A few doors further up the street are six **alms houses**, built in 1610 to house ex-soldiers.

Across the road is 15th-century **Tynte's Castle**, which originally had a defensive riverfront position. When the Blackwater silted up and changed course in the 17th and 18th centuries, the castle was left high and dry.

Built in 1220, **St Mary's Collegiate Church** incorporates elements of an earlier Danish church dating back to the 11th century. Inside there's a monument to Richard Boyle, who bought Raleigh's Irish estates and became the first earl of Cork; it shows him with his wife and 16 children. The churchyard is bounded by a fine stretch of the 13th-century **town wall** and one of the remaining turrets.

Beside the church, **Myrtle Grove** was once lived in by Sir Walter Raleigh, and retains some 16th-century features. The weather vane depicts the famous story of Raleigh, Elizabeth I, the puddle and the cloak.

Sleeping

Roseville (☎ 92571; rosevillebandb@eircom.net; New Catherine St; s/d €42.50/60; 🕑 mid-Jan–mid-Dec; **P**) In the heart of Youghal, this handsome old building has the mood of a country house and its own walled garden. Stylish rooms and a relaxed ambience are matched by the friendly welcome.

Aherne's (☎ 92424; www.ahernes.com; 163 North Main St; s/d €120/200; **P** 🔗) You get excellent value for the price at this charming four-star place. Rooms are individually decorated and there's a great sense of style and comfort.

Clonvilla Caravan & Camping Park (☎ 98288; clonvilla@hotmail.com; Clonpriest; camp sites €16; 🕑 Mar-Oct) This site, 4km out of town, has just 20 pitches. Facilities are basic, but it's quiet enough.

Eating

Aherne's Seafood Bar & Restaurant (☎ 92424; 164 North Main St; bar food €3.75-13.50, dinner menu €42; 🕑 bar food noon-10pm, dinner 6.30-9.15pm) If you're serious about food the only place to eat in Youghal is Aherne's, an award-winning restaurant justifiably famous for its terrific seafood menu. There's everything from chowder to hot buttered lobster; if the restaurant's too formal, sample fishy delights in the cosy bar.

Coffee Pot (☎ 92523; 77 North Main St; meals €5.50-15) This busy and basic coffee shop offers good-value sandwiches, burgers, mixed grills and scary-looking cream cakes.

Entertainment

Dancing Thru the Ages (☎ 92571; www.dancingthru theages.com; Mall Arts Centre; 🕑 8.30pm Tue & Wed Jun-Sep) Tickets are available for this new show from the Mall Arts Centre or the visitor centre. It is intended to put traditional Irish dancing in a modern light.

Getting There & Around

There are frequent Bus Éireann services to Cork (€7.90, 50 minutes, 13 daily) and Waterford (€13.50, 1½ hours, every hour).

Disc parking on the streets costs €0.60 per hour, but some of the car parks are free.

COUNTY CORK

WESTERN CORK

KINSALE

☎ 021 / pop 2257

Kinsale (Cionn tSáile) bursts with life and colour. Narrow winding streets, tiny houses, and bobbing fishing boats and yachts give it an extra-seductive picture-postcard feel. Its sheltered bay is guarded by a huge and startling star fort, just outside the town at Summercove.

Blessed by media visits from personalities such as Keith Floyd and Rick Stein, Kinsale has been labelled the gourmet centre of Ireland and, for such a small place, it certainly contains far more than its fair share of international-standard seafood restaurants.

Kinsale also attracts arty types. There are lots of crafty galleries and shops for buying treats and trinkets, and several celebs have houses here.

History

In September 1601 a Spanish fleet anchored at Kinsale was besieged by the English. An Irish army from the north, who had appealed to the Spanish King to help them against the English, marched the length of the country to liberate the ships, but were defeated in battle outside the town on Christmas Eve. For the Catholics, the immediate consequence was that they were banned from Kinsale; it would be another 100 years before they were allowed to go back. Historians now cite 1601 as the beginning of the end of Gaelic Ireland.

After 1601 the town developed as a shipbuilding port. In the early 18th century, Alexander Selkirk left Kinsale Harbour on a voyage that left him stranded on a desert island, providing Daniel Defoe with the idea for *Robinson Crusoe*.

Orientation

Most of Kinsale's hotels and restaurants are near the harbour and within easy walking distance, but there are a couple of restaurants out at Scilly, a peninsula to the southeast. A path continues from there to Summercove and Charles Fort. To the southwest, Duggan Bridge links Castlepark Marina and the scant ruins of James Fort to Pier Rd.

Information

Finishing Services (☎ /fax 477 3571; 71 Main St; per 30/60 min €3/5; ☼ 9am-5.30pm Mon-Fri & 10am-5pm Sat) Internet access.

Kinsale Bookshop (☎ 477 4244; kinsale@corkbookshop.ie; 8 Main St) Has all you need for a good read.

Kinsale Drycleaning & Laundry Co (☎ 477 2875; Market St; ☼ 9am-6pm Mon-Fri)

Tourist office (☎ 477 2234; kinsaletio@eircom.net; cnr Pier Rd & Emmet Pl; ☼ 9.30am-1pm & 2.15-5.30pm Mon-Sat Mar-Oct, daily Jul & Aug) On the harbourfront. You may find its opening hours flexible, especially in the quieter months. It has a free map detailing five walks in and around Kinsale lasting from one to two hours.

The post office and an Allied Irish Bank with ATM can both be found on Pearse St. Toilets are next to the tourist office.

Check out www.kinsale.ie for information about Kinsale.

Sights

MUSEUM

The small **museum** (☎ 477 7930; Market Sq; adult/concession €2.50/1.50; ☼ 10.30am-5pm Wed-Sat, 2-5pm Sun) is based in the 17th-century courthouse, which was used for the inquest into the sinking of the *Lusitania* in 1915. Naturally, the museum contains information relating to the disaster, as well as exhibits on topics as diverse as the 1601 Battle of Kinsale, and the eight-foot-tall Kinsale Giant.

CHARLES FORT

In Summercove, 3km east of Kinsale, stand the huge ruins of 17th-century **Charles Fort** (☎ 477 2263; adult/child €3.50/1.25; ☼ 10am-6pm Easter-Oct, 10am-5pm Nov-Easter, last admission 45 min before closing). This is one of the best-preserved 17th-century star-shaped forts in Europe, and is definitely worth a visit for its spectacular views alone. It was built in the 1670s to guard Kinsale harbour, and remained in use until 1921, when much of the fort was destroyed as the British withdrew. Most of the ruins you see inside date from the 18th and 19th centuries.

DESMOND CASTLE

This early-16th-century **tower house** (☎ 477 4855; Cork St; adult/child €2.75/1.25; ☼ 10am-6pm Tue-Sun mid-Apr–early Oct, last admission 45 min before closing) was occupied by the Spanish in 1601. Since then it has served as a prison for French

---

AAAAARRR, ME HEARTIES!

The swashbuckling story of pirate Anne Bonny (c 1697–c 1720) begins in County Cork. Anne's father William Cormac, an attorney in Kinsale, had a very visible affair with his maid, Mary Brennan. As a result, his legal work dried up, and he took Mary and their illegitimate daughter to start a new life in Charleston, South Carolina.

Tomboyish Anne ruled the roost. At 16, she fell for James Bonny and the couple wed, but William Cormac was disgusted by the match and cut her off without a penny. Anne and James left for New Providence, a rollicking 'pirates' paradise' in the Bahamas. Growing distant from her husband (possibly because of his new job as an informer), Anne then took up with 'Calico Jack' Rackham, a pirate renowned for his stripy trousers! The two eloped on a stolen ship, with Anne disguised in men's clothing.

Anne became a fully fledged pirate, boarding merchant ships, stealing booty, and wielding pistols, swords and cusswords with the best. In a strange twist, she developed a crush on a handsome young crew member. This turned out to be Mary Read, another woman disguised as a man, and the two became best friends.

Anne's life on the high seas ended in October 1720, when Jack's ship was attacked by pirate-hunter Captain Burnet. Anne and Mary were left to repel the boarders singlehandedly, as Jack and his men were too drunk to fight. Between firing bullets at Burnet, the disgusted women took potshots at their own crew, lying comatose below decks.

At trial, Anne and Mary were granted stays of execution when it was discovered they were both pregnant. Jack was sentenced to death and Anne's last words to him in prison were: 'I'm sorry to see you here, but had you fought like a man, you need not have been hanged like a dog.'

Mary died behind bars, but Anne Bonny vanishes without trace from the record. Theories abound: that her father took pity and bought her pardon; that a lover whisked her off to freedom; or, the favourite legend, that the pirate community rallied round, aiming their cannons at the governor's house with the message 'Let Anne Bonny go, or feel the thunder of pirate guns!'

---

and American captives, and as a workhouse during the Famine. It now houses a small **wine museum** relating the history of the Irish wine trade.

ST MULTOSE CHURCH

St Multose is the patron saint of Kinsale and this Church of Ireland **church** (rectory ☎ 477 2220; Church St) is one of Ireland's oldest, built around 1190 by the Normans on the site of a 6th-century church. Not much of the interior is original but the exterior is preserved beautifully. The graveyard has some interesting large family tombs, and several victims of the *Lusitania* sinking are also buried there. Inside, a flat stone carved with a strange, round-handed figure was traditionally rubbed by fishermen's wives to bring their husbands home safe from the sea. A guide is available for €2.50 at the entrance.

Activities

WALKING TOURS

The one-hour **Herlihy's Guided Tour** (☎ 477 2873; adult/child €5/1) leaves from outside the tourist office at 11.15am daily.

HARBOUR CRUISES

For sailings to Charles Fort, James Cove and up the Bandon River phone **Kinsale Harbour Cruises** (☎ 477 8946, 086 250 5456). Boats leave seven times a day during summer, five times a day at the weekend the rest of the year, from Denis Quay on Pier Rd, at the southern end of town. They cost €9/4.50 per adult/child seven to 16 years.

FISHING

Tackle can be hired at the **Hire Shop** (☎ 477 4884; 18 Main St) for €10 per day. For deep-sea fishing trips, contact **David Shorten** (☎ 087 214 2999).

Festivals & Events

Kinsale's **Festival of Autumn Flavours**, held in early October, highlights the town's gourmet reputation with tastings, meals, harbour cruises and loads of good food. Book ahead – see www.kinsalerestaurants.com.

Chilled-out entertainment is supplied on the late-October bank holiday weekend, courtesy of the **Kinsale Fringe Jazz Festival** – see www.kinsale.ie.

COUNTY CORK

Sleeping

BUDGET

Kinsale is geared towards the well-heeled. There are good bus links to Cork city, so you might consider staying in one of the bigger city's many hostels (see p211) and commuting.

Guardwell Lodge (☎ 477 4686; www.guardwell lodge.com; Guardwell; dm/s/d €17/28/55; ☐) This excellent Lodge is Kinsale's newest and cheapest accommodation option. It's parquet-floored throughout, clean as anything, and has intimate en-suite dorms (two- and four-bed affairs). There's also a good kitchen, dining room and a lounge with Internet access.

Garrettstown House Holiday Park (☎ /fax 477 8156; admin@garrettstownhouse.com; camp sites €15;

☼ May-Sep) This is the closest camp site and is in the grounds of an 18th-century estate. It's a peaceful setting but the park gets quite lively with families in summer. The site is 1.3km southwest of Ballinspittle (11km southwest of Kinsale) on the R600.

MIDRANGE

Rocklands House (☎ 477 2609; rocklandshouse@eircom .net; Compass Hill; s/d €80/90; ☐) Treat yourself to this top-of-the-range B&B, or to its self-catering cottage (enquire for terms). It's outside the town and high above the estuary, among beautiful hillside gardens. Even the rooms without estuary views are lie-back-and-dream quality, and the service is impeccable.

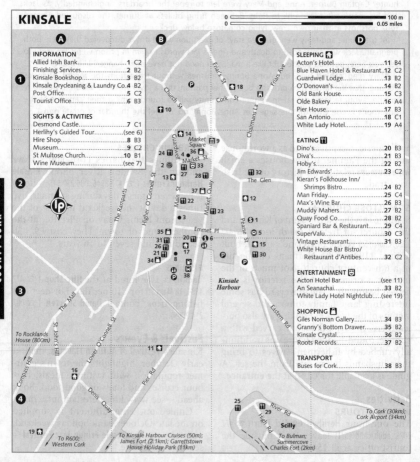

KINSALE

0 ———— 100 m
0 ———— 0.05 miles

INFORMATION	
Allied Irish Bank	1 C2
Finishing Services	2 B2
Kinsale Bookshop	3 B2
Kinsale Drycleaning & Laundry Co	4 B2
Post Office	5 C2
Tourist Office	6 B3

SIGHTS & ACTIVITIES	
Desmond Castle	7 C1
Herlihy's Guided Tour	(see 6)
Hire Shop	8 B3
Museum	9 C2
St Multose Church	10 B1
Wine Museum	(see 7)

SLEEPING	
Acton's Hotel	11 B4
Blue Haven Hotel & Restaurant	12 C2
Guardwell Lodge	13 B2
O'Donovan's	14 B2
Old Bank House	15 C3
Olde Bakery	16 A4
Pier House	17 B3
San Antonio	18 C1
White Lady Hotel	19 A4

EATING	
Dino's	20 B3
Diva's	21 B3
Hoby's	22 B3
Jim Edwards'	23 C2
Kieran's Folkhouse Inn/	
Shrimps Bistro	24 B2
Man Friday	25 C4
Max's Wine Bar	26 B3
Muddy Mahers	27 B2
Quay Food Co	28 B2
Spaniard Bar & Restaurant	29 C4
SuperValu	30 C3
Vintage Restaurant	31 B3
White House Bar Bistro/	
Restaurant d'Antibes	32 C2

ENTERTAINMENT	
Acton Hotel Bar	(see 11)
An Seanachai	33 B2
White Lady Hotel Nightclub	(see 19)

SHOPPING	
Giles Norman Gallery	34 B3
Granny's Bottom Drawer	35 B2
Kinsale Crystal	36 B2
Roots Records	37 B2

TRANSPORT	
Buses for Cork	38 B3

Market Square
Market St
The Glen
Kinsale Harbour
Emmet Pl
Scilly
River Rd
High Rd

To Rocklands House (800m)

To R600; Western Cork

To Kinsale Harbour Cruises (50m); James Fort (2.1km); Garrettstown House Holiday Park (11km)

To Bulman; Summercove; Charles Fort (2km)

To Cork (30km); Cork Airport (34km)

COUNTY CORK

Olde Bakery (☎ 477 3012; theoldebakery@oceanfree .net; 56 Lower O'Connell St; r €75; ✂) A short walk southwest of the centre is this very friendly house that was once the British garrison bakery. Rooms are a reasonable size and terrific breakfasts around a big kitchen table get everyone chatting.

O'Donovan's (☎ 477 2428; odonovans_bb@iolfree.ie; 8 Guardwell; s/d €35/64; ✂) Bright, fresh colours, simple, comfy rooms and a nice welcome, plus worthwhile advice on the town, make this central place deservedly popular.

San Antonio (☎ 477 2341; 1 Friar's St; s/d €42/64; ☯ Apr-Oct) This is another reasonably priced winner in a fine old house a short way up from the harbour. It has very comfy old-fashioned interiors and Jimmy, the owner, is a star…well, helpful.

TOP END

Pier House (☎ 477 4475; www.pierhousekinsale.com; Pier Rd; r €140) This superb B&B, set back from the road in its own private garden, is one of the best places in Ireland to rest your head. Pristine rooms, decorated with shell-and-driftwood sculptures, have hi-tech black-granite bathrooms attached – with power showers, underfloor heating and special non-misting mirrors! Four of them also have balconies and sea views. The whole place is wonderfully decorated and equipped, with bold artworks, modern furniture, a hot tub and sauna, and a barbecue if you fancy self-catering.

Old Bank House (☎ 477 4075; www.oldbank housekinsale.com; 11 Pearse St; s €130-155, d €170-215) Another spectacular option. Georgian elegance and style give a timeless quality to this top-of-the-range hotel. Beautiful *objets d'art* and paintings grace the walls, and the luxurious public rooms add a country-house ambience. The owners are lovely, and breakfasts, with home-made breads and jams, are superb.

Also recommended:

Blue Haven Hotel & Restaurant (☎ 477 2209; www.bluehavenkinsale.com; 3 Pearse St; s/d €140/220) Look for off-season deals at this central 'boutique' hotel, which adds all sorts of persuasive touches to its lavish sleigh-bedded rooms.

Acton's Hotel (☎ 477 2135; www.actonshotelkinsale .com; Pier Rd; s/d €180/240; ℗) This is a fairly pricey option, but rooms are well appointed and there's a good range of facilities, including swimming pool and fitness club.

White Lady Hotel (☎ 477 2737; wlady@indigo.ie; Lower O'Connell St; s/d €80/100) A modern upbeat hotel with comfortable rooms, restaurant, busy bar and night-club (see p226).

Eating

Kinsale's still-busy fleet of fishing vessels ensures that the town's restaurants have a high reputation for seafood. Meat eaters are not neglected, however, and you can also get cheap snacks and meals.

BUDGET

Diva's (☎ 477 3837; 40 Main St; snacks €3.70-5; ☯ 9am-7pm Mon-Sat, 11am-6pm Sun) A charming little oasis of affordable, healthy food, Diva's has a gently alternative mood. Coffee refills are the norm. There's a tasty choice of *panini*, including veggie options, with home-made cakes and brownies to follow.

Spaniard Bar & Restaurant (☎ 477 2436; www .thespaniard.ie; Scilly; lunch €5-9.50) This is a good old seafarers' bar on Scilly, with low ceilings and a peat fire. You can crack crab claws or settle for a sandwich at the bar, and there's a **restaurant** (mains €15-20; ☯ noon-6pm & 6.30-10pm Jun-Sep) during the summer. Monday and Wednesday are trad music nights all year round (six nights per week during the summer).

Dino's (☎ 477 4561; Pier Rd; mains €8-10; ☯ 8am-10.30pm) This no-fuss chipper and family restaurant is Kinsale's most convenient cheap fuel stop. Besides fish and chips, they do breakfasts (€5.50) and an all-day four-courser (€17.50).

Muddy Mahers (☎ 477 4602; www.muddymaher .com; 1 Main St; meals €9-15; ☯ noon-3pm & 6-9.30pm Mon-Fri, noon-9.30pm Sat & Sun) The big bar food-style meals here are good 'n' tasty. They include plenty of meat dishes, a veggie option, a great ocean chowder (€5.50), an even better fish pie (€10.50) and well-filled open baguettes (€6.75 to €9).

Kinsale has the **SuperValu** (Pearse St; ☯ 8.30am-9pm Mon-Sat, 10am-9pm Sun) supermarket, and the tremendously helpful **Quay Food Co** (☎ 477 4000; www.quayfood.com; Market Quay; ☯ 9am-6pm Apr-Sep, 9.30am-5.30pm Mon-Sat) for local produce and little luxuries.

MIDRANGE

Jim Edwards' (☎ 477 2541; www.jimedwardskinsale .com; Market Quay; bar meals €4-14.90, restaurant meals €17-29.50; ☯ bar 12.30-10pm, restaurant 6-10pm) Like

COUNTY CORK

TOP FIVE CORK CHEESES

- Gubbeen – in plain or smoked versions, this is recommended for Cork cheese newbies

- Ardrahan – a flavoursome farmhouse creation with a rich, nutty taste

- Hegarty's – there's a sharp bite to this raw-milk, 12-month-old cheddar

- Gabriel – a gruyère-style cheese with a lemony-pineapple tang

- Durrus – fine-food fans will fall for this creamy, fruity cheese

so many of the Kinsale places, this much-frequented eatery has bar food that is of restaurant standard. A steady Irish touch is nicely frothed with European influences. In the bar you may need to fight for attention amidst the clamour, but once served you'll want to stay all night. The restaurant specialises in steaks and fish, and does an excellent cold seafood platter of shellfish and salmon for €25.50.

White House Bar Bistro/Restaurant d'Antibes (☎ 477 2125; info@whitehouse-kinsale.com; Pearse St; bar meals €4.40-10, restaurant meals €17.50-26; ☺ bar noon-10pm, restaurant 6-10pm) The décor here is fairly standard, but the food is enjoyable at this busy central pub-restaurant. It doesn't try too hard to fit the 'gourmet' bill, instead it settles for efficient service and an unfussy menu.

Kieran's Folkhouse Inn/Shrimps Bistro (☎ 477 2382; Guardwell; bar mains €9-12, bistro mains €17-22; ☺ bar 12.30-10.30pm, bistro 6-10.30pm) A popular place done out in sunny colours, this inn also has a split food servery. The bar menu has choices ranging from snacks and sandwiches to heftier meals. Then there's the pricier seafood bistro, which also has a rather un-PC-sounding 'Safari Menu' for those sick of fish; it features ostrich, wild boar, kangaroo and crocodile – just don't tell the waiter to make it snappy.

TOP END

Vintage Restaurant (☎ 477 2502; www.vintage restaurant.ie; 50 Main St; mains €29-31.50; ☺ 6.30-10pm Apr-Oct) The Vintage is one of the real reasons that Kinsale deserves its gourmet label, with prices that are truly justifiable. Unbeatable dishes range from oyster starters to mains

of monkfish or sea bass; fish that demand a magic touch – and get it.

Bulman (☎ 477 2131; www.thebulman.com; Summer-cove; bar meals €4-9.50, mains €18-24; ☺ 12.30-9.30pm) This is seaside eating at its best. The Bulman is an escape from central Kinsale to an un-spoiled harbourside venue where informality is a style in its own right. Seafood excels here, with chowder or smoked salmon for lunch options, and with starters that add adventurous New World touches to sea bream and tiger prawns, among many choices.

Max's Wine Bar (☎ 477 2443; 48 Main St; lunch €4.50-9, dinner €16-25; ☺ 12.30-2.45pm & 6.30-10.30pm Mon & Wed-Sat, 1-3pm & 6.30-10pm Sun Mar-Oct) There's definitely an Irish-French crossover touch in both the surroundings and the subtle cuisine of this charming place, where exposed stone walls and burnished wooden tables reinforce Kinsale's unquestionable Brittany coast feel.

Hoby's (☎ 477 2200; 5 Main St; mains €18-25; ☺ 6-10.30pm) More excellent Irish-European cuisine is served at this very swish place, where subtle colours and thoughtful seating make you feel that it's all just for you.

Man Friday (☎ 477 2260; www.man-friday.net; cnr River & High Rds, Scilly; mains €20-28; ☺ 6.45-10.15pm Mon-Sat) Out of town at relaxing Scilly, this 28-year-old restaurant has outdoor seating with views across the harbour to Kinsale. Book ahead if you want a terrace table on balmy evenings. While excellent fish dishes are the norm, there are steak, lamb, duck and vegetarian options.

Entertainment

Spaniard Bar & Restaurant (☎ 477 2436; thespaniard@ eircom.net; Scilly) There's a regular Wednesday night trad session here at 9.30pm year round and music throughout the summer on Friday night and Sunday afternoon.

Acton's Hotel (☎ 477 2135; Pier Rd) Stages a terrific Sunday lunch-time jazz session (12.30pm to 2.30pm) featuring the famous Cork City Jazz Band.

An Seanachai (☎ 477 7077; www.anseanachai.com; 6 Market St) This big barn-like pub has trad music sessions on Tuesday, and there's a fairly stomping disco till late on Thursday, Friday and Saturday.

White Lady Hotel (☎ 477 2737; Lower O'Connell St) The nightclub has a breezy, youngish crowd at weekends and it runs '60s and '70s nights.

COUNTY CORK

Shopping

Giles Norman Gallery (☎ 477 4373; 45 Main St) There's a big selection of powerful and evocative black-and-white imagery here, mainly stunning landscapes, from a master of the genre. Prices, framed or unframed, start at about €25 and rise to hundreds of euros.

Granny's Bottom Drawer (☎ 477 4839; 53 Main St) A great range of exquisite Irish linen, damask and nightwear is sold at this cheerful shop.

Roots Records (☎ 477 4963; www.rootsrecords.ie; 1 Short Quay) This useful music shop has absolutely everything from trad to reggae.

Kinsale Crystal (☎ 477 4493; Market St) Exquisite work by an ex-Waterford craftsman who stands by the traditional 'deep-cutting, high-angle style' is available here. A napkin ring costs about €36, while large pieces are in the mid-hundreds.

Getting There & Away

Bus Éireann (☎ 450 8188) services connect Kinsale with Cork (€6.50, 50 minutes, 10 daily Monday to Saturday, five Sunday). The bus stops at the Esso garage on Pier Rd, near the tourist office.

Getting Around

You can hire bikes (€12 per day), including tandems, from the **Hire Shop** (☎ 477 4884; 18 Main St). For a taxi call **Kinsale Cabs** (☎ 477 2642).

CLONAKILTY

☎ 023 / pop 3432

Cheerful, brightly coloured Clonakilty is a bustling market town that knows how to look after its visitors. You'll find smart B&Bs, top restaurants and cosy pubs alive with great music.

Clonakilty is famous for two important Cork products. Firstly, it was the birthplace of Michael Collins (see boxed text, below), a matter of extreme pride to the community; a statue of the Big Fella stands on the corner of Emmet Square. Secondly, it's the source of the best black pudding in Ireland; for varieties based on 19th-century recipes, head for **Edward Twomey's** (☎ 33733; 16 Pearse St; puddings from €2.50).

History

Clonakilty received its first charter in 1292 but was refounded in the early 17th century by Richard Boyle, the first earl of Cork. He settled it with 100 English families and

---

MICHAEL COLLINS – THE 'BIG FELLA'

County Cork, and especially the Clonakilty area, has a close and deeply cherished association with Michael Collins, the 'Big Fella', commander-in-chief of the army of the Irish Free State that won independence from Britain in 1922.

Collins was born on a small farm at Woodfield near Clonakilty, the youngest of eight children, and went to school in the town. He lived and worked in London from 1906 to 1916, and then returned to Ireland where he took part in the Easter Rising. Thereafter Collins became a key figure in Irish Nationalism. He revolutionised the way the Irish rebels fought, organising them into guerrilla 'flying columns', and was the main negotiator of the 1921 Anglo-Irish Treaty that led to the Irish Free State, yet plunged the country into a brutal civil war.

Michael Collins was ambushed and killed by anti-treaty forces on 22 August 1922 at Beal-na-Bláth, near Macroom. He was on a tour of western Cork at the time. The site is marked by a stone memorial with a Gaelic inscription. Each year, a commemorative service is held on the anniversary of the killing. To visit the site follow the N22 west from Cork then after about 20km take the left turn (R590) to Crookstown. From there turn right onto the R585 to Beal-na-Bláth. The ambush site is on the left after 4km.

A useful map and leaflet *In Search of Michael Collins* (€4) can be obtained at Clonakilty tourist office, outlining places in the district associated with him. The excellent **Michael Collins Centre** (☎ 023-46107; www.reachireland.com, www.michaelcollinscentre.com; adult/child 10-16 €5/2; ☼ 10.30am-5pm Mon-Sat mid-Jun–mid-Sep) will give you a one- to 1½-hour tour of photos, letters and a reconstruction of the 1920s country lane where Collins was killed, complete with armoured vehicle. The centre is signposted off the R600 between Timoleague and Clonakilty. The **Clonakilty Museum** (Western Rd; admisstion €3; ☼ Jun-Aug) has some more memorabilia, including Collins' weapons and uniform. The museum is run on a voluntary basis: contact the tourist office for exact opening hours.

planned a Protestant town from which Catholics would be excluded. His plan ultimately failed: Clonakilty is now very Irish and very Catholic – the Presbyterian chapel has been turned into a post office.

From the mid-18th to mid-19th centuries over 10,000 people worked in the town's linen industry. The fire station stands on the site of the old linen market.

Orientation

Roads converge on Asna Square, which is dominated by a monument commemorating the 1798 Rising. Also in the square is the Kilty Stone, a piece of the original castle that gave Clonakilty (Clogh na Kylte, meaning 'castle of the woods') its name. Inchydoney Island is about 4km from the centre.

Information

Clon Cyber Café (☎ 21745; evitasadlowski@eircom .net; 37 Ashe St; €1/5 per 5/60min; ♥ 10am-6pm Mon-Sat, noon-6pm Sun) Internet access.

Library (Old Mill Library; ☎ 34275; Kent St; ♥ 10am-6pm Tue-Sat) For a €2.50 membership you can use the computers for free.

Tourist office (☎ 33226; info@corkkerrytourism.ie; Ashe St; ♥ 9am-6pm daily Jul & Aug, 9.15am-5pm Mon-Sat Sep-Jun) Has a good free map of the town.

Wash Basket (☎ 34821; Spiller's Lane; ♥ 9am-6pm Mon-Sat) Has a same-day laundry service.

The Allied Irish Bank on the corner of Pearse and Bridge Sts has an ATM. The post office is in the old Presbyterian chapel on Bridge St.

There are public toilets on the corner of Rossa and Kent Sts.

Sights & Activities

Of more than 30,000 ring forts scattered across Ireland, **Lisnagun** (Lios na gCon; ☎ 32565; www.liosnagcon.com; adult/child €5/3; ♥ by appointment only) is the only one that has been reconstructed on its original site. Complete with *souterrain* and central thatched hut, it gives a vivid impression of life in a 10th-century defended farmstead. To get there take the turning on the roundabout at the end of Strand Rd, signposted to Bay View House B&B. Follow the road uphill for 2km until you reach a T-junction. Turn right, then continue for about 800m before turning right again (signposted); the fort is a few hundred metres along the road.

West Cork Model Railway Village (☎ 33224; Inchydoney Rd; adult/child €6/3.50; ♥ 11am-5pm Feb-Oct) features not only a working replica of the West Cork Railway as it was during WWII, but superb miniature models of the main towns in western Cork – Clonakilty, Dunmanway, Kinsale and Bandonas – as they were in the 1940s. A **road train** (adult/child incl admission to Railway Village €10/5.50; ♥ Jun-Aug) leaves from the Railway Village on a 20-minute commentated circuit of the town.

The bay is good for **swimming**, albeit in a bracing sort of way. The sandy Blue Flag **beach** at nearby Inchydoney Island is good too, but watch for the dangerous riptide; when lifeguards are on duty a red flag indicates danger. The **West Cork Surf School** (☎ 086 869 5396; www.westcorksurfing.com; 2hr lesson €30) is also based there, should you fancy a ride on the waves.

Sleeping

Clonakilty Hostel (☎ 33525; fax 35673; Old Brewery Lane; dm/d €15/35; P &) This well-maintained place is at the end of a quiet cul-de-sac in one of the oldest parts of town. However, the building itself isn't well soundproofed, so noise can be a problem if it's busy.

Wytchwood (☎ 33525; wytchost@iol.ie; Old Brewery Lane; s/d from €50/70; P) Opposite the hostel and run by the same people, engaging Wytchwood is rooted in Clonakilty's past. The furnishings and dark wood add to the reflective mood.

Tudor Lodge (☎ 33046; tudorlodge1@eircom.net; MacCurtain Hill; s/d €40/65) Sitting pleasantly above it all is this pleasant, peaceful B&B where standards are kept up to scratch in spic-and-span rooms.

Bay View House (☎ 33539; bayviewhouse@eircom .net; Old Timoleague Rd; s/d €52/70) This modern house, with award-winning window boxes, offers impeccable B&B standards with frills, a genial welcome and some great breakfasts. Rooms 5 and 6, and the cosy little landing lounge, all have fantastic views over a barley/beet field that slopes down to Clonakilty Bay. There's also a 'garden suite', with private conservatory.

Emmet Hotel (☎ 33394; www.emmethotel.com; Emmet Sq; s/d €65/120) Refurbishment of Clonakilty's old Georgian hotel has retained its period charm. Rooms are simple, with a relaxing ambience, and O'Keeffe's Restaurant serves up a good selection of Irish food

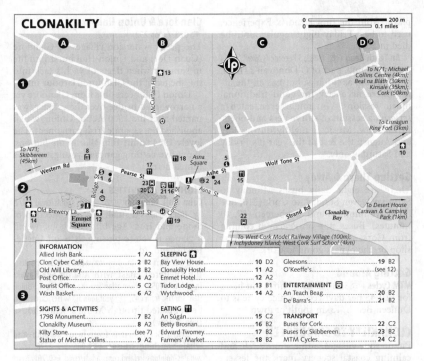

CLONAKILTY

INFORMATION	
Allied Irish Bank	1 A2
Clon Cyber Café	2 B2
Old Mill Library	3 B2
Post Office	4 A2
Tourist Office	5 C2
Wash Basket	6 A2

SIGHTS & ACTIVITIES	
1798 Monument	7 B2
Clonakilty Museum	8 A2
Kilty Stone	(see 7)
Statue of Michael Collins	9 A2

SLEEPING	
Bay View House	10 D2
Clonakilty Hostel	11 A2
Emmet Hotel	12 A2
Tudor Lodge	13 B1
Wytchwood	14 A2

EATING	
An Súgán	15 C2
Betty Brosnan	16 B2
Edward Twomey	17 B2
Farmers' Market	18 B2

Gleesons	19 B2
O'Keeffe's	(see 12)

ENTERTAINMENT	
An Teach Beag	20 B2
De Barra's	21 B2

TRANSPORT	
Buses for Cork	22 C2
Buses for Skibbereen	23 B2
MTM Cycles	24 C2

made from organic and local ingredients, served up with home-baked bread.

Desert House Caravan & Camping Park (☎ 33331; deserthouse@eircom.net; Coast Rd; camp site €11; ✆ Easter & May-Sep) This attractive park is 1.5km southeast of town on the road to Ring. It's on a dairy farm overlooking the bay.

Eating

Gleesons (☎ 21834; www.gleesons.ie; 3-4 Connolly St; lunch mains €13-16.50, dinner mains €17-25; ✆ 12.30-2.30pm Tue-Fri, 6-9.30pm Tue-Sat) Described by one reader as 'out of this world', Gleesons is Clonakilty's newest and best restaurant. The surrounds are nicely understated, with wood and slate décor, and the international menu is simple but perfectly prepared, using organic, fair trade and local seasonal food. The seafood is particularly tasty, or, for something that'll really stick to your ribs, how about a steak-and-Guinness pie?

An Súgán (☎ 33719; www.ansugan.com; 41 Wolfe Tone St; bar meals €5.50-11, mains €12-22; ✆ 12.30-6pm) Another top choice, this family-run eatery exudes style. There's a choice of traditional main bar and restaurant, or a more mod-

ern café-bar and outside courtyard. Seafood is the great thing here, from exquisite crab cocktail to a great selection of prawns, salmon, scallops and monkfish in a filo pastry basket.

Betty Brosnan (☎ 34011; 58 Pearse St; meals €5.50-10; ✆ 9am-5pm Mon, Tue, Thu-Sat, 9am-2.30pm Wed) A prime place for affordable yet satisfying snacks, this busy café offers lots of breakfast choices (€5.50 to €8), sandwiches, smoothies and yum puddings, and caters for coeliacs too. The upstairs gallery displays atmospheric black-and-white photos of the area.

Self-caterers should visit the Thursday **farmers' market** (McCurtain Hill; ✆ 10am-2pm Thu), which sells organic fruit and veg, herbs, smoked fish and local cheeses.

Entertainment

De Barra's (☎ 33381; www.debarra.ie; 55 Pearse St) A marvellous atmosphere, walls splattered with photos, press cuttings, masks and musical instruments, plus live music every night of the week (starting around 9.30pm) make this a busy pub. Noel Redding, bass

COUNTY CORK

player from the Jimi Hendrix Experience, used to be a Friday-night regular, until he died in 2003.

An Teach Beag (☎ 33883; 5 Recorder's Alley) This intriguing pub, part of O'Donovan's Hotel, is not as old as it looks, but has all the atmosphere necessary for good traditional music sessions. You might even catch a *scríocht*, a session of storytellers and poets, in full flow. Music is nightly during July and August; the rest of the year it's Friday and Saturday only.

Getting There & Away

There are eight daily buses Monday to Saturday, seven Sunday, to Cork (€10, one hour five minutes) and Skibbereen (€7, 40 minutes). Buses stop on Pearse St coming from Cork and across from Harte's Spar shop on the bypass going to Cork.

Getting Around

MTM Cycles (☎ 33584; 33 Ashe St) hires out bikes for €10/45 per day/week. A nice cycle is to Duneen Beach, 13km south of town.

CLONAKILTY TO SKIBBEREEN

Picturesque villages, a fine stone circle and calming coastal scenery mark the lesser-taken route from Clonakilty to Skibbereen. Rather than follow the main N71 all the way, when you get to Rosscarbery turn left onto the R597 at the far end of the causeway (signposted Glandore and Coppinger's Court).

Drombeg Stone Circle

On an exposed hillside, with green fields sweeping away down towards the coast, the Drombeg stone circle is superbly atmospheric. Its 17 uprights once guarded the cremated bones of an adolescent, discovered during a 1960s' excavation. The 9m-diameter circle probably dates from the 5th century AD, representing a sophisticated Iron Age update of an earlier Bronze Age monument.

Just beyond the stones are the remains of a hut and an Iron Age cooking pit, known as a *fulachta fiadh*. Experiments have shown that its heated rocks would boil water and then keep it hot for nearly three hours – enough time to cook hunks of meat.

Get there by taking the signposted left turn off the R597, approximately 4km west of Roscarbery.

Glandore & Union Hall

☎ 028 / pop 252

The pretty waterside villages of Glandore (Cuan Dor) and Union Hall burst into life in summer when fleets of yachts tack into the shelter of the Glandore Harbour inlet.

Union Hall, accessible from Glandore via a narrow road bridge over the estuary, was named after the 1800 Act of Union, which abolished the separate Irish parliament. The lovely 1994 family film *War of the Buttons*, about two battling gangs of youngsters, was filmed here.

SIGHTS & ACTIVITIES

Ceim Hill Museum (☎ 36280; adult/child €4/2; ☻ 10am-7pm) is a small private collection of Stone and Iron Age bits and bobs, worth a glance if you're passing. It is off Castletownshend Rd.

You can try a sea-kayaking trip round the sheltered coast with **Atlantic Sea Kayaking** (☎ 21058; www.atlanticseakayaking.com; Union Hall; 3hr trip from €45; ☻ year round), who can also be contacted through Maria's Schoolhouse (see below).

Colin Barnes runs four-hour **dolphin- and whale-watching cruises** (☎ 086 327 3226; www .whales-dolphins-ireland.com; adult/child €40/20) and shorter coastal trips from Reen Pier, about 3km beyond Union Hall. The best time of year for seeing cetaceans is between June and Christmas.

SLEEPING & EATING

Maria's Schoolhouse (☎ 33002; mariasschoolhouse@ eircom.net; Cahergal, Union Hall; dm €13, d with bathroom €50; P ☒) No longer owned by Maria but in safe hands, this outstanding hostel occupies a converted 19th-century schoolhouse of great character in peaceful surroundings. Year-round buffet breakfasts cost €6.50, and between June and August dinners are available on request (€24). The hostel can organise kayaking trips. To get there turn right after crossing the causeway into Union Hall and continue through the village following the sign for Skibbereen. It's signposted at the edge of town about 1km from the centre.

Meadow Camping Park (☎ 33280; the_meadow@ oceanfree.net; Rosscarbery road, Glandore; camp sites €16; ☻ Easter-mid-Sep) This small idyllic site, in a garden filled with trees and flowers, is 2km east of Glandore on the R597 to Rosscarbery.

Ardagh House & Restaurant (☎ 33571; Union Hall; s/d €40/64; mains €15.50-20; restaurant ⊗ daily Apr-Oct, Sat & Sun Nov-Mar; P 🖳) A friendly place by the harbour, Ardagh has bright sunny rooms. The popular restaurant does plentiful helpings of straightforward fish and meat dishes.

GETTING THERE & AWAY
Although buses do not pass through Glandor and Union Hall, they do stop in nearby Leap (3km north), and the hostel and most B&B owners will pick you up from here if you prearrange it.

SKIBBEREEN
☎ 028 / pop 2000
Skibbereen (Sciobairín) is a fine name to roll around the tongue. It's a typical market town – unvarnished, down-to-earth and warm hearted – with a busy Friday **market** (⊗ 12.30-2.30pm) and a steady influx of tourists stopping off on their way to western Cork.

History
Skibbereen was particularly badly affected during the Famine. Huge numbers of the local population emigrated or died of starvation, smallpox, dysentery, fever or typhus. 'The accounts are not exaggerated – they cannot be exaggerated – nothing more frightful can be conceived.' So wrote Lord Dufferin and GF Boyle, who journeyed from Oxford to Skibbereen in February 1847 to see if reports of the Famine were true. Their eye-witness account makes horrific reading; Dufferin was so appalled by what he saw that he contributed £1000 (about €100,000 in today's money) to the relief effort.

Orientation
The main landmark in town is a statue in the central square, dedicated to heroes of Irish rebellions against the British. From here, three roads branch off: Market St heads south past the post office to Lough Hyne and Baltimore; the principle shopping street, Main St, becomes Bridge St before heading west over the river to Ballydehob and Bantry; and North St heads towards the main Cork road.

Information
The **tourist office** (☎ 21766; skibbereen@skibbereen .corkkerrytourism.ie; North St; ⊗ 9am-7pm Jul & Aug,

9am-6pm Mon-Sat Jun & Sep, 9.15am-1pm & 2.15-5pm Mon-Fri Oct-May) has an excellent pamphlet, the *Skibbereen Trail* (€1.75), which takes you on a historical walking tour of the town; it's also available from newsagencies and the Heritage Centre.

There's an Allied Irish Bank with an ATM on Bridge St.

For Internet access head to the **Sutherland Centre** (☎ 21011; per hr €3; ⊗ 10am-5pm Mon-Fri), on the top floor of the **West Cork Arts Centre** (☎ 22090; North St; ⊗ 10am-6pm Mon-Sat), which hosts local art exhibitions.

Sights
Constructed on the site of the town's old gasworks, the small **Heritage Centre** (☎ 40900; www.skibbheritage.com; Old Gasworks Bldg, Upper Bridge St; adult/child €4.50/2.50; ⊗ 10am-6pm daily Jun-Sep, 10am-6pm Tue-Sat Easter-May & mid-Sep–Oct, last admission 5.15pm) houses a haunting exhibition about the Famine, where you can hear actors reading heart-breaking contemporary accounts. There's also a smaller exhibition about nearby Lough Hyne, the first marine nature reserve in Ireland, and a genealogical centre.

A visit here puts Irish history into harrowing perspective. The **Abbeystrewery Cemetery** is 1km east of the centre, on the N71 to Schull, and holds the mass graves of 8000 to 10,000 local people who died during the Famine.

Tours
Guided **historical walks** (☎ 40900, 087 930 5735; adult/child €4.50/2) of Skibbereen, lasting 1½ hours, leave from the Heritage Centre at 6.30pm on Tuesday and Saturday April to September. It's best to book.

Sleeping
Russagh Mill Hostel & Adventure Centre (☎ 22451; www.russaghmillhostel.com; Castletownshend Rd; camp sites €7, dm/d/f €13/30/40) This friendly, frenetic place is about 1.5km southeast of town on the R596, and occupies an atmospheric old corn mill that has preserved machinery. It caters mainly for schools groups, but everyone is made welcome. For about €25 you can sample some activities, including a day's kayaking on Loch Hyne or climbing instruction on the centre's climbing wall, taught by experienced kayakers and mountaineers.

> **SOMETHING SPECIAL**
>
> **Bridge House** (☎ 21273; Bridge St; s/d €30/65)
> We can guarantee you've never stayed any-
> where like *this* before! The charming owner,
> Mona Best, has turned her entire house into
> a work of art, filling the rooms with fabulous
> Victorian tableaux and period memorabilia;
> your poor, boggling brain just can't take
> it all in.
>
> If you're lost without a trouser press and
> a shoe-polishing service, this probably isn't
> the place for you. 'Eclectic', 'eccentric' and
> 'unique' are words that describe Bridge
> House, although they don't go far enough.
> Filmy material hangs over the beds in rooms
> strewn with counterpanes, satiny cushions
> and some interesting books. The whole place
> bursts at the seams with cherished clutter,
> crazed carvings, dressed-up dummies and
> stuff too weird to mention. There's a hearty
> nod to modernity in the bathroom, though,
> which contains a spanking-new spa bath.

Ilenroy House (☎ 22751; ilenroyhouse@oceanfree
.net; 10 North St; s/d €45/65) There are five excellent rooms in this old town house, which
has managed to retain its character in spite
of modernisation.

Eldon Hotel (☎ 22000; www.eldon-hotel.com;
Bridge St; d €130; P 🖳) There's a lot of history
in this attractive old hotel, where the walls
in the reception and bar are covered with
photographs and memorabilia of Michael
Collins, a friend of the hotel's owner of the
time. Collins ate his last meal here, before
being ambushed and killed at Beal na Bláth
(see p227). You can muse on the past in
comfy rooms.

Hideaway Camping & Caravan Park (☎ 22254;
the_hideaway@oceanfree.net; R596; camp sites €16;
🖳 late Apr–mid-Sep) This attractive park is
1km southeast of town on the road to
Castletownsend. There's a marshland bird
reserve nearby.

Eating

Ty Ar Mor (☎ 22100; www.tyarmor.com; 46 Bridge St;
lunch €9-15, dinner €35-47; 🖳 noon-2.30pm & 6.30-
9.15pm Jul & Aug) This brilliant award-winning
Breton restaurant offers the freshest fish,
such as turbot, black sole and John Dory,
as well as shellfish from the tank. Seafood
is the main thing, but lamb and steak also

feature, all done with inimitable flair. Phone
for opening times out of high season. Upstairs is the **Thai@Ty Ar Mor Noodle & Wine Bar**
(mains €6-15; 🖳 6.30-9pm Tue-Sat) with Thai staff
and décor.

Kalbo's Bistro (☎ 21515; 48 North St; snacks €4.50-
9, dinner mains €15-24; 🖳 noon-3pm & 6.30-9.30pm Mon-
Sat year round, plus 5.30-9.30pm Sun Jul & Aug) This
bustling place, with fresh flowers on the
tables, serves delicious soup, warm salads,
wraps and stir-fries at lunch-time. When
the candles come out, so does the varied
evening menu, which offers some particularly delish veggie options, alongside the
chicken, duck and salmon, like spicy roast
squash with leek risotto.

Porch Bar/Potter's Restaurant (☎ 22000; Bridge
St; bar snacks €3.20-14.90, dinner mains €14-23; bar food
🖳 noon-8pm year-round, restaurant 🖳 6-8pm Jun-Sep,
phone for winter hr) There's plenty of choice at
the Eldon Hotel's adjoining bar and restaurant, from strongly traditional dishes to
international cuisine, with local meat and
poultry and a great fish menu.

Getting There & Away

Bus Éireann services run to Cork seven
times daily Monday to Saturday, four on
Sunday, (€14, 1¾ hours), and twice daily to
Schull (€5.10, 30 minutes) from outside the
Eldon Hotel on Main St.

BALTIMORE

☎ 028 / pop 383
Picturesque Baltimore has its sailing hat
wedged at a jaunty angle, and a merry whistle on its lips. Its divine coastal setting, with
a pretty harbour dominated by the remains
of the Dún na Sead (Fort of the Jewels), is
the only sight, but there's nowhere better
on a sunny day. Watching the boats with a
pint of stout in your hand is a fantastically
lazy way to spend your time! It has a couple
of fine restaurants and lots of lively pubs to
complete the blissful picture.

Besides idlers, Baltimore is a magnet for
sailing folk, anglers, divers and visitors to
Sherkin and Clear Islands, meaning that the
population swells enormously during the
summer months. There's an information
board at the harbour.

Activities

There's some excellent diving to be had on
the reefs around Fastnet Rock, where the

waters are warmed by the Gulf Stream, and a number of shipwrecks lie nearby, between 10m and 40m down. **Aquaventures Dive Centre** (☎ 20511; www.aquaventures.ie; The Stonehouse B&B, Lifeboat Rd) charges €75 for one dive with gear rental, €50 if you have your own wetsuit and fins, and €35 without any rental. They also do diving/accommodation packages in the outdoorsy B&B attached; contact them for prices.

Baltimore Sailing School (☎ 20141) provides sailing courses (five days €295) from June to September for beginners and advanced sailors.

A white-painted landmark beacon (aka Lot's Wife) stands on the western headland of the peninsula and makes for a pleasant **walk**, especially at sunset.

Festivals & Events
Over the last full weekend of May, Baltimore stages a **seafood festival**. Jazz bands perform and pubs bring out the mussels and prawns.

Sleeping
If you come to Baltimore in summer without booking accommodation, make sure you've got a bivvy bag and a handy hedge to put it under!

Casey's of Baltimore (☎ 20197; www.caseys ofbaltimore.com; Skibbereen Rd; s/d €110/170; P) Ten of the 14 bedrooms here have estuary views so gorgeous you'll be caught looking for angels. Prise yourself from the windowsill to admire the lavish interiors, containing huge, cloud-like beds. Service is ever so friendly, and there are reasonable discounts offered in the off-season. Eating here is a delight as well (see right).

Fastnet House (☎ 20515; fastnethouse@eircom.net; Main St; s/d €50/70) Another super option, this early-19th-century house is just up from the main harbour. Worn stone steps lead up to calm, uncluttered rooms with big sunshiney windows. There's an easy-going ambience, and the lovely owners really do look after their guests.

Rolf's Holidays (☎ 20289; www.rolfsholidays.com; Baltimore Hill; dm €15, d €40-60; P) Upmarket Rolf's, in a rapidly expanding old farmhouse on the outside of town, does the lot: there are excellent-value bright clean dorms and private rooms, self-catering units, helpful staff, a charming café and restaurant, Café

Art, and the whole place is set in peaceful gardens. Rolf's is gay friendly.

Eating
Customs House Restaurant (☎ 20200; Main St; dinner €28-38; 7-10pm Wed-Sat Jul & Aug, closed Oct-Easter) A modest frontage belies the cool, contemporary interior of the Customs House, which adds to the area's reputation for gourmet food. There are good-value set dinners that feature subtle Italian and French meals of local seafood and fish, such as top-tasting red mullet and monkfish. Reservations are essential. Outside July and August, phone to check hours, as the restaurant only opens if there are enough bookings.

Chez Youen (☎ 20136; The Quay; dinner from €35; 6.30-10pm Jun-Aug, 6.30-10pm Thu-Sat Mar-May, Sep & Oct, 6.30-10pm Fri & Sat Nov-Feb) Terrific seafood is the rule in this Breton-inspired restaurant where the luscious shellfish platter (€55), containing lobster, prawns, brown crab, velvet crab, shrimps and oysters, really offers the chance of sampling shellfish at its best.

Café Art (☎ 20289; Baltimore Hill; baguettes €4-5, mains €14-18; 8.30am-9.30pm, closed Mon & Tue winter) You can order light pasta, salad or vegetarian meals (€5.50 to €11) at the relaxing café-restaurant–art gallery at Rolf's Holidays. There's a light European touch to all the food and an excellent wine list has been developed for the in-house wine bar. Hot dishes aren't served between 3pm and 6pm, but you can still get a sandwich if you're peckish.

Casey's of Baltimore (☎ 20197; sandwiches €3.50-8.80, mains €15-30; 12.30-2.30pm & 6.30-9.30pm) Even if you don't stay at Casey's you can call in for breakfast, sandwiches or full-on dinner, helped down by fantastic views. The seafood platters (€24) include mussels fresh from the hotel's own shellfish farm in Roaringwater Bay. Bar meals are served all day.

Getting There & Away
From Monday to Friday there are three buses per day from Skibbereen to Baltimore (€3.20, 20 minutes), with an extra two services daily during July and August. From May to mid-September, there are four buses on Saturday.

See p235 for the Schull–Clear Island–Baltimore ferry service.

COUNTY CORK

CLEAR ISLAND

☎ 028 / pop 150

With its lonely inlets, pebbly beaches, gorse and heather-covered cliffs, Clear Island (Oileán Cléire; also called Cape Clear Island) is an escapist's heaven. You'll need plenty of time to suck the full enjoyment from this rugged Irish-speaking (Gaeltacht) area, the most southerly inhabited island in the country. It's a place for quiet walks, hunting down standing stones, and bird-watching. Each year at the beginning of September, as the nights begin to shorten, the island hosts a week-long storytelling festival.

Facilities are few, but there are a couple of B&Bs, one shop and three pubs. The island has its own website at www.oilean -chleire.ie/index.htm.

Orientation & Information

The island is 5km long and just over 1.5km wide at its broadest point. It narrows in the middle where an isthmus divides the northern and southern harbours. There's a **tourist information post** (☎ 39100; ☼ 11am-1pm & 3-6pm May-Aug) beyond the pier, next to the coffee shop, which also has various leaflets.

You'll find public toilets down at the harbour.

Sights

The small **heritage centre** (☎ 39119; admission €2.50; ☼ 2.30-5pm Jun-Aug) has exhibits on the island's history and culture, and fine views looking north across the water to the Mizen Head Peninsula.

The ruins of 14th-century **Dunamore Castle**, the stronghold of the O'Driscoll clan, can be seen perched on a rock on the north-western side of the island (follow the track from the harbour).

Festivals & Events

The **Cape Clear Island International Storytelling Festival** (☎ 39116; http://indigo.ie/~stories; weekend ticket €50) brings hundreds of people to Clear Island for storytelling, workshops and walks. The event usually takes place over three days at the beginning of September. Book well ahead for tickets and accommodation as the festival is becoming more popular each year and there's limited availability.

Activities

BIRD-WATCHING

Cape Clear is one of the top bird-watching spots in Ireland, particularly for sea birds, including Manx shearwater, gannet, fulmar and kittiwake. The guillemot breeds on the island, but other birds head to and fro on hunting trips from the rocky outposts of the western peninsulas. Tens of thousands of birds can pass hourly, especially in the early morning and at dusk. The best time of year for twitching here is October.

The white-fronted, two-storey **bird observatory** is by the harbour (turn right at the end of the pier and it's 100m along). It's worth calling in to ask about any planned bird-watching trips.

For trips to Fastnet Rock or bird-watching boat trips phone **MVS Gaisceanán** (☎ 39182).

BirdWatch Ireland (www.birdwatchireland.ie) runs bird-watching field courses to Cape Clear; see the website for details.

OUTDOOR ACTIVITIES

For **guided walks** covering historical, archaeological or ecological aspects of the island phone ☎ 39157 (during summer); for natural history, phone ☎ 39193.

Courses

Comharchumann Chléire Teo (☎ 39119; ccteo@iol.ie) runs Irish-language courses for 11- to 18-year-olds (€650 for three weeks). For adult learners, **Ionad Foghlama Chléire** (☎ 39190; www .cleire.com) runs one- to 10-day programmes.

If there's anything you need to know about goat husbandry contact Ed Harper at **Cléire Goats** (☎ 39126; goat@iol.ie), based on a farm west of the church. He makes ice cream and cheese, available for tastings, and runs day- and week-long courses on goat keeping.

Sleeping & Eating

Accommodation on the island is satisfyingly simple and unfancy. Book ahead, especially between May and September.

There is a **camp site** (in summer ☎ 39136, in winter ☎ 39119; per person €7; ☼ Jun-Sep) and An Óige's **Cape Clear Island Hostel** (☎ 41968; anoige@ fenlon.net; Old Coastguard Station, South Harbour; dm €17 1st night, then €15; ▣), which is in a large white building at the south harbour.

Ask for directions to these two friendly B&Bs in typical island houses: **Ard Na Gao-**

ithe (☎ 39160; The Glen; s/d €30/60) and **Cluain Mara** (☎ 39153, 39172; www.capeclearisland.com; North Harbour; s/d €35/60), which also has self-catering cottages available.

In summer there's a chip van at the north harbour.

Other recommendations:

Siopa Beag (☎ 39099; North Harbour) Coffee shop and grocery store with a few supplies for self-caterers.

Ciarán Danny Mike's (☎ 39172; www.capeclearisland.ie; meals €7-12) Generous bar meals.

Getting There & Away

From Baltimore, the ferry **Naomh Ciarán II** (☎ 39159; www.capeclearferry.info) takes 45 minutes to cover the 11km journey to Clear Island and it's a stunning trip on a clear day. There are four boats per day between mid-July and mid-August, and at least two per day the rest of the year; return fares are €11.50/6.50 per adult/child and there are special family rates available. Bikes travel free of charge.

GOUGANE BARRA FOREST PARK

This is the most picturesque part of inland County Cork. The source of the River Lee is a mountain lake, fed by numerous silver streams. St Finbarre, the founder and patron saint of Cork, came here in the 6th century and established a monastery. He had a hermitage on the island in **Gougane Barra Lake** (Lough an Ghugain), which is now approached by a short causeway. The small, modern **chapel** on the island has fine stained-glass representations of obscure Celtic saints.

A road runs through the park in a loop and you can walk the network of paths and **nature trails** that are indicated on a signboard map.

Getting There & Away

In July and August there's one Saturday-only bus service that leaves Macroom at 8am and passes by the Gougane Barra Forest Park, returning at 4.40pm.

Driving from Cork to Bantry along the N22 and R584 you'll see a signpost for a park after Ballingeary. Returning to the main road afterwards and continuing west, you'll travel over the Pass of Keimaneigh and emerge on the N71 at Ballylickey, midway between the Beara Peninsula and the Sheep's Head Peninsula.

MIZEN HEAD PENINSULA

From Skibbereen the road continues west through Ballydehob, the gateway to the Mizen, and then on to the pretty village of Schull. Travelling on into the undulating countryside takes you through ever-smaller settlements, to the village of Goleen.

Even here the Mizen isn't done. Increasingly narrow roads head further west to spectacular Mizen Head itself and to the hidden delights of Barleycove Beach and Crookhaven. Without a decent map you may well reach the same crossroads several times.

Heading back from Goleen, you can bear off north to join the scenic coast road that follows the edge of Dunmanus Bay for most of the way to Durrus. At Durrus, one road heads for Bantry while the other turns west to Sheep's Head Peninsula.

SCHULL

☎ 028 / pop 693

Schull (pronounced skull) is a small fishing village where a few vessels still keep the trade alive. The harbour has the satisfying clutter of a working port, and water sports play their part in making Schull a busy tourist attraction. It's particularly busy during Calves Week, a sailing regatta usually held after the August bank holiday. Out of season it's even more attractive in some ways, with a strong local community.

A small Sunday **market** (☎ 27824; 🕓 10am-2pm Easter-Christmas) sells honey, cheese, plants and crafty things. It's held on the tennis courts in winter, and Pier Rd car park in summer and autumn.

Orientation & Information

Most shops and B&Bs line the long main street. Halfway along, a road to the left leads to the planetarium and hostel.

There's no tourist office, but a very useful booklet, *Schull: A Visitor's Guide*, can be obtained from hotels and some shops, and there's also a website – www.schull.ie.

The Allied Irish Bank branch at the top of Main St has an ATM and bureau de change.

Chapter One (☎ 27606; www.chapterone.ie; Main St) A co-operatively run book shop with a good general collection.

COUNTY CORK

Hurley's (☎ 28600; Main St; per 10/30/60 min €2/3/5; ⏱ 8am-8pm Mon-Fri) Internet access.

Schull Backpackers' Lodge (☎ 28681; www .schullbackpackers.com; Colla Rd; per 15 min €1) Internet access.

Sights

The Republic's only planetarium, the **Schull Planetarium** (☎ 28552; Colla Rd; ⏱ 3-5pm Tue, Thu & Fri, 7-9pm Mon & Sat Jul & Aug, 3-5pm Tue & 7-9pm Sat Jun), in the grounds of Schull Community College, has an 8m dome and a video and slide show. It was founded by a German visitor who was charmed by the town. A 45-minute **star show** (adult/child €5/3.50) starts an hour after opening time.

The planetarium is at the Goleen end of the village on the Colla road, just past Schull Backpackers' Lodge. You can also reach it by walking along the Foreshore Path from the pier.

Activities

There are a number of **walks** in the area including a serious 14km round trip up **Mt Gabriel**. The route is partly across open country that demands some skilled map and compass work in sometimes misty conditions. The mountain was once mined for copper, and there are Bronze Age remains and 19th-century mine shafts and chimneys. For a gentler stroll try the short Foreshore Path from the pier out to Roaringwater Bay and the many nearby islands. These walking routes and more are outlined in the publication *Schull: A Visitor's Guide*, and a small leaflet *Walks Around Schull*.

The helpful **Schull Watersport Centre** (☎ /fax 28554; The Pier; ⏱ 9.30am-6pm Mon-Sat Jun-Aug) hires out sailing dinghies (€50 per half-day) and snorkelling gear (€10 per day), and can arrange sea-kayaking sessions (three-hour session €30). Phone for opening times outside high season.

Divecology (☎ 28943; www.divecology.com; Cooradarrigan) runs courses and dives (€25) to wreck and reef sites.

For a fishing trip contact **Schull Angling Centre** (☎ 087 251 7452; mizen@eircom.net).

Horse and pony trekking and trap rides are available at the **Ballycumisk Riding School** (☎ 37246, 087 961 6969; Ballycumisk), found outside Schull on the way to Ballydehob, for €25 per hour.

Sleeping

Schull Backpackers' Lodge (☎ 28681; www.schullback packers.com; Colla Rd; dm/s €15/20, d €44-48; P ⌨) A wooded edge-of-town location adds to the charm of this timber lodge, where rooms are neat and comfy. There's also limited camping space. You can hire bikes (€11/60 per day/week) and book diving, kayaking and horse riding at the front desk. Internet access costs €1 per 15 minutes.

Adele's (☎ 28459; adeles@oceanfree.net; Main St; B&B s/d €27.50/55) The four rooms above the restaurant are small and simple, but good value, particularly if you grab one with sea views. Continental breakfasts come with a fab bread selection.

Schull Central (☎ 28227; Main St; s/d €40/60) Remarkably narrow hallways and stairs don't detract from this simple, well-kept and central house, where the owners exude kindness.

Glencairn (☎ 28007; malonetp@yahoo.com; Ardmanagh Dr; s/d €40/66; P) Excellent value is the norm at this friendly place, in a peaceful cul-de-sac 100m from Main St. There are some great little touches; Room No 4, the only non–en suite room, has dressing gowns to preserve your dignity while nipping to the detached private bathroom. Better still, there are biscuit barrels in all the rooms!

Grove House (☎ 28067; www.grovehouseschull.com; Colla Rd; s/d €90/130; ⏱ Easter-Nov; P) A beautifully restored ivy-covered mansion, this is the fanciest place to stay in Schull. The whole house is exquisitely decorated, including the large wooden-floored rooms, in an easygoing antiques-and-homemade-rugs style. You get to sample local food, like Gubbeen bacon and Schull eggs, for breakfast.

At the time of writing the **East End Hotel** (☎ 28101; Main St) was being completely refurbished. Phone for further information and prices.

Eating

Adele's (☎ 28459; www.adelesrestaurant.com; Main St; lunch €5-11.50; ⏱ 9.30am-8pm Tue-Sat, 11am-8pm Sun Jul & Aug, 9.30am-6pm Wed-Sat, 11am-6pm Sun Easter-Jun & Sep) A strong commitment to locally sourced and organic ingredients makes Adele's a top place for the taste buds. Hot, filling mains, like cottage pie and healthy stews, jostle with ciabattas, cheese plates and gourmet sandwiches to be chosen. The dazzling array of breads and cakes are baked

COUNTY CORK

fresh on the premises. There's an interesting wine list, a decent selection for veggies, and the staff are sweethearts.

Waterside Inn (☎ 28203; Main St; bar food €3-9, restaurant mains €16-25) Locals will stand by the claim that the chowder (€5.50) here is the best for a long way. Mains are seafood oriented too, with dishes such as pan-fried scallops doused in brandy and herb sauce.

TJ Newman's (☎ 27776; Main St; €4-8; ⏰ 9am-11pm) This nifty wine bar serves nibbles like soup, garlic bread and West Cork salamis and cheeses till late.

Picnickers are spoiled for choice: besides the supermarkets on Main St, try the **West Cork Gourmet Store** (☎ 27613; Main St), with a fantastic deli and selection of wines; or **Organic Oasis** (☎ 27886; Main St), which sells tasty and healthy foodstuffs to take away.

Getting There & Away
There are two buses daily from Cork to Schull (€14.50, 2½ hours), via Clonakilty and Skibbereen.

Boats for Clear Island and Sherkin Island leave from the pier in summer.

Getting Around
Parking in Schull is difficult in summer. There are three car parks, opposite the East End Hotel, behind the AIB, and at Pier Rd.

For bus and taxi services around the peninsula try **Betty Johnson's Bus Hire** (☎ 28410, 086 265 6078).

Bikes can be hired from Schull Backpackers' Lodge (see opposite).

WEST OF SCHULL TO MIZEN HEAD
☎ 028
If you're driving or cycling, take the coastal route from Schull to Goleen. On a clear day there are some great views out to Clear Island and Fastnet lighthouse. The landscape becomes wilder around the hamlet of Toormore. From Goleen, roads run out to thrilling Mizen Head and to the picturesque harbour village of Crookhaven.

Goleen
Tourism in the Goleen area has been handled well by the local community, with the Mizen Head Signal Station (see p238) being a token of their commitment and imagination.

SLEEPING & EATING
Fortview House (☎ 35324; fortviewhousegoleen@eircom.net; Gurtyowen, Toormore; s/d €45/90; ⏰ Mar-Oct; **P**) Out on its own, in terms of location, warmth *and* quality, this lovely house has five antique-filled, flower-themed bedrooms: lavender, daffodil, periwinkle, fuchsia and orchid. Hospitable hostess Violet has the most infectious laugh ever, and her breakfast choice is gourmet standard, with eggs from the 'happy, lazy hens' in the garden. To get there, head along the road that turns off the R592 for Durrus about 1km northeast of Goleen.

Heron's Cove (☎ 35225; www.heronscove.com; Goleen; s/d €40/80; **P**) A delightful location, on the shores of the tidal inlet of Goleen Harbour, makes this fine restaurant and B&B a top choice on the Mizen. Rooms have individual charm and several have balconies overlooking the inlet and the soothing turn of the tide. The **restaurant** (mains €17-25.50; ⏰ 7-9.30pm Apr-Oct, bookings only Nov-Mar) has an excellent menu of organic and local food, with fresh fish and shellfish featuring strongly, but with lamb, duckling and meat dishes too, and a vegetarian option.

GETTING THERE & AWAY
One bus daily goes to Goleen from Skibbereen (€8.20, one hour) via Schull, leaving Skibbereen at 7.45pm Monday to Saturday (two Sunday, at 11.30am and 1.05pm). In the other direction, buses leave Goleen at 7.45am and 5.30pm Monday to Saturday (Sunday at 1.35pm and 5.30pm). Buses travel no further down the peninsula than Goleen.

Crookhaven
Keep on beyond Goleen and you'll find Crookhaven, a place that is probably more easily reached by boat. In its heyday Crookhaven's natural harbour was an important anchorage. Mail from America was collected here, and sailing ships and fishing vessels found ready shelter.

On the opposite shore the gaunt remains of quarry buildings, closed in 1939, remain embedded in the hillside, the source of many tall tales by locals in response to curious questions from visitors. In summer there's a big yachting presence here and Crookhaven bustles with life. Off-season you can stop the world and get off.

Galley Cove House (☎ /fax 35137; www.galley covehouse.com; s/d €50/76; **P**) has terrific views across the ocean, and a cheerful welcome enhances the secluded location of this modern home, which is on the way to Crookhaven and is also handy for Barley Cove beach. The pine-floored rooms are clean, airy and filled with sea light.

Old Castle House (☎ 35900; s/d €35/70) has an exterior that looks grey and foreboding, but inside all is peace and harmony. The big sunny rooms have excellent views towards Spanish Point, and the place's isolated position gives it a real sense of peace. Find the only lane that continues through Crookhaven (marked as a cul-de-sac), then follow it 1km to the end.

O'Sullivan's Bar (☎ 35319; osullivans@crookhaven .ie; light snacks €3-8; ⊙ noon-8.30pm), located on the waterfront, is a lively place in summer. This cheery bar serves up sandwiches, soup and chowder and very tasty traditional desserts year round.

Crookhaven Inn (☎ 35309; main meals €6.50-11; ⊙ 12.30- 8pm Apr-Oct) is a pleasant bar that is located next to the sailing club and fills up with yachtspeople in summer. It does a decent line in food, with quiches, soups and seafood on offer.

Brow Head

This is the most southerly point on the Irish mainland and well worth the walk. As you leave Crookhaven, you'll notice a turn-off to the left marked 'Brow Head'. If travelling by car, park at the bottom of the hill and stretch your legs. The track is very rough and narrow and there's nowhere to pull over should you meet a tractor coming the other way. After about 1km the road ends. Continue on a walking track to Brow Head where you'll see an **observation tower**. This is the place from where Guglielmo Marconi transmitted his first message (to Cornwall) and received a reply.

Barleycove

Even though this is western Cork's finest beach, it never seems to get overcrowded. It's a great place for youngsters, with gorgeous stretches of golden sand, a safe area where a stream flows down to the sea, lifeguards in July and August, and a Blue Flag award marking the cleanliness of the water. Access is via a boardwalk and pontoon, which protect the surrounding wetlands from the impact of visitors' feet. There's a car park at the edge of the beach, on the south side of the causeway on the road to Crookhaven. If you can forgive the insensitivity of dumping buildings in this heavenly spot, **Barley Cove Beach Hotel** (☎ 35234; www.barleycovebeachhotel .com; Barley Cove; s/d €95/140; **P**) is a mere 200m away from the sand. The 11 rooms are simply done out, with calming beach views, and there's a pleasant bar-restaurant with outdoor seating. Self-caterers can opt for one of the hotel's holiday homes (high season from €750), with high-ceilinged rooms and cool wood-and-cream décor.

Mizen Head Signal Station

For the full Mizen experience, don't miss the **Mizen Head Signal Station** (☎ 35225, 35115; www.mizenhead.net; Mizen Head; adult/child 5-12 €6/ 3.50; ⊙ 10.30am-5pm mid-Mar–May & Oct, 10am-6pm Jun-Sep, 11am-4pm Sat & Sun Nov–mid-Mar). Apart from the thrill of standing on Ireland's most southwesterly point, the walk down to the Head and the fascinating displays inside the signal station make for a unique attraction.

At the top of the cliffs is **Fastnet Hall** where, amidst striking sculptures, there's plenty of information about local ecology, geology and history, and a flash new navigational-aids simulator that replicates actual ships' journeys.

From here, wander along protected walkways, steps and a spectacular **arched bridge** that spans a vast gulf in the cliffs. Far below, seals roll lazily in the dark water when the sea is calm. Beyond the bridge, and at the far point of the outer rock island, is the **signal station**, containing the keepers' quarters, engine room and radio room of the Mizen Head Fog Signal Station, completed in 1909 and de-staffed and automated in 1993. It complements Fastnet lighthouse and gives extra protection to Atlantic-bound ships. You can see how the keepers lived and how the station worked both before and after automation, but the real rush (even among crowds on a busy day) is the sense of so much Atlantic beneath vast skies.

Back at the top again, the **Mizen Café** is a good place for a bite after all the drama. If the station has whetted your appetite, you can learn more about the birds, whales and geology of the area on summer day-courses: contact Mizen Head for details.

NORTHSIDE OF THE PENINSULA

Although the landscape is less dramatic on this side of the peninsula, it's well worth driving along the coast road as there are great views out to Sheep's Head Peninsula and beyond to the magnificent Beara Peninsula.

Durrus

☎ 027

Gardeners will be impressed by **Kilravock Garden** (☎ 61111; Ahakista Rd; adult/child €5/3; ☼ noon-5.30pm May-Sep), which has been transformed over 15 years from a field to a feast of exotic plants by one dedicated couple. There's a Mediterranean section, a new Fern Walk, and some beautiful shrubs and trees. Check opening times by phone before visiting.

Dunbeacon Campsite (☎ 61246; camping@fishpublishing.com; camp sites €10; ☼ Easter–mid-Oct), about 5.5km southwest of Durrus on the R591, has tree-sheltered sites in a cracking location overlooking Dunmanus Bay.

Blairs Cove House (☎ 61127; blairscove@eircom.net; s/d €130/200; ☼ Mar-Oct) boasts an exquisite courtyard that is the focus of this Georgian house, where rooms and self-catering apartments display immense elegance and style in décor and furnishings. The **restaurant** (☼ 7.15-9.30pm Tue-Sat Mar-Oct) is in a chandeliered great hall and offers a superb set dinner (€48) with international influences. Booking is advised.

Good Things Café (☎ 61426; www.thegoodthingscafe.com; mains €11-22; ☼ 12.30-4.30pm & 7-8.30pm Wed-Mon mid-Jun–Aug) is an exceptionally popular scoffing place. It produces some great contemporary dishes from organic, locally sourced ingredients. Try the swiss chard, spinach and Durrus cheese pizza, fishcakes with coriander, or tasty West Cork fish soup.

BANTRY

☎ 027 / pop 3150

Vast blue Bantry Bay, framed by the craggy Caha Mountains, has an epic quality that you can't help but marvel at. The town's past is one of mixed fortunes – poverty and mass emigration were followed by unexpected prosperity when Gulf Oil built an oil terminal on Whiddy Island. A second source of riches also comes from the bay: you'll see Bantry oysters and mussels on the menu throughout the Cork region.

The town narrowly missed a big place in history during the late 18th century, when storms prevented a French fleet landing to join the United Irishmen's rebellion. A local Englishman, Richard White, was rewarded with a peerage for trying to alert the British military in Cork. His grand home is open to the public and this, along with a great exhibition devoted to the events of 1796, is now the town's main attraction. Before Irish independence, Bantry Bay was a major anchorage for the British navy.

Orientation & Information

The two main roads into Bantry converge on Wolfe Tone Square, where the large central concourse has been transformed into a super pedestrianised area complete with seats, fountains and a statue of Wolfe Tone himself (see p37).

The helpful **tourist office** (☎ 50229; Wolfe Tone Sq; ☼ 9am-6pm daily Jul & Aug, 9.15am-5pm Mon-Sat mid-Mar–Oct) is based in the old courthouse. There's a post office on Blackrock Rd, an Allied Irish Bank with ATM on Wolfe Tone Sq, and the **QuikKleen Launderette** (☎ 55858; ☼ 9am-6pm Mon-Fri) in a small courtyard off Barrack St.

Broadband Internet access is available at **Fast.net Business Services** (☎ 51624; New St; per 10/60 min €1/5; ☼ 9am-6pm Mon-Fri, 10am-5pm Sat).

Sights

With its melancholic air of faded gentility, 18th-century **Bantry House** (☎ 50047; www.bantryhouse.com; Bantry Bay; admission €10, gardens & French Armada Centre only €5, accompanied children free; ☼ 10am-6pm Mar-Oct) makes for a strange but interesting visit. The entrance is paved with mosaics from Pompeii, and French and Flemish tapestries adorn the walls. Upstairs, worn bedrooms look wanly out over an astounding view of the bay, and a huge library houses an ancient piano and the current owner's bass saxophone! It's possible to stay the night in the wings (see p240).

The **gardens** of Bantry House are its greatest glory. A vast lawn sweeps down towards the sea from the front of the house, and the formal Italian garden has an enormous 'Stairway to the Sky', offering spectacular views.

In the former stables is the **1796 French Armada Exhibition Centre**, with its powerful account of the doomed French invasion of Ireland, led by Wolfe Tone. The fleet was torn apart by storms; one frigate, *La*

COUNTY CORK

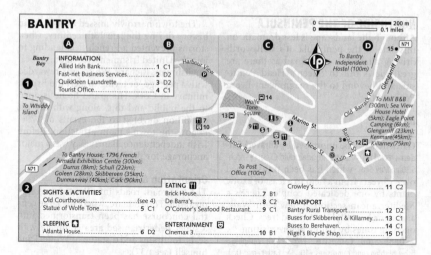

SIGHTS & ACTIVITIES
Old Courthouse.............................(see 4)
Statue of Wolfe Tone.......................5 C1

SLEEPING
Atlanta House.................................6 D2

EATING
Brick House....................................7 B1
De Barra's.....................................8 C2
O'Connor's Seafood Restaurant......9 C1

ENTERTAINMENT
Cinemax 3......................................10 B1

Crowley's......................................11 C2

TRANSPORT
Bantry Rural Transport...................12 D2
Buses for Skibbereen & Killarney....13 C1
Buses to Berehaven........................14 C1
Nigel's Bicycle Shop........................15 D1

Surveillante, was scuttled by its own crew and today lies 30m down in the bay. Sound effects, lights and models tempt you round; the 'tour' starts on the hour and half-hour, and lasts 30 minutes.

Bantry House is about 1km southwest of the centre on the N71.

Tours
George Plant Minibus Tours (☎ 50654, 086 239 8123; gplant@eircom.net) operates day trips to the Mizen Head Peninsula on Tuesday and Thursday (€20), the Beara Peninsula on Monday, Friday and Saturday (€25) and to Kenmare and Gougane Barra Forest Park (p235) on Wednesday (€20). Trips may depend on numbers wishing to take part.

Festivals & Events
The week-long **West Cork Chamber Music Festival** is held at Bantry House at the end of June and beginning of July. The house closes to the public during this time, although the garden, craft shop and tearoom remain open.

Sleeping
BUDGET
Bantry Independent Hostel (☎ 51050; bantryhostel@ eircom.net; Reenrour East; dm/d €11/24; Apr-Sep; P) In a quiet neighbourhood with its own peaceful garden, this is a pleasant IHH affair, with a big kitchen and women-only dorm. Follow Marino St from the town centre, then take the left fork up Old Barrack Rd to the top of the hill.

Eagle Point Camping (☎ 50630; www.eaglepoint camping.com; Glengarriff Rd, Ballylickey; camp sites €21; late Apr-Sep) An enviable location at the end of a promontory about 6km north of Bantry makes this a popular site. Most pitches have sea views, and there's direct access to the (pebbly) beaches nearby.

MIDRANGE
Mill (☎ 50278; Glengarriff Rd; www.themill.net; s/d €45/70; P) One of the best B&Bs in the west, this modern house on the immediate outskirts of town has great individuality. The delightful rooms are just part of it. There's a dinky kitchen for guests and, the spacious breakfast/dining room has a wonderful collection of Indonesian puppets and sunflower paintings to accompany terrific breakfasts. A laundry service is also available.

Atlanta House (☎ 50237; atlantaguesthouse@eir com.net; Main St; s/d €40/60) You won't get a more conveniently central place than this fine old town house, which has good-sized rooms, a pleasant welcome, and a reassuring sense of comfort and calm.

TOP END
Bantry House (☎ 50047; Bantry Bay; s/d €140/240; Apr-Oct; P) In an unexpected contrast to the rest of ghostly Bantry House, the guest accommodation is down-to-earth and has a warming mixture of antiques and contemporary furnishings. These east- and west-wing rooms, which overlook the wonderful Italian garden, are the place to luxuriate

COUNTY CORK

and dream away the hours. Enhance the dream by playing croquet, lawn tennis or billiards.

Sea View House Hotel (☎ 50073; www.seaview househotel.com; Ballylickey; s/d €110/170; P) Everything you'd expect from a luxury hotel – country house ambience, tastefully decorated public rooms, and extraordinarily snuggly bedrooms. The hotel's on the N71, 5km northeast of Bantry.

Eating

O'Connor's Seafood Restaurant (☎ 50221; Wolfe Tone Sq; lunch mains €5.50-10.50, dinner mains €18-26; ☾ noon-3pm & 6-9pm daily Jun-Aug, noon-3pm & 6-9pm Tue-Sun Sep-May; ☕) O'Connor's offers Bantry seafood at its best. The speciality here is mussels, with half a dozen differently prepared dishes (€11 to €13.50). It's all ultra-fresh; there's even a seawater tank for the restaurant's live lobsters and oysters.

De Barra's (☎ 51924; Wolfe Tone Sq; sandwiches & lunch dishes €3.50-9, dinner mains €16-23; ☾ 8.30am-10pm) A long-established Bantry eatery that offers a range of breakfasts, from a hefty 'working' version (€6.95) to a veggie choice (€5.25). Evening meals are meaty but with some good vegetarian, Thai and shellfish options.

Brick House (☎ 52501; The Quay; pizzas €7-14, mains €15-23; ☾ noon-3pm & 5-9pm Mon-Thu, noon-3pm & 6-10pm Fri & Sat, 1-10pm Sun) Generally rammed to the gills, this is a family favourite thanks to its cunningly divided menu. Kids can pig out on pizza, while their discerning parents feast on more adult fare, like roast monkfish in basil and orange sauce.

Entertainment

Crowley's (☎ 50029; Wolfe Tone Sq) is one of the best bars for music, with traditional music on Wednesday nights.

Cinemax 3 (☎ 55777; www.cinemaxbantry.com; The Quay) is a new three-screen cinema, showing blockbusters and a Tuesday art-house programme.

Getting There & Away

Bus Éireann (☎ 021-450 8188) has six buses daily Monday to Saturday (four Sunday) between Bantry and Cork (€14, 2½ hours). From mid-June to mid-September, there's one service daily to Killarney (€12, 2¼ hours) via Glengarriff and Kenmare.

The private **Berehaven bus** (☎ 70007) links Bantry to Castletownbere via Glengarriff. It leaves from the fire station in Wolfe Tone Square at noon and 5.50pm on Monday, and 3.45pm on Tuesday, Friday and Saturday (one way/return €8/15, one hour).

Bantry Rural Transport (☎ 52727; bantrybus@ eircom.ie; 5 Main St) runs a useful series of circular routes to Dunmanway, Durrus, Goleen, Schull, Skibbereen, and outlying villages. There's a set price of €4/6 one way/return. Services run on set days only. Phone for details.

Getting Around

Bicycles can be hired at **Nigel's Bicycle Shop** (☎ 52657; Glengarriff Rd) from €13/60 per day/week.

SHEEP'S HEAD PENINSULA

The least visited of Cork's three peninsulas, Sheep's Head has a rare charm of its own. There are wonderful seascapes to appreciate from the loop road running along most of its length. A good link road with terrific views, called the Goat's Path Rd, runs between Gortnakilly and Kilcrohane (on the north and south coasts respectively), over the western flank of Mt Seefin.

Walkers and cyclists will relish the chance to stretch their legs and enjoy the wild gorse, foxgloves and fuchsias in beautiful solitude.

Ahakista (Atha an Chiste) consists of a couple of pubs and a few houses stretched out along the R591. An ancient **stone circle** is signposted at the southern end of Ahakista where the road bends to the left; access is via a short pathway. The peninsula's other village is **Kilcrohane**, 6km to the southwest, beside a fine **beach**.

WALKING

The **Sheep's Head Way** is an 88km walking route around the peninsula, on roads and tracks where possible. Use Ordnance Survey maps 85 and 88 to navigate your way around it, and an up-to-date walking guidebook. There are no camp sites on Sheep's Head; camping along the route is only allowed with permission from the landowner.

Make time for an exhilarating stride to the summit of **Seefin** (345m), which begins at the top of the Goat's Path Rd, about 2km equidistant between Gortnakilly and Kilcrohane. At the roadside is an out-of-place imitation of Michelangelo's Pietá, and on the other side of the road is an inscribed slate bench, again in rather unsympathetic style. Follow the track that starts opposite the parking area on the south side of the Pietá. Keep to the path along the rocky spine of the hill until you reach a depression. Follow a path up a short, easy gully to the right of a small cliff and then continue, again on the rocky spine of the broad ridge, to a trigonometry point on the summit. Retracing your steps is not so obvious. From the trig point it's best to keep high along the broad ridge and not drift too far to the left.

Seefin is not a huge challenge. It's only about 1km to the summit and should take under an hour to get there. But it is still open country, where mist can easily descend, so go properly equipped. There's a path, but it fades out in places.

CYCLING

The 120km **Sheep's Head Cycle Route** runs from Ballylickey (north of Bantry), anticlockwise round the coastline of the Sheep's Head, back on to the mainland and down to Ballydehob. There are opportunities to take shortcuts or alternative routes (eg over the Goat's Path Rd, or along the coast from Ahakista to Durrus). The widely available brochure, *The Sheep's Head Cycle Route*, gives full details.

GETTING THERE & AWAY

Bantry Rural Transport (☎ 027-52727; 5 Main St) buses run a circular route on Tuesday and Thursday, leaving Bantry at 9.05am and going via the Goat's Path Rd to Kilcrohane and Durrus (one way/return €4/6).

BEARA PENINSULA (RING OF BEARA)

The Beara Peninsula (Mor Choaird Bheara) is the stuff of glossy tourist brochures; a sublime place of rock-studded mountains and green valleys, peppered with prehistoric stone circles, standing stones and old tombs. Its villages are as friendly and picturesque as you could wish for and an added bonus is the thrillingly wobbly cable car at the tip of the peninsula, which takes you and the sheep out to tiny Dursey Island.

Sitting insouciantly astraddle the Cork-Kerry border, Beara is less visited than the Ring of Kerry to the north. You can escape even further into the landscape by strapping on your hiking boots. There's exhilarating hill walking that requires some skill and commitment, as well as proper clothing and navigational experience.

The 196km **Beara Way** is a signposted walk linking Glengarriff with Kenmare (in Kerry) via Castletownbere, Bere Island, Dursey Island and the north side of the peninsula; for more details see p678. The 138km **Beara Way Cycle Route** takes a similar direction, passing on small lanes through all the villages on Beara. You can find maps and guidebooks in most of the main tourist offices in the area.

ORIENTATION & INFORMATION

A small northern part of the peninsula lies in Kerry but is dealt with here for the convenience of people travelling the Ring of Beara. Castletownbere in Cork or Kenmare in Kerry would make good bases for exploring the peninsula.

In theory you could drive the 137km around the coast in one day, but at the price of omitting a great deal. In particular you would miss the spectacular **Healy Pass**, which cuts across the peninsula to join Adrigole in Cork with Lauragh in Kerry.

The following towns are described in a route that assumes you are starting out from Glengarriff and working your way round the peninsula clockwise to Kenmare. There are tourist offices in Castletownbere and Glengarriff, open June to August only.

GLENGARRIFF

☎ 027 / pop 875

Glengarriff (Gleann Garbh) is an attractive village hidden deep in Bantry Bay, and has a very weird microclimate. Its sheltered position and shallow sea encourage lush, exotic plant growth. Explore the 'jungle' and Italianate gardens on Garinish Island, or wander through palm fronds in Bamboo Park (see p244).

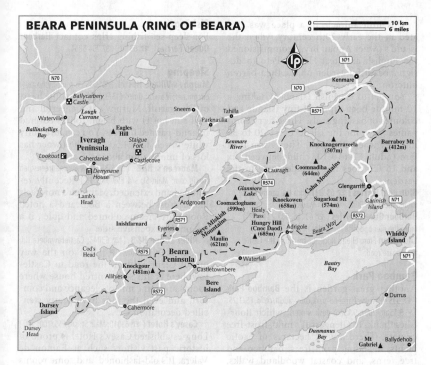

BEARA PENINSULA (RING OF BEARA)

The rough rocky Caha Mountains, in the backdrop, make for good hill walking. There are plenty of milder strolls too, in mature oak woodlands and through the coastal Blue Pool Amenity Area where, if you're lucky, you'll see seals loitering on the large rocks in the bay.

In the second half of the 19th century, Glengarriff became a popular retreat for prosperous Victorians, who sailed across from England to Ireland, took the train to Bantry, then chugged over to Glengarriff in a paddle steamer. By 1850 the road to Kenmare had been blasted through the mountains and the link with Killarney was established. Today Glengarriff lies on the main Cork to Killarney road; it draws the crowds in high season, but despite that there's still a satisfying back-country feel to the place.

Information

The **Fáilte Ireland tourist office** (☎ 63084; ☼ 9.15am-1pm & 2-5pm Jun-Aug) is in the main street. A useful alternative is the privately run **office** (☼ 10am-1pm & 2-6pm Mon-Sat Jun-Aug)

beside the Blue Pool Ferries terminal in the main street.

There's a small Allied Irish Bank on the main street, but no ATM. The post office/Spar Shop in the main street has a bureau de change.

Garinish (Ilnacullin) Island

The magical Italianate **garden** (☎ 63040; adult/senior & child €3.50/1.25; ☼ 9.30am-6.30pm Mon-Sat, 11am-6.30pm Sun Jul & Aug, 10am-6.30pm Mon-Sat, 11am-6.30pm Sun May, Jun & Sep, 10am-4.30pm Mon-Sat, 1-5pm Sun Mar & Oct, last admission 1hr before closing) on Garinish (also known as Ilnacullin) Island is a must. Exotic plants flourish in the rich soil and warm climate; the camellias, magnolias and rhododendrons especially provide a blaze of colour in a landscape usually dominated by greens and browns. There are good views from a **Grecian temple** at the end of a cypress avenue, and a panoramic spectacular from the top of the 19th-century **Martello tower**, built to watch out for a possible Napoleonic invasion. Other delights are the walled garden and giant tree ferns in the 'Jungle' area.

This little miracle of a place was created in the early 20th century, when the island's owner Annan Bryce commissioned the English architect Harold Peto to design a beautiful garden on the then-barren outcrop.

You get to Garinish Island by taking a 10-minute boat trip, past tiny islands and colonies of basking seals. Three ferry companies leave for the island every 20 to 30 minutes when it's open. The return boat fare (adult €7 to €10, child between six and 16 €5) does not include entry to the gardens:

Blue Pool Ferries (☎ 63333) From the centre of the village, near the Quills Woollen Market.

Harbour Queen Ferries (☎ 63116, 087 234 5861) From the pier opposite the Eccles Hotel.

Lady Ellen From Ellen's Rock, 1.6km along the Castletownbeare road.

Bamboo Park

Another great garden is the **Bamboo Park** (☎ 63570; www.bamboo-park.com; adult/child €5/1.25; ☻ 9.15am-7pm, 9.15am-dusk winter), which flourishes thanks to Glengarriff's mild, frost-free climate. There are 12 hectares of exotic plants, including palm trees, bamboo and tree ferns, and coastal woodland walks. Lining the waterfront are 13 ivy-covered stone pillars, the origin of which remains a mystery, even to locals.

Glengarriff Woods Nature Reserve

These 300-hectare oak and pine **woods** were owned by the White family of Bantry House in the 18th century. The thick tree cover maintains humid conditions that allow ferns and mosses to flourish. Look out especially for tiny white flowers on red stems rising from rosettes of leaves, these are rare kidney saxifrage.

The woodlands and bogs are also home to the Kerry slug, the 'aristocrat of slugs', a protected species found only here, in parts of Kerry and on the Iberian Peninsula. It's coffee-coloured with cream spots.

To get to the woods, leave Glengarriff on the N71 Kenmare road. The entrance is about 1km along on the left. A sign, just inside the gate, points across a footbridge to **Lady Bantry's Lookout**. It's a short, steep climb that brings you out on top of the world. There are other well-marked walks through the woods.

Fishing

For deep-sea fishing trips contact **Harbour Queen Ferries** (☎ 63116, 087 234 5861).

Sleeping

Murphy's Village Hostel (☎ 63555; murphyshostel@ eircom.net; Main St; dm/d €13/35) Right at the heart of Glengarriff, Murphy's is a cheerful and well-run hostel with bright rooms covered in hand-painted flowers. You can hire fluffy white towels for €1.50, and the owner has lots of information about the area.

Maureen's B&B (☎ 63201; www.maureensglen garriff.com; Main St; s/d €59/98; **P**) Recently revamped and extended, Maureen's now feels like a cross between a B&B and a hotel. Rooms are cream-coloured and quiet, if a tad on the expensive side.

River Lodge B&B (☎ 63043; Castletownbere Rd; s/d €40/70; ☻ Feb-Nov; **P**) Just on the way out of Glengarriff on the road to Castletownbere is this soft-centred house where rooms are a fine mix of elegance and comfort, and even the loos have pretty stencilled decoration.

Casey's Hotel (☎ 63010; Main St; s/d €55/100; **P**) Long-established Casey's Hotel is proud of historic past visitors such as Eamon de Valera. It's old-fashioned, and some rooms are a touch cramped, but you're treated with immense warmth and there's a restaurant, bar and new patio-garden to stretch out in.

Dowlings Camping & Caravan Park (☎ /fax 63154; Castletownbere Rd; camp sites €20; ☻ Easter-Oct) This highly welcoming park, about 1km west of Glengarriff on the Castletownbere road, is in an attractive woodland setting. Good amenities include a games room and a licensed bar that stages traditional music every night from June to August.

Eating

Martello Restaurant (☎ 63860; Garinish Ct, Main St; lunch mains €10-13.50, dinner mains €15-25; ☻ 12.30-3.30pm & 6.30-9.30pm Tue-Sat, 12.30-3.30pm Sun Jun-Aug, 6.30-9.30pm Thu-Sat, 12.30-3.30pm Sun Sep-May) Glengarriff's top eating place is the Martello, a smart but casual bistro serving up tasty grub. Try a chicken chilli pitta for a light lunch with a kick, or return later for local dishes like flambéed Bantry Bay scallops. Booking is advised.

Rainbow Restaurant (☎ 63440; Main St; mains €16-25, kid's meals €5) Local dishes are the fare here, with the emphasis on seafood. Try Bantry Bay mussels with white wine, seafood chowder, or scallops in smoked bacon sauce.

Hawthorn Bar (☎ 63315; Main St; bar food €3.50-8.50, mains €10-16) Stonking portions appear when you order at the refurbished Hawthorn. There are good-value burgers, pasta dishes, and platters of local fish.

Village Kitchen (☎ 63555; Main St) This cheery, relaxed little café in Murphy's Village Hostel was closed at the time of writing, but check if it's reopened.

Getting There & Away

A bus travels three times daily Monday to Saturday (twice Sunday) from Glengarriff to Bantry (€3.40, 25 minutes) and Cork (€14, 2½ hours). They are less frequent in the other direction to Adrigole and Castletownbere. From June to mid-September, two buses daily Monday to Saturday (one Sunday) go to Kenmare and Killarney. Buses stop outside Murphy's Village Hostel. For details of the private Berehaven bus service see p241.

Getting Around

Glengarriff Cabs (☎ 63060, 087 973 0741; glengarriff cabs@hotmail.com) also runs day trips; contact them for details.

GLENGARRIFF TO CASTLETOWNBERE

The landscape becomes more rugged and impressive as you head west from Glengarriff towards Castletownbere. On the highest hills, Sugarloaf and Hungry Hill, tall rock walls known as 'benches' snake backwards and forwards across the slopes; they can make walking on these mountains quite challenging, and dangerous in fog. Take a map (Ordnance Survey Discovery series 84 and 85 cover the area) and compass if venturing onto the hills, and seek advice locally.

Adrigole is a scattered strip of houses, ideal for walkers and sailors who like peace and quiet! The well-equipped **West Cork Sailing Centre** (☎ 027-60132; www.westcorksailing.com; The Boathouse) offers everything from instructional courses to family sailing holidays, and powerboat training to kayak hire. A half-day sailing course costs €90 for one person or €120 for two in July and August and there's about a 25% reduction in low season.

Hungry Hill Lodge (☎ 027-60228; www.hungry hilllodge.com; Adrigole; camp sites €13, dm €17, d €30-40; **P**) is a well-situated hostel with excellent facilities, just beyond Adrigole village. It's in a perfect location for walking and cycling.

CASTLETOWNBERE & AROUND

☎ 027 / pop 875

Tourism is not the first concern in Castletownbere (Baile Chais Bhéara), and as a result there's a refreshing appeal to the everydayness of the place. The town is home to one of Ireland's largest fishing fleets, and retains the atmosphere and bustle of a working port.

If you're carrying a copy of Pete McCarthy's bestseller, *McCarthy's Bar*, you may be excited to see the front-cover photo sitting in three dimensions on Main St! **McCarthy's Bar** is a great old grocery/pub, with frequent live music and a wicked wee snug inside the door.

The helpful **tourist office** (☎ 70054; www.beara tourism.com; Main St) is just outside the Church of Ireland.

The rather excitingly named **Beara Action Group** (☎ 70880; www.bearainfo.com; per 15/30/60 min €1/2/3.75) has Internet access. On Main St, you'll find a post office with a limited bureau de change, an Allied Irish Bank branch with an ATM, and a string of pubs. **O'Shea's Laundrette** (☎ 70994; Main St; ◷ 9am-6pm Mon-Sat) charges €8 per load.

Sights & Activities

The **Call of the Sea** (☎ 70835; www.callofthesea .com; North Rd; adult/child €4/2; ◷ 10am-5pm Mon-Fri, 1-5pm Sat & Sun Jun-Aug, phone for opening times outside these months) is a small museum with a nautical flavour, where the smuggling, mining, fishing and naval history of the Beara Peninsula is explored in a series of interesting, sometimes hands-on, exhibitions (try your skills at morse code!). It's on the R571 road running north from Castletownbere.

The impressive **Derreenataggart Stone Circle** of 10 stones is close to the roadside, about 2km from Castletownbere, and is reminiscent of the Drombeg Circle near Glandore. It's signposted at a turn-off to the right at the western end of town. There are a number of standing stones in the surrounding area.

COUNTY CORK

Beara Diving & Watersports (☎ 71682, 087 699 3793; www.bearadiving.com; The Square; ⏱ 10am-6pm Mon-Sat Jun–mid-Sep, noon-5pm Mon-Sat May, 10am-5.30pm Sat rest of year) run PADI courses and have boat dives (€48 with equipment) from Easter to mid-September, when you might even meet Dirk the friendly six-foot conger eel!

Sea Kayaking West Cork (☎ 70692; www.sea kayakingwestcork.com) can take you out for a paddle for €40 per half day.

Contact the tourist office for any **angling** information.

Dzogchen Beara Retreat Centre

This remote **Buddhist meditation and training centre** (☎ 73032; info@dzogchenbeara.org; www .dzogchenbeara.org; Garranes, Allihies) is about 8km southwest of Castletownbere on top of Black Ball Head. The solitude and inspiring views set the mood. Accommodation is available in self-catering cottages or the hostel. Visitors are welcome to attend sessions and the retreat offers regular seminars and study groups. It's necessary to enquire first by phone or email.

Sleeping

Rodeen B&B (☎ 70158; www.welcome.to/rodeen; s/d €40/70; ⏱ Mar-Oct; 🅿) A delightful haven, Rodeen B&B is tucked away above the eastern approaches to the town. The house has a sea view and is surrounded by gardens that are full of crumbling Delphic columns and other surprises. The rooms are comfy, bright and airy, and there's stylish artwork everywhere.

Harbour Lodge Hostel (☎ 71043; www.harbour lodge.net; Old Convent; per person sharing from €15; 🅿 ♿) This large building, situated off Main St, used to be a convent. It's a strange old place: just have a look at the refectory-like dining room! The rooms are worn but capacious, particularly the doubles, which have proper beds rather than the usual bunks.

Cametringane Hotel (☎ 70379; www.camehotel .com; The Harbour; s/d €70/140; 🅿) The best thing about this newly renovated hotel is the rooms with balconies, where you can sit in the sunshine and watch the boats on the harbour. Everything feels very fresh, and you also get a good view of Castletownbere. The hotel is on the far side of the harbour.

Eating

Olde Bakery (☎ 70869; oldebakerybeara@eircom.net; Castletown House; mains €12-20; ⏱ 5-9.30pm Tue-Sat, noon-9.30pm Sun) This is the best restaurant in town, and serves good-value portions of standard Irish grub. The seafood dishes are the strongest –try the prawns! – and the staff have steady reserves of patience and humour.

Castletownbere is short on good restaurants. You could also try **Murphy's Restaurant** (☎ 70244; Main St; meals €6.50-14; ⏱ 9am-9pm Mon-Sat year round, plus 9am-9pm Sun Jun-Oct), a busy place serving filling mixed grills and seafood platters.

Getting There & Away

Bus Éireann (☎ 021-450 8188) has one bus from Cork to Castletownbere (€16, 3¼ hours) on Monday, Wednesday, Friday and Sunday (plus another daily bus in July and August), via Bantry, Glengarriff and Adrigole. **Harringtons** (☎ 74003) runs a private bus between Cork and Castletown daily except Thursday; on Thursday, **O'Donoghue's** (☎ 70007) runs a bus instead. Buses leave from the Square.

DURSEY ISLAND

☎ 027 / pop 60

Tiny Dursey Island, at the end of the peninsula, is reached by Ireland's only **cable car** (adult/child return €4/1; ⏱ 9-11am, 2.30-5pm & 7-8pm Mon-Sat, 9-10am, 1-2pm, 4-4.30pm & 7-7.30pm Sun), which sways precariously 30m above Dursey Sound. Livestock take precedence over humans in the queue, and bikes are not allowed. The later times shown above are for returning only.

The island, just 6.5km long by 1.5km wide, is a wild bird and whale sanctuary, and dolphins can sometimes be seen swimming in the waters around it.

There's no accommodation on the island, but it's easy to find somewhere to camp. The **Beara Way** loops round the island for 11km, and the signal tower is an obvious destination for a shorter walk.

ALLIHIES & THE COPPER MINES

Copper-ore deposits were first identified on the far Beara in 1810. While mining quickly brought wealth to the Puxley family who owned the land, it brought low wages and dangerous, unhealthy working conditions for the workforce, which at one time numbered 1300 men, women and children. Experienced Cornish miners were brought into the area, and the dramatic ruins of engine houses replicate those of Cornwall's coastal tin mines. As late as the 1930s, over 30,000 tonnes of pure copper were being exported annually, but by 1962 the last mine was closed.

In Allihies (Na hAilichí), a small **tourist information kiosk**, beside the church, opens in the peak season. Allihies is served by the privately run **O'Donoghue's** (☎ 027-70007) bus company.

NORTHSIDE OF THE BEARA

Heading north and east from Allihies, a 23km coastal road, with hedges of fuchsias and rhododendrons, twists and turns all the way to **Eyeries**. This cluster of brightly coloured houses overlooking Coulagh Bay is often used as a film set. The town is also home to Milleens cheese, a popular brand throughout Ireland.

The coast road eventually rejoins the main road at the small village of **Ardgroom** (Ard Dhór). As you head east towards Lauragh, look for signs pointing right to the Ardgroom **stone circle**, an unusual Bronze Age monument with nine tall, thin uprights. At the end of a narrow approach lane there is rough parking. The circle is visible about 200m away and a path leads to it across bogland, although access may be problematic.

Lauragh (Laith Reach), situated northeast of Ardgroom, is in County Kerry. It's home to the **Derreen Gardens** (☎ 064-83103; adult/child €5/2; ⊙ 10am-6pm Apr-Oct), planted by the fifth Lord Lansdowne around the turn of the 20th century. Mossy paths weave through an abundance of interesting plants, including the spectacular New Zealand tree ferns and red cedars, that are normally found in rainforests.

From Lauragh, a serpentine road travels 11km south across **Healy Pass** and then down to Adrigole, offering spectacular views of the rocky inland scenery. About 1km west of Lauragh along the R572 is a road to **Glanmore Lake**, with the remains of an old hermitage on a tiny island in the middle. There are walking opportunities in the Glanmore Lake area, but gaining access may be problematic: ask locally for advice.

Sleeping & Eating
Glanmore Lake Hostel (☎ 064-83181; mailbox@ anoige.ie; Glanmore Lake; dm €15; ⊙ Jun-Sep) A timeless atmosphere and an engaging location at the wooded heart of Glanmore make this remote An Óige hostel an appealing place. It's in Glanmore's old National Schoolhouse, 5.6km from Lauragh. Take the road for Glanmore Lake and just keep going.

Inche's House (☎ /fax 027-74494; info@eyeries .com; Eyeries; s/d €40/64) A professionally run B&B just outside Eyeries, the comfortable modern rooms here are named after local hamlets. Hen and duck eggs fresh from the garden are served up for breakfast in the sunny conservatory, and you can also order evening meals, or book a cruise on the owners' boat *Tigger*.

Getting There & Away
The bus service is very limited. The No 282 bus runs between Kenmare and Castletownbere via Lauragh, twice daily Monday to Saturday in July and August only. Contact **Cork bus station** (☎ 021-450 8188) for times and prices.

NORTHERN CORK

Northern Cork lacks the glamour and romance of the county's south and west coast regions, but there is a pleasant sense of escape from the mainstream, and the area's towns and villages have a refreshing rural integrity. The area is popular for fishing and golf.

MALLOW & AROUND
pop 7091

Mallow (Mala) is a prosperous town located in the Blackwater Valley that caters for fans of fishing, golfing and horse racing. Visitors to its spa in the 19th century christened it the 'Bath of Ireland', although these days the comparison would seem pretty far-fetched. Today it's a sugar manufacturing and agricultural centre. It makes for a useful stop on the way west from Dublin.

At Buttevant, about 20km north of Mallow on the N20, are the ruins of a 13th-century **Franciscan abbey**. From Mallow to Killarney the landscape is nondescript,

COUNTY CORK

although you might want to divert to see the well-preserved remains of 17th-century **Kanturk Castle.**

A haven of peace, **Ard Na Laoi** (☎ /fax 022-22317; Bathview, Mallow; s/d €39/60; **P**) is a lovely house in garden surroundings and has big alluring rooms. The hallway and reception rooms have remarkable embossed

and painted tin ceilings, an American custom that was introduced by the original owner.

Buses run hourly every day between Mallow and Cork (€7.90, 35 minutes) and trains run every two hours (€8, 25 minutes). For Kanturk Castle you need your own transport.

County Kerry

Kerry is the Ireland we dream about, the Ireland of misty mountains, beckoning islands, mirrored lakes and the friendliest people on earth. The image may be overwhelmed at times by stagey helpings of sentimentality and kitsch, but Kerry gets close to matching the dream. It boasts some of Ireland's wildest terrain and is the location of its highest mountain, the 1041m Carrantuohil, at the heart of the magnificent Macgillycuddy's Reeks on the Iveragh Peninsula. Kerry's main tourist town of Killarney relishes its 250-year history as a centre of tourism. The price of all this conspicuous marketing is a year-round influx of visitors to the town, yet Killarney retains its natural charm while the flow of international visitors through its busy streets adds even more colour to an already strong local identity. In summer a convoy of tour buses trundles round the Iveragh Peninsula's coastal road, the Ring of Kerry. The good news for those who want to escape the crowds is that there are plenty of opportunities for walking, cycling and scenic driving on quieter roads.

Smaller than the Iveragh, but no less stunning, is Dingle Peninsula, with its outflung Blasket Islands and its shapely peaks such as Mt Brandon, Ireland's second-highest mountain at 951m. The northern part of County Kerry becomes flatter and far less dramatic as it stretches towards the River Shannon and the boundary with County Clare. Yet there is still much to enjoy in the county capital, Tralee, and in the charming writers' town of Listowel.

The smaller tourist centres of Kenmare and Dingle town have great individual appeal, and the Kerry's outlying villages (always, it seems, among hills or by the sea) reward time spent lingering.

HIGHLIGHTS

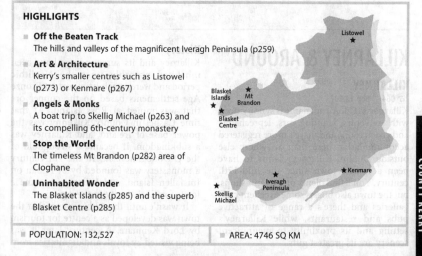

- **Off the Beaten Track**
  The hills and valleys of the magnificent Iveragh Peninsula (p259)

- **Art & Architecture**
  Kerry's smaller centres such as Listowel (p273) or Kenmare (p267)

- **Angels & Monks**
  A boat trip to Skellig Michael (p263) and its compelling 6th-century monastery

- **Stop the World**
  The timeless Mt Brandon (p282) area of Cloghane

- **Uninhabited Wonder**
  The Blasket Islands (p285) and the superb Blasket Centre (p285)

Listowel ★

Blasket Islands ★ · ★ Mt Brandon
★ Blasket Centre

★ Kenmare
★ Iveragh Peninsula
★ Skellig Michael

- **POPULATION: 132,527**
- **AREA: 4746 SQ KM**

COUNTY KERRY

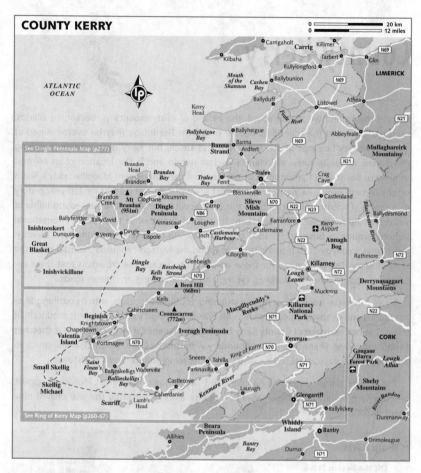

COUNTY KERRY

KILLARNEY & AROUND

KILLARNEY

☎ 064 / pop 12,807

Killarney's (Cill Airne) name is synonymous with souvenirs, jaunting cars, leprechauns and coach tours, and there's more registered accommodation here than anywhere else outside Dublin. Killarney claims to have been a tourist town since the mid-17th century. You'll find plenty of souvenir shops, but the town also boasts some excellent craft galleries and there's a range of attractive pubs and restaurants, while Killarney's setting and its proximity to magnificent scenery are its greatest gifts.

History

Killarney and its surroundings have been inhabited probably since the Neolithic period and were certainly important Bronze Age settlements based on the copper ore that was mined at Ross Island. At that time Cashel in County Kilkenny was the power base of Ireland, and Killarney was a subkingdom. It became a stronghold of the O'Donoghue clan. In the 7th century a monastery was founded by St Finian on Inisfallen Island, and Killarney became a focus for Christianity in the region.

It wasn't until the 18th century that the town was developed as a centre for tourism by Lord Kenmare. A century later it was being visited by royals and dignitaries from around Europe. Even Queen Victoria came, though as an enthusiast for the Scottish Highlands, most of which she owned, it's not known what she thought of Killarney.

Orientation

The centre of Killarney is the T-junction where New St meets High and Main Sts. As it heads south, High St becomes Main St then swings around to the left into East Avenue Rd where all the large hotels are. The national park is to the south, while the bus and train stations are to the east of the centre.

Information

BOOKSHOPS

Killarney Bookshop (☎ 34108; 32 Main St)
Pages Bookstore (☎ 26757; 20 New St)

CULTURAL CENTRES

Irish Roots Services (☎ 33506; info@irishrootsservices.com; Tralee Rd) Can help you trace your Irish ancestors and relatives.

EMERGENCY

The nearest accident and emergency unit is at Tralee Hospital (see p271). For emergencies, dial ☎ 999.

INTERNET ACCESS

Killarney Library (☎ 32655; Rock Rd) Free Internet access.
Leaders (☎ 39635; Beech Rd; per hr €2.95; ☹ 10am-6.30pm Mon-Sat)
WEB-Talk (☎ 37033; 12 Main St; per 10 min €1; ☹ 9am-11pm Mon-Sat, noon-9pm Sun) Also offers cheap phone calls abroad.

LAUNDRY

Park Laundry (☎ 35282; Park Rd; per load €10; ☹ 9am-6pm Mon-Sat)

LEFT LUGGAGE

Left-luggage office (☎ 37509; per bag per 12 hr €2; ☹ 7am-6.30pm Sat-Thu, 7am-7.30pm Fri) At the bus station; ask at the coffee shop in the station.

LIBRARIES

Killarney Library (☎ 32655; Rock Rd; ☹ 10am-5pm Wed, Fri & Sat, 10am-8pm Tue & Thu)

MONEY

Many banks have either a bureau de change or an ATM or both. There is a bureau de change in the tourist office.

POST

Killarney Post Office (☎ 31461; New St; ☹ 9am-5.30pm Mon & Wed-Sat, from 9.30am Tue)

TOILETS

There are public toilets at the main car park on Beech Rd.

TOURIST INFORMATION

Where Killarney (€5) is a good monthly 'what's on' guide found in many hotels, B&Bs, hostels and bookshops. It can also be obtained from the publishers, the **Frank Lewis Gallery** (☎ 34843; 6 Bridewell Lane).
Tourist office (☎ 31633; www.corkkerry.ie; Beech Rd; ☹ 9am-8pm Mon-Sat, 10am-6pm Sun Jul & Aug, 9am-6pm Mon-Sat, 10am-6pm Sun Jun & Sep, 9.15am-5.15pm Mon-Sat Oct-May) Busy but efficient.

Sights

ST MARY'S CATHEDRAL

Built between 1842 and 1855, this cruciform **cathedral** (☎ 31014; Port Rd), at the western end of New St in Cathedral Place, was designed by the architect Augustus Pugin and is a superb example of neo-Gothic revival architecture.

MUSEUM OF IRISH TRANSPORT

This **museum** (☎ 32638; Scott's Gardens, East Ave Rd; adult/child €5/2.50; ☹ 10am-6pm Jun-Aug, 11am-5pm Sep & Oct) is a diverting place with a collection of shiny old cars, bicycles and assorted odds and ends that include an 1844 Meteor Starley Tricycle found in a shop's unsold stock in 1961. Another exhibit is a 1910 Wolseley that was used by Countess Markievicz and WB Yeats. The museum is scheduled for relocation in 2006; phone for details.

OTHER SIGHTS

Situated at the northern end of High St is a **Famine memorial** to victims, which was erected by the Republican Graves Association in 1972. With a determination that reflects the implacable hope of a united Ireland, the inscription reads: 'This memorial will not be unveiled until Ireland is free.'

On Fair Hill is a **Franciscan friary**, built in the 1860s, displaying an ornate Flemish-style altarpiece and some impressive tile work. It has stained-glass work by Harry Clarke.

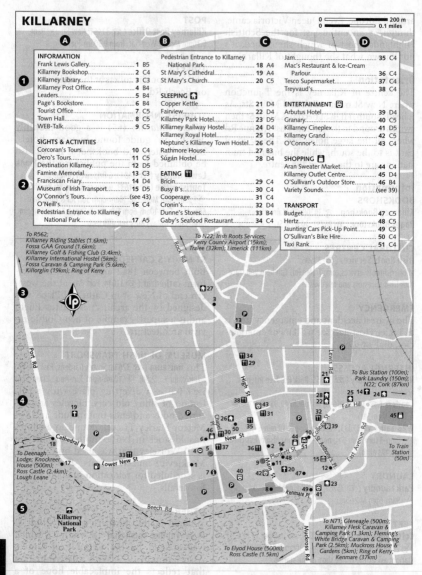

KILLARNEY

0 — 200 m
0 — 0.1 miles

INFORMATION	
Frank Lewis Gallery	1 B5
Killarney Bookshop	2 C4
Killarney Library	3 C3
Killarney Post Office	4 B4
Leaders	5 B4
Page's Bookstore	6 B4
Tourist Office	7 C5
Town Hall	8 C5
WEB-Talk	9 C5

SIGHTS & ACTIVITIES	
Corcoran's Tours	10 C4
Dero's Tours	11 C5
Destination Killarney	12 D5
Famine Memorial	13 C3
Franciscan Friary	14 D4
Museum of Irish Transport	15 D5
O'Connor's Tours	(see 43)
O'Neill's	16 C4
Pedestrian Entrance to Killarney National Park	17 A5

Pedestrian Entrance to Killarney National Park	18 A4
St Mary's Cathedral	19 A4
St Mary's Church	20 C5

SLEEPING	
Copper Kettle	21 D4
Fairview	22 D4
Killarney Park Hotel	23 D5
Killarney Railway Hostel	24 D4
Killarney Royal Hotel	25 D4
Neptune's Killarney Town Hostel	26 C4
Rathmore House	27 B3
Súgán Hostel	28 D4

EATING	
Bricín	29 C4
Busy B's	30 C4
Cooperage	31 C4
Cronin's	32 D4
Dunne's Stores	33 B4
Gaby's Seafood Restaurant	34 C4

Jam	35 C4
Mac's Restaurant & Ice-Cream Parlour	36 C4
Tesco Supermarket	37 C4
Treyvaud's	38 C4

ENTERTAINMENT	
Arbutus Hotel	39 D4
Granary	40 C5
Killarney Cineplex	41 D5
Killarney Grand	42 C5
O'Connor's	43 C4

SHOPPING	
Aran Sweater Market	44 C4
Killarney Outlet Centre	45 D4
O'Sullivan's Outdoor Store	46 B4
Variety Sounds	(see 39)

TRANSPORT	
Budget	47 C5
Hertz	48 C5
Jaunting Cars Pick-Up Point	49 C5
O'Sullivan's Bike Hire	50 C4
Taxi Rank	51 C4

To R562;
Killarney Riding Stables (1.6km);
Fossa GAA Ground (1.6km);
Killarney Golf & Fishing Club (3.4km);
Killarney International Hostel (5km);
Fossa Caravan & Camping Park (5.6km);
Killorglin (19km); Ring of Kerry

To N22; Irish Roots Services;
Kerry County Airport (15km);
Tralee (32km); Limerick (111km)

Rock Rd

Lewis Rd

To Bus Station (100m);
Park Laundry (150m);
N22; Cork (87km)

Fair Hill

Port Rd

High St

Chapel St

New St

College St

St Anthony's

East Avenue Rd

To Train
Station
(50m)

Cathedral Pl

To Deenagh
Lodge; Knockreer
House (500m);
Ross Castle (2.4km);
Lough Leane

Lower New St

Plunkett St

Main St

Kenmare Pl

Beech Rd

Killarney
National
Park

Muckross Rd

To Elyod House (500m);
Ross Castle (1.5km)

To N71; Gleneagle (500m);
Killarney Flesk Caravan &
Camping Park (1.3km); Fleming's
White Bridge Caravan & Camping
Park (2.5km); Muckross House &
Gardens (5km); Ring of Kerry;
Kenmare (37km)

Activities

You can **fish** for trout and salmon in the Rivers Flesk (per day €8) and Laune (per day €25); a state salmon licence (per day €15) is needed. Or you can fish brown trout for free in Killarney National Park's lakes. Information, permits, licences, and hire equipment can be obtained at **O'Neill's** (☎ 31970; 6 Plunkett St); it may look like a gift shop but is a long-established fishing centre.

Killarney Riding Stables (☎ 31686; Ballydowney; 1-/2-/3-hr rides €25/40/60) is 1.6km west of the centre on the R562. It's a huge and very well-run complex that offers four- and six-day rides through the Iveragh Peninsula for more experienced riders.

Killarney Golf & Fishing Club (☎ 31034; www.killarney-golf.com; Mahony's Point; green fees per person €50-85, club hire €25-35) is 4km west of town on the N72. There are three courses, two alongside Lough Leane and one with artificial lakes, and all with mountain views.

If you would like to watch some **Gaelic football** and you're in town during the football season, head for the Fossa GAA ground on the N72, 1.6km west of the centre.

Sleeping

BUDGET

Some hostels arrange pick-ups from the bus and train stations. It's advisable to book ahead in the summer.

Killarney Railway Hostel (☎ 35299; www.hoztel.com; Fair Hill; dm/d €13.50/36) A handy position close to the train and bus stations and the centre of town makes this a useful stopover. It's also extremely well equipped and has clean rooms and good kitchen facilities. Guests can take advantage of discounted tours of the Ring of Kerry (€20), Dingle Peninsula (€23.50) and Gap of Dunloe (€20) and bike hire (€12 per day).

Súgán Hostel (☎ 33104; Lewis Rd; dm/d €15/35) The recently refurbished Súgán still hangs on to its cheerful trail's-end atmosphere, while operating sensible guidelines when it comes to other guests' peace and quiet. It's ably run by Pa Sugrue, who has the inside track on how to have a good time in Killarney. You can even catch Pa performing on stage at O'Connor's (p254) in High St. Bike hire is €12 per day.

Neptune's Killarney Town Hostel (☎ 35364; www.neptuneshostel.com; Bishop's Lane, New St; dm/s/d €14/32/39; 💻) In a great central location, Neptune's is a fine great building with many rooms. It's a well-run, friendly place, and has a bureau de change and Internet access. Like the other hostels it can arrange various trips.

Killarney International Hostel (☎ 31240; anoige@killarney.iol.ie; Aghadoe House; dm €13-15, d €33-44; P 💻) Occupying a splendid 18th-century manor house overlooking lakes and forests, this An Óige hostel is 5km west of the centre and off the N72 to Killorglin. A complimentary bus service runs to and from the bus and train stations from June to September, and staff can arrange packed lunches, tours to the national park and bike hire (€12 per day).

Killarney Flesk Caravan & Camping Park (☎ 31704; www.campingkillarney.com; Muckross Rd; camp sites €19; 🕐 Easter-Sep) About 1.3km out of town on the N71 to Kenmare, the park is surrounded by woods and has great views of the mountains. There's a wide range of facilities, from a supermarket to bike hire.

Fossa Caravan & Camping Park (☎ 31497; www.camping-holidaysireland.com; Fossa; camp sites €15.50; 🕐 Easter-Sep) About 5.6km west of Killarney on the N72 Killorglin road, this park is in a relaxing spot among trees and has views of the Macgillycuddy's Reeks. There's also hostel accommodation starting from €12.

Fleming's White Bridge Caravan & Camping Park (☎ 31590; www.killarneycamping.com; White Bridge, Ballycasheen Rd; camp sites €19; 🕐 mid-Mar–Oct) This small site on the banks of the River Flesk is about 2.5km from town. It's in a delightful location and is enhanced even more by flower beds and sheltering woods. To get there head south out of town along Muckross Rd and turn left at Woodlawn.

MIDRANGE

There are dozens, if not hundreds, of B&Bs and guesthouses in Killarney. It can be difficult, however, to find a room from June to August when it's often best to let the tourist office find one for you for a €4 fee. New Rd, Rock Rd and Muckross Rd are good places to start looking.

Copper Kettle (☎ 34164; www.copperkettle.com; Lewis Rd; s/d €70/100; P) Under the same management as Fairview (see the boxed text, below), this very comfy place is all bright wood surrounds and lovely rooms. You need to head a few metres down the road to the Fairview for a big breakfast. Good discounts are available in the low season and midweek.

SOMETHING SPECIAL

Fairview (☎ 34164; www.fairviewkillarney.com; Lewis Rd; s/d €80/130; P ♿) One of Killarney's gems, this boutique hotel has exceptional standards without sacrificing the personal touch. There's a great sense of exclusivity without too much formality, and they don't miss a trick when it comes to comfort. Rooms are of the highest standard and delicious breakfasts are served with the courteous style that you won't always find in hotels charging twice as much. Good discounts are available in the low season and midweek.

Rathmore House (☎ 32829; rathmorehousekly@iol .ie; Rock Rd; s/d €46/75; **P**) Annual updating keeps things fresh, and there's a real Irish welcome at this long-established family-run place right at the entrance to town. Rooms are comfy and breakfasts are cheerful affairs.

Elyod House (☎ 36544; Ross Rd; s/d 55/70; **P**) This quietly located modern house is on the road to Ross Castle and a few minutes walk from town. Rooms are fresh and clean and the welcome is friendly.

TOP END

Killarney Park Hotel (☎ 35555; www.killarneypark hotel.ie; Kenmare Pl; s/d €220/360; **P**) Nicely detached from the tumult of Killarney, this hotel has beautiful surroundings and individually designed rooms. You can lounge in the library or frolic in the pool and spa.

Killarney Royal Hotel (☎ 31853; www.killarney royal.ie; College St; s/d €140/190; **P**) Spacious rooms with individuality in décor and furnishings make the Royal a spoil-yourself option at the heart of Killarney.

Eating

BUDGET

Cronin's (☎ 31521; 9 College St; mains €6.50-12.50; ☯ 9am-9.30pm) A great local favourite, Cronin's does no-nonsense meat and fish dishes with vegetarian options. It also does a roaring trade with its breakfasts and light lunches.

Busy B's (☎ 31972; 15 New St; snacks & meals €3.25-10; ☯ 11am-10.40pm) Fill up with everything from sandwiches to spaghetti bolognese, veggie burgers to baked spuds at this satisfying eatery. There's also a low-calorie menu complete with a points card to keep you on the right track.

Mac's Restaurant & Ice-Cream Parlour (☎ 35 213; 6 Main St; mains €3.50-12.50) The ice cream sold here is made on the premises and is delicious. You can get breakfasts and lunches as well.

Jam (☎ 31441; High St; sandwiches €3-5, meals €7.50; ☯ 8am-5pm Mon-Sat) Tasty sandwiches, salads and other simple dishes are served up in a bright environment at this little café.

Backstage of the clothes floor at **Dunnes Stores** (☎ 35888; New St) there's a well-stocked supermarket that has a fill-your-own salad and pasta counter. You can take-away for

about €3.50, if you're not too greedy. There is also a Tesco's supermarket on the corner of Beech Rd and New St.

MIDRANGE

Treyvaud's (☎ 33062; 62 High St; mains €15-24; ☯ noon-10.30pm Apr-Sep, check times rest of year) Treyvaud's is gaining a strong reputation for its inventive, subtle dishes that merge trad Irish with seductive European influences. From seafood chowder and beef and Guinness pie to gnocchi Sicilienne, you can ring the changes in a modish, uncluttered space.

Cooperage (☎ 37716; Old Market Lane; lunch €4-10.50, dinner mains €14-24; ☯ 12.30-3pm & 6-10pm) Studio chic at this modern restaurant is finessed with restrained background jazz. The food is modern Irish with a strong dash of Mediterranean. There are while-away lunch dishes such as julienne of venison, *fusilli* Florentine or subtle sandwiches. Dinner mains include flavoursome meat and game but there's always a choice of well-prepared fish, plus surprises such as grilled fillet of crocodile. There's a set menu for €21.

Brícín (☎ 34902; 26 High St; dinner mains €15-22; ☯ 6-9.30pm Mon-Sat mid-Mar–New Year) Countryside Kerry comes to town at this upstairs restaurant above a craft shop. There's an informal setting of individual eating areas and the food is a great mix of traditional Kerry cooking – the *boxty* (potato pancake) is especially good – with inventive influences.

TOP END

Gaby's Seafood Restaurant (☎ 32519; 27 High St; mains €24-32; ☯ 6-10pm Mon-Sat) Great food and fine service is the style at this smart restaurant with its strong French flair. They know how to treat prime fish here, but meat fanciers have beef and Kerry lamb as a choice. Cosy up to the open fire in the reception bar before settling down to pan-seared turbot or lobster in a magic sauce that includes cognac and cream. Dress well to go with the well-dressed food.

Entertainment

Many Killarney pubs have live music. At some it's traditional and often impromptu while at others it's a bit stagey.

O'Connor's (☎ 31115; 7 High St) A great venue for a mix of all things Irish. There's trad music, stand-up comedy (Pa Sugrue of

Súgán Hostel does a regular show here), readings and pub theatre. Entertainment starts at around 9.30pm most nights and 7pm on Sundays.

Arbutus Hotel (☎ 31037; College St) Great trad sessions fire up in the hotel's Buckley's Bar Wednesday to Sunday nights.

Killarney Grand (☎ 31159; Main St; ⊗ 8.30pm-late) A packed popular venue, the Grand's big bar has traditional music nightly from 9pm to 11pm, but the music can get a bit lost in the general racket. At 11pm, live bands take over and blast away with a mix of everything contemporary. There's a cover charge after 11pm.

Granary Bar (☎ 20075; Beech Rd) The Granary rocks every night with a range of trad, songwriters, rock, pub quizzes and karaoke. DJs burn until late on Friday and Saturday nights.

Gleneagle (☎ 36000; Muckross Rd) You can catch cabaret nightly during July and August at the Gleneagle, or bop late at O'D's Nightclub on Friday and Saturday nights.

Killarney Cineplex (☎ 37007; Kenmare Pl) If you want a break from Killarney Kulture, this four-screener has a good run of contemporary releases.

Shopping

Killarney has some excellent shops that balance the shamrock-shifting, booze-badge, T-shirt emporiums.

Variety Sounds (☎ 35755; 7 College St) A music shop with a fairly eclectic selection but with a good range of traditional music, instruments, sheet music and learn-to-play books.

Aran Sweater Market (☎ 39756; Plunkett St) Aran sweaters galore wrap round you at this well-stocked place.

Killarney Outlet Centre (☎ 36744; Fair Hill) This shopping mall has a number of shops including Lowe Alpine, Nike Factory Store and Blarney Woollen Mills, all selling brand-name clothing and other products at healthy discounts.

O'Sullivan's Outdoor Store (☎ 31282; New St) There's a general selection of activity gear at O'Sullivan's branches.

Getting There & Away
AIR
Kerry County Airport (☎ 066-9764644; www.kerry airport.com) is at Farranfore, about 15km north of Killarney along the N22 and then

about 1.5km along the N23. There are **Aer Arann** (☎ 0818 210210; www.aerarann.com) flights to Dublin and to Manchester (Monday, Wednesday and Friday) and daily **Ryanair** (☎ 0818 303030; www.ryanair.com) flights to Stanstead (twice daily Easter to October). Ryanair also has daily flights to Germany. There are car hire booths, a café and an ATM just outside the entrance door.

BUS
Bus Éireann (☎ 34777, 30011) operates from next to the train station, with regular links to Tralee (€7, 35 minutes, hourly), Cork (€14, two hours, 12 daily), Dublin (€20, six hours, four daily), Galway (€19, seven hours, four daily), Limerick (€14.50, 2¼ hours, four daily), Waterford (€20, 4½ hours, hourly) and Rosslare Harbour (€23, six to seven hours, two daily).

From June to mid-September, the Ring of Kerry has its own service, departing four times a day, Monday to Saturday, mid-September to May, and four times a day June to mid-September for Killorglin, Caherciveen and Waterville.

TRAIN
Killarney's **train station** (☎ 31067) is next to the bus station on Park Rd, east of the centre. Five trains a day go to Cork (€21, 2¼ hours) and Tralee (€8, 45 minutes). Some trains to Dublin, Waterford and Limerick are direct; others require a change at Mallow.

Getting Around
TO/FROM THE AIRPORT
Buses to and from the airport can be problematic. About 15 buses pass through Farranfore (€3.50), 1.5km from the airport along the N23. The less frequent service No 286 passes the airport. Check whether the bus is going to stop within the airport complex, or at the main road where it may need to be flagged down, if you're heading in to town. A shuttle bus meets German flights. A taxi to Killarney will cost about €25. The taxi rank in town in on College St.

CAR
The centre of Killarney can be thick with traffic at times. For car hire try **Avis** (☎ 36655) at the airport, **Budget** (☎ 34341) in Kenmare St and **Hertz** (☎ 34126) on Plunkett St.

BICYCLE

Bicycles are ideal for exploring the scattered sights of the Killarney area, many of which are accessible only by bike or on foot. Several places hire bikes at €12/70 per day/week including pannier bags, tool kit and maps. There's **O'Sullivan's Bike Hire** (☎ 31282), with several shops in town. The 18 New Street (Bishop's Lane) shop is best for arranging bike hire.

JAUNTING CAR

If you're not on two wheels, Killarney's traditional transport is the horse-drawn **jaunting car** (☎ 33358), which comes with a driver known as a jarvey. The pick-up point is on Kenmare Pl just past the town hall, but they also congregate in the N71 car park opposite Muckross House and at the Gap of Dunloe. Trips cost €25 to €57, depending on distance; traps officially carry four people.

AROUND KILLARNEY
Killarney National Park

Killarney's 10,236-hectare national park extends to the southwest of town, with two pedestrian entrances immediately opposite St Mary's Cathedral and others (for drivers) off the N71.

Enclosed within the park are beautiful Lough Leane (the Lower Lake or 'Lake of Learning'), Muckross Lake and the Upper Lake, as well as the Mangerton, Torc, Shehy and Purple Mountains. Areas of oak and yew woodland stretch for miles. This is wonderful walking and biking country, although there are also specific sights to see. A herd of red deer lives in the park and many species of bird can be spotted. In 1982 the park was designated a Unesco Biosphere Reserve.

An adventurous 55km cycle tour of the park (best undertaken on a dry day) is marked on the Around Killarney map (p256).

KNOCKREER HOUSE & GARDENS

Near the St Mary's Cathedral entrance to the park stands Knockreer House, surrounded by lovely gardens. The original 19th-century building burned down and the present incarnation dates from the 1950s. The house isn't open to the public,

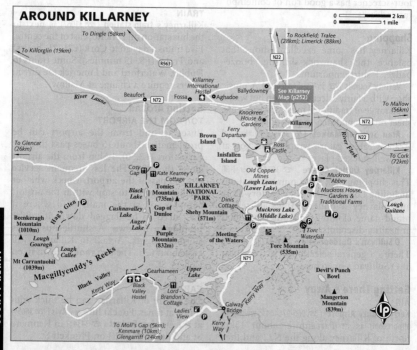

AROUND KILLARNEY

but you can walk around the gardens and there are great views across the valley and lakes to the mountains. To get to the house from the St Mary's Cathedral entrance, follow the path immediately to your right uphill for about 500m.

ROSS CASTLE

Restored by Dúchas, **Ross Castle** (☎ 35851; Ross Rd; adult/child €5/2; ⏰ 9am-6.30pm Jun-Aug, 9.30am-5.30pm Sep–mid-Oct & Mar-May, 9.30am-4.30pm Tue-Sun & bank holidays mid-Oct–mid-Nov; **P**)) dates back to the 14th century, when it was a residence of the O'Donoghues. It was the last place in Munster to succumb to Cromwell's forces.

According to prophecy, the castle would be captured only from the water, so in 1652 the Cromwellian commander, Ludlow, had floating batteries brought upriver from Castlemaine, then transported overland before being launched onto the lake. Seeing the prophecy about to be fulfilled, the defenders, having resisted the English siege from the land for months, surrendered promptly.

It's a 2.4km walk from the St Mary's Cathedral pedestrian park entrance to Ross Castle. If you're driving from Killarney, turn right opposite the Esso garage at the start of Muckross Rd, just past the roundabout. The castle is at the road end. Access is by guided tour only. There's a path leading through the woods from the castle to Muckross House.

INISFALLEN ISLAND

The first monastery on the island is said to have been founded by St Finian the Leper in the 7th century. The island's fame dates from the early 13th century when the Annals of Inisfallen were written here. The annals, now in the Bodleian Library, Oxford, England, remain a vital source of information on early Munster history. On the island, there are ruins of a 12th-century **oratory** with a carved Romanesque doorway, and of a later **monastery** built on the site.

You can hire boats from Ross Castle to row to the island. Alternatively, boatmen charge passengers around €8 each for the crossing. Some Gap of Dunloe boats and bus tours also stop at the island (see p258).

MUCKROSS ESTATE

The core of Killarney National Park is the Muckross Estate, which was donated to the

> **WARNING FOR CYCLISTS**
>
> If you're planning to cycle around Muckross Lake, note that you should do so only in an anticlockwise direction (from Muckross House towards the Meeting of the Waters and not vice versa). Nasty accidents involving broken limbs have occurred when two cyclists travelling at speed in opposite directions have collided on corners.

state by Arthur Bourn Vincent in 1932. **Muckross House** (☎ 31440; www.muckross-house.ie; adult/child/family €5.50/2.25/13.75; ⏰ 9am-6pm) has 19th-century fittings and you can inspect a variety of crafts, including bookbinding and stone cutting, in the basement. Guided tours are available but need to be pre-booked.

The beautiful gardens slope down to the lake and include an arboretum. A block behind the house contains a restaurant and craft shop. Jaunting cars wait outside to run you around the park.

Immediately east of Muckross House are the **Muckross Traditional Farms** (☎ 35571; adult/child/family €5.50/2.25/13.75, combined ticket with Muckross House €8.25/3.75/21; ⏰ 10am-7pm Jun-Sep, 1-6pm May, 1-6pm Sat, Sun & public holidays 21 Mar–Apr & Oct). These are reproductions from Kerry farmhouses of the 1930s complete with chickens, pigs, cattle and horses. You can walk around the circuit or save your legs and use the 'vintage coach' that shuttles between the buildings.

Muckross House is 5km from town on the N71 Kenmare road. Vehicle access is about 1km beyond the Muckross Park Hotel. During the summer a tourist bus leaves for the house at 1.45pm from outside O'Connor's pub in Killarney, returning at 5.15pm (return €8). The house is also included in some day tours of Killarney.

If you're walking or cycling to Muckross there's a cycle track alongside the Kenmare road for most of the first 2km. A path then turns right into Killarney National Park. Following this path, after 1km you'll come to **Muckross Abbey**, which was founded in 1448, and burned by Cromwell's troops in 1652. WM Thackeray called it 'the prettiest little bijou of a ruined abbey ever seen'. Muckross House is another 1.5km from the abbey ruins.

COUNTY KERRY

GAP OF DUNLOE

Geographically the Gap of Dunloe is outside the national park but, as most people start or end their visit to it in the park, details are included here. In high summer, the Gap is Killarney tourism at its full-blown worst. Every day cars and buses disgorge countless visitors at Kate Kearney's Cottage, who then proceed on a one-hour horse-and-trap ride through the Gap; no cars are allowed in summer. You could also walk through the Gap but it's not much fun in summer if you want to be alone. A trip there and back in a hackney carriage costs about €54 for four.

The best way to see the Gap is to hire a bike from Killarney and cycle to Ross Castle, then take the boat across the lakes to Lord Brandon's Cottage and cycle through the Gap and back into town via the N72 and a path through the golf course (including bike hire, about €22).

The boat ride alone justifies the trip. It lasts 1½ hours and passes through all three lakes, with lovely views of the surrounding mountains and of the Meeting of the Waters and Ladies' View, which was much enjoyed by Queen Victoria's ladies-in-waiting, who gave it its name. Lunches and teas are available at the 19th-century **Kate Kearney's Cottage** (☎ 44146; lunch mains €10-15) and **Lord Brandon's Cottage** (snacks €6.50).

Walking

There are numerous low-level walking opportunities around Killarney and there are several useful walking guidebooks to the area, available through such outlets as the **Killarney Bookshop** (☎ 34108; 32 Main St) and **Pages Bookstore** (☎ 26757; 20 New St). Hill walking on Macgillycuddy's Reeks and their neighbouring Mangerton Mountain and Purple Mountain, east of the Gap of Dunloe, should never be undertaken without having the skills to use a map and compass. Weatherproof and waterproof footwear and clothing are essential at all times of year.

There are several ways up Carrantuohil. Some require reasonable hill-walking ability; others are serious scrambling or rock-climbing routes. You can get a taste of the Reeks at close quarters by walking up the Hag's Glen, the beautiful approach valley that leads to the twin lakes of Callee and Gouragh below the north face of Carrantuohil.

The best approach is from a small car park at OS ref 836873 (Ordnance Survey Map Discovery Series No 78). It is reached from the N72 via Beaufort, to the west of Killarney. The car park is at a farm at the road's end; please pay the small fee if you come by car. From the car park the way lies alongside the Gaddagh River, which you need to ford in places. Great care is required if the river is in flood. It's just over 3km to the lakes.

The popular way to the summit of Carrantuohil from the lakes is via the Devil's Ladder, a gruelling trudge up a badly eroded gully path, southwest of the lakes. The ground is loose in places, and in wet conditions the way becomes very muddy.

Organised Tours

Guided two-hour **national park walks** (☎ 33471, 087 639 4362; www.killarneyguidedwalks .com; adult/child €7/3.50) leave at 11am daily from West End Corner at the end of New St and opposite St Mary's Cathedral. Evening walks can be arranged on request.

A REEK BY ANY OTHER NAME

Macgillycuddy's Reeks is the name of the magnificent group of mountains to the west of Killarney, contained between the Gap of Dunloe in the east and Lough Acoose in the west. The name Macgillycuddy derives from the Mac Gilla Muchudas, an ancient clan of the area. The word *reek* means pointed hill. To pronounce Macgillycuddy properly you may need to practice a few times. The accent is on the first syllable; the pronunciation should be 'Mak'lcuddy', roughly speaking of course.

The highest peak of the Reeks is Carrantuohil (1039m), whose name is said to translate rather boringly as 'reversed reaping hook', perhaps because of its curved outline. These are mountains of old red sandstone that were carved by minor glaciers into the elegant forms we see today. They're studded with awesome cliffs, the summits are buttressed by ridges of purplish rock, and the cupped valleys between are filled with glittering lakes. Their world is as wild as their name.

TOP FIVE ADVENTURES

- Climb **Carrantuohil** (opposite) or **Mt Brandon** (p282), but dress correctly and know how to use a map and compass.

- Try both your hands at rock climbing or canoeing at **Caherdaniel** (p266).

- Pack the seasickness pills and head for the **Skellig Islands** (p263). Who needs Himalayan trekking trips?

- Go horse riding along the western shores and beaches of the **Iveragh Peninsula** (right).

- Visit the **Blaskets** (p285). Not such a testing sea trip as the Skellig Islands, but a ticket to a timeless country in its own right.

A number of Killarney companies run daily day trips by bus around the Ring of Kerry (€20), the Gap of Dunloe (€20) and Dingle Peninsula (€25). Tours last from 10.30am until around 5.30pm. Half-day tours, taking in Aghadoe, Ross Castle, Muckross House and Torc Waterfall, also operate daily, as do bike tours and lake cruises. Some companies you might try are **O'Connor's Tours** (☎ 32456; 7 High St), **Dero's Tours** (☎ 31251; www.derostours.com; 22 Main St), and **Corcoran's** (☎ 36666; 8 College St). However, unless you're really pushed for time, these can be a bit rushed to do justice to the scenery.

Destination Killarney (☎ 32638; Scott's Gardens) and **Killarney Watercoach Cruises** (Deros; ☎ 31068) operate hour-long lake cruises with commentary from Ross Castle four times a day for €8/4 per adult/child. A number of private boat owners offer lake trips for the same price from near Ross Castle, but you won't find them around during winter.

Killarney to Kenmare

The N71 links Killarney to Kenmare, with spectacular lake and mountain scenery along the way. About 2km south of the entrance to Muckross House a path leads 200m to the pretty **Torc Waterfall**. After another 8km on the N71 you come to **Ladies' View**, with fine views along Upper Lake. There's another good viewpoint 5km further along at **Moll's Gap**.

RING OF KERRY

The Ring of Kerry, the 179km road circuit around the Iveragh Peninsula, is one of Ireland's best tourist attractions. Although it can be 'done' in a day by car or bus, or three days by bike, the more time you take the more you'll enjoy it. The stretch of road between Waterville and Caherdaniel in the southwest of the peninsula is reason enough for coming here. The Ballaghbeama Gap cuts across the peninsula's central highlands with some spectacular views and remarkably little traffic: it's perfect for a long cycle, as is the longer Ballaghisheen Pass to Waterville. See p679 for details of the 214km Kerry Way, which starts and ends in Killarney.

Tour buses approach the Ring in an anticlockwise direction. It's hard to know which or worse – driving around behind them or travelling in the opposite direction and meeting them on blind corners. Things get much quieter at the western end of the Iveragh Peninsula, when you leave the Ring of Kerry for the Skellig Ring, which is not used by the larger tour buses.

GETTING AROUND

From June to mid-September Bus Éireann operates a bus service to Waterville. Buses leave Killarney at 8.30am and 1.45pm Monday to Saturday, and 9.40am (late June, July and August only) and 12.45pm Sunday. Buses leave Killarney at 9.50am and 3pm Monday to Saturday the rest of the year. Buses stop at Killorglin, Glenbeigh, Kells, Caherciveen, and Waterville and back to Killarney. For details ring **Killarney bus station** (☎ 064-30011).

KILLORGLIN

☎ 066 / pop 3517

Travelling anticlockwise from Killarney, the first town on the Ring is Killorglin (Cill Orglan), which is famed for its annual Puck Fair Festival. Although there's not a great deal to see here, it's a pleasant town with a nice setting on the River Laune – the eight-arched bridge over the river was built in 1885. On the Killarney side of the river there's a handsome statue of King Puck himself. Killorglin has a reasonable choice of sleeping and eating options and a few pubs with live music.

There is a seasonal **tourist office** (☎ 976 1451; Iveragh Rd; ☻ 9.30am-7pm Apr-Oct).

RING OF KERRY

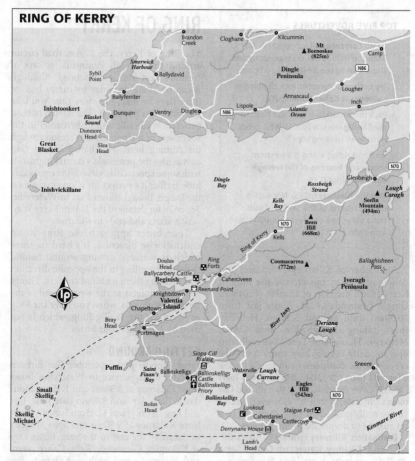

Festivals & Events

The lively three-day **Puck Fair Festival** (Aonach an Phuic) takes place during the second weekend in August. It is based around the custom of installing a billy goat (a poc, or puck), the symbol of mountainous Kerry, on a pedestal in the town, its horns festooned with ribbons. Everyone takes advantage of the special licensing hours and pubs stay open, notionally, until 3am. Accommodation is hard to come by if you have not booked in advance.

Sleeping

River's Edge (☎ 976 1750; coffeya@eircom.net; The Bridge; s/d €50/70; P) An unbeatable location right by the bridge over the River Laune

on the village side makes this an attractive stop. Rooms are smart and bright.

West's Holiday Park (☎ 976 1240; enquiries@ westcaravans.com; Killarney Rd; camp sites €15; ☼ Apr-Oct) This is a small site that is family-oriented and lies amid tree-lined fields. It has a pool, tennis court and children's play area, and is just under 2km from the bridge in Killorglin on the road to Killarney.

Eating & Drinking

If you're self-catering there's a useful supermarket with a help-yourself deli counter in the Square, Upper Bridge St.

Nick's Seafood Restaurant (☎ 976 1219; Lower Bridge St; mains €19-35, set dinner €40; ☼ 6.30-10pm daily May-Sep, Wed-Sun rest of year) French-Irish flair

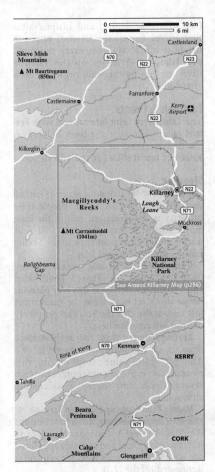

continues to keep this place a great favourite. Seafood gets the first class preparation it deserves – try moules or shellfish mornay – while you can choose the best Kerry beef and lamb or great vegetarian dishes as well, all in fine surroundings and set to stylish music. House wine is seductive and the main wine list well-sourced and extensive.

Bunkers Bar & Coffee Shop (☎ 976 1381; Iveragh Rd; mains €8-13.50; ☯ 11am-10pm) This combined pub-restaurant pays no dues to smart, trendy décor but offers a big choice of food from steak to chicken Kiev and also does breakfasts for about €6.50. You can eat in or take away.

La Deliziosa (☎ 979 0974; School Rd; lunch €5-7, mains €12-19; ☯ noon-2.30pm & 5pm-late) A well-run Italian restaurant with a good range of lunchtime pastas, pizzas and salads, with meat and fish dishes for dinner.

Clifford's Tavern (☎ 976 1539; Upper Bridge St) There's room to move in this spacious old pub that gets fairly packed on Friday and Saturday nights when there are trad music sessions.

Laune Bar (Lower Bridge St) The décor in this little street corner bar is unprepossessing, but there's a good Thursday night music session.

KERRY BOG VILLAGE MUSEUM

Found on the N70 between Killorglin and Glenbeigh and worth a quick pit stop is the **Kerry Bog Village Museum** (☎ 066-976 9184; adult/child/family €4.50/3.50/12; ☯ 9am-7pm Mar-Oct, 9am-6pm rest of year). It re-creates the buildings of a 19th-century bog village, typical of the small communities that carved out a precarious living in the harsh environment of Ireland's ubiquitous peat bogs during the 19th century. There are re-creations of the homes of the turfcutter, blacksmith, thatcher and labourer, and a dairy. Some Kerry Bog ponies are in a field behind the museum.

Red Fox (☎ 066-976 9288; Glenbeigh; meals €6-9.50) has a parking area bigger than the pub, which is always a sign that coach parties pile up on a good day, but there's reasonable nosh here, masquerading under names like 'turfcutter's delight', a steakburger by any other name.

CAHERCIVEEN

☎ 066 / pop 1300

You reach deep into the Iveragh Peninsula when you get to Caherciveen (Cathair Saidhthin). In 1815 there were reportedly only five houses here. Now the village is a refreshingly long straggling settlement with a refreshingly down-to-earth rural charm. Once a month there's a street market, overflowing with wonderful items, but the days on which it's held vary almost as much as the weather does.

Information

There are two banks, both with ATMs. The AIB bank has a bureau de change.

Java-site.ie On Line Coffee House (per 20 min €3) There's good Internet access and good conversation and coffee here.

Tourist office (☎ 947 2589; Community Centre; ☯ 9.30am-5pm Mon & Tue, Thu-Sun May-Aug)

COUNTY KERRY

Sights

O'CONNELL'S BIRTHPLACE

Daniel O'Connell, 'The Great Liberator', was born near here. On the eastern outskirts, as you approach from Kells, there's a bridge over the Carhan River. The ruins of O'Connell's birthplace can be seen on the east bank. On the west bank is a delightful little amenity area complete with a handsome bust of the great man. There are paths along the river, and various boards explain the area's wildlife.

The tourist office sells an *O'Connell Heritage Trail* leaflet (€2). The 6.5km trail takes about 2½ hours.

BARRACKS

This **heritage centre** is superbly situated in what was once the **Royal Irish Constabulary (RIC) barracks** (☎ 947 2777; adult/child €4/2; 10am-5pm Mon-Sat, 1-5pm Sun May-Sep). The building was burned down in 1922 by anti-Treaty forces, but was later reconstructed. It's a theatrical pile, oddly out of place for its surroundings. The story goes that the plans for the building got mixed up with ones intended for a barracks in India. There's a definite North West Frontier look.

The exhibits feature information on Daniel O'Connell, the Fenian Rising and other subjects of local and national interest. To get here, coming from the Kells end of town, turn right at the junction of Bridge and Church Sts.

BALLYCARBERY CASTLE & RING FORTS

Continue past the barracks and over the bridge for 2.4km to find the ruins of Ballycarbery Castle. Unfortunately, the castle is on private land and the only access is via the beach at the end of the road, and then only when the tide's out.

Along the same road are two stone ring forts. Leacanabuaile is the smaller one and dates from the 9th century. Cahergall, the larger, dates from the 10th century and has stairways on the inside walls, a beehive hut or *clochan*, and the remains of a house. It's accessible by foot. If driving you should leave your car in the parking area next to a stone wall and walk up the pathway.

Tours

From June to September you can join a two-hour **guided walk** (☎ 947 3186; adult/child €7/4) to archaeological and historic sites that leaves from the UN Bar, opposite the post office, at 11am every morning. **Boat Trips** (€15; Jun-Sep) on the Valentia River are run by the walk organiser each afternoon.

Festivals & Events

The **Caherciveen Celtic International Music Festival** takes place over the bank holiday on the first weekend in August. Contact the Killarney **tourist office** (☎ 31633) for details.

Sleeping

Sive Hostel (☎ 947 2717; sivehostel.com; 15 East End; dm €13-15, d €16-19) This small, simple IHH property is at the eastern end of the long main street. It has pleasant, well-kept dorms and rooms. Boat trips to the Skellig Islands can be arranged here.

O'Shea's B&B (☎ 947 2402; www.osheasbnb.com; Church St; s/d €35/60;) There's good value and a friendly welcome at this very pleasant house that's set back from the main street just east of the church. You can get plenty of local information here.

Keating's Corner (☎ 947 2107; josephinekeating@eircom.net; s/d with shared bathrooms €35/60;) Another good-value stopover is this pleasant corner pub. Rooms ramble through several floors and there's a welcoming atmosphere.

Mannix Point Camping & Caravan Park (☎ 947 2806; www.campinginkerry.com; Mannix Point; camp sites €17; mid-Mar–Sep) An invigorating place to stay, this nicely kept and superbly appointed site is a 15-minute walk west of town and is signposted off the N70.

Eating

Helen's Coffee Shop (☎ 947 2056; Main St; snacks €3.50-4) This is a cheerful gem of a place. You can choose from a range of coffee options as well as tasty soups and sandwiches, homemade cakes and confectionary, and all amid fresh, colourful surroundings.

Fertha (☎ 947 2023; 20 Main St; bar food €8.50-10) This spacious pub offers a range of steady dishes including roasts and poached salmon.

Entertainment

Two bars where there are good trad music sessions on various nights are An Bonnán Buí and Mike Murts.

VALENTIA ISLAND

☎ 066

Valentia Island (Oileán Dairbhre) may be only 11km long and 3km wide but it doesn't feel like an island, especially if you come by road. It needs at least a day's trip to appreciate its remote, timeless appeal.

Valentia was chosen as the site for the first transatlantic telegraph cable, and when the connection was made in 1858 it put Caherciveen in direct contact with New York, even though it had no connection with Dublin. The link worked for 27 days before failing, but went back into action some years later. The telegraph station was in operation until 1966.

Skellig Experience

Immediately across the bridge from Portmagee you'll see an interesting building with barrel roofs clothed in turf, a not entirely successful stab at replicating the vernacular buildings of the past. This is the **Skellig Experience** (☎ 947 6306; adult/child/family €4.40/2.20/10; ☽ 10am-6pm mid-Mar–mid-Nov) and it contains exhibitions on the life and times of the Skellig Michael monks, the history of the lighthouses on Skellig Michael, and the wildlife. If you're planning a trip to the Skelligs it's worth coming here for background information. If the weather's bad this may be as close as you get to the islands.

Getting There & Away

Most visitors reach Valentia Island via the bridge from Portmagee. From April to October, pedestrians, cyclists and motorists can also use the **ferry service** (☎ 947 6141) to Knightstown on Valentia Island from Reenard Point, 5km west of Caherciveen. The 10-minute crossing costs €5/7 one way/return for a car, €2/3 for a cyclist and €1.50/2 for a pedestrian. It operates 8.15am to 10pm Monday to Saturday, and 9am to 10.30pm Sunday.

SKELLIG ISLANDS

The Skellig Islands (Oileáin na Scealaga) are spectacular in the truest meaning of the word, and a boat trip to the islands, 12km out in the Atlantic Ocean, is one of the highlights of a trip to Ireland. The crossing can be rough, so brace yourself if you're a poor sailor. It's worth it. There are no toilets or shelter on Skellig Michael, the only island visitors are permitted to land on. Wear stout shoes and weatherproof clothing, including a waterproof jacket for the often wave-spattered boat trip, and bring something to eat and drink.

Activities

The Skelligs are a **bird-watching** paradise. Keep a sharp lookout during the boat trip and you may spot diminutive storm petrels, also known as Mother Carey's chickens, that dart above the water like swallows. Gannets, with savage beaks, imperious eyes and yellow caps, are unmistakable, not least because of their wing spans of 107cm. They dive like tridents into the sea to snatch fish from below the surface. Kittiwakes – small, dainty seabirds with black-tipped wings – are easy to see and hear around the covered walkway of Skellig Michael as you step off the boat. They winter at sea but then land in their thousands to breed between March and August. Further up the rock you'll see stubby-winged fulmars, with distinctive bony 'nostrils' from which they eject an evil-smelling green liquid if you get too close. Black-and-white guillemots and razorbills are also present. Look also for the delightful puffins with their multicoloured beaks and waddling gait. In May, puffins come ashore to lay a solitary egg at the far end of a burrow, and parent birds can be seen guarding their nests. Puffins stay only until the first weeks of August.

Skellig Michael

The 217m-high jagged rock of **Skellig Michael** (Archangel Michael's Rock), the larger of the two islands and a Unesco World Heritage site, looks like the last place on earth that anyone would try to land, let alone establish a community. Yet early Christian monks survived here from the 6th until the 12th or 13th century. They were influenced by the Coptic Church founded by St Anthony in the deserts of Egypt and Libya, and their determined quest for ultimate solitude led them to this remote, Atlantic edge of Europe.

The monastic buildings are perched on a saddle in the rock, some 150m above sea level, and are reached by 600 steps cut into the rock face. The astounding 6th-century oratories and beehive cells vary in size, the

COUNTY KERRY

> **WARNING**
>
> A notice on the island warns of 'an element of danger' in visiting Skellig Michael. It can certainly be an adventurous and sometimes tough trip, and definitely not a joyful experience for seasickness sufferers on rock-and-roll days. You also need to be sure-footed and must go carefully on the rocks and stone steps. Be careful when getting off the boat at the island.

largest cell having a floor space of 4.5m by 3.6m. The projecting stones on the outside have more than one possible explanation: steps to reach the top and release chimney stones, or maybe holding places for turf that covered the exterior.

Little is known about the life of the monastery, but there are records of Viking raids in AD 812 and 823. Monks were killed or taken away but the community recovered and carried on. Legend even says that one of these raiders, Olaf Tryggvesson, was converted by the monks and became Norway's first Christian ruler. In the 11th century a rectangular oratory was added to the site, but although it was expanded in the 12th century the monks abandoned the rock around this time, perhaps because of particularly ferocious Atlantic storms.

After the introduction of the Gregorian calendar in 1582, Skellig Michael became a popular spot for weddings. Marriages were forbidden during Lent, but since Skellig used the old Julian calendar a trip over to the islands allowed those unable to wait for Easter to tie the knot.

In the 1820s two lighthouses were built on Skellig Michael, together with the road that runs around the base.

You're asked to do your picnicking on the way up to the monastery, or at Christ's Saddle just before the last flight of steps, rather than among the ruins. This is to keep sandwich-loving birds and their droppings away from the monument.

Small Skellig

While Skellig Michael looks like two triangles linked by a spur, Small Skellig is longer, lower and much craggier. From a distance it looks as if someone had battered it with a feather pillow that burst. Close up you realise you're looking at a colony of 20,000 pairs of breeding gannets, the second-largest breeding colony in the world. Most boats circle the island so you can see them, and there may also be a chance of seeing basking seals. As Small Skellig is a bird sanctuary, no landing is permitted.

Getting There & Away

Because of concerns for the fragility of Skellig Michael there are limits on how many people can visit on the same day. There are 19 boats licensed to carry no more than 12 passengers each, so there should never be more than 250 people there at any one time. Because of these limits it's wise to book ahead in July and August, always bearing in mind that if the weather's bad the boats may not sail. Trips usually start around Easter, but high seas and bad weather can put them off until May.

Boats leave around 10am and return at 3pm. You can depart from either Portmagee (and even Caherciveen), Ballinskelligs or Derrynane. The boat owners try to restrict you to two hours on the island, which is the bare minimum, on a good day, to see the monastery, look at the birds and have a picnic. The crossing from Portmagee takes about 1½ hours and from Ballinskelligs it's about one hour (around €35 return from both places).

Some operators to try include **Owen Walsh** (☎ 066-947 6327, 947 6115), **Michael O'Sullivan** (☎ 066-947 4255), **Des Lavelle** (☎ 066-947 6124), **Sean and Sheila O'Shea** (☎ 066-947 5129) and **Patrick Casey** (☎ 066-947 2069). Most pubs and B&Bs in the area will point you in the right direction.

WATERVILLE
☎ 066 / pop 500

The popular beach resort of Waterville (An Coireán) is a triangle of pubs, restaurants and shops on a narrow bit of land between Ballinskelligs Bay and Lough Currane. Charlie Chaplin was probably the town's most famous visitor and there's an uncannily lifelike statue of him in his tramp's garb on the footpath above the beach.

Activities
Waterville House Golf Links (☎ 947 4102) charges a hefty €150 per round, or €80 before 8am and after 4pm Mondays to Thursdays; but

it is one of the most stunning links courses in the world and attracts serious golfers from all over.

There are lots of **angling** possibilities around Waterville. Lough Currane has free fishing for sea trout, while the River Inny is a breeding ground for wild salmon and trout. Sea angling offers the chance of catching mackerel, pollack and shark. The **Tadhg O'Sullivan tackle shop** (☎ 947 4433; Main St) has information.

Sleeping

There are several smart, luxury B&Bs on the way in to Waterville from the north. They are in the €70 to €100 range and cater to high-flying golfers, so prices stay fairly high.

Clifford's B&B (☎ 947 4283; cliffordbandb@eircom .net; Main St; s/d €35/60; ☿ Mar-Oct; (P)) This excellent-value, comfortable house is on the inland side of the main road at the southern end of town, but has clear views of the sea from the front upstairs rooms.

Butler Arms Hotel (☎ 947 4144; www.butlerarms .com; Main St; s/d €150/220; (P)) There are very comfy rooms in the older part of this long-established hotel or smart modern ones in an extension. The public rooms add a stylish tone and you can reflect on the spirit of Charlie Chaplin, who often stayed here.

Smuggler's Inn (☎ 947 4330; thesmugglersinn@ eircom.net; Cliff Rd; s €65, d €80-120; ☿ Apr-Oct; (P)) Standing in splendid isolation near the golf course and above a long, sandy beach, this pleasant guesthouse and restaurant has light and airy rooms with bright fittings. There are unquestionably spacious views from all points, but especially from sea-facing rooms and from the comfy sitting room.

Eating

Sheilin (☎ 947 4231; Top Cross; lunch €10, dinner mains €14-22; ☿ noon-3pm & 6-10pm) Located uphill from the foreshore road, this is the place for good seafood, including lip-smacking Valentia scallops.

Smuggler's Inn (☎ 947 4330; thesmugglersinn@ eircom.net; Cliff Rd; bar food €4.50-14, dinner mains €19-29; ☿ 8.30am-9.30pm Apr-Oct) Within sight and sound of the sea, especially through its floor-to-ceiling windows, it's no surprise that fish is a speciality at this restaurant.

Shellfish feature strongly and the baked salmon is delicious, while there's a tasty vegetarian platter.

SKELLIG RING

The Skellig Ring, in a Gaeltacht (Irish-speaking) area, is a scenic route that links Waterville with Portmagee via Ballinskelligs (Baile an Sceilg). It's signposted as you leave and is an enjoyable cycle route; however, there are lots of small unmarked roads, making it easy to get lost without a map; preferably use an Ordnance Survey one.

Sights

SIOPA CILL RIALAIG ART GALLERY

This splendid **gallery** (☎ 066-947 9324; cillrialaig@ easatclear.ie; Ballinskelligs; ☿ 10.30am-7pm Easter-Sep, 11am-5pm Thu-Sat rest of year), en route to Ballinskelligs, contains work by local and international artists, writers and composers. It is the shop window of the Cill Rialaig Project, which provides an international retreat for creative people. Free accommodation and free studio space at the retreat are available to people who are invited to donate work to the gallery at the end of their stay. Standards are very high and the result is as fine a collection of pieces as you'd find in a top Dublin gallery. Those wishing to apply to the project need to send a CV with pictures of their work and details of any exhibitions.

The gallery is by the roadside on the R566 – the thatched roofs are unmissable. There's a café in the gallery. Sit outside on a spectacular bench.

Ballinskelligs Priory & Bay

The sea and salty air are eating away at the atmospheric ruins of this medieval building, a monastic settlement that was probably associated with the monks of Skellig Michael after they left their rocky outpost during the 12th or 13th century. To reach it, and Ballinskelligs' fine little Blue Flag–award **beach**, continue past the post office down to Ballinskelligs Bay and walk to the remains from there. At the western end of the beach are the last remnants of a 16th-century **castle** stronghold of the McCarthys. Turn left at the junction after the post office for the castle.

Sleeping & Eating

Skellig Hostel (☎ 066-947 9229; Prior House; www.skellig hostel.com; dm €12-15, d €22.50-50; ☿ Easter-Sep; (P))

A genuine out-on-the-edge feel enhances this pleasant little place that's attached to the local shop. The mural on the end wall goes well with the very Irish tone.

Ballinskelligs Inn (Cable O'Leary's Pub; ☎ 066-947 9104; www.ballinskelligsinn.net; s/d €45/90; lunch €9, dinner €12-20; **P**) Comfy, recently refurbished rooms are on offer at this pleasant place, and meals are tasty and traditional. The pub draws a good local crowd.

CAHERDANIEL
☎ 066 / pop 335
Caherdaniel is neatly wedged between the sea and the foothills of Eagle Hill and has a delightful atmosphere because of it. There's an important historic house to enhance the cluster of buildings, and a couple of sandy beaches by the harbour add to the appeal.

Sights
DERRYNANE NATIONAL HISTORIC PARK
Having grown rich on smuggling with France and Spain, the O'Connells bought **Derrynane House** (☎ 947 5113; Derrynane; adult/child €2.75/1.25; ⏰ 9am-6pm Mon-Sat, 11am-7pm Sun May-Sep, 1-5pm Tue-Sun Apr & Oct, 1-5pm Sat & Sun Nov-Mar, last admission 45 min before closing) and the surrounding parkland.

The house is largely furnished with items relating to Daniel O'Connell, the campaigner for Catholic emancipation. Most amazing of all is the restored triumphal chariot in which O'Connell rode around Dublin after his release from prison in 1844.

There is a walking track through the surrounding wetlands from where you can spot wild pheasants and other birds. The grounds also include a sandy beach and **Abbey Island**, which can usually be reached on foot across the sand. The **chapel**, which O'Connell added to Derrynane House in 1844, is a copy of the ruined one on Abbey Island.

Look out for an **ogham stone**, a stone with carved notches representing the simple alphabet, called Ogham, of the ancient Irish. The Derrynane stone has several missing letters but may represent the name of a local chieftain. It is on the left of the road leading down to the house.

Activities
Caherdaniel competes with Valentia Island as the **diving** base for the Iveragh Peninsula.

Try **Activity Ireland** (☎ 947 5277; www.activity-ireland.com), which also organises a range of other outdoor activities including rock-climbing. **Derrynane Sea Sports** (☎ 947 5266) organises canoeing, windsurfing and water-skiing and operates from the beach from June to August.

Sleeping & Eating
Travellers' Rest Hostel (☎ 947 5175; www.caherdanielhostel.com; dm/d €14.50/34; **P**) Located right by the main road, opposite a garage, this is a charming little cottage-style hostel with cosy rooms and a pleasant kitchen area. Call at the garage if there's nobody about.

Kerry Way B&B (☎ 947 5227; www.caherdanielhostel.com; s/d €45/60; **P**) Run by the same people as Activity Ireland, this pleasant old house has good-sized en-suite rooms and a friendly atmosphere.

Olde Forge (☎ 947 5140; theoldforge@eircom.net; s/d €45/60; **P**) If Caherdaniel is too busy for you this well-positioned place with its great views and peaceful ambience is the ultimate escape. It's 1.2km east of Caherdaniel on the N70.

Glenbeg Caravan & Camping Park (☎ 947 5182; glenbeg@eircom.net; camp sites €17; ⏰ mid-Apr–early Oct) Overlooking a sandy beach and with great views across to the Beara Peninsula, this site can't be beaten for a genuine seaside location. It's 2.5km east of Caherdaniel on the N70.

Wave Crest (☎ 947 5188; www.wavecrestcamping.com; camp sites €18; ⏰ mid-Mar–mid-Oct) A superb setting and very well-kept facilities make this site, 1.6km southeast of Caherdaniel, popular with regulars. Booking during peak season is advised.

Glaise Rinn (☎ 947 5013; lunch €4-7; ⏰ May-Aug) A very useful pit stop located by the entrance to the Wave Crest camp site and offering baguettes with tasty deli fillings as well as home-made quiches and pizzas.

Blind Piper (☎ 947 5126; bar food €5.50-19 ⏰ noon-10pm Jun-Sep, noon-8pm rest of year) Even in summer the Piper does not lose its local atmosphere. There's a garden and outside seating. You can get all-day breakfast as well for €5.50 to €10.

STAIGUE FORT
This fort is a powerful evocation of late–Iron Age Ireland. Its 5m-high circular wall is up to 4m thick and is surrounded by a

large bank and ditch. Steps lead up to the interior wall and there are two small rooms in the walls. There was some reconstruction of the fort in the 19th century.

Staigue probably dates from the 3rd or 4th century. Despite having sweeping views down to the coast it can't be seen from the sea. It may have been a communal place of refuge, or a cultural and commercial centre where people came to celebrate, exchange goods and stage ceremonies. The sophistication of the building suggests that it may have been in the control of a chieftain's family.

The fort is near the village of Castlecove, about 4km off the N70, and is reached by a potholed country lane that narrows as it climbs to a road-end car park beside the site. Traffic jams can occur. This is a Dúchas site and access should be free, but there may be a (non-Dúchas) demand of about €2 for 'access' across private land.

KENMARE
☎ 064 / pop 2672
Picturesque Kenmare (Neidín) lives up to its romantic reputation more stylishly than does Killarney, and there is an elegance about its handsome central square and attractive buildings. It still gets very busy in summer all the same. The town stands where the delightfully named Finnihy, Roughty and Sheen Rivers empty into Kenmare River. For those with transport, Kenmare makes a pleasant alternative to Killarney as a base for visiting the Ring of Kerry and the Beara Peninsula.

Orientation & Information
In the 18th century Kenmare was laid out on an X-plan, with a triangular market square in the centre and Fair Green nestling in its upper V. To the south, Henry and Main Sts are the main shopping and eating/drinking thoroughfares, with Shelbourne St linking them at the southern end. Kenmare River stretches out to the southwest, and there are glorious views of the mountains.

The **tourist office** (☎ 41233; the Square; 9am-5pm May-Sep) provides a free heritage trail leaflet showing places of historic interest. The post office at the top of Henry St has some local walking maps and guides. It also has Internet access for €1 for 10 minutes. Kenmare has its own website, www.neidin.net.

The Allied Irish Bank, on the corner of Main and Henry Sts, and the Bank of Ireland in the Square have ATMs and bureaux de change. You'll find public toilets opposite the Holy Cross Church in Old Killarney Rd next to a car park. There's free parking around the central Square, but competition for spaces is fierce in summer.

Sights
The **Kenmare Heritage Centre** (☎ 41233; adult/child €2.70/1.30; 9.15am- 7pm Mon-Sat Jul & Aug, 9.15am-5.30pm Mon-Sat Easter-Jun & Sep) is reached through the tourist office. It recounts the history of the town from its founding as Neidín by William Petty-Fitzmaurice in 1670. Ask for the *Heritage Trail Map*. The centre also relates the story of the Kenmare Poor Clare Convent (still standing behind Holy Cross Church), which was founded in 1862 and provided local women with work as needlepoint lace-makers. Samples of their work are on display here and more can be seen upstairs in the **Kenmare Lace and Design Centre**. Also interesting in the heritage centre is the story of Margaret Anna Cusack (1829–99), the Nun of Kenmare and an early advocate of women's rights, who was eventually hounded out of Kenmare as a political agitator, then renounced Catholicism in favour of Protestantism and died, embittered, in Leamington, England. Watch out for the picture of Margaret Thatcher who claims descent from a Kerry washerwoman. Be just a little afraid…

Southwest along Market St and Pound Lane is a **stone circle**, with 15 stones ringing a boulder dolmen. The date is early Bronze Age. The context of this fine monument is rather marred by its suburban surroundings and the proximity of waste ground and a sewage treatment plant. There may be an admission fee of about €2 at busy times.

Holy Cross Church on Old Killarney Rd was built in 1864 and boasts a splendid wooden roof with 14 angel carvings. There are fine mosaics in the aisle arches and around the stained-glass window over the altar.

Activities
Kenmare Golf Club (☎ 41291; 18 holes Mon-Sat €42, Sun €50) has its entrance on the R569 to Cork, about 100m from the top of Main St.

You can hire snorkelling and diving gear from **Kenmare Bay Diving** (☎ 42238) in nearby Bonane. A half-day beginner's course costs €60.

Seafari River Cruises (☎ 83171; adult/child €16/8) departs from Kenmare Pier around Kenmare Bay on whale-, dolphin- and seal-watching trips. The company also hires out sailing, canoeing and windsurfing equipment. Reservations are advised.

Beach and mountain rides, as well as lessons for children and beginners, are offered by **Hazelwood Riding Stables** (☎ 41420), 3.2km southwest of Kenmare on the R571 to Lauragh.

Kenmare is ringed with lovely scenery, and short walks can be made along the river or into the hills. The Kerry Way (p679) passes through Kenmare.

Sleeping
BUDGET
Fáilte Hostel (☎ 42333; failtefinn@eircom.n; cnr Shelbourne & Henry Sts; dm/d €14/36; ⏰ Apr–Oct; Ⓟ) Excellent rooms and spick-and-span facilities characterise this pleasant hostel in a fine old building.

Ring of Kerry Caravan & Camping Park (☎ 41648; www.kerrycamping.com; Reen, Kenmare; camp sites €16-18; ⏰ Apr–Sep) Mountain and sea views enhance this beautiful site in wooded country. It's located 3.5km west of town and 1km down a side road off the north side of the Sneem road.

MIDRANGE
Hawthorn House (☎ 41035; www.hawthornhousekenmare.com; Shelbourne St; s/d €50/80; Ⓟ) A marvellous place to stay, this stylish house has lovely rooms, each with great individuality and charming touches such as fresh flowers and fruit every day.

Rose Cottage (☎ 41330; the Square; www.kenmare.net/rose-cottage; s/d €50/70; Ⓟ) A picturesque building set back from Fair Green, this old house was where the original Poor Clare nuns stayed when they arrived in Kenmare in 1861. It has charming rooms and elegant furnishings.

Whispering Pines (☎ 41194; wpines@eircom.net; s/d €40/80; ⏰ Mar–mid-Nov; Ⓟ) In a quiet location, this attractive bungalow offers immaculate rooms, a cheerful welcome and marvellous breakfasts.

Ashberry Lodge (☎ 42720; www.ashberrylodge.com; Sneem Rd; s/d €50/70; Ⓟ) Located on the N70 to Sneem, Ashberry Lodge is a pleasant

eight-minute walk from the centre of town. The modern house is set back from the road and has pleasant rooms and friendly owners. It's right on the Kerry Way walking route.

TOP END
Shelburne Lodge (☎ 41013; www.shelburne@kenmare.com; Cork Rd; s €80, d €100-160; ⏰ Apr–mid-Dec; Ⓟ) Run by the owners of Packies restaurant (see opposite), this handsome 18th-century Georgian house, set in suitably handsome grounds just under 500m from the town centre, really does treat you to splendid surroundings with each room individually styled. In keeping with the culinary connection, breakfasts are a feast of choices.

Eating
Kenmare has a deserved reputation for its fine range of eating places and there are some outstanding restaurants to back it up.

BUDGET
Purple Heather Bistro (☎ 41016; Henry St; lunch & snacks €4-15; ⏰ 10.45am-7pm Mon-Sat) A great atmosphere and comfy traditional décor make this popular place ideal for a relaxing chat. Enjoy a great range of tasty sandwiches, or Irish dishes with a dash of European cuisine. There are good vegetarian options, and the home-made desserts are a real flourish.

Jam (☎ 41591 Henry St; sandwiches €3-5, meals €7.50; ⏰ 8am-5pm Mon-Sat) A bustling, popular place, Jam does filling sandwiches, tasty salads and other dishes, as well as delicious cakes to go with your coffee. It's a great place to stock up for a picnic, too.

MIDRANGE
An Leath Phingin (☎ 41559; 35 Main St; mains €14-20; ⏰ 6-10pm Thu-Mon mid-Jan–mid-Nov) Irish by name it may be, but this excellent eatery is distinctly Italian-Irish cuisine at its best. The introductory reception area is Kerry; the upstairs restaurant is Italy. The food is sourced locally and ranges from pasta and risotto to oak-fire grilled salmon and Kerry lamb.

Horseshoe (☎ 41553; 3 Main St; mains €9-14; ⏰ 3-10pm Mon-Sat, 3-11pm Sun Apr–mid-Jan) Irish mood and style reigns at this charming place where even the chips are home-made. Tasty chowder, fish and meat dishes, good vegetarian options and no fancy touches are the thing here.

TOP END

Packies (☎ 41508; Henry St; mains €15.50-30; ☒ 6-9.30pm Tue-Sat mid-Mar–Oct, Fri & Sat Nov & Dec) Treat yourself to this award-winning restaurant where a sure touch with flavours creates an unbeatable merge of traditional Irish with Mediterranean flair, underpinned with tried-and-tested methods. Seafood matters here, and there's a strong bias towards organic produce. There's also chicken, lamb and tagliatelle choices and the setting is stylish, but not over the top.

Lime Tree Restaurant (☎ 41225; www.limetree restaurant.com; Shelbourne St; mains €16.50-22; ☒ 6.30-10pm) A beautiful old building framed by trees, and the interior exposed walls, panelling and a minstrel's gallery seating area all enhance the terrific food at this popular eatery. There's a fine choice of fish, meat and poultry, from the signature *En Papillote*, a selection of fish cooked in parchment paper, to free-range duck, oven-roasted with organic honey. Part of the 1st floor even doubles as a gallery of contemporary art.

Mulcahy's Restaurant (☎ 42383; 36 Henry St; mains €18-24, early menu €26-32; ☒ 6-10pm Wed-Mon) Mulcahy's brings world style to Kenmare, and the food is satisfyingly modernist, with sushi starters and Pacific Rim flair, but with inventive Irish touches. Vegetarians are well catered for and the wine list is worthy of big-city choice.

Entertainment

For good trad sessions try **Crowley's** bar in Henry Street while **Florry Batt's** in the same street sees a cheerful crowd and occasional singalongs. **Modo Bar** in Main Street cranks up the action for a club crowd.

Shopping

Kenmare has a fair mix of quality craft shops and souvenir centres. Most things are fairly pricey.

Nostalgia (☎ 41389; 27 Henry St) Superb antique linen and lace can be bought here, but for a price that matches the high quality.

PFK Gold & Silversmith (☎ 42590; 18 Henry St) Fine modern jewellery is on sale here. Expect to pay upwards of €80. The salt servers by the West Cork designer Marika O'Sullivan are a joy. PFK also takes commissions.

Soundz of Muzic (☎ 42268; 9 Henry St) Has a selection of Irish and contemporary music.

Kenmare Bookshop (☎ 41578; Shelbourne St) Has a wide range of books, including a strong Irish section with maps and guides.

Noel & Holland (☎ 42464; 3 Bridge St) Find that elusive favourite at this excellent second-hand bookshop that sells some rare editions and also has a terrific range of paperbacks, all neatly collated.

Getting There & Away

As well as the Ring of Kerry bus service, there's a twice-daily bus to Killarney (€6.35, 50 minutes) where you can change for Tralee. Every Friday afternoon a bus goes to Lauragh, Ardgroom and Castletownbere, while another service goes to Sneem. Buses stop outside Roughty Bar on Main St.

Getting Around

Finnegan's Cycle Centre (☎ 41083), opposite the Fáilte Hostel on Shelbourne St, is the Raleigh Rent-a-Bike dealer, with bikes costing €15/75 per day/week.

NORTHERN KERRY

The landscape of Northern Kerry is often dull compared with the glories of the Iveragh and Dingle Peninsulas, Killarney and Kenmare. There are some fascinating places all the same and they have enough compelling history to reward a few days' exploration. The coastal area is popular with Irish holiday-makers.

TRALEE

☎ 066 / pop 21,987

Tralee (Trá Lí) may be the county capital and its name may have a famous lilt to it, but this is a down-to-earth town with an authentic and appealing atmosphere of everyday Irish life. An expanding commercial and industrial hinterland does not detract from the compact centre, its handsome Georgian buildings and lively buzz. There's an excellent museum and several other attractions.

Founded by the Normans in 1216, Tralee has a long history of rebellion. In the 16th century the last ruling earl of the Desmonds was captured and executed here. His head was sent to Elizabeth I, who spiked it on London Bridge. The Desmond castle once stood at the junction of Denny St and the Mall, but any trace of medieval Tralee that

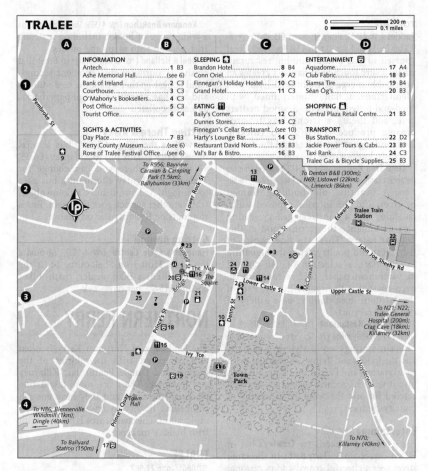

TRALEE

INFORMATION		
Antech...................................1 B3		
Ashe Memorial Hall..............(see 6)		
Bank of Ireland......................2 C3		
Courthouse.............................3 C3		
O'Mahony's Booksellers........4 C3		
Post Office..............................5 C3		
Tourist Office.........................6 C4		
SIGHTS & ACTIVITIES		
Day Place...............................7 B3		
Kerry County Museum.........(see 6)		
Rose of Tralee Festival Office..(see 6)		

SLEEPING		
Brandon Hotel........................8 B4		
Conn Oriel..............................9 A2		
Finnegan's Holiday Hostel.....10 C3		
Grand Hotel.........................11 C3		
EATING		
Baily's Corner.......................12 C3		
Dunnes Stores......................13 C2		
Finnegan's Cellar Restaurant...(see 10)		
Harty's Lounge Bar..............14 C3		
Restaurant David Norris.......15 B3		
Val's Bar & Bistro.................16 B3		

ENTERTAINMENT		
Aquadome............................17 A4		
Club Fabric..........................18 B3		
Siamsa Tíre..........................19 B4		
Séan Óg's.............................20 B3		
SHOPPING		
Central Plaza Retail Centre...21 B3		
TRANSPORT		
Bus Station..........................22 D2		
Jackie Power Tours & Cabs...23 B3		
Taxi Rank.............................24 C3		
Tralee Gas & Bicycle Supplies...25 B3		

survived the Desmond Wars was razed during the Cromwellian period.

The Rose of Tralee festival is in the last week of August.

Orientation
You'll find most things you need along the Mall and its continuation, Castle St. Elegant Denny St and Day Place are the oldest parts of town, with 18th-century buildings. Ashe St is home to the Courthouse, a solemn, fortresslike building. The tourist office is beyond the southern end of Denny St. The bus and train stations are a five-minute walk northeast of the town centre. The Square, just south of the Mall, is a pleasant open space with a contemporary style.

Information
On Castle St you'll find banks with ATMs and bureaux de change. The post office is on Edward St, which runs off Castle St. There's a left-luggage office at the train station costing €2.50 per item for 24 hours, and you'll find public toilets off Russell St. There's a big car park opposite the Brandon Hotel. It's handy for everything in the centre, with fixed rate all-day parking for €3.

Antech (☎ 719 1441; 40 Bridge St; per 10 min/1 hr €1/4) For Internet access; it also has cheap international calls, Western Union transfers, photocopying and free mobile top up.

O'Mahony's Booksellers (☎ 712 2266; Upper Castle St) Has a good selection of local and general books.

Tourist office (☎ 712 1288; www.shannon-dev.ie; ✆ 9am-7pm Mon-Sat, 9am-6pm Sun Jul & Aug, 9am-

6pm Mon-Sat Apr-Jun, Sep & Oct, 9am-1pm & 2-5pm Mon-Fri rest of year) At the back of Ashe Memorial Hall.

Tralee General Hospital (☎ 7126222; Boherboy) Has an accident and emergency unit.

Sights

Also in the Ashe Memorial Hall, but entered around the corner from the tourist office, is the **Kerry County Museum** (☎ 712 7777; Denny St; adult/child/family €8/5/22; ☺ 10am-6pm Easter-Sep, 10am-5pm Nov & Dec). It has an excellent series of permanent displays and interpretations of Irish historical events and trends, with emphasis on Kerry. At the time of writing the excellent 'temporary' **Antarctica Exhibition** celebrating Tom Crean from Annascaul (see p283), who accompanied Shackleton on an epic journey in Antarctica, was still going strong after several years. It deserves to become permanent, but there is an understandable commitment to new exhibitions. Also here is the **Geraldine Experience**, an enjoyable multimedia presentation re-creating life – and vague smells – of a walled town from 1450. You used to flit through on electronic 'carriages' but technology eventually foundered and now you can stroll round at your medieval leisure – a far more satisfying trip. Children love it and there's a commentary in various languages.

Between 1891 and 1953 a narrow-gauge **steam railway** connected Tralee with Dingle. The first short leg of the journey, from Tralee to Blennerville, was reopened and now operates from May to September. The train leaves **Ballyard station** (☎ 712 1064; adult/child €5/3; ☺ on the hour 11am-5pm, 20 min duration). You buy tickets on the train.

Blennerville used to be the chief port of Tralee, though it has long since silted up. A flour **windmill** was built here in 1800 but fell into disuse by 1880. It has been restored and is the largest working mill in Ireland or Britain. The modern **visitor centre** (☎ 712 1064; adult/child €5/3; ☺ 10am-6pm Apr-Oct) houses an exhibition on the grain-milling process and another on the thousands of emigrants who boarded 'coffin ships' for a new life in the USA from what was then Kerry's largest embarkation point. A 30-minute guided tour is included in the admission price. Blennerville Windmill is on the N86, 1km southwest of Tralee. One way to get there is by the steam railway.

Sleeping

Most B&Bs raise their prices by about €10 during the Rose of Tralee festival in late August.

Finnegan's Holiday Hostel (☎ 712 7610; www .finneganshostel.com; 17 Denny St; dm/d €16/40) Located in a fine old Georgian house, this hostel is pleasantly cavernous, but with some character. Rooms are spacious and the cooking and lounge facilities are quite good.

Denton B&B (☎ 712 7637; dentonbandb@eircom .net; Oakpark Rd; s/d €35/60; ℗) This spick-and-span modern house on the Listowel N69 road is great value and is only a short walk from the centre. There's a friendly welcome as well. Rooms are a reasonable size and immaculate, and breakfasts are generous.

Conn Oriel (☎ 712 5359; www.connoriel.com; 6 Pembroke Sq, Pembroke St; s/d €40/60; ℗) Another fine choice only 200m from the centre, this modern house has bright woodwork and cheerful rooms.

Grand Hotel (☎ 712 1499; info@grandhoteltralee .com; Denny St; s/d €70/120; ℗) The Grand's prices are a trifle grand, but this is a comfy, pleasantly old-fashioned place that still hangs on to a nice period feel in its public rooms. Bedrooms are a good size.

Brandon Hotel (☎ 712 3333; www.brandonhotel .ie; Princes St; s/d €105/160; ℗) If you want corporate big-hotel anonymity, then the Brandon is the place. Pricey but with good facilities, including a spa and leisure centre, the rooms are smart with bright pinewood surrounds.

Bayview Caravan & Camping Park (☎ 712 6140; bayviewtralee@eircom.net; Killeen; camp sites €14) This small park is in a pleasant tree-lined location and has good facilities. It's 1.5km north of the centre on the R556.

Eating

There are plenty of lunch-time places in Tralee and a couple of excellent restaurants and bar-food places.

Restaurant David Norris (☎ 718 5654; Ivy Tce; mains €16.50-22; ☺ 5-10pm Tue-Sat) Norris's flies the flag for the best of Tralee dining with consistent quality and flair. The décor is stylish and the menu is exciting. Even the bread and ice cream are made on the premises. Starters are terrific, from Cromane mussels to crisp-fried calamari. Grilled sirloin of Kerry beef on a black-pepper mash with

COUNTY KERRY

a tarragon cream sets the standard for lamb, duck and chicken mains. Vegetarians and fish fanciers always have delicious options.

Baily's Corner (☎ 712 6230; Ashe St; bar meals €4-7) This Limerick institution never falters. There's a cheerful bar menu offering tasty chowder, Irish stew and lasagne as well as sandwiches. A relaxed mid-morning scene gives way to a busy rest of the day.

Harty's Lounge Bar (☎ 25385; Lower Castle St; bar meals €4.50-8, mains €8-19) Recently transformed into a svelte modern bar, Harty's maintains a tradition of no-nonsense food, but with tagliatelle joining traditional shepherd's pie on the menu. You can get breakfast here too from €2.95 to €7.

Finnegan's Cellar Restaurant (☎ 718 1400; Finnegan's Holiday Hostel, 17 Denny St; lunch €3.20-8, mains €14-21.50; ☑ 5.30-11.30pm) It's mainly meat, lamb and poultry with an international touch at this attractive eatery that is in the basement kitchen and wine cellar of a classic Tralee Georgian house.

Val's Bar & Bistro (☎ 712 1559; Bridge St; mains €11.50-20; ☑ 12.30-2.30pm & 6.30-10.30pm) Dark wood, dark leather, chrome and low lights set the style at this trend-taster bar and bistro. The food has international touches and there are some worthwhile seafood dishes, as well as meat and poultry and a couple of decent vegetarian options.

Dunnes Stores (North Circular Rd) The perfect place for self-caterers.

Entertainment

Castle St is thick with pubs, many of them with live entertainment of one kind or another.

Baily's Corner (☎ 712 6230; Ashe St) Baily's maintains its popularity with traditional sessions. Local musicians perform original material on Sunday, Monday, Wednesday and Thursday.

Harty's Lounge Bar (☎ 25385; Lower Castle St) Ultra-modern surroundings suit the evening sessions of jazz, soft rock and mainstream at this modernised bar.

Seán Óg's (☎ 712 8822; Bridge St) Fair diddling trad is on at this popular 'drinking consultant' bar on Tuesday, Thursday and Sunday nights.

Club Fabric (☎ 712 4174; Godfrey Place) Tralee's club of the moment with the right mix of chill-out bar, upstairs level for 1970s and '80s faves, and a main disco for some floor-burning DJs.

Siamsa Tíre (☎ 712 3055; www.siamsat; Town Park; shows per person €22; booking office ☑ 9am-6pm Mon-Sat) In a pleasant location in the town park, near the tourist office, Siamsa Tíre (shee-am-sah tee-reh), the National Folk Theatre of Ireland, re-creates dynamic aspects of Gaelic culture through song, dance, drama and mime. There are several shows weekly May to September at 8.30pm. Winter shows range from dance to drama and mainstream musicals.

Aquadome (☎ 712 8899; www.aquadome.ie; adult/child €10/9; ☑ 10am-10pm Jul & Aug, phone for times rest of year) Tralee's landmark water fun centre has lagoons, water slides, sauna and steam room as well as plenty of water just to swim in.

Shopping

Central Plaza Retail Centre (the Square) A modern open mall with a good range of shops.

Getting There & Away

The **bus station** (☎ 712 3566) is next to the train station, east of the town centre. Daily Bus Éireann services connect Tralee with Dublin (€20.50, hourly), but you must change at Limerick. There are 10 buses daily Monday to Saturday, and eight on Sunday to Listowel (€6, 30 minutes). Bus No 40 runs daily to Waterford (€21.50, 5½ hours) via Killarney (€7, 35 minutes) and Cork (€15, five hours).

From the **train station** (☎ 712 3522) there's a service eight times a day to Cork (€27.50 2¼ hours) via Killarney (€8, 45 minutes). Trains to Dublin depart four times a day (€55, four hours). Change at Limerick Junction for Limerick (€23.50).

Getting Around

There's a taxi rank on the Mall, or try **Tralee Radio Taxis** (☎ 712 5451) or **Jackie Power Tours & Cabs** (☎ 712 9444). **Tralee Gas & Bicycle Supplies** (☎ 712 2018; Strand St) hires out bikes.

AROUND TRALEE
Crag Cave

This **cave** (☎ 714 1244; Castleisland; adult/child €6.50/4; ☑ 10am-6.30pm Jul & Aug, 10am-6pm mid-Mar–Jun, Sep-Nov) was discovered only in 1983 when problems with water pollution led to a search for the source of the local river. Although the cave entrance had been known for years, the system had never been explored until then. The 4km-long cave was opened to the public in 1989; admission is by a 30-minute guided tour. There are numerous remarkable formations including a large stalagmite shaped like a wine bottle in the 'Kitchen Cave', and the Crystal Gallery with its thousands of thin straw stalactites and a stalagmite shaped like a statue of the Madonna.

To get here, take the N21 to Castleisland from Tralee. The cave is signposted to the left – from here it's only 4km along a minor road. In July and August there's at least one bus a day Monday to Saturday between Tralee and Castlemaine, which stops in Castleisland.

Ardfert

☎ 066 / pop 861

Ardfert (Ard Fhearta) can be found about 7km northwest of Tralee on the Ballyheigue road. Most of **Ardfert Cathedral** (☎ 713 4711; adult/child €2/1; �9.30am-6.30pm May-Sep & Oct bank holiday weekend), which is owned by Dúchas, dates back to the 13th century. Additions were made in the 15th and 17th centuries. Set into one of the interior walls is an effigy, said to be of St Brendan the Navigator, who was educated in Ardfert and founded a monastery here. There are ruins of two other churches – 12th-century Templenahoe and 15th-century Templenagriffin – in the grounds, and there's a small visitor centre with an exhibition on the cathedral's history. The continuing work on shoring up the cathedral will take many years, and access to the interior is by guided tour only.

Turning right in front of the cathedral and going 500m down the road brings you to the extensive remains of a **Franciscan friary** dating from the 13th century but with 15th-century cloisters.

In July and August, Bus Éireann No 274 between Tralee and Ballyheigue stops in Ardfert at least once daily.

LISTOWEL

☎ 068 / pop 3999

Listowel (Lios Tuathail) is 15km south of Tarbert, from where a ferry crosses the Shannon Estuary to County Clare. It's an attractive and tidy Georgian town with a handsome central square, a large park and the scenic River Feale running along

its southern side. At its heart is a cluster of excellent literary and cultural venues including the Kerry Literary & Cultural Centre. The town has a great reputation for its literary connections to such accomplished writers as John B Keane, Bryan MacMahon, Maurice Walsh, George Fitzmaurice and Brendan Kennelly.

Orientation & Information

The Square is the main focus and at its centre is St John's Theatre and Arts Centre, formerly St John's Church, which houses the **tourist office** (☎ 22590; � 10am-1pm & 2-6pm Mon-Sat Jun-Sep). Church and William Sts, north from the Square, are where you'll find most pubs and restaurants, while a short walk down Bridge Rd to the south will take you to the river and Childers Park. The river can also be reached down the road alongside the castle.

There's a Bank of Ireland with an ATM and bureau de change in the Square. The post office is at the northern end of William St. Ó Hannán's Book Shop is opposite where William St joins Main St. A number of titles by local writers are also available from the bookshop at the Kerry Literary & Cultural Centre.

There's Internet access at the offices of **North Kerry Together** (☎ 21999; 58 Church St; per 15 min €1; � 9.30-5pm).

Parking in the main square is by discs bought at nearby shops. There's free parking downhill to the right of the castle.

Sights

Kerry Literary & Cultural Centre, with its audiovisual **Writers' Exhibition** (Seanchaí; ☎ 22212; www.kerrywritersmuseum.com; 24 the Square; adult/child €5/3; � 10am-5pm Jun-Sep, 10am-4.30pm Mon-Fri Oct-May), is an absolute gem that gives due prominence to a group of locally based writers of the highest calibre. In the centre, there are separate rooms each with simple, but haunting, tableau depicting the life of individual writers, whose recorded voices read excerpts from their works. Outside is a performance space where events are sometimes staged. The centre has a lift and there are toilets for the disabled.

St Mary's Church in the Square was built in 1829 in the neo-Gothic style. It has some lovely mosaic work over the altar and a vaulted roof with timber beams.

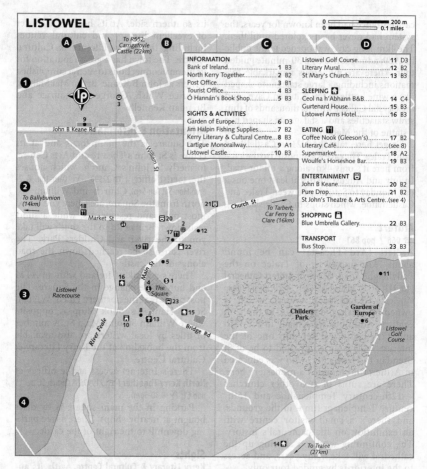

LISTOWEL

| 0 | 200 m |
| 0 | 0.1 miles |

INFORMATION
Bank of Ireland.............................**1** B3
North Kerry Together.....................**2** B2
Post Office...................................**3** B1
Tourist Office................................**4** B3
Ó Hannán's Book Shop..................**5** B3

SIGHTS & ACTIVITIES
Garden of Europe..........................**6** D3
Jim Halpin Fishing Supplies...........**7** B2
Kerry Literary & Cultural Centre.....**8** B3
Lartigue Monorailway....................**9** A1
Listowel Castle.............................**10** B3

Listowel Golf Course.....................**11** D3
Literary Mural...............................**12** B2
St Mary's Church..........................**13** B3

SLEEPING
Ceol na h'Abhann B&B.................**14** C4
Gurtenard House...........................**15** B3
Listowel Arms Hotel......................**16** B3

EATING
Coffee Nook (Gleeson's)...............**17** B2
Literary Café...............................(see 8)
Supermarket................................**18** A2
Woulfe's Horseshoe Bar................**19** B3

ENTERTAINMENT
John B Keane...............................**20** B2
Pure Drop....................................**21** B2
St John's Theatre & Arts Centre...(see 4)

SHOPPING
Blue Umbrella Gallery....................**22** B3

TRANSPORT
Bus Stop......................................**23** B3

Listowel Castle, behind the Kerry Literary and Cultural Centre, was built in the 12th century and was once the stronghold of the Fitzmaurice family, the Anglo-Norman lords of Kerry. The castle was the last in Ireland to hold out against the Elizabethan attacks during the Desmond revolt. What remains of the castle has been thoroughly restored.

In Childers Park is the **Garden of Europe**, opened in 1995. It has 12 sections representing 12 members of the EU of the day. There is a fine bust of the poet Schiller and, strikingly, there is Ireland's only public monument to those who died in the Holocaust, and to all victims of injustice.

On Church St there's the **literary mural** depicting well-known local writers.

Activities
Lartigue Monorailway (☎ 24393; John B Keane Rd; adult/child €6/3; ✆ 2-5pm May-Sep) was designed by Frenchman Charles Lartigue. This unique survivor of Victorian railway engineering operated between the town and Ballybunion on the coast. Engine and carriages sat on a single rail that ran through the centre of the train. The renovated section of line is quite short, but fascinating, and includes manual turnstiles at either end for swinging the train round.

Listowel Golf Course (☎ 21592; per 18 holes €30), on the banks of the River Feale, is about 2km west of the centre off the N69 to Tarbert. You can also walk through Childers Park and the 'Garden of Europe' to get there.

The River Feale provides many opportunities for angling year round. For permits and information contact **Jim Halpin Fishing Supplies** (☎ 22392; 24 Church St), which also sells angling equipment.

Festivals & Events

Writers' Week takes place each May. Details are available from **Writers' Week** (☎ 21074; writersweek@eircom.net; 24 the Square). Readings, poetry, music, drama, seminars, storytelling and many other events are held at various places around town. Past Writers' Weeks feature an impressive list of writers that in recent years has included Roddy Doyle, DBC Pierre, journalist Robert Fisk and Joe Simpson, author of the mountaineering epic *Touching the Void*, who has family connections in Listowel. Father to all of this marvellous tradition is the late John B Keane, probably the most famous writer associated with Listowel.

Sleeping

Gurtenard House (☎ 21137; gurtenardhouse@hotmail .com; Bridge Rd; s/d €40/70; P) Set in a peaceful location, a minute from the Square, this big, beautiful 200-year-old house pays no lip service to such things as TVs in the bedroom. With such huge windows, who needs it?

Ceol na h'Abhann B&B (☎ 21345; knstack@eircom .net; Tralee Rd; s/d €50/60; ⊗ mid-Apr–Oct; P) A great location on the banks of the River Feale makes this picturesque, thatched-roof house a great choice. Elegant surroundings and impeccable rooms are backed up with a charming welcome. It's just across the bridge, downhill from the centre, on the N69 Tralee road.

Listowel Arms Hotel (☎ 21500; the Square; www .listowelarms.com; s/d €75/120; P) Tucked away in a corner of the Square, the Georgian front of this long-established hotel belies its substantial size. Rooms are very comfortable and those at the back have a fine view of the river and racecourse. Public rooms are plush and relaxing and there's a restaurant.

Eating

There are several good eating places in Listowel, and for self-catering there's a supermarket in Market St.

Literary Café (☎ 22212; Kerry Literary & Cultural Centre, 24 the Square; lunch €6.50-9) A good place for a literary lunch or sandwich while digesting the centre's feast of literary delights.

Coffee Nook (Gleeson's; ☎ 21929; 40 Church St; snacks €3-6) An ideal little place for breakfast, coffee and cakes or light lunches, the Nook is local Listowel at its most unassuming.

Woulfe's Horseshoe Bar (☎ 21083; 17 Lower William St; lunch €5.50-8.50, dinner €17-24) Enjoy the cosiness of the downstairs bar or eat upstairs in an even cosier restaurant at this long-established place. The inventive menu offers meat, chicken and fish dishes with international touches.

Entertainment

Listowel has plenty of pubs, several with live music and traditional sessions during the week.

Pure Drop (☎ 23001; Church St) Traditional music at the weekend and good conversation at all times make this fine old place, with its dark wood and long bar, a local favourite.

John B Keane (37 William St) Owned by the family of the late writer of the same name, this small, unassuming bar features pub theatre every Tuesday and Thursday at 9.15pm during July and August.

St John's Theatre & Arts Centre (☎ 22566; the Square) The centre hosts drama, music and dance events year round.

Listowel Arms Hotel (Seisiún-Cois na Feile; ☎ 21500; the Square; adult/child €7/4) Every Thursday in July and August a performance of traditional song, music, dance and folklore is staged at the hotel.

Shopping

Blue Umbrella Gallery (21 Church St; ⊗ 10-6pm Tue-Sat) An arts and crafts cooperative that flies the flag for the visual arts in literary Listowel. There are changing exhibitions and lots of work for sale.

Getting There & Away

Buses run daily to Tralee (€5.70, 30 minutes, hourly and two-hourly middle of the day) and Limerick (€12.70, 1½ hours, four daily, one on Sunday). In July and August there are three buses daily to Ballybunion. Buses from Cork to the Cliffs of Moher and Galway also stop in Listowel three times a day (twice on Sunday). The bus stop is on the northern side of the Square.

COUNTY KERRY

AROUND LISTOWEL

Carrigafoyle Castle

A fine location above the Shannon Estuary adds to the romantic drama of this late-medieval castle. Built in the channel between the mainland and Carrig Island, its name comes from Carragain Phoill (Rock of the Hole). It was probably built at the end of the 15th century by the O'Connors, who ruled most of northern Kerry. It was besieged by the English in 1580, and retaken by O'Connor, but finally destroyed by Cromwell's forces in 1649. You can climb the spiral staircase to the top for a good view of the estuary.

You really need a car to get here. The castle is 2km west of the village of Ballylongford (Bea Atha Longphuirb), which is rarely served by bus from Listowel.

Tarbert

☎ 065 / pop 806

Tarbert is 16km north of Listowel on the N69. **Shannon Ferry Limited** (☎ 905 3124; one way/return bikes & foot passengers €4/6, cars €14/22, motorcycles €8/12; ☼ 7am-9.30pm Mon-Sat, 9am-9.30pm Sun Apr-Sep, 7.30am-7.30pm Mon-Sat, 10.30am-7.30pm Sun Oct-Mar) runs a 20-minute car ferry between Tarbert and Killimer in County Clare. It's useful if you want to avoid travelling through congested Limerick city. The ferry dock is 2.2km west of Tarbert and is clearly signposted. You join the queue and pay on board.

If you have a bit of time before you catch your ferry you should visit the **Tarbert Bridewell Jail & Courthouse** (☎ 36500; adult/child €5/2.50; ☼ 10am-6pm Apr-Oct). The exhibition features models and displays on the social and political conditions of the 19th century. From the jail you can take the **John F Leslie Woodland Walk**, a 3.8km walk along Tarbert Bay towards the mouth of the Shannon.

Bus Éireann No 13 runs to Tarbert from Tralee (€8.50, 55 minutes) via Listowel (15 minutes) once a day.

DINGLE PENINSULA

You step onto the Dingle Peninsula and things change. Kerry time becomes even slower and the world fills with shapely mountains and curving bays, long golden beaches and deep woods that lie like felt along the base of the rocky hills. There are still plenty of fellow visitors in summer, but you can find yourself happily alone on Dingle, where ring forts, beehive stone huts, burial chambers and standing stones punctuate a remarkable landscape.

Dingle is the main town. Ferries run from Dunquin to the now-unpopulated, and protected, Blasket Islands, off the tip of the peninsula. The Slea Head Drive touring route heads west from Dingle to Slea Head, Dunquin, Ballyferriter, Brandon Creek and back to Dingle. You could drive it in a day but it's worth taking your time.

Tours

There are a number of Dingle-based companies that operate tours of the peninsula for about €15 per person.

O'Connor's (☎ 087 248 8008) bus tours of Slea Head depart from the tourist office in Dingle at 11am daily.

Moran's Slea Head Tours (☎ 066-915 1155, 087 275 3333; Moran's Garage) leave from the pier in Dingle at 10am and 2pm daily.

Sciúird (☎ 066-51937; Fios Feasa) has 2½-hour archaeological tours (€15 per person) departing from Dingle at 10.30am and 5pm daily, but only if the demand merits it in the winter months. These tours explore the many remarkable prehistoric sites and monastic ruins of the peninsula. Check for departure point when booking.

DINGLE

☎ 066 / pop 1828

The attractive port of Dingle (An Daingean) makes a good base for exploring the Dingle Peninsula. The town has a famous resident dolphin that has long boosted an already steady tourist trade. Dingle's sizable fishing fleet gives the town a healthy down-to-earth edge, and fishing quays lie happily side-by-side with water sports and tourism offices.

Information

The banks on Main St have ATMs and bureaux de change.

Dingle Bookshop (☎ 915 2433; Green St) Has a good collection of new and used books, including books on travel and local interest.

Dingle Internet Café (☎ 915 2478; Lower Main St; per 30 min/1 hr €2.60/4; ☼ 10am-10pm May-Sep, 10am-6pm rest of year) Also offers cheap rate international calls.

Tourist office (☎ 915 1188; the Pier; ☼ 9am-7pm Jun-Sep, 9.15am-1pm & 2.15-5pm Oct-May) Helpful, but

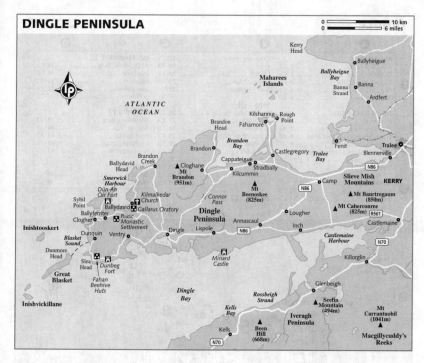

DINGLE PENINSULA

busy in summer, this place has plenty of information on the entire peninsula. It books accommodation for a €4 fee.

Sights

FUNGIE THE DOLPHIN

In the winter of 1984, Dingle fishing crews began to notice a solitary bottlenose dolphin that followed their vessels, jumped about in the water and sometimes leapt over smaller boats. Fungie the dolphin is now an international celebrity. Legend has it that no-one thought of running trips until a visiting American offered to pay a boatman to take him out to see Fungie. Free enterprise leapt the Atlantic faster than Fungie ever could.

Fungie still rules OK, and boats leave the pier daily year round for a one-hour dolphin-spotting trip; call **Dingle Boatmen's Association** (☎ 915 2626; adult/child €12/6). It's free if Fungie doesn't show, but he usually does. The association also runs a daily two-hour boat trip, leaving at 8am, for those who want to **swim with Fungie** (per person €25, plus wetsuit hire adult/child €25/15) but you need to book ahead. Wetsuits and snorkelling gear can also be hired from **Brosnan's** (☎ 915 1967; Coleen) and

from **Dingle Marine & Leisure Centre** (☎ 915 1344; www.dinglebaycharters.com; Strand St). You need to phone and arrange hire the day before.

DINGLE OCEANWORLD

This **aquarium** (☎ 915 2111; www.dingle-oceanworld .ie; Dingle Harbour; adult/child/family €10/6/27; ☼ 10am-8.30pm Jul & Aug, 10am-6pm May, Jun & Sep, 10am-5pm Oct-Apr), on the harbour road opposite the car park, had a complete refurbishment in 2005. You can see many types of local sea fish as they glide effortlessly in large tanks. Among the many features are a walk-through tunnel, a touch pool, a shark tank and an Amazon Jungle section complete with piranhas.

OTHER SIGHTS

Next to **St Mary's Church** in Green St is the **Trinity Tree**, an unusual three-trunked tree, representing the Holy Trinity, which has been carved with biblical characters. It looks like something out of a fairy tale.

Every second weekend in August the **Dingle Races** bring crowds from far and wide. The racetrack is opposite Ballintaggart Hostel, about 1.6km east of town on the N86.

COUNTY KERRY

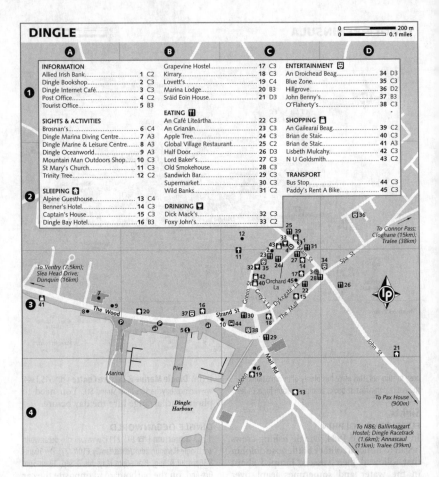

DINGLE

0 _____ 200 m
0 _____ 0.1 miles

INFORMATION		
Allied Irish Bank	1	C2
Dingle Bookshop	2	C3
Dingle Internet Café	3	C3
Post Office	4	C2
Tourist Office	5	B3

SIGHTS & ACTIVITIES		
Brosnan's	6	C4
Dingle Marina Diving Centre	7	A3
Dingle Marine & Leisure Centre	8	A3
Dingle Oceanworld	9	A3
Mountain Man Outdoors Shop	10	C3
St Mary's Church	11	C3
Trinity Tree	12	C2

SLEEPING		
Alpine Guesthouse	13	C4
Benner's Hotel	14	C3
Captain's House	15	C3
Dingle Bay Hotel	16	B3

Grapevine Hostel	17	C3
Kirrary	18	C3
Lovett's	19	C4
Marina Lodge	20	B3
Sráid Eoin House	21	D3

EATING		
An Café Liteártha	22	C3
An Grianán	23	C3
Apple Tree	24	C3
Global Village Restaurant	25	C2
Half Door	26	D3
Lord Baker's	27	C3
Old Smokehouse	28	C3
Sandwich Bar	29	C3
Supermarket	30	C3
Wild Banks	31	C2

DRINKING		
Dick Mack's	32	C3
Foxy John's	33	C2

ENTERTAINMENT		
An Droichead Beag	34	D3
Blue Zone	35	C3
Hillgrove	36	D2
John Benny's	37	B3
O'Flaherty's	38	C3

SHOPPING		
An Gailearaí Beag	39	C2
Brian de Staic	40	C3
Brian de Staic	41	A3
Lisbeth Mulcahy	42	C3
N U Goldsmith	43	C2

TRANSPORT		
Bus Stop	44	C3
Paddy's Rent A Bike	45	C3

The **Dingle Regatta**, a race in the harbour in traditional Irish *currach* canoes, is held at the end of August.

Activities

Hidden Ireland Tours (www.hiddenirelandtours.com) provides organised walking tours of the Dingle Peninsula.

Adventure Dingle (☎ 9152400; www.adventure dingle.com; Strand St) runs all sorts of adventure packages including rock climbing, sailing, horse riding, multiadventure and boat trips to the Blaskets, organised in conjunction with **Mountain Man Outdoor Shop** (☎ 915 2400; Strand St).

Snorkelling and scuba diving in Dingle Bay and around the Blasket Islands can be

arranged at **Dingle Marina Diving Centre** (☎ 915 2422) on the waterfront, near the harbour.

Ask at the tourist office for details of **sea fishing** trips, or call ☎ 915 1163. **Dingle Marine & Leisure Centre** (☎ 915 1344; Strand St) hires out fishing tackle. Four hours fishing costs €40 and all-day trips cost €80.

Long's Trekking Centre (☎ 915 9723; rides per hr €25) in Ventry has guided horse rides of the area.

Sleeping
BUDGET

Grapevine Hostel (☎ 9151434; www.grapevinedingle .com; Dykegate Lane; dm €14) Tucked away at the centre of town, this small, cosy hostel is well run and has pleasant rooms.

COUNTY KERRY

Lovett's (☎ 915 1903; Cooleen; dm/d €13/34) This is a small place in a family home and rooms are quite small, but it's well kept and there's a friendly attitude. It's handy for town in a quiet location.

Ballintaggart Hostel (☎ 915 1454; www.dingle accommodation.com; Racecourse Rd; camp sites €15, dm €15-18, d €56-70; ⊙ mid-Mar–Oct; P) A popular place, this old hunting lodge dates from 1703. It has excellent rooms and a great atmosphere. Out back there's a cobbled yard where there are giant soup urns, used when the building was a soup kitchen during the Famine years. The hostel is 1.6km east of Dingle on the N86. There's a free shuttle service to and from town, plus coin-operated Internet access.

MIDRANGE

Dingle has plenty of midrange B&Bs, but quite a few charge a bit too much for what has become, in a few cases, a take-it-or-leave-it service. There are, however, several 1st-class places.

Sráid Eoin House (☎ 915 1409; sraideoinhouse@ hotmail.com; John St; s/d €50/70; ⊙ mid-Apr–mid-Oct; P) A quiet location and a quiet house, with comfortable rooms that have a homelike atmosphere. It's close enough to the centre but feels comfortably out of town.

Marina Lodge (☎ 915 0800; www.dinglemarina lodge.com; s/d €60/90; P) A clean-cut building with neat, modern interiors, this hotel is near the harbour front and not too far from the centre of town.

Alpine Guesthouse (☎ 915 1250; www.alpine guesthouse.com; Mail Rd; s/d €60/90; P) This long-established, big guesthouse, on the outskirts of town as you come from the east, has decent rooms and straightforward breakfasts.

Kirrary (☎ 915 1606; Avondale; collinskirrary@eircom .net; s/d €55/74; P) You'll get plenty of chat and info at this cheerful place. Rooms are a reasonable size and breakfasts are hefty. Bike hire is available, and the family runs the three-hour archaeological tours to Slea Head (see p285).

TOP END

Pax House (☎ 915 1518; www.pax-house.com; Upper John St; s/d €70/140; P) From its highly individual décor, all bold colours and bright paintings, to the outstanding views over the estuary – you can catch Fungie in action from the fabulous balcony – Pax House is an absolute treat. It's just under 1km from the centre of town.

Captain's House (☎ 915 1531; captigh@eircom .net; the Mall; s/d €60/100; ⊙ mid-Mar–mid-Nov; P) A streamside garden and beautiful interior furnishings make this handsome house a great choice.

Dingle Bay Hotel (☎ 915 1231; www.dinglebayhotel .com; Strand St; s/d €100/150; P) It's business chic – and prices – at this hotel, but still a good base for visitors, with superb rooms full of light and bright woodwork, plenty of space and a good location for all the town has to offer.

Benner's Hotel (☎ 915 1638; www.dinglebenners .com; Main St; s/d €127/202; P) Prices drop by 20% in spring and autumn, and by nearly half in winter, at this long-established hotel, where old-fashioned style and modern amenities make a fine combination.

Eating

Dingle rings the changes on eating out, from no-frills cafés to some of the best restaurants in Kerry. For self-catering there's a big supermarket in Holyground. The garage just past the big roundabout on the eastern exit from town has a shop and sandwich bar.

BUDGET

An Café Liteártha (☎ 915 2204; Dykegate La; snacks €3-5; ⊙ 9am-6pm) Prices don't change much at this delightful place where you can relax at the back of an excellent bookshop engulfed in the spirit of literary Dingle.

John Benny's (☎ 915 1215; Strand St; snacks €3-5, mains €8.50-16; ⊙ 10am-9.30pm) Popular Benny's pub does good soup, chowder and sandwiches, or heftier dishes such as Irish stew or bacon and cabbage, as well as fish. Kids meals are between €4 and €7. There's good music here too (see p280).

An Grianán (☎ 915 1910; Green St; snacks €3-4) Wholefood and organic is the style at this shop, where there's a choice of sandwiches, pizza slices and other snacks. Special diets are catered for.

Apple Tree (☎ 915 0804; Orchard La; mains €4.50-10) A no-frills eatery that serves up breakfast and general meals including lasagne and quiche, all of it home cooked.

MIDRANGE

Global Village Restaurant (☎ 915 2325; Main St; mains €18-24; ⊙ 6-10pm) The owner-chef of this excellent restaurant is well travelled, and it shows in the mix of style, from modern European to Pacific Rim cuisine and adventurous dishes that include such specialities as roast skate in a tomato, saffron and cumin broth. Vegetarians are well catered for.

Wild Banks (☎ 915 2888; Main St; mains €18-26; ♥ 4-10pm Jun-Sep, 6-10pm Thu-Sun rest of year) There's imaginative modern Irish cuisine at this attractive restaurant that has a good choice of meat and fish dishes as well as such vegetarian delights as spinach and cheese roulade in filo pastry with tomato and red pepper sauce (€14.60). The set menu is €25.

Half Door (☎ 915 1600; John St; mains €22-35, set menu €25; ♥ 12.30-2pm Mon-Sat, 6-10pm Mon-Sun) You'll pay for the privilege at this outstanding seafood restaurant where fish and shellfish are superbly presented. But spoil yourself and go for lobster, or mussels in a garlic and wine sauce, or the seafood platter, hot or cold. There are meat and duck dishes too and the surroundings are suitably cosy.

Old Smokehouse (☎ 915 1061; cnr Main St & the Mall; lunch €6.50-9.50, dinner €15.50-22; ♥ noon-10pm) An attractive riverside location and unpretentious surroundings make this small restaurant a local favourite. Lunch can be hefty sandwiches or bangers and mash, while dinner offers traditional Irish meat and fish dishes with a vegetarian option.

Lord Baker's (☎ 915 1277; Lower Main St; bar menu €4-15.50, mains €16-28; ♥ 12.30-9.45pm Fri-Wed) You can't fail with this Dingle institution. Established as a pub in 1890 by local worthy 'Lord Baker', this big bar-restaurant has an excellent choice of meat and fish dishes from a splendid menu that wastes no energy on purple prose. The front bar has a cheerful turf fire. Dishes range from brill, monkfish and salmon to lobster, with Kerry lamb, steak and poultry dishes as well.

Drinking

Foxy John's (☎ 915 1316; Main St) It's hardware counter to the right, drinks to the left in this wonderful old pub, where even the characters on tap are still convincing.

Dick Mack's (☎ 915 1960; Green St) Celebrity status declares itself outside Dick Mack's

with the names of famous patrons engraved on the pavement for the rest of us to walk over. Dolly Parton, Charlie Haughey, Robert Mitchum and Julia Roberts are all there. Paul Simon merits a stone stool. Inside, the old shoe-repair section of the pub now makes leather belts.

Entertainment

John Benny's (☎ 915 1215; Strand St) Everything from lively trad and set dancing to blues and contemporary is on offer from 9.30pm Monday, Wednesday, Friday and Saturday at Benny's. There's good food here too.

O'Flaherty's (☎ 915 1983; Strand St) Summer-night trad sessions are popular at this big spacious bar, and sessions can spark up at any time of the year.

An Droichead Beag (Small Bridge Bar; ☎ 915 1723; Lower Main St) Traditional music kicks off at 9.30pm nightly at this pub by the bridge.

Blue Zone (☎ 915 0303; Green St; ♥ 6pm-1am) Dingle chill-out spot that also does a tasty line in pizzas and home-made ice creams and sorbets. There's a happy hour from 6pm to get you started and there's live music on Tuesday and Thursday from 10pm to 1am.

Hillgrove (☎ 915 1131) There's a break from traditional Dingle at the Hillgrove, off Spa Rd, where chart sounds rule nightly in summer and at weekends the rest of the year. Don't expect a blitz.

Shopping

An Gailearaí Beag (☎ 915 2976; Main St) Show-case for the work of the West Kerry Craft Guild, this charming shop has some fine items for sale, including ceramics, paintings, wood carvings, photography, Batik, jewellery, stained glass and much more.

N U Goldsmith (☎ 915 2217; Green St) Original jewellery by Niamh Utsch is on display at this stylish little gallery shop. Individual pieces start at €40 and keep rising.

Brian de Staic (☎ 915 1298; www.briandestaic .com; the Wood) Exquisite modern Celtic work by this local jewellery designer reflects the whole gamut of tradition and culture. The company also has a shop on Green St.

Lisbeth Mulcahy (☎ 915 1688; Green St) Beautiful scarves, rugs and wall hangings are created on a 150-year-old loom by this long-established designer. Also sold here are ceramics by her husband, who has a workshop west of Dingle (see p286).

Getting There & Away

Bus Éireann (☎ 712 3566) buses stop outside the car park behind the supermarket. There are five buses daily Monday to Saturday between Dingle and Tralee, and three on Sunday (€9). At least five buses a day Monday to Saturday depart Killarney for Dingle via Tralee (€11).

Two buses run daily Monday to Saturday, June to mid-September between Dingle, Ventry, Ballyferriter and Dunquin.

Getting Around

Dingle is easily navigated on foot. For a taxi call **Dingle Co-op Cabs** (☎ 915 1000), which can also give private tours of the peninsula.

There are several bike-hire places, including **Paddy's Rent A Bike** (☎ 915 2311; Dykegate St; per day/week €10/40) and **Foxy John's** (☎ 915 1316; Main St; per day/week €10/45).

NORTHSIDE OF THE PENINSULA

There are two routes from Tralee to Dingle, though they both follow the same road out of Tralee past the Blennerville Windmill. Near the village of Camp a right fork heads off to the Connor Pass, while the N86 via Annascaul takes you to Dingle more quickly. The Connor Pass route is much more beautiful and panoramic. At Kilcummin a road to the west heads to the relatively little-visited villages of Cloghane and Brandon and on to Brandon Point, with fine views of Brandon Bay.

Castlegregory

☎ 066 / pop 870

A small, rather scattered village, Castlegregory (Caislean an Ghriare) once rivalled Tralee as a busy local centre. A sand-strewn road heads north from the village along a broad spit of land between Tralee Bay and Brandon Bay to Rough Point. It's an intriguing place, flat, breezy and with terrific views across the water to Mt Brandon. Caravans and bungalows pepper the grassy dune land, and the flanking beaches are excellent venues for windsailing and surfing, although sets don't get too awesome. The Brandon Bay side is good for long boards and beginners, especially when there's a northerly swell. Wave-sailing is big here and there are major competitions staged at prime points with names such as Dumps and Mosies. Kite-surfing is also beginning to catch on.

Jamie Knox Watersports (☎ 713 9411; www .jamieknox.com; the Maharees) covers just about every aspect of surf-related sports. It's halfway along the peninsula.

Beyond Rough Point are the **Maharees Islands**. Illauntannig is the largest of these and is the site of a 6th-century monastery. Remains of the settlement include a stone cross, a church and beehive huts. Two small adjoining islands can be reached by foot from Illauntannig at low tide, but make sure you know exactly what the tide is doing. The islands are privately owned and were used to graze cows, but trips (taking about 10 minutes) can be arranged through Castle House or Harbour House in conjunction with a **scuba diving** trip. These waters have great underwater visibility and offer some of the best diving you're likely to get anywhere.

SLEEPING & EATING

Castle House (☎ 713 9183; www.caisleanti.com; s/d €45/70; P) Located at the northern edge of Castlegregory at the start of the road along the Rough Point peninsula, this handsome house has fine, big rooms. You can pop out the back and down a track to the beach in minutes. Trips to the Maharees Islands can be arranged, weather permitting.

Harbour House (☎ 713 9292; stay@iol.ie; Scraggane Pier; s/d €50/80; P) This busy place is in a great position right at the end of the peninsula 5km north of Castlegregory, near Kilshannig, overlooking the Maharees Islands. It's a popular diving centre and has excellent facilities including an indoor pool and a state-of-the-art fitness room. It provides Professional Association of Diving Instructors (PADI) diving instruction and takes divers to the waters around the Maharees.

Anchor Caravan Park (☎ 713 9157; www.caravan parksireland.net; camp sites €18; Easter-Sep) Wooded surroundings make this a sheltered place that has well-kept facilities. The park is on the R560 just east of Castlegregory.

Spillane's (☎ 713 9125; Maharees; bar meals €4.80-12.50, mains €11-22; 1-9.30pm mid-Mar–Nov) Very popular on weekends and during the high season, Spillane's churns the food out without losing quality. The steaks are huge and the fish is excellent. This is where the windsailing crew blast out on 'chocolate milkshake'. It's good for you.

GETTING THERE & AWAY

A year-round bus service leaves Tralee for Castlegregory on Friday only at 8.55am and 2pm, and returns at 10.35am. In July and early August there are also two services on Wednesday, leaving Tralee at 10.20am and 4.15pm, and returning at 11.05am and 5pm. There's no bus service along the peninsula.

Cloghane

☎ 066 / pop 268

Cloghane (An Clochán), on the southwestern edge of Brandon Bay, is a marvellous 'stop the world and get off' place. You'll leave with reluctance. There's a fine beach and a fascinating foreshore, and the road ends at far Brandon Point. There's terrific coastal and mountain walking and the best way up Mt Brandon starts from here.

Cloghane has an **information centre** (☎ 713 8277; ⏰ daily May-Sep, Sat & Sun rest of year) at the southern entrance to the village where you can buy the excellent *Cloghane and Brandon Walking Guide* (€3.80) with details of all the trails you'll see signposted. Those interested in the region's many archaeological sites should ask about guided walks or buy the equally excellent *Loch a'Dúin Archaeological and Nature Trail* (€3.80).

There is a post office in the village shop, attached to Mount Brandon Hostel.

Immediately opposite the information centre, **St Brendan's Church** has a stained-glass window showing the Gallarus Oratory and Ardfert Cathedral.

CLIMBING MT BRANDON

At 951m, **Mt Brandon** (Cnoc Bhréannain) is Ireland's second-highest mountain. It's made up of a beautiful series of high summits that lie along the edge of a spectacular series of east-facing cliffs and steep ridges above a rocky lake-filled valley. An ascent of the mountain is a serious all-day trip. You should be well-equipped with weatherproof clothing and mountain boots, even in summer. Above all you should be experienced in the use of a map (Ordnance Survey Map No 70) and compass because thick mist can develop quickly, as can wind and rain. Allow at least six to seven hours there and back.

A popular route from the west is the Saint's Rd, which starts at Kilmalkedar Church (see p287) but can be more easily started at OS reference 435095, 1km east of the hamlet of An Baile Breac, itself 4km northeast of Kilmalkedar. It is a straightforward 6km slog there and back and is fairly well marked, although you'll definitely need good compass work in mist.

The classic way up Mt Brandon starts from Faha road-end (OS reference 493120) above Cloghane. (You can drive or cycle there, although it's a steep option for bikes. If you walk this road section it adds a couple of hours onto the six-hour there-and-back climb from Faha.) To reach Faha take the turn left, signposted 'Cnoc Bhréanainn', about 200m northeast of Cloghane school, and follow the narrow lane to a T-junction. Go left here until you reach a car parking area at the road end (2km from Cloghane). For walkers, a shorter option than the road is to take the path that starts in Cloghane village, opposite the thatched pub, Tigh Tomsi. This can be very overgrown, however. From the road-end car park at Faha, the route there and back to the summit of Brandon is a fairly tough 7km.

Walk left up the track above the car park and follow the obvious path onto the open mountain and past a grotto. The rocky path is very clear. Occasional guide poles mark the way along a rising grassy ridge, with a magnificent line of cliffs and ridges ahead. The path contours around rocky slopes and then descends into the glaciated wilderness at the valley head, from where it winds its way between great boulders and slabs. Far too many yellow painted arrows on the rocks point the way. (Some guidance is sensible, but any more yellow paint and this beautiful wilderness will resemble a no-parking zone.)

When the back wall is reached, the path zigzags very steeply to the rim of the great cliffs. Turn left at the top and head for the summit of Mt Brandon, marked by a trigonometry point, or pillar (used for Ordnance Survey mapping calculations), a wooden cross and the remains of Teampaillin Breanainn (St Brendan's Oratory). The views in clear weather from the summit are beyond words. The edge of the cliffs is sudden, so care should be taken at all times. You can continue along the edge of the cliffs to the subsidiary summits and to Brandon Peak, 2km south, but this will add a couple of

---

TOM CREAN – ANTARCTIC HERO

County Kildare may boast the great polar explorer Ernest Shackleton as a native son, but Kerry has its own polar hero, Tom Crean, who was a key member of several early Antarctic expeditions.

Crean (1877–1938) came from Annascaul on the Dingle Peninsula. At age 15 he signed up with the British Navy, and in later life was a member of three of the four British Antarctic expeditions in the vessels *Discovery* (1901–04), *Terra Nova* (1910–13) and *Endurance* (1914–16).

Both Robert Falcon Scott and Shackleton saw Tom Crean as a crucial member of their expeditions, and Shackleton's letters to Crean reflect immense warmth and liking for the Kerryman, whose physical and mental strengths were outstanding. When the *Endurance* was trapped and crushed in ice and the crew sailed in small boats to Elephant Island, Shackleton chose Crean as one of the small crew that continued on the epic 800-mile sea voyage from Elephant Island to South Georgia to bring help to their stranded companions.

Tom Crean also served throughout WWI and retired in 1920. Shackleton wanted Crean to accompany him on his final expedition on the *Quest* in 1921, but he declined. He had spent more time in Antarctica than either Scott or Shackleton. He opened his pub, the South Pole, at Annascaul, married and had three daughters. Crean's later life was quiet and unassuming, like the man himself, but his remarkable achievements have become increasingly recognised both at home and abroad. His name lives on in the title of the Crean Glacier on South Georgia and Mt Crean in Victoria Land, Antarctica.

---

hours. Retracing your way down requires care and concentration on the initial steep zigzags. The rest of the way back to Faha is freewheeling.

CONNOR PASS & AROUND

At 456m, the Connor (or Conor) Pass is the highest in Ireland and offers spectacular views of Dingle Harbour to the south and Mt Brandon to the north. On a foggy day you'll see nothing but the road just in front of you. There's a car park near the summit. When visibility is good take the path up behind it to see the peninsula spread out below you.

SLEEPING & EATING

Mount Brandon Hostel (☎ 713 8299; www.mount brandonhostel.com; dm €17, s/d €26/38; P) At the heart of Cloghane, this smart place has delightful rooms and a terrific four-person apartment (€350 per week). Out front is the local post office, shop and café with Internet access (€1 per 10 min).

Benagh (☎ 713 8142; mcmorran@eircom.net; s/d €30/60; P) There's a very fair deal all round at this friendly house that is in a superb position overlooking Brandon Bay. You can watch the mud banks melt into the tide and then reappear six hours later. Guided walks can be arranged from here and the owners have great knowledge of local archaeology and ecology.

O'Connors (☎ 713 8113; Cloghane; s/d €40/70; meals €14-20; P) At this classic village pub that does decent food, you can get an evening meal between 7pm and 8pm, but you should book. It also does camping (€8 per person).

Crutch's Hillville House Hotel (☎ 713 8118; macshome@iol.ie; Connor Pass Rd; s/d incl breakfast €50/100; mains €17.50-23.50; P) An experience in itself, this handsome old house stands in glorious isolation amid trees, 6km from Cloghane on the road to Castlegregory. There's a cheerful welcome and a sense of gracious but easy living. There are four-poster beds in most of the bright and airy rooms. The restaurant offers excellent traditional Irish food with modern flair.

GETTING THERE & AWAY

On Fridays only, bus No 273 leaves Tralee at 8.55am and 2pm for Cloghane (1¼ hours). Returning, it leaves Cloghane at 10.05am and 3.10pm.

TRALEE TO DINGLE VIA ANNASCAUL

For drivers this route has little to recommend it other than being faster than the Connor Pass route. By bike it's less demanding. On foot the journey constitutes the first three days of the Dingle Way (p678).

The main reason to pause in Annascaul (Abhainn an Scáil), also spelled Anascaul, is to visit the **South Pole Inn** (☎ 066-915 7388;

COUNTY KERRY

Main St; bar meals €6.50-12; ☺ noon-8pm Easter-Sep) by the river, on your way to or from Dingle. It commemorates villager Tom Crean (see p283), who went to the South Pole with Robert Falcon Scott and Ernest Shackleton. You can study the memorabilia and read up on his expeditions while tucking into your lunch. The pub has traditional music on Wednesday, Friday, Saturday and Sunday nights.

KILLARNEY TO DINGLE VIA CASTLEMAINE
☎ 066

The quickest route between Killarney and Dingle is by going through Killorglin and Castlemaine. At Castlemaine the R561 heads west to Dingle, soon meeting the coast and passing Inch on the way to joining the main Tralee road to Dingle.

At least three Bus Éireann buses between Tralee and Dingle stop at Lispole, Annascaul and Inch daily. Seven buses between Tralee and Killorglin stop at Castlemaine from Monday to Saturday, with four buses on Sunday.

Mt Caherconree
About 11km west of Castlemaine is the turn-off for Mt Caherconree, one of the higher mountains on the peninsula at 825m. The road ends at Camp on the northern side of the peninsula. About 4km along this road coming from the south is an Iron Age promontory fort that may have been built by Cúror MacDáine, king of Munster. Whichever direction you come from, there are stunning views from this narrow, exposed and high (even a little scary) road that demands concentration from drivers; stop driving if you want to admire the views.

Phoenix Vegetarian Restaurant & Accommodation (☎ 976 6284; www.pheonixtyther@hotmail.com; Shanahill East, Castlemaine; camp sites incl shower €12, dm €12.50, d with/without bathroom €50/40; breakfast €10, lunch €4-7.50, dinner mains €7.50-16.50; P) always has something, or someone, of interest to see. It is a very original place, about 6km west of Castlemaine on the R561. It has its own organic garden and creative features. The owners will pick you up from Castlemaine by prior arrangement. Food is strictly vegetarian, and vegans are catered for too. If you wish to eat only, it's advisable to book.

Inch
The main attraction at Inch (Inse) is the 6km-long **sand spit** that runs into Dingle Bay – a location for the archetypal leprechaunish film *Ryan's Daughter* and the film of the more muscular *Playboy of the Western World*. The sand dunes once sheltered Stone Age and Iron Age settlements.

Cars are allowed on the beach, but be very careful because vehicles regularly get stuck in the wet sand. This is a hot surfing beach. It faces west and waves average 1m to 3m. **Sammy's Store** (☎ 915 8118), at the roadside entrance to the beach, was being virtually rebuilt at the time of writing. It is due to reopen as a food shop, licensed restaurant, tourist information point and Internet centre.

Camping (camp sites €10) is possible in the field opposite Inch Beach. Ask at Sammy's Store.

Inch Beach Guest House (☎ 915 8118/087 256 5700; www.inchbeachguesthouse.com; Inch; s/d €47/70) is a well-appointed, comfy place in a fine open setting above Inch Beach. It has been open for only a couple of years.

Caherbla House (☎ 915 8120; caherbla@eircom .net; Inch; s/d €30/55; P) is located just along the road from Inch on the way to Castlemaine. This is another B&B that deserves an award for fair dealing with singles as well as doubles. It offers good value in a modern house with a nice, friendly welcome and views to go with it. It's also on the Dingle Way walking route (see p678).

WEST OF DINGLE
The area west of Dingle takes in the Slea Head Drive along the R559. It has the greatest concentration of ancient sites in Kerry, if not in the whole of Ireland. To do the sites justice you should use one of the specialist guides on sale in the An Café Liteártha café-bookshop or the tourist office in Dingle town. The sites listed here are among the most interesting and easiest to find.

This part of the peninsula is a Gaeltacht (Irish-speaking) area. The landscape is dramatic, and can be more so in shifting mist, although full-on sea fog obliterates everything. When it does, just let all that bracing sea air wash over you.

For the most dramatic views it's best to follow the Slea Head drive in a clockwise direction. Cross the bridge west of Dingle and keep straight on to Ventry. Beyond Ventry the road hugs the coast past Dunbeg Fort and then round the rocky outposts of Slea Head and Dunmore Head. It is here that the offshore Blasket islands dominate the scene. The road continues north round the coast through Dunquin and Ballyferriter with widening views across glittering water to the lofty Mt Brandon and its outliers. Beyond Ballyferriter is the Gallarus Oratory and numerous other historic sites. North of here is a clutter of minor roads that lead in fascinating circles and to dead ends. From Gallarus the R599 turns north then east and southeast and so back to Dingle.

Ventry

☎ 066 / pop 460

The small village of Ventry (Ceann Trá) is next to a wide sandy bay.

A great base for exploring the area is **Ceann Trá Heights** (☎ 915 9866; ventry@iol.ie; s/d €45/65), a pleasant bungalow standing high above Ventry harbour. Rooms are comfy and breakfasts hearty.

Slea Head & Dunmore Head

Slea Head offers some of the Dingle Peninsula's best views, good walks and fine beaches. It is extremely popular with coach parties.

Dunmore Head is the most westerly point on the Irish mainland and the site of the wreckage in 1588 of two Spanish Armada ships.

About 7km south of Ventry on the road to Slea Head is the prehistoric **Dunbeg Fort**, perched on a cliff-top promontory with a sheer drop to the Atlantic. The fort has four outer walls of stone. Inside are the remains of a house and a beehive hut as well as an underground passage. On the inland side of the road is a car park and the **Stonehouse Restaurant** (☎ 915 9970; lunch €4.50-9.50, dinner mains €16.50-23), built in the Gallarus Oratory style. It has a pleasant choice of sandwiches, or more substantial meat, chicken and fish dishes, as well as vegetarian options.

The Slea Head area is dotted with **beehive huts**, **forts**, **inscribed stones** and **church sites**. The **Fahan huts** are on the inland side of the road a short distance further west from Dunbeg Fort. There are signs pointing the way from the road.

To visit the sights mentioned above you'll be charged about €2 to €3; it's unavoidable during the summer when there are attended kiosks. Comfort yourself with the thought that, given the chance, the original occupants of the sites would probably have charged as well.

Dunquin

About 3km north of Slea Head is the scattered village of Dunquin (Dún Chaoin) lying below breezy hills. A scenic road climbs through the mountains from Dunquin to Ventry. Dunquin is where you catch a boat to the Blasket Islands.

The superb **Blasket Centre** (Ionad an Bhlascaoid Mhóir; ☎ 915 6444; adult/child €3.50/1.25; 🕙 10am-7pm Jul & Aug, 10am-6pm Easter-Jun, Sep & Oct) is a brilliant example of how architecture and design can do justice to an awesome subject. This Dúchas-operated centre celebrates the lost lifestyle of the Blasket Islanders, and the Irish language and culture. The interiors are stunning; features replicate with great subtlety and drama a sense of sea and sky and the captivating uniqueness of the Blaskets. There's a café with Blasket Island views, and a small bookshop. Last admission is 45 minutes before closing.

The **Dunquin Hostel** (☎ 915 6121; mailbox@anoige .ie; dm/d €12/34; **P**) has a terrific location, near the Blasket Centre, and is not too far from the ferry departure point for Great Blasket Island. There are stunning views. Rooms are smart and there's a cheerful atmosphere.

By the junction with the road to the harbour is **An Portán B&B and Restaurant** (☎ 915 6212; www.anportan.com; s/d €32/51; lunch from €12, dinner €15-25; restaurant 🕙 Easter-Sep; **P**). An Portán has pleasant rooms in a complex separate from the restaurant. Meals are traditional Irish with an international flavour, and include such dishes as cajun cod in mango, salsa and lemon butter sauce.

BLASKET ISLANDS

The Blasket Islands (Na Blascaodaí), 5km out into the Atlantic, are the most westerly islands in Europe. At 6km by 1.2km, Great Blasket (An Blascaod Mór) is the largest and most visited, and is mountainous enough for strenuous walks, including a good one detailed in Kevin Corcoran's *Kerry Walks*. All of the Blaskets were inhabited at one time or another and there is evidence of Great Blasket being inhabited during the Iron Age and early Christian times. The last islanders left for the mainland in 1953 after the government and the remaining inhabitants agreed that it was no longer feasible to live in such remote and harsh conditions.

Two- and three-hour cruises around the islands can be booked through **Dingle tourist office** (☎ 066-915 1188; cruises €25).

There's no accommodation on the islands, but there are several accommodation options around Dunquin (see p285).

GETTING THERE & AWAY

Weather permitting, boats operate April to October (return adult/child €20/10, 20 minutes). Boats leave Dunquin every 30 minutes, 10am to 6pm. Check and double check on arrival when the last boat back is expected to leave.

Ballyferriter

Continuing north from Dunquin you pass the tiny settlement of Clogher from where the road turns east to reach Ballyferriter (Baile an Fheirtearaigh), named after Piaras Ferriter, a poet and soldier who emerged as a local leader in the 1641 rebellion and was the last Kerry commander to submit to Cromwell's army.

At Clogher is one of the most interesting potteries on the peninsula, the **Louis Mulcahy Pottery** (☎ 915 6229; Clogher, Ballyferriter; ☯ 9am-8pm Jul & Aug, 10am-5.30pm Mon-Sat, 11am-5.30pm Sun rest of year). Some pieces have been sold or given to such people as Bill Clinton and the Pope. Purchases can be delivered overseas from the shop.

Just before Ballyferriter proper, a road, signposted to Dún an Óir Ostán, leads northwest to **Ferriter's Cove** and its adjoining golf course. **Ceann Sibéal Golf Club** (☎ 915 6255; Ballyferriter; €45 Jun-Sep, €35 rest of year, plus club hire year round €15) is a wild and windy links course.

About 2.5km northeast of Ferriter's Cove, on the shores of the huge bay known as Smerwick Harbour, is **Dún an Óir Fort** (Fort of Gold), the scene of a hideous massacre during the 1580 Irish rebellion against English rule. The fort was held by Sir James Fitzmaurice, who commanded an international brigade of Italians, Spaniards and Basques. On 7 November, English troops under Lord

Grey attacked the fort and within three days the defenders surrendered. 'Then putt I in certeyn bandes who streight fell to execution. There were 600 slayne', said the poet Edmund Spenser, who was secretary to Lord Grey and patently not in a lyrical mood at the time.

To reach the site follow the road to Ferriter's Cove from the R559, and then after 1.3km, take the right fork at a Y-junction and go straight on, ignoring side tracks, until you come to a T-junction in another 1.4km. Turn right for another 1.3km, then right again and in about 300m you'll see a signpost to the fort. You can drive down the track, which was lavishly surfaced in the 1980s to accommodate the limousine of the then-President of Ireland, Charles Haughey, who officially opened the car park at the track's end. There's a handsome memorial sculpture by Cliodna Cussen here. The fort has been much eroded, but it's an atmospheric place.

Opposite the church at Ballyferriter is the **Dingle Peninsula Museum** (Músaem Chorca Dhuibhne; ☎ 915 6100; adult/child €2.50/1.50; ☯ 10am-6pm May-Sep, by appointment rest of year). It has displays on the ecology and geology of the Dingle Peninsula.

Just as you head east out of Ballyferriter, a side road on your left signposted 'Cuan Ard na Caithne/Smethwick Harbour' will take you to a fine beach about 1km from the main road.

Ferriter's Cove (☎ 915 6295; fcove@gofree.indigo .ie; Ballyyoughtra, Ballyferriter; s/d €40/55; **P**) is a bright and airy B&B where wooden floors and large rooms go with the freshness of the coastal location. To get there, follow the signs to the golf club and you'll see it on your left.

Free camping is possible near Ferriter's Cove but there are no facilities.

Riasc Monastic Settlement

The remains of this 5th- or 6th-century monastic settlement are quietly impressive and rather haunting. Excavations have revealed, among other finds, the foundations of an oratory first built with wood and later stone, a kiln for drying corn and a cemetery. Most interesting is a pillar with beautiful Celtic designs. The ruins are signposted as Mainistir Riaisc along a narrow lane off the R559, about 2km east of Ballyferriter.

Gallarus Oratory

Simple but stunning, this superb dry-stone oratory is in perfect condition, apart from a slight sagging in the roof, and has withstood the elements for some 1200 years. Traces of mortar suggest that the interior and exterior walls may have been plastered. Shaped like an upturned boat, it has a doorway on the western side and a small round-headed window on the eastern side. Inside the doorway are two projecting stones with holes that once supported the door.

The oratory is signposted off the R559 about 3km northeast of Ballyferriter and about 2km further on from the Riasc Settlement turn-off. If you arrive by car, note that the Gallarus Visitor Centre is a private venture. It charges for parking, an audiovisual presentation and for then passing through the centre to walk up to the oratory. Access to the oratory is actually free. The lane that runs inland from the main road leads in about 200m to a limited parking space from where a well-tended right-of-way leads to the oratory. Parking for Gallarus is problematic however and congestion in summer from vehicles on such a narrow road can also be a problem. All of this should be kept in mind by drivers.

Europe's most westerly camp site, **Oratory House Camping** (Campail Teach An Aragail; ☎ 915 5143; www.dingleactivities.com; Gallarus; camp sites €12; ☒ Easter–late Sep), is 300m from the Gallarus Oratory. It's a source of much local information on a mass of activities, walking especially.

Bus No 275 leaves Dingle at 9am and drops off at Gallarus 10 minutes later on Tuesday and Friday only. From Gallarus it picks up for Dingle at 1.25pm and 6.30pm.

Kilmalkedar Church

This 12th-century church was once part of a complex of religious buildings. The characteristic Romanesque doorway has a tympanum with a head on one side and a mythical beast on the other. There is an ogham stone, pierced by a hole, in the grounds, as well as a very early sundial. About 50m away is a two-storey building known as **St Brendan's House**, which is believed to have been the residence of the medieval clergy. At the time of writing the building was being restored. To the right of St Brendan's House is the start of the track known as the **Saint's Rd**, the traditional approach to Mt Brandon (see p282). Parking is very limited for both these sites.

From Gallarus Oratory the R559 goes north to the little village of Murreagh. The church is about 2km east of the village.

Following the R559 southeast for 8km from Kilmalkedar takes you back to Dingle.

Getting There & Away

Year round, two buses on Monday and three buses on Thursday operate from Dingle to Dunquin via Ventry Cross and Ballyferriter. June to September an additional two buses go from Dingle to Dunquin via Slea Head. Returns in all cases are from Dunquin via Ballyferriter and Ventry. For more details phone **Bus Éireann** (☎ 712 3566) in Tralee.

Counties Limerick & Tipperary

By their names alone Limerick and Tipperary seem to suggest every Irish cliché in the book; and all of it set to music, with rhyming couplets. Yet the reality is far richer, especially if you are looking for a rewarding mix of heritage sites, friendly towns and villages, svelte hills and sun-dappled woodland: a mix that offers a worthwhile alternative to the dramatic landscapes and sometimes plump romanticism of neighbouring Cork, Kerry and Clare.

Limerick and Tipperary make up a broad swathe of mainly farming country through which brimming streams and rivers wind their way against a backdrop of tawny hills. Limerick lies to the south of the inner estuary of the River Shannon, while landlocked Tipperary sprawls into the heart of Ireland.

Heritage fans and countryside lovers will delight in the region's Irish and Anglo-Irish history that is highlighted by prehistoric remains, medieval castles and ruined abbeys. From the formidable King John's Castle in Limerick city to Tipperary's Rock of Cashel, the region rings the changes on Ireland's vivid past with style.

Peaceful villages and pleasant market towns such as Clonmel and Cahir mix rural charm with cheerful modernity. For a touch of urban life with strong local colour, Limerick city continues to develop into a busy shopping centre full of upbeat restaurants and buzzing bars, and with a storming club and entertainment scene that features great local talent as well as visiting national stars.

HIGHLIGHTS

■ **Culture City**
A cultural trip to visit Limerick city's Georgian House (p292) and Hunt Museum (p292)

■ **Nature Calls**
The enchanting hills and woods of the Glen of Aherlow and the Galtee Mountains (p301)

■ **Fly by Night**
Great restaurants, trad music pubs, mainstream and alternative theatres and a club scene are all part of Limerick by night (p295)

■ **Medieval World**
The medieval architecture of Adare (p297), in County Limerick, or Fethard (p309), in County Tipperary

■ **History Rocks!**
The archaeological ruins and a taste of historic Ireland at the Rock of Cashel (p302)

★ Limerick
★ Adare
★ Rock of Cashel
★ ★ Fethard
★ Glen of Aherlow ★ Galtee Mountains

■ POPULATION: 261,412   ■ AREA: 6989 SQ KM

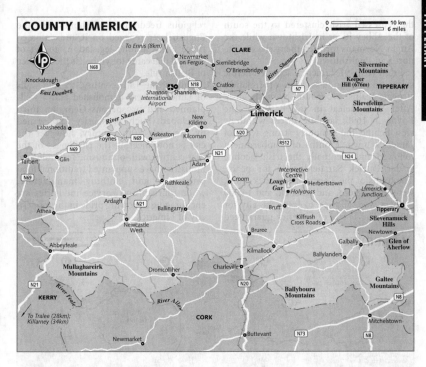

COUNTY LIMERICK

Limerick's low-lying farmland is framed on its southern and eastern boundaries by the swelling uplands of the Mullaghareirk, Galtee and Ballyhoura Mountains. Limerick city is cheerfully urban in contrast and has historic and cultural attractions in plenty to keep the visitor happily occupied for a day or two. About 10km south of the city lie the haunting archaeological sites around Lough Gur and just a few kilometres southwest is the village of Adare, with its plethora of medieval churches, castle ruins and 19th-century rusticity.

LIMERICK CITY
☎ 061 / pop 54,023
Limerick (Luimneach) has suffered too long from its hard-edged image as a bit of a rough old place. It is an image characterised by an uneasy reputation for crime and violence and by traditions of painful squalor, as portrayed graphically by Frank McCourt in his novel *Angela's Ashes*. The city has lifted itself, with some spirit, in recent times, however. Its central streets buzz with life and a busy shopping scene. Fine museums and galleries, and a thriving restaurant and pub-club culture, have enhanced Limerick's already warm heart. There's a slight hint of cosmopolitan style around the café-culture scene in the pedestrianised Cruise's St area off the north end of O'Connell St, while the refurbishment of Georgian houses, which match many of Dublin's finest, is a long-term aim.

History
Viking adventurers established a settlement on an island in the River Shannon in the 9th century. They fought with the native Irish for control of the site until Brian Ború's forces drove them out in 968 and established Limerick as the royal seat of the O'Brien kings. Brian Ború finally destroyed Viking power and presence in Ireland at the Battle of Clontarf in 1014. By the late 12th century invading Normans had supplanted the Irish. The two remained divided, and throughout the Middle Ages

the repressed Irish clustered to the south of the Abbey River in Irishtown while the Anglo-Normans fortified themselves to the north, in Englishtown.

From 1690–91, Limerick acquired heroic status in the endless saga of Ireland's struggle against occupation by the English. After their defeat in the Battle of the Boyne in 1690, Jacobite forces withdrew west behind the famously strong walls of Limerick town. Months of bombardment followed and eventually the Irish Jacobite leader Patrick Sarsfield sued for peace. The terms of the Treaty of Limerick, 1691, were then agreed, and Sarsfield and 14,000 soldiers were allowed to leave the city for France. The Treaty of Limerick guaranteed religious freedom for Catholics, but the English later reneged on it and enforced fierce anti-Catholic legislation, an act of betrayal that came to symbolise the injustice of British rule.

During the 18th century, the old walls of Limerick were demolished and a well-planned and prosperous Georgian town developed. Such prosperity had waned by the early 20th century, however the city is now meeting the challenges of the 21st century with optimism. Technological industries have supplanted traditional food processing and clothing manufacture, while tourism and service industries are encouraging a growing pride in the modern city of Limerick.

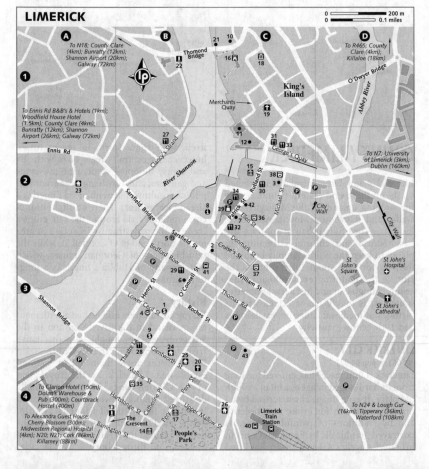

Orientation

Limerick straddles the Shannon's broadening tidal stream, where the river swings west to join the Shannon estuary. The city has a clearly defined grid of main streets. The central thoroughfare runs roughly north to south and its name changes, from Rutland St in the north to Patrick St, O'Connell St, The Crescent and Quinlan St. It then exits south along O'Connell Ave onto the Cork and Killarney roads. The main places of interest are clustered to the north on King's Island (the oldest part of Limerick and once part of Englishtown), to the south around The Crescent and Pery Sq (the city's noteworthy Georgian area), and along the riverbanks. The joint train and bus station lies southeast, off Parnell St.

Information

BOOKSHOPS

Eason (☎ 419 588; 9 O'Connell St) There are newspapers and magazines upstairs, and a good selection of books downstairs at this main street shop.
O'Mahony's (☎ 418 155; 120 O'Connell St) Ireland's largest independent bookshop has occupied these premises for over 100 years.

INTERNET ACCESS

Internet cafés come and go in Limerick, so it's a good idea to check at the tourist office. There's Internet access at Limerick City Library, but you usually need to book a 50-minute slot.
Netlink (☎ 467 869; 11 Sarsfield St; per 15 min €1) A fairly cramped place.

LAUNDRY

Superwash Launderette (☎ 414 027; 19 Ellen St; per load €8-16; ☻ 9-6pm Mon-Sat)

LEFT LUGGAGE

Limerick Train Station (☎ 217 331; Colbert Station, Parnell St; per item 24hr €2.50; ☻ 8am-6pm & 6.30-8.30pm Mon-Fri, 9.30am-6pm Sat & Sun)

LIBRARIES

Limerick City Library (☎ 407 501; The Granary, Michael St; ☻ 10am-5.30pm Mon & Tue, 10am-8pm Wed-Fri, 10am-1pm Sat)

MEDICAL SERVICES

Both hospitals have accident and emergency departments.
Midwestern Regional Hospital (☎ 482 219, 482 338; Dooradoyle)
St John's Hospital (☎ 415 822; John's Sq)

MONEY

Allied Irish and Ulster Banks, both on O'Connell St, have ATMs and bureaux de change. There's a handy ATM alongside the O'Connell St exit of the Arthur's Quay Shopping Centre.

POST

Main Post Office (☎ 316 777; Lower Cecil St)

TOILETS

Toilets (Arthur's Quay; admission €0.20)

TOURIST INFORMATION

Limerick Tourist Office (☎ 317 522; www.shannon regiontourism.ie; Arthur's Quay; ☻ 9.30am-1pm & 2-5.30pm Mon-Fri, 9.30am-1pm Sat) There is a Stena Line ferry information desk inside. Longer hours in peak season.

Dangers & Annoyances

History's rough handling of Limerick has left the modern city with a reputation for toughness and criminal violence. The latter should be seen in context, however. There is a 'gang' culture in the city, based increasingly on drug supplying, but its violence seems to be internecine and does not seem to affect mainstream life, or visitors. As with cities of any size, however, if you are out on the streets late at night, be alert and keep a low profile.

Sights

HUNT MUSEUM

Housed in the Palladian Custom House on the banks of the Shannon, this splendid **museum** (☎ 312 833; www.huntmuseum.com; Rutland St; adult/child €6.80/3.35; ☺ 10am-5pm Mon-Sat, 2-5pm Sun; ☺) contains probably the finest collection of Bronze Age, Iron Age and medieval treasures outside Dublin. All items are from the private collection of the late John and Gertrude Hunt, antique dealers and consultants, who gifted their collection to the nation in the 1970s. Exhibits are displayed in a succession of elegant galleries. Look out for the tiny, but exquisite, bronze horse by da Vinci, and a Syracusan coin thought to have been one of the '30 pieces of silver' paid to Judas for his betrayal of Christ. Cycladic sculptures, a Giacometti drawing and paintings by Renoir, Picasso and Jack B Yeats add to the feast. Guided tours are available. The museum has an in-house restaurant, DuCartes.

KING JOHN'S CASTLE

The massive curtain walls and towers of Limerick's showpiece **castle** (☎ 360 788; Nicholas St; adult/student/child €7/5.60/4.20; ☺ 9.30am-5.30pm Apr-Oct, 10.30am-4.30pm Nov-Mar, last admission 1hr before closing) are best viewed from the west bank of the River Shannon. The castle was built by King John of England between 1200 and 1212 on the site of an earlier fortification. It served as the military and administrative centre of the rich Shannon region.

Inside there are enjoyable exhibitions and audiovisual commentaries about the castle's history. Remnants of medieval siege mines and countermines, excavated Viking sites, reconstructed Norman features and artefacts offer graphic evidence of Limerick's colourful past. Check opening hours when you get to Limerick as times may be subject to change.

Across medieval Thomond Bridge on the other side of the river, the **Treaty Stone** marks the spot on the riverbank where the Treaty

---

BESIEGED BY SIEGES

It's small wonder that Limerick once developed a reputation for being a bit rough round the edges. The city was in and out of Irish history for centuries as competing interests fought over it. At times it seemed like Limerick was permanently under siege. It was besieged four times during the 17th century, with the final siege of 1690–91 (p289) setting the pattern for even rougher times for the native Irish. The sham of a treaty that followed was said to have been signed on the Treaty Stone (left) and the stone bears Virgil's Latin epithet on the City of Troy, 'An ancient city well-versed in the art of war'. Significantly, Virgil's additional phrase 'rich in resources' was omitted, although modern Limerick proves its relevance after all.

---

of Limerick was signed. Before you cross the bridge look out for the 18th-century **Bishop's Palace** (☎ 313 399; Church St; ☺ 10am-1pm & 2-4.30pm Mon-Fri) and the ancient **toll gate**.

GEORGIAN HOUSE & GARDEN

There is an engaging eeriness about the lofty, echoing rooms of the restored **Georgian House** (☎ 314 130; 2 Pery Sq; adult/child €5/3; ☺ 9.30am-4.30pm Mon-Fri), one of Limerick's finest treasures. A few plaster models in period dress enhance the marble, stucco and wall decorations in the main rooms, and the bare boards and dusty furnishings of the servants' quarters. Brace yourself for some tortuous but entertaining limericks on various wall plaques. The restored back garden leads to a coach house that contains a photographic memoir of Limerick and a small but quite evocative **Ashes Exhibition**, including a reconstruction of the childhood home of novelist Frank McCourt. An added pleasure is the **Carrol Collection**, the fascinating story of a leading Irish family illustrated with heirlooms and military memorabilia from the late 1700s to the 1920s.

LIMERICK CITY GALLERY OF ART

A happily random mix of traditional paintings covers every inch of wall space in the **Limerick City Gallery of Art** (☎ 310 633; Carnegie Bldg, Pery Sq; admission free; ☺ 10am-6pm Mon-Wed & Fri, 10am-7pm Thu, 10am-1pm Sat, 2-5pm Sun). The gallery is beside the peaceful People's Park, at the heart of Georgian Limerick. The permanent collection features work by Sean Keating and Jack B Yeats. Check out Keating's atmospheric *Kelp Burners* and Harry Kernoff's *The Turf Girl*; both infuse their traditional subjects with great energy and joy. The gallery also stages changing exhibitions of some fairly adventurous contemporary work that can sometimes set Limerick tongues wagging.

ST MARY'S CATHEDRAL
Limerick's ancient **cathedral** (☎ 310 293; Bridge St; admission by €2 donation; ☺ 9.30am-4.30pm Mon-Sat May-Nov, till 1pm Sat Dec-Apr) was founded in 1168 by Domhnall Mór O'Brien, king of Munster. Parts of the 12th-century Romanesque western doorway, the nave and aisles survive, and there are splendid 15th-century black-oak misericords (support ledges for choristers), unique examples of their kind in Ireland. It's worth checking if there are any musical events scheduled.

LIMERICK CITY MUSEUM
This small award-winning **museum** (☎ 417 826; Castle Lane; admission free; ☺ 10am-1pm & 2.15-5pm Tue-Sat) is beside King John's Castle. Exhibits include Stone Age and Bronze Age artefacts, the civic sword, samples of Limerick silver and examples of Limerick's lace- and kid-glove manufacturing, as well as a collection of paintings.

Tours
A two-hour **walking tour** (☎ 0876-353 648; per person €10; ☺ 2.30pm) of Limerick locations mentioned in Frank McCourt's novel *Angela's Ashes* starts and ends at the tourist office on Arthur's Quay. There is also a historical walking tour (☎ 318 106; www.iol .ie/~smidp/; 44 Nicholas St; per person €10; ☺ 11am & 2.30pm Mon-Fri) of Limerick. The start point is by arrangement.

Sleeping
BUDGET
At the time of writing there was a lack of hostels in Limerick city.

Courtbrack Hostel (☎ 302 500; info@summerwest .com; Courtbrack Ave; dm/s/d €22/28/49; ☺ Jun-Aug) A few minutes walk along Dock Rd from the Shannon Bridge, this useful place includes continental breakfast in its prices.

Jamaica Inn Holiday Hostel (☎ 369 220; www .jamaicainn.ie; Mount Levers, Sixmilebridge, Co Clare; dm €16-18, d €24-25; P ⊒) A good option, although it lies 13km northwest of the city. There are daily bus connections to Limerick and Shannon Airport. The bus stop is 200m from the hostel.

Cherry Blossom (☎ 469 449; www.cherryblossom limerick.com; 3 Alexandra Tce, O'Connell Ave; dm/s/d €20/30/50) An excellent budget choice, just south of the town centre, this is a bright and cheerful place that is ideal for all ages. It is well run and rooms are pleasant and bright. The larger rooms are dormitory-style with bunk beds. Light breakfast is included; full breakfast costs extra. Booking is advised.

Alexandra Guest House (☎ 318 472; info@alex andra.iol.ie; 5-6 Alexandra Tce, O'Connell Ave; s/d €35/65) There's an upbeat, caring attitude at this happily rambling house run by a member of the same family that operates the Cherry Blossom. Rooms are no-frills, but comfy. Light breakfast is included.

MIDRANGE
Alexandra Terrace on O'Connell Ave has several other B&Bs, all midrange in price. Ennis Rd, leading northwest towards Shannon, also has a selection of midrange B&Bs, although most are a kilometre or so from the centre.

Glen Eagles (☎ 455 521; gleneaglesbandb@eircom .net; 12 Vereker Gardens, Ennis Rd; s/d €43.50/62; ☺ Feb-Nov; P) Just 400m from the centre, Glen Eagles is in a peaceful cul-de-sac and has decent-sized, comfortable rooms and a cheerful welcome.

Hanratty's Hotel (☎ 410 999; hanrattyshotel@ hotmail.com; 5 Glentworth St; s/d €50/90; P) The oldest hotel in Limerick rather shows it round the edges. Period features survive; witness the elaborate chandelier in the stairwell. Some rooms are rather small.

Woodfield House Hotel (☎ 453 022; www.wood fieldhousehotel.com; Ennis Rd; s/d €85/145; P) The spacious bars and restaurant, and the comfortable bedrooms, of this out-of-town hotel create a pleasant country-house ambience in suburban Limerick. It's about 1.5km from the centre of town.

Railway Hotel (☎ 413 653; sales@railwayhotel.ie; Parnell St; s/d €46/80; P) Right across from the bus and train station, this long-established hotel keeps on keeping on. It has good-sized rooms, plus a bar and restaurant.

TOP END

Pery's (☎ 413 822; www.perys.ie; Glentworth St; s/d €100/160; ℗ ♿) The smooth Georgian façade of this modern hotel hides a glossy interior of bright tiling, wood and stainless steel fittings. Rooms are business standard and comfortable, and breakfasts are generous. Off-season discounts are available.

Clarion Hotel (☎ 469 555; www.clarionhotellimerick .com; r from €140; ℗ 💻) Limerick's waterfront showpiece hotel with all modernist accents and an internal landscape of chrome, glass and maple. Business and conference oriented but with everything for the tourist, including a health and leisure club, and in-house restaurant and bar.

Eating

Limerick has a reasonably good variety of eating places and there are a couple of outstanding restaurants.

BUDGET

Curragower Seafood Bar (☎ 321 788; Clancy's Strand; mains €4.50-12; ☽ noon-late) You can get cracking on delicious crab claws or sup tasty chowder from the simple but authentic menu of this great little bar on the west bank of the Shannon. There's a wonderful view of King John's Castle from the outside terrace; half-close your eyes on a sunny day and you could be by the seaside.

Chimes (☎ 319 866; Belltable Arts Centre, 69 O'Connell St; breakfast €4, mains €6-8; ☽ 8.30am-5pm Mon-Fri) The Belltable's basement café sidesteps the cultural diet and offers plump sandwiches and artful pastas.

Sails (☎ 416 622; 1st fl, Arthur's Quay, Patrick St; meals €6.50-8.50) A straightforward menu that includes salads, pasta and fish and chips at the heart of the Limerick shopping experience. There's a deli counter for takeaways.

Mojo Café Bar (☎ 410 898; 15 Patrick St; mains €4.50-10.50) It's main-street chic at this busy bar and eatery where sandwiches, *panini* (type of Italian sandwich) and wraps go for €5 to €7, and a good breakfast selection for €4 to €7. Lunch specials, such as savoury chicken pancake with trimmings, are €9.

French's (☎ 318 377; 6 Bedford Row; snacks €3-4.50) A neat little juice bar and creperie that offers tasty hot wraps, sandwiches and *panini* as well as crepes, from savoury to sweet. There's a great spread of smoothies, juices and coffees as well.

MIDRANGE

DuCartes (☎ 312 662; Hunt Museum, Rutland St; meals €4-12; ☽ 10am-5pm Mon-Sat, 2-5pm Sun) Window seats overlooking the Shannon add style to cultural lunches amid a swirl of tasteful chatter at the Hunt Museum's gallery-mode restaurant. On offer are tasty soups and sandwiches, grilled goat's cheese, Greek salads and other veggie options, as well as lamb and chicken dishes in tangy sauces.

Moll Darby's (☎ 411 511; George's Quay; mains €17.50-28.50; ☽ 5.30-11pm) Moll's by the river is nautical-themed, with stone floors, dark wood and exposed brickwork adding cosy intimacy. There's a mouthwatering choice, from starters such as Kenmare mussels with lemongrass and chilli, or crisp fried organic goat's cheese and spinach, to main dishes that include pan-seared monkfish, Connemara lamb and vegetarian choices such as couscous flavoured with curry and goat's cheese. An appealing three-course early bird deal costs €27.

Locke Bar (☎ 413 733; George's Quay; lunch mains €9.50) This popular riverside bar dishes out good helpings of Irish stew, chicken Kiev or fillet of cod for the busy local lunch crowd. There are comfy sofas indoors, and tables on an outdoor terrace beside the river.

TOP END

Green Onion (☎ 400 710; Old Town Hall, Rutland St; mains €15-23.50; ☽ noon-10pm Tue-Sat) Located in what was Limerick's old town hall, this is one of Limerick's coolest eateries and has cheerful staff and clientele to go with it. The lofty interior has been transformed into a vibrant red-and-blue dream space by the accomplished Bogside Artists from Derry. There's a set menu for €25 and main dishes ring the modern Irish changes from traditional meat, poultry and fish dishes to veggie tortillas and big open sandwiches. Try a dish of ultra-Irish colcannon: mashed potatoes with all sorts of tasty additions. There's an all-day menu and a great range of coffees for break time.

Freddy's Bistro (☎ 418 749; Theatre Lane; mains €18-26.50; ☽ 5.30-10pm Tue-Sat) A nice, peaceful location in a former coach house adds to the relaxed ambience of this consistently good restaurant. The menu combines a subtle mix of traditional and international cuisine ranging from Clonakilty Black Pudding croquettes with a seed mustard sabayon to a delicious seafood medley with a Chablis cream. A thoughtful wine list adds to the riches and there's a tempting early evening menu for €25.

Drinking & Entertainment

Limerick nightlife rocks as much as in any of Ireland's main cities. It's all the better for a few rough edges and reflects the city's vibrancy and contemporary outlook. Courtesy of local acts or visiting headliners, you'll find everything from trad Irish to trash rock, indie, chart, soul, reggae, drum 'n bass, jazz and classical, as well as theatre and stand-up comedy. Most clubs have strict door checks. The *Limerick Event Guide*, whose rather bland title translates cheerfully into the 'LEG', can be found for free in pubs, eateries and hotels all over town and is full of great info about the scene.

Dolan's Warehouse (☎ 314 483; www.dolanspub .com; 3/4 Dock Rd) One of Limerick's best venues promises an unbeatable gig list that has featured everyone from Evan Dando, Julia Turner and folk legends The Fureys, to the Trashcan Sinatras, as well as cutting edge stand-ups. The Warehouse is grafted on to the atmospheric Dolan's Pub, where you're guaranteed authentic trad music sessions most nights, though it can get very crowded.

Belltable Arts Centre (☎ 319 866; www.belltable .ie; 69 O'Connell St) Less funk and more fettuccini than Dolan's, the Belltable is a classy venue and a crucible for the arts in the midwest. It covers everything in theatre, visual arts, music, cinema and comedy – you're as likely to catch Voltaire's *Candide* as plays by John B Keane or Brecht. There's an art gallery too, and the Belltable's annual festival of fringe theatre, Unfringed (January and February), gets better every year.

Trinity Rooms (☎ 411 177; www.trinityrooms.ie; The Granary, Michael St) Three venues in one reflect the name of this big club-pub place. The Green Room front-of-house bar is open for food and drink all day, and has DJs and live bands after dark. The Quarter Club is a late-night chill-out lounge with R&B emphasis, and the Main Room blasts into the early hours with such acts as Moloko and a hot list of diva DJs. There's a Sunday night Comedy Clinic too, featuring top stand-ups.

University Concert Hall (UCH; ☎ 331 549; University of Limerick) Permanent home of the Irish Chamber Orchestra, the UCH adds lustre to Limerick's cultural scene with visits from world-class performers and regular concerts, opera, drama and dance events. It stays cutting edge, however, with stand-up guests, such as the genial and very fast Dara O'Briain and the outrageous Pat Shortt.

Nancy Blake's (☎ 416 443; Upper Denmark St) They still spread sawdust on the floor in this great old pub, and there's the backyard 'Outback' bar that rocks to regular music sessions on the weekend.

Cosmo Club (☎ 414 144; Vintage Club, Ellen St) A friendly gay and lesbian club at Limerick's long-established pub, the Vintage Club, this venue specialises in weekend entertainment. Saturday night is disco night from 9.30pm.

Mojo Café Bar (☎ 410 898; 15 Patrick St) Dishes out DJ fuelled rock, funk, indie, hip-hop, chart and retro for easy listening while you drink. Stays open Wednesday to Sunday nights until the early hours. Big screen TV caters for match fans.

Getting There & Away

AIR

Shannon Airport (☎ 712 000) in County Clare handles domestic and international flights. A taxi from Limerick city to the airport costs €28.

BUS

Bus Éireann (☎ 313 333; Parnell St) services operate from the bus and train station, a short walk south of the city centre. There are regular connections to Dublin (€15.50 one way, 1¼ hours), Tralee (€13.50, two hours), Cork (€14, one hour 50 minutes), Galway, Killarney, Rosslare, Donegal, Sligo, Shannon, Derry and most other centres. You can get off in Limerick at the bus stop on O'Connell St. There's a bureau de change at the Bus Éireann information desk.

TRAIN

There are regular trains to all the main towns from **Limerick Railway Station** (☎ 315 555; Parnell St): eight trains daily to Dublin (€40), two daily to Rosslare Harbour (€18), Cahir (€9.50) and Tipperary (€6.50), and one to Cork (€21). Other routes involve changing at Limerick Junction, 20km southeast of Limerick. Phone **Colbert station** (☎ 315 555) for details.

Getting Around

Regular buses connect Limerick's bus and train station with Shannon Airport (€5 one way). The airport is 26km northwest of Limerick, about 30 minutes by car.

Limerick is small enough to get around easily on foot or by bike. To walk across town from St Mary's Cathedral to the train station takes about 15 minutes.

Taxis are outside the tourist office, the bus and train station, and in Thomas St.

Scratch card parking discs (€1.50 per hour) are available from most newsagents and corner shops. Multistorey car parks around the city centre are open from 7.45am to 7pm (€1.50 per hour, €6 overnight).

Bikes can be hired at **Emerald Alpine** (☎ 416 983; www.irelandrentabike.com; 1 Patrick St; per day/week €20/80). The company will also retrieve or deliver a bike from anywhere in Ireland for €25. **McMahons Cycle World** (☎ 415 202; 30 Roches St; per day/week €15/70) is part of the national Raleigh Rent-a-Bike scheme. It charges €16 for retrieval or delivery at places outside Limerick, including Galway and Cork.

AROUND LIMERICK CITY

To the south of the city there's a clutch of outstanding historic sites that reward a day visit by car or a couple of days by bike. Only the larger villages are served by bus.

Lough Gur

The area around this horseshoe-shaped lake has many fascinating archaeological sites. To get there, leave Limerick on the N24 road south to Waterford. Look for a sign to Lough Gur indicating a right turn at the roundabout outside town. This takes you onto the R512. In about 18km you reach the superb **Grange Stone Circle**, known as the Lios, a 4000-year-old circular enclosure made up of 113 embanked uprights. It is the largest prehistoric circle of its kind in Ireland. There's roadside parking. Access to the site is free, but you may face a notice demanding a 'donation towards the cost and maintenance of the fence erected by the landowner to preserve this circle'. It's your call.

Around 1km further south along the R512, at Holycross garage and post office, a left turn takes you towards Lough Gur, past a ruined 15th-century **church** and a **wedge tomb** on the other side of the road.

Another 2km leads to a car park by Lough Gur, and the thatched replica of a Neolithic hut containing the **Lough Gur Interpretive Centre** (☎ 360 788; adult/child €5/3; ☀ 10am-5.30pm early May-late Sep; ℗). The centre has audiovisual presentations, and a small **museum** displaying a few Neolithic artefacts and a replica of the Lough Gur shield that's now in the National Museum in Dublin. The 700 BC shield is 72cm in diameter with six circles of raised bosses designed to weaken the impact of an enemy's sword.

There are short walks along the lake's edges that take you to burial mounds, standing stones, ancient enclosures and other points of interest. The whole area is ideal for picnics amid prehistory.

Kilmallock

☎ 063 / pop 1362

The scattering of medieval buildings confirms its status during the Middle Ages as Ireland's third-largest town, after Dublin and Kilkenny. Today the village lies sleepily beside the River Lubach, 26km south of Limerick, a world away from the city's urban racket. Kilmallock developed around a 7th-century abbey, and from the 14th to the 17th centuries it was the seat of the earls of Desmond.

Coming into Kilmallock from Limerick, the first thing you'll see (to your left) is a **medieval stone mansion** – one of 30 or so that housed the town's prosperous merchants and landowners. Further along, the street dodges around the four-storey **King's Castle**, a 15th-century tower house with a ground-floor archway through which the pavement now runs. Across the road, a lane leads down to the tiny **Kilmallock Museum** (☎ 91300; Sheares St; admission free; ☀ 2-5pm Mon-Fri). It houses a random collection of historical artefacts and a model of the town in 1597.

Beyond the museum and across the River Lubach are the impressive ruins of the 13th-century **Dominican priory**, which boasts a splendid five-light window in the choir.

Returning to the main street, head back towards Limerick city, then turn left into Orr St, which runs down to the 13th-century **Collegiate Church**. This has a round tower dating probably to an earlier, pre-Norman monastery on the site.

Further south along the main street, turn left (on foot, the road is one-way against you) into Wolfe Tone St. On the right, just before the bridge, you'll see a plaque marking the house where the Irish poet Aindrias Mac Craith died in 1795. Across the road, one of the pretty, single-storey cottages (the fifth one from the bridge) preserves a 19th-century interior. Obtain the key from next door.

On the other side of the main street in Emmet St is **Blossom Gate**, the one surviving gate of the original medieval town wall.

Kilmallock has an excellent facility in its **Friars' Gate Theatre and Arts Centre** (☎ 98727; www.friarsgate.net; Main St), where you can also find tourism information about the village. The centre hosts art exhibitions and has a fine little theatre in which it stages plays, music events and recitals.

If you're planning to stay for a bit, check out **Deebert House** (☎ 98106; www.deeberthouse .com; s/d €43.50/62; 🕑 Feb-Nov; 🅿). There are big, relaxing rooms in this fine Georgian house, which also has a charming garden and attached restaurant. It's best reached from the southern exit of the village by turning off down the road signed 'Tipperary'. Deebert House is on the corner at the next junction. Inquire about rates for the two self-catering apartments.

Two Bus Éireann buses run Monday to Saturday from Limerick to Kilmallock (€8.70, one hour).

ADARE & AROUND
☎ 061 / pop 1102

Picturesque ruins have made Adare a tourist honey pot and the wedding capital of west Ireland. This charming village on the River Maigue lies 16km southwest of Limerick on the busy N21, and the only thing that spoils it all is the torrent of cars and lorries that rattle through relentlessly. Yet, in spite of the cars, coaches and crowds, Adare's remarkable medieval buildings are a delight. The nuptial magic lies in the photo backdrops and the romance of handsome old churches. The main street is lined with thatched cottages that were created during the improving landlordship of the third earl of Dunraven in the 1820s. There's an interesting heritage exhibition, a pleasant riverside walk, which offers escape from the crowds, and some fine restaurants and cheerful pubs to support all the medievalism.

> **TOP FIVE WAYS TO RUIN YOUR DAY AT DUSK**
>
> There's nothing more satisfying than rambling round historic ruins, and Limerick and Tipperary have some of the finest in Ireland. Time your visits as dusk falls, when the mood is deliciously spooky. Try the following:
>
> **Athassel Priory** (near Cashel; p305) Ghostly in the gloaming.
>
> **Augustinian Friary** (Adare; p298) Delightful at nightfall.
>
> **Dominican Priory** (Kilmallock; opposite) Dignified at dusk.
>
> **Holy Trinity Churchyard** (Fethard; p309) Magic by moonlight.
>
> **Hore Abbey** (Cashel; p303) Brooding at batfall.

Information

The Allied Irish Bank (AIB) near the tourist office has an ATM and bureau de change.

Farrier's Internet Café (☎ 396 163; Main St; per 15 min €1.50) Next to Seán Collins pub.

Tourist office (☎ 396 255; Main St; Adare Heritage Centre; 🕑 9am-1pm & 2-5pm Mon-Sat, closed Jan) The friendly staff have plenty of advice and literature about Adare. Open slightly longer hours in peak season.

Sights
ADARE HERITAGE CENTRE

In the centre of the village is the **heritage centre** (☎ 396 666; Main St; adult/child €5/3.50; 🕑 9am-5pm). The centre's audiovisual presentation and exhibits explain the history and the medieval context of Adare's buildings in an entertaining way. At times during winter months the centre may close at 4pm.

RELIGIOUS HOUSES

Before the Tudor dissolution of the monasteries (1536–39), Adare had three flourishing religious houses, the remains of which can still be seen. In the village itself, next to the heritage centre, the dramatic tower and southern wall of the **Church of the Holy Trinity** date from the 13th-century Trinitarian priory that was restored by the first earl of Dunraven. Holy Trinity is now a Catholic church. There's a restored 14th-century **dovecote** down the side turning next to the church.

The ruins of a **Franciscan friary**, founded by the earl of Kildare in 1464, stand in the middle of Adare Manor golf course beside the River Maigue. Public access is assured, but let them know at the clubhouse that you intend to visit. A track leads away from the clubhouse car park for about 400m – watch out for flying golf balls. There's a handsome tower and a fine sedilia (row of seats for priests) in the southern wall of the chancel.

South of the village, on the N21, and close to the bridge over the River Maigue, is the Church of Ireland parish church, once the **Augustinian friary**, founded in 1316. It was also known as the Black Abbey. The interior of the church is pleasantly cavernous, but the real joy is the atmospheric little cloister.

A pleasant **riverside path**, with wayside seats, starts from just outside the friary gates. Look for a narrow access gap and head off alongside the river. After about 250m turn left along the road to reach the centre of Adare, where the main road intrudes noisily.

DESMOND CASTLE

Dating back to around 1200, this picturesque feudal ruin saw rough usage until it was finally wrecked by Cromwell's troops in 1657. By then it had already lost its strategic importance. Restoration work is endlessly 'in progress', but one day there may even be secure access. At present the castle can be viewed only from the always-busy main road, or more safely from the riverside footpath or the grounds of the Augustinian friary.

CELTIC PARK & GARDENS

About 8km northwest of Adare there's an interesting collection of re-created 'Celtic' structures (plus a few originals) on the site of an original Celtic settlement, at **Celtic Park** (☎ 394 243; Kilcornan; adult/child €6/free; ☺ 9.30am-6pm mid-Mar–Oct). There's also an extensive rose garden and tearoom.

ORGANISED TOURS

July to September a guide leads a daily 30-minute **historical tour** (☎ 396 666; Adare Heritage Centre; adult/child €5/3.50) of Adare, by prior arrangement. You can purchase a combined ticket for the heritage centre and the tour for adult/child €7.50/5.

Sleeping

Accommodation in Adare's big hotels is not cheap, but there are reasonable options to balance the high prices. An alternative is to stay in Limerick and then make a day visit.

Riversdale (☎ 396 751; Manor Court, Station Rd; s/d €35/65; ☺ mid-Mar–Nov; P) There's excellent value at this sparkling house, where good-sized rooms and hearty breakfasts set you up for the short stroll to the centre of the village. Station Rd has several other B&Bs as well.

Elm House (☎ 396 306; Mondellihy; s/d €40/60; P) A peaceful location 1km north of the village adds to this friendly B&B's cosy atmosphere. It has three rooms, one with en suite.

Curragh Lodge (☎ 396 329; curraghlodge@eircom .net; Askeaton Rd; s/d €30/58; P) This small, cheerful B&B is a five-minute walk from the centre of Adare along the quiet Askeaton Rd.

Dunraven Arms (☎ 396 633; www.dunravenhotel .com; Main St; s/d €170/190; P) There are tough prices for singles at this luxury-with-tradition hotel. Separate breakfast and service charges hike the bill even higher, although you do sleep amidst the lingering aura of such past guests as Irish presidents Robinson and McAleese, and Princess Grace of Monaco, who have all stayed here.

Adare Camping & Caravan Park (☎ 395 376; dohertycampingadare@eircom.net; Adare; camp sites €19) This sheltered, uncrowded site is about 4km south of Adare off the N21 and R519.

Eating

Blue Door (☎ 396 481; Main St; lunch mains €8-12, dinner mains €15-22; ☺ 11am-3pm & 6.30-10pm) There are mouthwatering lunches and a tempting evening menu at this delightful thatched-cottage restaurant. Delicious meat, chicken and fish dishes are supported by tasty vegetarian dishes such as spinach and ricotta tortellini with pesto sauce.

Wild Geese (☎ 396 451; Main St; mains €27; ☺ 6.30-10pm Tue-Sun May-Oct, Tue-Sat rest of year) A relaxing interior adds to the pleasure of this award-winning restaurant's imaginative menu. Offerings can include lobster ravioli or char-grilled tuna, as well as choice meat and poultry dishes. Roast rack of lamb is a speciality and there's a good choice of vegetarian dishes.

Seán Collins (☎ 396 400; Main St; mains €9) Cheer yourself up at this popular pub which has recently been refurbished, but with many of its original features retained. As well as bar meals, there are sandwiches for about €3.50.

Pink Potato & Pizza Blue (☎ 396 723; Main St; snacks €3-5, pizzas €8-16) Next door to Seán Collins and run by the same owners. You won't beat this place for sandwiches, burgers or chicken; tasty fish and chips costs €5.50.

Dovecot (☎ 396 449; Adare Heritage Centre, Main St; mains €8.50-11.50; ☒ 9am-5pm) This bright and airy cafeteria does sandwiches for €4, as well as Irish stew, shepherd's pie, quiche and salads.

Drinking

Seán Collins (☎ 396 400; Main St) A great local atmosphere, including Irish music on Sunday nights, is nicely spiced on Thursdays with one of the best karaoke nights around.

Bill Chawke Lounge Bar (☎ 396 160; Main St) Comfy traditional is the mood here; there's trad music every Thursday night and a sing-along on Friday nights.

Getting There & Away

Eleven Dublin–Adare buses per day call at Limerick and then Adare with an additional three per day from Limerick (return to Limerick €5.70). Eight buses per day leave Adare for Tralee and seven buses per day leave Adare for Killarney. For times contact **Limerick bus station** (☎ 313 333), pick up a timetable from the tourist office or check at the bus stop.

Getting Around

There's streetside parking, but the best bet is a free car park behind the heritage centre, although you're advised not to leave vehicles overnight.

COUNTY TIPPERARY

Landlocked Tipperary boasts the sort of fertile soil that farmers dream of. There's still an Anglo-Irish gloss to traditions here. Local fox hunts are still in full legal cry during the winter season and the villages can look like something out of the English shires. The central area of the county is low-lying, but rolling hills spill over from adjoining counties, while in the south the high tops of the Galtee Mountains give Tipperary an attractive context. The River Suir winds its way across the southern part of the county where most towns of interest are. The north is more subdued but has a pleasant away-from-it-all charm. Tipperary town is not the county's main settlement. Clonmel and Carrick-on-Suir are larger.

TIPPERARY TOWN
☎ 062 / pop 4546

Tipperary (Tiobrad Árann) has a name to conjure with but this down-to-earth market town has few pretensions. It is a busy place – its main street is heavy with traffic and it has a remarkably broad range of small shops. The nearby Slievenamuck Hills add scenic charm to Tipperary's landscape, and although the town has little to hold the tourist for long it is a useful base from which to explore the southern part of the county's gentle landscapes and rich heritage sites.

The **tourist office** (☎ 80520; Excel Heritage Centre, Mitchell St; ☒ 9.30am-5.30pm Mon-Sat) is reached via St Michael's St, a side street leading off the northern side of Main St. There's a car park (€0.70 per hour) and adjoining toilets alongside the Centre, with more toilets, including for the disabled, inside the Centre. On either corner of St Michael's St to the Centre there are banks with ATMs and bureaux de change. The post office is on Davis St, off the north side of Main St.

Sights & Activities

The tourist office is part of the larger **Excel Heritage Centre** (☎ 80520; www.tipperary-excel.com; Mitchell St; ☒ 9.30am-5.30pm Mon-Sat), a well-run facility that also houses a café, a local and family history centre, theatre, cinema, exhibition space and gift shop. There are changing art shows and other exhibitions on cultural themes, for which there is an entrance fee.

Midway along Main St there's a **statue of Charles T Kickham** (1828–82), a local novelist (author of *Knocknagow*, a novel about rural life) and Young Irelander. He spent four years in London's Pentonville Prison in the 1860s.

Sleeping

There's not a big choice in Tipperary, but standard B&Bs can be found on the N24 on either side of town.

Ach na Sheen (☎ 51298; gernoonan@eircom.net; Bansha Rd; s €38-42, d €68-76; P) An excellent choice, this place is on the immediate outskirts of town on the N24 Bansha–Cahir–Clonmel road. There's a cheerful family atmosphere, rooms are comfy, and breakfasts are filling.

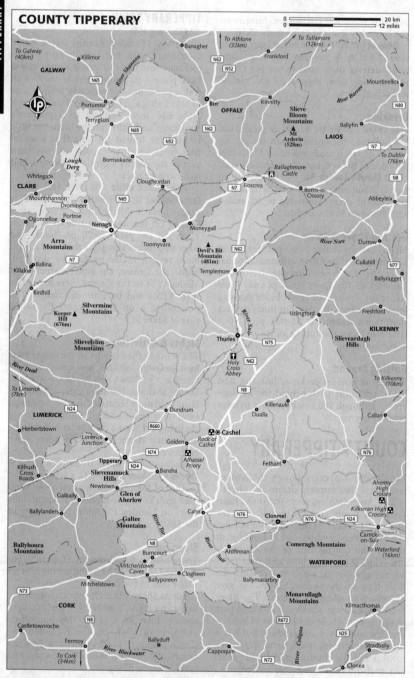

COUNTY TIPPERARY

There are two town centre hotels: the **Royal Hotel** (☎ 33244; Bridge St) and the **Times Hotel** (☎ 31111; Main St). Both charge €40/80 per single/double. Neither are very appealing, unless you're really pushed.

Eating

Pubs along Main St serve breakfast, tea and coffee, lunch and evening meals.

Papillon (☎ 31652; Davis St; mains €13.50-21.50; ⏰ 5.30-10pm) This pleasant restaurant raises the stakes – and the steaks – on Tipperary eating. Meat, Tipperary lamb and duck apart, there's an adventurous selection of fish and shellfish, including mussels in champagne and dill sauce, as well as vegetarian dishes.

Mary Hanna's (☎ 80503; Excel Heritage Centre, Mitchell St; mains €9-10; ⏰ 10am-5.30pm Mon-Sat) The Excel Heritage Centre's bustling in-house café offers meals and snacks all day, kicking off with a great choice of breakfasts (€4 to €9). There are tasty vegetarian options.

Entertainment

Tipperary Racecourse (☎ 51357; www.tipperaryraces .com; Limerick Rd) One of Ireland's leading tracks, it's 3km out of town and has regular meetings during the year. See the local press or phone the course for details. The course is within walking distance of Limerick Junction station. On race days there are minibus pick-ups from Tipperary town; phone for details.

Getting There & Away

Rafferty Travel (☎ 51555; Main St) does bookings for Bus Éireann and for Iarnród Éireann.

BUS

Most buses stop on Abbey St beside the river, except for the Rosslare Harbour bus, which stops outside the Supervalu supermarket on the link road. Bus Éireann runs up to 10 buses daily on the Limerick–Waterford express route. There's also one service a day on weekdays in each direction between Tipperary and Shannon in County Clare. Monday to Saturday, **Kavanagh's** (☎ 51563) runs services to Dublin via Cahir and Cashel. Buses leave at 7.45am from outside the Marian Hall at the northern end of St Michael's St.

TRAIN

To get to the station, head south along Bridge St. Tipperary is on the Waterford–Limerick Junction line. There are two daily services to Cahir, Clonmel, Carrick-on-Suir, Waterford and Rosslare Harbour, and multiple connections to Cork, Kerry, Waterford, Rosslare Harbour and Dublin from **Limerick Junction** (☎ 51406), barely 3km from Tipperary along the Limerick road.

GLEN OF AHERLOW & GALTEE MOUNTAINS

South of Tipperary are the shapely Slievenamuck Hills and Galtee Mountains, separated by the broad chequered valley of the Glen of Aherlow. A scenic drive through the Glen of Aherlow is signposted from Tipperary town. Between Tipperary and Cahir is Bansha (An Bháinseach), at the eastern end of the glen. The village marks the start of a 20km trip west to Galbally, an easy bike ride that takes in the best of the county's landscapes. It's a rewarding area for quiet walking, and has a good choice of rural accommodation.

Sleeping

Bansha House (☎ 54194; www.tipp.ie/banshahs.htm; Bansha; s/d €50/90; **P**) Period elegance and high ceilings characterise this Georgian country house in spacious grounds. There's a grand feeling of being away from it all here. The house is signposted and is 250m along a lane at the western entrance to Bansha.

Ballinacourty House Caravan & Camping Park (☎ 56559; www.camping.ie; Glen of Aherlow; camp sites €18; ⏰ mid-Apr–Sep) Set against a great backdrop of the Galtees, this attractive site is 10km from Bansha on the R663 to Galbally. It has excellent facilities, as well as a fine garden, restaurant, wine bar and tennis court.

Getting There & Away

Bus Éireann express No 55 from Limerick to Waterford via Tipperary town stops at Bansha five times daily. Contact **Rafferty Travel** (☎ 51555) in Tipperary town.

CASHEL

☎ 062 / pop 2403

Cashel (Caiseal Mumhan) is a major tourist destination, an unremarkable market town that is transformed by the dramatic Rock of Cashel and the clutch of historical religious buildings that crowns its breezy summit like a magical extension of the rocky landscape itself. A bypass on the Dublin–Cork route that opened in 2004 has eased some of the town's congestion by diverting heavy lorries, but there can still be fairly heavy traffic in the main streets at times. The Rock and its inspiring buildings stand loftily above it all. Reasonable photo opportunities for framing the Rock can be had on the road into town from the Dublin Rd Roundabout. Much better is to shoot from inside the ruins of Hore Abbey (see opposite). Cashel has a couple of other interesting attractions and a fair choice of pubs and eating places.

Information

AD Weblink (☎ 63304; 102a Main St; per 15 min €1.25) Internet access.

Book Nook (☎ 64947; 98-99 Main St) Has a good selection of local interest, general and travel books.

Car park (per hr/day €0.50/€2) Off Main St.

Cashel Heritage Centre (☎ 62511; www.cashel.ie; Town Hall, Main St; ✆ 9.30am-5.30pm mid-Mar–Oct, closed weekends Oct–mid-Mar) Helpful and efficient staff make this a great place to get information.

Police station (☎ 62866) Behind the post office at the bottom of Main St.

Sights

ROCK OF CASHEL

The **Rock of Cashel** (St Patrick's Rock; ☎ 61437; adult/child €5/2; ✆ 9am-7pm mid-Jun–mid-Sep, 9am-5.30pm mid-Mar–mid-Jun, 9am-4.30pm mid-Sep–mid-Mar, final admission 45 min before closing) is one of Ireland's most spectacular archaeological sites. The 'rock' is a prominent green hill, banded with limestone outcrops. It rises from a grassy plain on the outskirts of the town and bristles with ancient fortifications – the word 'cashel' is an anglicised version of the Irish word *caiseal*, meaning 'fortress'. Sturdy walls circle an enclosure that contains a complete round tower, a roofless abbey and the finest 12th-century Romanesque chapel in Ireland. For more than 1000 years the Rock of Cashel was a symbol of power, the seat of kings and churchmen who ruled over the region.

It's a five-minute stroll from the town centre to the rock. If driving use the car park at the foot of the rock (€2.50). There are a couple of parking spaces for disabled visitors only at the top of the approach road to the ticket office. The rock is a major draw for coach parties for most of

the year and is extremely busy during July and August.

History

In the 4th century the Rock of Cashel was chosen as a base by the Eóghanachta clan from Wales, who went on to conquer much of Munster and become kings of the region. For some 400 years it rivalled Tara as a centre of power in Ireland. The clan was associated with St Patrick, hence the rock's alternative name of St Patrick's Rock.

In the 10th century the Eóghanachta lost possession of the rock to the O'Brien, or Dál gCais, tribe under Brian Ború's leadership. In 1101, King Muircheartach O'Brien presented the Rock to the Church, a move designed to curry favour with the powerful bishops and to end secular rivalry over possession of the Rock with the Eóghanachta, by now known as the MacCarthys. Numerous buildings of all kinds must have occupied the Rock over the years, but it is the ecclesiastical relics that survived even the depredations of the Cromwellian army in 1647.

Hall of the Vicars Choral

The entrance to the Rock of Cashel is through this 15th-century building, once home to the male choristers who sang in the cathedral. It houses the ticket office. The exhibits in the adjoining undercroft include some very rare silverware, Bronze Age axes and **St Patrick's Cross**, an impressive, although eroded, 12th-century crutched cross with a crucifixion scene on one face and animals on the other. A replica stands outside, in the castle courtyard. The kitchen and dining hall upstairs contain some period furniture, tapestries and paintings beneath a fine carved-oak roof and gallery. A 20-minute audiovisual presentation on the rock's history runs every half hour. There are French, German and Italian showings as well as English.

The Cathedral

This 13th-century Gothic structure overshadows the other ruins. Entry is through a small porch facing the Hall of the Vicars Choral. The cathedral's western location is formed by the **Archbishop's Residence**, a 15th-century, four-storey castle that had its great hall built over the nave. Soaring above the centre of the cathedral is a huge, square tower with a turret on the southwestern corner.

Scattered throughout are monuments, panels from 16th-century altar tombs, and coats of arms. If you have binoculars, look for the numerous stone heads on capitals and corbels high above the ground.

Round Tower

On the northeastern corner of the cathedral is an 11th- or 12th-century round tower, the earliest building on the Rock of Cashel. It's 28m tall and the doorway is 3.5m above the ground – perhaps for structural rather than defensive reasons.

Cormac's Chapel

If the Rock of Cashel boasted only Cormac's Chapel, it would still be an outstanding place. This compelling building dates from 1127, and the medieval integrity of its trans-European architecture survives. It was probably the first Romanesque church in Ireland. The style of the square towers that flank it to either side may reflect Germanic influences, but there are haunting similarities in its steep stone roof to the 'boat-hull' shape of older Irish buildings, such as the Gallarus Oratory in County Clare and the beehive huts of the Dingle Peninsula.

The true Romanesque splendour is in the detail of the exquisite doorway arches, the grand chancel arch and ribbed barrel vault, and the outstanding carved vignettes that include a trefoil-tailed grotesque and a Norman-helmeted centaur firing an arrow at a rampaging lion. The chapel's interior is tantalisingly dark, but linger for a while and your eyes adjust. Inside the main door, on the left, is the sarcophagus said to house King Cormac, dating from between 1125 and 1150. Frescoes once covered the walls, but only vestigial elements of these survive. The southern tower leads to a stone-roofed vault or croft above the nave (no access).

HORE ABBEY

Cashel throws in another bonus for the heritage lover. This is the formidable ruin of 13th-century Hore Abbey, located in flat farmland just under 1km north of the Rock. Originally Benedictine and settled by monks from Glastonbury in England at the

end of the 12th century, it later became a Cistercian house, gifted to the order by a 13th-century archbishop who expelled the Benedictine monks after dreaming that they planned to murder him. The complex is enjoyably gloomy and from its interior there are superb photo ops of the Rock of Cashel with creative foregrounds, if you get it right.

BRÚ BORÚ

Cashel's award-winning heritage and cultural centre, **Brú Ború** (☎ 61122; www.comhaltas.com; 9am-5pm Jun-Sep, closed weekends Oct-May) is in a modern building next to the car park below the Rock of Cashel. The centre offers an absorbing insight into Irish traditional music, dance and song. It has a shop and café, but its main daytime attraction is **Sounds of History** (adult/child €5/3), an exhibition in a subterranean chamber where the story of Ireland and its music is told through imaginative audio displays. In the summer there is a **traditional show** (show €15, dinner & show €42; 9-11.30pm Tue-Sat Jun-Sep) in the centre's theatre.

OTHER SIGHTS

The **Cashel Heritage Centre** (☎ 61333; www.cashel.ie; Town Hall, Main St; admission free; 9.30am-5.30pm mid-Mar–Oct, closed weekends Oct–mid-Mar) is located in the town hall. It has a model showing what Cashel looked like in the 1640s. The Centre's website has useful information for visitors.

The **Cashel Folk Village** (☎ 62525; Dominic St; adult/child €3.50/1; 9.30am-7.30pm May-Oct, 10am-6pm Mar & Apr) is an intriguing exhibition of old buildings and shopfronts from around the town, plus local memorabilia.

The **Bolton Library** (☎ 61944; John St; adult/child €2/1.50; 9.30am-5.30pm Mon-Fri mid-Jan–mid-Sep) houses a splendid collection of books, maps and manuscripts from the dawn of printing onwards.

Sleeping

BUDGET

Cashel Holiday Hostel (☎ 62330; www.cashelhostel .com; 6 John St; dm €15-18, s €18-22, d €36-44) This is a friendly, central, budget option in a quiet, three-storey Georgian terrace off Main St. It has a recreation room, kitchen and laundry.

O'Brien's Holiday Lodge & Camping Park (☎ 61003; www.cashel-lodge.com; Dundrum Rd; camp sites €10, dm €15-18, s €30, d €50-6; P) This first-class

IHH hostel, in a converted coach house northwest of town, is friendly, relaxing, well equipped and has high-standard dorms and rooms and a camp site. Terrific views of the nearby Rock of Cashel and Hore Abbey are unbeatable bonuses.

MIDRANGE

Dominic St, on the way from Main St to the Rock of Cashel, has several quiet B&Bs with views of the rock.

Rockside House (☎ 63813; joyrocksidehouse@eircom .net; Rock Villas; s/d €60/80; P) A terrific location right beside the Rock, coupled with immaculate rooms and a warm welcome makes this B&B hard to beat.

Rockville House (☎ 61760; 10 Dominic St; s/d €38/52; P) Well-kept, brightly decorated rooms enhance this friendly place that is within a short distance of the Rock.

Abbey House (☎ 61104; teachnamainstreach@eircom .net; 1 Dominic St; s/d €43/70) Rooms are a touch cramped, but there's a cheerful mood at this bungalow opposite St Dominic's Friary and on the way to the Rock.

Ashmore House (☎ 61286; www.ashmorehouse .com; John St; s/d €60/70) This Georgian town house has big, high-ceilinged rooms, and is located in a quiet street just up from the Cashel Holiday Hostel.

Cashel Town B&B (☎ 62330; www.cashelbandb .com; 6 John St; s/d €35/70) Family rooms are especially bright and comfy, with spacious en suite facilities. It is run by the same

---

SOMETHING SPECIAL

Chez Hans (☎ 61177; Dominic St; starters €6.50-12.50, mains €28-45; ⏱ 6-10pm Tue-Sat) You'll go far to find a more enticing menu than the one at this long-established restaurant, located in an old chapel that has its barrel roof and stained glass intact. The style is understated, relaxed, unfussy and there's a subtlety about the often Mediterranean-influenced dishes. Tempting starters can include a risotto of wild mushrooms with duck confit and chorizo cream. Mains include a couple of delicious vegetarian dishes among the great choice of fish, meat and game. The wine list matches the cuisine for quality. There's an early-bird menu with two courses for €25, three courses for €30.

---

cheerful management as the Cashel Holiday Hostel next door.

TOP END

Cashel Palace Hotel (☎ 62707; www.cashel-palace.ie; Main St; s €140-155, d €195-240; P) There are right-royal rates at the Cashel Palace, a handsome red-brick, late–Queen Anne house. It was built in 1732 for a Protestant archbishop. Its rooms in the main building and a separate mews are luxurious. Some have views of the Rock, but it costs extra for the privilege.

Eating & Drinking

Cashel has several decent eateries and restaurants.

Café Hans (☎ 63660; Dominic St; mains €8-11; ⏱ noon-5.30pm) This recent addition to Cashel's eateries is run by the same family who run Chez Hans. There's a terrific selection of salads – try the chicken with Crozier blue cheese dressing – open sandwiches and fish, shellfish, lamb and vegetarian dishes, with a discerning wine selection and tingling desserts. The mood is relaxed and unpretentious.

Spearman's Bakery (☎ 61143; 97 Main St; sandwiches €3; ⏱ 9am-5.15pm Mon-Sat) Good home cooking characterises this pleasant café, where you can supplement your sandwiches with tasty soup (€3.30) or break for coffee and scrumptious cakes.

Bakehouse Bakery (☎ 61680; 7 Main St; meals under €7; ⏱ 9am-5pm) Head for this busy café for tea and coffee, breakfast or a light lunch. It's just across from the Cashel Heritage Centre. A local speciality is the tasty Cashel blue-cheese quiche. Full Irish breakfast costs €5.95.

Hannigan's (☎ 61737; Ladyswell St; mains €11-20) Filling, traditional food in a cosy pub atmosphere is the hallmark of Hannigan's. Get a bowl of Hannigan's Irish stew (€11) and you'll know you've been well fed.

Davern's (☎ 61121; 20 Main St) This bar is popular for a good chat. There's live music on certain nights, but it's best to check for details beforehand.

Getting There & Away

Bus Éireann runs six express buses daily between Dublin and Cork via Cahir and Fermoy. There are two buses daily on the Cork–Athlone route via Thurles, Roscrea and Birr. Tickets are available from the nearby Spar shop or you can buy them on the bus. The bus stop for Cork is outside the Bakehouse Bakery. The Dublin stop is opposite.

Kavanagh's (☎ 51563) has one bus daily to Dublin, leaving Cashel at 8.30am. From Dublin, it leaves George's Quay near Tara St Station at 6pm. It also does a twice-daily run between Cashel and Clonmel, departing from Cashel at noon and 6.35pm.

The nearest train stations are at Cahir and Thurles, where there are bus connections to Cashel.

Getting Around

McInerney's (☎ 61225) on Main St hires out bicycles (€10 per day), as do the two hostels (see p303). Cahir and Fethard are both within cycling distance.

AROUND CASHEL

The atmospheric – and deliciously creepy at dusk – ruins of **Athassel Priory** sit on the western bank of the River Suir 8km southwest of Cashel. The original buildings date from 1205, and Athassel became one of the richest and most important monasteries in Ireland. What survives is substantial: the gatehouse and portcullis gateway, the cloister and stretches of walled enclosure, as well as some medieval tomb effigies.

To get there take the N74 to the village of Golden, then head south, along the road signed Athassel Abbey, for 2km. Roadside parking is limited and very tight. The Priory is reached across often-muddy fields.

CAHIR

☎ 052 / pop 2794

Cahir (An Cathair; pronounced care) is 15km south of Cashel, at the eastern tip of the Galtee Mountains and on the banks of the River Suir. This pleasant country town is enhanced by its riverside location and its monolithic castle.

Orientation

Buses stop in Castle St near a large car park (€0.60 for two hours) alongside the river and castle. East of Castle St is the centre of town, the sloping square. It is surrounded by shops, pubs and cafés, and also has some parking.

Information

The AIB in Castle St has an ATM and bureau de change. The post office is north

of the square in Church St. There are toilets next to the tourist office.

Enterprise Centre (☎ 42616; Market Yard; per 5 min €1; ⏳ 9am-6pm Mon-Fri) Internet access; at the back of a courtyard off the upper side of the square.

Tourist office (☎ 41453; ⏳ 9.30am-6pm Mon-Sat Mar-Oct) Has leaflets and information about the town and area.

Cahir Castle

Cahir's awesome **castle** (☎ 41011; Castle St; adult/child €2.75/1.25; ⏳ 9am-7.30pm mid-Jun–mid-Sep, 9.30am-5.30pm Apr–mid-Jun & mid-Sep–mid-Oct, to 4.30pm mid-Oct–Mar) is feudal fantasy in a big way. A river-island site, rocky foundations, massive walls, turrets and towers, defences and dungeons are all there. This castle is one of Ireland's largest. Founded by Conor O'Brien in 1142, it was passed to the Butler family in 1375. The castle was surrendered to Cromwell in 1650 without a struggle; its solidity – or future usefulness – may have discouraged the usual Cromwellian 'deconstruction'. It is intact and formidable still, and was restored in the 1840s and again in the 1960s when it came under state ownership.

There's a short audiovisual show on other local sites of historic interest. The buildings within the castle are sparsely furnished, although there are small exhibitions. The real rewards come from simply wandering through this remarkable survivor of Ireland's medieval past.

Swiss Cottage

A pleasant riverside path from behind the car park meanders 2km south to Cahir Park and the **Swiss Cottage** (☎ 41144; Cahir Park; adult/child €2.75/1.25; ⏳ 10am-6pm mid-Apr–mid-Oct, 10am-1pm & 2-6pm Tue-Sun mid-Mar–mid-Apr, to 4.30pm Tue-Sun mid-Oct–mid-Nov). Also run by Dúchas, the Swiss Cottage is an exquisite thatched cottage orné, surrounded by roses, lavender and honeysuckle. It is the best in Ireland, and was built in about 1810 as a retreat for Richard Butler, 12th Baron Caher, and his wife. The design was by London architect John Nash, creator of the Royal Pavilion at Brighton and London's Regent's Park. The cottage-orné style emerged during the late 18th and early 19th centuries in England in response to the prevailing taste for the picturesque. Thatched roofs, natural wood and carved weatherboarding were characteristics, and most were built as ornamental features on estates.

There could not be a more lavish example of Regency Picturesque than the Swiss Cottage. It is more of a sizable house than a cottage, and has a basement kitchen and wine cellar, a ballroom and salon, and upper-floor bedrooms with balconies. The 30-minute (compulsory) guided tours are thoroughly enjoyable, although you may have to wait for one in the busier summer months.

Sleeping

Rectory (☎ 41406; faheyr@eircom.net; Cashel Rd; s/d €35/60; ☼ May-Sep; **P**) There are big rooms and big bathrooms in this fine and friendly Georgian house, tucked away off the busy main road about 1km from the town centre.

Ashling (☎ 41601; Cashel Rd; s/d €45/65; **P**) Located a short distance further on from the Rectory, this handsome bungalow has a charming and courteous atmosphere. The rooms are impeccable.

Apple Caravan & Camping Park (☎ 41459; www .theapplefarm.com; Moorstown; per adult/child May-Jun €5/3, Jun-Sep €5.50/3.50) This quiet camp site on a farm of mainly apple orchards is on the N24 between Cahir (6km) and Clonmel (9km). The place has a delightful appley ambience helped along by the delicious fruit and juices that are marketed here. There's free use of a tennis court and racquets.

Eating

Galileo Café (☎ 45689; Church St; pizza & pasta €6.50-10.50; ☼ noon-10pm) Lots of exposed stone and brick walls create a pleasant atmosphere at this Italian café-restaurant that also does salads (€3.50 to €5). You can bring your own wine.

Lazy Bean Café (☎ 42038; the Square; snacks €3.50-6.50; ☼ 9am-6pm Mon-Sat, 10.30am-6pm Sun) Busy, breezy little café that dishes out loads of tasty sandwiches, wraps, bagels and *panini*.

Getting There & Away

BUS

Cahir is on several **Bus Éireann** (☎ 062-51555) express routes, including Dublin–Cork, Limerick–Waterford, Galway–Waterford, Kilkenny–Cork and Cork–Athlone. There are eight buses per day Monday to Saturday, and six buses on Sunday to Cashel (€3.90,

15 minutes). Buses stop in the car park beside the tourist office.

Kavanagh's (☎ 062-51563) buses travel from Monday to Saturday between Tipperary town, Cashel and Dublin via Cahir.

TRAIN

Monday to Saturday, the Cork–Rosslare Harbour train stops once a day at Cahir, while the Dublin–Clonmel train stops twice. Contact **Thurles train station** (☎ 0504-21733) for details.

MITCHELSTOWN CAVES

The Galtee Mountains are mainly sandstone, but along the southern side runs a narrow band of limestone that has given rise to the **Mitchelstown Caves** (☎ 052-67246; Burncourt; adult/child/family €4.50/2/12.50; ☼ 10am-6pm) near Burncourt, 16km southwest of Cahir and signposted on the N8 to Mitchelstown (Baile Mhistéala). Superior to Kilkenny's Dunmore Caves and yet less developed for tourists, these caves are among the most extensive in the country.

There are nearly 2km of passages and spectacular chambers full of textbook formations with names such as The Pipe Organ, Tower of Babel, House of Commons and Eagle's Wing. The caves are dry in summer, but limestone leaks. If there's been heavy rain, bring a waterproof hooded jacket.

Call at English's farmhouse opposite the car park for tickets and a tour guide (a tour requires a minimum of two people).

Sleeping

Mountain Lodge Hostel (☎ 052-67277; Burncourt; adult/child €15/11; ☼ Apr-Sep; **P**) This An Óige hostel in an attractive one-time shooting lodge is 6km north of the caves, and is a handy base for exploring the Galtee Mountains. It lies to the north of the N8 Mitchelstown–Cahir road.

Getting There & Away

Daily **Bus Éireann** (☎ 062-51555) express buses from Dublin to Cork or Athlone drop off at the gate to Mountain Lodge Hostel, from where it's a 2km walk to the caves.

CLONMEL

☎ 052 / pop 15,739

Clonmel (Cluain Meala, 'Meadows of

Honey') is Tipperary's largest and busiest town. There's much more going on here than in neighbouring towns, but Clonmel retains its country town charm. Laurence Sterne (1713–68), author of *A Sentimental Journey* and *Tristram Shandy*, was a native of the town; but the commercial cheerleader for Clonmel was Italian Charles Bianconi (1786–1875), who at the precocious age of 16 was sent to Ireland by his father in an attempt to break his youthful liaison with a woman. Bianconi later channelled all his frustrated passion into setting up a coach service between Clonmel and Cahir; his company quickly grew to become a nationwide passenger and mail carrier. For putting Clonmel on the map, Bianconi was twice elected mayor.

Orientation

Clonmel's centre lies on the northern bank of the River Suir. Set back from the quays and running parallel to the river, the main street runs east–west, starting off as Parnell St and becoming Mitchell St and O'Connell St before passing under West Gate, where it changes to Irishtown and Abbey Rd. Running north from this long thoroughfare is Gladstone St, which has lots of shops and pubs.

Information

AIB (O'Connell St) Has an ATM and bureau de change.

Clonmel Library (☎ 24545; Emmet St; per 50 min €2; ☿ 10am-5.30pm Mon & Tue, 10am-8.30pm Wed & Thu, 10am-1pm & 2-5pm Fri & Sat) Internet access; it is advisable to book.

Post office (Emmet St)

Sophie's Bookshop (☎ 80752; 15 Mitchell St) Has a good selection of general and travel books as well as books of local interest.

Tourist office (☎ 22960; www.clonmel.ie; Sarsfield St; ☿ 9.30am-1pm & 2-5pm Mon-Fri) Offers lots of information and enthusiasm. Ask for the *Clonmel Heritage Trail* leaflet.

Sights

At the junction of Mitchell and Sarsfield Sts is the superb **Main Guard** (☎ 27484; Sarsfield St; adult/child €2/1; ☿ 9.30am-6pm mid-Mar–Oct), a Butler courthouse dating from 1675 and based on a design by Christopher Wren. Restored in recent years and with its handsome open arcade of sandstone columns reinstated, it is now open to the public.

In Nelson St, south of Parnell St, is the refurbished **County Courthouse** designed by Richard Morrison in 1802. It was here that the Young Irelanders of 1848, including Thomas Francis Meagher, were tried and sentenced to transportation to Australia.

West along Mitchell St (past the town hall with its statue commemorating the 1798 Rising) and south down Abbey St is the **Franciscan friary**. Inside, near the door, is a 1533 Butler tomb depicting a knight and his lady. There's some fine modern stained glass, especially in St Anthony's Chapel to the north.

Turn south down Bridge St and cross the river, following the road round until it opens out at **Lady Blessington's Bath**, a picturesque stretch of the river that is just right for picnicking.

A custom-made building houses **Tipperary South Riding County Museum** (☎ 25399; The Borstal, Market Place; admission free; ☿ 10am-5pm Mon-Fri, 10am-1pm & 2-5pm Sat). It has displays on the history of County Tipperary from Neolithic times to the present and hosts changing exhibitions.

Sleeping

Amberville (☎ 21470; amberville@eircom.net; Glenconnor Rd; s/d €40/60; P) North off Western Rd beside St Joseph's Hospital, this pleasant B&B is about 500m from the centre. It has five homely rooms.

Ashbourne (☎ 22307; ashbourn@iol.ie; Coleville Rd; s/d €43/66; P) The delightful accommodation in this handsome period house is best booked in advance. Ashbourne is south of the river on the other side of Gashouse Bridge. It has no outside sign.

Clonmel Arms Hotel (☎ 21233; theclonmelarms@ eircom.net; Sarsfield St; s/d €60/110; P) There are comfortable, fair-sized rooms with business-style standards at this long-established hotel that also has its own restaurant and popular bar.

Power's the Pot Caravan & Camping Park (☎ 23085; fax 23893; Harney's Cross; camp sites €18) This park has a Clonmel address even though it's 9km southeast in County Waterford on the northern slopes of the Comeragh Mountains. It's in a good location for exploring the Comeraghs. To get there, cross south over the river in Clonmel and then follow the road to Rathgormuck.

There are several B&Bs on Marlfield Rd, due west of Irishtown. These include **Benuala** (☎ 22158; benuala@indigo.ie; Marlfield Rd;

s €35, d €54-70; (P)), which has comfortable rooms, and **Hillcourt** (☎ 21029; www.hillcourt.com; Marlfield Rd; s/d €44/63; (P)), a pleasant bungalow with a garden for guests' use and discounts for children.

Eating

Angela's (☎ 26899; 14 Abbey St; meals €7.50-10; ⏰ 9am-5.30pm Mon-Fri, 9am-5pm Sat) This is the place for tasty and imaginative meals with a strong organic bias. Specials can include chicken risotto cakes with buffalo mozzarella, or char-grilled Toulouse sausages on a mustard mash with onion gravy. There are salads, soups, vegetarian options, filling bruschettas (€4 to €8.50) and great coffee, all in relaxing, unfussy surroundings.

Galileo (☎ 70855; 4 Gladstone St; meals €4.50-11; ⏰ noon-10pm Mon-Sat, 1-9pm Sun) An ideal little eatery where you can bring your own wine, and enjoy a great range of pizzas, pastas and salads as well as coffee and cakes.

Paddock Bar (Sarsfield St; lunch €8.50, mains €14-18; ⏰ 12.30-9.30pm) Inside the Clonmel Arms Hotel, this plush bar dishes up good-value pub meals, from smoked salmon to chicken curry.

Tierney's Pub (☎ 24467; 13 O'Connell St; snacks €5.50-16, mains €13-22) Award-winning Tierney's is dense with entertaining pub bric-a-brac. Its popular upstairs restaurant favours traditional dishes so expect steaks, grills, fish dishes and vegetarian possibilities, but with a dash of modernism.

O'Gorman's (☎ 21380; 61-62 O'Connell St; lunch €5.25; ⏰ 9am-5pm) This place is popular with locals and does breakfasts (€2.50 to €6.50), sandwiches and *panini* (€3.50 to €6.50), as well as lunch dishes such as lasagne and shepherd's pie. In the adjoining shop you can buy sandwiches to take away and it even has a bar.

Mulcahy's (☎ 25054; 47 Gladstone St; carvery €8.50-11, restaurant mains €15-20; ⏰ carvery 8.30am-5.30pm, restaurant 5.30-9.30pm) This vast, rambling, brightly decorated pub is a good place to lose yourself. It has a self-service carvery and there's everything from Irish beef to Moroccan ostrich in its restaurant, East Lane Café.

Entertainment

Clonmel has Tipperary's hottest pub and club music scene.

Gallery on Gladstone (Devane's; ☎ 28680; 13 Gladstone St; ⏰ 9.30pm-12.30am) Sparky line-ups are featured at the Gallery, which hosts visiting DJs, good local bands and occasional top tribute bands. There are live turns on Thursday and Sunday nights and chart mix disco on Friday and Saturday nights.

Mulcahy's (☎ 25054; 47 Gladstone St) Mulcahy's hosts Irish music in its bar on Wednesday, Friday and Saturday nights, while its Danno's nightclub, accessible from Market St, whisks up a froth of chart and retro on Saturday nights from 11pm to 2am.

Paddock Bar (☎ 21233; Sarsfield St) Live music on Thursday, Friday and Sunday nights.

Lonergan's (☎ 21250; 35-36 O'Connell St) Monday nights see trad music sessions at this very traditional pub in the heart of Clonmel's main street.

South Tipperary Arts Centre (☎ 27877; Nelson St) There's an excellent programme of art exhibitions, plays and films here, the focus of the arts in Tipperary.

SPORT

North of town is the **Powerstown Park Racecourse** (☎ 21422; Powerstown Park, Clonmel). It holds 13 meetings a year; call for details of fixtures.

Getting There & Away

BUS

Bus Éireann (☎ 051-79000) has two buses daily to Cork (€13.20), up to six to Dublin (€11.50), and a number of services to Waterford, Limerick and Kilkenny. The tickets can be bought at **Rafferty Travel** (☎ 22622; 45 Gladstone St) or at the train station where the buses stop. **Kavanagh's** (☎ 062-51563) has twice-daily buses between Cashel and Clonmel.

TRAIN

The **train station** (☎ 21982) is on Prior Park Rd. Head north along Gladstone St, past the Oakville Shopping Centre and it's just after the Statoil service station. Clonmel is on the Cork–Rosslare Harbour line, with one train a day Monday to Saturday. The Dublin–Clonmel train runs twice a day Monday to Saturday via Limerick Junction.

AROUND CLONMEL

Directly south of Clonmel, over the border in County Waterford, are the Comeragh Mountains. There's a scenic route south to Ballymacarbry and the Nire Valley. For more details, see p201.

The **East Munster Way** (see p679) passes through Clonmel. Heading east towards Carrick-on-Suir, the way follows the old towpath along the River Suir. At Sir Thomas Bridge it cuts south away from the river and into the Comeraghs and through Gurteen Wood to Harney's Crossroads. It rejoins the River Suir again at Kilsheelan Bridge, from where it follows the towpath all the way to Carrick-on-Suir. Going west from Clonmel, the way first leads south into the hills and then descends to Newcastle and the river once more. The route east is pleasant for a short there-and-back outing from Clonmel.

FETHARD

☎ 052 / pop 1388

Fethard (Fiodh Ard) is where keen medievalists will get carried away. This quiet little place, 14km north of Clonmel on the River Clashawley, has a good slice of its old walls still intact, as well as a fair sprinkling of other ruins. The generous width of the main street alone signifies medieval survival and conjures up images of boisterous markets and the delightful randomness of medieval 'town planning'.

Fethard has no official tourist office but you can get information and local leaflets from the helpful office of the **Tirry Community Centre** (☎ 31000; Barrack St). Ask for the walking-tour leaflet. Fethard has a useful website at www.fethard.ie. The post office is a few doors away from Barmor's shop. There's an ATM in Kenny's Foodmarket which is about 50m along the road from the Tirry Community Centre.

Sights

Fethard's **Holy Trinity Church** and **churchyard** (☎ 26643; Main St; admission free) lie within a captivating little time warp. The church is off Main St and is reached through a cast-iron gateway. To get inside you have to collect keys from Barmor's Shop, a few doors along from the entrance gate. The notice on the gate may direct you to Whyte's Foodstore, but that's just a test of initiative. It's Barmor's you want.

The main part of the building dates from the 13th century, but its ancient walls have been rather blighted by being covered with mortar for weatherproofing. The handsome west tower was added later and has had its sturdy stonework uncovered. It looks more like a fortified tower house and has savage-looking finials on its corner turrets. The interior of the church has an aisled nave and a chancel of typical medieval style, but it is sparsely furnished. A ruined chapel and sacristy adjoin the south end of the church. It is the context of the entire churchyard that is the real winner. Old gravestones descend in ranks to a refurbished stretch of medieval wall complete with a guard tower and a parapet, from where you can look down on the gentle River Clashawley between its green banks.

Close to the church in Main St is the 17th-century **town hall**, with some fine coats of arms mounted on the façade.

Fethard's main concentration of medieval remains (some of which have been incorporated into later buildings) are just south of the church at the end of Watergate St. Beside Castle Inn are the ruins of several fortified 17th-century **tower houses**. Just under the archway to the river bank and Watergate Bridge is a fine **sheila-na-gig** (see below) embedded in the wall to your left. You can stroll the river bank provided the resident geese are not in bullying mood. From here

---

SHAMELESS SHEILAS OR SYMBOLIC SHAMANESSES?

Sexually explicit stone images of women, known as sheila-na-gig, have long been a feature on the walls of church buildings and other old structures in Ireland. Theories about their origin are still debated. One suggestion is that they are a medieval concept brought to Ireland by the Normans and that they were placed on church walls as some kind of male-oriented warning against lust. Another suggestion is that they are ancient survivors of pre-Christian fertility symbolism that were simply incorporated into church buildings as recycled stonework. One English translation of the name is suggested as 'the old woman on her hunkers'. There are sheilas on display in the National Museum in Dublin. The village of Fethard once had four sheilas, but one was stolen from the wall of nearby Kiltinaban Church in 1990. In spite of a reward being offered for its return and Interpol being alerted, it has never been recovered.

the backs of the Abbey St houses, although much added to and knocked about in places, once again display the pleasing irregularities of typical medieval building style.

East along Abbey St is the 14th-century **Augustinian friary**, which is now a Catholic church, with some fine, medieval stained glass and another brazen **sheila-na-gig** in its east wall.

Sleeping & Eating

Gateway (☎ 31701; Rocklow Rd; s/d €33/50; **P**) Tucked away at the edge of the village, alongside the ruined 15th-century North Gate, this little house is a pleasant stopover with a genial welcome.

PJ Lonergan's (☎ 31447; Market Sq; lunch mains €8-9, salads €6-8; ☻ 12.30-2.30pm) Enjoy a relaxed lunch at this pleasant pub that offers a good selection of sandwiches (€4) as well as roast beef and lasagne.

Oriental Garden (☎ 32914; Market Sq; mains €8.50-21.50; ☻ noon-2pm & 5-10.30pm Mon-Sat, noon-2.30pm & 5-10.30pm Sun) Sophisticated cuisine at Fethard's Chinese eatery ensures a great selection of oriental favourites, including vegetarian dishes.

Getting There & Away

There's no public transport to Fethard but it would make a pleasant cycle from Cashel, 15km to the west.

CARRICK-ON-SUIR

☎ 051 / pop 5542

The friendly market town of Carrick-on-Suir (Carraig na Siúire), 20km east of Clonmel, boasted twice its present population during the late medieval period when it was a centre of the brewing and wool industries. The modern town is fairly quiet and unassuming, although the traffic flow can be relentless along the main street.

Carrick-on-Suir was quick to honour local boy Sean Kelly, one of the world's greatest cyclists in the late 1980s. The town square bears his name, as does the sports centre. Carrick is also the birthplace of the singing Clancy Brothers, who, with Tommy Makem and assorted Aran Island sweaters, did much to popularise folk music in the 1960s.

From Carrick-on-Suir the **East Munster Way** winds west to Clonmel before heading south into Waterford. For more details see p679.

Information

Heritage centre (tourist office; adult/child €3/2; ☻ 9.30am-5.30pm Mon-Sat May-Sep, 9.30am-5pm Mon-Fri Oct-Apr) You can park in the yard outside the tourist office.

Tourist office (☎ 640 200; ☻ 9.30am-5.30pm Mon-Sat May-Sep, 9.30am-5pm Mon-Fri Oct-Apr) Off Main St, through a narrow entranceway, an old church houses this helpful office, which has town maps and lots of material on Carrick and the district.

Sights

Carrick-on-Suir was once the property of the Butlers, the earls of Ormond, who built the **Ormond Castle** (☎ 640 787; Castle St; adult/child €2.75/1.25; ☻ 10am-6pm mid-Jun–early Sep) on the banks of the river in the 14th century. Anne Boleyn, the second of Henry VIII's six wives, may have been born here, though other castles also claim this distinction. The Elizabethan mansion next to the castle was built by the 10th earl of Ormond, Black Tom Butler, in a long-term anticipation of a visit by his cousin, Queen Elizabeth I, who rather thoughtlessly never turned up.

Some rooms in this Dúchas-owned edifice have fine 16th-century stuccowork, especially the Long Gallery with its depictions of Elizabeth and of the Butler coat of arms.

Sleeping & Eating

Fatima House (☎ 640 298; www.fatimahouse.com; John St; s/d €35/65; **P**) Pleasant rooms and charming service await at this guesthouse, situated about 500m west of the Greenside bus stop.

Carraig Hotel (☎ 641 455; www.carraighotel.com; Main St; s/d €75/130, bar snacks €4-12, mains €15-23; **P**) New rooms have been added and existing rooms updated, all to a very comfortable standard.

Carrick-on-Suir Caravan & Camping Park (☎ 640 461; www.carrickcamping.com; Kilkenny Rd; camp sites €16, caravan sites €18, extra person €3; ☻ Mar-Oct) This small friendly park has an adjoining shop and snack takeaway, and is only a few minutes' walk from the centre.

Park Inn (☎ 640 156; 1 New St; mains €10-22) A cut above the rest. Its pub is cosy and comfortable and there is a restaurant as well. The chef does clever things with monkfish and local salmon, as well as with lamb and beef.

Ormond Castle Restaurant (☎ 645 680; New St; breakfast €5-7, sandwiches €3-7, mains €8.50-14;

(☼ 9.30am-5.30pm Mon-Sat, 10am-4pm Sun) This is a good place for no-nonsense meals.

Most Main St pubs offer reasonably priced lunches.

Getting There & Away

BUS

Buses stop at Greenside, the park beside the N24 road. Follow New St north from Main St, then turn right.

Bus Éireann (☎ 879 000) has numerous buses to Carrick-on-Suir. Bus No 367 between Limerick (€13.70) and Waterford (€6.50) serves Tipperary town, Cahir, Clonmel and Carrick-on-Suir up to seven times daily, with connections to Galway and Rosslare Harbour. Bus No 7 from Clonmel to Dublin via Carrick-on-Suir and Kilkenny stops up to nine times daily, with connections to Cork.

TRAIN

The station is north of Greenside, off Cregg Rd. There are three trains a day Monday to Saturday to Dublin (€20). There are two trains a day Monday to Saturday to Waterford and Rosslare. Contact **Waterford train station** (☎ 051-317 899) for details.

ROSCREA

☎ 0505 / pop 5496

The pleasant little town of Roscrea (Ros Cré) is a useful stopover on the journey between Dublin and Limerick.

Roscrea owes its beginnings to a 5th-century monk, St Crónán, who set up a way station for the travelling poor. Most of the historical structures are on or near the main street, Castle St.

Tourist information is available from Roscrea Castle, a Dúchas-run 13th-century property in the town centre. There are substantial remains of a gatehouse, walls and towers, and inside the courtyard stands **Damer House**, the Queen Anne–style residence of the Damer family, which houses the **Roscrea Heritage Centre** (☎ 21850; Castle St; adult/concession €3.50/1.25; ☼ 10am-6pm Apr-Oct, Sat & Sun only Nov-Mar). The centre contains some interesting exhibitions, including one on the medieval monasteries of the midlands and another on early-20th-century farming life. There's a peaceful walled garden by the house.

The Bank of Ireland located in Castle St has an ATM.

Sleeping & Eating

Grant's Hotel (☎ 23300; www.grantshotel.com; Castle St; s/d €55/95; **P**) A classic country-town hotel and former coaching inn, Grant's has good modern facilities in fully restored, elegant and comfortable surroundings.

Lemon Tree Restaurant (lunch €15, dinner mains €18-20) Part of Grant's Hotel. Has a carvery and offers everything from ostrich and pheasant to salmon.

La Seranata (☎ 22431; The Mall; pizza & pasta €8-11; ☼ noon-10pm Mon-Sat, 1-9pm Sun) Lots of intimate little corners, exposed stonework, artworks and bright surroundings complement decent food in this cosy restaurant beside the river.

Quigley's Bakery (Roscrea Shopping Centre) Does great sandwiches for about €2.

Getting There & Away

Up to 13 **Bus Éireann** (☎ 01-836 6111) express buses stop at Roscrea between Dublin (two hours) and Limerick (one hour). There are daily buses to Sligo, Carrick-on-Shannon, Athlone, Thurles, Cahir, Cork and Shannon.

Dublin–Limerick trains stop at Roscrea twice a day Monday to Saturday, and once on Sunday (call ☎ 21823 for details).

AROUND ROSCREA

About 30km west of Roscrea along the N7 is the busy town of Nenagh with the ruins of **Nenagh Castle**. Nenagh is the gateway to the eastern shore of Lough Derg, a popular boating and fishing area.

About 9km northwest of Nenagh, on the R495, is the waterfront hamlet of **Dromineer**, a good place to sample lakeside life. There are plenty of visiting boats in summer and you can swim, fish or chart a yacht. Inquire at **Shannon Sailing** (☎ 067-24499; www.shannonsailing.com).

The **Dromineer Bay Hotel** (☎ 067-24114; www.dromineerbay.com; s/d €69/125; **P**) is a busy and attractive lakeside place with bright rooms. The hotel's **Crow's Nest Bar** (mains €11-19) does hefty sandwiches for €3 and the upstairs **Gillies Restaurant** (mains €14.50-31) offers enjoyable fish and meat dishes.

THURLES & AROUND

☎ 0504 / pop 6852

Thurles (Durlas) is a sizable market town 22km north of Cashel. It was founded by the Butler family during the 13th century. It is a down-to-earth place and is all the more pleasant for it. The centre of town is the long and spacious Liberty Square. It is rather traffic-bound, as in most modern towns, but has a lively air. At Thurles in 1884 the *Cumann Lúthchleas Gael*, the Gaelic Athletic Association (GAA), was founded and today the town's famous Semple Stadium rivals Croke Park Stadium in Dublin as a holy ground of Gaelic sport.

Tourist information can be found at **Lár na Páirc** (☎ 22702; http://tipperary.gaa.ie; Slievenamon Rd), the offices and shop of the GAA where there is also a fascinating **visitor centre** (adult/child €3/1.50; ✆ 10am-5pm Mon-Fri, plus Sat Apr-Sep) that tells the story of the Gaelic Games. Ask for the booklet *A Historical Walk of Thurles* which will guide you round the town.

The Cistercian **Holy Cross Abbey** (✆ 9am-8pm) lies 6km southwest of Thurles beside the River Suir. What survives today dates from the 15th century although the abbey was founded in 1168. The church was restored in the early 1970s and is now an active place of worship. The abbey contains two relics of the True Cross.

Sleeping & Eating

Hayes Hotel (☎ 22122; Liberty Sq; s/d €55/100; **P**) The one-time Commercial Hotel was where the foundation meeting of the GAA took place in 1884. The hotel is venerable and has pleasant rooms. The hotel restaurant (mains €12 to €19) does a roaring trade from morning till night with breakfast (€5) and lunch mains (€8 to €9) of reliable Irish fare, with vegetarian and pasta choices too.

County Kilkenny

Travellers guided by dreams of Irish greenery inevitably end up here. County Kilkenny is a beautiful grassy wonderland of virescent pastures, purling waterways, winding roads and mossy stone walls. Sheep graze amid stone hulks left by 15th-century monks, while highly esteemed restaurants are scattered throughout the county to gratify the peckish wanderer.

The Normans settled in this area, and gave Ireland one of its most beautiful cities, Kilkenny city, which captivates visitors with its medieval buildings and cosmopolitan pleasures. Along the Rivers Nore and Barrow, the arching bridges and tidy shop fronts of Inistioge and Graiguenamanagh frame Hollywood visions of Irish village life. Jerpoint Abbey and Kells Priory are two of Ireland's finest medieval monastic settlements. For walkers, the stretch of the South Leinster Way that crosses southern Kilkenny is rural Ireland at its prettiest.

The county is prone to quaint scenes. In Graiguenamanagh, old-timers step into a rustic old grocery-pub to buy fishing tackle and a pint of Guinness. Down the road, a solitary boy whiles time away whacking a ball at a barn with his hurling stick. At night, however, the current age reasserts itself as young professionals slide into the booths of trendy cafés and live rock music booms out of unpretentious pubs. You catch glimpses of such real-life details, and long after the castles and ruins have blurred, Kilkenny's unruffled spirit stays with you.

Kilkenny's history has long been linked with one Anglo-Norman family, the Butlers, earls of Ormond. They arrived in 1171 and made the region their own, promoting the Norman cause and then that of the English royal household. They were based in Kilkenny city.

COUNTY KILKENNY

HIGHLIGHTS

- **Swingin' Kilkenny Cats**
  Modern nightlife in medieval Kilkenny city (p315)

- **Peace, Brother**
  Peacefulness of Kells Priory (p324)

- **More Art than You Could Eat**
  Art and Medieval architecture at the Kilkenny Arts Festival (p319)

- **Rural Digs for Royalty**
  Country splendour at Foulksrath Castle (p327) and Ballyduff House (p325)

- **Country Idyll**
  Lazy days in charming Inistioge (p325) or Graiguenamanagh (p326)

★ Foulksrath Castle

★ Kilkenny

Graiguenamanagh ★

Kells Priory ★ ★ Ballyduff House

★ Inistioge

POPULATION: 75,366 | AREA: 1274 SQ KM

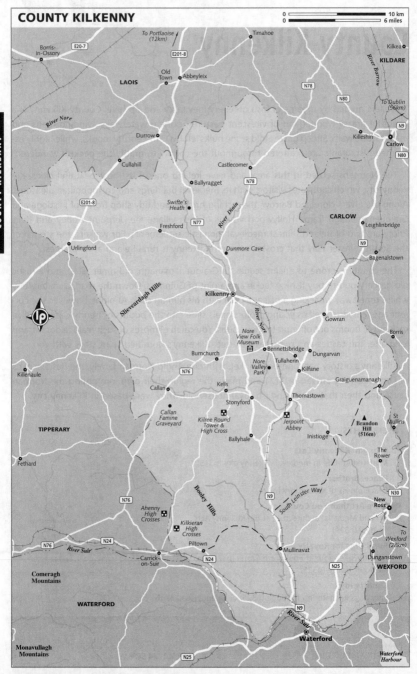

KILKENNY CITY

☎ 056 / pop 8594

Kilkenny has, shall we say, aged gracefully. It's frequently touted as a 'medieval city', but it's hardly plagued, and the people are a far cry from vassals. In fact, Kilkenny rates high among Ireland's most elegant and vibrant cities.

To be sure, much of Kilkenny's architectural charm owes a huge debt to the Middle Ages, when the city was a seat of political power. But time has not passed the city by. Kilkenny remains a cultural centre, renowned for its devotion to the arts. Its cobbled pedestrian passageways and old-fashioned shop fronts may look like the way to a mysterious time-warp realm, but in reality they lead to hip bars, fashion boutiques and chic restaurants. Kilkenny is clearly in the modern world, and it didn't sell out its traditional charms to get here.

Life is good in Kilkenny, which visitors are sure to appreciate. For a town – ahem, a *city* – of its modest size, Kilkenny's 60-odd licensed pubs and bars are more than adequate for the tippling needs of its citizens as well as the hordes of out-of-town merrymakers that show up each weekend. Along the High St, every odd address appears to be a pub, and visitors staying near the centre will have fun ambling from watering hole to watering hole.

Presiding over the town is a splendid medieval cathedral, named after St Canice (Cainneach or Kenneth), who founded a monastery here in the 6th century; hence the city's Irish name, Cill Chainnigh. The town's other 'must-see' attraction is its mighty castle – one of Ireland's finest – which sits majestically on a sweep in the Nore.

As if being medieval isn't enough, Kilkenny is also sometimes called the 'marble city' because of the local black limestone, which resembles a slate-coloured marble. This attractive stone is seen to most striking effect in the cathedral, and is used on floors and in decorative trim all over town. The people of Kilkenny call themselves 'Kilkenny Cats', which sounds innocent enough – until you realise this is a reference to the traditional nursery rhyme about two cats who clawed each other to death. Rest assured, this sort of thing doesn't happen on the streets of Kilkenny every day.

HISTORY

In the 5th century, St Kieran is said to have visited Kilkenny and, on the site of the present Kilkenny Castle, challenged the chieftains of Ossory to accept the Christian faith. Subsequently, St Canice established his monastery here. Kilkenny consolidated its importance in the 13th century under William Marshall, the earl of Pembroke and son-in-law of the Anglo-Norman conqueror Strongbow. Kilkenny Castle was built to secure a crossing point on the Nore.

During the Middle Ages, Kilkenny was intermittently the unofficial capital of Ireland, with its own Anglo-Norman parliament. In 1366 the parliament passed the so-called Statutes of Kilkenny, a set of Draconian laws aimed at preventing the assimilation of the increasingly assertive Anglo-Normans into Irish society. Anglo-Normans were prohibited from marrying the native Irish, taking part in Irish sports, speaking or dressing like the Irish or playing any Irish music. Any breach of the law was to result in the confiscation of Anglo-Norman property and death to the native Irish. Although the laws remained theoretically in force for over 200 years, they were never enforced with any great effect and did little to halt the absorption of the Anglo-Normans into Irish culture.

During the 1640s, Kilkenny sided with the Catholic royalists in the English Civil War. The 1641 Confederation of Kilkenny, an uneasy alliance of native Irish and Anglo-Normans, aimed to bring about the return of land and power to Catholics. After Charles I's execution, Cromwell besieged Kilkenny for five days, destroying much of the southern wall of the castle before Ormond surrendered. The defeat signalled a permanent end to Kilkenny's political influence over Irish affairs.

TOP FIVE RESTAURANTS IN COUNTY KILKENNY

- Lacken House (Kilkenny; p321)
- Motte Restaurant (Inistioge; p325)
- Waterside (Graiguenamanagh; p326)
- Hudsons (Thomastown; p325)
- Zuni (Kilkenny; p321)

ORIENTATION

At the junction of several major highways, Kilkenny straddles the River Nore, which flows through much of the county. St Canice's Cathedral sits on the northern bank of the River Bregagh (a tributary of the Nore) to the north of the town centre outside the town walls. Kilkenny's main thoroughfare runs southeast from the cathedral, past St Canice's Pl to Irishtown (where the common folk were once concentrated), then over the bridge, eventually becoming Parliament St. Kilkenny Castle, located on the banks of the River Nore, dominates the town's southern side.

INFORMATION

Bookshops

Kilkenny Book Centre (☎ 776 2117; 10 High St) This, the largest bookshop in town, stocks a range of titles and maps on Ireland, as well as periodicals.

Emergency

Police station (☎ 999, ☎ 22222; Dominic St)

Internet Access

C@fe Net (☎ 777 0051; 4 Patrick St; per hr €5;
🕑 7.45am-8pm Mon-Sat, 9am-6pm Sun)
Kilkenny e-centre (☎ 776 0093; 26 Rose Inn St; per hr €5; 🕑 10am-8pm Mon-Sat, 11am-7pm Sun)

Medical Services

Boots the Chemist (☎ 777 1222; 36-38 High St) Sells medicine and first-aid supplies.
St Luke's Hospital (☎ 775 1133; Freshford Rd)

Money

All of Ireland's big banks have branches, with ATMs, on High St.

Tourist Information

Tourist office (☎ 775 1500; Rose Inn St; www.south eastireland.com; 🕑 9am-5pm Mon-Sat Sep-Jun, 9am-6pm Mon-Sat, 11am-5pm Sun Jul & Aug) In the lovely stone Shee Alms House, the office sells excellent guides to the town and inexpensive walking maps of the county.

SIGHTS

Kilkenny Castle

On a lovely bend of the Nore stands **Kilkenny Castle** (☎ 772 1450; adult/child €5/2; 🕑 9.30am-7pm Jun-Sep, 10.30am-12.45pm & 2-5pm Oct-Mar, 10.30am-5pm Apr & May), one of Ireland's most magnificent fortresses and Kilkenny's premier tourist attraction. The first structure on this stra-

tegic site was a wooden tower built in 1172 by Richard de Clare, the Anglo-Norman conqueror of Ireland better known as Strongbow. In 1192 Strongbow's son-in-law, William Marshall, erected a stone castle with four towers, three of which still survive. The castle was bought by the powerful Butler family in 1391, and their descendants continued to live there until 1935. Maintaining such a structure became a big financial strain and most of the furnishings were sold at auction. The castle was handed over to the city in 1967 for the princely sum of £50 and is now administered by Dúchas.

The focus of the 40-minute guided tour is the **Long Gallery**, in the wing of the castle nearest the river. The gallery, which showcases stuffy portraits of the Butler family members over the centuries, is an impressive hall with high ceilings vividly painted with Celtic and Pre-Raphaelite motifs. Work to restore the castle to its Victorian splendour is ongoing, and more rooms are continuously being opened for the tours. Most of the furnishings are not original to the castle, although a few items have been purchased back by Dúchas. What you do see are Victorian antiques that would evoke gasps from viewers of the *Antiques Roadshow*.

The castle basement is also home to the **Butler Gallery** (☎ 776 1106; www.butlergallery .com; admission free), one of the country's most important art galleries outside Dublin. Small art exhibitions featuring the work of contemporary artists are held throughout the year. Also in the basement, the castle kitchen houses a popular summertime café. You can head directly to either the Butler Gallery or the café without paying the tour admission price.

About 20 hectares of **parkland** (admission free; 🕑 10am-8.30pm summer) extend to the southeast, with a Celtic cross–shaped rose garden, a fountain to the northern end and a children's playground to the south.

St Canice's Cathedral

Ireland's second-largest medieval cathedral (after St Patrick's in Dublin), **St Canice's Cathedral** (☎ 776 4971; stcanicecathedral@eircom.net; St Canice's Pl; admission €3; 🕑 9am-1pm & 2-6pm Mon-Sat, 2-6pm Sun Apr-Sep, 10am-1pm & 2-4pm Mon-Sat, 2-4pm Sun Oct-Mar) is a magnificent edifice in the

KILKENNY

0 ——————— 500 m
0 ——————— 0.3 miles

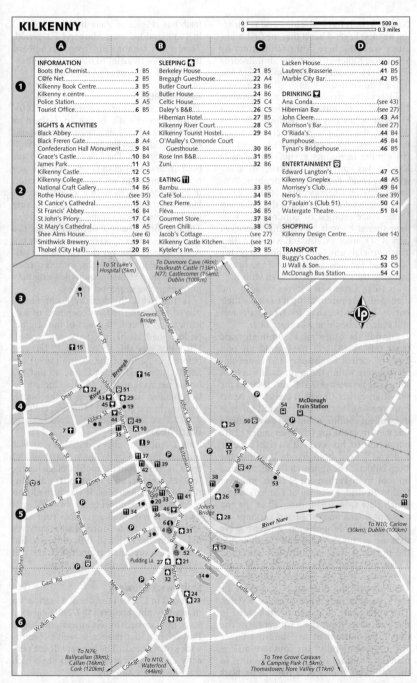

INFORMATION
Boots the Chemist...........................1 B5
C@fe Net..2 B5
Kilkenny Book Centre......................3 B5
Kilkenny e.centre............................4 B5
Police Station..................................5 A5
Tourist Office.................................6 B5

SIGHTS & ACTIVITIES
Black Abbey....................................7 A4
Black Freren Gate............................8 A4
Confederation Hall Monument.......9 B4
Grace's Castle................................10 B4
James Park.....................................11 A3
Kilkenny Castle..............................12 C5
Kilkenny College............................13 C5
National Craft Gallery.....................14 B6
Rothe House............................(see 35)
St Canice's Cathedral.....................15 A3
St Francis' Abbey...........................16 B4
St John's Priory.............................17 C4
St Mary's Cathedral.......................18 A5
Shee Alms House......................(see 6)
Smithwick Brewery........................19 B4
Tholsel (City Hall)..........................20 B5

SLEEPING 🏠
Berkeley House..............................21 B5
Bregagh Guesthouse......................22 A4
Butler Court...................................23 B6
Butler House..................................24 B6
Celtic House..................................25 C4
Daley's B&B...................................26 C5
Hibernian Hotel.............................27 B5
Kilkenny River Court......................28 C5
Kilkenny Tourist Hostel..................29 B4
O'Malley's Ormonde Court
  Guesthouse................................30 B6
Rose Inn B&B.................................31 B5
Zuni..32 B6

EATING 🍴
Bambu..33 B5
Café Sol..34 B5
Chez Pierre...................................35 B4
Fléva...36 B4
Gourmet Store...............................37 B4
Green Chilli...................................38 C5
Jacob's Cottage........................(see 27)
Kilkenny Castle Kitchen.............(see 12)
Kyteler's Inn.................................39 B5

Lacken House................................40 D5
Lautrec's Brasserie.........................41 B5
Marble City Bar.............................42 B5

DRINKING 🍸
Ana Conda..............................(see 43)
Hibernian Bar..........................(see 27)
John Cleere...................................43 A4
Morrison's Bar.........................(see 27)
O'Riada's......................................44 B4
Pumphouse...................................45 B4
Tynan's Bridgehouse......................46 B5

ENTERTAINMENT 🎭
Edward Langton's..........................47 C5
Kilkenny Cineplex..........................48 A5
Morrisey's Club.............................49 B4
Nero's......................................(see 39)
O'Faolain's (Club 51).....................50 C4
Watergate Theatre.........................51 B4

SHOPPING
Kilkenny Design Centre..............(see 14)

TRANSPORT
Buggy's Coaches...........................52 B5
JJ Wall & Son................................53 C5
McDonagh Bus Station..................54 C4

COUNTY KILKENNY

To St Luke's Hospital (5km)
To Dunmore Cave (4km); Foulksrath Castle (13km); N77; Castlecomer (16km); Dublin (100km)

New Rd
Castlecomer Rd
Greens Bridge
Greenbridge St
Vicar St
Bregagh
Inchbeg
River
Dean St
Abbey St
Parliament St
Blackmill St
Butts Green
Michael St
John's Quay
Wolfe Tone St
Bateman's Quay
High St
James St
Dominic St
Kickham St
Parnell St
Stephen St
Friary St
Kieran St
Butter Slip
Rose Inn St
The Parade
Pudding La
Patrick St
Ormonde St
New St
Gaol Rd
Walkin St
Maudlin St
Dublin Rd
John's Bridge
River Nore
Castle Rd
Castle Rd

McDonagh Train Station

To N10; Carlow (30km); Dublin (100km)

To N76; Ballycallan (8km); Callan (16km); Cork (120km)
College Rd
To N10; Waterford (44km)
To Tree Grove Caravan & Camping Park (1.5km); Thomastown; Nore Valley (11km)

Gothic style. It has had a long and fascinating history. Legend has it that the first monastery was built here in the 6th century by St Canice, Kilkenny's patron saint. Records show that a wooden church on the site was burned down in 1087.

The existing structure was raised between 1202 and 1285, but then endured a series of catastrophes and resurrections. The first disaster, the collapse of the church tower in 1332, was the consequence of one of the city's more intriguing events. Dame Alice Kyteler was convicted of witchcraft along with her maid. Dame Alice's nephew, William Outlawe, also was implicated. The unfortunate maid was burned at the stake, but Dame Alice escaped to London and William spared himself by offering to re-roof part of St Canice's Cathedral with lead tiles. Town officials unwisely took him up on the offer and the new roof proved too heavy, bringing the church tower down with it.

In 1650, Cromwell's forces defaced and damaged the church, using it to stable their horses. Repairs began in 1661, but there was still much to be done a century later.

Outside the cathedral, a 30m-high **round tower** (adult/child €2/1.50) rises amid an odd array of ancient tombstones and is the oldest structure within the grounds. It was built sometime between AD 700 and 1000 on the site of an earlier Christian cemetery. Apart from missing its crown, the round tower is in excellent condition and you can admire a fine view from the top (children under 12 are not permitted, however). It's a tight squeeze and you'll need both hands to climb the steep ladders. The approach to the cathedral on foot from Parliament St leads you over Irishtown Bridge and up St Canice's Steps, which date from 1614; the wall at the top contains fragmentary medieval carvings.

Inside, highly polished ancient **grave slabs** are set on the walls and the floor. On the northern wall, opposite the entrance, a slab inscribed in Norman French commemorates Jose de Keteller, who died in 1280; despite the difference in spelling he was probably the father of Alice Kyteler. The stone chair of St Kieran embedded in the wall dates from the 13th century. The fine 1596 monument to Honorina Grace at the western end of the southern aisle is made of beautiful local black limestone. In the southern transept, a handsome **black tomb** has effigies of Piers Butler, who died in 1539, and his wife, Margaret Fitzgerald. Tombs and monuments (listed on a board in the southern aisle) to other notable Butlers crowd this corner of the church.

Rothe House

The best surviving example of a 16th-century merchant's house in Ireland is **Rothe House** (☎ 772 2893; Parliament St; adult/child €3/1; ☺ 10.30am-5pm Mon-Sat, 3-5pm Sun Apr-Oct, 1-5pm Mon-Sat Nov-Mar). The fine Tudor house was built around a series of courtyards and now houses a museum with a sparse collection of local artefacts, including a well-used Viking sword found near here and a grinning head sculpted from a stone by a Celtic artist. The fine king-post roof of the 2nd floor is a meticulous and impressive reconstruction. A costume exhibit on the 1st floor is primarily good for mild laughs, with its cordon of oddly shaped mannequins looking very uncomfortable in period attire.

In the 1640s, the wealthy Rothe family played a part in the Confederation of Kilkenny, and Peter Rothe, son of the original builder, had all his property confiscated. His sister was able to reclaim it, but just before the Battle of the Boyne (1690) the family supported James II and so lost the house permanently. In 1850 a Confederation banner was discovered in the house. It's now in the National Museum, Dublin.

Black Abbey

This Dominican abbey on Abbey St was founded in 1225 by William Marshall and takes its name from the monks' black habits. In 1543, six years after Henry VIII's dissolution of the monasteries, it was turned into a courthouse. Following Cromwell's visit in 1650, it remained a roofless ruin until restoration in 1866. Much of what survives dates from the 18th and 19th centuries, but pieces of more ancient archways are still evident within the newer stonework.

Smithwick Brewery

Founded in 1710 on the site of a Franciscan monastery, this **brewery** (☎ 772 1014; Parliament St) is now owned by Guinness and brews Budweiser under licence as well as Smithwick's own brands. The brewery doesn't exactly encourage visitors; call to see which way the wind's blowing.

St Francis' Abbey, behind the brewery, was founded by William Marshall in 1232, but desecrated by Cromwell in 1650. The monks were reputed to be expert brewers.

National Craft Gallery

This **gallery** (☎ 776 1804; www.ccoi.ie; Castle Yard; admission free; ◷ 10am-6pm Apr-Dec, closed Sun Jan-Mar), opposite Kilkenny Castle, showcases contemporary Irish crafts. Its high-quality exhibitions highlight the diversity and imagination of crafts in contemporary Ireland. The emphasis is chiefly on ceramics, but exhibits regularly feature furniture, jewellery and weaving.

Other Sights

Shee Alms House, on Rose Inn St, was built in 1582 by local benefactor Sir Richard Shee and his wife to provide help for the poor. It continued as a hospital until 1740 but now houses the tourist office. The **Tholsel**, or City Hall, on High St was built in 1761 on the spot where Dame Alice Kyteler's maid, Petronella, was burned at the stake in 1324.

Next to the Tholsel is **Butter Slip**, a tunnel-like walkway that connects High St with Low Lane (now St Kieran's St). It was built in 1616 and once was lined with the stalls of butter vendors. Today it is home to a couple of restaurants and a sporting goods shop. With its arched entry and stone steps, Butter Slip is by far the most picturesque of Kilkenny's many narrow medieval corridors.

Black Freren Gate on Abbey St is the only gate from the old Norman city walls still standing, albeit with the help of metal bracing to ensure the safety of those who pass through. Crumbling sections of the old walls remain throughout the central city.

On the corner of Parliament St and the road leading down to Bateman's Quay, the **Confederation Hall monument** beside the Bank of Ireland marks the site where the national Parliament met from 1642 to 1649. Nearby is **Grace's Castle**, originally built in 1210, but lost to the family and converted into a prison in 1568, and then in 1794 into a courthouse, which it remains today. Rebels from the 1798 Rising were executed here. People taking part in one of Tynan Tours (see right) can enter to peek inside the cells.

Across the river stand the ruins of **St John's Priory**, which was founded in 1200 and was noted for its many beautiful windows until Cromwell's visit. Nearby, **Kilkenny College**, on John St, dates from 1666. Its students included Jonathan Swift and the philosopher George Berkeley, but it now houses Kilkenny's county hall.

TOURS

Central Kilkenny city is a small, walkable area, well-suited to comprehensive walking tours.

Tynan Tours (☎ 087 265 1745; www.tynantours .com; adult/student €6/5.50) conducts hour-long walking tours that meander through Kilkenny's narrow lanes, steps and pedestrian passageways. Smart, witty guides recount the intriguing stories these buildings might tell if they could talk. Tour groups meet at the tourist office several times daily March to October, less frequently the rest of the year. Call for times. Ask about a group rate if you're travelling with friends.

FESTIVALS & EVENTS

Kilkenny is rightly known as the festival capital of Ireland, with several world-class festivals throughout the year that attract thousands of people. The following festivals are staged throughout the year:

Kilkenny Rhythm & Roots (☎ 779 0057; www .kilkennyroots.com; early May) Over 30 different venues participate in hosting Ireland's biggest music festival, with country and 'old-timey' American roots music strongly emphasised.

Cat Laughs Comedy Festival (☎ 776 3416; (www .thecatlaughs.com; late May–early Jun) Cat Laughs is a much-acclaimed gathering of world-class comics.

Ultimate Frisbee Tournament (☎ 775 1500; iancud@hotmail.com; mid-Jun) This is an excellent weekend of booze, lunacy and an international competition in ultimate Frisbee.

Smithwick's Source at Kilkenny (www.smithwicks source.com; late July) Bob Dylan, Van Morrison, Bryan Ferry and many others have headlined at this huge music festival in Nowlan Park.

Kilkenny Arts Festival (☎ 775 2175; www.kilkenny arts.ie; late Aug) The city comes alive when theatre, cinema, music, literature, visual arts, children's events and street spectacles for 10 action-packed days. Accommodation at this time is like gold, and you're seriously advised to book far in advance.

SLEEPING

If you're arriving in town with no room booked, the tourist office runs an efficient accommodation booking system costing €4.

COUNTY KILKENNY

Budget

Kilkenny Tourist Hostel (☎ 776 3541; kilkenny hostel@eircom.net; 35 Parliament St; dm €13-18) You'll find the rooms clean and the staff friendly at this IHH hostel. It's on the main street of Kilkenny, within a few steps of half a dozen clubs and several good restaurants. Public spaces within the hostel are its true selling point, however. The kitchen is neat and has an atmospheric dining room, while the sitting room is outfitted with couches and a fireplace. Guests here are always well informed on Kilkenny nightlife and other happenings because the information board is updated daily.

Rose Inn B&B (☎ 777 0061; 9 Rose Inn St; s/d €30/60) Its furnishings are dated and rooms are a little dark during the day, but this pleasant little B&B opposite the tourist office is a serviceable cheapie. The place is central and quiet on the rear side of the building. If you're really looking to save money, inquire about dorm beds in the noisier front rooms.

Daley's B&B (☎ 776 2866; 82 John St; s €38-40; P) Looking very much the 20th century motor court, and hidden away behind a dense row of pubs and shops, Daley's is nothing fancy. It's an adequate cheapie, with decent rooms and a convenient location.

Tree Grove Caravan & Camping Park (☎ 777 0302; New Ross Rd; camp sites €11) This camping ground in a small park is 1.5km south of Kilkenny.

Midrange

Lacken House (☎ 776 1085; www.lackenhouse.ie; Dublin Rd; s/d €75/138; P) Just out of town, this beautiful Victorian-era guesthouse gets highly deserved praise from guests. The standard rate includes a superb breakfast; for a real treat, have a five-course dinner in the award-winning restaurant (ask about inclusive specials). More-expensive suites are also available.

Bregagh Guesthouse (☎ 772 2315; Dean St; s/d €45/85; P) Near St Canice's Cathedral, just off the main drag, this cheery home is welcoming and comfortably furnished with sturdy antiques. All rooms have a private bathroom.

Berkeley House (☎ 776 4848; www.berkeleyhouse kilkenny.com; 5 Lower Patrick St; s/d €59/108; P) In a stately Georgian building, half a block from High St, this hotel has a distinct air of

faded glory, though it's pretty comfortable. Breakfast is included.

Celtic House (☎ 776 2249; john376@gofree.indigo .ie; 18 Michael St; r €35-40) John and Angela Byrne's beautifully decorated home is just a short walk from the High St. The modern, airy guestrooms have private bathrooms. See if a room with a view of the castle is available.

Butler Court (☎ 776-1178; www.butlercourt.com; Patrick St; s/d €60/120) Not to be confused with the much grander Butler House, a few doors away, this basic little lodging offers spotless rooms at a modest price.

O'Malley's Ormonde Court Guesthouse (☎ 777 1003; omalleysguesthouse@eircom.net; Ormonde Rd; s €35-60, d €60-90; P) O'Malley's is not especially picturesque, with a large parking lot in front, but the place is run by friendly people and located just two blocks from High St. The rooms have en suites, are simply furnished and clean, and breakfast is included.

Top End

Butler House (☎ 772 2828; www.butler.ie; 16 Patrick St; d €250-400; P) You can't stay in Kilkenny Castle, but this is surely the next best thing. It once was home of the Earls of Ormonde (who built the nearby castle) and is now a luxurious hotel. The house has all the aristocratic trappings you'd expect, including sweeping staircases, marble fireplaces, an art collection and impeccably trimmed gardens. Rooms have elegant contemporary furnishings.

Hibernian Hotel (☎ 777 1888; www.kilkenny hibernianhotel.com; 1 Ormonde St; d €200-280; P) In a stolid Victorian building that once housed a bank, the Hibernian exudes grand hotel swank and has a stately bar.

Kilkenny River Court (☎ 772 3388; www.kil rivercourt.com; John St; r per person from €110; P) Along the Nore, by the bridge, this new hotel treats guests to plush rooms and a full range of modern amenities. The riverside terrace is a choice spot for a drink when the weather's fine.

Zuni (☎ 772 3999; www.zuni.ie; 26 Patrick St; s/d Sun-Thu €70/100, Fri & Sat €100/160; P) In a 1902 building that once served as a playhouse, Zuni has an ultramodern, minimalist design with lots of clean lines, muted lighting and not a flower in sight. It also has its own restaurant.

EATING
Cafés
Café Sol (☎ 776 4987; William St; lunch €6-10, dinner mains €15-23; ⏰ 10am-10pm Mon-Sat) Bright, warm and cheery, with yellow walls and numerous windows, this place evokes a sunny Mediterranean escape from wet and windy Ireland. It's an excellent place to go for simple lunches and eclectic, creative dinners.

Gourmet Store (☎ 777 1727; 56 High St; sandwiches €3; ⏰ 9am-6pm Mon-Sat) In this crowded little deli, terrific takeaway sandwiches packed with fresh, mouthwatering ingredients make the stomach growl as you wait for your order.

Chez Pierre (☎ 776 4655; 17 Parliament St; mains €3-8; ⏰ 10am-5pm) It's relaxed and unpretentious, which is why lunching locals love this French café. The menu offers an open-faced leek and Parma ham sandwich that'll brighten up the middle of your day, as well as an assortment of sandwiches, soups and sweets.

Kilkenny Castle Kitchen (☎ 772 1450; Kilkenny Castle; mains €4-10; ⏰ noon-5pm Jun-Aug) The castle's surprisingly humble café, looking very much the country kitchen, is a good place for lunch or delicious cakes; you don't have to fork out the castle admission charge to eat here.

Restaurants
Lacken House (☎ 776 1085; Dublin Rd; set 4-course €43, set 5-course €50; ⏰ 6-9pm daily Jun-Oct, Tue-Sat Nov-May) Touted as the best local restaurant for many years, Lacken House dishes out appetising original creations like pork with cider potato, and ostrich fillet with aubergine caviar.

Marble City Bar (☎ 776 1143; 66 High St; lunch €4-8, dinner €4-13; ⏰ food served 10am-8.30pm) In a city full of culinary bright spots, this stylishly mod bar manages to stand out. Tasty and smart-looking roasts, pastas, cod and chips are a good notch above the usual bar-food standards. Very nice for the price.

Lautrec's Brasserie (☎ 776 2720; 9 St Kieran's St; pizzas €9-12, mains €19-26; ⏰ 6-10pm Sun-Thu, 6-11pm Fri & Sat) Here's a romantic little spot with candle lit tables that's perfect for parties of two. Lautrec's eclectic offerings include pizzas, pastas and surf-and-turf mainstays, but everything is prepared and served with artistic flair.

Fléva (☎ 777 0021; 84 High St; lunch €10-14, dinner €18-26; ⏰ 12.30-2.30pm & 6-10pm Tue-Sat) The food in this airy and colourful restaurant could be described as 'fléva-ful'. The nightly menu might include a delectable roast rack of lamb or a zesty Cajun monkfish.

Zuni (☎ 772 3999; 26 Patrick St; lunch €11-17, dinner €19-30; ⏰ 12.30-2.30pm Tue-Sat, 6.30-10pm Mon-Sat, 1-3pm & 6-9pm Sun) Among Kilkenny's most attractive and busiest restaurants, Zuni deftly handles an impressive range of international dishes. Thai chicken, spinach tagliatelle, lamb rump and even kangaroo all vie for a spot in your stomach.

Edward Langton's (☎ 776 5133; 69 John St; mains €6-21; ⏰ noon-10pm Mon-Sat, noon-9pm Sun) Langton's is an enormous, snazzy pub with an award-winning restaurant. The varied crowd – well-dressed old-timers, belligerent hurling fans, trendy blondes gossiping at the bar – is as interesting as the food is good. Surf-and-turf dishes get creative, contemporary treatment here.

Bambu (☎ 777 0699; Butter Slip Lane; lunch €8-11, dinner €12-19; ⏰ 12.30-11pm) At the end of medieval Butter Slip, this stylish Thai restaurant comes as a pleasant surprise. Noodles and curries are fresh and snappy and just the ticket if you've had all the surf-and-turf you can take.

Jacob's Cottage (☎ 779 1220; 1 Ormonde St; lunch €8-15, dinner €16-28; ⏰ 12.30-3pm & 6.30-10pm) Part of the Hibernian Hotel, Jacob's is a polished operation, where competent staff put some fine, imaginative cuisine on the table. Irish staples are joined by some Mediterranean and southeast Asian touches.

Green Chilli (☎ 778 6990; 8 John St; mains €10-14; ⏰ 6pm-midnight Mon-Sat, 5-11pm Sun) The late hours at this Indian spot are ideal for hungry bar hoppers seeking spicy sustenance.

Kyteler's Inn (☎ 772 1064; 27 St Kieran's St; mains €9-20; ⏰ noon-10pm) Dame Alice Kyteler's old house, built in 1224, is one of the tourist magnets in town. Dame Kyteler, if you don't already know, went through four husbands, all of whom died in suspicious circumstances. She was rumoured to have sacrificed cockerels and consorted with the devil. Having acquired some powerful enemies, she was charged with witchcraft in 1324. The food here is not known for its greatness, but this is a fun place to hang out. For a real witchin' experience, sit in the solid stone basement, which feels like a dungeon.

DRINKING

O'Riada's (27 Parliament St) Here's an unassuming favourite, where the only dashes of flash are an electric light and a TV set. The joint fills up and gets pretty lively when there's a game on the tube, but most of the time it's just the best local along Kilkenny's main street.

Pumphouse (☎ 776 3924; 26 Parliament St) With live rock groups many nights a week, the Pumphouse is one of Kilkenny's livelier bars. When there's no band, music comes from a free jukebox that doesn't have a bad song on it. The Pumphouse typically draws a 20-something crowd, but old-timers won't feel uncomfortable here. Smokers hang out on the roof.

Ana Conda (☎ 777 1657; Parliament St) A frequent winner in local polls, Ana Conda has forged a unique, nonplussed hipness with Friday night céilidh sessions and Saturday night rock shows. The covered beer garden is popular among smokers.

Tynan's Bridgehouse (☎ 772 1291; St John's Bridge) Conversation is generally audible in this grand old Georgian pub, which recently celebrated its 300th birthday. The building has settled a bit over the years, and its sloping ceilings and tilting walls will make you think you're drunk before you are. After a few pints everything sort of straightens itself out.

John Cleere (☎ 776 2573; 22 Parliament St) This pub is well known for its regular productions of plays and for its poetry readings. It's also becoming one of Kilkenny's best rock venues, with touring alternative acts frequently passing through. You might also be able to catch a traditional Irish music session here.

Hibernian Bar (☎ 777 1888; Hibernian Hotel, Patrick St) Few things are as sublime as sinking into a plush leather couch in this swanky hotel bar. The high ceilings and soothing dark-wood trim make suitable environs for a sophisticated afternoon drink.

ENTERTAINMENT

For information on local events, check out the weekly *Kilkenny People* newspaper. A good website is www.whazon.com.

Cinema & Theatre

Kilkenny Cineplex (☎ 772 3111; Fair Green, Gaol Rd) This is Kilkenny's only multiplex cinema, with four screens all showing the latest releases.

Watergate Theatre (☎ 776 1674; www.watergatekilkenny.com; Parliament St) This theatre hosts drama, comedy and musical performances.

John Cleere (☎ 776 2573; 22 Parliament St) Besides poetry readings and music events, this pub also stages small productions.

Nightclubs

O'Faolain's (☎ 776 1018; John St; admission €8-10) Far and away Kilkenny's most dynamic club, O'Faolain's has three levels and the remains of an old church inside. It stays open till 2am and has live DJs most nights, starting around 10.30pm. Friday and Saturday the venue hosts Club 51, a popular club night in town.

Edward Langton's (☎ 776 5133; 69 John St; admission Tue/Sat €7/13) With resident DJs on Tuesday and Saturday nights, Langton's is the most popular club in town. It gets packed to the rafters.

Morrison's Bar (☎ 777 1888; 1 Ormonde St; ☼ 5pm-1am) In the cellar of the Hibernian Hotel there's this stylish hideaway, with its atmospheric lighting and snazzy *belle époque* décor. DJs spin an eclectic mix for a local professional crowd.

Morrisey's Club (☎ 777 0555; 40 Parliament St; admission €8; ☼ 8pm-late Thu-Sun) In a basement a few doors up from the Kilkenny Tourist Hostel, this disco usually doesn't really get cranking until around 10pm (those who show up earlier get in free). Bands sometimes play here. Sunday night draws an 18-and-up crowd.

Nero's (☎ 772 1064; 25 St Kieran's St; admission €8; ☼ 11.30pm-3am Thu-Sun) Next door to Kyteler's Inn, Nero's is a big and popular two-storey disco where the DJs are in tune with the latest trends.

Sport

James Park (☎ 772 1214; Freshford Rd; dog races ☼ 8pm Wed & Fri) Good fun is to be had on race night. Kilkenny may be sophisticated, but its residents aren't above putting a few euros on a fleet-footed greyhound.

SHOPPING

Kilkenny has a reputation as one of Ireland's cultural and artistic centres. Yet, there's really not much of a gallery scene here, and overall Kilkenny is not much of a shopper's mecca.

Kilkenny Design Centre (☎ 776 1804; www.kilkennydesign.com; Castle Yard) Across The Parade from Kilkenny Castle are the elegant former castle stables (1760), which have been tastefully converted into the Kilkenny Design Centre. There's an outstanding collection of Irish goods and crafts for sale, with potters, knitters, goldsmiths and silversmiths among the centre's many shopkeepers. Behind the shop, through the arched gateway, is Castle Yard, lined with the studios of various local craftspeople.

GETTING THERE & AWAY
Bus
Bus Éireann (☎ 776 4933; www.buseireann.ie) operates out of McDonagh bus station, on the corner of Dublin Rd and John St, and provides at least five daily services to and from Dublin (one way/return €10/12, two hours). There are three services daily (two on Sunday) to and from Cork city (one way/return €14/22, three hours). Bus Éireann also picks up and drops off passengers at the very central C@Fé Net on St Patrick's St.

Buggy's Coaches (☎ 444 1264), based in Castlecomer, runs a service from Kilkenny to Foulksrath Castle (and the An Óige hostel), Ballyragget, Dunmore Cave and Castlecomer. Buses (€2, 20 minutes) leave the Parade at 11.30am and 5.30pm Monday to Saturday; they leave from the Kilkenny Tourist Hostel at 8.25am and 3pm.

Train
McDonagh train station (☎ 772 2024) is on Dublin Rd, northeast of the town centre via John St. Daily trains link Dublin (Heuston Station) with Waterford via Kilkenny (adult one way/return €20/26, student return €16, two hours). For details of departure times phone ☎ 01-836 6222 or check www.irishrail.ie.

GETTING AROUND
JJ Wall & Son (☎ 772 1236; 86 Maudlin St) rents out bikes at €15 per day. The circuit round Kells, Inistioge, Jerpoint Abbey and Kilfane makes a fine day's ride. There's no deposit, but you'll need to present photo identification.

For a cab, call **Danny's Taxis** (☎ 223 8887).

CENTRAL KILKENNY

The area south – and most notably southeast – of Kilkenny city is graced with comely country towns and eye-popping scenic roads overlooking the rich, green Barrow and Nore Valleys. It's best to nudge out to the riverside towns of Graiguenamanagh and Inistioge, where the scenery is tops. This is prime walking country, with beautiful trails running alongside the rivers and between the towns.

BENNETTSBRIDGE & AROUND
☎ 056 / pop 922
In a scenic setting on the Nore, Bennettsbridge is an arts and crafts hotbed, with two of Ireland's most renowned potteries. In a big mill by the river is **Nicholas Mosse Irish Country Shop** (☎ 772-7105; www.nicholasmosse.com; ☺ 9am-6pm Mon-Sat, 1.30-5pm Sun), a pottery that specialises in handmade spongeware – creamy-brown pottery that's covered with sponged patterns. The shop also sells linens and other handmade craft items, and there's a tea shop upstairs known far and wide for its excellent scones.

In the centre of town, the **Bridge** (☎ 972 9156; www.bridgepottery.com; Chapel St; ☺ 1-6pm Tue-Fri, 11am-6pm Sat) is the studio-shop of Mary O'Gorman and Mark Campden, award-winning potters who craft warm-coloured pottery and personalised plates.

Almost 2km north of Bennettsbridge on the R700 road to Kilkenny, **Stoneware Jackson Pottery** (☎ 27175; www.stonewarejackson.com; ☺ 10am-6pm Mon-Sat) produces groovy pots, jugs, tea sets and even lamps.

On the other side of the Nore is **Dyed in the Wool** (☎ 27684; Bennettsbridge; ☺ 10am-6pm Mon-Fri, noon-6pm Sat & Sun). This knitwear factory sells its wares in some of Ireland's best design stores. Fetching chenille hats for the ladies are a forte.

About 2km west of Bennettsbridge, near the hamlet of Danesfort, is the **Nore View Folk Museum** (☎ 27749; Danesfort Rd; admission free; ☺ 10am-6pm Jun-Sep, 2.30-5.30pm Oct-May). It's a privately owned folk museum displaying local items of interest, including old farming tools and other bric-a-brac.

Nore Valley Camping & Caravan Park (☎ 972 7229; http://norevalleypark.tripod.com; Annamult; day admission adult/child €2.50/2; camp sites €16; ☺ 9am-7pm

Mon-Sat Mar-Oct) is a 5-acre farm that suits kids and campers. Kids can bottle-feed lambs and goats, cuddle rabbits, play in a fort and jump on a straw bounce. There is a tearoom and picnic area. If you're coming into Bennettsbridge from Kilkenny along the R700, turn right just before the bridge; the park is signposted.

Calabash Bistro (☎ 772 7850; Chapel St; starters €4-9, mains €19-25; 🕑 6-9.30pm Thu-Mon, closed mid-Feb–mid-Mar) is opposite the bridge in town. This is a stylish eatery that treats its guests to creative Irish cuisine, like fillet steak on chive potato cakes, and mustard-glazed duck breast.

KELLS & AROUND

Kells (not to be confused with Kells in County Meath) is a mere widening of the road, a hamlet with a fine stone bridge on a tributary of the Nore. However, in Kells Priory, the village has one of Ireland's most impressive and romantic monastic sites. The village is 13km south of Kilkenny city.

Kells Priory

This is the best sort of ruin, where visitors are free to explore as they like, whenever they like, with no tour guides, tours, ropes or restrictions. At dusk on a vaguely sunny day the old priory is simply beautiful. Most days you stand a chance of exploring the site alone, with only the company of bleating sheep.

The earliest remains of this gorgeous monastic site date from the late 12th century, while the bulk of the present ruins date from the 15th century. In a sea of rich farmland, a protective wall, carefully restored, connects seven dwelling towers. Inside the walls are the remains of an Augustinian abbey and the foundations of some chapels and houses. It's unusually well fortified for a monastery and the heavy curtain walls hint at a troubled history. Indeed, within a single century from 1250, the abbey was twice fought over and burned down by squabbling warlords.

There's no charge for visiting and no set opening hours. The ruins are 800m east of Kells on the Stonyford road.

Kilree Round Tower & High Cross

About 2km south of Kells (signposted from the priory car park) there's a 29m-high round tower and a simple early high cross, which is said to mark the grave of a 9th-century Irish high king, Niall Caille. He's supposed to have drowned in the King's River at Callan some time in the AD 840s while attempting to save a servant, and his body washed up near Kells. His final resting place lies beyond the church grounds because he wasn't a Christian.

Callan Famine Graveyard

About 10km west of Kilree, and signposted off the main road 2km south of Callan, is a **cemetery** where the local victims of the Great Famine are buried. It isn't much to look at, but the unmarked graves are a poignant reminder of the anonymity of starvation.

THOMASTOWN & AROUND

☎ 056 / pop 1704

Thomastown is a small market town nicely situated by the Nore. Unfortunately the Dublin–Waterford road (N9) runs right through the centre, and the traffic can be horrific. Named after Welsh mercenary Thomas de Cantwell, Thomastown has some fragments of a medieval wall and the partly ruined 13th-century **Church of St Mary**. Down by the bridge, **Mullin's Castle** is the sole survivor of the 14 castles that were originally here.

At the edge of town, there's a craft shop at **Grennan Mill Craft School** (☎ 792 4557; Waterford road; 🕑 9am-5pm Mon-Sat).

Jerpoint Abbey

About 1.5km southwest of Thomastown is **Jerpoint Abbey** (☎ 24623; Hwy N9; adult/child €2.75/1.25; 🕑 9.30am-6.30pm Jun-Sep, 10am-4pm Oct-May), one of Ireland's finest Cistercian ruins. It was established in the 12th century and has been partially restored. The fine tower and cloister are late 14th or early 15th century. Fragments of the cloister are particularly interesting, with a series of often amusing figures carved on the pillars. There are also stone carvings on the church walls and in the tombs of members of the Butler and Walshe families. Faint traces of a 15th- or 16th-century painting remain on the northern wall of the church. This chancel area also contains a tomb thought to be that of Felix O'Dullany, Jerpoint's first abbot and bishop of Ossory, who died back in 1202.

According to local legend, St Nicholas (or Santa Claus) is buried near the abbey. While retreating in the Crusades, the knights of Jerpoint removed his body from Myra in modern-day Turkey and reburied him in the **Church of St Nicholas** to the west of the abbey. The grave is marked by a broken slab decorated with a carving of a monk.

A few kilometres from Jerpoint Abbey, in the town of Stonyford, and housed in an old stone-walled farm building is the nationally renowned **Jerpoint Glass Studio** (☎ 24350; enquiries@jerpointglass.com; Stonyford; ☺ 9am-6pm Mon-Fri, 10am-6pm Sat, noon-5pm Sun). Many of the pieces produced here are extremely beautiful. You can watch glass-blowers at work 9am to 5pm Monday to Thursday and 9am to 2pm Friday.

Kilfane

The village of Kilfane, 3km north of Thomastown on the Dublin road, has a small, ruined **13th-century church** and **Norman tower**, 50m off the road and signposted. The church has a remarkable stone carving of Thomas de Cantwell called the Cantwell Fada or Long Cantwell. It depicts a tall, thin knight in detailed chain-mail armour brandishing a shield decorated with the Cantwell coat of arms.

Kilfane Glen & Waterfall (☎ 24558; admission €5; ☺ 11am-6pm daily Jul & Aug, 2-6pm Sun Apr, Jun & Sep) is a pretty spot with wooded paths winding through its wild 6-hectare gardens, which date from the 1790s. An elaborately decorated thatched cottage is worth hiking to. The top part of the garden is replete with works by Irish artists. Kilfane Glen is 2km north of town along the N9.

Sleeping & Eating

Ballyduff House (☎ 775 8488; ballyd@gofree.indigo .ie; Thomastown; s/d €51/76, ☺ Mar-Oct; Ⓟ) Here's fine Irish country living at an affordable price. This 18th-century manor is set in wooded grounds overlooking the River Nore. Children are welcome.

Hudsons (☎ 779 3900; Station Rd, Thomastown; set dinner €25; ☺ 6-10pm Tue-Sun) This Thomastown restaurant is atmospheric, friendly and contemporary. Modern classics such as grilled meats, seared salmon and Caesar salad make regular appearances on a daily menu that emphasises fresh local ingredients.

Getting There & Away

Bus Éireann (☎ 64933) operates daily buses between Dublin and Waterford with stops at Gowran and Thomastown. One service daily links Waterford with Longford via Thomastown and Kilkenny. Buses stop outside O'Keeffe's supermarket on Main St. From Kilkenny, the fare to Thomastown is €6/8 one way/return.

The train station is 1km west of town past Kavanagh's supermarket.

INISTIOGE

☎ 056 / pop 714

The little village of Inistioge (in-ish-teeg) is picture-perfect. It has a 10-arch stone bridge spanning the Nore, a tranquil square and antiquated shop signs. Somewhere so inviting could hardly hope to escape the attention of cinema location scouts: Inistioge's film credits include *Widow's Peak* (1993), *Circle of Friends* (1994) and *Where the Sun Is King* (1996). With a scenic stretch of the South Leinster Way coursing through town, this is a good base for exploring the region on foot, by bike or motor vehicle.

Approximately 1km south, on Mt Alto, is **Woodstock Park**. The hike up is well worth the effort for the panorama of the valley below, and the heavily forested park itself is a beauty, with acres of gardens, picnic areas and trails. For more fine walks, follow the riverbank and climb any of the surrounding hills.

Woodstock Arms B&B (☎ 775 8440; www.wood stockarms.com; Inistioge; s/d €40/60) The interior of this pub has been rather plainly remodelled, but on a warm day you'll want to have a pint on the front patio, overlooking the pretty square. This is also a B&B, with utilitarian but sparkly clean rooms, all with bathroom.

Motte Restaurant (☎ 775 8655; Plas Newydd Lodge; set dinner €37; ☺ 7-9.30pm Tue-Sat) This beautiful country restaurant has a delightful contemporary Irish menu. It's very welcoming and relaxed, and diners can linger over cordials and conversation long after supper is over.

Getting There & Away

Infrequent buses operate between New Ross and Kilkenny, calling in at Inistioge on the way.

COUNTY KILKENNY

WALKING COUNTY KILKENNY

South Leinster Way slices through the hilly southern part of County Kilkenny, from Graiguena-managh through Inistioge, down to Mullinavat and westward to Piltown. It looks attractive on the map, but in reality much of it is paved highway, and not particularly good for walking. Stick with the prettiest part, a stretch of some 13km, beginning on the River Barrow. It links Graigue and Inistioge, two charming villages with amenities for travellers. In either village you can reward yourself with a top-notch meal.

Alternatively, along this path branch off onto **Brandon Way** (4km south of Graigue), which scales **Brandon Hill** (516m). The broad moorland summit is easily reached and affords a lovely view of the Blackstairs Mountains and Mt Leinster to the east. A return trip from Graigue is a fairly relaxed 12km walk.

The trail down **River Barrow** from Graigue to St Mullins is equally beautiful, with a firm path wending past canals and through some wooded country and pleasant grassy picnic areas. **St Mullins** itself is an interesting destination (see below).

GRAIGUENAMANAGH

☎ 059 / pop 1620

Graiguenamanagh (greg-na-mana) is a picturesque town on a lovely stretch of the Barrow, 23km southeast of Kilkenny. The town's best feature is its six-arch stone bridge that is illuminated at night. Along the river there's a lovely wooded walk, of about 1½ hours, to St Mullins, just a few kilometres downstream from town, and another up Brandon Hill (516m), about 6km away.

Dating back to 1204, **Duiske Abbey** (☎ 24238 ⌚ 10am-5pm Mon-Fri year round, 2-5pm Sat & Sun Jun & Aug) was once Ireland's largest Cistercian abbey. It has now been completely restored and its pleasantly simple, whitewashed interior is in everyday use. Its name comes from the Irish *Dubh Uisce* (Black Water), a tributary of the Barrow. Inside the abbey, to the right of the entrance, is the Knight of Duiske, a 14th-century, high-relief carving of a knight in chain mail who's reaching for his sword. On the floor nearby, a glass panel reveals some of the original 13th-century floor tiles, now 2m below the present floor level. In the grounds stand two early high crosses, brought here for protection in the last century. The smaller Ballyogan Cross has panels on the eastern side depicting the crucifixion, Adam and Eve, Abraham's sacrifice of Isaac, and David playing the harp. The western side shows the massacre of the innocents.

Around the corner, the **Abbey Centre** (⌚ 10am-1pm & 2-5pm Mon-Fri) houses a small exhibition of Christian art, plus pictures of the abbey in its unrestored state.

Waterside (☎ 792 4246; www.watersideguesthouse .com; Quay Graiguenamanagh; s/d from €57/94, set dinner €32; ⌚ restaurant 6.30-9.30pm Mon-Sat, 12.30-2.30pm & 6.30-9.30pm Sun), in a converted stone warehouse, is a three-star hotel that overlooks the River Barrow. Breakfast is included with accommodation; dinner is optional. Off the lobby is one of the county's most exceptional restaurants (try the venison fillet). The hotel offers many specials.

Anchor Bar (☎ 792 4207; Lower Main St; s/d €30/60), just a few paces from the river, is also a B&B and does quite serviceable pub grub day and night.

For fishing tackle, canned vegetables and a pint of Guinness, head to **Mick Doyle's** or **Mick Ryan's**, two old pubs on Abbey St that admirably attempt to address their customers' basic needs.

ST MULLINS

A tranquil spot just a few kilometres downstream from Graiguenamanagh, St Mullins (on the County Carlow line) is good for a relaxing getaway, a picnic, or as rewarding destination on a long walk from Graigue. The river snakes through here in the shadow of Brandon Hill, and from it a trail winds uphill to the ruined hulk of an old monastery surrounded by the graves of 1798 rebels. A 9th-century Celtic cross, badly worn down over the centuries, still stands beside the monastery. Nearby, St Moling's Well is a holy well that seems to attract spare change.

Mulvarra House (☎ 051-424 936; www.mulvarra .com; s/d €40/68) is a B&B just up the hill from the river. It's modern and comfortable, a good base for exploring the area.

NORTHERN KILKENNY

The rolling green hills of northern County Kilkenny are perfect for leisurely drives with a picnic lunch stowed away in the backseat of the car. There's not a whole lot going on in this part of the county, but the picturesque towns of Ballyragget and Castlecomer are sure to tempt the traveller to pull over for a brief stroll. Dunmore Cave is the most frequently visited sight in these parts, and the hostel at Foulksrath Castle is reason enough to work the area into your plans for a night or so.

CASTLECOMER & AROUND
☎ 056 / pop 2319

Comely Castlecomer is on the gentle River Dinin, some 18km north of Kilkenny. The town became a centre for anthracite mining after the fuel was discovered nearby in 1636; the mines closed for good in the mid-1960s. The anthracite was widely regarded as being Europe's best, containing very little sulphur and producing almost no smoke.

About 8km west of Castlecomer is Ballyragget, with an almost-intact square tower in the 16th-century **Butler Castle** (closed to the public).

Almost 2km south of Ballyragget is **Swifte's Heath**, home to Jonathan Swift during his school years in Kilkenny. The 'e' was evidently dropped from the name before the satirist gained notoriety as the author of *Gulliver's Travels* and *A Modest Proposal*.

Foulksrath Castle (☎ 67674; foulksrath@eircom .net; Ballyragget; dm €13-14; P) is a busy An Óige hostel near Ballyragget with a superb setting, and surely rates among Ireland's best budget accommodations. Buggy's Coaches runs to Kilkenny most days.

Getting There & Away
The **Bus Éireann** (☎ 64933) bus stops outside Houlihan's in Castlecomer. **Buggy's Coaches** (☎ 444 1264) runs a service from Kilkenny to Castlecomer; four buses leave in each direction Monday to Saturday (€2, 25 minutes).

DUNMORE CAVE

Striking calcite formations emblazon **Dunmore Cave** (☎ 056-67726; Ballyfoyle; adult/child €2.75/1.25; ⏰ 10am-5pm Mar-Oct, 10am-7pm summer; 10am-4.30pm winter), some 10km north of Kilkenny on the Castlecomer road (N78). According to sources, marauding Vikings killed 1000 people at two ring forts near here in AD 928. When survivors hid in the caverns, the Vikings tried to smoke them out by lighting fires at the entrance. It's thought that they then dragged off the men as slaves and left the women and children to suffocate. Excavations in 1973 uncovered the skeletons of at least 44 people, mostly women and children. They also found coins dating from the AD 920s but none from a later date. One theory suggests that the coins were dropped by the Vikings (who often carried them in their armpits, secured with wax) while enthusiastically engaged in the slaughter. However, there are few marks of violence on the skeletons, lending weight to the theory that suffocation was the cause of death.

The cave is well lit and spacious. After a steep descent you enter caverns full of stalactites, stalagmites and columns, including the 7m Market Cross, Europe's largest freestanding stalagmite. It's damp and cold in the cave, so wear a sweater. The compulsory guided tours are worthwhile.

Buggy's Coaches (☎ 056-444 1264) runs four buses a day Monday to Saturday (return €4) from the Parade in Kilkenny, dropping you off 1km from the cave.

COUNTY KILKENNY

Central South

CENTRAL SOUTH

Lush farmland, rolling hills, magnificent Georgian homes and vast tracts of bog make up the four midland counties of Kildare, Carlow, Laois and Offaly. Scratch the surface and you'll find a region shaped by its ancient pagan past, its monastic settlements, its planters and its waterways.

Many of the best attractions are within easy reach of Dublin. The remarkably laid-back National Stud in Kildare gives you the chance to come muzzle to muzzle with some of the country's most famous ex-racehorses. Castletown House, the architectural forerunner of the White House, is one of Ireland's most impeccable country homes. A little further afield is the restored Georgian town of Birr, home to a historic castle and a giant 19th-century telescope used to map the moon.

Other highlights include Europe's biggest dolmen, just outside Carlow town; the elegant Moone High Cross in Kildare; and most impressive of all, Clonmacnoise, Ireland's most important monastic site, on the banks of the River Shannon.

HIGHLIGHTS

■ **Horses Galore**
The hysteria of the Curragh racecourse (p333), and watching future winners being born at the Irish National Stud (p334)

■ **Most Perfect Town**
Birr's (p346) Georgian splendour, its castle, and its top-quality restaurants

■ **The Best Damned Monastery in Ireland**
Sailing on a Viking ship (p480) to Ireland's finest monastic site, Clonmacnoise (p351)

■ **Who Ya Gonna Call?**
Ghostbusting at Leap Castle (p349), Ireland's most haunted building

■ **Environmental Action**
Learning about Ireland's peat bogs before they end up as garden compost, on the Clonmacnoise & West Offaly Railway Bog Tour (p351) and at the Bog of Allen Nature Centre (p333)

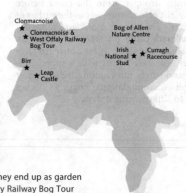

■ POPULATION: 332,395

■ AREA: 6301 SQ KM

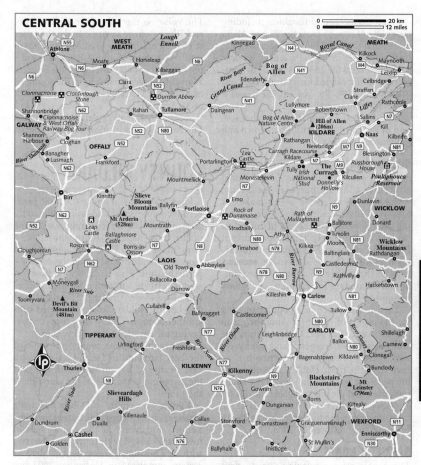

CENTRAL SOUTH

GRAND & ROYAL CANALS

The Grand and Royal Canals revolutionised transport in Ireland in the 18th century, but their heyday was short-lived and the railways soon superseded them. Today they're favoured for cruising and fishing, and for their easy walking and cycling.

For history, canal maps, ecology and coarse fishing information, try the *Guide to the Grand Canal of Ireland* and the *Guide to the Royal Canal of Ireland*, both sold in tourist offices and bookshops in the region.

GRAND CANAL

The Grand Canal threads its way from Dublin to Robertstown in County Kildare, where one branch continues west through Tullamore before joining the River Shannon, while the other turns south to join the River Barrow at Athy; a total of 130km in all.

The canal passes through relatively unpopulated countryside. Flowers, fens, picturesque villages and 36 finely crafted locks line the journey; if you're lucky you'll see otters. Near the village of Sallins, the graceful seven-arched **Leinster Aqueduct** carries the canal across the River Liffey, while further south sections of the River Barrow are particularly delightful.

Huge engineering difficulties, including the riddle of how to cross the Bog of Allen, meant that the canal took 23 years to build, finally opening in 1779. Passenger services continued until the 1850s. A trickle of commercial traffic carried turf, porter, coal and grain until 1960; the last shipment was a bargeful of Guinness!

For detailed information on the section of the canal between Robertstown and Lullymore, see p332.

ROYAL CANAL

Fourteen years behind the Grand Canal and duplicating its purpose, the 145km Royal Canal was always a loss-maker. It follows Kildare's northern border, passing an impressive backdrop of historical landmarks and stately homes, including St Patrick's College in Maynooth and Castletown House. There's a massive **aqueduct** near Leixlip, before it joins the River Shannon at Cloondara (or Clondra) in County Longford.

The canal has become a popular amenity for thousands of residents along the north Kildare commuter belt. Consequently, bus and rail services are good, and a leisurely walk between Leixlip and Maynooth is an easy day trip from Dublin. Although the towpaths are open all the way to the Shannon, the canal itself is navigable only as far as Abbeyshrule in County Longford. At the time of writing, the final stretch was due to be completely restored by 2006.

BARGES & BOATS

The canals offer a relaxing way to drift across the country; you can hire narrow boats at several locations. Two-/eight-berth boats cost about €650/1000 in September and about €1200/1600 in July and August.

Barrowline Cruisers (☎ 0502-25189; www.barrow line.ie; Vicarstown Inn, Vicarstown, Co Laois) Grand Canal and River Barrow.

Canalways (☎ 045-524 646; www.canalways.ie; Rathangan, Co Kildare) Grand Canal and River Barrow.

Leisureways Holidays (☎ 01-822 5034; www.leisure ways.com; Twelfth Lock, Dublin) Royal Canal.

WALKING THE TOWPATHS

Canal towpaths are ideal for leisurely walkers and there are numerous access points along both canals. Robertstown is a good starting point for long-distance rambles.

The village is the hub of the Kildare Way and River Barrow towpath trails, the latter stretching all the way to St Mullin's, 95km south in County Carlow. From there it's possible to connect with the South Leinster Way at Graiguenamanagh, or the southern end of the Wicklow Way at Clonegal, north of Mt Leinster.

A variety of leaflets detailing the paths can be picked up at most regional tourist offices.

COUNTY KILDARE

Kildare (Cill Dara) is one of the most prosperous counties in Ireland, with fertile soil, a growing population of commuters and some of the most lucrative thoroughbred stud farms in the world. The multimillion-pound bloodstock industry thrives in the county – partly because Irish law levies no taxes on stud fees (thanks to former prime minister and horse owner Charles J Haughey), and also because Kildare town is twinned with another famous horse-breeding centre, Lexington-Fayette in Kentucky, USA.

Geographically, the county has some of the best farmland in Ireland, as well as a vast swathe of bog to the northwest and the sweeping grasslands of the Curragh to the south.

Kildare's proximity to Dublin has made it an increasingly appealing option for commuters, and many of the county's main towns are choked with traffic and overrun with new housing developments. A bypass system completed in December 2003 has eased traffic congestion somewhat.

MAYNOOTH

☎ 01 / pop 10,151

The university gives Maynooth (Maigh Nuad) a vibrant edge. The small town has a pretty tree-lined main street with stone-fronted houses and shops, and easy access to the Royal Canal.

Orientation & Information

Main St runs east–west, while Leinster St runs south to the canal and the train station (accessed via a couple of footbridges).

Tech Store (☎ 629 1747; info@techstore.ie; Unit 5, Glenroyal Shopping Centre; per hr €5; 🕑 11am-11pm Mon-Fri, noon-8pm Sat & Sun) Surf the Internet here.

Sights
ST PATRICK'S COLLEGE
St Patrick's College & Seminary (☎ 628 5222; Main St) has been turning out Catholic priests since 1795. Ironically, it was founded by the English in an attempt to steer Irish priests away from the dangerous ideals of revolution and republicanism being taught in France. The college joined the National University in 1910 and currently has about 5500 students. However, the number of young men studying for the priesthood has fallen dramatically during recent years. At the time of writing there were only 60 seminarians.

The college buildings are impressive – Pugin had a hand in designing them – and well worth an hour's ramble. You enter the college via Georgian Stoyte House, where the **accommodation office** (☎ 708 3576; ☽ 8.30am-5.30pm & 8-11pm Mon-Fri, 8.30am-12.30pm & 1.30-11pm Sat & Sun) sells booklets (€4) for guiding yourself around. There is also a small **science museum** (admission by donation; ☽ 2-4pm Mon-Fri, 3-5pm Sun Apr-Sep). The college grounds contain a number of lofty Georgian and neo-Gothic buildings, gardens and squares, but the highlight of the tour has to be the College Chapel. Pull open the squeaky door and you enter the world's largest choir chapel, with stalls for more than 450 choristers and some magnificent ornamentation.

MAYNOOTH CASTLE
Near the entrance to St Patrick's College you can see the ruined gatehouse, keep and great hall of 13th-century **Maynooth Castle** (☎ 628 6744; maynoothcastle@opw.ie; admission free; ☽ 10am-6pm Mon-Fri, 1-6pm Sat & Sun Jun-Sep, 1-5pm Sun Oct), home of the Fitzgerald family. The castle was dismantled in Cromwellian times, when the Fitzgeralds moved to Kilkea Castle (see p337). Entry is by a 45-minute guided tour only; there's a small exhibition on the castle's history in the keep.

Activities
Leixlip, on the River Liffey between Maynooth and Dublin, is an important **canoeing** centre and the starting point of the Irish Sprint Canoe Championships and annual 28km International Liffey Descent Race (usually the first Saturday in September). Just to spice things up, the Electricity Sup-

ply Board releases 30 million tonnes of water into the river just before the races. For more information on canoeing in Ireland, try www.irishcanoeunion.com.

Sleeping
Maynooth is only 30 minutes from Dublin airport and makes a convenient base for your first or last night in Ireland if you want to avoid the city.

NUI Maynooth (☎ 708 6200; www.maynooth campus.com; s/d €26/44, with bathroom from €63/86; (P)) The university campus has a variety of good-value rooms, mostly in the modern north campus. Singles and apartments in the south campus, where the accommodation office is, are strewn around the courts and gardens of atmospheric St Patrick's College. Availability is higher in the summer months.

Glenroyal Hotel & Leisure Club (☎ 629 0909; www.glenroyal.ie; Straffan Rd; s/d from €115/168; (P) (⪧)) This modern hotel is tailored to corporate clients and weddings but also provides excellent facilities for the passing tourist. Although the design is a little predictable, rooms are spacious and spotless, and there are *two* swimming pools.

Moyglare Manor (☎ 628 6351; www.moyglare manor.ie; R157; s/d €160/260; (P)) This charming 18th-century manor, 3.5km north of Maynooth, is one of Ireland's best country houses. Despite the sumptuous decoration and period furniture (including some curtained four-poster beds), the atmosphere is incredibly relaxed and the excellent restaurant (open 12.30pm to 2.30pm Sunday and Monday, plus 7pm to 9pm daily, set menu €50) is open to nonresidents.

Eating
Stone Haven (☎ 629 1229; stonehavenrest@eircom .net; 1 Mill St; mains €12-15; ☽ 5-9.30pm Tue-Sun) The cut-stone walls and warm orangey alcoves give this restaurant, set in a 200-year-old building, a friendly atmosphere. The modern menu has some adventurous choices, including kangaroo and ostrich, and there are good veggie options.

Coffee Mill (☎ 601 6594; Mill St; lunch €4-6; ☽ 9am-5pm Mon-Sat) A favourite local lunching place tucked away in a basement, the Coffee Mill serves a good selection of deli-style lunches, interesting sandwiches, home-made cakes and hotplate dishes.

CENTRAL SOUTH

Getting There & Away

Dublin Bus (☎ 01-873 4222; www.dublinbus.ie) runs a service to Maynooth (€2.10) every 25 minutes from Pearse St in Dublin.

Maynooth is on the main Dublin–Sligo line, with regular trains in each direction: to Dublin (€2.70, 45 minutes, seven per day Monday to Friday, three Saturday, four Sunday); to Sligo (€33.50, two hours 40 minutes, two per day Monday to Saturday, three Sunday).

AROUND MAYNOOTH

Celbridge

Castletown House is a huge Palladian **mansion** (☎ 628 8252; adult/child €3.50/1.25; 🕑 10am-6pm Mon-Fri, 1-6pm Sat & Sun Easter-Sep, 10am-5pm Mon-Fri, 1-5pm Sun Oct, 1-5pm Sun Nov, last admission 1hr before closing), one of Ireland's finest. A lengthy tree-lined avenue leads up to the imposing façade, and the exquisite interior has been completely restored. Entry is by one-hour guided tour only.

The house was built between 1722 and 1732 for William Conolly, a humble publican's son who became speaker of the Irish House of Commons and the richest man in Ireland. It was designed by Alessandro Galilei, and his avant-garde building (a central block flanked by curved curtain walls) soon became the model for many of Ireland's country houses, and eventually the White House!

There are two follies in the grounds commissioned by Conolly's widow, Katherine, to give employment to the poor after the 1739 famine. The **obelisk** can be seen from the Long Gallery at the back of the house, while the Heath-Robinsonesque **Wonderful Barn**, six teetering storeys wrapped by an exterior spiral staircase, is on private property just outside Leixlip. At the time of writing, there was a scandalous plan to build 476 houses around it.

Bus Nos 120 and 123 run from Dublin to Celbridge (€3, 30 minutes, every half-hour Monday to Friday, hourly Saturday, six buses Sunday).

Larchill Arcadian Gardens

The **gardens** (☎ 628 7354; www.larchill.ie; Kilcock; adult/child €7.50/5.50; 🕑 noon-6pm Tue-Sun Jun-Aug, noon-6pm Sat & Sun Sep) are Europe's only example of a mid-18th-century *ferme ornée* (ornamental farm). A 40-minute walk takes you through beautiful landscaped parklands, passing eccentric follies (including a model of the Gibraltar fortress and a shell-decorated tower), gazebos and a lake. Children will be chuffed with the adventure playground, maze and rare-breed farm animals.

The gardens are 5km north of Kilcock on Dunsaughlin Rd (R125).

STRAFFAN

☎ 01 / pop 332

Teeny Straffan is famous for its luxurious hotel, the K Club (see the boxed text, opposite), but there are a few gentle entertainments to be had too.

The **Steam Museum & Lodge Park Walled Garden** (☎ 627 3155; www.steam-museum.ie; adult/concession €7.50/5; 🕑 2-6pm Wed-Sun Jun-Aug) traces the history of steam power and the Industrial Revolution. The collection includes working steam engines from breweries, distilleries, factories and ships. Next door, the 18th-century walled garden contains a sweet-scented rosery, best seen in July and August.

Just down the road at the **Straffan Butterfly Farm** (☎ 627 1109; www.straffanbutterflyfarm.com; Ovidstown; adult/child €7/4; 🕑 noon-5.30pm Jun-Aug), you can wander through a tropical greenhouse full of enormous exotic butterflies, or peer at the stick insects, bird-eating spiders and reptiles kept safely behind glass.

Bus Éireann Nos 120 and 123 run from Dublin (via Maynooth) to Celbridge (€3.50, 40 minutes, every half hour Monday to Friday, hourly Saturday, six buses Sunday).

BOG OF ALLEN

Stretching like a brown, dusty desert through Kildare, Laois and Offaly, the Bog of Allen is Ireland's best-known raised bog, and once covered much of the midlands. Unfortunately, in a pattern repeated across Ireland, the peat is rapidly being turned into potting compost and fuel. For details of the Clonmacnoise & West Offaly Railway Bog Tour, see p351. The Bog of Allen Nature Centre is further along the Grand Canal.

ALONG THE GRAND CANAL

Heading west from Straffan, there are some interesting sites as you follow the banks of the Grand Canal. Just past Clane it's worth making the short detour to tiny, tranquil **Robertstown**. This picturesque village has

---

THE 2006 RYDER CUP & THE K CLUB

In September 2006, for the first time, the **Ryder Cup** (www.europeantour.com) will be held in Ireland. For one wild weekend, the world's golfing cognoscenti will descend on the tiny village of Straffan for the biennial tournament, which sees the best US golfers pitted against the best of the Europeans.

The cup will be hosted by the **K Club** (Kildare Hotel & Country Club; ☎ 601 7200; www.kclub.ie; Straffan; d €395-445, ste €625-3800; **P**), a Georgian estate and golfers' paradise, and one of the most fabulous hotels in Europe. Its first golf course, designed by Arnold Palmer, is one of the best in Ireland and has been the home of the European Open since 1995. A second championship course was opened in 2003 and, despite the added fairways and the stiff green fees (up to €250), you'd be well advised to book in advance.

Any self-respecting golf fanatic will at least have a drink at the bar; but if you were thinking of wallowing in luxury at the hotel during the Ryder Cup, think again – accommodation was fully booked by the end of 2004.

---

remained largely untouched and is dominated by the now-dilapidated Grand Canal Hotel, built in 1801. It's a good place to start a canal walk (see p330).

Just southwest of Robertstown and at the centre of the Kildare flatlands, the **Hill of Allen** (206m) was a strategic spot through the centuries due to its 360-degree view. Today the top is marked by a 19th-century folly and the ruins of some Iron Age fortifications said to mark the home of Fionn McCumhaill.

Further west you'll find the interpretive **Bog of Allen Nature Centre** (☎ 045-860 133; www.ipcc.ie; R414, Lullymore; suggested donation €5; 9.30am-5pm Mon-Fri), a run-down institution recently taken over by the charitable Irish Peatland Conservation Council who intend to completely revamp it. The centre traces the history of bogs and peat production, and has the largest carnivorous plant collection in Ireland – sundews, butterworts and pitcher plants, all native to bogs.

For an excellent family day out, visit the friendly **Lullymore Heritage & Discovery Park** (☎ 045-870 238; www.lullymorepark.com; Lullymore; adult/child €9/8; 9.30am-6pm Mon-Fri, 11am-6pm Sat & Sun Easter-Oct, 11am-6pm Sat & Sun Nov-Easter), about 1km south of the Bog of Allen Nature Centre. A woodland trail leads you past various dwellings (including Neolithic huts, a Famine-era house and an enchanting fairy village), and there's crazy golf, a road train and an adventure park. The Funky Forest, an indoor adventure playground, opened in 2005, so there's entertainment even if it's raining.

For information on hiring narrow boats on the canal, see p330.

NEWBRIDGE & THE CURRAGH
☎ 045 / pop 15,749

The fairly unremarkable town of Newbridge (Droichead Nua) is known for its silverware, and you can visit the **Newbridge Silverware Showroom** (☎ 431 301; www.newbridgecutlery.com; 9am-5.15pm Mon-Sat, 11am-5pm Sun). However, the town is infinitely more famous as the gateway to the Curragh, one of the country's largest pieces of unfenced fertile land and the centre of the Irish horse industry. In the past, the area housed a large internment camp, but all that remains is Curragh Camp, a large barracks used by the Irish army.

Today the Curragh is renowned for its **racecourse** (☎ 441 205; www.curragh.ie; admission around €20; mid-Apr–Oct), the oldest and most prestigious in the country. Even if you're not a horsey type, it's well worth experiencing the passion, atmosphere and general craic of a day at the races, which can verge on mass hysteria. If you miss the chance to have a flutter, you can still see some action: if you get up early or pass by in the late evening, you'll see the thoroughbreds exercising on the wide-open spaces surrounding the racecourse.

The N7 runs through the Curragh between Newbridge and Kildare town. The No 123 Dublin–Naas (twice daily Monday to Saturday), No 124 Dublin–Mountmellick (one daily Monday to Saturday) and No 126 Dublin–Kildare (12 daily Monday to Saturday, seven Sunday) buses stop in Newbridge and at Curragh Camp (€7, one hour).

The Dublin–Kildare **train** (☎ 01-836 6222) runs from Heuston train station and stops in Newbridge (€10.50, 30 minutes, about every hour between 6.15am and 10.45pm Monday to Saturday, seven trains Sunday).

CENTRAL SOUTH

CHRISTY MOORE: THE TRADITION MOVES ON *by Stuart Cooper*

A native of Newbridge, County Kildare, Christy Moore is one of Ireland's best-known, and certainly best-loved, singers in the traditional mode. Combining a ready wit and puckish charm with his undoubted talent, he has produced more than 20 solo albums of breathtaking diversity and scope.

The causes he has championed – travellers, anti-nuclear protests, South Africa, Northern Ireland – might give one the wrong impression: Christy is equally at home singing tender love songs ('Nancy Spain'), haunting ballads ('Ride On'), comic ditties ('Lisdoovarna') and bizarre flights of lyrical fancy ('Reel in the Flickering Light'). He was also influential as a member of Planxty and Moving Hearts, as Ireland experimented during the 1970s and 1980s with its traditional musical forms to combine folk, rock and jazz in a heady and vibrant fusion.

Born in 1945, Moore grew up the son of a grocer and was influenced early in his musical career by a traveller, John Riley. He was denied the musical opportunities he craved in Ireland and left in 1966 for England, where he quickly became popular on the British folk scene in Manchester and West Yorkshire.

Moore's first big break came with *Prosperous* (named after the Kildare town), on which he teamed up with the legendary Donal Lunny, Andy Irvine and Liam O'Flynn. They went on to form Planxty and record three ground-breaking albums.

Among all the phoney Oirishness, Moore stands out as the genuine article: passionate, provocative and distinctive. He has built an international reputation as a writer and interpreter of a living tradition, at the head of the table of Irish traditional music.

Recommended listening: *The Christy Moore Collection, 81-91.*

KILDARE TOWN

☎ 045 / pop 5694

Kildare is a small cathedral and market town, strongly associated with one of Ireland's best-loved saints, St Brigid. Its busy triangular square is a pleasant place outside rush hour.

Information

The **Tourist Office & Heritage Centre** (☎ 521 240; kildaretownheritagecen@ireland.com; Market House, Market Sq; ☯ 9.30am-1pm & 2-5.30pm Mon-Sat May-Sep, 10am-1pm & 2-5pm Mon-Fri but subject to change Oct-Apr) also features a **multimedia exhibition** (admission €1), outlining Kildare's history. Check out www.kildare.ie for plenty of information about the town.

Sights

ST BRIGID'S CATHEDRAL

The solid presence of 13th-century **St Brigid's Cathedral** (☎ 521 229; Market Sq; admission by donation; ☯ 10am-1pm & 2-5pm Mon-Sat, 2-5pm Sun May-Sep) looms over Kildare Sq. Look out for a fine stained-glass window inside that depicts the three main saints of Ireland: Patrick, Brigid and Colmcille. The church also contains the restored tomb of Walter Wellesley, Bishop of Kildare, which disappeared soon after his death in 1539 and was only found again in 1971. One of its carved figures has been variously interpreted as an acrobat or a sheila-na-gig.

The 10th-century **round tower** (admission €4) in the grounds is Ireland's second highest at 32.9m, and one of the few that you can climb, provided the guardian is around. Its original conical roof has been replaced with an unusual Norman battlement. Near the tower is a **wishing stone** – put your arm through the hole and touch your shoulder and your wish will be granted. On the north side of the cathedral are the restored foundations of an ancient **fire temple** (see the boxed text, opposite

IRISH NATIONAL STUD & JAPANESE GARDENS

Do not miss the **Irish National Stud** (☎ 521 617; www.irish-national-stud.ie; Tully; adult/child €9/4.50; ☯ 9.30am-6pm mid-Feb–mid-Nov, last admission 5pm), about 3km south of Kildare, which was founded by Colonel Hall Walker (of Johnnie Walker whiskey fame) in 1900. He was remarkably successful with his horses, but his eccentric breeding technique relied heavily on astrology: the fate of a foal was decided by its horoscope and the roofs of the stallion boxes opened on auspicious occasions to reveal the heavens and duly influence the horses' fortunes. Today the immaculately kept centre is owned and managed by the Irish government. It breeds high-quality stallions to mate with mares from all over the world.

There are guided tours of the stud every hour on the hour, with access to the intensive-care unit for newborn foals. If you visit between February and June, you might even see a foal being born. Alternatively, the foaling unit shows a 10-minute video with all the action. Afterwards you can visit the small but interesting **Irish Horse Museum**, which examines the role horses have played in Irish life. Also fascinating are the stables and paddocks, where the centre's most famous tenant lives. 'Sire of sires', 21-year-old Indian Ridge, has a straw allergy and is bedded on shredded paper. He covers 75 mares a season for €75,000 each, and is insured for over €25 million.

Next door, the delightful **Japanese Gardens** (☎ 522 963; admission incl in Irish National Stud) are considered to be the best of their kind in Europe. Created between 1906 and 1910, they trace the journey from birth to death through 20 landmarks, including the Tunnel of Ignorance, the Hill of Ambition and the Gateway to Eternity.

Also on the grounds is **St Fiachra's Garden** with a mixture of bog oak, gushing water, replica monastic cells and an underground crystal garden of dubious distinction. Both gardens are great for a relaxing stroll, provided it isn't raining, and if it is, the large visitor centre houses a café, shop and children's play area. A tour of the stud and gardens takes about three hours.

Lying outside the site, behind the museum, are the ruins of a 12th-century **Black Abbey**. Just off the road back to Kildare is **St Brigid's Well**, where five stones represent different aspects of Brigid's life.

Sleeping

Martinstown House (☎ 441 269; www.martinstown house.com; The Curragh; s/d €140/220; 🕑 mid-Jan–mid-Dec; P) This beautiful 18th-century country manor is built in the 'strawberry hill' Gothic style and set in a 200-acre estate surrounded by trees. The house has a terrific atmosphere and rooms so elegant they're off limits to small children. If there are enough guests, the restaurant serves a very generous set dinner (€55), with fruit and veg from the house's walled garden; you're welcome to second helpings. Room rates drop considerably for stays of two nights or more.

Silken Thomas (☎ 522 232; fax 520 471; Market Sq; s/d €30/65; P) This popular 18th-century town house is a good-value central option with a variety of new and newly refurbished rooms. It's nothing special but makes a convenient place to rest your head.

Curragh Lodge Hotel (☎ 522 144; fax 521 247; s/d €50/100; P) You'll find this conventional Irish hotel about 800m south of town on the N7, the main Dublin road. It's child-friendly, with standard but comfy rooms, a reliable restaurant and regular evening entertainment in the bar.

ST BRIGID

St Brigid is one of Ireland's best-known saints, hailed as an early feminist but also known for her compassion, generosity and beauty. She was a strong-willed character: according to legend, when her father chose her an unwanted suitor, she pulled out her own eye to prove her resolve never to wed. After she had taken her vows, and was mistakenly ordained a bishop rather than nun, her beauty was miraculously restored.

Brigid founded a monastery in Kildare in the 5th century for both nuns and monks, which was unusual at the time. Its most bizarre feature, however, was a perpetual fire tended by 20 virgins. The fire burned continuously until 1220 when the Bishop of Dublin stopped the tradition, citing it as 'un-Christian'. The restored fire pit can be seen in the grounds of St Brigid's Cathedral where a fire is lit on 1 February, St Brigid's feast day.

Brigid was a tireless traveller, and as word of her many miracles spread, her influence stretched across Europe. One legend claims that the medieval Knights of Chivalry chose St Brigid as their patron, and that it was they who first chose to call their wives 'brides'.

Brigid is remembered by a simple reed cross first woven by her to explain the redemption to a dying chief. The cross, said to protect and bless a household, is still found in most rural homes.

Eating

Kristianna's Bistro (☎ 522 985; Market Sq; mains €12-17; ☼ noon-3pm Tue-Fri & Sun & 6-9pm Thu-Sun) This understated restaurant serves a good variety of simple, modern, French-influenced food, like steak Bordelaise, in generous proportions. Seafood is the speciality of the house and well worth trying.

Silken Thomas (☎ 522 232; Market Sq; mains €12-20, carvery lunch €9; ☼ carvery 12.30-3pm, restaurant 6-10pm Wed-Mon) This celebrated pub is a Kildare institution and has a reasonable carvery lunch as well as a more refined restaurant. Bar food is served all day in a not-so-authentic old-world atmosphere of low ceilings, dim lights and open fires.

Getting There & Away

Bus Éireann's Dublin–Ennis express service stops in Kildare (€9, one hour, hourly from Dublin 7.30am to 6.30pm, hourly from Kildare 10am to 7pm). The slower No 126 Dublin–Kildare bus (1½ hours, 12 daily Monday to Saturday, seven Sunday) occasionally stops outside the Irish National Stud and Japanese Gardens; from Dublin, the 9.30am service Monday to Saturday, and the 10am and noon services on Sunday stop there.

The Dublin–Kildare **train** (☎ 01-836 6222) runs from Heuston train station and stops in Kildare (€12, 30 minutes, approximately every 30 minutes Monday to Saturday, 12 trains Sunday).

ATHY

☎ 059 / pop 6049

Strategically placed at the junction of the River Barrow and the Grand Canal, the Anglo-Norman settlement of Athy (Áth Í; a-*thigh*) is a pleasant, unhurried town, but ruined in parts by the imposition of some modern eyesores.

Athy was founded in the 12th century and later became an important defence post. Many of the town's older buildings remain, including the impressive **White's Castle**, a tower built in 1417 to house the garrison. The castle is next to Crom-a-boo Bridge, named after what must be the world's worst battle cry, hollered by the local Geraldine family.

The **Tourist Office & Heritage Centre** (☎ 863 3075; Emily Sq; per 15 min €1; ☼ 10am-5pm Mon-Fri, 2-4pm Sat & Sun May-Oct, 10am-5pm Mon-Fri Nov-Apr)

has Internet access (one computer). The **heritage centre** (adult/child €3/2) traces the history of Athy and has a fascinating exhibit on Antarctic explorer Sir Ernest Shackleton (1874–1922), who was born in nearby Kilkea. On display is one of Shackleton's sledges, acquired from New Zealand where he sold it to pay off his debts!

The post office is on Duke St.

Activities

Athy is a popular centre for coarse, salmon and trout fishing. For equipment and information try **Griffin Hawe Hardware** (☎ 863 1221; www.griffinhawe.ie; 22 Duke St; ☼ 9.30am-5pm Mon-Sat).

Sleeping & Eating

Coursetown House (☎ 863 1101; fax 863 2740; Stradbally Rd; s/d €60/100; P ⑤) This 200-year-old farmhouse is dripping with character and charm and set in beautifully manicured gardens. Just 3km from town on the R428, seek it out for its excellent-value, cool-white-linen rooms and warm atmosphere. There's a big breakfast choice, including a low-fat cooked Irish alternative.

Café de Paor (☎ /fax 863 3155; Emily Sq; mains €5-8; ☼ 9am-5pm Mon-Sat) Good town-centre eating is hard to find. If you're stuck for lunch, you could try the small place, with laminated 1980s-style menus and food to match – there's very little else.

Getting There & Away

Bus Éireann (☎ 01-836 6111) has six buses daily Monday to Saturday (five Sunday) in either direction between Athy and Dublin (one way/return €10/11.50, 1½ hours).

JJ Kavanagh & Sons (in Dublin ☎ 01-679 1549; www.jjkavanagh.ie) runs three buses daily Monday to Saturday (two Sunday) between Dublin (Gresham Hotel, O'Connell St) and Clonmel, stopping in Athy (€5, 1¼ hours).

A circular community **bus service** (☎ 059-863 4758) runs from Athy through Kilkea, Castledermot, Moone, Ballitore and back to Athy five times a day (single trip €3).

DONNELLY'S HOLLOW TO CASTLEDERMOT

This 25km stretch south towards Carlow contains some interesting detours to tiny towns bypassed by the unlovely N9.

CENTRAL SOUTH

Donnelly's Hollow

Dan Donnelly (1788–1820) is revered as Ireland's greatest bare-knuckle fighter of the 19th century. He's also the stuff of legend – his arms were so long, he could supposedly tie his shoelaces without having to bend down! This spot, 4km west of Kilcullen on the R413, was his favourite battleground, and the obelisk at the centre of the hollow details his glorious career.

Ballitore

pop 716

Ballitore is the only planned and permanent Quaker settlement in Ireland, founded by incomers from Yorkshire in the early 18th century. A small **Quaker Museum** (☎ 059-862 3344; ballitorelib@kildarecoco.ie; Mary Leadbeater House, Main St; admission by donation; ◷ noon-5pm Tue-Sat year round, plus 2-6pm Sun Jun-Sep), in a minute and higgledy-piggledy restored house, documents the lives of the community through a folk collection. There's a Quaker cemetery and Meeting House, and a modern **Shaker Store & Tearoom** (☎ 059-862 3372; www.shakerstore.ie; Main St; ◷ 10am-6pm Mon-Fri, 2-6pm Sat & Sun) that sells exquisitely simple wooden toys and furniture.

About 2km west is **Rath of Mullaghmast**, an Iron Age hill fort and standing stone where Daniel O'Connell, champion of Catholic emancipation, held one of his 'monster rallies' in 1843.

Moone

pop 372

Just south of Ballitore, the unassuming village of Moone is home to one of Ireland's most magnificent high crosses. The unusually tall and slender **Moone High Cross** is an 8th- or 9th-century masterpiece, which displays its carved biblical scenes with the confidence and exuberance of a comic strip. The cross can be found 1km west of Moone village in an atmospheric early Christian churchyard.

The charming 18th-century **Moone High Cross Inn** (☎ 0502-24112; www.moonehighcross.com; Bolton Hill; s/d €45/80; ℗), 2km south of Moone, has a few simple en-suite rooms decorated in quaint country-house style. The quirky bar downstairs serves good lunches (€6 to €10) and there's a proper **restaurant** (mains €13-25; ◷ 6-8.45pm), which uses local and organic ingredients. The inn revolves around a Celtic theme, celebrating pagan festivals and

hoarding healing stones, lucky charms and even a 'love stone' in the outside courtyards. It has regular Friday trad sessions and a *sea-nachaí* (traditional storyteller) from 9pm on the third Saturday of the month.

Kilkea Castle

Built in the 12th century, **Kilkea Castle Hotel & Golf Club** (☎ 059-914 5156; www.kilkeacastle.ie; Castledermot; s/d standard €175/225, deluxe €225/280; ℗ ⚹) is Ireland's oldest continuously inhabited castle and has a resident ghost, an air of romance and a long, bloody history. It was once the second home of the Maynooth Fitzgeralds, and the grounds are supposedly haunted by Gerald the Wizard Earl, who rises every seven years from the Rath of Mullaghmast to free Ireland from its enemies – a pretty good trick considering he was buried in London.

The castle was completely restored in the 19th century and is now an exclusive hotel and golf club. Among its exterior oddities is an **Evil Eye Stone**, high up at the back of the castle. Thought to date from the 14th or 15th century, it depicts some very weird goings-on between nightmarish creatures in an 'ithyphallic condition'. No-one seems to agree on the tableau: one figure is variously described as a woman, St Anthony or a gargoyle-headed creature! Take a pair of binoculars and try to figure it out.

The interior decoration is a bit garish but service is excellent, there's a health and fitness centre and the **restaurant** (set dinner €50) is open to nonresidents.

The castle is 5km northwest of Castledermot on the Athy road.

Castledermot

pop 1123

Castledermot was once home to a vast ecclesiastical settlement, but all that remains of St Diarmuid's 9th-century **monastery** is a 20m round tower topped with a medieval battlement. Nearby are two well-preserved, carved 10th-century granite high crosses, a 12th-century Romanesque doorway and a medieval Scandinavian 'hogback' gravestone, the only one in Ireland. Reach the ruins by entering the rusty turnstile on Main St, then walking up the tree-lined avenue to St James' church. At the southern end of town, the ruins of an early 14th-century **Franciscan friary** can be seen by the road.

CENTRAL SOUTH

ffrench's Schoolhouse Restaurant (☎ 059-914 4099; www.theschoolhouse.ie; Main St; s/d €35/70; ☷ restaurant 7-9pm Thu-Sat, 12.30-2.30pm Sun; P) is an intimate inn based, as the name suggests, in a 1920s school. Five simple, elegant rooms are decorated with Victorian and Georgian fixtures and fittings, and are TV-free. The business has changed hands recently, but top-quality organic restaurant meals, served in a mellow atmosphere, are still on offer.

COUNTY CARLOW

Carlow (Ceatharlach), Ireland's second-smallest county, has an understated charm. The pace of life is unhurried, the locals are genuinely glad to see you and the undulating farmland has a beauty all of its own. Dotted around the county are strings of quietly picturesque villages such as Rathvilly, Leighlinbridge and Borris, which have scarcely changed in the past hundred years. The most dramatic chunk of history in these parts is Europe's biggest dolmen, just outside Carlow town.

The scenic Blackstairs Mountains dominate the southeast: their king, Mt Leinster (796m), is one of Ireland's premier hanggliding sites, with stunning views from the summit.

CARLOW TOWN
☎ 059 / pop 13,218

The winding streets and lanes of Carlow have the general upbeat air of a place on the cusp of greater things to come. Buildings are being renovated, trendy cafés and bars are opening up, and there is plenty of nightlife. The town also has its fair share of historic buildings, though not much remains of its medieval foundation.

Orientation & Information

Dublin St is the city's principal north–south axis, with Tullow St, the main shopping street, running off it at a right angle. The County Carlow Museum was being renovated at the time of writing and was due to reopen in 2007: ask the tourist office for details. The post office is on the corner of Kennedy Ave and Dublin St. Take a look at

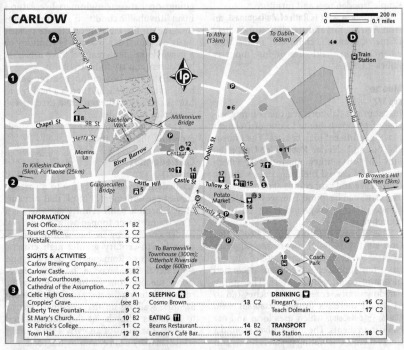

CARLOW

0 ———— 200 m
0 ———— 0.1 miles

To Athy (13km)
To Dublin (68km)
Train Station
Marlborough St
Chapel St
98 St
Bachelor's Walk
Millennium Bridge
Henry St
Morrins La
River Barrow
Centaur St
Dublin St
College St
To Killeshin Church (5km); Portlaoise (25km)
Graiguecullen Bridge
Castle Hill
Castle St
Tullow St
To Browne's Hill Dolmen (3km)
Station Rd
Potato Market
Kennedy Ave
To Barrowville Townhouse (300m); Otterholt Riverside Lodge (600m)
Coach Park
Bus Station

INFORMATION	
Post Office	1 B2
Tourist Office	2 C2
Webtalk	3 C2

SIGHTS & ACTIVITIES	
Carlow Brewing Company	4 D1
Carlow Castle	5 B2
Carlow Courthouse	6 C1
Cathedral of the Assumption	7 C2
Celtic High Cross	8 A1
Croppies' Grave	(see 8)
Liberty Tree Fountain	9 C2
St Mary's Church	10 C2
St Patrick's College	11 C2
Town Hall	12 B2

SLEEPING ⌂	
Cosmo Brown	13 C2

EATING ⊞	
Beams Restaurant	14 B2
Lennon's Café Bar	15 C2

DRINKING ⌑	
Finegan's	16 C2
Teach Dolmain	17 C2

TRANSPORT	
Bus Station	18 C3

CENTRAL SOUTH

www.carlowtourism.com for information about the town and its surroundings.
Tourist office (☎ 913 1554; cnr Tullow & College Sts; ⏱ 9.30am-1pm & 2-5.30pm Mon-Fri year round, 10am-5.30pm Sat Jun-Aug) A useful source of information.
Webtalk (☎ 913 9721; 44 Tullow St; per hr €5; ⏱ 9.30am-6pm Mon-Sat) Internet access.

Sights

If you're feeling more thirsty than energetic, you could visit the **Carlow Brewing Company** (☎ 913 4356; www.carlowbrewing.com; The Goods Store, Station Rd; admission €4.75). This small microbrewery has been phenomenally successful since it opened in 1998, with its O'Hara Stout winning first prize at the International Brewing Industry Awards just two years later. Tours include a glass of the prize-winning black stuff. Visits by prior arrangement only.

Activities

The River Barrow is popular with canoeists, kayakers and rowers. **Adventure Canoeing Days** (☎ 087 252 9700; info@gowiththeflow.ie) does weekend white-water river trips (€45) and rents canoes (€50 per day) year round. Advance bookings are recommended.

Walking Tour

Start your walk at the tourist office on College St. Just to the right is the elegant Regency Gothic **Cathedral of the Assumption (1)** that dates from 1833. The cathedral was the brainchild of Bishop Doyle, a staunch supporter of Catholic emancipation. His statue

inside includes a woman said to represent Ireland rising up against her oppressors. The church also has an elaborate pulpit and some fine stained-glass windows.

Next door is **St Patrick's College (2)**, Ireland's first post-penal seminary. Opened in 1793 (but now closed to the public), it is thought to have been in use for longer than any other seminary in the world.

Walking north along College St then turning left on Dublin St, you'll come to the impressive **Carlow Courthouse (3)**, at the northern end of Dublin St. Designed by William Morrisson in 1830, this elegant building is modelled on the Parthenon and is considered to be one of the most impressive courthouses in the country. Carlow got it through an administrative mix-up – the building was originally intended for Cork.

Walk down Dublin St and turn right into Centaur St and past the **Town Hall (4)**, dating from 1884. When you reach the river, cross the **Millennium Bridge (5)** and walk across the park to 98 St where you'll find the **Celtic high cross (6)** that marks the mass **Croppies' Grave (7)**. Here 640 United Irish rebels were buried following the bloodiest fighting of the 1798 Rising. The name 'croppie' came from the rebels' habit of cropping their hair to indicate their allegiance.

Distance: 2.5km
Duration: one hour

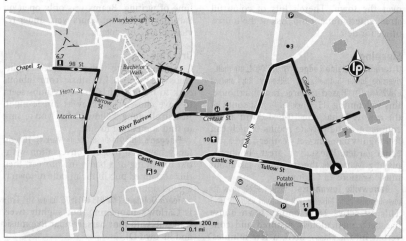

From here turn into Maryborough St and walk south to the five-arched **Graiguecullen Bridge (8)**, thought to be the oldest and lowest bridge over the River Barrow. Cross the bridge and continue east to the ruins of 13th-century **Carlow Castle (9)**, built by William de Marshall on the site of an earlier Norman motte-and-bailey fort. The castle survived Cromwell's attentions but succumbed to the grand plans of a certain Dr Middleton, who decided to convert it into a lunatic asylum. In an effort to remodel the interior, he blew up most of the castle in 1814. All that is left is a single wall flanked by two towers.

Continue up Castle Hill and take the fork to your left onto Castle St. On your left you'll see **St Mary's Church (10)**, built in 1727 (the tower and spire were added in 1834), with a number of statues by Richard Morrison.

Walk on up Tullow St, the town's principal shopping thoroughfare, and take the second right into Potato Market. At the end of the lane is a small square. The bronze statue in the middle of the fountain is the **Liberty Tree (11)**, designed by John Behan to commemorate the 1798 Rising.

Festivals & Events

Every summer (usually in mid-June) Carlow town celebrates the 10-day **Éigse Arts Festival** (☎ 914 0491; eigsecarlow@eircom.net), when Irish and international artists, musicians, film-makers, writers and performers take over the town. There's lots of colourful street entertainment too. Ask at the tourist office for details.

Sleeping

Otterholt Riverside Lodge (☎ 913 0404; otterholt_riverside_lodge@hotmail.com; Kilkenny Rd; dm/s/d €18/25/40; P) Based in a large, rambling house, this welcoming IHH hostel is just south of the centre. It has one 10-bed dorm and a couple of rustic private rooms (which can feel slightly damp in wet weather), and a riverside garden. The staff are great – bodhrán-playing Martin is the person to ask about music sessions in Carlow.

Barrowville Townhouse (☎ 914 3324; www.barrowvillehouse.com; Kilkenny Rd; s/d from €50/80; P) This attractive 18th-century town house has been meticulously restored and converted into a classy B&B, a few minutes'

walk south of town. The rooms are extremely comfortable and the atmosphere is relaxed and friendly.

Cosmo Brown (☎ 914 1384; info@cosmobrown.com; 10 Tullow St; r €140; ♿) This brand new hotel on Carlow's main street has spacious modern rooms (prices include nightclub admission!) and a stylish attitude. Deep leather sofas, ambient light and hip music attract a trendy young crowd to the bar (mains €6 to €9; food served noon to 3pm and 5pm to 7.30pm) and restaurant (mains €8 to €14; open noon to 3pm and 5.30pm to 8.30pm) downstairs.

Eating

Lennon's Café Bar (☎ 913 1575; lennonscafebar@eircom .net; 121 Tullow St; lunch €5-10; ☉ 10am-5pm) Tantalise your tastebuds with a noontime feast from Lennon's in-demand café, where gourmet sandwiches (like honey-roast ham with apricot chutney) and mouthwatering hot lunches lead to big hungry scrums. The snug window seats are by far the nicest in the fairy-lit interior.

Beams Restaurant (☎ 913 1824; 59 Dublin St; set dinner €40; ☉ 7.30-9.30pm Sat) Housed in an 18th-century coach house, this is one of Carlow's best restaurants, with a French chef serving up delectable modern Irish cuisine. Menus are created from home-grown vegetables and local fish, meat and game, and are supported by a cheeky little wine list. It also looks after veggies and advertises itself as coeliac-friendly. At the time of writing, Beams was only open on Saturday nights, but hours were under review; phone for details.

Drinking

Carlow has wall-to-wall pubs, several nightclubs and plenty of live music from dubious rock to traditional Irish. Many pubs seem to have chosen Thursday as music night. Just stroll along Tullow St and you're sure to find something to suit.

Finegan's (☎ 914 0458; Potato Market) If you fancy having a proper conversation without the twang of a banjo in your ear, then this acclaimed pub in the middle of town is a good option.

Teach Dolmain (☎ 913 0911; 76 Tullow St) This is Carlow's happening, but slightly twee, trad pub with four bars, regular live music and its own DJ.

Getting There & Away

BUS

Bus Éireann (☎ 01-836 6111) operates the Dublin to Carlow (one way/return €9.50/10.50, 1½ hours), and Carlow to Waterford (€9.50/ 10.50, 1½ hours) services, with 10 buses daily Monday to Saturday and seven on Sunday in both directions.

JJ Kavanagh & Sons (☎ 914 3081; www.jjkavanagh .ie) has 11 buses per day Monday to Friday, 10 Saturday, nine Sunday to Dublin (€9) and Waterford (€8). There are two buses daily Monday to Saturday to/from Kilkenny (€4.50, 45 minutes) and to Portlaoise (€6, one hour); the latter also stops in Athy (€4.50, 35 minutes).

From September to June, there is a Monday to Friday college run between Carlow and Newbridge (€6, 1¾ hours) that stops in Athy (€4.50, 35 minutes), Kildare (€6, one hour) and the Curragh (€6, 1¼ hours).

Buses for both companies leave from the bus station located at the eastern end of Kennedy Ave.

TRAIN

The **train station** (☎ 913 1633; Station Rd) is to the northeast of town. Carlow is located on the Dublin–Waterford line with five trains daily in each direction Monday to Saturday (four Sunday). One way to Dublin or Waterford (both 1¼ hours) costs €12 Monday to Thursday, €14.50 Fridays and Sundays.

AROUND CARLOW TOWN
Browne's Hill Dolmen

This 5000-year-old granite monster is Europe's largest **portal dolmen** and one of Ireland's most famous. The capstone alone weighs well over 100 tonnes and would originally have been covered with a mound of earth. The dolmen is 3km east of town on the R726 Hacketstown road; a path leads round the field to the dolmen. There's no public transport. **Tips Cabs** (☎ 087-244 0621) charges about €10 to €15 from Carlow, including a 20-minute wait.

Killeshin Church

Once the site of an important monastery with one of the finest round towers in the country, this medieval masterpiece was destroyed early in the 18th century by a farmer worried that it might collapse and kill his cows! The ruins of a 12th-century church remain, including a remarkable doorway said to date from the 5th century. Look out for the wonderful bearded face on the capstone. Killeshin Church is 5km west of Carlow on the R430. There's no public transport, but you could take a taxi: **Tips Cabs** (☎ 087 244 0621) charges about €10 to €15 from Carlow, including a 20-minute wait.

BORRIS
☎ 059 / pop 580

This seemingly untouched Georgian village has a luscious mountain backdrop and traditional main street. Borris is full of character, with plenty of friendly bars well known for their music. **O'Shea's** (☎ 977 3106), a genuine pub, hardware and grocery shop, still has its maze of tightly packed shelves, spare parts hanging from the ceiling and horse feed by the bar stools.

Sights & Activities

At the opposite end of the village from the graceful 16-arch railway viaduct is the dramatic **Borris House** (☎ 977 3105), a beautiful Tudor-style residence and one of Ireland's most majestic stately homes. Group tours by appointment only, price negotiable.

If you're feeling energetic, Borris is a starting point for the **Mt Leinster Scenic Drive** (it can also be walked) and is also on the South Leinster Way (see p679). Alternatively, there's a lovely 10km walk along the **River Barrow towpath** to picturesque Graiguenamanagh, just inside County Kilkenny.

Sleeping & Eating

Step House (☎ 977 3209; www.thestephouse.com; Main St; s/d €60/90; ⊗ mid-Mar–mid-Dec; **P**) This Georgian home situated right in the centre of town makes a charming place to stay, with comfortable rooms overlooking a large garden. Unfortunately, because of fragile antiques, it's not suitable for children.

Lorum Old Rectory (☎ 977 5282; www.lorum.com; Kilgreaney; s/d from €95/150; ⊗ Mar-Nov; **P**) Halfway between Borris and Bagenalstown is this historic manor house overlooked by the Blackstairs Mountains. It's a warm and welcoming guesthouse with comely character, wonderful organic cooking (a six-course dinner costs €40; closed for dinner Sunday) and peacocks roaming the croquet lawn. Cyclists are treated with sympathy, as the family also run biking holidays in the area.

CENTRAL SOUTH

SOMETHING SPECIAL

Moongate (☎ 977 3669; www.moongatesite.com; Tom Duff, Borris; per night/2 nights/week €1750/2450/4200, dinner €33; P) This awesome and eccentric guesthouse set in the lee of Mt Leinster is the perfect spot for a party or a weird and wonderful weekend. The whole place is a feast for the senses with lavish interiors decorated with an eclectic mix of salvaged materials, including chairs from the Scala cinema in Kings Cross, a door from Kabul, a wooden sculpture from a Filipino convent and, if you believe the owners, a light from the *Titanic*. The bedrooms are all individually themed (the Venetian Master is the best) and dinner is served communally at one long table. The only snag is that Moongate takes bookings for groups only (minimum of eight people, maximum 15).

Getting There & Away

Michael Kilbride (☎ 051-423 633) operates two buses daily Monday to Saturday between Borris and Kilkenny, leaving at 8am and 2.15pm from Borris, and noon and 6pm from Kilkenny (one way/return €4/6, one hour).

MT LEINSTER

At 796m, Mt Leinster offers some of Ireland's finest **hang-gliding**. It's also worth the hike up for the panoramic views over Counties Carlow, Wexford and Wicklow. To get there from Borris, follow the Mt Leinster Scenic Drive signposts 13km towards Bunclody in County Wexford (see p188). It takes a good two hours on foot or 20 minutes by car.

SOUTH LEINSTER WAY

Southwest of Clonegal, on the northern slopes of Mt Leinster, is the tiny village of **Kildavin**, the starting point of the South Leinster Way. For details see p679.

COUNTY LAOIS

Most people see Laois (pronounced leash) as a faint blur outside the car window as they zoom along the N7 or N8. But get off the main roads, and you'll discover the hidden corners of Ireland's heartland: pleasant heritage towns, the unspoiled Slieve Bloom Mountains and a patchwork of rivers and walkways. For all you need to know about the county, check out www.laoistourism.ie.

PORTLAOISE

☎ 0502 / pop 3482

Portlaoise's two main edifices are known locally as the 'nuts and bolts' – the large mental asylum and maximum-security prison. Unless you're planning to lose the plot or commit murder, there's very little to keep you here as a visitor. However, the Slieve Bloom Mountains to the west (p344) and the impressive Rock of Dunamaise to the east (opposite) are well worth a visit.

Information

Dunamaise Arts Centre (☎ 63355; Church St; per hr €5; 8.30am-5.30pm Mon-Sat) Has Internet access.

Tourist office (☎ 21178; James Fintan Lawlor Ave; 9.30am-1pm & 2-5.15pm Mon-Fri Oct-May, Mon-Sat Jun-Sep) In the shopping-centre car park beside the bypass – to get there from Main St, cut through Lyster's Lane beside the Bank of Ireland.

Sleeping & Eating

Heritage Hotel (☎ 78588; www.theheritagehotel.com; Jessop St; s/d from €95/160; P) This giant complex is the town's newest and plushest hotel with understated décor and a good variety of rooms. There's a fitness centre with saunas and a pool, a choice of three bars, and two restaurants.

Spago (Heritage Hotel; mains €12-18; 5-9.30pm Wed-Sun) An Italian-style bistro in the Heritage Hotel.

Fitzmaurice (Heritage Hotel; mains €16-22; 5.30-9.30pm Mon, Tue, Fri-Sun Sep-May, 5.30-9.30pm daily Jun-Aug) A refined eatery in the Heritage Hotel.

Kitchen & Foodhall (☎ 62061; Hyand's Sq; mains €7-10; 9am-5.30pm Mon-Sat; ♿) This is a wonderful place serving up delicious deli-style goodies and some great vegetarian options; not to mention the killer portions of home-made cake. Bright, cheery and child-friendly.

Entertainment

Dunamaise Arts Centre (☎ 63355; www.dunamaise.ie; Church St) The county's purpose-built theatre and arts centre presents a varied programme of national and international performing and visual arts, comedy and films.

Getting There & Away
BUS
Portlaoise is on one of the busiest main roads, at the junction of the N8 and N7. **Bus Éireann** (☎ 01-836 6111) runs 19 buses daily that pass from Dublin through Portlaoise (one way/return €11.10/18, 1½ hours) on their way to Cashel, Cork, Limerick and Kerry. It is also on the Waterford–Kilkenny–Carlow–Athlone–Longford route (two buses daily in each direction Monday to Saturday, one Sunday).

JJ Kavanagh & Sons (☎ 056-883 1106; www .jjkavanagh.ie) runs two buses daily Monday to Saturday to Carlow (€6, one hour) and Kilkenny (€6.50, 1½ hours).

TRAIN
Just 50 minutes from Dublin on the main line to Tipperary, Cork, Limerick and Tralee, Portlaoise is serviced by 12 daily trains from Dublin (single/return €17.50/23.50). The **train station** (☎ 21303; Railway St) is a five-minute walk north of the town centre.

ROCK OF DUNAMAISE
The Rock of Dunamaise is an arresting sight dramatically perched on a craggy limestone outcrop. It was first recorded on Ptolemy's map of AD 140 and suffered successive waves of Viking, Norman, Irish and English invasion and occupation. Cromwell's henchmen finally destroyed the site in 1650.

The ruins are undergoing some badly needed restoration and, for now, require a dose of imagination. However, the views from the summit are spectacular on a clear day. If you're lucky you'll be able to see Timahoe round tower to the south, the Slieve Blooms to the west and the Wicklow Mountains to the east.

The rock is situated 6km east of Portlaoise along the Stradbally road. **JJ Kavanagh & Sons** (☎ 056-883 1106) runs two buses per day Monday to Saturday from Portlaoise to Kilkenny via the Rock (€5.50, 10 minutes). Otherwise, **Portlaoise Taxi Service** (☎ 0502-62270) will take you out there for about €16 return.

STRADBALLY
pop 1178
The pretty village of Stradbally, 10km southeast of Portlaoise, is home to the newly renovated **Stradbally Steam Museum &**

Narrow Gauge Railway (☎ 0502-25154; www.irish steam.ie). It is a haven for steam enthusiasts, with a collection of lovingly restored fire engines, steam tractors and steamrollers. During the August bank-holiday weekend the museum hosts a two-day rally where the 40-hectare estate of Stradbally Hall is taken over by steam-operated machinery and vintage cars. Following a revamp, a grand opening is due to take place in late spring 2006; at the time of writing, opening hours and prices were still to be decided.

The 1895 Guinness Brewery steam locomotive in the village is used six times annually for a day trip to Dublin. You can also take trips on the **narrow-gauge railway** (adult/child €5/2; ⏱ 2.30-5pm Sun & Mon bank holiday weekends Easter-Oct).

JJ Kavanagh & Sons (☎ 056-883 1106) runs Portlaoise–Kilkenny buses that pass through Stradbally (from Portlaoise €3, 15 minutes, two daily Monday to Saturday).

Stradbally is also on **Bus Éireann's** (☎ 01-836 6111) Waterford–Longford service (two buses daily Monday to Saturday, one Sunday), which also passes through Kilkenny, Carlow, Portlaoise and Athlone. A one way/return fare from Portlaoise costs €2.50/4.50.

EMO COURT
Giant sequoia trees line the avenue leading to the unusual, green-domed **Emo Court** (☎ 0502-26573, 086-810 7916; Emo; adult/child €2.75/1.25, grounds free; ⏱ 10.30-6.30pm Tue-Sun mid-Jun–mid-Sep, last admission 5.45pm, grounds open daylight hrs year round). The impressive house was designed by James Gandon (architect of Dublin's Custom House) in 1790 and was originally the country seat of the first earl of Portarlington. After many years as a Jesuit novitiate, the house, with its elaborate central rotunda, was impressively restored. Access is only possible through the one-hour guided tour.

The extensive grounds contain over 1000 different trees and shrubs from all over the world, and are littered with Greek statues. The grounds are ideal for a picnic or for a long walk through the woodlands to Emo Lake.

Emo is about 13km northeast of Portlaoise, just off the main Portlaoise–Dublin road, which has frequent daily buses in both directions.

CENTRAL SOUTH

CENTRAL SOUTH

PORTARLINGTON & AROUND

☎ 0502 / pop 3260

Portarlington (Cúil an tSúdaire) grew up under the influence of French Huguenot and German settlers and has some fine 18th-century buildings, although many have been terribly neglected. The 1851 **St Paul's Church** (admission free; ☽ 7am-7pm), on the site of the original 17th-century French church, was built for the Huguenots, some of whose tombstones stand in a corner of the churchyard.

About 4km east of town are the impressive ivy-covered ruins of 13th-century **Lea Castle** on the banks of the River Barrow, once the stronghold of Maurice Fitzgerald, second baron of Offaly. The castle consists of a fairly intact towered keep with two outer walls and a twin-towered gatehouse. Access is through a farmyard 500m to the north off the main Monasterevin road (R420).

Portarlington is on the main railway lines between Dublin and Galway, Limerick, Tralee and Cork, with hourly trains daily in both directions. For details, contact **Portlaoise train station** (☎ 0502-21303). There are no bus services.

MOUNTMELLICK

☎ 0502 / pop 2525

Mountmellick is a quiet Georgian town 10km north of Portlaoise on the River Owenass. It was renowned for its linen production in the 19th century and owes much of its history to its Quaker settlers. A looped heritage trail, beginning in the square, leads you on a walking tour of the most important landmarks. There's a display of superbly subtle Mountmellick work (nature-inspired white-on-white embroidery) at the new **heritage museum** (☎ 24525; www.mountmellickdevelopment .com; Mountmellick Development Association, Irishtown; admission €3; ☽ 9am-1pm Mon-Fri).

Mountmellick is on **Bus Éireann's** (☎ 01-836 6111) Waterford–Longford route (two buses daily Monday to Saturday, one Sunday). Bus No 124 travels to and from Dublin (one way/return €11.10/18, two hours, one bus Monday to Saturday) via Newbridge, Kildare and Portlaoise.

MOUNTRATH

☎ 0502 / pop 1331

Another once-prosperous 18th-century linen hotspot, Mountrath is now a sleepy village. Both St Patrick and St Brigid are sup-posed to have established religious houses here, although no trace of either remains.

Today, the local place of pilgrimage is the 6th-century monastery of St Fintan at Clonenagh, 3km east on the Portlaoise road. Its claim to fame is **St Fintan's Tree**, a large sycamore with a groove filled with water in one of its lower branches and said to have healing properties.

Ballyfin House (8km north of Mountrath) is an architectural treasure, designed by Richard Morrison in 1850. It's undergoing extensive restoration work in order to reopen as an exclusive hotel in 2010, and was closed to visitors at the time of writing.

You can stay at **Roundwood House** (☎ 32120; roundwood@eircom.net; Slieve Blooms Rd; s/d €100/150, cottage/forge/coach house per week €250/320/500; ☽ Feb-Dec), a superb 17th-century Palladian villa. It makes a wonderfully original overnight stop, with its unceremonious atmosphere and superb service. The **restaurant** (set dinner €45; ☽ 8pm sitting Tue-Sat) serves a delicious, traditional five-course meal (residents only). Self-catering accommodation is also available in the sensitively restored coach house, forge and cottage inside the grounds. The house is 5km outside Mountrath.

Mountrath is on the main **Bus Éireann** (☎ 01-836 6111) Dublin–Limerick route, with up to 14 buses daily in each direction.

SLIEVE BLOOM MOUNTAINS

One of the best reasons for visiting Laois is to explore the Slieve (shlee-ve) Bloom Mountains. Although not as spectacular as other Irish ranges, their sudden rise from a great plain, and the absence of visitors, make them disproportionately attractive. You'll get a real sense of being away from it all as you tread the deserted mountaintop blanket bogs, moorland, pine forests and isolated valleys.

The highest point is Mt Arderin (528m), south of the Glendine Gap on the Offaly border, from where, on a clear day, it's possible to see the highest points of all four of the ancient provinces of Ireland. East is Lugnaquilla in Leinster, west is Nephin in Connaught, north is Slieve Donard in Ulster, and southwest is Carrantuohil in Munster.

If you're planning a walking tour, Mountrath to the south and Kinnitty to the north, are good bases. For leisurely walking, **Glenbarrow**, southwest of Rosenallis, has an interesting trail by the cascading River Barrow. Other spots to check out are **Glendine Park**, near the Glendine Gap, and the **Cut mountain pass**.

You can pick up a *Laois Walks Pack* (€2), which has information on more than 30 waymarked walks around the county, from the tourist office or the **Laois Leader** (☎ 61900; Peppers Ct) in Portlaoise.

The **Slieve Bloom Way** (p679) is a 77km signposted trail that does a complete circuit of the mountains, taking in most major points of interest. You can walk alone, or from May to October you could join a guided group walk (per person €5) organised by the **Slieve Bloom Walking Club** (☎ 0509-37299; www.slievebloom.ie).

WESTERN LAOIS

About 3km west of Borris-in-Ossory, once a major coaching stop, is **Ballaghmore Castle** (☎ 0505-21453; www.castleballaghmore.com; Ballaghmore; adult/child €5/3; ☺ 10am-5pm). This square tower fortress from 1480 is soaked in atmosphere with heavy, creaking wooden doors, cold stone walls and a mysterious sheila-na-gig. It's all faithfully restored and available to rent for €2000 per week. If that's out of your budget, you could stay in the grounds at **Manor Guest House** (s/d €70/120) and self-catering **Rose Cottage** (per week €500).

ABBEYLEIX

☎ 0502 / pop 2379

Abbeyleix (abbey-*leeks*), 14km south of Portlaoise, is a pretty tree-lined heritage town with neat houses and a lot of traffic. The original settlement, which grew up around a 12th-century Cistercian monastery, wasn't here at all: local 18th-century landowner Viscount de Vesci remodelled the village and moved it to its present location, bribing the inhabitants to move by giving them half an acre of land apiece. During the Famine, de Vesci proved a kinder landlord than many, and the fountain obelisk in the square was erected as a thank you from his tenants.

Sights

In an echo-filled old school building at the northern end of Main St is **Heritage House** (☎ 31653; adult/child €4/2; ☺ 10am-5pm Mon-Sat, 1-5pm Sun Mar-Oct, 9am-5pm Mon-Fri Nov-Feb). The museum details the town's colourful history, and contains some examples of the Turkish-influenced carpets woven in Abbeyleix from 1904 to 1913 – they even created some for the *Titanic*.

De Vesci's mansion, **Abbeyleix House**, was designed by James Wyatt in 1773. It's 2km southwest of town on the Rathdowney road, but is not open to the public.

Sleeping & Eating

Preston House (☎ /fax 31432; Main St; s/d €80/140) This ivy-clad town house has very comfy accommodation in what was once an old school; breakfasts are served in the former headmaster's office!

Abbeyleix Manor Hotel (☎ 30111; www.abbey leixmanorhotel.com; s/d €75/130; P) This is the town's newest accommodation, with an ugly motel-like exterior but good-value, spacious rooms. If you fancy a bit of local culture, Malachi's Bar on the ground floor has regular traditional music sessions.

Farren House Farm Hostel (☎ 34032; www.farm hostel.com; dm €15; P &) In a restored limestone grain loft on a working family farm (tours available), this quirky independent hostel has cosy en-suite rooms. Marty and Wendy Phelan can provide breakfast and dinner, if you warn them in advance. The hostel is out in the sticks, 3km from Ballacolla; attempting to find it without directions may leave you lost, tearful and mentally broken, so phone first.

Preston House café-restaurant (Preston House, Main St; lunch mains €10-14, dinner mains €18-32; ☺ 11am-6pm Tue-Thu, 7-8.30pm Thu-Sat) This wine-and-Wedgwood country-style place is an excellent upmarket pit stop with some wonderful vegetarian choices, although the staff seem a little stressed at busy times.

Drinking

Morrissey's (☎ 31233; Main St) This half-pub, half-shop and former travel agency and undertaker is a bit of a local legend and the winner of the 2004 National Heritage Pub of the Year award. In the half-light you can cradle a pint at the sloping counter while you soak up the atmosphere in the ancient pew seats in front of the potbelly stove.

Getting There & Away

Abbeyleix is on the **Bus Éireann** (☎ 01-836 6111) route between Dublin (one way/return €16/22.50, 1¾ hours) and Cork with six buses daily in each direction.

CENTRAL SOUTH

SOMETHING SPECIAL

Castle Durrow (☎ 0502-36555; www.castledurrow.com; d €200-340; **P**) Even if you can't stay here, it's well worth nipping into this elegantly restored mansion for a coffee or light lunch (€10) on the terrace or a walk through the 30 acres of gardens and woodland. The excellent restaurant (set menu €45; open 7pm to 8.45pm), supplied by the castle's organic kitchen garden, is also open to nonresidents.

Bedrooms are individually decorated (Lady Hannah's room is particularly nice), with super views over the grounds. Master rooms are medieval in spirit, with four-poster beds and sensuous crushed-velvet covers. Deluxe rooms are more contemporary, with sleigh beds and sharp-lined cherrywood furniture. The above-it-all beamed attic rooms have unusual oriental twists.

Unlike some antique-stuffed museum-type houses, children are made very welcome here, with their own playroom and comfortable, well-designed family rooms. It's worth calling ahead and enquiring about special offers.

Bernard Kavanagh (☎ 056-883 1189) runs one bus daily in each direction from Monday to Saturday between Portlaoise and Abbeyleix (€4, 20 minutes). The bus leaves from Abbeyleix at 9.55am to go to Portlaoise; and it leaves Portlaoise at 8.05pm to return to Abbeyleix.

TIMAHOE
pop 517

Tiny Timahoe casts a real charm, even if it's nothing more than a handful of houses around a grassy triangle. Across a tinkling stream, and straight out of a fairytale, is a tilting 30m-tall **round tower** – all it needs is Rapunzel to complete the picture. The tower, with its unusual carved Romanesque doorway (bring binoculars for a proper look), is all that remains of a 12th-century monastery.

Timahoe is 10km northeast of Abbeyleix on the R426. From Portlaoise, **JJ Kavanagh & Sons** (☎ 056-883 1106) runs two buses a day Monday to Saturday to Kilkenny via Timahoe (€4, 25 minutes); or you could take a **taxi** (☎ 0502-30042; about €20) from Abbeyleix.

DURROW
pop 1164

Neat rows of houses surround Durrow's manicured green. On the western side stands the unmissably imposing gateway to 18th-century **Castle Durrow**, a large Palladian villa. The castle is now an upmarket hotel (see the boxed text, above).

Durrow is 10km south of Abbeyleix, and is accessible by bus (Dublin–Cork route) from the town (€3, 10 minutes, six buses daily in each direction).

COUNTY OFFALY

The county's pride and joy is the ecclesiastical city of Clonmacnoise, one of Ireland's most famous sights. But Offaly's lowlands are dotted with monastic ruins, and its towns are steeped in history.

Geographically, Offaly is dominated by the low-lying bogs that stretch across the county. Enormous expanses like the Bog of Allen and the Boora Bog, where peat is extracted on an industrial scale, are horribly scarred, while Clara Bog is remarkably untouched and recognised internationally for its plant and animal life.

To the east the rugged and sometimes desolate Slieve Bloom Mountains (p344) provide excellent walking, while fishing and water sports are popular on the mighty River Shannon and the meandering Grand Canal. Access www.offaly.ie for more information.

BIRR
☎ 0509 / pop 3590

Birr is a little gem, with beautifully restored Georgian streets, classy accommodation options and excellent restaurants. To top it off, Birr Castle, with its fascinating science centre and gorgeous gardens, sits placidly in the centre.

History

Birr started life as a 6th-century monastic site founded by St Brendan. By 1208 the town had acquired an Anglo-Norman castle, home of the O'Carroll clan who reigned over the surrounding territory.

During the Plantation of 1620, the castle and estate were given to Sir Laurence Parsons, who changed the town's fate by carefully laying out streets, establishing a glass factory and issuing a decree that anyone who 'cast dunge rubbidge filth or sweepings in the forestreete' would be fined four pennies. He also banned barmaids, sentencing any woman caught serving beer to the stocks! The castle has remained in the family for 14 generations, and the present earl and his wife still live on the estate.

Orientation

All the main roads converge on Emmet Square; in one corner, Dooly's Hotel, dating from 1747, was once a coaching inn on the busy route to the west.

Information

The post office is in the northeastern corner of Emmet Sq.

Ely O'Carroll Tourism (☎ 20923; www.elyocarroll .com; Brendan St; ☒ 9.30am-5.30pm Mon-Fri) Provides visitor information, along with the tourist office.

Tourist office (☎ 20110; Brendan St; ☒ 9.30am-1pm & 2-5.30pm Mon-Sat mid-May–Aug)

Sights

BIRR CASTLE

It's easy to spend half a day rambling through the grounds and gardens of **Birr Castle** (☎ 20336; www.birrcastle.com; adult/child €9/5; ☒ 9am-6pm). The castle itself, however, is a private home and cannot be visited. Most of the present building dates from around 1620, with additional alterations made in the early 19th century. Extra fortifications were also added at this stage to placate a local Protestant woman, Mrs Legge, who was convinced the papists were about to rise up and kill the castle residents in their beds.

The 50-hectare castle surroundings are famous for their magnificent **gardens** set around a large artificial lake. They hold over 1000 species of shrubs and trees from all over the world, including a collection from the Himalayas and China. Here you'll also find the world's tallest box hedges, planted in the 1780s and now standing some 12m high.

The Parsons were a remarkable family of pioneering Irish scientists, and their work is documented in the **historic science centre** (admission incl in grounds ticket; ☒ 9am-6pm).

Exhibits include the massive **telescope** built by William Parsons in 1845. The 'leviathan of Parsonstown', as it was known, was the largest telescope in the world for 75 years and attracted a wide variety of scientists and astronomers. It was used to map the moon's surface, and made innumerable discoveries, including the spiral galaxies. After the death of William's son, the telescope, unloved and untended, slowly fell to bits. A huge restoration scheme in the 1990s rebuilt the telescope: it's now fully operational, and demonstrations are held three times daily in high season.

OTHER BUILDINGS & MONUMENTS

Birr has no shortage of first-class Georgian houses; just stroll down tree-lined **Oxmantown Mall**, which connects Rosse Row and Emmet St, or **John's Mall**, to see some of the best examples.

The tourist office hands out a free towntrail leaflet that details the most important landmarks, including a **statue** of the third earl of Rosse, the megalithic **Seffin Stone** (said to have marked the centre of Ireland) and **St Brendan's Old Churchyard**, reputedly the site of the saint's 6th-century settlement.

Activities

A beautiful tree-lined **riverside walk** runs east along the River Camcor from Oxmantown Bridge to Elmgrove Bridge.

If you're feeling more energetic, **Birr Outdoor Education Centre** (☎ 20029; birroec@eircom.net; Roscrea Rd) offers hill walking, rock climbing and abseiling in the nearby Slieve Blooms, as well as canoeing and kayaking on local rivers.

Birr Equestrian Centre (☎ 21961; fax 20479; Kingsborough House; treks per hr €20), 3km outside Birr on the Clareen Road, runs pony treks in the surrounding farmland and forests.

Sleeping

There are no budget accommodation options in town; the nearest hostel is 12km away in Banagher.

Walcot B&B (☎ 21247; walcot@hotmail.com; cnr Oxmantown Mall & Ross Row; s/d from €60/100) Wonderful friendly service and delightful rooms make this Georgian town house a winner. It's located right in the centre of town but set back off the road; the four elegant rooms overlook a tranquil private garden.

Maltings Guesthouse (☎ 21345; themaltingsbirr@ eircom.net; Castle St; s/d €50/75; P) Based in an old malt storehouse once used by Guinness, this is a terrific option right by the castle and the River Camcor. The 13 tastefully decorated rooms are very good value and there's a popular restaurant downstairs.

Stables Guesthouse (☎ 20263; www.thestables restaurant.com; Oxmantown Mall; s/d €55/90) Located on one of Birr's finest streets, this graceful Georgian town house is full of character. Rooms are spacious and luxuriously decorated, service is sound and there's a smashing restaurant, too.

Croghan Lodge & Bothy (☎ 20023; www.birr castle.com; Birr Castle surrounds; lodge/bothy per week €420/440; P) These self-catering cottages, which have private entrances to the glorious castle gardens, are good options if you'd like to stay and explore the area for longer. The lodge sleeps four people, the rather chintzy bothy sleeps five. Both are fully restored and completely refitted with all modern conveniences. Bookings are made by the week, running from Saturday to Saturday.

Eating

Stables (☎ 20263; www.thestablesrestaurant.com; Oxmantown Mall; mains €19-28; 🕒 6-9pm Thu-Sat, 12.30-3pm Sun; 🕭) In a converted stable yard at Stables Guesthouse, this restaurant is esteemed by diners from all over the county. It's celebrated for its cuisine and its character, efficient staff and relaxed ambience. Swing by for traditional Sunday lunch or for dinner, where Irish favourites like lamb, steak and monkfish appear in sauces guaranteed to set the tastebuds dancing.

County Arms Hotel (☎ 20791; countyarmshotel@ eircom.net; Railway Rd; dinner €30; 🕭) This place is good for a quick bar lunch or a refined evening meal. The restaurant serves a praiseworthy mix of Irish and French cuisine, and sources most of its vegetables from its own garden and greenhouses.

Riverbank (☎ 21528; riverbankrest@msn.com; Riverstown; lunch mains €5-9, dinner mains €12-20; 🕒 12.30-2.30pm & 5.30-10pm Tue-Sun) A favourite haunt for locals, this wonderful restaurant has earned plenty of rave reviews for its superb, freshly prepared dishes. It's 1.5km south of town on the banks of the River Brosna.

Thatch (☎ 20682; thethatchcrinkill@eircom.net; Crinkill; set dinner €40; 🕒 Tue-Sat) Only 2km south-

east of Birr, this gorgeous 200-year-old thatched pub is a real find. The old-world atmosphere might not be to everyone's taste, but the food is excellent, ranging from traditional Irish beef and crabmeat, to modern dishes like fillet of ostrich or honey-and-lemon roast duck – chances are they'll have to roll you out of there. Dinner reservations are vital.

Emma's Café & Deli (☎ 25678; 31 Main St; snacks €2-5; 🕒 9.30am-6pm Mon-Sat, 12.30-5.30pm Sun) This delicious-smelling deli-cum-caff is the newest eating venue in town, and is good for a low-key lunch. Huddle around wooden tables, or lounge on the huge L-shaped sofa in the window to scoff organic soup, sandwiches and warm, jammy scones.

Entertainment

Birr has a vibrant nightlife with music spilling out the doors of many of its pubs.

Craughwell's (☎ 21839; Castle St) Stop for a snootful at Craughwell's, renowned for its rollicking traditional session on Friday night and impromptu sing-along sessions on Saturday.

Market House Tavern (☎ 20180; Market Sq) Birr's most modern bar is a couple of giant strides away from the typical Irish pub. The Tavern is all pale wood and shiny lights, and is popular with younger drinkers in the evenings.

Melba's Nite Club (☎ 20032; Emmet Sq; 🕒 Fri-Sun) In the basement of Dooly's Hotel, this is the town's only nightclub, and on a Saturday it gives a fine anthropological insight into the typical dancing and mating habits of rural Ireland.

Birr Theatre & Arts Centre (☎ 22911; www.birr theatre.com; Oxmantown Hall) Plays are mainly amateur-dramatics productions, but there are also regular summer films (tickets are €7 for nonmembers, screening at 8pm Tue), impressive musical events and occasional interesting photographic exhibitions on offer, too.

Getting There & Away

Birr is found on the Bus Éireann Dublin–Portumna route, which also serves Tullamore and Maynooth. There's only one direct service in each direction, leaving Birr at 7am and Dublin at 4pm Monday to Friday (€13, 2½ hours). Buses run every day to Athlone (€7.90, 50 minutes, six daily Mon-

I AIN'T AFRAID OF NO GHOST!

Ireland's most haunted castle lies southeast of Birr between Kinnitty and Roscrea (in Tipperary). **Leap Castle** (☎ 0509-31115; seanfryan@oceanfree.net; R421; admission €6; ☼ 10am-5pm) was originally an O'Carroll family residence, keeping guard over a crucial route between Munster and Leinster. The castle was the scene of many dreadful deeds, and has quaint features like dank dungeons, a 'Bloody Chapel' and an oubliette, from which (allegedly) three cartloads of bones were removed in the 1920s. It's famous for its eerie apparitions – the most renowned inhabitant is the 'smelly ghost', a spirit that leaves a horrible stench behind after sightings.

The castle was looted and burned down last century, but has been mostly renovated. The current owner, Sean Ryan, is pleased to show people round, although it's best to phone ahead to make sure he's in. Banquets with traditional Irish music sessions can be arranged for groups of more than 20 (€65 per head).

There's no public transport to the castle but **Paddy Kavanagh** (☎ 090-647 4839; pkmail@eircom .net) runs private tours from Athlone; contact him to make arrangements. The price will vary depending on the number of people, how long you plan to stay etc, but you are looking at about €25 per person.

day to Saturday, three Sunday) and there's one bus to Limerick (€13.50, 1½ hours) from Birr at 7.20am Monday to Friday.

Kearns Transport (☎ 0509-22244; www.kearns transport.com) runs services via Birr on its Dublin–Portumna route. To Dublin, there are three buses daily Sunday to Thursday, four on Friday and two on Saturday; from Dublin, there are three buses daily Friday to Monday, and two on Tuesday, Wednesday and Thursday (one way €8).

All buses stop in Emmet Sq and you can usually get up-to-date information from the newsagencies nearby.

KINNITTY

☎ 0509 / pop 503

Kinnitty is a dinky, dreamy little village that makes a good base for the Slieve Bloom Mountains (see p344). Driving out of Kinnitty, the roads across the mountains to Mountrath and Mountmellick, both in County Laois, are particularly scenic. There's a seasonal **tourist information point** (☼ Tue-Fri Jun-Aug), with walking information, in the community centre.

Look out for the bizarre **stone pyramid** in the village graveyard behind the Church of Ireland. In the 1870s, Richard Bernard commissioned this scale replica of the Cheops pyramid in Egypt for the family crypt.

The shaft of the 9th-century **Kinnitty High Cross** was nabbed by Kinnitty Castle in the 19th century and is now displayed on the hotel's terrace. Adam and Eve and the Crucifixion are clearly visible on either face.

Sleeping & Eating

Kinnitty Castle (☎ 37318; www.kinnittycastle.com; s/d from €155/240) This former O'Carroll residence, rebuilt in neo-Gothic style in the 19th century, is one of Ireland's most renowned castles. Set on a vast estate, it is now a luxury hotel much in demand for weddings: Ozzy Osbourne's son Louis married here in 2003. You can act the lord and try your hand at falconry or archery; relax in the gatehouse spa; or do a spot of ghost-hunting (the castle is said to be haunted by a friendly monk). The top-quality restaurant (mains €20 to €28) is open to nonresidents and there is traditional music in the Dungeon Bar every Friday and Saturday evening at 10pm. The castle is 3km southeast of town.

Ardmore House (☎ 37009; www.kinnitty.net; The Walk; s/d €45/70; ☼) Brass beds, turf fires and home-made brown bread are the order of the day at this lovely Victorian stone farmhouse. Rooms two and five have views of the weird pyramid and the heathery mountains. If you're a rambler, ask about their four-day walking packages. The B&B is set off the main road, about 200m east of Kinnitty.

BANAGHER & AROUND

☎ 0509 / pop 1789

Banagher is a great little spot on the banks of the River Shannon, fast becoming a boaters' favourite thanks to its buzzing new marina. The town has a wonderful easy-going atmosphere, some impressive fortifications on the west bank of the river and an intriguing literary history.

CENTRAL SOUTH

Charlotte Brontë had her honeymoon in Banagher in 1854. Thirteen years earlier, Anthony Trollope, fresh from inventing the pillarbox, took up a job as a post-office clerk in the village; in his spare time he managed to complete his first novel, *The Macdermots of Ballycloran*.

Information

Tourist office (☎ /fax 52155; crankhouse@utvInternet .ie; Crank House, Main St; ☺ 9am-1pm & 2-5pm Mon-Fri) Inside an unusual bow-fronted Georgian town house, this helpful office provides information about Banagher and the surrounding region. Internet access is also available for €2/3.50/6 per 15/30/60 minutes.

Sights

Sited at a crossing point over the River Shannon, Banagher was a place of enormous strategic importance during turbulent times. **Cromwell's Castle** was built in the 1650s, but modified during the Napoleonic Wars, when **Fort Eliza** (a five-sided gun battery whose guardhouse, moat and retaining walls can still be seen), a military **barracks** and **Martello Tower** were also built.

St Paul's Church contains a resplendent stained-glass window originally intended for Westminster Abbey.

About 3km south of Banagher in Lusmagh is **Cloghan Castle** (☎ 51650; Lusmagh; per person €6, tour minimum €25; ☺ tour by prior arrangement only), in use for nearly 800 years. The castle has seen more than its fair share of bloodshed, beginning life as a McCoghlan stronghold and later becoming home to the mighty O'Carroll clan. Today the castle consists of a well-preserved Norman keep and an adjoining 19th-century house full of interesting antiques and armaments. The tour takes about an hour. There's no bus service.

Enclosed by an overgrown castellated wall, 16th-century **Clonony Castle** is sited around 12km out on the road to Shannonbridge. Stories that Henry VIII's second wife, Anne Boleyn, was born here are unlikely to be true, but her cousins Elizabeth and Mary Boleyn are buried beside the ruins.

About 8km south of Banagher on the County Galway side of the border is **Meelick Church**, one of the oldest churches still in use in Ireland.

Activities

Between April and October, hire canoes for trips on the River Shannon or Grand Canal from **Shannon Adventure Canoeing Holidays** (☎ /fax 51411; advcanoe@iol.ie; The Marina; 2-person canoe & camping equipment per week/weekend €312/150). It's cheaper outside summer months and if you have your own camping equipment.

A number of companies rent out beefier cruisers; prices shown are for high season: **Carrick Craft** (central reservations ☎ 01-278 1666; www.carrickcraft.com; The Marina) Four- to eight-person berths ranging from €926 to €2700 per week. **Silverline Cruisers** (☎ 51112; www.silverlinecruisers .com; The Marina) Two-/four-/six-/eight-person berths from €700/1035/1390/2140 per week.

Sleeping & Eating

Crank House Hostel (☎ 51458; fax 52155; Crank House, Main St; dm €14) This IHH is the only hostel in the region and has a variety of decent two- and four-bed rooms, a washing machine and fully equipped kitchen.

Brosna Lodge Hotel (☎ 51350; www.brosnalodge .com; Main St; s/d €45/85; P) A family-run hotel in the centre of town with 14 decent-sized, plainly furnished rooms that offers good value for money. The restaurant (mains €9 to €16) is popular with locals and has access to a large garden in good weather.

Vine House (☎ 51463; Main St; mains €8-12; ☺ noon-11pm Apr-Sep, 6-11pm Oct-Mar) Good food, good atmosphere and good conversation have earned this pub and restaurant a well-deserved reputation as one of the best eateries on the River Shannon. It's a relaxed place and always busy during the summer with drop-in trade from the river.

Heidi's Traditional Irish Coffee Shop (☎ 956 2680; mains €4-10; ☺ 9am-6pm Mon-Thu, 8am-8pm Fri-Sun) Tucked behind the tourist office, Heidi's serves breakfasts, snacks and light lunches in an informal setting. Check out the huge tea-towel collection!

Entertainment

JJ Hough's (☎ 51893; Main St) If you feel like stretching your vocal chords, this pretty, vine-draped 'singing pub' is a local legend for its traditional sessions.

Getting There & Away

Kearns Transport (☎ 22244; www.kearnstransport .com) includes Banagher on its daily Portumna–Dublin service (€8 from Dublin).

SOMETHING SPECIAL

Charlotte's Way (☎ 53864, 087 246 7411; The Hill; s/d €35/60) With out-of-the-ordinary prices, and a fantastic welcome, this stately yellow Georgian home at the top end of town is one of Ireland's few true bargains.

Bought as a wreck and lovingly restored, the former rectory now offers six luxurious en-suite rooms, containing huge comfy beds decked out with Irish linen, and bathrooms with power showers. Gorgeous breakfasts star eggs fresh from the hens outside. There's a big basement room where families will feel at home, and free babysitting can be arranged.

Your accommodation comes with a good dollop of history, explained in interesting home-made pamphlets. A honeymooning Charlotte Brontë was a frequent visitor and, after her death, her husband Arthur lived here as the rector. The house is reputedly haunted by his second wife, Mary Bell. But friendly Jack the dog will keep you safe from spooks.

SHANNONBRIDGE

☎ 090 / pop 353

Shannonbridge gets its name from a narrow 16-span 18th-century bridge that crosses the river into County Roscommon. It's a small, sleepy village with just one main street and two pubs.

You can't miss the massive 19th-century **fortifications** on the western bank, where heavy artillery was installed to bombard Napoleon in case he was cheeky enough to try to invade by the river. The fort has now been converted into the **Old Fort Restaurant** (☎ 967 4973; mains €19-28; 5-9.30pm Wed-Sat, 12.30-2.30pm Sun year round, plus 5-9.30pm Tue & Sun Jul & Aug), which serves high-class versions of old Irish favourites like poached salmon and wild boar.

Clonmacnoise & West Offaly Railway Bog Tour

This is a strange attraction that should be experienced: join the 45-minute **Bog Tour** (Bord Na Móna; ☎ 967 4450; bograil@bnm.ie; adult/child €6.50/4.50; 10am-5pm Apr–early Oct) which runs on a narrow-gauge railway line once used to transport peat. The diesel locomotive moves through the Bog of Allen at around 10km per hour – slow enough to take in the landscape and its special flora, which has remained unchanged for thousands of years, and to learn about peat-cutting and archaeological intrigues.

Trips leave on the hour, with tickets available from the on-site coffee shop; though it's advisable to book ahead.

To get there from Shannonbridge, follow the R357 towards Cloghan for about 5km, then take the signposted left turn and follow the road for another 3km.

CLONMACNOISE

☎ 090 / pop 316

Superbly placed overlooking the River Shannon, **Clonmacnoise** (☎ 967 4195; adult/child €5/2; 9am-7pm mid-May–mid-Sep, 10am-6pm mid-Sep–Oct & mid-Mar–mid-May, 10am-5pm Nov–mid-Mar, last admission 45 min before closing) was one of Ireland's most important monastic cities. The site is enclosed in a walled field and contains numerous early churches, high crosses, round towers and graves in astonishingly good condition. The surrounding marshy area is known as the Shannon Callows, home to many wild plants and one of the last refuges of the seriously endangered corncrake.

History

Roughly translated, Clonmacnoise (Cluain Mhic Nóis) means 'Meadow of the Sons of Nós'. The marshy land would have been impassable for early traders, who instead chose to travel by water or on *eskers* (raised ridges formed by glaciers). When St Ciarán founded a monastery here in AD 548 it was the most important crossroads in the country – the intersection of the north–south River Shannon, and the east–west Esker Riada (Highway of the Kings).

The giant ecclesiastical city had a humble beginning and Ciarán died just seven months after building his first church. Over the years Clonmacnoise grew to become an unrivalled bastion of Irish religion, literature and art and attracted a large lay population. Between the 7th and 12th centuries, monks from all over Europe came to study and pray here, helping to earn Ireland the title of the 'land of saints and scholars'. Even the high kings of Connaught and Tara were brought here for burial.

Most of what you can see today dates from the 10th to 12th centuries. The monks would have lived in small huts scattered in and around the monastery, which would probably have been surrounded by a ditch or rampart of earth.

The site was burned and pillaged on numerous occasions by both the Vikings and the Irish. After the 12th century it fell into decline, and by the 15th century it was home only to an impoverished bishop. In 1552 the English garrison from Athlone reduced the site to a ruin: 'Not a bell, large or small, or an image, or an altar, or a book, or a gem, or even glass in a window, was left which was not carried away.'

Among the treasures that survived the continued onslaughts are the crosier of the abbots of Clonmacnoise in the National Museum, Dublin, and the 12th-century *Leabhar na hUidhre* (The Book of the Dun Cow), now in the Royal Irish Academy in Dublin.

Information

There's an on-site museum and coffee shop, and a **tourist office** (☎ 967 4134; ⏰ 10am-5.45pm Easter-Oct) just by the entrance. If you want to avoid the crowds it's a good idea to visit early or late; the tiny country lanes nearby are rammed full of coaches in summer.

Sights

MUSEUM

The three beehivelike structures near the entrance are a museum echoing the design of the early monastic dwellings. The centre's 20-minute audiovisual show is an excellent introduction to the site.

The exhibition area contains the original high crosses (replicas have been put in their former locations outside), and various artefacts uncovered during excavation, including silver pins, beaded glass and an ogham stone. It also contains the largest collection of early Christian graveslabs in Europe. Many are in remarkable condition with inscriptions clearly visible, often starting with *oroit do* or *ar* (a prayer for).

HIGH CROSSES

Well done to the museum for their moody display: there's a real sense of drama as you descend to the foot of the sandstone **Cross of the Scriptures**, one of Ireland's finest. It's

very distinctive, with unique upward-tilting arms and richly decorated panels depicting the Crucifixion, the last judgement, the arrest of Jesus, and Christ in the tomb. A couple of figures with natty beards have been interpreted as Abbot Cólman and King Flann, who erected the cross.

Only the shaft of the **North Cross**, which dates from around AD 800, remains. It is adorned by lions, convoluted spirals and a single figure, thought to be the Celtic god Cerrunnos, or Carnunas, who sits in a Buddhalike position. The richly decorated **South Cross** has mostly abstract carvings – swirls, spirals and fretwork – and, on the western face, the Crucifixion.

CATHEDRAL

The biggest building at Clonmacnoise, the cathedral, was originally built in AD 909, but was significantly altered and remodelled over the centuries. Its most interesting feature is the intricate 15th-century Gothic doorway with carvings of St Francis, St Patrick and St Dominic. A whisper carries from one side of the door to the other, and this feature was supposedly used by lepers to confess their sins without infecting the priests.

The last high kings of Tara – Turlough Mór O'Connor (died 1156) and his son Ruairí, or Rory (died 1198) – are said to be buried near the altar.

At the time of writing, the cathedral was undergoing extensive restoration work, hopefully to be completed by mid-2006.

TEMPLES

The small churches are called temples, a derivation of the Irish word *teampall* (church). The little, roofed church is **Temple Connor**, still used by Church of Ireland parishioners on the last Sunday of the summer months. Walking towards the cathedral, you pass the scant foundations of **Temple Kelly** (1167) before reaching tiny **Temple Ciarán**, reputed to be the burial place of St Ciarán, the site's founder.

The floor level in Temple Ciarán is lower than outside because for centuries local farmers have been taking clay from the church to protect their crops and cattle. The floor has been covered in slabs, but handfuls of clay are still removed from outside the church in the early spring.

Near the temple's southwestern corner is a *bullaun* (ancient grinding stone), supposedly used for making medicines for the monastery's hospital. Today the rainwater that collects in it is said to cure warts.

Continuing round the compound you come to 12th-century **Temple Melaghlin**, with its attractive windows, and the twin structures of **Temple Hurpan** and **Temple Doolin**.

ROUND TOWERS
Overlooking the River Shannon is the 20m-high **O'Rourke's Tower**. Lightning blasted the top off the tower in 1135, but the remaining structure was used for another 400 years.

Temple Finghin and its round tower are on the northern boundary of the site, also overlooking the Shannon. The building dates from around 1160 and has some fine Romanesque carvings. The unusual herringbone-patterned tower roof is the only one in Ireland that has never been altered. Most round towers became shelters when the monasteries were attacked, but this one was probably just used as a bell tower since the doorway is at ground level.

OTHER REMAINS
Beyond the site's boundary wall, 500m east through the modern graveyard, is the secluded **Nun's Church**. From here the main site, including the towers, is invisible. The church has wonderful Romanesque arches with minute carvings; one has been interpreted as Ireland's earliest sheila-na-gig, but is more probably an acrobat.

To the west of the site, on the ridge near the car park, is a motte with the oddly shaped ruins of a 13th-century **castle**.

Sleeping
Kajon House (☎ /fax 967 4191; www.kajonhouse.cjb .net; Creevagh; d from €55; ☒ Feb–Oct; ℗) The chatty, genial hosts here welcome you with a pot of tea and a warm scone; there's such a relaxed atmosphere that you're instantly put at ease. Comfortable modern rooms have squashy beds, shared by the odd teddy bear! This is one of the closest places to stay to Clonmacnoise: just 1.5km from the ruins on the road signposted to Tullamore.

Meadowview (☎ 967 4257; meadowviewaccom@ eircom.net; Clonmacnoise; s/d from €40/60) Even closer is this new dormer bungalow, set back off the road about 1km from the entrance to

the ruins. They're friendly folk here too, and rooms are bright, airy and have an en suite.

Glebe Caravan & Camping Park (☎ 643 0277; www.glebecaravanpark.ie; Clonfanlough; camp sites €14; ☒ Easter–mid-Oct) This caravan park, 5km east of Clonmacnoise, is on a beautiful 3-hectare site. Amenities include a modern shower and toilet block, TV and games room, laundry, kitchen and playground.

Getting There & Away
Clonmacnoise is 7km north of Shannonbridge and about 24km south of Athlone. **Bus Éireann** (☎ 01-836 6111) operates 15 buses daily from Dublin to Athlone (€10.50, two hours), but after that things can get more complicated.

Paddy Kavanagh (☎ 087 240 7706) in Athlone runs private tours to Clonmacnoise and to the Bog Railway, accompanied by poetry and song. Prices are subject to variation depending on the number of people and how long you want to be at the site, so contact him to make arrangements.

There are river cruises to Clonmacnoise from Athlone in County Westmeath (see p480).

A **taxi** (☎ 647 4400) from Athlone will cost roughly €45, including an hour's wait.

TULLAMORE
☎ 0506 / pop 10,270
Tullamore (Tulach Mór), Offaly's county town, suffered two strange setbacks in its history. In 1764, the earl drowned in a freak accident. As his son was only six months old at the time, and unable to grant new building leases until he was of legal age, the town went into a Sleeping Beauty–style slumber for the next 21 years. It was rudely awakened by a second freak accident, when a hot-air balloon crashed in 1785 and burnt down most of the town.

In the long run, the effect was negligible: Tullamore is Ireland's fastest-growing town today. It's famous for smooth Tullamore Dew whiskey; although production has moved to County Tipperary, you can still visit the old distillery on the banks of the Grand Canal and have a snifter of the amber liquid. The other big sight is the magnificent Charleville Forest Castle.

Tullamore has one other claim to fame: Ireland's last public execution took place in 1865 at Tullamore Gaol.

CENTRAL SOUTH

Information

Post office (O'Connor Sq)

Tourist office (☎ 52617; tullamoredhc@eircom.net; Bury Quay; 🕙 9am-6pm Mon-Sat, noon-5pm Sun May-Sep, 10am-5pm Mon-Sat, noon-5pm Sun Oct-Apr) Inside the Tullamore Dew Heritage Centre.

Sights

CHARLEVILLE FOREST CASTLE

Spires, turrets, clinging ivy and creaking trees combine to give this extraordinary structure an eerie Gothic feel. **Charleville Forest Castle** (☎ 23040; www.charlevillecastle.com; admission for 1 or 2 people €16, per additional person €6; 🕙 regular tours Jul & Aug, by appointment Sep-Jun) was the family seat of the Burys, who commissioned the design in 1798 from Francis Johnston, one of Ireland's most famous architects. The interior is spectacular, with stunning ceilings and one of the most striking Gothic-revival galleries in Ireland. The kitchen block was built to resemble a country church. There's an ornate stable yard nearby, and ancient oak trees fill the extensive grounds.

Admission is by 35-minute tour only. If you'd like to help restore this gem, you can join groups of international volunteers; contact the castle for details. The entrance is on Charleville Rd, south of town on the road to Limerick.

TULLAMORE DEW HERITAGE CENTRE

Located in a canalside warehouse, the **heritage centre** (☎ 25015; www.tullamore-dew.org; Bury Quay; adult/child €5/3.20; 🕙 9am-6pm Mon-Sat, noon-5pm Sun May-Sep, 10am-5pm Mon-Sat, noon-5pm Sun Oct-Apr) tells the story of Tullamore Dew whiskey and the importance of the Grand Canal in the town's development. There are 'interactive' exhibits – have a go at coopering or raking malt – and some interesting snippets about the town, like the story of the terrible hot-air balloon disaster of 1785. At the end of your visit, you get to sample a glass of the golden liquor.

Activities

For information on hiring narrow boats on the canal, see p330.

Sleeping & Eating

Moorhill Hotel (☎ 21395; www.moorhill.ie; Clara Rd; s/d €68/100; P) Think 'boutique': this Victorian retreat is newly renovated, charming and eager to impress. If you don't fancy

trailing into town, there's a classy French-Irish restaurant (open noon to 3pm Monday to Friday, noon to 3.30pm Sunday, 6.30 to 10pm Wednesday to Saturday), also open to nonresidents, on the premises. The house is set amid chestnut trees about 3km north of town on the N80.

Bridge House Hotel & Leisure Club (☎ 22000; www.bridgehouse.com; Bridge St; s/d €109/178; P) Tullamore's long-established hotel has undergone a massive face-lift and upgraded its facilities to include a range of comfy, if fussy, rooms with Jacuzzi-equipped bathrooms. There's a giant leisure club with pool, gym and outdoor spa. Its bars and restaurant (mains €10 to €15; open 12.30pm to 2.30pm daily, 5.30pm to 10pm Monday to Saturday, 5.30pm to 9pm Sunday) are always busy and serve a mix of grills and steaks.

Señor Rico (☎ 52839; Patrick St; pizza & pasta €10-16; 🕙 noon-2.30pm & 6-11pm Mon-Fri, 6-11pm Sat, 2-10.30pm Sun) This proper-napkins Italian restaurant is Tullamore's best eatery. It's a busy, family-orientated place, with fast service and decently priced dishes. The speciality is charcoal steak with aubergine, tomato and garlic; but there are plenty of other options, including some tasty seafood.

Getting There & Away

BUS

Bus Éireann (☎ 21431) stops at the train station, south of town. From Tullamore there are seven buses daily each way Monday to Friday (one Saturday and Sunday) on the route to Dublin (€13, 2½ hours), one daily Monday to Friday and Sunday to Portumna (€11.20, 50 minutes), and two daily (one Sunday) on the route between Waterford (€17.50, 3¼ hours) and Athlone (€7, 40 minutes).

Kearns Transport (☎ 0509-22244; www.kearnstransport.com) runs services to Tullamore on its Dublin–Portumna route. To Dublin, there are three buses per day Sunday to Thursday, four on Friday and two on Saturday; from Dublin, there are three buses per day Friday to Monday, and two on Tuesday, Wednesday and Thursday (one way from Tullamore €7).

TRAIN

There are nine trains daily Monday to Saturday (seven Sunday) to Dublin (€21, 1¼ hours) and eight daily Monday to Saturday (five Sunday) to Galway (€23.50, 1¾ hours).

DURROW ABBEY

Founded by St Colmcille (also known as St Columba) in the 6th century, **Durrow Abbey** is most famous for producing the illustrated *Book of Durrow*. The 7th-century text is the earliest of the great manuscripts to have survived – a remarkable feat considering it was recovered from a farm where it was dipped in the cattle's drinking water to cure illnesses. It can be seen today at Trinity College, Dublin.

The site contains five early Christian gravestones and Durrow's splendid 10th-century **high cross**, whose complex, high relief carvings depict the sacrifice of Isaac, the Last Judgement and the Crucifixion; it was possibly created by the same stonemason who carved the Cross of the Scripture at Clonmacnoise. In December 2003 the government bought the site and moved the gravestone and cross into the nearby Protestant church for protection. At the time of writing, the church was being reroofed (with a view to turning it into a visitor centre) and was inaccessible to visitors, but access should be improved by late 2006.

The path north past the church leads to **St Colmcille's Well**, a place of pilgrimage marked by a small cairn of stones.

Durrow Abbey is 7km north of Tullamore down a long lane west off the N52 Kilbeggan road.

County Clare

Clare (An Clár) sits quietly between Galway to the north and Kerry to the south, unmoved by the starry reputations of those two famous Irish counties. Yet Clare wins hands down when it comes to startling landscape and dramatic prehistoric artefacts. It may not boast the great mountains of Galway and Kerry, nor their corrugated coastlines, but there are few more compelling landscapes in all of Ireland than the Burren of north Clare, with its swooping hills of raw limestone and its mosaic of vividly coloured wild flowers. Here you'll find the bare bones of ancient burial chambers, the curving walls of Iron-Age castles, medieval tower houses and remote beaches. At the Cliffs of Moher, Clare can claim one of the world's great sea-cliff spectaculars.

The eastern part of Clare offers a relaxing alternative of wooded hills, glittering lakes and quiet waterways. Only the flat and featureless south of the county lacks the landscape magic, yet there is still much of interest in the lonely dwindling peninsula that runs southwest to the dramatic Loop Head, and in resorts such as Kilrush and Kilkee, or along the Shannon shoreline with its strange mix of medieval castles and its huge airport.

Many of Clare's towns and villages retain their traditional charm. The county town of Ennis has an engaging network of narrow streets, while villages such as Milltown Malbay and Kilfenora have grand old pubs that host traditional music sessions on various evenings. Two villages define Clare's keynote attractions: Doolin on the breezy west coast draws music lovers and backpackers, while lovely Ballyvaughan, on the southern shores of Galway Bay, is an ideal base for exploring the Burren.

HIGHLIGHTS

■ **A Monumental Monument**
The Burren's magical hills and ancient sites such as Poulnabrone Dolmen (p383)

■ **Can't Stop the Music**
Music from Ireland's finest musicians in the pubs of Ennis (p361) or Doolin (p379), or at Ennis's Glór centre (p361)

■ **Time Standing Still**
Peaceful Ballyvaughan (p382) on the Burren coast of Galway Bay, and the lonely Loop Head peninsula (p372)

■ **Diamonds in the Rough**
Quiet Clare villages of Corofin (p386), Kilfenora (p385) and Ennistymon (p374)

■ **History Bites!**
Feasting on history at Bunratty Castle's medieval banquets (p365)

Map labels: Ballyvaughan, Doolin, Poulnabrone Dolmen, Kilfenora, Ennistymon, Corofin, Ennis, Bunratty Castle, Loop Head

---

■ POPULATION: 103,277 | ■ AREA: 3147 SQ KM

ENNIS & AROUND

ENNIS

☎ 065 / pop 18,830

Ennis (Inis), Clare's main town, is a busy commercial centre and is ideally placed for reaching all parts of the county. It lies on the banks of the River Fergus, which runs east, then south into the Shannon Estuary.

History

The town's medieval origins are indicated by its irregular, narrow streets. Its most important historical site is Ennis Friary, founded in the 13th century by the O'Briens, kings of Thomond, who also built a castle here in the 13th century. Much of the wooden town was destroyed by fire in 1249 and again in 1306, when it was razed by one of the O'Briens.

In the town centre, the Square, is a **Daniel O'Connell monument**. His election to the British parliament by a huge majority in 1828 forced Britain to lift its bar on Catholic MPs and led to the Act of Catholic Emancipation a year later. The 'Great Liberator' stands on an extremely high column, so far above the rest of us you would hardly know he was there.

Eamon de Valera was *teachta Dála* (TD; member of the Irish Parliament) for Clare from 1917 to 1959. There's a **bronze statue** of him near the **courthouse**.

Orientation

The old town centre is on the Square, and the principal streets – O'Connell St, High St (becoming Parnell St), Bank Pl and Abbey St – radiate from there. The large but fairly mundane cathedral (1843) is at the southern end of O'Connell St.

Information

You can change money at the Bank of Ireland (which also has an ATM) and Ulster Bank, both on the Square. The post office is on Bank Place, northwest of the Square.

Abbey News Agency (36 Abbey St) Good selection of newspapers, local and international. It also sells Ordnance Survey maps.

De Valera Library (☎ 682 1616; Harmony Row; ☼ 10am-5.30pm Mon, Wed & Thu, 10am-8pm Tue & Fri, 10am-2pm Sat) Offers one hour of free Internet access. Also has dedicated email screens for short-term use.

Dimension X (☎ 689 3767; 4 Lower Market St; per 30 min €1; ☼ 10.30am-9pm) Decent Internet point.

Edgecom Computing (☎ 684 8642; 3 River Lane; per 15 min €0.75; ☼ 10am-10pm Mon-Sat, noon-10pm Sun) Has Internet access, but is slightly cramped.

Ennis Bookshop (☎ 682 9000; 13 Abbey St) Good for maps and books of local interest.

Ennis Tourist office (☎ 682 8366; www.shannonregion tourism.ie; Arthur's Row; ☼ 9.30am-5.30pm Jun-Sep, 9.30am-1pm & 2-5.30pm Mon-Sat Apr-May & Oct, 9.30am-1pm & 2-5.30pm Mon-Fri Nov-Mar) Very helpful and efficient. Can book accommodation for a €4 fee.

Youth Information Bureau (☎ 682 4137; Carmody St; ☼ 9am-5.30pm Mon-Fri, 10am-3pm Sat) General remit to advise young people, mainly on local matters. It has email, photocopying and other services.

Sights

ENNIS FRIARY

Just north of the Square is **Ennis Friary** (☎ 682 9100; Abbey St; adult/child €1.50/0.75; ☼ 10am-6pm Jun–mid-Sep, 10am-5pm Apr, May & mid-Sep–Oct). It was founded by Donnchadh Cairbreach O'Brien, king of Thomond, sometime between 1240 and 1249, though a lot of the present structure was completed in the 14th century. Partly restored, it has a graceful five-section window dating from the late 13th century, and a McMahon tomb (1460) with alabaster panels depicting scenes from the Passion. There are informative guided tours.

CLARE MUSEUM

In the same building as the tourist office is this absorbing **museum** (☎ 682 3382; Arthur's Row; admission free; ☼ 9.30am-5.30pm Jun-Sep, closed Sun Apr, May & Oct, closed weekends Nov-Mar). The 'Riches of Clare' exhibition tells the story of Clare from 6000 years ago to the present day using original artefacts and audiovisual presentations. It also relates the development of the submarine by Clare-born JP Holland.

Festivals & Events

Fleadh Nua (☎ 684 2988 during week of event only, ☎ 086 8260 3000 rest of year; ceoltrad@eircom.net) is a lively traditional music festival held in May, with singing, dancing and workshops.

Sleeping

BUDGET

Abbey Tourist Hostel (☎ 682 2620; www.abbey touristhostel.com; Harmony Row; dm €14-16, s/d €25/40) A well-run place, this old building stands alongside the River Fergus. Rooms are big and well equipped, and rates include a light breakfast. There's a kitchen and a laundry.

COUNTY CLARE

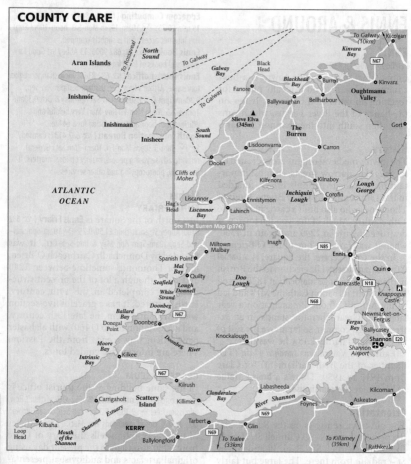

COUNTY CLARE

The hostel minibus arranges pick-ups from Shannon Airport for five people or more (€5 each) and you can arrange day trips round the Burren and other locations. Summer bike hire is €14/70 per day/week.

Aín Karem (☎ 682 0024; 7 Tulla Rd; s/d €40/57; P) Northeast of the centre, this modern two-storey house is pleasantly furnished and rooms are standard size. It's a bit further out from town, but buses stop outside.

MIDRANGE
Laurel Lodge (☎ 682 1560; Clare Rd; s/d €50/70; P) Very handy for town and set back from the busy Bunratty Rd, this big, well-run place has good-sized rooms and serves excellent breakfasts.

Four Winds (☎ 682 9831; Clare Rd; s/d €45/70; ☷ mid-Mar–mid-Oct; P) This is a pleasant house with decent rooms. There's a nice back garden. The friendly and chatty owners accept credit cards.

Newpark House (☎ 682 1233; www.newparkhouse .com; Tulla Rd; s/d €60/80; ☷ Easter-Oct; P) A beautiful country house dating from 1650, Newpark is 2km north of Ennis. Rooms are full of character and there are all sorts of fine furnishings. To get here go along the Scarriff road (R352) and turn right at the Roselevan Arms.

TOP END
Old Ground Hotel (☎ 682 8127; www.flynnhotels.com; O'Connell St; s/d €110/140; P) Rates drop by up to

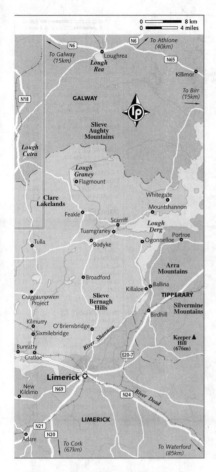

30% during low season at this marvellous old hotel, an Ennis institution. The building dates from the 18th century. With its own walled gardens, bars and restaurant, rambling corridors and busy public rooms, it brings a great sense of ease.

Temple Gate Hotel (☎ 682 3300; www.templegate hotel.com; the Square; s/d €120/170; P) You won't get a more central location than at this modern hotel. There are good discounts at quiet times. It also offers short-break deals. Rooms are plush and the public rooms have appealing mock-gothic trimmings.

West County Hotel (☎ 682 8421; www.lynchhotels .com; Clare Rd; s/d €75/130; P &) About 10 minutes south of the town centre, this updated modern hotel has excellent rooms and all

facilities are business standard. It handles a lot of conference business, but there's still a sense of individuality. There's a swish leisure suite and swimming pool.

Eating

Ennis has a good mix of restaurants, cafés and bars that serve food. For self-catering, Dunnes on O'Connell St has everything you'd need.

BUDGET

Glór Café (☎ 684 3103; Friar's Walk; mains €3.75-8.50; ☻ 10am-5pm Mon-Sat) It's worth dropping in to the café at Glór, the local arts centre, for a fresh, tasty range of filled rolls, ciabattas, wraps and salads, or a plate of beef-and-Guinness stew.

Hal Presto (1 Old Barrack St; sandwiches €4-7; ☻ 8am-7pm Mon-Thu, 8am-11pm Fri & Sat) Bringing a cheerful hint of continental style to Ennis, this café offshoot of fancier restaurant Hal Pino's does a good line in bagels and wraps, including vegetarian options, as well as soups and salads. There's also good coffee and real leaf teas, and on Friday and Saturday nights there's a wine bar and tapas scene.

Ennis Gourmet Store (☎ 684 3314; 1 Old Barrack St; snacks €4-9.50; ☻ 9am-7pm Mon-Sat, noon-6pm Sun) This place has a tasty range of sandwiches and baguettes with distinctive Mediterranean fillings. Its salads have a sunny style as well. The shop also sells a great choice of cheeses, preserves and other treats and has some excellent wines.

Brandon's Bar (☎ 682 8133; O'Connell St; lunch mains €8-10; ☻ food served 12.30-4pm) Brandon's is a great old pub that dishes up Irish stew as well as baguettes, sandwiches and wraps (€3 to €5.50).

O'Brien's Irish Sandwich Bar (☎ 682 2655; 5-6 Salthouse Lane; sandwiches €3.50-6.50) Takeaway culture and an all-day supply of sandwiches and wraps keep this place busy.

MIDRANGE

Poet's Corner Bar (☎ 682 8127; Old Ground Hotel, O'Connell St; lunch €4-9, dinner mains €8-10; ☻ 12.30-9pm) This famous old bar has a deserved reputation for its tasty dishes from strongly traditional boiled bacon and cabbage with parsley sauce, to chicken supreme and pasta. The great surroundings are vintage Clare.

Henry's (☎ 682 2848; Abbey St; lunch €4-9, dinner mains €11-13; ☻ 10.30am-10.30pm Mon-Sat) A cool,

COUNTY CLARE

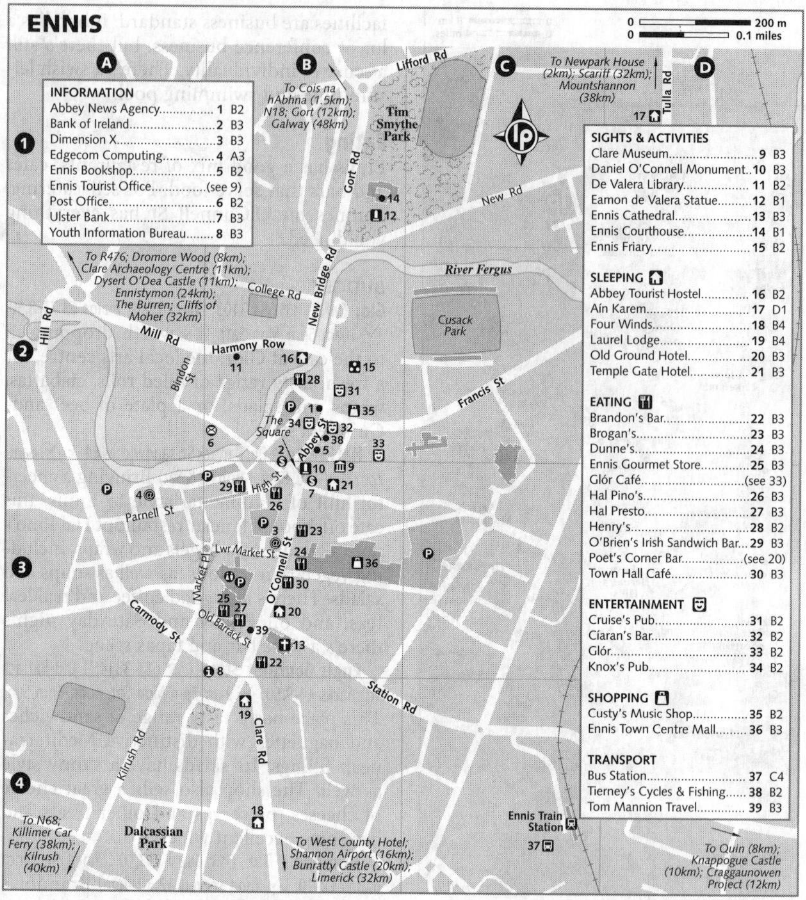
ENNIS
0 200 m
0 0.1 miles
INFORMATION
Abbey News Agency 1 B2
Bank of Ireland 2 B3
Dimension X 3 B3
Edgecom Computing 4 A3
Ennis Bookshop 5 B2
Ennis Tourist Office (see 9)
Post Office 6 B2
Ulster Bank 7 B3
Youth Information Bureau 8 B3
SIGHTS & ACTIVITIES
Clare Museum 9 B3
Daniel O'Connell Monument 10 B3
De Valera Library 11 B2
Eamon de Valera Statue 12 B1
Ennis Cathedral 13 B3
Ennis Courthouse 14 B1
Ennis Friary 15 B2
SLEEPING
Abbey Tourist Hostel 16 B2
Aín Karem 17 D1
Four Winds 18 B4
Laurel Lodge 19 B4
Old Ground Hotel 20 B3
Temple Gate Hotel 21 B3
EATING
Brandon's Bar 22 B3
Brogan's 23 B3
Dunne's 24 B3
Ennis Gourmet Store 25 B3
Glór Café (see 33)
Hal Pino's 26 B3
Hal Presto 27 B3
Henry's 28 B2
O'Brien's Irish Sandwich Bar 29 B3
Poet's Corner Bar (see 20)
Town Hall Café 30 B3
ENTERTAINMENT
Cruise's Pub 31 B2
Cíaran's Bar 32 B2
Glór 33 B2
Knox's Pub 34 B2
SHOPPING
Custy's Music Shop 35 B2
Ennis Town Centre Mall 36 B3
TRANSPORT
Bus Station 37 C4
Tierney's Cycles & Fishing 38 B2
Tom Mannion Travel 39 B3
To Cois na hAbhna (1.5km); N18; Gort (12km); Galway (48km)
Lifford Rd
Tim Smythe Park
To Newpark House (2km); Scariff (32km); Mountshannon (38km)
Tulla Rd
Gort Rd
New Rd
To R476; Dromore Wood (8km); Clare Archaeology Centre (11km); Dysert O'Dea Castle (11km); Ennistymon (24km); The Burren; Cliffs of Moher (32km)
River Fergus
College Rd
New Bridge Rd
Cusack Park
Hill Rd
Mill Rd
Harmony Row
Bindon St
Francis St
The Square
Abbey St
High St
Parnell St
Lwr Market St
Market Pl
O'Connell St
Carmody St
Old Barrack St
Station Rd
Kilrush Rd
Clare Rd
To N68; Killimer Car Ferry (38km); Kilrush (40km)
Dalcassian Park
To West County Hotel; Shannon Airport (16km); Bunratty Castle (20km); Limerick (32km)
Ennis Train Station
To Quin (8km); Knappogue Castle (10km); Craggaunowen Project (12km)

sunny café, this is a great place by the river for morning coffee, and lunch or evening meal choices from sandwiches to crisp salads and pizzas. There's a gentle international touch to the food.

Brogan's (☎ 682 9859; 24 O'Connell St; lunch mains €8-10, dinner mains €14-24; 🕑 10am-10pm) A big pub that stretches a long way back from the street. Food is straightforward Irish with plenty of meat, lamb and chicken dishes and the lunchtime clatter is nicely subdued. On the corner of Cooke's lane.

TOP END

Town Hall Café (☎ 682 8127; O'Connell St; lunch mains €5-14, dinner mains €15-24; 🕑 10am-4.45pm & 6-10pm) Ennis's handsome old town hall has been converted into this stylish eatery where you can relax over coffee, or lunch on such treats as Clare Coastline chowder scented with dill, goujons of chicken in a tortilla, or vegetarian spring rolls amid artworks and elegant décor. Dinner offers such fine treats as sesame-crusted sea bass, as well as beef and lamb and a vegetarian choice, all with international touches.

Hal Pino's (☎ 684 0011; 7 High St; mains €15-28; 🕑 5-10.30pm) From its smart and colourful exterior to the art-gallery dash of its upstairs restaurant, this is a stylish place and has attentive staff. They use local produce, and everything is prepared with an emphasis on flavour. Mains range from spicy tiger prawns in a coconut and chilli crust to pan-seared venison. Salmon, beef and pheasant are also featured and the fish menu ranges from mussels in garlic to monkfish, while the vegetarian menu has a generous half-dozen options. There are special menus ranging from €25 to €35.

Drinking & Entertainment

As the capital of a renowned music county, Ennis is not short of pubs with good music and other outlets for traditional culture as well as some contemporary clubs. The best sessions follow the best musicians, and pub scenes can change every now and then.

Brogan's (☎ 682 9859; 24 O'Connell St) One of the real trad session scenes at the time of writing, Brogan's sees a great gang of musicians ripping the roof off from about 9pm on Tuesday, Thursday, Friday and Sunday. On the corner of Cooke's Lane.

Brandon's Bar (☎ 682 8133; O'Connell St) Still holds its own for traditional sessions, on Monday nights especially; starts from about 9.30pm. During the day it serves food (see p359). Brandon's also stages live music, including blues, rock and contemporary.

Cruise's Pub (☎ 684 1800; Abbey St) Cruise's friendly bar is another good place for traditional music, with sessions nightly from 9.30pm.

Cíaran's Bar (☎ 684 0180; Francis St) This small, cosy place is popular with the local football crowd and has Irish music every night except Tuesday.

Glór (☎ 684 3103; www.glor.ie; Friar's Walk) Clare's flagship cultural centre, in a smart modern building, features the best of art, traditional music, theatre, dance and film. There's a strong Irish bias but the Glór buzz is international and terrific acts such as Ladysmith

Black Mambazo have been here. There's a big auditorium, a smaller studio, and an exhibition space for mainly contemporary painting, sculpture, ceramics and photography. Films are smack up-to-date.

Cois na hAbhna (☎ 682 0996; Gort Rd) This centre of traditional music is hallowed ground, housed in a custom-built pentagonal hall 1.5km north of town along the N18. There's a music session from 8.30pm to 11pm on Wednesday year round (€3) and on Saturday from 8.30pm to 10.30pm June to September (€3), with a full-blown *oíche céilidh* (music and dancing) one Saturday per month (€7). If you go along, be assured – you'll be up and dancing before you know it. The centre has an outstanding music archive and a good selection of tapes, books and records for sale.

Knox's Pub (☎ 682 2871; Abbey St) Knox's gives it all its got if you're looking for chart sounds, DJs riffing, full-on football mega-screen action and a generally bouncing crowd. Mr Knox, the original coffee, wine and spirits merchant, might even recognise some of the authentic old fittings that have survived. Knox's is open until midnight Monday to Wednesday, 1.30am Thursday, 1.45am Friday and Saturday, and 1am Sunday.

Shopping

On Saturday morning, there is a market at the Market Place. For general shopping, use the huge Ennis Town Centre mall, which contains Dunne's supermarket and can be entered halfway down O'Connell St.

Custy's Music Shop (☎ 682 1727; Francis St) The top place for a terrific stock of mainly Irish music, instruments, other musical items and general info about the scene. The CD range covers it all.

STRIKING A CHORD IN CLARE

Most visitors love the merest echo of Irish music, but the famous pub *seisún* (music session) can often be something of a staged affair; the best are impromptu, the very best are the regular get-togethers of local musicians and singers. There's a legion of superb local musicians who can light up any evening in every corner of Clare, often in a remote village bar or local hall. You can also get closer to the culture by visiting specialist music shops, such as Custy's in Ennis, and Irish cultural centres such as Glór and Cois na hAbhna (see above).

Famous Clare names of Irish music include the piper Willie Clancy, the fiddler Tommy Peoples, and Micho, Gus and Pakie Russell of Doolin. Modern Clare musicians who have gained worldwide acclaim include accordion player Sharon Shannon, who comes from near the village of Corofin. A singer whose voice is the essence of those western shores and islands is the Aran Island singer Lasairfhíona Ní Chonaola, who is a luminous performer of *sean-nós* (old style) songs in Irish.

Getting There & Away

BUS

The **bus station** (☎ 682 4177) is beside the train station. Buses run from Ennis to Limerick (€8.50, 40 minutes) up to 16 times a day Monday to Saturday (15 on Sunday). There are 12 direct buses daily to Dublin (€15, four hours) Monday to Saturday (10 on Sunday), 14 daily to Galway (€11, two hours), 12 daily to Cork (€15.50, three hours) and up to 15 a day (10 on Saturday and Sunday) to Shannon Airport (€5.50, 50 minutes).

TRAIN

From **Ennis station** (☎ 684 0444), direct trains for Dublin (€40, three hours) via Limerick leave several times a day Monday to Saturday, once on Sunday. There are frequent trains between Dublin and Limerick, 37km southeast of Ennis; check with **Limerick train station** (☎ 061-313 333).

Getting Around

For a taxi call **Burren Taxis** (☎ 682 3456) or pick one up at the taxi stands at the train station and beside the Daniel O'Connell Monument.

Tierney's Cycles & Fishing (☎ 682 9433; 17 Abbey St) has well-maintained mountain bikes costing €20/80 per day/week to hire, which includes a helmet, lock and repair kit. **Tom Mannion Travel** (☎ 682 4211; 71 O'Connell St) can fix you up with anything from a car to a motor home.

Parking is fairly good in Ennis. There's a big car park behind the tourist office in Friar's Walk and one alongside the river just off Abbey St. It's pay and display for about €1 per hour.

AROUND ENNIS

North of Ennis is the early Christian site of Dysert O'Dea; to the southeast are several fine castles.

GETTING AROUND

Local and express buses cover most areas around Ennis, but their frequency varies; many buses run only May to September (some only July and August) and on certain days. Before making plans confirm times and destinations with **Ennis bus station** (☎ 065-682 4177).

You can pick up the express bus service between Galway and Limerick in Ennis (up to 14 times daily) to get to Clarecastle, Newmarket-on-Fergus and Bunratty, but many stops on the route are 'request only'. Bus No 334 also operates daily to Limerick via Clarecastle, Newmarket-on-Fergus and sometimes Bunratty. On weekdays an infrequent service goes northwest to Ennistymon, then south along the coast to Kilkee.

Dysert O'Dea

On the Corofin road (R476), 11km north of Ennis, is **Dysert O'Dea**, the site where St Tola founded a monastery in the 8th century. The church and high cross, the White Cross of St Tola, date from the 12th or 13th century. The cross depicts Daniel in the lion's den on one side and a crucified Christ above a bishop carved in relief on the other. Look for carvings of animal and human heads in a semicircle on the southern doorway of the Romanesque church. There are also the remains of a 12m-high round tower.

In 1318 the O'Briens, who were kings of Thomond, and the Norman de Clares of Bunratty fought a pitched battle nearby, which the O'Briens won, thus postponing the Anglo-Norman conquest of Clare for some two centuries. The 15th-century O'Dea Castle nearby houses the **Clare Archaeology Centre** (☎ 065-683 7401; Corofin; adult/concession/family €4/3.50/10; ☺ 10am-6pm May-Sep). A 3km history trail around the castle passes some two dozen ancient monuments – from ring forts and high crosses to an ancient cooking site.

East of Dysert O'Dea off the N18 is **Dromore Wood** (☎ 065-683 7166; Ruan; admission free; visitor centre ☺ 10am-6pm mid-Jun–mid-Sep, wood ☺ daylight hours). This Dúchas nature reserve encompasses some 400 hectares as well as the ruins of the 17th-century O'Brien Castle, two ring forts and the site of Kilakee church.

GETTING THERE & AWAY

From mid-May to September, **Bus Éireann** (☎ 065-682 4177) runs one bus from Limerick (20 minutes), which leaves Ennis for Corofin and Ennistymon at 2.25pm Monday to Saturday and 12.25pm Sunday, passing Dysert O'Dea (€3.50) en route. The rest of the year, a bus departs Ennis on the same route at 3pm Monday to Saturday.

Quin
☎ 065 / pop 427

Quin (Chuinche), a tiny village 10km south-east of Ennis, was the site of the Great Clare Find of 1854 – the most important discovery of prehistoric goldwork in Ireland. Sadly, only a few of the several hundred torques, gorgets and other pieces, discovered by labourers working on the Limerick to Ennis railway, made it to the National Museum in Dublin: most were sold and melted down. The source of this and much of ancient Ireland's gold may have been the Wicklow Mountains.

The Franciscan friary **Quin Abbey** (☎ 684 4084; admission free; ☾ 10.30am-6pm Mon-Fri, 11.30am-5pm Sat & Sun May-Oct) was founded in 1433 using part of the walls of an older de Clare castle built in 1280. Despite many periods of persecution, Franciscan monks lived here until the 19th century. The last friar, Father Hogan, who died in 1820, is buried in one corner. The splendidly named Fireballs McNamara, a notorious duellist and member of the region's ruling family, is also buried here. An elegant belfry rises above the main body of the abbey, and you can climb the narrow spiral staircase to look down on the fine cloister and surrounding countryside.

Beside the friary is the 13th-century Gothic **Church of St Finghin**.

Abbey Tavern & Ardsolus Restaurant (☎ 682 5525; snacks €5.25-10, dinner mains €16-24; ☾ restaurant 6-9.30pm Wed-Sat) is at the centre of the village overlooking Quin Abbey. Bar meals are decent value and the restaurant cooks up traditional meat and fish dishes, with tasty stir-fries and herbed tagliatelle for vegetarians.

Knappogue Castle
About 3km southeast of Quin is **Knappogue Castle** (☎ 061-368 103; adult/child/family €6/3/16; ☾ 9.30am-4pm Apr-Oct). It was built in 1467 by the McNamaras, who held sway over a large part of Clare from the 5th to mid-15th century and built 42 castles in the region. Knappogue's walls are intact, and it has a fine collection of period furniture and fireplaces.

When Oliver Cromwell came to Ireland in 1649, he used Knappogue as a base, which is one of the reasons it was spared from destruction. The McNamara family regained the castle after the Restoration in 1660.

There's a small souvenir shop in the courtyard. Knappogue also hosts **medieval banquets** (☎ 061-360 788; adult/child under 9/child 9-12 €49/25/37; ☾ 6.30pm Apr-Oct). For medieval banquets at Bunratty Castle, see p365. Knappogue, unlike Bunratty, lays on knives and forks.

Craggaunowen Project
For a sense of Irish history visit the **Craggaunowen Project** (☎ 061-367 178; adult/child/family €7.50/4.50/19.50; ☾ 10am-6pm May-Aug). Located around 6km southeast of Quin, the project includes re-created ancient farms, dwellings such as a *crannóg* (artificial island) and a ring fort, plus real artefacts including a 2000-year-old oak road, and other items such as Tim Severin's leather boat, the *Brendan*, in which he crossed the Atlantic in 1976–77. Craggaunowen Castle is a small, well-preserved McNamara fortified house. With lots of animals, some rare, this is a good place for travellers with children.

The Craggaunowen Project also has a pleasant little café. Nearby Cullaun Lake is a popular boating and picnic spot, and there are forest trails.

EASTERN & SOUTHEASTERN CLARE

Away from the Atlantic coast and the rugged Burren uplands, Clare rolls gently eastward through low-lying green countryside that is given emphasis by the occasional range of smooth hills. The county's eastern boundary is the River Shannon and the long, wriggling inland waterway of Lough Derg, which stretches 48km from Portumna in County Galway, to just south of Killaloe. Lakeside villages such as Mountshannon seem a million miles away from the rugged, romantic west of Clare, but this is a delightful, intimate, country-side of water and woods and panoramic views. Southeastern Clare, where the Shannon swells into its broad estuary, is a plain landscape dotted with farms and small villages, but with the dramatic Bunratty Castle as a major attraction. Between Bunratty and Ennis lies the great entry point: Shannon Airport.

COUNTY CLARE

SHANNON AIRPORT

☎ 061

Shannon, Ireland's second-largest airport, used to be a vital fuelling stop on the transatlantic air route, as piston-engine planes barely had enough range to make it across the Atlantic to the European mainland. If you fly into Shannon (Sionainn), the extensive runways and numerous departure gates recall its successful past. The airport seems likely to expand its routes even more with the growth of budget airlines.

The world's first duty-free shop opened at Shannon in 1947; today, duty free is only available to those flying beyond the EU.

Information

In Shannon Town Centre (an enclosed shopping mall in the fairly featureless town of Shannon) there are two banks (Ulster Bank and Allied Irish Bank) and a post office. There's a bureau de change by the departure check-in. It opens at about 6am. There's a laptop plug-in at the Estuary Restaurant. Parking at Shannon's huge car parks costs €1 for 15 minutes or €2.50 per hour. Commit your car's position to memory or you'll never find it again.

Aer Rianta (☎ 712 000) This desk provides airport and flight information. Next door to the tourist office.

Bank of Ireland (☎ 471 100) Open from the first flight (about 6.30am) to 5.30pm.

Internet point (per 15 min €1.50) Outside the Hughes & Hughes Bookshop.

Tourist office (☎ 471 664; ☽ 6.30am-6pm May-Sep, 7am-5.30pm Oct-Apr) In the arrivals hall.

Sleeping

There's accommodation 3km from the airport in Shannon, Ireland's only 'new town' that was built from scratch, in this case to serve the airport.

Moloney's B&B (☎ 364 185; 21 Coill Mhara St; s/d €35/60; ℗) Rooms are spick-and-span and there's a friendly welcome at this Shannon stopover. Coming from the airport you need to turn right off the main drag at the big roundabout by the town centre. Keep on past the centre and at a crossroads go left down a slip road. Continue left past a school and the Shannon Leisure Centre. At the next junction go right, and then take the first left.

Shannon Great Southern Hotel (☎ 471 122; www.gshotels.com; r €155) This big modern hotel

directly in front of the airport terminal is ideal if you're taking an early flight. There can be discounts at times. There's a security barrier at the entrance.

Eating

Shannon Knights Inn (☎ 361 045; Shannon Town Centre; meals €3-9) Reasonable, if standard, food is available at this large pub in the centre of town.

Café 2000 (☎ 361 992; Shannon Town Centre; lunch €4-8; ☽ 8am-6pm Mon-Fri, 8am-5pm Sat) Smack bang at the heart of Shannon's big shopping mall, this busy café offers tasty lunches and sandwiches.

Getting There & Around

AIR

For general inquiries, call the airport authority, **Shannon Airport** (☎ 712 000). Airlines with direct flights to Shannon include **Aer Lingus** (☎ 715 400), **British Airways** (☎ 1800 626 747), **Delta Air Lines** (☎ 1800 768 080), **Ryanair** (☎ 0818 303 030), **Flybe** (☎ 1890 925 532) and **Continental** (☎ 712 670)

BUS

There are 18 **Bus Éireann** (airport ticket office ☎ 474 311) services daily to Ennis and 11 on Saturday and Sunday (€5.50, 50 minutes). The ticket office in the airport opens at 7am, and the first bus leaves at 8am. There are also services to major centres including Limerick (€5.50, 40 minutes, eight daily Monday to Saturday, 10 on Sunday), Galway (€14, two hours, up to 12 daily Monday to Saturday, one on Sunday) and Dublin (€15.50, three hours, 15 daily Monday to Friday, 12 on Saturday, six on Sunday).

TAXI

A taxi to the centre of Limerick or Ennis costs about €28 if booked at the taxi desk inside the airport. You may pay more at the outside rank. The taxi desk opens with first flights.

BUNRATTY

☎ 061

The castle at Bunratty (Bun Raite), which overlooks the Shannon Estuary, is in excellent condition and well worth a look, but it's a prime tourist attraction and is besieged by coach tours from April to September. However, the entire package is extremely worthwhile, more so if you go early in the day.

There's a small **visitor information office** (☎ 364 321; 🕑 9am-5.30pm Mon-Fri all year, 9am-5.30pm Sat & Sun mid-May–Sep) in Bunratty Village Mills, opposite the castle. It has a bureau de change and beside it is an ATM.

Bunratty Castle & Folk Park

The Vikings built a fortified settlement on this spot, a former island surrounded by a moat. Then came the Normans, and Thomas de Clare built the first stone structure on the site in the 1270s.

There's a joint-entry-fee option to both **Bunratty Folk Park** and **Bunratty Castle** (☎ 361 511; adult/child/family Apr-Sep €11/7/27, Oct-Dec €9/6/21, Jan-Mar €11/6/21; 🕑 9am-6.30pm Jun-Aug, 9.30am-5.30pm Sep-May, last admission 4pm). The present castle is the fourth incarnation to occupy the location beside the River Ratty. It was built in the early 1400s by the energetic McNamara family, but fell shortly thereafter to the O'Briens, kings of Thomond, in whose possession it remained until the 17th century. Admiral Penn, father of William Penn the Quaker founder of the US state of Pennsylvania and the city of Philadelphia, lived here for a short time.

A complete restoration was carried out more recently, and today the castle is full of fine 14th- to 17th-century furniture, paintings and wall hangings.

MEDIEVAL BANQUETS

The Great Hall hosts **medieval banquets** (☎ 360 788; adult/child under 9/child 9-12 €50/25/38; 🕑 5.30pm & 8.45pm), replete with harp-playing beauties, court jesters and food á la the Middle Ages, all washed down with mead, a kind of honey wine. You eat with your fingers. The banquets are very popular with coach parties so it's advisable for independent travellers to book well ahead. The whole thing is thoroughly enjoyable, taken in the right spirit.

The banquets at Knappogue Castle (p363) and Dunguaire Castle (in Galway, p417) are generally smaller and quieter affairs.

BUNRATTY FOLK PARK

The **folk park** (adult/child May-Sep €7/4.50, Oct-Dec €7/4, Jan-Apr €6/3.50) adjoins the castle. It is a reconstructed traditional Irish village with cottages, a forge and working blacksmith, weavers and buttermakers. There's a complete village street with post office, pub and small café. Some buildings were transplanted here from old settlements on what is now the site of Shannon airport. Peat fires glow romantically in the hearths and there's a persuasive feel to it all.

The **Traditional Irish Night** (bookings ☎ 360 788; adult/child under 9/child 9-12 €42/21/32; 🕑 7-9.30pm May-Oct) is held in a barn in the folk park, serving up music, dancing, wine, Irish stew, apple pie and soda bread and lashings of true Irish hospitality.

Sleeping

Bunratty's hotels tend to be expensive, but there are a couple of good-value B&Bs.

Rockfield House (☎ 364 391; Hill Rd; s/d €40/60; Ⓟ) High above the throng, but only minutes away from it all, this fine big house has excellent rooms, and you can even have the benefit of an electric blanket on chilly nights. Breakfasts are generous too.

Tudor Lodge (☎ 362 248; Hill Rd; s/d €50/70; Ⓟ) Located even further away, but still only a few minutes stroll from the centre, this handsome house among trees has excellent rooms.

Ashgrove House (☎ 369 332; www.ashgrovehouse .com; Low Rd; s/d €50/64; Ⓟ) Also well clear of the centre but a bit further away, this comfy and welcoming place has lots of little personal touches and treats.

Eating

Durty Nelly's (☎ 364 861; Bunratty House Mews; bar meals €5-12, restaurant mains €20) Nelly's churns out the food with a flourish. Bar meals range from toasted sandwiches to poached salmon salad. The Oyster Restaurant (open noon to 10.30pm) downstairs and Loft (open 6pm to 10.30pm Monday to Saturday) upstairs do a roaring trade. You can then walk it off at Bunratty Castle, which is next door.

Blarney Woollen Mills (☎ 364 321; Bunratty Village Mills; mains €5.50-11; 🕑 9am-6pm) Amid all the shopping extravaganza, this 1st-floor cafeteria-style restaurant serves a limited, but generally tasty, choice of dishes such as Irish stew and vegetable lasagne.

Drinking & Entertainment

Durty Nelly's (☎ 364082) Nelly's manages to keep doing the business with some style and you feel that you're still in the world of the nearby Folk Park. Even when topped up with tourists in summer, the local element still stands out and there's music every night starting at 10pm. Durty Nelly's also serves food.

Mac's Bar (☎ 361 511; Bunratty Folk Park) This engaging place is part of the Folk Park village. It has traditional music on Wednesday, Friday, Saturday and Sunday evenings June to September, and on weekends the rest of the year. You can still get there when the rest of the park is closed.

Shopping
Avoca Cottage (☎ 364 029) Crammed full of tweeds, crafts and woollen clothes, plus Waterford crystal and Belleek pottery, this outlet is situated just across the river from Durty Nelly's. Prices tend to reflect the high-profile tourism of Bunratty.

Blarney Woollen Mills (☎ 364 321; Bunratty Village Mills) This store stocks every 'Irish gift' you might conceive of, including Irish jumpers, Irish linen and Tipperary crystal, souvenirs and CDs.

Getting There & Away
Up to eight Bus Éireann services run directly from Limerick to Bunratty, stopping outside the Fitzpatrick Bunratty Shamrock Hotel. Bunratty is also served by up to 17 daily buses (10 on Sunday) on the Shannon Airport–Limerick route. Contact **Limerick bus station** (☎ 061-313 333) for times.

Buses travelling south through Bunratty leave Ennis daily from 10.12am onwards. Contact **Ennis bus station** (☎ 065-682 4177) for more details.

KILLALOE & BALLINA
☎ 061 / pop 1623
Killaloe (Cill Da Lúa) is picturesque Clare at its finest. It lies on the western banks of lower Loch Deirgeirt, the southern extension of Lough Derg, where the loch narrows at one of the principal crossings of the River Shannon. The village lies snugly against the Slieve Bernagh Hills that rise abruptly to the west. The Arra Mountains create a fine balance to the east and all of Lough Derg is at hand. The village is also on the 180km East Clare Way. A fine old 13-arch bridge spans the river, linking Killaloe with Ballina in County Tipperary. Some of the better pubs and restaurants of the area are in Ballina. From Killaloe, the Shannon is navigable all the way north to Lough Key in County Sligo, and in summer the town is jammed with weekend sailors.

Orientation & Information
The narrow street running from the river on the Killaloe side is Bridge St, which turns right and becomes Main St. The **tourist office** (☎ 376 866; the Lock House, Bridge St; ☽ 10am-6pm May–mid-Sep) is beside Shannon Bridge in Killaloe. Below, in the same building, free Internet access is available at **Killaloe Library** (☎ 376 062; ☽ 10am-1.30pm & 2.30-5.30pm Mon, Tue & Thu, 10am-5.30pm & 6.30-8pm Wed & Fri, 10am-2pm Sat).

The AIB bank at the bottom of Church St has an ATM. There's parking on both sides of the river, although space can be limited in high summer and at weekends.

There are toilets on the Killaloe side in the car park.

Sights & Activities
Killaloe Cathedral (St Flannan's Cathedral; ☎ 376 687; Limerick Rd) dates from the early 13th century and was built by the O'Brien family on top of a 6th-century church. Inside, magnificent carvings decorate the Romanesque southern doorway. Next to the doorway is the shaft of a stone cross, known as Thorgrim's Stone. It dates from the early Christian period and is unusual in that it bears both the old Scandinavian runic and Irish ogham scripts. In the cathedral grounds is St Flannan's Oratory, of 12th-century Romanesque design.

The **Killaloe & Brian Burú Exhibition Centre** (☎ 376 866; Lock House, Bridge St; adult/child €3/1.50; ☽ 10am-6pm May-Sep) has exhibits on local history and the cathedral.

Whelan's Foodstore (☎ 376 159; Church St, Killaloe) has a substantial selection of newspapers and magazines.

For all your fishing needs go to **TJ's Angling Centre** (☎ 376 009; Main St, Ballina). You can rent fishing tackle for €10 per day.

For boat hire try **Whelan's Boat Hire** (☎ 087 679 0771) which rents out 19ft lake boats for €15/50 per hour/day, including all equipment and fishing rods. For a lake cruise, the **Spirit of Killaloe** (☎ 086 814 0559), a 15m, 50-seater, covered vessel complete with bar and snack bar, does hour-long trips for €9.

Sleeping
There are lots of B&Bs in the area, but it's a popular getaway spot so call ahead.

Kincora House (☎ 376 149; www.kincorahouse.com; Church St, Killaloe; s/d €40/70) A friendly, comfy place that has a great sense of being at the heart of Killaloe.

Lakeland House (☎ 375 658; trudyryan@eircom .net; Boher Rd, Ballina; s/d €50/70; P) Nicely tucked away up a hillside road, this comfy, well-kept place has pleasant rooms and a big lounge for guests.

Waterman's Lodge (☎ 376 333; www.watermans lodge.ie; Ballina; s/d €100/190; P ⚲) In a great location on the Ballina side of the bridge, this attractive hotel faces downriver. Rooms have a satisfying country-house feel and there are handsome lounges and a restaurant.

Eating

Gooser's Bar & Eating House (☎ 376 791; Main St, Ballina; bar food €9.50-24, dinner mains €18-28; ☺ noon-10pm Mon-Sat, 12.30-9.30pm Sun) Only the masses of fellow foodies on busy weekends diminishes the Gooser's experience. This is a hugely popular place, noted for its terrific selection of fish, including delicious monkfish and a hefty seafood platter (€38), equally choice meat and poultry dishes, plus a discerning wine list.

Simply Delicious (☎ 375 335; Main St, Ballina; breakfast €6-7.50, lunch mains €6.50-9; ☺ 8.30am-5pm) Down-to-earth and friendly, this is a great local favourite that offers tasty lunch dishes, sandwiches and salads. It's open for filling breakfasts, including a vegetarian option.

Molly's Bar & Restaurant (☎ 376 632; Main St, Ballina; mains €10-24; ☺ food served noon-10pm) A riverside pub eatery, Molly's gets very busy. It offers strong Irish standards such as bacon and cabbage, but also does Greek salad, pastas, pizzas and filling baguettes (€7).

Waterman's Lodge (☎ 376 333; Ballina; P ⚲) The lodge restaurant offers á la carte meals for about €48.

Drinking & Entertainment

Most pubs provide some kind of music during the week.

Molly's Bar (☎ 376 632; Main St, Ballina) Serves up the sounds, as well as food, with chart selects and '80s favourites. There's a disco Saturday and Sunday all year and also on Friday from May to September.

Crotty's Bar (☎ 376 965; Main St, Killaloe) Tucked away in a courtyard behind the Crotty grocery store, this plain local pub provides traditional music on some weekends.

Anchor Inn (☎ 376 108; Bridge St, Killaloe) The cheerful Anchor Inn stages traditional music sessions on Wednesday night, and there's live music at weekends.

Getting There & Away

There are two **Bus Éireann** (☎ 313 333) buses a day Monday to Saturday from Limerick to Killaloe (€5, 45 minutes). The bus stop is outside the cathedral.

KILLALOE TO MOUNTSHANNON

The journey north to Mountshannon alongside Lough Derg is scenic and relaxing. To get to Mountshannon from Killaloe take the Scarriff (An Scairbh) road.

About 1.5km north of Killaloe, **Beal Ború** is an earthen mound or fort said to have been Kincora, the palace of the famous Irish king Brian Ború, who defeated the Vikings at the Battle of Clontarf in 1014. Traces of Bronze Age settlement have been found. With its commanding view over Lough Derg, this was obviously a site of strategic importance.

About 4km north of Killaloe is the **University of Limerick Activity Centre** (☎ 061-376 622; www.ulac.ie; Two Mile Gate; ⚲). Here individuals and groups can learn water-based skills including canoeing, sailing and windsurfing. Land-based activities include archery, orienteering and forest games. There's a very impressive, high-rig frame on which to get to grips with rope work. A weekend water-based skills course costs from €185 per person. Weekend courses for families cost €600.

About 4.5km north of Killaloe is Cragliath Hill, which has another fort, **Griananlaghna**, named after Brian Ború's great-grandfather, King Lachtna.

Sleeping & Eating

Lantern House (☎ 061-923 034; www.lanternhouse .com; Ogonnelloe, Killaloe; s/d €44/80; P) Located about 9km north of Killaloe, and in a superb location overlooking Lough Derg, this modern house has high standards of service. There's a restaurant (mains €12 to €24; open 6pm to 9pm mid-February to October) attached that offers distinctive modern Irish cuisine. Booking is advised.

Kincora Hall Hotel (☎ 061-376 000; www.kincora hall.com; Killaloe; s/d €120/198; P) This handsome hotel sits right on the lochside and has its own marina. There's a comfy away-from-it-all feel to everything; rooms are big and are stylishly done out and there's a plush library for relaxing. The bar has an appealing menu of dishes (€4.50 to €16.50) such

COUNTY CLARE

as chowder and stir-fry, and the in-house restaurant (three-course dinner €35, mains €13.50 to €22.50) is noted for its tasty desserts.

Lough Derg Holiday Centre (☎ 061-376 777; www.loughderg.net; Scarriff Rd, Killaloe; camp sites €20; ☺ mid-May–mid-Sep) Located 5km north of Killaloe, near the loch shore, this is the place to go if you're into fishing and water sports. You can organise most of these activities from the site.

MOUNTSHANNON & AROUND
☎ 061 / pop 309

The attractive village of Mountshannon (Baile Uí Bheoláin), on the southwestern shores of Lough Derg, was founded in 1742 by an enlightened landlord to house a largely Protestant community of flax workers.

The harbour is host to a fair number of angling boats, and visiting yachts and cruisers in summer. It is the main centre for trips to Holy Island, one of Clare's finest early Christian settlements. There's great fishing here, mainly for brown trout, pike, perch and bream. Ask at B&Bs about boat hire and equipment.

There are toilets by the harbour.

Holy Island
Lying 2km offshore from Mountshannon, Holy Island (Inis Cealtra) is the site of a **monastic settlement** thought to have been founded by St Cáimín in the 7th century. On the island you'll see a round tower that is over 27m tall (though missing its top storey). You'll also find four old chapels, a hermit's cell and some early Christian gravestones dating from the 7th to 13th centuries. One of the chapels has an elegant Romanesque arch. Inside the chapel is an inscription in old Irish, which translates as 'Pray for Tornog, who made this cross'.

The Vikings treated this monastery roughly in the 9th century, but under the subsequent protection of Brian Ború and others it flourished.

From Mountshannon you can take a cruise around the island with **Ireland Line Cruises** (☎ 375 011; Killaloe; adult/child €7/4.50; ☺ late Apr–Oct). Trips can also be arranged from Mountshannon through the **East Clare Heritage Centre** (☎ 921 351, 921 615; Tuamgraney), about 10km southwest on the R352.

Sleeping & Eating
Derg Lodge (☎ 927 319, 927 180; bridgebarbb@mail .com; Whitegate Rd, Mountshannon; s/d €30/50; ℗) This pleasant four-room B&B is about 500m from the village. It hires boats for €35 per day, €65 with a gillie (boatperson).

Oak House (☎ 927 185; howemaureen@eircom.net; Mountshannon; s/d €42/64; ℗) Just 200m north of the village, this distinctive house is an angler's paradise. You can hire boats for €16 per day and there's plenty of fishing lore available. Rooms have a cosy lodgelike ambience, and the lovely garden overlooking Lough Derg has recently been extended and landscaped superbly.

Mountshannon Hotel (☎ 927 162; Main St, Mountshannon; s/d €50/80; ☺ Mar–Oct) Things are a touch old fashioned in this little hotel, but it has a pleasant atmosphere and there's a busy and popular bar and restaurant (lunch meals €3.50 to €18).

Lakeside Caravan & Camping Park (☎ 927 225; www.lakesideireland.com; Mountshannon; camp sites €16; ☺ May–Oct) This spacious park has a fine lakeside location and hires out boats and equipment for windsurfing, rowing and sailing. From Mountshannon, head north along the Portumna road (R352) for 2km and take the first turn-off on the right.

Rob's An Cupán Caifé (☎ 927 275; Main St; dinner mains €13-16; ☺ 10.30am-9pm May-Aug, 12.30-9pm Sep-Apr, closed Tue) This café-restaurant has a charmingly intimate atmosphere. It does Irish, continental and vegetarian breakfasts (€7.50 to €9) and sandwiches (€3.50 to €5) and lunch dishes including salads and stir-fries for about €9.

Getting There & Away
On weekdays, **Bus Éireann** (☎ 313 333) bus No 345 runs twice daily from Limerick to Killaloe and continues to Scarriff (8km southwest of Mountshannon). On Wednesday and Saturday only, bus No 346 from Limerick (departing at 1.15pm) to Whitegate via Scarriff runs to Mountshannon (1½ hours). Buses stop outside Keane's on the main street.

NORTH TO GALWAY
North of Mountshannon, the R352 follows Lough Derg to Portumna in Galway. Inland is an area known as the Clare Lakelands, based around Feakle, where numerous lakes offer good coarse fishing.

SOUTHWESTERN & WESTERN CLARE

Loop Head on Clare's southwestern tip meets the Atlantic face to face. In stormy weather massive waves thunder in and obliterate with huge bursts of spray the great cliffs that lie between the Head and the seaside resort of Kilkee. Southeast of Kilkee on the Shannon estuary is the attractive town of Kilrush. North of Kilkee the road (N67) edges away from the coast, but there are some worthwhile detours to beaches where Spanish Armada ships were wrecked over 400 years ago. Kilkee, White Strand, Spanish Point and Lahinch all have good beaches.

North of Lahinch the road hugs the coast again across the neck of Hag's Head to reach the spectacular Cliffs of Moher, one of Ireland's most iconic tourist attractions. Beyond lies that great centre of Irish music, the village of Doolin, lying scattered across a rugged, exposed landscape at the edge of the Atlantic and on the southern threshold of the magical Burren.

North and northwest of Ennis, the Doolin and Burren areas are approached through pleasant settlements such as Corofin, Kilfenora and Ennistymon.

This region is great for cycling, and two signposted routes are the Loop Head Cycleway and West Clare Cycleway.

Getting There & Away

BOAT

Shannon Ferry Limited (☎ 905 3124; www.shannon ferries.com) runs a 20-minute car ferry from Killimer, across the Shannon Estuary, to Tarbert in County Kerry. You pay on board. See p276 for fares and times.

BUS

There are infrequent local bus services to the coastal towns and villages; some buses run from Limerick, while others are on express routes from Galway or Tralee. Services are more frequent May to September. Phone the **Ennis bus station** (☎ 065-682 4177) or **Limerick bus station** (☎ 061-313 333) for exact times and fares.

Bus Éireann express bus No 15 terminates in Ennis or Ennistymon. It runs through Doolin, Lisdoonvarna, Lahinch, Miltown Malbay, Kilkee and Kilrush. The Killarney–Galway bus No 50 stops in Ballyvaughan, Lisdoonvarna, Doolin, the Cliffs of Moher, Lahinch, Miltown Malbay, Doonbeg, Kilkee and Kilrush. Bus No 333 travels between Limerick, Ennis, Ennistymon, Lahinch, Milton Malbay, Quilty, Doonbeg, Kilkee and Kilrush.

Bus No 336 between Kilkee and Limerick travels via Kilrush and Ennis four times a day Monday to Saturday (three on Sunday) late June to August, and twice a day rest of the year. Bus No 337 runs three times daily between Limerick and Lisdoonvarna, passing through Ennis, Ennistymon, Lahinch, Liscannor, the Cliffs of Moher and Doolin, from mid-May to September. The rest of the year it goes twice daily.

KILRUSH

☎ 065 / pop 2699

Kilrush (Cill Rois) is an engaging small town that overlooks the Shannon Estuary and the hills of Kerry to the south. The main street, Frances St, runs directly to the harbour. It is more than 30m wide, reflecting Kilrush's origins as a port and market town in the 19th century, when there was much coming and going between land and sea. It has the western coast's biggest **marina** (www.kilrushcreek marina.ie) located at Kilrush Creek.

Kilrush's tourist office (☎ 905 1577; 2 Frances St; ☯ 9.30am-1pm & 2-5.30pm Mon-Sat, 10am-2pm Sun Jun–early Sep) has plenty of information about the area. In Market Sq there's an ACC bank with ATM and on Frances St you'll find an Allied Irish Bank with an ATM and the post office. The **Internet Bureau** (☎ 905 1061; Frances St; per 10 min €2) is at the very bottom of Frances St.

COUNTY CLARE'S TOP FIVE PUBS

- Eugene's (p374; Ennistymon) – a terrific talkers' pub.
- Vaughan's Pub (p385; Kilfenora) – the place to sing and dance your feet off.
- Poet's Corner Bar (p359; Ennis) – offers great food in literary company.
- Crotty's Pub (p370; Kilrush) – timelessness personified.
- Brogan's (p361; Ennis) – one of the sparkiest trad music scenes around.

COUNTY CLARE

Sights & Activities

St Senan's Catholic church, on Toler St, contains eight detailed examples of stained glass by well-known artisan Harry Clarke. East of town is **Kilrush Wood**, which has some fine old trees and a picnic area.

Vandeleur Walled Garden (☎ 905 1760; adult/child €5/2; ☽ 10am-6pm Apr-Oct, 10am-5pm Nov-Mar) is a remarkable 'lost' garden. It was the private domain of the wealthy Vandeleur family, merchants and landowners who engaged in harsh eviction and forced emigration of local people in the 19th century. The gardens lie within a large walled area and have been redesigned and planted with colourful and unusual plants. There are woodland trails around the area and the reception has a coffee shop.

Near the marina is **Kilrush Creek Adventure Centre** (☎ 905 2855; www.kcac.nav.to; Kilrush Creek; ☽ 10am-4.30pm). It offers a range of activities including archery, windsurfing, kayaking, sailing and power boating (nonresident multiactivity is €30/50 for a half/full day) plus accommodation.

Weather permitting, you can do a two- to 2½-hour dolphin-watching trip on Shannon Estuary with **Dolphin Discovery** (☎ 905 1327; www.discoverdolphins.ie; Cappa, Kilrush; adult/child €18/9). Boats leave from Kilrush Creek Marina.

Sleeping

Katie O'Connor's Holiday Hostel (☎ 905 1133; katieoconnors@eircom.net; Frances St; dm/d €15/32; ☽ mid-Mar–Oct) This fine old main-street house dates from the 18th century, and was one of the town houses of the Vandeleur family. It's an atmospheric place with pleasant rooms, and there are nice touches such as panels with historical details of Kilrush.

Hillcrest View (☎ 905 1986; www.hillcrestview .com; Doonbeg Rd; s/d €50/70; P) This large house, at the top of the hill where the Doonbeg road climbs out of Kilrush, is about 1km from the centre. It has lavish furnishings, and breakfast is served in a pleasant conservatory.

Dolphins Pass (☎ 905 1822; jemesbandb@esatclear .ie; Aylevarroo, Kilrush; s/d €35/55; ☽ Jul-mid-Sep; P) Watch ruby-red sunsets flood the headlands, or spot dolphins from this bright and relaxed modern house overlooking Kilrush Creek, 3km west of town.

Eating

Kelly's Bar & Restaurant (☎ 905 1811; 26 Henry St; lunch €7-8, dinner mains €12.50-20; ☽ 11am-9pm Mon-Sat, 12.30-9pm Sun) This delightful pub-restaurant has polished dark woodwork and snug seating, with its handsome bar as the main focus. It does tasty sandwiches (€4.50 to €8) including a hefty double-decker, as well as pastas, stir-fries and traditional Irish dishes.

Coffey's (☎ 905 1104; Market Sq; sandwiches €3, pizzas €6.50-16; ☽ 10am-5pm Tue-Sat) This cheerful and busy place on the main square serves breakfasts all day, decent sandwiches and pizzas, plus fish and chips from a takeaway section.

Drinking & Entertainment

Crotty's Pub (☎ 905 2470; Market Sq) Brimming with character, Crotty's has an old-fashioned high bar, tiled floors and a series of snugs decked out with traditional furnishings, including a kitchen complete with old range. You can enjoy music on Tuesday, Thursday and Saturday nights.

Kelly's Bar & Restaurant (☎ 905 1811; 26 Henry St) As well as being a good place to eat, Kelly's is great for just a drink and it has occasional music sessions.

Getting There & Around

For information on buses to and from Kilrush, see p369.

You can hire bikes at **Gleeson's Cycles** (☎ 905 1127; Henry St; per day/week €20/80, day deposit €40).

SCATTERY ISLAND

This uninhabited, windswept, treeless island, 2.5km southwest of Cappa pier, is the site of a Christian settlement founded by St Senan in the 6th century. Its 36m-high **round tower** is one of the tallest and best preserved in Ireland, and the entrance is at ground level instead of the usual position high above the foundation. There are remains of five **medieval churches**, including a 9th-century cathedral.

An exhibition on the history and wildlife of the island is housed in the Scattery Island Visitor Centre. Admission is free.

Getting There & Away

The harbour at Cappa village near Kilrush is where you catch the boat to Scattery Island. To get there turn left at the bottom of Frances St in Kilrush and follow the road for 2km.

Scattery Island Ferries (☎ 065-905 1327) runs boats from Kilrush Creek Marina to the island (return adult/child €12/6, 20 minutes, mid-June to mid-September). There's no strict timetable as the trips are subject to tidal and weather conditions. There's a stay of about an hour on the island. You can buy tickets at the small kiosk at the marina.

KILKEE
☎ 065 / pop 1260

During the summer, Kilkee's wide semicircular bay is thronged with day-trippers and holiday-makers, mainly from Clare and Limerick. Kilkee (Cill Chaoi) first became popular in Victorian times when rich Limerick families built seaside retreats here. Today, it is well supplied with guesthouses, amusement arcades and takeaways. Its exhilarating beach and good-natured atmosphere make it an enjoyable stop.

Information
Bank of Ireland (O'Curry St) Has an ATM.
Post office (O'Connell St) Across from the library.
Tourist office (☎ 905 6112; O'Connell St; ☒ 9.30am-5.30pm)Just up to the left from the seafront.

Sights & Activities
Many visitors come for the fine sheltered **beach** and the **Pollock Holes**, natural swimming pools in the Duggerna Rocks to the south of the beach. **St George's Head** to the north has good cliff walks and scenery, while south of the bay the **Duggerna Rocks** form an unusual natural amphitheatre. Further south is a huge **sea cave**. These sights can be reached by driving to Kilkee's West End area and following the coastal path.

Kilkee is a well-known **diving** centre. There are shore dives from the Duggerna Rocks fringing the western side of the bay, and boat dives on the Black Rocks further out. Experience and local knowledge or guidance is strongly advised. Right at the tip of the Duggerna Rocks is the small inlet of Myles Creek, out from which there's excellent underwater scenery. **Kilkee Diving & Watersports Centre** (☎ 905 6707; kilkee@iol.ie; George's Head, Kilkee) by the harbour has tanks and other equipment for hire and runs Professional Association of Diving Instructors (PADI) courses.

Sleeping
There are plenty of guesthouses in Kilkee, though during the high season they are usually a little more expensive than in other areas. At busy times you may have to take whatever the tourist office can get you.

Stella Maris Hotel (☎ 905 6455; info@stellamaris hotel.com; O'Connell St; s/d €55/120; ℗) A complete refurbishment in 2003 has given this long-established hotel a range of good-sized rooms that have bright décor and good facilities.

Bayview (☎ 905 6058; bayview3@eircom.net; O'Connell St; s/d €40/64; ℗) A very central guesthouse with lots of little personal touches, Bayview has good views over the bay from its front rooms. There's a 50% discount for children under 10.

Kilkee Thalassotherapy Centre & Guest House (☎ 905 6742; www.kilkeethalasso.com; Grattan St; s/d €50/100; ℗) If you really want to get to grips with all that buzzing sea air and seaweed, this smart place offers a seaweed bath (€18), body scrub (€36) and detox body wrap (€80) among its various treatments. The guesthouse is part of the complex and rooms are as smart as the rest of the place.

Kilkee Hostel (☎ 905 6209; O'Curry St; dm €14; ☒ Jun-Sep) This well-run place is only 50m from the seafront and is right at the heart of the village. There's a well-equipped kitchen and a laundry room.

Green Acres Caravan & Camping Park (☎ 905 7011; Doonaha, Kilkee; camp sites €20; ☒ early Apr–Sep) Located beside the Shannon, 6km south of Kilkee on the R487, this is a small peaceful park.

Eating
Myles Creek (☎ 905 6771; O'Curry St; snacks €2.75-8.50, mains €7.50-16.50; ☒ 9am-9pm) Join the locals and summer visitors at this popular place that dishes out unpretentious, filling dishes including roast lamb, lasagne and chicken curry.

Old Bistro (☎ 905 6898; O'Curry St; mains €17-23; ☒ summer) A bold black, yellow and red frontage draws you in to this popular and welcoming eatery that features fresh local seafood, as well as meat and vegetarian choices.

Pantry (☎ 905 6576; O'Curry St; lunch mains €6-7, dinner mains €11-15) There are plenty of fast-food outlets, but this busy café stands out for its delicious home-made food and reasonable prices.

Entertainment

Myle's Creek (☎ 905 6771; O'Curry St) Music plays every night from June to August in this down-to-earth place, and at weekends the rest of the year. In summer, especially, it sees a happy crowd enjoying a mix of mainstream sounds and live groups.

Mary O'Mara's (☎ 905 6286; O'Curry St) For a more traditional music scene this is the place to be on Wednesday and Friday nights in July and August.

Getting There & Away

For information on buses to and from Kilkee, see p369.

KILKEE TO LOOP HEAD

The land from Kilkee south to Loop Head is flat and rather nondescript, but spectacular coastal cliffs make up for it and there is a rewarding sense of escape from the mainstream. It's good cycling country and there are coastal walks. Care should be taken near the cliff edges, which can drop away suddenly.

Carrigaholt

☎ 065 / pop 100

On 15 September 1588, seven tattered ships of the Spanish Armada took shelter off Carrigaholt (Carraig an Chabaltaigh), a tiny village inside the mouth of the Shannon Estuary. One, probably the *Annunciada*, was torched and abandoned, sinking somewhere out in the estuary. Today Carrigaholt has a safe beach, and the substantial remains of a 15th-century McMahon castle with a square keep overlook the water.

To view resident bottlenose dolphins (there are about 120 pods in the Shannon Estuary), head for **Dolphinwatch** (☎ 905 8156; www.dolphinwatch.ie; Carrigaholt; adult/child €18/9). Opposite the post office, Dolphinwatch runs two-hour trips in the estuary from April to October, weather permitting.

Long Dock (☎ 905 8106; West St; snacks €4.50-11, mains €8.50-22; ⏲ food served 11am-9pm) is a cosy pub-cum-restaurant that has won national awards for its food and its music. Stone walls and floors and a welcoming fire are only the start. Fresh fish is the thing here; there are tasty meat and chicken dishes, but all that sea air will persuade you to eat fish.

Morrissey's Village Pub (☎ 905 8041; West St) hasn't changed much in a long time and is

all the better for it. Get your feet ready for music and dancing Tuesday, Friday, Saturday and Sunday in summer, and Tuesday and Saturday in winter.

Loop Head

On a clear day, Loop Head (Ceann Léime), Clare's southernmost point, has magnificent views south to the Dingle Peninsula crowned by Mt Brandon (951m), and north to the Aran Islands and Galway Bay. There are bracing walks in the area and a long hiking trail running along the cliffs to Kilkee. When the winds blow, or *blast* as they often do, take great care near the abrupt edge of the cliffs, especially when the grass is wet.

KILKEE TO ENNISTYMON

North of Kilkee, there's a growing sense that you're heading into Ireland's fabled 'West'. The N67 runs inland for some 32km until it reaches Quilty. Take the occasional lane to the west and search out unfrequented places such as White Strand, north of Doonbeg. **Ballard Bay** is 8km north of Doonbeg, where an old telegraph tower looks over some fine cliffs. **Donegal Point** has the remains of a promontory fort. There's good fishing all along the coast, and safe beaches at Seafield, Lough Donnell and Quilty.

Getting There & Away

From May to September Bus Éireann's express Galway–Killarney–Cork bus No 50 stops three times a day (twice on Sunday) at Doolin, Cliffs of Moher, Liscannor, Lahinch, Miltown Malbay and Doonbeg. From mid-June to late August an extra bus runs on Monday to Saturday as far as Lahinch. From Monday to Saturday bus No 333 connects Doonbeg, Quilty, Spanish Point, Miltown Malbay and Lahinch with Kilrush and Kilkee. Contact **Ennis bus station** (☎ 065-682 4177) for times and fares.

Doonbeg

☎ 065 / pop 596

Doonbeg (An Dún Beag) is a tiny seaside village about halfway between Kilkee and Quilty. Near the mouth of the Doonbeg River, another Armada ship, the *San Esteban*, was wrecked on 20 September 1588. The survivors were later executed at Spanish Point. **White Strand** (Trá Ban) is a quiet beach, 2km long and backed by dunes.

SLEEPING & EATING

For campers there are often spots on the side roads around Doonbeg that make a good pitch, with glorious sunsets as a bonus.

An Tinteán (☎ 905 5036; www.antintean.com; Main St; s/d €55/80; P &) There's a great welcome at this central house where rooms have individuality and where there's always a good flow of conversation and information.

San Esteban (☎ 905 5105; www.anicebandb.com; Rhynagonnaught; s/d €60/80; P) An out-of-the-way location makes this delightful house a winner for its sea views and its comfy rooms. To get here you need to escape from the main road at the northern end of the village.

Olde Kitchen Restaurant (Igoe Inn; ☎ 905 5039; Main St; mains €14-20; 🕑 6.30-9.30pm) There's good seafood here and there's music in the bar on Saturday nights during July and August.

Miltown Malbay

☎ 065 / pop 1517

Like Kilkee, Miltown Malbay was a resort favoured by well-to-do Victorians, though the town isn't actually on the sea: the beach is 2km south at Spanish Point. Miltown Malbay has a thriving music scene, and every year hosts a **Willie Clancy Irish Music Festival** (☎ 708 4148) as a tribute to a native son and one of Ireland's greatest pipers. The festival is usually the first week in July, when the town is overrun with wandering minstrels, the pubs are packed, and Guinness is consumed by the bucket load. There are workshops and classes underpinning the whole event and there's much music in the surrounding villages.

Old-fashioned style and service at **Ocean View Restaurant** (O'Loughlin's; ☎ 708 4649; Main St; mains €7-17; 🕑 9am-10pm) backs up solid traditional food. They do good Irish breakfasts (€6). Next door is O'Loughlin's Bar, which has traditional music and sing-along nights on Friday and Sunday in summer.

The name over the door is 'Lynch', but who's complaining? **O'Friel's Bar** (☎ 708 4275; the Square) is a genuine old-style place, where the legendary Willie Clancy used to play and where there are traditional sessions on Saturday and Sunday nights.

Lahinch

☎ 065 / pop 625

Lahinch (Leacht Uí Chonchubhair) is unashamedly resort land – full of fast-food joints and amusement arcades, but lively enough, and with a world-class golf course. The town sits on protected Liscannor Bay and has a fine beach, which draws big crowds in summer.

The tourist office, **Lahinch Fáilte** (☎ 708 2082; www.lahinchfailte.com; the Dell; 🕑 9am-8pm May-Oct, 9am-5pm Nov-Apr), is off the northern end of Main St and is part of a well-stocked gift shop. There's an ATM outside the tourist office and the office has a bureau de change.

The surfing can be good at any time of year. **Lahinch Surf Shop** (☎ 708 1543; www.lahinch surfshop.com; Old Promenade) has gear and can put you in touch with surf instructors.

Lahinch Surf School (☎ 960 9667; www.lahinch surfschool.com; Beach Hut Lahinch Prom; adult/child €30/20) offers two-hour surfing lessons and also does full weekend course packages for €169.

Lahinch Seaworld Leisure Centre (☎ 708 1900; the Promenade; adult/child €7/5; 🕑 10am-9.30pm Mon-Fri, 10am-7pm Sat & Sun, to 10pm Jun-Aug) has a collection of fish species from the surrounding seas on show in tanks, and the complex has a 25m pool for the human species to play in.

SLEEPING & EATING

Lahinch Hostel (☎ 708 1040; www.visitlahinch.com; Church St; dm/d €17/40) An excellent well-run hostel that has clean, bright rooms. It's close to the beachfront and has laundry facilities.

Atlantic Hotel (☎ 708 1049; www.atlantichotel.ie; s/d €85/140; P) It's resort chic at this fine old hotel right in the main street. The updated rooms are cosy and there's still a pleasant air of bygone times in the reception rooms and bars. Bar food (€3.50 to €9) is inventive and features some good seafood choices, with additional and pricier meat and chicken dishes. The restaurant does a three-course dinner for €29.

Lahinch Caravan & Camping Park (☎ 708 1424; camp sites €14; 🕑 May-Sep) A pleasant and fairly quiet place that's close to the beach and only 200m south of the village, this site has good amenities.

Mrs O'Brien's Kitchen (☎ 708 1020; Main St; mains €5-13) You won't beat Mrs O'Brien's for good, straightforward food and cheerful service. Pizzas, chicken wings, chowder and a salad platter are among the choices and you can start the day with a really big breakfast special (€9).

COUNTY CLARE

ENNISTYMON

☎ 065 / pop 881

Don't be fooled by the fairly unexceptional main street of Ennistymon (Inis Díomáin), 3km inland from Lahinch. Step under the archway just down from the bridge, at the south end of Main Street, and you'll find the town's fabulous glory, the **Cascades**, the stepped falls of the River Inagh. After heavy rain the falls roar, beer-brown and foaming, and you risk getting drenched on windy days in the flying drizzle.

There are no other attractions to match the river, but Ennistymon is a pleasant town with a couple of excellent pubs and good sleeping options.

The **library** (☎ 707 1245; ☽ 10am-1.30pm & 2.30-5.30pm Mon, Tue & Thu, 10am-5.30pm Wed & Fri, 10am-2pm Sat), just down from the Square, offers free Internet access. The Bank of Ireland, in Parliament St, has a bureau de change and an ATM.

Sleeping & Eating

Station House (☎ 707 1149; cahilka@indigo.ie; Ennis Rd; s/d €44/62; ℗) There's excellent value on offer at this big modern house about 500m south of the centre. Rooms are a good size and it's in a quiet location.

Falls Hotel (☎ 707 1004; falls@iol.ie; s/d €91/142; ℗ 🖧) This handsome Georgian house, built on the ruins of an O'Brien castle, is a real treat. The view of the Cascades from the entrance steps is stunning, and there are walks around the 20 hectares of wooded

gardens. Rooms are big and comfortable and there's a restaurant.

Connie's Café (☎ 087 786 3815; Parliament St; lunch mains €8-10; ☽ 9am-6pm) Hearty breakfasts (€6) are also available at this breezy and busy little café, where you can get a lunch of steak, chicken and pasta or Irish stew, as well as sandwiches and salads. There's also a supermarket next door if you are self-catering.

Byrne's Restaurant (☎ 707 1080; Main St; mains €15-25; ☽ 6.30-9.30pm Mon-Sat) Handsome views of the Cascades enhance the bright, contemporary surroundings of this fine restaurant, where modern Irish cuisine – baked turbot with basil and goat's cheese mash, for example – is the style. There's a three-course early bird option starting at €18.50 from 6.30pm to 7.30pm Monday to Friday.

Entertainment

Eugene's (☎ 707 1777; Main St) An experience not to be missed, Eugene's is a true talkers' pub. It's intimate, cosy and has a trademark collection of visiting cards covering its walls, alongside photographs of famous writers and musicians; not to forget the *Father Ted* crew (see the boxed text, left). There is also a truly stunning collection of whiskey (Irish) and whisky (Scottish) over which you can smoothly debate their competing qualities.

Cooley's House (☎ 707 1712; Main St) Another great talking pub, but with music most nights in summer and on Wednesday in winter. Wednesdays are trad music nights.

Getting There & Away

Bus Éireann's No 15 bus from Limerick runs four times a day Monday to Saturday and once on Sunday stopping at Ennistymon (€10.70, 30 minutes) in front of Aherne's on Church St. Contact the bus stations in **Ennis** (☎ 065-682 4177) or **Limerick** (☎ 061-313 333) for details.

LISCANNOR & AROUND

☎ 065 / pop 352

This small, seaside village overlooks Liscannor Bay where the road (R478) heads north to the Cliffs of Moher and Doolin. Liscannor (Lios Ceannúir) has given its name to a type of local stone, slatelike and with a rippled surface, that is used for floors, walls and even roofs.

PASSIONATE POET & FAMOUS FATHERS

Ennistymon has more than its fair share of cultural associations. The Welsh poet Dylan Thomas lived at what is now the Falls Hotel (see above) when the house was the family home of his wife Cáitlín McNamara. Just gazing at the great falls from the front door must have tumbled his mind into roaring rhythms. There's plenty of Thomas memorabilia, and a Dylan Thomas Bar, at the hotel. At the other end of the scale is the cast of Ireland's groundbreaking TV comedy *Father Ted,* who spent a lot of time in the local area while filming the series. They also stayed at the Falls and were patrons of Eugene's marvellous bar (see right).

John Philip Holland (1840–1914), the inventor of the submarine, was born in Liscannor. He emigrated to the USA in 1873, and wistfully hoped that his invention would be used to sink British warships.

Sleeping & Eating

Moher Lodge Farmhouse (☎ 708 1269; www.cliffsofmoher-ireland.com; s/d €40/66; ⊙ Apr-Oct; P) There's Irish hospitality at its finest at this big bungalow in a great position overlooking open countryside and the sea. It's 3km northwest of Liscannor, close to the Cliffs of Moher.

Sea Haven (☎ 708 1385; fax 708 1474; s/d €45/64) This exceptionally neat-as-a-pin bungalow is on high ground south of town.

Vaughan's Anchor Inn (☎ 708 1548; Main St; lunch mains €12-14, dinner mains €18-23; ⊙ noon-9.30pm) Noted for its excellent seafood, Vaughan's is a busy place. You can settle for tasty lunch sandwiches or a vegetarian dish, but there's also leg of lamb and fresh salmon and scallops and a terrific sea platter that will make you want to live by the sea forever.

Getting There & Away

From May to September, Bus Éireann's Killarney to Galway express bus No 50 stops at Liscannor. Bus No 337 between Limerick and Lisdoonvarna stops daily year round. Contact the **Ennis bus station** (☎ 065-682 4177) or **Limerick bus station** (☎ 061-313 333) for times and fares.

HAG'S HEAD

Forming the southern end of the Cliffs of Moher, Hag's Head is a dramatic place from which to view the cliffs.

There's a huge sea arch at the tip of Hag's Head and another arch visible to the north. The signal tower on the Head was erected in case Napoleon tried to attack on the western coast of Ireland. The tower is built on the site of an ancient promontory fort called Mothair, which has given its name to the famous cliffs to the north.

CLIFFS OF MOHER

One of Ireland's most famous sights, the Cliffs of Moher (Aillte an Mothair, or Ailltreacha Mothair) rise to a height of 203m. They are entirely vertical and the cliff edge is abrupt. Where access is permitted there's a protecting wall. On a clear day the views are

tremendous; the Aran Islands stand etched on the waters of Galway Bay, and beyond lie the hills of Connemara in western Galway.

Be warned, however: this is a honey-pot destination besieged by visitors and tour coaches and its ease of access, right beside the main road, has turned it into something of a 'sightseeing circus'. Don't expect to commune with the elements in solitary glory. It was once possible to hike along less-crowded sections of the cliff top, but for some years now, access to the north has been discouraged, although you can head south towards Hag's Head – with infinite care when close to the cliff edge. At the time of research the planning go-ahead had been given for a reception and interpretive centre to be embedded into the hillside beside the car park.

Information

There's a bureau de change, a small café and a gift shop full of souvenirs at the **visitor centre** (☎ 065-708 1171; ⊙ 9am-8pm Jul & Aug, 9am-7pm Jun, 9am-6.30pm May & Sep, 9.30am-6pm Apr, 9.30am-5pm Oct-Mar). The car park costs €4, but there's room to turn round before the entrance booth if you decide all that thin air isn't worth it.

Getting There & Away

Bus Éireann No 337, from Limerick to Lisdoonvarna, stops at the Cliffs of Moher three times a day from mid-May to late September and once daily the rest of the year, as does the express bus from Galway to Kilrush. Contact **Ennis bus station** (☎ 065-682 4177) for details.

THE BURREN

The Burren region is one of those compelling places that will captivate you and may never let go. It stretches across northern Clare, from the Atlantic coast to Kinvara in County Galway, a unique limestone landscape that was shaped beneath ancient seas, and then forced high and dry during some great geological cataclysm. The sea is not muted here by offshore islands or muffled promontories, as it sometimes is on the more picturesque coasts of Kerry and Galway. In the Burren, land and sea seem to merge into one vast, exhilarating space beneath huge skies.

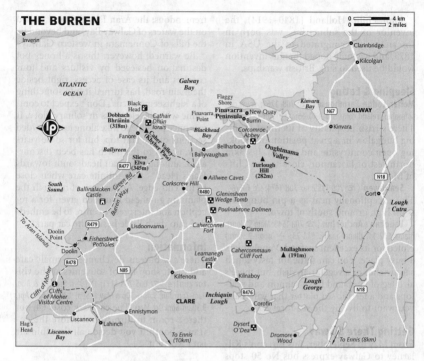

THE BURREN

Boireann is the Irish term for 'rocky country', a plain but graphic description of the Burren's acres of silvery limestone karst pavements. The pavements, known as 'clints', lie like huge, scattered bones across the swooping hills. Between the seams of rock lie narrow fissures, known as 'grykes'. Their humid, sheltered conditions support exquisite wild flowers in spring, lending the Burren its other great charm: brilliant, if ephemeral, colour amid so much arid beauty. There are also fascinating villages to enjoy, especially along the coast and in the south Burren. These include Doolin on the west coast, and Ballyvaughan in the north, on the shores of Galway Bay. The Burren's coastline is made up of rocky foreshores, occasional beaches and bare limestone cliffs, while inland lies a haunting landscape of rocky hills peppered with ancient burial chambers and medieval ruins.

Large areas of the Burren, about 40,000 hectares in all, have been designated as Special Areas of Conservation. Apart from being against the law, it makes ecological sense not to remove plants or to damage walls,

ancient monuments or the landscape itself. Visitors are also asked to resist the temptation to erect 'sham' replicas of dolmens and other monuments, however small.

Information

The nearest information point is the **Cliffs of Moher Visitor Centre** (☎ 065-708 1171), but don't expect too much in-depth information. Generally there is a wealth of literature about the Burren and it's best to trawl the bookshops of Ennis and any local heritage centres for long-standing, but still relevant, publications such as Charles Nelson's *Wild Plants of The Burren and the Aran Islands* (€12.79). The Tír Eolas series of foldout maps, *A Rambler's Guide & Map* (€5), shows antiquities and other points of interest. The Burren *Journey* books by George Cunningham are excellent for local lore, but you may have to search for them.

Archaeology

The Burren's bare limestone hills were once lightly wooded and covered in soil. Towards the end of the Stone Age, about

6000 years ago, nomadic hunter-gatherers began to develop a settled lifestyle of farming and hunting. They cleared the woodlands and used the hills for grazing. Over the centuries, much soil was eroded and the limestone bones of the country became increasingly exposed.

Despite its apparent harshness, the Burren supported quite large numbers of people in ancient times and has over 2500 historic sites. Chief among them is the 5000-year-old Poulnabrone Dolmen, the framework of a Neolithic/Bronze Age chamber tomb, and one of Ireland's iconic ancient monuments.

There are around 70 such tombs erected by the Burren's early settlers. Many of these tombs are wedge-shaped graves, stone boxes tapering both in height and width and about the size of a large double bed. The dead were placed inside, and the whole structure was covered in earth and stones. Gleninsheen, south of Aillwee Caves, is a good example.

Ring forts dot the Burren in prodigious numbers. There are almost 500, including Iron Age stone forts such as Cahercommaun near Carron.

In later times, many castles in the area were built by the region's ruling families, and these include Leamanegh Castle near Kilfenora, Ballinalacken Castle near Doolin and Gleninagh Castle on the Black Head road.

Many ring forts and stone walls have been bulldozed out of existence.

Flora & Fauna
Soil may be scarce on the Burren, but the small amount that gathers in the cracks is well drained and rich in nutrients. This, together with the mild Atlantic climate, supports an extraordinary mix of Mediterranean, Arctic and Alpine plants. Of Ireland's native wild flowers, 75% are found here, including a number of beautiful orchids, the creamy-white burnet rose, the little starry flowers of mossy saxifrage and the magenta-coloured bloody cranesbill.

The Burren is a stronghold of Ireland's most elusive mammal, the weasel-like pine marten. They're rarely seen, although there are certainly some living in the Caher Valley. Badgers, foxes and even stoats are common throughout the region. Otters and seals haunt the shores around Bellharbour, New Quay and Finavarra Point.

The estuaries along this northern coast are rich in bird life and frequently attract Brent geese during the winter. More than 28 of Ireland's 33 species of butterfly are found here, including one endemic species, the Burren green.

As always, modern farming and 'land-improvement' grants have had their effect on the Burren. Weedkillers, insecticides and fertilisers favour grass and little else, often fatally undermining fragile ecological systems.

Walking
'Green roads' are the old highways of the Burren, crossing hills and valleys to some of the remotest corners of the region. Many of these unpaved roads were built during the Famine as part of relief work, while some date back possibly thousands of years. They're now used mostly by hikers and the occasional farmer. Some are signposted, but there is an element of footpath blockage and neglect these days in spite of much publicity being given to walking and to 'official' walking routes.

The Burren Way (see p678) runs down through the Burren from Ballyvaughan to Doolin and then inland along mainly paved lanes, since cliff access around the Cliffs of Moher has been restricted.

Guided nature, history, archaeology and wilderness walks cost about €15 and are available through **Burren Hill Walks** (☎ 065-707 7168; burrenhillwalks@eircom.net; Corkscrew Hill, Ballyvaughan), **Burren Wild** (☎ 087 877 9565; www.burrenwalks.com; Bealaclugga), or **Burren Walking Weekends** (☎ 065-707 7037; hylandsburren@eircom.net; Ballyvaughan).

Getting There & Away
Various buses pass through the Burren. From Limerick, bus No 337 runs three times daily (twice on Sunday) from late May to September, once daily the rest of the year. It connects with Ennis, Ennistymon, Lahinch, Liscannor, the Cliffs of Moher, Doolin and Lisdoonvarna. Express bus No 50 connects Galway with Ballyvaughan, Lisdoonvarna, Lahinch, Kilkee and Tralee. It runs three times daily (twice on Sunday) from late May to late September. From mid-June to late August an extra bus runs Monday to Saturday as far as Lahinch. Bus No 423 runs from Galway to Kinvara, Ballyvaughan, Black

Head, Fanore, Lisdoonvarna and Doolin. It runs three times daily (once on Sunday) from late May to late September. The rest of the year it runs once a day from Monday to Saturday. Also see Tours on p394.

For precise times and other details of buses to the Burren area, ring the **Ennis bus station** (☎ 065-682 4177), **Limerick bus station** (☎ 061-313 333) or **Galway bus station** (☎ 091-562 000).

Getting Around

The best way to see the Burren is on foot or by cycling; good mountain bikes are available in Doolin from **Aille River Hostel** (☎ 065-707 4260).

DOOLIN

☎ 065 / pop 200

Doolin, or Fisherstreet as it is also known, stretches for several kilometres along the road. Despite its remoteness and its tree-less, often windswept surroundings, it has some of the best music pubs in the west, a couple of decent restaurants and cafés, and plenty of good hostels and guesthouses. It's also an excellent base for the Burren, which lies just to the north. There are ferries to the Aran Islands (see opposite).

Doolin is extremely popular among backpackers and music lovers, and at night the pubs are filled with a cosmopolitan crowd. The downside is that Doolin is on the conventional coach trip trail and the 'backpacker' tour bus trail. Never the twain shall meet, but it all adds to the fun, if you like company and people-watching. In the high season it can be difficult to get a bed, so you should definitely book ahead.

Orientation & Information

Doolin is made up of three parts. Coming from the north along the R479 you first reach Doolin Catholic church on the left, then after less than 1km you'll find the upper village, known as Roadford, with a shop, restaurant and cafés, hostels and two pubs. Then there's a slightly bigger gap before reaching Fisherstreet, the lower village, which has the popular Paddy's Doolin Hostel, more shops and O'Connor's pub. It's another 1.5km to the harbour and the ferry to the Aran Islands.

There are no post office or banks in Doolin, but a mobile bank visits on Thursday. You can change money and travellers cheques in Fisherstreet at Paddy's Doolin Hostel. The nearest ATM is in Ennistymon.

Activities

The Doolin area is popular with cavers. The **Fisherstreet Potholes** are nearby, and **Poll na gColm**, 5km northeast of Lisdoonvarna, is Ireland's longest cave, with over 12km of mapped passageways. See www.cavingireland.org for more details.

The rocks to the north of Doolin Harbour are honeycombed with an unusual system of undersea caves called the **Green Holes of Doolin**. They're the longest known undersea caves in temperate waters. Nondivers can look, with care, into Hell, a large gash in the rocks, north of the harbour and about 50m from the sea. The gash is about 6m wide, and the heaving water at the bottom leads to a maze of submarine passages.

To explore the caves mentioned here, caving experience and use of full equipment are essential.

Sleeping

BUDGET

Sleeping places in Doolin are generally of a good standard and the choice is wide.

Aille River Hostel (☎ 707 4260; ailleriver@eatclear.ie; Roadford, Doolin; camp sites €13, dm/d €13/29; ◯ mid-Mar–Dec; [P]) In a picturesque spot by the river in the upper village, this converted 17th-century farmhouse is a great choice. It has been renovated, but in keeping with its great traditional character. There are turf fires, hot showers, free laundry and good company. There's Internet access for €1.50 per 15 minutes.

Rainbow Hostel (☎ 707 4415; www.rainbowhostel.com; Roadford, Doolin; dm/d €13/28; [P]) Another good choice, this smart and friendly place is in a convenient location near McGann's pub in the upper village.

Paddy's Doolin Hostel (☎ 707 4006; www.doolinhostel.com; Fisherstreet, Doolin; dm/d €14/36; [P]) Better known as Paddy Moloney's, this is a busy place and a great gathering point for backpackers.

Nagles Doolin Caravan & Camping Park (☎ 707 4458; ken@doolincamping.com; camp sites €15; ◯ Apr-Sep) With full-on views of the Cliffs of Moher, and Doolin only a short distance away, this is a pleasant site. It's open to the elements, so pin those pegs down.

MIDRANGE

Doolin Cottage (☎ 707 4762; caroldoolin@hotmail.com; Roadford; s/d €30/50; ☷ Mar-Oct; P) This charming little house has a peaceful and friendly atmosphere and is excellent value. It's just behind the Aille River Hostel.

Rainbow's End (☎ 707 4900; rainbowhostel@eircom .net; Roadford; s/d €40/60; P) There's lots of exposed wood and light and airy rooms at this friendly family-run place that is owned by the owners of Rainbow Hostel.

Cullinan's Guest House (☎ 707 4183; www .cullinansdoolin.com; s/d €60/80; P) Stylish surroundings and comfortable rooms are the hallmark of Cullinan's. The in-house restaurant (below) will tempt you as well.

Doonmacfelim House (☎ 707 4503; www.doon macfelim.com; Roadford, Doolin; s/d €55/68; P) Doolin has lots of big detached guesthouses and this is a good one. Rooms are nicely done out and breakfasts are hearty. There's a bit of history as well: prehistoric artefacts were found on the surrounding property.

Seaview House (☎ 707 4826; www.ireland-doolin .com; s/d €60/80; P) Located on high ground above the south end of the village, this big house has fine views, and rooms are bright and a good size.

Two other good options among Doolin's many B&Bs and guesthouses, and with similar prices, are **Killilagh House** (☎ 707 4392; killilaghhouse@esatclear.ie; Roadford) and **Atlantic View House** (☎ 707 4189; Pier Rd).

TOP END

Aran View House (☎ 707 4061; www.aranview.com; Coast Rd, Doolin; s/d €70/110; ☷ May-Sep; P) Just outside the village on its northern edge is this handsome Georgian hotel. Rooms are spacious and there are great sea views. The hotel has its own restaurant, and it has an excellent range of fish and meat dishes for €16 to €25.

Eating

For self-catering there's the fairly well-stocked Doolin Deli, just down from O'Connor's pub on the road to the pier.

Cullinan's (☎ 707 4183; mains €20-26; ☷ 6-9pm Thu-Tue) Attached to the guest house of the same name, this excellent restaurant offers delicious seafood as well as meat and poultry dishes, including tasty lamb cutlets. Vegetarians are well catered for too. The cuisine is modern Irish, but with good traditional accents, and French touches here and there.

Local smoked salmon, goat's cheese and scallops are on the menu, and there's a popular early bird option for €27.

Doolin Café (☎ 707 4795; Roadford, Doolin; mains €15-22; ☷ 10am-10pm) There's a great atmosphere at this friendly café-restaurant where you can get hefty breakfasts from 10am onwards, as well as lunch and evening meals. The menu covers everything from fish to tasty vegetarian dishes.

O'Connor's (☎ 707 4168; Fisherstreet, Doolin; sandwiches €3.50, mains €10-17) Music and Irish pub grub are the things here. There's a big, busy coach trade in summer.

McGann's (☎ 707 4133; Roadford, Doolin; mains €10-15) It's standard pub grub again at Mc-Gann's where there's usually a crowd.

Drinking & Entertainment

Doolin is renowned for Irish music, and you can hear it almost every night in summer, in the company of a lot of other people, and on most nights in winter.

O'Connor's (☎ 707 4168; Fisherstreet, Doolin) This favourite packs them in and has a great atmosphere when the traditional music, singing and drinking are all in full swing. Pub grub is also available.

McGann's (☎ 707 4133; Roadford, Doolin) Mc-Gann's has all the classic touches of a full-on Irish music pub with the action often spilling out onto the street. Food is also served here.

MacDiarmada's (☎ 707 4700; Roadford, Doolin) Also known as MacDermott's, it sees more of a local crowd with a younger set beering up at weekends. Music sessions are up to Doolin standards.

Shopping

Doolin's Traditional Music Shop, next to the Doolin Deli and just down from O'Connor's Pub, has a good selection of traditional music CDs.

Getting There & Away

BOAT

Doolin is the ferry departure point to the Aran Islands. Ferries are operated daily, April to September, by **Doolin Ferries** (☎ 707 4455, 707 5555; www.doolinferries.com; the Pier, Doolin).

It takes around 20 minutes to cover the 8km to Inisheer, the smallest and closest of the three Aran Islands (return €25). There are around five sailings daily, beginning at 10am. The last ferry returns from Inisheer at 5pm.

The first ferry to Inishmór, the largest island, leaves Doolin Harbour at 9am and the last ferry from Inishmór departs at 4pm (return €35, 50 minutes).

Other ferries with similar prices and schedules are run by **Aran Island Fast Ferries** (☎ 707 4550; www.aranislandsfastferries.com; the Pier, Doolin).

Ferries also run to the small island of Inishmaan (return €30). Booking for all ferries is strongly advised.

BUS

Buses stop by the Rainbow Hostel in Roadford, Paddy's Doolin Hostel in Fisherstreet, and the Rainbow Hostel near McGann's pub. There are buses between Doolin and Ennis, Limerick, Galway and Dublin. For details, see p377.

Getting Around

The **Aille River Hostel** (☎ 707 4260; Roadford, Doolin) hires out bikes for €10 per day (€8 for hostel guests).

LISDOONVARNA

☎ 065 / pop 917

Lisdoonvarna (Lios Dún Bhearna), often just called 'Lisdoon', is well known for its mineral springs. For centuries people have been visiting the local spa to swallow its waters, or to bathe in them. The town was once a centre for *basadóiri* (matchmakers) who, for a fee, would fix a person up with a mate. Most of the mainly male hopefuls would hit town in September, feet shuffling, cap in hand, after the hay was in. Today, true matchmaking is unlikely, but the **Lisdoonvarna Matchmaking Festival** (www.matchmakerireland.com), held throughout September and early October, is a great excuse for daftness, drinking, merrymaking, music and, of course, moneymaking.

Orientation & Information

Lisdoonvarna is essentially a one-street town with a square in the centre from where you turn west for Doolin and the coast. The town has plenty of shops, pubs, B&Bs and smart hotels with some fine restaurants, but no bank or ATM. You can, however, change money at the post office on Main St to the north.

There's Internet access at the **Internet Café** (☎ 707 5005; Main St; per 20 min €2; ☒ 9am-6pm Mon-Sat).

Sights

SPA WELLS HEALTH CENTRE

At the southern end of town is Ireland's only working **spa** (☎ 707 4023; Main St; sulphur bath €30; ☒ 10am-6pm Jun-Sep). It has a sulphur spring, a Victorian pump house, massage room, sauna and mineral baths, all in an agreeable, wooded setting. The iron, sulphur, magnesium and iodine in the water are supposed to be good for rheumatic and glandular complaints. You can drink the water, but it's not exactly a vintage-wine tasting experience. Modern treatments include wax bath, aromatherapy and reflexology.

BURREN SMOKEHOUSE VISITOR CENTRE

You can learn about the ancient Irish art of oak-smoking salmon from a video (four languages) at the **visitor centre** (☎ 707 4432; www.burrensmokehouse.ie; Kincora Rd; admission free; ☒ 10am-5pm Apr-May, 9am-6pm Jun-Oct, 10am-4pm Nov-Mar). Delicious smoked salmon in all its guises is on sale, with free tastings to gently reel you in. Excellent coffee takeaways are also available. The complex has an art and craft gallery and sells stylish clothes. Tourist information is available. The centre is on the edge of Lisdoonvarna on the Kincora road (N67).

SOMETHING SPECIAL

Sheedy's Country House Hotel & Restaurant (☎ 707 4026; www.sheedys.com; Sulphur Hill, Lisdoonvarna; s/d €100/150; ☒ Mar-Oct; ℙ) Sheedy's would be a top choice anywhere. The hotel stands in a splendid location in attractive grounds that have a number of endearing features. (Check out the imaginative potager, well-kept vegetable and herb plots, that lie just in front of the house.) There is a sense of gracious, yet informal, living inside the house where rooms are individually and stylishly designed and the public areas are full of character. The bar menu (meals €4.50 to €15) has a terrific seafood choice and the restaurant (dinner mains €19 to €28) offers modern Irish cuisine at its best, enhanced by an excellent wine list. An added bonus is the good information on local walking that can be had, and the personable and friendly owners can even arrange guides.

Sleeping & Eating

Prices in some establishments may go up during September's Matchmaking Festival.

Carrigann Hotel (☎ 707 4036; www.gateway-to-the-burren.com; Doolin Rd; s/d €75/110; P) A relaxing atmosphere and bright, comfy rooms make this a good out-of-centre choice. The hotel offers walking packages with environmental themes and with guide supplied. Its restaurant (bar meals €3.50 to €16.50, dinner mains €14 to €20) has a wide range of meat and fish dishes with an international theme.

O'Loughlin's (☎ 707 4038; Main St; s/d €30/55; Apr-Oct) O'Loughlin's is an unpretentious, friendly B&B with an apparent maze of roomsthat are plain, but good value.

Royal Spa Hotel (☎ 707 4288; Main St; bar meals €7.50-15.50) There's a good choice of bar food ranging from pizzas to vegetarian lasagne in this pleasant main-street bar.

Irish Arms (☎ 707 4207; Main St; meals €9.50-12.50) This pub flies the flag for Ireland and the Glasgow Celtic football club. The food is good, solid pub fare.

Getting There & Around

From Limerick, bus No 337 runs three times daily (twice on Sunday) from late May to September, once daily the rest of the year. It connects with Ennis, Ennistymon, Lahinch, Liscannor, the Cliffs of Moher, Doolin and Lisdoonvarna. Express bus No 50 connects Galway with Ballyvaughan, Lisdoonvarna, Lahinch, Kilkee and Tralee. It runs three times daily (twice on Sunday) from late May to late September. From mid-June to late August an extra bus runs Monday to Saturday as far as Lahinch. Bus No 423 runs from Galway to Kinvara, Ballyvaughan, Black Head, Fanore, Lisdoonvarna and Doolin. It runs three times daily (once on Sunday) from late May to late September. The rest of the year it runs once a day from Monday to Saturday.

FANORE

☎ 065 / pop 150

Fanore (Fan Óir), 5km south of Black Head, is less a village and more a stretch of coast with a shop, a pub, and a few houses scattered along the main road (R477). It has a fine sandy beach with an extensive backdrop of dunes. It's the only safe beach between Lahinch and Ballyvaughan.

There's extensive parking and there are toilets open in summer.

There's a fairly well-stocked shop, **Siopa Fan Óir** (☎ 707 6131; Fanore; 9am-9pm summer, 9am-7pm winter), just across from O'Donohue's pub, where you can buy fishing tackle.

Sleeping & Eating

There are few accommodation options and eateries in the Fanore area.

Rocky View Farmhouse (☎ 707 6103; www.rockyviewfarmhouse.com; s/d €35/60; P) A charming place at the heart of the coastal Burren, this detached house reflects the special character of the area in its fresh, airy rooms. Organic food is used, and vegetarian and vegan diets are catered for. Here too is the Harebell Centre, devoted to holistic and healing workshops. Phone for details of the workshops.

O'Donohue's (☎ 707 6119; snacks €3.50) This pub, 4km south of the beach, offers no-nonsense soup and sandwiches along with its no-frills genuine local character. It has music on Saturday nights and hosts some of the sessions for the Lisdoonvarna Matchmaking Festival in September. There are no other bars along this stretch of coast.

Siopa Fan Óir Tea Room is next to the shop and craft gallery of the same name.

Getting There & Away

Bus No 423 runs from Galway to Kinvara, Ballyvaughan, Black Head, Fanore, Lisdoonvarna and Doolin. It runs three times daily (once on Sunday) from late May to late September. The rest of the year it runs once a day from Monday to Saturday.

BLACK HEAD & CATHAIR DHÚN IORAIS

Black Head, Clare's northwesternmost point, is a wild and exhilarating headland of limestone that descends steeply to the sea. The main road curves around Black Head just above the sea and there is an automatic lighthouse at the head's northern tip. There's good shore **angling** for pollock, wrasse, mackerel – and sea bass if you're lucky – from the rocky platforms near sea level. These can be fatally dangerous waters, even for those with long-standing local knowledge. Even in apparently calm conditions, absolute care must be taken when near sea level.

An exhilarating outing is the climb up Black Head to the Iron Age **ring fort of Cathair Dhún Iorais**. There's no path, so it's essential to take a map (*Ordnance Survey Discovery Series No 51*) and compass. The ground is very rocky in places, so strong footwear is essential. Be prepared for wet, windy and potentially cold conditions, even in summer. It's a steep 1.5km to the fort.

Start from just above the lighthouse on the northern tip of Black Head. There's limited parking on the inland side of the road. Head due south up the rocky hillside from the road, negotiating between rock shelves, to reach an old green track. Cross the track and continue directly to where things level off and Cathair Dhún Iorais stands amid a sea of limestone pavements. It's not the most dramatic of ring forts, but the setting is magnificent. The views to Galway and Connemara are breathtaking in clear weather.

From the fort you can bear southeast to skirt the limestone cliffs that run in an unbroken wall to the west. This takes you onto the broad shoulder that leads south, in 1.3km, to the summit of **Dobhach Bhráinín**, one of the highest points in the Burren at 318m. Again, skilled use of map and compass is essential in case of sudden mist, when careless descent from Dobhach Bhráinín may land you above the cliffs. It's best to return to the fort and descend the way you came.

BALLYVAUGHAN & AROUND
☎ 065 / pop 201

All the charm of the Burren is distilled into its favoured location, Ballyvaughan (Baile Uí Bheacháin), where the hard land of the hills gives way to a quiet leafy corner of Galway Bay. It makes an excellent base for visiting the northern part of the Burren. You'll be reluctant to leave.

The centre of the village is at the junction of the N67 and the coastal R477. Going south and inland on the N67 brings you to the centre of the Burren, Aillwee Caves, Poulnabrone Dolmen and Lisdoonvarna. Turning west leads you to the magnificent coast road (R477), Black Head and south towards Doolin. Going northeast on the N67, you reach Kinvara and County Galway.

Just west of the junction, on the R477, is the quay and Monk's Bar. The quay was built in 1829 at a time when boats traded with the Aran Islands and Galway, exporting grain and bacon and bringing in turf – a scarce commodity in the Burren.

A few metres past the harbour, a signposted track leads to a seashore bird hide from where there is a good view of tidal shallows. If driving, you'll find a car park and another access path to the bird hide a few metres further on.

Information
Linnane's Village Stores (☎ 707 7077; villagestores@eircom.net) in Ballyvaughan has an excellent **tourist information centre** (⊙ 9am-6pm). There are no banks in Ballyvaughan. The nearest ATM is at Ennistymon.

Corkscrew Hill
About 6km south of Ballyvaughan on the Lisdoonvarna road is a series of severe bends up Corkscrew Hill (180m). The road was built as part of a Great Famine relief scheme in the 1840s. From the top there are spectacular views of the northern Burren and Galway Bay, with Aillwee Mountain and the caves on the right, and Cappanawalla Hill on the left, and with the partially restored 16th-century Newtown Castle, erstwhile residence of the O'Lochlains, at its base. From here, the route to Lisdoonvarna is through boggy, fairly characterless countryside.

Sleeping
There are no hostels in Ballyvaughan; the closest is Johnston's Independent Hostel in Kinvara, County Galway (see p417).

Rusheen Lodge (☎ 707 7092; www.rusheenlodge.com; Lisdoonvarna Rd; s/d €68/96; P) Outstanding is the only word for this beautifully appointed house that outclasses many top hotels elsewhere. Stylish, imaginative furnishings add to the general comfort. It's about 750m south of the village on the N67.

Hyland's Burren Hotel (☎ 707 7037; www.hylandsburren.com; Main St; s/d €85/130; P) An appealing place, this central hotel has fine, spacious rooms and manages to retain a local feel alongside its corporate image. There's a bar and restaurant. Ask for the hotel's *Walks* leaflet and for information about guided walks.

Stonepark House (☎ 707 7056; Bishops Quarter; s/d €30/46, d with bathroom €50; ⊙ Mar-Sep; P) Stonepark is a small B&B in a peaceful location just over 2km along the Kinvara road.

COUNTY CLARE

Things are pleasantly old fashioned and the welcome is kind and gentle.

Eating

Tea Junction (☎ 707 7289; Main St; lunch dishes €3-7; ☺ 9am-6pm mid-Mar–Oct, Wed-Sun Nov–mid-Mar) It's all tasty soups, sandwiches and baguettes at this delightful place that also does breakfasts (€4 to €7.75), including a filling vegetarian option.

O'Brien's (☎ 707 7003; Main St; mains €9-16; ☺ 12.30-8.30pm) A few doors down from Hyland's Hotel, this is a relaxed pub and restaurant. Seafood is a speciality and toasted sandwiches are a stopgap during the day.

Monk's Bar & Restaurant (☎ 707 7059; the Old Pier; mains €11-15; ☺ noon-8pm) Famed for its delicious seafood, Monk's is a cheerful, spacious and comfortable place. The harbour's just across the road to put you in the mood for oysters, mussels or crab claws. There's meat and vegetarian specials too.

Entertainment

O'Brien's (☎ 707 7003; Main St) The place for a bit of Ballyvaughan bopping at the Thursday to Sunday night discos. There is also a restaurant.

Monk's Bar (☎ 707 7059; the Old Pier) Runs live music sessions Saturday night all year and mid-week and Saturday night June to August. Food is also available.

Ólólainn (o-*loch*-lain) (Main St) A tiny place on the left as you head down to the pier, Ólólainn is the place for a timeless moment or two in old-fashioned snugs.

Getting There & Away

For information on bus services see p377. The Spar supermarket is the Bus Éireann agent.

Getting Around

There are bikes for hire for €12 per day at John Connolle's, opposite the post office and filling station.

CENTRAL BURREN

The road through the heart of the Burren, the R480, runs south from Ballyvaughan to Leamanegh Castle, where it joins the R476, which runs southeast to Corofin, and northwest to Kilfenora. Travelling south from Ballyvaughan (on the N67), turn east before Corkscrew Hill at the Aillwee

Caves sign. The road goes past Gleninsheen Wedge Tomb, Poulnabrone Dolmen and into some harsh but inspiring scenery.

Aillwee Caves

A good place to spend a rainy afternoon or to take children is the extensive limestone **Aillwee Caves** (☎ 065-707 7036; www.aillweecave.ie; Ballyvaughan; adult/child/family €8.50/4.50/22; ☺ from 10am Jan-Nov, by appointment Dec). The main passage penetrates for 600m into the mountain, widening into larger caverns, one with its own waterfall. The caves were carved out by water some two million years ago. Near the entrance are the remains of a brown bear, extinct in Ireland for over 10,000 years. You can only go into the cave as part of a guided tour. There are six tours daily (phone for exact times); the last tour departs at 5.30pm in summer. Try to visit early in the day before the crowds arrive. There's a cheese- and honey-making centre and there are craft shops, a restaurant and café on site.

Gleninsheen Wedge Tomb

One of Ireland's most famous prehistoric grave sites, Gleninsheen lies beside the R480 just south of Aillwee Caves. It's thought to date from 4000 to 5000 years ago. A magnificent gold torque (a crescent of beaten gold that hung round the neck) was found nearby in 1930 by a young boy called Paddy Dolan, who was hunting rabbits. Dating from around 700 BC, the torque is reckoned to be one of the finest pieces of prehistoric Irish craftwork and is now on display at the National Museum in Dublin. The gate giving access to the Gleninsheen tomb may well be locked. Just inside the gate is a handsome memorial to Paddy Dolan, complete with gold-coloured torque inlay.

Poulnabrone Dolmen

Also known as the Portal Tomb, Poulnabrone Dolmen is one of Ireland's most photographed ancient monuments – a trademark tourist icon. The dolmen (a large slab perched on stone uprights) stands amid a swathe of rocky pavements, for all the world like some surreal bird of prey about to take off. The capstone weighs five tonnes. The site is 8km south of Aillwee and is visible from the R480. A path leads to it from the roadside.

Poulnabrone was built over 5000 years ago. It was excavated in 1986, and the remains

ROCK LEGENDS

The geology of the Burren may seem like a load of old rocks, but there is immense drama and excitement in the primeval adventures that produced the exquisite landscape that we see today. The Burren is the most extensive limestone region, or karst (after the original Karst in Slovenia), in Ireland or Britain. It consists almost entirely of limestone, except for a cap of mud and shale that sits on the higher regions.

During the Carboniferous period 350 million years ago, this whole area was the bottom of a warm and shallow sea. The remains of coral and shells fell to the sea bed, and coastal rivers dumped sand and silt on top of these lime deposits. Time and pressure turned the layers to stone, with limestone below and shale and sandstone above.

Massive shifts in the earth's crust some 270 million years ago buckled the edges of Europe and forced the sea bed above sea level, at the same time bending and fracturing the stone sheets to form the long, deep cracks so characteristic of the Burren today, each one a stone trench crammed full of wild flowers, nurtured on tenuous soil and a microclimate of sweet, damp air.

During numerous Ice Ages, glaciers scoured the hills, rounding the edges and sometimes polishing the rock to a shiny finish. The glaciers also dumped a thin layer of rock and soil over the region. Huge boulders were carried by the ice, incongruous aliens on a sea of flat rock. Seen all over the Burren, these 'glacial erratics' are often a visibly different type of rock.

---

of 16 people were found, as well as pieces of pottery and jewellery. Radiocarbon dating suggests that they were buried between 3800 and 3200 BC. When the dead were originally entombed here, the whole structure was partially covered in a mound of earth, which has since worn away.

Caherconnell Fort

Located about 1km south of Poulnabrone, **Caherconnell Fort** (☎ 708 9999; adult/child/family €5/3/12; ☽ 9.30am-6.30pm Jul & Aug, 10am-5pm Mar-Jun, Sep-Oct; **P**) is a convenient stop-off, where you can get a paid-for peek at a well-preserved *caher* or walled homestead of the late Iron Age–Early Christian period. The evolution of these defensive settlements may have reflected territorialism and competition for land among a growing, settling population. The drystone walling of the fort is extremely well preserved. There is a visitor centre with audio-visual presentation and information on other monuments.

Carron & Cahercommaun Cliff Fort

The tiny village of Carron ('Carran' on some maps; 'An Carn' in Gaelic), a few kilometres east of the R480, is a delightfully remote spot. It was the birthplace of Michael Cusack, founder of the Gaelic Athletic Association. Signposted at the T-junction near the church is the remote **Burren Perfumery & Floral Centre** (☎ 065-708 9102; Carron; admission free; ☽ 9am-7pm Jun-Sep, 9am-5pm Oct-May). It uses wild flowers of the Burren to produce its scents, and it's the only handicraft perfumery in Ireland. There's a free audiovisual presentation on the flora of the Burren.

Below Carron lies one of the finest *turloughs* in Ireland. It's known as the Carron Polje. Polje is a Yugoslav term used universally for these shallow depressions that flood in winter and dry out in summer, when the lush grass that flourishes on the surface is used for grazing.

About 3km south of Carron and perched on the edge of an inland cliff is the great stone fort of Cahercommaun. It was inhabited in the 8th and 9th centuries by people who hunted deer and grew a small amount of grain. There are the remains of a souterrain (underground passage) leading from the fort to the outer cliff face. To get there, go south from Carron and take a left turn for Kilnaboy. After 1.5km a path on the left leads up to the fort.

Clare's Rock Hostel (☎ 065-708 9129; www.clares rock.com; Carron; dm/d €12/17; **P**) is an imposing building in grey exposed stone. It has big spacious rooms and excellent facilities. If you stay you can hire bikes for about €11 per day. From April to October, **Cassidy's Croide na Boirne Pub** (☎ 065-708 9109; Carron; bar mains €4.50-9.50) serves up a good range of tasty dishes all with witty names and descriptions, several reflecting the pub's previous incarnation as a British RIC station, and then as a Garda barracks. Parts of the old furnishings are incorporated into the bar and there are traditional music sessions every Saturday, and music and set dancing on Friday and Saturday nights.

KILFENORA

☎ 065 / pop 361

Kilfenora (Cill Fhionnúrach) lies on the southern fringes of the Burren, 8km southeast of Lisdoonvarna. It's a small place, like its diminutive 12th-century cathedral. There are several high crosses in its churchyard.

Sights

BURREN CENTRE

The **Burren Centre** (☎ 708 8030; www.theburren centre.ie; Main St; adult/child/family €5.50/3.50/15; ☼ 9.30am-6pm Jun-Aug, 10am-5pm mid-Mar–May, Sep & Oct) has a series of entertaining and informative displays on every aspect of the Burren past and present. There's a tea room and a shop that sells local products.

KILFENORA CATHEDRAL

In the past the ruined 12th-century cathedral at Kilfenora was an important place of pilgrimage. St Fachan (or Fachtna) founded the monastery here in the 6th century, and it later became the seat of Kilfenora diocese, the smallest in the country.

The cathedral is the smallest you're ever likely to see. Only the ruined structure and nave of the more recent Protestant church are actually part of the cathedral. The chancel has two primitive carved figures on top of two tombs.

HIGH CROSSES

Kilfenora is best known for its high crosses, three in the churchyard and a large 12th-century example in the field about 100m to the west.

The most interesting one is the 800-year-old **Doorty Cross**, standing prominently to the west of the church's front door. It was lying broken in two until the 1950s, when it was re-erected. A panel in the churchyard does an excellent job of explaining the carvings that adorn the crosses.

Sleeping & Eating

Carraigliath (☎ 708 8075; eimeorhowlwy@eircom.net; Kilfenora; s/d €35/55) This big detached house

is just along the R476 Lisdoonvarna road from Kilfenora centre. There's a great, generous welcome here and you may well hear the strains of excellent Irish music – most of the family play instruments.

Mrs Mary Murphy (☎ 708 8040; Main St; s/d €35/55; ☼ mid-Feb–Nov) Located right on the main street, this family home is a quietly welcoming place with unfussy rooms.

Vaughan's Pub (☎ 708 8004; Main St; mains €9-12; ☼ 10am-9pm) Bar meals cover a good range of seafood and meat dishes and local produce is a strong feature. Classic Irish dishes such as beef-and-Guinness stew are backed by alternatives such as lasagne and vegetarian quiche. At the time of research, plans were underway for Vaughan's to build a hostel, called Shepherd's Rest Hostel, next door.

Linnane's (☎ 708 8157; Main St; bar meals €3-9) You can get sandwiches at Linnane's, but there's rib-sticking soup and other Irish standards too in a bar that makes no concessions to modernism.

Entertainment

Vaughan's Pub (☎ 708 8004; Main St) Vaughan's has a big reputation in Irish music circles. There's music in the bar every night during the summer and on several nights the rest of the year. The adjacent barn is the scene of terrific set-dancing sessions on Thursday and Sunday nights.

Linnane's (☎ 708 8157; Main St) Linnane's gears up for a big night of Irish music on Wednesdays in summer and at weekends most of the year.

THE PARISH POPE

Pope Benedict XVI is a parish priest in County Clare. He may not be immediately aware of it and he may not be calling in just yet, but the 2005 successor to Pope John Paul II is the bishop of the diocese of Kilfenora and Killaloe, and is thus parish priest to a number of churches. In 1883 the Holy See united Kilfenora and Kilmacduagh with Galway. Because Kilfenora was within the province of Cashel, the Bishop of Galway and Kilmacduagh was only appointed as the 'Apostolic Administrator' of Kilfenora on behalf of the Pope, who is therefore, technically, the Bishop of Kilfenora.

Getting There & Away

Bus Éireann's service No 333 leaves Ennis at 3pm Tuesday to Thursday and Saturday, stopping at Kilfenora. Bus No 337 leaves Ennis at 2.25pm Monday to Saturday mid-May to September. Check with the **Ennis bus station** (☎ 065-682 4177) for times.

COROFIN & AROUND

☎ 065 / pop 382

Corofin (Cora Finne), also spelled Corrofin, is a quiet, friendly village on the southern fringes of the Burren. The surrounding area features a number of *turloughs*. There are several O'Brien castles in the area, two being on the shores of nearby Inchiquin Lough.

Corofin is home to the interesting **Clare Heritage Centre** (☎ 683 7955; www.clareroots.com; Church St; adult/concession €4/2; 🕙 10am-6pm mid-May–Oct). It has a display covering the period around the Potato Famine. Over 250,000 people lived in Clare before the Famine; today the county's population stands at about 91,000 – a drop of some 64%. In a separate building nearby, the **Clare Genealogical Centre** (☎ 683 7955; 🕙 9am-5.30pm Mon-Fri) has facilities for people researching their Clare ancestry.

About 4km northwest of Corofin, on the road to Leamanegh Castle and Kilfenora (R476), look for the small town of **Kilnaboy**. The ruined church here is well worth seeking out for the sheila-na-gig over the doorway (see the boxed text, p309).

Sleeping & Eating

Lakefield Lodge (☎ 683 7675; mcleary.ennis@eircom .net; Ennis Rd; s/d €45/62; 🕙 Mar-Oct) A very well-run place near the southern edge of the village. There are comfy rooms and a great welcome at this pleasant bungalow. Credit cards are accepted.

Shamrock & Heather (☎ 683 7061; bmkearney@ eircom.net; Station Rd; s/d €44/62; 🕙 Mar-Oct) Another welcoming place just a few minutes from the village centre. Rooms are immaculate and of adequate size at this small bungalow.

Restaurant Le Catelinais (☎ 683 7425; mains €18-24; 🕙 5.30pm-late Tue-Thu) Being tucked away in Corofin enhances the experience at this serene little restaurant, where the relaxing mood is matched by a fine merging of modern Irish and international cuisine. Early bird menu is €23.

Bofey Quinn's (☎ 683 7321; Main St; bar snacks €3.50-8.50, dinner €9-18; 🕙 noon-11pm) Busy Bofey's does a wide range of seafood, meat and poultry dishes, as well as pastas and pizzas. Both bar and restaurant are friendly places without fancy trappings. There are good traditional music sessions round the big table on Monday, Tuesday and Wednesday nights from March to October, and on Wednesday night the rest of the year.

Getting There & Away

Bus Éireann's service No 333 leaves Ennis at 3pm for Corofin, Monday and Friday only. Bus No 337 leaves Ennis at 2.25pm Monday to Saturday mid-May to September. Check with the **Ennis bus station** (☎ 065-682 4177) for times.

NORTHERN BURREN

There's low farmland stretching south from County Galway until it meets the bluff limestone hills of the Burren, which begin west of Kinvara and Doorus in County Galway. Here the road forks, going inland to Carron or along the coast to Ballyvaughan.

From Oranmore in County Galway to Ballyvaughan, the coastline wriggles along small inlets and peninsulas; some, such as Finavarra Point and New Quay, are worth a detour.

Inland near Bellharbour is the largely intact Corcomroe Abbey, while the three ancient churches of Oughtmama lie up a quiet side valley. Galway Bay forms the backdrop to some outstanding scenery: bare stone hills shining in the sun, with small hamlets and rich patches of green wherever there's soil.

GETTING THERE & AWAY

June to mid-September, Bus Éireann No 50, between Galway and Cork, passes through Kinvara and Ballyvaughan twice daily. Bus No 423 between Galway and Doolin also stops in those two places; there are up to three buses daily, May to September, and one bus a day Monday to Saturday the rest of year. Check the details with **Galway** (☎ 091-562 000) or **Ennis bus station** (☎ 065-682 4177).

New Quay & the Flaggy Shore

New Quay (Ceibh Nua), on the **Finavarra Peninsula**, is about 1km off the main Kinvara–Ballyvaughan road (N67) and is reached by turning off the N67 at Ballyvelaghan Lough 3km north of Bellharbour.

It's worth stopping at the shoreside **Linnane's Bar** (☎ 065-707 8120; New Quay; mains €10-22) for its fresh seafood. For centuries this area was famous for its oysters; shellfish are still processed here and you can buy them from the little processing works behind the pub.

The **Flaggy Shore**, west of New Quay, is a particularly fine stretch of coastline where limestone terraces step down to the restless sea. About 500m west of Linnane's, at a crossroads, is **Russells Ceramics** (☎ 065-707 8185; Newquay), which specialises in *raku* (Japanese lead-glazed earthenware) work. The pottery shop has a range of other art and craft work for sale.

Turn right at the crossroads for the Flaggy Shore. The road hugs the shoreline going west, then curves south past **Lough Muirí**, where you're likely to see a number of wading birds, as well as swans. There are said to be otters in the area. At a T-junction just past the lough, a right turn leads to a rather dingy-looking **Martello tower** on Finavarra Point. There's nothing drab about the history. Defensive Martello towers were another example of paranoia over the Napoleonic threat, even this far west.

Bellharbour

No more than a crossroads with some thatched holiday cottages and a pub, Bellharbour (Beulaclugga) is about 8km east of Ballyvaughan. There's a pleasant **walk** along an old green road that begins behind the modern Church of St Patrick, 1km north up the hill from the Y-junction at Bellharbour, and threads north along Abbey Hill.

Inland from here are the ruins of Corcomroe Abbey, the valley and churches of Oughtmama, and the interior road that takes you through the heart of the Burren.

Corcomroe Abbey

The beautiful and atmospheric Corcomroe, a former Cistercian abbey 1.5km inland from Bellharbour, lies in a small, tranquil valley surrounded by low hills. It is a marvellous place, one of the finest buildings of its kind. It was founded in 1194 by Donal Mór O'Brien. His grandson, Conor na Siudaine O'Brien (died 1267), king of Thomond, is said to occupy the tomb in the northern wall, and there's a crude carving of him below an effigy of a bishop armed with a crosier, the pastoral staff that was carried by a bishop or abbot. The surviving vaulting in the presbytery and transepts is very fine and there are some striking Romanesque carvings scattered throughout the abbey.

Oughtmama Valley

Small ancient churches lie hidden in this lonely, deserted valley. To get there turn inland at Bellharbour, then go left at the Y-junction. In just under 1km you reach a house amid trees, on the right at Shanvally. A rough track leads inland from just beyond the house for about 1.5km to the churches. Roadside parking is very limited, but there is a large roadside area about 400m before Shanvally, back towards the Y-junction, with views of Corcomroe. The churches at **Oughtmama** were built in the 12th century by monks in search of solitude. It's a hardy walk up **Turlough Hill** behind the chapels, but the views are tremendous. Near the summit are the remains of a **hill fort**.

COUNTY CLARE

County Galway

The ragged, untamed beauty of County Galway evokes the ancient allure of Ireland's west. Remote sandy beaches claw at the sea and at times feel like the ends of the earth. Persistent sea breezes stir the passions, or at least mess with your hair, while a calming diffuse light draws out the landscape's palette of rusty browns, moody greens and multifarious blues. Islands just a few miles off the coast feel like they are centuries away.

Connemara, largely a Gaeltacht region, is a patchwork of bogs, windswept hills and shifting beaches that are superb for hiking, biking and driving. To get away from it all and explore prehistoric forts, the rugged Aran Islands and placid Inishbofin are easy ferry rides away. The complexities of modern Ireland – its prosperity, its quickening pace, its heightened stress levels – have not yet touched these isolated spits of land. Eastern Galway is very different from the rest of the county, with the same rolling farmlands you'll see in the Midlands, and a paucity of visitor amenities and attractions means less tourism and, possibly, a very authentic glimpse of modern Irish country life.

While the rural parts are clearly what make County Galway one of Ireland's most magnetic destinations, its culturally dynamic city is what separates Galway from other, equally scenic parts of Ireland. Galway city is a potent fusion of healthy elements: it's arty, romantic, youthful and eccentric. Its cosmopolitan qualities are balanced by an intimate, closed-in feel. Some of Galway city's charm has rubbed off on Clifden, Connemara's beach resort capital. Excellent seafood restaurants can be found in the smallest coastal communities.

HIGHLIGHTS

- **Sláinte!**
  Galway city's pubs and clubs (p396)

- **Slow it Down**
  The quaint fishing village of Roundstone (p411)

- **The Quiet Life**
  Taking it slow on Inishmaan (p403) or Inisheer (p405)

- **Coastal Reveries**
  The wild shore and terrain of Connemara (p406) will stir your imagination

- **Ancient Ways**
  Ancient ring forts of Dún Aengus (p401) on Inishmór

★ Connemara
★ Roundstone
Galway city ★
Inishmór ★ Inishmaan ★★
Inisheer

■ POPULATION: 208,801 ■ AREA: 3760 SQ KM

COUNTY GALWAY

GALWAY CITY

☎ 091 / pop 65,774

The romantic city of Galway has claimed many a traveller's heart, and it isn't difficult to understand why. The city offers little in terms of sightseeing opportunities, but more than compensates with spirit and atmosphere. This is a walkable city that successfully melds old world grace and contemporary panache.

Galway has long been a magnet for creative types and wayfarers. A curved, cobbled High St, lined with stone shop fronts, bohemian cafés and enticing pubs, is closed to auto traffic much of the time and generally swarms with a festive crowd. Buskers and performance artists – many of them genuinely entertaining – break the pedestrian flow year round. The River Corrib roils with unexpected ferocity beneath Galway's stone bridges, and one can work up a healthy thirst strolling its banks and the picturesque canals that carve up the west side of town.

Of course, Galway's real appeal is its nightlife. Pubs and clubs come in all shapes and sizes. Your basic time-worn local, where the Guinness is poured slowly and the music is not amplified, will satisfy anyone who simply fancies a pint and some jovial company. But Galway is perhaps best known for its multilevel 'superpubs', with room after room of loud-talking, hard-drinking university students and party-mad tourists. Of late, Galway's after-dark scene is enhanced by a growing number of sleek lounges and dance clubs that reflect Ireland's increasingly cosmopolitan tastes. Theatre is another traditional strength.

That Dubliners can reach Galway in three hours helps augment the crowds every weekend, and the city's summer festivals – particularly Galway Race Week in July – draw multitudes of visitors. Advance accommodation booking is often necessary during these times.

Galway is an ideal stop before exploring Connemara and the Aran Islands.

HISTORY

Galway grew from a small fishing village in the Claddagh area at the mouth of the River Corrib to become an important walled town when the Anglo-Normans, under Richard de Burgo (also spelled de Burgh or Burke), captured territory from the local O'Flahertys in 1232. The Irish word for 'outsiders' or 'foreigners' is *gaill*, which may be the origin of the city's name in Irish, Gaillimh. The town walls were built by the Anglo-Normans from around 1270.

In 1396, Richard II granted a charter to the city, effectively transferring power from the de Burgos to 14 merchant families or 'tribes' – hence the informal sobriquet 'City of the Tribes', by which Galway is still known. These powerful families were mostly English or Norman in origin, and clashes with the leading Irish families of Connemara were frequent. At one time the city's western gate bore the prayer and warning: 'From the fury of the O'Flahertys, good Lord deliver us.' To ensure the ferocity was kept outside, the city fathers warned in the early 16th century that no uninvited 'O' or 'Mac' should show his face on Galway's streets.

English power throughout the region waxed and waned, but the city maintained its independent status under the ruling merchant families, who were mostly loyal to the English Crown. Galway's relative isolation encouraged a huge trade in wine, spices, fish and salt with Portugal and Spain. At one point the city rivalled Bristol and London in the volume of goods passing through its docks.

Galway's faithful support of the English Crown led to its downfall with the arrival of Cromwell. The city was besieged in 1651 and fell in April 1652. Cromwell's forces under Charles Coote wreaked their usual havoc, and Galway's long period of decline began. In 1691 the city chose the wrong side again, and William of Orange's forces added to the destruction. The important trade with Spain was almost at an end and, with Dublin and Waterford taking most of the sea traffic, Galway stagnated until its revival in modern times.

ORIENTATION

Galway's tightly packed town centre lies on both sides of the River Corrib, which connects Lough Corrib with the sea. Most of the commercial businesses are on the river's eastern bank, while there are a number of good pubs and restaurants on the west side.

From Eyre Sq, the meandering main shopping street starts as Williamsgate St, becomes

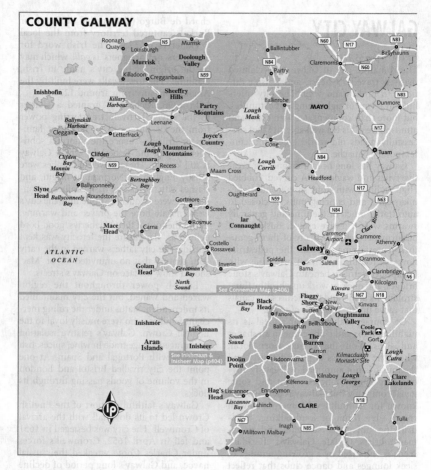

COUNTY GALWAY

See Connemara Map (p406)

See Inishmaan & Inisheer Map (p404)

William St and then Shop St, before splitting into Mainguard St and High St. Just east of Eyre Sq is the combined bus and train station, north of which is the tourist office.

Immediately to the west of Galway is the faded beach resort of Salthill, with some good B&Bs just 10 minutes' walk from central Galway.

INFORMATION
Bookshops
Charlie Byrne's (☎ 561 766; The Cornstore, Middle St) A huge collection of second-hand and discounted books.
Eason's (☎ 562 284; Shop St) Superstore with a large, general-interest selection and Galway's biggest periodicals rack.
Kenny's Bookstore & Gallery (☎ 562 739; High St) The best shop in town for Irish literature and nonfiction,

Kenny's is also one of the leading antiquarian bookshops in the country. The shop features old maps, prints and an art gallery.

Internet Access
Internet cafés charging around €5 per hour can be found on blocks immediately off the High St. They seem to come and go, but the following have been around a while.
Celtel e.centre (☎ 566 620; Kinlay House hostel, Merchant's Rd)
net@ccess (☎ 569 772; Old Malt shopping arcade, High St)

Laundry
Wash and fold service runs about €8 per load at **Laundrette** (☎ 584 524; 4 Sea Rd) and **Bubbles Inn Laundrette** (☎ 563 434; 19 Mary St).

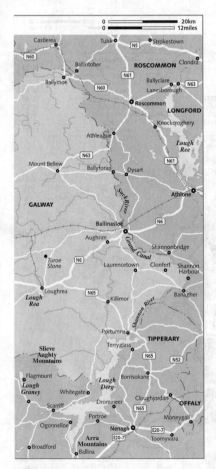

Money
Irish banks all have branches with ATMs in the city centre. The banks open 10am to 4pm Monday to Friday (to 5pm Thursday). The post office and tourist office change money.

Allied Irish Bank (Lynch's Castle, Shop St)
Bank of Ireland (2 branches on Eyre Sq)

Post
The post office on Eglinton St opens 9am to 5.30pm Monday to Saturday.

Telephone
Pay phones are located on the main pedestrian mall and on the southern side of Eyre Sq. Eircom callcards are sold in convenience stores and supermarkets.

Tourist Information
Ireland West Tourism (☎ 563 081; Forster St; ⏰ 9am-6pm daily Easter-Sep, 9am-6pm Mon-Fri, 9am-noon Sat Oct-Easter) North of Eyre Sq, this is a large information centre that can help set up accommodation locally, as well as organise bus tours and ferry trips outside the city. A row of telephones is available for free calls to local car rental agencies.

Travel Agencies
Usit (☎ 565 177; www.usit.ie; 16 Mary St) Travellers can arrange plans throughout Ireland and abroad.

SIGHTS
Collegiate Church of St Nicholas of Myra
The graceful stone edifice in the heart of town is the **Collegiate Church of St Nicholas of Myra** (☎ 564 648; Market St; admission by donation €3; ⏰ 9am-5.45pm Mon-Sat, 1-5pm Sun Apr-Sep, 10am-4pm Mon-Sat, 1-5pm Sun Oct-Mar). It's Ireland's largest medieval parish church still in use, and it's a beauty, with a curious pyramidal spire. The church also has some awfully intriguing lore, and it's surely Galway's most important monument.

The structure dates to 1320, and although it has been rebuilt and enlarged over the centuries, much of the original form has been retained. Reputedly, Christopher Columbus worshipped in the church in 1477. One theory postulates that Columbus' purpose in visiting Galway had something to do with tales of St Brendan's 6th-century voyage to America (see p418). Incidentally, St Nicholas, for whom the church was named, is the patron saint of sailors.

After Cromwell's victory, the church suffered the usual indignity of being used as a stable. Much harm was done and damaged stonework is still visible today. But St Nicholas' church was relatively fortunate: 14 other Galway churches were razed to the ground.

The church has numerous finely worked stone tombs and memorials. The two church bells date from 1590 and 1630. Parts of the floor are paved with gravestones from the 16th to 18th centuries, and the Lynch Aisle holds the tombs of the powerful Lynch family. A large block tomb in one corner is said to be the grave of James Lynch, a mayor of Galway in the late 15th century who condemned his son, Walter, to death for killing a young Spanish visitor. As the tale goes, none of the townsfolk would act as executioner

GALWAY

0 — 200 m
0 — 0.1 miles

INFORMATION		
Allied Irish Bank	(see 18)	
Bank of Ireland	1	D3
Bank of Ireland	2	D2
Bubbles Inn Laundrette	3	C2
Celtel e.centre	4	D3
Charlie Byrne's	5	C4
Eason's	6	C3
Ireland West Tourism	7	D2
Kenny's Bookstore & Gallery	(see 41)	
Laundrette	(see 44)	
net@ccess	(see 64)	
Post Office	8	C3
Usit	9	C3

SIGHTS & ACTIVITIES		
Augustinian Church	10	A4
Browne's Doorway	11	D2
Collegiate Church of St Nicholas of Myra	12	B3
Franciscan Abbey	13	B2
Galway Cathedral	14	A2
Galway City Museum	15	B4
Island Ferries Ticket Office	16	D3
Lynch Memorial Window	17	B3
Lynch's Castle	18	C3
Nora Barnacle House	19	B3
Spanish Arch	20	B5
Town Hall	21	B2

SLEEPING		
Barnacle's Quay Street House	22	B4
Eyre Square Hotel	23	D3
Galway Arms Inn	24	B4
Grange B&B	25	B3
Great Southern Hotel	26	D3
Kinlay House	27	D3
Salmon Weir Hostel	28	C2
Skeffington Arms Hotel	29	C3
Sleepzone	30	D2
Spanish Arch Hotel	31	B4
St Martin's B&B	32	B4

EATING		
Bananaphoblacht	33	B4
Busker Brownes	34	B4
Café du Journal	35	B4
Couch Potata's	36	C3
Druid Lane Restaurant	(see 56)	
Food 4 Thought	37	C3
Goya's	38	B4
Home Plate	39	B3
Kirwan's Lane Creative Cuisine	40	B4
Malt House	41	C4
McDonagh's	(see 31)	
Nimmo's	42	B5
Oscar's Restaurant	43	A4

DRINKING		
Crane Bar	44	A4
Front Door	45	B4
King's Head	46	C3
Monroe's Tavern	47	A4
Quays	48	B4
Róisín Dubh	49	A4
Séhán Ua Neáchtain	50	B4
Taaffe's Bar	51	C3
Tig Coili	52	C3

ENTERTAINMENT		
An Taibhdhearc na Gaillimhe (Galway Theatre)	53	C4
Blue Note	54	A4
cuba	55	D2
Druid Theatre	56	B4
GPO	57	C2
Karma	(see 29)	
Living Room	58	B4
Town Hall Theatre	59	B2

SHOPPING		
Bridge Mills	60	B4
Corn Store	(see 65)	
Design Concourse Ireland	61	B4
Eyre Square Centre Entrance	62	D3
Mulligan Records	63	C3
O'Maille	64	C4
River Deep Mountain High	65	C4
Thomas Dillon's Claddagh Gold	66	B4

TRANSPORT		
Abbey Cabs	67	C2
Bus Nestor	(see 7)	
Bus Station	68	D3
City Link	(see 7)	
Galway Taxis	69	B4
Michael Nee Coaches	(see 7)	
Taxi Rank	(see 2)	

To University; Coolavalla (0.5km); Villa Nova (0.5km); N59; Westport (66km); Clifden (68km)

To Renmore; Ballybrit Racecourse (3km);N6; Ballyloughane Caravan & Camping Park (5km); Airport (10km); Dublin (180km)

To Salthill (0.5km); Clare Villa (0.5km); Adare Guesthouse (0.5km); St Jude's (1.5km); Spiddal (16km); Rossaveal (32km)

To Devondell (0.75km)

To Aran Islands Ferry Pier

and the mayor was so dedicated to upholding justice that he personally acted as hangman, after which he went into seclusion. Outside on Market St, north of the church, is a stone plaque on the **Lynch Memorial Window**, complete with skull and crossbones beneath it, which relates this legend and claims to be the spot where the gallows stood.

At the end of the southern transept is the empty frame that is said to have once held an icon of the Virgin Mary. It was supposedly whisked off to Győr in western Hungary in the 17th century by an Irish bishop sent packing by Cromwell.

Nora Barnacle House

Nora Barnacle (1884–1951), the wife of James Joyce, lived in this nondescript little **house** (☎ 564 743; 8 Bowling Green; admission €2; 🕑 10am-5pm mid-May–mid-Sep, or by arrangement) for several years. The great author visited his future wife here on many occasions, beginning in 1909 and again several times during the summer of 1912. The humble abode is now a museum dedicated to the couple, with some letters and photographs among furniture arranged to suggest Nora and her bespectacled companion are due back in at any moment.

Lynch's Castle

Parts of the old, stone town house called **Lynch's Castle** (cnr Shop & Upper Abbeygate Sts), which in some circles is considered the finest town castle in Ireland, date back to the 14th century. Most of the surviving structure dates from around 1600. The Lynch family was the most powerful of the 14 ruling Galway 'tribes', and members of the family held the position of mayor no fewer than 80 times between 1480 and 1650.

Lynch's Castle has numerous fine stone features on its façade, including the coats of arms of Henry VII, the Lynches and the Fitzgeralds of Kildare, as well as gargoyles, which are unusual in Ireland. The castle is now a branch of the Allied Irish Bank, and you can enter the foyer to peer into an old fireplace and withdraw money from the ATM.

Spanish Arch

Near the river, east of Wolfe Tone Bridge, the **Spanish Arch** (1584) appears to have been an extension of Galway's old city walls. The arch may have been a passage through which ships entered the city to unload their goods – often wine and brandy from Spain.

A 1651 drawing of Galway clearly shows its extensive city walls. But since the visits of Cromwell in 1652 and William of Orange in 1691, and the subsequent centuries of neglect, the walls have almost completely disappeared. (If such walls are of interest, another surviving portion has been fully incorporated into the design of a modern shopping mall, Eyre Square Centre.)

Next to the arch, the small, rundown **Galway City Museum** (☎ 567 641; Spanish Pde; adult/child €2/1; 🕑 11am-1pm & 2-5pm Wed-Sun) is a delightfully disorganised collection of artefacts, including some military items from the War of Independence. Mainly, though, the museum's appeal comes from rummaging through what feels like a cellar full of historic curios.

Galway Cathedral

Looming magnificently over the River Corrib, **Galway Cathedral** (☎ 563 577; Gaol Rd; admission by donation €3; 🕑 8am-6pm) is a huge, imposing structure, dedicated to the late Cardinal Richard Cushing of Boston in 1965. The exterior design isn't to everyone's taste, but the interior, with its high, curved arches and central dome, has a simple, solid elegance. The cathedral's full name is a mouthful: the Catholic Cathedral of Our Lady Assumed into Heaven and St Nicholas. From the Spanish Arch, a pleasant riverside path runs upriver and across the Salmon Weir Bridge to the cathedral.

Eyre Square

Galway's central public square, undergoing much needed restoration at the time of writing, is a fine spot of municipal greenery that's suitable for people-watching, dog-walking or eating a takeaway lunch. It's framed by a busy crossroad, where cars, taxis, buses and pedestrians zigzag the lanes on their way to other parts of town. The eastern side of the square is taken up almost entirely by the Great Southern Hotel, a large, grey, limestone pile that was recently restored to its former Victorian glory.

The western side of the square has **Browne's Doorway** (1627), a fragment from the home of one of the city's merchant rulers. It looks like the remains from a carpet-bombing, but is a classy touch nevertheless.

A **statue** of the Galway-born writer Pádraic O'Conaire (1883–1928), a well-known hell-raiser, has long graced the north side of the square. Here's hoping Pádraic survives the restoration project!

Salmon Weir

Salmon Weir Bridge crosses the River Corrib just east of the cathedral. Upstream is the great weir where the waters of the Corrib cascade down one of their final descents before reaching the sea in Galway Bay. The weir controls the water levels above it, and when the salmon are running you can often see shoals of them waiting in the clear waters before making the rush upstream.

The salmon and sea-trout seasons are usually February to September, but most fish pass through the weir during May and June. To obtain fishing permits and to book a time you must write to the manager at **Galway Fisheries** (☎ 562 388; Nun's Is, Galway) several months ahead of your visit.

TOURS

Hopping aboard a bus tour is the easiest way to see nearby scenery like Connemara, the Burren or the Cliffs of Moher. You can book tours with the following companies at the tourist office in Galway or near the Salthill Promenade. Similarly, a boat trip from Galway will get you right into the heart of Lough Corrib.

Corrib Princess (☎ 592 447; www.corribprincess.ie; Woodquay; adult/family €12/25; ☻ May-Oct) Runs 1½-hour cruises on the River Corrib and Lough Corrib. The boat departs from Woodquay, just beyond Salmon Weir Bridge.

Lally Coaches (☎ 562 905; www.lallytours.com; Spiddal; adult/student €25/20) Offers bus tours of Connemara or the Burren and Cliffs of Moher. Tours leave from the tourist office.

O'Neachtain Tours (☎ 553 188; www.galway.net/pages/oneachtain-tours; Spiddal; adult/student €25/20) Runs daily, year-round coach tours departing from the tourist office to Connemara or the Burren and Cliffs of Moher.

FESTIVALS & EVENTS

Galway is festive any time of year, but the city and surrounding communities kick it up a few notches for frequent festivals. During the events, laws are usually suspended, permitting pubs to remain open 24 hours a day (many restaurants also stay open). Also see p417 for the Galway Hookers races and for events related to the Oyster Festival (p416).

The following are the highlights of Galway's calendar:

Cúirt Poetry & Literature Festival (☎ 565 886; Apr) Literati from around the EU converge on Galway for poetry slams and theatrical performances.

Galway Arts Festival (☎ 566 577; www.galwayartsfestival.ie; mid-Jul) During this two-week extravaganza of theatre, music, art and comedy, the city parties round-the-clock.

Galway Film Fleadh (☎ 751 655; www.galwayfilmfleadh.com; Jul) One of Ireland's biggest film festivals, it is held around the same time as the arts festival.

Galway Race Week (☎ 753 870; late Jul/early Aug) Horse races in Ballybrit, 3km east of the city, are the centrepiece of this week-long, round-the-clock bacchanalia.

Galway International Oyster Festival (☎ 527 282; oysters@iol.ie; last week of Sep) Oyster-slurping is accompanied by lots of partying.

SLEEPING

To fully take advantage of Galway's easy living, try to get a room in the city itself, rather than in nearby Salthill (which involves a 10- to 20-minute walk to the centre). There are many B&Bs west of the Corrib within a few minutes' stroll along pretty streets to the heart of town. July and August are particularly busy times, but most weekends can involve some calling around if you've not booked ahead.

Budget

Kinlay House (☎ 565 244; www.kinlayhouse.ie; Merchant's Rd; dm €15-18, s/d €45/54) Modern and brightly lit Kinlay House is a convenient base. It's just half a block off Eyre Sq and has clean, spacious rooms. Continental breakfast is included. Guests can book bus tours at the reception desk, and coaches pick up and drop off passengers in front of the building. There's an Internet café downstairs.

Sleepzone (☎ 566 999; www.sleepzone.ie; Bóthar na mBan; dm €13-18, s/d €30/45) The rooms are tidy and utilitarian, and the staff are generally friendly at this modern hostel. Guests have free use of the Internet, and tours can be arranged at the front desk. Sleepzone is about a five-minute walk from Eyre Sq.

Barnacle's Quay Street House (☎ 568 644; www.barnacles.ie; 10 Quay St; dm €12-22, d €54) If location is your top priority, this hostel is Galway's best value. It's in a repurposed 16th-century town house right on the pedestrian mall. It is surrounded by all the pubs, restaurants and cafés you came to Galway for. Rooms are modernised (with no hint of the building's medieval history) and a kitchen is available for self-catering. A light breakfast is included.

Salmon Weir Hostel (☎ 561 133; 3 St Vincent's Ave; dm/d €15/38) This clean, medium-sized hostel has a 3am curfew for late-night revellers. All rooms have shared bathroom.

Ballyloughane Caravan & Camping Park (☎ 755 338; galwcamp@iol.ie; Ballyloughane Beach, Renmore; camp sites €10; ☼ Apr-Sep) This family-run camping ground is clean, peaceful and secure, and its beachside location gives it good views across the bay. It's off the Dublin road (N6), 5km from Galway.

Midrange

St Martin's B&B (☎ 568 286; 2 Nun's Island Rd; s/d €35/70) Mary Sexton's homey abode has a pre-eminent location, with back-window views overlooking the Corrib and the William O'Brien Bridge and a simple garden that reaches the river bank. It's in a well-kept, older town house, and the home cooking, comfortable rooms, central location and Mary's friendliness put it at the top of the list.

Grange B&B (☎ 530 160; Smith St; s/d €40/60) The Grange is a fine choice, with a desirable central location upstairs from a taco restaurant. All rooms have a private bathroom and the High St is just a couple of blocks away.

St Jude's (☎ 521 619; www.st-judes.com; 110 Lower Salthill; ☼ closed mid-Dec–mid-Jan; Ⓟ) This absolutely gorgeous family home has elegantly furnished guestrooms (all en suite) and does a stellar breakfast. It's near the beach in Salthill, about a 10-minute walk to central Galway.

Devondell (☎ 528 306; www.devondell.com; 47 Devon Park, Lower Salthill; s/d €45/90; Ⓟ) It's not central, but Berna Kelly's B&B makes up for it with excellent breakfasts, and tea and scones in the afternoon. All rooms are en suite.

Coolavalla (☎ 522 415; coolavalla@eircom.net; 22 Newcastle Rd; s/d €48/66; ☼ Mar-Nov; Ⓟ) A little way beyond the West Side action, Coolavalla is a stately two-storey home operated by a nice family. It has four guestrooms, most with shared bathroom. The five-minute walk down to the heart of town is not at all unpleasant.

Clare Villa (☎ 522 520; clarevilla@yahoo.com; 38 Threadneedle Rd; s/d €50/70; ☼ Mar-Oct; Ⓟ) There are six clean, comfy rooms, all of which have showers, at this modern B&B near the beach.

Galway Arms Inn (☎ 565 444; cnr Lower Dominick & Mill Sts; d €50-80) Above a pub facing the William O'Brien Bridge, this nondescript inn has 11 simple but neat rooms. It's no beauty, but is very central. Breakfast is included.

Villa Nova (☎ 524 849; 40 Lower Newcastle Rd; s/d €43/70; Ⓟ) In a quiet recess along the main road towards the university, Villa Nova is a friendly B&B. All its four rooms have private bathrooms.

Top End

Great Southern Hotel (☎ 564 041; www.greatsouthern hotelgalway.com; Eyre Sq; d €110; Ⓟ) The monumental Great Southern Hotel presides over Eyre Sq as though it was the city's most important edifice, and if it's not that it is certainly Galway's pre-eminent accommodation. A recent makeover has the rooms looking spiffy and modern, complete with extras from saunas and fitness rooms to bars and restaurants.

Spanish Arch Hotel (☎ 569 600; www.spanisharch hotel.ie; Quay St; d €90-145) On the main drag, this 20-room hotel manages to feel both historic and modern. Guests will feel well cared for amid antique furnishings and designer opulence.

Skeffington Arms Hotel (☎ 563 173; www.skeff ington.ie; Eyre Sq; d €70-140; Ⓟ €8.50) The 'Skeff', overlooking Eyre Sq, has spacious and slightly pompous rooms. This is a modern, full-service hotel in a classic old building with an attractive pub-nightclub. Breakfast is included.

Eyre Square Hotel (☎ 569 633; www.byrne-hotels -ireland.com; Eyre Sq; d €79-139) This large, fully refurbished hotel offers enticing extras for stylin' tourists, like hair dryers and trouser presses. Off the lobby are a snazzy café and a swanky pub.

Adare Guesthouse (☎ 582 638; www.adarebedand breakfast.com; 9 Father Griffin Pl; s/d €55/90; Ⓟ) The Adare is in a large, barn-like house overlooking a children's playground. It's convenient, tidy, furnished almost completely in pine, and just a five-minute walk from the centre. All rooms have private bathroom.

EATING
Restaurants

Home Plate (☎ 561 475; 13 Mary St; mains €4-10; ☯ noon-8pm Mon-Sat) smart and homey, Home Plate serves up high-quality, hearty meals in heaping quantities. It's the best deal in town, whether you crave roasted meat, a ciabatta sandwich or one of a variety of vegetarian omelettes.

Oscar's Restaurant (☎ 582 180; Upper Dominick St; mains €17-27; ☯ 5.30pm-late Tue-Sun) The flamboyant and fun atmosphere at Oscar's doesn't overshadow the first-rate, adventurous cooking. Southeast-Asian ingredients season such dishes as char-grilled supreme of chicken with sweet-and-sour sauce, and dishes are arranged like three-dimensional paintings.

Nimmo's (☎ 561 114; Long Walk; mains €14-26; ☯ 7-10pm Tue-Sat, 1-4pm & 6-10pm Sun) Hidden behind the Spanish Arch, Nimmo's is romantic and dimly lit for a special evening out. The menu is creative, with a strong seafood bias.

McDonagh's (☎ 565 001; 22 Quay St; fish & chips €7; ☯ noon-3pm & 5-10pm Mon-Sat) Galway's best chipper is always crowded. Cod, plaice and haddock lathered in a tasty batter are churned nonstop out of the fryer.

Malt House (☎ 567 866; High St; mains €17-20; early set dinner €20; ☯ 12.30-3pm & 6.30-10.30pm Mon-Sat) One of Galway's more traditional restaurants is the Malt House, with a formal dining room that beams with well-seasoned pride. Dinner here assures capably handled Irish standbys from the sea and the land.

Kirwan's Lane Creative Cuisine (☎ 568 266; Kirwan's Lane; lunch mains €10-14, dinner mains €18-25; ☯ noon-2pm & 6-10pm Mon-Sat) A stylish bistro with devoted followers, Kirwan's Lane spruces up Irish cuisine with judicious use of Asian ingredients. Seafood is a strength. Reservations are advised.

Druid Lane Restaurant (☎ 563 015; 9 Quay St; lunch mains €8-13, dinner mains €15-24; ☯ 5pm-late Tue-Sat) An intimate, tastefully decorated restaurant, Druid Lane serves imaginative, modern Irish dishes. Pastas, roasts and seafood anchor the menu, and the wine list is extensive.

Couch Potata's (☎ 561 664; 40 Upper Abbeygate St; mains €8-11; ☯ noon-9.30pm) The baked potatoes churned out in this unassuming eatery are tastily endowed with heaped portions of chicken strips, bolognaise sauce, chilli con carne, or curry. One potato, served with a tossed salad, will fill you up.

Cafés

Goya's (☎ 567 010; 2 Kirwan's Lane; dishes €4-9; ☯ 9.30am-6pm Mon-Sat) The cake is supreme in Goya's, a Galway treasure that's hidden on a narrow walkway. You can also get a light lunch or a frothy espresso and while away an hour or so in the friendly environs.

Bananaphoblacht (☎ 561 478; 56 Lower Dominick St; snacks €2-5; ☯ 9am-10pm) Don't be scared off by the weird splattered-banana name. This place is Galway's artiest, hippest little café, where fair-trade espressos are poured daily and live acoustic music is performed Sunday night.

Busker Brownes (☎ 563 377; Upper Cross St; dishes €10; ☯ 10.30am-11.30pm Mon-Thu, 10.30-12.30am Fri & Sat, 12.30-11.30pm Sun) A café-bar that manages to offer comfort in a suave lounge environment, Busker Brownes does top-notch pub fare and hangover breakfasts. With tables beside the front windows, this is also a nice spot for coffee and the morning paper.

Food 4 Thought (☎ 565 854; Lower Abbeygate St; mains €4-7; ☯ 8am-6pm Mon-Sat, 11.30am-4pm Sun) For organic and vegetarian sandwiches and dishes, head to this casual establishment. It's also a worthy stop for baked goods and espresso drinks.

Café du Journal (☎ 568 426; Quay St; mains €4-9; ☯ 10am-6pm winter, 10am-10pm summer) Arty deep-thinkers and French expats congregate here for zesty sandwiches, strong coffee and animated conversation.

DRINKING

Visitors will notice that Galway has two, somewhat separate hubs for entertainment, divided by the river. The greatest concentration of pubs and clubs, around the pedestrian drag, is slightly more touristy but certainly worth a thorough investigation. Among the superpubs and sleek lounges are some graceful old watering holes. The west side, while not necessarily quieter, has a local feel and attracts a slightly hipper crowd. Either way, you can't go wrong, and the river is no obstacle to taking in pubs and clubs from both sides.

Séhán Ua Neáchtain (☎ 568 820; 17 Upper Cross St) Known simply as Neáchtains, this dusty old pub has a truly fabulous atmosphere and attracts a mix of eccentrics and working people.

Róisín Dubh (☎ 586 540; Upper Dominick St) Appearing like a reliable local boozer, Róisín Dubh is better known as *the* place to see new rock-and-roll talents before they get too big for such intimate venues. On occasion it's also good for traditional music.

Crane Bar (☎ 587 419; 2 Sea Rd) An atmospheric old pub west of the Corrib, the Crane is good for a quiet pint even when a top-notch *céilidh* (traditional music session) session is on. Head upstairs where the action is.

Quays (☎ 568 347; Quay St) One of Galway's most famous pubs, the Quays is another enormous tavern with an endless series of atmospheric rooms and passageways. There are some great vantage points from which to watch the upbeat crowd or the live music (traditional to pop) that's on most nights.

Front Door (☎ 563 757; High St) This is Galway's best pub for an afternoon pint, thanks to its easy-going regulars and a row of high windows casting a most pleasing light.

King's Head (☎ 566 630; 15 High St) This is a superpub fashioned from a 17th-century stone pub. Beyond its narrow frontage it opens up way back to a small stage. Rock bands play most nights, and a popular jazz session takes place Sunday morning.

Tig Coili (Mainguard St) Just off High St is this den of civility, where 5pm sessions always draw a crowd.

Taaffe's Bar (☎ 564 066; 19 Shop St) Well-loved for its nightly Irish music sessions, which begin at 5pm, the pub itself is nothing to marvel at, having been stripped of some of its charm when remodelled.

Monroe's Tavern (☎ 583 397; Upper Dominick St) A reliable spot for traditional music and ballads, Monroe's is the only pub in the city to offer set dancing (Tuesday).

ENTERTAINMENT

The free *Galway Advertiser* includes listings of what's on in the city. It's available every Thursday at the tourist office and newsstands around town, and copies get snatched up fast.

TOP FIVE COUNTY GALWAY PUBS

- Séhán Ua Neáchtain, Galway (opposite)
- O'Dowd's, Roundstone (p412)
- Teach Ósta, Inishmaan (p405)
- Crane Bar, Galway (above)
- Róisín Dubh, Galway (opposite)

Nightclubs

Clubs generally get cranking around 11pm and don't wind down till around 2am. Admission prices vary according to the nightly programme.

cuba (☎ 565 991; www.cuba.ie; Eyre Sq; admission €5-15; 🕙 8pm-late) Upstairs from Bar 903, cuba draws exuberant crowds for DJs and live bands.

Blue Note (☎ 589 116; 3 West William St) DJs spin most nights in this slightly jazzy club, and an interesting mix of students and tourists come here for drinking and dancing. The beer garden is popular in summer (and among smokers year round). There's usually no cover charge.

Living Room (www.thelivingroom.ie; 🕙 till 2am Thu-Sun) A young, well-heeled crowd is attracted to the Living Room's retro décor, DJs and, in the early evening, televised sporting events.

GPO (☎ 563 073; 21 Eglinton St; admission €6-10) Trendy 20-somethings flock here for 1980s and house grooves. Cheap drinks are no deterrent either.

Karma (☎ 563 173; www.karma.ie; Eyre Sq; admission €10-15; 🕙 11pm-late Thu-Sun) Galway's most sophisticated nightclub attracts a young, smartly dressed professional crowd (a dress code ensures it). The space really is gorgeous. The club is downstairs in the Skeffington Arms Hotel.

Theatre

Druid Theatre (☎ 568 617; www.druidtheatre.com; Chapel Lane) The long-established Druid is famed for its experimental works by young Irish playwrights.

Town Hall Theatre (☎ 569 777; Courthouse Sq) On the corner of St Vincent's Ave, this theatre tends to feature Broadway or West End shows and visiting singers.

An Taibhdhearc na Gaillimhe (☎ 562 024; Middle St) Perhaps not of much interest to non-Irish-speakers, this Galway Theatre stages plays in Irish.

SHOPPING

Speciality stores are more Galway's style. Following are a few standout shops in the city centre.

Design Concourse Ireland (☎ 566 927; Kirwan's Lane; 🕙 closed Sun) Head here to familiarise yourself with contemporary Irish design in jewellery, tableware, greeting cards and high fashion in Donegal tweed.

Mulligan Records (☎ 564 961; 5 Middle St) Drop into this record store for Irish music and folk music from around the world; it does mail order.

O'Maille (☎ 562 696; 16 High St; ☺ closed Sun) If it's cold and damp out, nothing will suit you better than Irish woollens. This is the best shop in town for such things as tweed caps, Aran sweaters, and traditional long-sleeved undershirts just like grampaw used to wear.

River Deep Mountain High (☎ 563 938; Middle St) This is one of the better places for outdoor clothing and equipment.

Thomas Dillon's Claddagh Gold (☎ 566 365; 1 Quay St) The memento of choice for many visitors to Galway is a Claddagh ring in silver or gold. Before making your purchase you can learn a bit about the tradition of these rings here and see some vintage examples in Dillon's back-room 'museum'.

When the weather is good, Galway's Farmer's Market can be an exuberant festival in its own right. Organic farmers and hippy craft vendors line up along Churchyard St every Saturday morning.

There are a few general purpose shopping centres: the big Eyre Square Centre, southeast of Eyre Sq; Bridge Mills, in an old mill building by the river at the western end of William O'Brien Bridge; and the Cornstore on Middle St.

GETTING THERE & AWAY
Air
British Airways has limited services to **Galway Airport** (☎ 800 491 492; www.galwayairport .com; Carnmore) from London, Manchester and Glasgow.

Aer Arran (www.aerarran.com) has cheap flights between Galway and London Luton, Edinburgh, Manchester and Birmingham, as well as to Lorient in France.

Bus
From the **bus station** (☎ 562 000), just off Eyre Sq, there are frequent Bus Éireann services to all major cities in the Republic and the North. The one-way fare to Dublin (3¾ hours) is €13.

A lot of the private companies are also well represented.

Bus Nestor (☎ 797 484; busnestor@eircom.net) runs five to eight daily services to Dublin (€10), going via Dublin airport. Buses leave from outside the tourist office every couple of hours or so between 6.30am and 5.25pm.

Hourly buses to Dublin (€12) and Dublin airport (€17), run by **City Link** (☎ 564 163; www.citylink.ie), depart from the tourist office daily.

Michael Nee Coaches (☎ 095-51082) runs two or three daily services to towns throughout Connemara. Buses depart from Forster St in Galway, just across from the tourist office.

Train
From **Ceannut Station** (☎ 564 222), just off Eyre Sq, there are up to five trains daily to/from Dublin's Euston Station (one way from €28, three hours). Connections with other train routes can be made at Athlone (one hour).

GETTING AROUND
To/From the Airport
A bus runs daily Monday to Saturday between the airport and Galway bus station (€3.25). It leaves the airport at 1.25pm, and leaves the bus station at 12.50pm. A taxi to/from the airport costs about €18.

Bicycle
Most hostels, including Kinlay House and Salmon Weir Hostel, hire out bikes. At **Europa Bicycles** (☎ 563 355; Hunter's Bldg; ☺ Mon-Sat), on Earl's Island opposite Galway Cathedral, bikes cost €10 for 24 hours.

Bus
You can walk to almost everything in Galway and even out to Salthill, but there are regular buses from Eyre Sq. Bus No 1 runs from Eyre Sq to Salthill.

Car
Drivers will need parking discs to park on the street; these are available from the tourist office and from newsagencies. The car park just over William O'Brien Bridge is next to the garda station.

Taxi
Taxi ranks are located on Eyre Sq, on Bridge St, and next to the bus/train station. You can also catch a cab by dropping by a taxi office. Try **Abbey Cabs** (☎ 569 469; Eyre St) or **Galway Taxis** (☎ 561 111; Mainguard St).

ARAN ISLANDS

☎ 091

Among the most compelling reasons for a trip to Galway is the chance to sail off to the rugged Aran Islands, which are a short boat ride from the mainland but can feel centuries removed. At their best, these stark, rocky outcrops are atmospheric, dramatic but slightly subdued. Earthen paths that weave through small fields partitioned by stone walls are conducive to long, contemplative walks. When the islands succeed in lulling the visitor to their ancient tempo, time spent following these dense stone mazes creeps by very slowly and it's strangely satisfying.

However, the islands aren't well suited to large numbers of tourists, and a maddening crowd does show up in July and August. Inishmaan and Inisheer are sublime any time of year, but especially in the early spring, when erratic weather draws out the islands' subtle colours and keeps the number of visitors down.

Inishmór, the largest island and most easily accessible from Galway, features one of Ireland's most important and impressive archaeological sites. There's generally more fun to be had on Inishmór, with tourists cruising its dusty roads on bikes and making merry in its pubs and restaurants. But Inishmór is the least appealing island in many ways. It is less beautiful, and Kilronan, its small capital, suffers from crass commercialism and even traffic congestion.

Geologically speaking, the islands are an extension of the limestone escarpment that forms the Burren, and they look it. The outer periphery of the islands resembles cracked grey pavement that gives way, as the islands rise, to shallow topsoil on which buttercups, daisies and spring gentian naturally take root. The small pastures, so solidly fenced in, are covered with a very soft grass that would be irresistibly tempting for an afternoon nap if it weren't for random heaps of cow dung scattered about. The western edges of Inishmaan and Inishmór are dramatic, perfectly vertical cliffs jutting 50m to 100m above a tumultuous surf.

The ancient forts on the islands – most notably Dún Aengus on Inishmór and Dún Chonchúir on Inishmaan – are some of the oldest archaeological remains in Ireland, and exploring them freely is a rare delight. The islands also have a few *clocháns* (dry stone beehive huts), resembling igloos made of stone, in which early Christian monks retreated.

Services are limited on the islands. There are no ATMs and restaurants tend to shut during the winter. Be sure to seek advice on such matters when you book accommodation, and plan accordingly.

HISTORY

Almost nothing is known about the people who built the massive Iron Age stone structures on Inishmór and Inishmaan. These sites are commonly referred to as 'forts', but are actually believed to have served as pagan religious centres. In folklore, the forts are said to have been built by the Firbolgs, a Celtic tribe who invaded Ireland from Europe in prehistoric times.

It is believed that people came to the islands to farm, which would have presented a major challenge. The topsoil was rarely more than a foot deep, if that, and it was laden with stones. As a matter of necessity the early settlers began building the 1600km of stone walls we see today, which put extracted stones to good use (the stone walls keep precious dirt from blowing off to sea and help regulate livestock grazing habits). These early islanders augmented their soil by hauling seaweed and sand up from the shore. People also fished the surrounding waters on long *currachs* (rowing boats made of a framework of laths covered with tarred canvas), which still remain as a symbol of the Aran Islands.

Christianity reached the islands remarkably quickly, and some of the earliest monastic settlements were founded by St Enda (Éanna) in the 5th century. Any remains you see today are later, from the 8th century onwards. Enda appears to have been an Irish chief who converted to Christianity and spent some time studying in Rome before seeking out a suitably remote spot for his monastery.

From the 14th century, control of the islands was disputed by two Gaelic families, the O'Briens and the O'Flahertys. The English took over during the reign of Elizabeth I, and in Cromwell's times a garrison was stationed here.

As Galway's importance waned, so too did that of the islands. Isolation permitted the islanders to maintain a traditional lifestyle well into the 20th century. Irish is still very much the local tongue, and until the 1930s people wore traditional Aran dress: bright-red skirts and black shawls for women, baggy woollen trousers and waistcoats with colourful belts (or *crios*) for men. The classic cream Aran sweater knitted in complex patterns originated here. These days some older women on Inishmaan still wear shawls and skirts.

BOOKS & MAPS

The elemental nature of life on the islands has always attracted writers and artists. The dramatist JM Synge (1871–1909) spent a lot of time on the islands, and his play *Riders to the Sea* (1905) is set on Inishmaan. His book *The Aran Islands* (1907) is the classic account of life here and is readily available in paperback.

The American Robert Flaherty came to the islands in 1934 to film *Man of Aran,* a dramatic account of daily life. It became a classic and there are regular screenings of it in Kilronan on Inishmór.

The islands have produced their own talent, particularly the writer Liam O'Flaherty (1896–1984) from Inishmór. O'Flaherty, who wandered around North and South America before returning to Ireland in 1921 and fighting in the Civil War, wrote several outstanding novels, including *Famine.*

The mapmaker Tim Robinson has written a wonderful two-volume account of his explorations on Aran called *Stones of Aran: Pilgrimage* and *Stones of Aran: Labyrinthe.* His *The Aran Islands: A Map and Guide* is superb.

Two other excellent publications in paperback are *The Book of Aran,* edited by Anne Korf and published by Tír Eolas, consisting of articles by 17 specialists covering diverse aspects of the islands' culture, and *Aran Reader* (Lilliput Press), edited by Breandán and Ruairí O hEither, with essays by various scholars on the islands' history, geography and culture.

GETTING THERE & AWAY

Air

All three islands have landing strips, in case you are short on time or susceptible to seasickness. The mainland departure point is Connemara regional airport at Minna, near Inverin (Indreabhán), about 35km west of Galway. A connecting bus from outside the Galway tourist office costs €3 one way. The flights take just 10 minutes.

Aer Arann (☎ 593 034; www.aerarannislands.ie) offers return flights to any of the islands five times daily (hourly in summer) for €44/25/37 per adult/child/student. Groups of four can ask about group rates.

Boat

There's at least one boat a day heading out to the Aran Islands. Around Galway's Eyre Sq there are several Island Ferries offices that'll set you up with a boat ride as well as accommodation if you need it. Galway's tourist office will do the same.

Island Ferries (☎ 568 903, 572 273; www.aranislandferries.com) is the biggest ferry line, and the only one to operate daily year round. Boats leave from Rossaveal (return per adult/child/student €19/10/15), about 40km west of Galway, which makes for a quick crossing (about 40 minutes). The return Galway–Rossaveal bus trip costs €5/2.50 per adult/child and leaves Galway's Kilroy House Hostel 1½ hours before the ferry's scheduled departure. If you are driving to Rossaveal, you can park your car in the car park near the Island Ferries office.

Ferries to Aran Island also operate from Doolin (p379).

GETTING AROUND

The islands of Inisheer and Inishmaan are small enough to explore on foot, but to see larger Inishmór bikes are the way to go. You can also arrange transport on Inishmór with any of the small tour vans or pony traps.

Island Ferries (☎ 568 903, 572 273; www.aranislandferries.com) runs inter-island services. Connections may require a trip back to Rossaveal from October to April.

INISHMÓR

☎ 099 / pop 1281

The vast majority of visitors to the Aran Islands don't make it beyond Inishmór (Árainn). Understandably, the attraction is ancient Dún Aengus, the spectacular stone crescent at the edge of the island's sea cliffs. Tourism has had an impact on this island though, as should be abundantly clear once you disembark from the ferry in Kilronan. An armada of tour vans will be lined up to greet you, offering a ride round the sights (not a bad idea if you're just doing a quick day trip), and in summer the little town's narrow streets gridlock just before and after the arrival of a ferry. The best way around town is aboard a hired bicycle or in a small pony trap. After climbing the hill west of Kilronan, the island's main settlement, the arid landscape is dominated by stone walls and boulders, scattered buildings and the odd patch of deep-green grass and potato plants.

Orientation

Inishmór is 14.5km long and a maximum of 4km wide, running northwest to southeast. All ferries and boats arrive and depart from Kilronan (Cill Rónáin) on the southeastern side of the island. The airstrip is 2km further southeast of town. One principal road runs the length of the island, with many smaller lanes and paths of packed dirt and stone leading off it.

Information

The **tourist office** (☎ 61263; ◷ 11am-1pm & 2-5pm Mon-Fri, 10am-1pm & 2-5pm Sat & Sun), on the waterfront west of the ferry pier in Kilronan, can help with accommodation and planning your visit, and can also change money. The **Bank of Ireland** (◷ 10am-12.30pm & 1.30-3pm Wed), north of the village centre, has no ATM.

Sights

Inishmór has three impressive stone forts, believed to be around 2000 years old. Chief among them, two-thirds of the way down the island from Kilronan and perched on the edge of the sheer southern cliff, is one of the most amazing archaeological sites in the country, **Dún Aengus** (Dún Aonghasa; ☎ 61008; adult/child €1.20/0.50; ◷ 10am-6pm). It has a remarkable *chevaux de frise*, a dense arrangement of defensive stone spikes around the exterior of the fort that surely helped deter ancient armies considering invading the site. If you go at a quieter time, such as late evening, when there are fewer visitors, you won't forget the sight and sound of the powerful swells pounding the cliff face. There are no guard rails and the winds can be strong, so be careful; tourists have been blown off and killed on the rock shelf below. Of course, that won't keep people

from creeping on hands and knees to the precipice for a peek over the edge.

Along the road between Kilronan and Dún Aengus is the smaller **Dún Eochla**, a perfectly circular fort. Directly south of Kilronan and dramatically perched on a promontory is **Dún Dúchathair**, surrounded on three sides by cliffs.

The ruins of numerous stone churches trace the island's monastic history. The small **Teampall Chiaráin** (Church of St Kieran), with a high cross in the churchyard, is near Kilronan. To the southeast, near Cill Éinne Bay, is the early-Christian **Teampall Bheanáin** (Church of St Benen). Past Kilmurvey is the perfect **Clochán na Carraige**, an early-Christian stone hut that stands 2.5m tall, and various small early-Christian ruins known rather inaccurately as the **Na Seacht dTeampaill** (Seven Churches), consisting of a couple of ruined churches, monastic houses and some fragments of a high cross from the 8th or 9th century. To the south is **Dún Eoghanachta**, another circular fort. Near the airstrip are the sunken remains of a church said to be the site of **St Enda's Monastery** in the 5th century.

There's a fine beach at **Kilmurvey**, west of Kilronan, and it's pleasant to stay here away from the bustle of Kilronan. Before the beach, in the sheltered little bay of **Port Chorrúch**, up to 50 grey seals make their home, sunning and feeding in the shallows.

To have a more informed appreciation of the island, stop in at **Ionad Árann** (Aran Heritage Centre; ☎ 61355; www.visitaranislands.com; Kilronan; adult/child €5.50/4; ◷ 11am-1pm & 2-5pm Mon-Fri, 10am-1pm & 2-5pm Sat & Sun). Just off the main road leading out of Kilronan, the centre offers a useful introduction to the geology, wildlife, history and culture of the three islands. The admission fee includes a viewing of Robert Flaherty's 1934 film *Man of Aran*, screened three times daily. The centre also has a coffee shop.

Sleeping

The **tourist office** (☎ 61263) can help book rooms, and a number of places to stay are near enough from the pier to check out before deciding.

HOSTELS

Mainistir House Hostel (☎ 61169; www.mainistir housearan.com; Mainistir; dm €12, s/d €35/50) This appealing 60-bed hostel, on the main road north of Kilronan, is a fun place for young travellers, and for families as well. The private rooms are very colourful and neatly designed. It has a large kitchen, and bicycles for hire. Fresh morning pastries, bed linen and free pick-up are included in the rates.

Artist's Lodge Hostel (☎ 61456; Kilronan; dm €10) It doesn't look exactly 'artistic', but this small and modern house is exceptionally clean and has good ocean views.

An Aharla Hostel (☎ 61305; Kilronan; dm €12) In a laid-back former farmhouse, quietly positioned in a grove of trees (a rarity on these islands), An Aharla has two four-bed dorms. Conveniently, Joe Watty's Bar is just paces away.

Kilronan Hostel (☎ 61255; www.kilronanhostel .com; Kilronan; dm €14) This clean, friendly hostel is a short walk from the pier. The floors have been insulated, so although the hostel is above Tí Joe Mac's pub, you hear very little noise. Breakfast is included, and guests can hire bikes for the day (€10).

B&BS

Kilmurvey House (☎ 61218; www.kilmurveyhouse. com; Kilmurvey; s/d €40/70; ♈ Apr-Sep) On the path leading to Dún Aengus is this grand 18th-century stone mansion. It's a beautiful setting, and the rooms are well maintained and have private bathrooms. Meals (dinner €22) are finely crafted with home-grown vegetables and fresh fish and meats. A short walk from the house is a nice beach for swimming.

St Brendan's House B&B (☎ 61149; stbrendans aran@eircom.net; Kilronan; s/d €25/50) A cheerful old house with views of the Kilronan harbour, it's a little rough around the edges, but the hospitality makes up for it. Guests can get lower rates if taking shared bathroom or passing on breakfast.

Man of Aran Cottage (☎ 61301; www.manofaran cottage.com; Kilmurvey; s/d €45/74; ♈ Mar-Oct) It was built for the 1930s film of the same name, but this thatched B&B doesn't trade merely on past glories. Age has worn some of its ersatz sheen, and the place feels genuinely homey. Best of all, owners Joe and Maura Wolfe provide hospitality and fine cooking. Guests can hire bikes and tool around Kilmurvey Bay.

Pier House Guest House (☎ 61416; www.galway .net/pages/pierhouse; Kilronan; s/d €35/70) The first building you'll see as you come off the pier

is this modern B&B, with a pleasant sitting room, and phones and TVs in the rooms.

Cregmount House (☎ 61139; Creggakeerain, Kilronan; s/d €50/64; ♈ May-Sep) At the northwestern end of the island, 9km from Kilronan, Cregmount House is a pleasant, three-room B&B with views across Galway Bay.

An Crúgán (☎ 61150; www.ancrugan.com; Kilronan; s/d €50/66; ♈ Apr-Sep; **P**) Located off the main road north of Kilronan, An Crúgán has six well-appointed rooms, and bikes for hire. This place also has a two-bedroom cottage (€450 to €550 per week) that's available year round.

Eating

Mainistir House Hostel (☎ 61169; buffet €12; ♈ 8pm-close summer, 7pm-close winter) The island's most interesting spot for dinner is, remarkably, in this hostel. Mainistir House serves flavourful, organic, largely vegetarian buffet dinners. The joint's popular, so book ahead.

Man of Aran Cottage (☎ 61301; Kilmurvey; sandwiches from €2.50, set dinner €25; ♈ noon-3pm Jun-Sep, 7.30pm-close daily) Idyllic and homey Man of Aran serves fresh fish and flavourful organic vegetables and herbs, which the owners grow in their garden. It offers light lunches during the summer, and full dinners in the evening. Reservations required.

Dún Aonghasa (Aran Fisherman Restaurant; ☎ 61104; Kilronan; mains €7-18; ♈ 12.30-4pm & 5-9pm) A general-purpose restaurant with an extensive menu that will please the entire family. Fish features prominently, but there are also pizzas and sandwiches on offer.

For self-catering there's a Spar supermarket in Kilronan.

Drinking

Tigh Fitz (☎ 61213; Killeaney) Near the airport, 1.6km from Kilronan, this jovial pub has traditional sessions every weekend and does excellent bar food during the summer months.

Joe Watty's Bar (Kilronan) The best pub in Kilronan is Joe Watty's, where a traditional session is on most nights. It's on the road heading north of town. Pub food is served.

Shopping

A hand-knitted Aran sweater is top of many people's shopping lists when visiting the islands. In Kilronan, **Carraig Donn Woollen Shop** (☎ 61123; Kilronan), near the old pier, will gladly accommodate this need.

Getting Around

Aran Cycle Hire (☎ 61132; per day €10), near the pier, hires out good bikes. You can also bring your own bicycle on the ferry.

Numerous minibuses greet tourists as they disgorge from the ferry. They offer 2½-hour tours of the island's principal sights for €10. It's not a bad way to see everything if you're just on the island for a few hours, but if you have more time walking and cycling will give you a better sense of the place.

In summer, pony traps with a driver are available for a return trip between Kilronan and Dún Aengus, costing €30 for up to four people. If they're not waiting by the pier, walk to the tourist office and ask where they're stationed.

INISHMAAN

☎ 099 / pop 200

This is a sweet spot. Indeed, the cows here groan with what must be the pure pleasure of grazing in such a peaceful place. (Cows elsewhere just moo.) Early Christian monks, seeking solitude but not wishing to displease their refined sense of natural beauty, were drawn to Inishmaan (Inis Meáin), as was the author JM Synge, who spent five summers here over a century ago. The island they knew largely survives today: endless, snaking stone walls up to 2m high; docile farm animals; warm-hearted Irish speakers; impressive old forts; startling cliffs; and a welcomed respite from the fast-paced modern world. To their credit, the islanders here are mildly indifferent to the prospect of attracting tourist euros, so visitor facilities are limited.

Inishmaan is about 5km long by 3km wide. Walking is a fine way to get around.

Orientation & Information

Most of Inishmaan's buildings are spread out along the road that runs east–west across the centre of the island. The principal boat landing is on the eastern side of the island, while the airstrip is in the northeastern corner. In An Córa, the helpful **Inishmaan Island Co-operative** (☎ 73010), northwest of the pier and post office, dispenses tourist information.

Sights

The chief archaeological site is **Dún Chonchúir**, a massive oval-shaped stone fort built on a high point and offering fine views of the island and the sea. It's similar to Dún Aengus on Inishmór, but is completely round and built inland overlooking a limestone valley. Chonchúir's age is a bit hazy: it's thought to have been built sometime between the 1st and 7th centuries.

Teach Synge (☎ 73036; admission €3; ☑ by appointment), a thatched cottage on the road just before you head up to the fort, is where the writer JM Synge spent his summers between 1898 and 1902.

Cill Cheannannach is a rough 8th- or 9th-century church, south of the pier. The well-preserved stone fort **Dún Fearbhaigh**, a short distance west, dates from the same era.

At the desolate western edge of the island, **Synge's Chair** is a lookout at the edge of a sheer limestone cliff with the pounding surf from Gregory's Sound booming below. In a well-chosen spot the cliff ledge is often sheltered from the wind, so do like Synge did and find a comfortable seat to take it all in.

On the walk out to Synge's Chair a sign points the way to a **clochán**, hidden behind a house and shed. It's a small, domed monk dwelling that vaguely resembles a beehive. Needless to say, stark little huts such as this one did not represent the 'easy life'.

In the east of the island, about 500m north of the boat landing stage, is **Trá Leitreach**, a safe, sheltered beach.

Sleeping & Eating

Most B&Bs serve evening meals, usually using organically grown food. They generally cost around €20.

An Dún (☎ 73047; anduninismeain@eircom.net; s/d €38/64) Opposite the entrance to Dún Chonchúir, modern An Dún has comfortable en-suite rooms and a sauna. It serves very hearty set dinners (€20) and nonguests are welcome, though you must make a reservation. An Dún also has a handy little grocery shop, good for packing essentials for your day hike.

Máire Mulkerrin (☎ 73016; s/d €25/40) Elderly Mrs Mulkerrin is a local icon in her skirts and shawls and with her quiet, dour demeanour. She keeps a cosy home, filled with faded family photos, and her stove keeps the kitchen warm all day. Breakfast is included.

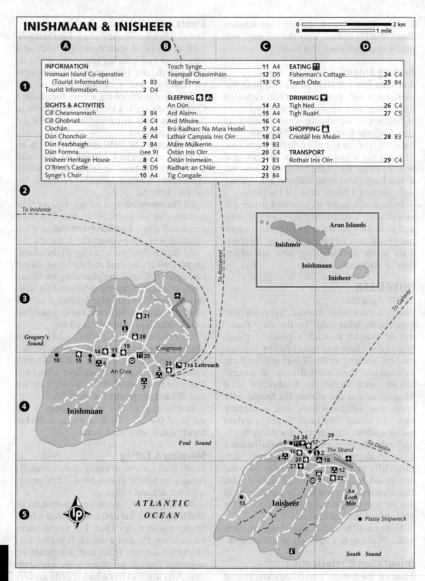

INISHMAAN & INISHEER

0 ———————— 2 km
0 ———————— 1 mile

INFORMATION
Inismaan Island Co-operative
(Tourist Information)......................**1** B3
Tourist Information...........................**2** D4

SIGHTS & ACTIVITIES
Cill Cheannannach.............................**3** B4
Cill Ghobnait....................................**4** C4
Clochán..**5** A4
Dún Chonchúir..................................**6** A4
Dún Fearbhaigh.................................**7** B4
Dún Formna..............................(see 9)
Inisheer Heritage House.....................**8** C4
O'Brien's Castle.................................**9** D5
Synge's Chair..................................**10** A4

Teach Synge....................................**11** A4
Teampall Chaoimháin........................**12** D5
Tobar Éinne.....................................**13** C5

SLEEPING 🏠 🛆
An Dún...**14** A3
Ard Alainn..**15** A4
Ard Mhuire.......................................**16** C4
Brú Radharc Na Mara Hostel...............**17** C4
Lathair Campala Inis Oírr...................**18** D4
Máire Mulkerrin................................**19** B3
Óstán Inis Oírr..................................**20** C4
Óstán Inismeáin................................**21** B3
Radharc an Chláir.............................**22** D5
Tig Congaile.....................................**23** B4

EATING 🍴
Fisherman's Cottage..........................**24** C4
Teach Ósta.......................................**25** B4

DRINKING 🍷
Tigh Ned..**26** C4
Tigh Ruaírí.......................................**27** C5

SHOPPING 🛍
Cniotáil Inis Meáin............................**28** B3

TRANSPORT
Rothair Inis Oírr................................**29** C4

To Inishmór

To Rossaveal

To Galway

Aran Islands

Inishmór

Inishmaan

Inisheer

Gregory's
Sound

Creigmore

An Córa

Trá Leitreach

Inishmaan

To Doolin

Foul Sound

The Strand

An
Loch
Mór

ATLANTIC
OCEAN

Inisheer

• Plassy Shipwreck

South Sound

Tig Congaile (☎ 73085; tigcongaile@eircom.net;
Moore Village, Inishmaan; s/d €38/66; dishes €4-20; ☻ restaurant 10.30am-9pm) This hotel-restaurant is not
far from the pier, and does brisk business
among folks hopping briefly off the ferry
boats. Guatemalan-born Vilma Conneely
adds unexpected diversity to the local dining
scene, making the most of limited local ingre-

dients. She does a fine sea vegetable soup and
her vegetable and herb quiche is wonderful.
Guestrooms are modern and comfortable.

Ard Alainn (☎ 73027; s/d €25/50; ☻ May-Sep) Ard
Alainn, signposted just over 2km from the
pier, has five simple rooms all with shared
bathroom. Hostess Maura Faherty's breakfasts will keep you going all day.

Óstán Inismeáin (☎ 73020; bfaherty@iol.ie; s/d €58/ 90) At the northern end of the island, out on the bare limestone flats, this modern, motel-like building has 10 en-suite rooms, a pub and a large formal dining room. Bar food (€5 to €9) and á la carte plates (€13 to €32) showcase the freshest of ingredients. Room rates drop significantly when summer is over.

Teach Ósta (☎ 73003; mains €7-12; ☽ noon-late) This terrific little pub hums with life on summer evenings and supplies snacks, sandwiches, soups and seafood platters. The lack of a garda on the island means the pub can keep going into the wee hours (food service stops around 7pm).

Shopping

The knitwear factory **Cniotáil Inis Meáin** (☎ 73 009) exports fine woollen garments to some of the world's most exclusive shops. You can buy the same sweaters here, at the source.

INISHEER

☎ 099 / pop 300

What's most instantly mind-boggling about Inisheer (Inis Oírr) is that this is a *very* small island for so *many* stone walls. From an arriving ferry, the island appears caught within a massive stone fishing net. At its highest point stand the ruins of a 15th-century castle, which preside over small clover-covered fields and a small village. There's a small sandy beach next to the pier.

Only 8km off the coast from Doolin in County Clare, Inisheer is the smallest of the three Aran Islands. There isn't much to do here, although at night the pubs sometimes get cranking and are known to stay open far past midnight. Days spent wandering the maze of fields are good for soul-searching and working up a thirst for a few pints. Despite a regular ferry service and proximity to the mainland, the absence of major archaeological sites and tourist amenities keeps the number of visitors down, making Inisheer rather special.

Information

In July and August a small kiosk at the harbour provides tourist information 10am to 6pm daily. There's no ATM or bank.

Sights

Most sights are in the north of the island. The 15th-century **O'Brien's Castle** (Caislea'n

Uí Bhriain) overlooks the beach and harbour. It was built within the remains of a ring fort called **Dún Formna**, dating from as early as the 1st century. Nearby is an 18th-century signal tower. On the Strand (An Trá) is the 10th-century **Teampall Chaoimháin** (Church of St Kevin), with some gravestones and shells remaining from an ancient rubbish dump.

West of the beach and pier, **Inisheer Heritage House** (☎ 75021; Inisheer; admission €1; ☽ 2-4pm Jul & Aug) is a traditional stone-built thatched cottage with some interesting old photographs. It also has a craft shop and café.

Cill Ghobnait (Church of St Gobnait), southwest of Inisheer Heritage House, is a small 8th- or 9th-century church named after Gobnait, who fled here from Clare when trying to escape an enemy who was pursuing her. A 2km walk southwest of the church leads to the **Tobar Éinne** (Well of St Enda).

The signposted 10.5km **Inisheer Way** is a recommended walk. The eastern road to the lighthouse is more popular, but the coast around the western side is wilder. On the eastern shore is the rusting hulk of the *Plassy*, a freighter wrecked in 1960 and thrown high up onto the rocks. The uninhabited lighthouse (1857) on the island's southern tip, with its neat enclosure, is off limits.

Sleeping & Eating

Brú Radharc Na Mara Hostel (☎ 75024; maire. searraigh@oceanfree.net; dm €12, B&B €30; ☽ Mar-Oct) This spotless Independent Holiday Hostels of Ireland (IHH) hostel near the pier has ocean views, kitchen facilities and bikes for hire. It's next to a pub. The owners of the hostel also run the adjacent B&B, with basic en-suite rooms.

Radharc an Chláir (☎ 75019; bridpoil@eircom.net; s/d €38/70) This pleasant B&B near O'Brien's Castle has views of the Cliffs of Moher and Galway Bay. You'll need to book several weeks ahead, as hostess Brid Poil's home cooking draws many repeat visitors. Guests can hire bikes and arrange evening meals costing (€20).

Ard Mhuire (☎ 75005; unamcdonagh@hotmail.com; d €60; ☽ closed 10 Dec–10 Jan) You'll see this house when you turn left off the pier. It's home to the Conneely family, who have refurbished the guestrooms and put on a fine breakfast (dinner can also be arranged). No credit cards.

Óstán Inis Oírr (☎ 75020; www.ostaninisoirr.com; s/d €33/63; ☺ Apr-Sep) This modern hotel, just up from the Strand, has homely en-suite rooms, and serves hearty meals in its pub and **restaurant** (mains €6-12; ☺ 9am-9pm).

Fisherman's Cottage (☎ 75073; mains €12-20; ☺ Apr-Oct) Cosy Fisherman's Cottage, near the pier, specialises in tasty, fresh seafood and organically grown vegetables.

Láthair Campála Inis Oírr (Inisheer Camp Site; ☎ 75008; camp sites €5; ☺ May-Sep) This is a basic camping ground overlooking the windswept Strand, and it has showers.

Drinking

Tigh Ned (☎ 75004) A mixed crowd comes to this welcoming, unpretentious place for its lively, traditional music.

Tigh Ruairí (☎ 75020) Rory Conneely's atmospheric and friendly old hostel presents live music sessions.

Also, there's a friendly pub at the Óstán Inis Oírr hotel.

Getting Around

Bikes are available for hire from **Rothair Inis Oírr** (☎ 75033; per day €8). The IHH hostel also hires out bicycles.

CONNEMARA

If the name conjures images of wonderfully wild and eerily desolate landscapes, then Connemara (Conamara) lives up to expectations. Immediately northwest of Galway city, it's a vivid patchwork of rusty bogs, lonely valleys, pale grey mountains and small black lakes that shimmer when the sun shines. At its heart are the Maumturk Mountains and the grey, quartzite peaks of the Twelve Bens, with an alluring network of scenic trails. The coastal road west of Spiddal (R336) skirts a tortuous series of small bays and inlets, and connects a succession of Gaeltacht (Irish-speaking) villages and seaside resorts.

The region's towns, roads and nature areas offer a host of appealing choices for the multitudes who holiday here. Clifden, Connemara's largest resort, is beautifully set, even if the town itself lacks any special appeal. The nearby coast, however, is flat-out gorgeous. Tiny Roundstone is a sweet, sweet spot if you avoid the summer crowds.

The withered blacktop through Roundstone Bog is otherworldly and bumpy. The windswept sandy beaches and twisting scenic roads around Letterfrack will delight cyclists and walkers. The northernmost town of Leenane, on Killary Harbour, is charming, sleepy and uneventful. The Loch Corrib is good for a boat ride and especially for fishing. Inishbofin is a dream.

A cursory bus tour from Galway hardly does Connemara justice. A two- or three-day driving trip is rushing it. Four or five days would satisfy. Connemara's true devotees, who number in the thousands, easily while away a month or two here every year.

One of the most important Gaeltacht areas in the country begins just west of Galway city around Barna and stretches westwards through Spiddal and Inverin, and along much of the coast as far as Cashel. Ireland's national Irish-language radio station, Radio na Gaeltachta, is based at Costello. The Irish-language weekly newspaper, *Foinse* (Source), is published in Spiddal.

If you intend any detailed exploration, the excellent *Connemara: Introduction and Gazeteer*, by Tim Robinson, is a must. *Connemara: A Hill Walker's Guide*, by Robinson and Joss Lynam, is also invaluable.

GETTING THERE & AROUND

Driving is a real pleasure in Connemara, though you'll need to be careful on the narrow roads lined with stone walls just waiting to scrape the sides of your car. Heading west from Galway you have two options: the coast road (R336) through Salthill, Barna and Spiddal, or the inland route (N59) through Oughterard, which leads directly to the heart of Connemara. The journey from Maam Cross northwest to Leenane (R336) or northeast to Cong (R345) takes you through Joyce country, a stunning mountainous region. The trip north along Lough Inagh Valley past the Twelve Bens and around Kylemore Lake is difficult to surpass. Many road signs in this area are in Irish only, so note the Irish place names (in parentheses) as you read the following text.

Bus Éireann (☎ 091-562 000; www.buseireann.ie) is the Republic's principal bus line and serves most of Connemara, with many buses originating in Galway. Check with the bus station there for times and fares. Services can be sporadic, and many buses operate May

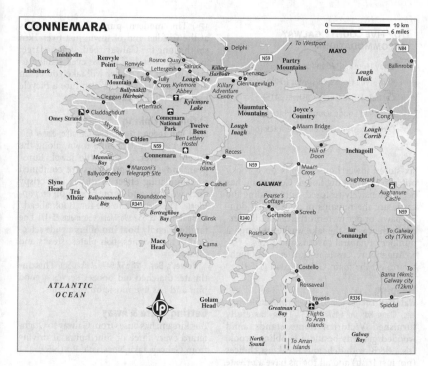

CONNEMARA

to September only or July and August only. Some drivers will stop in between towns if arranged at the beginning of the trip.

Michael Nee Coaches (☎ 095-51082) is an independent line that specifically serves Connemara, with daily buses beginning in Galway and connections within the area. The Galway stop is just opposite the tourist office. Connemara towns served include Maam Cross, Recess, Cashel, Clifden, Letterfrack, Tullycross and Cleggan. If you're going somewhere in between towns (a hostel in the countryside) you might be able to arrange a drop-off with the driver.

OUGHTERARD
☎ 091 / pop 2364

The small town of Oughterard (Uachtar Árd), 27km along the main road from Galway to Clifden, calls itself the 'Gateway to Connemara'. And sure enough, immediately west of town, the countryside opens up to sweeping panoramas of lakes, mountains and bogs that get more spectacular the further west you travel. Oughterard itself is a pleasant little town and due to its prox-imity to Lough Corrib (see p408) it's one of Ireland's principal angling centres. Most travellers are just passing through, as the coast is a mere hour's drive from here.

Nearby attractions include Aughanure Castle to the southeast and the lovely drive along the Glann Rd by Lough Corrib to a vantage point overlooking the Hill of Doon.

Information
In addition to heaps of tourism brochures and assistance with booking tours and ac-commodation, the **tourist office** (☎ 552 808; www.oughterardtourism.com; Main St; ⊙ 9.30am-5.30pm Mon-Fri, 10am-2pm Sat) offers Internet access at €4.70 per hour. The **Bank of Ireland** (Main St) has an ATM and bureau de change, and the post office is on Main St, just east of Market Sq.

Aughanure Castle
Built in the 16th century, this bleak **fortress** (☎ 552 214; adult/child €2.75/1.25; ⊙ 10am-6pm daily Jun–early Sep, 10am-6pm Sat & Sun early Sep–Oct) was home to the Fighting O'Flahertys. The clan controlled the region for hundreds of years after they fought off the Normans. The

six-storey tower house stands on a rocky outcrop overlooking Lough Corrib and has been extensively restored. Surrounding the castle are the remains of an unusual double bawn or perimeter fortification. Underneath the castle, the lake washes through a number of natural caverns and caves.

Aughanure Castle is 3km east of Oughterard, off the main Galway road (N59).

Sleeping

Waterfall Lodge (☎ 552 168; www.waterfalllodge .net; Glann Rd; s/d €45/70; **P**) This tastefully furnished Victorian home stands amid wooded gardens beside a babbling brook. It's a B&B, with delicious breakfast choices (not just Irish) and all rooms have a private bathroom.

Currarevagh House (☎ 552 312; www.currarevagh .com; s/d €92/184; ⊙ Apr-Oct; **P**) You'd be hard pressed to find a more romantic place than this 19th-century mansion on the shore of Lough Corrib, just outside Oughterard. It's renowned for its exquisite five-course dinners (€40 for nonguests, reduced for guests) and quality accommodation.

Fairybridge Cottage (☎ 552 855; g53@family homes.ie; Tonwee, Oughterard; s/d €27/54; **P**) This compound of kitschy thatched cottages is a fantasy land for little girls and nostalgic leprechauns. It's genuinely cosy and in a pretty spot, up a country road near the lake (take the high road about 1.5km from town). Families with children should stay in the self-catering family hut.

Jolly Lodger (☎ 552 682; jollylodger@eircom.net; Main St; s/d €25/50) Although modernised, this two-storey, greystone town house retains many of its original 19th-century features. It's a B&B with excellent breakfasts and en-suite rooms.

Oughterard's Canrawer House (☎ 552 388; canrawer@indigo.ie; Station Rd; dm €14-17; ⊙ Feb-Oct;

P) This modern, purpose-built hostel is at the Clifden end of town, just over 1km south along the Galway road. It has a large, airy kitchen and, if you've ever wanted to learn to fish, the owner will take you on an organised trip. You can also hire a bicycle here (€15/70 per day/week).

Eating & Drinking

River Run Lodge (☎ 552 697; Glann Rd; dinner €30; ⊙ 6.30-9.30pm) Just outside town, along the Owenriff River, is this little jewel. European and Asian ingredients are combined to scintillating effect in dishes like crispy duck wontons and *darne* of salmon *en papillotte*. Desserts are to die for. Book ahead.

Boat Inn (☎ 552 196; Market Sq; mains €5-17) The family-friendly Boat Inn offers a wide selection of sandwiches, fish plates, steaks and pizzas.

Power's Bar (☎ 557 047; Market Sq) This intimate, thatched old boozer serves a good pint and has live music on weekends.

Getting There & Away

Bus Éireann has buses from Galway to Oughterard every three or four hours. If driving from Galway, take Newcastle Rd (N59).

LOUGH CORRIB

Lough Corrib, the Republic's largest lake (it's over 48km long and covers some 200 sq km), virtually cuts off western Galway from the rest of the country and encompasses over 360 islands. On the largest one, Inchagoill, there's a monastic settlement that visitors can get to from Oughterard or Cong.

Lough Corrib is world famous for its salmon, sea trout and brown trout, and the area attracts legions of anglers from all over the world in season. The highlight of the **fishing** year is the mayfly season, when zillions of the small lacy bugs hatch over a few days (usually in May) and drive the fish and anglers into a frenzy. The hooks are baited with live flies, which join their cousins dancing on the surface of the lake. The main run of salmon doesn't begin until June. The owner of **Oughterard's Canrawer House** (☎ 552 388; Station Rd, Oughterard) is a good contact for information and boat hire. You can buy fishing supplies from **Thomas Tuck** (☎ 552 335; Main St, Oughterard; ⊙ 9am-6.30pm Mon-Sat).

Inchagoill Island

The largest island on Lough Corrib and some 7km northwest of Oughterard, Inchagoill is a lonely place hiding many ancient remains. Most fascinating is an obelisk called **Lia Luguaedon Mac Menueh** (Stone of Luguaedon, Son of Menueh) marking a burial site. It stands about 75cm tall, near the Saints' Church, and some people claim that the Latin writing on the stone is the oldest Christian inscription in Europe – apart from those in the catacombs in Rome.

Teampall Phádraig (St Patrick's Church) is a small oratory of a very early design with some later additions. The prettiest church is the Romanesque **Teampall na Naoimh** (Saints' Church), probably built in the 9th or 10th century. There are carvings around the arched doorway.

The island can be reached by boat from Oughterard (or Cong in County Mayo). **Corrib Cruises** (☎ 092-46029; www.corribcruises.com) sails from Oughterard to Inchagoill Island (€13/6 per adult/child) and on to Cong (€20/9). Departures are at 11am, 2.45pm and 5pm May to October.

LOUGH INAGH VALLEY
☎ 091

The journey north along the Lough Inagh Valley, just north of Hwy N59, is one of the most scenic in Ireland. There are two fine approaches up valleys from the south, starting on either side of Recess, and the sweep of Derryclare and Inagh Loughs accompanies you most of the way. On the western side are the brooding **Twelve Bens**, while just beyond the valley on the northern side is the picturesque drive beside Kylemore Lake.

Towards the northern end of the valley, a track leads off the road west up a blind valley, which is also well worth exploring.

Sleeping

Ben Lettery Hostel (☎ 51136; Ballinafad, Recess; dm €11.50-15; ☺ Mar-Nov; [P]) You'll wake up to the sound of sheep bleating at this spotless HI hostel. On the main Clifden road, in the heart of the Connemara wilderness, it is an excellent base to explore the Twelve Bens and Lough Inagh Valley. It's a friendly place, with a tidy and homey kitchen and living room. The hostel is 8km west of Re-

cess and 13km east of Clifden. Michael Nee Coaches will stop here if you arrange it with the driver.

Lough Inagh Lodge (☎ 34706; www.loughinagh lodgehotel.ie; Recess; d €161-264; [P]) About 7km north of Recess on the R344 is the atmospheric, Victorian Lough Inagh Lodge, an upmarket country-house hotel. It's a worthwhile place to stop for a light meal, particularly in good weather. The location is magnificent and there's a path in front of the lodge down to the lake. Pets are welcome.

CLIFDEN
☎ 095 / pop 1925

Clifden (An Clochán), the capital of Connemara, is beautifully set at the head of narrow Clifden Bay, where the River Owenglin tumbles into the sea. Its Victorian houses and needle-sharp church spires appear inviting as one approaches the town on the coast highway, and the surrounding countryside promises leisurely walks through woods and along the Sky Road towering above the shore. Clifden's central area can seem a little dragged down by tourism, and the town has a vaguely jaded feel to it, but its numerous hotels and easy transit access (it's about 80km from Galway city) make it a useful stop. Certainly it is convenient for travellers intent on enjoying the sea and the Twelve Bens. Some of the most appealing accommodations are in the town's scenic outskirts.

Information

The **tourist office** (☎ 21163; ☺ 10am-5pm Mon-Sat Sep-Jun, daily Jul & Aug) is on Galway Rd, while the post office is on Main St. For Internet access try **Two Dog Internet Café** (☎ 22186; Church Hill; per hr €5) and wash those dirty clothes at **Shamrock Washeteria** (Market Sq). There are banks with ATMs around Market Sq.

Activities

Heading directly west from Clifden's Market Sq, the **Sky Road** takes you on a loop out to a town known as Kingston and back to Clifden through some rugged, stunningly beautiful coastal scenery. The round trip of about 12km can easily be walked or cycled. To take advantage of Clifden's multitude of superb walking and cycling possibilities get a copy of Map 31 in the OS Discovery Series.

An essential stop is the **Connemara Walking Centre** (☎ 21379; walkwest@indigo.ie; Market St; ⊗ Mar-Sep), where you can buy books and maps outlining the area's walking routes. The centre also runs guided walking trips exploring local sites of historical, geographical and natural interest. A day's walk costs €20; longer walks are available.

Errislannan Riding Centre (☎ 21134; info@connemara-tourism.org; Ballyconneely Rd) thrills kids and adults, with docile Connemara ponies for hire. Guides lead rides along the beach and up into the hills and lessons are available. Rates depend on type and length of ride you want to take. The centre is about 3.5km south of Clifden on the R341.

Sleeping
HOSTELS

Brookside Hostel (☎ 21812; brooksidehostel@eircom.net; Fairgreen; dm €12-15; ⊗ Mar-Oct; P) The River Owenglin trickles past this IHH hostel in a quiet spot off the bottom of Market St.

Clifden Town Hostel (☎ 21076; seancth@eircom.net; Market St; dm €14, r from €22; P) A friendly establishment, this central IHH property has 34 beds in bright spick-and-span rooms.

B&BS & HOTELS

Quay House (☎ 21369; www.thequayhouse.com; Beach Rd; s/d €105/160; ⊗ mid-Mar–mid-Nov) Location and history make this a charmed spot. The harbour master used to live in this house right on the water, but it was converted into a choice little hotel long ago. Rooms are large and warmly furnished with antiques, and some have working fireplaces and views of the harbour. Breakfast is included.

Abbeyglen Castle (☎ 21201; www.abbeyglen.ie; Sky Rd; s/d €189/278; ⊗ closed Jan; P) The swells stay here, where it is possible to land a private helicopter. But even your humble tourist looking for a splurge will feel entirely welcome, relaxed and pampered in the historic home of Clifden founder John d'Arcy. Rooms are immense and sumptuously furnished, though you'll want to divide your time between the dining room, the chummy pub and the snooker table.

Mallmore House (☎ 21460; www.mallmorecountryhouse.com; Ballyconneely Rd; d €60-70; ⊗ Mar-Sep; P) This restored Georgian manor house is a top choice for Clifden. It's set in 14 hectares of woodland about 2km from town,

and its spacious rooms are elegantly furnished. The super breakfasts include pancakes and smoked salmon. Unbeatable for the price.

Ben View House (☎ 21256; www.house4rent.ie/BenView; Bridge St; s/d €32/60) This 19th-century town house is a family-run B&B and retains a lot of homey, comfy and antiquated charm. It's very central.

Foyle's (☎ 21801; www.foyleshotel.com; Main St; s/d €70/140; ⊗ Jun-Aug) Clifden's oldest hotel, Foyle's has 28 en-suite rooms with all mod cons. It has a patio garden and a lively pub.

Kingstown House (☎ 21470; fax 21530; Bridge St; s/d €44/64) There are eight rooms, most with private bathroom, in this large, hospitable guesthouse in the town centre.

Eating & Drinking

Signal Restaurant (☎ 22946; Clifden Station House; dinner mains €18-26; ⊗ 6.30-9.30pm Wed-Sun) In the atmospheric old train station this class act has earned a devoted following. The menu abounds with savoury and vegetarian delights. The Connemara mountain lamb is cooked to perfection and served with oven-roasted vegetables. In the old station waiting room, a more casual diner serves less expensive fare and is more suitable for families.

Mitchell's Restaurant (☎ 21867; Market St; lunch €7-12, dinner mains €16-25; ⊗ noon-10pm Mar-Oct) Mitchell's is a small and homey spot for a quality seafood dish or Irish stew. It's particularly good for a light lunch, served all day till 5pm.

Two Dog Café (☎ 22186; 2 Church Hill; dishes €4-7) Clifden's hip spot is loved best for its fresh-baked goods, but the *panini* (type of Italian sandwich) and the tortilla wraps are all fresh and delicious as well. This is the place to go for good, strong coffee. The upstairs Internet terminals make this Europe's westernmost Internet café.

EJ Kings (☎ 21330; Market Sq; mains €12-21; ⊗ 10.30am-9pm) A busy old pub, EJ Kings serves soups, salads and a fine Irish stew. It's a good choice for family dining.

D'Arcy Inn (☎ 21146; Main St; mains €8-15; ⊗ 10.30am-late) Sandwiches and seafood are the staples in this friendly old pub. Live music and poetry readings give the joint added pep some nights.

Fogerty's (☎ 21427; Market St; mains €16-23; ⊗ 5.30-10pm Thu-Tue) Fogerty's, in a thatched stone house, ladles out traditional Irish and seafood dishes in its warm, traditional environs.

Lowry's Bar (☎ 21347; Market St) The traditional pleasures of Lowry's extend from the age-old look of the place and the *céilidh* (traditional music) sessions that cheer things up most nights. Pub food is served.

Getting There & Away

Buses stop on Market St near the library. For Bus Éireann information phone the **bus station** (☎ 091-562 000) in Galway.

Michael Nee Coaches (☎ 51082) runs between Clifden (from the square) and Galway (one way/return €10/13) three times daily, June to September. During the same period there are two buses daily to Cleggan (twice weekly from October to May), from where the ferry sails to Inishbofin.

Getting Around

A one-way traffic system operates in the town centre. Walking will get you around town. **John Mannion & Son** (☎ 21160; Bridge St) is a Raleigh agent and hires out bicycles for €10 per day. The Connemara Walking Centre can also arrange bike hire.

CLIFDEN TO ROUNDSTONE

The R341 skirts the coast from Clifden to the beautiful harbour town of Roundstone, passing some spectacular scenery along the way. Fine beaches include **Mannin Bay**, between Clifden and Ballyconneely, and **Trá Mhóir** (Great Beach), a lovely expanse of white sand. Trá Mhóir is off the highway, but well worth the slight detour. To get there, turn off at Ballyconneely, heading south towards the Connemara Golf Club. You will pass the ruins of **Bunowen Castle** before reaching the shore.

An alternate route between Clifden and Roundstone is via the bog road, which connects with the N59 east of Clifden. The old road is a bumpy ride, but passes through the eerie, rust-collared wilderness of Roundstone Bog. Locals who believe the bog is haunted won't drive this road at night (indeed, the roughness of the road is reason enough to avoid it after dark). In summer, you might see men manually cutting turf (blanket bogs cannot be cut mechanically). It takes about 10 to 15 minutes to drive through the bog.

ROUNDSTONE

☎ 095 / pop 424

Surely Roundstone (Cloch na Rón), a small fishing village with a narrow main street coursing through tidy rowhouses, shops and tempting pubs, is the most idyllic hamlet in Connemara. The harbour, in a dark recess along Bertraghboy Bay, is home to lobster boats and traditional *currachs* with their tarred canvas bottoms stretched over wicker frames. The people of Roundstone seem to enjoy the good life and are friendly to strangers. They have fine beaches and hill walking within easy reach, and they eat and drink well. Roundstone's pleasures are well known, however, and in the summer the road through town gets clogged with artery-clenching traffic.

Just south of the centre is a **craft complex**, in Michael Killeen Park, with various small factory shops selling everything from teapots to sweaters. One of the more interesting shops is Malachy Kearns' **Roundstone Musical Instruments** (☎ 35808; ☺ 9am-9pm daily Jul-Sep, 9am-6pm Mon-Sat Oct-Jun). Kearns is a maker of the *bodhrán*, the hand-held goatskin drum used in traditional Irish music. His shop also sells tin whistles, harps and inexpensive booklets filled with Irish ballads.

Looming above the staunch stone pier is **Mt Errisbeg** (298m), the only significant hill along this section of coastline. The pleasant walk from Roundstone to the top takes about two hours. Follow the small road past O'Dowd's pub in the centre of the village. From the summit are wonderful views across the bay to the distant humps of the Twelve Bens.

South of town, off the road to Ballyconneely (R341), are the magnificent **white beaches** of Gurteen (or Gorteen) Bay and Dog's Bay.

Sleeping

Angler's Return (☎ 31091; www.bodhran.com/index2 .htm; Toombeola; d €90; ☺ Mar-Nov; P) Folks who fish naturally gravitate here, but there are those who just enjoy a tranquil break amid beautiful gardens and the beauty of Bertraghboy Bay. This B&B is a few miles out of Roundstone, along R341. Most of the cosy rooms have shared bathrooms, and the home is not suitable for children under four.

St Joseph's (☎ 35865; www.connemara.net/stjosephs; Main St; s/d €40/70; ☺ closed late Dec; P) Christina

Lowry's excellent, central B&B offers a warm welcome and good views over the harbour. Rooms have private bathroom and dinner can be arranged.

Gurteen Beach Caravan & Camping Park (☎ 35882; Roundstone; camp sites €20) This peaceful camp site is in a great spot 2km west of town near the beach, and has full facilities.

Eating & Drinking
O'Dowd's (☎ 35809; Main St; mains €9-21; ✆ noon-10pm) The romantic idea of a well-worn and very comfortable old pub matches up with O'Dowd's. Its adjoining restaurant is known far and wide for tasty food, which can also be ordered from the bar. It has an extensive menu of pasta, fish, meat and vegetarian dishes, and views over the harbour. Reservations are required for seating in the restaurant.

CLAGGAGHDUFF & OMEY ISLAND
The deeply indented coastline north of Clifden brings you to the tiny village of **Claddaghduff** (An Cladach Dubh), which is signposted off the road to Cleggan. If you turn west here down by the Catholic church you will come out on **Omey Strand**, and at low tide you can drive or walk across the sand to **Omey Island**, a low islet of rock, grass and sand with a few houses for the island's population of 20. During the summer, horse races are held on Omey Strand.

CLEGGAN
☎ 095 / pop 303
Cleggan (An Cloiggean) is a small fishing village, 16km northwest of Clifden, which visitors pass through en route to Inishbofin island. This is a good headquarters for horse riding on sandy beaches, and many pony-loving families choose to stay a week here in an old farmhouse cottage.

To get straight to the heart of Ireland's wild west, visit **Cleggan Riding Centre** (☎ 44746), which can set up a variety of horseback adventures, including a three-hour trek to Omey Island via the sandy causeway. Prices depend on what sort of trek you decide to take.

Sleeping
Cleggan Farm Holiday Cottages (☎ 44648; http:// homepage.eircom.net/~cleganfarmhols; cottages per week €135-474; **P**) Six stone farmhouses, which sleep between two and 10 people, ooze rustic charm without being precious. Prices are much lower during autumn and winter, but restrictions include a Saturday-to-Saturday time frame and extra charge for use of power and heat. It's great for family holidays but make reservations well in advance.

INISHBOFIN
☎ 095 / pop 173
The nocturnal inhabitants of Inishbofin stay up late and sleep in late for the simple reason that there's not much going on during the day and there are no cops on the island to enforce closing times at the pub. During the day, this means the island is a haven of tranquillity. A visitor will surely benefit from walking or biking the narrow, deserted lanes through green pastures and past sandy beaches, farm animals and seals. At night, it means Inishbofin has damn good craic.

Inishbofin is just 9km out in the Atlantic from Cleggan. It's compact – 6km long by 3km wide – and the highest point is a mere 86m above sea level. Just off the northern beach is **Lough Bó Finne**, from which the island gets its name. Bó finne means 'white cow'.

St Colman exiled himself to Inishbofin in AD 664, after he fell out with the Church over its adoption of a new calendar. He set up a monastery, supposedly northeast of the harbour, where the more recent ruins of a small 13th-century **church** still stand. Grace O'Malley, the famous pirate queen who was based on Clare Island, used Inishbofin as a base in the 16th century. Cromwell's forces captured Inishbofin in 1652 and built a star-shaped prison for priests and clerics. Many died or were killed; one bishop was reputedly chained to Bishop's Rock near the harbour and drowned as the tide came in.

Information
Inishbofin's small post office has a grocery shop as well as a currency-exchange facility. Pubs and hotels will usually change travellers cheques.

Sleeping & Eating
You can pitch a tent on most unfenced ground, but not on or near the beaches.

Inishbofin Island Hostel (☎ 45855; www.inish bofin-hostel.ie; dm €12, d €32-36; ✆ Apr-Oct) In an old farmhouse, this fine IHH hostel offers panoramic views and camping (€7 per person). It's 500m up from the ferry dock.

Doonmore Hotel (☎ 45804; www.doonmorehotel .com; d €76-110; ☵ Apr-Sep) Close to the harbour, Doonmore has comfortable, unpretentious rooms in both its modern extension and the original building. You can eat in the dining room, where seafood is the speciality, costing around €25.

Day's Hotel (☎ 45809; d €60-90; ☵ Apr-Oct) This modest, comfortable hotel has turf fires and a dining room looking out over the harbour. The food (mains €14 to €20) is creative, with excellent fresh fish.

Day's Bar (☎ 45829) Adjoining Day's Hotel, this welcoming pub supplies inexpensive food and a lively atmosphere. Traditional *ceilidh* sessions are held several nights a week.

Getting There & Away

Ferry trips from Cleggan to Inishbofin take 30 to 45 minutes. Sometimes dolphins follow the ferries. A nondescript kiosk on the Cleggan pier dispenses information.

Island Discovery (☎ 45894, 45819; nikolaj@indigo .ie) runs daily from Cleggan to Inishbofin. The trip costs €15 return.

Inishbofin Ferries (☎ 45903, 45806, 45831; inishbofinferry@eircom.net) operates the *Galway Bay* twice daily April to October, and three times daily June to August. The fare is €15 return. This line also runs the older *Dún Aengus* mail boat (11.30am Monday to Saturday year round).

Getting Around

Inishbofin Cycle Hire (☎ 45833), at the pier, hires out bicycles for €15 per day.

LETTERFRACK & AROUND

☎ 095 / pop 150

Founded by Quakers in the mid-19th century, Letterfrack (Leitir Fraic) is ideally situated for explorations of Connemara National Park, Renvyle Point and Kylemore Abbey. The village is barely more than a crossroads with a few pubs and B&Bs, but the setting is wooded and very pretty. Letterfrack is 15km northeast of Clifden on the N59.

There's some fine scenery along the coast north of Letterfrack, especially from Tully Cross east to Lettergesh and Salruck. **Glassillaun Beach** is a breathtaking expanse of pure white sand. There are other fine beaches at **Gurteen** and at **Lettergesh**, where the beach horse-racing sequences for John Ford's 1952 film *The Quiet Man* were shot.

Leisurely **walks** can be enjoyed all along the coast and around Renvyle Point to Derryinver Bay. An excellent hill walk, which takes four to five hours each way, starts from the post office at Lettergesh and heads up Binn Chuanna and Maolchnoc and then down to Lough Fee. A 4km walk from Letterfrack to the peak of Tully Mountain takes 30 minutes and affords wonderful ocean views.

On Glassillaun Beach, to the northeast, is **Scuba Dive West** (☎ 43922; www.scubadivewest.com; Letterfrack), offering courses and diving on the surrounding coast and islands. A full day with guide and equipment costs €99/145 for shore/boat diving.

Kylemore Abbey & Lake

A few kilometres east of Letterfrack, towards the northern end of the Lough Inagh Valley, stands **Kylemore Abbey** (☎ 41146; adult/child €7/4; ☵ 9am-5.30pm). The castlelike, 19th-century neo-Gothic mansion was built for a wealthy English businessman, Mitchell Henry, after he spent his honeymoon in Connemara and fell in love with the region. During WWI, a group of Benedictine nuns left Ypres in Belgium and eventually set up in Kylemore, turning the place into an abbey.

Today, the nuns run an exclusive convent boarding school here and some sections of

---

SOMETHING SPECIAL

Old Monastery Hostel (☎ 41132; www .oldmonasteryhostel.com; Letterfrack; dm/d €12/32; Ⓟ) Magnificent, but decidedly rustic, this stone house, built in the 1840s, is in the woods 400m up a dirt road from the Letterfrack crossroads. It is truly atmospheric, if you're up for the bohemian life. Upkeep and restoration of the old building is ongoing, but it's being done gracefully, with attractive rough edges kept intact. Rooms are very basic. Camping (€9 per person) is permitted, bikes can be hired (€10 per day) and some evenings there's a vegetarian buffet (€10). Afterwards, guests can retreat to a faded parlour, lit by candles and a fireplace. Connemara National Park is literally just a few paces away.

the abbey are open to the public. There's also a craft shop and garden tearoom. The building is impressive, and the setting overlooking Kylemore Lake is beautiful, but the abbey interior is a fairly limited showpiece of stuffy furniture and the like. Without paying admission, you can take a walk around the lake and surrounding woods.

Be sure to come hungry, as the Abbey's **restaurant** (9.30am-5.30pm) serves up savoury stews and mouthwatering baked goods.

Sleeping & Eating

Renvyle House Hotel (☎ 43511; www.renvyle.com; Renvyle; d €100-225; **P**) This 56-room converted country house, once owned by the poet Oliver St John Gogarty, is the best place in the area to have a drink or snack or relax after a walk along the peninsula. You can also stay here, although during July and August rates are quite high.

Renvyle Beach Caravan & Camping (☎ 43462; Renvyle; camp sites €16; Easter-Sep) This camping ground, 1.5km west of Tully Cross, is in a beautiful location with direct access to the sandy beach.

Pangur Ban (☎ 41243; Letterfrack; mains €15-21; noon-3pm & 6-10pm) Well worth a modest splurge, this thatched-cottage restaurant, 100m west of the Letterfrack crossroads, serves terrific roasts and fish plates. Specials include a venison stew cooked in Guinness.

Getting There & Away

Bus Éireann (☎ 091-562 000) No 420 runs year round between Galway and Clifden, calling at Salruck, Lettergesh, Tully Church, Kylemore, Letterfrack, Cleggan and Claddaghduff en route.

CONNEMARA NATIONAL PARK

Immediately southeast of Letterfrack, **Connemara National Park** (☎ 095-41054; Letterfrack; adult/child/family €2.75/1.25/7; 10am-6.30pm Jun, 9.30am-6.30pm Jul & Aug, 10am-5.30pm Apr, May, Sep & Oct) spans about 2000 hectares of bog, mountain and heath. The headquarters and visitor centre are housed in old buildings just south of the crossroads in Letterfrack.

The park encloses a number of the **Twelve Bens**, including Bencullagh, Benbrack and Benbaun. The heart of the park is **Gleann Mór** (Big Glen), through which flows the River Polladirk. There's fine walking up the glen and over the surrounding mountains.

There are two- to three-hour guided **nature walks** on Monday, Wednesday and Friday in July and August, leaving the centre at 10.30am. Bring good boots and rainwear. There are also short, self-guided walks and, if the Bens look too daunting, you can hike up **Diamond Hill** nearby.

The visitor centre offers an introduction to the park's flora, fauna and geology, and visitors can scrutinise maps and various trails here before heading out into the park. Seeing the exhibits on bog biology and the video *Man and the Landscape* will make walking the park a more rewarding experience. It has an indoor eating area and rudimentary kitchen facilities for walkers.

LEENANE & KILLARY HARBOUR

☎ 095
The small and sleepy village of Leenane (also spelled Leenaun) makes a scenic stopover for travellers heading north to County Mayo. Leenane's name in Irish, An Líonán, means 'ravine', referring to the way the sea slices its way into narrow Killary Harbour. Mussel rafts dot the long, narrow harbour, which looks like a fjord but may not actually have been glaciated. It's 16km long and over 45m deep in the centre. **Mt Mweelrea** (819m) towers over its northern shores.

The village boasts both a cinematic and literary connection. It was the location for *The Field* (1989), based on John B Keane's poignant play about a tenant farmer's ill-fated plans to pass on a rented piece of land to his son. The village's name made it onto the literary map with the success in London and New York of Martin McDonagh's play *The Beauty Queen of Leenane*.

There's no bank or ATM, but the post office changes foreign currency.

Activities

The well-run **Killary Adventure Centre** (☎ 43411; www.killary.com; Leenane; half/full day €37/68; 10am-1pm & 2-5pm), 3km west of Leenane on the N59, offers activities in just about every adventure (and other) sport you can think of, including canoeing, sea kayaking, sailing, rock climbing, clay-pigeon shooting, wind surfing, waterskiing and archery, to name just a few. You can stay in the lodgings and live the action lifestyle a few days.

From Nancy's Point, about 2km west of Leenane, **Killary Cruises** (☎ 091-566 736; www.killarycruises.com; adult/child €18/8; 4 cruises daily Apr-Oct) offers 1½-hour cruises of Killary Harbour aboard a catamaran. Ask about cocktail cruises and family rates.

There are several excellent **walks** from Leenane, including one to **Aasleagh Waterfall** (Eas Liath), about 3km away on the northeastern side of Killary Harbour. Also from Leenane, the road runs west for about 2km along the southern shore. Where the highway veers inland, walkers can continue on an old road along the shore to Rosroe Quay.

Sleeping

Killary Adventure Centre (☎ 43411; www.killary.com; dm €14-30, lodge s/d €45/90; **P**) The adventure centre has clean, darn near-sterile dorm rooms, as well as a restaurant and bar with a great view of Killary Harbour.

Sleepzone Connemara (☎ 42929; www.sleepzone.ie; dm €13-18, s/d €30/45; **P**) Near the adventure centre, this old country house has been converted into a hostel with many modernised private rooms, mostly en suite. Sleepzone offers a daily shuttle service to and from Galway (€5).

Killary House (☎ 42254; www.connemara.com/killaryhouse; Leenane; d €50-60; **P**) On a working farm just a short walk from Leenane, this cosy B&B is very family friendly. The front rooms have views of the bay, while the rear ones look up to the hills behind.

Eating

Blackberry Cafe (☎ 42240; Leenane; mains €16-23; Apr-Sep) A splash of contemporary style in a remote location, Blackberry Cafe's calling card is fresh seafood.

Gaynor's (Leenane; mains €2-7) Offering sandwiches and light meals, Gaynor's is a traditional Irish pub where the farmers and other locals come for a quiet drink and to catch up on each other's news.

SPIDDAL TO MACE HEAD

If you elect to drive the slow route from Galway along the coast into Connemara, you'll pass through many little towns, some worth stopping in and some merely deserving a toot on the horn. Many people come to these parts specifically to fish the nearby lakes and sea. Just 17km west of Galway, Spiddal (An Spidéal) is an attractive little settlement with a couple of good pubs in case you're already thirsty. At the Galway city end of the village is the Irish-language **Connaught College** (Coláiste Chonnacht; ☎ 091-553 383; www.colaistechonnacht.com; Spiddal), founded in 1910.

A few kilometres west of Spiddal, the scenery starts to become more dramatic, with parched fields delineated by low stone walls rolling to a ragged shore. **Carraroe** (An Cheathrú Rua) is famous for its fine beaches, including the **Coral Strand**, which is composed entirely of shell and coral fragments. Equally well known is University College Galway's **Irish Language Centre** (Áras Mháirtín Uí Chadhain; ☎ 091-595 101; treasanimhaoil@eircom.net; An Cheathrú Rua). It offers four-week courses in the Irish language for all levels, and can arrange accommodation. Contact the centre to discuss prices.

Lettermore, **Gorumna** and **Lettermullen** islands are low and bleak, with a handful of farmers eking out an existence from tiny, rocky fields. Fish farming is big business in these parts.

Near Gortmore, along the R340, is **Pearse's Cottage** (Teach an Phiarsaigh; ☎ 091-574 292; Hwy R340; adult/family €1.50/4.25; 10am-6pm daily Easter & mid-Jun–mid-Sep, 10am-5pm Sat & Sun spring & autumn). Pádraig Pearse (1879–1916) lead the Easter Rising with James Connolly in 1916. After the revolt he was executed by the British. Pearse wrote some of his short stories and plays in this cottage.

Continuing along the R340 brings you to **Carna**, a small fishing village from which there are nice walks out to **Mweenish Island** or north to Moyrus and out to **Mace Head**. It's a lovely journey from here heading north on the R340.

Sleeping & Eating

The following special places are worth hitting the brakes for if you aren't planning to make Roundstone or beyond by nightfall. Many have multiday and fishing packages.

Ballynahinch Castle Hotel (☎ 095-31006; www.ballynahinch-castle.com; Recess; d €190-260; **P**) This gorgeous hotel, southwest of Recess, is quite a treat. B&B and fishing packages are available. If just driving through, stop by for a drink in the bar and a stroll on the grounds.

Cashel House Hotel (☎ 095-31001; www.cashel-house-hotel.com; Cashel; d €170-280; **P**) At the head of Cashel Bay, this gorgeous old house is a

---

JOE HEANEY & SEAN-NÓS SINGING

One of Ireland's greatest *sean-nós* (old style) singers was Joe Heaney, born near Carna in Connemara in 1919. The Carna area, in fact, has long been famous for its excellent singing families, chief among them the McDonagh family, who lived near Joe Heaney when he was a boy.

In this part of Connemara the soil is rocky, and most of the locals cull a modest sustenance from the sea. The hard life comes through in the region's song, which is decidedly melancholic. Many of the songs can be characterised as laments, but some are in fact protest songs. Heaney had many 'anti-landlord' tunes in his repertoire, and opposition to the British military is evident in many *sean-nós* classics.

Heaney spent most of his adult life overseas. He moved first to Scotland, then to London, before ending up in the USA, where he lived the last 20 years of his life. He died in 1984. Unable for many years to support himself as a singer, Heaney worked as a doorman in a New York apartment building. In the 1970s, the talk show host Merv Griffin lived in the building and invited Heaney to appear on his show, which gave Heaney's music career a much needed boost. Many regard Heaney as an ambassador who helped spread the *sean-nós* tradition far beyond the small community of Carna.

Heaney himself modestly credited Dara Bán Mac Donnchadha, of the McDonagh clan, with being the greatest *sean-nós* performer. If curious about other *sean-nós* singers, start by visiting the Cló Iar-Chonnachta website (www.cic.ie), which has a thorough index and sells CDs.

32-room hotel surrounded by 17 hectares of woodland and gardens. It has a stable of Connemara ponies and riding lessons are available. There's even a small private beach.

Zetland Country House Hotel (☎ 095-31111; www.zetland.com; Cashel Bay; s/d €130/190) This secluded, 19th-century manor has panoramic views and is in a tranquil setting overlooking Cashel Bay. Rooms are princely, and facilities include an excellent seafood restaurant (dinner €50) and a tennis court.

Spiddal Caravan & Camping Park (☎ 091-553 372; fax 553 976; Spiddal; car & tent €11, cyclists & hikers €4.50; ⊗ mid-Mar–Oct) This riverside camping ground is on the R336, 18km west of Galway and about 1.5km west of Spiddal village. It's also signposted in Irish as 'Pairc Saoire an Spidéil'. Its modern facilities include a toilet block, laundry and free showers.

SOUTH OF GALWAY CITY

The coast south of Galway City is scenic and relaxed and has many sites worth visiting. The tranquil monastic settlement and round tower at Kilmacduagh is worth making a special effort to visit, and the quaint coastal town of Kinvara is a good place to stay overnight if you're looking to slow things down a bit. Most travellers pass through en route to or from County Clare,

but you can also visit on a day trip from Galway.

CLARINBRIDGE & KILCOLGAN
☎ 091 / pop 2081

Some 16km south of Galway, Clarinbridge (Droichead an Chláirin) and Kilcolgan (Cill Choglán) come alive during the **Clarinbridge Oyster Festival** (www.clarenbridge.com), held during the second weekend of September. However, the oysters are at their best in the summer, beginning in May. Clarinbridge is also good for rummaging the antique stores along the highway.

Moran's Oyster Cottage (☎ 976 113; The Weir, Kilcolgan; 6 oysters €12, mains €13-20; ⊗ noon-10pm Mon-Sat, 10am-10pm Sun) is signposted near the post office just north of Kilcolgan. This wonderful thatched pub and restaurant overlooks narrow Dunbulcaun Bay, where the famous Galway oysters are reared. Expertly shucked oysters and sublime smoked salmon are specialities.

Paddy Burke's Oyster Inn (☎ 796 107; Clarinbridge; 6 oysters €10, mains €10-24; ⊗ 12.30-10pm) is an old-fashioned, thatched inn by the bridge. Paddy's is famous for its long association with the oyster festival and for its seafood.

Getting There & Away
Clarinbridge is on the main Galway–Gort–Ennis–Limerick road (N18) and is served

by numerous Bus Éireann buses from Galway. Kilcolgan is also on the N18; Moran's Oyster Cottage is about 1.5km to the west.

KINVARA
☎ 091 / pop 430

The quiet village of Kinvara (Cinn Mhara) is a delight. It's tucked away on the southeastern corner of Galway Bay, with a small stone harbour that's home to a number of Galway hookers (traditional sailing boats). The village is endowed with a castle and several sanguine taverns.

Dunguaire Castle

This **castle** (☎ 637 108; adult/child €4/2; ☯ 9.30am-5.30pm May-Oct) was erected around 1520 by the O'Hynes clan and is in excellent condition after extensive restoration. It is widely believed that the castle occupies the former site of the 6th-century royal palace of Guaire Aidhne, the king of Connaught. Dunguaire's owners have included Oliver St John Gogarty (1878–1957), poet, writer, surgeon, Irish Free State senator and known to many as the wildest wit in Dublin.

A medieval banquet is held in the castle. These banquets are an intimate affair, with music, storytelling, and a hearty chicken dinner costing €40, with two sittings a night (5.30pm and 8.45pm) May to October. Mead, a medieval beer, is also served.

Festivals & Events

Fleadh na gCuach (Cuckoo Festival; late May) A music festival.
Cruinniú na mBáid (Gathering of the Boats; 2nd weekend in Aug) A celebration of Galway's traditional hooker boats.

Sleeping & Eating

Doorus House (☎ 637 512; doorushouse@kinvara.com; Doorus, Kinvara; dm €15; P) This lovely An Óige hostel is 6km northwest of Kinvara, signposted off the main road to Ballyvaughan (N67). It's an old mansion once owned by Count Floribund de Basterot, who entertained here such notables as WB Yeats, Lady Augusta Gregory, Douglas Hyde and Guy de Maupassant. Rooms are basic and spotless.

Johnston's Independent Hostel (☎ 637 164; Main St, Kinvara; dm €14; ☯ Jul & Aug; P) Johnston's is a quaint, medium-sized hostel (24 beds) up the hill from the harbour. Showers and laundry cost extra.

Burren View (☎ 637 142; burrenviewdorrus@eircom .net; Doorus, Kinvara; d €65; ☯ May-Oct; P) About 6km northwest of Kinvara, it's in a scenic spot on a peninsula with views of Galway Bay and the Burren. You can swim at a nearby Blue Flag beach.

Keough's (☎ 637 145; Main St, Kinvara; mains €8-12; ☯ 10am-10pm) This friendly local, where you'll sometimes hear Irish spoken, serves up a fresh battered cod and pints of the good stuff.

Getting There & Away

Late May to late September, Bus Éireann's Galway–Killarney bus No 50 stops in Kinvara three to four times daily Monday to Saturday, and twice on Sunday. Bus No 423, linking Galway with towns in County Clare, stops in Kinvara. For more details contact **Galway bus station** (☎ 091-562 000).

GORT & AROUND
☎ 091 / pop 1795

Gort's a real honest-to-gosh working town, but there's not much to hold the common traveller's interest. Head out to the surrounding countryside to gawk at some well-known literary sights, including two of special interest to fans of poet WB Yeats.

A 16th-century Norman tower known as **Thoor Ballylee** (☎ 631 436; Peterswell; adult/child €4/2; ☯ 10am-6pm Mon-Sat May-Sep) was the summer home of WB Yeats from 1922 to 1929. It was the inspiration for one of Yeats' best-known works, *The Tower*. The restored 16th-century tower contains the poet's furnishings and you can see an audiovisual presentation on his life. From Gort take the Loughrea road (N66) for about 3km and look for the sign.

About 3km north of Gort is **Coole Park** (☎ 631 804; exhibits €3; ☯ 10am-5pm Apr-Sep). It was the home of Lady Augusta Gregory, co-founder of the Abbey Theatre and a patron of Yeats. An exhibit focuses on the literary importance of the house and the flora and fauna of the surrounding nature reserve. The main attraction on the grounds is the **autograph tree**, on which many of Lady Gregory's esteemed literary guests carved their initials.

About 5km southwest of Gort is the extensive monastic site of **Kilmacduagh**. Beside a small lake is a well-preserved round tower,

COUNTY GALWAY

the remains of a small, 14th-century cathedral (Teampall Mór MacDuagh), an oratory dedicated to St John the Baptist, and various other little chapels. The original monastery is thought to have been founded by St Colman MacDuagh at the beginning of the 7th century. The 34m-high round tower leans some 60cm from the perpendicular and the doorway is 8m above ground level. There are fine views over the Burren from here and you can visit any time.

There are regular buses from Galway to Gort, but you'll need a car or bike to get to the sights.

EASTERN GALWAY

Lough Corrib separates Eastern Galway from the dramatic landscape of Connemara and the county's western coast, and this region is markedly different. Eastern Galway is relatively flat, and its underlying limestone has given it a well-drained, fertile soil that is ideal for farming. Eastern Galway has more in common with the midlands. It is the largest section of the county, but does not have many sites or towns of significant interest to tourists.

GETTING THERE & AWAY

Bus Éireann (☎ 091-562 000) express buses from Galway serve Ballinasloe and Loughrea; local bus No 427 connects Galway, Ballinasloe and Loughrea with Portumna.

BALLINASLOE

☎ 0509 / pop 5977

The biggest town in eastern Galway, Ballinasloe (Béal Átha na Sluaighe) is on the main Dublin–Galway road (N6). The town is pleasant enough, but during the eight days at the start of October the **Ballinasloe Horse Fair** attracts horse buyers and sellers and merrymakers in great numbers.

Around 6km southwest of town on the N6, Aughrim was the site of a crucial victory by William of Orange over the Catholic forces of James II in 1691. It was the bloodiest battle ever fought on Irish soil. The **Battle of Aughrim Visitor Centre** (☎ 73939; Aughrim; adult/child €4/3; ⏰ 10am-6pm Tue-Sat, 2-4pm Sun Jun-Aug) helps put it into perspective within the framework of the 'War of the

---

DID ST BRENDAN DISCOVER AMERICA?

It is little known outside Ireland, but some scholars believe that the Irish missionary Brendan – widely referred to as 'the Navigator' – sailed to America in the 6th century, long before Leif Ericson or Christopher Columbus set foot in the New World. Improbable though it may seem, there are some intriguing indications that Irishmen did travel across the Atlantic long ago.

According to legend, St Brendan (AD 484–577), who is buried at Clonfert, led a seven-year journey in a fleet of *currachs* to a place he referred to as the Land of Promise. Scholars have suggested this magical place could have been anywhere from the Canary Islands to Newfoundland, and some have even theorised that Brendan may have gone no further than an island a short distance off the coast of Ireland. Nevertheless, by the 11th century, a Latin text called the *Navigatio Sancti Brendani* recorded a lengthy account of Brendan's voyage that suggested his party sailed west, across the North Atlantic. It is not unlikely that Columbus himself would have been familiar with the *Navigatio,* and he may have drawn inspiration from it.

Apart from the lack of supporting evidence that Brendan travelled so far, naysayers have generally pointed to the inadequacy of the tiny *currach* for sailing the cold and turbulent North Atlantic – the same sea that brought down the *Titanic* in 1912. But in 1976, the British navigator Tim Severin reconstructed a traditional *currach* and launched off the coast of Ireland in an attempt to prove that such a journey was actually possible. The following spring, after several months sailing from island to island, Severin landed at Newfoundland.

In the early 1980s, some carvings were discovered in West Virginia – far south of Newfoundland – that included Old Irish writing in the Ogham alphabet. These carvings were determined to date from as early as the 6th century. Again, this discovery fails to support claims that Brendan himself reached the Americas, but certainly promotes the notion that early Irish seafarers, sailing in humble *currachs*, successfully crossed the Atlantic.

TRAVELLING LIKE TRAVELLERS

You can still travel the west of Ireland the old-fashioned way – in a horse-drawn Travellers' caravan. Into the West is a tour company (based at Cartron House Farm in eastern Galway) that can set you up with a tubular wooden trailer of the type the Travelling people once used. These caravans accommodate up to five people and have been updated slightly and include modest furnishings, beds, and a washbasin. You'll also get a mild-mannered draught horse, advice on how to manage your trip, and a detailed itinerary. Basically, the entire kit and caboodle is yours for one week (starting on Wednesday or Saturday). You'll travel a few hours each day, and you'll have your choice of family farms to stop at for the night. Contact **Cartron House Farm** (☎ 90-974 5211; cartronhouse@hotmail.com; Ballinakill, Kylebrack, Loughrea; per week €560-740) for more information

Two Kings'. Signposts from the interpretive centre indicate the actual battle site.

Hyne's Hostel (☎ 73734; Aughrim, Ballinasloe; dm €12-15; P), close to the centre, is an IHH property. It only has 12 beds, so book ahead in summer or when the horse fair is on. It hires out bikes and can arrange pick-up.

CLONFERT CATHEDRAL

About 21km southeast of Ballinasloe, off the R256, is the tiny 12th-century cathedral at Clonfert. It's on the site of a monastery said to have been founded in AD 563 by St Brendan the Navigator (see opposite), who is believed to be buried here. The main attraction is the six-arch Romanesque doorway, adorned with surreal human heads.

LOUGHREA & AROUND

☎ 091 / pop 4001

Loughrea (Baile Locha Riach) is a large, busy market town 26km southeast of Galway. It gets its name from the little lake at the southern end of town. Not to be confused with St Brendan's Church on Church St, which is now a library, **St Brendan's Catholic Cathedral** (☎ 841 212; Barrack St; admission free; ☉ 11.30am-1pm &

2-5.30pm Mon-Fri), dating from 1903, is renowned for its Celtic-revival stained glass, furnishings and marble columns. Interestingly, Loughrea has a functioning medieval **moat**, which runs from the lake at Fair Green near the cathedral to the River Loughrea north of town. It's the only one left in Ireland.

Near Bullaun, 7km north of Loughrea, is the remarkable **Turoe Stone**, a phallic standing stone covered in delicate La Téne-style relief carvings. It dates from between 300 BC and AD 100. There are similarly carved stones in Brittany, associated with La Téne Celts (late Iron Age). The stone wasn't set here originally, but was found at an Iron Age fort a few kilometres away.

PORTUMNA

☎ 0509 / pop 1928

In the southeast corner of the county, the lakeside town of Portumna is an attractive village and a popular base for boating and fishing on **Lough Derg**. Impressive **Portumna Castle** (☎ 41658; Castle Ave; adult/child €2/1; ☉ 10am-6pm Apr-Oct) was built in 1618 by Richard de Burgo (or Burke) and boasts an elaborate, geometrically laid-out garden.

Counties Mayo & Sligo

It doesn't take much effort to get good and lost in predominantly pastoral Mayo and Sligo. Set in a hypnotic landscape of vast peat bogs, bubbling streams, deserted beaches, sparkling loughs and myth-infused mountains, it's possible to walk for hours without seeing any more signs of intelligent life than sheep chewing thoughtfully by the roadside. This is particularly true of Mayo's isolated corners, the remote islands off its coast and the stunning mountains north of Sligo town.

Despite the peace and tranquillity, neither county has had an easy existence. Famine, war and pestilence – you name it, poor old Mayo and Sligo have endured it. Both counties were hit especially hard by the Potato Famine, which saw their populations slashed by starvation and mass emigration. Even today, Mayo suffers from its prolonged shortage of population and chronically sluggish economy.

Sligo, on the other hand, has a powerful cultural string to its bow: the WB Yeats factor. The county has been immortalised many times over by the poet's emotive verse, as well as by the paintings of his brother Jack. It's easy to understand the siblings' obsession; the county has a heady natural beauty and a particularly rich vein of folklore, encouraged by improbably high numbers of prehistoric sites scattered on every hillside. The county's cultural legacy is also continued with gusto in Sligo Town. There are few better places in the northwest for music, theatre and galleries.

Together, Mayo and Sligo make a delightful detour from the well-beaten tourist trail to the south. Theirs is a wildly beautiful landscape and a deeply ingrained sense of identity that needs none of the artificial authentication so often seen elsewhere in Ireland.

HIGHLIGHTS

- **Meet the Ancestors**
  Keeping in company with cairns at spooky Carrowkeel Passage Tomb Cemetery (p448)

- **Island Escape**
  Ruggedly remote Achill Island (p431) off western Mayo

- **Mountain Pilgrimage**
  Holy but temperamental Croagh Patrick (p428)

- **Adrenaline Rush**
  Superb surf at Strandhill Beach (p447)

- **Sing Along**
  Raising a glass, and your voice, at Matt Molloy's pub in Westport (p427)

Strandhill ★

Carrowkeel ★

Achill Island ★

Croagh Patrick ★ ★ Westport

■ POPULATION: 175,600 | ■ AREA: 7195 SQ KM

COUNTY MAYO

Humble Mayo (Maigh Eo) sits demurely alongside the more travelled counties of Galway and Sligo. It does not court the tour-bus races, nor boast of its endless pristine beaches, idyllic islands and sweeping agrarian landscapes. And therein lies the county's great appeal. Travellers eager for an intimate peek into a more traditional, introspective Ireland need not stray far here.

Mayo's modesty may in part be due to its past, which has been anything but kind. The ravages of the Potato Famine – which provoked the woeful refrain 'County Mayo, Mayo, God help us!' – were harshest here,

and the emigration that it provoked still plagues the county. The modernisation of its infrastructure and the creation of employment opportunities are a slow, ongoing process, but Mayo's future is certainly looking brighter than its past ever did.

CONG

☎ 094 / pop 185

Being a picture-postcard country village is all in a day's work for pretty Cong (Cung). Ever since it was selected by Hollywood in 1951 to represent the quintessential Irish rural town, it has celebrated its own chocolate-box quaintness. We're talking, of course, of *The Quiet Man*, filmed here over 10 weeks by John Ford and starring

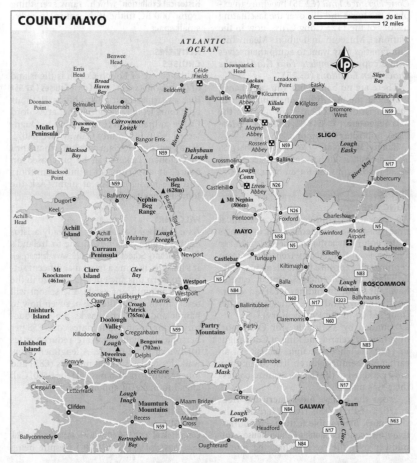

John Wayne and Maureen O'Hara. Cong has made a big deal of its links with the film, and there are plenty of reminders scattered throughout of that momentous summer.

It's also home to some important monastic ruins and a gloriously over-the-top castle, and offers some tempting activities, including lake cruises and lessons in falconry.

Cong is just east of the border with County Galway and lies on the narrow isthmus between Lough Corrib and Lough Mask, 5km north.

Information

The **tourist office** (☎ 954 6542; Abbey St; ☽ 10am-6pm Mar-Nov) is in the old courthouse building opposite Cong Abbey. Get a copy of the *Cong Heritage Trail* (€2.35) brochure to explore the town and discover the fascinating history of the 1123 Cong Cross, now in the National Museum in Dublin. Meanwhile film fanatics may want to equip themselves with a copy of *Complete Tour Guide to the Quiet Man Locations* (€3.25).

There are no banks, but you can change money at the post office on Main St or in the tourist office. There is an ATM in the **Gala Superstore** (☎ 954 6485; Circular Rd; ☽ 7am-10pm), opposite O'Connor's.

Hungry Monk Café (☎ 954 6866; Abbey St; ☽ 10am-6pm Mar-Oct) has Internet access for €1.50 for 15 mins, €5 for an hour.

Sights

CONG ABBEY

An evocative reminder of ecclesiastical times past, the weathered shell of Cong's 12th-century **Augustinian abbey** (admission free; ☽ dawn-dusk) is scored by wizened lines from centuries of exposure to the elements. Nevertheless, several finely sculpted features have survived, including a carved doorway, windows and lovely medieval arches (touched up in the 19th century).

Founded by Turlough Mór O'Connor, high king of Ireland and king of Connaught in 1120, the abbey occupies the site of an earlier 6th-century church. The community once gathered in the **Chapter House** to confess their sins publicly.

From the abbey, moss-encrusted trees guard a path to the river. Here lies the site's most memorable feature – a diminutive 16th-century **Monk's Fishing House** built midway over the river so that the monks

could haul their catch straight up through a hole in the floor. There would have once been a cord to a bell in the kitchen, letting the cooks know to get the pot on.

QUIET MAN HERITAGE COTTAGE

Wwest of the tourist office is the **Quiet Man Heritage Cottage** (☎ 954 6089; Circular Rd; adult/child/student €3.75/2/3; ☽ 10am-5pm Mar-Oct). In a life-imitating-art exercise so twisted it begs a map, the cottage attempts to re-create the exact set John Ford used to film many of the interior shots of *The Quiet Man* in Hollywood. Never mind that original cottages such as this one were his inspiration but, hey, the people want Hollywood. The cottage also contains a regional **Archaeological & Historical Exhibition**, which crams everything from 7000 BC to the 19th century in a very small space.

Activities

CRUISES

In the centre of Lough Corrib is the island of Inchagoill (see p409). **Corrib Cruises** (☎ 954 6029; www.corribcruises.com; Cong) offers 1½-hour boat tours from Lisloughrey Pier at Ashford Castle to Inchagoill (€15) and on to Oughterard (€20) in County Galway (see p407). Tours leave at 11.15am and 3pm from April to October. Tickets can be purchased on board. It also runs 45-minute minitours and live-music cruises at night. Ask the tourist office for details.

FALCONRY

As if Ashford Castle wasn't already aristocratic enough, it is now home to Ireland's first **Falconry School** (☎ 954 6820; www.falconry.ie). It's hard to imagine a more magnificent setting to learn this ancient art. Set deep in the castle's magnificent estate, the school will teach anyone over the age of seven how to handle and fly Harris hawks. An introductory lesson lasting 45 minutes costs €55 per person, although there are reduced rates for two or more people. A lengthier 'hawk walk' lesson lasts for 90 minutes (€85) and longer hunts are also possible for €140. Call ahead to make an appointment.

Sleeping

BUDGET

Cong Hostel (☎ 954 6089; www.anoige.ie; Quay Rd; Lisloughrey; dm/d/q €15/40/74; ℗) Despite being a 2km trek from the village, alongside the camping ground, this large rambling hostel has good facilities, large grounds and a sociable atmosphere. It's affiliated with both An Óige and Independent Holiday Hostels of Ireland (IHH). It screens *The Quiet Man* nightly.

Cong Caravan & Camping Park (☎ 954 6089; info@quietman-cong.com; Quay Rd, Lisloughrey; camp/caravan sites €15/20) About 2km east of town off the Galway road (R346) and close to Lough Corrib, this agreeable camping ground is like a self-contained village. The long list of amenities includes a laundry, a shop, and boat and bike hire.

MIDRANGE

Michaeleen's Manor (☎ 954 6089; www.quietman -cong.com; Quay Rd, Lisloughrey; s/d €45/60; **P**) If you've never seen the film that immortalised Cong, this *Quiet Man* obsessed B&B opposite the hostel will soon enlighten you. And once you've watched it on DVD in the privacy of your own room, you can appreciate better the memorabilia inside, and minibridge on which to mimic *Quiet Man* scenes outside. There's also a hot tub and tennis court.

River Lodge (☎ /fax 954 6057; the Lane; s/d €30/60; Mar-Oct; **P**) Overlooking the river in a rough-plastered Georgian house, this homely B&B has five en-suite rooms and a pleasant garden to relax in. It accepts credit cards.

Lydon's Lodge (☎ 954 6053; lydonslodge@eircom .net; Circular Rd; s/d incl breakfast €50/100; Mar-Oct; **P**) This rambling family-run lodge by the river has comfy but plain rooms and a laid-back bar with an open fire and occasional music.

Danagher's Hotel (☎ 954 6028; fax 954 6495; Abbey St; s/d €50/80) Near the town's main junction, this is a gaudily painted old-style bar-cum-hotel with 11 reasonable rooms. The hotel also has the requisite bar and serves traditional Irish fare. However, its slogan 'No place for a Quiet Man' doesn't bode well for light sleepers!

Eating

Fennel Seed (☎ 954 6004; Ryan's Hotel, Main St; mains €15-25, bar food €8.50-12; 7-10pm Mon-Sat, 1-7pm Sun) Two chefs used to cooking for the upper-crust at Ashford Castle have brought their culinary skills to the village, with great success. The dining room combines elegance and hominess. The Connemara lamb shank

---

SOMETHING SPECIAL

Ashford Castle (☎ 954 6003; www.ashford .ie; Ashford; r from May-Sep €417, Oct-Apr €225-305; gardens adult/child €5/2.50; **P** 💻) Once owned by the Guinness family, this glorious Victorian castle is now one of the top luxury hotels in the world, a fairy-tale place surrounded by an enchanted wood and shielded on three sides by a glistening moat. There are plenty of activities, from horse riding to golf, archery to falconry (see opposite). Ford and his actors stayed here during the filming of *The Quiet Man* (the film is shown 24 hours a day on a hotel TV channel). Before leaving, add your name to the guestbook, which reads like a celebrity's who's who. Nonresidents can walk about the 350 acres of parkland surrounding the castle (for a fee) from 9am to 5pm.

---

is recommended, but vegetarians are also catered for. Also above-average bar food is served until 7pm daily.

Quiet Man Coffee Shop (☎ 954 6034; Main St; soup €4, snacks around €6; 10.30am-6pm Apr-Nov) As authentic as you could hope for, this friendly little coffee shop has been in the family for generations. It's scattered with dusty photos from the film in which family members were extras. It sells appetising home-made fare, including sandwiches, snacks, scones and pies.

Hungry Monk (☎ 954 6866; www.cong-ireland .com; Abbey St; sandwiches €6.50-8, salads €8.50-14; 10am-6pm Mar-Oct; 💻) This contemporary little coffee shop offers a more daring menu of delicious salads and light meals. You can tuck into such fresh combinations as pear, blue cheese and bacon salad, followed by the best coffee in town.

Getting There & Away

Monday to Saturday **Bus Éireann** (☎ 096-71800; www.buseireann.ie) bus No 51 from Galway to Ballina stops at Cong (one way/return €9/12) and at Ashford Castle gates in the early afternoon.

If you're travelling by car or bike further into County Mayo, eschew the main N84 to Castlebar and take the longer, but much more attractive, route west to Leenaun (starting with the R345) and north to Westport via Delphi.

Getting Around

Bikes can be hired from **O'Connor's** (☎ 954 6008; Main St; per day €15), the combined Esso station, Spar supermarket and craft shop by the northern entrance to town.

AROUND CONG

Caves

The Cong area is honeycombed with limestone caves, each of which – in true Irish style – has a colourful legend or story to its credit.

One of the best is **Pigeon Hole**, a deep limestone gash in pine forest about 1.5km west of Cong. It can be reached by road or by the walking track from across the river. Steep and slippery stone steps lead down into the cave, where subterranean water flows in winter. Keep an eye out here for the white trout of Cong – a mythical woman who turned into a fish to be with her drowned lover.

About 200m east of the dry canal on the road to Cross (R346) is a woodland path to **Kelly's Cave** (now closed to explorers), supposedly hideout to a famous 18th-century fugitive. Also a short distance to the west, though trickier to find, is the water-filled **Captain Webb's Hole**. This deep swallow hole lays claim to the grisliest legend in the area. Two centuries ago, a local villain nicknamed Captain Webb for the deformity of his hands and feet, is said to have lured a succession of 12 unfortunate women here, stripped them naked and hurled them into the hole's soggy depths to die. His would-be 13th victim however was a canny lass. She asked Webb to look away as she undressed, then promptly pushed him to his own watery grave.

Circles & Graves

The weathered remains of **Cong Stone Circle** stick up like rotten teeth in a field about 1.5km northeast of Cong just east off the Neale road (R345). About 3.5km east of Cong, north off the Cross road (R346), is the overgrown **Ballymacgibbon Cairn**, supposedly the site of a legendary Celtic battle of Moytura (take the track signposted and watch for a stile to your right).

Neale

It was near this unassuming little village, 6km northeast of Cong, that the word boycott was first born. The miserly landlord's agent Captain Charles Boycott was demanding impossibly high rents and evicting the poorest families. However, he got his comeuppance when the workers famously 'boycotted' work and let his crops rot.

If you take the turn-off at the northern end of the village, you will find the curious carved stone known as the **Gods of the Neale** about 200m east of the main road, through an unsigned gateway on the left. This mysterious slab, which is dated 1757, is carved with figures of a human, animal and reptile.

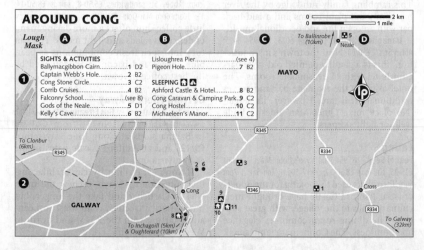

AROUND CONG

0 — 2 km
0 — 1 mile

Lough Mask

To Ballinrobe (10km)
To Neale

MAYO

SIGHTS & ACTIVITIES
Ballymacgibbon Cairn................1 D2
Captain Webb's Hole................2 B2
Cong Stone Circle....................3 C2
Corrib Cruises.........................4 B2
Falconry School....................(see 8)
Gods of the Neale....................5 D1
Kelly's Cave.............................6 B2
Lisloughrea Pier....................(see 4)
Pigeon Hole............................7 B2

SLEEPING
Ashford Castle & Hotel.............8 B2
Cong Caravan & Camping Park..9 C2
Cong Hostel...........................10 C2
Michaeleen's Manor.............11 C2

To Clonbur (6km)
R345

To Inchagoill (5km) & Oughterard (10km)

GALWAY

Cong

R346

R345

R334

Cross

R334

To Galway (32km)

WESTPORT

☎ 098 / pop 5315

Mayo's tourist honey pot, the genteel country town of Westport (Cathair na Mairt), is all about atmosphere. In the daytime, its broad Georgian streets and elegant lime-flanked riverside mall evoke an air of well-to-do times past. Meanwhile the night-time spirit bristles with *joie de vivre*, bubbling its way along the cheek-by-jowl pubs of Bridge St. A short distance west is the town's pretty harbour, Westport Quay, on the shores of Clew Bay and an ideal location for a leisurely meal or pint at sundown.

The town's unusual layout unfurls from the octagonal square, and slopes down to the River Carrowbeg. The first settlement was built around an O'Malley castle, but it disappeared beneath the demolish-and-build spree that was the Georgian era. The new town was designed by 18th-century architect James Wyatt with a little help from Georgian superstar Richard Castle.

Tourists aren't the only ones to note Westport's attractiveness: in 2004 it was named Ireland's tidiest town and the tourist board has also designated it a Heritage Town.

Orientation & Information

Westport consists of two parts: the town proper and Westport Quay on Clew Bay, just outside town on the road to Louisburgh (R335).

Allied Irish Bank (Shop St) ATM and bureau de change.

Bank of Ireland (North Mall) Near the post office.

Bookshop (☎ 26816; Bridge St; ☾ 11am-6pm) Good selection of OS maps and books on Ireland.

Gavin's Video & Internet Cafe (☎ 26461; Bridge St; per hr €6; ☾ noon-10pm) Internet access.

Gill's Launderette (☎ 25819; James St; from €5.35; ☾ 9am-6pm Mon-Sat) Will recycle your dirty laundry.

P Dunning (☎ 25161; James St; per hr €5; ☾ 9am-midnight) Cyber-pub with Internet access.

Tourist office (☎ 25711; www.irelandwest.ie, www.visitmayo.com, www.westporttourism.com; James St; ☾ 9am-6pm Mon-Sat, 10am-6pm Sun Jul & Aug, 9am-5.45pm Mon-Sat Apr-Jun & Sep, 9am-12.45pm & 2-5pm Mon-Fri rest of year) Best in the county.

Sights

WESTPORT HOUSE & COUNTRY PARK

If you can cultivate tunnel vision, the charms of this glorious country **mansion** (☎ 25430; www.westporthouse.ie; Quay Rd; admission to house & gardens adult/child/concession €11.50/6.50/7.50,

attractions cost extra; ☾ 11.30am-5pm Mar-Oct, Sat & Sun only Nov-Feb; Ⓟ)) may still outshine its commercial overhaul of recent years. Once one of the country's most dignified country homes, built in 1730, it has since sold its soul to become a kind of stately-home theme-park hybrid. A fake 'dungeon' sits below the house, unnerving waxworks dot the upper galleries, plastic swans drift on the elegantly landscaped lake, and a minirailway and water slides are tucked into the once tranquil gardens. Admittedly it's great if you have kids, though you may still question the extortionate entrance fee.

Head out of Westport on Quay Rd towards Croagh Patrick and Louisburgh. After 1km, just before Westport Quay, take a small road to the right and through the grand gateway.

OCTAGON MONUMENT

This memorial was erected in 1845 in honour of eminently forgettable George Clendening, a local banker. Until 1922, his statue stood upon the podium, but it was decapitated during the Civil War. In 1990 a Roman-looking statue of St Patrick complete with serpent-entwined staff replaced the unfortunate capitalist.

WESTPORT HERITAGE CENTRE

This small **heritage centre** (☎ 25711; James St; adult/concession/family €3/1/6; ☾ 9am-5pm Mon-Fri May-Sep) within the tourist office has a painstaking model of Westport and multilingual explanations of its history.

CLEW BAY HERITAGE CENTRE

This **heritage centre** (☎ 26852; the Quay; adult/concession/child €3/2/free; ☾ 10am-5pm Mon-Fri, 3-5pm Sun Jul & Aug, 10am-5pm Mon-Fri Jun & Sep, 10am-2pm Mon-Fri Apr, May & Oct), on the pier in Westport Quay, has a collection of local artefacts, including a spinning wheel presented to Maud Gonne, Yeats' unwilling muse.

Activities

GUIDED WALKS

Tours of the town (adult/child €5/free) begin at the clock at the top of Bridge St at 8pm Tuesdays and Thursday July and August.

FISHING

For information about fishing, enquire at **Hewetson** (☎ 26018; Bridge St; ☾ Mon-Sat).

HORSE-RIDING

Carrowholly Stables (☎ 27057; www.carrowholly -stables.com; Carrowholly) has horses and ponies at the ready for guided treks. It's 3km north, next to Westport Golf Club, off the N59 to Newport. You could also try **Drummindoo** (☎ 25616; www.anu.ie/drummindoo; Knockranny; ☒ Mon-Sat Apr-Sep, Sat only Oct-Mar), 1.5km out of town towards Castlebar.

Sleeping

BUDGET

Old Mill Holiday Hostel (☎ 27045; oldmillhostel@ eircom.net; Barrack Yard, James St; dm/d/tr €16.50/45/49.50; ☒ closed Christmas) A winner for charm and convenience, this converted mill is tucked right behind the tourist office. The IHH property has exposed stone walls, well-kept dorms and inviting communal areas that make for a laid-back social vibe.

Abbeywood Hostel (☎ 25496; www.abbeywood house.com; Newport Rd; dm €16-20, d/q €48/80; ☒ daily May-Sep, weekends only Oct-Apr; ℗ ▢) Set back from the road on the northern end of town is this characterful old house and gardens, originally part of a monastery. It still boasts some stained glass, wood floors and high ceilings. A light breakfast is available daily.

Parkland Caravan & Camping Park (☎ 27766; camping@westporthouse.ie; Westport House, Quay Rd; camp sites €25; ☒ mid-May–early Sep) Let your imagination go, and camping on the sprawling Westport estate can feel akin to being an evicted tenant or lowly groundsman. However, the site's wide-open areas and proximity to funfair-like attractions at the house make it a hit for families with young children.

MIDRANGE

Westport overflows with B&Bs, yet they in turn overflow with guests at weekends year round. The tourist office books rooms, or you can take pot luck on Altamount St or Quay Rd towards the harbour.

St Anthony's (☎ 28887; www.st-anthonys.com; Distillery Rd; s/d €40/80; ℗) Welcoming guests for almost four decades, this genteel B&B sits demurely under cover of a large hedge and thick creepers inhabited by birds' nests. The interior is just as easy on the eye, with six simple but elegant rooms; two even have Jacuzzi-style baths.

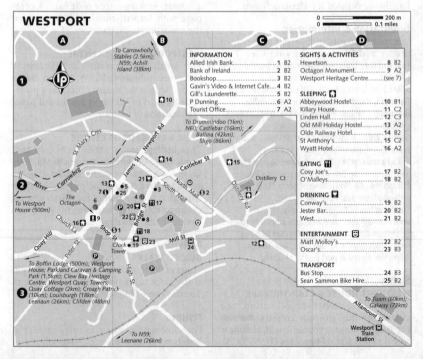

WESTPORT

0 _____ 200 m
0 _____ 0.1 miles

INFORMATION	
Allied Irish Bank	1 B2
Bank of Ireland	2 B2
Bookshop	3 B2
Gavin's Video & Internet Cafe	4 B2
Gill's Launderette	5 B2
P Dunning	6 A2
Tourist Office	7 A2

SIGHTS & ACTIVITIES	
Hewetson	8 B2
Octagon Monument	9 A2
Westport Heritage Centre	(see 7)

SLEEPING ⌂	
Abbeywood Hostel	10 B1
Killary House	11 C2
Linden Hall	12 C3
Old Mill Holiday Hostel	13 A2
Olde Railway Hotel	14 B2
St Anthony's	15 C2
Wyatt Hotel	16 A2

EATING ⋔	
Cosy Joe's	17 B2
O'Malleys	18 B2

DRINKING ▽	
Conway's	19 B2
Jester Bar	20 B2
West	21 B2

ENTERTAINMENT ▦	
Matt Molloy's	22 B2
Oscar's	23 B3

TRANSPORT	
Bus Stop	24 B3
Sean Sammon Bike Hire	25 B2

Boffin Lodge (☎ 26092; www.boffinlodge.com; Quay Rd; s/d €45/80; P) About 500m west of town and close to the harbour is this lovely home with cosy bedrooms and attentive service. The name refers not to egg-heads but rather Inishbofin islanders landing at the harbour.

Killary House (☎ 27457; killaryhouse@msn.com; 4 Distillery Ct; s/d €40/70; P) Tucked away in a quiet cul-de-sac, formerly home to an 18th-century distillery, this characterful B&B has four en-suite rooms, each warmly decorated and well appointed.

Linden Hall (☎ 27005; lindenhall@iol.ie; Altamount St; s/d €40/70) This is an attractive three-storey town house with spacious rooms and welcoming owners.

TOP END

Olde Railway Hotel (☎ 25166; www.anu.ie/railway hotel; the Mall; s/d from €95/150; P) 'One of the prettiest, comfortablist inns in Ireland', declared English novelist William Thackeray when he stayed here in 1834. And things haven't changed that much since. You'd be hard pressed to find a hotel oozing more old-world charm, nor stuffed so full of quirky antiques, collectables and hunting trophies.

Wyatt Hotel (☎ 25027; www.wyatthotel.com; the Octagon; s/d €80/160; P) Other than its position smack in the middle of town, it's the quality of service that really distinguishes this pleasant hotel. Rooms are comfortable though characterless, and guests have free access to a local swimming pool.

Eating

Quay Cottage (☎ 26412; www.quaycottage.com; the Harbour; mains €16-25; ☾ 6-11pm Tue-Sat) Serving seafood hauled straight from the harbour boats, this delightful restaurant is rich in salty-dog charm, with lobster pots hanging from the roof beams. There are a few meat and vegetarian dishes offered 'for landlubbers' too. It's located by the gates to Westport House.

Towers (☎ 26534; the Harbour; mains €9-17; ☾ noon-9.30pm) This wonderfully cosy pub is housed in a former coastguard station with an odd turreted design, faux-Tudor features, rough stone and stained glass. It serves up a terrific menu of local produce, heaping plates high with locally caught seafood and other Irish specialities.

Cosy Joe's (☎ 28004; Bridge St; sandwiches €4-7, mains €6.50-10; ☾ noon-7pm) This bar sets out to mix trendy new décor with its cosy old image; what is consistently good is its hearty menu of superior pub grub.

O'Malley's (☎ 27307; Bridge St; mains €11-20; ☾ 6-10pm Thu-Tue) The 'Around the World' menu served above the youthful pub of the same name has an incredible array of dishes culled from many different cuisines, including Italian, Thai and Mexican.

Drinking

Pub crawlers have a straight shot of it down Bridge St.

West (☎ 28984; Bridge St) You'd be forgiven for thinking the bar is magnetic here, going on the number of punters fastened to it. All ages are drawn to this revamped pub-bar, undeterred by its modern makeover and pop-rock soundtrack.

Jester Bar (☎ 29255; Bridge St) A more select, too-cool-for-school crowd frequent this bar-cum-club, which opts for more urban grooves and hip hop.

Conway's (☎ 26145; Bridge St) With its dark-wood walls, wizened clientele and friendly banter, Conway's is the place for a relaxed pint and good conversation. It's in stark contrast to the Saturday-night meat market next door at O'Malley's.

O'Malley's (☎ 27307; Bridge St) The venue of choice for hens' parties and roaming stags, hell bent on drinking themselves to a good time. A rush-hour traffic jam awaits anyone trying to reach the bar and enjoy its wide variety of multicoloured drinks.

Entertainment

Matt Molloy's (☎ 26655; Bridge St) Many visitors to Westport come solely to set foot inside this tiny but celebrated old pub. Owned by Matt Molloy of the Chieftains it attracts the cream of Irish trad, and music nights see an astonishing number of people squeezing into its wooden-floored interior.

Oscar's (☎ 29200; Mill St; admission €2.50; ☾ 11.30pm-2.30am Thu-Sat) This is where the night ends for Westport's more energetic revellers. It's a snazzy two-level nightclub where beautiful young things sashay till late.

Getting There & Away

Bus Éireann (☎ 096-71800) travels to Achill (€5.60, 30 minutes, two daily), Ballina (€10,

1¼ hours, five daily), Cork (€23, 6¼ hours, five daily), Dublin (€16, five hours, five daily), Galway (€13, two hours, eight daily) and Sligo (€15, two hours, four daily). Buses depart from and arrive at the Mill St stop. There are limited services on Sunday.

The **train station** (☎ 25253) is 800m from the town centre. There are three daily connections (four on Sunday) to Dublin (adult/child €28/14, 3¾ hours) via Athlone.

Getting Around

For a cab call **Moran's Executive Taxis** (☎ 25539) or **O'Toole Taxis** (☎ 087-243 2600). **Sean Sammon Bike Hire** (☎ 25471; James St) hires out bikes for €10 per day.

AROUND WESTPORT
Croagh Patrick

St Patrick couldn't have picked a better spot for a pilgrimage than this conical mountain (also known as 'the Reek') towering to the southwest of Westport. If the weather is clear, the tough two-hour climb rewards with a stunning view of Clew Bay's innumerable sandy islets, seemingly writhing in whirls and eddies, like froth in a gargantuan bathtub.

It was on Croagh Patrick where Ireland's patron saint fasted for 40 days and nights, and where he reputedly banished venomous snakes. Climbing the 765m holy mountain is an act of penance for thousands of pilgrims on the last Sunday of July (Reek Sunday). The truly contrite make the trek along Tóchar Phádraig (Patrick's Causeway), the original 40km route from Ballintubber Abbey, and ascend the mountain barefoot.

The trail taken by less contrite folk begins beside Campbell's pub in the village of Murrisk (Muraisc), west of Westport. There's no mistaking the route. At the start of the path you'll find a **visitor centre** (☎ 098-64114; croaghpatrick@ireland.com; ⊗ 11am-5pm Mar-Oct).

Opposite the car park is the **National Famine Memorial**, a spine-chilling sculpture of a three-masted ghost ship wreathed in swirling skeletons, commemorating the lives lost on so called 'coffin ships' employed to escape the Famine (1845–49). The path down past the memorial leads to the scant remains of **Murrisk Abbey**, founded by the O'Malleys in 1547.

Louisburgh & Around

☎ 098 / pop 207

The small village of Louisburgh (Cluain Cearbán) was founded under curious circumstances in 1795. Based on a simple four-street system known as the Cross, the whole town was designed and built as a living memorial to a relative of the first marquess of Sligo, Lord Altamont (John Browne to you and me): his kinsman was killed at the Battle of Louisburgh in Nova Scotia, 1758.

Visit the **Granuaile Visitors Centre** (☎ 66134; Church St; adult/child/concession €3.50/1.50/2.50; ⊗ 10am-6pm Mon-Sat) for a quick glimpse into the life and times of Grace O'Malley (Gráinne Ní Mháille or Granuaile, 1530–1603) the infamous pirate queen of Connaught.

There are some excellent Blue Flag **beaches** in the vicinity: Old Head Beach is particularly sandy and safe. It's found 4km from Louisburgh, just off the main road to Westport.

Old Head Forest Caravan & Camping Park (☎ 087-648 6885; Old Head, Louisburgh; camp sites €12; ⊗ Jun-Sep) is a medium-sized camping park in woodland, a short walk from its namesake beach, where there is a pier and a slipway with a lifeguard on duty.

Bus Éireann (☎ 096-71800) bus No 450 links Westport and Louisburgh (€6.50, 35 minutes, five daily Monday to Saturday) via Murrisk.

Killadoon

Panoramic ocean views and vast sandy beaches, almost always empty, can be found at the tiny village of Killadoon. It's reached by a narrow coastal road heading south from Louisburgh or by turning west off the R335 at Cregganbaun.

Bus Éireann (☎ 096-71800) bus No 450 from Westport and Louisburgh continues to Killadoon up to three times daily. The trip takes about 15 minutes.

Doolough Valley

The R335 scenic route from Westport and Leenane (County Galway) via Louisburgh and Delphi travels through the stunning Doolough Valley. It's wildly beautiful, not least because of the lonely expanse of **Doo Lough** (Dark Lake) with the **Mweelrea Mountains** behind. At the southern end of the lake **Bengorm** rises to 702m. The landscape changes from baize-green and sparkling wet stone to a forbidding grey as shadows envelop everything when cloud banks spread in from the Atlantic.

During the Famine, the valley was the scene of tragedy when some 600 men, women and children walked from Louisburgh to Delphi Lodge hoping that the landlord would offer them food. Help was flatly refused and, on the return journey, around 400 perished. There's a rough-cut stone cross memorial to the unfortunate souls along the road.

DELPHI

☎ 095

It's no accident that one of the country's top spas chose to locate itself in Delphi. This starkly beautiful swathe of mountainous moorland is ideal get-away-from-it-all territory. Miles from any significant settlements, you can toss aside that mobile phone, forget your troubles and set about the serious business of relaxing.

The area was named by its most famous resident, the second Marquess of Sligo, who was convinced that the land strongly resembled the area around Delphi, Greece.

Delphi Lodge (☎ 42222; www.delphilodge.ie, www.delphi-salmon.com; Leenane; s/d €125/190, with lake view €165/270; P 💻) feels more like a congenial house party than a hotel. This lakeside Georgian lodge is a popular retreat for well-heeled fishermen, walkers and seekers after tranquillity. It was once the sporting lodge of the Marquis of Sligo.

Delphi Mountain Resort & Spa (☎ 42987, 42208; www.delphiescape.com; Leenane; s/d with breakfast & activities from €180/290; P 💻) is built from rough-cut stone and honey-coloured wood. This world-class spa-hotel hits the perfect note between modern chic and rustic glow – even if the exterior somewhat resembles a hobbit hole. Day programmes for non-guests cost from €80 to €230.

Delphi Adventure Centre (☎ 42307; www.delphi adventureholidays.ie), alongside the lodge, offers over 25 outdoor activities – from hill walking to raft building to cross-country assault courses.

CLARE ISLAND

☎ 098 / pop 200

Clew Bay reputedly has 365 islands – one for every day of the year. However, the largest by far is mountainous Clare Island, 5km

offshore at the mouth of the bay. Dominated by rocky **Mt Knockmore** (461m), the island is a terrific place for **walking** and **climbing** on a clear day. It also has several safe, sandy beaches to its credit.

The island has the ruins of the Cistercian **Clare Island Abbey** (c 1460) and **Granuaile's Castle**, both associated with the piratical Grace O'Malley. The tower castle was her stronghold, although it was altered considerably when the coastguard took it over in 1831. Grace is said to be buried in the small abbey, which contains a stone inscribed with her family motto: 'Invincible on land and sea.'

The island is also one of the dwindling number of places where you can find **choughs**, which look like blackbirds but have red beaks.

Sleeping & Eating

Bay View Hotel & Hostel (☎ 26307; carlogradyci@ eircom.net; dm/s/d €15/30/60, s/d with bathroom €45/90; ☼ May-Oct) The island's only hotel overlooks the harbour with a sunset view of the mainland that is simply sublime. A revamp in 2005 will eventually see prices rise. It also has a basic self-catering hostel next door.

Cois Abhainn (☎ 26216; Toremore; s/d €30/60; ☼ May-Oct) Alternatively, for that 'ends-of-the-earth' feeling, you could head to the windswept southwestern corner of the island, 5km from the harbour. This B&B has sensational views of Inishturk Island. Not all rooms are en suite.

If you're just going for the day, consider taking your own food, though pub grub is available at the Bay View Hotel, and B&Bs do evening meals (from €15).

Getting Around

You can hire **bikes** (☎ 25640) from opposite the pier for €10 per day. The same family offers the island's only taxi service.

Getting There & Away

The nearest mainland point is Roonagh Quay, 8km west of Louisburgh. **Clare Island Ferries** (☎ 28288, 087-241 4653; www.clareislandferry .com) and **O'Malley's Ferries** (☎ 25045, 086 877 7390) make the 25-minute trip from Roonagh (€15/5 per adult/child return). There are eight sailings daily in July and August, and from three to five daily in May, June and September; call for the October to April schedule.

INISHTURK ISLAND

☎ 098 / pop 98

Still further off the beaten track is ruggedly beautiful Inishturk, which lies about 12km off Mayo's western coast. It is a sparsely populated and little visited island, despite the two **sandy beaches** on its eastern side, impressive **cliffs**, wonderful **flora and fauna**, and a rugged, hilly landscape ideal for **walking**. It's a terrific getaway.

Accommodation and meals are available at the colourful **Concannon's B&B** (☎ 45520; s/d incl breakfast & dinner €50/100), a short walk from the ferry, and the more remote but scenically positioned **Teach Abhainn** (☎ 45510; s/d €30/50; dinner €25), a working farm 1.5km west of the harbour.

John Heanue operates a **ferry** (☎ 45541, 086 202 9670; Roonagh) from Roonagh Quay (adult/child return €25/12.50, 11am and 6.30pm). There is also a twice weekly service to Cleggan in County Galway; call for details of departure times.

NEWPORT

☎ 098 / pop 530

The first thing you notice about this small 18th-century town, 12km north of Westport, is the elegant seven-arch viaduct spanning the River Newport. Trains once rattled across the pedestrianised walkway, plying the route from Westport to Achill Sound from 1892 to 1936.

Newport (Baile Uí Fhiacháin) is a popular base for **fishing** in the nearby loughs and Clew Bay. The town is also at one end of the Bangor Trail (see p434).

The post office and bureau de change are across the river. There are no banks.

Sleeping & Eating

Newport House (☎ 41222; www.newporthouse.ie; Main St; s €132-201, d €216-332; dinner €58; ☺ Mar-Sep; P ⌨) This magnificent Georgian mansion, smothered by crimson ivy, is one of the top country hotels in Ireland. Every room in the hotel is beautifully appointed and includes breakfast, but Newport House is especially known for its contemporary Irish cuisine and a vintage wine list that will make you drool. The bar is also worth checking out, even if you're not a guest.

Anchor House (☎ 41178; maureenanchorhouse@ hotmail.com; The Quay; s/d €35/60; ☺ Mar-Oct; P) A wonderful riverfront B&B with spot-less rooms and friendly hosts, the upstairs rooms have river-view balconies. Turn down the lane next to Newport House.

Getting There & Away

A **Bus Éireann** (☎ 096-71800) service runs between Achill Island (€8.50, one hour) and Westport (€4, 20 minutes) via Newport once a day, Monday to Saturday. There are extra buses in July and August. The bus stop is outside Chambers Newsagent.

NEWPORT TO ACHILL ISLAND

Burrishoole Abbey

From a distance, the eerie shell of this wind-battered **abbey** (admission free; ☺ dawn-dusk) resembles a 2D film set. It was founded in 1486 by the Dominicans. However, in a strange twist of fate, the abbey actually plunged the surrounding devout community into holy hot water, when Rome threatened them with excommunication for not consulting them on its creation.

About 2.5km northwest towards Achill a sign points the way, from where it's a further 1km.

Rockfleet Castle

Also known as **Carrigahowley**, this bluff 15th-century tower is one of the most tangible spots to be associated with 'pirate queen' Grace O'Malley. She married her second husband, Richard an-Iarrain (unfortunately nicknamed 'Iron Dick' Burke) to gain control of this castle, and famously fought off an English attack here. The tower is in a quiet outlet of Clew Bay. Turn south at the sign about 5km west of Newport on the Achill road.

Mulrany & Curraun Peninsula

This elongated hillside village (An Mhala Raithní, also called Mulranny) is a great spot to try counting the approximately 365 saucer-sized islands that grace Clew Bay. Mulrany stands on the isthmus with Bellacragher Bay and boasts a stunning, wide Blue Flag **beach**. Take the steps opposite the Great Western Parklands Hotel, or the path beside the Top service station.

Sleeping

Midrange accommodation is best on Achill, but a few forlorn B&Bs with spectacular views can be found in Mulrany.

Traenlaur Lodge (☎ 098-41358; www.anoige.ie; Lough Feeagh, Newport; dm €15; ⓨ Jun-Sep) A gorgeous An Óige hostel in a former fishing lodge with its own harbour on Lough Feeagh, it's often full of walkers resting their weary feet from the Western Way or Bangor Trail, which meet here. It is 8km from Newport, signposted from the Achill road.

Great Western Parklands Hotel (☎ 098-36000; N59, Mulrany; s/d €160/200; (P) (🖳) (♿)) To universal delight, this grand old dame of the railway-group golden days recently reopened after decades of dereliction. Established in 1897, it was once a playground for Ireland's great and good. Even in the 1960s, it attracted stars like John Lennon and Yoko, to whom a suite is dedicated. The hotel boasts one of the most magical coastal views in Ireland, rooms have fresh up-to-the-minute décor, and bonus features include a swimming pool.

ACHILL ISLAND
☎ 098 / pop 958

Ireland's largest off-shore island, Achill (An Caol), is ringed by breathtaking cliff scenery and rocky headlands. When the wind is up, waves lash the exposed rocks so hard that they throw up little white clouds of spume that drift across the coastal road. Yet the island also shelters safe sandy coves, broad expanses of blanket bog and rolling mountains, all crammed into its 147 sq km. Although it's a rather bleak place in winter, the summer sets the island alight with purple heather, rhododendrons and wildflowers. Achill's sprinkling of holiday chalets (some nicknamed the Toblerones), hotels and camping grounds also fill in summer months.

The island is joined to the mainland (the Curraun Peninsula) by a swing bridge, and the village of Keel is the island's main centre of activity.

Information

Most of the villages have a post office and O'Malley's Spar supermarket in Keel doubles as a post office and has an ATM. There are no banks but mobile banks visit the various villages (the tourist office has times) and there's another ATM at the craft shop beside Sweeney's supermarket.

INTERNET ACCESS

Achill & Curraun IT Centre (Coiste Forbartha Áitiúil Acla; ☎ 43292; Keel; per hr €6; ⓨ 9am-5pm Mon-Fri;

THE GREAT WESTERN GHOST TRAIN

A spooky footnote can be added to the Great Western Railway's short-lived history in Achill Sound. Local folklore likes to tell how a 17th-century prophet named Brian Rua O'Cearbhain had a vision that one day 'carts on wheels, blowing smoke and fire' would run here, and that their first and last journeys would carry corpses.

Chillingly, just as work was completed on the railway line to Achill in 1894, tragedy struck when 32 young locals were drowned in Clew Bay, and the very first train from Westport to Achill carried the bodies back to their grieving families. The prophecy reared its ugly head four decades later when the railway had already ceased to run. Ten migrant workers from Achill were killed in a fire at Kirkintilloch, Scotland in 1937. The railway line was reopened for one last run to bring the bodies back for burial.

(P)) An educational centre with over a dozen Internet terminals, 1km from Keel (signposted off road to Slievemore). **Mayo County Library** (☎ 20910; Achill Sound; per 30 min €1.50; ⓨ 2-7pm Tue-Wed, 11am-4pm Fri & Sat) Allows nonmembers to check their email.

TOURIST INFORMATION

Fáilte Ireland (☎ 45384; www.ireland.ie; Cashel; ⓨ 9am-5.45pm Jul & Aug) A seasonal tourist office in a cabin opposite the main tourist office.
Tourist office (☎ 47353; www.achilltourism.com, www.visitachill.com; Cashel; ⓨ 9am-6pm Mon-Fri Jul & Aug, 9am-5pm Sep-Jun) The best source of information on the island, this locally run office is beside the petrol station in Cashel.

Sights
SLIEVEMORE DESERTED VILLAGE

The eerie remains of this deserted village at the foot of Slievemore Mountain are a poignant reminder of a lost way of life. Until the mid-19th century, the village was divided between permanent inhabitants and transhumance farmers (known here as 'booleying'), but as the Potato Famine took grip, starvation forced the villagers to the sea and its sources of food.

DOOAGH

This village is where Don Allum, the first person to row across the Atlantic Ocean in

www.lonelyplanet.com

ACHILL ISLAND

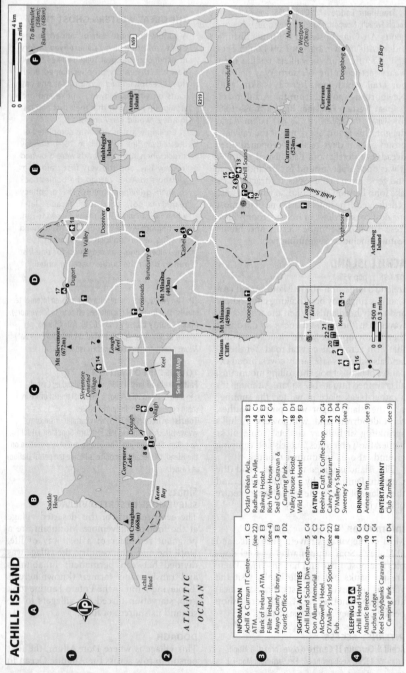

To Belmullet (38km); Ballina (48km)

N59

To Westport (20km)

Clew Bay

Mulrany

Annagh Island

Owenduff

R319

Curraun Hill (524m)

Achill Sound

Curraun Peninsula

Doogbeg

Inishbiggle Island

Achill Sound

Cloghmore

Achillbeg Island

15

13

2

19

3

The Valley

Dooniver

18

Dugort

17

Slievemore Deserted Village

Mt Slievemore (672m)

Doogah

Dooagh

8

16

10

Pollagh

Corrymore Lake

Mt Croaghaun (668m)

Saddle Head

ATLANTIC OCEAN

Achill Head

Keem Bay

Bunacurry

Crossroads

Castle

4

Mt Minaun (403m)

Mt Minaun (459m)

Minaun Cliffs

Dooega

7

14

Lough Keel

Keel

See Inset Map

Lough Keel

1

9 20 22 21

11 16

5

12

Keel

0   500 m
0   0.3 miles

0   4 miles
0   2 km

INFORMATION
Achill & Curraun IT Centre......**1** C3	
ATM...............................(see **22**)	
Bank of Ireland ATM..............**2** E3	
Fáilte Ireland.....................(see **4**)	
Mayo County Library.............**3** E3	
Tourist Office.....................**4** D2	

SIGHTS & ACTIVITIES
Achill Island Scuba Dive Centre....**5** C4	
Don Allum Memorial................**6** C2	
McDowell's Hotel..................**7** C1	
O'Malley's Island Sports..........(see **22**)	
Pub...............................**8** B2	

SLEEPING 🏠
Achill Head Hotel.................**9** C4	
Atlantic Breeze...................**10** C1	
Fuchsia Lodge....................**11** C4	
Keel Sandybanks Caravan & Camping Park.....**12** D4	
Ostán Oileán Acla.................**13** E3	
Radharc Na h-Aille................**14** C1	
Railway Hostel...................**15** E3	
Rich View House..................**16** C4	
Seal Caves Caravan & Camping Park.....**17** D1	
Valley House Hostel...............**18** D1	
Wild Haven Hostel................**19** E3	

EATING 🍴
Beehive Craft & Coffee Shop......**20** C4	
Calvey's Restaurant..............**21** D4	
O'Malley's Spar..................**22** D4	
Sweeney's.......................(see **2**)	

DRINKING
Annexe Inn......................(see **9**)	

ENTERTAINMENT
Club Zamba......................(see **9**)	

both directions, landed in September 1982 in his 6m-long plywood boat, dubbed the *QE3*, after 77 days at sea. The **Pub** (that's its name) has memorabilia marking the feat, and there's a memorial opposite.

Activities

While parts of Achill's coastline are lashed by merciless waves, it also shelters a few lovely bays with hardly a ripple. Often deserted, the sandy **beaches** at Keel, Dooega, Keem, Dugort and Golden Strand (Dugort's other beach) are all of Blue Flag quality, and the ones at Dooagh and Dooniver are just as sandy.

The island is a wonderful place for **walking** and even the highest point (Mt Slievemore, 672m) presents no problems. It can be climbed from behind the deserted village, and from the top there are terrific views of Blacksod Bay. A longer climb would take in Mt Croaghaun (668m), Achill Head and a walk atop some of the highest cliffs in Europe. Achill Tourism produces a bilingual *Guide to Walking in Achill* (€3.50) detailing 14 walks.

Sea-angling gear is sold by **O'Malley's Island Sports** (☎ 43125; Keel), which can also arrange boat and bike hire. **Tony Burke** (☎ 47257; tm burke@eircom.net) also organises deep-sea angling trips. With its clear waters Achill is a good diving spot and **Achill Island Scuba Dive Centre** (☎ 087 234 9884; www.achilldivecentre.com; Purteen Harbour, Keel) offers training and equipment hire.

Windsurfing is also popular, and **Gareth Allen** (☎ 43958; windwise@hotmail.com; Bunacurry) hires out gear and runs courses. Other activities include rock climbing, canoeing and surfing. Richie O'Hara at **McDowell's Hotel** (☎ 43148; Slievemore Rd), southwest of Dugort, gives instruction and hires out canoes and surfboards (€15 per hour). Kite-surfing is increasingly spotted off-shore, though there's nowhere to hire gear.

Less energetic activities include summer painting classes run by **O'Dálaigh** (☎ 36137; www.achillpainting.com), and courses in archaeology with enthusiasts from **Achill Archaeological Field School** (☎ 43564; www.achill-fieldschool.com; Achill Folklife Centre).

Special Events

Traditional Irish music can be heard for miles around in the first two weeks of Au-

gust, during the **Scoil Acla Festival** (☎ 43063). The event also promotes Irish dancing, culture and music through numerous workshops (swiftly relocating to pubs come the evening).

Sleeping

BUDGET

Valley House Hostel (☎ 47204; www.valley-house .com; the Valley; camp sites/dm/d €12/13/32, f from €39.50; **P**) Put a hostel in an atmospheric old house, with a licensed bar and nearby beaches, and you're onto a winner. But Valley House has still more going for it – its infamous history. In 1894, the landlady was brutally attacked by a local man and JM Synge based *The Playboy of the Western World* on his misadventures. The subsequent film *Love and Rage* (1999) was also partially shot here. Take the road to Keel and turn right (northeast) at the Bunacurry junction signposted for Dugort.

Wild Haven Hostel (☎ 45392; Achill Sound; dm/d €15/40; ⌚ Apr-Oct; **P**) The island's cosiest, but smallest, hostel (there are only four dorm beds!) is a beautifully furnished house with home-made quilts and a roaring fire. It's over the bridge on the left behind the parish church.

Rich View House (☎ 43462; richviewhostel@ hotmail.com; Keel; s/d incl breakfast €15/30) Facilities at this relaxed hostel-cum-home-stay are simple, even scarce, but the jolly live-in owner is extremely knowledgeable about Achill and quick to invite guests to the pub.

Keel Sandybanks Caravan & Camping Park (☎ 094-903 2054; www.achillcamping.com; Keel; camp sites €10; ⌚ mid-May–mid-Sep) This sand-box camping ground is beside Keel Strand, a Blue Flag beach, and a short stroll from the town.

Budget travellers could also consider:
Railway Hostel (☎ 45187; Achill Sound; camp sites/dm €6/11; **P**) The old station house now serves as a no-frills hostel, just before the bridge.
Seal Caves Caravan & Camping Park (☎ 43262; Dugort; camp sites €12; ⌚ May-Sep) Terrific site on the island's remote northern side. Two Blue Flag beaches nearby.

MIDRANGE

Atlantic Breeze (☎ 43189; atlanticbreeze01@hotmail .com; Pollagh, Keel; s/d €30/56; ⌚ Apr-Oct; **P**) This award-winning B&B has three rooms, a personable host and lovely views from its conservatory.

Achill Head Hotel (☎ 43108; www.achillhead .com; Pollagh, Keel; s/d €65/100; **P**) This medium-sized hotel has 19 modern rooms, some with rather grandiose four-poster beds and patchwork-style quilts. The hotel is in the heart of Keel and close to the seafront, though not so well located as its website would have you believe.

Fuchsia Lodge (☎ 43350; fuchsialodge@eircom.ie; Keel; s/d €40/60; **P** **&**) This popular and convenient B&B opposite Rich View House is one of few open all year round. It has four cosy bedrooms, including two connecting rooms ideal for a family.

Radharc Na h-Aille (☎ 43378; radharcnahaille@ hotmail.com; Slievemore, Keel; s/d €35/60; ☺ Jul-Sep; **P**) If you don't mind the spooky location alongside the cemetery and deserted village below Slievemore, this family-friendly B&B is a cosy choice. A baby-sitting service can be arranged.

Óstán Oileán Acla (☎ 45138; www.achillisland hotel.com; s/d incl breakfast €60/80; **P**) Big new waterfront hotel perched by the swing bridge across to the island, with restaurant, bar and outdoor seating with stunning views across the sound.

Eating

Calvey's Restaurant (☎ 43158; Keel; mains €6-18; ☺ 6-10pm Mon-Sat) This award-winning restaurant serves up a mix of fresh local seafood and meat from its attached butchery. Its signature dish is local lamb, but there are also a few nonmeat dishes for vegetarians.

Beehive Craft & Coffee Shop (☎ 43134; Keel; snacks around €7; ☺ 10.30am-6pm Apr-Oct; **P**) As much a craft shop as a café, the Beehive dishes up wonderful home-made soups served with brown scones and a more sinful selection of home-baked cakes.

If you're camping or hostelling, stock up at **Sweeney's** (☎ 45211) supermarket, just across the bridge as you enter Achill, or at **O'Malley's Spar** (☎ 43125) supermarket in Keel. Most hotels serve lunch or dinner to nonguests.

Drinking & Entertainment

From May to September most pubs and hotels have music.

Annexe Inn (☎ 43268; Keel) This cosy little pub delivers the best traditional music sessions all year round. It has music almost nightly in July and August, and weekends the rest of the year.

Club Zamba (☎ 43108; Achill Head Hotel, Pollagh, Keel) This is a summer-only hotel-nightclub that is strung with video screens and swirling lights. It has a text-message request-service to the DJ, so it's no good using the old 'not my kind of music' excuse to avoid dancing.

Getting There & Around

A **Bus Éireann** (☎ 096-71800) bus runs across the island from Dooagh, taking in Keel, Dugort, Dooega and Achill Sound before crossing to Mulrany, Newport, Westport and finally Ballina (see p438), Monday to Saturday year round. Check the current schedule with the tourist office.

On Thursdays in July and August, Bus Éireann operates a day tour around Achill from Westport (€20), departing at 10.30am and returning at 5.45pm.

Bikes can be hired from **O'Malley's Island Sports** (☎ 43125; Keel).

BANGOR ERRIS

☎ 097 / pop 265

This unexceptional little village is the start or end point for the 48km **Bangor Trail**, which connects Bangor (Bain Gear) and Newport. It's an extraordinary hike that takes walkers through some of the bleakest, most remote countryside in Ireland. Unfortunately, you'll need several 1:50,000 OS maps to cover the trail.

Hillcrest House (☎ 83494; hillcresthouse@eircom .net; Main St; s/d €30/60), a well-kept though brusque B&B, is the village's best spot to bed down.

Monday to Saturday **Bus Éireann** (☎ 096-71800) runs once daily (twice daily in July and August) from Ballina to Bangor Erris and Belmullet (€11, 1½ hours), then south to Blacksod Point.

MULLET PENINSULA

☎ 097

Unspoilt and virtually ignored by most visitors, this bleak, sparsely populated peninsula juts 30km out into the Atlantic where it is exposed to the worst of its ravages. On kinder days, it is well worth checking out, as the eastern, more sheltered, side is home to some of Ireland's most pristine beaches. The peninsula is Irish speaking and the functional little town of **Belmullet** (Béal an Mhuirthead) is the main settlement.

Information

Atlantek Computers (☎ 82255; Carter Sq; per hr €6; ⏰ 10am-6pm Mon-Sat) For Internet access.

Bank of Ireland (Carter Sq) Has an ATM and bureau de change.

Erris Tourist Office (☎ 81500; Barrack St; ⏰ 9.30am-4.30pm Mon-Fri Easter-Sep) Close to Belmullet's central roundabout.

Post office (Main St)

Blacksod Point & Around

The road south from Belmullet loops round the tip of the peninsula to rejoin itself at Aghleam. Near the point are the remains of an old **church**, and the view across the bay takes in the spot where *La Rata Santa Maria Encoronada*, part of the 1588 Spanish Armada, came in and was later burned by its captain.

The road to Blacksod Point passes **Elly Bay**, a pleasant beach and a favourite haunt of bird-watchers. Further south it passes stunning **Mullaghroe Beach**. In the early years of the 20th century, a whaling station operated at Ardelly Point, just north of here.

The weather centre here determined the eventual date for the D-Day Normandy Landing.

Sleeping & Eating

Western Strands Hotel (☎ 81096; westernstrands hotel@eircom.net; Main St, Belmullet; s/d €38/62) There's a consistently cheerful mood at this central hotel-cum-guesthouse. Rooms are straightforward without being flashy, and good food is available in the bar.

Chez Nous (☎ 82167; chez_nous_belmullet@esat clear.ie; Church Rd, Belmullet; s/d €42/60; ⏰ Mar- Dec; P) Wonderfully snug rooms with cheerful colour schemes can be found at this modern B&B 500m from the town's central roundabout; take the road signposted Garda.

Getting There & Around

Monday to Saturday **Bus Éireann** (☎ 096-71800) runs once daily (twice daily in July and August) from Ballina to Bangor Erris and Belmullet (€11, 1½ hours), then south to Blacksod Point.

McNulty's Coaches (☎ 81086; Chapel St), with an office near the Belmullet post office, runs buses to Castlebar at 8.15am Monday to Wednesday and Friday, returning at 5.30pm on the same days. The 1¾-hour trip costs €9/13 one way/return.

POLLATOMISH

☎ 097 / pop 150

Pretty little Pollatomish (Poll an Tómais), also spelled Pullathomas, sits in a serene bay some 16km east of Belmullet, signposted on the road to Ballycastle (R314). There's a pleasant sandy **beach** and walks up to **Benwee Head** from where there are terrific views.

The owners of the cosy **Kilcommon Lodge Hostel** (☎ 84621; www.kilcommonlodge.net; Pollatomish; dm/d €11/28; P) deserve a medal for their attentive service. The building also boasts good facilities, a drying room and garden filled with quirky bric-a-brac, including whale's bones. Evening meals are available.

BALLYCASTLE & AROUND

☎ 096 / pop 250

Fifty years ago, just one megalithic tomb was recorded in the region around Ballycastle (Baile an Chaisil). Now, the area claims one of the greatest concentrations of such tombs in Europe. It is also blessed with breathtaking coastal scenery. The pretty village consists of one sloping street.

Céide Fields

A famous wit once described archaeology as being all about 'a series of small walls'. Well it's not often that such walls have had experts hopping up and down with such excitement as at Céide Fields (Achaidh Chéide), 8km west of Ballycastle.

During the 1930s, a local man, Patrick Caulfield, was digging in the bog when he noticed a lot of piled-up stones buried beneath it. About 40 years later, his son Seamus, who had become an archaeologist on the basis of his father's discovery, began extensive exploration of the area. What he, and later others, uncovered was the world's most extensive Stone Age monument, consisting of stone-walled fields, houses and megalithic tombs – reckoned to total about half a million tonnes of stone. Astonishingly, five millennia ago a thriving farming community lived here, growing wheat and barley, grazing sheep and cattle, and fencing off land with an impressive level of planning.

Even for nonarchaeologists, the award-winning **Interpretive Centre** (☎ 43325; R314; adult/child under 6/student/concession €3.50/free/1.25/2.50; ⏰ 10am-6pm Jun-Sep, 10am-5pm mid-Mar–May, Oct &

Nov, groups only rest of year), in a glass pyramid overlooking the site, gives a fascinating glimpse into the past of 5500 years ago. However, it's recommended that you take a guided tour of the site itself, or it may seem nothing more than, well, a series of small walls.

Downpatrick Head

The landscape northeast of Ballycastle is one of wave-gouged rock and glistening surf. High cliffs culminate in the precarious rock stack **Dun Briste** severed from the mainland at Downpatrick Head. The headland also has a blowhole that occasionally shoots up plumes of water.

Sleeping & Eating

Céide House (☎ 43105; denise@ceidehouse.com; Main St; s/d €25/50) This ex-pub offers excellent value B&B in the village centre. Its cosy breakfast room is splashed with murals by friends and family, and retains private stalls from its days as a pub-restaurant.

Mary's Cottage Kitchen (☎ 43361; Lower Main St; mains €5-9; ☼ 10am-3pm Mon-Sat Oct-Mar, 10am-6pm Apr-Sep) This cosy grey-stone cottage bakery serves light meals, cakes and ambrosial apple and rhubarb pies. The leafy rear garden is a cherry on top. Mary sometimes extends hours in summer to make evening meals.

Getting There & Away

Bus Éireann (☎ 71800) No 445 runs between Ballycastle and Ballina (€9, one hour) twice a day, Monday to Saturday, stopping outside Katie Mac's pub.

KILLALA & AROUND

☎ 096 / pop 650

The town itself is pretty enough, but Killala (Cill Alaidh or Cill Ála) is more famous for its namesake Bay nearby, and its role in the French invasion and rebellion of Wolfe Tone in 1798.

It's claimed that St Patrick founded Killala, and the Church of Ireland cathedral sits on the site of the first Christian church. The 25m round tower still looms over the town's heart; it was struck by lightning in 1800 and the cap was later rebuilt. A seasonal **tourist office** (☎ 32166; ☼ 10am-5pm Jun-Sep) is located 500m outside town on the Ballina road.

Rathfran Abbey

The remains of this remote Dominican friary, dating from 1274, can be both tranquil and downright eerie. The silence is broken only by the cawing of crows and the whistling wind. In 1590 the friary was burned by the English, but the resilient monks stayed nearby until the 18th century.

Take the R314 road north out of Killala and, after 5km and crossing the River Cloonaghmore, turn right. After another 2km turn right at the crossroads.

Moyne Abbey

This 15th-century Franciscan impressive structure was also torched by Richard Bingham in the 16th century. It's a scramble across private farmland to reach its lonely ruin. If you fancy a shot at it, the abbey is 3km north of Rosserk Abbey; you'll see it on the right across a field.

Breastagh Ogham Stone

This lonely lichen-covered stone, the height of a basketball champ, is etched with an obscure ogham script but the weathered markings are all but invisible. It's in a field left of the R314 just past the turning for Rathfran Abbey. Cross the ditch where the sign points to the stone.

Kilcummin & Lackan Bay

Flush with revolutionary fervour and eager to hurt the English in their own backyard, on 22 August 1798 more than 1000 French troops commanded by General Humbert landed at Kilcummin in Killala Bay. It was hoped (or rather promised by Irish patriot Wolfe Tone) that their arrival would inspire the Irish peasantry to revolt against the English.

A right turn off the main R314 is signposted for Kilcummin. On the R314 just after the turning to Lackan Bay a **sculpture** of a French soldier helping a prostrate Irish peasant marks the place where the first French soldier died on Irish soil. Lackan Bay **beach** is a stunning expanse of golden sand, ideal for young children.

Getting There & Away

The Ballina–Ballycastle bus runs once or twice a day Monday to Saturday, stopping outside McGregor's newsagency. Ring **Bus Éireann** (☎ 71800) for details.

BALLINA

☎ 096 / pop 9478

The bustling town of Ballina (Béal an Átha; balli-*nagh*) is the largest in the county, and a good base for exploring northern Mayo. Its densely packed streets retain traces of Victorian and Edwardian elegance, and two comely bridges link the town's two halves over the River Moy.

Information

Atlantek Computers (☎ 70658; Circular Rd; per hr €6; ☽ 10am-6pm Mon-Sat) An Internet café.

Bank of Ireland (Pearse St) With ATM and bureau de change.

Moy Valley Resources (☎ 70848; Cathedral Rd; per hr €9; ☽ 9am-1pm & 2-5.30pm) Internet access in same building as the tourist office.

Post office (O'Rahilly St) On the southern extension of Pearse St.

Tourist office (☎ 70848; Cathedral Rd; ☽ 10am-5.30pm Mon-Sat Apr-Oct) Across the River Moy from the centre.

Ulster Bank (Pearse St) With ATM and bureau de change.

Sights

The megalithic **Dolmen of the Four Maols**, 2000 BC, is behind the train station and connected with a bloody tale of a murdered bishop and four hangings. Alongside the cathedral are the scarce remains of a 15th century **Augustinian Friary**.

Activities

In season you'll see green-garbed waders heading for the River Moy in droves. This is one of the most prolific **salmon-fishing** rivers in Europe, and you can often see the scaly critters jumping in the Ridge (salmon pool), with otters and grey seals in pursuit.

A list of fisheries and permit contacts is available at the tourist office. The season is February to September, but the best fishing is June to August. Equipment is available from the tackle shops by the Ridge.

Lough Conn, southwest of Ballina, is an important brown-trout fishery, and there's no shortage of places with boats and *ghillies* (guides) round the lake. Pontoon is a good base for **trout fishing** in both Lough Conn and Lough Cullin.

Special Events

One of the best outdoor parties in the country, the town's annual knees-up is the **Ballina Street Festival** (☎ 79814; www.ballinastreetfestival .ie), which lasts for a full two weeks in early July. On Heritage Day, during the festival, shop fronts and townsfolk don 19th-century garb.

Sleeping

BUDGET

Suncroft (☎ 21573; suncroftbb@eircom.net; Cathedral Close; s/d €35/60; ℗) Smack in the town centre with a charming view of the cathedral's backside, this five-room house (four with en suite) is a very amiable place to bed down in.

Belleek Caravan & Camping Park (☎ 71533; lenahan@indigo.ie; Ballina; camp sites €15; ☽ mid-Mar–mid-Sep) This well-manicured, grassy site is a 1st-class choice for campers. You'll find it 2.5km from Ballina, 300m off the Killala road.

MIDRANGE & TOP END

Lismoyne House (☎ 70582; lismoynehouse@wattle web.com; Francis St; s/d €35/65; ☽ Mar-Nov) This genteel town house has such authentic old-world charm that it's surprising to find a young couple running it. It's favoured by fishermen, and has a quiet ambiance broken only by the tick-tock of the grandfather clock. It's a mere fly-fisherman's cast from both bus and train station.

Belleek Castle (☎ 22400; www.belleekcastle.com; s/d from €91/140; ☽ Apr-Dec; ℗) A fabulously over-the-top neo-Jacobean manor, set deep in woodland outside Ballina. Organic foodies will love the restaurant, romantics the four-poster beds, and amateur historians the armoury.

Eating

Dillon's Bar & Restaurant (☎ 72230; Dillon's Tce; mains €14-25; ☽ food served 3-9pm Mon-Thu, 12.30-9pm Fri-Sun) This pub-restaurant's vine-covered cobbled courtyard makes it everybody's favourite find. The menu exploits local produce, and the al fresco seating is a bonus in summer. Turn right at the south end of Pearse St and enter an arch to your left.

Murphy Bros (☎ 22702; Clare St; bar food €8-19, restaurant mains €10-20; ☽ 12.30-2.30pm & 5-9.30pm; ℗) Bigger and brasher than Dillon's, this excellent pub-restaurant is a short walk north of the tourist office. Its speciality is salmon – poached, grilled, baked or smoked. Nab a spot on the 1st-floor balcony for a romantic river view.

Drinking & Entertainment

Pub-crawlers will be kept busy in Ballina, which has some 60 watering holes to tick off. Many have traditional music sessions on Wednesday and Friday evenings.

Broken Jug/The Music Box (☎ 73097; O'Rahilly St) Enormous wooden doors lead into this cavernous pub, furbished with barrel-tables and plenty of private nooks. Friday and Saturday see its Music Box nightclub open for business.

An Bolg Buí (Yellow Belly; ☎ 22561; Tolan St) This well-worn, all-wood pub by the bridge is a great spot to savour a pint in peace. Except, that is, for Wednesdays when you can expect traditional music.

Getting There & Away

Bus Éireann runs services from the **bus station** (☎ 71800; Kevin Barry St) to Achill Island (€13.50, two to three hours, two daily), Sligo (€11.50, 1½ hours, five daily) and Dublin (€16, 3¾ hours, six daily).

Trains to Dublin (€28, 3¾ hours, three daily) leave from the **train station** (☎ 71818; Station Rd), at the southern extension of Kevin Barry St. Ballina is on a branch of the main Westport–Dublin line, so you'll have to change at Manulla Junction.

AROUND BALLINA
Rosserk Abbey

Dipping its toes into the River Rosserk, a tributary of the Moy, this handsome Franciscan abbey dates from the mid-15th century. There's an eye-catching double piscina (perforated stone basin) in the chancel: look for the exquisite carvings of a round tower and several angels. Rosserk was destroyed by Richard Bingham, the English governor of Connaught, in the 16th century.

Leave Ballina on the R314 for Killala and after 6.5km turn right at the sign and then left at the next crossroads. Continue for 1km, then turn right.

North Mayo Sculpture Trail

This trail of 15 outdoor sculptures essentially follows the R314 from Ballina to Blacksod Point. It was inspired by the discoveries at Céide Fields and was inaugurated in 1993 to mark 5000 years of Mayo history. Leading artists from eight different countries were commissioned to create sculptures reflecting the beauty and wilderness of the northern Mayo countryside.

The North Mayo Sculpture Trail (Tír Sáile) is a 60-page book detailing each sculpture. It's available from tourist offices and bookshops. The trail is about 90km and walkable.

CROSSMOLINA & AROUND

☎ 096 / pop 935

The unexceptional little town of Crossmolina (Crois Mhaoiliona), 13km west of Ballina, nuzzles the northern shores of **Lough Conn**. It's a quiet retreat for anyone looking to fish or attempt the two-hour climb up **Mt Nephin** (806m). There's a Bank of Ireland with an ATM opposite Hiney's pub.

Sights

It's a rough 800m scramble over farmland to reach the ruined **Errew Abbey**, but you'll be rewarded by the picturesque location cupped on three sides by mirror-like Lough Conn. The disintegrating remains include a 13th-century house for Augustinian monks built on the site of a 7th-century church.

Take the Castlebar road south, and 1km past the heritage centre turn left at the sign and keep going for 5km. The entrance is by a farm.

GETTING IN TOUCH WITH YOUR NAME

If your family name is Barrett, Brennan, Dogherty, Doyle, Foy, Gallagher, Harkin, Henry, Kelly, Lavelle, McNulty or McNicholas, there's a more than strong chance that your people originally hailed from north Mayo. You can get in touch with your roots at the **North Mayo Family History Research & Heritage Centre** (☎ 31809; Castlebar Rd; ☒ 9.30am-4pm Mon-Fri Apr-Sep; ℗), beginning with an initial assessment (€75). Attached is a piecemeal **museum** (adult/student museum €4/2, museum & garden €8/3; ☒ 10am-6pm Mon-Fri, 2-6pm Sat & Sun Apr-Sep) of old farm machinery and domestic implements. The tea room spills into walled gardens from Enniscoe House. There's also a resident blacksmith, who gives two-week courses in the trade. The centre is 3km south of Crossmolina towards Castlehill.

Sleeping & Eating

Enniscoe House (☎ 31112; www.enniscoe.com; Castle-hill; d €164-200; dinner €45; ☻ Apr-Oct; **P**)) Even the vines struggle to climb the enormous flanks of this magnificent 18th-century mansion. Its Victorian walled garden is only a tiny portion of the sprawling estate, which includes wild woodland walks and large grassy expanses.

Lake View House (☎ 31296; lakeviewhouse@oceanfree.net; Ballina Rd; s/d €40/56; ☻ Apr-Oct; **P**)) One of a string of B&Bs on the road from Ballina, this modern spot is 500m east of the town centre. It has six spick-and-span rooms, and boat hire for water-bound folk.

Hiney's (☎ 31202; Main St; meals around €9) A great old pub behind a modern thatched doorway, Hiney's serves gargantuan helpings of bar food all day.

Getting There & Away

There are regular **Bus Éireann** (☎ 71800) buses to Ballina and Castlebar. The bus stop is outside Hiney's.

CASTLEBAR & AROUND

☎ 094 / pop 10,290

Thriving Castlebar (Caisleán an Bharraigh's) is no great shakes in itself, but it draws a goodly number of visitors en route to nearby attractions.

The town's place in Irish history was cemented in 1798, when General Humbert's outnumbered army of French revolutionary soldiers and Irish peasants pulled off an astonishing victory. The ignominious cavalry retreat of the British became known as the Castlebar Races.

The attractive village green, known as the Mall, was once the Lucan family's cricket ground. Lord Lucan notoriously disappeared after the murder of his children's nanny in 1974, and hasn't been seen since.

Orientation & Information

The main thoroughfare changes its name from Ellison St to Main St to Thomas St as you head north. The Mall is to the east.

Allied Irish Bank (Main St) ATM and bureau de change.

Chat'rnet (☎ 903 8474; Linenhall St; per hr €3.60; ☻ 10.30am-10.30pm) Internet café opposite the tourist office.

Tourist office (☎ 902 1207; Linenhall St; ☻ 9.30am-1pm & 2-5.30pm May-Sep) West off the northern end of Main St.

Una's Laundrette (☎ 902 4100; New Antrim St) Round the corner from the tourist office.

Sights

NATIONAL MUSEUM OF COUNTRY LIFE

Before entering this enlightening **museum** (☎ 903 1755; www.museum.ie; Turlough Park, Turlough; admission free; ☻ 10am-5pm Tue-Sat, 2-5pm Sun; **P** &), take a guess how many uses Irish country-dwellers might once have had for straw. Quadruple that figure, and it's likely to still fall pitifully short of the truth. Visitors here are guaranteed to leave with a profound respect for the resourcefulness and cultural richness of agricultural Ireland. Indeed the museum, which opened in 2001, has won awards for the engaging way in which it explores the folk life and folklore of the Irish countryside from 1850 to 1950.

The extensive lakeside grounds invite picnics, and part of Turlough's 19th-century manor is open for snooping. Interesting demonstrations and workshops are organised for Wednesdays and Sundays – see the website for schedules.

The museum is signposted off the N5, 5km northeast of Castlebar.

TURLOUGH ROUND TOWER

The impenetrable 9th-century tower calls to mind the fairy story Rapunzel with its single lofty window. It stands on a hilltop by a ruined 18th-century church, a short distance northeast of the National Museum of Country Life.

MICHAEL DAVITT MEMORIAL MUSEUM

Housed in a pre-penal church where the man himself was christened and buried is this small but passionate **museum** (☎ 903 1022; Straide; adult/child €3.20/1.30; ☻ 10am-6pm Apr-Sep, 10am-5pm Oct-Mar; **P**) devoted to the life of Michael Davitt (1846–1906). He was a Fenian and zealous founding member of the Irish National Land League. Davitt's family was brutally evicted from his childhood home here.

Take the N5 east and turn left onto the N58 to Straide (Strade on some maps). It's 16km from Castlebar.

BALLINTUBBER ABBEY

The history of this delightful little **abbey** (☎ 903 0934; btuabbey@eircom.net; Ballintubber; admission free; ☻ 9am-midnight; **P**) reads like a collection of far-fetched folk tales. Commonly referred to as 'the abbey that refused to die', this is the only church in Ireland founded by an Irish king that is still in use. It was set up in 1216 next to the site of an earlier church founded by St Patrick after he came down from Croagh Patrick.

The abbey was burned by Normans, seized by James I and suppressed by Henry VIII. The nave roof was only restored in 1965 after the original was burned down by Cromwell's soldiers in 1653. Mass was outlawed and priests hunted down. Yet worship in the roofless remains continued against all the odds.

Take the N84 south towards Galway and after about 13km turn left at the Campus service station; the abbey is 2km along.

Sleeping & Eating

Imperial Hotel (☎ 902 1961; www.imperialhotel castlebar.com; the Mall; s/d Sun-Thu €65/110, Fri & Sat €75/130; mains €7-15) Established in 1795, Castlebar's oldest hotel still has a good dose of old-world character, reflected in its chequered floors and cosy old bar. Its spacious rooms, however, have been revamped to a wholly modern standard.

Rose Garden (☎ 902 1162; rosegdn@eircom.net; the Mall; s/d €38/60) This spick-and-span B&B is run by a friendly, house-proud family and it's conveniently close to the town centre.

Café Rua (☎ 902 3376; New Antrim St; mains €7-10; 9.30am-6pm Mon-Sat) This bright little coffee shop wins loyal support for its down-home menu of Irish dishes, including champ, made with mashed potatoes and onions. It does a mean breakfast too.

Getting There & Around

Bus Éireann (☎ 096-71800) travels to Westport (adult/child €4/2.65, 20 minutes, 10 daily), Dublin (€16/13, 4¾ hours, one daily) and Sligo (€14/9, 1½ hours, three daily). Services on Sunday are less frequent. Buses stop outside Flannelly's pub in Market St.

McNulty's Coaches (☎ 097-81086) runs a service from Castlebar to Belmullet at 5.30pm Monday to Wednesday and Friday). The 1¾-hour trip costs €9/13 one way/return.

The Westport–Dublin train stops at Castlebar (€28, 3¼ hours) three times daily. The station is just out of town on the N84 towards Ballinrobe.

KNOCK
☎ 094 / pop 595
Catholic Ireland's answer to Lourdes and Fatima was once a downtrodden rural village. However, that all changed in 1879. A divine apparition propelled this little settlement to become one of the world's most sacred Catholic shrines. Pilgrims come to Knock (Cnoc Mhuire) in ever-increasing numbers, but be warned: religion is big business here and the village is crammed with hawkers looking to cash in on the fervent, almost medieval piety of pilgrims.

The Knock Marian Shrine consists of several churches and shrines in the town centre. Nearby are clustered shops, restaurants and the **tourist office** (☎ 938 8193; 10am-6pm May-Sep). There's a **Bank of Ireland** (10.15am-12.15pm Mon & Thu May-Oct, Mon only rest of year) with an ATM.

Sights
CHURCH OF THE APPARITION
The story goes thus: in drenching rain during the evening of 21 August, two young Knock women were startled by a vision of Mary, Joseph and St John the Evangelist freeze-framed in dazzling white light against the southern gable of the parish church. They were soon joined by 13 more villagers, and together gazed at the heavenly apparition for hours as the daylight faded.

A Church investigation quickly confirmed it as a bona fide miracle, and a sudden rush of other Vatican-approved miracles followed as the sick and disabled claimed amazing recoveries upon visiting the spot. Today, dutiful worshippers are always found praying at the modern chapel enclosing the scene of the apparition. Seemingly floating above the altar are ethereal sculptures of the apparition, carved from snow-white marble. Near the church is the enormous spiky-topped **Basilica of Our Lady, Queen of Ireland**.

KNOCK FOLK MUSEUM
A short stroll from the basilica, this petite **museum** (☎ 938 8100; www.knock-shrine.ie; adult/ child/concession €4/3/3.50; 10am-6pm May-Oct, call ahead Nov-Apr) does its best to encapsulate the Knock phenomenon. It follows the story from the first witnesses, through the miraculous cures, the repeated Church investigations and finally to the visit of Pope John

Paul II on the event's centenary. One striking photograph shows rows of crutches left behind by miraculously cured pilgrims.

Sleeping

Pilgrims periodically swamp Knock, so there is no shortage of digs.

Aisling House (☎ 938 8558; Ballyhaunis Rd; s/d from €30/60; P) You'll be made to feel like a member of the family at this homey B&B, which offers spacious rooms with fussy décor about 500m east of town.

Belmont Hotel (☎ 938 8122; www.belmonthotel .ie; s/d €55/90; P ☐) A dignified old-world hotel with a conservative atmosphere, about 800m southeast of the shrine.

Knock Caravan & Camping Park (☎ 938 8100; fax 938 8295; Claremorris Rd; camp/caravan sites €10/17.50; ☺ Apr-Oct) This pocket-sized but well tended camping ground is only a five-minute walk uphill from the shrine, sheltered by woodland.

Getting There & Away

Knock Airport (☎ 936 7222; www.knockairport.com), 15km north of the N17, has daily flights to Dublin (Aer Arann), London Stansted (Ryanair), Gatwick (Easyjet and Ryanair), Manchester (BMI Baby) and Birmingham (BMI Baby and MyTravelLite). There are also five-weekly flights to Liverpool (Aer Arann). A €10 development fee is payable on departure.

Bus Éireann service No 21 connects Knock's town centre with Westport (€9, one hour), Castlebar (€7, 45 minutes), Athlone (€13, 1¾ hours) and Dublin (€16, four hours) three times daily (once Sunday).

Getting Around

A shuttle bus service is run by **Bus Éireann** (☎ 096-71800) to and from Knock airport and Charlestown (€4, 20 minutes), where connections can be made.

COUNTY SLIGO

Despite its pipsqueak size, County Sligo (Sligeach) packs as much poetry, myth and folklore into its lush landscape as you'd expect of a small country. This was the place that most inspired the Nobel laureate, poet and dramatist William Butler Yeats (1865–1939), whose mother was born

---

TOP FIVE PEEPS INTO PREHISTORY

- Creepy cairns of Carrowmore (p446)
- Groundbreaking archaeology at Céide Fields (p435)
- Vast monuments of Carrowkeel (p448)
- Legendary Queen Mab's Knocknarea Cairn (p446)
- Well-preserved Creevykeel Goort Cairn (p451)

---

into a well-to-do Sligo family. Much of his writing is infused with the county's wild landscapes, bitter history and rich folklore. And it's easy to see why. Here lie the largest number of prehistoric sites in Ireland, and some of the most impressive. And looming over the county are the unlikely twins of Knocknarea and Benbulben – two flat-topped mountains that look like something from *The Lost World*.

SLIGO TOWN

☎ 071 / pop 18,475

Self-confident Sligo is one of the liveliest and culturally active towns in the northwest. Its centre simmers with a lucky-dip of galleries, musical bars, cosmopolitan restaurants and untamed nightlife, all within a short saunter of the River Garavogue.

Information

Bank of Ireland (Stephen St) ATM and bureau de change.

Cafe Online (☎ 914 4892; 1 Calry Court, Stephen St; per hr €3.50; ☺ 10am-11pm Mon-Sat, noon-11pm Sun) It's possible to plug your laptop into the broadband connection here.

Cygo Internet Cafe (☎ 914 0082; 19 O'Connell St; per 15 min €1; ☺ 10am-9pm Mon-Fri, 10am-7pm Sat, 2-6pm Sun) At the back of the arch.

Keady Laundrette (☎ 916 9791; 3 Lower Pearse Rd; from €8; ☺ 9am-6pm Mon-Sat) Next-day laundry service.

Keohane's Bookshop (☎ 42597; Castle St) Stocks maps and books by and about Yeats.

North-West Regional Tourism office (☎ 916 1201; www.irelandnorthwest.ie; Temple St; ☺ 9am-6pm Mon-Fri, 10am-6pm Sat & Sun Jun-Sep, 9am-5pm Mon-Fri Oct-May) South of the centre.

Post office (Wine St)

Ulster Bank (Stephen St) ATM and bureau de change.

COUNTIES MAYO
& SLIGO

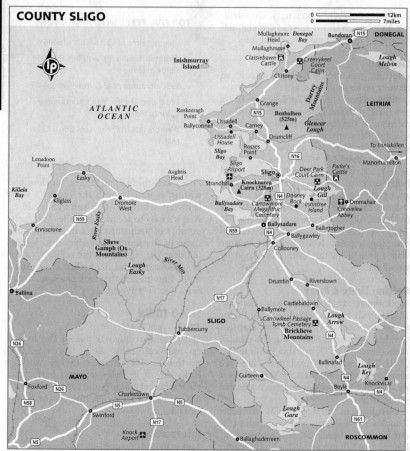

Sights

SLIGO COUNTY MUSEUM

The main appeal of this **museum** (☎ 914 1623; Stephen St; admission free; ⌚ 10.30am-12.30pm & 2.30-4.30pm Mon-Sat Jun-Sep, 2-5pm Tue-Sat Apr, May & Oct) is the Yeats room. There are photographs, letters and newspaper cuttings connected with the poet WB Yeats, and drawings by Jack B Yeats, his brother. The room across the hall contains a prison apron dress worn by Countess Constance Markievicz (see p450) after the 1916 Rising.

MODEL ARTS & NILAND GALLERY

In contrast to its imposing 19th-century facade, the interior of Sligo's excellent **gallery** (☎ 914 1405; www.modelart.ie; the Mall; admission free; ⌚ 10am-5.30pm Tue-Sat, 11am-4pm Sun; ♿) is pleasantly airy and contemporary. The wide-ranging collection includes works by Charles Lamb and Sean Keating as well as Jack B Yeats, one of Ireland's most important modern artists (who said he never painted anything without putting a thought of Sligo into it). The gallery also hosts a rich schedule of travelling exhibitions, readings, film and music events.

SLIGO ABBEY

The handsome husk that is Sligo's **abbey** (☎ 914 6406; Abbey St; adult/child €2/1.25; ⌚ 10am-6pm mid-Mar–Oct, 9.30am-4.30pm Fri-Sun Nov–mid-Mar) has enjoyed the best and worst of luck. It was first built by the town's founder, Maurice

FitzGerald, around 1252 for the Dominicans, but it burned down in the 15th century and was rebuilt. Friends in high places then saved the abbey from the worst ravages of the Elizabethan era, and rescued the only sculpted altar to survive the Reformation. However, the abbey's fortunes reversed when it was put to the torch in 1641, and subsequently raided for stone. The doorways reach only a few feet high at the abbey's rear: mass graves from years of famine and war swelled the ground-level here.

COURTHOUSE
The extravagant Gothic architecture of the courthouse sticks out like a sore thumb on Teeling St. Modelled on the Law Courts in London, it's a palpable reminder of the other power that once ruled this land.

YEATS BUILDING
On the corner of Lower Knox and O'Connell Sts, near Hyde Bridge, the Yeats Building hosts the annual **Yeats International Summer School** (☎ 914 2693; www.yeats-sligo.com), a two-week gathering of scholars in August. The rest of the year it houses the hit-and-miss **Sligo Art Gallery** (☎ 914 5847; Lower Knox St; admission free; ☑ 10am-5pm Mon-Sat), with travelling exhibitions.

Across the bridge, there's a **statue** of the poet himself, wrapped in his words.

Sleeping
BUDGET
Eden Hill Holiday Hostel (☎ 914 3204; edenhill@eircom.net; Pearse Rd; camp sites per person €8, dm €12-14, d €32-36; **P**) Sharing honours as best hostel in Sligo, this converted Victorian home is run by a Christian society and has a bubbly atmosphere, spotless dorms and an enormous communal kitchen. It's 1.5km from the station, but pick up may be arranged.

Harbour House (☎ 917 1547; www.harbourhouse.com; Finisklin Rd; dm €18, s/d €25/40) If you prefer mod-cons to quirkiness, then you'll be more than happy with this excellent, well-equipped IHH hostel less than 1km northwest of the centre. It offers a little budget luxury, in the form of colourful en-suite rooms each with private TV.

White House Hostel (☎ 914 5160; fax 914 4456; Markievicz Rd; dm €14; **P**) To stay closer to the action and mingle with more fellow hos-

tellers, you could try this laid-back central spot. It has 43 beds in a faded, unexciting house by the river.

MIDRANGE
B&Bs line the various approach roads into Sligo town.

Pearse Lodge (☎ 916 1090; pearselodge@eircom.net; Pearse Rd; s €38-45, d €60; **P**) A delightfully warm, youthful and well groomed B&B, with six cheerful rooms, a garden and a terrific breakfast menu including smoked salmon, pancakes and vegetarian options. Good family choice.

St Ann's (☎ 914 3188; Pearse Rd; d €66; **P** 🐾) With an al-fresco swimming pool (unheated), neatly snipped topiary and frilly feminine rooms, this well maintained B&B comes highly recommended.

Lissadell (☎ 916 1937; Mail Coach Rd; s/d €45/68; **P**) This immaculate B&B has welcoming but unobtrusive owners, and is a 10-minute walk southeast of town on the N16 Dublin road. Its breakfast menu is refreshingly high in vitamins, and low in grease.

Clarence Hotel (☎ 914 2211; clarencehotel@eircom.net; Wine St; s/d €63/126; **P**) This small grey-stone hotel is one of Sligo's best in its price range and one of scant central options. It was closed for renovation at time of writing. Call ahead.

TOP END
Southern Hotel (☎ 916 2101; www.sligosouthernhotel.com; Strandhill Rd; s/d €97/150; **P** 🖳 ♿) The courtly gardens of this elegant hotel border the bus and train stations. Its boldly coloured interior manages to combine superb facilities (including swimming pool, plasma TV and broadband Internet access) with comfortable charm.

Eating
Coach Lane (☎ 916 2417; Donaghy's Pub, 1-2 Lord Edward St; mains €14-28; ☑ 5.30-11pm) Top-class Irish and international cuisine is available at this slinky restaurant over a pub. The seafood includes juicy Lissadell clams and mussels, and there are some intriguing wild-card specials. Roast Tipperary ostrich anyone?

Garavogue/Cafe Bar Deli (☎ 914 0100; 15-16 Stephen St; bar food €8-9, restaurant mains €9-14; ☑ lunch noon-3pm, bar food 3-6pm, restaurant 6-11pm) Tables fill a well-lit atrium in Cafe Bar Deli,

SLIGO

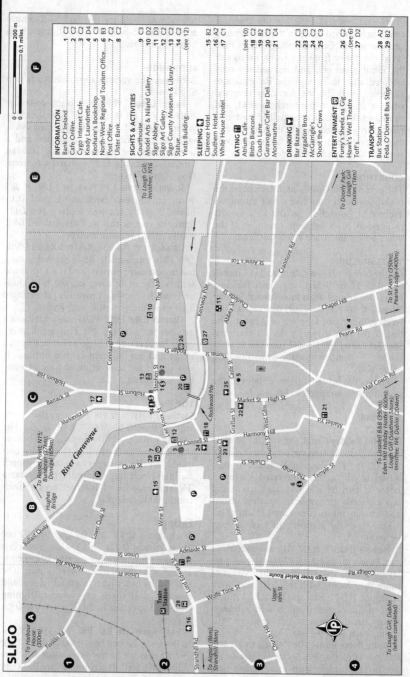

INFORMATION	
Bank Of Ireland	1 C2
Cafe Online	2 C2
Cygo Internet Cafe	3 C2
Keady Laundrette	4 D4
Keohane's Bookshop	5 C3
North-West Regional Tourism Office	6 B3
Post Office	7 C2
Ulster Bank	8 C2

SIGHTS & ACTIVITIES	
Courthouse	9 C3
Model Arts & Niland Gallery	10 D2
Sligo Abbey	11 D3
Sligo Art Gallery	12 C2
Sligo County Museum & Library	13 C2
Statue	14 C2
Yeats Building	(see 12)

SLEEPING	
Clarence Hotel	15 B2
Southern Hotel	16 A2
White House Hostel	17 C1

EATING	
Atrium Cafe	(see 10)
Bistro Bianconi	18 C2
Coach Lane	19 B2
Garavogue/Cafe Bar Deli	20 C2
Montmartre	21 C4

DRINKING	
Bar Bazaar	22 C3
Hargadon Bros	23 C2
McGarrigle's	24 C3
Shoot the Crows	25 C3

ENTERTAINMENT	
Furey's Sheela na Gig	26 C2
Hawk's Well Theatre	(see 6)
Toff's	27 D2

TRANSPORT	
Bus Station	28 A2
Feda O'Donnell Bus Stop	29 B2

above popular bar Garavogue. And if you don't fancy the pasta-and-pizza menu here, the bar below serves gourmet pub grub. There is also riverside seating for fair-weather days.

Bistro Bianconi (☎ 914 1744; 44 O'Connell St; mains €12-18; ☽ 12.30-2.30pm & 5.30-10pm Mon-Sat) It's hard to resist the delicious aromas wafting from this bustling Italian bistro. It has three-dozen varieties of pizza alone, not to mention pasta and risotto. The open kitchen lets guests see the chefs in action.

Montmartre (☎ 916 9901; Market Yard; mains €14-25; ☽ 5-11pm Tue-Sun) This sleek little French restaurant oozes Gallic panache, and cooks up some truly exquisite dishes including some vegetarian options. With pristine table linen, suited waiters and elegant stemware, this is the place to best impress.

Atrium Cafe (☎ 914 1405; Model Arts & Niland Gallery; sandwiches & snacks €4-8; ☽ 10am-4pm Tue-Sat, 11am-3pm Sun) To enjoy a healthy bite while hob-nobbing with the Sligo art set, head to this gourmet gallery café.

Drinking

Sligo enjoys some of the best night-time fun in Ireland's northwest, with impromptu sessions striking up at every opportunity, although the town also has a reputation for late-night wildness.

Bar Bazaar (☎ 914 4749; 34 Market St; ☽ 10am-6pm Mon-Sat) County Sligo's best spot for a caffeine fix, this cosmopolitan little coffee shop offers everything from organic black tea to barleycup lattes, and sinful Irish-cream milkshakes.

Shoot the Crows (☎ 916 2554; www.shootthe crows.ie; Castle St) Painted with enigmatic murals and dotted with skulls, this long, dimly lit bar attracts a young, arty clientele and has traditional music sing-alongs on Tuesdays and Thursdays.

Hargadon Bros (☎ 917 0933; 4 O'Connell St) This battered old bar could bottle and sell nostalgia, which it has by the bucket-load. Its dark wood interior is like a stage set, with 19th-century bar fixtures, snugs, nooks and crannies inviting conspiracy. There's music on Thursdays but otherwise this is a talkers' and dreamers' pub.

McGarrigle's (☎ 917 1193; O'Connell St) Cavernous McGarrigle's has dimly lit snugs downstairs, and an alternative-music bar upstairs. You'd think the bar was in imminent danger of falling given the faithful punters that always seem to be propping it up.

Garavogue (☎ 914 0100; 15-16 Stephen St; admission after 11pm €5) Garavogue's low-slung sofas, cube stools and hula-hoop bar make it one of Sligo's trendiest haunts. It's also one of Sligo's gay-friendly joints, and there's often live jazz.

Entertainment

Furey's Sheela na Gig (☎ 914 3825; Bridge St) Named after a Gaelic fertility symbol of a naked woman, this old-style bar is Irish traditional band Dervish's local watering hole, and has superb traditional music most nights.

Hawk's Well Theatre (☎ 61526; www.hawkswell .com; Temple St) This well-regarded theatre presents a varied programme of concerts, dance and drama.

Toff's (☎ 916 1250; Kennedy Pde; admission €7-10; ☽ 11pm-4am Thu-Sun) One of several slick nightclubs that shimmy with youthful energy, getting increasingly wild as the night wears on. The riverside boulevard often takes the overflow.

Getting There & Away

AIR

From **Sligo Airport** (☎ 916 8280; www.sligoairport .com; Strandhill Rd) there are direct Aer Arann flights to Dublin twice daily from €30 (40 minutes).

BUS

Bus Éireann (☎ 916 0066) leaves from the terminal below the train station, on Lord Edward St. Destinations include Ballina (adult/child €11.50/7.50, 1½ hours, five daily), Castlebar (€14/9, 1½ hours, three daily), Dublin (€16/10, four hours, four daily) and Westport (€15/10, two hours, twice daily). Services are less frequent on Sunday.

Feda O'Donnell (☎ 074-954 8114) operates a service between Crolly (County Donegal) and Galway via Donegal town and Sligo town twice daily (three times Friday). The buses leave by Lyon's on the corner of Wine and Quay Sts.

TRAIN

Trains leave the **station** (☎ 916 9888) for Dublin (€24, 3¼ hours, three daily) via Boyle, Carrick-on-Shannon and Mullingar.

Getting Around

Local buses run to Strandhill (€2.50, five to seven daily) and sometimes continue to the airport if you ask nicely, while a taxi costs about €14. **Feehily's Taxis** (☎ 914 3000) and **Elliot's Taxi** (☎ 914 1111) offer a 24-hour service.

AROUND SLIGO TOWN
Rosses Point

☎ 071 / pop 774

This long, foot-shaped headland was the scene of a bloody battle between two Irish warlords in 1257. Rosses Point (An Ros) is now a picturesque seaside resort with a lovely Blue Flag beach.

ACTIVITIES

Established in 1894, **County Sligo Golf Course** (☎ 917 7134; www.countysligogolfclub.ie; Rosses Point) is still one of Ireland's most challenging and renowned links courses, attracting golfers from all over Europe. Its position on the peninsula is simply stunning. Green fees are from €68 Monday to Friday and €83 Saturday and Sunday; less in the winter.

SLEEPING & EATING

Oyster View (☎ 917 7201; s/d €50/70) This faded B&B on the waterfront is a favourite with golfers, so book ahead. It's a short walk from the point, and bear several restaurants.

Yeats Country Hotel (☎ 917 7211; www.yeats countryhotel.com; s/d €75/130; P) Commanding prime position at point's end, this dignified three-star hotel mostly attracts golfers and families. It has large rooms, sea views and a leisure centre with swimming pool.

Greenlands Caravan & Camping Park (☎ 917 7113; noelineha@eircom.net; camp sites €10; ☼ Easter–mid-Sep) Peering over the Atlantic from the point's extreme, this site manages to feel isolated despite its proximity to local amenities. It borders the golf course (mind your heads!) and has easy access to two safe beaches.

Waterfront (☎ 917 7122; mains €11-22; ☼ 5-10pm) This aptly named pub-restaurant faces the estuary and Oyster Island. It cooks up excellent Irish and European dishes, including vegetarian, but it is the fresh seafood platters that are really worth writing home about.

Carrowmore Megalithic Cemetery

The largest Stone Age cemetery in Ireland and the second-biggest in Europe, **Carrow-**

more (☎ 916 1534; adult/child/concession €2/1/1.25; ☼ 10am-6pm Easter-Sep; P) impresses for its variety as well as its scale. Everywhere you look the gently rolling hills are beaded with stone circles, passage tombs and dolmens.

Attempts to date the site have had both diverse and divisive results. The conventional wisdom is that the site pre-dates Newgrange in County Meath by some 700 years, however one study astonished everybody by suggesting the oldest tomb was built around 5400 BC. Over the years, many of the stones have been destroyed, and several remaining stones are on private land.

The delicately balanced dolmens were originally covered with stones and earth, so it requires some effort to picture what this 2.5km-wide area might once have looked like. To help (or some would say hinder) the imagination, the Dúchas-operated site has launched a decapitated reconstruction of one cairn, caged by wire and sliced open by a gaping entrance. An exhibit in the roadside visitor centre gives the full lowdown on this fascinating site.

To get there, leave town by Church Hill and continue south for 5km; the route is clearly signposted.

Knocknarea Cairn

It's easy to see why this eye-catching cairn grave, 2km northwest of Carrowmore, is so deeply mired in myth. Perched high atop its limestone plateau (328m), the enormous stone heap seems to be looking over your shoulder everywhere you dare tread in its ancestral backyard.

Around 1000 years younger than Carrowmore, the cairn is popularly believed to be the grave of legendary Queen Maeve (Queen Mab in Welsh and English folk tales). The 40,000 tonnes of stone have never been excavated, despite speculation that a tomb on the scale of the one at Newgrange lies buried below.

Leave Sligo as though for Carrowmore, then follow signs to Knocknarea. Or from Carrowmore, continue down the road, turn right by a church then follow signs. From the car park it's a 45-minute walk to the summit and views to knock your socks off.

Deer Park Court Cairn

Just a 10-minute walk from the car park through pine-scented forest leads to this enigmatic court tomb (also called Maghera-ghanrush). Dating from around 3000 BC, the crumbling structure is comparable to a crude human form, with a large belly-like central court and several protruding burial chambers positioned as though the head and legs.

Take the N16 east from Sligo and turn onto the R286 for Parke's Castle. Almost immediately, turn left at the Y-junction onto a minor road for Manorhamilton. Continue for 3km to the car park, then follow the trail for 50m before veering right up a small hill.

Strandhill

☎ 071 / pop 1000

The great Atlantic rollers that sweep into the long red-gold beach by Strandhill (An Leathras), 8km west of Sligo off the R292 airport road, have made it a **surfing** mecca of international renown. Its handy 24-hour surfcam (www.strandhillsurfcam .com) brings enthusiasts scurrying whenever the surf's good. Enquire at **Perfect Day Surf Shop** (☎ 087-202 9399; www.perfectdaysurfing .com) for gear and lessons.

There's also a **golf course** (☎ 916 8188; www .strandhillgc.com) and some **seaweed baths** (☎ 916 8686; Shore Rd; s/tw bath €18/22; ⏲ 11am-8pm) for lovers of dry land. A few kilometres towards Sligo, there is a point from which, at low tide, you can walk to **Coney Island**: its New York namesake was supposedly named by a man from Rosses Point.

Strandhill Lodge & Hostel (☎ 916 8313; Shore Rd; dm/d €15/30; P) is a cheerful budget haunt, the place to mingle with kindred surfing spirits. It has 33 beds distributed between dorms of different sizes, plus a self-catering kitchen and a few twins.

Ocean View Hotel (☎ 916 8115; www.ovhotel .com; Main St; s/d €93/136; ⏲ Mar-Nov; P) is a courteous little mock-Tudor hotel on the main road, in the shadow of Knocknarea's limestone plateau. The modern rooms are exquisitely kept and there's a good restaurant. Prices drop outside July to August.

Strandhill Caravan & Camping Park (☎ 916 8111; fax 916 8396; camp sites €12; ⏲ mid-Apr–Sep) is ideally positioned by the long beach, separated only by grassy dunes. This large flat camp site has 100 sites and good facilities.

Strand House Bar (☎ 916 8140; Shore Rd), aside from being a terrific pub, is a great place to

glean the surfing low-down, as it is run by three Irish champions. There's a seafood restaurant above.

Getting There & Away

Bus Éireann (☎ 916 0066) buses run from Sligo to Strandhill and Rosses Point (€2.50, five to seven daily), but there's no public transport to other places of interest in the area. While it's possible to walk to Carrowmore and Knocknarea from town, it's a long day's return trek.

SOUTH OF SLIGO TOWN

Collooney

☎ 071 / pop 620

But for an extravagant castle and boyish monument to war hero Bartholomew Teeling, Collooney (Cúil Mhuine) is an unremarkable village. The mossy **monument**, at the village's northern end, commemorates Teeling's single-handed charge against an English gunner, winning Humbert's French-Irish army passage to Longford. Sadly his efforts were ill-rewarded as the army was soon defeated, and 500 Irishmen, including Teeling, ruthlessly executed.

The county's oldest inhabited castle, **Markree Castle** (☎ 916 7800; markree@iol.ie; Collooney; s/d €99/165; dinner €38.50; P ⏲) is now a three-star hotel near the village, signposted from the roundabout. It's topped by showy battlements, more for fancy than fortification, and a whimsical Gothic façade. The castle has remained in the Cooper family since Cromwell's time, hosting such figures as Charles Kingsley and WB Yeats. It's said that Mrs Alexander wrote the hymn 'All Things Bright and Beautiful' after her stay here.

Ballymote

☎ 071 / pop 980

This pretty little town merits a visit if only to see the immense ivy-covered shell of **Ballymote Castle** (Tubbercurry road). It was from this early-14th-century castle, fronted by formidable drum towers, that O'Donnell marched to disaster at the Battle of Kinsale in 1601.

In a remote spot 3km northwest of Ballymote, the **Irish Raptor Research Centre** (☎ 918 9310; www.eaglesflying.com; Portinch, Ballymote; adult/ child/student €7/4/6; ⏲ Apr-Oct; P) is the country's largest sanctuary for birds of prey, home to everything from lightning-fast falcons to canny vultures. The team puts on 45-minute flying displays at 11am and 3pm.

Temple House (☎ 918 3329; www.templehouse.ie; Ballymote; s/d €85/170; dinner €35; ⊗ Apr-Nov; **P**), a glorious Georgian mansion, offers luxury digs amid a 1000-acre estate, freckled white with sheep, graced by a glassy lake and home to a 13th-century Knights Templar castle. The house is packed with period décor, dusty natural-history collections and decapitated hunting trophies. It's 4km northwest of Ballymote, close to the N17.

Mill House (☎ 918 3449; Ballymote; s/d €35/60; **P**) in the town centre is an attentive B&B with a tennis court, beautiful gardens and exceptional breakfasts.

Carrowkeel Passage Tomb Cemetery

With a God's-eye view of the county from high in the Bricklieve Mountains, there's little wonder why this hill-top site was sacred in prehistoric times. The windswept location is simultaneously uplifting and downright eerie, dotted with around 14 cairns, dolmens and the scattered remnants of other graves. It's possible to squeeze into at least one limestone chamber, although bigger folk are liable to get stuck. The place has been dated to the late Stone Age (3000 to 2000 BC).

West off the N4 road, Carrowkeel is closer to Boyle than Sligo town. If coming from the latter, turn right in Castlebaldwin, then left at the fork. The site is 2km uphill from the gateway. You can take an Athlone bus from Sligo and ask to dismount at Castlebaldwin.

Coopershill House (☎ 071-916 5108; www.coopers hill.com; Riverstown; d €202; 5-course dinner from €45; ⊗ Apr-Oct; **P**) is a grey-stone mansion that seems to exist in a world of its own, an idyllic Georgian retreat in an estate speckled by wildflowers, alive with birdsong and home to a deer farm. Most of the eight bedrooms have lovely canopy beds. Riverstown, close to Carrowkeel, is halfway between Sligo and Boyle.

Tubbercurry

☎ 071 / pop 1170

Sleepy Tubbercurry (Tobar an Choire), also spelled Tobercurry, is shaken awake in mid-July, when the week-long **South Sligo Summer School** (☎ 912 0912; www.sssschool .org) celebrates Irish music and dance with infectious gusto. Try your hand at anything from the tin whistle to an Irish jig, or simply enjoy the eruption of local concerts and recitals.

Easky & Enniscrone

☎ 096 / pop 880

Easky (Eascaigh) has scant remains of a 15th-century castle, but most visitors come for the year-round surfing. For details contact the **Easky Surfing & Information Centre** (Irish Surfing Association; ☎ /fax 49428; www.isasurf.ie) on the main street.

Further west at Enniscrone (Innis Crabhann), a stunning Blue Flag **beach** known as the Hollow stretches its sandy arm for 5km.

SLEEPING

Atlantic Caravan & Camping Park (☎ 36132; atlanticcaravanpk@eircom.net; Enniscrone; camp sites

---

SOMETHING SPECIAL

Sinking into a sea-water bath and slathering yourself with seaweed may sound like madness. And, granted, you'll look and feel much like a sea-monster crossed with a merperson. But for the enlightened, a trip to **Kilcullen Seaweed Baths** (☎ 36238; bathhouse@eircom.net; Enniscrone; bath s/tw €17/30, massage €25; ⊗ 10am-9pm May-Oct, noon-8pm Mon-Fri, 10am-8pm Sat & Sun Nov-Apr) is the last word in luxury. Seaweed baths have been part of Irish homeopathy for centuries and are considered a cure for rheumatism and arthritis, even hangovers. Although some claims are unproven, one thing's for sure – a single session wallowing in the soupy waters will leave your skin feeling baby-soft. Seaweed's silky oils contain a massive concentration of iodine, a key presence in most moisturising creams.

Several seaweed baths have recently reappeared on the west coast, notably at Strandhill and Bundoran. However, the Edwardian baths at Kilcullen beat them hands down for character: here you'll find the original gigantean porcelain baths, stout brass taps and coffin-like steam baths to enhance the already surreal experience.

from €10; ☯ Mar-Sep) This sandy little two-star camping ground is wonderfully located next to the Hollow beach.

Getting There & Away
Bus Éireann's (☎ 071-916 0066) express No 23 to Sligo from Dublin (€16, 3¾ hours) and No 64 between Galway (€13, 2¼ hours) and Derry (€18, three hours) stop outside Quigley's in Collooney. The Saturday only, Sligo–Castlerea bus No 460 stops at Collooney (€3, 15 minutes), Ballymote (€5, 30 minutes) and Tubbercurry (€7, 40 minutes). Local buses run from Sligo to Collooney, Monday to Saturday. From Easky and Enniscrone, buses run four times daily (once on Sunday) to Sligo (€8/9, 50/65 minutes) and Ballina (€5/2.50, 30/15 minutes).

The Sligo train stops at Collooney and Ballymote en route to Dublin (both €24, three times daily, four Friday). Call **Sligo station** (☎ 071-916 9888) for times.

LOUGH GILL
The mirror-like 'Lake of Brightness', Lough Gill is home to as many legends as fish; one that can be tested easily is the story that a silver bell from the abbey in Sligo was thrown into the lough and only those free from sin can hear it pealing. No, you didn't hear it (but neither did we!). A return trip of 48km takes in most of this lough southeast of Sligo as well as Parke's Castle, which, though in County Leitrim, is included here.

Dooney Rock
This huge limestone knoll bulges awkwardly upward by the lough's southern shore. Yeats immortalises it in *The Fiddler of Dooney*. There's a good lake view from the top, and tranquil woodland walks below its fissured flanks.

Leave Sligo south on the N4, but turn left at the sign to Lough Gill. Another left at the T-junction brings you onto the R287 towards Dooney car park.

Innisfree Island
This pint-sized island (Inis Fraoigh) lies tantalisingly close to the lough's southeastern shore. Its air of tranquillity so moved Yeats that he famously wrote *The Lake Isle of Innisfree*:

I will arise and go now, and go to Innisfree,
And a small cabin build there, of clay and wattles made;
Nine bean rows will I have there, a hive for the honey bee,
And live alone in the bee-loud glade.

Continue east from Dooney Rock and turn left at the crossroads. After 3km turn left again for another 3km. A small road leads down to the lake.

Creevelea Abbey (County Leitrim)
A short riverside walk from Dromahair village leads to the ruinous remains of this unfortunate Franciscan friary. A monument to bad timing, the abbey was founded just a few decades before the orders were suppressed in 1539. Yet, despite being gutted by fire on several occasions, desecrated by Richard Bingham and later Cromwell, the hardy monks kept coming back. The cloister has some curious carvings of St Francis, one displaying stigmata and another preaching to birds.

From Innisfree, return to the R287 and follow signs to Dromahair and the abbey.

Parke's Castle (County Leitrim)
The tranquil surrounds of **Parke's Castle** (☎ 071-916 4149; Fivemile Bourne; adult/concession €2.75/1.25; ☯ 10am-6pm mid-Mar–Oct; **P**), with swans drifting by on Lough Gill and neat grass cloaking the old moat, belies the fact that its early Plantation architecture was created out of an unwelcome English landlord's insecurity and fear.

The thoroughly restored, three-storey castle forms part of one of the five sides of the bawn, which also has three rounded turrets at its corners. Join one of the entertaining guided tours after viewing the 20-minute video.

From Creevelea Abbey, continue east along the R287, turn left towards Dromahair and continue northwards. To return to Sligo from Parke's Castle turn west onto the R286.

Getting There & Away
BOAT
The **Rose of Innisfree** (☎ 071-916 4266, 087-259 8869; adult/child €12/6) offers live recitals of Yeats' poetry accompanying music during

1½-hour cruises on Lough Gill that run from Parke's Castle at 12.30pm, 1.30pm, 3.30pm, 4.30pm and 6.30pm, July and August. It also runs cruises in April, May, June, September and October, but you'll need to call ahead for the schedule.

CAR & BICYCLE
Leave Sligo east via the Mall past the hospital, then turn right off the N16 onto the R286, which leads to the northern shore of Lough Gill and round to Innisfree. The southern route is less interesting until you reach Dooney Rock.

NORTH OF SLIGO TOWN
Drumcliff & Benbulben
One of the most recognisable hills in Ireland, the limestone plateau of Benbulben (525m) thrusts flatly upwards like a giant upturned bathtub, 7km north of Sligo. The most westerly of the Dartry Mountains, its high plateau is astonishingly flat and its near-vertical sides are scored by vein-like rivulets that give it an almost wizened look.

Its rare beauty was not lost on WB Yeats. Even in death, it seems the poet had an eye for inspirational locations. Though Yeats died in 1939 in Menton, France, he had requested: 'If I die here, bury me up there on the mountain, and then after a year or so, dig me up and bring me privately to Sligo'. True to his wishes, although later than planned in 1948, his body was interred in the churchyard at Drumcliff, where his great-grandfather had been rector.

Yeats' grave is next to the Protestant church's doorway, and his youthful bride Georgie Hyde-Lee is buried alongside. Almost three decades her senior, Yeats was 52 when they married. The poet's epitaph is from his poem *Under Ben Bulben*:

Cast a cold eye
On life, on death.
Horseman, pass by!

In the 6th century, St Colmcille chose the same location for a monastery. You can still see the stumpy remains of the **round tower**, which was struck by lightning in 1936, on the main road nearby. Also in the churchyard is an extraordinary 11th-century **high cross**, etched with intricate biblical scenes.

EXTREME COPYRIGHT

We might take plagiarism seriously these days, but we ain't got nothing on the early Irish church. What might incur a hefty fine and slap on the wrist in the modern day cost the lives of 3000 men in battle in the year AD 561. The aptly named 'Battle of the Book' took place in Cooldrumman, near Drumcliff, after St Colmcille (or Columba) provoked rage by copying rare religious manuscripts. The matter initially went to the local king to settle, who famously declared 'to every cow its calf, to every book its copy', siding against St Colmcille. But the matter persisted, and the battle commenced. It's said that the ensuing loss of life drove St Colmcille to devote himself to saving as many souls as had been lost in the bloody battle. Thus he founded the Drumcliff monastery and set about spreading Christianity far and wide.

In summer, the **church** projects a 15-minute audiovisual on Yeats, St Colmcille and Drumcliff. There's also a little tea shop in which to browse books, pick up local ceramics and peruse novelty shamrock badges.

Glencar Lough
As well as **fishing**, the attraction of this lake is the beautiful **waterfall** signposted from all directions. Yeats refers to this picturesque spot in *The Stolen Child*. The surrounding countryside is best enjoyed by walking east and taking the steep trail north to the valley. From Drumcliff it's less than 5km to the lake, and there's a **Bus Éireann** (☎ 071-60060) service from Sligo. Call for details.

Lissadell House
Pretty it is not. However, don't let the grim, slab-like, exterior of **Lissadell House** (☎ 087-629 6928; www.lissadellhouse.com; Drumcliff; adult/child €6/3; ⏰ 11am-6pm May-Sep; 🅿) put you off or you'll miss out on a fascinating peek into the life of one of Ireland's most colourful families.

The house itself was built by Sir Robert Gore-Booth back in 1830, when Greek Revival style was in vogue. The interior has all the pomp missing from the bunker-like exterior. However, the family itself is remembered more for its activism than for its affluence.

Sir Robert took to calling himself 'Count Markiewicz', an affectation that passed onto his famous granddaughter Constance Gore-Booth (1868–1927). She was a committed activist for Irish independence, and earned a death sentence (later commuted) for her part in the Easter Rising. In 1918 she became the first woman elected to the British House of Commons but – like most Irish rebels – refused to take her seat.

Her sister Eva was just as fiery a character, an ardent suffragette and poet. The sisters' friendship with WB Yeats was commemorated by him in the poem *In Memory of Eva Gore-Booth and Con Markievicz*.

The light of evening, Lissadell,
Great windows, open to the south,
Two girls in silk kimonos, both
Beautiful, one a gazelle.

The 45-minute guided tour is filled with stories of the family's adventures, quirks and peccadillos. The murals of domestic servants standing alongside family members in the dining hall are just one illustration of how they liked to thumb their noses at convention.

Lissadell was sold in 2003, along with much of its finery, but happily fell to a couple for whom its restoration is a labour of love.

To get there, follow the N15 north from Sligo and turn west at Drumcliff, just past Yeats Tavern.

Streedagh

From the village of Grange, signs point towards Streedagh Beach, a grand crescent of sand that saw some 1100 sailors perish when three ships from the Spanish Armada were wrecked nearby. Swimming is dangerous, but the beach is ideal for horse riding. **Island View Stables** (☎ 916 6156; islandview@ eircom.net; Grange) charges €15 per hour.

Mullaghmore

The delightful **beach** at Mullaghmore (An Mullach Mór) is a sweeping arc of dark-golden sand and shallow waters, wide and safe. Mind you, it wasn't so safe for poor old Lord Mountbatten. It was in this bay that the IRA rigged his boat with explosives and assassinated him in 1979.

The road loops around Mullaghmore Head, where wide shafts of rock slice into the Atlantic surf. It also passes the rather smug-looking **Classiebawn Castle** (closed to the public) a neo-Gothic turreted pile built for Lord Palmerston in 1856 and later home to the ill-fated Lord Mountbatten.

Creevykeel Goort Cairn

Shaped like a lobster's claw, this intriguing prehistoric **court tomb** (admission free; ☉ dawn-dusk) encloses several burial chambers. The structure was originally constructed around 2500 BC, with several more chambers added later. Once in the unroofed oval court, smaller visitors can duck under the stone-shielded entrance to reach the site's core. You'll find the tomb north of Cliffony on the N15.

WORTH THE TRIP

If access was easier to arrange, a visit to **Inishmurray Island** would be a must. Early-Christian remains sit cheek-by-jowl with fascinating pagan relics on this uninhabited isle. There are three well-preserved **churches**, Christmas pudding–shaped **beehive cells** and **open-air altars**. The old monastery is surrounded by a thickset oval wall. It was founded in the early 6th century by St Molaise, and his wooden statue once stood in the main church, but is now in the National Museum in Dublin.

The pagan relics were also assembled by Inishmurray monks. There's a collection of cursing stones: those who wanted to lay a curse did the Stations of the Cross in reverse, turning the stones as they went. There were also separate burial grounds for men and women, and a strong belief that if a body was placed in the wrong ground it would move itself during the night.

Only 6km separates Inishmurray from the mainland, but there's no regular boat service, and the lack of a harbour makes landing subject to the weather. Excursions can be arranged for €25 to €30 return with **Lomax Boats** (☎ 071-916 6124; Mullaghmore) or **Joe McGowan** (☎ 071-916 6267; Streedagh Point) in July and August. Trips can also be arranged throughout the spring and autumn, but get a group together as you'll be asked to cough up a collective €300 for the boat hire.

Sleeping & Eating

Serenity B&B (☎ 071-914 3351; Doonierin; d €70; **P**)
If you like peace, quiet and sigh-inducing
views you'll have few quibbles with this
homy B&B, 1km southwest of Yeats' grave.
It enjoys a delicious vantage point from
which to watch the changing moods of
Benbulben and Drumcliff Bay.

Benwiskin Centre (☎ 071-917 6721; www.ben
wiskincentre.com; Ballintrillick; dm/f €15/50; **P** &)
Located in the nether reaches of the county,
4km east of Cliffony, this superb hostel-
cum-community-centre justifies the effort
of reaching it with impeccable en-suite
dorms, a leafy garden and warmly coloured
décor. Book ahead in summer. Take the lane
by Creevykeel and follow signs.

Celtic Farm Hostel (☎ 071-916 3337; Derry Rd,
Grange; dm/d €13/30; **P**) With more of a personal touch than Benwiskin, this cosy 12-
bed IHH hostel is run by an affable host
in attractive countryside about 1km north
of Grange.

Benbulben Farm (☎ 071-916 3211; hennigan@
eircom.net; Barnaribbon, Drumcliff; s/d €40/60; ☾ Apr-
Sep; **P**) This isolated farmhouse B&B, 2km
north of Drumcliff, has a wonderful location treading on the toes of Benbulben.

Yeats Tavern (☎ 071-916 3117; N15, Drumcliff;
mains €8-17; ☾ noon-9.30pm; **P**) An army of
businessfolk, locals and tourists converge
on this vast pub-restaurant, about 300m
north from Yeats' grave, for meals. It buzzes
with a platoon of scurrying waiters and has
a huge menu catering to every taste.

Getting There & Away

Regular **Bus Éireann** (☎ 071-916 0066) buses
run from Sligo to Drumcliff (€3, 15 minutes), Grange (€4, 20 minutes) and Cliffony
(€5, 25 minutes), as most buses to Donegal
and Derry follow the N15. In Drumcliff the
bus stop is near the church, in Grange it's
outside Rooney's newsagency, and in Cliffony it's O'Donnell's Bar. The tourist office
has schedules.

Central North

The six counties (Cavan, Monaghan, Roscommon, Leitrim, Longford and Westmeath) of the central north are Ireland's rough diamonds. While they may never lure the same hordes as the west or south, the scarcity of tour buses and the unspoiled countryside make the region all the more attractive.

Water is a common feature, with the wondrous Shannon threading its way through the landscape. The lively towns of Carrick-on-Shannon and Athlone splash across the river like two big kids playing: hire a boat from either place and explore the river at a leisurely pace. Anglers will appreciate the great lakes of Counties Monaghan and Cavan, where the fishing is mighty.

Stately buildings include Strokestown Park House and Famine Museum, which provide a vivid glimpse into Ireland's colonial history, and Belvedere House, a more personal story of madness.

In this little-visited region, far from the feet of a thousand tourists, enchantment still exists: see the seven wonders of the magical Fore Valley, or visit Cruachan Aí, Europe's most important Celtic royal site, where the landscape is spattered with barrows, cairns and standing stones. Be careful where you tread: one woman and her cow are said to have entered a cave at the site and appeared the next day in Sligo!

HIGHLIGHTS

- **Most Historic Hotel**
  Eccentric accommodation at Glaslough's Castle Leslie (p464)

- **Lazing on the River...**
  Cruising down the Shannon–Erne Waterway (p473)

- **The Famine in a Nutshell**
  Two perspectives on the Famine at the Strokestown Park House and Famine Museum (p466)

- **Best Family Attraction**
  The hands-on King House Interpretive Centre (p467) in Boyle where children get to dress up, bang drums and build buildings

- **Bohemian Athlone**
  A gourmet meal (p481) in this culinary centre and a pint at Ireland's oldest bar, Sean's Bar (p481)

★ Glaslough

Boyle ★   ★ Shannon-Erne Waterway

★ Strokestown Park House and Famine Museum

Athlone ★

- POPULATION: 291,638
- AREA: 9302 SQ KM

CENTRAL NORTH

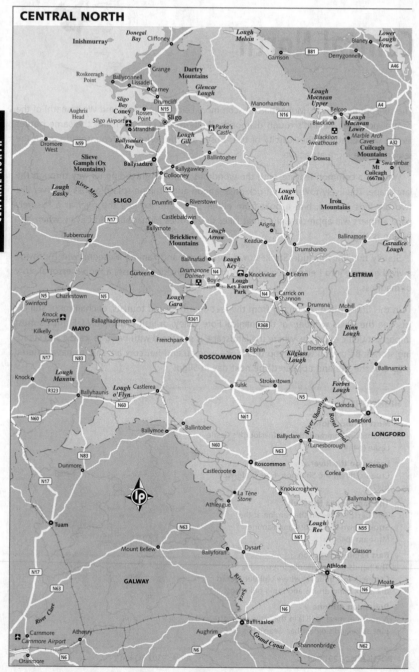

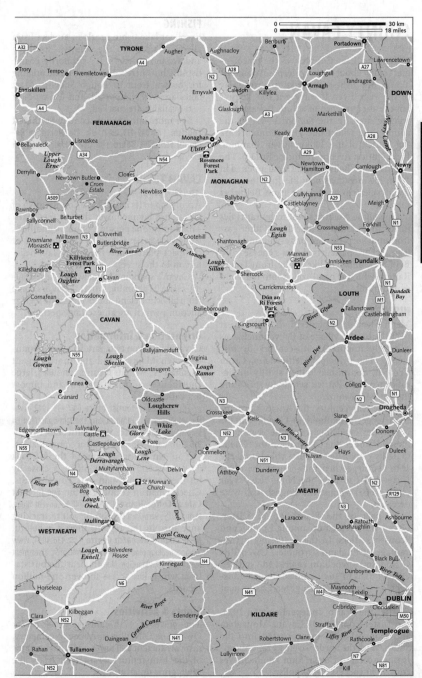

COUNTY CAVAN

Cavan, the 'Lake Country', is the place anglers smile about in their sleep – it contains almost one fish-stuffed lake for every day of the year. Even if waving a rod doesn't appeal, the presence of so much water and wildlife may. In the far northwest of the county, the wild Cuilcagh Mountains are the source of the 300km River Shannon, the mightiest river in Ireland or Britain. The Ballinamore–Ballyconnell Canal, opened in 1994, has breathed new life into the area: try a cycle trip or a cruise from Belturbet marina.

One of the country's best restaurants lies in the tiny hamlet of Blacklion. Other gastronomic surprises are prize-winning Corleggy, a hard pasteurised goat's cheese from Belturbet, and feta-like Boilie from Lough Ramor, which is hand-rolled into balls and stored in oil.

HISTORY

Magh Sleacht, a plain in the northwest near the border village of Ballyconnell, was a hugely important 5th-century druidic centre. The principal Celtic deity, Crom Cruaich, diminished rather swiftly in significance as St Patrick set about spreading the Christian word.

In the 12th century, the Anglo-Normans tried to get a foothold in Cavan, but the landscape foiled them and the region remained under the control of the Gaelic O'Reilly clan. The O'Reillys ruled until the 16th century, when they joined the other Ulster lords to fight the Nine Years' War (1594–1603) against the English and were defeated.

As part of the Plantation of Ulster, Cavan was divided up among English and Scottish settlers. In the 1640s, taking advantage of England's troubles, Owen Roe O'Neill led a rebellion against the settlers. O'Neill died in 1649 – poisoning was suspected – in Clough Oughter Castle near Cavan.

After the War of Independence in 1922, the Ulster counties of Cavan, Monaghan and Donegal were incorporated into the South. With the border so close, republicanism is strong in Cavan: Sinn Féin achieves consistent success at the polls.

FISHING

Excellent lake fishing reels in anglers from all over Europe to the county's southern and western borders. It's primarily coarse fishing, but there's also some game angling for brown trout in Lough Sheelin. Most lakes are well signposted, and the types of fish available are marked.

For more information, contact **North West Tourism** (☎ 049-433 1942) or the **Northern Regional Fisheries Board** (☎ 049-37174), both in Cavan town.

CAVAN TOWN
☎ 049 / pop 3538

According to its natives, the county town of Cavan has boomed over the last few years. Thankfully, one person's boom is another's tranquil escape: Cavan is still the sort of compact place where strangers say 'hello' to you in the street.

Cavan's sparkling crystalware is a speciality, as are its gleaming horses – visitors come from all over Ireland and overseas for regular auctions, which are an exciting spectacle.

Orientation & Information

Cavan centres on two parallel streets, country town Main St and the more elegant Farnham St, with its Georgian houses, large courthouse and garda station, and imposing cathedral.

If the **Cavan tourist office** (☎ 433 1942; www.cavantourism.com; Farnham St; 🕒 9am-5pm Mon-Fri May–mid-Oct) is closed, **Sligo tourist office** (☎ 071-916 1201) can help you book accommodation.

You can change money at the **ACC Bank** (91 Main St), and the post office is close by on the corner of Main and Townhall Sts. Check email in comfort at the **Ego Internet Café & Coffee House** (☎ 437 3488; Convent Bldgs, Main St; 🕒 9am-7pm Mon-Sat). If you're tracking ancestors in the region, there's a helpful **Genealogical Research Centre** (☎ 436 1094; www.cavangenealogy.com; Cana House, Farnham St; assessment fee €45; 🕒 9.30am-5pm Mon-Fri) near the bus station, which has access to over one million records.

Sights & Activities

The **grave** of 17th-century rebel leader Owen Roe O'Neill is in Abbey St cemetery, near an ancient **bell tower** – all that remains of the 13th-century Franciscan friary the town grew up around.

Fire destroyed the old Cavan Crystal factory in 2003, but it's been replaced by the shining new **Cavan Crystal Showroom** (☎ 433 1800; www.cavancrystaldesign.com; Dublin Rd; admission free; ☼ 9.30am-6pm Mon-Fri, 10am-5pm Sat, noon-5pm Sun), which sells the famous crystal and local crafts. The showroom is about 2km southeast of the town centre on the N3.

Cavan Equestrian Centre (☎ 433 2017; www.cavan equestrian.com; Ballyhaise Rd) is the largest in the country, with showjumping events most weekends and auctions six times a year. All the pretty horses are situated 1.5km north of town off the N3.

If you feel safer on a nonliving steed, try a **canoeing course** on the River Erne: check the notice board in Louis Blessing's pub (right) for details.

Sleeping

Glendown House (☎ 433 2257; www.glendownhouse .com; 33 Cathedral Rd; s/d €35/60; ℗) In a country full of genial welcomes, it takes a lot for one place to stand out – but this one really does. Tom and Eileen Flynn make their warm, sunshiny home feel like your home too, pepping up weary guests with chat, tea and biscuits. If you've overdosed on fried breakfasts, there's a wonderful fruit-and-yoghurt alternative. It's gay-friendly.

Cavan Crystal Hotel (☎ 436 0600; www.cavan crystalhotel.com; Dublin Rd; s/d from €120/190; ℗) All your senses are wooed at this plush 85-room hotel. It's filled with a delicious woody aroma, decorated in striking contemporary style (with sublime Cavan Crystal chandeliers), contains a fine restaurant, and there're an 18m swimming pool and a beauty clinic for ultimate pampering. As you'd expect, the bedrooms are immaculate, with subtle lighting and the snuggest of beds.

Glenlara House (☎ 433 1136; Swellan; s/d €37/60; ☼ Jun-Sep; ℗) This spooky-looking manor is situated on the shores of Swellan lake, with gardens sweeping right down to the water. Rooms are old-fashioned but comfortable, with restful views, and anglers are offered private fishing on the grounds. It's 1.5km from the corner of College and Wolfe Tone Sts in town, at the end of a long drive (signposted).

Farnham Arms Hotel (☎ 433 2577; fax 436 2606; Main St; s/d/tr €70/110/150; ℗) A typical provincial hotel, the Farnham Arms is a little battered at the edges, but it's slap in the centre of

town. The lounge serves carvery lunches, while the bar has good all-day hot snacks and sandwiches. Meals cost from €7 to €11.

Eating

Ego Internet Café & Coffee House (☎ 437 3488; Convent Bldgs, Main St; ☼ 9am-7pm Mon-Sat; ▯) Insinuate yourself onto the huge sofa by the window and watch the world go by. Food is served by friendly faces: pick from hot pita sandwiches, salads and baked potatoes, or take a quiet moment to dribble over the ice-cream menu. You can also check your email on one of the two computers.

Side Door (☎ /fax 433 1819; thesidedoor@tjgavigan .com; Drumalee Cross; mains €14-22; ☼ 5.30-10.30pm Tue-Sat, 5.30-9.30pm Sun) Sited out of town, the Side Door is a colourful candlelit restaurant with a funky sax-and-strings soundtrack. It entices couples, families and bunches of friends with its seafood specialities, pizzas, fajitas and steaks.

Manna Café (☎ 437 7777; Thomas Ashe St; mains €3-8; ☼ 8.30am-6pm Mon-Sat) 'Sit, Relax, Gossip' – these are the Three Commandments at this rustic lunch-time spot near the tourist office. Select a coffee, homemade salad or hot special, settle yourself indoors or out, and get chatting.

Melbourne Bakery (☎ 436 1266; Main St; mains €6-9; ☼ 9.30am-5.30pm Mon-Fri) Almost opposite Ego is this old-world bakery-canteen. Shallow booths offer a degree of privacy, but that's not why you'd come here – it's full of all kinds of folk, from harassed mums to tea-swigging builders, and it's fascinating just to watch and listen…if you can tear your thoughts away from the cream buns.

Drinking

Louis Blessing's (☎ 433 1138; 92 Main St) Happily untouched for years, authentic Louis Blessing's is one of those great Irish pubs that also doubles as a grocery shop. Tucked into a small courtyard off Main St, it attracts a real mixture of people.

McMahons Café Bar (☎ 436 5484; www.mcma honscafebar.com; Main St) Cavan's newest drinking hole makes a dramatic impact, with a long, thin, terraced interior, funky cocktails and late-night pizza servings. Like moths to candles, the town's 18 to 25 year olds flitter towards the blue-neon lights…

Abbey Bar (☎ 433 1650; Coleman Rd) At the opposite end of the spectrum, the Abbey is an unreconstructed old-men's pub, with lots of dark wood, tatty seats and a row of proper characters having slightly surreal conversations and slowly draining the place dry.

Getting There & Around

Buses arrive at and depart from the small **bus station** (☎ 433 1353; Farnham St; ⏲ 7.30am-8.30pm Mon-Sat).

Cavan is on the Dublin–Donegal, Galway–Belfast and the Athlone–Belfast bus routes. Buses to Dublin (€10.50, two hours, 7am to 8pm Monday to Saturday, 8am to 8pm Sunday) leave on the hour. There are buses to Belfast (€18, three hours, two per day Monday to Saturday, one Sunday), to Galway (€18, 3¼ hours, two per day Monday to Saturday, one Sunday) and to Donegal (€13.90, 2¼ hours, four daily).

Bus Éireann also has services running to various small towns throughout the county: for example, there are four services daily to Bawnboy, Ballyconnell and Belturbet; and buses leave every hour on the hour to Virginia, Kells, Dunshaughlin, Navan and Cootehill.

Taxis can be ordered on ☎ 433 1172 or ☎ 433 2876.

AROUND CAVAN TOWN
Lough Oughter & Killykeen Forest Park

With its tortuous outline, Lough Oughter lies across the map like a splatter of spilt liquid. Rod-wielding anglers congregate for coarse fishing, but it's also good for naturalists, walkers and anyone wanting to vanish into a landscape of shining waters and cathedral-like aisles of trees. It's best accessed via **Killykeen Forest Park** (☎ 049-433 2541; killykeen@coillte .ie; car €5, pedestrian & cyclist free), 12km northwest of Cavan, where various nature trails lead you through the woods and along the shore.

Many of the low overgrown islands in the lake were *crannógs* (fortified, artificial islands; see the boxed text, p463), the most spectacular being **Clough Oughter Castle**, a 13th-century circular tower perched on a tiny speck of land. It was used as a lonely prison, then as a stronghold by rebel leader Owen Roe O'Neill, who was (probably) poisoned there in 1649, before it was destroyed by Cromwell's army in 1653. Although the castle lies out of reach over the water, it's worth getting near for the sheer loveliness of the view: go on foot via the forest trails,

or get a closer look by car by turning left out of the Killykeen park exit and following the narrow road running north from the village of Garthrattan.

You can stay on the peaceful shores of Lough Oughter in the self-catering **Killykeen Forest Chalets** (☎ 049-433 2541; killykeen@coillte.ie; 4/6 people for 3 nights €310/380; P), a touch of Scandinavia in the wilds of Ireland. The complex is signposted off the N3.

Butlersbridge & Cloverhill

These two places are so tiny that if you blink you'll miss them. The pretty hamlet of Butlersbridge (6km north of Cavan) is plonked right on top of the River Annalee and makes a pleasant spot to stop for a riverside picnic. If making sandwiches sounds like hard work, pop into the **Derragarra Inn** (☎ /fax 049-433 1003; mains €8-14), a raspberry-red, ivy-covered pub with a beer garden, live music at weekends, and well-priced bar food (one woman was so excited by her succulent pie, she showed it to everyone in the queue!).

At Cloverhill (9km north of Cavan), the main attraction is gourmet grub at the award-winning **Olde Post Inn** (☎ 047-55555; www.theoldepostinn.com; mains €23-28, 5-course dinner €45; ⏲ 6.30-9.30pm Tue-Sat, 12.30-3pm & 6.30-8.30pm Sun). The meaty menu revolves around old Irish favourites, such as suckling pig, venison, pheasant and steak, served with inventive sauces. If you eat too much, flop into one of the nine comfortable rooms (singles/doubles €50/80) upstairs.

Another pleasant place to rest your head is **Fortview House** (☎ 049-433 8185; fortviewhouse@hotmail.com; Drumbran; s/d €43/62), a friendly, modern working farm particularly suitable for families and fishermen. Food is home-grown, so you know you're getting the freshest fodder possible. From Butlersbridge take the N54 to Cloverhill, turning right just after the Olde Post Inn. The farm is a further 2km along this lane.

Belturbet
☎ 049 / pop 1295

This old-fashioned inland settlement, 16km northwest of Cavan, is a fisherman's favourite. It's also a busy base for cruise boats, thanks to its plum position on the Shannon–Erne Waterway, and the start of many a cycle trip along the mighty canal and river system.

Emerald Star (☎ 952 2933; www.emeraldstar.ie) has several hire boats that you can sail between Belturbet and Belleek. A four-berth boat costs from €1540 per week in the high season.

Hire bicycles and get route advice from Padraig Fitzpatrick at **Fitz Hire** (☎ 952 2866, 086-804 7521; fitzhire@eircom.net; Bridge St; per day/week €15/45). For an additional €10 per bike, you can cycle one way along the waterway and have Padraig collect your bikes from your final destination.

Volunteers have restored the old **Belturbet Railway Station** (☎ 952 2074; www.belturbet -station.com; Railway Rd; adult/child/student €2.50/1.30/2; ◷ 9.30am-5pm Jun-Sep). It's probably one for train enthusiasts only, although there are occasional vintage rallies and children's activity days.

For accommodation options, see the previous Cloverhill section (opposite).

Bus Éireann (☎ 433 1353) bus No 30 runs through Belturbet, stopping outside the post office (on the Diamond) six times per day Monday to Saturday (four Sunday). The main towns on this route are Dublin (€13, two hours), Cavan (€3, 15 minutes) and Donegal (€16, 2¼ hours).

SOUTHERN CAVAN

Ballyjamesduff
☎ 049 / pop 871

Breeze into Ballyjamesduff to visit the **Cavan County Museum** (☎ 854 4070; ccmuseum@tinet.ie; Virginia Rd; adult/child €3/1.50; ◷ 10am-5pm Tue-Sat year round, 2-6pm Sun Jun-Oct), located inside a grim-looking former convent. Highlights include the Pighouse Collection (18th-, 19th- and 20th-century costumes and folk items), a 1000-year-old boat excavated from Lough Erril, a stone carved with swirling La Tène artwork, and two medieval sheila-na-gigs. There's also a large feature on Gaelic sports: saintly types should swot up on the hurling rules, as apparently it's 'the game they play in heaven'.

In mid-June, you can make a pig of yourself at the three-day **Ballyjamesduff International Pork Festival** (☎ 854 5972), a bacon-based bash with pig racing, a giant spit roast, pork-inspired cooking competitions and music.

Lough Sheelin
☎ 049

Game fishermen sit patiently alongside the tree-lined banks of Lough Sheelin, particularly in May and June when the trout fishing is at its best. It's also a pleasant area for horse riding, walking or splashing about in boats far from, well, anything.

You can find places to stay at opposite ends of the 6km-long lough – in the villages of Finnea (in County Westmeath) and Mountnugent (about 24km south of Cavan).

Ross House (☎/fax 854 0218; www.ross-house.com; Mountnugent; s/d €45/70; P) is a refined period farmhouse in mature grounds on the lake's edge with a sauna, Jacuzzi, tennis, horse riding (€15 per hour) and boat hire (€13 per day) to entice you. Rooms are good value; several have their own conservatories and an extra sense of space. You can also arrange to eat evening meals at the house.

Crover House Hotel (☎ 854 0206; www.croverhouse hotel.ie; Mountnugent; €80/130; P) has fantastic panoramic lake views from the bedrooms, and you can become a part of the soothing scenery by hiring a boat from the hotel's private jetty. A golf course, private gardens and restaurant are also on offer. Kids will be fascinated by the indoor wishing well.

WESTERN CAVAN

This rarely visited area is dominated by the beautiful backdrop of the Cuilcagh Mountains, straddling the border with the North. Surprisingly, the remote village of Blacklion is alive with determined gourmets, drawn by the presence of one of Ireland's best chefs.

GETTING THERE & AWAY

There are few buses serving this isolated fragment of the county. The express Donegal–Dublin buses pass through Ballyconnell, Bawnboy and Swanlinbar four times daily. The Galway–Belfast bus goes via Sligo and stops in Blacklion four times Monday to Saturday (twice Sunday). Contact **Bus Éireann** (☎ 433 1353) in Cavan for more information.

Ballyconnell
☎ 049 / pop 1072

The best thing about Ballyconnell is its splendid isolation, ideal if you want to flee from your hectic lifestyle. The Shannon–Erne Waterway, which passes through the village, adds an extra dimension of peacefulness.

Cavan's only hostel, **Sandville House** (☎ 952 6297; sandville@eircom.net; tent/dm/d €10/15/30; ◷ Easter-Oct; P), demonstrates just how tranquil this area is: many guests come here on spiritual

CENTRAL NORTH

SOMETHING SPECIAL

Jampa Ling Buddhist Centre (☎ 952 3448; www.jampaling.org; Owendoon House, Bawnboy; dm/s/d €32/39/68) Those in search of enlightenment or time out, casual travellers and the plain curious have been coming to Jampa Ling (Place of Loving Kindness) since it opened over a decade ago. The centre, in a lovely pastoral setting, has two dorms and three doubles (the price includes full board) or self-catering accommodation (€16/8 per adult/child), surrounded by a walled garden, a lake and almost six hectares of woodland. As a Buddhist retreat centre it primarily offers courses (from about €45 per day) in Galupa Buddhism, philosophy and meditation, though you don't have to take part in a course to stay here. One of the unique things about Jampa Ling is that a Panchen Lama, a revered senior figure in Tibetan Buddhism, is resident here year round and visitors may avail themselves of his wisdom over a cup of chai tea! The centre occasionally hosts weekends on everything from yoga to medicinal and culinary herbs and visitors can stay as long as they like. This is truly a special place.

---

retreats. Campers are welcome, the kitchen is well equipped, and in nippy weather there's a real peat fire in the sitting room. It's set in silent fields 5km southeast of the village (signposted off the R200). The Dublin to Donegal bus stops on request at the Slieve Russell Hotel; if you call the hostel beforehand, they can arrange to pick you up from there.

Slieve Russell Hotel (☎ 952 6444; www.quinn hotels.com; Cranaghan; s/d €130/240; P 🖳) offers an entirely different kind of relaxation. This legendary hotel, 2km southeast of town, was built by a local millionaire, and features marble columns, fountains, restaurants, bars, a 20m pool and an 18-hole golf course. Spa treatments range from the well known (Jacuzzi, steamroom, sauna) to the wacky (flotation tanks, herb sauna, salt grotto). Rates include breakfast.

If the Slieve Russell is beyond your budget, slip into **An Crannog** (☎ /fax 952 6545; Cranaghan; s/d €45/65; 🖳), a modern buttercup-yellow bungalow next door. Rooms are very comfy, with far-ranging views over the Cavan countryside, and there's a pleasant garden.

Pólo D (☎ 952 6228; polod@oceanfree.net; Main St; 3-course dinner €35; ⏱ 6.30-9.30pm Wed-Sat), at the northern end of Main St, is one of Cavan's best eateries. It's based in an old-world cottage, with uneven floors and doorways built for hobbit-sized folk. Sadly, it's stopped opening at lunch-time, but still serves substantial evening meals such as crispy smoked duck and grilled salmon.

Blacklion

☎ 071 / pop 166

The area between Blacklion and Dowra is spotted with prehistoric monuments, including the remains of a cashel (ring fort) and the ruins of several sweathouses, used mostly in the 19th century. However, the main reason to come to Blacklion is FOOD.

Gourmets from all over Ireland and beyond make the pilgrimage to **MacNean House & Bistro** (☎ 985 3022; fax 985 3404; Main St; dinner menu €55; ⏱ restaurant 6-9pm Thu-Sat, noon-2.30pm & 6-9pm Sun; P 🕭), a much-fêted restaurant run by award-winning TV chef Neven Maguire. The food is outstanding: feast on delights such as crab ravioli, succulent lamb with truffle juice, or excellent veggie treats including avocado spring rolls, before polishing off one of Maguire's to-die-for desserts. The 10-room B&B (singles/doubles €50/90) is one of the few accommodation options in Blacklion.

The Sligo–Belfast buses stop in Blacklion four times every day from Monday to Saturday (twice Sunday). The bus stop is in front of Maguire's pub.

Cuilcagh Mountain Park

The border between Eire and Northern Island runs along the ridge of Mt Cuilcagh, the distinctive summit of the park. Its lower slopes are important protected peatland habitats. The visitor centre and the park's biggest attraction, the **Marble Arch Caves**, lie a short hop over the border from Blacklion, in County Fermanagh (see p667).

Cavan Way

You can walk the 26km Cavan Way (p678), which runs between the villages of Blacklion and Dowra, in a day. Southwards, it takes you through an area known locally as the Burren, which is dotted with prehistoric monuments; past the Shannon Pot, source of Ireland's longest river; then by road to Dowra, passing over the Black Pigs Dyke, an ancient fortification which once divided Ireland in two.

EASTERN CAVAN

Heading east from Cavan town, you move into the heart of drumlin country. Many of the towns in this area, such as **Virginia** (*ver*-ginee), were laid out as 17th-century Plantation estates.

GETTING THERE & AWAY

Bus Éireann (☎ 01-836 6111) express buses on the Dublin–Donegal route pass through Virginia, but only pick up going north and drop off going south. Bus No 109 from Dublin to Cavan stops in Virginia (€11, 1¾ hours, hourly). A Cavan–Dundalk bus passes through Kingscourt (€8.50, one hour) on Tuesday and Thursday. There's also a Dublin–Navan–Kingscourt (€11, 1¾ hours) service, with two buses per day Monday to Saturday (one Sunday).

Kingscourt

☎ 042 / pop 1307

If you're swinging through Kingscourt, stop at **St Mary's Catholic Church** where there are some superb 1940s stained-glass windows by artist Evie Hone.

Just to the northwest of the village is 225-hectare **Dún an Rí Forest Park** (☎ 966 7320; car/ pedestrian €5/free), good for breaking up a car journey if the kids have started throttling each other. There are four colour-coded forest walks (all under 4km long), with picnic places, deer-spotting opportunities and a wishing well.

The stately **Cabra Castle** (☎ 966 7030; www .manorhousehotels.com; s/d €150/250), about 3km out of Kingscourt on the Carrickmacross road, was put together in the 19th century, since Cromwell battered the original Cabra Castle to pieces. The current owners have decked it out with plush period furnishings. The 80 rooms have super views over the hotel's vast parkland; a top-notch restaurant and a nine-hole golf course are on site; and at the time of writing, building work (to be completed by summer 2006) had just begun on a gym complex and marriage hall.

COUNTY MONAGHAN

Few visitors ever pass through Monaghan (Muineachán), which bulges with tiny rounded hills like the bubbles in badly pasted wallpaper. These are drumlins, lumps of debris left by retreating glaciers during the last Ice Age, and in among them are more lakes, fewer than in neighbouring Cavan, but still enough to make a fisherman grin.

Patrick Kavanagh (1905–67), one of Ireland's most respected poets, was born in Inniskeen. His long poem *The Great Hunger* (1942) blasts away the earlier clichés of Anglo-Irish verse and shows Ireland's poor farming communities as they were: half-starved, 'broken-backed' and sexually repressed.

Monaghan is noted for its lace, and this eye-straining craft continues in Clones and Carrickmacross, centres of the industry since the early 19th century.

History

Unlike much of Ulster, Monaghan was mostly left alone during the Ulster Plantation. After the Cromwellian wars, though, local chieftains were forced to sell their land for a fraction of its true value, or it was simply seized and redistributed to Cromwell's soldiers. The new settlers levelled the forests and built numerous no-frills Protestant towns and villages. Disapproving of Irish pastoral farming methods, they introduced arable farming. The linen industry later became very profitable.

Monaghan's historical ties with Ulster were severed by the partition of Ireland in

---

FEARSOME ENGINES

If Monaghan's regular, drumlin-scattered landscape and somnolent settlements leave you thirsting for sound, speed and adrenalin-fuelled sensation, visit **Rally School Ireland** (☎ 047-89098; www.rallyschoolireland .ie; Gola, Scotstown; half-/full-day course from €215/320). Slap on a helmet, leap into one of the school's front-, rear- or 4-wheel-drive rally cars, and turbo round a specially designed track. Personal tutors instruct you on safety and technique before and during the drive. Bookings are essential.

CENTRAL NORTH

1922 and, though republicanism is quite strong, it's not as visible as you may expect. A number of towns have Sinn Féin bookshops and advice centres.

MONAGHAN TOWN
☎ 047 / pop 5717
It may be the county town, but Monaghan is more down-to-earth than a limbo-dancing mole: people here live their lives utterly unaffected by tourism. The main visitor attraction is the county museum, containing a worthy regional collection. It's also pleasant just to wander the streets admiring the elegant 18th- and 19th-century limestone buildings.

The MacMahon family ruled this area for centuries: in Convent Lake, just behind St Louis Convent, there is a small overgrown *crannóg* that served as the family headquarters in the 14th century. After the turbulent wars of the 16th and 17th centuries, the town was settled by Scottish Calvinists.

Monaghan lies 141km northwest of Dublin, but just 8km from the border with Northern Ireland.

Orientation & Information
Monaghan is squashed between two small lakes, Peter's Lake to the north, and Convent Lake in the southwest. Its principal streets form a rough arc, broken up by the town's three main squares. From east to west these are Church Sq, the Diamond (the Ulster name for a town square) and Old Cross Sq.

To the west of this arc, at the top of Park St, are Market Sq and the **tourist office** (☎ 81122; www.monaghantourism.com; 6 Castle meadow Ct; ☼ 9am-5pm Mon-Fri May–mid-Oct). The post office is on Mill St. A one-way traffic system operates through the centre of town. For help with genealogies, write to the **Monaghan Ancestral Research Group** (☎ 82304; 6 Tully St).

Sights & Activities
Monaghan County Museum & Gallery (☎ 82928; comuseum@monaghancoco.ie; 1-2 Hill St; admission free; ☼ 10am-1pm & 2-5pm Tue-Fri, 11am-1pm & 2-5pm Sat) is an excellent regional museum, containing exhibits from the Stone Age to modern times. Its crowning glory is the 14th-century **Cross of Clogher**, an oaken altar cross encased in decorative bronze panels. Other impressive finds include the Lisdrumturk and Altar-tate Cauldrons, medieval *crannóg* artefacts, and some frightening articles relating to the border with the North (including knuckle-dusters, cudgels, and the most calligraphic death threat you're ever likely to see).

There are several eye-catching edifices scattered about town. The **Dawson Monument** (1857), in Church Sq, is a hefty obelisk commemorating one Colonel Dawson's unfortunate demise in the Crimean War. Overlooking it is the Gothic **St Patrick's Church** and a stately Doric **courthouse** (1829). Even more striking is the **Rossmore Memorial** (c 1875), a Victorian drinking fountain that dominates the Diamond – it certainly beats the average office water cooler for pomp.

Just out of the centre of town on the Dublin road is another piece of Victorian whimsy, **St Macartan's Catholic Cathedral** (1861). It's said to be architect JJ McCarthy's finest building, and the mock-14th-century design and teetering 77m-high needle-sharp spire certainly make you stop and stare.

Fishing is the main activity in town. Contact Dick Kernan at **Venture Sports** (☎ 81495; 71 Glaslough St) for permits, tackle and local knowledge.

Sleeping
Four Seasons Hotel (☎ 81888; www.4seasonshotel .ie; Coolshannagh; r €138; **P**) Unconnected to the similarly named international chain, this is a large, modern hotel with good facilities, including a Jacuzzi, sauna and gym. Service is affable, and it's less than 1km from town on the N2.

Glendrum House (☎ 82347; Cootehill Rd, Drumbear; s/d €40/65; **P**) There are five comfortable rooms in this gay-friendly, modern home, a 10-minute walk from the town centre (on the R188).

Lakeside Hotel (☎ 83599; fax 82291; North Rd; s/d €60/120) This recently refurbished Georgian hotel, beside Peter's Lake, is a five-minute walk from town on the Derry road. The downstairs bar sometimes puts on tribute acts (like Tom Jones impersonators), which can be hilariously funny. Enjoy!

Eating
Mediterraneo (☎ 82335; 58 Dublin St; mains €12-20; ☼ 5.30-10.30pm Wed-Sat, 5.30-10pm Sun) The two-sittings system on busy nights shows you just how popular this colourful bistro is. There's

CENTRAL NORTH

LAKE ESCAPES

Favoured by renegades, rebels and reclusive royal residents, *crannógs* (meaning 'small islands built with young trees') were the escapists' homes of choice. These artificial islands, particularly popular in times of political instability, had a surprisingly long life, and were made throughout the 6th to the 17th centuries.

Overgrown now with trees and brambles, it's sometimes hard to see *crannóg* remains as the amazingly dogged pieces of engineering that they are. Using the simplest tools, the islands were built from scratch from layers of wood, peat, stone, heather and soil. *Crannóg* dwellers made access even trickier by palisading the islands, and by using zigzagging causeways or submerged stepping stones as a front path. Sometimes canoe-like boats were the only way to get across.

Crannógs were used as defended farmsteads, craft centres and storage places for valuables (for example, during 9th-century Viking raids). They were important rebel hide-outs during the Nine Years' War: the English realised this, and made *crannógs* a serious target in their northerly Irish assaults.

There are over 1200 *crannógs* in Ireland (mainly in Cavan, Monaghan, Leitrim and over the border in Fermanagh), but few have been properly excavated. Those that have give tantalising glimpses of *crannóg* life: manacled, mutilated skeletons of slaves and hostages, for example, highlight their turbulent histories.

---

a good fish selection, as well as decent Italian staples including pizza and pasta. Reserve at the weekend, and turn up on time.

Andy's Bar & Restaurant (☎ 82277; www.andys monaghan.com; 12 Market St; lunch €8, mains €14-20, set dinner €28; ☺ 4-10.15pm Tue-Fri, noon-10.15pm Sat, 3.30-10pm Sun) You can barely see Andy's Bar for the plaudits that plaster its exterior. Most of these relate to its dark, old-fashioned interior and top-quality beer, but the humungous pub roasts and monkfish served in lemon oil deserve a wholehearted mention too.

Paramount (☎ 77333; 30 Market St; mains €16-22, 3-course dinner €35; ☺ 6.30-10pm Wed-Mon) This classy, minimalist restaurant over Cooper's pub serves excellent seafood and steak, and there are always two or three veggie options on the menu.

Greedy (☎ 83333; 8a the Diamond; sandwiches €4-6; ☺ 9am-6pm Mon-Sat) Tucked down an alley, this new coffee-and-sandwich bar is perfect for a light (by Irish standards) lunch. Its *panini* (Italian sandwiches) and pastries are made from fresh local produce – although the location of Monaghan's olive farm is still a mystery.

Drinking & Entertainment

Sherry's (☎ 81805; 24 Dublin St) Walking into Sherry's, one of Monaghan's oldest bars, is like stepping back into a spinster's parlour of the 1950s. The old tiled floor, beauty board and dusty memorabilia probably haven't been touched in decades.

Market House (☎ 38158; www.themarkethouse.ie; Market St) This shiny arts venue has really given the town a cultural heart. It hosts traditional, classical and jazz music concerts, poetry readings and drama events, and shows the occasional film (€5). Contact the centre for details.

Getting There & Around

From the **bus station** (☎ 82377; North Rd), there are numerous daily intercity services within the Republic and into the North. These include 12 Monday to Saturday (seven Sunday) to Dublin (€10.50, two hours); six to Derry (€11.90, two hours) via Omagh; five (four Sunday) to Belfast (€10.70, two hours); and nine (eight Sunday) to Armagh (€5.80, 40 minutes). There are also frequent daily local services to the nearby towns of Castleblayney, Ballybay, Carrickmacross and Ardee.

McConnon's (☎ 82020) private bus company runs buses to Dublin (single/return €8/12, two Monday to Friday, one Saturday and Sunday), which serve Castleblayney, Carrickmacross and Slane en route. They leave from outside Ronaghan's chemist on Church Sq.

ROSSMORE FOREST PARK

The atmospheric **Rossmore Forest Park** (☎ 047-433 1046; car/pedestrian €5/free; ☺ Jul & Aug) was originally the home of the Rossmore family;

you can still see their pet cemetery and the crumbling entrance stairway and buttresses of their 19th-century castle.

Along with forest walks and pleasant picnic areas, the park contains several giant redwoods (some of the tallest trees in Ireland), a fine yew avenue and Iron Age tombs. A gold collar (known as a lunula) from 1800 BC was found here in the 1930s and is now on display in the National Museum in Dublin. The park is located 3km southwest of Monaghan on the Newbliss road (R189).

GLASLOUGH

☎ 047 / pop 726

Glaslough is a quaint little place of cut-stone cottages, 9km northeast of Monaghan. It was once the estate village for the magnificent **Castle Leslie** (see the boxed text, below), a 19th-century Italianate mansion overlooking the nearby lake. Within the grounds is the **Greystones Equestrian Centre** (☎ 88100), where you can ride horses (€30 per hour) through 40km of trails in the demesne.

Don't leave the village without stopping at **J & W Wright** (☎ 88106; Thu & Sat), a bar and grocery shop with old-fashioned petrol pumps outside. It's perfectly intact and untouched since the 1950s.

CLONES & AROUND

☎ 047 / pop 1721

Patrick McCabe's dark novel *The Butcher Boy* was set in Clones (Cluain Eois), and

Neil Jordan's 1997 film of the book was shot on location here, with many of the townspeople appearing as extras. Another famous son is the 'Clones Cyclone', former featherweight boxer Barry McGuigan, who sent the town into ecstasies by winning the world championship in 1985.

Madness, murder and fisticuffs aside, Clones was once the site of an important 6th-century monastery that later became an Augustinian abbey.

The bus stop, post office and banks are in the central Diamond. There's no tourist office, but you can pick up information at the **Ulster Canal Stores** (☎ 52125; Cara St; 9am-5pm Mon-Fri year round, 10am-6pm Sat, 2-6pm Sun May-Sep).

Sights

Besides spotting scenes from *The Butcher Boy* film, most sights in town are ecclesiastical. There's a well-preserved 10th-century **high cross** on the Diamond, decorated with the stories of Adam and Eve, Daniel in the lion's den, and Cain slaying Abel.

Along with the remains of the **abbey** founded by St Tiernach on Abbey St, there's a truncated 22m-high **round tower** in the cemetery south of town, from the early 9th century. Nearby is the supposed burial place of Tiernach himself, a chunky 9th-century **sarcophagus** with worn animal-head carvings.

Sleeping & Eating

Hilton Park (☎ 56007; www.hiltonpark.ie; Clones; s/d with park view €150/250, with lake view €165/300; Apr-

---

SOMETHING SPECIAL

Castle Leslie (☎ 88109; www.castleleslie.com; s €160-220, d €270-370) Always a mecca for rock stars and actors (Mick Jagger infamously spent an extended period *in situ*), trade has stepped up a notch since Sir Paul McCartney's wedding to Heather Mills here in 2002. The secret arrangement was comically blurted to the press by innocent eccentric Sir John Leslie, fourth baronet to the estate. At 88 Sir John is no stranger to the media himself: his passion for dancing to house music has taken him to raves in Ibiza and has been the subject of TV documentaries.

The castle's 14 atmospheric rooms each have a unique character and history to tell – and Sir John will be only too pleased to fill you in. The gorgeous Red Room, used by WB Yeats, contains the first bath plumbed in Ireland; and in Uncle Norman's Room, guests claim to have been levitated in the Gothic four-poster bed from Brede House (reputedly the most haunted house in England). Room rates depend on whether they have a garden or lake view; whichever you choose, you can be sure of odd stories galore. There is a minimum two-night stay on weekends, and children under 18 are not allowed.

Candlelit dinner (from €52) at the castle is a sumptuous, communal affair (also open to non-guests), with frequent gourmet and themed nights. Guests can also fish on the estate's private lake (boat hire is €35 per day).

Sep) This glamorous country home is the antidote to 21st-century cares. The interior was transformed into an Italianate palazzo in the 1870s, and its sumptuous rooms are studded with elegant stained glass and antiques. Top-class food (dinner €48), much of it grown in the estate's organic gardens, is served in regal surroundings, and there's an 18-hole golf course so you can walk off the calories. Hilton Park is 5km south of Clones along the L46 towards Scotshouse.

Glynch House (☎ /fax 54045; marthaog@eircom .net; Newbliss; s/d €50/100; **P**) Martha O'Grady's Georgian home makes a lavish stopover, with antique furnishings, real log fires, and a welcome perfected over a period of 36 years! Rooms seem to induce a good night's sleep, with comfy wooden beds and soothing views of fields and cows. Glynch House is 7km from Clones on the Newbliss road (R183).

Lennard Arms Hotel (☎ 51075; thelennardarms hotel@eircom.net; the Diamond, Clones; s/d €40/70; **P**) A plain, homespun country hotel, Lennard Arms offers simple comfort in refurbished rooms. Snacks and more substantial meals are available all day from the bar, which is decorated with old photos of boxing champ Barry McGuigan.

Getting There & Around

Bus Éireann (☎ 82377) runs a service from Clones to Monaghan (€4.30, 30 minutes, five buses Monday to Saturday, one Sunday), with connections on to Castleblayney, Carrickmacross, Slane and Dublin.

Ulsterbus (☎ 048-9066 6630) has one direct service per day between Clones and Belfast (€6.20, 2¾ hours), and another service that requires a change in Monaghan, running Monday to Friday.

McConnon's (☎ 82020) runs a bus to Dublin (€8, two hours), leaving Clones at 8.20am Monday to Saturday, which stops in Monaghan, Castleblayney, Carrickmacross and Slane.

Collins Coaches (☎ 042-966 1631) operates a bus to Dublin (€10, 2½ hours) at 7.45am from Monday to Saturday, and at 5.45pm on Sunday that stops at various towns including Carrickmacross.

CARRICKMACROSS & AROUND
☎ 042 / pop 1964

The coolest thing about Carrickmacross (Carraig Mhachaire Rois) is that it's the birth-place of comedy god Ardal O'Hanlon, better known as Father Dougal McGuire in the TV series *Father Ted*. O'Hanlon's first novel *The Talk of the Town* was set in 'Castlecock', a thinly disguised version of the town.

Carrickmacross was first settled by early English and Scottish Planters, and today consists of one wide street dotted with some elegant Georgian houses. Delicate Carrick-macross lace, an industry revived in 1871 by the St Louis nuns, is a world-famous export. The sleeves of Princess Diana's wedding dress were trimmed with Carrickmacross lace.

Sights & Activities

In town, a local cooperative runs the **Carrickmacross Lace Gallery** (☎ 62506; Market Sq; ⊗ 9.30am-5.30pm Mon-Fri), which has gossamer-like designs for sale.

Harry Clarke, Ireland's most renowned stained-glass artist, was responsible for 10 of the windows in **St Joseph's Catholic Church** (O'Neill St).

There's fishing in many of the lakes around Carrickmacross, including Loughs Capragh, Spring, Monalty and Fea: contact **Peader O'Brien** (☎ 966 3207) for angling information.

Dún an Rí Forest Park is 5km southwest towards Kingscourt (see p461 for further details).

Sleeping & Eating

Food in Carrickmacross is limited to dubious takeaways and pub meals.

Lodge (☎ 966 1833, 087-680 1650; Parnell St; s/d €40/70) This is the best B&B in town, centrally situated and stuffed with big fat comfy beds. Breakfasts feature local produce and the largest pots of tea in Ireland, and there are trying-hard details, such as like the water cooler on the landing, but it's a tad overpriced.

Getting There & Away

Four **Bus Éireann** (☎ 01-836 6111) routes connecting Dublin with Letterkenny, Derry, Armagh and Portrush pass through Carrickmacross (€11, two hours, 11 daily Monday to Saturday, six Sunday).

Collins Coaches (☎ 966 1631) runs a service to Dublin (€9, five daily Monday to Friday, four Saturday, two Sunday).

McConnon's (☎ 047-82020) has a bus service that passes through Carrickmacross on its

CENTRAL NORTH

Dublin–Monaghan–Clones route, with two buses per day on weekdays (€7 to Dublin) leaving Carrickmacross at 7.15am and 9.35am, and on Saturday at 9.35am.

The bus stop is outside O'Hanlon's shop on Main St.

INNISKEEN

☎ 042 / pop 310

Acclaimed poet Patrick Kavanagh (1904–67) was born in the village of Inniskeen (Inis Caoin), which lies 10km northeast of Carrickmacross. Fans will be fascinated by the **Patrick Kavanagh Rural & Literary Resource Centre** (☎ /fax 937 8560; www.patrickkavanaghcountry .com; adult/child €5/3; ⏰ 11am-4.30pm Tue-Fri year round, 2-6pm Sat Jun-Sep, 2-6pm Sun mid-Mar–Nov), housed in the old parish church where the poet was baptised. It's a wonderful building, with its upturned 'fisherman's boat' ceiling, and the staff there have a passion for Kavanagh that is infectious. Even if you don't know much about the poet, the centre is an excellent introduction to his life and work.

A local actor leads groups on a **literary tour** (☎ /fax 937 8560; adult/child €7/5) of the area on request, including Brennan's pub, which was Kavanagh's watering hole, or you can buy a copy of the *Patrick Kavanagh Trail Guide* (€0.70) from the resource centre and guide yourself.

Elsewhere in Inniskeen, the **round tower** is all that is left of the 6th-century **St Daig Monastery**.

COUNTY ROSCOMMON

Fins rather than feet would be an advantage in Roscommon – one-third of the county is bog! Large lakes bathe the countryside, and to the east and west lie the mighty River Shannon and the River Suck. As you'd guess, fishing is a major draw, but there are plenty of other intriguing attractions.

The cheerful town of Boyle is worth a stopover, especially for the unique King House Interpretive Centre, a winner with the kids. Strokestown Famine Museum was Ireland's first attempt to explain the horrors of the 1840s potato blight to itself and is vital visiting. At the Arigna Mining Experience, a stone's throw from the pretty village of Keadue in the north, you can descend into the pit to see the narrowest mine tunnels in Europe.

Roscommon contains a massive number of megalithic tombs, ring forts and mounds – over 5000 of the things. The most important complex is around the Cruachan Aí Visitor Centre in Tulsk.

STROKESTOWN & AROUND

☎ 078 / pop 631

Strokestown (Béal na mBuillí), about 18km northeast of Roscommon town, is worth at least a half-day visit for its grand estate and Famine Museum. The incredibly broad main street in town was deliberately designed by one of the early Mahons to be Europe's widest.

Over the May Bank Holiday weekend, Gaelic and English poetry and music are read and played at the **International Poetry Festival** (☎ 947 4123; www.strokestownpoetry prize.com).

Strokestown Park House & Famine Museum

At the end of Strokestown's main avenue are three Gothic arches, beyond which is the very impressive **Strokestown Park House and Famine Museum** (☎ 33013; www.strokestown park.ie; adult/child/family €12.50/5.70/28; ⏰ 10am-5.30pm Mar-Oct).

The original 12,000-hectare estate was granted by King Charles II to Nicholas Mahon for his support in the English Civil War. Nicholas' grandson Thomas commissioned Richard Cassels to build him a Palladian mansion in the early 18th century. Over the centuries, the estate decreased along with the family's fortunes. When it was eventually sold to a local garage in 1979, it had been whittled down to 120 hectares. The estate was bought as a complete lot, so virtually all of its contents are intact.

Admission to the house is by a 50-minute **guided tour** (⏰ 11.30am, 2pm & 4pm Mon-Fri, plus 5pm Sat & Sun), providing an intriguing glimpse into the Anglo-Irish Ascendancy and taking in a galleried kitchen with state-of-the-art clockwork machinery, and a child's bedroom complete with 19th-century toys and fun-house mirrors.

The lovely **walled garden**, the result of a 10-year restoration project, contains the longest herbaceous border in Ireland and Britain, a riot of rainbow colours in summer. A maze and electronic sound garden are in development in the pleasure gardens.

In direct and deliberate contrast to the splendour of the house and its grounds is the harrowing **Strokestown Famine Museum**, a must for anyone seeking to understand the devastating 1840s potato blight. The museum takes an unblinking look at the pitiful starvation of the poor, and the ignorance, callousness and cruelty of those who were in a position to help. In Strokestown the landlord Major Denis Mahon simply evicted starving peasants who couldn't pay their rents, chartering boats to transport them away from Ireland. Almost 600 of these 1000 emigrants died on the overcrowded 'coffin ships'; perhaps unsurprisingly, Mahon was assassinated in 1847. The museum also does a sterling job of opening visitors' eyes to contemporary famine around the world.

Cruachan Aí Visitor Centre

Around the village of Tulsk stand 60 ancient national monuments – standing stones, barrows, cairns and fortresses – which give the area an eerie, atmospheric charge. This landscape and its sacred structures, which have lain largely undisturbed for the past 3000 years, form one of the most important Celtic royal sites in Europe. Audiovisual displays and informative panels at the **Cruachan Aí Visitor Centre** (☎ 071-963 9268; www.cruachanai.com; adult/child €5/2.75; ☉ 9am-6pm Mon-Fri, 11am-6pm Sat, 2-6pm Sun Apr-Sep, 9am-5pm Mon-Fri Oct-Mar) explore its importance. The centre can also give you a map and let you know the current status of access to the (privately owned) sites.

According to the legend of *Táin Bó Cúailnge* (see the boxed text, p552), bolshy, bull-baiting Queen Maeve (Medbh) had her palace at Cruachan. The Oweynagat Cave (Cave of the Cats), believed to be the entrance to the Celtic otherworld, is also situated here.

Tulsk is 10km west of Strokestown on the N5.

BOYLE & AROUND

☎ 071 / pop 2205

Found at the feet of the Curlew Mountains, spirited little Boyle (Mainistir na Búille) has a punchy trio of attractions: Boyle Abbey, deemed one of the finest Cistercian

churches in Ireland; the hands-on King House Interpretive Centre; and the superb 4000-year-old Drumanone Dolmen.

It's well worth turning up for the 10-day **Boyle Arts Festival** (www.boylearts.com) in the last week of July, which has an impressive programme of music, theatre, storytelling and contemporary Irish art exhibitions.

Maureen O'Sullivan, American film actress and Mia Farrow's mum, was born in a house on Main St opposite the Bank of Ireland in 1911.

History

The history of Boyle is the history of the King family. In 1603 Staffordshire-born John King was granted land in Roscommon with the aim of 'reducing the Irish to obedience'. Over the next 150 years, through canny marriages and cold-blooded conquests, his descendants made their name and fortune, becoming one of the largest landowning families in Ireland; the town grew around their estate.

King House was built in 1730, and in 1780 the family moved to the grander Rockingham House, built in what is now Lough Key Forest Park, and which was destroyed by fire in 1957.

Information

The **tourist office** (☎ 966 2145; cnr Military Rd & Main St; ☉ 10am-5.30pm Mon-Sat Jun-early Sep) is in King House. When it's closed, calls are diverted to Galway tourist office, or you can seek assistance from the friendly staff at the **Úna Bhán Tourism Centre** (☎ 966 3033; www.unabhan .net; ☉ 9am-6pm May-Aug, closed weekends Sep-Apr), also in King House.

There's a National Irish Bank branch with an ATM on the corner of Bridge and Patrick Sts and a Bank of Ireland at the eastern end of Main St. The post office is on Carrick Rd, south of the river.

Sights & Activities
KING HOUSE INTERPRETIVE CENTRE

One of the most inspired museums in the country is the **King House Interpretive Centre** (☎ 966 3242; kinghouseboyle@hotmail.com; Main St; adult/child/family €5/3/15; ☉ 10am-6pm Apr-Sep) – and to think that it was almost flattened to make a car park! Sinister-looking dummies from various eras tell the turbulent history of the Connaught kings, and of the town of Boyle and the King family, including a rather grim tale of tenant eviction during the Famine. Kids will especially enjoy King House: they can try on ancient Irish cloaks, brooches and leather shoes, write with a quill, play a regimental drum, and even 'build' a vaulted ceiling from specially designed blocks.

After the King family moved to Lough Key, the house became a military barracks for the fearsome Connaught Rangers from 1788 until Irish independence in 1922. The county council bought the property in 1987, and spent several years and €3.8 million turning it into this splendid centre.

BOYLE ABBEY

Down by the rushing River Boyle is the finely preserved **Boyle Abbey** (☎ 966 2604; adult/concession €2/1; ☼ 10am-6pm Easter-end Oct, last admission 45 min before closing), founded in 1161 by monks from Mellifont, County Louth. Its stones capture the transition from Romanesque to Gothic, best seen in the nave, where a set of arches in each style face each other. Unusually for a Cistercian building, carved animals and rather rigid little figures decorate the capitals to the west. After the Dissolution of the Monasteries, the abbey was occupied by the military and became Boyle Castle; the stone chimney on the southern side of the abbey (once the refectory) dates from that period.

Guided tours of the abbey are available on the hour until 5pm.

LOUGH KEY FOREST PARK

The most beautiful public parkland in the northern counties is 350-hectare **Lough Key Forest Park** (☎ 966 2363; car/pedestrian €5/free; ☼ Apr-Sep), 3km east of Boyle on the N4. Out of season, it's a quietly romantic spot: Lough Key is full of scattered islands, several with picturesque ruins including a 12th-century abbey on tiny Trinity Island, and a 19th-century castle on Castle Island. Bring on the sunshine and ice creams, and its character changes – it makes a great family day out, with a child-pleasing wishing chair, bog gardens, fairy bridge and viewing tower over the lake. Deer roam about, and there are several marked walking trails.

If you fancy something more energetic, contact **Lough Key Boats** (☎ 086-816 7037; www.loughkeyboats.com; ☼ 11am-7pm Jun-Aug), who provide several watery entertainments in-cluding water-skiing lessons (€50 per hour), on-the-hour commentated boat trips aboard the *Trinity* (€10/5 per adult/child), rowing-boat hire (€10/50 per hour/day), and fishing advice (record-breaking pike have been caught here).

The park was once part of the Rockingham estate, owned by the King family from the 17th century until 1957. Rockingham House, designed by John Nash, was destroyed by a fire in the same year; all that remains are some stables, outbuildings and tunnels leading to the lake – built to hide the servants from view!

DRUMANONE DOLMEN

This superb portal dolmen, one of the largest in Ireland, measures 4.5m by 3.3m and was constructed before 2000 BC. It can be tricky to find: follow Patrick St west out of town for 2km, then bear left at the junction signposted to Lough Gara. Follow this road for another kilometre, passing under a railway arch. A sign indicates the path across the railway line.

DOUGLAS HYDE INTERPRETIVE CENTRE

The life of Dr Douglas Hyde (1860–1949), poet, writer and the first president of Ireland, is celebrated at the **Douglas Hyde Interpretive Centre** (Gairdín an Craoibhín; ☎ 094-987 0016; Frenchpark; admission free; ☼ 2-5pm Tue-Fri, 2-6pm Sat & Sun May-Sep). Outside the political arena, Hyde cofounded the Gaelic League in 1893 and spent a lifetime gathering Gaelic poems and folklore that might otherwise have been lost forever.

The centre is housed in the former Protestant church at Frenchpark, 12km southwest of Boyle on the R361.

ARIGNA MINING EXPERIENCE

Ireland's first and last coal mine (1600s to 1990) is remembered at the award-winning **Arigna Mining Experience** (☎ 964 6466; www.arigna miningexperience.ie; Derreenavoggy; adult/child €8/5; ☼ 10am-6pm mid-Mar–Dec, 10am-6pm Mon-Fri Jan-mid-Mar), set in the hills above Lough Allen. The highlight is the 40-minute underground tour, which takes you 400m down to the coal face. Tours are led by ex-miners, who really bring home the gruelling working conditions and dangers of their job. The breathtaking views of the valley look even more spectacular when you emerge

HARP & SOUL

The blind harpist, composer and whiskey drinker Turlough O'Carolan (1670–1738), celebrated as the last of the Irish bards, is associated with northeast Roscommon and southwest Leitrim.

O'Carolan spent most of his time in Mohill (County Leitrim) where his patron Mrs MacDermott-Roe lived; a sculpture on the main street of the town commemorates the association. His declining years were spent in the pretty village of Keadue (County Roscommon), where the 10-day **O'Carolan International Harp Festival** (☎ 071-964 7204; www.keadue.harp.net) is held in his honour around the August Bank Holiday. The poet is buried just outside the village in Kilronan church, which preserves a 12th-century doorway. To get to the church, head west from Keadue on the R284 to Sligo.

O'Carolan is credited with composing the tune of 'The Star-Spangled Banner'.

---

from the darkness. Wear sturdy shoes for the tour, as it can be quite wet and muddy underfoot.

ARIGNA MINERS WAY & HISTORICAL TRAIL

Covering 118km of north Roscommon, east Sligo and mid-Leitrim, these well-signposted tracks and hill passes cover the routes taken by miners on their way to work. A guidebook with detailed maps is available from local tourist offices or the **Arigna Miners Way & Historical Trail office** (☎ 078-47212; www.arignaminerswayandhistoricaltrail.com; Keadue Presbytery, Keadue).

Sleeping & Eating

Abbey House (☎ 966 2385; Abbeytown Rd; s/d €40/64; ✷ Mar-Oct; (P)) This large, family-friendly Victorian house has a fantastic position right in the grounds of Boyle Abbey. Rooms are time-worn but spacious, and overlook either the abbey or the mature back garden with its splashing stream.

Riversdale House (☎ /fax 966 7012; jpburke@indigo.ie; Knockvicar; d €64; ✷ Jun–mid-Aug; (P)) This rambling Georgian house, on a 21-hectare working farm, is the former home of film star Maureen O'Sullivan. It has three spacious rooms and residents can fish or hire

boats (€20 per day) on Lough Key, accessible directly from the house by private road. It's located 12km northeast of Boyle on the R285.

Royal Hotel (☎ 966 2016; fax 966 4949; Bridge St; s/d €55/100; (P)) In the town centre, this 18th-century country hotel is old-fashioned and downright odd! Despite fairly recent renovations, the place feels as though it's from another era, or possibly planet; that's not to say it's bad, just don't expect the slickness of a modern chain hotel. Some of the 22 plain but comfy rooms overlook the river, and there's a restaurant with a good Chinese menu.

Lough Key Caravan & Camping Park (☎ 966 2212; camp sites €12; ✷ May-Aug) This camp site is situated right inside the picturesque Lough Key Forest Park. Facilities are good, and include a recreation room, laundrette and children's play area.

Chambers (☎ 966 3614; the Crescent; mains €14-24; ✷ 6-10pm Tue-Sun) At the top end of the Crescent, above the Moving Stairs pub, this restaurant serves the highest quality 'modern Irish cuisine'. The wide choices are good news for lovers of meat, fish and vegetables, and most produce is sourced locally and is fresh as a flower. Specials, such as wild boar, and ostrich served with rösti potatoes, are on offer at weekends.

Stone House Café (Bridge St; lunch €3.50-6; ✷ 9.30am-6pm Mon-Fri, 10am-6pm Sat Jun-Aug, till 5pm Mon, Tue, Thu-Sat, till 3pm Wed Sep-May) This interesting, curvy-walled little building on the river was once the gate lodge to Frybrook House (closed). It's smashing for lunch, with a range of soups, *panini* and puddings, and has a fab view of the water rushing past.

Drinking & Entertainment

Moving Stairs (☎ 966 3586; the Crescent) Undoubtedly the most lively evening joint, the Moving Stairs is the pub to go for a range of music – jazz, traditional and rock, depending on the night. It also has excellent bar meals from the same kitchen as Chambers restaurant.

Wynne's Bar (☎ 086-821 4736; Main St) This quaint pub in the centre of town has bought a bunch of jarringly new seat covers, but the rest of the décor (and its heart and soul) remains that of an old man's pub. Its trad music session, from 10pm on Friday, is the most respected in Boyle – come early if you want to sit down.

Clark's (☎ 966 2064; Patrick St) Fill your weekend with music by dropping in here for the Saturday-night session. It's a large, newly renovated place, with cheery staff serving at the bar.

Getting There & Around

From almost outside the Royal Hotel on Bridge St, **Bus Éireann** (☎ 916 0066) buses leave for Sligo (€9, 50 minutes, six Monday to Saturday, four Sunday) and Dublin (€16, three hours, five Monday to Saturday, four Sunday).

Boyle **train station** (☎ 966 2027) is on Elphin St. Trains leave three times daily to Sligo (€9, 40 minutes) and Dublin (€21, three hours) via Mullingar.

You can order a taxi on ☎ 966 3344 or ☎ 966 2119.

ROSCOMMON TOWN
☎ 090 / pop 1623

Samba, soccer, Latin dance classes, and mass in Portuguese have become as familiar as bingo in Roscommon (Ros Comáin), thanks to the influx of around 600 Brazilians who came to work here in the 1990s. Exotic South American influences aside, this county town has a small but stately centre, with several sights worth a gander.

Information

The local **tourist office** (☎ 662 6342; www.ireland west.ie; John Harrison Hall, the Square; 10am-1pm & 2-5pm Mon-Sat Jun-Aug) is next door to the post office, and there's a Bank of Ireland in the Square.

Sights & Activities

Roscommon County Museum (☎ 662 5613; the Square; adult/child €2/1; 10am-3pm Mon-Fri Jun–mid-Sep), in the former Presbyterian church, contains some interesting pieces, including an inscribed 9th-century slab from St Coman's monastery and a medieval sheila-na-gig from Rahara. The unusual Star of David window supposedly represents the Trinity.

The Norman **Roscommon Castle**, built in 1269, was almost immediately destroyed by Irish forces. Its turbulent 'knocked-down, get-put-up-again' history continued until the final surrender to Cromwell in 1652. The massive walls and round bastions,

standing alone in a field to the north of town, look mighty impressive as you approach…although the castle's as hollow as an Easter egg inside!

Pay a quick visit to the 13th-century **Dominican priory**, off Circular Rd, at the southern end of town, to see its unusual 15th-century carving of eight *gallóglí* ('gallowglasses', mercenary soldiers). Waving seven swords and an axe, they protect an earlier effigy of the priory's founder, Felim O'Conor, set in the north wall.

Roscommon is lent dignity by the proud buildings lining its central square. Slap in the centre is the former courthouse (now the Bank of Ireland), opposite the enormous **old jail**, where in the 18th century 'Lady Betty', who had murdered her lodger, evaded death by taking on the job of public executioner. Despite objections, everything but the façade was demolished a decade ago to make way for a dismal shopping arcade.

Ask at the tourist office for a map of the **Suck Valley Way**, a 75km walking trail along the River Suck. The river offers some of the best mixed fishing in Ireland, with rudd, tench, pike and perch in abundance. En route you may pass **La Tène Stone** in Castlestrange, 7km southwest of town on the R366, an Iron-Age spiral-inscribed stone, one of only four in the country from this period.

Sleeping & Eating

Gleeson's Guesthouse (☎ 662 6954; www.gleesons townhouse.com; Market Sq; s/d from €55/100; P) There's a wonderfully warm welcome at this listed 19th-century house, set back from the Square in its own tree-studded, fairy-lit courtyard. The 20 comfortable rooms have pine furnishings and are decorated in bright Mediterranean colours. Eamonn and Mary Gleeson never seem to sit still: they also run a bustling café (sandwiches and snacks €3.50 to €8), which is open from 8am till 6pm, and the Manse restaurant (lunch mains €8 to €11, dinner mains €16 to €23, four-course dinner €30), serving hearty homespun menus based primarily on beef, duck and fish. The restaurant is open from 12.30pm till 2.30pm and from 6.30pm till 9.30pm.

Tatler Hotel (☎ 662 5460; tatler@iol.ie; Main St; s/d €40/70) The service can be slow, but it's well worth waiting: this hotel, over a busy central pub, has 12 surprisingly nice rooms with subtle furnishings and decent bathrooms. Adjoining Jono's Bar packs them in at lunch-time for the humungous carvery lunches and chunky sandwiches (€6 to €8).

Abbey Hotel (☎ 662 6250; www.abbeyhotel.ie; Abbeytown; s/d €100/180; P ⬜) This 18th-century manor at the start of the Galway road is posh. Try to get one of the five rooms in the old house, most of which have big four-poster beds and antique furniture. The new fitness centre and pool will keep the health-conscious happy.

Comfy Coffee Café (☎ 087-683 3794; Main St; snacks €3-8; ⏱ 9am-6pm Mon-Sat, 1-5pm Sun) Roscommon's newest café is a hectic lunch-time spot, run by a frazzled but friendly young team. In addition to serving speciality coffees, salads, *panini* and all-day brekky, it plans to host live traditional music – pop in to see what's going on.

Drinking & Entertainment

JJ Harlow's (☎ 663 0869; the Square) Converted from a family drapery, this old-style bar has retained shelves full of provisions and hardware items, but the effect is more oddball

---

SOMETHING SPECIAL

Castlecoote House (☎ 666 3794; www.castle cootehouse.com; Castlecoote; s/d from €110/180) About 8km southwest of Roscommon, gorgeous Castlecoote House is just too romantic for words! A wreck when the present owners bought it in 1997, it has since been restored to supreme heights of 18th-century elegance, with added 21st-century luxuries including spa baths. The five rooms have rich antique furnishings and views over the orchard, croquet lawn, ruined castle or river; a couple also have four-poster beds and chandeliers. It's very good value for this amount of history and beauty.

From Roscommon town, take the R366 signposted to Fuerty and follow it to Castlecoote. As you go over the bridge into the village, the double gates of Castlecoote House are to the right of the road. Let them know you're coming, otherwise you may find the gate locked.

---

museum than hideous theme pub. It has cosy snugs, and if you're sick of hearing diddly-dee music, you may enjoy the bluegrass on Wednesday and jazz on Sunday evenings.

Roscommon Arts Centre (☎ 662 5824; www.ros commonartscentre.ie; Circular Rd) There's an impressive programme of independent cinema and touring comedy, theatre and music at this auditorium.

Getting There & Around

Bus Éireann (☎ 071-916 0066) express buses between Westport (€14, 2¼ hours) and Dublin (€16, three hours) via Athlone stop in Roscommon three times daily (once on Sunday). Buses stop in front of Regan's Guesthouse on the Square.

Roscommon train station is in Abbeytown, just west of the town centre near the Galway road; there are three trains daily (four Friday) on the line from Dublin (€34.50, two hours) to Westport (€21, 1½ hours).

Order taxis on ☎ 087-979 1406.

COUNTY LEITRIM

Vast portions of Leitrim (Liatroim), split almost in two by Lough Allen, are composed of two parts H and one part O: it's said that land here is sold by the gallon, and they're only half joking. Leitrim suffered hugely from emigration because of its terrible soil fertility. Even today it has the smallest population (around 25,800) of all the counties – but on the bright side, it has the most pubs per capita in Ireland!

Besides people-free lakes and drumlins, Leitrim contains delightful Carrick-on-Shannon. On a summer's day, the small town's marina heaves with ice cream–eating pleasure-seekers. It's the Shannon's main boating centre: pick up a cruiser and get exploring.

CARRICK-ON-SHANNON
☎ 071 / pop 1842

Carrick-on-Shannon (Cora Droma Rúisc; known simply as Carrick) is a thriving, buzzing, captivating little town, particularly delightful on a sunny day. It's become a major marina, thanks to the completion of the Shannon–Erne Waterway in 1994, which put the town on the tourist map.

Aquatic pursuits aside, Carrick has some above-par examples of early-19th-century architecture on St George's Terrace. Have a glance at **Hatley Manor**, home of the St George family; the **Old Courthouse**, now the seat of the county council, whose underground tunnel led convicts from the dock to the (demolished) jail; and newly refurbished **Market Yard**.

Orientation & Information

Carrick's main L-shaped layout – Main St, then the right-angled turn onto Bridge St – is in Leitrim, but the town straddles the border and some of it lies over the bridge in County Roscommon.

The **tourist office** (☎ 962 0170; www.leitrim tourism.com) has been in disarray after a fire destroyed its Old Barrel Store premises on the Marina. At the time of writing it was hoping to move back there for 2006, but opening times (probably 9.30am to 5pm Monday to Friday May to mid-October, 9am to 5pm Friday and Saturday year round) were not confirmed: contact the office for information. If open, ask about the walking-tour booklet, which takes in Carrick's places of interest.

There's an Allied Irish Bank branch at the top of Main St. The post office is on Bridge St, opposite Flynn's Corner House bar. Gartlan's Newsagents has an **Internet café** (☎ 962 1103; gartlans@eircom.net; Bridge St; 9.30-5.30 Mon-Sat) above it, costing €2/3/6 per 15/30/60 minutes.

Sights & Activities

COSTELLO CHAPEL

The sombre **Costello Chapel** (Bridge St), measuring a tiny 5m by 3.6m, is Europe's smallest. It was built by Edward Costello in 1877, distraught at the early death of his wife Mary. Both husband and wife now lie inside the grey limestone interior, dimly lit by a single stained-glass window. Their embalmed bodies were placed in lead coffins, which sit on either side of the door under slabs of glass. If the door is locked, ask the tourist office to open it.

LEITRIM DESIGN HOUSE

If you've money to spend, take it to the **Leitrim Design House** (☎ 965 0550; www.leitrim designhouse.com; Market Yard; 10am-6pm Mon-Sat), which sells sinfully gorgeous items of furniture, jewellery, textiles, glass and stationery gathered from over 60 studios around the county.

BOATING & FISHING

The 110-seater boat **Moon River** (☎ 962 1777; www.moon-river.net; the Quay) runs one-hour cruises on the Shannon. There are one or two sailings per day (€10/5 per adult/child) between Easter and October, rising to four sailings during June, July and August: check the information board on the quay for details. The boat also has late-night cruises – see opposite.

The annual regatta run by **Carrick Rowing Club** (☎ 962 0532) takes place on the first Sunday in August and draws a big crowd.

For information on fishing, contact the **Carrick-on-Shannon Angling Association** (☎ 962 0489; Gortmor House, Lismakeegan).

Several cruiser-hire companies are based in Carrick, see opposite for details.

Sleeping

Carrick is a popular weekend and hen- or stag-night destination for Dubliners; accommodation fills up quickly, so book ahead. Camping is free on the Roscommon side of the riverbank, though there are no facilities. Tokens for the showers at the nearby Marina can be purchased from the Marina office.

Hollywell (☎ 962 1124; hollywell@esatbiz.com; Liberty Hill; s €55-75, d €96-135; mid-Jan–mid-Dec; P) Without hesitation, this beautiful ivy-covered Georgian country house, on the Roscommon side of the river, is Carrick's best place to stay. The spacious, restful bedrooms contain huge beds and two of them have splendid views of the Shannon and its ever-changing light. The owners are charming and full of local knowledge; they put on superb breakfasts too, with freshly baked bread and homemade bits and pieces. Because of the old furnishings and its proximity to the water, the house isn't suitable for children.

Bush Hotel (☎ 962 0014; www.bushhotel.com; Main St; s/d €79/149; P) This centrally located, family-run hotel is an old stagecoach inn with lots of character. The 60 rooms are something of a mixed bag, but ongoing renovations should mean they all end up refreshed. If traffic noise annoys you, ask for a room at the back overlooking the garden. The hotel buzzes with activity: there's an all-day coffee shop and restaurant, and since the town's cinema closed there have been regular film screenings here.

An Oiche Hostel (☎ 962 1848; Bridge St; dm €20; Ⓟ) You may have to pet your way through sick animals to get to this small new hostel, which is set above a vet's surgery at the bottom of Bridge St. There are four single-sex dorms (no private rooms) that are comfortable if on the pricey side, and a small kitchen and sitting room.

Eating

Cryan's (☎ 962 0409; Bridge St; mains €10-15; ⊗ noon-3.30pm Mon-Sat & 7-9.30pm Thu-Sat) An old-fashioned kitsch restaurant with tasselled lamps and banquettes, Cryan's serves lashings of all things traditional, from bacon and cabbage to schoolboys' favourite sherry trifle. It's good, solid, tasty stuff, with portions that are large even by Irish standards, and is served with amazing cheer. The attached pub has recommended traditional music sessions on Saturday and Sunday nights.

Wheats (☎ 965 0525; Market Yard; snacks €3-5; ⊗ 9am-6pm Mon-Sat) This tiny café serves coffees, smoothies and healthy homemade breads, salads and wraps to take away or to eat in at the carved wooden bar.

Coffey's Pastry Case (☎ 962 0929; Bridge St; mains €4-7; ⊗ 8.30am-7pm Mon-Sat, 9.30am-7pm Sun) Straight out of the 1970s, Coffey's is a cheap, self-service coffee shop–cum-bakery with considerable retro charm. Upstairs tables overlook the river.

Vittos (☎ 962 7000; josephinecoen@yahoo.co.uk; Market Centre; mains €12-20; ⊗ 12.30-2.30pm & 7-9.30pm Thu-Tue) Vittos is an Italian restaurant serving traditional Irish dishes alongside the pasta and pizzas. It's all very clean and cosy, with lots of wood and candlelit tables. If you don't want to dine in, there's a takeaway attached.

Also recommended:

Shannon View House (☎ 962 0594; Liberty Hill; s/d €40/70) A jolly pink family-run home with six light, bright rooms. Nos 1, 2 and 3 have smashing river views. Just over the bridge on the Roscommon side of the river.

Four Seasons (☎ 962 1333; Main St; s/d €35/70) Courteous, centrally located B&B.

Aisleigh (☎ 962 0313; www.aisleighguesthouse.com; Dublin Rd; s/d €45/75) If central locations are booked out, try your luck along the N4. The most impressive B&B is this large modern house with a sauna for guests.

Drinking & Entertainment

Carrick cinema has closed down, but at the time of writing the Bush Hotel was hosting a mobile cinema approximately once a fortnight, open to nonguests. Contact it for information.

Flynn's Corner House (☎ 962 1139; cnr Main & Bridge Sts) Flynn's is a great, authentic pub with a good drop of Guinness and live music on Friday night. Savour it before it's modernised.

Moon River (☎ 962 1777; www.moon-river.net; the Quay; admission €10) Dancers with sea legs could try the 'Party Night' on this 110-seater cruiser, complete with local singers or bands. Boarding is at 11.30pm on Saturday nights; the boat then sets sail along the Shannon until 3am, returning to dry land between 1.30am and 2am for those who want to get off.

Also recommended:

Oarsman Bar & Boathouse Restaurant (☎ 962 1139; Bridge St; mains €11-15) Upmarket pub grub and seafood are served all day at this cavernous watering hole.

Lemongrass (☎ 962 0320; www.victoriahall.ie; Victoria Hall, Quay Rd; mains €14-20; ⊗ 12.30-10pm) Part of the popular Asian food chain, it's worth dropping in here just to admire the building (a graceful old parochial hall) and the 1980s photos of Carrick hung around the mezzanine.

Getting There & Away

The bus stop is outside Coffey's Pastry Case near the bridge. **Bus Éireann** (☎ 01-836 6111, 916 0066) express service No 23 between Dublin (€16, 2¾ hours) and Sligo (€11, one hour) stops here six times in each direction Monday to Saturday (five Sunday). The service stops at several large towns en route, including Boyle, Longford and Mullingar.

The **train station** (☎ 962 0036) is a 15-minute walk over on the Roscommon side of the river. Turn right across the bridge, then left at the service station onto Station Rd. Carrick has three trains daily to Dublin (€21, 2¼ hours) and Sligo (€13, 55 minutes), with an additional one to Sligo on Friday.

AROUND CARRICK-ON-SHANNON
Shannon–Erne Waterway

A far-sighted renovation project, completed in 1994, saw the creation of a symbolic link between southern and northern Ireland, when the 19th-century Ballyconnell–Ballinamore Canal was reopened as the Shannon–Erne Waterway. It joins Ireland's two main river systems (the Shannon and the Erne) to create an amazing 750km network of rivers, lakes and artificial navigations.

The waterway stretches from the River Shannon beside the village of Leitrim, 4km north of Carrick-on-Shannon, through northwestern County Cavan to the southern shore of Upper Lough Erne, just over the Northern Ireland border in County Fermanagh.

You too can join the happy throngs of people and pleasure-crafts: Carrick-on-Shannon is the boat-hire capital, with several companies based at the Marina. It's easy sailing – the canal's 16 locks are fully automated, you don't need a licence, and all of the hire companies give full instructions on handling your boat before you leave. Make sure you take a chart of the waterway (available from bookshops and boat-hire companies) with you, showing the depths and locations of locks. High-season prices are given below.

Carrick Craft (central reservations ☎ 01-278 1666, Carrick office ☎ 071-962 0236; www.carrickcraft.com; the Marina, Carrick-on-Shannon) Hires out four- to eight-berth cruisers, with high-season prices ranging from €926 to €2700 per week.

Crown Blue Line (☎ 071-962 7634; www.crownblueline.com; the Marina, Carrick-on-Shannon) A four-/six-/eight-berth boat costs from €1555/2450/2955 per week.

Emerald Star (☎ 071-962 0234; www.emeraldstar.ie; the Marina, Carrick-on-Shannon) Owned by the Crown Blue Line, with similar prices.

Leitrim Way

The Leitrim Way begins in Drumshanbo and ends in Manorhamilton, a distance of 48km. For more detailed information get a copy of *Way-Marked Trails of Ireland*, by Michael Fewer, from the tourist office.

COUNTY LONGFORD

County Longford (An Longfort) is a quiet farming county that goes about its daily business untroubled by tourism. Most visitors come here for the fishing round Lough Ree and Lanesborough, but there are one or two unusual places worth a visit near Longford town.

If you fancy a walking holiday with a difference, consider exploring the region

on the towpath of the 145km-long **Royal Canal** (p330), which runs from Dublin to meet the River Shannon near Clondra, west of Longford.

One of the three biggest portal **dolmens** in Ireland, with an improbably balanced top stone, lies at Aughnacliffe in the north; it's thought to be around 5000 years old.

Longford suffered massive emigration during the Famine of the 1840s and 1850s, and it's never really recovered. Many Longford migrants went to Argentina, where one of their descendants, Edel Miro O'Farrell, became president in 1914.

LONGFORD & AROUND
☎ 043 / pop 6831

Longford, the county town, is solidly workaday with few fripperies and baubles to interest the visitor. However, you may like to stop here for a breath of sanity after the tourist overkill further west, and to visit the county's two biggest attractions, which are within easy striking distance.

Information

The relatively newly opened **Longford tourist office** (☎ 42577; www.longfordtourism.com; 45 Dublin St; ☺ 9am-5.30pm Mon-Sat) contains a rather nice coffee shop.

Sights

Discreetly hidden 15km southwest of Longford on a broad stretch of bogland is **Corlea Trackway Visitor Centre** (☎ 22386; Keenagh; adult/child €3.50/1.25; ☺ 10am-6pm Apr-Sep), well worth an afternoon's excursion. Corlea bog is extremely important archaeologically, as it contains the only example of Irish timber trackway *(togher)* dateable to about 148 BC. An 18m stretch is on view in a specially designed hall. There's an interesting 45-minute tour detailing the bog's unique flora and fauna, how the track was discovered, and methods used to preserve it. Head south from Longford on the Ballymahon road (R397).

Carrigglas Manor (☎ 48135; house tour adult/child €10/7.50, museum & garden only €5/2.50; ☺ 11am-5pm Sun-Fri Jun–mid-Aug, house tours at noon, 2pm, 3pm & 4pm) is a wonderful castellated Gothic manor house – grim and forbidding from the outside, but with a sumptuous interior – which has been the home of the Lefroy family since it was built in 1837. A youthful Thomas Lefroy had a dalliance with Jane Austen in 1796, and the hero of *Pride and Prejudice,* Mr Darcy, is said to have been based on him. You can tour the house, visit the Victorian costume and lace museum in the Palladian yard buildings, or stroll the 18th-century pleasure gardens. Phone first to check the house is open. Carrigglas Manor is 5km northeast of Longford on the R194 to Granard.

Sleeping & Eating

Viewmount House (☎ 41919; www.viewmounthouse .com; Dublin Rd; s/d €50/90; P) Another sensitively restored Georgian residence, this B&B, about 1km out of town, is the pick of the Longford crop. Five peaceful bedrooms, filled with period antiques and solid wooden beds, look out over a handsome garden. Breakfast is served in the eggshell-blue vaulted dining room; alternatives to the Irish fry include homemade muesli and pecan-topped pancakes. There's a tiny restaurant (dinner €50) in the former coach house, open to nonguests. The restaurant is open from 6pm till 9pm.

Aubergine Gallery Café (☎ 48633; 1 Ballymahon St; mains €12-18; ⏱ noon-5.30pm Tue, noon-8pm Wed & Thu, noon-4pm & 6-9.30pm Fri & Sat, 2-8pm Sun) Upstairs, above the Market Bar, is this young and cheerful restaurant. Dishes are mainly contemporary Mediterranean affairs, and there are several good veggie options.

Chilli Peppers Café (☎ 42577; 45 Dublin St; ⏱ 9am-5.30pm Mon-Sat) Inside the tourist information office, Chilli Peppers is good for a decent lunch, with dishes (soup, sandwiches and hot specials) served in a light and airy exhibition space.

Getting There & Away

Longford **train station** (☎ 45208), off New St, has trains to Dublin (€18.50, one hour and 40 minutes, four daily) and Sligo (€16.50, 1¼ hours, three daily Monday to Saturday, four Sunday), with an extra one to Sligo on Friday.

Bus Éireann (☎ 090-648 4406) operates services from Longford to Athlone (€9, one hour, six daily Monday to Saturday), Carrick-on-Shannon (€7.50, 40 minutes, six daily Monday to Saturday, five Sunday), Dublin (€12, two hours, 13 daily Monday to Saturday, 11 Sunday), Galway (€16, 2½ hours, three daily Monday to Saturday, one Sunday) and Sligo (€10.50, 1½ hours,

six daily Monday to Saturday, five Sunday). Buses stop outside Longford train station.

COUNTY WESTMEATH

Characterised by lakes and rich pasture land, Westmeath (An Iarmhí) is noted more for its beef than its scenic splendour – but don't have a cow, man. Of all the central northern counties, there's probably more to distract the visitor here than anywhere else.

Around Mullingar you'll find everything from a devilish whiskey distillery to the miraculous Fore Valley. Bohemian Athlone is stuffed with history *and* gourmet restaurants: gorge mind and body in one pretty town. Regular river trips explore Viking-rich Lough Ree; in the other direction, they sail to Clonmacnoise (County Offaly) – the best possible way to arrive at Ireland's most important early-Christian site.

MULLINGAR

☎ 044 / pop 8824

Mullingar (An Muileann gCearr) is a prosperous market town. Nearby are teeming lakes of fish, and a preserved bog to delight all you naturalists. The town itself is one of the few places outside Dublin that James Joyce visited: Mullingar gets brief mentions in both *Ulysses* and *Finnegans Wake.* Nearby sections of the **Royal Canal** (p330) are being restored; so far, several kilometres of towpaths have been opened in either direction from Mullingar.

Information

Market House tourist office (☎ 48650; cnr Mount & Pearse Sts; ⏱ 9.30am-5.15pm Mon-Fri Jun-Sep) is central but seasonal. For year-round information, contact **East Coast & Midlands Tourism** (☎ 48761; www.eastcoastmidlands.ie; Dublin Rd; ⏱ 9.30am-1pm & 2-5.30pm Mon-Fri), about 1.5km east of town.

For access to the Internet, try **Ndirox Ventures** (☎ 33821; ndiroxventur@yahoo.com; 57/59 Austin Friar St; per 15/60min €1.50/5; ⏱ 9am-10pm Mon-Sat, noon-9.30pm Sun).

There are several banks on the main street (which changes name five times), including an ACC Bank branch at the start of Oliver

CENTRAL NORTH

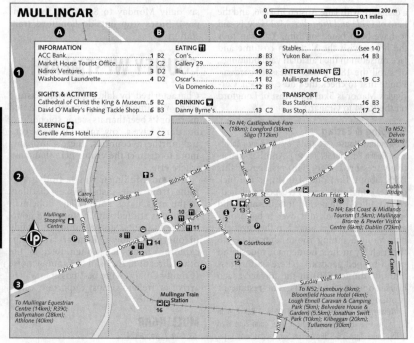

MULLINGAR

INFORMATION	
ACC Bank	1 B2
Market House Tourist Office	2 C2
Ndirox Ventures	3 D2
Washboard Laundrette	4 D2

SIGHTS & ACTIVITIES	
Cathedral of Christ the King & Museum	5 B2
David O'Malley's Fishing Tackle Shop	6 B3

SLEEPING	
Greville Arms Hotel	7 C2

EATING	
Con's	8 B3
Gallery 29	9 B2
Ilia	10 B2
Oscar's	11 B2
Via Domenico	12 B3

DRINKING	
Danny Byrne's	13 B3

Stables	(see 14)
Yukon Bar	14 B3

ENTERTAINMENT	
Mullingar Arts Centre	15 C3

TRANSPORT	
Bus Station	16 B3
Bus Stop	17 C2

Plunkett St. The post office is to the west on Dominick St. The **Washboard Laundrette** (☎ 43045; Dublin Bridge; ☼ 8.45am-6.15pm Mon-Sat) charges €6.90 per machine.

Sights

Mullingar is known for its pewterware. At the **Mullingar Bronze & Pewter Visitor Centre** (☎ 48791; www.mullingarpewter.com; Great Down, the Downs), you can tour the **factory floor** (☼ 9.30am-4pm Mon-Thu, 9.30am-12.30pm Fri) and see artisans turning the silvery-grey metal into cups, bowls and *objets d'art*. Two large **gift shops** (☼ 9.30am-6pm Mon-Fri, 10am-6pm Sat) sell crystal, pottery and textile pieces. The centre is about 6km southeast of Mullingar on the Dublin road (N4).

The **Cathedral of Christ the King** was built just before WWII and has large mosaics of St Anne and St Patrick by Russian artist Boris Anrep. There's a small **ecclesiastical museum** (☎ 48338; adult/child €1.25/0.65; ☼ 3-4pm Sat & Sun Jul & Aug) over the sacristy, entered from the side of the church, which contains vestments worn by St Oliver Plunkett.

Activities

Trout fishing is popular in the loughs around Mullingar, including White, Mt Dalton and Pallas Lakes, and Loughs Owel, Derravaragh, Glore, Lene, Sheelin and Ennell – where the largest trout (11.9kg) ever caught in Ireland was landed in 1894. The fishing season runs from 1 March or 1 May (depending on the lake) to 12 October. All the lakes except Lough Lene are controlled by the **Shannon Regional Fisheries Board** (☎ 48769).

For further information contact **East Coast & Midlands Tourism** (☎ 48761) or the helpful **David O'Malley's Fishing Tackle Shop** (☎ 48300; 33 Dominick St), both in Mullingar. O'Malley's can supply gillies and fishing tackle. For Lough Derravaragh contact **Mr Newman** (☎ 71206); for Lough Owel, **Mr Doolan** (☎ 42085); for Lough Sheelin, **Mr Reilly** (☎ 043-81124); and for Lough Ennell, **Mrs Hope** (☎ 40807), **Mr Roache** (☎ 40314) or **Mr Gavigan** (☎ 086-828 6849).

Mullingar Equestrian Centre (☎ 48331; www.mullingarequestrian.com; Athlone Rd), southwest of Mullingar on the Athlone road (R390), offers riding packages starting at €80 (for lesson, lunch and a two-hour cross-country ride).

Swimming is possible in Loughs Ennell, Owel and Lene (which has a Blue Flag award and lifeguards on duty in July and August), but Derravaragh is very deep and has no shallows.

Sleeping

There are very few central B&Bs: most are on the approach roads from Dublin and Sligo.

Bloomfield House Hotel (☎ 40894; www.bloomfieldhouse.com; Tullamore Rd; s/d €95/170; P) Nicely located near Lough Ennell, 4km from town, this rambling, old-fashioned hotel was fully refurbished in 2004 and a new extension added. Rooms are inoffensively decorated, with the suites (with four-poster beds) being particularly sumptuous. The hotel has a spa and leisure centre attached, with a full range of therapies. Accommodation and treatment packages are on offer.

Lynnbury (☎ 48432; Tullamore Rd; s/d from €50/80) This 200-year-old Georgian farmhouse is beautifully located in secluded grounds, 3km south of town. It has interesting sports facilities, including a tennis court, snooker table and table tennis. Bedrooms don't have en suites, but several of them do have good views of Lough Ennell.

Greville Arms Hotel (☎ 48563; www.grevillearmshotel.com; Pearse St; s/d €80/140; P) Kids will love charging around this mazelike old-world country hotel, which seems to have staircases and landings everywhere. Its 40 rooms are a little loud décor-wise, but they're spacious and the service is extremely good-natured. The hotel is mentioned briefly in James Joyce's *Ulysses*.

Lough Ennell Caravan & Camping Park (☎/fax 48101; eamon@caravanparksireland.com; Tudenham; camp sites €15; ☼ Apr-Sep; P) Eight hectares of woodland surround this peaceful camp site, where facilities include a playground and coffee shop. It's right on the shore of Lough Ennell, and is within walking distance of Belvedere House. The site is 5km south of town on the N52 to Tullamore.

Eating

Gallery 29 (☎ 49449; corbetstown@eircom.net; 16 Oliver Plunkett St; lunch mains €4-9, dinner mains €14-22; ☼ 9am-6pm Tue-Sat) This funky café, with wooden floors and wild flowers, doubles as a gallery space for artwork gathered on the owner's travels. By day it serves delicious *panini*, crepes and homemade desserts, and at night there's a short but imaginative menu. Vegetarians are well catered for.

Ilia (☎ 40300; 28 Oliver Plunkett St; light meals €4-10; ☼ 9am-6pm Mon-Sat) Croissants, full Irish, pancakes with maple syrup, bacon and eggs, muesli…this is Mullingar's most popular spot for breakfast, and when you look at the huge choice you can understand why. Combine with good fresh coffee and a rack of newspapers, and you may end up sitting here till lunch-time.

Via Domenico (☎ 49480; 15 Dominick St; pizzas €6-10, mains €10-20; ☼ 9am-9pm Mon-Sat, noon-9pm Sun) Ignore the checked tablecloths and unflattering lighting in this patisserie-cum-café: the food is where it's at. Join the crowds to sample Via Domenico's superb lasagne or char-grilled salmon, or indulge in a mouthwatering profiterole or feather-light pavlova.

Con's (☎ 40925; 22 Dominick St; mains €6-9; ☼ noon-3pm) Hordes of hungry diners materialise from nearby shops and offices and descend on this bustling pub at lunch-time, for huge carvery lunches and hearty sandwiches.

SOMETHING SPECIAL

Temple House & Health Spa (☎ 0506-35118; www.templespa.ie; s/d €235/430; ☼ Tue-Sun; P ▯) For the ultimate in pampering try this luxurious retreat, where even the birds seem to turn down the tweeting. The 250-year-old house is set in 40 hectares of grounds, on the site of an ancient monastery. There are eight impeccably decorated en suite rooms; when you're not taking advantage of the massage and beauty treatments, you'll be desperate to return to their calming colours and panoramic country views. The spa is also open to nonguests, with a boggling number of packages – pampering days start at €115.

Food is locally sourced (with herbs fresh from the garden) and transformed into imaginative dishes. Special dietary needs are catered for, and 'health spa' doesn't mean 'no alcohol' – you may be pleased to hear that a wine list accompanies the dinner menu.

Temple House is just off the N6, 1.5km west of Horseleap.

Oscar's (☎ 44909; 21 Oliver Plunkett St; pizzas €14, mains €15-25; ⏰ 6-9.30pm daily plus 12.30-1.45pm Fri) For the weirdest pizza toppings imaginable, visit this colourful eatery where you can pep up the cheese-and-tomato with Clonakilty black pudding and chilli mango!

Drinking & Entertainment

Yukon Bar (☎ 40251; 11 Dominick St) The fortuneteller at this pub is a real draw: have your future foretold from 4pm until closing time Monday to Friday. There's also a Monday- and Thursday-night soul, blues and rock session in the front bar, while the small venue at the back, Stables, has occasional gigs.

Danny Byrne's (☎ 43792; 27 Pearse St) This renovated pub has a strangely cosy mock-antique interior, although cosiness flies out of the window when football and rugby matches are shown on the two vast TV screens. There's traditional music on Wednesday nights.

Mullingar Arts Centre (☎ 47777; www.mullingar artscentre.ie; County Hall, Lower Mount St) The centre runs a regular programme of music, comedy, drama and art exhibitions. Phone for details.

Getting There & Away

Bus Éireann (☎ 01-836 6111) runs services to Athlone (€9, one hour, two Monday to Saturday, one Sunday), Ballina (€16, three hours, three Monday to Saturday, four Sunday) and Dundalk (€14.50, 2½ hours, two Monday to Saturday, one Sunday). There's also a very frequent commuter service to and from Dublin (€11.50, 1½ hours), reduced at weekends to around eight buses on Saturday and five on Sunday. All stop at Austin Friar St and the train station.

The **train station** (☎ 48274) sees three or four trains daily in each direction on the line from Dublin (€15, one hour) to Sligo (€18.50, two hours).

SOUTH OF MULLINGAR
Belvedere House & Gardens

Aptly named **Belvedere** (Beautiful View; ☎ 044-49060; Mullingar; adult/child €8/4.50; ⏰ 10am-5pm May-Aug, 10.30am-6pm Mar, Apr, Sep & Oct, 10.30am-4pm Nov-Feb), a handsome hunting lodge with 65 hectares of gardens, overlooks sparkling Lough Ennell. But what a bastard its builder was! Lord Belfield, the first earl, had a true talent for unpleasantness: shortly after Bel-

vedere was finished in 1740, he accused his wife and younger brother Arthur of adultery. She was placed under house arrest for 30 years, and Arthur was jailed in London for the rest of his life. Meanwhile, the earl lived as a wild bachelor infamous for his 'debauchery and dissipation'. On his death, his wife emerged dressed in the fashion of three decades earlier, still protesting her innocence.

Lord Belfield also found time to fall out with his other brother George, who built a home nearby. Ireland's largest folly, a ready-made 'ruin' called the **Jealous Wall**, was commissioned by the earl so he wouldn't have to look at George's swankier mansion.

The house, designed by Richard Cassels, contains some inventive audiovisual displays, and delicate rococo plasterwork in the upper rooms. The **gardens**, with their follies, Victorian glasshouses and lakeshore setting, make for wonderful walking on a sunny day, and they stay open until 9pm in summer. Kids will enjoy tram rides around the grounds, which hold an **animal sanctuary** full of donkeys, ponies and goats, and a **Falconry Centre** with owls, hawks, falcons and eagles, and summer flying displays.

Belvedere House is 5.5km south of Mullingar on the N52 to Tullamore.

Lough Ennell

The lough is renowned for its brown trout and coarse fishing. It's also the area where Jonathan Swift first dreamed up *Gulliver's Travels* (1726); hence the name of the **Jonathan Swift Park** where both **Lilliput Boat Hire** (☎ 044-26167; lilliputboathire@ireland.com; boat hire per day €20) and the **Lilliput Adventure Centre** (☎ /fax 044-26789; www.lilliputadventure.com) are based. The latter organises kayaking, gorge walking and abseiling courses; a day's mixed-activity package including a night's dorm accommodation costs €45. The park is 10km south of Mullingar on the N52.

There are several places to stay near the shores of the lake (see p477).

Kilbeggan
☎ 0506
SIGHTS & ACTIVITIES
Locke's Distillery

Between crafty workers stealing slugs of booze and the 10% that evaporated as 'the angels' share', it's a wonder that any whiskey at all came out of **Locke's Distillery** (☎ /fax 32134; www.lockesdistillerymuseum.com; Kilbeggan; adult/concession/child €5/4/free; �9am-6pm Apr-Oct, 10am-4pm Nov-Mar). A sterling restoration job has made this 18th-century whiskey producer a great visitor attraction, particularly for fans of industrial archaeology. You can marvel at huge lumps of machinery, visit a cooper's room and warehouse, and listen to the creaks and groans of the working mill wheel on a 50-minute guided (or self-guided) tour. Lunch and snacks are served at the adjoining coffee shop, whiskey at the bar.

Kilbeggan Races

Try to back a winner at the **Kilbeggan Races** (☎ 32176; www.kilbegganraces.com; adult/child €18/free), Ireland's only National Hunt course, where there are evening meetings approximately once a fortnight from May to September.

NORTH OF MULLINGAR
Crookedwood & Around

Crookedwood is a small village on the shores of Lough Derravaragh. The 8km-long lake is associated with the tragic legend of the children of Lir, who were transformed into swans here by a jealous stepmother.

About 3km west of Crookedwood is the **Multyfarnham Franciscan friary**. In the present church, the remains of a 15th-century church still stand, and there are outdoor Stations of the Cross set beside a stream.

East of Crookedwood, a small road leads 2km to the ruins of the fortified 15th-century **St Munna's Church**, built in a lovely location on the site of a 7th-century church founded by St Munna. Keys to the church are available from the nearby bungalow.

Tullynally Castle Gardens

The seat of the Pakenham family is the impressive Gothic revival **Tullynally Castle** (☎ 044-61159; www.tullynallycastle.com; Castlepollard; gardens adult/child €5/2.50; � 2-6pm Jun-Aug). The castle is closed to visitors, but you can roam 12 hectares of gardens and parkland containing ornamental lakes, a Chinese and a Tibetan garden and a wonderful stretch of 200-year-old yews.

To get here, take the N4, then the R394 to Castlepollard. From there the castle and gardens are signposted 2km to the northwest.

Fore Valley

The Fore Valley, a green, gorgeous area near the shores of Lough Lene, is great for exploring by bicycle or on foot. In AD 630, St Fechin founded a monastery just outside the village of Fore. There's nothing left of this early settlement, but three later buildings in the valley are closely associated with 'seven wonders' said to have occurred here.

The **Fore Abbey Coffee Shop** (☎ 044-61780; fore abbeycoffeeshop@oceanfree.net; � 11am-6pm daily Jun-Sep, 11am-5pm Sat & Sun year round), on the edge of Fore village, contains a heady combination of home-baked goodies and information leaflets, and there's a 20-minute video about the wonders. Guided tours of Fore can be arranged by phoning the coffee shop in advance.

From Mullingar, take the N4 then the R394 northeast to Castlepollard. The road to Fore is signposted from there.

THE SEVEN WONDERS OF FORE

The oldest of the three buildings is St Fechin's Church, containing an early-13th-century chancel and baptismal font. Over the cyclopean entrance is a huge lintel stone carved with a Greek cross and thought to weigh about 2.5 tonnes. It's said to have been put into place by St Fechin's devotions – the wonder of the **Stone Raised by Prayer**.

A path runs from the church to the attractive little anchorite cell – the **Anchorite in a Stone** – which dates back to the 15th century and was lived in by a succession of hermits. The Seven Wonders pub in the village holds the key.

On the other side of the road near the car park is St Fechin's Well, filled with **Water that Will Not Boil**. Cynics should beware of testing this claim, as it's said that if you try it, doom will come to your family! Nearby is a branch from the **Tree that Will Not Burn**; the coins pressed into it are a more contemporary superstition.

Further over the plain are the extensive remains of a 13th-century Benedictine priory, the **Monastery of the Quaking Scraw**, miraculous because it was built on what once was a bog. In the following century it was turned into a fortification, hence the loophole windows and castlelike square towers. The western tower is in a dangerous state – keep clear.

The last two wonders are the **Mill Without a Race** and the **Water that Flows Uphill**. The mill site is marked, and legend has it that St Fechin caused water to flow uphill, towards the mill, by throwing his crosier against a rock near Lough Lene, about 1.5km away.

ATHLONE
☎ 090 / pop 7354

The county town of Athlone (Baile Átha Luain) has something of a split personality. It has been a garrison town for 300 years, and its eastern half has a hard-edged, no-nonsense feel. Cross the river to the jokingly named 'Left Bank', and you enter a world of painted houses, interesting antique and knick-knack shops, tempting restaurants and twisting streets, all hiding behind the mighty bulk of the castle.

Popular boat tours along the powerful River Shannon run either north to Loch Ree (the 'Lake of Kings') or south to Clonmacnoise, the best way to arrive at the site.

Athlone has always been important historically because of its strategic position at a crossing point on the Shannon. It's a confident, booming town, with a campaign underway to have it promoted to city status – watch this space.

Orientation & Information

Athlone is on the main Dublin–Galway road (N6), and the River Shannon flows through the town from Lough Ree. Major landmarks are Athlone Castle and Sts Peter and Paul Cathedral, prominently located on the western ('Left') bank of the river.

The **tourist office** (☎ 649 4630; Athlone Castle; ⏰ 9.30am-1pm & 2-5.15pm Mon-Fri May-Sep) is inside the castle guardhouse. It's well supported by the **information office** (☎ 647 3173; Lloyds Lane; ⏰ 9am-5pm) run by the local chamber of commerce.

Check email at the **Lost Highway** (☎ 649 2696; www.thelosthighway.org; cnr O'Connell & Pearse Sts; per hr €4; ⏰ 10am-10pm Mon-Sat, 2-10pm Sun).

The Bank of Ireland is at the start of Northgate St, just up from Custume Pl. The post office is on Barrack St beside the cathedral.

Sights & Activities
ATHLONE CASTLE VISITOR CENTRE

The Normans built their **castle** here in 1210, at this important crossroads formed by the river and the ford across it. Over the centuries it was much squabbled over, particularly during the turbulent 17th cen-

tury. In 1690 the Jacobite town survived a siege by Protestant forces, but a year later it fell, under a devastating bombardment of 12,000 cannonballs, to William of Orange's troops. Major alterations to the castle took place between the 17th and 19th centuries.

The **Athlone Castle Visitor Centre** (☎ 649 2912; adult/child/family €5.50/1.60/12; ⏰ 10am-4.30pm May-Sep) contains displays on the 1691 Siege of Athlone; the flora and fauna of the Shannon, and its hydroelectricity role; an old gramophone that belonged to John McCormack (1884–1945), a native of Athlone and one of the greatest tenors of all time; and a military and folk museum, the highlight of which are two sheila-na-gigs. An hour is probably enough time to take it all in.

RIVER CRUISES

Between May and September, two companies have appealing trips on the River Shannon.

Viking Tours (☎ 086-262 1136; vikingtours@ireland .com; 7 St Mary's Pl) offers cruises on a replica Viking longship, with helmets, swords and shields on board so that kids can get into the plunder-and-pillage spirit. They sail north to Lough Ree (adult/child/family €10/8/32, 1½ hours), departing from the Strand roughly four times per day; and south to Clonmacnoise (adult/child/family €17/10/50, 4½ hours) in County Offaly, leaving a couple of times per week. Schedules vary depending on how many reservations are received, so phone or ask at the tourist office.

MV Ross (☎ 087-609 5857; fax 647 4386; Jolly Mariner Marina, Coosan) also runs 1½-hour cruises on Lough Ree (€10/6 per adult/child); phone for schedules.

FISHING

Information and permits are available from the very friendly **Strand Tackle Shop** (☎ 647 9277; powell@iol.ie; the Strand), on the eastern bank of the river opposite the castle.

Sleeping

Bastion B&B (☎ 649 4954; www.thebastion.net; 2 Bastion St; s €35-45, d €60) This is just the most fantastic B&B! With twisting wooden staircases, cactus collections, eclectic bits of artwork and odd curios, you literally don't know what to expect around the corner. The five rooms (three en suite) are crisp, clean and cool, with white walls and bedspreads, neatly folded fluffy towels, and bright Indian hangings. Sunshine and big fat sofas fill the funky lounge-breakfast room. Breakfast is a serve-yourself buffet, with cereal, fruit, fresh bread and a cheeseboard.

Prince of Wales Hotel (☎ 647 6666; www.theprince ofwales.ie; Church St; s/d from €70/130; P ☐) Athlone's newest and most upmarket option on the eastern bank opened in 2004 after a three-year redevelopment scheme. Restful chocolate-and-cream bedrooms have the latest gizmos such as DVD and CD players, and the black marble bathrooms have special non-misting mirrors so you can admire yourself after your power shower.

Lough Ree Lodge (☎ 647 6738; www.athlone hostel.ie; Dublin Rd; dm/s/d incl breakfast €16/25/40; ☺ May-Sep; P ☐) This modern hostel, situated 1km out of town, normally houses students during term time. Rooms are simple but spotless, although many overlook a busy road, and there're a large kitchen, pool table, TV lounge and Internet access (€1 per 15 minutes). If you don't fancy the walk into town, there's a shuttle bus service (€1.50 return, every 15 minutes).

Eating

Athlone is gaining a well-deserved reputation as a centre of culinary excellence. Most of the best restaurants and cafés are behind the castle.

Left Bank Bistro (☎ 649 4446; www.leftbankbistro .com; Fry Pl; mains €18-25; ☺ noon-5pm & 5.30-10.30pm Tue-Sat) This airy, sophisticated bistro at the bottom of Bastion St is probably the town's best restaurant. Dishes come from all over the globe, with particular emphasis on the Orient and the Mediterranean, and the menu is ever-changing to keep up with new foodie trends. It also has a huge wine choice.

Le Chateau (☎ 649 4517; lechateau@eircom.net; Peter's Port; mains €15-24; ☺ 12.30-10pm) There's a cosy old-world atmosphere about Le Chateau, housed in a former church behind the castle, and that extends to the menu. Roast beef and rack of lamb are traditional staples and you'll find no place better to eat them.

Olive Grove (☎ 647 6946; www.theolivegrove.ie; Custume Pl; mains €15-22; ☺ noon-4pm & 5.30-10pm Tue-Sun) This colourful, informal restaurant by the river serves all kinds of everything. It has a modern Irish menu with 'world' influences, which results in some interesting food combinations: how about a starter of mozzarella sticks with spicy peach salsa (€6.50)?

Kin Khao Thai (☎ 649 8805; kinkhaothai@eircom .net; Abbey Lane; express lunch €9.95, dinner mains €17-25; ☺ 12.30-2.30pm Wed-Sat, 1.30-2.30pm Sun, 5.30-9.30pm daily) Succulent green and ruby curries and spicy stir-fries are served up at this genuine Thai restaurant, located on the 1st floor of a higgledy-piggledy yellow building. There's a specials menu of family favourites, including the wonderfully named 'Crying Tiger' (beef served with hot-hot chillies), and at least five veggie options. Opening hours are shorter during low season.

There are two quality cafés on Bastion St: **Slice of Life** (☎ 649 3970; Bastion St; mains €3-7; ☺ 9am-6pm Mon-Sat), which serves really tasty hot specials, pizza slices and sandwiches at bargain-basement prices; and brand-new **Foodies** (☎ 649 8576; Bastion St; sandwiches €3-6; ☺ 9am-6pm Mon-Sat), with is wooden floors and a soothing old stove, where you can have good coffee, cakes, sandwiches and a civilised read of the newspaper.

Drinking & Entertainment

Sean's Bar (☎ 649 2358; Main St) Something of a legend, this is *officially* Ireland's oldest pub! (Well, that's what they told us...) Though the old bus seats have gone, the interior is suitably down-at-heel with log fires, uneven floors, sawdust and a rickety piano. You can catch live music most nights in summer from the riverside beer garden.

Dean Crowe Theatre (☎ 649 2129; www.dean crowetheatre.com; Chapel St) This sizable, refurbished theatre has wonderful acoustics, and runs a broad programme of theatrical and musical events year round; call for details.

Getting There & Around

The **bus depot** (☎ 648 4406) is beside the train station. Express buses stop there on many east–west routes. There are 15 buses daily to Dublin (€10.50, two hours) and Galway (€10.50, 1¼ hours); three from Monday to Saturday (one Sunday) to Westport (€13.50, 2¾ hours) in County Mayo; and three Monday to Saturday (one Sunday, an extra bus Friday) to Mullingar (€9, one hour).

From **Athlone train station** (☎ 647 3300), there are nine trains daily Monday to Saturday (seven Sunday) to Dublin (€18, 1¾ hours); three daily (plus an extra train Friday) to Westport (€18, two hours); and six Monday to Saturday (four Sunday) to Galway (€17.50, 1¼ hours). The train station is on the eastern

CENTRAL NORTH

CENTRAL NORTH

SOMETHING SPECIAL

Wineport Restaurant (☎ 648 5466; www.wineport.ie; mains €24-29, dinner menu €55; ☺ 5-10pm Wed-Sat, 12.30-9pm Sun) This outstanding restaurant, in a sweet-smelling cedar lodge on the lake's edge, showcases chef Feargal O'Donnell's award-winning modern Irish cuisine and carefully chosen wines. The atmosphere is surprisingly relaxed and it's a family-friendly place with a decent children's menu.

There are 10 magnificent contemporary bedrooms (€250), each with a west-facing balcony over the lake so you can revel in the sunsets. Furnishings include Egyptian-cotton duvets, flat screen TVs, Bose stereos and specially commissioned walnut furniture. Sensuous sandstone bathrooms are extra large, and have floor heating for warm-toed luxury. Each room is named after a wine or champagne, and you get to sample the tipple of your chosen room when you arrive. You can also summon a masseur for a stress-busting massage or facial (€50 to €75).

Boat hire can be arranged for a day's jaunt around the lake or a trip across to Glasson golf course.

From Athlone follow the N55 northeast, turning left at the Dog & Duck pub just beyond Ballykeeran; Wineport is 1.5km along this lane, near Glasson.

---

bank on Southern Station Rd. To get there, follow Northgate St up from Custume Pl. Its extension, Coosan Point Rd, joins Southern Station Rd near St Vincent's Hospital.

You can order a taxi on ☎ 647 4400.

AROUND ATHLONE
Lough Ree
Many of Lough Ree's 50-plus islands were once inhabited by monks and their ecclesiastical treasures, drawing Vikings like flies to a honeypot. Hare Island has delivered up two large treasure-hoards of gold ingots and arm rings, possibly buried by the superbly named King Olaf Scabbyhead, scourge of the lake in the 10th century.

These days, its visitors are less bloodthirsty, with sailing, trout fishing and bird-watching the most popular pastimes: the lough attracts many migratory birds that come here to nest, particularly swans, plovers and curlews.

Glasson
☎ 090 / pop 816
The petite, picturesque village of Glasson (Village of the Roses) consists of only one main street, but is well worth a visit for its good restaurants, lively pubs and its proximity to Lough Ree. Glasson is 8km northeast of Athlone on the N55.

SLEEPING & EATING
Glasson Stone Lodge (☎ 648 5004; s/d from €45/65; ☺ Mar-Dec; P) This friendly modern house, built to blend in with its surroundings, is the only B&B in the village centre. The five pine-furnished, wooden-floored rooms are

decent sized and comfy, and breakfast contains home-baked goodies.

Glasson Village Restaurant (☎ 648 5001; mains €19-24, 3-course dinner €34; ☺ 6-9.30pm Tue-Sat, 12.30-2.30pm Sun) People travel for miles to get a table in this award-winning restaurant at the northern end of the village. In a stone cottage that originally housed a garda barracks, it specialises in fresh local produce and seafood.

Grogan's (☎ 648 5158; mains €8-17; ☺ food noon-4pm & 5.30-9pm Mon-Sat, 4-8pm Sun) In the village centre, this pub is the real thing: an authentic old man's bar and lounge with peat fires and a great atmosphere. Smiling staff serve good seafood and hearty pub grub that really is a cut above the usual. Wednesday and Sunday are traditional music nights.

GETTING THERE & AWAY
Bus Éireann (☎ 647 3322) service No 466 from Athlone to Longford has two trips daily from Monday to Saturday, stopping outside Grogan's pub.

Goldsmith Country
Poet, playwright and novelist Oliver Goldsmith (1728–74), author of *The Vicar of Wakefield*, is closely associated with the area northeast of Athlone running alongside the eastern shore of Lough Ree. The *Lough Ree Trail: a Signposted Tour,* by Gearoid O'Brien, is available from the tourist offices in Athlone and Mullingar. This 32km tour is ideal for cycling, and runs through Glasson, around the shores of Lough Ree and into County Longford, also noting sites connected with Goldsmith.

County Donegal

If counties were kids, then Donegal would be the wild child at the back of the bus. Ireland's second-largest county (after Cork) is an intoxicating mix of unbridled bravado and daredevil extremes. It exists in exaggerated isolation, severed from the rest of the Republic by the extended finger of County Fermanagh. But even before history and politics conspired to cut the region off, Donegal was a stubbornly independent land, largely ignored by those in Dublin's distant driving seat.

Half-measures do not get much of a look in here, especially when describing the county's famously fickle weather. A spring trip to Donegal doesn't so much blow away the cobwebs as blast them to oblivion. Wind and rain can strike like raging tempests, yet each outburst leaves behind a glistening born-again landscape of exquisite and quite astonishingly guileless beauty. Meanwhile in summer, the shining sun surpasses itself, driving you to question the geographical fact that you're further north than Newfoundland.

And then there's the scenery: even superlatives fall short of Donegal's soul-stirring landscapes. The county outdoes anywhere else in Ireland for its sheer physical drama and unspoilt splendour. Inland, it hosts some of the country's highest peaks and wildest heathland. But if Donegal's mountainous heart is spectacular, then its vast coastline – the longest of any Irish county – is simply dazzling. Precipitous cliffs, wind-whipped peninsulas and tawny beaches characterise its stunning Atlantic shores. When the weather is kind, Donegal's better beach resorts can rival any in Europe, and make perfect destinations for a summer getaway. However, whenever you come, and for whatever purpose, be assured that this untamed land is never, ever dull.

HIGHLIGHTS

- **Take to the Hills**
  The alpine magic around the Glen Gesh Pass (p496)
- **King of the Castle**
  A quirky mansion in the heart of the glorious national park of Glenveagh (p503)
- **Cliff-top Vertigo**
  Europe's highest sea cliffs, Slieve League (p494)
- **Musical Pub**
  The atmosphere, trad and stout in the renowned Leo's Tavern (p501) near Gweedore
- **Ancient Encounter**
  The views from Grianán of Aileách (p520) hilltop ringfort

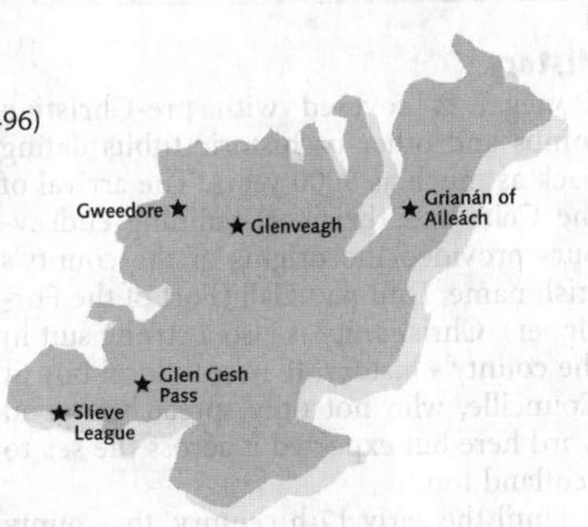

- POPULATION: 137,575
- AREA: 3001 SQ KM

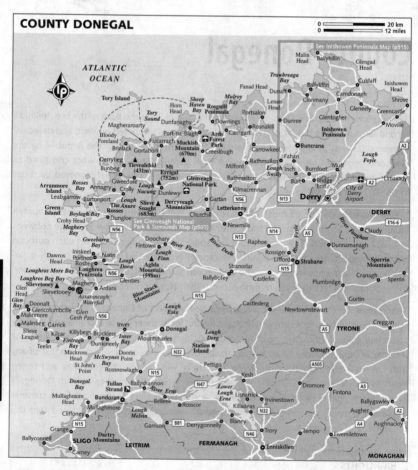

History

Donegal is covered with pre-Christian tombs and other prehistoric titbits dating back as much as 9000 years. The arrival of the Celts and their fort-building endeavours provided the origins of the county's Irish name, Dun na nGall (Fort of the Foreigner). Christianity is also a strong suit in the county's history, thanks to local boy St Colmcille, who not only spread the good word here but exported it across the sea to Scotland too.

Until the early 17th century, the county was roughly divided between two clans, the O'Donnells and the O'Neills, but the Plantation of Ulster that followed their defeat and flight from Ireland reduced the county to a subservient misery. The partition of Ireland in 1921 compounded Donegal's isolation, as it was cut off from Derry, which it served as a natural hinterland. Despite major efforts by the government to offer incentives to industry- and job-creating schemes, Donegal remains largely underdeveloped.

Climate

In many ways, Donegal seems to defy its northerly location; its thermometers rarely drop below zero, and in summer the temperature can top 25°C. This is largely due to the warm caress of the Atlantic Gulf Stream along the county's vast coastline. But when the winter winds and heavy rain are ripping through your semiprotective parka, it doesn't really matter that the 'official' temperature is a balmy 4°C – it can feel arctic. Conversely, when the summer gauge shows that it's less than 20°C, you'll soon find yourself stripping down to your swimsuit.

Language

Roughly one-third of the county lies in the Gaeltacht, where Irish is the lingua franca and road signs challenge the reader to perform linguistic gymnastics to get the right pronunciation. Donegal Irish has a markedly different pronunciation from that spoken elsewhere, and even native speakers from southern Ireland can have difficulty understanding the local vernacular. Before you panic and rush out to do a crash course in Irish, however, be assured that virtually everyone speaks English and will do so without hesitation. It would behove you, though, to familiarise yourself with the Irish place names; although we use English transliterations, their Irish names are included in brackets.

Getting There & Away

Isolation is the leitmotif of Donegal's existence, especially in terms of transportation. There is no rail service to the county and the bus is your main option if you don't have your own car.

Donegal Airport (☎ 074-954 8284; www.donegal airport.ie; Carrick Finn) has daily flights to/from Dublin (from €30, 50 minutes) daily, and flights to Glasgow Prestwick (€57, Friday and Sunday). It's in the townland of Carrick Finn (Charraig Fhion) about 3km northeast of Annagry along the northwestern coast, which makes it somewhat inconvenient for travellers going to the south of the county. There is no public transportation to the airport, so you'll have to get there by your own steam; there are car-rental desks in the terminal.

Getting Around

Although you can get around County Donegal by bus, it's a time-consuming endeavour. Private bus company **Lough Swilly** (in Letterkenny ☎ 074-912 2863, in Derry ☎ 028-7126 2017) has a six-day Runabout unlimited travel pass costing around €30/21/23 per adult/child/student, but it's only valid during July and August.

This is very much walking and cycling country. Plenty of Donegal walking guides can be found in tourist offices and larger bookshops. Recommended companions include *New Irish Walks: West and North* by Tony Whilde and Patrick Simms (Gill & Macmillan), and *Hill Walkers' Donegal* by David Herman (Shanksmare Publications), which have details of many walks mentioned in this chapter.

When driving, be prepared for switchback roads, directions only in Irish, signs hidden behind vegetation, signs pointing the wrong way, signs with misleading mileage or no signs at all. Most of all, prepare yourself for the lunatic boy-racers that seem to plague Donegal's roads.

DONEGAL TOWN

☎ 074 / pop 2455
This snoozy little town was once a stamping ground to the great Irish chieftains, the O'Donnells, top dogs in the northwest from the 15th to 17th centuries. These days it's a far more sedate spot, hugging the innermost edge of Donegal Bay, into which flows the River Eske. If you're coming from the south, chances are you'll arrive here and it makes a pleasant pit stop en route to the north of Donegal.

INFORMATION

Bank of Ireland (the Diamond) One of several banks with ATM and bureau de change.
Blueberry Cybercafe (☎ 972 2933; the Diamond; per hr €6; ☽ 9am-7.30pm Mon-Sat) Internet café above the Blueberry Tearoom. It's an honour system: you fill in a chit with your times and pay downstairs.

TOP FIVE SCENIC RIDES

- Rosguill's roller coaster **Atlantic Drive** (p511)

- Inishowen's isolated **Inis Eoghain 100** (p514)

- Vertiginous heights of **Horn Head** (p507)

- Lingering arc through stunning **Glenveagh** (p502)

- Snaking switchbacks of **Glen Gesh Pass** (p496)

Four Masters Bookshop (☎ 972 1526; the Diamond)
A good spot for books, maps and travel guides. Doubles as
a gift shop.
Post office (Tirchonaill St) North of the Diamond.
Tourist office (☎ 972 1148;
donegal@irelandnorthwest.ie; the Quay; ☼ 9am-6pm
Mon-Sat, noon-4pm Sun Jul & Aug, 9.30am-5.30pm Mon-
Sat Sep-Jun) South of the Diamond.

SIGHTS
Donegal Castle
Shielded on two sides by a bend of the Eske,
the Dúchas-operated **Donegal Castle** (☎ 972
2405; Castle St; adult/student/senior €3.50/1.25/2.50;
☼ 10am-6pm mid-Mar–Oct, 9.30am-4.30pm Nov-Dec)
remains an imperious monument to both
Irish and English might. Built by the
O'Donnells in 1474, it served as the seat
of their formidable power until 1607, when
the English decided to be rid of pesky Irish
chieftains once and for all. Even in defeat, Rory O'Donnell was no pushover,
however. To stop the English getting their
grubby hands on it, he torched his own
castle before fleeing to France in the infamous Flight of the Earls. Their defeat
paved the way for the Plantation of Ulster
by thousands of newly arrived Scots and
English Protestants, thereby creating the
divisions that still afflict the island to this
very day.

The castle was rebuilt in 1623 by Sir Basil
Brooke, along with the adjacent three-story
Jacobean house. There are information
panels on the top floor that chronicle the
history of the castle.

Diamond Obelisk
In 1474 Red Hugh O'Donnell and his wife,
Nuala O'Brien, founded a **Franciscan friary**
by the shore south of town. It was accidentally blown up in 1601 by Rory O'Donnell
while laying siege to an English garrison,
and little remains. What makes it famous
is that four of its friars, fearing that the arrival of the English meant the end of Celtic
culture, chronicled the whole of known
Celtic history and mythology from 40 years
before the Flood to AD 1618 in *The Annals of the Four Masters*, still one of the
most important sources of early Irish history. The **obelisk** (1937), in the Diamond,
commemorates the work, copies of which
are displayed in the National Library in
Dublin.

Donegal Railway Heritage Centre
Hardcore railway buffs will best appreciate this **heritage centre** (☎ 972 2655; www.county
donegalrailway.com; Tirchonaill St; adult/child €3.50/2;
☼ 10am-5pm Mon-Fri, noon-5pm Sat, 2-5pm Sun Jun-
Sep, 10am-5pm Mon-Fri Oct-May), in the former
train station northeast of the centre. It tells
the history of the steam railway that ran
from Ballyshannon to Derry until 1959.
Visitors can also clamber aboard the restored *Drumboe*.

ACTIVITIES
Boat Trips
A fantastic way to explore the highlights of
Donegal Bay is to take one of the boat tours
run by **Donegal Bay Waterbus** (☎ 972 3666; www
.donegalbaywaterbus.com; Donegal Pier; adult/child €10/5).
The 1¼-hour tour covers everything from
seal-inhabited coves to an island manor,
oyster farm and a ruined castle. The tour
runs up to five times daily during the summer and at least once a day the rest of the
year, depending on the weather. Call to
check departure times.

Fishing
Permits are required for fishing in many
of the local rivers. Kit and information are
available from **Doherty's** (☎ 972 1119; Main St;
☼ 9am-6pm Thu-Tue).

SLEEPING
B&Bs are plentiful around Donegal town,
and the tourist office can assist with making bookings.

Budget
Donegal Town Independent Hostel (☎ 972 2805;
www.donegalhostel.com; Killybegs Rd, Doonan; dm/d
€13/31; Ⓟ) Gaudily painted dorms are on
offer at this clean, friendly IHH hostel,
1.2km northwest of town off the Killybegs
road (N56). It's far enough out to be quiet,
but still within walking distance of town.
Pick up can be arranged.

Bluestack Centre (☎ 973 5564; www.bluestack
mountains.com/centre; Drimarone; dm/f €15/40; Ⓟ) This
is a remote country hostel-cum-community
centre with squeaky-clean rooms and a basketball court. It's also a handy point for hikers tackling the Bluestack Mountains. It's
often left unmanned, however, so call ahead.
It's 7km north of town, signposted from the
roundabout northwest of town.

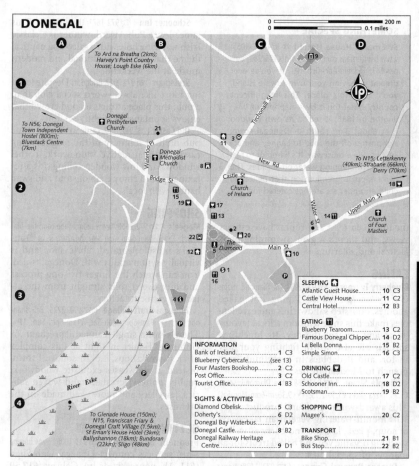

Midrange

Atlantic Guest House (☎ 972 1187; Main St; s/d from €35/45; P) A youthful family, with children bombing around on toy bikes, run this busy old guesthouse near the Diamond. It has 16 dated but pleasant rooms, five of which have a bathroom.

Castle View House (☎ 972 2100; Waterloo Pl; s/d €30/60) This riverside B&B peers up at the castle's back side. It's a simple place, with straightforward rooms, courteous owners and shared bathrooms.

Ard na Breatha (☎ 972 2288; www.ardnabreatha .com; Drumrooske Middle; s/d €55/80; P) Despite a neither-here-nor-there location, this is a terrific little guesthouse, 2.4km out of town signposted off the road to Lough Eske. It

has modern rooms furnished to the highest standard and charming service. The restaurant is open for dinner at weekends.

Glenade House (☎ 972 3186; glenadehouse@eircom .net; 27 Glebe Crest; s/d €35/56; P) If you want a family friendly B&B, look no further. This modern house is set above town in a quiet cul-de-sac, where kids can be found playing whenever school's out. Take the road next to Super Valu.

Top End

Central Hotel (☎ 972 1027; centralhotel@eircom.net; the Diamond; s/d €75/140) Other than the predictable comfort and mod cons of a large establishment, this terracotta-fronted hotel's principal attraction is its position plump in

SOMETHING SPECIAL

St Ernan's House Hotel (☎ 074-972 1065; www.sainternans.com; R267; s/d €175/280, dinner €42; ☿ mid-Apr–Oct; **P**) If you've ever dreamt of having your own private island, you'll love this place. This magnificent country hotel (built by a nephew of Wellington in 1836) is set on its own wooded islet about 3km south of Donegal town, signposted off the road to Laghey and accessible via a causeway. It's hard not to feel serene with lapping water on all sides. The owners put a premium on that peace, so children under six are not catered for.

the town centre. A few rooms have estuary views, and there's a gym, swimming pool, Jacuzzi and solarium.

EATING

Blueberry Tearoom (☎ 972 2933; the Diamond; mains €5-8; ☿ 9am-7pm Mon-Sat) Piping hot baked goodies, doorstep sandwiches and excellent pies make this snug tearoom a local favourite at any time of the day. Its lunchtime specials are also worth fighting your way in for, and it dabbles in everything from French to Mexican dishes.

Simple Simon (☎ 972 2687; the Diamond; soups €1.25, pizza slices €1.50-2.75; ☿ 9.30am-6pm Mon-Sat) This award-winning natural-products shop sells mouth-watering vegetarian takeaways of soup, pizza, lasagne and curry as well as stocking organic veg and baked treats for all manner of special diets.

Famous Donegal Chipper (☎ 972 1428; Upper Main St; fish & chips €7; ☿ 12.30-11.30pm Thu-Tue) They're not kidding: this brightly daubed chippie enjoys an enviable reputation for its freshly fried fish and chips.

La Bella Donna (☎ 972 5790; Bridge St; mains €9-20; ☿ noon-5pm & 7-9.30pm) For a relaxing sit-down meal, this stylish new Mediterranean restaurant excels in almost perfect lunchtime panini and authentic Italian espresso.

DRINKING

Numerous pubs are within a stone's throw of the Diamond, and commonly attract many musicians. Check the Thursday edition of the *Donegal Democrat* for details of what's going on around town.

Schooner Inn (☎ 972 1671; Upper Main St) This James Joyce Pub Award–winner is a classic Irish watering hole with a salty-dog nautical theme that puts on traditional and modern music at the weekend.

Scotsman (☎ 972 2022; Bridge St) Despite looking more like a well-worn social club than a pub, this place attracts a good crowd that enjoys spontaneous nightly sessions.

Old Castle (☎ 972 1062; Castle St) A grey-stone pub built in mimicry of the neighbouring castle with attractive stonework, corbel windows and low wooden ceiling. It's a relaxing spot to enjoy a sip of stout and swap banter with locals.

SHOPPING

Magee's (☎ 972 2660; www.mageeshop.com; the Diamond; ☿ 9.30am-6pm Mon-Sat) Magee's is Donegal's most celebrated fabric shop and is virtually synonymous with Donegal tweed. You can watch the finger-twisting process and buy tweed rolls straight from the attached garment factory.

Donegal Craft Village (☎ 972 2225; Ballyshannon Rd; ☿ 9am-6pm Mon-Sat, 11am-6pm Sun; **P**) There's not a single canned leprechaun or Guinness T-shirt in sight at this complex of craft workshops, 1.5km south of town. Instead, it showcases exquisite woodwork, quality pottery, crystal, hand-woven fabrics, jewellery and more – all made on the premises.

GETTING THERE & AWAY

Frequent **Bus Éireann** (☎ 913 1008; www.buseireann.ie) services connect Donegal with Sligo (€11, 1¼ hours, six daily), Galway (€17.50 3½ hours, two to three daily) and Killybegs (€6, 35 minutes, three daily) to the west; Derry (€11.50, 1½ hours), Enniskillen (10, 1¼ hours) and Belfast (€16, 3½ hours) in the North; and Dublin (€16, four hours, six daily) in the southeast. The bus stop is on the western side of the Diamond.

Private coaches operated by **Feda O'Donnell** (☎ 954 8114; www.fedaodonnell.com) run to Galway (single/return €15/22, 3½ hours, twice daily, three on Friday and Sunday) via Ballyshannon, Bundoran and Sligo. Departures are from the tourist office. Fares within Donegal range from €6 to €10.

McGeehan Coaches (☎ 954 6150; www.mcgeehan coaches.com) runs buses to Dublin (single/ return €16.50/23, four hours, one daily, two Monday, Friday, Saturday and Sunday) from in front of the garda barracks across from the tourist office.

GETTING AROUND

The **Bike Shop** (☎ 972 2515; Waterloo Pl) is a good bet for cycle hire (€10/60 per day/week). The owner is friendly and knowledgeable and will help you plan a cycling itinerary.

AROUND DONEGAL TOWN

LOUGH ESKE

Despite its optimistic name, meaning 'Lake of the Fish', this picturesque spot northeast of Donegal town isn't the fishpond it once was, but it's still terrific territory for **cycling** or **walking** over the majestic Blue Stack Mountains.

Sleeping & Eating

Ardeevin Guest House (☎ 074-972 1790; seanmc ginty@eircom.net; Lough Eske; s/d €50/70; P) Of the scattered B&Bs that ring the lough, this is our favourite. Running for 40 years, it has evolved into a large rambling house with charming rooms and an old-fashioned garden overlooking the lough and mountains. It's 4km north of town off the Letterkenny road (N15). Take the second left after the Skoda car dealership and follow the signs.

Harvey's Point Country Hotel (☎ 074-972 2208; www.harveyspoint.com; Harvey's Point; s €89-199, d €178-290, 4-course dinner €50; P 🖳) Great as a romantic retreat or executive sanctuary, this superb country hotel sprawls along the brink of the lough. The wide variety of rooms include top-of-the-range suites the size of a footy field, beds the size of goalposts and private Jacuzzi that would fit half the team. The French-inspired cuisine at its restaurant is rightly praised by foodies. Harvey's is 6km north of Donegal town.

Getting There & Away

From the Diamond leave Donegal on the N56 to Killybegs. About 300m past the bridge, turn right following the signs to Harvey's Point. The ring road eventually joins the N15 to northeast Donegal, so it makes a convenient cycling trip.

ROSSNOWLAGH

☎ 071 / pop 50

The old-world resort of Rossnowlagh (Ross Neamblach), southwest of Donegal town, has a dazzlingly white Blue Flag beach, which extends for nearly 5km and is a great **surfing** spot. While the beach attracts plenty of holiday-makers, you'll never have to battle for space to put your beach towel down, nor is there any trace of an amusement arcade.

Deep in the adjacent forest is a **Franciscan friary** (☎ 985 1342; admission free; ☽ 10am-8pm Mon-Sat) with tranquil gardens; the way of the cross takes you through a hillside smothered with rhododendron to spectacular hill-top views.

Smugglers Creek (☎ 985 2367; smugcreek@eircom .net; Rossnowlagh; s/d €45/90; ☽ Easter-Oct; P) is perched dramatically on the hillside above the bay. This pub, restaurant and guesthouse is justifiably popular for its excellent food and sweeping views. Room No 4 has the best vantage point and a balcony into the bargain.

Sand House Hotel (☎ 985 1777; www.sandhouse -hotel.ie; Rossnowlagh; s €90-160, d €180-320; ☽ Feb-Dec; P 🖴) is a truly splendid beach getaway. Once an extravagant 19th-century fishing lodge, this enormous old hotel sits directly by the sea and seems to enjoy a permanent atmosphere of gaiety.

BALLYSHANNON

☎ 071 / pop 2230

The pretty little V-shaped town of Ballyshannon (Béal Átha Seanaidh, meaning 'the ford entrance of the hill slope') crawls up a steep incline above the River Erne. It's a world away from the tacky excess of nearby Bundoran, and makes a more tranquil base to explore the coastline.

Orientation & Information

Ballyshannon's centre, north of the river, has two main streets converging below the distinctive clock tower of Gallogley Jewellers: looking uphill, Main St runs left and Market St to the right. There's an **AIB** (Market St) with an ATM and a **post office** (Market St) near the junction.

Sights & Activities
ALLINGHAM'S GRAVE

As a kid, the poet William Allingham (1824–89) scribbled his first attempts at verse on a window in the AIB bank on

Castle St where his dad was the manager. The wordsmith, who is best remembered for his poem *The Fairies*, is now buried in the graveyard beside **St Anne's Church**, the grave marked simply 'poet'. The church is signposted left off Main St after Dorrian's Imperial hotel.

ABBEY MILLS

Waterwheels have been harnessing the river's power for centuries at **Abbey Assaroe** (☎ 985 8966; Abbeylands; admission free; ❤ 11am-7pm Jun-Sep, 2.30-7pm Sun Oct-May; Ⓟ). The site was founded in the late 12th century by Cistercian monks from County Roscommon. Now restored to working order, the mills are open as a heritage centre. Take the road to Rossnowlagh (R231) and after 2km, signs indicate Abbey Mills on the left.

A one-hour walking tour called **Ballytour** (☎ 985 2822; www.geocities.com/ballytour; adult/child incl drink €8/4; ❤ Jul-Sep) leaves from the bridge. Call for the schedule.

Festivals & Events
BALLYSHANNON FOLK & TRADITIONAL MUSIC FESTIVAL

This exuberant celebration of traditional music arrives for the last weekend in July or the first in August. The schedule is available online at www.ballyshannonfolk festival.com.

Sleeping & Eating

Rockville House (☎ 985 1106; rockvillehouse@eircom .net; Belleek Rd; s/d €35/60; Ⓟ) This genteel 17th-century country house stands on a solitary hillock about 500m from the centre, and overlooking the River Erne. Service is cheerful and rooms are very pleasant.

Breesy Centre (☎ 982 2925; www.breesycentre.com; Cashelard; dm/d/q €18/50/60; Ⓟ ♿) If you've got wheels and the will to find it, this remote country hostel has spanking new en-suite dorms and a tranquil village setting 6km northeast of Ballyshannon. The neighbouring pub claims to be where British PM Tony Blair first tasted Guinness. Head north on the N15, turn east after 5km and continue 1km towards Cashelard.

Dorrian's Imperial (☎ 985 1147; www.dorrians imperialhotel.com; Main St; s/d €80/140) Trimmed with blood-red ironwork and daubed with pastel colours, this grand old hotel dominates a broad chunk of lower Main St. It

has 26 carefully maintained rooms, a leisure centre and understated, ageing décor.

Lakeside Caravan & Camping (☎ 985 2822; lakesidecentre@eircom.net; Beleek Rd; camp sites €15 ❤ Mar-Sep) Nestling on the shore of Assaroe Lake, this four-star camping ground is worth the trip. It's especially well equipped for kids. From Ballyshannon, take the N3 for 1km towards Beleek.

Shannon's Corner (☎ 985 1180; Main St; mains €6-10; ❤ 8.30am-4.30pm) In-the-know locals pile into this down-home bistro, opposite the Thatch Pub, for its home-cooked lunches and smashing sarnies.

Drinking

Two deservedly popular pubs are **Finn McCool's** (☎ 985 2677; Main St), a 'traditional drinking emporium' that hosts twice-weekly traditional music, and the impossibly quaint **Thatch Pub** (Bridge St), which is just off the top of Main St, and draws as many photographers as it does punters.

Getting There & Away

There are regular daily **Bus Éireann** (☎ 074-912 1309) services to Bundoran (€2.10, 10 minutes), Sligo (€9, 50 minutes), Galway (€17.50, 3½ hours), Donegal (€5.10, 25 minutes), Derry and Dublin (via Enniskillen, Cavan and Navan). The bus station is between the bridge and the Gallogley Jewellers clock tower.

Feda O'Donnell (☎ 074-974 8114) buses depart from opposite the bus station, for Donegal (€5, 15 minutes), Letterkenny (€6, one hour), en route to Gweedore (€6, 2¼ hours) twice daily, four times on Friday. For Sligo (€6, 45 minutes) and Galway (€15, three hours) they leave from outside Maggie's Bar, south of the river near the roundabout, twice daily, three Friday and Sunday.

BUNDORAN
☎ 071 / pop 1680

Surfing has been the surprise saviour of the much-maligned seaside resort of Bundoran (Bun Dobhráin). Long one of Ireland's tackiest holiday resorts, a kitsch assortment of half-baked fairground rides, flashing arcades, fast-food diners and overpriced B&Bs, the town has nonetheless been riding a new wave of popularity as one of Europe's premier surfing spots. If you're a confirmed landlubber, there are far better places to visit.

The seasonal **tourist office** (☎ 984 1350; bundoran@irelandnorthwest.ie; The Bridge, Main St; 🕑 10am-5pm Mon-Fri mid-Mar–Sep, 10am-4pm Fri & Sat Oct–mid-Mar) is opposite the Holyrood Hotel. The post office is a further 120m south; the AIB Bank on Main St has an ATM and bureau de change.

Activities

SURFING & KITE-SURFING

The boarding bug has caught on in a big way in Bundoran. The breaks of Tullan Strand, just north of the town centre, offer some of the best surfing in Europe, and Bundoran hosts the annual Irish National Surfing Championships, which are usually held in April. For more information, check out the website of **Irish Surfing Association** (www.isa.ie).

The superb **Donegal Adventure Centre** (☎ 984 2418; www.donegal-holidays.com; Bay View Ave) rents gear and runs all-year surf tuition but also offers a range of other programmes, from kayaking to gorge walking. It also has accommodation for those on courses.

One step further, **Bundoran Surf Co** (☎ 984 1968; www.bundoransurfcompany.com; 🕑 9.30am-7pm) offers lessons in kite-surfing and power-kiting. A day-long lesson costs €120. The company also rents standard surf gear (board and wetsuit €30 per half day) and gives surf lessons (€30 for up to three hours).

HORSE RIDING

Homefield Equestrian Trails (☎ 984 1288; www.donegalequestrianholidays.com; Bayview Ave) is an excellent adventure centre and hostel that, among other activities, organises horse-riding along the beach and instructional courses. A half-day trail costs €45, but shorter rides are also possible.

WATER ACTIVITIES

If you'd rather let the kids burn off some energy while you fit in some serious pampering, **Waterworld** (☎ 984 1172; www.waterworldbundoran.com; adult/child under 8 €8.50/3.50) on the seafront has a swimming pool complete with water slides, and some decidedly more relaxing seaweed baths at **Aquamara** (☎ 984 1173; baths from €18; 🕑 11am-7pm). See p448 for more Irish seaweed therapy.

Sleeping

There are plenty of hotels scattered about town, although overpricing is the norm in summer.

Homefield Hostel (☎ 984 1288; homefield@indigo.ie; Bayview Ave; dm/d €18/40; P) Although you'd never guess it from outside, this 260-year-old building was once Viscount Enniskillen's holiday play pad, and later served as an altogether more restrained convent. The six-bed dorms and private rooms are in good nick and there are lots of cosy lounges.

Gillaroo Lodge (☎ 984 2357; www.gillaroo.net; Sligo Rd; s/d €38/60; P 💻) Outdoorsy people and fisher-folk will feel right at home in this excellent two-storey B&B; it's close to the beach and has plenty of fishy facilities, including boat hire and tackle storage. Plus it's beautifully cared for and friendly to boot.

Grand Central Hotel (☎ 984 2722; www.grandcentralbundoran.com; Main St; s/d €90/140, mains €12-18) Despite décor that brings to mind a posh pub, this large, professional hotel is plum in Bundoran's centre and has a recommended restaurant.

Eating

La Sabbia Wine & Oyster Bar (Homefield Equestrian Trails; ☎ 984 2253; Bayview Ave; mains €12-20; 🕑 6-10pm) This affordable Mediterranean bistro is bursting with colour and charm, with tables spilling out onto the front porch. It's a breath of fresh air following the predictable quickie meal options in the town centre.

Le Chateaubrianne (☎ 984 2160; Sligo Rd; set meals €34-40; 🕑 6.30-9.30pm Tue-Sat, 12.30-3.30pm Sun; P) Posing as an elegant Georgian home, this welcoming restaurant is worth seeking out for its imaginative French and modern Irish cuisine using fresh local seafood and game; vegetarians are catered for.

Entertainment

There's a youthful energy to the nightlife in Bundoran, which absorbs the post-beach euphoria nightly in summer. A string of identical pubs line the main street, while unsophisticated nightclubs abound. **Dome** (☎ 984 2430; East End; 🕑 midnight-4am Fri-Sun) gets the biggest following for its guest DJs.

Getting There & Away

Bus Éireann (☎ 074-912 1309) buses stop on Main St. There are direct daily services to Sligo (€8, 45 minutes), Galway (€17.50,

---

PILGRIMAGE TO LOUGH DERG

In summer, tens of thousands of devotees from all walks of Irish life make the millennia-old pilgrimage to peaceful **Station Island**. Located in the middle of Lough Derg, east of Donegal town, St Patrick himself is thought to have fasted here. The traditional three-day retreat starts with a 24-hour vigil; one meal (of dry bread and black tea) a day is permitted; and everyone is expected to complete the Stations of the Cross in bare feet, having fasted from the preceding midnight. In recent years, the focus has changed slightly to embrace stressed-out urbanites in search of the ultimate peaceful haven. Indeed anyone over 14 years is allowed on the island, but you should be a genuine pilgrim to participate. Shorter one-day pilgrimages are also run from the end of April.

Further information is available from the **Priory** (☎ 071-986 1518; www.loughderg.org; St Patrick's Purgatory, Pettigo). The pilgrims reach the island by boat from St Patrick's Purgatory, about 7km north of Pettigo, but outside the pilgrim season there's no regular service to the island. During the busiest pilgrim season (1 June to 15 August), **Bus Éireann** (☎ 01-836 6111) runs special services to Lough Derg from Dublin, Galway, Sligo and Ballyshannon. Call for details.

2¼ hours), Donegal (€3.50, 40 minutes) and more. **Ulsterbus/Translink** (☎ 028-9066 6630; www.ulsterbus.co.uk) has three services daily Monday to Friday (one Saturday) to Belfast (€17.50, 3½ hours) via Enniskillen (€12.50, 1¼ hours). **Feda O'Donnell** (☎ 074-974 8114) buses from Crolly (€6, 2½ hours) travelling to Galway (€14, three hours) stop in Bundoran outside the Holyrood Hotel twice daily, three times on Friday and Sunday.

SOUTHWESTERN DONEGAL

MOUNTCHARLES TO BRUCKLESS

Apart from a scattering of pubs and cafés in Mountcharles and Dunkineely, there are few places to eat, so stock up before leaving Donegal or Killybegs.

Mountcharles
☎ 074 / pop 430

The shiny-green **pump** at the top of this hillside village was once the backdrop for stories of fairies, ghosts, historic battles and mythological encounters. For it was at this point that local boy Séamus MacManus, a poet and *seanachaí* (storyteller) of international repute, practised the ancient art in the 1940s and 1950s.

Mountcharles (Moin Séarlas) is the first settlement along the coastal road (N56) west of Donegal town. About 2km south of the village is a safe, sandy beach.

Dunkineely
☎ 074 / pop 353

The dozy little village of Dunkineely (Dún Cionnfhaolaidh or Dún Cionnaola) is situated a little further west. From here, a minor road runs down the improbably thin finger of land poking into the sea at **St John's Point**. There's a beach with a little bit of sand and sweeping coastal views, and the waters around the point are a prime diving site.

Blue Moon Hostel (☎ 973 7264; bluemoonhostel@eircom.net; Main St; camp sites per person €5, dm/d €10/24; P) is an IHO hostel that looks unexceptional, though its three-tier bunk beds are comfy enough and it offers two kitchens, a washer-dryer and plenty of information on local goings-on such as deep-sea diving and sea-angling.

Seaview House (☎ 973 7252; anneshovlin9a@eircom.net; St John's Point; s/d €35/56; P) is an excellent modern B&B with panoramic views to either side from atop St John's Point. It's family friendly but there are only two rooms so book ahead. It's midway along the promontory, 6km from Dunkineely.

Bruckless
☎ 074 / pop 180

The scattered settlement of Bruckless (An Bhroclais) is the next stop about 2km west of Dunkineely. Horse riding and pony trekking are available at **Deane's Equestrian Centre** (☎ 973 7160; deanesequestrian@eircom.net; Darney, Bruckless), including lessons, five-minute rides for children (€3.50) and longer excursions (adult/child from €16/20).

Gallagher's Farm Hostel (☎ 973 7057; camp sites €17, dm €13.50; **P**) is an excellent farmhouse hostel with a familial atmosphere. Gallagher's has 18 beds in converted outbuildings. It is halfway between Dunkineely and Bruckless. Campers have separate facilities, but all have access to the laundry, picnic area and table tennis. The hostel has a list of walks in the area.

Bruckless House (☎ 973 7071; bruc@bruckless .com; d €120; ☺ Apr-Sep; **P**) is fronted by a traditional cobbled farmyard, and is home to a stud farm for Connemara ponies. This luxury, ivy-clad, Georgian B&B is simply gorgeous. The interior is furnished with antique oriental influences. It's signposted off the main road approximately 3km after Dunkineely.

Getting There & Away

Bus Éireann (☎ 972 1008) No 490 leaves Donegal for Killybegs (€3.50, 35 minutes) four times daily from Monday to Saturday, stopping near the Village Tavern in Mountcharles, the Inver post office, Bruckless and the Dunkineely Furniture Centre in Dunkineely.

KILLYBEGS

☎ 074 / pop 1395

A fishy fragrance announces your arrival at Killybegs (Ceala Beaga), Ireland's most important fishing port and home to a large fishmeal processing plant. It's a predictably popular stop for deep-sea angling, but is also a convenient base for the spectacular cliff scenery beyond Kilcar.

The community-run **tourist office** (☎ 973 2346; Quay St; ☺ 9.30am-1.30pm & 2-5.30pm Mon-Fri) is in a cabin near the harbour. The **Bank of Ireland** (Main St) has an ATM and bureau de change.

Sights & Activities

A right turn in town up a steep hill brings you to St Mary's Church, outside which stands the extraordinary **tombstone of Niall Mór MacSweeney**, head of the MacSweeney clan, one of Donegal's ruling families before 1607. It clearly depicts a chain-mailed warrior with a plumed helmet, his battle-axe raised and sword at the ready. This warlike figure is a *gallowglass*, Scottish mercenaries who first came to the north and west of Ireland in the late 13th century.

Several operators offer fishing expeditions with the opportunity to catch pollock, cod and whiting. **Brian McGilloway** (☎ 973 1144; www.killybegsangling.com) runs fishing trips (per person with/without rod & tackle around €50/60). The **Harbour Store** (☎ 973 1569; the Harbour), by the wharf, sells fishing gear.

The wild, secluded **Fintragh Bay**, about 3km west and down a big-dipper of a road, is fun to explore and the water is clean and safe for swimming.

Sleeping

Ritz (☎ 973 1309; www.theritz-killybegs.com; Chapel Brae; s/d/tr/q €30/50/60/80; **P** &) As budget haunts go, this central place really is 'The Ritz'. It boasts the independence of an IHO hostel with the privacy and comfort of a hotel. Top features include an enormous modern kitchen, colourful en-suite rooms with TV and cosy common areas. A light breakfast is included. It's a good family choice.

Lupra Lodge (☎ 973 2135; Fintra Rd; s/d €40/60; ☺ Apr-Sep; **P**) A quirky carousel-shaped bungalow in pleasant gardens about 1km from town, this friendly B&B is worth the trip. Indeed, sensitive noses will appreciate its distance from the harbour's distinctive aroma.

Tara Hotel (☎ 974 1700; www.tarahotel.ie; Main St; s/d €80/110; ☐ &) Not just *in* the town centre, this swanky new hotel practically *is* the town centre. It's characterised by stylish minimalist décor, many seafront rooms with all the frills (including TV with Internet). Ask for one of six sea-view rooms with balcony (costing €10 extra in summer).

Eating

22 Main Street (☎ 973 2876; www.22mainstreet.com; Main St; mains €10.50-16.50; ☺ 5-10pm) Mediterranean-style bistro in the heart of the town, offering seafood, pizza and several good veggie options. You'll find it through an archway opposite the Bank of Ireland.

Kitty Kelly's (☎ 973 1925; Kilcar Rd; mains €16-25; ☺ 6.30-9.30pm Easter-Sep, Thu-Sun Oct-Mar) Run by a gregarious local celebrity, this russet-coloured cottage restaurant feels much like an intimate dinner party. It also enjoys high praise for its seafood and converted farmhouse setting, 5km west of Killybegs. Reservations recommended.

COUNTY DONEGAL

Getting There & Away

Bus Éireann (☎ 912 1008) service No 492 to Donegal (€6, 30 minutes) from Killybegs runs four times daily Monday to Saturday. Bus No 490 heads west to Kilcar (€4, 20 minutes) and Glencolumbcille (€8, 45 minutes) once daily Monday, Wednesday and Friday, and twice on Tuesday, Thursday and Saturday. In July and August an extra bus runs daily, and buses continue to Malinmore twice daily, Monday to Saturday.

McGeehan Coaches (☎ 954 6150) runs from Glencolumbcille to Dublin (€17.50, 4½ hours, one to two daily). Extra buses are laid on in summer. It also runs to Glencolmcille (€5, one hour).

KILCAR & AROUND

☎ 074 / pop 260

Kilcar (Cill Chártha) and neighbouring Carrick (An Charraig) make good bases to explore the breathtaking coastline of southwestern Donegal, and not least the stunning sea cliffs at Slieve League. Kilcar is also famous for the manufacture of Donegal tweed. Just outside Kilcar is a small, sandy beach.

Tourist information is available from the community centre, **Aísleann Cill Cartha** (☎ 973 8376; Main St; ⏲ 9am-5.30pm Mon-Fri), which also has an Internet connection (€5 per hour). There are no banks. The post office is off Main St past O'Gara's pub.

Sights

STUDIO DONEGAL

Beside the community centre is the **Studio Donegal** (☎ 973 8194; www.studiodonegal.ie; The Glebe Mill, Kilcar; admission free; ⏲ 10am- 5.30pm Mon, 9am-5.30pm Tue-Thu, 9.30am-5pm Fri), a tweed factory that sometimes allows visitors upstairs to see spinners and weavers in action. In its shop you can buy tweed at prices not to be sniffed at.

SLIEVE LEAGUE

Suffers of vertigo should avoid Slieve League like the plague. Even driving up to these spectacular polychrome sea cliffs, the highest in Europe dropping some 600m into the sea, is a hair-raising – but exhilarating – experience. From the car park, there's a path skirting up around the near-vertical rock face to the aptly named **One Man's Pass**.

Take the turn-off signposted Bunglass from the R263 at Carrick, 5km northwest of Kilcar, and continue beyond the narrow track signposted Slieve League to the one that's signposted Bunglass.

Activities

Three walks that start in Kilcar are collectively known as the **Kilcar Way**. From Teelin, experienced walkers can spend a day walking north via Bunglass and the cliff-top One Man's Path – not for the faint hearted – to Malinbeg, near Glencolumbcille. It shouldn't be attempted in windy conditions or if bad weather is likely to impede visibility.

Sleeping & Eating

Dún Ulún House (☎ 973 8137; dunulunhouse@eircom .net; Coast Rd; camp sites €10, dm €15-22.50, s/d €30/60; **P**) The sweeping view down to a ruined ringfort is what strikes you first about this combined B&B, hostel and camping ground, 1km west of the village. Accommodation is simple but homy, while the unusual little camping ground is ensconced in the tiered hillside; a tiny shower-toilet block is nearby.

Derrylahan Hostel (☎ 973 8079; derrylahan@eircom .net; Derrylahan, Kilcar; camp sites €12, dm/d €12/32; **P**) Another top option for hostellers and campers, this friendly IHH hostel is some 3km west of the village. It's a working farm, with poultry pecking around the yard outside. The dorms are well worn but comfortable, there are plentiful cooking facilities and a 20-person group house. Pick-ups can be arranged.

Restaurant Teach Barnaí (☎ 973 8160; Main St; mains €12-25; ⏲ 6-10pm, noon-3pm Sun) 'Barney's House' is a superb little restaurant dotted with rustic household paraphernalia and brass carriage lamps, and serving local seafood with a continental twist.

Getting There & Away

Bus Éireann (☎ 912 1309) service No 490 connects Kilcar and Carrick with Killybegs and Glencolumbcille once daily Monday to Friday (twice daily Saturday, once Sunday). In July and August an extra bus runs daily Monday to Saturday. **McGeehan Coaches** (☎ 954 6150) runs a daily service from Glencolumbcille to Dublin stopping at Carrick and Kilcar. There are extra buses in summer.

GLENCOLUMBCILLE

☎ 074 / pop 255

The beauty of Glencolumbcille (Gleann Cholm Cille, 'Glen of Columba's Church') is in stark contrast to the desolate landscapes that precede it as you travel westward from Killybegs and Kilcar. The dark turf bog gives way to a lush green valley that has been inhabited since 3000 BC and you'll find plenty of Stone Age remains throughout the collection of tiny settlements. It is believed that the 6th-century St Colmcille (Columba) founded a monastery here (hence the valley's name) and incorporated Stone Age standing stones called *turas* into Christian usage by inscribing them with a cross.

At midnight on **Colmcille's Feast Day** (9 June) penitents begin a walkabout of the *turas* and the remains of Colmcille's church before attending Mass at 3am in the local church.

Information

The **Lace House** (☎ 973 0116; Cashel; ☺ 10am-6pm Mon-Sat, 1-5pm Sun Apr, Jun & Sep–mid-Nov, 9.30am-9pm Mon-Sat, noon-6pm Sun Jul & Aug) craft shop dispenses limited tourist information. There are no banks but the post office has a bureau de change.

Sights & Activities

FOLK VILLAGE MUSEUM & HERITAGE CENTRE

A museum with a mission, this **folk centre** (☎ 973 0017; www.glenfolkvillage.com; Doonalt; adult/concession/child €2.75/2.30/2; ☺ 10am-6pm Mon-Sat, noon-6pm Sun Easter-Sep; P) 3km west of the village, by the beach, was established by the forward-thinking Father James McDyer in 1967 to freeze-frame traditional folk life for posterity. It's housed in a huddle of replicated thatched cottages of the 18th and 19th centuries, with genuine period fittings. The *shebeen* (illicit drinking place) sells unusual local wines (made from ingredients such as seaweed and fuchsias) alongside marmalade and whisky truffles. Admission includes a tour.

MALINMORE ADVENTURE CENTRE

Overlooking Malin Bay, this recently revived **adventure centre** (☎ 973 0003; Malinmore, Glencolumbcille) offers canoeing, snorkelling, fishing, orienteering, boat trips and more. It's affiliated with the Glencolumbcille Hotel.

BEACHES

There are two sandy beaches with brisk waves in **Doonalt**, west of Columbcille. Another gorgeous little beach can be found at **Malinbeg**, a perfect sheltered bay bitten out of low cliffs and filled with firm red-tinged sand.

Courses

Oideas Gael (☎ 973 0248; www.oideas-gael.com; ☺ mid-Mar–Oct), at the Foras Cultúir Uladh (Ulster Cultural Foundation) 1km west of the village centre, offers a range of adult courses in the Irish language and traditional culture, from Donegal dancing to *bodhrán* (hand-held goatskin drum) playing. Weekend/week-long courses with accommodation cost €95/190 per person.

Sleeping

Dooey Hostel (☎ 973 0130; camp sites/dm/d €7/12/25; P) Once the flagship property of the IHO, this ageing hostel still has character in spades and a decent view to boot. Built into the hillside, it has an earthy feel compounded by the bulging rock and dripping greenery lining its inner corridor. Facilities are primitive but plentiful (including six kitchens), and a group house for 20 is available. Drivers should take the turn beside the Glenhead Tavern for 1.5km; walkers can take a short cut beside the Folk Village.

Malinbeg Hostel (☎ 973 0006; www.malinbeghostel.com; Malinbeg, Glencolumbcille; dm/d €12/30; P) Altogether more comfort-orientated than Dooey, modern Malinbeg is also within striking distance of a beautiful beach. It scores extra points for spotless en-suite rooms, and proximity to a food store and restaurant. Call ahead for a pick-up.

Corner House (☎ 973 0021; Cashel, Glencolumbcille; s/d €33/50; P) Flowery rooms that are a tad dated but nonetheless cosy are on offer at this long-running B&B close to the centre. Each bedroom has its own shower.

Glencolumbcille Hotel (Óstán Ghleann Cholm Cille; ☎ 973 0003; www.glenhotel.com; s/d €49/80; P) This canary-coloured hotel stands amid the rolling countryside, with its own golf course slowly taking shape at its rear. Its 40 classy rooms are extremely spacious. For something special, request the suite facing the coast. To get there, continue past the folk museum towards Malinbeg.

COUNTY DONEGAL

Eating

An Chistin (The Kitchen; ☎ 973 0213; Glencolumbcille; mains €10-22; ⓨ 9.30am-9.30pm Easter-Oct) You won't find a better spot to chow down than this café-restaurant attached to Oideas Gael. It serves up a surprisingly gourmet selection, including superb seafood, to a soundtrack of mellow jazz.

Silver Strand House (☎ 973 0220; Malinbeg; mains €15-20; ⓨ 9am-9.30pm May-Sep; Ⓟ) For those staying towards the tip of Malinbeg, this catch-all restaurant by the beach proffers a great fisherman's platter so you can sample most of the local haul.

Shopping

Glencolumbcille Woollen Mill (☎ 973 0070; www .rossanknitwear-glenwoolmill.com; Malin More; ⓨ 10am-8pm Mar-Oct, 10am-5.50pm Nov-Feb) This is the place to stock up on woollies. Rossan knitwear is manufactured locally, but you can also pick up Donegal tweed jackets, caps and ties alongside lamb's-wool scarves and shawls. It's 3km southwest of Cashel.

Lace House (☎ 973 0116; Cashel, Glencolumbcille) As well as dispensing tourist information, the Lace House sells Rossan knitted garments, jackets and rugs.

Getting There & Away

Bus Éireann (☎ 912 1309) service No 490 leaves for Killybegs (see p494) daily with an extra service on Saturday and in July and August.

McGeehan Coaches (☎ 954 6150) leaves from Biddy's Pub near Killybegs (€5, one hour) and Dublin (€20, five hours, twice daily). McGeehan also runs to Ardara, Dungloe and Glenties.

MAGHERY & THE GLEN GESH PASS
☎ 074 / pop 640

A tiny village on the northern edge of the peninsula, Maghery has a picturesque waterfront, and if you follow the strand westward, you'll get to a rocky promontory full of caves. During Cromwell's 17th-century Irish Destruction Tour, 100 villagers sought refuge here but all except one were discovered and massacred.

About 1.5km east of Maghery is **Assarancagh Waterfall**, beyond which is the beginning of a 10km marked trail to the **Glen Gesh Pass** (Glean Géis, meaning 'glen of the swans'), one of the most beautiful spots in Europe. It's almost alpine in appearance;

cascading mountains and lush valleys dotted with isolated farmhouses and small lakes. If you're driving, you can get to the pass directly from Glencolumbcille by following the road signs for Ardara.

ARDARA
☎ 074 / pop 580

Most visitors come to scenically positioned Ardara (Árd an Rátha) simply to boost their winter wardrobe, for this small heritage town represents the heart of Donegal's knitwear and hand-woven tweed tradition. But there are other reasons to come, not least its proximity to the spaghetti-switchbacks of the beautiful Glen Gesh Pass.

Tourist information is available from the Triona Design visitor centre (opposite). On the Diamond there's an Ulster Bank with an ATM; the post office is a short walk away on Main St.

Festivals & Events

The trad-music **Cup of Tae Festival** (www.cupof taefestival.com) takes place at the end of April or early May. It includes a school of music, as well as dancing and story telling.

Sleeping & Eating

Drumbarron Hostel (☎ 954 1200; the Diamond; dm/d €12/26) This Georgian-style two-storey house is furnished with comfortable bunk beds, brightened up with modern art and equipped with a large kitchen. Knock at the B&B opposite if there's nobody in the hostel.

Drumbarron House (☎ 954 1200; the Diamond; s/d €35/50) In the family for three generations, this large B&B is both courteous and cosy. It's currently run by an artist, who has a private studio at the back of the house.

Green Gate (☎ 954 1546; www.thegreengate-ireland .com; Ardvally, Ardara; s/d from €40/70; Ⓟ) Seemingly too good to be true, this idyllic hilltop B&B is spread out over several restored thatched cottages and has sweeping views down to the bay and fearless rabbits lolloping around. Follow the tiny pictorial signs of a gate beyond Woodhill House.

Woodhill House (☎ 954 1112; www.woodhillhouse .com; d €90-130; Ⓟ) This 17th-century manor house is rich in history and legend alike. The courtly gardens are a huge bonus, and its cosy restaurant has a wine list to leave any connoisseur drooling. It's 400m southeast of the centre.

COUNTY DONEGAL

Nancy's Bar (☎ 954 1187; Front St; mains €8-12) If this delightful little pub were any more homy, the clientele would all be seated around the fire in slippers. It almost feels as though you're sitting in Nancy's living room. The bar serves superb seafood and chowder that will not disappoint. It's also the best place in town to savour a quiet pint or two.

Entertainment

Corner House (☎ 954 1736; the Diamond) A good spot to listen to an Irish music session (nightly from June to September) while savouring a drop or two of the black stuff.

Shopping

Ardara is a great place to stock up on winter woollens and warm tweed. There are half a dozen outlets specialising in local knitwear.

Triona Design (☎ 954 1422; Main St; ✆ 9am-8pm Jun-Sep, 9am-6pm Oct-May) has weavers beavering away in the shop and are fully versed in the profession's rich history.

Kennedy's (☎ 954 1106; Front St) You could also try this place, which is uphill from the Diamond.

Getting There & Away

In July and August, **Bus Éireann** (☎ 912 1309) service No 492 from Killybegs (€4, 25 minutes) stops three times daily Monday to Friday, in each direction, outside O'Donnell's in Ardara. The rest of the year these buses run once on Tuesday and Thursday, and twice on Monday, Wednesday and Friday. June to mid-September **McGeehan Coaches** (☎ 954 6150) runs a service to Dublin (€17.50, 4½ hours) twice daily via Donegal (€4, 50 minutes).

Getting Around

Don Byrne's of Ardara (☎ 954 1638; Main St), east of the centre, rents bikes for €15/60 per day/week.

DAWROS HEAD

This peninsula north of Ardara glistens with a multitude of tiny lakes cupped by gentle, undulating hills. The twin resort towns of **Narin** and **Portnoo** also tend to be swamped with summer weekenders, attracted by the beautiful wishbone-shaped Blue Flag beach at Narin.

The beach's sandy tip points towards the protective bulk of **Iniskeel** island, and at low tide you can walk out to this island. St Connell, a cousin of St Colmcille, founded a monastery here in the 6th century. Hardly any trace of the monastery remains but the island is nevertheless studded with interesting early medieval Christian remains.

Another adventurous diversion is to track down Lough Doon, 3km south of Narin, in the centre of which sits the 2000-year-old **Doon Fort**, a fortified oval settlement. To reach the fort, you need to hire a rowing boat (around €8) from an adjacent farm. Pick a day that's not too windy.

If the fort whets your appetite for archaeology, pay a visit to the **Dolmen Eco-Tourism Centre** (☎ 074-954 45010; www.dolmencentre.ie; Kilclooney; ✆ 9am-5pm Mon-Fri), which can point you towards several other prehistoric sites, including a delightful tortoise-like passage tomb a short walk up a track left of the church.

Also on the peninsula, hemmed in by grassy dunes, is **Tramore Beach**. In 1588 part of the Spanish Armada ran aground here. The survivors temporarily occupied O'Boyle's Island in Kiltoorish Lake, but then marched to Killybegs, where they set sail again in the *Girona*. The *Girona* met a similar fate that year in Northern Ireland, with the loss of over a thousand crew.

Sleeping

Tramore Beach Caravan & Camping Park (☎ 074-955 1491; campbella@eircom.net; Rosbeg; small/large tents €10/12) The remote place has 24 sandy camp sites sheltered amid dunes, just a short hop from the beach. Take the road from Ardara to Narin then turn left, following the signposts to Tramore Beach.

Narin and Portnoo have B&Bs aplenty, which are generally open from April to September.

Carnaween House (☎ 074-954 5122; Narin; s/d €35/60; ✆ May-Sep; P) This B&B bags prime position overlooking the beach, and has four pleasant rooms (with shower).

Getting There & Away

From Monday to Saturday in July and August, **Bus Éireann** (☎ 074-912 1309) service No 492 runs between Killybegs and Portnoo (€9, 55 minutes, twice daily).

GLENTIES

☎ 074 / pop 790

This parish-pump town prides itself in being a long-time performer in the Irish Tidy Towns competition. For travellers, however, the attraction of Glenties (Na Gleannta) is in its beautiful location at the foot of two valleys with a southern backdrop laid on by the Blue Stack Mountains. It's a good spot for **fishing** and there are some cracking **walks** in the surrounding countryside.

A **summer school** (www.patrickmacgill.com) is held in August in honour of plucky Patrick MacGill (1891–1963), the 'navvy poet' who was sold by his parents at a hiring-fair, later escaped and eventually ended up writing for the English *Daily Express*. Glenties is also linked with playwright Brian Friel, whose play (and later star-studded film), *Dancing at Lughnasa*, is set in the town.

On the main street there's a Bank of Ireland, with an ATM and bureau de change, and a post office.

St Connell's Museum & Heritage Centre (☎ 955 1227; Main St; adult/child €2.50/1; ☿ 10am-1pm & 2-4.30pm Mon-Fri Apr-Sep), beside the old courthouse at the western end of town, has a fusty ragbag of local artefacts. Also worth checking out is the tent-shaped modern **church**, through a guillotine-like gate opposite the museum.

Sleeping & Eating

Campbell's Holiday Hostel (☎ 955 1491; campbellshostel@eircom.net; Glenties; dm/d €13/30; ☿ Apr-Oct; **P**) A smashing hostel with colour-coded six-bed dorms and comfortable doubles, plus a couple of kitchens and a laundry. It's located on the left behind the museum as you enter from Ardara town on the N56.

Avalon (☎ 955 1292; Glen Rd; s/d €35/50; **P**) No-nonsense B&B with a chatty host, Avalon is scenically positioned about 500m from the centre of town. It offers four bedrooms (three with shower). Credit cards are accepted.

Highlands Hotel (☎ 955 1111; highlandhotel@eircom.net; Main St; s/d €52/96; mains €7-18) This laid-back country hotel dominates the western end of town. It serves excellent all-day food in substantial proportions using the freshest of produce.

Entertainment

Paddy's Bar (☎ 955 1158; Main St) Paddy's is a comely old watering hole whose walls reverberate to the sound of traditional music several nights a week, and nightly in July and August.

Limelight (☎ 955 1118; Main St; admission €2.50) This youth-driven club, attached to Molloy's Bar, absorbs revellers from a 20-mile radius every Friday and Saturday. The music sticks to a predictable pattern of pop and hits of yesteryear.

Getting There & Away

Bus Éireann (☎ 912 1309) service No 492 from Killybegs stops off in Glenties (€7, 45 minutes) one to two times daily Monday to Friday.

McGeehan Coaches (☎ 954 6150) runs a service from Dungloe to Dublin via Glenties (€17.50, 4¼ hours, twice daily).

FINN VALLEY & AROUND

Off the beaten track, even by Donegal standards, the Finn valley makes a serene escape for fishing, hill walking or cycling. The River Finn is a good **salmon-fishing** river. There's also good **hill walking** on the Blue Stack Mountains and along the Ulster Way, but you do need to be equipped with maps and provisions. Finn Farm Hostel (opposite) can dispense maps and advice for the area. A long, one-day trek could start from the hostel and end at Campbell's Holiday Hostel in Glenties.

The main town is **Ballybofey** (bally-*boh*-fay; Bealach Féich), linked to adjoining **Stranorlar** by an arched bridge over the Finn. There's a locally run **tourist office** (☎ 074-913 2377; Main St; ☿ 9am-5pm Mon-Fri) in the Ballybofey Balor Theatre. In Ballybofey's Protestant church is the **grave** of Isaac Butt (1813–79), founder of the Irish Home Rule movement.

Fintown (Baile na Finne), 30km northwest overlooking Lough Finn, is a mere cluster of houses and pubs dotting the main road. However, it's home to the renovated narrow-gauge **Fintown Railway** (☎ 074-954 6280; Fintown; adult/child €5/2; ☿ 12.30-4.30pm Thu-Sat, 1-5.30pm Sun Jun-Sep), which runs short scenic excursions alongside Lough Finn. It's best to call ahead though, as the railway has struggled for funding in recent years.

Sleeping & Eating

Finn Farm Hostel (☎ 074-913 2261; Cappry, Ballybofey; camp sites/dm/d €8/12/30; ℗) An informal IHO hostel on a working farm. It is enthusiastically involved in reviving dying musical traditions, so it's common to hear musicians practising here. It also offers horse-riding lessons and organised walks. Finn Farm is about 2km from Ballybofey; the turning is signposted simply 'Hostel' off the N15 Donegal road.

Getting There & Away

Bus Éireann (☎ 074-912 1309) express service No 64 between Galway (€17, 4¾ hours) and Derry (€7, 35 minutes) via Sligo (€12, two hours), Donegal (€6, 30 minutes) and Letterkenny (€5, 25 minutes) stops up to six times daily in Ballybofey. Local buses connect Ballybofey with Killybegs and also Letterkenny.

McGeehan Coaches (☎ 074-954 6150) runs a Glencolumbcille (€8, 1¾ hours) to Letterkenny (€5, 35 minutes) service Monday to Saturday that stops in front of the Fintown post office at 1.20pm (at 4.45pm heading for Glenties, Ardara, Killybegs, Kilcar and Glencolumbcille).

The **Feda O'Donnell** (☎ 074-974 8114) bus from Crolly to Galway stops in Ballybofey (€16, three hours, twice daily, three Friday and Sunday).

NORTHWESTERN DONEGAL

There are few places in Ireland that are more savagely beautiful than northwestern Donegal. Humans have been unable to tame the landscape, which varies from wild and bleak to the breathtakingly spectacular. The stretch of land between Dungloe and Crolly is a bleak, rocky Gaeltacht known as the Rosses (Na Rossa) containing numerous tiny lakes and a coastline of clean, sandy beaches. Further west, between Bunbeg and Dunfanaghy, the scenery is softer but more stunning – to many visitors, this is the epitome of what unspoilt Ireland should look like. Offshore, the islands of Arranmore and Tory are both beautiful and fascinating to those eager for a glimpse of a more traditional way of life.

DUNGLOE & AROUND

☎ 074 / pop 945

'Sweet Dungloe' (An Clochán Liath), immortalised in the song by Emmet Spiceland Ballad Group, is a busy little bow-shaped town and capital of the Rosses. Apart from hosting the popular Mary from Dungloe festival, however, it is only of interest as a base to explore the area.

The **tourist office** (☎ 952 1297; ☯ 10am-2pm & 3-6pm Mon-Sat, 11am-5pm Sun Jun-Sep) is off Main St behind the Bridge Inn. The **Bank of Ireland** (Main St) has an ATM and bureau de change. The **post office** (Quay Rd) is off Main St.

Activities

Fishing for salmon and trout is popular and you can get tackle and permits from **Bonner's** (☎ 21163; Main St). The nearest good beach is 6km southwest of town at **Maghery Bay**.

Kevin Tobin runs the local **Dooey Surf School** (Scoil na dTonn; ☎ 952 2468; www.dooeysurf school.com; 2hr lesson €25).

Festivals & Events

Crooner Daniel O'Donnell, pin-up to pensioners across England and Ireland, returns to his home town to host the 10-day **Mary from Dungloe Festival** (☎ 952 1254; www.maryfrom dungloe.info) in late July/early August. Thousands pack the town for all kinds of revels culminating in a pageant where this year's 'Mary' is selected.

Sleeping & Eating

Atlantic Guesthouse (☎ 952 1061; www.atlantichouse dungloe.com; Main St; s/d €35/70) Smack in the middle of town, this is a sugary-coloured guesthouse with a finger in many pies – video rental, youthful bar, and more. Its 10 en-suite rooms are well-kept, and the atmosphere laid-back.

Utopia Guest Accommodation (☎ 956 1875; utopiaga@eircom.net; Church Rd; s/d €35/70; ☯ Apr-Sep; ℗) It might not be a mythical paradise, but this six-room riverside B&B certainly is a tempting prospect thanks to its spotless rooms, al fresco decking and barbecue out the back.

Riverside Bistro (☎ 952 1062; Main St; mains €14-20; ☯ 12.30-3pm & 6-10pm) A lively French theme pervades this colourful little bistro, which is a good spot for candle-lit dinners and a choice of surprisingly daring Irish and international dishes, including a few for vegetarians.

Getting There & Away

Dungloe is served by several private companies but not Bus Éireann.

McGeehan Coaches (☎ 954 6150) runs a service from Dungloe to Dublin (€17.50, 4½ hours, two daily, three Sunday) via Glenties (€4, 30 minutes) and Donegal (€6, one hour).

Lough Swilly (☎ 912 2863) runs a Dungloe to Derry service (single €18, three hours, three daily Monday to Friday, one Saturday) via Burtonport, Crolly, Bloody Foreland, Falcarragh and Letterkenny.

Feda O'Donnell (☎ 974 8114) runs twice weekly from Annagry (Anagaire) to Killybegs via Dungloe (€5, 1¼ hours, 8.10am on Monday and 2.40pm on Sunday), Glenties and Ardara. Returning it runs twice on Friday only, stopping in Dungloe at 8.45pm and 10.30pm.

BURTONPORT

☎ 074 / pop 345

This pocket-sized port village is the embarkation point for Arranmore Island. For a rather anonymous little place, Burtonport (Ailt an Chorráin) has attracted some famously off-the-wall characters. In the 1970s, the Atlantis commune was established here, and practised a primal therapy that earned them the nickname 'the Screamers'. Eventually they relocated to the Colombian jungle. Later, the Silver Sisters chose Burtonport to live out their Victorian lifestyle, complete with Victorian dress.

For fishing trips contact **Inishfree Charters** (☎ 954 2245) or you can approach the cabins by the pier.

Cois Na Mara (☎ 954 2079; timothydoherty@hotmail .com; Main St; dm/d €12.50/30; ☷ Mar-Oct; P) is a handsome canary-yellow Victorian house that's difficult to miss. It welcomes all-comers with a mix of hostel-like accommodation and easy-going B&B, close to the middle of town.

The giant fibreglass lobster clinging precariously to the outer wall at **Lobster Pot** (☎ 954 2012; Main St; mains €10-20; ☷ noon-2pm & 6-9.30pm) is an unsubtle clue as to the menu: freshly netted seafood. Its aptly named 'Titanic' shellfish and fish platter is big enough to sink the heartiest appetite.

Lough Swilly (☎ 912 2863) buses stop in Burtonport en route from Dungloe to Derry.

ARRANMORE

☎ 074 / pop 900

Blessed by dramatic cliff faces, sea caves and clear sandy beaches, the small island of Arranmore (Árainn Mhór) lies a short ferry trip from the mainland. Measuring just 9km by 5km, the island has been inhabited since the Early Iron Age (800 BC), and a prehistoric triangular fort can be seen on the southern side. The western and northern parts are wild and rugged, with few houses to disturb the sense of isolation. The **Arranmore Way** circles the island (allow three to four hours) and off the southwestern tip is **Green Island**, a bird sanctuary. You'll hear mostly Irish spoken here, although most islanders are bilingual.

Sleeping & Eating

Arranmore Hostel (☎ 952 0015; www.arranmorehostel .com; Leabgarrow; dm/d €14/32) A short walk left of the ferry, and beautifully positioned next to a beach, is this civilised 30-bed hostel. Originally a post office, its owners live off-site so call ahead.

Bonner's Ferryboat Restaurant (☎ 952 0532; Leabgarrow; s/d €45/80, mains around €10) This café-cum-B&B is also just around the corner from the ferry. It's in a convenient spot although there are cheaper places close by.

A new 23-room hotel was also set to open in late 2005 near the beautiful beach at Aphort Strand, charging around €50/80 per single/double.

Entertainment

The island's all-night festivities are renowned. Pubs often open 24 hours a day to sate thirsty fishermen, and reverberate to the pleasant sound of traditional-music sessions.

Getting There & Around

The **Arranmore Ferry** (☎ 952 0532; www.arainnmhor .com/ferry) plies the 1.5km from Burtonport to Leabgarrow (adult/student/child return €10/8/5, 25 minutes, seven Sunday, eight Monday to Saturday July and August, three Sunday, five Monday to Saturday September to June). It also takes cars (€27 return).

Once there, you can save your legs by taking an island tour with **O'Donnell Taxis** (☎ 087-260 6833).

GWEEDORE & AROUND

☎ 074 / pop 1390

The Irish-speaking district of Gweedore (Gaoth Dobhair) is commonly used as a base for trips to Tory Island or Glenveagh National Park. Its rugged coast, dotted with white, sandy beaches, was once an attraction in itself, though it has since been overrun by holiday-home mania. Consequently, Derrybeg (Doirí Beaga) and Bunbeg (Bun Beag) virtually run into each other along the R257, while a few kilometres east on the R258, Gweedore, is scattered along the roadside with no clear core.

Thankfully, the developers haven't yet ventured inland. Away from the coast, habitations are few and far between, and the only feature breaking up the bleak landscape is the presence of dozens of small fishing lakes.

On the main road in Bunbeg there's an National Irish Bank with an ATM and bureau de change, while Derrybeg has a post office. Ferries depart Bunbeg for Tory Island (see p505).

Activities

The most beautiful walking trail in the area is the **Tullagobegley Walk** (Siúlóid Tullagobegley), a historical trample over **Tievealehid** (Taobh an Leithid; 431m), which was used for centuries by locals carrying corpses to the 13th-century graveyard in Falcarragh. The 5½-hour walk begins at Lough Nacung (Loch na Cuinge), just east of Gweedore off the N56. The path brings you past some 19th-century silver mines to Keeldrum, a small townland on the outskirts of Gorta-

hork, before finishing up at the Tullagobegley graveyard in Falcarragh.

Unfortunately, the walk is not waymarked so we strongly advise that you carry an OS Sheet 1 of the area.

Sleeping & Eating

Screag an Iolair Hostel (☎ 954 8593; isai@eircom .net; Tor, Crolly; dm/d €15/35; ☺ Mar-Oct) This is an enchanting little farmyard hostel enveloped in the remote, rocky landscape 5km above Crolly, southwest of Gweedore on the N56. It combines unforced rustic charm with knowledgeable owners who welcome guests as old friends – highly recommended.

Bunbeg House (Teach na Céidhe; ☎ 953 1305; www .bunbeghouse.com; s/d €50/76) Originally a corn mill, this B&B sits directly by Bunbeg harbour where ferries leave for Tory. It's a cosy place filled with wood panelling and rattan furniture, and was immortalised in Tony Hawke's much-loved *Round Ireland with a Fridge* travelogue.

Óstán Radharc na Mara (Seaview Hotel; ☎ 953 1159; boylec@iol.ie; Bunbeg; s/d €60/100; P) On the main road, this newly revamped hotel has 40 spacious en-suite rooms.

Attached to Óstán Radharc na Mara, **Tábhairne Hughie Tim** (mains around €8; ☺ 1-9.30pm) whips up good bar food, or you can dine á la carte in the elegant **Gola Bistro** (mains €20-28; ☺ 6-10pm).

Entertainment

You never know who'll drop by for a sing along at **Leo's Tavern** (☎ 954 8143; Meenaleck, Crolly), Donegal's most famous pub. It is owned by Leo and Baba Brennan, parents of

COUNTY DONEGAL

THE BUNGALOW BLITZ

Donegal's scenery is renowned for the raw, ragged beauty that makes it seem almost indomitable. Yet even here in Ireland's most isolated corner, the coastline is falling prey to an insidious invasion – a bungalow blight. Developers are falling over themselves to take advantage of – many would say mar – the area's natural beauty.

Around two-thirds of construction undertaken in Donegal today is aimed at the second-home market. Already, almost a quarter of the county's homes lie empty for much of the year. And while beautiful stone-walled, slate-roofed and thatched cottages waste away, locals too are opting for the comforts of modern housing. Indeed, far from mourning the loss of their ancestral homes, many admit that the old cottages are too strong a reminder of the hard times suffered by generations of their forebears. It's a tragic loss for such cottages to be replaced with hoards of identikit homes that invite names like 'Legoland' and 'Little Belfast'.

While the casual traveller can do little to stem the tide, we recommend staying in renovated cottages and traditional town houses wherever possible to encourage their upkeep.

Máire, Ciaran and Pól, who were the core of the group Clannad. Another sibling, Enya, needs no introduction to fans of contemporary Irish music. The pub glitters with gold, silver and platinum disks and various other mementos of the successful kids. It is in the townland of Meenaleck, about 3km south of Gweedore on the road to Crolly; it's well signposted.

Getting There & Away
Feda O'Donnell (☎ 954 8114) runs a service twice daily (three Friday and Sunday) from Gweedore to Letterkenny (€5, 1½ hours), Donegal (€6, 1¾ hours), Sligo (€10, 3¼ hours) and Galway (€20, 5½ hours).

DUNLEWY & AROUND
☎ 074 / pop 695
Blink and you could miss the tiny village of Dunlewy (Dún Lúiche), sitting at the foot of Mt Errigal beside Lough Dunlewy.

Sights & Activities
DUNLEWY LAKESIDE CENTRE
The catch-all **lakeside centre** (Ionad Cois Locha; ☎ 953 1699; www.dunleweycentre.com; Dunlewy; admission to house & grounds or boat trip adult/child/student €5.50/3.50/4.50, combined ticket €9/6/7.50; ☑ 10.30am-6pm Mon-Sat, 11am-7pm Sun Easter-Oct) offers something for everybody, especially kids. On the one hand, it reconstructs the home of the last local weaver, who died in 1975. On the other, it's an activity centre with a petting zoo, lakeside walks, pony trekking, and, best of all, excellent boat trips with a storyteller who vividly brings local history, geology and ghoulish folklore to life. In summer there are traditional music concerts. There's also a good café with a turf fire and craft shop.

MT ERRIGAL & THE POISONED GLEN
Scree-scarred Mt Errigal (752m) is one of Ireland's highest peaks. It looms over Dunlewy, seemingly daring walkers to attempt the tough but beautiful climb to its conical peak. Anyone keen to take on the challenge should pay close attention to the weather. It's a dangerous climb on misty or wet days, when the mountain is shrouded in cloud and visibility is minimal.

There are two paths to the summit: the easier route, which covers 5km and takes around two hours; and the more difficult

3.3km walk along the northwestern ridge, which involves scrambling over scree for about 2½ hours. Details of both routes are available at the Dunlewy Lakeside Centre.

Legend has it that the stunning ice-carved rock-face of Poisoned Glen got its sinister name when the ancient one-eyed giant king of Tory, Balor, was killed here by his exiled grandson, Lughaidh, whereupon the poison from his eye split the rock and poisoned the glen. The less interesting truth, however, lies in a cartographic gaffe. Locals were inspired to name it An Gleann Neamhe (the Heavenly Glen), but when an English cartographer mapped the area, he carelessly marked it An Gleann Neimhe – the Poisoned Glen.

The R251 has several viewpoints overlooking the glen. It's possible to walk through it, although the ground is rough and boggy. From the lakeside centre a return walk along the glen is 12km and takes two to three hours. Just watch out for the green lady – the resident ghost!

Sleeping
Errigal Hostel (☎ 953 1180; www.errigalhostel.com; Dunlewy; dm/d €15/36; P) Just 2km north of Dunlewy at the base of Mt Errigal, this long-popular An Óige hostel was slated to be entirely rebuilt by September 2006. Ring ahead to check it has reopened.

Radharc an Ghleanna (☎ 953 1835; radharcang@hotmail.com; Moneymore, Dunlewy; s/d €35/60; P) The four comfy rooms at this farm B&B are slathered in icing-like Artex, while the view over the lough and to the Poisoned Glen is eye-popping. It's down a small lane a short drive east of the hostel.

GLENVEAGH NATIONAL PARK
Lakes cluster like dew in the mountainous valley of **Glenveagh National Park** (Pairc Naísúnta Ghleann Bheatha; glenveaghnationalpark@duchas.ie; admission free; ☑ 10am-6pm Feb-Nov, last admission 5pm), one of the most beautiful spots in Ireland. Alternating between great knuckles of rock, green-gold swathes of bog and scatterings of oak and birch forest, the 16,500-sq-km protected area makes wonderful walking country. It is also home to a variety of wildlife, including the golden eagle, which was hunted to extinction here in the 19th century but was reintroduced in 2000.

Yet such serenity came at a heavy price. The land was once farmed by 244 tenants, who were forcibly evicted by landowner John George Adair in the winter of 1861 following what he called a 'conspiracy' but really because their presence obstructed his vision for the valley.

Adair put the final touches on his paradise (1870–73) by building the spectacular lakeside Glenveagh Castle, while his better half, wife Adelia, introduced two things that define the national park's appearance: the herd of red deer and the rhododendrons. Green fingers and a love of animals notwithstanding, the Adair name still meets with dripping scorn. However, a rather poetic revenge was enacted when Adair's body was to be buried in 1885. As the funeral cart rolled up to his grave, it's said they found a donkey already occupying his would-be home for eternity.

If anything, things got even more surreal after Adair's death. The castle was briefly occupied by the IRA in 1922. Then in 1929 the property was acquired by Kingsley Porter, professor of art at Harvard University, who mysteriously disappeared in 1933 (presumed drowned, but rumoured

to have been spotted in Paris afterwards). Six years later the estate was bought by his former student, Henry McIlhenny, once described by Andy Warhol as 'the only person in Philadelphia with glamour'. In 1975 he sold the whole kit and caboodle to the Irish government and it is now administered by Dúchas, the Heritage Service.

The park features nature trails along lakes, through woods and blanket bog, as well as a viewing point that's a short walk behind the castle.

The **Glenveagh Visitor Centre** (☎ 074-913 7090; Churchill) has a 20-minute audiovisual display on the ecology of the park and the infamous Adair. The restaurant serves hot food and snacks, and the reception sells the necessary midge repellent, as vital in summer as walking boots and waterproofs are in winter. Camping is not allowed.

Glenveagh Castle

This delightfully showy **castle** (adult/concession/child €3/2/1.50; ☺ 10am-6pm Easter- Nov) was modelled in miniature on Scotland's Balmoral Castle. Henry McIlhenny made it a

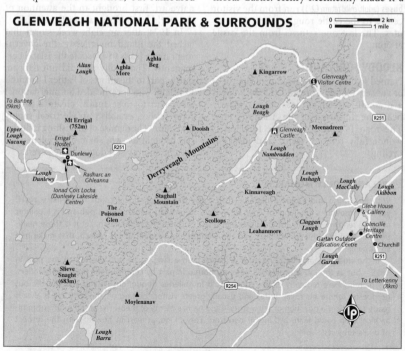

GLENVEAGH NATIONAL PARK & SURROUNDS

characterful home with liberal reminders of his passion for hunting deer. In fact you'll be hard pressed to find a single room without a representation – or even the remains – of a stag.

An entertaining guided tour takes in a series of flamboyantly decorated rooms that look as if McIlhenny just left them. The most eye-catching, including the tartan-and-antler-covered music room and the pink candy-striped room demanded by Greta Garbo whenever she stayed here, are in the round tower. The drawing room has a splendid 300-year-old Adams-style fireplace bought by McIlhenny from the Ards estate near Dunfanaghy.

The exotic gardens are similarly spectacular. They were nurtured for decades and boast a host of terraces, an Italian garden, a walled kitchen garden, and the Belgian Walk, built by Belgian soldiers who stayed here during WWI. Their cultured charm is in marked contrast to the wildly beautiful landscape that enfolds the area.

The last guided tours of the castle leave about 45 minutes before closing time. **Minibuses** (adult/child return €2/1) run from the visitor centre to the castle roughly every 15 minutes. The last one returns from the castle at 6pm.

BLOODY FORELAND

Named for the crimson colour of the rocks at sunset, Bloody Foreland (Cnoc Fola) is a dramatic stretch of coast that regularly bears the full brunt of the Atlantic's fury. The road to and around the foreland is wonderfully remote, scenic and ideal for cycling.

Foreland Heights (☎ 074-953 1785; foreland heights@hotmail.com; Bloody Foreland, Gweedore; s/d €50/72; ☿ Apr-Sep; P) is hardy little 12-room hotel standing at the head of the foreland, with extraordinary views of the cliffs and crashing ocean.

TORY ISLAND

☎ 074 / pop 190

Swept by sea winds and stung by salt spray, the remote crag of Tory Island (Oileán Thóraigh) has taken its fair share of batterings. With nothing to shield it from savage Atlantic squalls, it's a tribute to the hardiness of its inhabitants that the island has been inhabited for over 4500 years. Although it's only 11km north of the mainland, the rough sea has long consolidated the island's staunch independence.

So it's no surprise that Tory is one of the last places in Ireland that holds onto, rather than simply paying lip service to, traditional Irish culture. The island has its own dialect of Irish and even has an elected 'king'. However, the island is perhaps best known for its unique art form, known as naïve art, first brought to the attention of the world by English painter Derek Hill.

In 1974, after an eight-week storm that lashed the island mercilessly, the government made plans to evacuate the island permanently. Thankfully this did not happen, due in part to the efforts of Father Diarmuid Ó Peícín, who spearheaded an international campaign to raise funds, create a proper ferry service, establish an electrical supply and more. The demise of the fishing industry has brought its own share of problems, but the community still doggedly perseveres.

IRELAND'S ONLY MONARCH

With an earring and a blue fisherman's cap, Patsy Dan Rogers doesn't look much like a royal, yet he is known as the 'King' of Tory. He lives in an ordinary house, runs a pub and is a painter of some renown – hardly the qualities that one associates with a monarch. Yet it is these qualities, coupled with his friendliness and the warmth and wisdom of his speech, that make him so popular.

If the truth be told, he is more of a mayor than a king, as he was elected to the post in 1995 – but as the job is unsalaried he is supported in part by contributions from the islanders. His paintings are regularly exhibited and sold in galleries throughout Ireland and the UK, but he doesn't ignore his royal duties and usually greets visitors getting off the ferry. He is always ready to answer a question or tell a story – and he has plenty of them. The world's current monarchical crop could learn a thing or two from Tory's king, at least in how to earn the respect of one's subjects!

The island has just one pebbly beach and two recognisable villages: West Town (An Baile Thiar), containing most of the island's facilities; and East Town (An Baile Thoir). Its eastern end is dominated by jagged quartzite crags like colossal keys, while the southwest slopes down to wave-washed bedrock.

Sights & Activities

Cottages mingle with ancient ecclesiastical treasures in West Town. St Colmcille is said to have founded a monastery here in the 6th century, and reminders of the early church are scattered throughout the town. One example is the T-shaped **Tau Cross**, which stands with its two arms open beside the pier, seemingly welcoming passengers from the ferry. Also nearby is a **round tower**, with a circumference of nearly 16m, built of warmly coloured beach-stones and rough granite, with a round-headed doorway high above the ground.

The island is a wondrous place for **birdwatching**: over 100 species of sea bird inhabit the island, and among the cliffs in the northeast you can see colonies of puffin (around 1400 are thought to inhabit the island).

Art from the Tory **school of primitive painters**, whose work is also known as naïve art and generally depicts island life, has been exhibited around Europe. The most accomplished was James Dixon, who was inspired by (or rather thought he could do better than) the English artist Derek Hill (see p511) in the 1960s. You can see and buy the artists' work in the **Dixon Gallery** (☎ 916 5420) by the hotel.

Sleeping & Eating

Most island B&Bs go unmarked so listen carefully when asking directions.

Teach Bhillie (☎ 916 5145; www.toraigh.net; West Town; s/d €25/40) From the ferry, walk 300m left to this unmarked, yellow B&B. It contains spartan but spotless rooms enlivened with bright splashes of colour, and welcomes guests with genuine warmth. Bikes may be rented next door.

Graceanne Duffy's (☎ 913 5136; East Town; s/d €30/56, dinner €13; 🕑 May-Oct) An approved B&B in the smaller of Tory's two villages, Graceanne's has three simple but comfy bedrooms (two with showers) and uses organically grown food.

Óstán Thóraigh (☎ 913 5920; www.toryhotel.com; West Town; s/d €70/110, mains €8; Ⓟ) Located by the pier, this is a modern, 14-room hotel where you can stay in pastel-coloured rooms, get the low-down on Tory from helpful staff, and enjoy good pub food or full meals. It also has a club for island music and dance (see below).

Entertainment

Club Soisialta Thóraigh (Tory Social Club; ☎ 916 5121; West Town) The island's social life revolves around this merry club, which presents regular *céilidhs* (traditional music and dancing sessions).

Óstán Thóraigh (☎ 913 5920; West Town) The pub at this hotel is a relaxed place to enjoy a drop of the black stuff, swap stories and listen to traditional music sessions.

Getting There & Away

Bring waterproofs for the trip – it can be a wild ride. **Donegal Coastal Cruises** (Turasmara Teo; ☎ 953 1340) runs boats to Tory (adult/student/child return €22/16.50/11) from Bunbeg (daily June to September, Monday to Friday October to May) and Magheraroarty (two daily June to September, with an extra trip daily July and August), which is reached by turning off the N56 at the western end of Gortahork near Falcarragh. The road is signposted Coastal Route/Bloody Foreland.

There's also a seasonal service from Portna-Blagh, 2km east of Dunfanaghy (same price, Wednesday July and August).

Call ahead, as weather and tides affect sailings. It's not uncommon for travellers to be stranded on the island in bad weather.

Getting Around

Bike hire is available from **Rothair ar Clós** (☎ 916 5614) in West Town for €10 per day.

FALCARRAGH & AROUND

☎ 074 / pop 850

The Irish-speaking Falcarragh (An Fál Carrach) and neighbouring Gortahork (Gort an Choirce) are plain little settlements, although there's a good beach nearby. The Bank of Ireland at the eastern end of Main St has an ATM and bureau de change, and the post office is at Main St's western end.

The 19th-century police barracks now houses **Falcarragh Visitor's Centre** (An tSean Bheairic; ☎ 918 0888; 🕑 9am-5pm Mon-Fri, noon-5pm Sat & Sun), which has tourist information and a café, plus a few display cases on the local bobby.

COUNTY DONEGAL

Sights & Activities

It's 4km to the windswept **beach**; follow the signs marked Trá from either end of Main St. The beach is superb for walking, but currents make swimming unsafe.

The grey bulk of **Muckish Mountain** (670m) dominates the coast between Dunfanaghy and the Bloody Foreland. The top has sweeping views to Malin Head and Tory Island. It can be climbed from southeast of Falcarragh by way of the inland road through Muckish Gap.

Sleeping & Eating

Óstán Loch Altan (☎ 913 5267; www.ostanlochaltan .com; Gortahork; s/d €55/110, mains €14-21; **P**) This bold 38-room hotel has entertainment at weekends. Its rooms lack personality, but make up for it with comfort. The restaurant (open from April to October) dishes up decent local fare.

Cuan-na-Mara (☎ 913 5327; crisscannon@hotmail .com; Ballyness, Falcarragh; s/d €30/55; ☉ Jun-Sep; **P**) This plain-faced bungalow B&B has four decent rooms, and a view that encompasses Ballyness Bay and Tory Island. It's located about 1km west of town.

Maggie Dan's (☎ 916 5022; www.maggiedans.ie; An Phanc, Gortahork; pizzas €5-9; ☉ 6pm-midnight; **P**) A little bit of bohemia in the countryside, you're just as likely to hear chat on poetry as pizza in this excellent little eatery.

Entertainment

Falcarragh and Gortahork have a string of good music pubs, but the pick of the bunch is **Teach Ruairi** (☎ 913 5428; Beltany, Gortahork), a traditional bar about 1km west of Gortahork, signposted off the Gweedore road. There is live traditional music most nights, and the atmosphere is as authentic as can be.

Getting There & Away

The **Feda O'Donnell** (☎ 954 8114) bus from Crolly stops on Main St twice daily, Monday to Saturday (three Friday and Sunday). From Falcarragh it travels on to Letterkenny (€5, one hour) and Galway (€20, 5¼ hours).

The **John McGinley** (☎ 913 5201) bus leaves for Dublin at 7.25am daily (€16, five hours) with extra trips Monday, Thursday, Friday and Sunday. The **Lough Swilly** (☎ 912 2863) Dungloe-to-Derry bus (€6, 2½ hours) stops in Falcarragh twice daily Monday to Friday, three times on Saturday.

DUNFANAGHY & AROUND

☎ 074 / pop 295

Easily the most attractive village along this stretch of coast, Dunfanaghy is unassumingly elegant, thanks to its partly Presbyterian heritage that sets it apart from other villages in the area. Even today, the village is roughly 50% Protestant, and their numbers inflate during the holidays when Northerners descend on the place for seaside fun.

Dunfanaghy is blessed with the fabulous **Killyhoey Beach**, a wide, sandy, virtually empty beach that leads right into the heart of the village. **Marble Hill Beach**, about 3km east of town in Port-na-Blagh, is more secluded but very popular, and is usually crammed in summer.

Information

The Allied Irish Bank, opposite the Carrig Rua Hotel, has no ATM, but you'll find one in Ramsey's Shop on the waterfront.

Movie World (☎ 913 6532; Main St; per hr €6; ☉ 5-10pm) Has evening Internet access.

Post office (Main St; ☉ 9am-1pm & 2-5.30pm Mon-Sat) Has a bureau de change.

Sights

DUNFANAGHY WORKHOUSE

This grim building, with bricked-up windows, was the local workhouse, and built to keep and employ the destitute. Conditions were deliberately harsh. Men, women, children and the sick were separated from one other, and their lives were dominated by gruelling work. Dunfanaghy's workhouse was soon inundated with starving people as the Famine took grip. Just two years after it opened in 1845, it accommodated some 600 people – double the number originally planned.

The workhouse, west of the centre up past the post office, is now a **heritage centre** (☎ 913 6540; simmonsjanis@hotmail.com; Main St; adult/child/concession €4.25/2/3; ☉ 10am-5pm Mon-Fri, noon-5pm Sat & Sun mid-Mar–Sep), which tells the history of 'Wee Hannah's' and her passage through the institution.

DUNFANAGHY GALLERY

Just up the road from the heritage centre, **Dunfanaghy Gallery** (☎ 913 6224; Main St; admission free; ☉ 10am-6pm Mon-Sat) started life as a fever hospital. Nowadays it houses art and crafts.

HORN HEAD

The towering headland of **Horn Head** (Corrán Binne) has some of Donegal's most spectacular coastal scenery and plenty of birdlife. Its dramatic quartzite cliffs rear over 180m high, and the view from their tops is heart-pounding. Take care in bad weather, however, as the route can be perilous.

An alternative route is to go by bike or car from the Falcarragh end of Dunfanaghy. The road circles the headland and offers tremendous views on a fine day: Tory, Inishbofin, Inishdooey and tiny Inishbeg islands to the west; Sheep Haven Bay and the Rosguill Peninsula to the east; Malin Head to the northeast; and even the coast of Scotland.

ARDS FOREST PARK

This forested **park** (admission free), about 3km southeast of Dunfanaghy off the N56, is crisscrossed by many marked nature trails varying in length from 2km to 13km. It covers the northern shore of the Ards Peninsula and there are walks to its clean beaches. In 1930 the southern part of the peninsula was taken over by Capuchin monks; the grounds of their friary are open to the public.

DOE CASTLE

The early 16th-century **Doe Castle** (Caisléan na dTuath; Creeslough) was the stronghold of the Scottish MacSweeney family until it fell into English hands in the 17th century. The castle is picturesquely sited on a low promontory with water on three sides and a moat hewn out of the rock on the landward side. The best view is from the Carrigart-to-Creeslough road. The interior isn't open to the public, unless you can sweet-talk a key from the neighbouring house.

The castle is around 16km from Dunfanaghy on the Carrigart road and is clearly signposted.

MUCKISH MOUNTAIN

The distinctive shape of Muckish Mountain (670m) – when it's not shrouded in the cloud and mist that locals call *smir* – is an eye-catching landmark and a good climb. You can get to it via the village of **Creeslough**, 11km south of Dunfanaghy on the N56, and home to an extraordinary **modern church**, resembling a half-melted sugar cube, whose snowy bulk is intended to mirror the mountain's shape. To get to Muckish, take

a right about 2km northwest of the village and continue for about 6km, where a rough track begins the ascent.

Activities

WALKING

For an exhilarating hike, take the road from Dunfanaghy towards Horn Head until the bridge. After crossing, go through the gate on your left and stroll along the track until you reach the dunes. A well-beaten path will lead you to the magnificent **Tramore Beach**. Turn left and follow it to the end, where you can find a way up onto a path leading north to **Pollaguill Bay**. Continue to the cairn at the end of the bay and follow the coastline for a stupendous view of the 20m **Marble Arch**, carved out by the sea.

A shorter walk begins at Marble Hill Beach in Port-na-Blagh. Take the path on the left side of the beach past the cottage and work your way about 500m through the brush and along the top of the cliff until you reach **Harry's Hole**, a small crevice in the cliff that is popular with daredevil kids, who dive 10m into the water below.

GOLF

Dunfanaghy Golf Club (☎ 913 6335; www.dunfanaghy .com) is a stunning waterside 18-hole links course just outside the village on the Port-na-Blagh road.

HORSE RIDING

This is a terrific way of exploring the expansive beaches and surrounding countryside. It can be arranged through **Arnold's Hotel** (☎ 913 6208; www.irish-trailriding.com, www.dunfanaghy stables.com; Main St; per hr €25), which also offers wildlife-watching, fishing, painting, photography and even writing holidays.

SEA ANGLING & DIVING

Richard Bowyer (☎ 913 6640; Port-na-Blagh) organises sea-angling trips from the small pier in Port-na-Blagh between Easter and September. Local diving trips are also run by **Diveology** (☎ 086-809 5737; www.diveology.com).

WINDSURFING & KITE-SURFING

Windsurfing lessons and gear rental are available through the following.
Marble Hill Windsurfing (☎ 913 6231; the Cottage, Marble Hill, Port-na-Blagh; ☼ daily Jul & Aug, by appointment May, Jun & Sep) Lessons start from €40.

Breezypoint Kitesurf Donegal (☎ 087-667 3932; ericgreenberg@hotmail.com; Breezy Point, Craig, Creeslough) Offers one-/three-day kite-surfing lessons for €115/300.

Sleeping

Corcreggan Mill Cottage Hostel (☎ 913 6409; www.corcreggan.com; Dunfanaghy; camp sites per person €8, dm €12-15, d €35-40; P) The most unique budget accommodation in the northeast, IHH hostel Corcreggan Mill has private rooms in a 120-year-old mahogany railway car and dorms in the 200-year-old former kiln house. The hostel is 4km southwest of Dunfanaghy on the Falcarragh road (N56). Buses stop outside. Sadly, however, the mill was up for sale in mid-2005, so call ahead to ensure it remains open.

Whins (☎ /fax 913 6481; www.thewhins.com; Kill, Dunfanaghy; s/d €35/60; P) The Whins wins the prize for the most welcoming B&B in town; its rooms are decorated with panache, there's a roaring fire, wide choice of superb breakfasts and gorgeous garden. It is about 750m south of the village overlooking the golf course. Credit cards are accepted.

Rosman House (☎ /fax 913 6273; www.rosman house.ie; Figart, Dunfanaghy; s/d €45/60; P) A more old-fashioned B&B with six flowery, spotless rooms can be found at this working farm close to the workhouse.

Arnold's Hotel (☎ 913 6208; www.arnoldshotel .com; Main St; s €89-110, d €118-160; ☼ mid-Mar–Nov; P) Open since 1922, Arnold's is a self-assured, 30-room hotel overlooking the waterfront in Sheep Haven Bay. Strewn with deep armchairs and backed by neatly trimmed terrace gardens it is a relaxing place to stay. However, it also offers all manner of activity holidays (see the website).

Eating

Muck 'n' Muffins (☎ 913 6780; Main Sq; sandwiches & snacks €5-6; ☼ 10am-5pm Mon-Sat, 11am-5pm Sun, wine bar from 8pm Aug, Fri & Sat Sep-Jul) A 19th-century rough-stone grain store now hosts this three-storey café and craft shop by the waterfront. The perfect place for a quick informal lunch, it serves a good chicken fajita, tempting cakes and muffins. When things are busy, it reopens later as a wine bar, serving tapas and cheeseboards.

Mill (☎ 913 6985; www.themillrestaurant.com; Figart, Dunfanaghy; 3-course dinners €37; ☼ 7-9pm Tue-Sun Mar-Dec) To really treat yourself, make a bee-line for this award-winning restaurant, set in an attractive old flax mill just beyond the town on the Falcarragh road. Book ahead. It also offers a high-class B&B.

Cove (☎ 913 6300; Rockhill, Port-na-Blagh; 4-course dinner €40; ☼ 6-10pm Wed-Mon, 1-4pm Sun) Inventive fish and meat dishes are cooked up at this excellent little restaurant, set in minimalist elegance within a former coastguard cottage in Port-na-Blagh.

Getting There & Away

Feda O'Donnell (☎ 954 8114) buses from Crolly (€5, 40 minutes) to Galway (€20, five hours) stop in Dunfanaghy square twice daily Monday to Saturday, three Friday and Sunday.

John McGinley (☎ 913 5201) buses to Dublin stop in Dunfanaghy (€16, 4¾ hours). The **Lough Swilly** (☎ 912 2863) Dungloe-to-Derry bus stops in Dunfanaghy (€7, 1½ hours) twice daily Monday to Friday, three times on Saturday.

EASTERN DONEGAL

LETTERKENNY

☎ 074 / pop 7965

Hillside Letterkenny (Leitir Ceanainn) was given a huge shot in the arm after Derry, 34km northeast, was cut off from its hinterland by the partition of Ireland, and is now Donegal's largest town. Apart from a buzzing student-driven nightlife and new cultural vigour, there's little to snag travellers' interest for long. However it makes a good base to explore middle and eastern Donegal, especially if you're reliant on public transportation.

Orientation

Main St, said to be the longest high street in Ireland, runs from Dunnes Stores at one end to the courthouse at the other, and divides into Upper and Lower Main Sts. At the top of Upper Main St there is a Y-junction: High Rd veers left, while Port Rd goes right to the bus station and the road out to Derry.

Information

AIB (Main St) Bank branch with ATM.

Bank of Ireland (Main St)

Cyberworld (☎ 912 0440; Lower Main St; per 15min €2) Internet café below Four Lanterns Chinese takeaway.

Duds 'n' Suds Laundrette (☎ 912 8303; Pearse Rd; load from €8)

Northwest Tourist Office (☎ 912 1160; www.done galdirect.ie; Neil Blaney Rd; ☧ 9am-5pm Mon-Fri, noon-3pm Sat & Sun Jun-Aug, 9am-5pm Mon-Fri Sep-May; Ⓟ) Run by Fáilte Ireland (Irish Tourist Board), has great information but is located about 1km southeast of town at the end of Port Rd; you can walk there from the roundabout where the buses stop. Alternatively, there's a good website at www.destinationletterkenny.com.

Post office (Upper Main St)

Sights & Activities

Dominating the town's hillside profile, the enormous Gothic-style **St Eunan's Cathedral** (1901) thrusts skyward on Sentry Hill Rd (take Church Lane up from Main St) and contains much intricate Celtic carving.

The lacklustre **Donegal County Museum** (☎ 912 4613; donegalcountymuseum@eircom.net; High Rd; admission free; ☧ 10am-12.30pm & 1-4.30pm Mon-Fri, 1-4.30pm Sat), on the left past the leisure centre, is housed in part of Letterkenny's old workhouse. It has a collection of dense information boards and a meagre clutch of local archaeological finds, including Iron Age stone axe heads and early Christian material.

There are some salmon and trout rivers and lakes surrounding Letterkenny. Equipment and information is available from **Top Tackle** (☎ 916 7545; 55 Port Rd; ☧ 9.30am-5.30pm Mon-Sat).

Festivals & Events

The **Letterkenny Festival** (☎ 912 7856) is a four-day international festival of music and dance held at the end of August. In 2006, however, it will be sidelined by Ireland's biggest competition and celebration of traditional music, the **Fleadh** (www.fleadh2006.com), which comes to town in mid- to late August. The festival, which changes town every few years, will bring around 200,000 visitors and accommodation is likely to be booked months in advance. Expect music everywhere you go.

Sleeping

Port Hostel (☎ 912 5315; www.porthostel.ie; Port Rd; camp sites €20, dm €15, d €36-40; Ⓟ) Expect to be invited to pub-crawls and barbecues with the gregarious owners of this secluded IHO hostel, tucked away behind the An Grianán Theatre. There's no pressure to join in the fun though, and the sprawling gardens also provide a peaceful escape.

Pearse Road Guesthouse (☎ 912 3002; Pearse Rd; s/d €35/60; Ⓟ) Eight spotless and newly decorated rooms are available at this handsome town house, surrounded by office blocks and business parks; it's just a short amble down the hill from Main St.

Castle Grove House Hotel (☎ 915 1118; www .castlegrove.com; Ramelton Rd; s/d €95/160; Ⓟ) Ignore Letterkenny's slew of swanky business hotels. The place for a luxurious stay is this grandiose Georgian manor 5km out toward Ramelton. Its enormous estate rolls down unimpeded to the estuary and the impossibly neat lawn seems cut with nail clippers. Award-winning Irish/French food in its restaurant clinches the deal.

Cove Hill House (☎ 912 1038; Port Rd; s with/without bathroom €40/35, d €60/50; Ⓟ) This B&B has a comfortable just-like-grandma's feel to it, crammed with homey clutter and nuzzled by a beautiful garden. Credit cards are accepted. It's behind the theatre and next to Port Hostel.

Quality Hotel (☎ 912 2977; www.qualityhotelletter kenny.com; 29-45 Main St; s/d €59/118) The crimson-and-black exterior suggests a pub, but this professional hotel's 85 rooms are of the same cardboard cut-out quality to be found at any decent chain hotel. The real appeal is in its location, bang in the middle of Main St. Parking costs extra.

Eating

Simple Simon (☎ 912 2382; simplesimon@eircom.net; Oliver Plunkett Rd; soups & salads €3-6.50; ☧ 9am-6pm Mon-Sat) 'Genetically modified' is a dirty term at this passionate natural-products shop and attached café. The on-site bakery produces delightful treats for every special diet imaginable and it stocks a good selection of organic veggies into the bargain.

Galfees (☎ 912 8535; Main St; baps & baguettes €3.50-6, Irish breakfast €4.50-6.50; ☧ 9am-6.30pm Mon-Sat, 10.30am-5.30pm Sun) A more sinful selection of snacks and cakes is on offer at this gourmet café at the upper end of Main St. It also dishes up artery-stopping breakfasts and terrific coffees.

Yellow Pepper (☎ 912 4133; 36 Lower Main St; dinner mains €8-17; ☧ noon-10pm) It looks like a chain restaurant outside, but this popular little spot is family run, and proud of it. The building was once a late-19th-century shirt factory, and retains original flooring and pillars. It has a reputation for excellent fish.

COUNTY DONEGAL

Brewery (☎ 912 7330; Upper Main St; bar food around €8, mains €14-20; ☒ 3-9pm) There's a choice between great bar food downstairs or enormous platters upstairs at this mellow pub-restaurant overlooking the small square.

Entertainment

Cottage Bar (☎ 912 1338; 49 Upper Main St) Locals flock to this character-laden pub with a low ceiling so heavily hung with bric-a-brac that you'll find yourself wanting to stoop. A beautiful open fire and Thursday night music sessions sweeten the deal.

Bar Mono (☎ 917 7911; 21 Lower Main St) The cheap booze, high-energy music and sparkling glass and chrome all bring out a glint in the eye of Mono's cheeky clientele. Its slogan says it all: Three bars, two floors and one big party.

Old Orchard Inn (☎ 912 1615; High Rd) With a flowery patio garden and outdoor heating, this pub opposite the museum is a popular port of call on fair-weather days. There's often live rock in the attached nightclub.

An Grianán Theatre (☎ 912 0777; www.angrianan.com; Port Rd) An Grianán Theatre is both a community theatre and major arts venue for the northwest, presenting national and international drama, comedy and music. It also has a good café and bar.

Getting There & Away

Letterkenny is a major bus hub for northwestern Ireland. The bus station is by the roundabout at the junction of Ramelton Rd and the Derry road. It will look after luggage for €2.

Bus Éireann (☎ 912 1309) express bus No 32 runs to Dublin (€16, four hours) six times daily (four on Sunday) via Omagh (€11, one hour) and Monaghan (€13, 1¾ hours). The Derry (€7, 35 minutes) to Galway (€14.50, 4¾ hours) bus No 64 stops at Letterkenny three times daily (twice on Sunday) before continuing to Donegal (€7.90, 50 minutes), Bundoran (€11.50, 1½ hours), Sligo (€12, 2¼ hours) and Galway. The Derry to Cork (€26, 8½ hours) express bus No 53, via Letterkenny, Sligo, Galway and Limerick, runs three times daily (once on Sunday).

John McGinley (☎ 913 5201) buses run twice daily Sunday to Thursday (three times Friday, once on Saturday) from Annagry to Dublin (€15, 3¾ hours) through Letterkenny and Monaghan.

Lough Swilly (☎ 912 2863) has regular services from Derry (€6.60, one hour) to Dungloe (€8, two hours), via Letterkenny and Dunfanaghy, as well as direct to Letterkenny.

Feda O'Donnell (☎ 954 8114) runs a bus from Crolly (€5, 1½ hours) to Galway (€16, four hours) twice daily via Letterkenny, Donegal, Bundoran and Sligo. Buses stop on the road outside the bus station.

McGeehan Coaches (☎ 954 6150) runs a service from Letterkenny to Glencolumbcille (€10, 2¼ hours) daily except Sunday.

Getting Around

Taxis can be ordered from **A Cabs** (☎ 912 2272). There are taxi stands on Main St opposite the square, and opposite the bus station.

AROUND LETTERKENNY

One of the largest waterwheels in Ireland can be found alongside these painstakingly restored **Newmills Corn & Flax Mills** (☎ 074-912 5115; Churchill Rd, Newmills; adult/concession/child €2.75/2/1.25; ☒ 10am-6.30pm May-Sep, last tour 5.45pm; **P** ⓺), 6km southwest of Letterkenny. The site, which is Dúchas-run, has a visitor centre explaining the hows and whys of corn and flax milling. There's a riverside walk to a 19th-century flax-worker's cottage and forge.

LOUGH GARTAN
☎ 074

The patriarch of Irish monasticism, St Colmcille (or Columba), was born near the glassy Lough Gartan, 17km northwest of Letterkenny.

Colmcille Heritage Centre

This **heritage centre** (☎ 913 7306; Gartan; adult/concession €2/1.50; ☒ 10.30am-6.30pm Mon-Sat, 1-6.30pm Sun, Easter & early May-late Sep), on the shore of Lough Gartan, is Colmcille's Hall of Fame, with a lavish display on the production of illuminated manuscripts.

Colmcille's mother, on the run from pagans, supposedly haemorrhaged during childbirth and her blood is believed to have changed the colour of the surrounding Gartan Clay from brown to pure white. Ever since, the clay has been regarded as a charm. Ask nicely and the staff may produce some from under the counter.

On the way to the heritage centre you'll also see signs to the ruins of **Colmcille's Abbey** and to the hillside location of the **saint's** birthplace, marked by a hefty cross. Also here is an intriguing prehistoric tomb strewn with greening coppers. It's popularly known as the Flagstone of Loneliness, on which Columba supposedly slept. The chunky slab was once believed to cure homesickness.

To reach the heritage centre, leave Letterkenny on the R250 road to Glenties and Ardara. After a few kilometres, turn right on the R251 to Churchill village and follow the signs. Alternatively, from Kilmacrennan on the N56, turn west and look for signs.

Gartan Outdoor Education Centre

Courses including rock climbing, sea kayaking, sailing, windsurfing, hill climbing and more are offered for both adults and children at this adventure centre (☎ 913 7032; www.gartan.com; Gartan, Churchill). It's located 18km northwest of Letterkenny, and set in its own 35-hectare estate on the shores of Lough Gartan.

Glebe Gallery & House

There are many reasons to visit Regency-built Glebe House (☎ 913 7071; Churchill; adult/concession/child €2.75/2/1.25; ☽ 11am-6.30pm Easter, Sat-Thu only mid-May–Sep; P ⅙), operated by Dúchas on the shore of Lough Gartan. Not least is the house itself: once a rectory, then a hotel, it was bought by the widely travelled artist Derek Hill in 1953, and has since been turned into a sumptuously decorated mansion, alive with colour, flair and an evident love of all things exotic.

Glebe is best known for its astonishing art collection, including works by Picasso, Landseer, Hokusai, Jack B Yeats and Kokoschka among others. The wonderfully folksy kitchen is full of paintings by the Tory Island artists (see p505), including the 'king', Patsy Dan Rodgers. The woodland gardens are also wonderful. A guided tour of the house takes about 45 minutes.

DOON WELL & ROCK OF DOON

In centuries past wells were commonly believed to cure afflictions and judging by the shimmering rosaries, multicoloured rags and trinkets bejewelling nearby bushes, many still believe this to be true of Doon Well (Tobar an Duin). Despite its decoration, the well itself looks more like a kitchen cupboard than a wishing well.

A sign points to the overgrown Rock of Doon (Carraig an Duin), which has some far-reaching views. This is where the O'Donnell kings were crowned – presumably so they could get a squiz at what they were inheriting.

Take the signposted turn-off from the N56 just north of Kilmacrennan. The well and rock are about 1.5km north of the village.

LIFFORD & AROUND
☎ 074 / pop 1395

Nudging the border by Strabane in County Tyrone, the dwindling town of Lifford (Leifear) was formerly the judicial capital of Donegal. While its powerful past is long gone, its spirit lives on in the daunting 18th-century courthouse. The building has been converted into an excellent heritage centre (☎ 914 1733; www.liffordoldcourthouse.com; adult/concession €5/3; ☽ 10am-4.30pm Mon-Fri, 12.30-4.30pm Sun; P) with creepily lifelike re-creations that use actors' faces projected onto waxworks. In this manner, Manus O'Donnell tells the story of Donegal's Gaelic chieftains and several bonafide trials are re-enacted in the austere courtroom (including that of Napper Tandy, John 'half-hanged' McNaughten and the Lord Leitrim murder). A guard will take you down to the prison cells, accompanied by sounds of banging doors and ominous footsteps, to be locked up for sheep-stealing or the like.

Getting There & Away

Bus Éireann's (☎ 912 1309) express service No 32 from Dublin (€16, 3¼ hours) to Letterkenny (€6.50, 20 minutes) stops in Lifford up to five times daily. Local buses connect Lifford with Letterkenny, Ballybofey and Strabane.

NORTHEASTERN DONEGAL

ROSGUILL PENINSULA
☎ 074

Rosguill is one of the most beautiful peninsulas in the county. The best way to explore its rugged splendour is by driving, cycling, or even walking, the 15km Atlantic Drive, signposted to your left as you come into the sprawling village of Carrigart (Carraig Airt) from the south. There are plenty of pubs in the village to cure your thirst and a

COUNTY DONEGAL

nice, secluded beach at **Trá na Rossan**. On no account should you swim in Boveeghter or Mulroy Bay – both are unsafe. The summer crowds don't linger here, though, preferring instead to travel 4km northward to the fishing village of **Downings**.

There's plenty of merriment in Downings' pubs, which are often packed with holidaymakers from the North, while nearby Rosapenna Golf Club is a favourite with golfers.

Activities

The superb links of **Rosapenna Golf Club** (☎ 915 5301; Downings; hotel guest/nonguest green fee €30/50), designed by St Andrew's Old Tom Morris in 1891 and remodelled by Harry Vardon in 1906, is one of the outstanding seaside courses in Ireland. The scenery is spectacular as is the layout, which can challenge even the lowest handicapper.

Sleeping

Casey's Caravan Park (☎ 915 5301; rosapenna@eircom .net; Downings; camp sites €15; ☼ Apr-Sep) You won't get closer to the Blue Flag beach than at this extremely popular camp site right beside the dunes. It's also conveniently close to the village's heart. Book ahead.

Trá na Rosann Hostel (☎ 915 5374; www.anoige .ie; Downings; dm €15; ☼ Jun-Sep) Knockout views and a terrific atmosphere are the biggest draws at this chalet-like former hunting lodge, now an An Óige hostel. The one drawback is that it's 6km east of Downings and you'll have to hitch if you don't have your own wheels.

Dun Roamin (☎ 915 5716; www.littlebandb.com; Rosapenna, Downings; s €30-38, d €60; ☼ Apr-Sep; P) This modern hillside B&B has glorious sea views from its long conservatory-style breakfast room. Its three rooms are cheerily decorated, and have every convenience. Follow the sign to the youth hostel shortly before reaching Downings.

Downings Bay Hotel (☎ 915 5586; www.downings bayhotel.com; Downings; s/d €60/100; P &) Outside the summer months, this newly revamped beachside hotel offers great deals on its 40 immaculate rooms. They have all the spaciousness and mod cons of an executive city hotel, for a reasonable midrange price tag.

Beach Hotel (Óstán na Trá; ☎ 915 5303; beach hoteldonegal@eircom.net; Downings; s/d €40/80; ☼ Apr-Oct; P) For more of a personal touch, come to this family-run hotel, which has 20 pristine rooms close to the beach. Ask for one of the new rooms, most of which have sea views.

Rosapenna Hotel & Golf Club (☎ 915 5301; www .rosapenna.ie; Downings; s/d €115/190; ☼ Mar-Oct; P) The showiest hotel on the peninsula, with swimming pool and tennis courts to its credit, can be worth the expense for golfers because guests can benefit from a whole array of special offers. It sits alone and aloof to the south of Downings.

Eating

Old Glen Bar & Restaurant (☎ 915 5130; Glen, Carrigart; mains €14-21; ☼ 6-11pm) This wonderful pub is classic Irish countryside, entirely authentic and serves a sensational pint. At the back of the pub, though, modernity rules with a contemporary restaurant serving up a fabulous menu of fish, seafood and meat. The tiny hamlet of Glen is signposted off the R245 between Creeslough and Carrigart, about 6km south of the latter.

Downings Bay Hotel (☎ 915 5586; bar food €11-20, restaurant mains €16-25; ☼ restaurant 6-9.30pm) The evening restaurant fare and all-day bar food are both of above-average calibre at this beachside hotel. The Thai curry is recommended.

Getting There & Around

A local bus connects Carrigart and Downings, but it's of limited use for visitors. You do need your own transport for this area.

FANAD PENINSULA

The second-most northern point in Donegal, Fanad Head thrusts out into the Atlantic to the west of Rosguill. The peninsula's question-mark shape (obligingly dotted by Inch Island) curls around the watery expanses of Mulroy Bay to the west, and Lough Swilly to the east, the latter trimmed by high cliffs and sandy beaches. Most travellers stick to the peninsula's eastern flank, visiting the beautiful beach and excellent golf course at Portsalon, and quiet heritage towns of Rathmelton and Rathmullan. Accommodation is relatively limited, so book ahead in summer.

The **Lough Swilly** (☎ 074-912 2863) bus leaves Letterkenny twice daily for Milford (€3.50, one hour) and continues from Milford to Portsalon (€9, 35 minutes, morning bus only).

Portsalon & Fanad Head

Once named the second most beautiful beach in the world by British newspaper the *Observer*, the tawny-coloured Blue Flag beach in Ballymastocker Bay, which is safe for swimming, is the principle draw of tiny Portsalon (Port an tSalainn). However, it's closely followed by the marvellously scenic **Portsalon Golf Club** (☎ 915 9459; Portsalon).

Knockalla Caravan & Camping Park (☎ 074-915 9108; Portsalon; camp sites €14-18; ☯ mid-Mar–mid-Sep) is a short walk from the beach on the lower slopes of Knockalla Mountain and fills up quickly in summer. It has a kitchen, a laundry, a shop, a games room and an outdoor play area.

It's another 8km to the lighthouse on the rocky tip of Fanad Head, the best part of which is the scenic drive there. Driving the rollercoaster road that hugs the cliffs back to Rathmullan, you'll pass the early 19th-century **Knockalla Fort**, built to warn of any approaching French ships.

Rathmullan

☎ 074 / pop 515

The somnolent little port of Rathmullan (Ráth Maoláin) has a tranquillity about it that belies the momentous events that took place here from the 16th to 18th centuries.

In 1587, Hugh O'Donnell, the 15-year-old heir to the powerful O'Donnell clan, was tricked into boarding a ship here and taken to Dublin as a prisoner. He escaped four years later on Christmas Eve and, after unsuccessful attempts at revenge, died in Spain, aged only 30. In 1607, despairing of fighting the English, Hugh O'Neill, the earl of Tyrone, and Rory O'Donnell, the earl of Tyrconnel, boarded a ship in Rathmullan harbour and left Ireland for good. This decisive act, known as the Flight of the Earls, marked the effective end of Gaelic Ireland and the rule of Irish chieftains. Large-scale confiscation of their estates took place, preparing for the Plantation of Ulster with settlers from Britain. At time of writing, authorities were planning an event in 2007 to mark the 400th anniversary of the Flight of the Earls.

Wolfe Tone (see p37) was captured in Rathmullan following the 1798 Rising.

SIGHTS

The location is more exciting than the contents of the small **Rathmullan Heritage Centre** (☎ 915 8229; Rathmullan Pier; adult/concession/child €5/3/2; ☯ 10am-1pm & 2-5pm Thu-Sat, noon-5pm Sun Easter-Sep), which explains the Flight of the Earls in a series of text-heavy displays. It's housed in a squat early 19th-century British fort of Lego-like simplicity.

A short amble from the heritage centre, the picturesque Carmelite **Rathmullan Friary** is so covered in vines that it would probably crumble should they be taken away. It was founded around 1508 by the MacSweeneys, and was still used in 1595 when English commander, George Bingham, raided the place and took off with the communion plate and priestly vestments. Bishop Knox then renovated the friary in 1618 in order to use it as his own residence.

SLEEPING & EATING

Dinner at the hotels costs from €40 to €45; there are several pubs in town serving bar food.

Knoll (☎ 915 8241; Main St; s/d €30/60; P) This genteel black-and-white house was built to house the commander of the North Atlantic Fleet in 1780, and has since been reincarnated as everything from a police station to a post office. Happily for travellers, it now houses a cosy three-room B&B, fronted by beautifully maintained gardens.

Rathmullan House (☎ 915 8188; www.rathmullan house.com; s/d €105/210; P ☐ ☙) Just north of town, on the shores of Lough Swilly, this luxurious country house boasts an indoor heated swimming pool, a sauna and tennis courts, and is set in a beautifully wooded garden by the water. There's even a special 'pooch-friendly' room complete with a bed for Fido.

Fort Royal (☎ 915 8100; www.fortroyalhotel.com; s/d €122/184; ☯ Apr-Oct; P) This more down-to-earth but equally exclusive waterside hotel has 15 old-fashioned rooms, a wonderful restaurant and rambling gardens that feel as old as the house, built in 1805. It has its own beach, tennis court and pitch-and-putt course.

GETTING THERE & AWAY

The **Lough Swilly** (☎ 912 2863) bus from Letterkenny arrives in Rathmullan (€4.80, 45 minutes, twice daily) en route to Milford and Portsalon (morning bus only).

COUNTY DONEGAL

Rathmelton

☎ 074 / pop 1050

If you approach the peninsula from its eastern flank, the first town you come to is the genteel heritage town of Rathmelton (Ráth Mealtain, also commonly called Ramelton). Handsome Georgian houses and rough-walled stone warehouses cluster picturesquely around the river here. Nowadays there are few signs of life other than a mini traffic jam crossing the narrow bridge, but Rathmelton was once a thriving town. The hush descended when its local railway was rerouted to Letterkenny and has remained ever since.

The **National Irish Bank** (the Mall), by the River Lennon, has a bureau de change but no ATM. The **post office** (Castle St) is off the Mall.

SIGHTS

Housed in a restored warehouse on the riverfront, the **Donegal Ancestry Family Research Centre & Heritage Centre** (☎ 915 1266; www.donegal ancestry.com; the Quay; adult/concession/child €4/2.50/2; ☻ 9am-4.30pm Mon-Thu, 9am-4pm Fri) has an exhibition on the history of Rathmelton, and also does genealogical research. It costs €15 for an initial consultation.

Coming from Letterkenny turn right at the river and follow it round for about 400m. The ruined **Tullyaughnish Church**, on the hill, is also worth a visit because of the Romanesque carvings in the eastern wall, which were taken from a far older church on nearby Aughnish Island, on the River Lennon.

SLEEPING & EATING

Lennon Lodge Hostel (☎ 915 1227; Market Sq; s/d with breakfast €25/50; ℗) This is a hostel-hotel hybrid with self-catering facilities, a laundry, a large common room and TVs in every room. The attached lounge-bar also has live music Thursday to Sunday nights, and regular darts competitions.

Crammond House (☎ 915 1055; Market Sq; s with/ without breakfast €35/30, d €58/53; ☻ Apr-Oct; ℗) An old-fashioned welcome is found at this sedate Georgian terrace house at the northern end of Rathmelton.

Donegal Shore (☎ 915 2006; www.donegalshore .com; s/d €31/62; ℗) This bright little bungalow has five just-like-home bedrooms, down a quiet lane 1km south of town off the R245 to Letterkenny. The owner is a trained chef and dinner is often available. Credit cards are accepted.

Fraoc bán Frewin (☎ 915 1246; flaxmill@indigo .ie; s/d €90/140; ℗) A sheltered Victorian rectory in a state of excellent preservation, just south of town towards Letterkenny (if coming from Letterkenny, turn right just before entering the village). Not suitable for small children. Three of the four rooms have a private lounge.

Bridge Bar (☎ 915 1119; Bridgend; mains €13-18; ☻ 6-11pm) On the other side of the river, the Bridge Bar is a lovely old pub decorated with shiny red shutters, hanging baskets and pebble-dashed walls. It has a cosy 1st-floor restaurant with good seafood dishes, such as roasted swordfish.

Mirabeau Steak House (☎ 915 1138; the Mall; mains €9-18; ☻ 6-10pm) This dimly lit restaurant claims the old living room of a Georgian house on the riverfront. The cuisine is French with an emphasis on steak and seafood, and portions are colossal.

GETTING THERE & AWAY

Lough Swilly (☎ 912 2863) buses connect Rathmelton with Letterkenny (€2.85, 30 minutes, three times daily from Monday to Saturday).

INISHOWEN PENINSULA

The sprawling Inishowen (Inis Eoghain) Peninsula, with Lough Foyle to the east and Lough Swilly to the west, stretches just far enough out into the Atlantic to win Ireland's northernmost point: Malin Head. The landscape is typically Donegal: rugged, desolate and mountainous. Ancient sites abound, as do traditional thatched cottages, roofless stone-walled ruins and pristine sandy beaches. Tourist offices in Donegal, Letterkenny and Derry have free leaflets about walks in the Inishowen area, complete with maps.

A stunning scenic drive, the **Inis Eoghain 100**, is clearly signposted round the peninsula. It is well worth following, despite making for some very interesting cliff-top manoeuvres with oncoming traffic.

The peninsula is a European Special Area of Conservation and home to over a hundred species of migrating and indigenous birds.

The towns in the next section are part of a route that follows the road west of Derry up the coast of Lough Foyle to Moville and then northwest to Malin Head, before head-

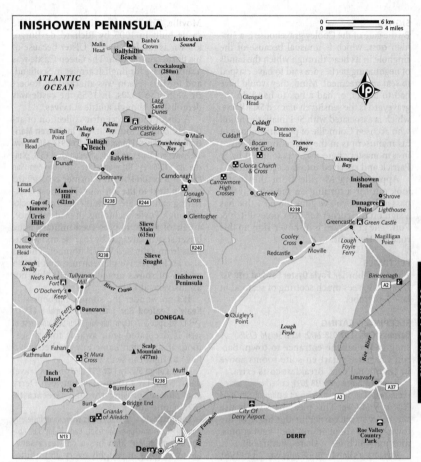

INISHOWEN PENINSULA

COUNTY DONEGAL

ing down the western side to Buncrana. If you're coming from Donegal, the peninsula can be approached from the southwest by turning off for Buncrana on the N13 road from Letterkenny to Derry.

Muff to Moville

The tiny village of Muff (Mugh), only 8km north of Derry, has pubs offering food and music, and a fair share of Northern visitors. Northeast of Muff, along the coast, there are larger pubs catering to the same market. Horse riding is available at **Lenamore Stables** (☎ 074-938 4022).

North of Muff at **Quigley's Point** (Rinn Mic Coigus) there are good views across Lough Foyle to County Derry.

Lough Swilly (☎ 912 2863) runs up to nine buses daily from Derry to Carndonagh via Muff (€1.95, 15 minutes), with almost as many to Shrove that also go through Muff. There's no Sunday bus on either route.

Moville & Around
☎ 074 / pop 1465

Now a sleepy seaside town, Moville (Bun an Phobail) was once a busy port where emigrants set sail for America. The **coastal walkway** from Moville to Greencastle takes in the stretch of coast where the steamers used to moor. There's **fishing** off the pier for mackerel, mullet and coalfish.

Main St has several banks with ATMs and the post office.

SIGHTS

By the gate of the Cooley gravehouse is a 3m-high **cross**, which is unusual because of the ringhole in its head through which the hands of negotiating parties are said to have clasped to seal an agreement. Mind, they would have had to be tall, or had a box to hand. In the graveyard is the sensitively named **Skull House**, which is associated with St Finian, the monk who accused Colmcille of plagiarising one of his manuscripts in the 6th century. He lived in a monastery here that was founded by St Patrick and survived into the 12th century.

Approaching Moville from the south, look out for a turning on the left – if you pass a church, you've gone too far – that has a sign on the corner for the Cooley Pitch & Putt. The graveyard is just over 1km up this road on the right.

FESTIVALS

The cross-border **Foyle Oyster Festival** (☎ 938 2753; Main St) sees much scoffing of seafood in late September.

SLEEPING & EATING

Barron's Café (☎ 938 2472; Main St; s/d €25/50) A snug spot near the entrance to town, Barron's has five smart en-suite rooms above its traditional café. Breakfast costs extra.

Naomh Mhuíre (☎ 938 2091; catherinemcgroarty@eircom.net; Main St; s with/without bathroom €30/25, d €60/50; ☺ Mar-Sep) This pleasant town house sits on a street corner in the heart of the town. It has six plain but well-kept rooms, most of which use a shared bathroom.

McNamara's Hotel (☎ 938 2010; Main St; s/d €35/60, mains €7-14; P ☺) Off the bottom of Main St, McNamara's is a family-run, 60-room establishment with dog-eared rooms and paisley bedspreads, but with a restaurant and friendly service good enough to forgive its shortcomings. It was to be renovated (and prices raised) some time in 2006.

GETTING THERE & AWAY

Lough Swilly (☎ 912 2863) runs four buses daily Monday to Saturday to Moville (€6.50, 45 minutes) from Derry.

Greencastle

☎ 074 / pop 570

Seals can be spotted bobbing their smooth heads hopefully in the busy little fishing port of Greencastle (An Cáisleán Nua), north of Moville. The town gets its name from the castle built in 1305 by Richard de Burgo, known as the Red Earl of Ulster because of his florid complexion. The Green Castle was a supply base for English armies in Scotland, and for this reason was attacked by Robert Bruce in the 1320s. In 1555 the castle was demolished, though a little survives.

A disarmingly eccentric collection of artefacts can be found at the **Inishowen Maritime Museum & Planetarium** (☎ 938 1363; www.inishowenmaritime.com; museum adult/child €5/3, planetarium €10/6; ☺ 10am-6pm Mon-Sat, noon-6pm Sun Apr-Sep, to 5pm Oct-Mar), in a former coastguard station next to the harbour. The most fascinating exhibits are from the sunken wrecks of Lough Foyle, including, in pride of place, a pair of perfectly preserved military-issue boxer shorts salvaged by marine archaeologists from a ditched WWII bomber! There's also an impressive planetarium that runs a variety of shows aimed primarily, but not exclusively, at kids.

It's no wonder the simple, harbour-side **Kealy's Seafood Bar** (☎ 938 1010; mains €11-27; ☺ 12.30-3pm & 7-10pm Jun-Aug, Thu-Sun only rest of year) is decorated with awards for its seafood: if the catch came any fresher you'd have to fight the seals for it.

Five **Lough Swilly** (☎ 912 2863) buses travel daily, Monday to Saturday, between Derry and Shrove, passing through Greencastle (€7.50, one hour).

Lough Foyle (☎ 938 1901; www.loughfoyleferry.com; ☺ 7.20am-10pm Mon-Sat, 9am-10pm Sun Apr-Sep, to 8pm Oct-Mar) also has a car-ferry service to Magilligan roughly every 25 minutes from outside the museum. Single fares cost €9/4.50/2/1 per car/motorbike/adult/child, and the crossing takes just 15 minutes. It runs every 15 minutes from 7.20am Monday to Saturday and 9am Sunday year round. The last ferry is at 9.50pm, April to September, and 7.50pm, October to March.

Inishowen Head

A right turn outside Greencastle leads to Shrove; a sign indicating Inishowen Head is 1km along this road. It's possible to drive or cycle part of the way, but it's also an easy walk to the headland, from where you can see (on a clear day) the Antrim coast as far as the Giant's Causeway. A more demanding walk continues to the sandy beach of **Kinnagoe Bay**.

Culdaff & Around

☎ 074 / pop 180

Several ancient sites surround the sleepy, secluded, resort village of Culdaff (Cúil Dabhcha), which can be visited from the main Moville to Carndonagh road (R238).

SIGHTS & ACTIVITIES

Sheep now wander the remains of the **Clonca Church & Cross**. Inside, an intricately carved tombstone sporting a sword and hurling-stick motif was erected by one Magnus MacOrristin. The carved lintel over the door is thought to come from an earlier church. Outside, the remains of the cross show the miracle of the loaves and fishes on the eastern face and geometric designs on the sides.

Look for the turn-off to Culdaff, on the right if coming from Moville, on the left after about 6km if coming from Carndonagh. The Clonca Church & Cross are 1.5km on the right behind some farm buildings. A necklace of around 30 prehistoric stones embroiders a farmer's field east of Clonca Church. From Clonca, continue along the road until you reach a T-junction with a modern church facing you. Turn right here and after about 500m turn left (no sign). The **Bocan Stone Circle** is inside the first heather-covered field on the left.

The plain stumpy-armed **Carrowmore High Crosses** are all that remain of an ancient monastic site straddling a small lane. One is basically a decorated slab showing Christ and an angel, while the other is a taller, unadorned cross.

From Bocan Stone Circle and Clonca Church, retrace the route back to the main Carndonagh to Moville road and turn left, then almost immediately right.

Culdaff has a beach that's good for **swimming** and **windsurfing** and, from Bunagee Pier, **sea angling** and **diving** are popular.

SLEEPING & EATING

McGrory's Bar (☎ 937 9104; www.mcgrorys.ie; Culdaff; s/d €65/110; P) There's hardly any reason to look elsewhere as McGrory's has first-rate music, traditional Irish food (in its bar and Art-Deco restaurant) and lodgings all under the same roof. On Tuesday and Friday from 10pm it hosts regular traditional music sessions that continue well into the night, while the attached Mac's Backroom Bar often attracts big-name musicians.

Malin Head

☎ 074

The knobbly bulk of Malin Head (Cionn Mhálanna) feels like it's at the end of the earth, let alone the northern tip of Ireland. It's here, on rocky, weather-beaten **Banba's Crown** (Fíorcheann Éireann) that the northernmost tip of the mainland drops to the sea.

The cumbersome cliff-top **tower** here was built in 1805 by the British admiralty and later used as a Lloyds signal station. The ugly concrete huts were used by the Irish army in WWII as lookout posts. To the west from the fort-side car park, a path leads to **Hell's Hole**, a chasm where the incoming waters crash against the rocky formations. To the east a longer headland walk leads to the **Wee House of Malin**, a hermit's cave in the cliff face.

The wind is so brutal on Malin Head that it's hard to imagine birds flying far without falling flat on their feathery behinds, yet several endangered species thrive here. Not least, this is one of the few places in Ireland where you can still hear the call of the endangered corncrake in summer. Other birds to look out for are choughs, snow bunting and puffins.

The pretty Plantation village of **Malin** (Málainn), on Trawbreaga Bay 14km south of Malin Head, is centred on a tri-cornered village green and shaded by copper beeches. A circular walk from the green takes in **Knockamany Bens**, a local hill with terrific views, as well as **Lagg Presbyterian Church** (3km from Malin), the oldest church still in use on the peninsula. Children will love the massive sand dunes at Five Fingers Strand, another 1km beyond the church.

SLEEPING & EATING

Malin Head Hostel (☎ 937 0309; dm/d €13/32; Mar-Oct; P) A clean, friendly 20-bed IHH hostel with free hot showers and an organic garden where you can buy fruit and vegetables. There's also aromatherapy and reflexology treatments (€35/45 per reflexology/full-body massage). Local buses stop here.

Sandrock Holiday Hostel (☎ 937 0289; sandrock hostel@eircom.net; Port Ronan Pier, Malin Head; dm €10; P) Visitors are welcomed like family at this perennially popular IHH hostel on the western side of the headland. It's situated in a rocky bay, where seafood can sometimes be bought straight off the boats. Sandrock has 20 remarkably cosy beds, laundry facilities, pick-up and bike hire.

COUNTY DONEGAL

Malin Hotel (☎ 937 0606; www.malinhotel.ie; Malin; s/d from €65/110, mains €9-15; ⊗ restaurant 6-10pm, bar food 12.30-3pm) This civilised old-style hotel beside the village green has lavishly decorated rooms, a good restaurant and entertainment at the weekend.

Seaview Tavern (☎ 937 0117; Ballygorman) This tavern trumpets itself as Ireland's most northerly restaurant, grocery shop and, more bizarrely, filling station. It's a rather glorified title for an ordinary place, but it does have sweeping coastal views.

GETTING THERE & AWAY

The best way to approach Malin Head is by the R238/242 from Carndonagh, rather than up the eastern side from Culdaff. **Lough Swilly** (☎ 912 2863) operates a bus that runs on Monday, Wednesday and Friday at 11am between Derry and Malin Head via Carndonagh (€4, 30 minutes); on the same days a bus leaves Carndonagh at 3pm for Malin Head. There are three buses from Derry to Malin Head on Saturday.

Carndonagh

☎ 074 / pop 1675

Carndonagh (Cardomhnach), surrounded by hills on three sides, is a busy commercial centre serving the local farming community.

The helpful, locally run **Inishowen tourism office** (☎ 937 4933; www.visitinishowen.com; Chapel St; ⊗ 9.30am-5.30pm Mon-Fri Sep-May, 9.30am-7pm Mon-Fri, 11am-4pm Sat Jun-Aug), southwest of the Diamond, also sells fishing licences for all of Donegal. There are three banks on the Diamond and AIB has an ATM; the post office is in the shopping centre half-way down Bridge St towards the Donagh Cross.

SIGHTS

Once an important ecclesiastical centre, Carndonagh has several early Christian stone monuments. Not least, the delightful 7th-century **Donagh Cross** stands under a shelter by an Anglican church at the Ballyliffin end of town. It's carved with a darling short-bodied, big-eyed figure of Jesus, seemingly smiling impishly. Flanking the cross are two small pillars, one showing a man, possibly Goliath, with a sword and shield, the other, David and his harp. In the graveyard there's a pillar with a carved marigold on a stem and nearby a crucifixion scene.

SLEEPING & EATING

Ashdale House (☎ 937 4017; ashdalehouse@eircom .net; s/d €40/60; ⊗ Mar-Nov; Ⓟ) This large family home, 1km out of town on the road towards Malin, is recommended.

Arch Inn (☎ 937 3209; the Diamond; snacks around €5) In the main square, the Arch does good soup and sandwiches by day and hosts a traditional music session on Sunday evening.

If you're off to Malin Head for the day or going on to the camping ground at Clonmany, stock up with provisions at the Costcutter supermarket in the large shopping centre on Bridge St.

GETTING THERE & AWAY

A **Lough Swilly** (☎ 912 2863) bus leaves Buncrana for Carndonagh (€5.30, 45 minutes) three times daily except Tuesday, Wednesday (once) and Sunday (no service). On weekdays they return from Carndonagh three times daily. Lough Swilly also runs a bus between Derry (€8, 55 minutes) and Malin Head via Carndonagh daily Monday, Wednesday and Friday (three times Saturday).

Ballyliffin & Clonmany

☎ 074 / pop 705

For such a diminutive and remote seaside resort, cheerful Ballyliffin (Baile Lifin) does a roaring summer trade. It has a handful of good hotels, which somehow soak up an army of Northern Irish holiday-makers, who come to play golf on the two championship 18-hole courses, and enjoy the local beaches. Both villages have post offices but no banks.

SIGHTS

About 1km north of Ballyliffin is the lovely, sandy expanse of **Pollan Strand**, but, unfortunately, the crashing breakers make it unsafe for swimming. A walk along the dunes to the north of this beach brings you to **Doagh Island** (now part of the mainland), where the matchbox ruin of 16th-century **Carrickbraghey Castle** (Carraic Brachaide) is still battered by the ocean.

Also on the island is the enthusiastically thrown together **Doagh Famine Village** (☎ 937 8078; Doagh Island, Inishowen; adult/child €6/4; ⊗ 10am-5.30pm Easter-Sep) in a reconstructed village of thatched cottages. It runs a terrific tour packed with entertaining titbits about a disappearing way of life, and takes a refreshing approach to the Famine by making insightful comparisons with famine-stricken countries today. Tea and scones are included in the admission fee.

The other beach is at **Tullagh Strand**. It's great for an exhilarating walk and, although swimming is possible, the current can be strong and it isn't recommended when the tide is going out. There are walks to **Butler's Glen** and **Dunaff Head** from Clonmany.

ACTIVITIES
With two championship courses, **Ballyliffin Golf Club** (☎ 937 6119; Ballyliffin; green fees weekday/weekend Old Links €50/55, Glashedy €65/75) is easily one of the best place to play golf in Donegal. The scenery is so beautiful that it can distract even the most focused golfer.

SLEEPING & EATING
As more high-class hotels arrive, the more Ballyliffin's popularity is increasing. A high-class spa hotel is also tipped to open in late 2005 (see www.ballyliffinlodge.com).

Tullagh Bay Camping & Caravan Park (☎ 937 8997; Tullagh Bay; camp sites €14; ☯ Easter-Sep) About 5km from Clonmany, this windy but flat park is ideal for the bucket-and-spade brigade as it's just behind the vast, dune-backed Tullagh Strand.

B&Bs line the 2km stretch of road between Ballyliffin and Clonmany.

Rossaor House (☎ 937 6498; Ballyliffin; s €45-50, d €70-80; Ⓟ) It's worth the extra few euros to stay at this above-average B&B just outside town. Quite apart from its wonderful views, pristine rooms and leafy little garden, where else can you request home-produced honey on your freshly baked scones?

Doherty's Pollan Beach Hotel (☎ 937 8840; www.pollanbeachhotel.com; Shore Rd; s €70-80, d €110-130; Ⓟ ▯ ⚅) One of several flashy new hotels in town, this immaculately maintained place has two outstanding features: its position overlooking the wide sandy beach, about 1.5km from the town centre, and its hugely popular restaurant.

GETTING THERE & AWAY
Lough Swilly (☎ 912 2863) buses run between Clonmany and Carndonagh (€3.45, 20 minutes); see opposite for details.

Clonmany to Buncrana
There are two routes from Clonmany to Buncrana: the scenic coastal road via the Gap of Mamore and Dunree Head; and the speedier inland road (R238). The awesome **Gap of Mamore** (elevation 262m) descends dramatically between Mamore Hill and Croaghcarragh on its way to Dunree (An Dún Riabhach), where the **Guns of Dunree military museum** (☎ 074-936 1817; www.dunree.pro.ie; ☯ 10.30am-6pm Mon-Sat, 1-6pm Sun Jun-Sep, 10.30am-4.30pm Mon-Fri, 1-6pm Sat & Sun Oct-May) sits on a rocky outcrop in a 19th-century fort.

Buncrana
☎ 074 / pop 3420
Sugary-coloured pubs, greasy-spoon diners and shops cluster along Buncrana's main street, which, during winter, quietly awaits the summer hordes that converge from Derry. A 5km sandy beach on the shores of Lough Swilly is the town's main attraction, but there are a couple of worthwhile sights to distract you from working on your tan.

INFORMATION
A broadband Internet café was set to open at Tullyarvan Mill in late 2005.
Bank of Ireland (Lower Main St) ATM and bureau de change.
Post office (Upper Main St)
Tourist office (☎ 936 2600; Derry Rd; ☯ 11am-3.30pm Fri, 11.30am-2pm Sat) Seasonal; 1km south of the town centre.
Ulster Bank (Upper Main St) ATM and bureau de change.
Valu Clean (☎ 936 2570; Lower Main St; laundry from €6) Laundry service.

SIGHTS
The community-run **Tullyarvan Mill** (☎ 936 1613; tullyarvan@eircom.net; Carndonagh Rd; admission free; ☯ 10am-5pm May-Sep; Ⓟ) is a community centre, craft shop and tearoom 1km north of town on the River Crana. Since it was built in the mid-18th century, the building has been used for such diverse incarnations as a seaweed-extraction centre, cornmill and hattery. Its riverside gardens make a good picnic spot. It's also worth visiting for its music evenings in summer. Head north out of town on the R238 and follow the signs.

At the northern end of the seafront the early-18th-century six-arched Castle Bridge leads to **O'Docherty's Keep**, a tower house built by the O'Dochertys, the local chiefs, in 1430. It was burned by the English and then rebuilt for their own use. At its side is the manor-like **Buncrana Castle**, built in 1718 by John

Vaughan, who also constructed the bridge; Wolfe Tone was imprisoned here following the unsuccessful French invasion in 1798. Walking 500m further from the keep (turn left and stick to the shoreline) brings you to **Ned's Point Fort** (1812), built by the British and now under siege from graffiti artists.

SLEEPING & EATING

B&Bs abound, but they can fill up quickly during August.

Tullyarvan Mill (☎ 936 1613; tullyarvan@eircom.net; Carndonagh Rd; dm €15-20; ☺ year round; P ⬜ ♿) Call ahead to check if this showcase new hostel is open: a long-awaited community-run project built by the 18th-century mill, it looks set to open by September 2006. Expect beautiful riverside gardens, and a few private doubles.

Town Clock Guest House (☎ 936 2146; 6 Upper Main St; s/d €25/50, mains €5-15; ☺ food served 8.15am-8pm Mon-Thu, to 9pm Fri & Sat, 10.30am-9pm Sun) This no-nonsense place, bang in the centre, has straightforward, spacious rooms. Breakfast can be gleaned in the downstairs café, which serves a range of dishes and snacks (including vegetarian) from lasagne to toasties.

Lake of Shadows Hotel (☎ 936 1005; www.lakeof shadows.com; Grianán Park; s/d €48/96; P) A fine Victorian façade brings to mind past generations coming to 'take the sea air' here. Its 23 modern but fading, flowery rooms help maintain the image. To get here from Main St, head down Church St towards the bay.

Cranberry (☎ 936 3990; Upper Main St; snacks & sandwiches around €6) A terrific little fly-by-day restaurant to grab snacks and light meals on the go.

ENTERTAINMENT

Atlantic Bar (☎ 932 0880; Upper Main St) Dating from 1792, the Atlantic is Buncrana's oldest pub.

Zone (Upper Main St) Of the few nightclubs in town, Zone attracts the best visiting DJs, despite being daubed in nursery hues of pink and blue.

GETTING THERE & AROUND

From Buncrana, **Lough Swilly** (☎ 912 2863) buses run several times daily to Derry and less often to Carndonagh.

Lough Swilly Ferry services now run from Buncrana to Rathmullan (30 minutes, nine daily, single car/motorbike/adult/concession €12/6/3/2) from mid-June to September. Pick up a current timetable at the tourist office.

South of Buncrana

FAHAN

A monastery was founded in Fahan by St Colmcille in the 6th century. Among its ruins is the beautifully carved, 7th-century **St Mura Cross** in the graveyard beside the church. Each face is decorated with a cross, in intricate Celtic weave, and the barely discernible Greek inscription is the only one known from this early Christian period.

GRIANÁN OF AILEÁCH

This amphitheatre-like stone **fort** (admission free; ☺ 10am-6pm; P) encircles the top of Grianán Hill like a halo, 18km south of Buncrana near Burt, signposted off the N13. In many ways it's a very theatrical place, offering eye-popping views of the surrounding loughs and all the way to distant Derry. And its mini-arena can resemble a circus whenever a tour bus rolls up and spills its load inside the 4m-thick walls.

The fort may have existed at least 2000 years ago, but it's thought that the site itself goes back to pre-Celtic times as a temple to the god Dagda. Between the 5th and 12th centuries it was the seat of the O'Neills, before being demolished by Murtogh O'Brien, king of Munster. You might wonder how a fort demolished 800 years ago could look so complete – well, between 1874 and 1878 an amateur archaeologist from Derry reconstructed it, and it's mostly what you see now.

The merry-go-round–shaped **Burt Church** at the foot of the hill was modelled, by Derry architect Liam McCormack, on the fort and built in 1967.

The 19th-century church of Christchurch at Burt, on the N13 about 300m south of the turn-off to the fort, houses the Grianán of Aileách Visitor Centre. However, the centre has been shut for renovations in recent years and it's unclear when – or if – it will reopen.

INCH ISLAND

Few tourists make it to tranquil Inch Island, accessible from the mainland by a causeway, but it does have plenty of birdlife, including a sanctuary for swans, two small beaches and the remains of an old fort. **Inch Island Stables** (☎ 074-936 0335) organises horse-riding lessons and trips around the island.

Counties Meath & Louth

Nowhere else in Ireland are history and mythology woven into such a rich tapestry of explosive fact and wonderful fiction than in the adjoining counties of Meath and Louth. Scattered throughout the low coastal landscape are the memories and monuments of an extraordinary story that began with the earliest Irish at Newgrange and Loughcrew, continued on with the early Christians at Monasterboice, Mellifont and Kells and climaxed in the dramatic and bloody struggle between the native people and the waves of invaders from across the Irish Sea. Those battles left scars in Drogheda, along the River Boyne and, most tellingly, in the border that runs an invisible line across Carlingford Lough.

More beautiful and most terrible of all, however, is the other great story of this rich green land, known in folklore as the Plain of Murtheimne; it is the *Táin Bó Cúailnge* (Cattle Raid of Cooley), the Iron Age saga that is considered one of the great epics of world literature. The epic's dramatic climax occurred on Louth's beautiful Cooley Peninsula, but throughout the area you will find places that owe their names to the legendary heroes and battles of that time.

If history is poetry, then the present is prose, and Meath and Louth are becoming increasingly urbanised in the face of the rapid, largely unplanned growth of Dublin. New housing, new roads and greater opportunities for industry and tourism are proving to be unstoppable forces, adding a new and potentially traumatic chapter to an already long tale.

HIGHLIGHTS

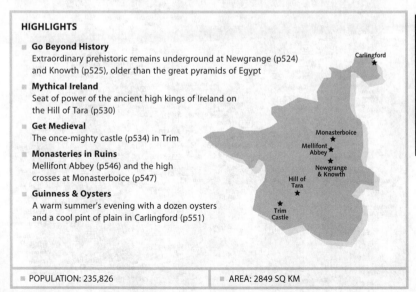

- **Go Beyond History**
  Extraordinary prehistoric remains underground at Newgrange (p524) and Knowth (p525), older than the great pyramids of Egypt

- **Mythical Ireland**
  Seat of power of the ancient high kings of Ireland on the Hill of Tara (p530)

- **Get Medieval**
  The once-mighty castle (p534) in Trim

- **Monasteries in Ruins**
  Mellifont Abbey (p546) and the high crosses at Monasterboice (p547)

- **Guinness & Oysters**
  A warm summer's evening with a dozen oysters and a cool pint of plain in Carlingford (p551)

COUNTIES MEATH & LOUTH

Carlingford

Monasterboice

Mellifont Abbey

Newgrange & Knowth

Hill of Tara

Trim Castle

- POPULATION: 235,826   ■ AREA: 2849 SQ KM

COUNTY MEATH

In the original Gaelic divisions of Ireland, Meath (An Mhí) was Mide, 'the Middle Kingdom' and one of five provinces. The seat of the high kings until the 6th century, it is still known as the Royal County. Basically, Meath was a fairly heavy hitter in Irish affairs.

These days, Meath's influence doesn't extend far beyond agricultural matters, but in that domain it still packs a solid punch: a farm in Meath is worth two in any other county, so goes the old saying. The fecund earth has attracted settlers since earliest times, and Meath's principal attractions are its ancient sites in the Boyne Valley and among the isolated hills of Tara and Slane.

The county's towns have experienced rapid growth in the last decade, as Dubliners searching for affordable housing have swallowed their pride and gone to live among the culchies of Navan, Trim and Kells. For the locals, the arrival of so many smelly Dubs is a mixed blessing: they bring plenty of cash, but they also bring traffic jams and horrific housing developments that threaten to engulf the county.

HISTORY

Meath's rich soil, laid down during the last Ice Age, attracted settlers as early as 8000 BC. They worked their way up the banks

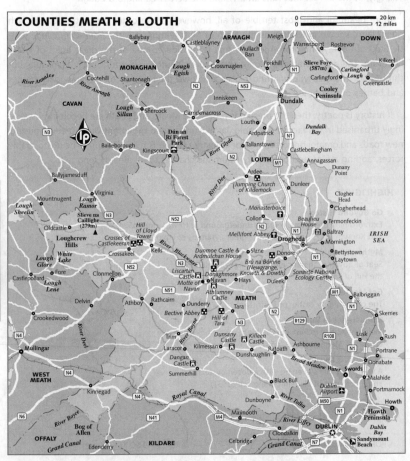

COUNTIES MEATH & LOUTH

of the River Boyne transforming the landscape from forest to farmland. The extensive necropolis at Brú na Bóinne, dating from when the pyramids where still but a dream, lies on a meandering section of the Boyne between Drogheda and Slane. There's a group of smaller passage graves in the Loughcrew Hills near Oldcastle. For a thousand years the Hill of Tara was the seat of power for Irish high kings (*ard ríthe*; pronounced ard-ree-huh), until the arrival of St Patrick in the 5th century. Later, Kells became one of the most important and creative monastic settlements in Ireland and lent its name to the famed *Book of Kells*, a 9th-century illuminated manuscript now displayed in Trinity College, Dublin.

THE COAST

Meath's mere 10km of coastline includes a number of small resorts with wide expanses of sand dunes and safe beaches popular with Dubliners and people from Drogheda and Dundalk. From the Elizabethan **Maiden Watchtower**, in Mornington at the mouth of the Boyne, there are fine views of Drogheda, 5km to the west, and the Boyne Estuary.

Laytown is a busy little seaside town with golf, tennis and good windsurfing. It hosts an annual **horse-racing festival** on the beach in mid-August. Outside Laytown, on the road to Julianstown (the R150), is **Sonairte National Ecology Centre** (☎ 041-982 7572; The Ninch; adult/child/student €3.20/1.30/1.90; ☒ 9am-5pm Mon-Fri, 11am-5pm Sat, 11am-6pm Sun), beside the River Nanny. It has an organic garden, a nature trail, adventure playground and exhibits displaying the use of wind, water and solar power. In the gift shop you can buy wine made from the centre's own organically grown grapes.

Just 1km north of Laytown is **Bettystown**, whose claim to fame is that the magnificent 8th-century Tara Brooch was found in a box on the beach here in 1850. The only link between the brooch and Tara is that the magnificent ornamentation and preciousness of its materials seem to indicate a wealthy, if not royal, association with the high kings, who were based in Tara. It's now on display in the National Museum in Dublin. There is a long strand on the edge of the village, which is very popular in summer, affording long walks and, if you can overcome the pollution, some pretty good swimming.

Sleeping & Eating

Beach Lodge (☎ 041-988 7866; www.beachlodge.ie; Golf Links Rd, Bettystown; s/d €45/80) Four beautifully appointed rooms with fabulous views of the sea and the local golf links make this a pretty good choice in the area.

Neptune Beach (☎ 041-982 7107; www.neptune beach.ie; Bettystown Beach; s/d €120/160) The classy option in Bettystown has just had a much-needed refurb, which has left it looking pretty good. There are a variety of different-sized rooms with a selection of views: you'll pay more for a sea view, a Jacuzzi and a suite. Breakfast is included.

Bacchus at the Coastguard (☎ 041-982 8251; Bayview, Bettystown; mains from €14; ☒ 6-11pm Tue-Sat, noon-7pm Sun) As you might expect, seafood is the speciality here and the place has a big reputation.

Getting There & Away

Bus Éireann (☎ 041-983 5023; www.buseirann.ie) runs at least four buses each day along the coast, stopping at Laytown and Bettystown. From the coast to Drogheda costs €2.50/4.50 one way/return, and to Dublin €8.20/11.

The coast is served by regular **trains** (☎ 01-836 6222) on the Dublin–Belfast line: eight a day Monday to Thursday and Saturday, nine on Friday and four on Sunday. Dublin to Laytown costs €9/13 one way/return and takes 20 minutes. Belfast to Laytown is €23/33 and takes a bit over 1½ hours.

BRÚ NA BÓINNE

One of Ireland's genuine five-star attractions, the extensive Neolithic necropolis known as Brú na Bóinne (the Boyne Palace) is one of the most extraordinary sites in

COUNTIES MEATH & LOUTH

TOP FIVE SLEEPS IN MEATH & LOUTH

- Rossnaree (Newgrange, County Meath; p526)
- Ghan House (Carlingford, County Louth; p553)
- Woodtown House (Athboy near Trim, County Meath; p536)
- Lennoxbrook (Kells, County Meath; p539)
- Smarmore Castle (Ardee, County Louth; p548)

Europe. A thousand years older than Stonehenge, this is a powerful and evocative testament to the mind-boggling achievements of prehistoric humans.

This necropolis was built to house the VIP corpses – no ordinary Joes or Janes here. Its tombs were the largest artificial structures in Ireland until the construction of the Anglo-Norman castles 4000 years later. The area consists of many different sites, the three principal ones being Newgrange, Knowth and Dowth.

Over the centuries the tombs decayed, were covered by grass and trees and were plundered by everybody from Vikings to Victorian treasure hunters, whose carved initials can be seen on the great stones of Newgrange. The countryside around them is littered with countless other ancient mounds (tumuli) and standing stones.

The entire complex, including the three main passage tombs (of which only Newgrange and Knowth are accessible) can be visited as part of a tour run by the **Brú na Bóinne visitor centre** (☎ 041-988 0300; www.heritage ireland.ie; Donore; adult/student/family €2.75/1.50/7, visitor centre, Newgrange & Knowth €8.80/4.10/6.30; ⏲ 9am-6.30pm Jun-Sep, 9.30am-5pm Oct-Apr), a superb interpretive centre with an extraordinary series of interactive exhibits on the passage tombs and prehistoric Ireland in general. It is located south of the River Boyne and 2km west of Donore.

You should allow plenty of time to visit this unique centre. If you're only planning on taking the guided tour of the interpretive centre, give yourself about an hour. If you plan a visit to Newgrange or Knowth, allow at least two hours. If, however, you want to visit all three in one go, you should plan at least half a day. In summer, particularly at the weekend, and during school holidays, the place gets very crowded, and you will not be guaranteed a visit to either of the passage tombs; call ahead to book a tour and avoid disappointment. In summer, the best time to visit is mid-week or early in the morning.

Newgrange

From the surface **Newgrange** (visitor centre & Newgrange adult/student/senior €5/2.50/3.80) is a somewhat disappointing, flattened, grass-covered mound about 80m in diameter and 13m high. But underneath lies the finest Stone Age passage tomb in Ireland and one of the most remarkable prehistoric sites in Europe. It dates from around 3200 BC, predating the great pyramids of Egypt by some six centuries. The purpose for which it was constructed remains uncertain. It could have been a burial place for kings or a centre for ritual – although the alignment with the sun at the time of the winter solstice also suggests it was designed to act as a calendar.

The name derives from 'new granary' (the tomb did in fact serve as a repository for wheat and grain at one stage), although a belief more popular in the area is that it comes from the Irish for 'Cave of Gráinne', a reference to a Celtic myth taught to every Irish child. The story of *The Pursuit of Diarmuid and Gráinne* tells of the illicit love between the wife of Fionn McCumhaill (or Finn McCool), leader of the Fianna, and Diarmuid, one of his most trusted lieutenants. When Diarmuid was fatally wounded, his body was brought to Newgrange by the god Aengus in a vain attempt to save him, and the despairing Gráinne followed him into the cave, where she remained long after he died. This suspiciously Arthurian-type legend (for Diarmuid and Gráinne read Lancelot and Guinevere) is undoubtedly untrue, but it's still a pretty good story. Newgrange also plays another role in Celtic mythology, as the site where the hero Cúchulainn was conceived.

Over time, Newgrange, like Dowth and Knowth, deteriorated and was even quarried at one stage. There was a standing stone on the summit until the 17th century. The site was extensively restored in 1962 and again in 1975.

A superbly carved kerbstone with double and triple spirals guards the tomb's main entrance. The front façade has been reconstructed so that tourists don't have to clamber in over it. Above the entrance is a slit or roof box, which lets light in. Another beautifully decorated kerbstone stands at the exact opposite side of the mound. Some experts say that a ring of standing stones encircled the mound, forming a Great Circle about 100m in diameter, but only 12 of these stones remain – with traces of some others below ground level.

Holding the whole structure together are the 97 boulders of the kerb ring, designed to stop the mound from collapsing outwards. Eleven of these are decorated with motifs similar to those on the main entrance stone, although only three have extensive carvings.

The white quartzite was originally obtained from Wicklow, 70km to the south – in an age before horse and wheel it was transported by sea and then up the River Boyne – and there is also some granite from the Mourne Mountains in Northern Ireland. Over 200,000 tonnes of earth and stone also went into the mound.

You can walk down the narrow 19m passage lined with 43 stone uprights, some of them engraved, which leads into the tomb chamber about one-third of the way into the colossal mound. The chamber has three recesses, and in these are large basin stones that held cremated human bones. Along with the remains would have been funeral offerings of beads and pendants, but these were stolen long before the archaeologists arrived.

Above, the massive stones support a 6m-high corbel-vaulted roof. A complex drainage system means that not a drop of water has penetrated the interior in 40 centuries.

At 8.20am during the winter solstice (19 to 23 December), the rising sun's rays shine through the slit above the entrance, creep slowly down the long passage and illuminate the tomb chamber for 17 minutes. There is little doubt that witnessing this is one of the country's most memorable, even mystical, experiences; be sure to add your name to the list that is drawn by lottery every October 1. Even if you miss out, there is a simulated winter sunrise for every group taken into the mound.

Knowth

Northwest of Newgrange, the burial mound of **Knowth** (Cnóbha; visitor centre & Knowth adult/child/student €3.80/1.50/2.50; May-Oct) was built around the same time and seems set to surpass its better-known neighbour, both in the extent and the importance of the discoveries made here. It has the greatest collection of passage-grave art ever uncovered in Western Europe. Under excavation since 1962, it recently opened to the public at last.

Modern excavations at Knowth soon cleared a 34m passage leading to the central chamber, much longer than the one at Newgrange. In 1968 a second 40m passage was unearthed on the opposite side of the mound. Although the chambers are separate, they're close enough for archaeologists to hear each other at work. Also in the mound are the remains of six early-Christian souterrains (underground chambers) built into the side. Some 300 carved slabs and 17 satellite graves surround the main mound.

Human activity at Knowth continued for thousands of years after its construction, which accounts for the site's complexity. The Beaker folk, so called because they buried the dead with drinking vessels, occupied the site in the Bronze Age (c 1800 BC), as did the Celts in the Iron Age (c 500 BC). Remnants of bronze and iron workings from these periods have been discovered. Around AD 800 to 900 it was turned into a *ráth* (earthen ring fort), a stronghold of the very powerful Uí Néill (O'Neill) clan. In 965, it was the seat of Cormac Mac-Maelmithic, later Ireland's high king for nine years. The Normans built a motte and bailey here in the 12th century. In about 1400 the site was finally abandoned. Further excavations are likely to continue at least for the next decade, and one of the thrills of visiting Knowth is being allowed to watch them at work.

Dowth

The circular mound at **Dowth** (Dubhadh, meaning 'dark') is similar in size to Newgrange – about 63m in diameter – but is slightly taller at 14m high. It has suffered badly at the hands of everyone from road builders and treasure hunters to amateur archaeologists, who scooped out the centre of the tumulus in the 19th century. For a time, Dowth even had a teahouse ignobly perched on its summit. Relatively untouched by modern archaeologists, Dowth shows what Newgrange and Knowth looked like for most of their history. Because it's unsafe, Dowth is closed to visitors, though the mound can be viewed from the road. Excavations began in 1998 and will continue for years to come.

There are two entrance passages leading to separate chambers (both sealed), and a 24m early-Christian souterrain at either end, which connect up with the western passage.

NEWGRANGE FARM

Here is one for the kids. Situated a few hundred metres down the hill to the west of Newgrange tomb is a 135-hectare **working farm** (☎ 041-982 4119; www.newgrange farm.com; Newgrange; adult €7, family €12-30; ☻ 10am-5.30pm Mon-Fri, 2-5.30pm Sun Easter-Sep, 2-5.30pm Sat Jul & Aug). The truly hands-on, family-run farm allows visitors to feed the ducks and lambs and tour the exotic bird aviaries. Charming Farmer Bill keeps things interesting, and demonstrations of threshing, sheepdog work and shoeing a horse are absorbing. Sunday at 3pm is a very special time when the 'sheep derby' is run. Finding jockeys small enough isn't easy, so teddy bears are tied to the sheep's backs. Visiting children are made owners of individual sheep for the race.

This 8m-long passage leads into a small cruciform chamber, in which a recess acts as an entrance to an additional series of small compartments, a feature unique to Dowth. To the southwest is the entrance to a shorter passage and smaller chamber.

North of the tumulus are the ruins of **Dowth Castle** and **Dowth House**.

Sleeping

There are a couple of really beautiful B&Bs in the area.

Glebe House (☎ 041-983 6101; fax 984 3469; Dowth; r €120) A magnificent 17th-century, wisteria-clad country house that's near the Dowth burial mound and has gorgeous rooms with open, log fires. It is 7km west of Drogheda. Children under 10 are not welcome.

Mattock House (☎ /fax 041-982 4592; s/d €35/50) About 2km east of Slane, near the Newgrange mound, is a modern farmhouse with large, comfortable rooms and a breakfast that struggles to fit on the plate. Access is off the N51.

Tours

Brú na Bóinne is one of the most popular tourist attractions in Ireland, and there is a plethora of organised tours transporting busloads of eager tourists to the interpretative centre.

Highly recommended is the superbly informative tour run by **Mary Gibbons** (☎ 01-283 9973; www.newgrangetours.com; tour & admission €35). Tours depart from Buswells Hotel, Molesworth St, at 10am; Dublin Tourism Centre, Suffolk St, at 10.15am; Royal Dublin Hotel, O'Connell St, at 10.30am Monday to Friday, and take in the whole of the Boyne Valley, including Newgrange and the Hill of Tara (p530). Eamonn P Kelly, the Keeper of Irish Antiquities at the National Museum in Dublin, described it as 'the authentic tour of Ireland's history'. The expert guides offer a fascinating insight into Celtic and pre-Celtic life in Ireland.

Bus Éireann (☎ 01-836 6111; www.buseireann.ie; adult/child/student & senior €27/17.55/25.20; Mon-Thu, Sat & Sun) runs Newgrange and the Boyne Valley tours departing from Busáras in Dublin at 9.30am, returning at approximately 5.45pm. The tours are cheaper between October and December.

Getting There & Away

Newgrange, Knowth and Dowth are all well signposted. Newgrange lies just north of the River Boyne, about 13km southwest of Drogheda and around 5km southeast of Slane; Dowth is between Newgrange and Drogheda; while Knowth is about 1km northwest of Newgrange, or almost 4km by road.

From Drogheda, **Bus Éireann** (☎ 01-836 6111) runs a service that drops you off at the gates of the interpretive centre (€1.45, 20 minutes, six daily 10.15am to 4pm). You can also catch Bus Éireann from Dublin

---

SOMETHING SPECIAL

Rossnaree (☎ 041-982 0975; rossnaree@eircom .net; Newgrange; s/d €90/140, dinner €45) At a sharp corner on the narrow road between Donore and Slane, just south of the Brú na Bóinne visitor centre, is this magnificent Palladian-style country house overlooking the Boyne and surrounded by a working farm. The bedrooms are simply exquisite, as is the cooking – dinner is an experience in itself (and must be booked the day before). The house is a terrific destination for anglers, who can try their luck for salmon and brown trout in the river. The legend of Fionn and the Salmon of Knowledge is said to have taken place in this very spot (see the boxed text, opposite).

FIONN & THE SALMON OF KNOWLEDGE

One of the best-known stories in the Fenian Cycle tells of the old druid Finnegan who struggled for seven years to catch a very slippery salmon that, once eaten, would bestow enormous wisdom on the eater, including the gift of foresight. The young Fionn McCumhaill arrived at his riverside camp one day looking for instruction, and no sooner did the young hero arrive, than Finnegan managed to land the salmon. As befits the inevitable tragedy of all these stories, Finnegan set the fish to cook and went off for a bit, ordering Fionn to keep an eye on it without eating so much as the smallest part. You'd think that after all these years of labour Finnegan could have put off his errand until after dinner, but it wasn't to be: as Fionn turned the fish on the spit a drop of hot oil landed on his thumb, which he quickly put in his mouth to soothe. Finnegan returned, saw what had happened and knew that it was too late; he bade Fionn eat the rest of the fish and so it was that Fionn acquired wisdom and foresight.

(one way/return €7.20/12.20, 1½ hours, one daily). Visitors are bussed from the centre to the sites.

SLANE

☎ 041 / pop 823

The pretty village of Slane (Baile Shláine) grew in support of the enormous castle whose grounds dominate everything around; the massive grey gate to the privately owned castle lies southwest of the town centre, which is made up of pleasant 18th-century stone houses and cottages. At the junction of the main roads are four identical houses facing each other: local lore has it that they were built for four sisters who had taken an intense dislike to one another and kept watch from their individual residences.

Orientation & Information

Slane is perched on a hillside overlooking the River Boyne, at the junction of the N2 and N51, some 15km west of Drogheda. At the bottom of the hill to the south, the Boyne glides by under a narrow bridge. The hairpin turn on the northern side of the bridge is considered to be one of the most dangerous in the country as there is a steep hill preceding it; fatal accidents occur there on an all-too-regular basis. If you are driving, be extra careful.

The helpful, community-run **tourist office** (☎ 988 4055; info@meathtourism.ie; Main St; ⏱ 9.30am-5pm Mon, Thu & Sat) is directly opposite the Conyngham Arms Hotel.

Sights

HILL OF SLANE

About 1km north of the village is the Hill of Slane, a fairly plain looking mound that only stands out for its association with a thick slice of Celto-Christian mythology. According to the legend, St Patrick lit a paschal (Easter) fire here in AD 433 to proclaim Christianity throughout the land. Patrick's fire infuriated Laoghaire, the pagan high king of Ireland, who had expressly ordered that no fire be lit within sight of the Hill of Tara. Thankfully – at least for the future of Irish Christians – he was restrained by his far-sighted druids, who warned that 'the man who had kindled the flame would surpass kings and princes.' Laoghaire went to meet Patrick and question him, and all but one of his attendants – a man called Erc – greeted Patrick with scorn. And here the story *really* gets far-fetched.

During the meeting, Patrick killed one of the king's guards and summoned an earthquake to subdue the rest. After his Herculean efforts, Patrick calmed down a little and plucked a shamrock from the ground, using its three leaves to explain the paradox of the Holy Trinity – the union of the Father, the Son and the Holy Spirit in one Godhead. Laoghaire wasn't convinced, but he agreed to let Patrick continue his missionary work; Patrick's success that day – apart from keeping his own life, starting an earthquake and giving Ireland one of its enduring national symbols – was good old Erc, who was baptised and later became the first bishop of Slane. To this day, the local parish priest lights a fire here on Holy Saturday.

The Hill of Slane originally had a church associated with St Erc and, later, a round tower and monastery, but only an outline of the foundations remains. Later a motte and bailey were constructed and are still visible on the western side of the hill. A ruined church, tower and other buildings once formed part of an early-16th-century Franciscan friary. On a clear day, from the top of the tower, which is always open, you can see the Hill of Tara and the Boyne Valley, as well (it's said) as seven Irish counties.

St Erc is believed to have become a hermit in old age, and the ruins of a small Gothic **church** (15 Aug) mark the spot where he is thought to have spent his last days, around AD 512 to 514. It's on the northern riverbank, behind the Protestant church on the Navan road, and lies within the private Conyngham estate.

SLANE CASTLE

The private residence of Lord Henry Conyngham, earl of Mountcharles, **Slane Castle** (988 4400; www.slanecastle.ie; adult/child/family €7/5/20; noon-5pm Sun-Thu May-Jul) is west of the centre along the Navan road and is best known in Ireland as the setting for major outdoor rock concerts in its natural amphitheatre.

Built in 1785 in the Gothic Revival style by James Wyatt, the building was altered later by Francis Johnson for George IV's visit to Lady Conyngham. She was allegedly his mistress, and it's said the road between Dublin and Slane was built especially straight and smooth to speed up the randy king's journeys.

U2 fans may recognise the castle from the cover of their 1984 album *The Unforgettable Fire*, which was recorded here. Seven years later, a *really* unforgettable fire gutted most of castle, whereupon it was discovered that the earl was underinsured. A major fundraising drive – of which the summer concerts were a part – led to a painstaking restoration and the castle finally reopened for tours in 2001.

LEDWIDGE MUSEUM

If farm labourers' cottages from the 19th-century float your boat, you will enjoy a visit to the **Ledwidge Museum** (982 4544; www.francis ledwidge.com; Janesville; admission €2.60; 9am-1pm & 2-7pm Apr-Sep, 9am-1pm & 2-4.30pm Mon-Fri Oct-Mar), the birthplace of poet Francis Ledwidge (1891–1917), who died on the battlefield at Ypres. It is about 1.5km northeast of Slane on the Drogheda road. A keen political activist, Ledwidge was thwarted in his efforts

to set up a branch of the Gaelic League in the area; in the course of an argument, he vented his spleen in verse:

Oh! What a pleasant world 'twould be
How smoothly we'd step thro' it
If all the fools who mean no harm
Could manage not to do it.

We know his pain.

Sleeping & Eating

Slane Farm Hostel (/fax 988 4985; www.slanefarm hostel.ie; Harlinstown House, R163 Navan road; dm/s/d €16/30/40) These former stables, built by the Marquis of Conyngham in the 18th century, have been converted into a fabulous hostel that is part of a working farm surrounding Harlinstown House (where the owners reside). Our readers have consistently raved about this place and we heartily concur.

Conyngham Arms Hotel (982 4155; www.con ynghamarms.com; Slane; s/d €65/120; mains €9-13; noon-8pm) This fairly elegant 19th-century hotel maintains that village-inn feel and look. The four-poster bed in each room is a real treat; breakfast is included. The hotel's restaurant serves up a menu of solid favourites such as roast chicken with stuffing, bacon and cabbage and the like.

Boyle's Licensed Tea Rooms (982 4195; Main St; snacks from €3; 10am-5pm) This marvellous teashop and café lies behind an equally beautiful shop front with gold lettering. The menu – written in 12 languages – is strictly of the tea-and-scones type, but people come here for the ambience, which is straight out of the 1940s.

Getting There & Away

Bus Éireann (01-836 6111) services to Dublin (one way/return €7.50/11.50, 45 minutes, five daily) stop in front of the sweet shop on the main Derry road, and at Conlon's Shop near the crossroads for buses to Drogheda (one way €2, 35 minutes) and Navan (one way €1.50, 30 minutes), both of which run six a day Monday to Saturday and five on Sunday.

SLANE TO NAVAN

Along the 14km journey southwest on the N51 from Slane to Navan there are a few manor houses, ruined castles, round towers and churches dotted throughout; don't get too excited however as they're not nearly as impressive as sites elsewhere in Meath.

Dunmoe Castle lies down a badly signposted cul-de-sac to the south, 4km before reaching Navan. This D'Arcy family castle is a 16th-century ruin with good views of the countryside and of the impressive redbrick **Ardmulchan House** (closed to the public), on the opposite side of the River Boyne. Cromwell is supposed to have fired at the castle from the riverbank in 1649, and local legend holds that a tunnel used to run from the castle vaults under the river. Near Dunmoe Castle is a small overgrown chapel and graveyard with a crypt containing members of the D'Arcy family. Ardmulchan House, though somewhat dilapidated, is still used as a private residence.

You can't miss the fine 30m round tower and 13th-century church of **Donaghmore**, on the right 2km nearer Navan. The site has a profusion of modern gravestones, but the 10th-century tower with its Crucifixion scene above the door is interesting, and there are carved faces near the windows and the remains of the church wall.

NAVAN

☎ 046 / pop 3406

You won't want to waste too much time in Navan (An Uaimh), Meath's county town. It's a busy enough place, serving as the crossroads between the busy N3 Dublin road and the N51 between Drogheda and Westmeath, which is good for local business but bad for aesthetics. You might find yourself here changing buses. If you do, you should know that Sir Francis Beaufort – the guy who devised the internationally accepted scale for wind strengths – was born here, and if that's not enough of an incentive then the clincher should be Europe's largest lead and zinc mine, Tara, about 3km out of town on the Kells road.

If you need local information, the **tourist office** (☎ 902 1581; Railway St; ☻ 9.30am-12.30pm & 1.30-5pm Mon-Sat) is in the town library about 500m southwest of Market Sq.

Sleeping

There are plenty of B&Bs around town should you decide to stay.

Killyon House (☎ 907 1224; www.killyonguest house.ie; Dublin Rd, Navan; s/d from €45/70) From the

front, this is another charming suburban home, but inside it is a gorgeous home with handsome period furniture and beds. The breakfast room, which overlooks the garden that stretches down to the Boyne, is about as idyllic a place to munch into a home-cooked breakfast as we've seen anywhere in the whole country.

Athlumney Manor (☎ 907 1388; www.athlumney manor.com; Athlumney, Duleek road R153; s/d €45/66) This super B&B about a mile out of town is the best around; a large, modern house with well-appointed, comfortable rooms.

Eating

Hudson's Bistro (☎ 902 9231; 30 Railway St; 4-course dinner €30; ☻ 6-10pm Tue-Sat) With a growing reputation as one of the best restaurants in all of Meath, the wide-ranging menu has a tendency to overreach itself at times, but the solid classics – steak, fish and poultry – are lip-smackingly good.

Ryan's Pub (☎ 902 1154; 22 Trimgate St; bar food from €4; ☻ noon-8pm) This lovely old pub serves great pub grub, including brown bread with smoked salmon.

Getting There & Away

Bus Éireann (☎ 01-836 6111) has services almost hourly on the Dublin–Cavan–Donegal route, which stop in Navan and go to Kells (one way/return €3.50/4.50, 15 minutes). Navan is only 50 minutes from Dublin (€8.50/11), and is also on the Dundalk (€10/13.50, 1¼ hours) to Galway route (€16/22, 3¼ hours), with one bus daily stopping at Drogheda (€5/8, 35 minutes). All buses stop in front of the Mercy Convent on Railway St and in Market Sq.

Getting Around

You can order a taxi from **Navan Cabs** (☎ 902 3053), and ranks are on Market Sq and in front of the shopping centre on Kennedy Rd.

AROUND NAVAN

The impressive and relatively intact **Athlumney Castle** lies about 2km southeast of town. It was built by the Dowdall family in the 16th century with additions made a hundred years later. After King James' defeat at the Battle of the Boyne, Sir Lancelot Dowdall set fire to the castle so as to ensure that James' conqueror, William of Orange, would never shelter or confiscate his home. He watched the blaze from the opposite bank of the river before leaving for France and then Italy. As you enter the estate, take a right toward the Loreto Convent, where you can pick up the keys to the castle. In the convent yard is another **motte**, which at one time it had a wooden tower on it.

There are some pleasant **walks** around Navan, particularly the one following the towpath that runs along the old River Boyne canal towards Slane and Drogheda. On the southern bank, you can go about 7km as far as Stackallen and the Boyne bridge, passing Ardmulchan House and, on the opposite bank, the ruins of Dunmoe Castle (see p529). Going beyond the bridge towards Slane is trickier as the path is rough and in some places switches to the opposite side of the bank, with no bridge for you to cross over.

Close to the Kells road (N3), 5km northwest of Navan, is the large ruin of a castle that once belonged to the Talbot family. **Liscartan Castle** is made up of two 15th-century square towers joined by a hall-like room.

TARA

It's Ireland's most sacred stretch of turf, a place at the heart of Irish history, legend and folklore. It was the home of the mystical druids, the priest-rulers of ancient Ireland who practised their particular form of Celtic voodoo under the watchful gaze of the all-powerful goddess Maeve (Medbh). Later it was the ceremonial capital of the high kings – 142 of them in all – who ruled until the arrival of Christianity in the 6th century. It is also one of the most important ancient sites in Europe, with a Stone Age passage tomb and prehistoric burial mounds that date back up to 5000 years. The **Hill of Tara** (Teamhair) may look like a bumpy pitch 'n' putt course, but its historic and folkloristic significance is immense: it is Ireland's own Camelot. So what does the government plan to do with it? Run a nine-mile section of the N3 through it in an act of state-sponsored vandalism that has left critics apoplectic. One archaeologist has likened the plan to 'ripping a knife from a Rembrandt.'

You won't see much, but there's plenty to imagine. The Celts believed that Tara was the sacred dwelling of the gods and the gateway to the otherworld. The passage grave was thought to be the final resting place of the Tuatha de Danann, the mythical fairy folk – who were real enough, only

they weren't pixies and brownies but earlier, Stone Age arrivals on the island.

As the Celtic political landscape began to evolve, the druids' power was usurped by warlike chieftains who took kingly titles; there was no sense of a united Ireland so at any given time there were countless *rí tuaithe* (petty kings) controlling many small areas. The king who ruled Tara, though, was generally considered the big kahuna, the high king, even though his direct rule didn't extend too far beyond the provincial border. The most lauded of all the high kings was Cormac MacArt, who ruled during the 3rd century.

The most important event in Tara's calendar was the three-day harvest *feis* (festival) that took place at Samhain, a precursor to modern Halloween. During the festival, the high king pulled out all the stops: grievances would be heard, laws passed and disputes settled amid an orgy of eating, drinking and all-round partying.

When the early Christians hit town in the 5th century, they targeted Tara straight away. Although the legend has it that Patrick lit the paschal fire on the Hill of Slane (see p527), some people believe that Patrick's incendiary act took place on Tara's sacred hump. The arrival of Christianity marked the beginning of the end for Celtic pagan civilisation, and the high kings began to desert Tara, even though the kings of Leinster continued to be based here until the 11th century.

In August 1843, Tara saw one of the greatest crowds ever to gather in Ireland. Daniel O'Connell, the 'Liberator' and leader of the opposition to union with Great Britain, held one of his 'monster rallies' at Tara, and up to 750,000 people came to hear him speak.

With so much history, archaeology and legend wrapped up in such a place, it seems genuinely incredible that the government would even consider building a road through it. However, traffic congestion in this part of Meath has hit critical point and a solution is desperately overdue. We hope that the solution is found elsewhere but we fear the worst: go now before the site is ruined forever.

Sights

TARA VISITOR CENTRE

The former Protestant church (with a window by the well-known artist Evie Hone) is home to the impressive **Tara Visitor Centre** (☎ 046-902 5903; www.heritageireland.ie; Navan; adult/child/family €2/1/5.50; ☙ 10am-6pm May-Oct, last admission 5.15pm), where a 20-minute audiovisual presentation about the site, *Tara: Meeting Place of Heroes*, is shown. During summer the tour from here is a must, as the anecdotes really bring the mounds and relics to life (see p532).

RÁTH OF THE SYNODS

The names applied to Tara's various humps and mounds were adopted from ancient texts, and mythology and religion intertwine with the historical facts. The Protestant church grounds and graveyard spill onto the remains of the **Ráth of the Synods**, a triple-ringed fort supposedly where some of St Patrick's early meetings (synods) took place. Excavations of the enclosure suggest that it was used between AD 200 and 400 for burials, rituals and living quarters. Originally the ring fort would have contained wooden houses surrounded by timber palisades.

During a digging session in the graveyard in 1810, a boy found a pair of gold torques (crescents of beaten gold hung around the neck), which are now in the National Museum in Dublin. Later excavations brought a surprise when Roman glass, shards of pottery and seals were discovered, showing links with the Roman Empire, even though the Romans never extended their power into Ireland.

The poor state of the enclosure is due in part to a group of British 'Israelites' who in the 1890s dug the place up looking for the Ark of the Covenant, much to the consternation of the local people. The Israelites' leader claimed to see a mysterious pillar on the enclosure, but unfortunately it was invisible to everyone else. After they failed to uncover anything, the invisible pillar moved to the other side of the road but, before the adventurers had time to start work there, the locals chased them away.

ROYAL ENCLOSURE

To the south of the church, the **Royal Enclosure** (Ráth na Ríogh) is a large, oval Iron Age hill fort, 315m in diameter and surrounded by a bank and ditch cut through solid rock under the soil. Inside the Royal Enclosure are smaller sites.

Mound of the Hostages

This bump (Dumha na nGiall) in the northern corner of the enclosure is the most ancient known part of Tara and the most visible of the remains. Supposedly a prison cell for hostages of the 3rd-century king Cormac MacArt, it is in fact a small Stone Age passage grave dating from around 1800 BC and later used by Bronze Age people. The passage contains some carved stonework, but it's closed to the public.

The mound produced a treasure trove of artefacts, including some ancient Mediterranean beads of amber and faïence (glazed pottery). More than 35 Bronze Age burials were found here, as well as a mass of cremated remains from the Stone Age.

Cormac's House & the Royal Seat

Two other earthworks found inside the enclosure are Cormac's House (Teach Cormaic) and the Royal Seat (Forradh). Although they look similar, the Royal Seat is a ring fort with a house site in the centre, while Cormac's House is a barrow, or burial mound, in the side of the circular bank. Cormac's House commands the best views of the surrounding lowlands of the Boyne and Blackwater Valleys.

Atop Cormac's House is the phallic **Stone of Destiny** (Lia Fáil), originally located near the Mound of the Hostages and representing the joining of the gods of the earth and the heavens. It's said to be the inauguration stone of the high kings, although alternative sources suggest that the actual coronation stone was the Stone of Scone, which was removed to Edinburgh, Scotland, and used to crown British kings. The would-be king stood on top of it and, if the stone let out three roars, he was crowned. The mass grave of 37 men who died in a skirmish on Tara during the 1798 Rising is next to the Stone.

ENCLOSURE OF KING LAOGHAIRE

South of the Royal Enclosure is the **Enclosure of King Laoghaire** (Ráth Laoghaire), a large but worn ring fort where the king, a contemporary of St Patrick, is supposedly buried dressed in his armour and standing upright.

BANQUET HALL

North of the churchyard is Tara's most unusual feature, the **Banquet Hall**, or Teach

Miodhchuarta (meaning 'house of mead-circling'; mead, which was a popular tipple, is fermented from honey). This rectangular earthwork measures 230m by 27m along a north–south axis. Tradition holds that it was built to cater for thousands of guests during feasts. Much of this information about the hall comes from the 12th-century *Book of Leinster* and the *Yellow Book of Lecan*, which even includes drawings of it.

Opinions vary as to the site's real purpose. Its orientation suggests that it was a sunken entrance to Tara, leading directly to the Royal Enclosure. More recent research has uncovered graves within the compound, and it's possible that the banks are in fact the burial sites of some of the kings of Tara.

GRÁINNE'S FORT

Gráinne was the same daughter of King Cormac who was betrothed to Fionn Mc-Cumhaill (Finn McCool) but eloped with Diarmuid ÓDuibhne, one of the king's warriors, on her wedding night and became the subject of the epic *The Pursuit of Diarmuid and Gráinne*. See p524 for more about the legend. **Gráinne's Fort** (Ráth Gráinne) and the northern and southern **Sloping Trenches** (Claoin Fhearta) off to the northwest are burial mounds.

Tours

Mary Gibbons (☎ 01-283 9973) has an excellent Boyne Valley tour that includes the Hill of Tara as well as Brú na Bóinne.

Bus Éireann (☎ 01-836 6111) tours to Newgrange and the Boyne Valley sometimes include a visit to Tara.

See p526 for prices and departure times.

Drinking

O'Connell's (☎ 046-902 5122; Skryne) An unspoilt and atmospheric country pub with all the essentials – a nice, open fire, friendly service and plenty of local lore on the walls. It is in Skryne, not far from Tara.

Getting There & Away

Tara is 10km southeast of Navan just off the N3 Dublin-to-Cavan road. **Bus Éireann** (☎ 01-836 6111) services linking Dublin and Navan pass within 1km of the site (€8, 40 minutes, hourly Monday to Saturday and four times on Sunday). Ask the driver to drop you off at the Tara Cross and then follow the signs.

AROUND TARA

About 5km south of Tara on the Dunshaughlin to Kilmessan road is **Dunsany Castle** (☎ 046-902 5198; www.dunsany.net; Dunsany; adult/child/senior €15/free/7.50; ⏰ 9am-1pm Mon-Fri May-Jul or Jun-Aug). It's the residence of the lords of Dunsany, former owners of the lands around Trim Castle. The Dunsanys are related to the Plunkett family, the most famous Plunkett being St Oliver, who was executed and whose head is kept in a church in Drogheda. As it's very much a lived-in property, opening hours vary in accordance with the family's schedule; major refurbishment has kept hours limited even further. Call for details.

There's an impressive private art collection and many other treasures related to important figures in Irish history, such as Oliver Plunkett and Patrick Sarsfield, leader of the Irish Jacobite forces at the siege of Limerick in 1691. A number of upstairs bedrooms have been restored and are now included in an expanded tour (though the charge to visit these is extra). Maintenance and restoration are ongoing (as it would be in a castle built in 1180!) and different rooms are open to visitors at different times.

Housed in the old kitchen and in part of the old domestic quarters is a **boutique** (⏰ 10am-5pm) that proudly sells the Dunsany Home Collection, featuring locally made table linen and accessories, as well as various articles for the home designed by Lord Dunsany himself, who is something of a well-known artist and designer.

About 1.5km northeast of Dunsany is the ruined **Killeen Castle**, the seat of another line of the Plunkett family. The 1801 mansion was constructed around a castle built by Hugh de Lacy, Lord of Meath, originally dating from 1180. It comprises a neo-Gothic structure between two 12th-century towers. It is closed to the public.

According to local lore, the surrounding lands were divided at one point between the two Plunkett branches by a race. Starting at the castles, the wives had to run towards each other and a fence was placed where they met. Luckily for the Killeen womenfolk, their castle was on higher ground and they made considerable gains as they ran down-hill towards their Dunsany counterparts.

TRIM

☎ 046 / pop 1447

The delightfully sleepy town of Trim (Baile Átha Troim, meaning 'town at the ford of the elder trees') doesn't get too many visitors these days, but at one time it was a major player in local affairs and a cursory exploration of the town will reveal some inviting relics of its medieval past, none more so than the very obvious and very big castle that was Ireland's largest Anglo-Norman fortification. The medieval town was a busy jumble of streets, and once had five gates and as many as seven monasteries in the immediate area.

Hard to imagine nowadays, but a measure of Trim's importance was that Elizabeth I genuinely considered building Trinity College here, only for it to be built 'just outside' the city walls of Dublin. One student who did go to school here – at least for a short time – was Arthur Wellesley, the duke of Wellington, who studied in Talbot Castle and St Mary's Abbey. Not content with claiming a bit of his education, local legend has it that the duke was born in a stable round these parts, which then explains the duke's famous exclamation that

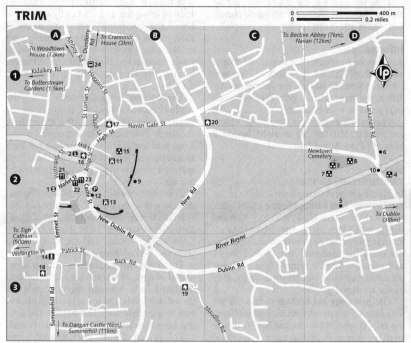

simply being born in a stable doesn't make one a horse. If he did say it – which is hardly definite – he didn't mean it *literally:* for stable and horse read Ireland and Irish, for he was in fact born in Dublin. The local burghers dedicated a **Wellington column** at the junction of Patrick and Emmet Sts, which was less a tribute to his cool views on his own birth and more to the fact that his impressive career did actually benefit Ireland. After defeating Napoleon at the Battle of Waterloo, the Iron Duke went on to become prime minister of Great Britain and in 1829 passed the Catholic Emancipation Act, which repealed the last of the repressive penal laws.

Trim was home to the county jail, giving rise to the ditty: 'Kells for brogues, Navan for rogues and Trim for hanging people'.

Information

Among the brochures for sale in the **tourist office** (☎ 943 7111; Mill St; ☉ 9.30am-5.30pm Mon-Sat, noon-5.30pm Sun May-Sep, 9am-5pm Mon-Sat Oct-Apr) is the handy little *Trim Tourist Trail* (€3) walking-tour booklet.

The **post office** (cnr Emmet & Market Sts; ☉ 9.30am-6pm Mon-Fri, 9.30am-1pm Sat) is right beside a branch of the Allied Irish Bank.

Sights

TRIM HERITAGE CENTRE

Immediately next to the tourist office is the informative **Trim Heritage Centre** (☎ 943 7227; Mill St; adult/child/student €3.20/1.90/2.20; ☉ 10am-5pm Mon-Sat, noon-5.30pm Sun Apr-Sep), which has an exhibit known as *The Power and the Glory*, outlining the medieval history of Trim in audiovisuals. The 20-minute film is shown six times daily and focuses on delights such as the medieval plague of rats.

The **genealogy and heritage section** (☎ 943 6633; Castle St; initial consultation €20, personalised family tree €95; ☉ 9am-5pm Mon-Thu, 9am-2pm Fri) of the heritage centre is in the town hall. Here, under the expert guidance of local historian Noel French (who also penned the *Trim Tourist Trail* booklet), there's an extensive genealogical database for people trying to trace Meath ancestors.

TRIM CASTLE

Where now the glories of Babylon? Proof of Trim's medieval importance, Hugh de Lacy founded **Trim Castle** (King John's Castle;

☎ 943 8619; adult/student €3.20/1.20, grounds only €1.20/0.50; ☉ 10am-6pm May-Oct) in 1173, but Rory O'Connor, said to have been the last high king of Ireland, destroyed this motte and bailey within a year. De Lacy did not live to see the castle's replacement, and the building you see today was begun around 1200. It has hardly been modified since then. A keen eye might recognise the castle from Mel Gibson's 1996 movie *Braveheart*, in which it served as a 'castle double' for the castle at York. The interesting historical coincidence is that Queen Isabella's real lover, Roger de Mortimer, Earl of March, actually lived in the castle between 1316 and 1320.

Although King John visited Trim in 1210 to bring the de Lacy family into line – hence the building's alternative name of King John's Castle – he never actually slept in the castle. On the eve of his arrival, Walter de Lacy locked it up tight and left town, forcing the king to camp in the nearby meadow.

Throughout Anglo-Norman times the castle occupied a strategic position on the western edge of the Pale, the area where the Anglo-Normans ruled supreme; beyond Trim was the volatile country where Irish chieftains and lords fought with their Norman rivals and vied for position, power and terrain.

Trim was conquered by Silken Thomas in 1536 and again in 1647 by Catholic Confederate forces, opponents of the English Parliamentarians. In 1649 it was taken by Cromwellian forces, and the castle, town walls and Yellow Steeple were damaged.

The grassy two-hectare enclosure is dominated by a massive stone keep, 25m tall and mounted on a Norman motte. Inside are three lofty levels, the lowest one divided in two by a central wall. Just outside the central keep are the remains of an earlier wall.

The principal outer-curtain wall, some 500m long, and for the most part still standing, dates from around 1250 and includes eight towers and a gatehouse. The finest stretch of the outer wall runs from the River Boyne through Dublin Gate to Castle St. The outer wall has a number of sally gates from which defenders could exit to confront the enemy.

Within the northern corner was a church and, facing the river, the Royal Mint, which produced Irish coinage (called 'Patricks' and 'Irelands') into the 15th century. The Russian cannon in the car park is a trophy from the Crimean War and bears the tsarist double-headed eagle.

In 1465, Edward IV ordered that anyone who had robbed or 'who was going to rob' should be beheaded and their heads mounted on spikes and publicly displayed as a warning to other thieves. In 1971, excavations in the castle grounds near the depression south of the keep revealed the remains of 10 headless men, presumably the hapless (or wannabe) criminals.

The castle was closed to the public in 1995, but reopened in 2000 under the care of Dúchas, the Heritage Service. You can now visit the restored keep (by guided tour only) and the rest of the castle grounds.

TALBOT CASTLE & ST MARY'S ABBEY

Across the River Boyne from the castle are the ruins of the 12th-century Augustinian **St Mary's Abbey**, rebuilt after a fire in 1368 and once home to a wooden statue of Our Lady of Trim, which was revered by the faithful for its miraculous powers. Cromwell's soldiers set fire to the statue in front of their injured commander, General Croot, a rather poignant slap in the face of Catholic belief. Just in case the locals didn't get the symbolism of the gesture, the soldiers destroyed the abbey as well. An artists' rendition of the statue is by the roadside in front of the ruins.

Part of the abbey was converted in 1415 into a fine manor house by Sir John Talbot, then viceroy of Ireland; it came to be known as **Talbot Castle**. The Talbot coat of arms can be seen on the northern wall. Talbot went to war in France, where in 1429 he was defeated by none other than Joan of Arc at Orleans. He was taken prisoner, released and went on fighting the French until 1453. He was known as 'the scourge of France' or 'the whip of the French', and Shakespeare wrote of this notorious man in Henry VI: 'Is this the Talbot so much feared abroad/That with his name the mothers still their babes?'

Talbot Castle was owned in the early 18th century by Esther 'Stella' Johnson, the mistress of Jonathan Swift. She bought the manor house for £65 sterling and lived there for 18 months before selling it to Swift for a tidy £200 sterling; he lived there for a year. Swift was rector of Laracor, 3km southeast

of Trim, from around 1700 until 1745 when he died. From 1713 he was also – and more significantly – dean of St Patrick's Cathedral in Dublin.

Just northwest of the abbey building is the 40m **Yellow Steeple**, once the bell tower of the abbey, dating from 1368 but damaged by Cromwell's soldiers in 1649. It takes its name from the colour of the stonework at dusk.

A part of the 14th-century town wall stands in the field to the east of the abbey, and includes the **Sheep Gate**, the lone survivor of the town's original five gates. It used to be closed daily between 9pm and 4am, and a toll was charged for sheep entering to be sold at market.

NEWTOWN

About 1.5km east of town on Lackanash Rd, Newtown Cemetery contains an interesting group of ruins. What had been the **parish church** of Newtown Clonbun contains the late-16th-century tomb of Sir Luke Dillon, chief baron of the Exchequer during the reign of Elizabeth I, and his wife Lady Jane Bathe. The effigies are known locally as 'the jealous man and woman', perhaps because of the sword lying between them.

Rainwater that collects between the two figures is claimed to cure warts. Place a pin in the puddle and then jab your wart. When the pin becomes covered in rust your warts will vanish. Some say you should leave a pin on the statue as payment for the cure.

The other ruins here are Newtown's **Cathedral of Sts Peter and Paul**, and the 18th-century **Newtown Abbey** (Abbey of the Canons Regular of St Victor of Paris). The cathedral was founded in 1206 and burned down two centuries later. Parts of the cathedral wall were flattened by a storm in 1839, which also damaged sections of the Trim Castle wall. The abbey wall throws a superb echo back to **Echo Gate** across the river.

Southeast of these ruins, and just over the river, is the **Crutched Friary**. There are ruins of a keep, and traces of a watchtower and other buildings from a hospital set up after the crusades by the Knights of St John of Jerusalem, who wore a red crutch, or cross, on their cassocks. **St Peter's Bridge**, beside the friary, is said to be the second-oldest bridge in Ireland. **Marcy Regan's** (Lackanash Rd, Newtown Trim), the small pub beside the bridge, claims to be Ireland's second-oldest pub.

WORTH THE TRIP

'The most imaginative garden in Ireland' is how *House & Garden* magazine described the multi-award-winning **Butterstream Gardens** (☎ 046-943 6017; Kildalkey Rd; admission €5.50; ⏰ 11am-6pm Apr-Sep) on the western outskirts of Trim. Surprisingly it's still something of a hidden treasure often overlooked by visitors to Ireland. Designed and planted solely by the owner, Butterstream comprises a series of carefully integrated 'rooms' each with their own character and style. You will find a stream garden, obelisk garden, pool garden, kitchen garden and hot-coloured garden all side by side. Ideal for a gentle afternoon stroll, this place is a feast for the eyes and nose alike.

Sleeping

BUDGET

Bridge House Tourist Hostel (☎ 943 1848; silver sue@eircom.net; Bridge St; dm/d €20/40) Travellers from all corners of the globe chill out in Bridge House's stylish TV room, built out of an old cellar. The large, comfortable doubles are the best option.

MIDRANGE

Woodtown House (☎ 943 5022; woodtown@iol.ie; Athboy; s/d €43/70) It's well worth the 12km trip on the R154 north out of Trim to stay at this very special country house. The perfectly restored 18th-century interiors compete with the beautiful, tree-filled grounds for your attention. You can get a high-quality dinner (€28) in the elegant dining room.

Highfield House (☎ 943 6386; www.highfieldguest house.com; Maudlins Rd; s/d €50/72) This elevated, elegant 18th-century country house has seven exquisite bedrooms that have been restored to their former grandeur – with a few modern touches thrown in for extra comfort. It's like waking up in the gilded age, only with central heating.

Tigh Cathain (☎ 943 1996; www.tighcathaintrim .com; Longwood Rd; s/d €44/66) A Tudor-style country house about 1km southwest of the town centre, there are three lovely bedrooms (the pink, yellow and blue rooms) decorated with the appropriately dominant colour scheme. The house is surrounded by a large, handsome garden.

Brogan's Guesthouse (☎ 943 1237; www.brogans .ie; High St; s/d €45/72) Brogan's has been taking care of its guests since 1915, both in the handsome pub downstairs and in the 14 en-suite rooms, eight in the converted stables out the back and the rest in the main building, which these have been recently refurbished and win our comfort vote, although the stables are further from the madding crowds in the bar. If you're looking for central accommodation, this is the best in town.

White Lodge (☎ 943 6549; www.whitelodgetrim .com; New Rd; s/d €40/60) This is a modern, 1950s American–style house that makes use of a lot of polished oak – in the floors, the furniture and the fittings. The light-filled rooms are quite spacious. It's 500m east of the centre at the northern end of New Rd.

Crannmór House (☎ 943 1635; www.crannmor .com; Dunderry Rd; s/d €46/68) Five acres of rolling farmland and paddock surround this converted period residence about 2km along the road to Dunderry.

TOP END

Castle Arch Hotel (☎ 943 1516; www.castlearchhotel .com; Summerhill Rd; r €130) Formerly the Wellington, Trim's fanciest hotel has 18 well-equipped rooms and an overall modern feel punctuated by period touches such as antique dressers and headboards. Primarily aimed at the business traveller and the top-end leisure traveller (golfers are particularly targeted), this is pretty much what you'd expect from a high-end small-town hotel.

Eating

Most pubs do decent pub grub and there are a couple of OK cafés, but don't hold your breath for quality restaurants.

Franzini O'Brien's (☎ 943 1002; French Lane; mains €12-20; ⏰ 6.30-9.30pm Tue-Sat, 5-8.30pm Sun) The exception that proves the rule, this modern café-bar, with a great location overlooking the castle, has raised the standards of cuisine in Trim. The fairly broad menu – it's best described as Irish-international – changes regularly, but you're always going to find noodle, meat and pasta dishes.

If you're looking for something on the go, try **Watson's Elementary Café** (Market St; mains €5; ⏰ 9am-5pm Mon-Sat), a quality greasy spoon, or **Pastry Kitchen** (☎ 943 8902; Market St; snacks around €3; ⏰ 7.30am-5.30pm Mon-Sat, 10am-2pm

Sun), a great early-morning spot for sandwiches and selected hot plates.

Getting There & Away

Bus Éireann (☎ 01-836 6111) runs a very regular service between Dublin and Trim (one way/return €7.40/9.90, one hour, every 15 minutes). Buses stop in front of Tobin's newsagent at the northern end of Haggard St.

AROUND TRIM

There are a couple of evocative Anglo-Norman remains in the area around Trim. Some 7.5km northeast of Trim on the way to Navan is **Bective Abbey**, founded in 1147 and the first Cistercian offspring of magnificent Mellifont Abbey in Louth. The remains seen today are 13th- and 15th-century additions and consist of the chapter house, church, ambulatory and cloister. In 1543, after the Dissolution of the Monasteries, it was used as a fortified house, and the tower was built.

In 1186, Hugh de Lacy, Lord of Meath, began demolishing the abbey at Durrow in County Offaly in order to build a castle. A workman, known both as O'Miadaigh and O'Kearney, was offended by this desecration, lopped off de Lacy's head and fled. Although de Lacy's body was interred in Bective Abbey, his head went to St Thomas' Abbey in Dublin. A dispute broke out over who should possess all the bodily remains, and it required the intervention of the pope to, well, pontificate on the matter, with a ruling in favour of St Thomas' Abbey.

Some 12km northwest of Trim, on the road to Athboy, is **Rathcairn**, the smallest Gaeltacht (Irish-speaking) district in Ireland. Rathcairn's population is descended from a group of Connemara Irish speakers, who were settled on an estate here as part of a social experiment in the 1930s.

Six kilometres southeast of Trim, on the road to Summerhill, stands **Dangan Castle**, built by the Wellesley family, and the boyhood home of the duke of Wellington. The castle is also supposed to have been the birthplace of Don Ambrosio O'Higgins (1720–1801), the Spanish viceroy of Peru and Chile at the end of the 18th century. His son, Bernardo O'Higgins, went on to become the liberator of Chile, and Santiago's main thoroughfare is named after him (he was also the founder of Argentina's navy, and Buenos Aires has a number of statues in his honour). The mansion's current state is the result of the efforts of Roger O'Conor, its last owner, who set it alight on a number of occasions between 1808 and 1809 for the insurance money.

KELLS

☎ 046 / pop 2362

Kells is best known for the magnificent, illuminated manuscript that bears its name, and which so many visitors queue to see on their visits to Trinity College in Dublin. Generally, they don't make the trip to where it was stashed for the guts of 600 years, from the end of the 9th century until its removal by the Church in 1541. Frankly, they're not missing all that much, and apart from the best remnants of the monastic site that housed the *Book of Kells* – some interesting high crosses and a 1000-year-old round tower – there's not a lot to see or do here.

Orientation & Information

The N3 from Dublin to Cavan almost bypasses the town. Turning south at Cross St brings you down to Farrell St, where you'll find most of the pubs and shops. The **tourist office** (☎ 924 9336; Headfort Pl; ⊙ 10am-5.30pm Mon-Sat, 1.30-5.30pm Sun May-Sep, 10-5pm Mon-Fri Oct-Apr) is in the heritage centre behind the town hall. Kells Hostel is also helpful with queries. There's also a **Bank of Ireland** (John St) and a **post office** (Farrell St).

Sights

KELLS HERITAGE CENTRE

Spread across two detail-packed floors, the town's **heritage centre** (☎ 924 9336; Headfort Pl; adult/concession/family €4/3/12; ⊙ 10am-5.30pm Mon-Sat, 1.30-5.30pm Sun May-Sep, 10am-5pm Mon-Fri Oct-Apr) has a 12-minute audiovisual on the monastic era and it sets the tone for the exhibits. On the ground floor is a replica of the Market Cross (the real one is outside), while upstairs is a rather beautiful copy of the area's most famous object, the *Book of Kells*, which was brought here from the monastery on Iona in Scotland in 807 after a Viking raid. Two touch-screens allow you to leaf interactively through the entire book. One (paltry) advantage to viewing this interactive copy over seeing the original (and its copy) in Trinity College, Dublin, is that here there are no guards hurrying you along after a two-second glimpse; you can take your time and get a proper sense of the book's awesome beauty. Surrounding the book are various 6th- to 12th-century relics and artefacts, as well as a scale model of the town in the 6th century.

ROUND TOWER & HIGH CROSSES

When the Protestant church of **St Columba** (admission free; ☉ 10am-1pm & 2-5pm Mon-Sat, services only Sun), west of the town centre, was constructed in the grounds of the old monastic settlement, the anti-Catholic reformers were making the mother of all political statements about which branch of the divided church was going to be top dog.

The churchyard has a 30m-high, 10th-century **round tower** on the southern side. It's without its conical roof but is known to date back at least as far as 1076, when Muircheartach Maelsechnaill, the high king of Tara, was murdered in its confined apartments.

Inside the churchyard are four 9th-century high crosses in various states of repair. The **West Cross**, at the far end of the compound from the entrance, is the stump of a decorated shaft with scenes of the baptism of Jesus, the Fall of Adam and Eve, and the Judgement of Solomon on the eastern face, and Noah's ark on the western face. All that is left of the **North Cross** is the bowl-shaped base stone.

Near the tower is the best preserved of the crosses, the **Cross of Patrick and Columba**, with its semilegible inscription 'Patrici et Columbae Crux' on the eastern face of the base. Above it are scenes of Daniel in the lions' den, the fiery furnace, the Fall of Adam and Eve and a hunting scene. On the opposite side of the cross are the Last Judgement, the Crucifixion, and riders with a chariot and a dog on the base.

The other surviving cross is the unfinished **East Cross**. On the eastern side is a carving of the Crucifixion and a group of four figures on the right arm. The three blank, raised panels below these were prepared for carving, but the sculptor apparently never got round to the task.

ST COLMCILLE'S HOUSE

From the churchyard exit on Church St, **St Colmcille's House** (admission free; ☉ 10am-5pm Sat & Sun Jun-Sep) is left up the hill, among the row of houses on the right side of Church Lane. It is usually open in the summer; otherwise, pick up the keys from **Mrs Carpenter** (☎ 924 1778; 1 Lower Church View), at the brown-coloured house as you ascend the hill.

This squat, solid structure is a survivor from the old monastic settlement. Its name is a misnomer, as it was built in the 10th century and St Colmcille was alive in the 6th century. Although its use is unclear, experts have suggested that it was used as a scriptorium, a place where monks illuminated books. The original entrance to the 1000-year-old building was over 2m above ground level. Inside, a very long ladder leads to a low attic room under the roof line.

MARKET CROSS

Until 1996, the **Market Cross** had stood for centuries in Cross St, at the heart of the town centre, where it was said to have been placed by none other than Jonathan Swift. Besides inviting the pious admiration of the faithful, the cross was used as a gallows in the aftermath of the 1798 revolt; the British garrison hanged rebels from the crosspiece, one on each arm so the cross wouldn't fall over. But what 1000 years of foul weather and the sacrilegious British wouldn't do, a careless bus driver did with one bad turn-and-reverse in 1996: topple the cross. However the story doesn't end there. The cross was eventually repaired, but plans to erect it in the heritage centre were dumped after locals objected to having to pay to see what they'd seen for free all their lives; instead, the cross was erected outside the centre. Our favourite part of the story, though, is that you can pay to see a replica inside the centre, but you'll have to walk by the real thing to do so.

On the eastern side of the Market Cross are depictions of Abraham's sacrifice of Isaac, Cain and Abel, the Fall of Adam and Eve, guards at the tomb of Jesus and a wonderfully executed procession of horsemen. On the western face, the Crucifixion is the only discernible image. On the northern side is a panel of Jacob wrestling with the angel.

Sleeping

Kells Hostel (☎ 924 9995; www.kellshostel.com; The Carrick, Cavan Rd; dm €14-18) This IHH hostel on the Cavan road, about 200m uphill from the bus stop, has large eight-bed and six-bed dorms, some with an en suite. It's a fairly modern place and has benefited from a recent renovation that has seen the addition of a laundry and pool table.

Headfort Arms Hotel (☎ 924 0063; www.headfort armshotel.com; John St; s/d €70/120) Plain and businesslike, the Headfort Arms has 18 well-appointed rooms that will do the job if all you're looking for is a place to lay your head and get ready for tomorrow's meeting. Although there's a nightclub attached, you'll sleep noise-free; the Vanilla Pod restaurant (below) is part of the hotel but run by different management.

Eating

Vanilla Pod (☎ 924 0084; Headfort Arms Hotel, John St; mains €11-17; ⏲ 5.30-10pm Mon-Fri, 5.30-11pm Sat & Sun) A bistro-style restaurant with a something-from-everywhere-for-everyone approach to cooking, Vanilla Pod calls its cuisine contemporary, which really means taking a little bit of Chinese *bok choi* and using it to garnish the Irish spring lamb that comes after the goats' cheese crostini…you get the picture. And it works.

Ground Floor (☎ 924 9688; Bective Sq; mains €15-22; ⏲ 5.30-11pm Mon-Sat, 5.30-10pm Sun) You can get home-made burgers, sizzling steaks, Mexican fajitas and a host of other dishes from around the globe at this funky eatery. It is adorned with local artwork and staffed by a friendly bunch who manage that rare gift of doing things right but in a relaxed manner.

Penny's Place (☎ 924 1130; Market St; sandwiches from €5; ⏲ 9am-6pm Mon-Sat) Brown bread with-

---

SOMETHING SPECIAL

Lennoxbrook (☎ 924 5902; s/d €50/70) Live like a country squire for a night. Pauline Mullan is the fifth generation of her family to live in this wonderful, 200-year-old farmhouse outside Kells. She'll treat you as one of the family and give you the run of this beautifully designed and restored house. The four bedrooms are all decorated in a luxurious but restrained fashion, with patterned wallpaper and period furniture. Dinner (€22) in the elegant dining room is a must. Lennoxbrook is 5km north of Kells on the N3.

---

out equal is the speciality at this excellent café with home-made food.

Drinking

O'Shaughnessy's (☎ 924 1110; Market St) This pub features lots of rustic timber and is always choc full of chattering locals.

Blackwater Inn (☎ 924 0386; Farrell St) Another favourite with regular Irish music sessions.

Monaghan's (☎ 924 9995; The Carrick, Cavan Rd) Monaghan's is favoured by a younger crowd; it often has music at the weekend.

Getting There & Away

Bus Éireann (☎ 01-836 6111) has services from Dublin to Kells and Cavan (one way/return €9/12.20, one hour, almost hourly from 7am to 10pm). Buses stop in front of the church on John St and near the hostel (by request only); times are posted at the stop. There are also regular services running to Navan (€3.10/4.50, 15 minutes) and Drogheda (€6.30/8.90, 1½ hours, 12 daily).

AROUND KELLS
Hill of Lloyd Tower

The 30m **tower** (☎ 924 0064; adult/child €2/1.50; ⏲ by appointment) on the Hill of Lloyd is visible from behind the hostel in Kells, and it's easy to see why it became known as the 'inland lighthouse'. Built in 1791 by the earl of Bective, in memory of his father, it has been renovated and if it's open you can climb to the top, or picnic in the surrounding park. The tower is 3km northwest of Kells, off the Crossakeel road.

Crosses of Castlekeeran

Lost in the ruins of an ancient hermitage, through a farmyard about 2km further down the Crossakeel Rd toward Loughcrew, are the **Crosses of Castlekeeran** (admission free; ⏲ 24hr). They're not overly impressive in themselves – three plainly carved, early-9th-century crosses (one in the river) – but there's something invitingly peaceful about the quiet, overgrown cemetery that surrounds them. The **ruined church** in the centre has some early grave slabs and an ogham stone.

LOUGHCREW CAIRNS

With Brú na Bóinne, a bone fide Unesco World Heritage Site, in the neighbourhood, it's just too hard to compete. Which is precisely why the 30-odd Stone Age passage graves strewn about three summits of the Loughcrew Hills are so wonderful: they're hard to get to and relatively few people ever bother. What's more, once you make the effort you can hang around as long as you like and explore at your leisure. Interested? You should be.

The hills, also known as Slieve (Sliabh) na Caillighe and the Mountains of the Witch, are northwest of Kells near Oldcastle. From here there are some splendid views of the surrounding countryside, east and south to the plains of Meath and north into the lake country of Cavan. The main passage graves are grouped on three summits – Carnbane East (194), Carnbane West (206m) and Patrickstown (279m) – although the last has been so ruined by 19th-century builders that there's little to see.

Like Brú na Bóinne, the graves were all built around 3000 BC, but, unlike their better-known and better-excavated peers, were used right up to the Iron Age, at least until 750 BC. As at Newgrange, larger stones in some of the graves are decorated with spiral patterns. Archaeologists have unearthed bone fragments and ashes, stone balls and beads. Some of the graves look like large piles of stones, while others are less obvious, their cairn having been removed.

Carnbane East

Carnbane East has a cluster of sites; Cairn T is the biggest at about 35m in diameter and has numerous carved stones. One of its outlying kerbstones is called the Hag's Chair and is covered in gouged holes, circles and other markings. You need the gate key to enter the passageway and a torch to see anything in detail. It takes about half an hour to climb Carnbane East from the car park. From the summit on a reasonably clear day, you should be able to see the Hill of Tara to the southeast, while the view north is into Cavan, with Lough Ramor to the northeast and Lough Sheelin and Oldcastle to the northwest.

The key to Cairn T is held by the coffee shop at the **Loughcrew Historic Garden Visitor Centre** (☎ 049-854 1060; ⊙ noon-5pm mid-Mar–Sep, 1-4pm Sun Oct–mid-Mar). At other times, you can make arrangements to get the key from **Loughcrew House** (☎ 049-854 1356), about 1km away, but only during sociable hours and

never after 5pm, as this is a private home. A deposit of €50 or a driver's licence (or passport) is required to secure the key.

Carnbane West

From the same car park, it takes about an hour to reach the summit of Carnbane West, where Cairn D and L are both some 60m in diameter. Cairn D has been disturbed in an unsuccessful search for a central chamber. Cairn L, northeast of Cairn D, is also in poor condition, though you can enter the passage and chamber where there are numerous carved stones and a curved basin stone, in which human ashes were placed.

Cairn L is administered by the **Heritage Service** (☎ 01-6476915), which only gives out the key to those with an authentic research interest.

COUNTY LOUTH

'The Wee County', as Ireland's smallest is often called, is a sobriquet borne with pride round these parts. Louth may indeed be tiny, but it packs a mean little punch. The two principal towns of the northeast, Drogheda and Dundalk, give the county more than a hint of industrial flavour, but the real attractions here are pastoral: from the prehistoric and monastic sites north and east of the Boyne Valley to the lonely and beautifully scenic Cooley Peninsula north of Dundalk.

HISTORY

As part of the ancient kingdom of Oriel, Louth is the setting for perhaps the most epic of all Irish mythological tales, the *Táin Bó Cúailnge* (Cattle Raid of Cooley), which includes a starring role for Ireland's greatest mythological hero, Cúchulainn (see the boxed text, p552). *The Táin*, by Thomas Kinsella, is a modern version of this compelling and bloody tale.

Louth is home to a number of monastic ruins dating from the 5th and 6th centuries; the monastery at Monasterboice and the later Cistercian abbey at Mellifont, both near Drogheda, are Louth's most interesting archaeological sites.

The arrival of the Normans in the 12th century ushered in a period of great change and upheaval: attracted by the fertile plains of the Boyne, the Anglo-Norman gentry set about subduing the local population and building mighty houses and castles. The Norman invaders were responsible for the development of Dundalk and the two towns, on opposite banks of the Boyne, which united in 1412 to become what is now Drogheda.

DROGHEDA
☎ 041 / pop 28,333

Drogheda's past is rich and storied, its future may be bright, but its present leaves a lot to be desired. This once fortified town straddling the River Boyne has a clutch of fine old buildings, a handsome cathedral

and a riveting museum that offers at least a partial insight into its eventful past, while an ongoing spate of development and a rising population of Dublin commuters have slowly begun to breathe new life into the place, but for now Drogheda remains in a charmless limbo.

Besides the aforementioned sights, your main reason for visiting is that Drogheda plays a strong supporting role for the world-class attractions that surround it in the Boyne Valley, as well as being the main transport hub for the area.

History

This bend in the Boyne has always been desirable, right back to the Danes who built a

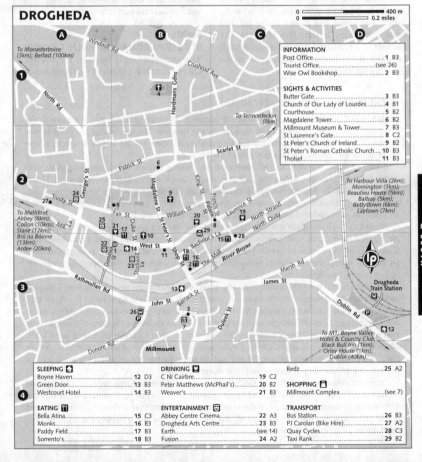

DROGHEDA

INFORMATION
Post Office	1 B3
Tourist Office	(see 26)
Wise Owl Bookshop	2 B3

SIGHTS & ACTIVITIES
Butter Gate	3 B3
Church of Our Lady of Lourdes	4 B1
Courthouse	5 B2
Magdalene Tower	6 B2
Millmount Museum & Tower	7 B3
St Laurence's Gate	8 C2
St Peter's Church of Ireland	9 B2
St Peter's Roman Catholic Church	10 B3
Tholsel	11 B3

To Monasterboice (3km); Belfast (100km)
To Termonfeckin (8km)
To Harbour Villa (2km); Mornington (3km); Beaulieu House (5km); Baltray (5km); Bettystown (6km); Laytown (7km)
To Mellifont Abbey (8km); Collon (10km); Slane (12km); Brú na Bóinne (13km); Ardee (20km)
To M1; Boyne Valley Hotel & Country Club; Black Bull Inn (1km); Orley House (1km); Dublin (40km)
Drogheda Train Station
Dublin Rd
Millmount

SLEEPING 🏠			DRINKING 🍷			Redz	25 A2
Boyne Haven	12 D3		C Ní Cairbre	19 C2			
Green Door	13 B3		Peter Matthews (McPhail's)	20 B2		SHOPPING 🛍	
Westcourt Hotel	14 B3		Weaver's	21 B3		Millmount Complex	(see 7)

EATING 🍴			ENTERTAINMENT 🎭			TRANSPORT	
Bella Atina	15 C3		Abbey Centre Cinema	22 A3		Bus Station	26 B3
Monks	16 B3		Drogheda Arts Centre	23 B3		PJ Carolan (Bike Hire)	27 A2
Paddy Field	17 B3		Earth	(see 14)		Quay Cycles	28 C3
Sorrento's	18 B3		Fusion	24 A2		Taxi Rank	29 B2

COUNTIES MEATH & LOUTH

fortified settlement here around 910. In the 12th century, the Normans added a bridge and expanded the two settlements forming on either side of the river. They also built a large defensive motte-and-bailey castle on the southern side at Millmount. By the 15th century, Drogheda was one of Ireland's four major walled towns and a major player in Irish affairs.

Drogheda made the European headlines in 1649 as the scene of Cromwell's most notorious Irish slaughter (see the boxed text, below) and things went from bad to worse in 1690 when the town backed the wrong horse at the Battle of the Boyne and surrendered the day after the defeat of James II.

Despite a boom in the 19th century when Drogheda became a textile and brewing centre, the town has never really hit full stride and today it struggles to break the shackles of a century-long torpor, although the current economy is starting to make some big differences.

Orientation & Information

Drogheda sits astride the River Boyne with the principal shopping area on the northern bank along West and Laurence Sts. The area south of the river is residential, dull and dominated by the mysterious Millmount mound. The main road to Belfast skirts round the town to the west. There's terrible traffic congestion in the city centre and disc parking (€1 per hour) is in operation throughout the town. Discs can be bought in newsagents and other shops.

Post office (West St) Next to the Westcourt Hotel.

Tourist office (☎ 983 7070; www.drogheda-tourism .com; Mayoralty St; ☼ 9.30am-5.30pm Mon-Fri, to 5pm Sat) On the northern side of the river, just off the docklands. There is a second office in the Millmount Museum.

Wise Owl Bookshop (☎ 984 2847; The Mall; ☼ 9am-5pm Mon-Sat) Has a good range of books.

Sights

ST PETER'S ROMAN CATHOLIC CHURCH

The shrivelled little head of the martyr St Oliver Plunkett (1629–81) is the main draw

---

GREAT PROTECTOR TURNS DESTROYER

England's first democrat and protector of the people is an Irish nightmare, and the name Oliver Cromwell (1599–1658) is still used to scare children at bedtime. The feeling was mutual, it seems: Cromwell may have been devoted to fighting tyranny at home but he wasn't averse to a little bit of death and destruction on this side of the Irish Sea.

Cromwell hated the Irish. To him, they were treacherous infidels, a dirty race of papists who had sided with Charles I during the Civil War. When 'God's own Englishman' landed his 12,000 troops at Dublin in August 1649, he immediately set out for Drogheda, a strategic fort town and bastion of royalist support. It was his first engagement in Ireland, and he was determined to 'make an example' of the town so as to discourage further resistance.

When Cromwell arrived at the walls of Drogheda, he was met with the resistance of 2300 men led by Sir Arthur Aston, who boasted that 'he who could take Drogheda could take hell'. After a week's planning, Cromwell demanded the town's surrender and Aston duly refused. Cromwell let fly with heavy artillery, mostly heavy cannon, and after two days the walls were breached. Hell, it seems, was next.

In order to set a terrifying example to any other town that might resist his armies, Cromwell ordered that the defenders of the town be spared no quarter. Over a period of hours, an estimated 3000 were massacred, mostly royalist soldiers but also priests, women and children. Aston was bludgeoned to death with his own leg and in the most gruesome incident of a very bloody tale, about 100 terrified locals hiding in the tower of St Peter's Church of Ireland were killed when the tower was set alight. Of the survivors, many were captured and sold into slavery in the Caribbean; the genetic presence of red hair on some Barbadians is commonly attributed to the sexual intermingling of African and Irish slaves.

Cromwell defended his action as God's righteous punishment of treacherous Catholics, and he was quick to point out that he had never ordered the killing of non-combatants: it was the 17th century's version of 'collateral damage'. Despite the fact that Cromwell's army behaved pretty much like any destructive army of the times, his name still provokes hatred in Ireland, nowhere more so than in Drogheda.

of the 19th-century **Catholic church** (West St), which is actually two churches in one: the first, designed by Francis Johnston in classical style and built in 1791; and the newer addition, built in the Gothic style visible today. Plunkett's head – from which the rest of him was separated following his hanging in 1681 – is in a glittering brass-and-glass case in the north transept.

ST LAURENCE'S GATE

Astride Laurence St, the eastwards extension of the town's main street, is St Laurence's Gate, the finest surviving portion of the city walls and one of only two surviving gates from the original 11.

The 13th-century gate was named after St Laurence's Priory, which once stood outside the gate; no traces of it now remain. The gate consists of two lofty towers, a connecting curtain wall and the entrance to the portcullis. This imposing pile of stone is not in fact a gate but a barbican, a fortified structure used to defend the gate, which was further behind it. When the walls were completed in the 13th century, they ran for 3km round the town, enclosing 52 hectares.

MILLMOUNT MUSEUM & TOWER

Across the river from town, in a village-like enclave amid a sea of dull suburbia, is Millmount, an artificial hill overlooking the town. Although it may have been a prehistoric burial mound along the lines of nearby Newgrange, it has never been excavated. There is a tale that it was the burial place of Amergin, a warrior-poet who arrived in Ireland from Spain around 1500 BC. Throughout Irish history, poets have held a special place in society and have been both venerated and feared.

The Normans constructed a motte-and-bailey fort on top of this convenient command post overlooking the bridge. It was followed by a castle, which in turn was replaced by a **Martello tower** (admission as part of the museum) in 1808. The tower played a dramatic role in the 1922 Civil War – there are fine views over the town from the top.

It was at Millmount that the defenders of Drogheda, led by the governor, Sir Arthur Ashton, made their last stand before surrendering to Cromwell. Later, an 18th-century English barracks was built round the base, and today this has been converted

to house craft shops, museums and a restaurant, though the courtyard retains the flavour of its former life.

A section of the army barracks is now used as the **Millmount Museum** (☎ 983 3097; www .millmount.net; Millmount; adult/child/student/family €4.50/2.50/3.50/11.50; ☺ 10am-6pm Mon-Sat, 2.30-5.30pm Sun), with interesting displays about the town and its history. Displays include three wonderful late-18th-century guild banners, perhaps the last in the country. There is also a room devoted to Cromwell's siege of Drogheda and the Battle of the Boyne. The pretty, cobbled basement is full of gadgets and kitchen utensils from bygone times, including a cast-iron pressure cooker and an early model of a sofa bed. There's also an excellent example of a coracle (type of small boat). Across the courtyard, the **Governor's House** opens for temporary exhibitions.

You can drive up to the hilltop or climb Pitcher Hill via the steps from St Mary's Bridge.

The 13th-century **Butter Gate**, just northwest of Millmount, is the only genuine town gate to survive. This tower, with its arched passageway, predates the remains of St Laurence's Gate by about a century.

OTHER BUILDINGS

Tholsel (cnr West & Shop Sts), an 18th-century limestone town hall, is now occupied by the Bank of Ireland.

North of the centre is **St Peter's Church of Ireland** (William St), containing the tombstone of Oliver Goldsmith's uncle Isaac, as well as another on the wall depicting two skeletal figures in shrouds, dubiously linked to the Black Death. This is the church whose spire was burned by Cromwell's men, resulting in the death of 100 people seeking sanctuary inside. Today's church (1748) is the second replacement of the original destroyed by Cromwell. It stands in an attractive close approached through lovely wrought-iron gates. Note the old 'Blue School' of 1844 on one side. Off Hardmans Gardens is the rather charming and more recent **Church of Our Lady of Lourdes**.

At the time of writing, the modest 19th-century **Courthouse** (Fair St) was being renovated. It is home to the sword and mace presented to the town council by William of Orange after the Battle of the Boyne.

Topping the hill behind the main part of town is the **Magdalene Tower**, dating from the 14th century, the belltower of a Dominican friary founded in 1224. Here, England's King Richard II, accompanied by a great army, accepted the submission of the Gaelic chiefs with suitable ceremony in 1395; but peace lasted only a few months and his return to Ireland led to his overthrow in 1399. The earl of Desmond was beheaded here in 1468 because of his treasonous connections with the Gaelic Irish. The tower is reputed to be haunted by a nun.

Sleeping

Most of the B&Bs are slightly out of town; the only centrally located options are the hostel and a business hotel.

BUDGET

Green Door (☎ 983 4422; www.greendoor.hostel.com; 47 John St; dm/d €16.50/63) A clean and tidy hostel only 150m from the bus station on the south side of the Boyne, the Green Door has large dorms and comfortable private rooms, all with an en suite. It is also a great resource of info for travellers.

MIDRANGE

Orley House (☎ 983 6019; www.orleyhouse.com; Bryanstown, Dublin Rd; s/d €45/70; **P**) A pretty good B&B about 2km out of town on the Dublin road; the rooms are extremely comfortable and breakfast is in a sun-filled conservatory (if it's not pouring rain, that is).

Harbour Villa (☎ 983 7441; Mornington Rd; s/d €40/70; **P**) This place is 2km along the river towards the sea on the Mornington road. It overlooks the estuary and has small but pleasant rooms.

Boyne Haven (☎ /fax 983 6700; Bryanstown, Dublin Rd; s/d €55/95; **P**) Definitely an upscale B&B, with loads of space and a great breakfast, this excellent establishment is on the Dublin road.

TOP END

Boyne Valley Hotel & Country Club (☎ 983 7737; www.boyne-valley-hotel.ie; Stameen, Dublin Rd; s/d €85/160; **P**) Beer built this exquisite 18th-century mansion on 16 acres of pristine, landscaped grounds including a small golf course and swimming pool. The huge rooms have magnificent views of the Boyne. If you're after something special, go no further.

Westcourt Hotel (☎ 983 0965; www.westcourt.ie; West St; s/d €65/135; **P**) In the most convenient spot in town is smack in the middle of West St, opposite the Catholic church, this recently refurbished hotel is plenty comfortable but won't win awards for style. No matter, as this is primarily a business hotel – breakfast and car parking are included in the rate.

Eating

Drogheda dining is all about eating, not eating well. With only one or two exceptions, there's little here to tickle your taste buds besides the usual fare of pub grub and indifferent dishes poorly prepared.

BUDGET

Monks (☎ 984 5630; 1 North Quay; mains €6-9; ☽ 8.30am-6pm Mon-Sat, 10.30am-5pm Sun) At the southern end of Shop St, on the corner of North Quay, this lovely espresso bar and café is a local institution. The sandwiches are inventive and the coffees good.

Paddy Field (☎ 984 2680; Unit 1, West St; mains €7-9; ☽ 9am-6pm Mon-Sat) This cleverly named, Asian-owned Irish café does a roaring trade in Irish breakfasts before inviting punters to go for its mildly Asian lunch dishes – chicken wings with sweet chilli sauce and the like.

MIDRANGE

Sorrento's (☎ 984 5734; 41 Shop St; mains €8-15; ☽ 6.30-11pm Tue-Sun) At this Italian restaurant simple, quality pasta and meat dishes are the order of the day. Try the *arancini*, a delicious rice and cheese starter.

Black Bull Inn (☎ 983 7139; www.blackbull.ie; Dublin Rd; sandwiches €6-8, dinner mains €10-20; ☽ noon-10pm) About 1km along the Dublin road this pub was once winner of the regional Pub of the Year title and it still gets the local vote. The adventurous menu satisfies virtually every taste, whether you're looking for a giant beefburger or Chinese marinated breast of duck.

Bella Atina (☎ 984 4878; the Mall; mains €9-13; ☽ 6-10.30pm Mon-Sat) A newish Italian restaurant with a growing reputation for solid dishes from the Old Country.

Drinking

C Ní Cairbre (Carberry's; ☎ 984 7569; North Strand) A proper old-style pub like they don't make anymore, Carberry's is the best watering hole in town and the perfect spot to while away an evening. There's musical accompaniment to your musings most nights. It gets busy on weekend nights and Sunday afternoon.

Peter Matthews (McPhail's; ☎ 984 3168; Laurence St) More popular with those barely old enough to enjoy a legal drink, McPhail's (as it's better known here) favours a poppy, chart-oriented soundtrack to the evening's entertainment. Some nights feature live music, mostly cover bands.

Weavers (☎ 983 2816; 82-83 West St) Another popular destination for Drogheda's young party crowd, who load up on alco-pops and pass notes to the DJ requesting a shout-out for their friend's 21st birthday party.

Entertainment

Besides the pub and the late-night club, entertainment options are a little thin on the ground.

Fusion (☎ 983 5166; www.fusiononline.ie; 12 George's St) The beer garden is a big pull here, as is the fairly animated disco from Thursday to Sunday nights with a mix of '60s, rock, funk and dance music.

Earth (☎ 984 5561; Westcourt Hotel, Stockwell St; admission €6, Sat €10) A popular nightclub in the basement of the Westcourt Hotel, Earth keeps them dancing by not going too far beyond the boundaries, so you can expect a fairly uptempo mix of charty stuff and classic floor-fillers.

Redz (☎ 983 5331; 79 West St) A small, chilled-out bar at the front hides a big club out back at this new nightspot. DJs and live bands play on different nights.

Abbey Centre Cinema (☎ 983 0188; Abbey Shopping Centre) This two-screen cinema is at the back of the shopping centre, off West St.

Drogheda Arts Centre (☎ 983 3946; Stockwell Lane) Theatrical and musical events are staged in the municipal building.

Shopping

The **Millmount complex** (Millmount) has a number of craft studios where you can buy all sorts of *objets d'art*. There is also a **jewellery studio** (☎ 984 1960), **ceramic potter** (☎ 984 6065), **decorative glassworks** (☎ 984 5018) and studio where you can buy **hand-painted silks** (☎ 984 1245). Call to arrange a viewing of the work; some of it is of extremely high quality.

Getting There & Away

BUS

Drogheda is only 48km north of Dublin, on the main M1 route to Belfast. The bus station is just south of the river on the corner of John St and Donore Rd. This is one of the busiest bus routes in the country, and **Bus Éireann** (☎ 983 5023) regularly serves Drogheda from Dublin (one way/return €7.20/12.20, one hour, every 30 minutes between 7.30am and 4pm, every 15 minutes between 4pm and 7pm, and every 30 minutes thereafter until 11pm). Drogheda to Dundalk is another popular route (€6.30/10.80, 30 minutes, hourly from 6.45am to 11.45pm daily).

There is also a daily Dundalk to Galway bus (€16.20/22.10, 4¾ hours) departing Drogheda at 11.10am Monday to Thursday and Saturday, and 4.30pm Friday and Sunday, which stops at Athlone, from where you can make connections to Limerick, Sligo and Donegal.

TRAIN

The **train station** (☎ 983 8749) is just south of the river and east of the town centre, off the Dublin road. Drogheda is on the main Belfast-to-Dublin line and there are five or six express trains (and many slower ones) daily each way, with five on Sunday (€11.20, 30 minutes to Dublin; €22, 1½ hours to Belfast). This is the best line in Ireland, with excellent on-board service.

The train crosses the river just downstream from Drogheda on Sir John McNeill's mid-19th-century Boyne Viaduct, a fine piece of engineering that dominates the seaward view.

Getting Around

Drogheda itself is infinitely walkable, and many of the surrounding region's interesting sites are within easy cycling distance. **PJ Carolan** (☎ 983 8242; 77 Trinity St; per day €16) offers good bikes. **Quay Cycles** (☎ 983 4526; 11a North Quay; per day €15), near the bridge, also rents bikes.

There's a taxi rank on St Laurence St, near Laurence Gate.

AROUND DROGHEDA

There are a number of stellar attractions around Drogheda. Mellifont and Monasterboice are two famous monastic sites, a few kilometres north of town, that are definitely worth the visit. Drogheda is also a good base for exploring the Boyne Valley. If you're travelling on to Dundalk and into Northern Ireland, you can go for one of three routes: the quicker but duller M1; the circuitous inland route via Collon and Ardee, along which you can also visit Monasterboice and Mellifont; or the scenic coastal route that leads you up to Carlingford.

Beaulieu House

Before Andrea Palladio and the ubiquitous Georgian style that changed Irish architecture in the early decades of the 18th century, there was the Anglo-Dutch style, a simpler, less ornate look that is equally handsome. **Beaulieu House** (☎ 041-984 5051; www.beaulieu.ie; Beaulieu; house & garden €10, garden only €5; ☉ 11am-5pm Mon-Fri May-Sep), about 5km east of Drogheda on the Baltray road, is a particularly good example of the style and – apparently – the first unfortified mansion to be built in Ireland, which doesn't say a lot for neighbourliness up to that time. It was built between 1660 and 1666 on lands confiscated from the Plunkett family (the headless Oliver's family) by Cromwell and given to the Marshall of the Army in Ireland, Sir Henry Tichbourne. The red-brick mansion, with its distinctive steep roof and tall chimneys, has been owned by the same family ever since.

Besides admiring the house and elegant gardens, the real draw is the superb art collection spread about the stunning interior, a motley collection of lesser Dutch masters to 20th-century Irish painters.

Mellifont Abbey

In its Anglo-Norman prime, **Mellifont Abbey** (☎ 041-982 6459; www.heritageireland.ie; Tullyallen; adult/student/family €2/1/5.50; ☉ 10am-6pm May-Oct) was the Cistercians' first and most magnificent centre in the country. Although the ruins are highly evocative and worth exploring, they don't do real justice to the site's former significance.

In the mid-12th century, Irish monastic orders had grown a little too fond of the good life and were not averse to a bit of corruption. In 1142, Malachy, bishop of Down (later canonised for his troubles) was at the end of his tether and he invited a group of hardcore monks from Clairvaux in

France to set up shop in a remote location, where they would act as a sobering influence on the local monks. The Irish monks didn't quite get on with their French guests, and the latter soon left for home. Still, the construction of Mellifont – from the Latin *mellifons* (honey fountain) – continued and within 10 years nine more Cistercian monasteries were established, and Mellifont was eventually the mother house for 21 lesser monasteries. At one point as many as 400 monks lived here.

Mellifont not only brought fresh ideas to the Irish religious scene, it also heralded a new style of architecture. For the first time in Ireland, monasteries were built with the formal layout and structure that was being used on the Continent. Only fragments of the original settlement remain, but the plan of the extensive monastery can easily be traced. Like many other Cistercian monasteries, the buildings clustered round an open cloister.

To the northern side of the cloister are the remains of a principally 13th-century cross-shaped church. To the south, the chapter house has been partially floored with medieval glazed tiles, originally found in the church. Here also would have been the refectory, kitchen and warming room – the only place where the austere monks could enjoy the warmth of a fire. The eastern range would once have held the monks' sleeping quarters.

Mellifont's most recognisable building, and one of the finest pieces of Cistercian architecture in Ireland, is the lavabo, an octagonal washing house for the monks. It was built in the early 13th century and used lead pipes to bring water from the river. A number of other buildings would have surrounded this main part of the abbey.

After the Dissolution of the Monasteries, a fortified Tudor manor house was built on the site in 1556 by Edward Moore using materials scavenged from the demolition of many of the buildings. In 1603, this house was the scene of a poignant and crucial turning point in Irish history. After the disastrous Battle of Kinsale, the vanquished Hugh O'Neill, last of the great Irish chieftains, was given shelter here by Sir Garret Moore until he surrendered to the English Lord Deputy Mountjoy. After his surrender, O'Neill was pardoned but, despairing of his position, fled to the Continent in 1607 with other old-Irish leaders in the Flight of the Earls. In 1727 the site was abandoned altogether.

The visitor centre next to the site describes monastic life in detail. The ruins are about 1.5km off the R168, the main Drogheda to Collon road. A back road connects Mellifont with Monasterboice. There is no public transportation to the abbey.

Monasterboice

Just off the M1 motorway to Belfast, about 8km north of Drogheda, is **Monasterboice** (Mainistir Bhuithe; admission free; ☉ sunrise-sunset), an intriguing monastic site containing a cemetery, two ancient church ruins, one of the finest and tallest round towers in Ireland and two of the best high crosses. The site can be reached directly from Mellifont via a winding route along narrow country lanes.

Down a leafy lane and set in sweeping farmland, Monasterboice has a special atmosphere, particularly at quiet times. The original monastic settlement at Monasterboice is said to have been founded by St Buithe, a follower of St Patrick, in the 4th or 5th century, although the site probably had pre-Christian significance. St Buithe's name somehow got converted to Boyne, and the river is named after him. It's said that he made a direct ascent to heaven via a ladder lowered from above. An invading Viking force took over the settlement in 968, only to be comprehensively expelled by Donal, the Irish high king of Tara, who killed at least 300 of the Vikings in the process.

There's a small gift shop outside the compound. There are no set hours but come early or late in the day to avoid the crowds.

HIGH CROSSES

The high crosses of Monasterboice are superb examples of Celtic art. The crosses had an important didactic use, bringing the gospels alive for the uneducated – cartoons of the Scriptures, if you like. Like Greek statues, they were probably brightly painted, but all traces of colour have long disappeared.

The cross near the entrance is known as **Muirdach's Cross**, named after a 10th-century abbot. The subjects of the carvings have not been positively identified. On the eastern face, from the bottom up, are thought to

be: the Fall of Adam and Eve, the murder of Abel, David and Goliath, Moses bringing water from the rock to the waiting Israelites and the three wise men bearing gifts to Mary and Jesus. The Last Judgement is at the centre of the cross with the risen dead waiting for their verdict, and further up is St Paul in the desert.

The western face relates more to the New Testament, and from the bottom depicts the arrest of Christ, Doubting Thomas, Christ giving a key to St Peter, the Crucifixion in the centre, and Moses praying with Aaron and Hur. The cross is capped by a representation of a gabled-roof church.

The **West Cross** is near the round tower and stands 6.5m high, making it one of the tallest high crosses in Ireland. It's much more weathered, especially at the base, and only a dozen or so of its 50 panels are still legible. The more distinguishable ones on the eastern face include David killing a lion and a bear, the sacrifice of Isaac, David with Goliath's head, and David kneeling before Samuel. The western face shows the Resurrection, the crowning with thorns, the Crucifixion, the baptism of Christ, Peter cutting off the servant's ear in the garden of Gethsemane, and the kiss of Judas.

A third, simpler cross in the northeastern corner of the compound is believed to have been smashed by Cromwell's forces and has only a few, straightforward carvings. Photographers should note that this cross makes a great evening silhouette picture, with the round tower in the background.

The **round tower**, minus its cap, stands in a corner of the complex. It's still over 30m tall but is closed to the public. In 1097, records suggest, the tower interior went up in flames, destroying many valuable manuscripts and other treasures. The church ruins are from a later era and of less interest.

ARDEE

☎ 041 / pop 3568

A leading contender for most attractive town in Louth (the competition is pretty poor), Ardee (Baile Átha Fhirdhia) only stands out because it has two castles on its main street – Ardee Castle to the south and Hatch's Castle to the north. Otherwise, this fairly sleepy market town on the narrow River Dee shouldn't distract you for any longer than it takes to get through it.

History

Ardee's colourful history is mostly tied up with the mythology of the *Táin Bó Cúailnge* (see the boxed text, p552), most notably the tragic tale of Cúchulainn and his foster brother Ferdia. After an almighty duel, Cúchulainn fatally wounded his beloved Ferdia with the *gae bolga*, a five-pronged weapon given to him by the demigod Lug. Cúchulainn's grief was such that he never fully recovered. It is one of the most beautiful stories of the Cooley cycle.

In the 12th century, the area was turned into a barony and the town remained in English hands until taken by the O'Neills in the 17th century. James II had his headquarters here for two months in 1689, prior to the Battle of the Boyne.

Sights & Activities

A square tower dating from the 13th century, **Ardee Castle** (☎ 685 3805; adult/child €1.50/0.75; ☼ 9am-5pm Mon-Sat Jun-Oct) was an important outpost on the edge of the English Pale. It later became a courthouse and now houses a museum on the town's history, as well as a coffee shop and craft units. The smaller **Hatch's Castle** also dates from this time, and from Cromwellian times until 1940 it remained in the hands of the Hatch family. It's still a private residence.

The riverbank can be explored around the ford, where there's a well-tended **riverside walk** with an impressive **bronze sculpture** of Cúchulainn and Ferdia.

Sleeping & Eating

Carraig Mor (☎ 685 3513; www.carraigmor.com; Blakestown; s/d €43/60; **P**) This family-run modern bungalow has five well-appointed rooms, four with an en suite. It is just 2km south of Ardee on the N2.

Smarmore Castle (☎ 685 7167; www.smarmore castle.com; Smarmore, Ardee; s/d from €70/110; **P**) One part medieval fortress and one part luxurious country home, this 14th-century castle has been converted into a very smart boutique hotel. The six rooms, from the four-postered Viscount's Room in the castle tower to the family-friendly Count's Room, all offer a range of experiences, from courtly knight to country gent. There's also a pretty decent fitness centre on the premises. It is situated 6km south of Ardee.

Rolf's Bistro (☎ 685 7949; 52 Market St; main course €15-25; ☼ 5.30-10.30pm Mon-Sat, 5-9pm Sun) Paul Svender's Swedish-influenced cuisine – how about prawn toast with caviar followed by beef Lindstrom (minced meat with capers and beetroot)? – might have been too much of a challenge for Ardee's taste buds were it not for the fact that the menu mixes in plenty of other dishes more familiar to Irish palates.

AROUND ARDEE
Jumping Church of Kildemock

One thunderous night in February 1715, St Catherine's Church in Kildemock mysteriously jumped sideways so as to avoid being the final resting place of an excommunicated member of the flock. No, not really, but that's the explanation the locals prefer to the far more prosaic *real* reason: the heavy storm caused a wall to shift inwards from its foundations. Frankly, we agree: the Jumping Church of Kildemock sounds so much better than the Church with Dodgy Foundations.

Louth

North of Tallanstown (but the turn-off is just south of town), the county's namesake is an insignificant little place with some mildly interesting remains. **St Mochta's** is a small 11th- or 12th-century church with an enclosure and stone roof. St Mochta, a British follower of St Patrick, founded a monastery here in the early 6th century. Nearby is the church of a 15th-century Dominican friary, sometimes called Louth Abbey.

Ardpatrick

To the east of Louth village are Ardpatrick and Ardpatrick House, home of Oliver Plunkett. There's a mound here where he is supposed to have illegally ordained priests. It was also a good vantage point to spot any advancing English soldiers.

THE COAST ROAD

While the most visually rewarding route between Drogheda and Dundalk is the minor inland road via Mellifont and Collon, the coastal route is also scenic. The latter heads off north under the railway viaduct, passes Baltray with its championship golf course, and continues on quiet country roads to Termonfeckin.

Termonfeckin

☎ 041 / pop 503

The sleepy little village of Termonfeckin (Tearmann Féichín) was, until 1656, the seat and castle of the medieval and then Protestant primate of Armagh. The 15th-century **castle** (admission free; ☉ 10am-6pm), or tower house, is in a good state of preservation; it has two small corbel-vaulted alcoves and an anticlockwise spiral staircase (most go clockwise). Its most unusual feature is the excellent corbelled roof on the third floor, built using the same technique as that used in the main chamber of the passage grave at Newgrange (see p524) 4000 years earlier! From the village, follow the road to Seapoint Golf Club, take the first left, then the first right. You need to get the key from across the road.

The town got its name from the 6th-century monastery founded here by St Féichín of Cong, County Mayo. All that remains are some gravestones, and a 10th-century **high cross** on the left as you enter the churchyard.

Clogherhead

☎ 041 / pop 906

About 2km further north is the busy seaside and fishing centre of **Clogherhead** (Ceann Chlochair), with a good, shallow Blue Flag beach. Around the town there are enjoyable **walks** along the coast (partially marred by vistas of caravan parks) or out to **Port Oriel**, an attractive little harbour with views of the Cooley Peninsula and the Mourne Mountains further north. During the summer, Port Oriel is home to a fleet of trawlers and smaller fishing boats.

On the southern side of the headland is **Red Man's Cave**. At low tide a reddish fungus becomes visible, covering the cave walls. According to folklore, a group of people fleeing from Cromwell hid in the cave. A barking dog revealed the hideout and the people were slaughtered, their blood splashing on the walls, where it remains to this day. The cave is hard to find, so it's sensible to ask a local for directions, but even if you don't find it, the walk is satisfying enough.

Castlebellingham

☎ 042 / pop 721

Northwest of Annagassan, the coast road joins the busy main N1 at Castlebellingham, only 12km south of Dundalk. The village grew up around its 18th-century mansion, which from a visitor's point of view is something of a disappointment after the imposing castellated entrance.

Buried in the local graveyard is Dr Thomas Guither, a 17th-century physician supposed to have reintroduced frogs to Ireland by releasing imported frog spawn into a pond in Trinity College, Dublin. Frogs, along with snakes and toads, had supposedly received their marching orders from St Patrick a thousand years earlier.

SLEEPING

Bellingham Castle (☎ 937 2176; www.bellingham castle.com; Castlebellingham; s/d €75/130) The castle in the title is somewhat of a misnomer, referring to an earlier building that was burnt down by the troops of James II, but it is a better lure for guests than 'house', which it most certainly is, albeit a pretty grand 18th-century one. The rooms are large, well-appointed and very comfortable, but it lacks an atmosphere, probably because it caters to corporate gigs and weddings.

DUNDALK

☎ 042 / pop 27,385

Tough, uncompromising Dundalk is a reminder of a bygone age, when Irish towns couldn't care less about looking pretty for the nice tourists and just went about the hard business of eking out a living. Louth's dour county town – which takes its name from Dún Dealgan, a prehistoric fort that was reputedly the home of the hero Cúchulainn (see the boxed text, p552) – is a charmless place, with few historic sites and not much else to see or do. Some use it as a base for exploring the surrounding border country – the (almost invisible) frontier with Northern Ireland is only 13km away.

The town grew under the protection of a local estate controlled by the de Verdon family, who were granted lands here by King John in 1185. In the Middle Ages, Dundalk was at the northern limits of the English-controlled Pale, strategically located on one of the main highways heading north.

Orientation & Information

Northbound traffic sweeps round to the east of the town centre. The main commercial streets are Clanbrassil and Park Sts. The **tourist office** (☎ 933 5484; Jocelyn St; ☉ 9am-5pm

Mon-Fri year around, plus 9am-1pm & 2-5.30pm Sat Jun–mid-Sep) is next to Louth County Museum. There are also boards and maps with tourist information dotted around town. The main post office is on Clanbrassil St.

Sights

The **Courthouse** (cnr Crowe & Clanbrassil Sts) is a fine neo-Gothic building with large Doric pillars designed by Richard Morrison, who also designed the courthouse in Carlow. In the front square is the stone **Maid of Éireann**, commemorating the Fenian Rising of 1798.

St Nicholas' Church (Church St), also known as the Green Church, is the burial site of Agnes Burns, elder sister of Robert, the Scottish poet. She married the local rector, and the monument was erected by the townspeople to honour them both. The 15th-century tower to the right of the church entrance is the oldest structure on the site.

The richly decorated **St Patrick's Cathedral** was modelled on King's College Chapel in Cambridge, England. In front of it is the **Kelly Monument** (Jocelyn St), in memory of a local captain drowned at sea in 1858. Also here is the interesting **County Museum** (☎ 932 7056; Jocelyn St; adult/concession €4/2.50; ☉ 10.30am-5.30pm Mon-Sat, 2-6pm Sun, closed Mon Oct-Apr). Different floors in the museum are dedicated to the town's early history and archaeology and to the Norman period. One floor deals with the growth of industry in the area from the 1750s right up to the 1960s and the cult classic Heinkel Bubble Car, which was manufactured in the area.

At the eastern end of Jocelyn St is the Seatown area of Dundalk with its **castle** (really a friary tower) and a sail-less **windmill**, the tallest in Ireland. If you arrive in Dundalk by train, you pass the 1820 **garda station** (police station; St Dominick's Pl) on the way into town. Its first prisoner is believed to have been its architect, who misappropriated funds and was arrested for nonpayment of bills.

Sleeping

Rosemount (☎ /fax 933 5878; Dublin Rd; s/d €40/80) Homely and beautifully maintained, this wonderful little B&B stands out for its rich and colourful garden carefully nurtured by its owners. They apply the same care to the guestrooms, which are well-appointed and usually adorned with flowers from the garden.

Innisfree Guesthouse (☎ 933 4912; Carrick Rd; www.innisfreeguesthouse.com; s/d from €40/64; P) An early-20th-century town house with a convivial, friendly atmosphere and a handful of comfortable rooms.

Ballymascanlon House Hotel (☎ 937 1124; fax 937 1598; Carlingford Rd; s/d €108/160) This is a manorhouse hotel with a swimming pool, squash courts, a superb 18-hole golf course and other sporting facilities. On the grounds of the hotel, up by the 5th green of the golf course (there's a signposted trail for non-golfers), is the fine Giant's Load Proleek Dolmen and Gallery Grave. It's 6km north of Dundalk on the way to Carlingford.

Eating

Dundalk is hardly a culinary hot spot. There are, however, a couple of exceptions.

Cube (☎ 932 9898; www.cuberestaurant.ie; 5 Roden Pl; lunch mains €10, dinner mains from €20; ☉ 12.30-3pm Mon-Fri, 5.30-10.30pm Mon-Sat) A chic, minimalist interior sets a stylish tone for what is a superb menu of largely Irish dishes given an imaginative, international once-over: lobster ravioli with poached cream, chives and beluga caviar, followed by locally farmed wild-boar sausages adorned with apple and buttered mash, is one particularly inviting option. Highly recommended.

No 32 (☎ 933 1113; www.no32.ie; 32 Chapel St; set menu €26, mains €18-32; ☉ 5.30-10pm Mon-Sat) Another superb, stylish restaurant set to raise the dining bar in Dundalk. It serves the usual suspects – pasta, chicken, lamb etc – but it's the way they're done that makes this place worth seeking out.

Drinking & Entertainment

Several good pubs are found on and around Park St.

Toal's Bar (☎ 933 2759; 7 Crowe St) This is one of the nicer pubs in town, with plenty of character…and characters. It has recently been refurbished.

McKeown's (☎ 933 7931; 16 Clanbrassil St) Superpubs and modern themed bars may be the future, but the old-style Irish boozer is alive and well, if this wonderfully atmospheric place is anything to go by.

Spirit Store (☎ 935 2697; George's Quay) This wonderful little bar, about 3km out of town by the harbour, was originally your typical harbour saloon full of small drinking corners and snugs, but it has been taken over, painted in bright colours and turned into one of the hippest joints in the whole country. It is a favourite fixture on the Irish and international singer-songwriter touring schedule – you're liable to see something great at least once a week. A terrific night out.

Getting There & Away

BUS

Bus Éireann (☎ 041-982 8251) runs an almost hourly service to Dublin (one way/return €9.90/13.10, 1½ hours) and a less-frequent one to Belfast. The **bus station** (☎ 933 4075; Long Walk) is near the shopping centre. There are plenty of local buses and daily connections to centres nationwide.

TRAIN

Clarke Train Station (☎ 933 5521), a few hundred metres west of Park St on Carrickmacross Rd, has trains daily to Dublin (€15.70, one hour, 10 daily) on the Dublin–Belfast line.

Getting Around

The **Cycle Centre** (☎ 933 7159; 44 Dublin St; per day €13), opposite the Dundalk Shopping Centre south of the town centre, hires out bikes.

Local taxi companies include **A-1 Cabs** (☎ 932 6666; 9 Crowe St) and **Five Star Cabs** (☎ 933 6000; 74 Clanbrassil St).

COOLEY PENINSULA

When over-eager scribes and cynical tourist brochures wax lyrical about misty mountains and landscapes steeped in myth and history, the reality is inevitably a little bit disappointing. There's been many a square inch of type devoted to describing the Cooley Peninsula in similarly elegiac terms, and there is an arresting beauty in the forested slopes rising out of the dark waters of Carlingford Lough up to the naked hilltops of moorland that grow further into the Mourne Mountains.

But there's something unsettling about the place too. Isolated and remote, the Cooley Peninsula may be a political part of the Republic, but its spirit is in the wilds of South Armagh, a fiercely independent territory that is deeply suspicious of outsiders, and a bastion of Republican support. It's a tradition rooted in legend, for Cooley is the setting for a large part of Ireland's most famous epic fable, the *Táin Bó Cúailnge* (see the boxed text, p552).

Carlingford

☎ 042 / pop 1329

Near Carlingford (Cairlinn), the Cooley Peninsula's mountains and views display themselves to dramatic effect. This pretty village, with its cluster of narrow streets and whitewashed houses, nestles on Carlingford Lough, beneath Slieve Foye (587m). Hard though it is to believe, not much of this was appreciated until the late 1980s, when the villagers got together to show what can be done to revive a dying community. The story of their efforts is vividly told in the heritage centre.

The Mourne Mountains are just a few kilometres north across the lough.

INFORMATION

The **tourist office** (☎ 937 3033; www.carlingford.ie; 🕒 10am-5.30pm Mon-Sat, 11am-5.30pm Sun Apr-Sep, 11am-5pm Mon-Fri Oct-Mar) is right next to the bus stop on the waterfront.

SIGHTS

Holy Trinity Heritage Centre

The **heritage centre** (☎ 937 3454; Churchyard Rd; adult/concession €1.50/1; 🕒 10am-12.30pm & 2-4.30pm Mon-Fri, noon-4.30pm Sat & Sun) is in the former Holy Trinity Church. The information boards are encased within closable doors so that the centre can double as a concert hall outside visiting hours. A mural shows what the village looked like in its heyday, when the Mint and Taafe's Castle were right on the waterfront. A short video describes the village history and explains what has been done to give it new life in recent years.

King John's Castle

Carlingford was first settled by the Vikings, and in the Middle Ages became an English stronghold under the protection of the castle, which was built on a pinnacle in the 11th to 12th centuries to control the entrance to the lough. On the western side, the entrance gateway was built to allow only one horse and rider through at a time. King John's name stuck to quite a number of places in Ireland, given that he spent little time in or near any of them! In 1210 he spent a couple of days here en route to a battle with Hugh de Lacy at Carrickfergus Castle in Antrim. It's suggested that the first few pages of the Magna Carta, the world's first constitutional bill of rights, were drafted while he was here.

Other Sights

Near the disused station is **Taafe's Castle**, a 16th-century tower house that stood on the waterfront until the land in front was reclaimed to build the short-lived train line. The **Mint**, in front of the hostel near the square, is of a similar age. Although Edward IV is thought to have granted a charter to a mint in 1467, no coins were produced here. The building has some interesting Celtic carvings round the windows. Near it is the **Tholsel**, the only surviving gate to the original town, although much altered in the 19th century when its defensive edge was softened in the interests of letting traffic through.

West of the village centre are the remains of a **Dominican friary**, built around 1305 and used as a storehouse by oyster fishermen after 1539.

Carlingford is the birthplace of Thomas D'Arcy McGee (1825–68), one of Canada's founding fathers. A bust commemorating him stands opposite Taafe's Castle.

ACTIVITIES

Táin Trail

Carlingford is the starting point for the 40km Táin Trail, making a circuit of the Cooley Peninsula through the Cooley Mountains. The route is a mixture of surfaced roads, forest tracks and green paths. For more information contact the local tourist office (p551) or the **Dundalk tourist office** (☎ 933 5484).

Cruises

Carlingford Pleasure Cruises (☎ 937 3239; adult/child €10/5) runs one-hour cruises between May and September; there's no set time as departure depends on the tides.

FESTIVALS & EVENTS

In mid-August the pubs are packed from morning to midnight when the village is overrun by 20,000 visitors to the **Oyster Festival**, with funfairs, live bands and buskers alongside the official oyster-opening competitions and tastings.

Almost every weekend from June to September, Carlingford goes event-crazy: there are summer schools, medieval festivals, leprechaun hunts and homecoming festivals.

SLEEPING & EATING

Carlingford is a far nicer option for a night's sleep than Dundalk, but it gets pretty

---

TÁIN BÓ CÚAILNGE (CATTLE RAID OF COOLEY)

This remarkable tale of greed and war is one of the oldest stories in any European language and the closest thing Ireland has produced to the Greek epics. The story goes that Queen Maeve (Medbh), the powerful ruler of Connaught, was jealous because she couldn't match the white bull owned by her husband, Ailill. She heard tales of the finest bull in Ireland, the brown bull of Cooley, and became determined to rectify the situation.

Maeve gathered her armies and headed for Ulster, where she conspired with her druids to place the Ulster armies under a spell. A deep sleep descended on them, leaving the province undefended. The only obstacle remaining was the boy warrior Cúchulainn, who tackled Maeve's soldiers as they tried to ford the river at Ardee in County Louth. Cúchulainn killed many of them and halted their advance. Maeve eventually persuaded Cúchulainn's foster brother and close friend, Ferdia, to take him on, but he was defeated after a momentous battle and died in Cúchulainn's arms.

The struggle continued across Louth and onto the Cooley Peninsula, where many place names echo the ensuing action. Sex rears its head regularly in the *Táin*, for Maeve was more interested in her chief warrior, Fergus, than in her husband. At various spots in the saga, they sneak off to make love, and in one instance Ailill steals the sword of the distracted Fergus, to shame him and show how careless he is.

While Maeve's soldiers were being despatched in all sorts of ways by Cúchulainn, Maeve had managed to capture the brown bull and spirit it away to Connaught. The wounded Cúchulainn defeated her armies, but the bull was gone. In the end, the brown bull killed Ailill's white bull and thundered around Ireland leaving bits of his victim all over the place. Finally, spent with rage, he died near Ulster at a place called Druim Tarb (Ridge of the Bull). Cúchulainn and Ulster then made peace with Maeve, and thus the saga ended.

crowded during the summer, especially at weekends: book well in advance. As for food, you won't go far wrong: seafood dominates virtually every menu and the standards are deliciously high.

Beaufort House (☎ 937 3879; www.beauforthouse .net; Ghan Rd; r from €45; P) This stylish, multi-award-winning B&B with stunning front-lawn views of the lough is along the road towards the pier. Their main business is taking care of guests, which they do with considerable comfort, but they also run a yacht charter and sea school.

Oystercatcher Lodge & Bistro (☎ 937 3989; www .theoystercatcher.com; Market Sq; s/d from €55/90; mains from €15; ⊙ 6.30-9.30pm Mon-Sat, 5-8.30pm Sun) Renowned for the superb quality of its oysters, this terrific restaurant does fish just right and has a policy of not using warm-water fish – unlike many Irish restaurants. If you want to avoid the fruits of the sea, the succulent rack of Cooley lamb is divine. Upstairs are seven well-appointed rooms that ensure the high standards of the whole place.

McKevitt's Village Hotel (☎ 937 3116; www .mckevittshotel.com; Market Sq; s/d €60/90; P) With 17 recently renovated rooms all kitted out in light creams and whites, this hotel offers quality accommodation, as well as a lovely bar that draws lots of locals and a well-respected restaurant where, naturally, seafood rules.

Carlingford Adventure Centre (☎ 937 3100; www.carlingfordadventure.com; Tholsel St; s/d €25/50) The leading adventure centre in Carlingford teaches rock climbing, orienteering, hill walking and windsurfing to groups, so the dorm rooms are almost exclusively reserved for the gaggle of school kids that flood here during the summer. Individual travellers not put off by the racket downstairs are put up in singles and doubles (all with en suite) on the second floor.

Kingfisher Bistro (☎ 042-937 3151; Ghan Rd; mains €13; ⊙ 12.30-10.30pm Mon-Sat) Oysters and a pint of Guinness are a match made in heaven. This small, excellent restaurant at-

---

SOMETHING SPECIAL

Ghan House (☎ 937 3682; www.ghanhouse .com; Main Rd; s/d from €65/170; 5-course dinner €47; ⊙ 7-9.30pm Mon-Sat, 12.30-4pm Sun) This magnificent Georgian house in a gloriously isolated spot, about 2km outside the village just off the Dundalk road, is the kind of place you'll struggle to leave. There are only four guestrooms in the main house, each immaculately decorated with period antiques and original artworks. Contemporary touches such as mini-hifis, bottled waters and modern bathrooms merely highlight the house's superior class. A new wing with eight newer rooms isn't as handsome. The exceptional restaurant features a classical menu of traditional dishes; there's also a cookery school on the premises.

---

tached to the heritage centre does wonders with all kinds of seafood, not just the stuff you slurp out of shells.

DRINKING & ENTERTAINMENT
O'Hares (☎ 937 3106; Newry St) Behind the old-style grocery at the front is a classic, stone-floor pub where a peat fire burns and drinkers sit in animated conversation over a cool pint. The owners have done a little modernising in recent years, adding a new bar and an outdoor seating area that means more visitors and more noise, but thankfully the older parts were left intact. There's music here throughout the summer.

Carlingford Arms (☎ 937 3418; Newry St) The most popular pub in town is nothing special, but it draws a good and lively crowd throughout the busy summer months; there's often live music.

GETTING THERE & AWAY
Bus Éireann (☎ 933 4075) has services to Dundalk (one way/return €4.60/6, 50 minutes, six a day Monday to Saturday). There are no Sunday services.

Belfast

Belfast is buzzing. Massive investment combined with the optimism engendered by the peace process have transformed the city into a boom town, and its old bombs and bullets reputation has given way to a designer Belfast, typified by hip hotels like TENsq and Malmaison, elegant restaurants like Roscoff and Michael Deane, and the trendy boutiques that line Lisburn Rd.

Redevelopment continues apace as Victoria Sq, Europe's biggest urban regeneration project, is set to add a massive city-centre shopping mall to a list of tourist attractions that includes imposing Victorian architecture, an attractive waterfront lined with modern art, foot-stomping music in packed-out pubs and the UK's second-biggest arts festival.

The city that gave birth to the *Titanic* has also launched more than a few titanic hangovers. Belfast boasts a vibrant nightlife and plenty of good places to eat – a colourful new wave of stylish bars and gourmet restaurants has emerged to complement the splendid Victorian pubs that have been a mainstay of the city's social life for decades.

The city is compact and easy to get around, with most points of interest within easy walking distance of each other. Classic Belfast experiences include the Victorian delights of City Hall and the Crown Liquor Saloon; a climb to the top of Cave Hill for the view; a hike along the Lagan Towpath for lunch at a riverside pub; the 21st-century attractions of the shiny new Odyssey Complex; and taking a tour around the powerful political murals of West Belfast.

There are still reminders of the Troubles, and the passions that have torn Northern Ireland apart over the decades still run deep. Despite occasional setbacks, there is an atmosphere of determined optimism that will hopefully propel Belfast towards a peaceful future.

HIGHLIGHTS

- **City Lights**
  The craic in Belfast's traditional pubs (p577)

- **Fine Dining**
  Dining out in style at Roscoff (p575) or Restaurant Michael Deane (p575)

- **Culture Vulture**
  A black-taxi tour of the murals (p565) in West Belfast

- **Stroll in the Park**
  Hikes along the Lagan Towpath (p569)

- **Blast from the Past**
  The DeLorean DMC at the Ulster Transport Museum (p592)

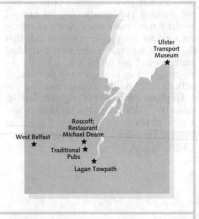

Ulster Transport Museum ★

West Belfast ★

Roscoff; Restaurant Michael Deane ★

Traditional ★ Pubs

Lagan Towpath ★

- POPULATION: 277,000
- AREA: 115 SQ KM

HISTORY

Belfast is a relatively young city, with few reminders of its pre-19th-century history. The
city's name comes from Beál Feirste (Mouth
of the Sandbank), a reference to the shallow
ford at the mouth of the River Farset (now
channelled through a culvert) where it flowed
into the River Lagan. In 1177 the Norman
John de Courcy built a castle here and a small
settlement grew up around it. Both were destroyed 20 years later, and the town did not
begin to develop in earnest until 1611 when
Baron Arthur Chichester built a castle and
promoted the growth of the settlement.

The early-17th-century Plantation of
Ulster brought in the first waves of Scottish and English settlers, followed in the
late 17th century by an influx of Huguenots
(French Protestants) fleeing persecution in
France, who laid the foundations of a thriving linen industry. More Scottish and English settlers arrived, and other industries
such as rope-making, tobacco, engineering
and ship-building developed.

During the 18th and 19th centuries Belfast was the one city in Ireland that felt
the full force of the Industrial Revolution.
Sturdy rows of brick terrace houses were
built for the factory and shipyard workers,
and a town of around 20,000 people in 1800
grew steadily into a city of 400,000 by the
start of WWI, by which time Belfast had
nearly overtaken Dublin in size.

The partition of Ireland after WWI gave
Belfast a new role as the capital of Northern Ireland. It also marked the end of the
city's industrial growth, although decline
didn't really set in until after WWII. With
the outbreak of the Troubles in 1969, the
city saw more than its fair share of violence
and bloodshed, and shocking news images
of terrorist bombings, murders and security forces brutality made Belfast a household name around the world. The mayhem
reached its peak in the 1970s but continued
through the 1980s until the 1994 cease-fire.
Violence continues to rumble on, but at a
much lower level, consisting mostly of in-
fighting between paramilitary factions.

The cease-fire and the 1998 Good Friday
Agreement raised hopes for the future, and
Belfast has seen a huge injection of money,
especially from the EU. Massive swathes
of the city centre have been (or are being)
redeveloped, unemployment is low, house
prices continue to rise faster than in any
other UK city, and tourism is really taking off.

ORIENTATION

Belfast sits at the head of Belfast Lough,
straddling the lower reaches of the River
Lagan and hemmed in to the west by the
steep slopes of Black Mountain and Cave
Hill. The city centre lies on the west bank
of the Lagan, with the imposing City Hall

BELFAST IN...

One Day
Start your day with breakfast in one of the many cafés on Botanic Ave – **Maggie May's** (p576)
will do nicely – then stroll north into the city centre and take a free guided tour of **City Hall**
(p560). Nose around the shops on Donegall St and Royal Ave, then have lunch in **White's Tavern**
(p574) before phoning for a black-taxi tour of the **West Belfast murals** (p565). Ask the taxi driver
to drop you off near the Waterfront Hall, and walk north along the Lagan waterfront to **Lagan
Lookout and the Bigfish** (p563), then head back towards Donegall Sq for dinner at **Deane's
Brasserie** (p575) or **Roscoff** (p575).

Two Days
On your second day take a quick look at **Queen's University** (p564), wander around the Early
Ireland exhibit in the **Ulster Museum** (p565) and stroll through the **Botanic Gardens** (p565),
then walk south along the river for lunch at **Cutter's Wharf** (p577). In the afternoon either
continue walking south along the Lagan Towpath to **Shaw's Bridge** (p569) and catch a bus
back to town, or return to the Lagan Lookout and take a **boat trip** (p570) on the river. Spend
the evening doing a pub crawl of traditional bars such as the **Crown Liquor Saloon** (p561) and
the **Duke of York** (p579).

BELFAST

in Donegall Sq as a convenient central landmark. The principal shopping district is north of the square along Donegall Pl and Royal Ave. North again, the once run-down area around Donegall St and St Anne's Cathedral forms the bohemian Cathedral Quarter.

South of Donegall Sq, the so-called Golden Mile stretches for 1km along Great Victoria St, Shaftesbury Sq and Botanic Ave to Queen's University and the leafy suburbs of South Belfast. This area has dozens of restaurants and bars and most of the city's midrange accommodation. Northwest of Donegall Sq, Divis St leads across the Westlink Motorway to the Falls Rd and West Belfast. East of the river rise the huge yellow cranes of the Harland & Wolff shipyards in East Belfast.

The Europa BusCentre and Great Victoria St train station are behind the Europa Hotel on Great Victoria St, 300m southwest of City Hall (access through Great Northern Mall); the Laganside BusCentre is near the Albert Memorial Clock Tower, 600m northeast of City Hall. Central train station (which isn't very central!) is 800m east of City Hall on East Bridge St.

Steam Packet ferries dock at Donegall Quay, 1km north of City Hall. The Stena Line car-ferry terminal is 2km north of the city centre, and the P&O Irish Sea ferry terminal is 5km north of the city centre (see p590).

Maps

The Belfast Welcome Centre provides a free map of the city centre. The *Collins Belfast Streetfinder Atlas* (£3.50) is more detailed and includes a full index of street names. Most detailed of all, but in the form of an unwieldy folded sheet, is the Ordnance Survey of Northern Ireland's 1:12,000 *Belfast Street Map* (£4.99).

INFORMATION
Bookshops

Bookfinders (☎ 9032 8269; 47 University Rd, South Belfast; ⏲ 10am-5.30pm Mon-Sat) A studenty second-hand bookshop and book-finding service with a gallery and café at the back.

Bookshop at Queen's (☎ 9066 6302; 91 University Rd, South Belfast; ⏲ 9am-5.30pm Mon-Fri, 9am-5pm Sat) Opposite Queen's University.

Eason (☎ 9023 5070; 20 Donegall Pl; ⏲ 9am-5.30pm Mon-Wed, Fri & Sat, to 9pm Thu) Books, magazines and stationery.

Stationery Office Bookshop (☎ 9023 8451; 16 Arthur St; ⏲ 9am-5pm Mon-Fri, 10am-4pm Sat) Good for Ordnance Survey maps, street plans and Lonely Planet guidebooks.

Waterstones (☎ 9024 0159; 44-46 Fountain St; ⏲ 9am-6pm Mon-Wed, Fri & Sat, to 9pm Thu, 12.30-5.30pm Sun) Café on the 1st floor.

Emergency

For national emergency phone numbers, see Telephone inside the front cover.

Rape Crisis & Sexual Abuse Centre (☎ 9024 9696)

Samaritans (☎ 0845 790 9090; www.samaritans .org.uk)

Victim Support (☎ 0845 303 0900; www.victim support.org)

Internet Access

You can use British Telecom's blue, Internet-enabled phone boxes around Donegall Sq and at Central Station, for 10p a minute (50p minimum).

Belfast Welcome Centre (☎ 9024 6609; www.goto belfast.com; 47 Donegall Pl; per 15 min/hr £1/3)

Linen Hall Library (☎ 9032 1707; cnr Fountain St & Donegall Sq; per 30 min £1; ⏲ 9.30am-5.30pm Mon-Fri, 9.30am-4.30pm Sat) One computer on each floor; ask at desk before using.

net-one (☎ 9032 5400; Great Northern Mall, Great Victoria St; per 15 min £1; ⏲ 9am-11pm Mon-Fri, 10am-10pm Sat, 11am-9pm Sun) Twelve PCs; in mall leading to Europa BusCentre.

Revelations (☎ 9032 0337; 27 Shaftesbury Sq; per 15 min £1; ⏲ 10am-10pm Mon-Fri, 10am-6pm Sat, 11am-7pm Sun) Eighteen PCs, laptop access, printers available. Concession rate of £1 per 20 minutes for holders of student and hostelling ID cards.

Laundry

Expect to pay around £4 to £5 total to wash and dry one load.

Globe Drycleaning & Laundrette (37 Botanic Ave)

Mike's Laundrette (46 Agincourt Ave, South Belfast)

Whistle Laundrette (160 Lisburn Rd, South Belfast) Offers service washes only; no self-service.

Left Luggage

Because of security concerns, there are no left-luggage facilities at Belfast's airports, train stations and bus stations. However, most hotels and hostels allow guests to leave their bags for the day, and the **Belfast Welcome Centre** (☎ 9024 6609; www .gotobelfast.com; 47 Donegall Pl) also offers a daytime left-luggage service.

Libraries

Belfast Central Library (☎ 9050 9150; Royal Ave; 🕑 9.30am-8pm Mon & Thu, 9.30am-5.30pm Tue, Wed & Fri, 9am-1pm Sat)

Linen Hall Library (☎ 9032 1707; cnr Fountain St & Donegall Sq; 🕑 9.30am-5.30pm Mon-Fri, 9.30am-4.30pm Sat)

Medical Services

Accident and emergency services are available at these hospitals:

City Hospital (☎ 9032 9241; 51 Lisburn Rd)

Mater Hospital (☎ 9074 1211; 45-51 Crumlin Rd) Near the junction of Antrim Rd and Clifton St.

Royal Victoria Hospital (☎ 9024 0503; Grosvenor Rd) West of the city centre.

Ulster Hospital (☎ 9048 4511; Upper Newtownards Rd, Dundonald) Near Stormont Castle.

For advice on medical and dental emergencies, call NHS Direct on ☎ 0845 4647 (available 24 hours).

Money

There are plenty of ATMs around town. There are currency-exchange facilities at the **Belfast Welcome Centre** (☎ 9024 6609; www.gotobelfast.com; 47 Donegall Pl) on Castle Pl and Shaftesbury Sq, and the following branches of Thomas Cook:

Thomas Cook City centre (☎ 9088 3900; 11 Donegall Pl; 🕑 9am-5.30pm Mon-Wed, Fri & Sat, 10am-5.30pm Thu); Belfast International Airport (☎ 9442 2536; 🕑 5.30am-9.30pm Mon-Fri, 5.30am-midnight Sat & Sun) Times vary slightly in winter and during the summer peak to reflect flight activity.

Post

Bedford St post office(16-22 Bedford St)

Botanic Gardens post office (cnr University Rd & College Gardens, South Belfast)

Main post office (12-16 Bridge St; 🕑 9am-5.30pm Mon-Sat)

Shaftesbury Sq post office (1-5 Botanic Ave)

Tourist Information

Belfast Welcome Centre (☎ 9024 6609; www.gotobelfast.com; 47 Donegall Pl; 🕑 9am-7pm Mon-Sat, noon-5pm Sun Jun-Sep, 9am-5.30pm Mon-Sat Oct-May) Provides information about the whole of Northern Ireland, and books accommodation anywhere in Ireland and Britain. Services include left luggage (not overnight), currency exchange and Internet access.

Cultúrlann MacAdam ÓFiaich (☎ 9096 4188; 216 Falls Rd; 🕑 9am-5pm Mon-Fri) Tourist information desk in West Belfast.

Fáilte Ireland (Irish Tourist Board; ☎ 9032 7888; www.ireland.travel.ie; 53 Castle St; 🕑 9am-5pm Mon-Fri year round, 9am-12.30pm Sat Jun-Aug) Can book accommodation in the Republic of Ireland.

Tourist information desks Belfast City Airport (☎ 9045 7745; 🕑 5.30am-10pm); Belfast International Airport (☎ 9442 2888; 🕑 24hr)

Travel Agencies

STA Travel (☎ 9024 1469; 92-94 Botanic Ave; 🕑 9.30am-5.30pm Mon-Fri, 10am-5pm Sat)

Thomas Cook (☎ 9088 3900; 11 Donegall Pl; 🕑 9am-5.30pm Mon-Sat, Fri & Sat, 10am-5.30pm Thu)

Trailfinders (☎ 9027 1888; 47-49 Fountain St; 🕑 9am-7pm Mon-Fri, 9am-6pm Sat, 10am-6pm Sun)

usit NOW (☎ 9032 4073; 13b Fountain Centre, College St; 🕑 9.30am-5pm Mon-Fri, 9.30am-12.30pm Sat)

DANGERS & ANNOYANCES

Even at the height of the Troubles, Belfast wasn't a particularly dangerous city for tourists, and today you're less at risk from crime here than you are in London. You should, however, keep away from the so-called 'interface areas' – near the Peace Lines in West Belfast, Crumlin Rd and the Short Strand (just east of Queen's Bridge) – after dark; if in doubt about any area, ask at your hotel or hostel.

One irritating legacy of the Troubles is the absence of left-luggage facilities at bus and train stations. You will also notice a much more obvious security presence than elsewhere in the UK and Ireland, in the form of armoured police Land Rovers, fortified police stations, and security doors on some shops (mostly outside the city centre) where you have to press the buzzer to be allowed in. There are doormen on many city centre shops.

If you want to take photos of fortified police stations, army posts or other military or quasi-military paraphernalia, get permission first to be on the safe side. In the Protestant and Catholic strongholds of West Belfast it's best not to photograph people without permission: always ask first and be prepared to accept a refusal. Taking pictures of the murals is not a problem.

You're unlikely to get into furious political or religious arguments in Belfast pubs because both topics are usually avoided with outsiders. In staunchly single-minded pubs of either persuasion, outsiders are often studiously avoided.

BELFAST

BELFAST

INFORMATION

Belfast Central Library	1 D2
Belfast Welcome Centre	2 D4
Bookfinders	(see 84)
Bookshop at Queens	3 C7
Botanic Gardens Post Office	4 C7
City Hospital	5 C6
Eason	6 D3
Fáilte Ireland	7 D3
Globe Drycleaning & Laundrette	8 D6
Main Post Office	9 D3
Mater Hospital	10 C1
Mike's Laundrette	11 C7
Net-one	12 C4
Revelations	(see 89)
Shaftesbury Square Post Office	13 D6
STA Travel	14 D6
Stationery Office Bookshop	15 D4
Thomas Cook	16 D3
Trailfinders	17 D4
usit Now	18 D3
Waterstones	19 D4
Whistle Laundrette	20 B8

SIGHTS & ACTIVITIES

Albert Memorial Clock Tower	21 E3
Bank of Ireland Building	22 D2
Bigfish Sculpture	23 E2
Botanic Gardens	24 D8
City Hall	25 D4
Clarendon Building	26 E1
Clifton House	27 C1
Commercial Building	28 D3
Custom House	29 E2
Falls Rd People's Taxis	30 C3
Former Methodist Church	(see 52)
Harbour Commissioner's Office	31 E2
Lagan Boat Tours	(see 23)
Lagan Lookout Visitor Centre	32 E2
Life Cycles	33 C3
Linen Hall Library	34 D4
Lord Kelvin Statue	35 C7
Methodist Church	36 C6
Northern Bank Building	37 D3
Northern Bank Building	38 D3
Ormeau Baths Gallery	39 D5
Palm House	40 D7

Pearl Assurance Building	41 D4
Queen's University	42 D7
Robinson & Cleaver Building	43 D4
Royal Courts of Justice	44 E4
Scottish Provident Building	45 D4
Shankill Rd People's Taxis	46 D2
Sinclair Seamen's Church	47 E2
Sinclair Store	48 D2
St Anne's Cathedral	49 D2
St George's Market	50 E4
Tropical Ravine	51 D8
Ulster Bank	52 D4
Ulster Bank	53 E3
Ulster Museum	54 C8
Union Theological College	55 D7
W5	56 F2

SLEEPING

Ark	57 D7
Arnie's Backpackers	58 C7
Belfast International Youth	
Hostel	59 C6
Benedicts	60 C6
Botanic Lodge Guesthouse	61 D6
Camera Guesthouse	62 B8
Crescent Town House	63 D6
Days Hotel	64 C5
Dukes Hotel	65 C7
Eglantine Guesthouse	66 B8
Europa Hotel	67 C4
Jury's Inn	68 C4
Linen House	69 D2
Madison's	70 D6
Malmaison Hotel	71 E3
Malone Lodge Hotel	72 B8
Marine Guesthouse	73 B8
Tara Lodge	74 D6
TENsq	75 D4
Travelodge	76 D4
Wellington Park Hotel	77 C8

EATING

Altos	78 D3
Ann's Pantry	79 D3
Apartment	80 D4
Archana	81 D5
Ba Soba	82 D2

▲ 10

▼ 0   400 m

▼ 0   0.2 miles

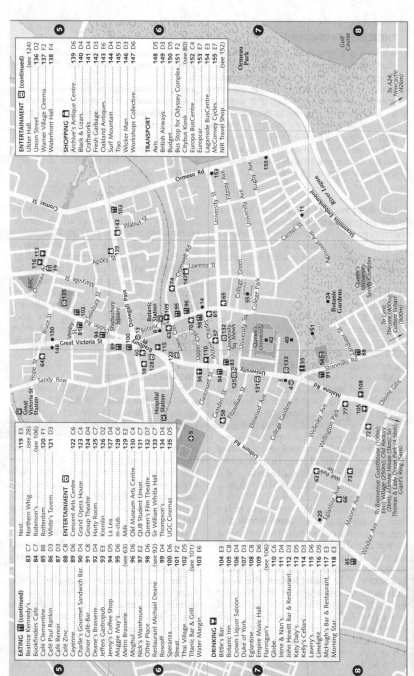

THE ICEBERG COMETH?

Will the city that launched the *Titanic* become the city that lassoed an iceberg? Belfast artist Rita Duffy hit the headlines in 2005 with a plan to tow an iceberg from Arctic waters to Belfast Lough and moor it there as a sort of art installation.

To her, the sinking of the *Titanic* marked the beginning of Belfast's decline; the iceberg would symbolise all that has sunk Belfast, in particular the sectarian conflict that has blighted the city for decades. She hopes that as the months pass, the gradually melting berg will symbolise the possibility of a thaw in the hardened attitudes on both sides of the sectarian divide, and the melting of the currently frozen peace process.

A company has been set up to look at the practicalities of realising the iceberg project, which has the backing of Belfast's mayor and Pulitzer-prize-winning poet Paul Muldoon. If the plan ever becomes a reality, it will probably not happen until 2008 at the earliest.

One thing you will find difficult to avoid in Belfast pubs is the continuing and eye-watering popularity of smoking. While some restaurants have nonsmoking areas, you will almost always catch a whiff of tobacco fumes.

SIGHTS
City Centre
CITY HALL
The Industrial Revolution transformed Belfast in the 19th century, and its rapid rise to muck-and-brass prosperity is manifested in the extravagance of **City Hall** (☎ 9027 0456; www .belfastcity.gov.uk; Donegall Sq; admission free; ☺ guided tours 11am, 2pm & 3pm Mon-Fri, 2.30pm Sat Jun-Sep, 11am & 2.30pm Mon-Fri, 2.30pm Sat Oct-May). Built in classical Renaissance style in fine, white Portland stone, it was completed in 1906 and paid for from profits of the gas supply company. Controlled by unionists throughout most of its existence, City Hall received its first ever Sinn Féin lord mayor in Alex Maskey, who served in the post in 2002–03. It is equipped with facilities for the disabled.

The hall is fronted by a statue of a rather dour 'we are not amused' **Queen Victoria**. The bronze figures on either side of her symbolise the textile and shipbuilding industries, while the child at the back represents education. At the northeastern corner of the grounds is a statue of **Sir Edward Harland**, the Yorkshire-born marine engineer who founded the Harland & Wolff shipyards, and served as mayor of Belfast in 1885–86. To his south stands a memorial to the victims of the *Titanic*. The **Marquess of Dufferin** (1826–1902), whose career included postings as ambassador to Turkey, Russia, Paris and Rome, governor-general of Canada and viceroy to India, has an ornate, temple-like memorial flanked by an Indian and a Turkish warrior, on the western side of the City Hall.

The highlights of the free **guided tour** of City Hall include the sumptuous, wedding-cake Italian marble and colourful stained glass of the entrance hall and rotunda, an opportunity to sit on the mayor's throne in the council chamber, and the idiosyncratic portraits of past lord mayors. Each lord mayor is allowed to choose his or her own artist, and the variations in personal style are intriguing.

LINEN HALL LIBRARY
Opposite City Hall, on North Donegall Sq, is the **Linen Hall Library** (☎ 9032 1707; www.linen hall.com; 17 North Donegall Sq; admission free; ☺ 9.30am-5.30pm Mon-Fri, 9.30am-1pm Sat; ☒). Established in 1788 to 'improve the mind and excite a spirit of general inquiry', the library was moved from its original home in the White Linen Hall (the site is now occupied by City Hall) to the present building a century later. Thomas Russell, the first librarian, was a founding member of the United Irishmen and a close friend of Wolfe Tone – a reminder that this movement for independence from Britain had its origins in Belfast. Russell was hanged in 1803 after Robert Emmet's abortive rebellion.

The library houses some 260,000 books, more than half of which are part of its important Irish and local-studies collection. The political collection consists of pretty much everything that has been written about Northern Irish politics since 1966. The library also has a small **café** (☺ 10am-4pm Mon-Fri, 10am-12.30pm Sat) and all the daily newspapers.

OTHER DONEGALL SQUARE BUILDINGS

On West Donegall Sq is the ornate **Scottish Provident Building** (1897–1902). It's decorated with a veritable riot of fascinating statuary, including several allusions to the industries that assured Victorian Belfast's prosperity, as well as sphinxes, dolphins and lions' heads. The building was the work of the architectural partnership of Young & MacKenzie, who counterbalanced it in 1902 with the red sandstone **Pearl Assurance Building** on East Donegall Sq. Also on the east side of the square is the Classical Greek portico of the former **Methodist Church** (1847), now occupied by the Ulster Bank.

On the north side of square is the equally fine **Robinson & Cleaver Building** (1888), once the Royal Irish Linen Warehouse and later home to Belfast's finest department store. There are 50 busts adorning the façade, representing patrons of the Royal Irish Linen company – look out for Queen Victoria and the Maharajah of Cooch Behar, both former customers.

CROWN LIQUOR SALOON

There are not too many historical monuments that you can enjoy while savouring a pint of beer, but the National Trust's **Crown Liquor Saloon** (☎ 9027 9901; 46 Great Victoria St; admission free; ⏰ 11.30am-11pm Mon-Sat, 12.30-10pm Sun) is one. Belfast's most famous bar was refurbished by Patrick Flanagan in the late 19th century and displays Victorian decorative flamboyance at its best (your man was looking to pull in a posh clientele from the new-fangled train station and Grand Opera House across the street).

The exterior (1885) is decorated with ornate and colourful tiles, and a mosaic of a crown on the floor outside the entrance, while the interior (1898) sports a mass of stained and cut glass, marble, ceramics, mirrors and mahogany, all atmospherically lit by genuine gas mantles. A long, highly decorated bar dominates one side of the pub, while on the other is a row of ornate wooden snugs. The snugs come equipped with gunmetal plates (from the Crimean War) for striking matches, and bell-pushes that once allowed drinkers to order top-ups without leaving their seats (alas, no more).

Above the Crown is **Flannigan's** (☎ 9027 9901), another interesting bar with *Titanic* and other maritime memorabilia.

GRAND OPERA HOUSE

One of Belfast's great Victorian landmarks is the **Grand Opera House** (☎ 9024 1919; www.goh .co.uk; Great Victoria St), across the road from the Crown Liquor Saloon. Opened in 1895, and completely refurbished in the 1970s, it suffered grievously at the hands of the IRA, having sustained severe bomb damage in 1991 and 1993. It has been suggested that as the Europa Hotel next door was the home of the media during the Troubles, the IRA brought the bombs to them so they wouldn't have to leave the bar.

The interior has been restored to over-the-top Victorian pomp, with swirling wood and plasterwork, purple satin in abundance, and carved elephant heads in the auditorium. See also p589.

THE ENTRIES

The oldest part of Belfast, around High St, suffered considerable damage from WWII bombing. The narrow alleyways running off High St and Ann St, known as the Entries, were once bustling commercial and residential centres: **Pottinger's Entry** had 34 houses in 1822.

Joy's Entry is named after Francis Joy, who founded the *Belfast News Letter* in 1737, the first daily newspaper in the British Isles (and still in business). One of his grandsons, Henry Joy McCracken, was executed for supporting the 1798 United Irishmen's revolt.

The United Irishmen (see p37) were founded in 1791 by Wolfe Tone in Peggy Barclay's tavern in **Crown Entry**, and used to meet in Kelly's Cellars (1720; p578) on Bank St, off Royal Ave. White's Tavern (1630; p578), on **Wine Cellar Entry**, is the oldest pub in the city and is still a popular lunch-time meeting spot.

QUEEN'S SQUARE

At the east end of High St is Belfast's very own leaning tower, the **Albert Memorial Clock Tower**. Erected in 1867 in honour of Queen Victoria's dear departed husband, it is not so dramatically out of kilter as the more famously tilted tower in Pisa but does, nevertheless, lean noticeably to the south – as the locals say, 'Old Albert not only has the time, he also has the inclination.' Recent restoration work has stabilised its foundations and left its Scrabo sandstone masonry sparkling white.

RED HAND OF ULSTER

According to legend, the chief of a war party approaching the Ulster coast decreed that the land would belong to the first man to lay his right hand upon it. One particularly competitive chap lopped off his own right hand with his sword and lobbed it to the shore, thus claiming Ulster as his own. The O'Neill clan later adopted the Red Hand as their emblem and it went on to become the symbol of the Irish province of Ulster.

You'll see the Red Hand of Ulster in many places: on the official Northern Irish flag, in the Ulster coat of arms, above the entrance to the Linen Hall Library on Donegall Sq, and laid out in red flowers in the garden of Mount Stewart House in County Down (p602).

Many of the buildings around the clock tower are the work of Sir Charles Lanyon, Belfast's pre-eminent Victorian architect. The white stone building immediately north of the clock tower was completed in 1852 by Lanyon as head office for the **Northern Bank**.

South of the tower on Victoria St is the Malmaison Hotel (1868), formerly two seed warehouses – look for the friezes of exotic birds, plants and nut-munching squirrels on the left half of the façade.

Cathedral Quarter

The district north of the centre around St Anne's Cathedral, bounded roughly by Donegall, Waring, Dunbar and York Sts, has been promoted in recent years as Belfast's Left Bank, a bohemian district of restored red-brick warehouses and cobbled lanes lined with artists' studios, design offices, and new bars and restaurants. It's home to the Cathedral Quarter Arts Festival (see p571).

Built in imposing Hiberno-Romanesque style, **St Anne's Cathedral** (☎ 9033 2328; Donegall St; admission free, donations accepted; 🕓 10am-4pm Mon-Sat; ♿) was started in 1899 but did not reach its final form until 1981. As you enter you'll see the black and white marble floor is laid out in a maze pattern – the black route leads to a dead end, the white to the sanctuary and salvation. The 10 pillars of the nave are topped by carvings symbolising aspects of Belfast life; look out for the Freemasons' pillar (the central one on the right, or south side). In the south aisle is the tomb of unionist hero Sir Edward Carson (1854–1935). The stunning mosaic of *The Creation* in the baptistry contains 150,000 pieces of coloured glass; it and the mosaic above the west door are the result of seven years' work by sisters Gertrude and Margaret Martin.

A 10-minute walk northwest from the cathedral along Donegall St and Clifton St leads to **Clifton House** (2a Hopewell Ave, Carlisle Circus), built in 1774 by Robert Joy (Henry Joy McCracken's uncle) as a poorhouse, and the finest surviving 18th-century building in Belfast. It now houses a nursing home.

Walk south from the cathedral along Donegall St and you'll see the elegant Georgian **Commercial Building** (1822) ahead, easily identified by the prominent name of the Northern Whig Printing Company, with a modern bar on the ground floor. Opposite is the **Northern Bank Building**, the oldest public building in the city, which started life as the single-storey Exchange in 1769, became the Assembly Rooms with the addition of an upper storey in 1777, and was remodelled in Italianate style in 1845 by Charles Lanyon to become a bank.

Turn left along Waring St to find the most flamboyant legacy of Belfast's Victorian era, the grandiose **Ulster Bank** (1860) building. Closed to the public at the time of writing, this Italianate extravaganza has iron railings decorated with the Red Hand of Ulster and Irish wolfhounds, soaring columns and sculpted figures depicting Britannia, Justice and Commerce.

To the west of the cathedral, at the junction of Royal Ave and North St, is the **Bank of Ireland Building** (1929), a fine example of Art Deco architecture. The former **Sinclair Store** (1935), diagonally opposite the bank, is also in Deco style.

Laganside & Victoria Square

The ambitious **Laganside Project** to redevelop and regenerate the centre of Belfast saw the building of the Waterfront Hall, British Telecom's Riverside Tower and the Belfast Hilton in the 1990s. Projects completed since then include several clusters of riverside apartments, the Lanyon Quay office development next to the Waterfront Hall and the restoration of listed buildings such as McHugh's bar on Queen's Sq, the ornate Victorian warehouses now housing the Malmaison Hotel on Victoria St, and the Albert Memorial Clock Tower.

Future plans include the £300 million redevelopment of **Victoria Sq** (www.victoriasquare.com), whose centrepiece will be a shopping mall topped by a vast glass dome (due for completion in 2007); and the even bigger £1 billion regeneration project known as **Titanic Quarter** (www.titanicquarter.com), which plans to develop the long-derelict shipyards and docklands of East Belfast over the next 15 to 20 years.

CLARENDON DOCK
Near the ferry terminal on Donegall Quay is the Italianate **Harbour Commissioner's Office** (1854). The striking marble and stained-glass interior features art and sculpture inspired by Belfast's maritime history. The captain's table built for the *Titanic* survives here – completed behind schedule, it never made it on board. Guided tours of the office are available during the Belfast Summer in the City festival. It's also open during European Heritage Weekend, which usually takes place in October or November.

Sinclair Seamen's Church (☎ 9086 8568; Corporation Sq; admission free; ☿ 2-4pm Wed, 11.30am-7pm Sun), next to the Harbour Commissioner's Office, was built by Charles Lanyon in 1857–58 and was intended to meet the spiritual needs of visiting sailors. Part church, part maritime museum, it has a pulpit in the shape of a ship's prow (complete with red and green port and starboard lights), a brass ship's wheel and binnacle (used as a baptismal font) salvaged from a WWI wreck and, hanging on the wall behind the wheel, the ship's bell from HMS *Hood*.

North of the Harbour Commissioner's Office is the restored Clarendon Dock. Leading off it are the dry docks where Belfast's ship-building industry was born – No 1 Dry Dock (1796–1800) is Ireland's oldest, and remained in use until the 1960s; No 2 (1826) is still used occasionally. Between the two sits the pretty little **Clarendon Building**, now home to the offices of the Laganside Corporation.

CUSTOM HOUSE SQUARE
South along the river is the elegant **Custom House**, built by Lanyon in Italianate style between 1854 and 1857; the writer Anthony Trollope once worked in the post office here. On the waterfront side the pediment carries sculpted portrayals of Britannia, Neptune and Mercury. Custom House Sq and Queen's Sq were redeveloped in 2004–05, and now form a pedestrianised public space linking the city centre to the riverbank.

Looking across the River Lagan from the Custom House, East Belfast is dominated by the huge yellow cranes of the Harland & Wolff shipyards. The modern Queen Elizabeth Bridge crosses the Lagan just to the south, but immediately south again is **Queen's Bridge** (1843) with its ornate lamps, Sir Charles Lanyon's first important contribution to Belfast's cityscape.

LAGAN WEIR & LOOKOUT
Across the street from the Custom House is *Bigfish* (1999), the most prominent of the many modern artworks that grace the riverbank between Clarendon Dock and Ormeau Bridge. The giant ceramic salmon is covered with tiles depicting the history of Belfast.

It sits beside **Lagan Weir**, the first stage of the Laganside Project, completed in 1994. Years of neglect and industrial decline had turned the River Lagan, the original lifeblood of the city, into an open sewer flanked by smelly, unsightly mudflats. The weir, along with a programme of dredging and aeration, has improved the water quality so much that salmon, eels and sea trout now migrate up the river.

The **Lagan Lookout Visitor Centre** (☎ 9031 5444; 1 Donegall Quay; adult/child £1.50/0.75; ☿ 11am-5pm Mon-Fri, noon-5pm Sat, 2-5pm Sun Apr-Sep, 11am-3.30pm Tue-Fri, 1-4.30pm Sat, 2-4.30pm Sun Oct-Mar) offers a state-of-the-art explanation of how the weir works and why it was needed, with interactive computers to bring things to life. The centre also has displays on the progress of the entire Laganside Project.

For details of the boat tours that depart from here, see p570.

ODYSSEY COMPLEX
The Odyssey Complex is a huge sporting and entertainment centre on the eastern side of the river across from Clarendon Dock. The complex features a hands-on science centre, a 10,000-seater sports arena (home to the Belfast Giants ice-hockey

team), a multiplex cinema with an IMAX screen, a video-games centre and a dozen restaurants, cafés and bars.

Also known as whowhatwherewhenwhy, **W5** (☎ 9046 7700; www.w5online.co.uk; adult/child/family £6/4/15; ☽ 10am-5pm Mon-Thu, 10am-6pm Fri & Sat, noon-6pm Sun, last admission 1hr before closing; ☒) is an interactive science centre aimed at children of all ages. Kids can compose their own tunes by biffing the 'air harp' with a foam rubber bat, try to beat a lie detector, create cloud rings and fire tornadoes, and design and build their own robots and racing cars.

The Odyssey Complex is a five-minute walk across the weir from the Lagan Lookout. The Airbus No 600 service between Europa BusCentre and Belfast City Airport stops at the complex (70p, 10 minutes) between 6pm and 10pm only, departing every 20 minutes Monday to Saturday, every 40 minutes Sunday; the rather inconspicuous bus stop is on Sydenham Rd.

LANYON PLACE
A five-minute walk south from the Lagan Lookout leads to Lanyon Pl, the Laganside Project's flagship site, dominated by the 2235-seat Waterfront Hall (p580). Across Oxford St lie the neoclassical **Royal Courts of Justice** (1933), bombed by the IRA in 1990 but now emerging from behind the massive security screens that once concealed them.

South of the courts is the elegant Victorian **St George's Market** (☎ 9043 5704; cnr Oxford & May Sts; admission free; ☽ 6am-1pm Fri, 10am-4pm Sat), built in 1896 for the sale of fruit, butter, eggs and poultry, and the oldest continually operating market in Ireland. Restored in 1999, it now sells fresh flowers, fruit, vegetables, meat and fish, plus general household and second-hand goods on Friday, and hosts a farmers' market on Saturday. The Ha'penny Fair, with antiques and collectables, arts and crafts, is held on the first Sunday of the month.

South of the Centre
The Golden Mile – a 1km strip of pubs and restaurants – stretches south from the city centre to the University district, and is the focus for much of Belfast's nightlife. The Mile is not confined to one street, but takes in Great Victoria St and Bedford St/Dublin St, which converge on Shaftesbury Sq and

Bradbury Pl, then continues along Botanic Ave and University Rd.

Citybus Nos 8A, 8B and 8C run from East Donegall Sq along Bradbury Pl and University Rd to Queen's University.

ORMEAU BATHS GALLERY
Housed in a 19th-century public bath-house, the **Ormeau Baths Gallery** (☎ 9032 1402; www.obgonline.net; 18a Ormeau Ave; admission free; ☽ 10am-5.30pm Tue-Sat) is Northern Ireland's principal exhibition space for contemporary visual art. The gallery stages changing exhibitions of work by Irish and international artists, and has hosted controversial showings of works by Gilbert and George, and Yoko Ono. The gallery is a few blocks south of Donegall Sq.

QUEEN'S UNIVERSITY
If you think that Charles Lanyon's Queen's College (1849), a Tudor Revival building in red brick and honey-coloured sandstone, has something of an Oxbridge air about it, that may be because he based the design of the central tower on the 15th-century Founder's Tower at Oxford's Magdalen College. Northern Ireland's most prestigious university was founded by Queen Victoria in 1845, one of three Queen's colleges (the others were in Cork and Galway) created to provide a non-denominational alternative to the Anglican Church's Trinity College in Dublin. In 1908 the college became the Queen's University of Belfast, and today its campus spreads across some 250 buildings. Queen's has around 24,000 students and enjoys a strong reputation in medicine, engineering and law.

Just inside the main entrance is a small **visitor centre** (☎ 9033 5252; www.qub.ac.uk/vcentre; University Rd; admission free; ☽ 10am-4pm Mon-Sat May-Sep, 10am-4pm Mon-Fri Oct-Apr; ☒) with exhibitions and a souvenir shop. You can arrange a guided tour by phoning in advance.

The university quarter is an attractive district of quiet, tree-lined streets. Georgian-style **University Sq** (1848–53), on the northern side of the campus, is one of the most beautiful terraced streets in Ireland. Opposite its eastern end is the grand, neo-Renaissance **Union Theological College** (1853), originally the Presbyterian College and yet another Lanyon design. It housed the Northern Ireland Parliament from the partition of Ireland until 1932, when the Parliament Buildings at Stormont were opened.

BOTANIC GARDENS

The green oasis of Belfast's **Botanic Gardens** (☎ 9032 4902; Stranmillis Rd; admission free; ⏲ 7.30am-sunset) is a short stroll away from the university. Just inside the Stranmillis Rd gate is a statue of Belfast-born William Thomson, **Lord Kelvin**, who helped lay the foundation of modern physics and invented the Kelvin scale that measures temperatures from absolute zero (-273°C or 0°K).

The gardens' centrepiece is Charles Lanyon's beautiful **Palm House** (admission free; ⏲ 10am-noon & 1-5pm Mon-Fri, 2-5pm Sat, Sun & bank holidays, closes 4pm Oct-Mar), built in 1839 and completed in 1852, with its birdcage dome, a masterpiece in cast-iron and curvilinear glass. Nearby is the unique **Tropical Ravine**, a huge red-brick greenhouse designed by the garden's curator Charles McKimm and completed in 1889. Inside, a raised walkway overlooks a jungle of tropical ferns, orchids, lilies and banana plants growing in a sunken glen. It has the same opening hours as Palm House.

ULSTER MUSEUM

If the weather washes out a walk in the Botanics, head instead for the nearby **Ulster Museum** (☎ 9038 3000; www.ulstermuseum.org.uk; Stranmillis Rd; admission free; ⏲ 10am-5pm Mon-Fri, 1-5pm Sat, 2-5pm Sun). Don't miss the **Early Ireland gallery**, a series of tableaux explaining Irish prehistory combined with a spectacular collection of prehistoric stone and bronze artefacts that help provide a cultural context for Northern Ireland's many archaeological sites. The exhibits are beautifully displayed – the Malone Hoard, a clutch of 16 polished, Neolithic stone axes discovered only a few kilometres from the museum, looks more like a modern sculpture than a museum exhibit.

Other highlights include the **Industrial History gallery**, based around Belfast's 19th-century linen industry, and the **Treasures of the Armada**, a display of artefacts and jewellery recovered from the 1588 wreck of the *Girona* and other Spanish Armada vessels. Among the treasures is a ruby-encrusted golden salamander.

The centrepiece of the Egyptian collection is the **mummy of Princess Takabuti**. She was unwrapped in Belfast in 1835, the first mummy ever to be displayed outside Egypt; more recently, her bleached hair has led the locals to dub her 'Belfast's oldest bleached blonde'.

The top floors are given over to 19th- and 20th-century **Irish and British art**, notably the works of Belfast-born Sir John Lavery (1856–1941), who became one of the most fashionable and expensive portraitists of Victorian London.

West Belfast

Though scarred by three decades of civil unrest, the former battleground of West Belfast is one of the most compelling places to visit in Northern Ireland. Recent history hangs heavy in the air, but the old Victorian slums and most of the 1960s tower blocks have been replaced by greatly improved public housing, and there is a noticeable feeling of optimism and hope for the future.

The main attractions are the powerful murals that chart the history of the conflict as well as the political passions of the moment, and for visitors from mainland Britain there is a grim fascination to be found in wandering through the former 'war zone' in their own backyard.

West Belfast grew up around the linen mills that propelled the city into late 19th-century prosperity. It was an area of low-cost, working-class housing and even in the Victorian era was divided along religious lines. The advent of the Troubles in 1968 solidified the sectarian divide, and since 1970 the ironically named 'Peace Line' has separated the Loyalist and Protestant Shankill district from the republican and Catholic Falls.

Despite its past reputation the area is safe to visit. The easiest way to see West Belfast is on a black-taxi tour (see p570). The cabs visit the more spectacular murals as well as the Peace Line (where you can write a message on the wall) and other significant sites, while drivers provide a colourful commentary on the history of the area.

There's nothing to stop you visiting under your own steam, either walking or using the shared black taxis along the Falls or Shankill Rds (see p566). Alternatively, bus Nos 10A to 10F from Queen St will take you along the Falls Rd; bus Nos 11A to 11D from Wellington Pl go along Shankill Rd.

FALLS ROAD

Although the signs of past conflict are inescapable, the Falls today is an unexpectedly lively, colourful and optimistic place. Local

---

PEOPLE'S TAXIS

The black taxis that cruise along the Falls and Shankill Rds in West Belfast have more in common with Turkey's 'dolmuş' minibuses than the black cabs of London. These are shared taxis that operate along fixed routes, departing only when full, then dropping off and picking up passengers as they go, more like buses than traditional taxis.

Indeed, the 'People's Taxis', as they became known, were introduced in the 1970s to replace local bus services that had been disrupted or cancelled as a result of street riots at the height of the Troubles. The drivers' associations that run the taxis are community-based ventures that provided much-needed employment during difficult times, and often gave jobs to ex-internees and prisoners who could not find work elsewhere.

About 30 years on, the black taxis are an accepted part of Belfast's public transport infrastructure. There is even a black taxi 'bus station' under construction on Castle St. However, those on the unionist side allege that the Falls Rd taxis channel funds to the IRA, while republicans make similar claims about the Shankill taxis and Loyalist paramilitaries.

Falls Rd taxis (with green licence discs) depart from the corner of King and Castle Sts. During the day a sign in the windscreen shows their route; after 5.30pm the first person in the queue dictates the destination. You can hail a taxi anywhere; when you want to get out, knock on the window, then pay the driver from the footpath.

Shankill taxis (with orange licence discs) depart from North St. You can hail them at bus stops; when you want to get out, say 'next stop' to the driver, and pay before you get out. Fares on both services range from around 70p to £1 per person.

---

people are friendly and welcoming, and community ventures such as Conway Mill, the Cultúrlann centre and black-taxi tours are drawing increasing numbers of tourists into the area.

The focus for community activity is the Irish language and cultural centre **Cultúrlann MacAdam ÓFiaich** (☎ 9096 4180; www.culturlann.ie; 216 Falls Rd; ⏰ 9am-5.30pm Mon-Fri, 10am-5.30pm Sat). Housed in a red-brick, former Presbyterian church, it's a cosy and welcoming place with a tourist information desk, a shop selling a wide selection of books on Ireland, crafts, and Irish music tapes and CDs, and an excellent café-restaurant (see p577). The centre also has an art gallery and a theatre that stages music, drama and poetry events.

A few blocks away is **Conway Mill** (☎ 9024 7276; www.conwaymill.org; 5-7 Conway St; admission free; ⏰ 10am-4pm Mon-Fri), a 19th-century flax mill that now houses more than 20 small shops and studios making and selling arts, crafts and furniture, and an exhibition on the mill's history.

Common images seen in the republican murals for which the Falls Rd is famous include the phoenix rising from the flames (symbolising Ireland reborn from the flames of the 1916 Easter Rising), the face of hunger striker Bobby Sands, and

scenes and figures from Irish mythology. Common mottoes include 'Free Ireland', 'Brits Out' and the Irish 'Caisc 1916' (Easter 1916) and 'Tíocfaídh Ár Lá' ('Our Day Will Come', a republican slogan).

The main areas for republican murals are Falls Rd, Beechmount Ave, Donegall Rd, Shaw's Rd and the Ballymurphy district in West Belfast; New Lodge Rd in North Belfast; and Ormeau Rd in South Belfast.

If you're interested in Northern Ireland's mural tradition, look out for the books *Drawing Support: Murals in the North of Ireland* and *Drawing Support 2: Murals of War and Peace* by Bill Rolston, and the Mural Directory website (www.cain.ulst.ac.uk/murals).

SHANKILL ROAD

Although the Protestant Shankill district (from the Irish *sean chill,* meaning 'old church') has received less media and tourist attention than the Falls, it also contains many interesting murals. The people here are just as friendly, but the Shankill has a rather foreboding atmosphere that contrasts with the more outgoing feel of the Falls Rd. Loyalist communities seem to have more difficulty in presenting their side of the story than the republicans, who have a far more polished approach to propaganda and PR.

Whereas the Falls Rd murals are often artistic and rich in symbolic imagery, the Shankill ones are generally more militaristic and defiant in tone. The Loyalist battle cry of 'No Surrender!' is everywhere, along with red, white and blue painted kerbstones, paramilitary insignia and images of King Billy (William III, Protestant victor over the Catholic James II at the Battle of the Boyne in 1690), usually shown on a prancing white horse. You will also see the Red Hand of Ulster, sometimes shown as a clenched fist (the symbol of the UFF), and references to the WWI Battle of the Somme in 1916 (in which many Ulster soldiers died; it is seen as a symbol of Ulster's loyalty to the British crown, in contrast to the republican Easter Rising of 1916). Common mottoes include 'Quis Separabit' (Who Shall Divide Us?), the motto of the UDA; and the defiant 'We will maintain our faith and our nationality'.

To reach Shankill Rd on foot, set off north from City Hall along Donegall Pl and Royal Ave, then turn left on Peter's Hill and keep straight on across the Westlink dual carriageway.

Beyond Shankill Rd, about 500m up Glencairn Rd, is **Fernhill House: The People's Museum** (☎ 9071 5599; Glencairn Rd; adult/child £2/1; ⊙ 10am-4pm Mon-Sat, 1-4pm Sun). A re-creation of a 1930s Shankill house, the museum has exhibitions detailing the history of the Shankill district, the Home Rule crisis, the two World Wars and the Orange Order. To get there, take bus No 11B, 11C or 11D from Wellington Pl, at the northwest corner of Donegall Sq.

Suburbs
CAVE HILL COUNTRY PARK
The best way to get a feel for Belfast's natural setting is to view it from above. In the absence of a private aircraft, head for **Cave Hill** (368m), which looms over the northern fringes of the city. The view from its summit takes in the whole sprawl of the city, the docks and the creeping fingers of urbanisation along the shores of Belfast Lough. On a clear day you can even spot Scotland lurking on the horizon.

The hill was originally called Ben Madigan, after the 9th-century Ulster king, Matudhain. Its distinctive, craggy profile, seen from the south, has been known to locals for two centuries as 'Napoleon's Nose' – it supposedly bears some resemblance to Bona-

parte's hooter, but you might take some convincing. On the summit is an Iron Age ring fort known as McArt's Fort where members of the United Irishmen, including Wolfe Tone, looked down over the city in 1795 and pledged to fight for Irish independence.

You can climb to the summit from **Cave Hill Country Park** (☎ 9077 6925; Antrim Rd; admission free; ⊙ 7.30am-dusk), which spreads across the hill's eastern slopes. There are several waymarked walks in addition to the summit trail, and an adventure playground for kids aged three to 14 years.

To get there, take bus Nos 1A to 1H from West Donegall Sq to Belfast Castle or Belfast Zoo.

BELFAST CASTLE
Built in 1870 for the third Marquess of Donegall, in the Scottish Baronial style made fashionable by Queen Victoria's recently built Balmoral, the multiturreted pomp of **Belfast Castle** (☎ 9077 6925; www.belfastcastle.co.uk; Antrim Rd; admission free; ⊙ 9am-10pm Mon-Sat, 9am-5.30pm Sun) commands the eastern slopes of Cave Hill. It was presented to the City of Belfast in 1934.

Extensive renovation between 1978 and 1988 left the interior comfortably modern rather than intriguingly antique, and the castle is now a popular venue for wedding receptions. Upstairs is the **Cave Hill Visitor Centre** (admission free) with displays on the folklore, history, archaeology and natural history of the park. Downstairs is the Cellar Restaurant and a small **antiques shop** (⊙ noon-10pm Mon-Sat, noon-5pm Sun).

Legend has it that the castle's residents will experience good fortune only as long as a white cat lives there, a tale commemorated in the formal gardens by nine portrayals of cats in mosaic, painting, sculpture and garden furniture.

BELFAST ZOO
Belfast Zoo (☎ 9077 6277; Antrim Rd; adult/child Apr-Sep £7/3.60, Oct-Mar £6/3, children under 4, senior & disabled visitors free; ⊙ 10am-7pm Apr-Sep, 10am-4.30pm Oct-May, last admission 2hr before closing) is one of the most appealing zoos in Britain and Ireland, with spacious enclosures set on an attractive, sloping site; the sea lion and penguin pool with its underwater viewing is particularly good. Some of the more unusual animals include tamarins, spectacled bears

BELFAST

and red pandas, but the biggest attractions are 'Jack' the white tiger, the ultra-cute meerkats and the colony of ring-tailed lemurs.

MALONE HOUSE

Malone House (☎ 9068 1246; Upper Malone Rd; admission free; ☒ 9am-5pm Mon-Sat, noon-5pm Sun) is a late-Georgian mansion in the grounds of Barnett Demesne. Built in the 1820s for local merchant William Legge, the house is now used mainly for social functions and conferences, with art exhibitions staged in the Higgin Gallery. The surrounding gardens are planted with azaleas and rhododendrons, with paths leading down to the Lagan Towpath (see boxed text, opposite).

The house is about 5km south of the centre; take bus No 8A or 8B to Dub Lane, Upper Malone Rd.

SIR THOMAS & LADY DIXON PARK

Sir Thomas & Lady Dixon Park (Upper Malone Rd; admission free; ☒ 7.30am-dusk year round) consists of rolling meadows, woodland, riverside fields and formal gardens. The main draw is its spectacular **Rose Garden**, which contains more than 20,000 blooms. Among other displays, a spiral-shaped garden traces the development of the rose from early shrub roses up to modern hybrids; the roses are in bloom from late July. The park also contains a walled garden, a Japanese-style garden, a children's playground and a café.

The park is 1.5km south of Malone House.

GIANT'S RING

This huge **prehistoric earthwork** (admission free; ☒ 24hr), nearly 200m in diameter, is a circular Neolithic ritual complex with a dolmen (known as the Druid's Altar) in the centre. Prehistoric rings were commonly believed to be the home of fairies and consequently treated with respect, but this one was commandeered in the 19th century as a racetrack, the 4m-high embankment serving as a natural grandstand. The site is 6.5km south of Belfast city centre, off Milltown Rd near Shaw's Bridge.

STORMONT

The dazzling white neoclassical façade of **Parliament House** at Stormont is one of Belfast's most iconic buildings. For 40 years, from its completion in 1932 until the introduction of direct rule in 1972, it was the seat of the parliament of Northern Ireland. More recently, from November 1999 to October 2002, it hosted the devolved Northern Ireland Assembly. In the North, 'Stormont' carries the same connotation as 'Westminster' does in Britain and 'Washington' in the USA – the seat of power.

The building occupies a dramatic position at the end of a rising, 1.5km-long avenue and is fronted by a defiant statue of the arch-unionist Sir Edward Carson. Parliament House is not open to the public, but you are free to walk in the extensive grounds, and you can take a virtual tour at www.niassembly.gov.uk. Nearby 19th-century **Stormont Castle** is, like Hillsborough in County Down, an official residence of the Secretary of State for Northern Ireland.

Stormont is 8km east of the city centre, off the A20 Newtonards road. Take bus No 4A or 4B from West Donegall Sq.

WALKING TOUR

Distance: 4km
Duration: one hour

This walk leads through the heart of West Belfast from the city centre to Milltown Cemetery. Starting from **City Hall** go north along Donegall Pl and turn left on Castle St. Keep straight ahead along Divis St.

As you cross the busy Westlink dual carriageway, the first indication that this is no ordinary suburb you are entering is the army observation post atop the infamous **Divis Tower**. The security forces took over the top two floors of the tower block in the 1970s, and still use the post to monitor people's movements. When you get closer you'll see posters and graffiti calling for the 'Demilitarisation of the Divis'.

As you pass the Divis Tower, look to the right along the side street opposite and you'll see the beginning of the so-called **Peace Line**, the 6m-high wall of corrugated steel, concrete and chain link that has divided the Protestant and Catholic communities of West Belfast for 35 years. Begun in 1970 as a 'temporary measure', it has now outlasted the Berlin Wall, and zigzags for some 4km

---

LAGAN TOWPATH

Part of Belfast's Laganside redevelopment project has been the restoration of the towpath along the west bank of the River Lagan. You can now walk or cycle for 20km along the winding riverbank from central Belfast to Lisburn. The Belfast Welcome Centre provides a leaflet with a detailed map (*The Lagan and Lough Cycle Way*).

A shorter walk (10km) that you can easily do in half a day starts from Shaw's Bridge on the southern edge of the city. Take bus No 8A or 8B from East Donegall Sq to the stop just before the Malone Roundabout (where Malone Rd becomes Upper Malone Rd). Bear left at the roundabout (signposted Outer Ring A55) and in five minutes or so you will reach the River Lagan at Shaw's Bridge.

Turn left and follow the cycle/walkway downstream on the left bank of the river (waymarked with red No '9' signs). After 30 minutes you will arrive at the most attractive part of the walk – **Lagan Meadows**, a tree-fringed loop in the river to the right of the path, and a good place for a picnic on a summer's day. Another half-hour will bring you to **Cutters Wharf** (see p577), a great place for a lunch break. From the pub it's another hour of pleasant walking to Lagan Weir in the city centre.

---

from the Westlink to the lower slopes of Black Mountain. These days the gates in the wall remain open during the day, but most are still closed from 5pm to 8am. There are now around 20 such barriers in Belfast, the most recent having been built in the Short Strand area of East Belfast in 2002.

Next, you pass the **Solidarity Wall**, a collection of murals expressing republican sympathies with, among others, the Palestinians, the Kurds and the Basques. Conway St, on the right at the Celtic Bar, leads to **Conway Mill**.

On the corner with Sevastopol St is the red-brick **Sinn Féin headquarters**, with its famous mural of a smiling Bobby Sands, the hunger striker who was elected as MP for West Belfast just a few weeks before he died in 1981. The text reads, in Sands' own words, 'Our revenge will be the laughter of our children'. A few blocks further on, on the right between Waterford St and Springfield Rd, look out for the **Ruby Emerald Take-Away** at 105 Falls Rd – it was on the pavement outside this shop (known as Clinton's Hot Food from 1996 to 2003) that the historic handshake between Sinn Féin leader Gerry Adams and US president Bill Clinton took place in November 1995.

On the left now are the artwork railings of the **Royal Victoria Hospital**, which has a well-earned reputation for expertise in the treatment of gunshot wounds; the wavy form of the railings mimics the structure of DNA, and the portraits (laser-cut in sheet steel) chart the progress of a human life.

Just beyond the hospital is the **Cultúrlann MacAdam ÓFiaich** cultural centre.

All along the Falls Rd you'll see republican murals, as well as memorials in honour of people who have died during the conflict. At Islandbawn St on the right, the **Plastic Bullet Mural** commemorates the 17 people, including eight children, who were killed by plastic baton rounds (now banned) fired by the security services. Two streets on, on the right, is **Beechmount Ave**, with a huge 'Free Ireland' mural. Look at the street name – a hand-painted sign reads 'RPG Avenue'. 'RPG' stands for 'rocket-propelled grenade', and the street earned its nickname because it offered a line of sight for IRA rocket attacks on the security forces base in nearby Springfield Rd.

Another 15 minutes of walking will take you past the **City Cemetery** and Falls Park to **Milltown Cemetery** where the 1981 hunger strikers are buried. You'll see lots of green Hs attached to lamp posts (in memory of the H-blocks at the Maze prison where the hunger strikers were incarcerated); at Hugo St, opposite the City Cemetery, there's a large mural entitled 'St James's Support the Hunger Strikers'.

Return by the same route or catch any bus or taxi back to the city centre. There's a bus stop across the road from the Milltown Cemetery entrance.

BELFAST FOR CHILDREN

W5 (p563) is the city's biggest draw for kids – it's hard to drag them away once they get started on the hands-on exhibits – and the **Odyssey Complex** houses other attractions including a video-games arcade, a ten-pin bowling rink and an IMAX cinema. **Belfast Zoo** (p567) is a perennial favourite, and the Ulster Museum (p565) also has plenty of exhibits and special events designed for children of all ages.

For outdoor fun, head for the **Botanic Gardens** (p565), or the adventure playground in **Cave Hill Country Park** (p567). Or you can try crazy golf with a difference at **Pirates Adventure Golf** (☎ 9048 0220; 111a Dundonald Rd; adult/child £5/3.50; ☉ 10am-10pm), a landscaped, 36-hole course decked out with waterfalls, fountains and a giant pirate ship.

Sweeties may not be at the top of parents' shopping lists these days, but you might be prepared to make an exception for **Aunt Sandra's Candy Factory** (☎ 9073 2868; www.irishcandyfactory.com; 60 Castlereagh Rd; ☉ 9.30am-5pm Mon-Fri, 10am-4.30pm Sat). This 1950s-style shop sells fudge, candy, chocolates, toffee apples and other traditional sweets which have been made by hand – you can get a tour of the workshop before buying the goods.

Out of town but near enough for a day trip, you'll find the **Ulster Folk & Transport Museums** (p592), and the **Ark Open Farm** (p603), both of which are hugely popular with kids.

The free monthly *Whatabout?* booklet (available from the Belfast Welcome Centre) has a 'Family Fun' section, which lists events and attractions of interest to travellers with children. If you're in town in late May, look out for the **Belfast Children's Festival**, which is packed with cultural and educational events.

TOURS

You can find full details of organised tours at the Belfast Welcome Centre. If you want to hire a personal guide, call the Welcome Centre or contact the **Northern Ireland Tourist Guide Association** (☎ 9042 6019; www.bluebadgeireland.org; half-/full-day tours £65/120).

Boat Tours

Lagan Boat Company (☎ 9033 0844; www.laganboatcompany.com; adult/child £6/5) offers two 1¼-hour boat tours: the **River Lagan Tour** (☉ 2pm & 3.30pm Mon, 12.30pm, 2pm & 3.30pm Mon-Thu May-Oct, 12.30pm & 2pm Fri-Sun Apr & May, 12.30pm & 2pm Sat &

Sun Nov & Dec) heads upstream to Stranmillis, departing from the Lagan Lookout. The **Titanic Tour** (☉ 12.30pm, 2pm & 3.30pm Fri-Sun May-Oct) explores the docks and shipyards downstream of the weir, departing from Donegall Quay near the *Bigfish* sculpture and picking up passengers at the Odyssey Complex.

You can book through the **Belfast Welcome Centre** (☎ 9024 6609); call to confirm times.

Bus Tours

Belfast City Sightseeing (☎ 9062 6888; www.city-sightseeing.com; per person £8) Runs one-hour open-top bus tours that visit City Hall, the Albert Clock, the Botanic Gardens, and the Falls Rd and Crumlin Rd murals in West Belfast. There are departures from Castle Pl every 30 minutes from 10am to 4pm year round and to 4.30pm March to October (every 15 minutes at weekends March to October).

Belfast International Youth Hostel (☎ 9032 4733; www.minicoachni.co.uk; 22 Donegall Rd; tour per person £8) Has been recommended by many readers for its two-hour minibus tour that takes in the city centre, Belfast Castle and the Falls and Shankill Rds. Tours depart from the hostel daily at 10.30am and 12.30pm Monday to Friday.

Cycling Tours

Life Cycles (☎ 9043 9959; www.lifecycles.co.uk; 36-37 Smithfield Market; per person £15) Offers three-hour guided tours (minimum five people) of the city centre, South Belfast and the Lagan Towpath. The cost includes bike and helmet rental. Call to arrange a tour at least one day in advance.

Taxi Tours

Black-taxi tours of West Belfast's murals – known locally as the 'bombs and bullets' tours – are being offered by an increasing number of taxi companies and local cabbies. These can vary in quality and content, but in general they're an intimate and entertaining way to see the sights and can be customised to suit your own interests. There are also historical taxi tours of the city centre. For a one-hour tour expect to pay £25 total for one or two people, and £8 per person for three to six.

The two most recommended companies are: **Black Taxi Tours** (☎ 9064 2264, toll-free ☎ 0800 052 3914; www.belfasttours.com) and **Original Belfast Black Taxi Tours** (☎ 0780 091 8468). Call and they will pick you up anywhere in the city centre; the front gate of City Hall is the traditional pick-up spot.

Walking Tours

Bailey's Historical Pub Tours (☎ 9268 3665; www
.belfastpubtours.com; tour £6; ⏱ 7pm Thu, 4pm Sat
May-Sep) has a two-hour tour (not including
drinks) taking in six of the city's historic
pubs, departing from the Crown Dining
Rooms, above the Crown Liquor Saloon
on Great Victoria St.

The following three tours all depart from
the **Belfast Welcome Centre** (☎ 9024 6609):

Belfast City Centre Walk (☎ 9049 1469; tour £4;
⏱ departs 2pm Fri Jun-Oct) A 1½-hour tour that explores
the architecture and history of the Victorian city centre and
Laganside.

Blackstaff Way (☎ 9029 2631; tour £5; ⏱ departs
11am Sat Jun-Oct) A fascinating 1½-hour historical tour
through the city along the route of the Blackstaff River,
which was channelled underground in 1881.

Old Town: 1660-1685 (☎ 9023 8437; tour £4;
⏱ departs 2pm Sat Jun-Oct) A 1½-hour tour following
the line of the old town walls of Belfast, exploring the
origins of the city.

FESTIVALS & EVENTS

The Belfast City Council organises **Summer in the City** (☎ 9027 0222; www.belfastcity.gov
.uk/events), a programme of events from May
to September covering everything from
classical and traditional music concerts to
community events and the Lord Mayor's
Show. Several buildings are opened to the
public for guided tours.

March

St Patrick's Carnival (☎ 9031 3440; www.feilebelfast
.com) A celebration of Ireland's national saint marked by
various community festivals and culminating in a grand
city-centre carnival on 17 March.

Belfast Film Festival (☎ 9032 5913; www.belfastfilm
festival.org) A week-long celebration of Irish and international film-making held in late March.

May

Belfast Marathon (☎ 9027 0345; www.belfastcity
marathon.com) First Monday in May. Runners from across
the globe come to compete but it's also a people's event,
with a walk and fun run as well.

Cathedral Quarter Arts Festival (☎ 9023 2403;
www.cqaf.com) Twelve days of drama, music, poetry,
street theatre and art exhibitions in and around the
Cathedral Quarter. Held in early May.

August

Féile an Phobail (☎ 9031 3440; www.feilebelfast
.com) Said to be the largest community festival in Ireland,

the Féile takes place in West Belfast over 10 days in early
August. Events include an opening carnival parade, street
parties, theatre performances, concerts and historical tours
of the City and Milltown cemeteries.

October

Belfast Festival at Queen's (☎ 9066 7687; www
.belfastfestival.com) The UK's second-largest arts festival
held in and around Queen's University during three weeks
in late October and early November.

Halloween Carnival (☎ 9027 0222; www.belfastcity
.gov.uk/events) Held from 27 to 31 October, with special
events across the city, including a carnival parade, ghost
tours and fireworks.

December

Christmas Festivities (☎ 9027 0222; www.belfastcity
.gov.uk/events) A range of events from late November to
31 December, including carol singing, lamplight processions, a street carnival and a huge outdoor ice rink at the
Odyssey Complex.

SLEEPING

From backpacker hostels to the Belfast
Hilton, the range of places to stay is now
wider than ever. The traditional accommodation scene – red-brick B&Bs in
the leafy suburbs of South Belfast and
city-centre business hotels – has been lent
a splash of colour in the form of stylish
hotel-restaurant-nightclub combos (such as
Benedicts and Madisons) and elegant but
expensive boutique hotels set in refurbished
historic buildings (eg TENsq and the Malmaison Hotel).

Most of Belfast's budget and midrange
accommodation is south of the centre, in
the university district around Botanic Ave,
University Rd and Malone Rd. This area is
also crammed with good-value restaurants
and pubs, and is mostly within a 20-minute
walk of City Hall. You can expect to pay
around £7 to £11 for a dorm bed in a hostel, approximately £40 to £55 for a double
room in a good B&B or guesthouse, and
about £60 to £90 for a double in a luxurious
midrange hotel. The top end and more expensive midrange places attract a business
clientele during the week, and usually offer
lower rates at weekends (Friday to Sunday
nights).

Book ahead in summer or during busy
festival periods. The Belfast Welcome
Centre will make reservations for a fee
of £2.

City Centre

BUDGET

Linen House (Paddy's Backpackers; ☎ 9058 6400; www.belfasthostel.com; 18-20 Kent St; dm £6.50-9, s/d £15/24; P ✗ ⬜) This independent hostel is housed in a former linen factory in the Cathedral Quarter, about a 15-minute walk from the ferry terminal. It comes well recommended by readers, though it lacks the cosy personal feel of Arnie's (right) and the Ark (see right). It has two big kitchens, a laundry and a basement games room.

Belfast International Youth Hostel (☎ 9031 5435; www.hini.org.uk; 22-32 Donegall Rd; dm £9.50-10.50, s/d £18/28; ✗ ⬜ ♿) Belfast's modern HINI hostel is conveniently sited on the Golden Mile, which means it can be a bit noisy at night when the pubs and clubs empty. Recently expanded to cope with extra demand, the hostel has a kitchen, laundry, café and free linen. Take bus No 9A or 9B from East Donegall Sq or Great Victoria St (across from the Europa BusCentre) to Bradbury Pl.

MIDRANGE

Jury's Inn (☎ 9053 3500; www.jurysdoyle.com; Fisherwick Pl, Great Victoria St; r £85-99; ✗) Jury's bland modernity is more than made up for by its top location (only three minutes from City Hall) and good value – fixed room rates apply for anything up to three adults, or two adults and two kids; booking more than 30 days in advance can get rates as low as £39. Breakfast is optional, but costs £8 extra.

Two more chain hotels with flat-rate rooms that can be recommended on price and location rather than character are:

Days Hotel (☎ 9024 2494; www.dayshotelbelfast.co.uk; 40 Hope St; r £60-80; P ✗)

Travelodge (☎ 9033 3555; www.travelodge.co.uk; 15 Brunswick St; r £49; ✗)

TOP END

Malmaison Hotel (☎ 9022 0200; www.malmaison -belfast.com; 34-38 Victoria St; r from £135; ✗) The Malmaison chain of boutique hotels has transformed two beautifully restored Italianate warehouses (originally built for rival firms in the 1850s, and formerly the McCausland Hotel) into a luxurious haven of king-size beds, deep leather sofas and roll-top baths big enough for two, all done up in a decadent décor of black, red, dark chocolate and cream. The kind of hotel where you don't want to leave your room.

TENsq (☎ 9024 1001; www.tensquare.co.uk; 10 South Donegall Sq; d £160-200; P) The designer name says it all – 'ten square' is a former bank building to the south of City Hall that has been given a luxurious feng-shui makeover with dark lacquered wood, cream carpets and low-slung futon-style beds. Magazines such as *Cosmopolitan* and *Conde Nast Traveller* drool over the sumptuous linen and toiletries, and the list of former guests includes Bono, Moby and Brad Pitt.

Europa Hotel (☎ 9032 7000; www.hastingshotels .com; Great Victoria St; s/d from £120/175; P ✗) Belfast's most famous landmark has shaken off its 1970s reputation as the world's most bombed hotel and is now better known as the place where Bill Clinton stayed during his famous visits to Belfast in 1995 and 1998. The monumental, almost Stalinist façade conceals a fully renovated and very comfortable business hotel.

South Belfast

To get to places on or near Botanic Ave, take bus No 7A or 7B from Howard St; for places on or near University and Malone Rds take bus No 8A or 8B from East Donegall Sq; for places close to Lisburn Rd take bus Nos 9A or 9B from East Donegall Sq.

BUDGET

Botanic Lodge Guesthouse (☎ /fax 9032 7682; 87 Botanic Ave; s/d £25/40; ✗) The Botanic is one of the university district's best B&B bargains, a handsome red-brick house where all rooms have TV and a basin, but most bathrooms are shared; the two en-suite doubles cost £45. Winner of the Brighter Belfast Best Guesthouse Award 2004.

Arnie's Backpackers (☎ 9024 2867; www.arnies backpackers.co.uk; 63 Fitzwilliam St; dm £7-8.50; ✗) This long-established hostel is set in a quiet terrace house in the university area, with plenty of lively bars and restaurants nearby. It has basic laundry and cooking facilities and is a bit on the cramped side, but travellers recommend it as a friendly and fun place to stay.

Ark (☎ 9032 9626; www.arkhostel.com; 18 University St; dm £9.50, s/d £22/36; ✗ ⬜) This is a cosy, compact hostel in a pleasant terrace house in a quiet street, with comfortable dorms, a small sitting room, kitchen and laundry facilities. This is a good place to look for temporary work, and long-term accommodation is available.

Elms Village (☎ 9038 1608; qehor@qub.ac.uk; 78 Malone Rd; tw £19-24; ✗) Available from late June to early September, this modern university hall of residence in leafy South Belfast offers standard student rooms with 24-hour reception. Rates include bed linen but not towels, and there are cooking and laundry facilities. Take bus No 8A or 8B from East Donegall Sq.

MIDRANGE

Old Rectory (☎ 9066 7882; info@anoldrectory.co.uk; 148 Malone Rd; s/d £42/60; P ✗) A lovely red-brick Victorian villa set back from the road in peaceful, leafy gardens, this former rectory has four spacious bedrooms, a comfortable drawing room, and posh breakfasts (venison sausages, scrambled eggs with smoked salmon, freshly squeezed OJ). It's a 10-minute bus ride from the centre – the inconspicuous driveway is on the left, just past Deramore Park South. Handy for genealogy buffs researching at the nearby public records office.

Benedicts (☎ 9059 1999; www.benedictshotel.co.uk; 7-21 Bradbury Pl; s £50-60, d £60-75; ✗) Set bang in the middle of the Golden Mile, Benedicts is a modern, style-conscious hotel at the heart of Belfast's nightlife. The rooms are above a huge Gothic bar and restaurant (where you also have breakfast), so don't expect peace and quiet till after 1am.

Crescent Town House (☎ 9032 3349; www.crescent townhouse.com; 13 Lower Cres; s £55-85, d £75-105; ✗ ⚇) Another stylish hotel with a perfect location, the Crescent is an elegant Victorian town house transformed into a den of designer chic, with its finger on the pulse of the city's party zone. Rooms have silky, Ralph Lauren–style décor.

Madison's (☎ 9050 9800; www.madisonshotel.com; 59-63 Botanic Ave; d £70-80; ✗ ⚇) This swish place successfully rolls a designer hotel, bar-restaurant and nightclub into one sharply styled package, pulling in a mixed crowd of tourists, business people and clubbers who just don't want to go home.

Bienvenue Guesthouse (☎ 9066 8003; bienvenue guesthouse@aol.com; 8 Sans Souci Park; s/d £42/55; P ✗ ⌨) Set in a grand Victorian house in a very quiet side street off Malone Rd, the Bienvenue's four en-suite rooms offer hotel-standard accommodation, with period antiques (including a half-tester bed in one room), direct-dial phones, 24-hour reception and daily newspapers.

Marine Guesthouse (☎ 9066 2828; www.marine guesthouse3star.com; 30 Eglantine Ave; s/d £40/55; P ✗) The family-friendly Marine is a large, detached red-brick villa set on a quiet, leafy side street, offering homely B&B in eight spacious en-suite rooms.

Camera Guesthouse (☎ 9066 0026; camera_gh@ hotmail.com; 44 Wellington Park; s/d £48/64; ✗) A cosy, welcoming Victorian B&B with an open fire in the drawing room, the Camera is set in yet another of South Belfast's peaceful, tree-lined terraces. Breakfasts are prepared using organic produce.

Dukes Hotel (☎ 9023 6666; www.welcome-group .co.uk; 65-67 University St; s/d £65/70; ✗) The red-brick Victorian look and Addams Family–style corner tower belie the fact that this is a thoroughly modern place – the 12 bedrooms have been done up in Art Deco style, and the Chinese owners have had the feng-shui experts in so your room should be brimming with positive energy.

Tara Lodge (☎ 9059 0900; www.taralodge.com; 36 Cromwell Rd; s/d £63/70; ✗ P) This B&B is a cut above your average South Belfast guesthouse, with its stylish, minimalist décor, friendly, efficient staff, delicious breakfasts and 18 bright and cheerful bedrooms (with plans for 15 more). Great location too, on a quiet side street just a few paces from the buzz of Botanic Ave.

TOP END

Wellington Park Hotel (☎ 9038 1111; www.welling tonparkhotel.com; 21 Malone Rd; s £75-120, d £80-132; P ✗ ⚇) A modern makeover with sunny yellow décor and designer frills has made the Wellie Park into a family-friendly, business-friendly place that appeals to a wide range of people, and provides all those little luxuries that make you want to come back – overstuffed sofas, bathrobes and slippers, newspapers delivered to your room. The best rates are available by booking online.

Malone Lodge Hotel (☎ 9038 8000; www.malone lodge.com; 60 Eglantine Ave; s £65-95, d £89-119, apt £99-129; P ✗) The centrepiece of an elegant Victorian terrace, the Malone Lodge has pulled in many plaudits for its luxurious but homely rooms, good food and pleasant,

---

AIRPORT ACCOMMODATION

Park Plaza Hotel (☎ 9445 7000; www.park plazabelfast.com; Belfast International Airport, Aldergrove; s/d £75/90; P ✗) Immediately opposite the terminal at Belfast International Airport, the 106-room Park Plaza has a business centre, conference facilities and free courtesy transport to the city centre.

Park Avenue Hotel (☎ 9065 6520; www .parkavenuehotel.co.uk;158HolywoodRd;s/d£75/95; P) The classy 56-room Park Avenue is the nearest hotel to Belfast City Airport (3km away), and 3km east of the city centre.

---

helpful staff. It also offers five-star self-catering apartments (one-, two- and three-bedroom).

Outside the Centre

Farset International (☎ 9089 9833; www.farsetinter national.co.uk; 446 Springfield Rd; s/d £30/40; P ✗) This is a community-run venture in West Belfast, best described as a posh hostel. The bright and cheerful modern complex is set in its own grounds overlooking a small lake, and has 38 en-suite rooms with TV. Rates don't include breakfast (£4 extra per person); you can eat in the restaurant or use the self-catering kitchen.

Dundonald Touring Caravan Park (☎ 9080 9100; www.theicebowl.com; 111 Old Dundonald Rd, Dundonald; camp/caravan sites £9/16; ⊙ Mar-Sep) This small site (22 pitches) in a park next to the Dundonald Icebowl is the nearest camping ground to Belfast, 7km east of the city centre and south of the A20 road to Newtownards.

EATING

In the last five years Belfast's restaurant scene has been totally transformed by a wave of new restaurants whose standards compare with the best eating places in Europe.

City Centre

The main shopping area north of Donegall Sq becomes a silent maze of deserted streets and steel shutters after 7pm, but during the day the many pubs, cafés and restaurants do a roaring trade.

BUDGET

Café Paul Rankin (☎ 9031 5090; 27-29 Fountain St; snacks £1.50-4; ⊙ 7.30am-6pm Mon-Wed, Fri & Sat,

7.30am-9pm Thu) Owned by Northern Ireland's top celebrity chef, this café serves quality coffee, cakes, focaccia, soups, pastas and salads, with comfy benches and sofas for lounging on.

Café Renoir (☎ 9032 5592; 5 Queen St; mains £3-5; ⊙ 9am-5pm Mon-Sat) A café that tempts in hungry shoppers with decent coffee, home-baked bread and a range of filling vegetarian and wholefood dishes.

Ann's Pantry (☎ 9024 9090; 29-31 Queen's Arcade; snacks £1-4; ⊙ 9am-5.30pm Mon-Sat) A tiny bakery set incongruously at the end of an arcade of jewellery shops, Ann's serves superb home-made soups, pies, cakes and mix-your-own sandwiches to take away or sit (OK, squeeze) in.

Charlie's Gourmet Sandwich Bar (☎ 9024 6097; 48 Upper Queen St; £2-3) Another good place for cheap, healthy and filling sandwiches.

MIDRANGE

Apartment (☎ 9050 9777; 2 West Donegall Sq; mains £7-9; ⊙ food served noon-9pm Mon-Sat, noon-6pm Sun) The hottest spot on Donegall Sq – sit in a big brown leather sofa and gaze out at City Hall, or gaze in at all the beautiful people, while tucking into a menu of lightly prepared Mediterranean and Asian fusion cuisine such as a warm salad of crispy squid, chorizo and baby potatoes with lemon and rocket aioli.

White's Tavern (☎ 9024 3080; 2-12 Wine Cellar Entry; mains £4-7; ⊙ food served noon-6pm Mon-Sat) Historic White's, on a cobbled alley between Rosemary and High Sts, has an upstairs dining room decked out in warm brick, wood and copper, serving down-to-earth pub food such as baked potatoes, fish dishes, Irish stew, and sausage and champ. It's also a good place for a pint.

Morning Star (☎ 9023 5986; 17 Pottinger's Entry; mains £5-10; ⊙ food served noon-9pm Mon-Sat) This former coaching inn is famed for its eat-

---

TOP FIVE BELFAST RESTAURANTS

- Beatrice Kennedy's (p577)
- Cayenne (p576)
- Jeffers Gastropub (opposite)
- Restaurant Michael Deane (opposite)
- Roscoff (opposite)

---

all-you-can lunch buffet (£4). The upstairs restaurant features traditional Irish beef (big 700g steaks cost £14), mussels, oysters and eels, as well as more unusual things like Irish-farmed ostrich. It's not a bad place for a drink either.

Altos (☎ 9032 3087; Anderson McCauley Bldg, Fountain St; mains £6-10; ☺ 10am-5pm Mon-Wed, 10am-8pm Thu, 10am-6pm Fri & Sat) This arty, high-ceilinged bistro has giant modern art canvases on the walls. The menu is Mediterranean-Asian-Irish fusion, with the likes of crispy chilli beef, and focaccia with roast veggies and pesto; breakfast is served until 11.15am.

TOP END

Roscoff (☎ 9031 1150; 7-11 Linenhall St; mains £16-22, 2-/3-course lunch £16/20; ☺ noon-2.15pm Mon-Fri, 6-10.30pm Mon-Sat) A muted décor in shades of slate blue, white and dark grey, with polished wood floors and white linen, puts the food squarely centre stage in this sophisticated and smoothly-run restaurant. Part of the Paul Rankin stable, Roscoff takes inspiration from Irish produce and French cuisine, with some intriguing dishes such as crispy braised pigs' cheeks with sherry lentils and roast crêpes, oxtail ravioli with truffled creamed leeks, and 'assiette of offal'.

Deane's Brasserie (☎ 9056 0000; 34-40 Howard St; mains £11-16, 2-course lunch £13; ☺ noon-3pm & 5.30-11pm Mon-Sat) The street-level brasserie beneath Restaurant Michael Deane (see right) is a big, bustling testimonial to the pulling power of fine food. It is packed to the gills day and night with diners enjoying the 'lite' version of the Michelin-starred eatery upstairs.

Cathedral Quarter & Around

John Hewitt Bar & Restaurant (☎ 9023 3768; 51 Donegall St; mains £5-7; ☺ food served noon-3pm Mon-Sat, noon-6pm Fri) Named for the Belfast poet and socialist, this is a modern pub with a traditional atmosphere and a well-earned reputation for excellent food. The menu changes weekly, but includes inventive dishes such as broccoli and Cashel blue cheese fritter with salad and roasted shallot mayo. It's also a great place for a drink.

Nick's Warehouse (☎ 9043 9690; 35-39 Hill St; mains £9-17; ☺ food served noon-3pm Mon-Fri, 6-9.30pm Tue-Sat) A Cathedral Quarter pioneer (opened in 1989), Nick's is an enormous red-brick and blonde-wood wine bar and

---

SOMETHING SPECIAL

Restaurant Michael Deane (☎ 9033 1134; 34-40 Howard St; 2-course dinner £33; ☺ 7-9.30pm Wed-Sat) Chef Michael Deane heads the kitchen in Belfast's only Michelin-starred restaurant, where he takes the best of Irish and British produce – beef, game, lamb, seafood, even black pudding – and gives it the gourmet treatment. Signature dishes include roast scallops with potato bread, black pudding, cauliflower and brown butter, and Irish salmon with salt cod, red pepper, creamed leek and langoustine and champagne velouté. The restaurant (upstairs from Deane's Brasserie) is a romantic, regency boudoir of marble, mirrors, taffeta and crisp, carpet-length table linen, frequented by local and international celebrities – past patrons include rock band U2, TV foodie Loyd Grossman and Belfast-born actor James Nesbitt. The nine-course tasting menu costs £59.

---

restaurant buzzing with happy drinkers and diners. The menu is strong on inventive seafood and veggie dishes, such as char-grilled tuna with mango and cucumber salad and mandarin syrup, and parsley risotto with black olive tapenade, and the wine list is excellent.

Ba Soba (☎ 9058 6868; 38 Hill St; mains £6-11; ☺ noon-2.30pm Mon, noon-11pm Tue-Sat) Bright and breezy Ba Soba is an Asian noodle bar, dishing up fragrant, steaming bowls of Japanese *ramen* (noodle broth), prawn tempura, Thai warm salad, Malaysian curry and a host of other oriental dishes.

Jeffers Gastropub (☎ 9023 2448; 3 Skipper St; mains £13-16; ☺ noon-3pm Mon-Fri, 6-10pm Tue-Sat) This intimate designer pub is aimed more at diners than drinkers, with gourmet dishes such as tartlet of Irish goats' cheese with cured ham and thyme, and crispy cod with risotto of monkfish, chorizo and herbs to tempt the palate in the evening. The lunch menu is upmarket pub grub – beef-and-ale pie with mash, venison sausages with parsnip purée – and beer drinkers are not forgotten; choose from Irish Legbiter ale, Czech Budvar and Belgian Hoegaardern.

McHugh's Bar & Restaurant (☎ 9050 9999; 29-31 Queen's Sq; lunch £5-7, dinner £8-12; ☺ noon-10.30pm Mon-Sat, noon-9pm Sun) This restored pub is a highlight of the Laganside redevelopment project, and boasts one of the city's best bar-restaurants, serving traditional pub grub downstairs and fancier dishes in the restaurant upstairs. The house speciality is oriental stir-fries cooked in a flaming wok. You can also come here for a well-earned drink.

Odyssey Complex

There are a dozen or so eating places in the Odyssey Complex.

Streat (☎ 9045 0807; Odyssey Pavilion; sandwiches £3; ⏰ 9.30am-10pm Mon, 9.30am-11pm Tue & Wed, 9.30am-midnight Thu & Fri, 10.30am-midnight Sat, 11.30am-11pm Sun) One of a city-wide chain, the Streat is a comfortable, modern café serving good coffee, sandwiches and snacks with an Irish twist – where else would you find a champ bar? – and makes a good spot for a pre- or post-cinema cappuccino.

Titanic Bar & Grill (☎ 9076 6990; Odyssey Pavilion; mains £7-12; ⏰ noon-10pm) It was only a matter of time before someone opened a restaurant themed on the *Titanic*, and here it is – ocean-liner décor, lots of artefacts and old photographs, and a menu that's heavy on the seafood. Very family-friendly, with colouring-in stuff and other things to keep the kids occupied.

Golden Mile North

Cayenne (☎ 9033 1532; 7 Ascot House, Shaftesbury Sq; mains £14-18; ⏰ noon-2.15pm Mon-Fri, 6-10.15pm Mon-Thu, 6-11.15pm Fri & Sat) Behind an anonymous frosted-glass façade lurks a funky, award-winning restaurant clad in conceptual art, and serving quality Irish produce prepared with an Asian or Mediterranean twist. Cayenne is owned and operated by TV celebrity chef, Paul Rankin.

Speranza (☎ 9023 0213; 16-19 Shaftesbury Sq; mains £9-12; ⏰ 5-11.30pm Mon-Sat, 3-10pm Sun) A local institution – it's been around for more than 20 years – Speranza is a big, buzzing Italian restaurant that complements the traditional pizzas and pastas with more sophisticated dishes. It doesn't take reservations – join the queue for a pager, then head upstairs for a drink and they'll buzz you when your table's ready.

Archana (☎ 9032 3713; 53 Dublin Rd; mains £6-9; ⏰ noon-2pm & 5pm-midnight Mon-Sat, 5-11pm Sun) A cosy and unpretentious Indian restaurant, Archana offers a good range of vegetarian

dishes from its separate 'Little India' menu. The *thali* – a platter of three curries with naan bread, pakora and dessert – is good value at £13/8 for the meat/veggie version.

Thai Village (☎ 9024 9269; 50 Dublin Rd; mains £8-10; ⏰ noon-2.30pm & 6.30-11pm Mon-Sat, 5.30-11pm Sun) This candle-lit nook serves tasty, and very nearly authentic (spot the bottled chilli sauce and supermarket mushrooms), Thai food, including an excellent selection of vegetarian and vegan dishes. A one-course lunch special costs £7.

Water Margin (☎ 9032 6888; 159-161 Donegall Pass; mains £9-14; ⏰ noon-11pm) You can worship at the altar of Cantonese cuisine in this stylishly converted church, a five-minute walk west of Shaftesbury Sq. Expect authentic Chinese food from the Cantonese chefs and friendly, professional service.

Jenny's Coffee Shop (☎ 9024 9282; 81 Dublin Rd; mains £3-5; ⏰ 9am-5.30pm Mon-Sat) Try out this pleasant little café-sandwich bar serving tasty and filling student nosh.

Golden Mile South

Moghul (☎ 9032 6677; 62a Botanic Ave; mains £6-9; ⏰ noon-2pm & 5-11pm Mon-Thu, 5pm-midnight Fri & Sat, 5-11pm Sun) A traditional Indian restaurant aiming at the student market, Moghul has good-value specials like the weekday lunch *thali* (£4 for two curries, rice and naan bread) and Friday's all-you-can-eat buffet (£6). Grab a table by the window and watch the world go by on Botanic Ave.

Metro Brasserie (☎ 9032 3349; 13 Lower Cres; mains £10-15; ⏰ noon-3pm Mon-Sat, 6-9.30pm Mon-Thu, 6-10pm Fri & Sat, 5-9pm Sun) Located in the Crescent Town House, Metro is a bright and lively wine bar and brasserie with low ceilings, wood floors and wrought-iron railings, with a menu offering French and Asian flavours. The early-bird menu, served 5.45pm to 7.15pm, offers a two-/three-course dinner for £12/14.50.

Maggie May's (☎ 9032 2662; 50 Botanic Ave; mains £3-5; ⏰ 8am-10.30pm Mon-Sat, 10am-10.30pm Sun) This is a homely little café with two rows of cosy wooden booths, colourful murals of old Belfast, and a host of hungover students wolfing down huge fried breakfasts at lunchtime.

Other Place (☎ 9020 7200; 79 Botanic Ave; mains £6-8; ⏰ 8am-11pm) This is another student favourite where you can linger over the Sunday papers amid red-brick, orange-pine

Beatrice Kennedy's (☎ 9020 2290; 44 University Rd; mains £13-16; ☽ 5-10.30pm Tue-Sat, 12.30-2.30pm & 5-8.30pm Sun) This is where Queen's students take their parents for a posh dinner – candle-lit Edwardian drawing-room décor of burgundy, bottle green and bare red brick, with polished floorboards, starched white linen, and brown leather chairs, and a simple menu of superb cuisine, including home-made bread and ice cream. Enjoy dishes such as crisp, airy prawn tempura with cashew nuts, seared salmon with linguine, sun-blush tomatoes, olives and green beans, and a luscious apple crumble with crushed walnut and cinnamon ice cream. There's a separate vegetarian menu, and from 5pm to 7pm you can get a two-course dinner for £12.

and antique *objets*, or damp down a rising hangover with big plates of lasagne, cajun pitta or home-made hamburger.

University

Café Clementine (☎ 9038 2211; 245 Lisburn Rd; mains £9-13; ☽ 9.30am-4.30pm Sun & Mon, 9.30am-10.30pm Tue-Sat) The décor may be pale but interesting – cream walls and curvy plywood chairs with a flash of silvered wallpaper, and red table tops adding a splash of colour to its cheeks – but the menu is rich and full of strong flavours. Dishes include chunky smoked-haddock chowder, and aubergine and shiitake mushroom tart with chilli lime mayo. Enjoy outdoor tables in summer, and an early-bird two-course dinner for £14 including a glass of wine.

Conor Café-Bar (☎ 9066 3266; 11a Stranmillis Rd; mains £8-15; ☽ 9.30am-11pm, dinner from 5pm) Set in the glass-roofed former studio of William Conor, a Belfast artist, this is a relaxing place for a drink or a meal after a visit to the Botanic Gardens or Ulster Museum. The dining area is light and airy, the bar dominated by a portrait of Conor himself, and the menu offers a range of pasta, salads and daily specials such as pan-fried duck breast with braised red cabbage and apple in a cinnamon plum jus.

Bookfinders Cafe (☎ 9032 8269; 47 University Rd; mains £4-5; ☽ 10am-5.30pm Mon-Sat) Tucked away at the back of the bookshop, this is the sort

of smoky, bohemian café where you would expect to find poetry readings…and, during the Belfast Festival (see p571), you do. It's famed among local students for its excellent soup of the day and range of vegetarian dishes.

Café Zinc (☎ 9068 2266; 12 Stranmillis Rd; mains £4-7; ☽ food served 10am-2.30pm Mon-Sat, 5-9pm Mon-Wed, 5-10pm Thu & Fri, 10am-7pm Sun) Brushed steel, blonde wood and sharp styling complement Café Zinc's good-value bistro menu offering everything from bar snacks and sandwiches to steaks and hearty veggie dishes.

Outside the Centre

Cutters Wharf (☎ 9080 5100; Lockview Rd, Stranmillis; lunch £7-9, dinner £8-14; ☽ food served noon-10pm) One of the few bar-restaurants in Belfast with a waterside setting, Cutters Wharf has a terrace overlooking the River Lagan where you can enjoy excellent bar meals – try steak-and-stout sausages with champ and onion gravy, or roast vegetable fettucini – while watching sculls and eights from the nearby rowing club messing about on the river. The colourful, California-themed restaurant upstairs also enjoys river views.

An Caife (☎ 9096 4184; Cultúrlann MacAdam ÓFiaich, 216 Falls Rd; snacks £2-5, dinner mains £6-11; ☽ 9am-9pm Sun-Wed, 9am-1pm Thu-Sat) If you're exploring West Belfast, drop in to the café in the Irish language and arts centre for some good home-cooked food – the menu includes stews, soups, pizzas, cakes, scones and fresh pastries. The evening á la carte menu extends to stir fry of Dublin Bay prawns, chicken with mushroom and tarragon sauce, and strudel of roast Mediterranean vegetables.

DRINKING

Bars are to Belfast what art galleries are to Florence – a distillation of the city's culture and one of the main reasons for visiting. The pub scene is lively and friendly, with the older traditional pubs complemented – and increasingly threatened – by a rising tide of stylish designer bars.

Standard opening hours are 11am or 11.30am to 11pm Monday to Saturday, though pubs with an entertainment licence stay open to 1am or 1.30am, and 12.30pm to 11pm Sunday; some pubs remain closed all day Sunday.

The worst thing about drinking in Belfast is getting past the bouncers on the door –

the huge number of security staff employed in the city means that polite, well-trained doormen are a rarity. Some of the flashier bars have a dress code, usually no training shoes, no jeans and no baseball caps (so that the security cameras can get a clear shot of your face!). A few even specify 'No political tattoos'.

City Centre

Crown Liquor Saloon (☎ 9024 9476; 46 Great Victoria St) Belfast's most famous bar has a wonderfully ornate Victorian interior. Despite being a tourist attraction (see p561), it still fills up with crowds of locals at lunch-time and in the early evening.

Robinson's (☎ 9024 7447; 38-40 Great Victoria St) Next door to the Crown, this is a theme pub spread over four floors with music most nights – from traditional music in **Fibber Magee's** to the latest DJs in the **Mezzanine** club. In the basement is **BT1**, a wine bar aimed at Belfast's young professionals.

Irene & Nan's (☎ 9023 9123; 12 Brunswick St) Named after two pensioners from a nearby pub who fancied themselves as glamour queens, I & N's typifies the new breed of Belfast bar, dripping with designer chic and tempting your taste buds with an in-bar bistro. It's a laid-back place with a 1950s retro theme, good food and good cocktails.

Morning Star (☎ 9023 5986; 17 Pottinger's Entry) One of several traditional pubs hidden away in the pedestrian alleys off High St, the Morning Star dates back to at least 1810 when it was mentioned in the *Belfast News Letter* as a terminal for the Dublin to Belfast stage coach. It has a big sweeping horseshoe bar, and cosy snugs for privacy.

White's Tavern (☎ 9024 3080; 1-4 Wine Cellar Entry) Established in 1630 but rebuilt in 1790, White's claims to be Belfast's oldest tavern (unlike a pub, a tavern provided food and lodging). In those days the River Blackstaff had not been hidden underground and sailing ships would have been moored next to White's – the murals opposite the pub show life here in the 18th century. There's live music most nights, with traditional sessions Monday and Tuesday.

Kelly's Cellars (☎ 9032 4835; 1 Bank St) Kelly's is Belfast's oldest pub (1720), and was a meeting place for Henry Joy McCracken and the United Irishmen when they were planning the 1798 Rising. The story goes that Mc-

Cracken hid behind the bar when British soldiers came for him. The pub features folk and blues bands on Friday and Saturday nights.

McHugh's Bar & Restaurant (☎ 9050 9999; 29-31 Queen's Sq) Built in the early 1700s and restored at a cost of £2 million in 1998, this is the oldest surviving building in Belfast. McHugh's is now a popular bar-restaurant with live music (mostly rock and cover bands) on Friday and Saturday nights and traditional music on Wednesday.

Bittle's Bar (☎ 9031 1088; 103 Victoria St) A cramped and staunchly traditional bar that occupies Belfast's only 'flat iron' building, Brittle's is a 19th-century triangular redbrick building decorated with gilded shamrocks. The wedge-shaped interior is covered in paintings of Ireland's literary heroes by local artist Joe O'Kane. Pride of place on the back wall is taken by a large canvas depicting Yeats, Joyce, Behan and Beckett at the bar with glasses of Guinness, and Wilde pulling the pints on the other side.

Cathedral Quarter & Around

John Hewitt Bar & Restaurant (☎ 9023 3768; 51 Donegall St) The John Hewitt is one of those treasured bars that have no TV and no gaming machines; the only noise here is the murmur of conversation. The bar has gained a reputation for its music sessions – jazz on Friday, folk several nights a week – and is also a venue during the annual Cathedral Quarter Arts Festival (p571).

Northern Whig (☎ 9050 9888; 2 Bridge St) A stylish modern bar set in an elegant Georgian printing works, the Northern Whig's airy interior is dominated by three huge Socialist-Realist statues rescued from Prague in the early 1990s. Its relaxing sofas and armchairs in fashionable chocolate and café-au-lait colours encourage serious afternoon loafing, though the pace hots up considerably after 5pm on Friday and Saturday.

TOP FIVE TRADITIONAL PUBS

- Bittle's Bar (above)
- Crown Liquor Saloon (left)
- Duke of York (opposite)
- Kelly's Cellars (left)
- Morning Star (left)

Duke of York (☎ 9024 1062; 11 Commercial Ct) Hidden away down an alley in the heart of the city's former newspaper district, the snug, traditional Duke was a hang-out for print workers and journalists and still pulls in a few hacks. One claim to fame is that the Sinn Féin leader, Gerry Adams, worked behind the bar here during his student days.

Rotterdam (☎ 9074 6021; 54 Pilot St) Ahh, those three little words that mean so much to the dedicated barfly – cramped, smoky and dark. The Rotterdam is a purist's pub, unrepentantly old-fashioned, wonderfully atmospheric, and famed for the quality of its live music sessions. Jazz, folk, rock or blues plays most nights, and in summer the tables – and the gigs – spill outdoors.

Golden Mile & University

Eglantine (☎ 9038 1994; 32 Malone Rd) The 'Eg' is a local institution, and widely reckoned to be the best of Belfast's student pubs. It serves good beer and good food, and there are DJs spinning most nights except Tuesday, which is the big music and entertainment quiz night. Expect to see the odd stag and hen party stagger through at weekends.

Botanic Inn (☎ 9050 9740; 23-27 Malone Rd) The 'Bot' is the second pillar of Malone Rd's unholy trinity of student pubs, along with the 'Eg' and the 'Welly Park' (Wellington Park). The latter has sadly been renovated into airport-departure-lounge anonymity, but the Bot is still a wild place, with dancing in the upstairs Record Club Wednesday to Saturday (people queue down the street to get in), live folk music in the downstairs bar on Wednesday, and big-screen sport when there's a match on.

Limelight & Katy Daly's (☎ 9032 5942; 17-19 Ormeau Ave) This combined pub and club is a popular venue for live rock bands and indie music, and is recommended locally as the best place for a good old-fashioned, head-banging night out.

Lavery's (☎ 9087 1106; 14 Bradbury Pl) Managed by the same family since 1918, Lavery's is a vast, multilevel, packed-to-the-gills boozing emporium, crammed with drinkers young and old, from students to tourists, businessmen to bikers. The Back Bar has acoustic music on Wednesday and live indie and alternative bands on Thursday, while the

Middle Bar has a DJ every night and the top floor hosts local and guest DJs playing mainstream dance on Saturday (bit of an underage crowd, though).

Empire Music Hall (☎ 9024 9276; 42 Botanic Ave) A converted late-Victorian church with three floors of entertainment, the Empire is a legendary live-music venue, preaching jazz (in the Basement Bar) and stand-up comedy (in the main hall) on Tuesday, blues on Thursday and live bands – tribute bands are a favourite – Friday and Saturday.

Globe (☎ 9050 9848; 36 University Rd) This popular student pub seems to be the karaoke capital of Belfast, with sing-it-yourself sessions almost every night; the pseudo-1970s décor goes well with the wild retro sessions on Wednesday nights. During the afternoons, sport is the order of the day with football or rugby blaring on half a dozen giant screens.

ENTERTAINMENT

The Belfast Welcome Centre issues *Whatabout?*, a free monthly guide to Belfast events. The Thursday issue of the *Belfast Telegraph* has the Nightlife section with club listings, and the Metro section in Friday's *Irish News* covers everything from music to art exhibitions and special events. *Art.ie* is another free monthly that covers the arts scene throughout the whole of Northern Ireland.

The *Big List* (www.thebiglist.co.uk) is a weekly freesheet, published on Wednesday, that covers pubs, clubs and music events in Northern Ireland, although the emphasis is heavily on Belfast. The *Belfast Beat* is a free monthly guide listing what's on where each day of the week. The website www.whereto tonight.com is another useful guide to events and venues.

Cinemas

Queen's Film Theatre (☎ 9097 1097; www.qftbelfast .info; 20 University Sq) A two-screen art-house cinema close to the university, and a major venue for the Belfast Film Festival.

UGC Cinemas (☎ 0870 155 5176; www.ugccinemas .co.uk; 14 Dublin Rd) A convenient city-centre 10-screen multiplex.

Warner Village Cinemas (☎ 0870 240 6020; www .warnervillage.co.uk; Odyssey Pavilion) Belfast's biggest multiplex, with 12 screens and stadium seats throughout; part of the Odyssey Complex.

BELFAST

Gay & Lesbian Venues

Belfast's compact but tentatively expanding gay scene is concentrated in the Cathedral Quarter.

Kremlin (☎ 9080 9700; www.kremlin-belfast.com; 96 Donegall St; admission £4-9; ⊗ 4pm-1am Mon, 4pm-3am Tue-Thu, noon-4am Fri & Sat, noon-3am Sun) Gay-owned and operated, the Soviet-kitsch-themed Kremlin is the heart and soul of Northern Ireland's gay scene. A statue of Lenin guides you into Tsar, the pre-club bar, from where the Long Bar leads into the main clubbing zone, Red Square. There's something going on seven nights a week, but Revolution on Saturday (doors open 8pm) is the flagship club night.

Milk (☎ 9027 8876; www.clubmilk.com; Tomb St) Monday's Forbidden Fruit hardcore club night at Milk presents an extravaganza of drag and cabaret acts hosted by the Kremlin's outrageous drag queen Baroness Titti von Tramp.

Union Street (☎ 9031 6060; www.unionstreetpub .com; 8-14 Union St) A stylish modern bar with retro styling – lots of bare brick and dark wood, and check out the Belfast sinks in the loo – Union Street pulls in a mixed gay and straight crowd, attracted by the laid-back atmosphere and good food. Host to Slosh, a weekly gay club night (till 2.30am).

Some gay-friendly pubs include the **Nest** (☎ 9032 5491; 22-28 Skipper St) and the **John Hewitt** (☎ 9023 3768; 51 Donegall St).

Live Music

Waterfront Hall (☎ 9033 4400; www.waterfront.co .uk; Lanyon Pl) The impressive 2235-seat Waterfront is Belfast's flagship concert venue, hosting local, national and international performers from pop stars to symphony orchestras.

Odyssey Arena (☎ 9073 9074; www.odysseyarena .com; 2 Queen's Quay) The home stadium for the Belfast Giants ice-hockey team is also the venue for big entertainment events like rock and pop concerts, stage shows and indoor sports.

Ulster Hall (☎ 9032 9685; www.ulsterhall.co.uk; Bedford St) The 1862 Ulster Hall is a popular venue for a range of events including rock concerts, lunch-time organ recitals, boxing bouts and performances by the excellent Ulster Orchestra.

Crescent Arts Centre (☎ 9024 2338; www.cres centarts.org; 2-4 University Rd) The Crescent hosts some excellent concerts, from New York jazz to top-rate Irish music, and there's a regular night club (10pm to late, admission £5) on the first Saturday of each month, offering a wide range of live music and entertainment. The Crescent also stages a 10-day literary festival called Between the Lines each March, and a dance festival, City Dance, in June.

Queen's University (☎ 9033 5337; www.music .qub.ac.uk; University Rd) The university's School of Music stages free lunch-time recitals on Thursday and regular evening concerts in the beautiful, hammer beam–roofed **Harty Room** (School of Music, University Sq), and occasional performances in the larger **Sir William Whitla Hall** (University Rd). You can download a programme from the website – click on the Events link on the home page, and then Music@Queens.

King's Hall (☎ 9066 5225; www.kingshall.co.uk; Lisburn Rd) Northern Ireland's biggest exhibition and conference centre hosts a range of music shows, trade fairs and sporting events. It's accessible by any bus along Lisburn Rd or by train to Balmoral Station.

Nightclubs

Club hours are generally 9pm to 3am, with no admittance after 1am.

Milk (☎ 9027 8876; www.clubmilk.com; Tomb St; admission £3-10; ⊗ daily) Set in a converted red-brick warehouse, Milk is one of Belfast's hottest and most sophisticated clubs (dress code: no effort, no entry), where you can dance every night of the week. Monday is gay night Forbidden Fruit, Tuesday is student night (free admission before midnight with student ID), disco, house and electro on Friday and resident and guest DJs on Saturday playing funk, rap and R&B.

La Lea (☎ 9023 0200; www.lalea.com; 43 Franklin St; admission £2-5; ⊗ from 9pm Wed-Sat) Billed as Belfast's most prestigious nightclub, La Lea caters to a cocktail-sipping, style-conscious over-23 crowd (which translates as 'no students'), with a strict door policy to keep out the riff-raff. Impressive décor with space-age lighting and huge Cambodian stone heads.

Thompson's (☎ 9032 3762; www.clubthompsons .com; 3 Patterson's Pl, Arthur St; admission £3-5; ⊗ Tue-Sun) The best night at Thompson's is Friday's Groovilicious, with DJs laying down

(Continued on page 589)

OLIVER STREWE

Tile mosaic at the entrance to the Crown Liquor Saloon (p561), Belfast

OLIVER STREWE

Enjoying a drink in Belfast (p577)

Previous Page: Carrick-a-Rede Rope Bridge (p646), County Antrim

GARETH MCCORMACK

Europa Hotel (p562), Belfast

MARTIN MOOS

Shopping in Belfast (p589)

RICHARD CUMMINS

Irish staples – soda bread and Guinness

Rotunda, City Hall (p560), Belfast

Lagan Weir (p563), Belfast

Red deer (p64)

RICHARD MILLS

Puffin (p64)

RICHARD MILLS

Gannet (p64)

DAVID TIPLING

Nasturtiums growing on a stone wall, County Kerry (p249)

MANFRED GOTTSCHALK

Original growth forest, Killarney National Park (p256), County Kerry

Native heather, Killarney region (p250), County Kerry

Grey seal (p64)

Relaxing in a pub on High St, Galway city (p396)

Cooling off with a beer in County Cork (p204)

Old Guinness bottles at the Guinness Storehouse, Dublin (p100)

One of the many pubs in Ennis (p361), County Clare

JONATHAN SMITH

Talking celluloid over a drink at the Irish
Film Institute (p139), Dublin

Gastronomic offerings (p128), Dublin

OLIVER STREWE

Café culture (p396), Galway city

RICHARD CUMMINS

Selection of Irish cheeses

Olive oil loaf and Ireland's famous soda bread

Hearty Irish fare

Fruit and vegetable stall in Dublin

(Continued from page 580)

everything from electro-funk to breakbeat
to classic acid house; Wednesday's Funka-
rama is student night with hip hop, funk
and classic R&B.

QUB Student Union (☎ 0870 241 0126; www.qub
su-ents.com; Mandela Hall, Queen's Students Union,
University Rd; ☻ Sat) The student union has
various bars and music venues, and in
Shine (www.shine.net) it can boast one of the
city's best club nights – many visiting clubbers have recommended it – with resident
and guest DJs pumping out harder, heavier
dance music than most of Belfast's other
clubs. Student or photo ID required.

m-club (☎ 9023 3131; Manhattan Bar, 23-25 Bradbury
Pl; admission £2-8; ☻ Mon & Thu-Sat) Belfast's biggest club, m-club offers a wild student night
on Thursday (admission £2) and pulls in a
slightly older crowd with Friday's Groovy
Train ('70s disco music) and Saturday's Ab-
solution (dance). Monday is 'rehab night'
with £2 admission and drinks promos.

Sport

Rugby, soccer, Gaelic football and hockey
are played through the winter, cricket and
hurling through the summer. International
rugby and soccer matches take place at
Windsor Park (☎ 9024 4198; off Lisburn Rd), south
of the centre; bus Nos 9A and 9B go that
way. You can see Gaelic football and hurling at **Roger Casement Park** (☎ 9070 5868; An-
dersonstown Rd) in West Belfast. Take bus No
10A, 10B or 10C.

The Belfast Giants ice-hockey team draws
big crowds to the **Odyssey Arena** (☎ 9073 9074;
www.odysseyarena.com; 2 Queen's Quay) at the Odyssey Complex; the season is September to
March.

The **Sports Council** (☎ 9038 1222; www.sportni
.net) provides information on a range of
sporting events.

Theatre & Opera

Grand Opera House (☎ 9024 1919; www.goh.co.uk;
2-4 Great Victoria St; ☻ box office 8.30am-6pm Mon-Sat,
8.30am-9pm Thu) This grand old venue plays
host to a mixture of opera, popular musicals,
and comedy shows. The box office is across
the street on the corner of Howard St.

Lyric Theatre (☎ 9038 1081; www.lyrictheatre.co.uk;
55 Ridgeway St; ☻ box office 10am-7pm Mon-Sat) Located on the riverside south of the Botanic

Gardens, the Lyric stages serious drama
and is a major venue for the Belfast Festival
at Queen's (see p571). Hollywood star Liam
Neeson first trod the boards here.

Group Theatre (☎ 9032 9685; Bedford St; ☻ box office noon-3pm Mon-Fri) This theatre, located above
the foyer in the Ulster Hall, stages work by
local companies from September to June.

Old Museum Arts Centre (☎ 9023 3332; www.old
museumartscentre.org; 7 North College Sq; ☻ box office
9.30am-5.30pm Mon-Sat, 9.30am-7pm before a performance) The Old Museum stages an exciting
programme of drama and comedy, with
occasional prose and poetry readings and
dance performances.

SHOPPING

For general shopping you'll find all the
usual high-street chains and department
stores in the compact central shopping
area north of City Hall. Items particular to
Northern Ireland that you may like to look
out for include fine Belleek china, linen
(antique and new) and Tyrone crystal.

Newer shopping districts include the
ultra-hip Lisburn Rd (from Eglantine Ave
out to Balmoral Ave) – a straggling strip
of red-brick and mock-Tudor façades lined
with fashion boutiques, interior design
shops, art galleries, delicatessens, espresso
bars, wine bars and chic restaurants – and
the unexpected concentration of designer
fashion shops (about a dozen of them) on
Bloomfield Ave in East Belfast.

Wicker Man (☎ 9024 3550; 14 Donegall Arcade;
☻ 9am-5.30pm Mon-Wed, Fri & Sat, 9am-9pm Thu, 1-5pm
Sun) This shop sells a wide range of contemporary Irish crafts and gifts, including silver
jewellery, glassware and knitwear.

Craftworks (☎ 9024 4465; 40 Bedford St; ☻ 9.30am-
5.30pm Mon-Wed, Fri & Sat, 9.30am-8.30pm Thu) At
this specialist of top-quality crafts from all
over Ulster, you'll find beautifully made designer knitwear, linen shirts, leather-wear,
ceramics, *bodhráns* (traditional goatskin
drums), textiles and jewellery.

Workshops Collective (☎ 9020 0707; 1a Lawrence
St; ☻ 10am-5.30pm Mon-Fri, 11am-4pm Sat) You can
buy paintings, sculpture, furniture and
crafts direct from the artist at this collection
of arts and crafts studios housed in an old
mews courtyard near the university.

Fresh Garbage (☎ 9024 2350; 24 Rosemary St;
☻ 10.30am-5.30pm Mon-Wed, Fri & Sat, 10.30am-8pm
Thu) Easily recognised by the glumfest of

BELFAST

goths hovering outside the door, this place has been around for 20 years but remains a cult favourite for hippie and goth clothes and Celtic jewellery.

Oakland Antiques (☎ 9023 0176; 135 Donegall Pass; ✆ 10am-5.30pm Mon-Sat) Donegall Pass, east of Shaftesbury Sq, has six antiques shops. Oakland is the biggest, with a huge collection of Georgian, Victorian and Edwardian furniture, silver, porcelain and clocks.

Archive's Antique Centre (☎ 9023 2383; 88 Donegall Pass; ✆ 10.30am-5.30pm Mon-Fri, 10am-6pm Sat) This is a warren of curios and collectables spread over three floors, with Irish silver, brass, pub memorabilia, militaria, books and light fittings.

Tiso (☎ 9023 1230; 12-14 Cornmarket; ✆ 9.30am-5.30pm Mon, Tue, Fri & Sat, 10am-5.30pm Wed, 9am-8pm Thu) Make tracks to Tiso for hiking, climbing and camping gear and outdoor clothing.

Surf Mountain (☎ 9024 8877; 12 Brunswick St; ✆ 9am-5.30pm Mon-Sat) Yo dude – come and join the goatee-stroking, nad-scratching crew checking out Surf Mountain's skate and snowboard gear.

Black & Lizars (☎ 9032 1768; 8 Wellington Pl; ✆ 9am-5.30pm Mon-Sat) The place to go for all your photographic needs, both film and digital.

Other good places to shop for Irish crafts and traditional Irish music include **Cultúrlann MacAdam ÓFiaich** (☎ 9023 9303; 216 Falls Rd; ✆ 9am-5.30pm Mon-Fri, 10am-5.30pm Sat) and **Conway Mill** (☎ 9024 7276; 5-7 Conway St; ✆ 10am-4pm Mon-Fri).

GETTING THERE & AWAY
Air
There are direct flights from Dublin and most British cities to the convenient **Belfast City Airport** (☎ 9093 9093; www.belfastcityairport .com; Airport Rd). Most flights from the Republic, Britain, Amsterdam, Brussels and New York land at **Belfast International Airport** (☎ 9448 4848; www.bial.co.uk; Aldergrove), 30km northwest of the city. For details of flights and fares, see p695.

The only airline office in Belfast is **British Airways** (☎ 0845 722 2111; 1 Fountain Centre, College St).

Boat
The giant catamaran car ferries operated by **Steam Packet Company** (☎ 0870 552 3523; www .steam-packet.com) and serving the Isle of Man, Heysham and Liverpool (England) dock at

Donegall Quay, a short distance from the city centre.

The terminal for **Stena Line** (☎ 0870 520 4204; www.stenaline.co.uk) car ferries from Stranraer in Scotland is 2km north of the city centre; head north along York St, and turn right into Dock St (just past the Yorkgate Centre). Other car ferries to and from Scotland dock at Larne, 30km north of Belfast (see p697).

Norse Merchant Ferries (☎ 0870 600 4321; www .norsemerchant.com) between Belfast and Liverpool dock at the Victoria terminal, 5km north of town. Take the M2 motorway north and turn right at junction No 1.

For more information on ferry routes and prices, see p697.

Bus
Belfast has two bus stations. The main Europa BusCentre is behind the Europa Hotel and next door to Great Victoria St Station, reached via the Great Northern Mall beside the hotel. It's the main terminus for buses to Derry, Dublin and destinations in the west and south of Northern Ireland. The smaller **Laganside BusCentre** (Oxford St), near the river, is mainly for buses to County Antrim, eastern Down and the Cookstown area.

There are **information desks** (✆ 7.45am-6.30pm Mon-Fri, 8am-6pm Sat) at both bus stations, where you can pick up regional bus timetables, and you can contact **Translink** (☎ 9066 6630; www.translink.co.uk) for timetable and fares information.

Typical one-way fares from Belfast:

Service	Fare	Duration	Frequency
Armagh	£6.20	1¼	hourly Mon-Fri, eight daily Sat, three Sun
Ballycastle	£8.20	2¾	four daily Mon-Fri, two Sat
Bangor	£2.70	¾	half-hourly Mon-Sat, eight Sun
Derry	£8.80	1¾	hourly Mon-Sat, six Sun
Dublin	£13.10	3	seven daily Mon-Sat, six Sun
Downpatrick	£4.30	1	at least hourly Mon-Sat, five Sun
Enniskillen	£8.60	1	hourly Mon-Sat, four Sun
Newcastle	£5.60	1¼	13 daily Mon-Fri, nine Sat, six Sun

Eurolines (☎ 9033 7002) runs a daily coach service between Belfast and London (one way/return £70/107, 14½ hours) via the Stranraer ferry, Dumfries, Carlisle, Preston, Manchester and Birmingham. The ticket office is in the Europa BusCentre.

For information on bus fares, durations and frequencies in Ireland, see p700.

Train

Trains to Dublin and all destinations in Northern Ireland depart from Belfast's **Central Station** (East Bridge St), east of the city centre. Trains for Portadown, Lisburn, Bangor, Larne Harbour and Derry depart from **Great Victoria St Station** (Great Northern Mall), next to the Europa BusCentre.

For information on fares and timetables, contact **Translink** (☎ 9066 6630; www.translink.co.uk). The **NIR Travel Shop** (☎ 9023 0671; Great Victoria St Station; 9am-5pm Mon-Fri, 9am-12.30pm Sat) books ferries, Dublin Rail Breaks and Scotland Rail Breaks (for Glasgow and Edinburgh).

Typical train fares from Belfast:

Service	Fare	Duration	Frequency
Bangor	£3.10	½	half-hourly
Derry	£8.20	2¼	8 daily
Dublin	£22	2	8 daily
Larne Harbour	£3.90	1	hourly
Newry	£6.30	¾	7 daily
Portrush	£6.80	1¾	8 daily

On Sundays you can buy a Sunday Day Tracker ticket (£4.50), which allows unlimited travel on all scheduled train services within Northern Ireland.

For more information on the train network in Ireland, see p704.

GETTING AROUND

Belfast possesses that rare but wonderful thing – an integrated public-transport system, with buses linking both airports to the central train and bus stations and to the ferries.

To/From the Airports

Belfast International Airport is 30km northwest of the city. The AirBus service (No 300) connects it with the Europa BusCentre (one way/return £6/9, 30 minutes, every 30 minutes) between 6am and 10.30pm. A taxi costs about £25.

The more convenient Belfast City Airport is only 6km northeast of the centre. There's a shuttle bus from the terminal to nearby Sydenham train station, where you can catch a train to Central Station (£1.20, 10 minutes, every 30 minutes), Botanic Station in the popular university area, or Great Victoria St (15 minutes). The AirLink Bus (No 600) links the terminal with the Europa BusCentre (£2, 20 minutes, every 40 minutes) between 6.30am and 10pm. The taxi fare to the city centre is about £7.

For details of the Airporter bus linking both airports to Derry, see p635.

To/From the Ferry Terminals

You can walk from Donegall Quay to City Hall in about 15 minutes. Alternatively, Laganside BusCentre is only a five-minute walk away, where you can catch the Airlink bus (No 600) to Central Station, Donegall Sq and the Europa BusCentre (70p). There is no public transport to the Stena Line and Norse Merchant ferry terminals.

Trains to the ferry terminal at Larne Harbour depart from Great Victoria St Station (see p652).

Bicycle

National Cycle Network route No 9 runs through central Belfast, mostly following the western bank of the River Lagan.

You can hire bikes from **McConvey Cycles** (☎ 9033 0322; www.mcconveycycles.com; 183 Ormeau Rd; 9am-6pm Mon-Sat, till 8pm Thu) and **Life Cycles** (☎ 9043 9959; www.lifecycles.co.uk; 36-37 Smithfield Market; 10am-5.30pm Mon-Sat) for around £10 a day, or £40 a week.

Bus

Metro (☎ 9066 6630; www.translink.co.uk) operates the bus network in Belfast. An increasing number of buses are low-floor, 'kneeling' buses with space for one wheelchair.

Buy your ticket from the driver (change given); fares range from £1 to £1.50 depending on distance. The driver can also sell you a 3-2-1 Day Ticket (£3), giving unlimited bus travel within the City Zone all day Monday to Saturday. Cheaper versions allow travel any time after 10am Monday to Saturday (£2), or all day Sunday (£1).

Most city bus services depart from various stops on and around Donegall Sq, at

City Hall. You can pick up a free bus map (and buy tickets) from the **Metro kiosk** (8am-5.30pm Mon-Fri) at the northwest corner of the square.

If you plan on using city buses a lot, it's worth buying a **Smartlink Travel Card** (available from the Metro kiosk, the Belfast Welcome Centre, the Europa and Laganside BusCentres). The card costs an initial fee of £1.50, plus 90p per journey – you can get it topped up with as many journeys as you want, as often as you want. Alternatively, you can get seven days' unlimited travel for £14.50. When you board the bus, you simply place the card on the ticket machine, and it automatically issues a ticket.

If you arrive by train at Central Station, your rail ticket entitles you to a free ride into the city centre on any Metro, Airlink or Ulsterbus No 500 service.

Car & Motorcycle

A car can be more of a hindrance than a help in Belfast, as parking is restricted in the city centre. For on-street parking between 8am and 6pm Monday to Saturday you'll need to buy a ticket from a machine; the cost is 25p per 15 minutes and there's a maximum stay of one hour. For longer periods, head for one of the many multistorey car parks that are dotted around the city centre.

Major car hire agencies in Belfast:

Avis (www.avisworld.com) City (9024 0404; 69-71 Great Victoria St); Belfast City Airport (9045 2017); Belfast International Airport (9442 2333)

Budget (www.budget-ireland.co.uk) City (9023 0700; 96-102 Great Victoria St); Belfast City Airport (9045 1111); Belfast International Airport (9442 3332)

Europcar (www.europcar.com) City (9031 3500; 159-161 University St); Belfast City Airport (9045 0904); Belfast International Airport (9442 3444)

Hertz (www.hertz.co.uk) Belfast City Airport (9073 2451) Belfast International Airport (9442 2533)

The Ireland-wide agency **Dooley Car Rentals** (9445 2522; www.dooleycarrentals.com; 175 Airport Rd, Belfast International Airport, Aldergrove) is reliable and offers good rates – around £155 a week for a compact.

Taxi

For information on the black cabs that ply the Falls and Shankill Rds, see p566. Regular black taxis have yellow plates back and front (£2.50 minimum fare) and can be hailed on the street.

Minicabs are cheaper but you have to order one by phone. Companies to call include **Fona Cabs** (9023 3333), **Value Cabs** (9080 9080) and **Sure Cabs** (9076 6666).

Train

There are local trains every 20 or 30 minutes connecting Great Victoria St and Central Stations via City Hospital and Botanic Stations. There's a flat fare of £1 for journeys between any of these stops.

AROUND BELFAST

LISBURN & AROUND

The southwestern fringes of Belfast extend as far as Lisburn (Lios na gCearrbhach), 12km southwest of the city centre. Like Belfast, Lisburn grew rich on the proceeds of the linen industry in the 18th and 19th centuries. This history is celebrated in the excellent **Irish Linen Centre & Lisburn Museum** (9266 3377; Market Sq; admission free; 9.30am-5pm Mon-Sat), housed in the fine 17th-century Market House.

The museum on the ground floor has displays on the cultural and historic heritage of the region, while upstairs the award-winning 'Flax to Fabric' exhibition details the fascinating history of the linen industry in Northern Ireland – on the eve of WWI Ulster was the largest linen-producing region in the world, employing some 75,000 people.

There are plenty of audiovisual and hands-on exhibits – you can watch weavers working on Jacquard looms and even try your hand at spinning flax.

Lisburn Tourist Information Centre (9266 0038; Lisburn Sq; 9.30am-5pm Mon-Sat) is on the town's newly renovated main square.

Bus No 21 from Belfast's Europa BusCentre, and Nos 523 and 532 from Queen St, go to Lisburn (£2, 30 minutes, hourly), or catch the train (£2.50, 30 minutes) from either Belfast Central or Great Victoria St Stations.

ULSTER FOLK & TRANSPORT MUSEUMS

Two of Northern Ireland's finest **museums** (9042 8428; www.magni.org.uk; Cultra, Holywood; per museum adult/child £5/3, combined ticket for both £6.50/3.50; 10am-6pm Mon-Sat, 11am-6pm Sun Jul-Sep, 10am-5pm Mon-Fri, 10am-6pm Sat, 11am-6pm Sun Mar-Jun, 10am-4pm

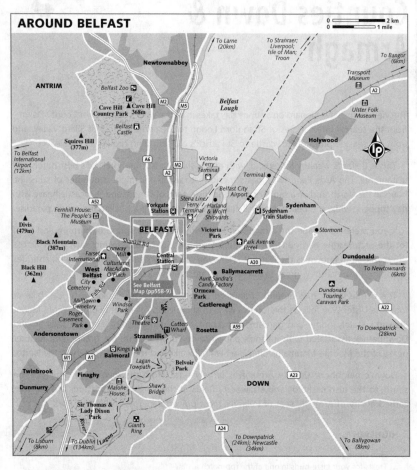

AROUND BELFAST

Mon-Fri, 10am-5pm Sat, 11am-5pm Sun Oct-Feb) lie close to each other on either side of the A2.

On the south side is the Folk Museum, where farmhouses, forges, churches and mills, and a complete village have been reconstructed, with human and animal extras combining to give a strong impression of Irish life over the past few hundred years. From industrial times, there are red-brick terraces from 19th-century Belfast and Dromore. In summer, thatching and ploughing are demonstrated and there are characters dressed in period costume.

On the other side of the road is the Transport Museum, a sort of automotive zoo with displays of captive steam locomotives, rolling stock, motorcycles, trams, buses and cars.

Highlight of the car collection is the stainless steel–clad prototype of the ill-fated DeLorean DMC, made in Belfast in 1981. The car was a commercial disaster but achieved fame in the *Back to the Future* films.

Most popular is the SS *Titanic* display, which includes the original design drawings for the *Olympic* and *Titanic*, photographs of the ship's construction and reports of its sinking. Most poignant are the items of pre-sailing publicity, including an ad for the return trip that never was.

Buses to Bangor stop nearby. Cultra Station on the Bangor train line is within a 10-minute walk. There are car parks at the rural, town and transport sections, but then there's a lot of walking.

BELFAST

Counties Down & Armagh

The view from Slieve Donard on a sunny day takes in all the varied treasures of County Down – from the seal-haunted shores of Strangford Lough to the secluded fold of Silent Valley, and from the seaside prom of Newcastle to St Patrick's old stamping ground of Lecale.

This is Belfast's wealthy hinterland, with its fair share of Northern Ireland's best hotels and restaurants. The Ards Peninsula boasts the lowest rainfall and highest number of sunshine hours in the North, and on a summer weekend the resorts of Bangor and Newcastle heave with day trippers, while the beaches of Ballyhalbert and Tyrella are a bucket-and-spade paradise.

If you prefer to escape the crowds, choose midweek in the spring or autumn and head for the picturesque harbour towns of Portaferry and Strangford, facing each other across the scenic strait known as the Narrows. Here you can enjoy peaceful coastal walks, antiques shopping in Greyabbey, great seafood restaurants and welcoming pubs.

The gentle landscapes around Strangford Lough are ideal for exploring by car, bike or foot (the Ulster Way follows the lough's western shore), and offer plenty of interest in Mount Stewart's stately home and gardens, Nendrum's ancient monastery, and the sites around Downpatrick associated with Ireland's patron saint. Further south, the granite and heather peaks of the Mourne Mountains offer the best hill walks and mountain scenery in the North.

Down's neighbour County Armagh is largely rural, from the low, rugged hills of the south, to the lush orchards and strawberry fields of the north. Its attractions are the trim cathedral city of Armagh, seat of Ireland's most powerful clergy, and Navan Fort.

HIGHLIGHTS

- **Fine Dining**
  Treats for your taste-buds in one of the top-notch restaurants in the pretty village of Hillsborough (opposite)

- **Country House**
  A stroll through the stately halls and exquisite gardens of Mount Stewart (p602) near Greyabbey

- **Chill Out**
  Winding down and watching the world go by in picturesque Portaferry (p600)

- **Country Hike**
  Hikes in the granite hills of the Mourne Mountains (p611)

- **Blast from the Past**
  The compact cathedral city of Armagh (p617) and nearby Navan Fort (p620)

Greyabbey ★
Hillsborough ★
Portaferry ★
Navan Fort ★ ★ Armagh
Mourne Mountains ★

| ■ POPULATION: 652,000 | ■ AREA: 4696 SQ KM |

COUNTY DOWN

CENTRAL COUNTY DOWN

South of Belfast is pastoral countryside, with only the rough moorland of Slieve Croob, southwest of Ballynahinch, breaking the flatness of the terrain. The attractive towns of Hillsborough and Banbridge lie on the main A1 road from Belfast to Newry.

Hillsborough

pop 2400

Hillsborough is a name familiar to British ears as the official residence of the Secretary of State for Northern Ireland – Hillsborough Castle is used to entertain visiting heads of state (US presidents George W Bush and Bill Clinton have both enjoyed its hospitality). It's also the Queen's official residence when she is in Northern Ireland.

The elegant little town of Hillsborough (Cromghlinn) was founded in the 1640s by Colonel Arthur Hill, who built a fort here to quell Irish insurgents. Fine Georgian architecture rings the square and lines Main St.

The **Hillsborough Tourist Information Centre** (☎ 9268 9717; tic.hillsborough@lisburn.gov.uk; the Square; ☽ 9am-5.30pm Mon-Sat year round, 2-6pm Sun Jul & Aug) is in the Georgian courthouse in the centre of the village.

SIGHTS & ACTIVITIES

The town's main attraction is **Hillsborough Castle** (☎ 9268 2244; Main St; adult/child £5/3.50; ☽ grounds & state rooms 11am-4.30pm Sat, mid-Apr–mid-Sep), a rambling, two-storey, late-Georgian mansion built in 1797 for Wills Hill, the first marquess of Downshire, and extensively remodelled in the 1830s and 1840s. The castle is closed to the public during official visits and state events.

At the bottom of Main St is a statue of Arthur Hill, fourth marquess of Downshire, opposite a tree-lined avenue leading to **St Malachy's Parish Church** (Main St; admission free; ☽ 9am-5.30pm Mon-Sat), one of Ireland's most splendid 18th-century churches, with twin towers at the ends of the transepts and a graceful spire at the western end.

Close to the church is **Hillsborough Fort** (☎ 9268 3285; Main St; admission free; ☽ 10am-7pm Tue-Sat, 2-7pm Sun Apr-Sep, 10am-4pm Tue-Sat, 2-4pm Sun Oct-Mar). It was built as an artillery fort by Colonel Hill in 1650 and remodelled as a Gothic-style tower house in 1758.

FESTIVALS

Each year around 10,000 people – plus 6000 oysters from Dundrum Bay – converge on the small village for a three-day **Oyster Festival** (www.hillsboroughoysterfestival.com; early Sep), a celebration of local food, drink and general good fun, which includes an international oyster-eating competition. A Norwegian man entered the Guinness Book of records in the 2004 competition having swallowed 187 oysters in three minutes (the existing record was 97). And yes, he topped them off with a few pints of stout.

SLEEPING & EATING

Fortwilliam Country House (☎ 9268 2255; www .fortwilliamcountryhouse.com; 210 Ballynahinch Rd; s/d £40/65; Ⓟ ☒) The house offers B&B in four luxurious rooms stuffed with period furniture – our favourite is the Victorian room, with its rose wallpaper, huge antique mahogany wardrobe and view over the garden. Breakfast includes eggs from the chickens in the yard, with the smell of home-baked wheaten bread wafting from the Aga. Book well in advance.

Plough Inn (☎ 9268 2985; 3 the Square; mains £12-15; ☽ bar lunches noon-2.30pm, bistro noon-2.30pm & 5-9pm, restaurant 6-9.30pm) This fine old pub, with its maze of dark wood-panelled nooks and crannies, has been offering 'beer and banter' since 1758, and also offers fine dining in the restaurant around the back. Stone walls, low ceilings and a roaring fireplace make a cosy setting for an adventurous menu that includes Japanese and Asian influences as well as the expected steak and seafood dishes.

Hillside Bar & Restaurant (☎ 9268 2765; 21 Main St; mains £6-10, 3-course dinner £25; ☽ bar meals noon-2.30pm & 5-9pm, restaurant 7-9.30pm Fri & Sat) This is a homely pub serving real ale (and mulled wine beside the fireplace in winter), with live jazz Sunday evenings and a dinky wee beer garden in a cobbled courtyard out the back. The upstairs restaurant offers formal dining, with crisp white table linen and sparkling crystal, and a menu offering dishes such as lobster tart, roast quail, venison and steak.

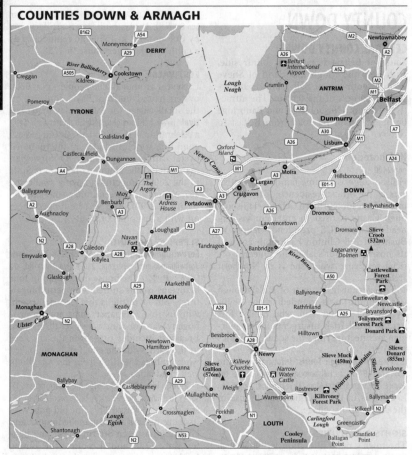

GETTING THERE & AWAY

Bus No 238 from Belfast's Europa BusCentre (£2.70, 25 minutes, at least hourly Monday to Saturday, five Sunday) to Newry stops at Hillsborough (15km southwest of Belfast) and Banbridge.

Banbridge & Around

Banbridge (Droíchead na Banna) is another handsome 18th-century town, whose fortunes were founded on the linen trade.

The town's broad main drag, Bridge St, climbs a steep hill from the bridge across the River Bann (from which the town takes its name) to the unusual **Downshire Bridge** at the top of the hill. A cutting was made in the middle of the street in the 19th century

to lower the crest of the hill and make the climb easier for the Royal Mail coaches, who had threatened to boycott the town because of the difficulty of scaling the incline.

On the opposite side of the river stands the **Crozier Monument**, which is adorned with four idiosyncratically sculpted polar bears. Captain Francis Crozier (1796–1848), a native of Banbridge, was commander of HMS *Terror* and froze to death in the Arctic during Sir John Franklin's ill-fated expedition in search of the Northwest Passage. Crozier lived in the fine blue and grey Georgian house across the road from the statue.

Banbridge is the starting point for the **Brontë Homeland Drive**, a signposted route

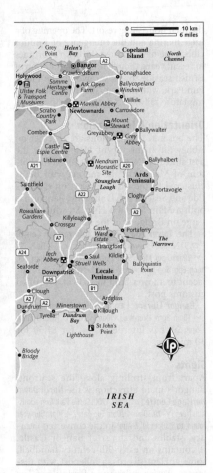

along the Bann valley to Rathfriland, 16km to the southeast. Patrick Brontë, father of the famous literary sisters, was born and brought up here, and the locals like to think that her father's tales of the Mourne Mountains inspired the bleak setting for Emily's classic *Wuthering Heights*. Milking this tenuous connection for all it's worth is the **Brontë Homeland Interpretive Centre** (☎ 4062 3322; Ballyroney; adult/child £3/2; ☽ noon-4.30pm Fri-Sun mid-Mar–Sep) in the former Drumballyroney School and Church, off the B10 road 13km southeast of Banbridge, where Patrick taught and preached. His birthplace is at Emdale, 6km west of here, near the B3 road between Rathfriland and Loughbrickland.

Bus No 238 from Belfast's Europa Bus-Centre (£4.60, 50 minutes, at least hourly Monday to Saturday, five Sunday) to Newry stops at Hillsborough and Banbridge (15km southwest of Hillsborough).

Saintfield & Around
Saintfield is a pretty and prosperous little town, a popular weekend destination for visitors from Belfast who come to browse its dozen or so antique shops and tearooms.

Rowallane Garden (☎ 9751 0131; Crossgar Rd, Saintfield; adult/child £3.10/1.30 Mar-Oct, admission free Nov-Feb; ☽ 10am-8pm May-Sep, 10am-4pm Oct-Apr, closed 24 Dec–1 Jan), 2km south of Saintfield, is renowned for its spectacular spring displays of rhododendrons and azaleas, which thrive behind a windbreak of Australian laurels, hollies, pines and beech trees. The walled gardens feature rare primulas, blue Himalayan poppies, plantain lilies, roses, magnolias and delicate autumn crocuses.

Saintfield is 16km south of Belfast, on the A7 Downpatrick road.

Legananny Dolmen
This is perhaps Ulster's most famous Stone Age monument. It's a strangely elegant tripod dolmen, looking as if some giant's hand has dropped the capstone delicately atop the three slim uprights. Its elevated position on the western slopes of Slieve Croob (532m) gives it an impressive view to the Mourne Mountains.

Legananny is a challenge to find without the aid of a 1:50,000 scale map. Heading south from Ballynahinch along the B7 to Rathfriland, go through the hamlets of Dromara and Finnis, then look out for a minor road on the left (signposted Legananny Dolmen). Continue for a further 3km, through a crossroads, and look for another road on the left (a signpost is there, but difficult to spot). Continue over the hill for 2km, then turn left again at a farm. There's a parking place 50m along, and the dolmen is 50m uphill on the adjacent farm track.

BELFAST TO BANGOR
The coastal region stretching east from Belfast to Bangor and beyond is commuter territory for the capital, and home to many of the North's wealthiest citizens – it's known locally as the 'Gold Coast'. The attractive **North Down Coastal Path** follows the shore from Holywood

SOMETHING SPECIAL

Old Inn (☎ 9185 3255; www.theoldinn.com; 15 Main St, Crawfordsburn; r £75-105; **P**) The picturesque Old Inn, in the pretty village of Crawfordsburn, was established in 1614, making it Ireland's oldest hotel. The part-thatched hostel has hosted many famous names through the centuries, including the young Peter the Great (tsar of Russia), Dick Turpin (highwayman), former US president George Bush Sr, and a veritable roll call of literary figures including Swift, Tennyson, Thackeray, Dickens, Trollope and CS Lewis. The rooms, ranging in atmosphere from chintzy to antique, have bags of character – for £200 a night you can rent your own private cottage, complete with log fire and four-poster bed – and the inn's oak-panelled **Restaurant 1614** (3-course dinner £26; ☽ 7-9.30pm Mon-Sat, 12.30-2.30pm Sun) is one of Northern Ireland's best.

train station to Bangor Marina (15km), and continues east to Orlock Point.

See also the Ulster Folk and Transport Museums (p592).

Crawfordsburn Country Park

Just over 3km west of Bangor, off the B20 at Helen's Bay, **Crawfordsburn Country Park** (☎ 9185 3621; South Bridge Rd, Helen's Bay; admission free; ☽ 9am-8pm Apr-Sep, 9am-4.45pm Oct-Mar) offers a number of woodland and coastal walks. **Grey Point Fort** (☎ 9185 3621; admission free; ☽ noon-4pm 1st Sat of month Apr-Sep) is an early-20th-century gun emplacement with command post and lookout station. The 30-tonne six-inch coastal defence gun has been trained on Belfast Lough since 1904, though never fired in anger.

Access to the park is by the B2 Belfast to Bangor bus or by train to Helen's Bay Station, a wonderful little Victorian station dating from 1865 and built by the Marquess of Dufferin, who owned the surrounding estate.

BANGOR

pop 57,700

Bangor is to Belfast what Brighton is to London – a seaside resort and party town where the city slickers go to let their hair down. The Belfast to Bangor train line was built in the late 19th century to connect the capital with the then flourishing resort. The opening of a huge marina and the emergence of a minor club scene have boosted the town's fortunes in recent years, though the kitsch tradition of British seaside towns survives in the Pickie Fun Park, with its swan-shaped pedalos and miniature railway.

Orientation & Information

The bus and train stations are together on Abbey St, at the top of Main St near the **post office** (☎ 9145 0150; 143 Main St). At the bottom of Main St is the marina with B&Bs clustered to the east and west on Queen's Pde and Seacliff Rd. Unusually, Bangor has both a Main St and a High St, which converge on Bridge St at the marina.

The **Tower House Tourist Information Centre** (☎ 9127 0069; www.northdown.gov.uk; 34 Quay St; ☽ 10am-7pm Mon, 9am-7pm Tue-Fri, 10am-4pm Sat, noon-6pm Sun Jul & Aug, reduced hrs rest of year) is adjacent to a tower built in 1637 as a fortified customs post.

Bangor Library (☎ 9127 0591; 80 Hamilton Rd; ☽ 10am-8pm Mon-Wed, 10am-5pm Fri, 10am-1pm & 2-5pm Sat) has Internet access for £1.50 for 30 minutes.

Sights

Apart from strolling along the seafront, Bangor's main attraction is the **North Down Heritage Centre** (☎ 9127 1200; Castle Park Ave; admission free; ☽ 10.30am-4.30pm Tue-Sat, 2-4.30pm Sun year round, to 5.30pm Jul & Aug) in the converted laundry, stables and stores of Bangor Castle. It contains an early-9th-century handbell, some ancient swords, a milepost with distances in Irish miles and a facsimile of *The Antiphonary of Bangor*, a small 7th-century prayer book and the oldest surviving Irish manuscript (the original is housed in Milan's Ambrosian Library). There's also an interesting section on the life of William Percy French (1854–1920), the famous entertainer and songwriter. The centre is in Castle Park, west of the train and bus stations.

The fishing village of Groomsport on the eastern edge of town has a picturesque harbour, overlooked by **Cockle Row Cottages** (☎ 9145 8882; admission free; ☽ 11.30am-5.30pm daily Jul & Aug, 1.30-5.30pm Mon-Fri, 1-5pm Sat & Sun Jun & 1-15 Sep, 1-5pm Sat & Sun May & 16 Sep–Oct), one of which is restored as a typical fisherman's home of 1910.

Sleeping

Cairn Bay Lodge (☎ 9146 7636; www.cairnbaylodge .com; 278 Seacliff Rd; s £35-40, d £70; P ⊠) This lovely, seaside, B&B villa overlooking Bally-holme Bay, east of the marina, oozes Edwardian elegance, with wood-panelled lounge and dining room, and five old-world en-suite bedrooms.

Bangor Bay Inn (☎ 9127 0696; www.bangorbayinn .com; 10-12 Seacliff Rd; s £45-65, d £65-90; P) This cosy 15-room hotel overlooking the marina combines business-class comfort with a homely atmosphere, a friendly bar and a good restaurant. The more expensive rooms have sunset views across the harbour.

Pierview House B&B (☎ 9146 3381; osborne1948@ aol.com; 28 Seacliff Rd; s/d £25/44; P ⊠) This B&B is only a short walk east of the tourist office. Some of the five bedrooms have sea views; the nicest have a bay window on the 1st floor with a comfy sofa from which to enjoy the view.

Clandeboye Lodge Hotel (☎ 9185 2500; www .clandeboyelodge.com; 10 Estate Rd; s £85-95, d £95-105; P ⊠) Looking a little like a modern, red-brick church set amid landscaped gardens on the southwest edge of town, the recently upgraded Clandeboye offers informal luxury – big rooms, bathrobes, champagne and chocolates – plus a log fire in winter and a drinks terrace in summer.

Eating

Genoa's (☎ 9146 9253; 1a Seacliff Rd; mains £9-17; ☺ 10.30am-2.30pm & 6-9.30pm Mon-Fri, 10.30am-10pm Sat, noon-8pm Sun) This is a cosy little nook of stone, brick and pine, tucked into the former Harbour Master's office across the street from the tourist office. The menu features local seafood, steak and venison, and there's a separate vegetarian menu.

Rioja (☎ 9147 0774; 119 High St; mains £8-13; ☺ noon-2.30pm & 5-9.30pm Mon-Fri, noon-10pm Sat & Sun) Enjoy a relaxed bistro with terracotta tiles and candle-lit tables offering a range of Spanish, French and Italian dishes including seared baby squid with a chilli-lentil broth, and braised lamb shank with a rosemary jus. It's unlicensed, so if you want a bottle of the eponymous wine, BYOB (corkage £1).

Shanks (☎ 9185 3313; The Blackwood, 150 Craw-fordsburn Rd; 3-course dinner £45; ☺ 12.30-2.30pm & 7-10pm Tue-Fri, 7-10pm Sat) This Michelin-starred restaurant, at the Blackwood Golf Club, has a Terence Conran interior decorated with David Hockney paintings, and a mouthwatering gourmet menu. Chef Robbie Millar uses Irish and French produce as well as game from the local Clandeboye estate to turn out dishes such as roast venison with chestnuts, apple, madeira and thyme, and fillet of beef with wild mushroom and truffle cappuccino.

Coyle's Restaurant (☎ 9127 0362; 44 High St; mains £8-13; ☺ 5-9pm Tue-Sat) Located upstairs from a busy music bar, this place is surprisingly intimate and inviting, with wood panelling, mirrored walls and subdued lighting. The menu focuses on well-prepared and well-presented local favourites such as potato and leek soup, shepherd's pie, lamb stew, and grilled lobster and chips.

Entertainment

Jenny Watts (☎ 9127 0401; 41 High St; ☺ 11-1am Mon-Sat, noon-11pm Sun) Bangor's oldest bar (established 1780) is a traditional pub with a beer garden out back. It pulls in a mixed-age crowd, offering folk music on Tuesday nights, easy listening on Thursday, clubbing (upstairs) on Friday and Saturday, and jazz on Sunday afternoon. It also serves good pub grub, and kids are welcome at meal times.

Café Ceol (☎ 9146 8830; 17-21 High St; admission £2-6; ☺ 7pm-1am Wed-Fri, 7pm-1.45am Sat) Bangor's biggest and busiest nightclub has recently been given a sleek and sexy makeover – new club venue Mint features dance, house, funk and R&B on Saturday nights, while Wednesday is student night (free entry with student ID). The main Café Ceol venue has an '80s night on Thursday and cheesy disco music on Friday.

Getting There & Away

Ulsterbus No B2 runs from Belfast's Laganside Bus Centre to Bangor (£2.70, 50 minutes, half-hourly Monday to Saturday, eight Sunday). From Bangor, bus No 3 goes to Donaghadee (£2, 25 minutes, hourly Monday to Saturday, five Sunday); bus No 6 goes to Newtownards (20 minutes, half-hourly).

There's also a regular train service to Bangor from Belfast Central Station (£3.50, 30 minutes, half-hourly).

ARDS PENINSULA

The low-lying Ards Peninsula (An Aird) is the finger of land that encloses Strangford Lough, pinching against the thumb of the

Lecale Peninsula at the Portaferry Narrows. The northern half of the peninsula has some of Ireland's most fertile farmland, with large expanses of wheat and barley, while the south is a landscape of neat fields, white cottages and narrow, winding roads. The eastern coast has some good sandy beaches.

Donaghadee
pop 4800

Donaghadee (Domhnach Daoi) was the main ferry port for Scotland until 1874, when the 34km sea-crossing to Portpatrick was superseded by the Stranraer–Larne route. Its harbour walls were designed by John Rennie in 1819 and completed by his son, Sir John Rennie, who also designed several of London's bridges. Now it's fast becoming a commuter town for Belfast.

The town claims to be home to Ireland's oldest pub – **Grace Neill's** (☎ 9188 4595; 33 High St), which dates from 1611. Among its 17th-century guests was Peter the Great, tsar and later emperor of Russia, who stopped for lunch in 1697 on his grand tour of Europe. In the 19th century, John Keats found the place 'charming and clean' but was 'treated to ridicule, scorn and violent abuse by the local people who objected to my mode of dress and thought I was some strange foreigner'.

From June to September **Nelson's Boats** (☎ 9188 3403; www.nelsonsboats.co.uk) runs boat trips to Copeland Island (adult/child £3/2, departure 2pm daily, weather permitting), which was abandoned to the birds at the turn of the 20th century. There are also sea-angling trips (£7 per person, departures at 10.30am and 7pm), with all tackle and bait provided.

SLEEPING & EATING
Herdstown House (☎ 9188 3773; 9 Hogstown Rd; s/d £25/45; P ✗) The old 18th-century farmhouse offers family-friendly B&B in a country setting, 1.5km west of Donaghadee on the A48 towards Newtownards.

Pier 36 (☎ 9188 446; 36 the Parade; lunch £7-9, dinner £11-16; ✆ food served noon-2.30pm & 6.30-9.30pm) An excellent pub with a big brick and terracotta dining room at the back, dominated by a yellow Raeburn stove that turns out home-baked bread and the daily roast. The hearty menu includes soups, stews, sausage and champ, mussels, seafood, steaks and a good range of veggie dishes.

Grace Neill's Bar & Grill (☎ 9188 4595; 33 High St; mains £9-14; ✆ food served noon-2.30pm & 5.30-9pm Mon, noon-2.30pm & 6-9.30pm Tue-Sat, 12.30-2.30pm & 5.30-8pm Sun) This bright, pleasant bistro in a modern building at the back of the old pub serves up Asian- and French-influenced dishes made with fresh Irish produce. You can also enjoy bar meals in the modern Library Bar, with its bookshelves, gas fire and leather sofas.

East Coast
The A2 runs along the east coast of the peninsula through the seaside villages and permanent caravan parks of Millisle, Ballywalter and Ballyhalbert, and the ugly fishing harbour of Portavogie. The best **beaches** are the Long Sand, immediately south of Ballywalter, and the seawater lagoon (enclosed by a stone dike for safe bathing) at Millisle.

Approximately 1.5km northwest of Millisle (Oileán an Mhuilinn) is **Ballycopeland Windmill** (☎ 9054 6552; Moss Rd; admission free; ✆ 10am-1pm Wed & Thu, 2-6pm Tue & Fri-Sun Jul & Aug), a late-18th-century corn mill that remained in commercial use until 1915 and has been restored to full working order.

Portaferry
pop 2300

Portaferry (Port an Pheire), a neat huddle of streets around a medieval tower house, is the most attractive town on the Ards Peninsula, looking across the turbulent Narrows to the matching tower house in Strangford. A renowned marine biology station on the waterfront uses the lough as an outdoor laboratory; you can investigate the local marine life yourself at the nearby Exploris aquarium. There are some good coastal walks, and in fine weather you can sit outside the pubs on the waterfront and watch the comings and goings of yachts and the ferry.

The **Portaferry Tourist Information & Visitor Centre** (☎ 4272 9882; tourism.portaferry@ards-council .gov.uk; Castle St; ✆ 10am-5pm Mon-Sat, 2-6pm Sun Easter-Sep) is in a restored stable near the tower house.

SIGHTS & ACTIVITIES
You can take a look at **Portaferry Castle** (admission free; ✆ 10am-5pm Mon-Sat, 2-6pm Sun Easter-Sep), a small 16th-century tower house beside the visitor centre, which together with the tower house in Strangford used to control sea traffic through the Narrows.

SOMETHING SPECIAL

Narrows (☎ 4272 8148; www.narrows.co.uk; 8 Shore Rd; s/d £70/90; **P** ⊠) One of our favourite places to stay in the whole of Northern Ireland, the award-winning Narrows has 13 stylish but unfussy, not-quite-minimalist bedrooms, all sunny and west-facing and every one of them with a sea view. The **restaurant** (lunch £6-9, dinner £11-15; ☽ noon-3pm daily, 7-9pm Mon-Thu, 7-9.30pm Fri, 6-9.30pm Sat, 6.30-8.30pm Sun) is as relaxed and informal as the accommodation, with top-quality food simply prepared, home-baked bread, and a good wine list. Dishes include local mussels in a white wine and cream broth, grilled lobster with garlic butter and asparagus, and slow-roasted pork belly with caramelised onions and puréed peas.

Next to the tower house is the outstanding state-of-the-art aquarium, **Exploris** (☎ 4272 8062; www.exploris.org.uk; Castle St; adult/child £6.50/3.75; ☽ 10am-6pm Mon-Fri, 11am-6pm Sat, noon-6pm Sun Apr-Aug, 10am-5pm Mon-Fri, 11am-5pm Sat, 1-5pm Sun Sep-Mar), with displays of marine life from Strangford Lough and the Irish Sea. Touch tanks allow visitors to stroke and hold rays, starfish, sea anemones and other sea creatures. Exploris also has a seal sanctuary where orphaned, sick and injured seals are nursed back to health before being released into the wild.

Walk up to **Windmill Hill** above the town, topped by an old windmill tower, for a good view over the Narrows to Strangford. The Vikings named this stretch of water Strangfjörthr, meaning 'powerful fjord', because when the tide turns, as it does four times a day, 400,000 tonnes of water per minute churn through the gap at speeds up to eight knots (15km/h). You get some idea of the current's remarkable strength when you see the ferry being whipped sideways by the tide.

There are pleasant **walks** along the shore, north to Ballyhenry Island (accessible at low tide), and south to the National Trust nature reserve of Ballyquintin Point, good for bird-watching, seal-spotting, or just admiring the view of the Mourne Mountains.

Des Rogers (☎ 4272 8297) and **John Murray** (☎ 4272 8414) organise fishing and bird-watching trips, as well as pleasure cruises on the lough (around £75/150 a half/full day) for up to six people.

SLEEPING & EATING

Barholm (☎ 4272 9598; www.barholmportaferry.co.uk; 11 The Strand; dm £12-13; ☽ year-round; **P**) You get hostel-style accommodation inside a Victorian house in a superb seafront location opposite the ferry slipway, with a spacious kitchen, laundry facilities and a big, sunny conservatory for breakfast (£3.75 extra). It's popular with groups, so be sure to book ahead.

Adair's B&B (☎ 4272 8412; 22 the Square; s/d £18/36; ⊠) Mrs Adair's friendly and good-value B&B is an anonymous-looking house right on the main square (there's no sign outside; look for No 22), with three spacious rooms – a single, a double and a family room.

Fiddler's Green (☎ 4272 8393; www.fiddlersgreen portaferry.com; 10-12 Church St; s/d £30/50; **P**) This popular pub and restaurant provides B&B in four homely bedrooms – one has a four-poster bed (£75 a night) – neatly decorated with pine furniture and paintings, and serves up a stonking cooked breakfast. The pub has traditional music sessions every Friday, Saturday and Sunday night, and the nautical-themed restaurant, the **Quarterdeck** (mains £7-12; ☽ 6-9pm Thu-Sun), offers seafood specials, char-grilled steaks, roast lamb and a handful of Far Eastern dishes.

Portaferry Hotel (☎ 4272 8231; www.portaferry hotel.com; 10 The Strand; s/d £70/110; **P** ⊠) Converted from a row of 18th-century terrace houses, this charming seafront hotel is as traditional and old-fashioned as the Narrows is hip and modern; ask for a room with a waterside view.

GETTING THERE & AWAY

Ulsterbus Nos 9 and 10 travel from Belfast to Portaferry (£4.90, 1¼ hours, nine daily from Monday to Saturday, three Sunday) via Newtownards, Mount Stewart and Greyabbey. More frequent services begin from Newtownards (some buses go via Carrowdore and don't stop at Mount Stewart and Greyabbey; check first).

The **ferry** (☎ 4488 1637) between Portaferry and Strangford sails every half-hour between 7.30am and 10.30pm Monday to Friday, 8am to 11pm Saturday and 9.30am to 10.30pm Sunday. The journey time is about 10 minutes. The one-way/same-day-return fares are £5.30/8.50 for a car and driver; £3.40/5.30 for motorcyclists and their bikes; and £1.10/1.80 for car passengers and pedestrians.

Greyabbey

pop 700

The village of Greyabbey is home to the splendid ruins of **Grey Abbey** (☎ 9054 6552; Church Rd; admission free; ❂ 10am-7pm Tue-Sat, 2-7pm Sun Apr-Sep, 10am-4pm Sat, 2-4pm Sun Oct-Mar). The Cistercian abbey was founded in 1193 by Affreca, wife of the Norman aristocrat John de Courcy (the builder of Carrickfergus Castle, see p653), in thanks for surviving a stormy sea-crossing from the Isle of Man. The small visitor centre explains Cistercian life with paintings and panels.

The abbey church, which remained in use as late as the 18th century, was the first in Ireland to be built in the Gothic style. At the east end is a carved tomb possibly depicting Affreca; the effigy in the north transept may be her husband. The grounds, overlooked by 18th-century Rosemount House, are awash with trees and flowers on spreading lawns, making this an ideal picnic spot.

Hoops Courtyard, off Main St in the village centre, has a cluster of 18 little shops selling antiques and collectables; opening times vary, but all are open on Wednesday, Friday and Saturday afternoons. **Hoops Coffee Shop** (☎ 4278 8541; Hoops Courtyard, Main St; mains £4-5; ❂ 10am-5pm Wed, Fri & Sat year round, daily in Jul & Aug) is a traditional tearoom, with outdoor tables in the courtyard in fine weather, serving good lunches and wicked cream teas.

An alternative lunch spot is the atmospheric **Wildfowler Inn** (☎ 4278 8260; 1 Main St; mains £5-7.50; ❂ food served noon-2.30pm & 6-9pm), a local pub crammed with wooden beams, copper jugs and ceramic tankards. Tasty bar meals include steaks, burgers, sausage and champ, grilled salmon, and huge, smoking stir-fries.

Mount Stewart House & Gardens

The magnificent 18th-century **Mount Stewart** (☎ 4278 8387; house & gardens adult/child £5.45/2.70; ❂ house noon-6pm daily Jul & Aug, noon-6pm Wed-Mon Sep, 1-6pm Mon & Wed-Fri, noon-6pm Sat & Sun May & Jun, noon-6pm Sat, Sun & public hols mid-Mar–Apr & Oct; ♿) is one of Northern Ireland's grandest stately homes. It was built for the marquess of Londonderry and is decorated with lavish plasterwork, marble nudes and priceless artworks – the portrait of the racehorse Hambletonian by George Stubbs is one of the most important paintings in Ireland.

Much of the landscaping of the beautiful **gardens** (gardens only £4.40/2.30; ❂ 10am-8pm May-Sep, 10am-6pm Apr & Oct, 10am-4pm Nov-Mar; ♿) was supervised in the early 20th century

---

LORD CASTLEREAGH

As you wander around Mount Stewart, spare a thought for Robert Stewart, Lord Castlereagh (1769–1822), whose childhood home this was. Despite going down in history as one of Britain's most accomplished foreign secretaries, during his lifetime he was enormously unpopular with the public who saw him as the spokesman for a violently repressive government. He was savagely attacked in print by liberal reformers, including Daniel O'Connell (see p37) – who denounced him as 'the assassin of his country' – and the poets Percy Bysshe Shelley and Lord Byron. The latter's notorious *Epitaph for Lord Castlereagh* could hardly be bettered for withering contempt:

Posterity will ne'er survey
A nobler scene than this:
Here lie the bones of Castlereagh;
Stop, traveller, and piss!

Castlereagh's father, the first marquess of Londonderry, primed his son's political career in 1790 by buying him a place in the Irish parliament as member for County Down. The campaign cost a cool £60,000, leaving the marquess unable to afford various planned improvements to Mount Stewart.

As Chief Secretary for Ireland in the government of William Pitt, Castlereagh was responsible for quelling the 1798 Rising and for passing the 1800 Act of Union. Later he served as foreign secretary during the Napoleonic wars, and represented Britain at the Congress of Vienna in 1815. Political success did not bring happiness however; while still in office, Castlereagh succumbed to paranoia and depression, and committed suicide by slitting his own throat with a letter knife.

by Lady Edith, wife of the seventh marquess, for the benefit of her children – the Dodo Terrace at the front of the house is populated with unusual creatures from history (dinosaurs and dodos) and myth (griffins and mermaids), accompanied by giant frogs and duck-billed platypuses. The 18th-century **Temple of the Winds** (🕑 2-5pm Sun Apr-Oct) is a folly in the classical Greek style built on a high point above the lough.

Mount Stewart is on the A20, 3km northwest of Greyabbey and 8km southeast of Newtownards. Buses from Belfast and Newtownards to Portaferry (see p601) stop at the gate. The ground floor of the house and most of the gardens are wheelchair accessible.

NEWTOWNARDS & AROUND
pop 27,800

Founded in the 17th century on the site of a 6th-century ecclesiastical centre, Newtownards (Baile Nua na hArda) today is a busy but unexceptional commercial centre. The **Ards Tourist Information Centre** (🕿 9182 6846; tourism@ards-council.gov.uk; 31 Regent St; 🕑 9.15am-5pm Mon-Fri, 9.30am-5pm Sat) is next to the bus station.

There's some fine 18th- and 19th-century architecture in the town, especially along Church St. Most striking of all is the 18th-century **Market House**, which once housed the town's prison – you can ask to see an original cell – and is now home to the **Ards Arts Centre** (🕿 9181 0803; Conway Sq; admission free; 🕑 9am-4pm Mon-Sat), which hosts changing art exhibitions. The square in front of Market House hosts a lively **market** every Saturday, and a traditional harvest fair in September.

The remains of **Movilla Abbey** and its 13th-century church have been almost swallowed up by the forest of gravestones in Movilla Cemetery (on Old Movilla Rd, on the B172 towards Millisle). There are some interesting Knights Templar grave slabs and Freemasonic memorials here.

The bus station is on Regent St, near the tourist office. Bus No 5 goes to Belfast (£2.10, 30 minutes, at least hourly Monday to Friday, nine Saturday, two Sunday), and Nos 9 and 10 run to Portaferry (see p601); some go via Mount Stewart and Greyabbey.

Scrabo Country Park
Newtownards is overlooked by the prominent landmark of Scrabo Hill, 2km south-

west of town. It was once the site of extensive prehistoric earthworks, which were largely removed during construction of the 41m **1857 Memorial Tower** (🕿 9181 1491; admission free; 🕑 10.30am-6pm Sat-Thu Apr-Sep) in honour of the third marquess of Londonderry. Inside there's a slide show on Strangford Lough and a 122-step climb to the superb viewpoint at the top of the tower – on a clear day you can see Scotland, the Isle of Man, and even Snowdon in Wales. The disused sandstone quarries nearby provided material for many famous buildings, including Belfast's Albert Memorial Clock Tower (see p561).

Somme Heritage Centre
The grimly fascinating **Somme Heritage Centre** (🕿 9182 3202; www.irishsoldier.org; 233 Bangor Rd; adult/child £3.75/2.75; 🕑 10am-5pm Mon-Fri, noon-5pm Sat & Sun Jul & Aug, 10am-4pm Mon-Thu, noon-4pm Sat Apr-Jun & Sep, 10am-4pm Mon-Thu, noon-4pm 1st Sat of month Oct-Mar) vividly illustrates the horrors of the WWI Somme campaign of 1916 from the perspective of men of the 10th (Irish), 16th (Irish) and 36th (Ulster) divisions. It's a high-tech show with short films and nothing celebratory about the exhibits, intended as a memorial to the men and women who died. A photographic display commemorates the suffragette movement and the part that women played in WWI.

The centre is 3km north of Newtownards on the A21 towards Bangor. The No 6 Bangor to Newtownards bus passes the entrance every half-hour or so.

Ark Open Farm
Opposite the Somme Heritage Centre, on the other side of the dual carriageway, is the **Ark Open Farm** (🕿 9182 0445; www.thearkopenfarm.co.uk; 296 Bangor Rd; adult/child £3.10/2.50; 🕑 10am-6pm Mon-Sat, 2-6pm Sun). Hugely popular with families, the farm has displays of rare breeds of sheep, cattle, poultry, llamas and donkeys. Kids get to stroke and hand-feed the lambs, piglets and ducklings.

STRANGFORD LOUGH
Connected to the open sea only by a 700m-wide strait (the Narrows) at Portaferry, Strangford Lough (Loch Cuan) is almost a lake. Its western shore is fringed by humpbacked islands – half-drowned mounds of boulder clay (called drumlins) left behind by ice sheets at the end of the last Ice Age.

On the eastern shore, the drumlins have been broken down by the waves into heaps of boulders that form shallow tidal reefs (known locally as 'pladdies').

Large colonies of grey seals frequent the lough, especially at the southern tip of the Ards Peninsula where the exit channel opens out into the sea. Birds abound on the shores and tidal mudflats, including brent geese wintering from Arctic Canada, eider ducks and many species of wader. Strangford Lough oysters are a local delicacy.

Castle Espie Wildfowl & Wetlands Centre

About 2km southeast of Comber, off the Downpatrick road (A22), is the **Castle Espie Wildfowl & Wetlands Centre** (☎ 9187 4146; www .wwt.org.uk; Ballydrain Rd, Comber; adult/child £4.60/2.75; ⊙ 10.30am-5pm Mon-Fri, 11am-5.30pm Sat & Sun Mar-Oct, 11am-4pm Mon-Fri, 11am-4.30pm Sat & Sun Nov-Feb). It's a haven for large gatherings of geese, ducks and swans – around 75% of the world's population of light-bellied brent geese spend the winter here – and a paradise for fledgling ornithologists. The best time to visit is in May and June, when the grounds are overrun with goslings, ducklings and cygnets.

SLEEPING & EATING

Anna's House B&B (☎ 9754 1566; www.annashouse .com; Tullynagee, 35 Lisbarnett Rd, Lisbane; s/d £35/60; P ⊠) Just west of Lisbane, Anna's is a secluded country house set in a superb garden with views over a little lake (free angling for residents). There are three en-suite rooms, and all the food is organic – the breakfast menu ranges from an Ulster fry through kippers or smoked salmon omelette to fresh fruit salad.

Old School House Inn (☎ 9754 1182; www.theold schoolhouseinn.com; Ballydrain Rd, Comber; s/d £45/65; P ⊠) Just south of Castle Espie on the road to Nendrum, the characterful Old Schoolhouse has 12 luxurious, modern rooms, each named for a former US president. The former classroom, now swathed in shades of deep claret and decorated with old musical instruments, houses an award-winning **restaurant** (3-course dinner £19; ⊙ 7-10pm Tue-Sat, 12.30-2.45pm Sun) serving local produce cooked in French country-kitchen style.

Old Post Office Tearoom (☎ 9754 3335; 191 Killinchy Rd, Lisbane; mains £2-5; ⊙ 9.30am-5pm Mon-Sat) The thatched cottage that once housed the village post office has been lovingly converted into a tearoom and art gallery with cream plaster, bare stone, pine furniture and a wood-burning stove. It serves great coffee and home-baked scones.

Nendrum Monastic Site

The Celtic monastic community of **Nendrum** (admission free; ⊙ 24hr) was built in the 5th century under the guidance of St Mochaoi (St Mahee). It is much older than the Norman monastery at Grey Abbey on the opposite shore and could not be more different. The scant remains provide a clear outline of its early plan. Foundations survive from a number of churches, a round tower, beehive cells and other buildings, as well as three concentric stone ramparts and a monks' cemetery, all in a wonderful island setting. A particularly interesting relic is the stone sundial that has been reconstructed with some of the original pieces. The minor road to Mahee Island from the lough's western shore crosses a causeway to Reagh Island and then a bridge guarded by the remains of 15th-century Mahee Castle.

The small **visitor centre** (☎ 9754 2547; admission free; ⊙ 10am-7pm Tue-Sat, 2-7pm Sun Apr-Sep, 1-6pm Sat, 2-4pm Sun Oct-Mar) screens an excellent video comparing Nendrum to Grey Abbey, and there's some interesting material about the concept of time and how we measure it, presented in child-friendly fashion.

The site is signposted from Lisbane, on the A20 5km south of Comber.

Killyleagh

pop 2200

Killyleagh (Cill O Laoch) is a former fishing village dominated by the impressive **castle** (closed to the public) of the Hamilton family. Built originally by John de Courcy in the 12th century, the Scottish Baronial-style reconstruction of 1850 sits on the original Norman motte and bailey. Outside the gatehouse, a plaque commemorates Sir Hans Sloane, the naturalist born in Killyleagh in 1660, whose collection was the basis for the founding of the British Museum (London's Sloane Square is named after him). The parish church houses the tombs of members of the Blackwood family (marquesses of Dufferin), who married into the Hamiltons in the 18th century.

SLEEPING & EATING

Killyleagh Castle Towers (☎ 4482 8261; www.killy leagh.com; High St; 4-person apt per week £245-295; **P**) If you ever fancied staying in a castle, Killyleagh's three gatehouse towers (complete with spiral staircases and roof terraces) are available for weekly rental, including use of the castle gardens, swimming pool and tennis court. The two smaller towers sleep four and the largest sleeps five.

Dufferin Coaching Inn (☎ 4482 8229; www.duffer incoachinginn.co.uk; 35 High St; s/d £37.50/65; **✗**) The Dufferin has six spacious en-suite rooms, some with four-poster beds, and a library-cum-reception area with many books on the region. The inn has two bars – the comfortably old-fashioned **Dufferin Arms** (bar meals £6-11) and the larger Stables Bar downstairs – and the cosy, candle-lit **Kitchen Restaurant** (mains £9-14; ☷ 5.30-8.30pm Mon-Thu, 5.30-9.30pm Fri & Sat, 12.30-2.30pm Sat & Sun). Bands play on Thursday, Friday and Saturday, with traditional sessions on Saturday afternoon.

GETTING THERE & AWAY

Bus No 11 runs from Belfast to Killyleagh (£3.70, one hour, 10 daily Monday to Friday, five Saturday, two Sunday) via Comber. No 14 continues from Killyleagh to Downpatrick (20 minutes, eight daily Monday to Friday, five Sunday).

DOWNPATRICK

pop 10,300

Downpatrick (Dún Pádraig) is named after Ireland's patron saint, who is associated with numerous places in this corner of Down – on St Patrick's Day (17 March) the town is crammed with crowds of pilgrims and revellers.

Downpatrick is County Down's administrative centre. It was settled long before the saint's arrival, his first church here being

---

> **TOP FIVE ROMANTIC HIDEAWAYS IN NORTHERN IRELAND**
>
> ▪ Bushmills Inn (p643)
> ▪ Clandeboye Lodge Hotel (p599)
> ▪ Malmaison Hotel (p572)
> ▪ Narrows (p601)
> ▪ Old Inn (p598)

---

constructed inside the *dún* (fort) of Rath Celtchair, an earthwork still visible to the southwest of the cathedral. The place later became known as Dún Pádraig, anglicised to Downpatrick in the 17th century.

In 1176 the Norman John de Courcy is said to have brought the relics of St Colmcille and St Brigid to Downpatrick to rest with the remains of St Patrick, hence the local saying, 'In Down, three saints one grave do fill, Patrick, Brigid and Colmcille'. Later the town declined along with the cathedral until the 17th and 18th centuries, when the Southwell family developed the old town centre you see today. The best of its Georgian architecture is centred on English St and the Mall, which lead up to the cathedral.

Orientation & Information

The bus station is on Market St (the main A25 road south towards Newcastle), on the southern edge of the town centre.

The **Downpatrick Tourist Information Centre** (☎ 4461 2233; www.kingdomsofdown.com; 53a Market St; ☷ 9.30am-7pm Mon-Sat, 2-6pm Sun mid-Jun–Sep, 9.30am-5pm Mon-Fri, 10am-5pm Sat Oct–mid-Jun) is in the St Patrick Centre, just north of the bus station.

Sights

SAINT PATRICK CENTRE

The Saint Patrick Centre houses a multimedia exhibition called **Ego Patricius** (I Am Patrick; ☎ 4461 9000; www.saintpatrickcentre.com; 53a Market St; adult/child £4.90/2.35; ☷ 9.30am-6pm Mon-Sat, 10am-6pm Sun Jun-Aug, 9.30am-5.30pm Mon-Sat, 1-5.30pm Sun Apr, May & Sep, 10am-5pm Mon-Sat Oct-Mar, 9.30am-7pm St Patrick's Day), charting the life and legacy of Ireland's patron saint. Occasionally filled with parties of school kids, the exhibition uses audio and video presentations to tell St Patrick's story, often in his own words (taken from his *Confession*, written in Latin around the year AD 450). At the end is a spectacular widescreen film that takes the audience on a swooping, low-level helicopter ride over the landscapes of Ireland.

DOWN CATHEDRAL

According to legend St Patrick died in Saul, where angels told his followers to place his body on a cart drawn by two untamed oxen, and that wherever the oxen halted, that was where the saint should be buried. They supposedly stopped at the church on the hill of Down, now the site of the Church of

Ireland's **Down Cathedral** (☎ 4461 4922; the Mall; admission free; ⏲ 9.30am-4.30pm Mon-Sat, 2-5pm Sun).

The cathedral is an agglomeration of 1600 years of building and rebuilding. Viking attacks wiped away all trace of the earliest churches, and the subsequent Norman cathedral and monasteries were destroyed by Scottish raiders in 1316. The rubble was used in a 15th-century construction finished in 1512, but after the Dissolution of the Monasteries, it was razed to the ground in 1541. Today's cathedral dates largely from the 18th and 19th centuries, with a completely new interior installed in the 1980s.

In the churchyard immediately south of the cathedral is a slab of Mourne granite with the inscription 'Patric', placed there by the Belfast Naturalists' Field Club in 1900, marking the traditional site of St Patrick's grave.

To reach the cathedral, go up the stairs to the right of the Saint Patrick Centre and turn left at the top, opposite Down County Museum.

DOWN COUNTY MUSEUM

Downhill from the cathedral is the **county museum** (☎ 4461 5218; www.downcountymuseum.com; the Mall; admission free; ⏲ 10am-5pm Mon-Fri, 1-5pm Sat & Sun), housed in the town's restored 18th-century jail. In a cell block at the back are models of some of the prisoners incarcerated there, and details of their sad stories. Displays cover the story of the Norman conquest of Down, but the biggest exhibit of all is outside – a short signposted trail leads to the **Mound of Down**, a good example of a Norman motte and bailey.

The **Mall** itself is the most attractive street in Downpatrick, with some lovely 18th-century architecture, including Soundwell School built in 1733 and a courthouse with a finely decorated pediment.

INCH ABBEY

This **abbey** (☎ 9023 5000; admission free; ⏲ 24hr), built by de Courcy for the Cistercians in 1180 on an earlier Irish monastic site, is visible across the river from the cathedral. The English Cistercians had a strict policy of nonadmittance to Irishmen and maintained this until the end in 1541. Most of the ruins are just foundations and low walls; the neatly groomed setting beside

the marshes of the River Quoile is its most memorable feature.

To get here head out of town for about 1.5km on the A7 Belfast road, then take the first left after crossing the river.

DOWNPATRICK & COUNTY DOWN RAILWAY

This working **railway museum** (☎ 4461 5779; www.downrail.co.uk; Market St; adult/child £4.50/3.50; ⏲ 2-5pm Sat & Sun late Jun–mid-Sep & Dec, St Patrick's Day, Easter, May Day, Halloween) runs steam-hauled trains over a restored section of the former Belfast to Newcastle line. There is a western terminus at Ballydugan, and a northern one close to Inch Abbey, plus a halt next to the grave of King Magnus Barefoot, a Norwegian king who died in battle on this spot in 1103. The ticket price includes a return journey on the train and a tour around the engine shed and signal cabin.

QUOILE COUNTRYSIDE CENTRE

A tidal barrier was built at Hare Island, 3km downstream from Downpatrick, in 1957 to control flooding. The waters enclosed by the barrier now form the Quoile Pondage Nature Reserve, whose ecology is explained at the **Quoile Countryside Centre** (☎ 4461 5520; www .ehsni.gov.uk; 5 Quay Rd; admission free; ⏲ reserve 24hr, visitor centre 11am-5pm daily Apr-Aug, 1-5pm Sat & Sun Sep-Mar). It's in a little cottage beside the ruins of **Quoile Castle**, a 17th-century tower house. There's **bird-watching hide** (⏲ 10am-4pm; ♿) on Castle Island, downstream from the centre.

GUITAR-MAKER TO THE GREATS

Belfast-born George Lowden has been creating guitars in Northern Ireland since the 1970s, and his hand-built instruments have gained a world-wide reputation for excellence – satisfied Lowden owners include Eric Clapton, Van Morrison, Richard Thompson, Mark Knopfler and the Edge. If you're interested in buying one, you can get a tour of the workshop at **Lowden Guitars** (☎ 4461 9161; www.georgelowden .com; 34 Down Business Park, Belfast Rd; ⏲ by prior arrangement Mon-Fri), which was relocated from Newtonards in 2004. However, don't count on getting any change out of £4000.

Sleeping & Eating

Denvir's Hotel & Pub (☎ 4461 2012; www.denvirshotel
.co.uk; 14 English St; s/d £32.50/55; **P**) Denvir's is
an old coaching inn dating back to 1642,
offering B&B in six characterful rooms
with pine floorboards, Georgian windows
and period fireplaces. The homely **restaurant** (mains £8-11; ☺ noon-2.30pm & 5.30-9pm) has
an enormous, original stone fireplace and
serves good wholesome dishes such as Irish
stew, shepherd's pie and local seafood, accompanied by fresh organic vegetables.

Rosebank (☎ 4461 7021; 108 Ballydugan Rd; s/d
£25/45; **P** ✕) You'll get a warm welcome
and a hearty breakfast at this luxurious
modern villa, set in open countryside about
4km southwest of the town centre on the
A25. All three rooms are neat as a pin, and
all have private bathrooms.

Mill at Ballydugan (☎ 4461 3654; www.ballydugan
mill.com; Drumcullen Rd, Ballydugan; s/d £60/75; **P**) This
giant, eight-storey, 18th-century mill build-
ing overlooking Ballydugan Lake has been
restored as a hotel and restaurant, and now
offers 11 atmospheric, en-suite bedrooms
with exposed beams and stone walls. It's 3km
southwest of Downpatrick, off the A25.

Getting There & Away

Downpatrick is 32km south of Belfast. Bus
Nos 15, 15A and 515 depart from the Europa BusCentre in Belfast for Downpatrick
(£4.30, one hour, at least hourly Monday
to Saturday, five Sunday). There's also an
express service, bus No 215 (45 minutes,
hourly Monday to Friday, eight Saturday).

Bus No 240 runs from Downpatrick to
Newry (£4.30, one hour, six daily Monday to Saturday, two Sunday) via Dundrum, Newcastle (£2.90, 25 minutes) and
Hilltown.

AROUND DOWNPATRICK

According to popular tradition, the young
St Patrick was kidnapped from Britain by
Irish pirates and spent six years as a slave
tending sheep (possibly on Slemish; see
p654) before escaping back home to his
family. After religious training, he returned
to Ireland to spread the faith and is said to
have landed on the shores of Strangford
Lough near Saul, northeast of Downpatrick.
He preached his first sermon in a nearby
barn, and eventually retired to Saul after
some 30 years of evangelising.

Struell Wells

These supposedly curative wells are traditionally associated with St Patrick – it is said
he scourged himself here, spending 'a great
part of the night, stark naked and singing psalms' immersed in what is now the
Drinking Well. He must have been a hardy
soul – the well-preserved but chilly 17th-
century bathhouses here look more likely
to induce ill health than cure it! The site
has been venerated for centuries, although
the buildings are all post-1600. Between the
bathhouses and the ruined chapel stands
the Eye Well, whose waters are said to cure
eye ailments.

The wells are in a scenic, secluded glen
2km east of Downpatrick. Take the B1 road
towards Ardglass, and turn left after passing the hospital.

Saul

On landing near this spot in AD 432, St
Patrick made his first convert: Díchú, the
local chieftain, who gave the holy man a
sheep barn (*sabhal* in Gaelic, pronounced
'sawl') from which to preach. West of Saul
village is the supposed site of the *sabhal*,
with a replica 10th-century **church and round
tower** built in 1932 to mark the 1500th anniversary of his arrival.

East of the village is the small hill of **Slieve
Patrick** (120m), with stations of the cross
along the path to the top and a massive
10m-high statue of St Patrick, also dating from 1932, on the summit. The hill is
the object of a popular pilgrimage on St
Patrick's Day.

Saul is 3km northeast of Downpatrick off
the A2 Strangford road.

LECALE PENINSULA

The low-lying Lecale Peninsula is situated east of Downpatrick, isolated by the
sea and Strangford Lough to the north,
south and east, and the marshes of the
Quoile and Blackstaff Rivers to the west.
In Irish it is Leath Chathail, or Cathal's
territory, a region of fertile farmland that
is fringed by fishing harbours, rocky bluffs
and sandy beaches.

Lecale is a place of pilgrimage for Van
Morrison fans – Coney Island, immortalised in his song of the same name, is between Ardglass and Killough in the south
of the peninsula.

Strangford

pop 550

Strangford (Baile Loch Cuan), a picturesque fishing village, is dominated by **Strangford Castle** (☎ 9023 5000; Castle St; admission free), a 16th-century tower house that faces its twin across the Narrows in Portaferry. To get inside, ask for the keys from Mr Seed across the road at 39 Castle St. At the end of Castle St is a footpath called the **Squeeze Gut** that leads over the hill behind the village, with a fine view of the lough, before looping back to Strangford via tree-lined Dufferin Ave (1.5km), or continuing around the shoreline to Castle Ward Estate (4.5km).

Strangford is 16km northeast of Downpatrick. See p601 for details of the car ferry between Strangford and Portaferry.

SLEEPING & EATING

Cuan (☎ 4488 1222; www.thecuan.com; the Square; s/d £50/80; P X) Just around the corner from the ferry slip, the Cuan is a nice old hotel with nine modern en-suite rooms. It also has a **restaurant** (mains £8-14; 7-9.30pm Mon-Sat, noon-2.30pm & 5-9pm Sun) serving local seafood, lamb and beef. A three-course set-menu dinner costs £40 for two, including a bottle of wine.

Castle Ward Estate Camp Site (☎ 4488 1680; 19 Castle Ward Rd; camp/caravan sites £7/12; mid-Mar–Sep) The entrance to this wooded, lough-shore National Trust site is separate from the main estate entrance (closer to Strangford village).

Lobster Pot (☎ 4488 1288; 9-11 the Square; bar meals £5-10, restaurant mains £9-12; noon-9pm Mon-Fri, noon-9.30pm Sat, noon-8pm Sun) This charmingly old-fashioned pub overlooking the harbour has a posh new bistro at the back, with green marble tables and linen napkins, serving excellent seafood – the house speciality is jumo scampi in a light, crispy batter. The weekday three-course lunch (£10) is great value, as is the Sunday carvery (£15 for three courses).

Castle Ward Estate

Castle Ward house enjoys a superb setting overlooking the bay to the west of Strangford, but has a something of a split personality. It was built in the 1760s for Lord and Lady Bangor – Bernard Ward and his wife, Anne – who were a bit of an odd couple. Their widely differing tastes in architecture resulted in an eccentric country residence – and a subsequent divorce. Bernard favoured the neoclassical style seen in the front façade and the main staircase, while Anne leant towards the Strawberry Hill Gothic of the rear façade, which reaches a peak in the incredible fan vaulting of her Gothic boudoir.

The house is now part of the National Trust's **Castle Ward Estate** (☎ 4488 1204; Park Rd; adult/child house & grounds £5.30/2.40, grounds only £3.70/1.70; house & wildlife centre 1-6pm daily Jun-Aug, 1-6pm Wed-Mon May, 1-6pm Sat, Sun & public hols mid-Mar–Apr, Sep & Oct, grounds 10am-8pm daily May-Sep, 10am-4pm daily Oct-Apr). In the grounds you can visit a Victorian laundry museum, the Strangford Lough Wildlife Centre, Old Castle Ward (a fine 16th-century Plantation tower) and Castle Audley (a 15th-century tower house).

Kilclief Castle

Square-jawed and thick-set, **Kilclief Castle** (☎ 9023 5000; Kilclief; admission free; 2-6pm Tue & Fri-Sun, 10am-1pm Wed & Thu Jul & Aug) guards the seaward entrance to the Narrows. This is the oldest tower house in the county, built between 1413 and 1441 for John Cely, the adulterous bishop of Down. It has some elaborate details and is thought to have been the prototype for Ardglass, Strangford and other castles in Lecale.

Kilclief is on the A2, 4km south of Strangford.

Ardglass

pop 2900

Ardglass (Ard Ghlais) today is a small village with a busy fishing harbour, but in medieval times it was a major port and an important trading centre. The legacy of its heyday is the seven tower houses, dating from the 14th to the 16th centuries, that punctuate the hillside above the harbour.

The only one open to the public is **Jordan's Castle** (☎ 9181 1491; Low Rd; admission free; 10am-1pm Tue, Fri & Sat, 2-6pm Wed & Thu Jul & Aug), a four-storey tower near the harbour, built by a wealthy 15th-century merchant at the dawn of Ulster's economic development. The castle now houses a local museum and a collection of antiques accumulated by its last owner.

Ardglass is on the A2, 13km south of Strangford.

SLEEPING & EATING

Margaret's Cottage (☎ 4484 1080; www.margarets cottage.com; 9 Castle Pl; d £40; P ⊠ ⌨) A dinky little flower-bedecked 18th-century cottage (with a modern upper floor), Margaret's is squeezed between Aldo's Restaurant and the ruins of Margaret's Castle. It now offers luxurious B&B accommodation, with four cosy rooms and an open fire in the lounge.

    Aldo's Restaurant (☎ 4484 1315; 7 Castle Pl; mains £9-11; ⊙ 5-10pm daily, plus 12.30-2pm Sun Jun-Aug, 5-10pm Thu-Sun, plus 12.30-2pm Sun Sep-May) A local institution, this cosy Italian restaurant serves excellent seafood, pasta and vegetarian dishes.

    Coneyisland Caravan Park (☎ 4484 1210; 75 Killough Rd; camp/caravan sites £6/10; ⊙ Apr-Nov) The nearest camping ground is this pleasant seaside site just west of Ardglass on the way to Killough.

SOUTH DOWN & THE MOURNE MOUNTAINS

Newcastle

pop 7200

The old-fashioned seaside resort of Newcastle (An Caisleán Nua) enjoys a superb setting on a 5km strand of golden sand at the foot of the Mourne Mountains. The little harbour at the south end of town once served the 'stone boats' that exported Mourne granite from the quarries of Slieve Donard, but the arrival of the railway in the 19th century saw the town's economy shift towards tourism.

    Nice setting, shame about the main street – on summer weekends it's a garish, traffic-choked strip of raucous amusement arcades and fast-food outlets. Nevertheless, the town has a great beach and is a good base for exploring the Mourne Mountains – on foot, by car or by public transport – and in the quiet of winter it regains something of its Victorian composure.

ORIENTATION

As you exit the bus station, Main St stretches ahead towards the mountains, becoming Central Promenade (with the tourist office on the left) and then South Promenade. Turning left out of the bus station leads to a mini-roundabout; straight ahead is the beach, to the right is Downs Rd and the youth hostel, and to the left is the Slieve Donard Hotel.

INFORMATION

Coffee-Net (☎ 4372 7388; 5-7 Railway St; per 30 min £1.50; ⊙ 9am-6pm Mon-Sat) Internet access in the coffee shop in the bus station.

Mourne Heritage Trust (☎ 4372 4059; www.mourne live.com; 87 Central Promenade; ⊙ 9am-5pm Mon-Fri) Books, maps and brochures on the Mourne region, plus information on walking in the Mournes.

Post office (☎ 4372 2651; 6 Railway St) Opposite the bus station.

Tourist information centre (☎ 4372 2222; new castle.tic@downdc.gov.uk; 10-14 Central Promenade; ⊙ 9.30am-7pm Mon-Sat, 1-7pm Sun Jul & Aug, 10am-5.30pm Mon-Sat, 2-5.30pm Sun Sep-Jun) Sells local-interest books and maps, and a range of traditional and contemporary crafts.

SIGHTS & ACTIVITIES

Newcastle's main attraction is the **beach**, which stretches 5km northeast to **Murlough National Nature Reserve** (admission free, car park £3 May-Sep; ⊙ 24hr), where footpaths and boardwalks meander among the grassy dunes, with great views back towards the Mournes.

    Back in town, **Tropicana** (☎ 4372 5034; Central Promenade; adult/child £2.60/2.10; ⊙ 11am-7pm Mon & Wed-Fri, 11am-5pm Tue & Sat, 1-5.30pm Sun Jul & Aug) is a family entertainment centre with outdoor heated fun pools, giant water slides, and paddling pools for toddlers.

    Stretching north of town is the **Royal County Down Golf Course** (☎ 4372 3314; www.royal countydown.org; green fees Mon-Fri/Sun £115/130 Apr-Oct, £55/65 Oct-Mar). The challenging Championship Links – full of blind tee-shots and monster rough – is one of the world's top 10 golf courses, and is open to visitors on Monday, Tuesday, Thursday, Friday and Sunday.

SLEEPING

Beach House (☎ 4372 2345; fax 4372 2817; 22 Downs Rd; s/d £45/70; P ⊠) Enjoy a sea view with your breakfast at the Beach House, an elegant Victorian B&B with three rooms (two en suite) and a balcony (open to all guests) overlooking the beach.

    Harbour House Inn (☎ 4372 3445; www.stone boatrestaurant.com; 4 South Promenade; s/d £30/50; P ⊠) Here is a family-friendly guesthouse with four en-suite rooms overlooking the old 'stone boat' harbour 2km south of the bus station. It also has a popular seafood restaurant.

Newcastle Youth Hostel (☎ 4372 2133; www.hini .org.uk; 30 Downs Rd; dm £11; ☺ 3 Jan–22 Dec) The hostel is only a few minutes' walk from the bus station, housed in an attractive 19th-century villa with sea views. It has 38 beds in four-, six- and seven-bed dorms, a kitchen, laundry and TV room.

Briers Country House (☎ 4372 4347; www.the briers.co.uk; 39 Middle Tollymore Rd; s £25-40, d £40-55; Ⓟ ✗) A peaceful farmhouse B&B with eight en-suite rooms in a country setting, and views of the Mournes, Briers just 1.5km northwest of the town centre (signposted off the road between Newcastle and Bryansford). Huge breakfasts – vegetarian if you like – and evening meals are available in its licensed restaurant.

Hastings Slieve Donard Hotel (☎ 4372 3681; www.hastingshotels.com; Downs Rd; s/d from £135/155; Ⓟ ✗) Established in 1897, the Slieve Donard is a grand, Victorian red-brick pile overlooking the beach, and claims Charlie Chaplin as a former guest. Add £20 to £40 to the room rate for a view of the sea or the Mournes, but ask for a discount in low season and you could get all that luxury for 60% of the full price.

Tollymore Forest Park (☎ 4372 2428; 176 Tully-branigan Rd; camp & caravan sites £9-13; ☺ year round) The nearest camp site is 3km northwest of the town centre, amid the attractive scenery of Tollymore Forest Park. You can hike there (along Bryansford Ave and Bryansford Rd) in 45 minutes.

EATING

Café Maud's (☎ 4372 6184; 106 Main St; mains £3-6; ☺ 9am-9.30pm) Maud's is a bright, modern café with picture windows presenting a view across the river to the Mournes. It serves good coffee, a range of tempting scones and sticky buns, and salads, crêpes, pizza and pasta.

Seasalt (☎ 4372 5027; 51 Central Promenade; lunch mains £5-8, 3-course dinner £21.50; ☺ 10am-6pm Tue-Sun, dinner at 7pm & 9pm Fri & Sat) Escape Newcastle's glut of junk food at this sunny bistro offering everything from organic soups to home-made beef-and-Guinness pie to local seafood. Dinner on Friday and Saturday is a bookings-only, two-sittings affair, with a superb Mediterranean/Asian fusion menu.

Percy French Bar & Restaurant (☎ 4372 3175; Downs Rd; mains £6-10; ☺ food served noon-9.30pm Mon-Sat, 12.30-9pm Sun) Themed after local composer William Percy French, this is an ap-pealing, low-raftered barn of a place, with sea views in summer and a roaring log fire in winter. The menu includes steaks, salads, Mexican and Italian dishes, with the choice of bar meals or a sit-down restaurant.

Strand Restaurant & Bakery (☎ 4372 3472; 53-55 Central Promenade; mains £4-8; ☺ 8.30am-11pm Jun-Aug, 9am-6pm Sep-May) The Strand has been around since 1930, and dishes up great home-made ice cream and cakes, as well as serving all-day breakfast (£1.50 to £4), lunch and dinner in its traditional, seaside, chips-with-everything restaurant.

Campers can stock up on provisions at the **Lidl Supermarket** (3 Railway St; ☺ 9am-7pm Mon-Wed & Fri, 9am-9pm Thu, 9am-6pm Sat, 1-6pm Sun) in the red-brick former train station beside the bus station.

SHOPPING

Hill Trekker (☎ 4372 3842; 115 Central Promenade; ☺ 10am-5.30pm Tue-Sun), at the far south end of town, sells hiking, climbing and camping equipment.

GETTING THERE & AROUND

The bus station is on Railway St. Ulsterbus No 20 runs to Newcastle from Belfast's Europa BusCentre (£5.60, 1¼ hours, 12 daily Monday to Friday, nine Saturday, seven Sunday) via Dundrum. Bus No 37 continues along the coast road from Newcastle to Annalong and Kilkeel (£2.80, hourly, 40 minutes).

Bus No 240 goes from Newry (£3.90, 40 minutes, six daily Monday to Saturday, two Sunday) to Newcastle (inland via Hilltown) and on to Downpatrick (£2.70, 40 minutes). You can also get to Newry along the coast road, changing buses at Kilkeel.

Wiki Wiki Wheels (☎ 4372 3973; 10b Donard St; ☺ 9am-6pm Mon-Sat, 2-6pm Sun) and **Ross Cycles** (☎ 4372 5525; Unit 9, Slieve Donard Shopping Centre, Railway St; ☺ 9.30am-6pm Mon-Sat, 2-5pm Sun), both near the bus station, hire out bikes for around £10/50 per day/week.

Around Newcastle

DUNDRUM

Second only to Carrickfergus as Northern Ireland's finest Norman fortress is **Dundrum Castle** (☎ 9181 1491; Dundrum; admission free; ☺ 10am-7pm Tue-Sat, 2-7pm Sun Apr-Sep, 10am-4pm Sat, 2-4pm Sun Oct-Mar), founded in 1177 by John de Courcy of Carrickfergus (see p653). The original castle was made largely of timber, but De Courcy's successor, Hugh de Lacy, added the massive circular keep in the first years of the 13th century, and the twin-towered gatehouse a few decades later. Occupied by the Maginnis family of Mourne from the 14th to the 17th centuries, it was finally captured by Cromwell who blew it up in 1652.

In mid-August, the streets of Dundrum village, below the castle, fill with musicians, jugglers, fire-eaters and clowns for the annual **All Ireland Busking Competition** (☎ 4375 1528; www.allirelandbuskingcompetition.com).

The **Buck's Head Inn** (☎ 4375 1868; 77-79 Main St; mains £7-10, 3-course dinner £25; ⏱ noon-2.30pm, 5-6.45pm & 7-9.30pm, closed Mon Oct-Apr) is a cosy, traditional restaurant with a modern gourmet menu that features Dundrum oysters, Mourne lamb, Down beef and a selection of vegetarian dishes.

Dundrum is 5km north of Newcastle. Bus No 17 from Newcastle to Downpatrick stops in Dundrum (£1.30, 12 minutes, 10 daily Monday to Friday, three Saturday, two Sunday).

TOLLYMORE FOREST PARK
This scenic **forest park** (☎ 4372 2428; Bryansford; car/pedestrian £4/2; ⏱ 10am-sunset), 3km west of Newcastle, has lengthy walks along the Shimna River and across the northern slopes of the Mournes. The **visitor centre** (⏱ noon-5pm daily Jun-Aug, noon-5pm Sat & Sun Sep-May), in 18th-century Clanbrassil Barn (it looks more like a church), has information on the flora, fauna and history of the park. Note: mountain-biking is not allowed in the park.

If the weather is wet, you can still go rock climbing at **hot rock** (☎ 4372 5354; www.hotrock wall.com; adult/child £3.50/2; ⏱ 10am-5pm Mon & Tue, 10am-10pm Wed-Fri, 10am-6pm Sat & Sun), the indoor climbing wall at Tollymore Mountain Centre. The entrance is on the B180, 2km west of the Tollymore Forest Park exit gate.

CASTLEWELLAN FOREST PARK
A less rugged outdoor experience is offered by **Castlewellan Forest Park** (☎ 4377 8664; Main St, Castlewellan; car/pedestrian £4/2; ⏱ 10am-dusk), with gentle walks around the castle grounds and trout fishing in its lovely lake (a daily permit costs £5).

Outside the park is **Mount Pleasant Horse Trekking Centre** (☎ 4377 8651; www.mountpleasant centre.com; Bannonstown Rd, Castlewellan; per hr £10-12), which caters for both experienced riders and beginners, and offers various guided treks into the park. Short rides, beach rides and pony trekking can also be arranged.

Mourne Mountains
The hump-backed granite peaks of the Mourne Mountains dominate the horizon as you head south from Belfast or Downpatrick towards Newcastle. This is one of the most beautiful corners of Northern Ireland, a distinctive landscape of yellow gorse, grey granite and whitewashed cottages, the lower slopes of the hills latticed with a neat patchwork of dry-stone walls cobbled together from huge, rounded granite boulders.

The hills were made famous in a popular song penned by Irish songwriter William Percy French in 1896, whose chorus, 'Where the Mountains of Mourne sweep down to the sea', captures perfectly their scenic blend of ocean, sky and hillside.

The Mournes offer the best hill walking and rock climbing in the North. Specialist guidebooks include *The Mournes: Walks* by Paddy Dillon and *A Rock-Climbing Guide to the Mourne Mountains* by Robert Bankhead. You'll also need an Ordnance Survey map, either the 1:50,000 Discoverer Series (Sheet No 29: *The Mournes*), or the 1:25,000 Outdoor Pursuits Series (*Mourne Country*).

HISTORY
The crescent of low-lying land on the southern side of the range is known as the Kingdom of Mourne. Cut off for centuries by its difficult approaches (the main overland route passed north of the hills), it developed a distinctive landscape and culture. Neither St Patrick nor the Normans – their nearest strongholds were at Greencastle and Dundrum – ventured here and until the coast road was built in the early 19th century the only access was on foot or by sea.

Apart from farming and fishing, the main industry was the quarrying of Mourne granite. The quarried stone was carried down from the hills on carts to harbours at Newcastle, Annalong and Kilkeel where 'stone boats' shipped it out; kerbstones of Mourne granite are found in Belfast, Liverpool, London, Manchester and Birmingham.

Smuggling provided a source of income in the 18th century. Boats carrying French spirits would land at night and packhorses would carry the casks through the hills to the inland road, avoiding the excise men at Newcastle. The Brandy Pad, an ex-smugglers' path from Bloody Bridge to Tollymore, is today a popular walking route (see opposite).

SIGHTS & ACTIVITIES

At the heart of the Mournes is the beautiful **Silent Valley Reservoir** (☎ 9074 6581; Silent Valley; car/motorcycle £3/2, adult/child pedestrian £1.50/0.50; ◷ 10am-6.30pm Apr-Sep, 10am-4pm Oct-Mar), where the Kilkeel River has been dammed to provide water for Belfast. There are scenic, way-marked walks around the grounds, a **coffee shop** (◷ 11am-6.30pm daily Jun-Aug, 11am-6.30pm Sat & Sun Apr, May & Sep) and an information centre. From the car park a shuttle bus (adult/child return £1.50/0.90) will take you another 4km up the valley to the Crom Dam. It runs daily in July and August, weekends only in May, June and September.

The dry-stone **Mourne Wall** was built between 1904 and 1922 to provide work during a period of high unemployment, and to enclose the catchment area of the Silent Valley and the Annalong River. The waters are diverted to the reservoir via a 3.6km-long tunnel beneath Slieve Binnian (habitation and livestock are banned within the catchment). The spectacular wall, 2m high, 1m thick and over 35km long, marches across the summits of 15 of the surrounding peaks, including the highest, Slieve Donard (853m).

If you fancy a shot at hill walking, rock climbing or canoeing, **Bluelough Mountain & Water Sports Centre** (☎ 4377 0715; www.mountain andwater.com; Grange Courtyard, Castlewellan) offers one-day, have-a-go sessions for individuals, couples and families (around £45 to £80 per person), and Sunday afternoon taster sessions (£10 per person).

FESTIVALS

The Mournes are the venue for various hiking festivals, including the **Mourne International Walking Festival** (www.mournewalking.co.uk) in late June, and the **Down District Walking Festival** in late July.

SLEEPING

Cnocnafeola Centre (☎ 4176 5859; www.cnocnafeola centre.com; Bog Rd, Atticall; dm £12-15; ◷ Feb–22 Dec; **P**) This modern, purpose-built hostel is in the village of Atticall 6km north of Kilkeel, off the B27 Hilltown road, and 3km west of the entrance to Silent Valley. It has a kitchen, laundry and restaurant.

Meelmore Lodge (☎ 4372 6657; www.meelmore lodge.co.uk; 52 Trassey Rd, Bryansford; camp sites per adult/child £3.50/2; **P**) Set on the northern slopes of the Mournes, 5km west of Bryansford village, Meelmore has a basic camp site with hot showers and a coffee shop.

GETTING THERE & AWAY

In July and August only, the Ulsterbus No 405 Mourne Rambler service runs a circular route from Newcastle calling at a dozen stops around the Mournes, including Bryansford (10 minutes), Meelmore (17 minutes), Silent Valley (35 minutes), Carrick Little (40 minutes) and Bloody Bridge (50 minutes). It departs hourly from 10am to 5pm (except 1pm) every day; a £4 all-day ticket allows you to get on and off as many times as you like.

Bus No 34A runs from Newcastle to the Silent Valley gates (30 minutes, four daily Monday to Friday, three Saturday, two Sunday), calling at Donard Park (five minutes) and Bloody Bridge (10 minutes).

Mournes Coast Road

The scenic drive south along the A2 coast road from Newcastle to Newry is the most memorable journey in Down. Annalong, Kilkeel and Rostrevor offer convenient stopping points from which you can detour into the mountains.

As in many parts of the North, someone has fixed signs bearing religious texts to many of the roadside telephone poles. Whoever it was has a sense of humour, though – one reading 'Prepare to meet thy God' appears just before a tricky S-bend.

ANNALONG

The harbour at the fishing village of Annalong (Áth na Long) desperately wants to be picturesque, with an early 19th-century **Corn Mill** (☎ 4376 8736; Marine Park; adult/child £1.90/1.05; ◷ 2-6pm Wed-Mon Apr-Oct, 3-5pm Wed-Mon Nov-Mar) overlooking the river mouth on one side. The effect is spoiled a bit by graffiti and ugly buildings on the other side.

The attractive **Harbour Inn** (☎ 4376 8678; 6 Harbour Dr; bar meals £5-8; ◷ food served 12.30-2.30pm, 5-8pm Sun-Fri, 12.30-9pm Sat) has an upstairs din-

---

CLIMBING SLIEVE DONARD

The rounded form of Slieve Donard (853m), the highest hill in Northern Ireland, looms above Newcastle like a slumbering giant. You can hike to the summit from various starting points in and around Newcastle, but remember – it's a stiff climb, and you shouldn't attempt it without proper walking boots, waterproofs and a map and compass.

On a good day the view from the top extends to the hills of Donegal, the Wicklow Mountains, the coast of Scotland, the Isle of Man and even the hills of Snowdonia in Wales. Two cairns near the summit were long believed to have been cells of St Donard, who retreated here to pray in early Christian times.

From Newcastle (9km, three hours)

This is the shortest but least interesting route. Begin at Donard Park car park, at the edge of town 1km south of the bus station. At the far end of the car park, turn right through the gate and head into the woods, with the river on your left. A gravel path leads up the Glen River valley to the saddle between Donard and Slieve Commedagh. From here, turn left and follow the Mourne Wall to the summit. Return by the same route.

From Bloody Bridge (10km, 3½ hours)

Start from the car park at Bloody Bridge on the A2 coast road 5km south of Newcastle (any bus to Kilkeel will drop you there). From here, an old smugglers' path called the Brandy Pad leads up the valley of the Bloody Bridge River past old granite workings to the saddle south of Slieve Donard. Turn right and follow the Mourne Wall to the summit; cross the wall first, as the best views are to your left. Return by the same route, or descend the Glen River (Rte 1) to Newcastle.

---

ing room with a great view across the harbour to the Mournes.

You can overnight at the **Cornmill Quay Hostel** (☎ 4376 8269; www.cornmillquay.com; Marine Park; dm adult/child £15/10, d £40; ✖ P), set in a pretty little cottage courtyard above the harbour.

KILKEEL

Kilkeel (Cill Chaoil, meaning 'church of the narrow place') takes its name from the 14th-century **Church of St Colman**, whose ruins stand in the graveyard across the street from the tourist office. The town has a busy commercial fishing harbour and a quayside fish market supplied by Northern Ireland's largest fishing fleet.

Kilkeel Tourist Office (☎ 4176 2525; kdakilkeel@ hotmail.com; 28 Bridge St; ☼ 9am-1pm & 2-5.30pm Mon-Sat) is on the main road through town.

For a bite to eat, try the deliciously fresh fish and chips at Neptune's Larder, on the road to the harbour.

GREENCASTLE

The square Norman keep of **Greencastle** (☎ 9181 1491; Cranfield Point; admission free; ☼ 2-6pm Tue & Fri-Sun, 10am-1pm Wed & Thu Jul & Aug) once guarded the entrance to Carlingford Lough.

Built in 1261 as a companion to Carlingford Castle on the opposite side of the lough in County Louth, it later served as a royal garrison until it was destroyed by Cromwell's forces in 1652.

Greencastle is at the end of a minor road 6km southwest of Kilkeel.

ROSTREVOR

Rostrevor (Caislean Ruairi) is a pretty Victorian seaside resort famed for its lively pubs. Each year in late July, folk musicians converge on the village for the **Fiddler's Green International Festival** (☎ 4173 9819; www.fiddlers greenfestival.com).

To the east is **Kilbroney Forest Park** (☎ 4173 8134; Shore Rd; admission free; ☼ 9am-10pm Jun-Aug, 9am-5pm Sep-May). From the car park at the top of the forest drive, a 10-minute hike leads up to the **Cloughmore Stone**, a 30-tonne granite boulder inscribed with Victorian graffiti, and a superb view over the lough to Carlingford Mountain.

There's a **camping ground** (☎ 4173 8134; kil broneypark@newryandmourne.gov.uk; camp/caravan sites £7/12; ☼ Apr-Oct) in Kilbroney Forest Park. For B&B try the central **An Tobar** (☎ 4173 8712; www.kilbroney.net; 2 Cherry Hill; s/d £27/44; P), a modern house with grand views, just northeast of the church.

The town is noted for its many pubs, most of which have regular live music. The best ones to eat in are the **Kilbroney** (☎ 4173 8390; 31 Church St) and the **Celtic Fjord** (☎ 4173 8005; 8 Mary St).

Warrenpoint
pop 13,500

Warrenpoint (An Pointe) is a Victorian resort at the head of Carlingford Lough, its seaside appeal somewhat diminished by the large industrial harbour at the west end of town. Its broad streets, main square and recently renovated prom are pleasant enough, though, and it has better sleeping and eating options than either Newry or Rostrevor.

The **Warrenpoint Tourist Information Centre** (☎ 4175 2256; Church St; 9am-5pm daily Jun-Aug, 9am-5pm Mon-Fri Oct-May) is in the town hall.

About 2km northwest of the town centre is **Narrow Water Castle** (☎ 9181 1491; admission free; 10am-1pm Tue, Fri & Sat, 2-6pm Wed & Thu Jul & Aug), a fine Elizabethan tower house built in 1568 to command the entrance to the Newry River.

SLEEPING & EATING

Whistledown & Finns (☎ 4175 4174; www.whistle down.co.uk; 6 Seaview; s/d £40/65) This waterfront guesthouse offers country-style accommodation in five en-suite rooms (ask for No 2, with its pine four-poster bed and bay window overlooking the sea), and a stylish bar and **restaurant** (mains £8-15; 12.30-3.30pm & 5.30-10pm).

Boathouse Inn (☎ 4175 3743; www.boathouseinn .com; 3 Marine Pde; s/d £45/70; P ⊠) Overlooking Warrenpoint's tiny marina, the Boathouse has 12 luxury en-suite rooms. It also offers two top-notch dining options: the **Boathouse Restaurant** (mains £9-13; 7-10pm), a chilled out, candle-lit bistro with a modern fusion menu, and the **Vecchia Roma** (mains £6-9; noon-2.30pm & 6-11pm), a traditional, checked-tablecloth-and-candle-in-a-chianti-bottle Italian restaurant.

Mariann's Place (☎ 4175 2085; cooper.stuart@ btconnect.com; 18 Upper Dromore Rd; s/d £24/38; P ⊠) Mariann's is a large modern B&B with views over the lough, about 500m north of the Square on the B7 Mayobridge road.

GETTING THERE & AWAY

Bus No 39 runs between Newry and Warrenpoint (£1.50, 20 minutes, at least hourly Monday to Saturday), with some services continuing to Kilkeel (one hour).

Newry
pop 22,975

Newry has long been a frontier town, guarding the land route from Dublin to Ulster through the 'Gap of the North', the pass between Slieve Gullion and the Carlingford hills, still followed by the main Dublin–Belfast road and railway. Its name derives from a yew tree (An tIúr) supposedly planted here by St Patrick.

The opening of the Newry Canal in 1742 – the first summit-level canal in the British Isles – linking the town with the River Bann at Portadown, made Newry into a busy trading port, exporting coal from Coalisland on Lough Neagh as well as linen and butter from the surrounding area.

Newry today is a major shopping centre, with a market on Thursday and Saturday, and makes a good base for exploring the Mourne Mountains, South Armagh and the Cooley Peninsula in County Louth.

INFORMATION

Newry Library (☎ 3026 4683; 79 Hill St; 9.30am-5pm Wed & Sat, 9.30am-6pm Mon & Fri, 9.30am-8pm Tue & Thu) Internet access for £1.40 per 30 minutes.

Tourist Information Centre (☎ 3026 8877; Town Hall, Bank Pde; 9am-5pm Mon-Fri year round, to 8pm Jul & Aug, plus 10am-4pm Sat Jun-Sep)

SIGHTS

So fierce was the rivalry between counties Down and Armagh in the 19th century, that when the new red-brick **town hall** was built in 1893 it was erected right on the border – on a three-arched bridge across the Newry River. The cannon outside was captured during the Crimean War (1853–56) and given to the town in memory of local volunteers who fought in the war.

The small **Newry & Mourne Museum** (☎ 3026 6232; Bank Pde; admission free; 10.30am-1pm & 2-4.30pm Mon-Fri) in the Arts Centre next to the town hall has an interesting display on the rediscovery of Bagenal's Castle.

Bagenal's Castle is the town's oldest surviving building, a 16th-century tower house built for Nicholas Bagenal, grand marshal of the English army in Ireland. Recently rediscovered, having been incorporated into more recent buildings, the castle is currently being restored and will house the Newry and Mourne Museum when the castle opens in late 2006.

The **Newry Canal** runs parallel to the river through the town centre, and is a focus for the city's redevelopment. A cycle path runs 30km north to Portadown, following the route of the canal. **Newry Ship Canal** runs 6km south towards Carlingford Lough, where the Victoria Lock has been restored to working order as part of a long-term project to reopen the whole canal to leisure traffic. Designed by Sir John Rennie, the civil engineer who designed Waterloo, Southwark and London Bridges in London, the ship canal allowed large, sea-going vessels to reach Albert Basin in the centre of Newry.

SLEEPING & EATING

Belmont Hall (☎ 3026 2163; www.belmont-hall.co.uk; 18 Downshire Rd; s £30-42.50, d £60-70; P ✗) Revel in Regency elegance at this lovingly restored Georgian villa, with 12 en-suite rooms, just 700m north of the town centre. The house has many period features including polished wooden floors, original coving and marble fireplaces.

Canal Court Hotel (☎ 3025 1234; www.canalcourt hotel.com; Merchants Quay; s/d £80/130; P ✗) You can't miss this huge, yellow building opposite the bus station. Although it's a modern hotel, it promotes a deliberately old-fashioned atmosphere, with leather sofas dotted around the vast wood-panelled lobby and a restaurant that veers dangerously close to chintzy.

Marymount (☎ 3026 1099; patricia.ohare2@btopen world.com; Windsor Ave; s/d £30/46; P) A modern bungalow in a quiet location up a hill off the A1 Belfast road, Marymount is only a 10-minute walk from the town centre. One of the three rooms has a private bathroom (twin £50).

Soho Place (☎ 3083 3333; 15 The Mall; mains £11-14; ✆ noon-5pm Mon, noon-9pm Tue-Thu, noon-10pm Fri & Sat, noon-8.30pm Sun) Currently the hottest item on Newry's dining-out menu, Soho Place ticks all the boxes on the Irish restaurant–style list – dark wood, burgundy walls, staff dressed all in black, and those circular rubber place mats from Habitat. Inventive Irish-Asian-Mediterranean cuisine, though portion control tends towards overkill – expect fishcakes the size of Belgium as a starter.

Café Krem (☎ 3026 6233; 14 Hill St; snacks £2-3; ✆ 8.30am-6pm Mon-Sat) A friendly, community atmosphere and the best coffee in town make Café Krem stand out from the crowd. There's also wicked hot chocolate, tasty *panini* (type of Italian sandwich) and a couple of big, soft sofas to sink into.

Brass Monkey (☎ 3026 3176; 1-4 Sandy St; mains £5.50-7; ✆ food served 12.30-2.30pm & 5-8pm) Newry's most popular pub, with Victorian brass, brick and timber décor, serves good bar meals ranging from lasagne and burgers to seafood and steaks.

GETTING THERE & AWAY

Newry BusCentre is on the Mall, opposite the Canal Court Hotel. Bus No 238 runs regularly to Newry from Belfast's Europa BusCentre (£6.20, 1¼ hours, at least hourly Monday to Saturday, five daily Sunday).

Bus No 44 runs from Newry to Armagh (£3.80, 1¼ hours, twice daily Monday to Saturday), and No 295 from Newry to Enniskillen (£8.20, 2¾ hours, twice daily Monday to Saturday, July and August only) via Armagh and Monaghan. Bus No 39 departs at least hourly for Warrenpoint (20 minutes) and Rostrevor (30 minutes), with 10 a day continuing to Kilkeel (£3, one hour).

The train station is 2.5km northwest of the centre, on the A25; bus No 341 goes there hourly from the bus station. Newry is a stop on the train service between Dublin (£12.30, 1¼ hours, eight daily) and Belfast (£6.90, 50 minutes, seven daily).

TOP 10 RESTAURANTS IN NORTHERN IRELAND OUTSIDE BELFAST

- Boathouse Inn (opposite)
- Genoa's (p599)
- Lime Tree (p636)
- Lobster Pot (p608)
- Manor Park Restaurant (p620)
- Narrows (p601)
- Old School House Inn (p604)
- Pier 36 (p600)
- Plough Inn (p595)
- Seasalt (p610)

COUNTY ARMAGH

SOUTH ARMAGH

Rural and staunchly republican, South Armagh is known to its inhabitants as 'God's Country'. But to the British soldiers stationed there in the 1970s it had another, more sinister nickname – 'Bandit Country'. With the Republic only a few miles away, South Armagh was a favourite venue for IRA cross-border attacks and bombings.

Although life now has regained some semblance of normality, here more than anywhere else in Northern Ireland you will be aware of the security forces' presence – the huge barracks at Bessbrook Mill and Crossmaglen, the hilltop watchtowers, soldiers on foot patrol in village streets, and the constant clatter of army helicopters. And the insignia of republican resistance are everywhere – Irish tricolours, IRA signs nailed to telephone poles, and the notorious 'sniper at work' signs (mock road signs showing the silhouette of a masked gunman).

That said, like anywhere else in the North, there's no reason for visitors to stay away from what is a lovely part of Ireland.

Bessbrook

pop 3150

Bessbrook (An Sruthán) was founded in the mid-19th century by Quaker linen manufacturer John Grubb Richardson as a 'model village' to house the workers at his flax mill. Rows of pretty terrace houses made from local granite line the two main squares, Charlemont and College, each with a green in the middle, and are complemented by a town hall, school, bathhouse and dispensary. It is said that Bessbrook was the inspiration for Bournville (near Birmingham in England), the model village built by the Cadbury family for their chocolate factory. Sadly the village atmosphere is marred a little by the massively fortified Bessbrook Mill army base. The helipad on top of the former mill building is reputedly the busiest in Europe, with anything up to 100 flights a day.

Just south of Bessbrook is **Derrymore House** (☎ 3083 8361; Bessbrook; adult/child £3/1.50; ☒ house 2-5.30pm Thu-Sat May-Aug, grounds 10am-7pm May-Sep, 10am-4pm Oct-Apr), an elegant thatched cottage built in 1776 for Isaac Corry, the Irish MP for Newry for 30 years. The Act of Union was drafted in the drawing room of the house in 1800. The surrounding parkland was laid out by John Sutherland (1745–1826), one of the most celebrated disciples of Capability Brown.

Bessbrook is 5km northwest of Newry. Bus No 41 runs from Newry to Bessbrook (15 minutes, hourly Monday to Saturday), while bus Nos 42 (to Crossmaglen) and 44 (to Armagh) pass the entrance to Derrymore House on the A25 Camlough road.

Ring of Gullion

The Ring of Gullion is a magical region, steeped in Celtic legend, centred on Slieve Gullion (Sliabh gCuilinn; 576m) where the Celtic warrior Cúchulainn is said to have taken his name after killing the dog (cú) belonging to the smith Culainn. The 'ring' is a necklace of rugged hills strung between Newry and Forkhill, 15km to the southwest, encircling the central whaleback ridge of Slieve Gullion. The unusual concentric formation is a geological structure known as a ring-dyke.

KILLEVY CHURCHES

Surrounded by beech trees, these ruined, conjoined **churches** (admission free; ☒ 24hr) were constructed on the site of a 5th-century nunnery that was founded by St Moninna. The eastern church dates from the 15th century, and shares a gable wall with the 12th-century western one. The west door, with a massive lintel and granite jambs, may be 200 years older still. At the side of the churchyard a footpath leads uphill to a white cross that marks St Moninna's holy well.

The churches are 6km south of Camlough, on a minor road to Meigh. Look out for a crossroads with a sign pointing right to the churches and left to Bernish Rock Viewpoint.

SLIEVE GULLION FOREST PARK

A 13km scenic drive through this **forest park** (admission free; ☒ 10am-dusk) provides picturesque views over the surrounding hills. From the parking and picnic area at the top of the drive you can hike to the summit of Slieve Gullion, the highest point in County Armagh, topped by two early-Bronze Age cairns and a tiny lake (1.5km round trip). The park entrance is 10km southwest of Newry on the B113 road to Forkhill.

MULLAGHBANE & FORKHILL
In the village of Mullaghbane (Mullach Bán), just west of Slieve Gullion, is **Thí Chulainn** (☎ 3088 8828; Mullaghbane; admission free; ۞ 9am-5pm Mon-Fri, 11am-12.30pm Sat), a cultural activities centre that promotes the Irish language, local folklore, traditional music and storytelling.

The pubs in nearby Forkhill hold traditional music sessions on Tuesday nights and alternate Saturdays, and a folk music festival in October.

Crossmaglen
pop 1600
Crossmaglen (Crois Mhic Lionnáin) is a strongly republican village just 4km inside the border, arranged around one of Ireland's biggest market squares. At the height of the Troubles the barracks at 'Cross' (or XMG, as it was known) was the most feared posting in the British Army. For today's visitors, however, it's a friendly place with a reputation for Gaelic football, horse breeding, and lively pubs known for their excellent music sessions.

You can get tourist information at **South Armagh Tourism Initiative** (☎ 3086 8900; www .south-armagh.com; 25-26 the Square; ۞ 9am-5pm Mon-Fri).

Murtagh's Bar (☎ 3086 1378; aidanmurtagh@ hotmail.com; 13 North St; s £20-25, d £40-50; ✗) offers good craic, traditional music, bar meals and B&B, while **Ma Kearney's** (☎ 3086 8944; 20 Newry St) serves bar meals all day and restaurant food for lunch and dinner Monday to Saturday. There's live music on Friday, Saturday and Sunday nights.

Bus No 42 runs from Newry to Crossmaglen (£3, 50 minutes, six daily Monday to Friday, four Saturday) via Camlough and Mullaghbane.

ARMAGH CITY
pop 14,600
The attractive little cathedral city of Armagh (Ard Macha) has been an important religious centre since the 5th century. Today it remains the ecclesiastical capital of Ireland, the seat of both the Anglican and Roman Catholic archbishops of Armagh and primates of all Ireland.

Armagh is associated with some prominent historical figures. James Ussher (1580–1655), Archbishop of Armagh, was an avid scholar who is best known for pinning down the day of the Creation to Sunday, 23 October 4004 BC by adding up the generations quoted in the Bible, a date which was accepted as fact until the late 19th century. His extensive library became the nucleus of the great library at Trinity College, Dublin. Jonathan Swift (1667–1745), Dean of St Patrick's Cathedral, Dublin, and author of *Gulliver's Travels,* was a frequent visitor to Armagh, while the architect Francis Johnston (1760–1829), responsible for many of Dublin's finest Georgian streetscapes, was born in the city.

History
When St Patrick began his mission to spread Christianity throughout Ireland, he chose a site close to Emain Macha (Navan Fort), the nerve centre of pagan Ulster, for his power base. In AD 445 he built Ireland's first stone church on a hill nearby (now home to the Church of Ireland cathedral), and later decreed that Armagh should have pre-eminence over all the churches in Ireland.

By the 8th century Armagh was one of Europe's best-known centres of religion, learning and craftwork. The city was divided into three districts (called 'trians'), centred around English, Scotch and Irish streets. Armagh's fame was its undoing, however, as the Vikings plundered the city 10 times between AD 831 and 1013.

The city gained a new prosperity from the linen trade in the 18th century, a period whose legacy includes a Royal School, an astronomical observatory, a renowned public library and a fine crop of Georgian architecture.

Information
Armagh City Library (☎ 3752 4072; Market St; ۞ 9.30am-5.30pm Mon, Wed & Fri, 9.30am-8pm Tue & Thu) Internet access for £1.50 per 30 minutes.
Tourist Information Centre (☎ 3752 1800; www .visitarmagh.com; 40 English St; ۞ 9am-5pm Mon-Sat year round, 1-5.30pm Sun Jul & Aug, 2-5pm Sun Sep-Jun) Part of the St Patrick's Trian complex.

Sights
ST PATRICK'S TRIAN
The old Presbyterian church behind the tourist office has been turned into a heritage centre and visitor complex known as **St Patrick's Trian** (☎ 3752 1801; 40 English St;

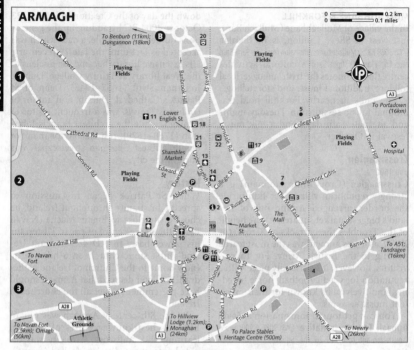

ARMAGH

INFORMATION		St Patrick's Church of Ireland Cathedral..**10** B2	Manor Park Restaurant.......................**17** C2
Armagh City Library.............................**1** C3		St Patrick's Roman Catholic Cathedral..**11** B1	
Tourist Information Centre....................**2** C2		St Patrick's Trian ....(see 2)	**ENTERTAINMENT**
			Armagh City Film House...................(see 19)
SIGHTS & ACTIVITIES		**SLEEPING**	Devlin's...**18** B1
Armagh County Museum......................**3** C2		Armagh City Hostel.............................**12** B2	Market Place Theatre & Arts Centre...**19** C2
Armagh Gaol.......................................**4** D3		Charlemont Arms Hotel........................**13** B2	Northern Bar....................................**20** B1
Armagh Planetarium............................**5** C1		De Averell House.................................**14** C2	Shambles Bar...................................**21** B2
Armagh Public Library..........................**6** B2			
Charlemont Place................................**7** C2		**EATING**	**TRANSPORT**
Courthouse..**8** C2		Breeze Bistro......................................**15** B3	Armagh BusCentre...........................**22** C2
Royal Irish Fusiliers Museum................**9** C2		Café Papa...**16** C3	

adult/child £4.50/2.75; ⌚ 10am-5pm Mon-Sat, 2-5pm
Sun). There are three exhibitions: the Armagh Story explores the history of Armagh
from pagan prehistory to the present day,
while Patrick's Testament takes an interactive look at the ancient *Book of Armagh*.
For the kids there's the Land of Lilliput
where Gulliver's adventures in Lilliput are
recounted by a gigantic model of Jonathan
Swift's famous creation.

ST PATRICK'S CHURCH OF IRELAND CATHEDRAL

The city's **Anglican Cathedral** (☎ 3752 3142; Cathedral Close; admission free, guided tours £2; ⌚ 9.30am-
5pm Apr-Oct, 9.30am-4pm Nov-Mar, guided tours 11.30am

& 2.30pm Mon-Sat Jun-Aug) occupies the site of St
Patrick's original stone church. The present
cathedral's ground plan is 13th-century but
the building itself is a Gothic restoration dating from 1834 to 1840. A stone slab on the
exterior wall of the north transept marks the
burial place of Brian Ború, the High King of
Ireland, who died near Dublin during the
last great battle against the Vikings in 1014.

Within the church are the remains of
an 11th-century **Celtic Cross** that once stood
nearby, and the **Tandragee Idol**, a curious
granite figure dating back to the Iron Age.
In the south aisle is a **memorial to Archbishop
Richard Robinson** (1709–94), who founded
Armagh's observatory and public library.

ARMAGH PUBLIC LIBRARY

The Greek inscription above the main entrance to **Armagh Public Library** (☎ 3752 3142; www.armaghrobinsonlibrary.org; 43 Abbey St; admission free; ⊙ 10am-1pm & 2-4pm Mon-Fri), founded in 1771 by Archbishop Robinson, means 'the medicine shop of the soul'. Step inside and you'd swear that the archbishop had just swept out of the door leaving you to browse among his personal collection of 17th- and 18th-century books, maps and engravings.

The library's most prized possession is a first edition of *Gulliver's Travels*, published in 1726 and annotated by none other than Swift himself. It was stolen in an armed robbery in 1999, but was recovered, undamaged, in Dublin 20 months later.

Other treasures of the library include Sir Walter Raleigh's 1614 *History of the World*, the *Claims of the Innocents* (pleas to Oliver Cromwell) and a large collection of engravings by Hogarth and others.

ST PATRICK'S ROMAN CATHOLIC CATHEDRAL

The other **St Patrick's Cathedral** (☎ 3752 2802; Cathedral Rd; admission free; ⊙ 8am-5pm, mass 10am Mon-Fri, 9am, 11am & 5.30pm Sun) was built between 1838 and 1873 in Gothic Revival style with huge twin towers dominating the approach up flight after flight of steps. Inside it seems almost Byzantine, with every piece of wall and ceiling covered in brilliantly coloured mosaics. The sanctuary was modernised in 1981 and has a very distinctive tabernacle holder and crucifix that seem out of place among the mosaics and statues of the rest of the church.

THE MALL

The Mall, to the east of the town centre, was a venue for horse racing, cock fighting and bull baiting until the 18th century when Archbishop Robinson decided it was a tad vulgar for a city of learning, and transformed it into an elegant Georgian park.

At its northern end stands the **courthouse**, rebuilt after being destroyed by a huge IRA bomb in 1993. It originally dates from 1809, designed by local man Francis Johnston, who later became one of Ireland's most famous architects. At the southern end, directly opposite the courthouse, is the forbidding **Armagh Gaol**. Built in 1780 to the design of Thomas Cooley, it remained in use until 1988.

The east side of the park is lined with handsome Georgian terraces. **Charlemont Place** is another creation of Francis Johnston, as is the portico fronting **Armagh County Museum** (☎ 3752 3070; the Mall East; admission free; ⊙ 10am-5pm Mon-Fri, 10am-1pm & 2-5pm Sat). The museum displays prehistoric axe heads, items found in bogs, corn dollies and strawboy outfits, and military costumes and equipment. Don't miss the gruesome cast-iron skull that once graced the top of the Armagh gallows.

The nearby **Royal Irish Fusiliers Museum** (☎ 3752 2911; the Mall East; admission free; ⊙ 10am-12.30pm & 1.30-4pm Mon-Fri) tells the story of the first regiment to capture one of Bonaparte's imperial eagle standards in 1811.

ARMAGH PLANETARIUM

The Armagh Observatory was founded by Archbishop Robinson in 1790 and is still Ireland's leading astronomical research institute. The Star Theatre at the nearby **Armagh Planetarium** (☎ 3752 3689; www.armagh planet.com; College Hill) was closed for refurbishment at the time of research, and is due to reopen in late 2006.

PALACE STABLES HERITAGE CENTRE

The Primate's Palace, overlooking the ruins of a 13th-century Franciscan friary on the southern edge of town, was built for Archbishop Robinson when he was appointed primate of Ireland in 1769. It now houses the local council, and the former stables are home to the **Palace Stables Heritage Centre** (☎ 3752 9629; Palace demesne; adult/child £4.50/2.75; ⊙ 10am-5pm Mon-Sat, noon-4pm Sun Jun-Aug, 10am-4pm Mon-Sat, noon-4pm Sun Sep-May), a set of tableaux illustrating how the archbishop's guests were entertained in the 18th century.

Sleeping

Armagh City Hostel (☎ 3751 1800; www.hini.org.uk; 39 Abbey St; dm/tw £13.50/32; ⊙ 8-11am & 5-11pm 3 Jan–22 Dec; P) This modern, purpose-built hostel, near the Church of Ireland Cathedral, is more like a small hotel than a youth hostel. There are six comfortable twin rooms complete with private bathroom, TV, and tea and coffee facilities, as well as 12 small dorms, a well-equipped kitchen, laundry, lounge and reading room.

De Averell House (☎ 3751 1213; www.deaverell house.net; 47 Upper English St; s/d £35/59; P ✗)

A converted Georgian town house with four spacious en-suite rooms and a self-catering apartment, De Averell is the town centre's best choice for comfort, friendliness and convenience.

Hillview Lodge (☎ 3752 2000; www.hillviewlodge .com; 33 Newtownhamilton Rd; s/d £30/50; P ☒) Just 1.5km south of Armagh, Hillview is a welcoming, family-run guesthouse with a self-contained accommodation block containing six appealing en-suite rooms with great countryside views. And there's a driving range next door to practice your golf swing.

Charlemont Arms Hotel (☎ 3752 2028; www .charlemontarmshotel.com; 57-65 English St; s/d £50/75; P ☒ ▣) This hotel dates from the 19th century, but has been renovated in charming period décor – oak-panelled dining room, Victorian fireplaces, flagstone-floored cellar restaurant. The bedrooms, in contrast, are modern and stylish.

Eating

Manor Park Restaurant (☎ 3751 5353; 2 College Hill, the Mall; mains £15-20; ☯ 5-10.30pm Tue-Sun, noon-2.30pm Sun) Crisp white linen and silver candlesticks complement a cosy olde-worlde décor of red-brick walls, parquet floors and Persian rugs in this atmospheric French restaurant. The menu runs the gastronomic gamut from frogs legs fricassee to *millefeuille* of monkfish and salmon, with a wine list as long as the Loire.

Breeze Bistro (☎ 3751 8051; 16-18 Market St; mains £5-8; ☯ noon-2.30pm & 6.30-10pm Mon, Tue & Thu-Sat, 5.30-9pm Sun) An informal, modern bistro with friendly staff, a Mediterranean-influenced menu and a dinky little outdoor terrace, Breeze is unlicensed – which means you're free to bring your own wine or beer.

Café Papa (☎ 3751 1205; 15 Thomas St; mains £4-8; ☯ 9am-5.30pm Mon-Sat, 6-9pm Sat) This café serves good coffee, cakes, home-baked bread and gourmet sandwiches, and does bistro dinners on Saturday evenings when you can bring your own wine.

De Averell House (☎ 3751 1213; 47 Upper English St; ☯ noon-2.30pm daily, 6-9.30pm Thu-Sat) The rustic basement restaurant at the De Averell offers a crowd-pleasing menu that includes steak, chicken, stir fries, fajitas, daily seafood specials, and a half-dozen vegetarian dishes.

Entertainment

The **Market Place Theatre & Arts Centre** (☎ 3752 1821; www.marketplacearmagh.com; Market St; ☯ box office 9.30am-4.30pm Mon-Sat) is Armagh's main cultural venue, with a 400-seat theatre, exhibition galleries, a restaurant, bar and café. Right next door is the **Armagh City Film House** (☎ 3751 1033; www.armaghfilmhouse.com; Market St).

The **Shambles Bar** (☎ 3752 4107; 9 Lower English St) and **Devlin's** (☎ 3752 3865; 23 Lower English St) are good places to catch live bands on a Saturday night. Locals recommend the **Northern Bar** (☎ 3752 7315; 100 Railway St), better known as Hughes' Bar, which has DJs on Friday, live bands on Saturday, and traditional music sessions on Tuesday.

Sport

You may be lucky enough to catch a game of **road bowling**, a traditional Irish game now played mostly in Armagh and Cork. Contestants hurl small metal bowls weighing 750g along quiet country lanes to see who can make it to the finishing line with the least number of throws. Games usually take place on Sunday afternoons in summer, with tournaments held at Easter and the August bank holiday. Ask for details at the Tourist Information Centre.

Getting There & Away

Ulsterbus No 251 runs from Belfast's Europa BusCentre (£6.20, 1¼ hours, hourly Monday to Friday, eight Saturday, three Sunday) to Armagh. Bus No 44 runs from Armagh to Newry (£3.80, 1¼ hours, twice daily Monday to Saturday), and No 295 runs to Enniskillen (£5.70, two hours, twice daily Monday to Saturday, July and August only) via Monaghan.

There are no direct services from Armagh to Derry – the fastest route (3½ hours) is via Belfast (bus Nos 251 and 212).

Armagh is a stop on the once-daily (except Saturday) bus No 278 from Portrush to Dublin (change at Monaghan) and the once-daily bus No 270 from Belfast to Galway.

AROUND ARMAGH CITY
Navan Fort

Perched atop a drumlin a little over 3km west of Armagh is Navan Fort (Emain Macha), the most important archaeological site in Ulster. It was probably a prehistoric provincial capital and ritual site, on a par with Tara in County Meath (see p530).

The Irish name Emain Macha means 'the twins of Macha', Macha being the same mythical queen or goddess after whom Armagh itself is named (from Ard Macha, 'heights of Macha'). The site is linked in legend with the tales of Cúchulainn – see p552 – and named as capital of Ulster and the seat of the legendary Knights of the Red Branch.

It was an important centre from around 1150 BC until the coming of Christianity; the discovery of the skull of a Barbary ape indicates trading links with North Africa. The main circular earthwork enclosure is no less than 240m in diameter, and encloses a smaller circular structure and an Iron Age burial mound. The circular structure has intrigued archaeologists. It appears to be some sort of temple, whose roof was supported by concentric rows of wooden posts, and whose interior was filled with a vast pile of stones. Stranger still, the whole thing was set on fire soon after its construction around 95 BC, possibly for ritual purposes.

The nearby **Navan Interpretative Centre** (☎ 3752 1800; 81 Killylea Rd, Armagh; adult/child £4.50/ 2.75; ☺ 10am-5pm Mon-Sat, 2-5pm Sun) places the fort in its historical context.

You can walk to the site from Armagh (45 minutes), or you can take the No 73 Ballygawley bus (10 minutes, seven daily Monday to Friday, three Saturday) to Navan village.

NORTH ARMAGH

North Armagh, 'the orchard of Ireland', is the island's main fruit-growing region, famed for its apples and strawberries. In May the countryside is awash with pink apple blossom.

Ardress House

Starting life as a farmhouse, **Ardress House** (☎ 3885 1236; 64 Ardress Rd; adult/child £3.30/1.70; ☺ 2-6pm Sat, Sun & public hols mid-Mar–Sep) was upgraded to a manor house in 1760. Much of the original neoclassical interior remains and the farmyard still functions with a piggery and smithy. The walled garden has been planted with a selection of the old apple varieties for which North Armagh's orchards are famous, and there are pleasant walks around the wooded grounds.

Ardress is 15km northeast of Armagh, on the B28 halfway between Moy and Portadown.

Argory

A fine country house above the River Blackwater, the **Argory** (☎ 8778 4753; Derrycaw Rd; adult/ child grounds & tour £4.50/2.40, grounds only per car £2.50; ☺ house 1-6pm daily Easter week & Jun-Aug, 1-6pm Sat, Sun & public hols mid-Mar–May & Sep–mid-Oct) retains most of its 1824 fittings; some rooms are lit by acetylene gas from the house's private plant. There are two formal gardens featuring roses, Victorian clipped-yew arbours and a lime walk by the river.

The Argory is 3.5km northeast of Moy on the Derrycaw road (off the B28), and 5km northwest of Ardress.

Oxford Island

Lough Neagh is the largest freshwater lake in the British Isles, big enough to swallow the city of Birmingham (West Midlands, UK, or Alabama, USA – either one would fit). Though vast (around 30km long and 14km wide), the lough is relatively shallow – never more than 9m deep – and is an important habitat for waterfowl. Its waters are home to the dollaghan, a sub-species of trout unique to Lough Neagh, as well as migratory salmon and eels on their way between the sea and the half-dozen rivers that flow into the lake.

Oxford Island National Nature Reserve protects a range of habitats – woodland, wildflower meadows, reedy shoreline and shallow lake margins – on the lough's southern edge, and is criss-crossed with walking trails, information boards and bird-watching hides.

The **Lough Neagh Discovery Centre** (☎ 3832 2205; www.oxfordisland.com; Oxford Island, Lurgan; admission free; ☺ 10am-6pm Mon-Sat, 10am-7pm Sun Apr-Sep, 10am-5pm Wed-Sun Oct-Mar) explains the ecology of the lough, and has a great little café with lake-shore views.

One-hour **boat trips** (☎ 3832 7573; adult/child £4/2; ☺ 1.30-6.30pm Sat & Sun Apr-Oct) on the lough depart from nearby Kinnego Marina, aboard the 10m cabin cruiser *Master McGra*.

Oxford Island is just north of Lurgan, signposted from Junction 10 on the M1 motorway.

Counties Derry & Antrim

The long sweep of coast from Carrickfergus, in County Antrim, round to Coleraine offers some of the most beautiful coastal scenery in Ireland – contrasting sea cliffs of black basalt and white chalk, caves and rock pinnacles and picturesque harbours, fern-fringed waterfalls hidden in lush green glens, and broad, sweeping beaches pounded by wild Atlantic surf.

In the middle lies the surreal geological centrepiece of the Giant's Causeway, its popularity challenged only by the test-your-nerve tightrope of the famous wire-rope bridge suspended above the sea at Carrick-a-Rede. Further east beyond Ballycastle, the cliffs of Fair Head offer fine walking with views over Rathlin Island to Scotland's Mull of Kintyre and the island hills of Islay and Jura. To its south lie the scenic Glens of Antrim, with the picturesque village of Cushendall and the picturesque old church of Layde, and the imposing castle of Carrickfergus.

The historic city of Derry, nestled by a broad sweep of the River Foyle, is County Derry's chief attraction. It is the only walled city in Ireland whose ramparts have survived intact, and a walk around it is one of the highlights of a visit to Northern Ireland. Derry's other draws include the powerful political murals in the Bogside district and the lively music scene in its many pubs.

Northeast along the coast there are vast sandy beaches at Magilligan Point, Portstewart and Portrush, with good surfing and windsurfing at the last two. And from the basalt escarpment of Binevenagh, which overlooks the coast here, superb views across Lough Foyle beckon you towards the blue-hazed hills of County Donegal.

HIGHLIGHTS

- **City Lights**
  Walking the city walls and pubs in the historic city of Derry (p625 and p633)

- **Distiller's Art**
  A tour of the Bushmills Distillery (p643) near the town of Bushmills

- **Scenic Stroll**
  A picnic and hike along the spectacular Causeway Coast to the Giant's Causeway (p644)

- **Adrenaline Rush**
  Tests of nerve as you tiptoe across the Carrick-a-Rede Rope Bridge (p646) near Ballycastle

- **Wildlife Encounter**
  Bird-watching and seal-spotting on wild Rathlin Island (p648)

★ Rathlin Island
★ Giant's Causeway   ★ Ballycastle
★ Bushmills
★ Derry

■ POPULATION: 532,000   ■ AREA: 4696 SQ KM

Getting There & Away

Translink (☎ 9066 6630; www.translink.co.uk) operates several bus services specially designed for tourists visiting the popular Antrim coast and Giant's Causeway areas.

The Antrim Coaster (bus No 252) links Coleraine with Larne (£8.20, 3¼ hours, two daily Monday to Saturday) via Portstewart, Portrush, Bushmills, the Giant's Causeway, Ballycastle and the Glens of Antrim. In summer one bus a day continues to/from Belfast's Europa BusCentre (£8.20, 4½ hours), departing Belfast at 9am (June to September only), and Larne at 10.15am and 3pm (year round). Southbound buses leave Coleraine at 9.55am (ending in Belfast June to September, in Larne October to April) and 3.40pm (Larne only). A Sunday service operates from July to September only.

From mid-June to mid-September the Causeway Rambler (bus No 402) links Bushmills Distillery and Carrick-a-Rede (£3.50, 25 minutes, seven daily) via the Giant's Causeway, Whitepark Bay and Ballintoy. The ticket allows unlimited travel in either direction for one day.

In July and August only the Bushmills Bus (No 177), an open-topped (weather permitting) double-decker, runs from Coleraine to the Giant's Causeway (one way/ day return £2.70/4, one hour, five daily) via Portstewart, Portrush, Portballintrae and Bushmills Distillery.

COUNTY DERRY

DERRY/LONDONDERRY

pop 83,100

The riverside city of Derry (or Londonderry – see boxed text, p625), the fifth largest in Ireland, is a pleasant surprise to many visitors. There's lots of fascinating history to absorb – a stroll around the 17th-century city walls is a must, as is a visit to the Tower Museum – and the city has a well-founded reputation for musical excellence, from traditional to cutting-edge contemporary.

Derry is also a good base for exploring Donegal's Inishowen peninsula, and for an excursion to the Grianán of Aileách, a spectacular stone fort dating back to 1700 BC, just 6km over the border in Donegal.

History

Elizabeth I, determined to conquer Ulster, sent English troops to garrison Derry in 1566. In 1600 a second, more successful attempt to secure the town was made against the O'Neills and O'Donnells.

Sir Cahir O'Doherty attacked Derry in 1608 and virtually wiped it out but in 1609 James I, determined to settle matters for good, granted land to English and Scottish settlers. The wealthy London guilds were put in charge of 'planting' Derry and building the city walls.

During the Civil War the city backed parliament and supported William of Orange against James II. In December 1688 Catholic forces led by the earl of Antrim arrived on the other side of the River Foyle. They sent emissaries into the city to discuss the crisis; in the meantime troops were being ferried across the river. On seeing this, some apprentice boys locked the city gates and then the Great Siege of Derry began.

For 105 days the Protestant citizens of Derry withstood bombardment, disease and starvation. By the time a relief ship burst through and broke the siege, an estimated quarter of the city's 30,000 inhabitants had died.

In the 19th century Derry was one of the main emigration ports to the USA, a fact commemorated by the sculptures of an emigrant family standing in Waterloo Place. It also played a vital role in the transatlantic trade in linen shirts; supposedly, local factories provided uniforms for both sides in the American Civil War. To this day Derry still supplies the US president with 12 free shirts every year.

In the late 1960s, predominantly Catholic Derry became a flashpoint for the Troubles. In recent years, however, the Bogside and the inner city have been redeveloped. Major projects that reflect a new confidence in the future include the big Foyleside, Quayside and Richmond Shopping Centres and the Millennium Forum.

Orientation

The old centre of Derry is the small walled city on the western bank of the River Foyle. At its heart is the square called The Diamond, with Shipquay, Ferryquay, Butcher and Bishop Sts converging

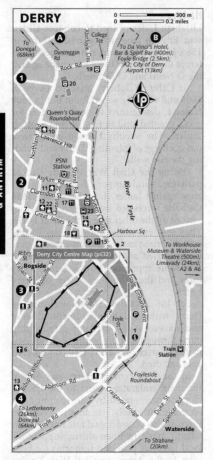

DERRY

0 —————— 300 m
0 —————— 0.2 miles

INFORMATION	
Derry Visitor & Convention Bureau..................	1 B3

SIGHTS & ACTIVITIES	
Foyle Cruises..................	2 B3
Free Derry Corner..................	3 A3
Hands Across the Divide..................	4 A4
Hunger Strikers' Memorial..................	5 A3
Long Tower Church..................	6 A4
St Eugene's Cathedral..................	7 A2

SLEEPING	
Abbey B&B..................	8 A3
City Hotel..................	9 A2
Clarence House..................	10 A2
Derry City Independent Hostel..................	(see 12)
Merchant's House..................	11 A2
Saddler's House..................	12 A2
Sunbeam House..................	13 A4
Travelodge..................	14 A2

EATING	
Exchange Wine Bar & Restaurant..................	15 A3
Mange 2..................	16 A2
Sandwich Co..................	17 A2
Tesco..................	(see 21)

DRINKING	
Mullan's Bar..................	18 A2

ENTERTAINMENT	
Earth@Café Roc..................	19 A1
Magee College..................	20 A1
Strand Multiplex..................	21 A2

SHOPPING	
Ogmiós..................	22 A2

TRANSPORT	
Airporter Bus Service..................	23 A2

on it. The bus station is just outside the walled city, but the train station is on the far bank of the River Foyle, across Craigavon Bridge.

Information

BOOKSHOPS

Bookworm (Map p632; ☎ 7128 2727; 18-20 Bishop St Within; 🕑 9.30am-5.30pm Mon-Sat) Good for books on Derry, the Troubles and Ireland generally. Has an in-store café.

Eason (Map p632; ☎ 7137 7133; Foyleside Shopping Centre, Foyle St; 🕑 9am-6pm Mon, Tue & Thu, 9am-9pm Wed & Fri, 9am-7pm Sat, 1-6pm Sun) The city's biggest bookshop, on Level 3 of the shopping centre.

Foyle Books (Map p632; ☎ 7137 2530; 12a Magazine St; 🕑 11am-5.15pm Mon-Fri, 10am-5pm Sat) Stocks a good selection of second-hand books.

INTERNET ACCESS

Central Library (Map p632; ☎ 7127 2310; 35 Foyle St; per 30 min £1.50; 🕑 9.15am-8pm Mon & Thu, 9.15am-5.30pm Tue, Wed & Fri, 9.15am-5pm Sat) Internet access.

MONEY

Bank of Ireland (Map p632; ☎ 7126 4992; 12 Shipquay St)

First Trust Bank (Map p632; ☎ 7136 3921; 15-17 Shipquay St)

Thomas Cook (Map p632; ☎ 7185 2552; 34 Ferryquay St)

POST

Branch post office (Map p632; Bishop St Within) A convenient branch inside the city walls.

Main post office (Map p632; Custom House St; 🕑 8.30am-5.30pm Mon, 9am-5.30pm Tue-Fri, 9am-12.30pm Sat)

TOURIST INFORMATION

Derry Visitor & Convention Bureau (Map p624; ☎ 7126 7284; www.derryvisitor.com; 44 Foyle St; 🕑 9am-7pm Mon-Fri, 10am-6pm Sat, 10am-5pm Sun Jul-Sep, 9am-5pm Mon-Fri, 10am-5pm Sat mid-Mar–Jun & Oct, 9am-5pm Mon-Fri Nov–mid-Mar) Covers all of Northern Ireland and the Republic as well as Derry.

Books accommodation throughout Ireland and has a bureau de change.

Sights

Derry's walled city is Ireland's oldest example of town planning. It is thought to have been modelled on the French Renaissance town of Vitry-Le-François, designed in 1545 by Italian engineer Hieronimo Marino; both are based on the grid plan of a Roman military camp, with two main streets at right angles to each other, and four city gates, one at the end of each street.

CITY WALLS

Built between 1614 and 1619, Derry's city walls were the last to be constructed in Europe, and the only city walls in Ireland to survive almost intact. They are about 8m high and 9m thick, with a circumference of about 1.5km. The four original gates (Shipquay, Ferryquay, Bishop's and Butcher's) were rebuilt in the 18th and 19th centuries, when three new gates (New, Magazine and Castle) were added. Derry's nickname, the Maiden City, derives from the fact that the walls have never been breached by an invader.

See p629) for a self-guided walk around the walls.

WALLED CITY

Just inside the Magazine Gate is the award-winning **Tower Museum** (Map p632; ☎ 7137 2411; Union Hall Pl; adult/child £4.20/1.60; ☺ 10am-5pm Mon-Sat, 2-5pm Sun Jul & Aug, 10am-5pm Tue-Sat & bank hol Mon Sep-Jun), where well-thought-out exhibits and audiovisuals lead you through the history of Derry from the founding of St Colmcille's monastery in the 6th century to the Battle of the Bogside in the 1970s. Allow a good two hours to do the museum justice.

There's a wonderful eyewitness account of Shane O'Neill and his soldiers arriving at the court of Elizabeth I to pledge allegiance to the Crown in 1562 (he later reneged):

DERRY-STROKE-LONDONDERRY

Derry/Londonderry is a town with two names. Derry is derived from the Gaelic word *doíre*, meaning 'oak grove'. The settlement was originally named Doíre Calgaigh (Oak Grove of Calgach), after a pagan warrior-hero, then in the 10th century it was renamed Doíre Colmcille (Oak Grove of St Colmcille), in honour of the 6th-century saint who established the first monastic settlement here.

In the following centuries the name was shortened and anglicised to Derrie or Derry. Then in 1613, in recognition of the Corporation of London's role in 'planting' the city with Protestant settlers, the city's name was changed to Londonderry. However, people continued to call it Derry, except in official documents.

When nationalists gained a majority on the city council in 1984, they voted to change its name from Londonderry City Council to Derry City Council. This infuriated unionists, and the name became a touchstone for people's political views. Nationalists always use Derry, and extremists often deface the 'London' part of the name on road signs. Staunch unionists insist on Londonderry, which remains the city's (and county's) official name, used in government publications, Ordnance Survey maps, rail and bus timetables and Northern Ireland Tourist Board (NITB) tourist literature.

On radio and TV, to avoid giving offence to either side, some announcers use both names together – 'Derry-stroke-Londonderry' – while the BBC uses Londonderry at its first mention in a report, and Derry thereafter. Road signs in Northern Ireland point to Londonderry, those in the Republic point to Derry (or Doíre in Irish).

A move to change the city's official name to Derry failed in the 1980s, but in November 2002 Sinn Féin councillors again proposed a motion to make the name Derry official. However, this would take an act of parliament, and could only be done by the Queen on recommendation of the Westminster government.

Luckily, not everyone takes the Derry/Londonderry controversy too seriously. One local journalist opted instead for the simpler 'Stroke City'! In fact, the majority of the people in Northern Ireland, no matter what their political persuasion, still use 'Derry' in everyday speech, which is why we are using the shorter version in this book.

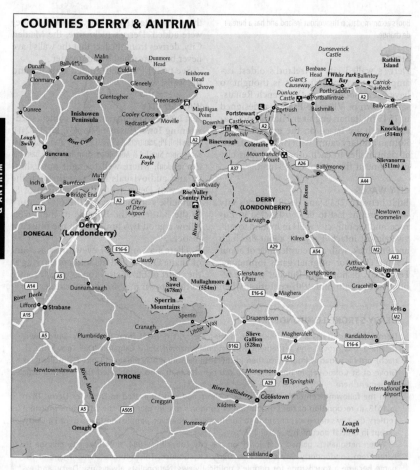

COUNTIES DERRY & ANTRIM

...armed with hatchets, all bare-headed, their hair flowing in locks on their shoulders, on which were yellow surplices dyed with saffron, or stained with urine, with long sleeves, short coats and thrum jackets, which caused as much staring and gaping among the English people as if they had come from China or America.

At the time of writing, a major new exhibition on the Spanish Armada in Ireland was being added to the Tower Museum.

Standing just outside the city walls opposite the Tower Museum, the neo-Gothic **Guildhall** (Map p632; ☎ 7137 7335; Guildhall Sq; admission free; ☽ 9am-5pm Mon-Fri) was originally built in 1890, then rebuilt after a fire in 1908. As the seat of the old Londonderry Corporation, which institutionalised the policy of discriminating against Catholics over housing and jobs, it incurred the wrath of nationalists and was bombed twice by the Irish Republican Army (IRA) in 1972. From 2000 to 2005 it was the seat of the Bloody Sunday Inquiry (see boxed text, opposite). The Guildhall is noted for the fine stained-glass windows, presented by the London Livery Companies, which adorn the Council Chamber. Guided tours are available in July and August.

The small, old-fashioned **Harbour Museum** (Map p632; ☎ 7137 7331; Harbour Sq; admission free; ☽ 10am-1pm & 2-4.30pm Mon-Fri), with models

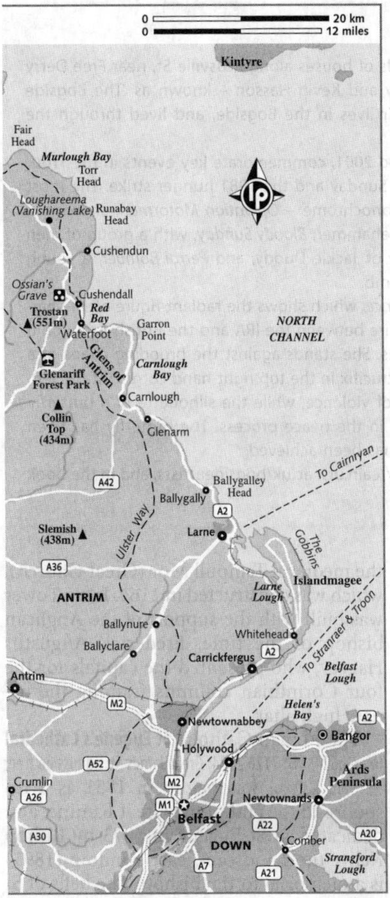

of ships, a replica of a *currach* – an early sailing boat of the type that carried St Colmcille to Iona – and the bosomy figurehead of the Minnehaha, is housed in the old Harbour Commissioner's Building next to the Guildhall.

Standing at the southern end of the walled city, **St Columb's Cathedral** (Map p632; ☎ 7126 7313; London St; adult/child £1.50/0.50; 🕒 9am-5pm Mon-Sat Easter-Oct, 9am-1pm & 2-4pm Mon-Sat Nov-Easter), built between 1628 and 1633, was the first post-Reformation church to be built in Britain or Ireland, and is Derry's oldest surviving building.

In the **porch** (under the spire, by the St Columb's Court entrance) you can see the original foundation stone of 1633 that records the cathedral's completion, inscribed:

> If stones could speake
> Then London's prayse
> Should sounde who
> Built this church and
> Cittie from the grounde

The smaller stone inset, inscribed '*In Templo Verus Deus Est Vereo Colendus*' (The True God is in His Temple and is to be truly worshipped), comes from the original Columban church built here in 1164.

Also in the porch is a hollow mortar shell fired into the churchyard during the Great Siege; inside were the terms of surrender. The neighbouring **chapter house** contains more historical artefacts, including paintings, old photos and the four huge padlocks used to secure the city gates in the 17th century.

BLOODY SUNDAY

On Sunday 30 January 1972, some 20,000 civilians marched through Derry protesting against internment without trial. It now seems clear that soldiers of the 1st Battalion of the Parachute Regiment opened fire on unarmed marchers. Fourteen people were shot dead, some shot in the back. None of those who fired the 108 bullets, nor the officers in charge, have been brought to trial or even disciplined; records have disappeared and weapons have been destroyed. The Widgery Commission investigation in 1972 failed to find anyone responsible.

Public dissatisfaction with the original investigation led to the massive **Bloody Sunday Inquiry** (www.bloody-sunday-inquiry.org.uk), headed by Lord Saville, which began in March 2000 and was drawing to a close at the time of writing; the inquiry received around 2500 witness statements. Its findings were due to be submitted to the government in the summer of 2005.

The **Bloody Sunday Trust** (Map p632; ☎ 7136 0880; www.bloodysundaytrust.org; 7-15 Foyle St; admission free; 🕒 9.30am-4pm Mon-Thu, 9.30am-3pm Fri) is a community-based history and education organisation that provides support for the families of Bloody Sunday. It is open to the public and has a range of photographic and audio exhibits on the events of that day.

THE BOGSIDE MURALS

The powerful murals that decorate the gable ends of houses along Rossville St, near Free Derry Corner, are the work of Tom Kelly, William Kelly and Kevin Hasson – known as 'The Bogside Artists'. The three men have spent most of their lives in the Bogside, and lived through the worst of the Troubles.

Their murals, mostly painted between 1997 and 2001, commemorate key events in the Troubles, including the Battle of the Bogside, Bloody Sunday and the 1981 hunger strike. The most powerful images are those painted largely in monochrome – *Operation Motorman*, showing a British soldier breaking down a door with a sledgehammer; *Bloody Sunday*, with a group of men led by local priest Father Daly carrying the body of Jackie Duddy; and *Petrol Bomber*, a young boy wearing a gas mask and holding a petrol bomb.

The most moving image is *The Death of Innocence*, which shows the radiant figure of 14-year-old schoolgirl Annette McGavigan, killed in crossfire between the IRA and the British Army on 6 September 1971, the 100th victim of the Troubles. She stands against the brooding chaos of a bombed-out building, the roof-beams forming a crucifix in the top right-hand corner. At the left, a downward-pointing rifle stands for the failure of violence, while the silhouette of a butterfly symbolises resurrection and the hope embodied in the peace process. The butterfly has been deliberately left unfinished until a lasting peace has been achieved.

The murals can be seen on the Internet at http://cain.ulst.ac.uk/bogsideartists, and in the book *Murals: The Bogside Artists* by William Kelly.

The **nave**, built in a squat, solid style known as Planter's Gothic, shares the austerity of many Church of Ireland cathedrals, with thick walls, small windows, and an open-timbered roof (from 1823) resting on corbels depicting the heads of past bishops and deans. The bishop's throne, at the far end of the nave, is an 18th-century mahogany chair in ornate, Chinese Chippendale style.

The **chancel**, and the stained-glass east window depicting the Ascension, date from 1887. The flags on either side of the window were captured from the French during the Great Siege; although the yellow silk has been renewed several times since, the poles and gold wirework are original.

OUTSIDE THE WALLS

As you enter the city across Craigavon Bridge, the first thing you see is the **Hands Across the Divide** monument. This striking bronze sculpture of two men reaching out to each other symbolises the spirit of reconciliation and hope for the future; it was unveiled in 1992, 20 years after Bloody Sunday.

Outside the city walls to the southwest is **Long Tower Church** (Map p624; ☎ 7126 2301; Long Tower St; admission free; ⊙ 9am-8.30pm Mon-Sat, 7.30am-7pm Sun), Derry's first post-Reformation Catholic church. Built in 1784 in neo-Renaissance style, it stands on the site of

the medieval Tempull Mor (Great Church), which was constructed in 1164. Long Tower was built with the support of the Anglican bishop of the time, Frederick Augustus Harvey, who presented the capitals for the four Corinthian columns framing the ornate high altar.

The Roman Catholic **St Eugene's Cathedral** (Map p624; ☎ 7126 2894; Great James St; admission free; ⊙ 9am-8.30pm) was begun in 1851 as a response to the end of the Great Famine, and dedicated to St Eugene in 1873 by Bishop Kelly; the handsome east window (1891) is a memorial to the bishop. The bells of St Eugene's still ring every night at 9pm as a reminder of the Penal Laws (in force from 1691 until the early 19th century) which forbade Catholics to attend mass and subjected them to a 9pm curfew.

BOGSIDE

The Bogside district, to the west of the walled city, developed in the 19th and early 20th centuries as a working-class, Catholic residential area. By the 1960s, its serried ranks of small, terrace houses had become an overcrowded ghetto of poverty and unemployment, a focus for the emerging civil-rights movement and a hotbed of nationalist discontent.

In August 1969, the three-day 'Battle of the Bogside' – a running street battle between local youths and the police – prompted the UK government to send British troops into Northern Ireland. The residents of the Bogside and neighbouring Brandywell district – 33,000 of them – declared themselves independent of the civil authorities, and barricaded the streets to keep the security forces out. 'Free Derry', as it was known, was a no-go area for the police and army, its streets patrolled by IRA volunteers. In 1972, the area around Rossville St witnessed the horrific events of Bloody Sunday (see boxed text, p627).

In recent years the area has been extensively redeveloped, the old houses and flats demolished and replaced with modern housing; the population is now down to 8000. All that remains of the old Bogside is **Free Derry Corner** (Map p624), at the intersection of Fahan and Rossville Sts, where the gable end of a terrace house painted with the famous 'You Are Now Entering Free Derry' slogan still stands. Nearby is the H-shaped **Hunger Strikers' Memorial** (Map p624).

The **Bloody Sunday Memorial** (Map p632), on Rossville St, is a simple granite obelisk that commemorates the 14 civilians who were shot dead by the British Army on 30 January 1972. The gable ends of the houses along Rossville St are decorated with murals painted by the Bogside Artists (see boxed text, opposite).

At the time of writing, the new **Museum of Free Derry** was due to open in Glenfada Park, just off Rossville St. It will chronicle the history of the Bogside and the civil-rights movement, and house an archive of documents, photographs and film footage relating to the area and its history.

THE WATERSIDE

Across the river from the walled city lies the largely Protestant Waterside district. At the height of the Troubles, many Protestants living in and around the Bogside moved across the river to escape the worst of the violence.

Here you'll find the **Workhouse Museum** (☎ 7131 8328; 23 Glendermott Rd; admission free; ☯ 10am-4.30pm Mon-Thu & Sat) housed in Derry's original 1840–1946 workhouse. Daily life at the workhouse for the 800 inmates was designed to encourage them to leave as soon as possible, alive or dead – one of

the exhibits is the grisly horse-drawn hearse used to carry away the corpses.

Other displays cover the Potato Famine, while the excellent Atlantic Memorial exhibition tells the story of the WWII Battle of the Atlantic and the major role that Derry played.

Walking Tour

Distance of Trail: 2km
Duration: 30 to 40 minutes

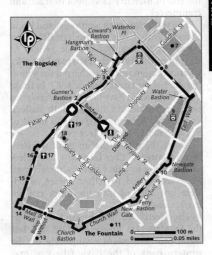

You can make a complete circuit of Derry's walled city, walking along the top of the walls, in around 30 minutes. There are frequent sets of steps where you can get on and off.

This walk starts from The Diamond, Derry's central square, dominated by the **war memorial (1)**.

From The Diamond, head along Butcher St to **Butcher's Gate (2)**. At the height of the Troubles the gate reverted to its original, 17th-century role, serving as a security checkpoint controlling entry to the city centre from the Bogside. Turn right before the gate and climb the steps up onto the top of the city walls.

Stroll downhill across **Castle Gate (3)**, added in 1865, to **Magazine Gate (4)**, named for the powder magazine that used to be close by. Inside the walls is the modern **O'Doherty's Tower** (5), based on a 16th-century castle that once stood nearby. It houses the excellent **Tower Museum** (6; p625). Outside the walls is the red-brick, neo-Gothic **Guildhall** (7; p626).

The River Foyle used to come up to the northeastern wall here, and the stretch from Coward's Bastion to the Water Bastion (demolished 1844) once had ships moored just outside. In the middle is the **Shipquay Gate** (8) built in 1805 to link the port with the market area. Symbols above the arch show the cornucopia (horn of plenty) and the rod of Mercury (a symbol of trade and commerce).

The walls then turn southwest and begin a steep climb beside the modern **Millennium Forum** (9) theatre and concert venue. At the top of the hill is the **Ferryquay Gate** (10), where the apprentice boys barred the gate at the start of the Great Siege of 1689. In those days there would have been a drawbridge as well as a padlock on the gate. Both padlock and key can be seen in the chapter house of St Columb's Cathedral (see p627).

Above the gate is the image of the Reverend George Walker (see item 16). Below in the arches to either side are metal rings; these were used to tether horses, which were not allowed into the inner city on market days.

The stretch of wall beyond overlooks the **Fountain** (11) housing estate, the last significant Protestant community on the western bank of the Foyle (the vast majority of Derry's Protestants have moved across the river to the Waterside area or further afield). A defiant mural proclaims 'Londonderry West Bank Loyalists Still Under Siege – No Surrender'. The round, brick-paved area on the ground outside New Gate is where a 10m-high bonfire is lit on the night before the annual Apprentice Boys' march.

Bishop's Gate (12), which bisects the southern flank of the wall, was rebuilt in 1789 for the 100th anniversary of the Siege. Bishop Harvey, a keen antiquarian, had a hand in the reconstruction and requested a triumphal arch in honour of King William III. During the Great Siege, it was here that King James II demanded the surrender of the city. The defenders replied with gunshots and a cry of 'There'll be no surrender!' – a phrase that staunch loyalists still cling to today.

Outside the gate on Bishop St Without is the one remaining turret of the 1791 **Old Gaol** (13). Theobald Wolfe Tone, founder of the United Irishmen, spent some time in prison here following the failed rebellion of 1798.

The **Double Bastion** (14) at the southwestern corner of the walls is dominated by an army observation tower, bristling with listening and watching devices and splashed with paint bombs hurled from below the walls by nationalist youths. The next section of wall is known as the **Grand Parade** (15), and offers an excellent view over the nationalist Bogside estate. The prominent murals were painted by a group known as the Bogside Artists (see boxed text, p628).

An empty plinth on **Royal Bastion** (16) marks the site of a monument to the Reverend George Walker, joint governor of the city during the Great Siege. The 27m-tall monument, erected in 1826 and seen by local nationalists as a symbol of unionist domination, was blown up by the IRA in 1973. The restored statue of Walker now stands in the memorial garden just behind the Apprentice Boys' Hall.

During the annual Apprentice Boys' march, an effigy of Robert Lundy used to be burnt at Royal Bastion. Lundy, the city governor before Walker, fled Derry at the start of the Siege and is still seen as a traitor by the loyalist community. In reply, Bogside Catholics used to stoke their fires with old shoes, clothes and anything else to produce an obnoxious smoke, in the hope that the loyalists would be smoked out.

Behind the Royal Bastion is the 1872 Church of Ireland **Chapel of St Augustine** (17), built on the site of St Colmcille's 6th-century monastery. A little further along is the **Apprentice Boys' Memorial Hall** (18), its windows protected by steel grilles and, like the army observation tower, splashed with paint bombs, and the grand Corinthian temple of the **First Derry Presbyterian Church** (19).

Just past the church is the Butcher's Gate, from where you can return to The Diamond, head down Magazine St to the Tower Museum, or descend Fahan St to the Bogside and the Bloody Sunday memorial.

Tours

City Tours (Map p632; ☎ 7127 1996; www.irishtour guides.com; 11 Carlisle Rd) Runs 1½-hour walking tours at 10am and 2pm daily, year round, starting at 11 Carlisle Rd. Tours cost £4 per person. It also offers tours of the Bogside and of Derry's murals.

Derry Visitor & Convention Bureau (Map p624; ☎ 7126 7284; 44 Foyle St) Offers 1½-hour guided walking tours of the walled city for £5/3.50 per adult/ concession. General-history tours depart from the centre at 11.15am and 3.15pm Monday to Friday in July and August, and at 2.30pm Monday to Friday November to June. The Living History tour on Friday afternoons covers Derry's role in the Troubles.

Foyle Cruises (Map p624; ☎ 7136 2857; Harbour Museum, Harbour Sq) Operates daily cruises on the Foyle estuary. Trips to Culmore Bay (1¼ hours) cost £6/4 per adult/child and depart at 2pm; evening cruises to Greencastle (four hours) with bar and entertainment cost £10/7 per adult/child, and depart at 8pm.

Northern Ireland Tours & Guides (☎ 7128 9051) Runs 1¼-hour Essential Walking Tours of historic Derry departing from the Guildhall, June to October (times by arrangement). These are tours for groups (£5 per person, minimum four) but individuals can phone to check if they can join an existing tour.

Festivals & Events

City of Derry Jazz Festival (www.cityofderryjazzfestival .com; early May) Five days of jazz at various venues.

Gasyard Wall Féile (☎ 7126 2812; early Aug) A cultural festival that features concerts, theatre and Irish-language events.

Féile na Samnha (www.derrycity.gov.uk/halloween; 27-31 Oct) The annual Halloween carnival, which has the entire city dressing up and partying in the streets.

Foyle Film Festival (www.foylefilmfestival.com; Nov) This week-long event is the North's biggest film festival.

Sleeping

It's best to book accommodation in advance during festival events.

BUDGET

Derry City Independent Hostel (Map p624; ☎ 7137 7989; www.derryhostel.com; 44 Great James St; dm/d £10/28; ☒ ▣) This small, friendly independent hostel is set in a Georgian town house, just a short walk north of the walled city. Rates include a continental breakfast and Internet access. There are laundry facilities, and a fifth night's stay is free. It's less than 10 minutes' walk from the bus station.

Derry City Hostel (Map p632; ☎ 7128 0280; derry citytours@aol.com; 4-6 Magazine St; dm £10-12.50, s/d £15/35; ▣ ☒) This family-friendly hostel is inside the city walls near Butcher's Gate, a five-minute walk from the bus station. It has a 24-hour reception, kitchen, dining room and restaurant. Dorm and singles rates exclude breakfast; doubles/twins have private bathroom and include breakfast.

MIDRANGE

Merchant's House (Map p624; ☎ 7126 9691; www .thesaddlershouse.com; 16 Queen St; s/d £25/45; ☒) Run by the same couple as the Saddler's House (below), this listed, Georgian-style town house is a gem of a B&B. It has an elegant lounge and dining room with marble fireplaces and antique furniture, TV and coffee-making facilities in all rooms, and home-made marmalade at breakfast. There are even bathrobes in the bedrooms. Call at the Saddler's House first to pick up a key.

Saddler's House (Map p624; ☎ 7126 9691; www .thesaddlershouse.com; 36 Great James St; s/d £25/45; ☒) Centrally located within a five-minute walk of the walled city, this friendly B&B is set in a lovely, Victorian town house. All seven rooms have private bathrooms, and you get to enjoy a huge breakfast in the family kitchen.

Abbey B&B (Map p624; ☎ 7127 9000; www.abbey accommodation.com; 4 Abbey St; s/d £30/50; ☒) There's a warm welcome waiting at this family-run B&B just a short walk from the walled city, on the edge of the Bogside. The brightly decorated rooms mostly have private bathrooms, and include family rooms with up to four beds.

Sunbeam House (Map p624; ☎ 7126 3603; sun beamhouse@hotmail.com; 147 Sunbeam Tce, Bishop St; s/d £28/48; ☒) This attractive red-brick terraced house is a five-minute walk south-west of the walled city. The four cheerfully decorated bedrooms are a bit on the small side, but there's nothing cramped about the hospitality. Or the size of the breakfasts!

Clarence House (Map p624; ☎ 7126 5342; clarence house@zoom.co.uk; 15 Northland Rd; s/d £30/50) A grand, red-brick Victorian town house, the Clarence opened as Derry's first ever B&B back in 1962. The chintzy, en-suite rooms are popular with visiting TV crews (the local BBC studio is just across the road).

Travelodge (Map p624; ☎ 0870 085 0950, from Republic of Ireland ☎ 1800 709 709; www.travelodge.co.uk;

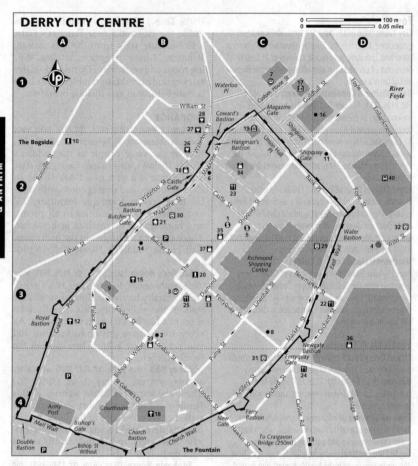

DERRY CITY CENTRE

22-24 Strand Rd; r £40-50; ⊠) Bland and characterless, but central and comfortable, the Travelodge offers a flat rate for rooms that take up to two adults and two children.

TOP END

Da Vinci's Hotel (☎ 7127 9111; www.davincishotel.com; 15 Culmore Rd; d £55-85, apt £67-160; P ⊠ ▣) This sleek boutique hotel on the west bank of the Foyle is the accommodation of choice for visiting celebrities, business people and politicians, offering spacious, stylish rooms and a hip cocktail bar and restaurant. It's located 1.5km north of the city centre. It also runs Da Vinci's Aparto-tel, a complex of 21 super-trendy, one- and two-bedroom serviced apartments closer

to the city centre at College Terrace, on Strand Rd.

City Hotel (Map p624; ☎ 7136 5800; www.gshotels.com/derry; Queen's Quay; s/d £67.50/90; P ⊠) Many of the rooms in this modern, stylish and business-oriented hotel have views over the river, and its central location puts it within easy walking distance of all the city's attractions. The website often has bargain midweek special offers.

Eating

Café Artisan (Map p632; ☎ 7128 2727; 18-20 Bishop St Within; mains £4-5; ◷ 9.30am-5.30pm Mon-Sat) This cool little caff is tucked away at the back of the Bookworm bookshop and serves delicious home-made soups, deli sandwiches, *panini* (type of Italian sandwich) and excellent cappuccinos.

Mange 2 (Map p624; ☎ 7136 1222; 2 Clarendon St; mains £11-15; ⏱ 11.30am-3pm & 5.30-10pm Mon-Fri, 10.30am-3pm & 5.30-10pm Sat & Sun) A candle-lit, Georgian-style dining room, with pale green walls and dark wood furniture, makes this an elegant venue for a splurge. The interesting fusion menu includes a handful of good veggie options, and there's an 'early bird' three-course dinner for two (£30 including a bottle of wine, 5.30pm to 6.30pm).

Fitzroy's (Map p632; ☎ 7126 6211; 2-4 Bridge St, 2nd entrance on Carlisle Rd; mains £7-12; ⏱ 10am-8pm Mon & Tue, 10am-10pm Wed, 9.30am-10pm Thu-Sat, noon-8pm Sun) Informal, bistro-style Fitzroy's does breakfast until 12.30pm, lunch to 5.30pm (mains £6), and then dinner, or you can just drop in for a coffee anytime. The menu offers Mediterranean and Asian flavours and caters well to vegetarians, and the set three-course dinner for £10 (7pm to 10pm Wednesday, Thursday and Friday) is excellent value.

Exchange Wine Bar & Restaurant (Map p624; ☎ 7127 3990; Queen's Quay; lunch £5-7, dinner £9-12; ⏱ noon-2.30pm & 5.30-10pm Mon-Sat, 5.30-9pm Sun) Dripping with designer chic in dark wood, stainless steel and coffee-coloured leather, the always-busy Exchange sports a good-value international menu that specialises in char-grilled chicken, steak and fish dishes. No reservations – it's first-come first-served.

Badger's Bar & Restaurant (Map p632; ☎ 7136 3306; 16-18 Orchard St; mains £5-6; ⏱ food served noon-7pm Mon-Thu, noon-9.30pm Fri & Sat, noon-4pm Sun) This convivial and family-friendly bar, decked out in stained glass and wood panelling, serves some of the best pub grub in the city, including a magnificent steak-and-Guinness pie. There's also a separate kids' menu.

Boston Tea Party (Map p632; 15 Craft Village; snacks £1-4; ⏱ 9am-5.30pm Mon-Sat) Home-made soups, very tasty sandwiches, freshly baked cakes, friendly service – what more could you want from a café?

Sandwich Co The Diamond (Map p632; ☎ 7137 2500; sandwiches & salads £3; ⏱ 9am-5pm Mon-Sat); Strand Rd (Map p624; 61 Strand Rd) White bread, brown bread, baguettes, *panini*, ciabatta – this place offers good-value, choose-your-own sandwiches and salads.

SELF-CATERING

Tesco (Map p624; ☎ 7137 4400; Quayside Shopping Centre, Strand Rd; ⏱ 9am-9pm Mon-Thu, 8.30am-9pm Fri, 8.30am-8pm Sat, 1-6pm Sun) Self-caterers can stock up at this big supermarket, just north of the walled city.

Drinking

Whatever you do in Derry, don't miss an evening in the city's lively pubs. They're friendly and atmospheric, mostly open until 1am, and are within easy walking distance of each other – there are six within dancing distance along Waterloo St.

Mullan's Bar (Map p624; ☎ 7126 5300; 13 Little James St) Mullan's is a good live-music venue, featuring jazz, blues and traditional sessions on Wednesday and Thursday nights, with a DJ Friday to Sunday. The lavish interior, stuffed with stained glass, polished wood, brass rails and bronze figures, was rebuilt after a petrol bomb set the roof on fire during the Troubles.

Bar (☎ 7127 9111; 15 Culmore Rd) This award-winning bar at Da Vinci's Hotel goes in for the monumentalism so loved by Irish bar designers, sporting a massive, polished wood bar topped with what can only be described as a triumphal arch. The mood is laid back, and food is available from noon to 5.30pm.

Peadar O'Donnell's (Map p632; ☎ 7126 2318; 63 Waterloo St) A backpackers' favourite, Peadar's goes for traditional music sessions every night starting about 11pm. It's done up as a typical Irish pub-cum-grocer down to shelves of grocery items, with a pig's head and hams hanging off the ceiling.

Other good traditional bars in Waterloo St include:

Gweedore Bar (Map p632; ☎ 7126 3513; 59-61 Waterloo St) Live bands every night.

Dungloe Bar (Map p632; ☎ 7126 7716; 41 Waterloo St) Irish music Thursday night, live bands Friday and Saturday, karaoke on Sunday.

Entertainment
CLUBS & LIVE MUSIC

Earth@Café Roc (Map p624; ☎ 7136 0556; 1 College Tce; admission free–£5) Derry's main nightclub and bar complex, close to the university, has music and moods to suit all tastes. The flagship Earth club has a student night on Tuesdays, chart hits and dance anthems on Fridays, and guest DJs on Saturdays. Stylish Café Roc is the neighbouring pre-club bar, with live bands on Monday nights, while the classical, candle-lit Suzie's Piano Bar offers the chance to relax with just a baby grand for background music.

Sandino's (Map p632; ☎ 7130 9297; www.sandinos .com; 1 Water St; admission free; ☯ 11.30am-1am Mon-Sat, 1pm-midnight Sun) This is a smoky, intimate Latin American–themed venue (named after Nicaraguan guerrilla leader Augusto Sandino), popular with up-and-coming local bands as well as visiting musicians. There's a live band on Friday and occasionally midweek, a DJ on Saturday night and a traditional Irish music session on Sunday afternoon at 4pm. There are regular theme nights, fundraising nights and political events. Check the website for events.

Spirit Bar (☎ 7127 9111; 15 Culmore Rd; admission free; ☯ from 8.30pm Fri-Sun) The Spirit Bar at Da Vinci's Hotel is *the* place to sip cocktails and be seen among Derry's 20- and 30-something in-crowd (there's a strict 23-and-over age limit). There's a '60s and '70s

night on Friday, chart hits and dance music on Saturday and Sunday.

CONCERTS, THEATRE & CINEMA

Millennium Forum (Map p632; ☎ 7126 4455; www .millenniumforum.co.uk; Newmarket St) Ireland's biggest theatre auditorium is a major venue for dance, drama, concerts, opera and musicals.

Nerve Centre (Map p632; ☎ 7126 0562; www.nerve -centre.org.uk; 7-8 Magazine St) The Nerve Centre is a multimedia arts centre started in the late 1980s to encourage young, local talent in the fields of music and film. The centre has a performance area, theatre, cinema, bar and café.

Playhouse (Map p632; ☎ 7126 8027; www.derry playhouse.co.uk; 5 Artillery St; ☯ box office 10am-4pm Mon-Fri) This community arts centre stages dance and theatre performances. It also houses the Context Gallery, which hosts exhibitions by local artists.

Waterside Theatre (☎ 7131 4000; The Ebrington Centre, Glendermott Rd) This theatre 500m east of the River Foyle stages concerts and plays about twice a week.

Magee College (Map p624; ☎ 7137 5679; www .ulster.ac.uk/culture; University of Ulster, Northland Rd) The college holds a variety of arts, theatrical and classical concert performances throughout the year.

Strand Multiplex (Map p624; ☎ 7137 3900; Quayside Shopping Centre, Strand Rd) Apart from Tuesday night screenings at the Nerve Centre, this seven-screen multiplex is the only cinema in town.

Shopping

Craft Village (Map p632; entrances from Shipquay St, Magazine St & Tower Museum) is a little courtyard with a handful of craft shops selling Derry crystal, hand-woven cloth, ceramics, jewellery and other local craft items.

Donegall Shop (Map p632; ☎ 7126 6928; 8 Shipquay St) Sells garments, tweeds and souvenirs.

Ogmiós (Map p624; ☎ 7126 4132; 34 Great James St) Stocks a good range of Irish-language books, traditional-music CDs, musical instruments, pottery, prints and jewellery.

Soundsaround (Map p632; ☎ 7128 8890; 22a Waterloo St) Has an excellent selection of traditional music on tape and CD.

McGilloway Gallery (Map p632; ☎ 7136 6011; 6 Shipquay St) A commercial gallery that deals in modern Irish paintings.

Whatnot (Map p632; ☎ 7128 8333; 22 Bishop St Within) An interesting little antique shop crammed with jewellery and collectables.

Austins (Map p632; ☎ 7126 1817; 2 The Diamond) Ireland's oldest department store, is a good place to shop for Irish linen.

Foyleside Shopping Centre (Map p632; ☎ 7137 7575; Orchard St) is a huge, four-level mall just outside the eastern city walls, which contains a Marks and Spencer, Virgin Megastore, Dixons and other high-street chain stores.

Getting There & Away

AIR

City of Derry Airport (☎ 7181 0784; www.cityofderry airport.com) is about 13km east of Derry along the A2 towards Limavady. There are direct flights daily to London Stansted (Ryanair), Dublin and Glasgow (British Airways), Birmingham and Manchester (Aer Arann).

BUS

The **bus station** (Map p632; ☎ 7126 2261) is on Foyle St, just northeast of the walled city.

Bus No 212, the *Maiden City Flyer*, is a fast and frequent service between Derry and Belfast (£9, 1¾ hours, every 30 minutes Monday to Saturday, seven Sunday), calling at Dungiven. Other useful Ulsterbus services include No 273 to Belfast (three hours) via Omagh (£6, 1¼ hours, five to eight daily); bus No 234 to Limavady and Coleraine (£5.90, one hour, five daily Monday to Saturday), continuing to Portstewart and Portrush twice daily (four daily during university vacations).

The **Airporter** (Map p624; ☎ 7126 9996; www .airporter.co.uk; Quayside Shopping Centre, Strand Rd) bus service runs direct from Derry to Belfast International (£15, 1½ hours) and Belfast City (£15, two hours) airports. There are 10 buses a day from Monday to Friday, five on Saturday and four on Sunday.

Ulsterbus services to the Republic include bus No 274 to Dublin (£14, 4½ hours, five or six daily) and No 296 to Cork (£18, 10¼ hours, one daily Monday to Friday) via Omagh and Enniskillen (change buses at Omagh and Longford). The Cork bus leaves Derry at 9am, arriving at 7.15pm. The bus from Cork leaves at 9.20am and arrives in Derry at 7.50pm.

Lough Swilly Bus Company (☎ 7126 2017) has an office upstairs at the bus station, and runs buses to Buncrana, Carndonagh, Dun-gloe, Letterkenny (£4.80, 10 daily Monday to Saturday) and Moville in County Donegal. The 10.15am bus to Carndonagh continues to Malin Head (£5.50, 1½ hours) on Monday, Wednesday, Friday and Saturday – a very scenic trip.

Bus Éireann (in Donegal ☎ 353-742 1309) service No 64 runs from Derry to Galway (£12.50, 5¼ hours, six daily Monday to Saturday, four on Sunday) via Letterkenny, Donegal and Sligo.

TRAIN

Derry's Waterside train station is on the eastern side of the River Foyle; a free shuttle bus (No 999) links it with the bus station on Foyle St. Trains to Belfast (£9, 2¼ hours, seven or eight daily Monday to Saturday, four on Sunday) are slower but more comfortable than the bus, and the section of line between Derry and Coleraine is very scenic. There are also frequent trains to Coleraine (45 minutes, seven daily), with connections to Portrush (1¼ hours).

Getting Around

Bus No 143 to Limavady stops near the airport, otherwise a taxi costs about £10.

Local buses leave from Foyle St, outside the bus station, where there are also shareable black cabs to outlying suburbs such as Shantallow. The **Derry Taxi Association** (☎ 7126 0247) and **Foyle Taxis** (☎ 7126 3905) operate from the city centre to all areas.

The Foyle Valley cycle route passes through Derry on the way to Strabane.

LIMAVADY & AROUND

pop 12,000

Enchanted by a folk tune played by a blind fiddler outside her window in 1851, Limavady resident Jane Ross (1810–79) jotted down the melody – then known as O'Cahan's Lament, and later as the Londonderry Air. She had written down for the first time the tune that came to be known around the world as *Danny Boy* – probably the most famous Irish song of all time.

Limavady was granted to Sir Thomas Phillips, the organiser of the Plantation of County Londonderry (see p35), by James I in 1612, after the last ruling chief, Sir Donnell Ballagh O'Cahan, was found guilty of rebellion. Its original Gaelic name Léim an Mhadaidh means 'The Dog's Leap' and refers to one of the O'Cahans' dogs that jumped a gorge across the River Roe to bring warning of an unexpected enemy attack.

The **tourist office** (☎ 7776 0307; 7 Connell St; ☺ 9am-5pm Mon-Fri Sep-Jun, to 5.45pm Jul & Aug) is northeast of the town centre in the Limavady Borough Council Offices. You can find Internet access at the café, Oven Door.

Sights

Today Limavady is a quiet, prosperous small town. There's not much to see in town except the **blue plaque** on the wall at 51 Main St, opposite the Alexander Arms, commemorating the home of Jane Ross. Limavady holds a **jazz and blues festival** (www .limavadyjazzandblues.com) in early June.

The lovely **Roe Valley Country Park**, about 3km south of Limavady, has riverside walks stretching for 5km either side of the River Roe, a world-renowned trout and salmon river. The area is associated with the O'Cahans, who ruled the valley until the Plantation. The 17th-century settlers saw the flax-growing potential of the damp river valley and the area became an important linen-manufacturing centre.

The **Dogleap Centre** (☎ 7772 2074; 41 Dogleap Rd; admission free; ☺ 9am-6pm daily Apr-Sep, 9am-5pm Mon-Fri Oct-Mar) houses a visitor centre and tearoom. Next door is Ulster's first domestic **hydroelectric power station**, opened in 1896; it opens on request at the visitor centre. The nearby **Weaving Shed Museum** (admission free; ☺ 1-5pm daily Jul & Aug, 1-5pm Sat & Sun May & Jun) contains old photographs and relics of the valley's flax industry. The scutch mill, where the flax was pounded, is a 20-minute walk away, along the river, past two watchtowers built to guard the linen when it was spread out in the fields for bleaching.

The park is clearly marked off the B192 road between Limavady and Dungiven. Bus No 146 from Limavady to Dungiven will drop you on the main road, but there's no weekend service. The park is about a 30-minute walk from the main road.

Sleeping & Eating

Gorteen House Hotel (☎ 7772 2333; www.gorteen .com; 187 Roe Mill Rd; s/d £48/65; ☐ P) A fine old country house off Roe Mill Rd, 1.5km south of Limavady town centre, the grandly renovated Gorteen House is popular with golf-

ers, and sports an impressive lobby and a lovely restaurant with a panoramic view of the hills.

Alexander Arms Hotel (☎ 7776 3443; 34 Main St; s/d £25/40; ☐ P ☒) A long-established hotel and pub dating from 1875, the centrally located Alexander Arms is now a friendly, family-run place that offers B&B and serves pub grub and restaurant meals.

Lime Tree (☎ 7776 4300; 60 Catherine St; mains £13-16; ☺ 6-9pm Tue-Fri, 6-9.30pm Sat) Limavady's top restaurant serves up fresh local produce, with an emphasis on fish dishes such as baked salmon supreme with a fresh herb crust, and seafood thermidor. There's also a three-course set menu (£20), and an early-bird menu (two/three courses £10.50/13.50) available before 7pm Tuesday to Friday.

Oven Door (☎ 7772 2411; 5 Market St; mains £3-5; ☺ 9am-5.30pm Mon-Sat) If you fancy a quick snack, this homely bakery has a comfy cafeteria at the back, serving good coffee, cakes and light meals. It's a local institution, patronised by a cross-section of the community, with a pleasantly old-fashioned feel.

Getting There & Away

Bus No 143 runs between Derry and Limavady almost hourly. There's no direct bus to Belfast from Limavady but connections can be made at Coleraine or Dungiven.

DUNGIVEN

The small market town of Dungiven (Dún Geimhin), 14km south of Limavady, has an interesting old priory and a good independent hostel. It's an easy stopoff if you're travelling between Belfast and Derry, and a

---

TOP FIVE B&BS IN NORTHERN IRELAND

- Anna's House (County Down; p604)
- Briers Country House (County Down; p604)
- Fortwilliam Country House (County Down; p604)
- Merchant's House (County Derry; p604)
- Whitepark House B&B (County Antrim; p604)

better base than Limavady for exploring the Sperrin Mountains. The Ulster Way passes nearby.

There's a tourist information desk in Dungiven Castle.

Sights

The remains of the Augustinian **Dungiven Priory**, off the A6 on the eastern edge of town, date back to the 12th century when it replaced a pre-Norman monastery.

In the chancel of the church is the magnificent **tomb of Cooey-na-Gal**, a chieftain of the O'Cahans who died in 1385. It's difficult to see in the dark of the blocked-off chancel, but the tomb bears figures of six kilted 'gallowglasses' (armed retainers), Scottish mercenaries hired by Cooey O'Cahan as minders – they earned him the nickname 'na-Gal' ('of the Foreigners'). It's topped by a beautifully sculpted canopy of Gothic tracery.

Near the entrance to the churchyard is a **bullaun**, a mossy, hollowed stone originally used by the monks for grinding grain, but now collecting rainwater and used as a site of pilgrimage and prayer by people seeking cures for illnesses. A nearby tree is covered in prayer rags left by visiting pilgrims.

Sleeping

Dungiven Castle (☎ 7774 2428; www.dungivencastle .com; Main St; dm/d £12/32; **P** 🖳 🖧) Renovated Dungiven Castle provides good hostel-style accommodation in 10-bed dorms, and en-suite doubles, twins and family rooms. Facilities include laundry, kitchen and free tea and coffee. Don't be put off by the car park and ugly buildings on the street side – the other side looks out across beautiful gardens to the Sperrin Mountains.

Flax Mill Hostel (☎ 7774 2655; www.flax-mill.com; Mill Lane, Derrylane; camp sites £3.50, dm £5.80; 🕙 Mar-Oct; **P** ✗) This converted 18th-century flax mill is 5km north of Dungiven, signposted off the B192 road to Limavady. The owners of this idyllic countryside retreat mill their own flour, grow their own organic veggies, weave their own textiles and generate their own electricity. There are 16 beds in three dorms and one double room; it's an extra £2.20 for breakfast. If you're travelling by bus, the owners will pick you up from Dungiven.

Getting There & Away

The hourly bus No 212 between Derry and Belfast stops on Main St in Dungiven, as does the No 246 Limavady (£2.40, 25 minutes, six daily Monday to Saturday, two Sunday) to Belfast service.

INLAND COUNTY DERRY

Inland County Derry, southeast of Dungiven across the Glenshane Pass, is staunch Protestant territory occupied by Plantation towns like Draperstown, Magherafelt and Moneymore, established by the London guilds in the 17th century with grants of land from William of Orange.

Draperstown

pop 1400

Draperstown was founded in the early 17th century by, surprise surprise, the Worshipful Company of Drapers. Today it is a neat little market town, home to the **Ulster Plantation Centre** (☎ 7962 7800; 50 High St; adult/child £3/1.50; 🕙 10am-5pm Mon-Sat, 1-5pm Sun Easter-Sep, 10am-4pm Mon-Fri Oct-Easter) whose multimedia exhibits tell the story of the Plantation from the 'Flight of the Earls' in 1603 to the Potato Famine of the mid-19th century. At the time of research the opening times were a little uncertain – best to phone ahead and check before going out of your way for a visit.

Draperstown can be reached from Dungiven by taking the Belfast bus No 212 to Glenshane Rd, Castledawson, then changing to No 182 (2¼ hours). Check the bus times locally.

Moneymore

pop 1200

Moneymore was also founded by the London Drapers, which installed Ulster's first piped water supply here in 1615. The country house of **Springhill** (☎ 8674 8210; 20 Springhill Rd; adult/child £4.10/2.20; 🕙 noon-6pm daily Jul & Aug, noon-6pm Sat, Sun & hols mid-Mar–Jun & Sep), 1.5km south of Moneymore on the B18, is an interesting example of early Plantation architecture. The original house was built around 1695 by the Lenox-Conynghams, settlers from Scotland, and enlarged by the addition of the wings in the 18th century. Inside are antique weapons, an important collection of costumes dating from the 18th to the early 20th centuries, and a friendly ghost called Olivia.

Ulsterbus Nos 110 and 210 between Belfast and Cookstown stop at Moneymore, a 20-minute walk from the house.

COASTAL COUNTY DERRY
Magilligan Point

The huge triangular spit of land that almost closes off the mouth of Lough Foyle is mostly taken up by a military firing range, and is home to a once-notorious prison. Still, it's worth a visit for its vast sandy beaches – **Magilligan Strand** to the west, and the 9km sweep of **Benone Strand** to the northeast. On the point itself, watching over the entrance to Lough Foyle, stands a **Martello tower**, built during the Napoleonic Wars in 1812 to guard against French invasion.

Benone Tourist Complex (☎ 7775 0555; 59 Benone Ave; camp sites £6.60-8.50, caravans £11-14.60; ☼ 9am-10pm Jul & Aug, 9am-dusk Apr-Jun & Sep, 9am-5pm Oct-Mar), adjacent to Benone Strand, has an outdoor heated pool, children's pool, tennis courts and putting green. Note that dogs are not allowed on the beach from May to September.

A **ferry** (in the Republic ☎ 074-938 1901; www .loughfoyleferry.com; car/motorcycle/pedestrian £6/3/1.50) runs between Magilligan Point and Greencastle in County Donegal all year round. The trip takes 15 minutes and runs every 15 minutes from 7.20am Monday to Saturday and 9am Sunday. The last ferry is at 9.50pm every day April to September and 7.50pm every day October to March.

Downhill

In 1774 the eccentric Bishop of Derry and fourth Earl of Bristol, Frederick Augustus Hervey, built himself a palatial home, Downhill, on the coast west of Castlerock. It burnt down in 1851, was rebuilt between 1873 and 1876, and finally abandoned after WWII. The ruins of the house now stand forlornly on a cliff top.

The original demesne covered some 160 hectares, which is now part of the Forest Service's **Downhill Forest** (admission free; ☼ 10am-dusk). The beautiful landscaped gardens below the ruins of the house are the work of celebrated gardener Jan Eccles, who became custodian of Downhill at the age of 60 and created the garden over a period of 30 years. She died in 1997 aged 94.

The main attraction here is the little **Mussenden Temple** (admission free; parking at Lion's Gate car/motorcycle £3.70/2.30; ☼ 11am-7.30pm daily Jul & Aug, 11am-6pm daily Jun, 11am-6pm Sat, Sun & hols Mar-May & Sep, 11am-5pm Sat & Sun Oct), built by the bishop to house his library or his mistress – opinions differ! He had an affair with the mistress of Frederick William II of Prussia well into his old age.

It's a pleasant, 20-minute walk to the temple from Castlerock, with fine views west to the beach at Benone and Donegal, and east to Portstewart and the shadowy outlines of the Scottish hills. Begin at the path along the seaward side of the caravan park; halfway there, you have to descend into a steep-sided valley and climb the steps on the far side of the little lake. On the beach below the temple, the bishop used to challenge his own clergy to horseback races, rewarding the winners with lucrative parishes.

On the main road 1km west of the temple, at the closed-down Downhill Hotel, the scenic **Bishop's Road** climbs steeply up through a ravine, and heads over the hills to Limavady. There are spectacular views over Lough Foyle, Donegal and the Sperrin Mountains from the **Gortmore** picnic area, and from the cliff top at **Binevenagh Lake**.

SLEEPING

Downhill Hostel (☎ 7084 9077; www.thedownhill hostel.com; 12 Mussenden Rd; dm/d £9/35, r £35 plus £5 per child; P) This beautifully restored late-19th-century house, tucked beneath the sea cliffs and overlooking the beach, offers very comfortable accommodation in three six-bed dorms and four double rooms. There's a well-stocked kitchen, laundry facilities and a big lounge with an open fire and a view of the sea. You can even paint your own mugs, plates and bowls in the neighbouring pottery. There are no shops in Downhill so bring supplies with you.

Castlerock

Castlerock is a small seaside resort with a decent beach. At the turn-off from the main coast road towards Castlerock is the late-17th-century **Hezlett House** (☎ 7084 8567; guided tour adult/child £3.70/2.20; ☼ 1-5pm Wed-Mon Jul & Aug, 1-5pm Sat & Sun Jun), a thatched cottage noted for its cruck-truss roof gables of stone and turf strengthened with wooden crucks, or crutches. The interior decoration is Victorian.

Bus No 134 between Limavady and Coleraine (10 to 12 daily Monday to Saturday) stops at Downhill and Castlerock, as does No 234 between Derry and Coleraine.

There are eight trains a day from Castlerock to Coleraine (10 minutes) and Derry (35 minutes) Monday to Saturday, and four on Sunday.

COLERAINE
pop 25,300
Coleraine (Cúil Raithin), on the banks of the River Bann, is an important transport hub and shopping centre for County Derry and the Causeway Coast. It was one of the original Plantation towns of County Londonderry, founded in 1613. The University of Ulster was established here in 1968, much to the chagrin of Derry, which had lobbied hard to win it.

Orientation & Information
The mostly pedestrianised town centre is on the east bank of the River Bann. From the combined train and bus station turn left along Railway Rd to find the **Tourist Information Centre** (☎ 7034 4723; colerainetic@btconnect.com; Railway Rd; ❂ 9am-5pm Mon-Sat) then turn right at King's Gate St for the main shopping area and **Coleraine Library** (☎ 7034 2561; Queen St; ❂ 10am-8pm Mon, Tue & Fri, 10am-5.30pm Wed & Thu, 10am-5pm Sat), which has public Internet access £1.50 per 30 minutes.

Sights
The tourist office has a *Heritage Trail* leaflet that will guide you around what little remains of the original Plantation town, including **St Patrick's Church**, parts of which date from 1613, and fragments of the town walls.

Just 1.5km south of the town centre, on the east bank of the river, is **Mountsandel Mount**, a mysterious mound that may have been an early-Christian stronghold or a later Anglo-Norman fortification. Nearby, a 7th-millennium-BC Mesolithic site has been excavated, revealing postholes, hearths and pits.

Sleeping
There's not much accommodation in the town centre; most B&Bs are on the fringes.

Town House (☎ 7034 4869; dale@townhouse.free serve.co.uk; 45 Millburn Rd; s/d £20/36; P ✗) The Town House B&B is a listed mid-19th-

century terrace house with large bedrooms and a homely atmosphere; originally built for a sea captain, it has been tastefully restored and furnished with antiques. It's a 10-minute walk west of the train and bus station.

Camus Country House (☎ 7034 2982; 27 Curragh Rd, Castleroe; s/d £30/50; P ✗) This lovely 17th-century house is on the site of an 8th-century monastery, and there's an old Celtic cross in the adjacent cemetery. The owner can organise fishing trips. It's signposted off the A54, west of the river and 5km south of town.

Getting There & Away
Ulsterbus No 218 links Coleraine to Portrush (£2, 20 minutes) and Belfast (£7.40, 1¾ hours, hourly Monday to Saturday, three on Sunday). Bus No 234 goes to Derry (£5.90, one hour, six to nine daily Monday to Saturday, two Sunday) via Limavady. See also p623.

There are regular trains from Coleraine to Belfast (£7.20, two hours) and Derry. A branch line links Coleraine to Portrush (£1.20, 12 minutes, hourly).

PORTSTEWART
pop 6500
When the English novelist William Thackeray visited the seaside and golfing resort of Portstewart (Port Stíobhaird) in 1842, he noted the 'air of comfort and neatness'. His assessment still rings true, and the place has a slightly upmarket feel that distinguishes it from populist Portrush, 6km farther east.

Orientation & Information
Central Portstewart consists of a west-facing promenade with a harbour at the north end. A coastal walk, paralleled by Strand Rd, continues south to the beach of Portstewart Strand.

The **tourist office** (☎ 7083 2286; Town Hall, The Crescent; ❂ 10am-1pm & 2-4.30pm Mon-Sat Jul & Aug) is in the library in the red-brick town hall at the south end of the promenade.

Sights & Activities
The broad, 2.5km-long beach of **Portstewart Strand** is a 20-minute walk south of the centre, or a short bus ride along Strand Rd. Parking (£4.50 per car) is allowed on the

firm sand, which can accommodate over 1000 cars.

In early May the **North-West 200 motorcycle race** (www.northwest200.fm) is run on a road circuit taking in Portrush, Portstewart and Coleraine. This classic race is one of the last to be run on closed public roads anywhere in Europe, and attracts up to 70,000 spectators; if you're not one of them, it's best to avoid the area on the race weekend.

The **Port Path** is a 10.5km coastal footpath (part of the Ulster Way) that stretches from Portstewart Strand to White Rocks, 3km east of Portrush.

Portstewart is within a few kilometres of three of Northern Ireland's top **golf courses** – Royal Portrush (green fees weekday/weekend £95/110), Portstewart (£65/85) and Castlerock (£50/70).

Sleeping

Don't even think about turning up without a booking during the North-West 200 weekend in May.

Causeway Coast Hostel (☎ 7083 3789; rick@causewaycoasthostel.fsnet.co.uk; 4 Victoria Tce; dm £8.50, d £22-26) This neat terrace house just northeast of the harbour has spacious four-, six- and eight-bed dorms plus three twin rooms. It has its own kitchen, laundry and a welcoming open fire in winter. Bus No 218 from Coleraine train and bus station stops nearby.

Anchorage Inn (☎ 7083 4401; .com; 87-89 The Promenade; s/d £50/70; **P** ✗) The inn's 20 en-suite rooms, some with sea views, provide comfortable, central B&B accommodation just a one-minute walk from the prom.

Cul-Erg B&B (☎ 7083 6610; culerg@btopenworld .com; 9 Hillside; s/d £30/50; ✗) This family-run B&B is in a modern, flower-bedecked terrace house just a couple of minutes' walk from the promenade. Warm and welcoming, it's set in a quiet cul-de-sac; the rooms at the back have a view of the sea.

Cromore Halt Inn (☎ 7083 6888; www.cromore .com; 158 Station Rd; s/d £45/75; **P** ✗) About 1km east of the harbour, on the corner of Station Rd and Mill Rd, Cromore has a dozen modern, businesslike rooms with satellite TV, phone and modem point, and a good restaurant.

Portstewart Holiday Park (☎ 7083 3308; 80 Mill Rd; camp sites £14; ☼ Mar-Oct) This is the nearest place to the promenade (a 15-minute walk

away) that you can pitch a tent. Coming from Coleraine on the A2, turn right at the Mill Rd/Strand Rd roundabout.

Eating & Drinking

Morelli's (☎ 7083 2150; 53 The Promenade; mains £3-7; ☼ 9am-11pm, food served to 8pm) This is a local institution that has been dispensing mouthwatering ice cream since 1911. This modern café dishes up pasta, pizza, sandwiches, omelettes, and fish and chips, as well as good coffee and cakes, and has a great view across the bay to Mussenden Temple, Benone Strand and Donegal.

Anchor Bar (☎ 7083 4401; 87-89 The Promenade; mains £7-11) Located at the Anchorage Inn, this is the liveliest of Portstewart's traditional pubs, famed for its Guinness and hugely popular with students from the nearby University of Ulster. It serves decent pub food, opens till late, has live music Thursday to Monday, karaoke on Tuesday and a quiz on Wednesday. There's also Skippers Bistro, which serves more substantial meals with a Mediterranean and Mexican menu.

Shenanigans Winebar & Restaurant (☎ 7083 6000; 78 The Promenade; mains £9-14; ☼ food served 12.30-2.30pm & 5-9.30pm Mon-Sat, 12.30-9.30pm Sun) Big, bright, brash and busy, Shenanigans has an international menu that ranges from Irish and Mexican through Indian to Chinese and Thai, with a fair selection of veg dishes. In addition to a restaurant, the complex has two bars – rustic O'Haras Bar is another popular student venue, with standing room only at weekends, while Bar 7 is more relaxed, serving coffee, cocktails and shooters.

Harbour Café (☎ 7083 4103; 18 The Promenade; mains £4; ☼ 9am-7pm Mon-Fri, 9am-8pm Sat) The local 'greasy spoon' is the place for reasonably priced breakfast fry-ups, filled rolls and light meals.

***

TOP FIVE VIEWPOINTS IN NORTHERN IRELAND

- Binevenagh Lake (p638)
- Fair Head (p649)
- Magho Cliffs (p666)
- Scrabo Hill (p603)
- Slieve Donard (p613)

Ashiana (☎ 7083 4455; 12a The Diamond; mains £5-8; ✆ 5-11pm Tue-Sun) This place offers a mixed menu of Indian and European dishes, with a good vegetarian selection.

Getting There & Away

Bus No 140 plies between Coleraine and Portstewart (£2, 17 minutes) roughly every half-hour (fewer on Sunday). Also see p623.

The nearest train station is at Portrush. See p642 for details.

COUNTY ANTRIM

PORTRUSH

pop 5700

The bustling seaside resort of Portrush (Port Rois) is bursting at the seams with holiday-makers in high season and, not surprisingly, many of its attractions are focused unashamedly on good, old-fashioned family fun. However, it is also one of Ireland's top surfing spots, and is home to the North's hottest nightclub.

Portrush Tourist Information Centre (☎ 7082 3333; Dunluce Centre, 10 Sandhill Dr; ✆ 9am-7pm mid-Jun–Aug, 9am-5pm Mon-Fri, noon-5pm Sat & Sun Apr–mid-Jun & Sep, noon-5pm Sat & Sun Mar & Oct) books accommodation and has a bureau de change.

Sights & Activities

Portrush's main attraction is the beautiful sandy beach of **Curran Strand** that stretches for 3km to the east of the town, ending at the scenic chalk cliffs of White Rocks.

The **Dunluce Family Entertainment Centre** (☎ 7082 4444; 10 Sandhill Dr; admission £3.50-4.50; ✆ noon-6.30pm Sat & Sun Apr & May, noon-5pm Mon-Fri, noon-6.30pm Sat & Sun Jun, 10.30am-6.30pm daily Jul & Aug, noon-5pm Sat & Sun Sep-Mar) is a hi-tech, indoor adventure playground especially for kids, with interactive games, a computerised treasure hunt and a 'turbo-tour' motion-simulator ride.

Waterworld (☎ 7082 2001; The Harbour; adult/child under 7 £4.50/1.50; ✆ 10am-8pm Mon-Sat, noon-8pm Sun), by the harbour, has indoor swimming pools, waterslides and spa baths for children to play in (family tickets are available), and ten-pin bowling (6pm to 10pm Monday to Friday, noon to 10pm Saturday, noon to 6pm Sunday). The Health Suite (sauna,

steam room and sunbeds) is included in the admission price.

Portrush Countryside Centre (☎ 7082 3600; Bath Rd; admission free; ✆ 10am-6pm Jun-Sep) has even more activities for kids, including marine-life exhibits, a touch pool, rock-pool rambles and fossil hunts (closed until further notice at time of research).

In summer, boats depart regularly for **cruises** or **fishing trips**; the tourist office has a list of operators. For horse riding contact the **Maddybenny Riding Centre** (☎ 7082 3394; Maddybenny Farm, Atlantic Rd; lessons & hacking per hr £10); beginners are welcome.

Portrush is famous as a **surfing** centre. The friendly **Troggs** (☎ 7082 5476; www.troggs .com; 88 Main St; ✆ 9am-5.30pm Tue-Sun) surf shop offers bodyboard/surfboard hire (£4/10 per day) and wetsuit hire (£5 per day), surf reports, an online guide to local beaches, and general advice. A two-hour lesson including equipment hire costs £25.

Sleeping

Places fill up quickly during summer so it's advisable to book in advance.

Alexandra Town House (☎ 7082 2284; www .alexandratownhouse.com; 11 Landsdowne Cres; s £25, d £45-60; **P** ✕) An elegant, four-storey terraced town house dating from 1901, the Alexandra has lots of nice features such as polished wood floors, period fireplaces and a rolltop bath. The more expensive rooms have superb views along the coast.

Clarmont (☎ 7082 2397; www.clarmont.com; 10 Landsdowne Cres; s/d £25/50; ✕) If the Alexandra is full, its next-door neighbour shares the great views, and has a décor that tastefully mixes period and modern. Ask for a bedroom with a bay window overlooking the sea.

Harbour Heights (☎ 7082 2765; www.harbour heightsportrush.com; 17 Kerr St; s/d £25/65; ✕ 💻) This place has everything a good guesthouse should have – smart, comfortable rooms, fluffy bathrobes, great food, and a stunning view over harbour and beach, plus knowledgeable owners who manage to be friendly and helpful without being in your face.

MaCools (☎ 7082 4845; www.portrush-hostel.com; 5 Causeway View Tce; dm/d £10/28; 💻) MaCools is a welcoming, independent hostel with 18 beds in single-sex dorms with sea views, and one private double room. There's laundry and cooking facilities (with free tea, coffee, herbs and spices) and bicycles for hire

(£5 per day). It's a 10-minute walk north of the train and bus station.

Peninsula Hotel (☎ 7082 2293; www.peninsula hotel.co.uk; 15 Eglinton St; s/d/t £40/60/75; 🕭) Just a short walk from the train station, the rooms at the Peninsula are modern, functional and, well…a bit heavy on the pink and orange. Rooms cost £10 more per person on Saturday nights, and breakfast isn't included.

Carrick Dhu Caravan Park (☎ 7082 3712; 12 Ballyreagh Rd; camp sites £12-15; 🕭 Apr-Sep) This is a small site with standard facilities, 1.5km west of Portrush on the A2 towards Portstewart.

Eating

Ramore Wine Bar (☎ 7082 4313; The Harbour; mains £6-12; 🕭 12.15-2.15pm & 5-10pm Mon-Sat, 12.30-3pm & 5-9pm Sun) A posher alternative to the neighbouring Harbour Bar, the stylish Ramore, with a huge curving bar, a better view of the harbour and a more upmarket menu, offers the likes of Thai chicken and prawn tempura.

Harbour Bar & Bistro (☎ 7082 2430; The Harbour; mains £8-11; 🕭 12.30-2.15pm & 5.30-10pm Mon-Sat, 12.30-3pm & 5.30-9pm Sun) Quality grub – juicy steaks, home-made burgers, spicy chicken, oriental dishes and vegetarian meals – and a harbour-side location make the Harbour one of Portrush's most popular eating places.

Coast (☎ 7082 3311; The Harbour; mains £5-8; 🕭 5-10pm Wed & Thu, 4.30-10.30pm Fri, 4-10.30pm Sat, 3-9.30pm Sun) Offering a third harbour-side choice, Coast does stone-baked pizzas, pastas and a range of steak, chicken and fish dishes.

Bread Shop (☎ 7082 3722; 21 Eglinton St; mains £3-6; 🕭 9am-5.30pm Mon-Sat) A combined bakery and café, the Bread Shop serves decent coffee, sandwiches, fish and chips and light meals.

55 Degrees North (☎ 7082 2811; 5 Causeway St), which opened too late to be fully reviewed, promises to be one of the north coast's most stylish and popular restaurants.

Entertainment

Kelly's Complex (☎ 7082 6611; www.kellysportrush .co.uk; 1 Bushmills Rd) The North's top clubbing venue regularly features DJs from London and Manchester, and attracts clubbers from as far afield as Belfast. Plain and small-looking from the outside, the Tardis effect takes over as you enter a wonderland of seven bars and three dance floors, with décor ranging from old-world wood and antiques to ultra-modern steel and mirrors. **Lush!@Kellys** (admission £3-15; 🕭 9pm-2am Wed & Sat) is, quite simply, one of the best club nights in the UK and Ireland. Don't miss it.

The complex, which is on the A2 just east of Portrush, beside the Golf Links Holiday Park, includes a hotel and restaurant.

Getting There & Around

The bus terminal is near the Dunluce Centre. Bus Nos 139 and 140 link Portrush with Coleraine (£2, 20 minutes) every 20 minutes or so. Bus No 172 runs to Ballycastle (£4.40, one hour, four daily Monday to Saturday, three Sunday) via Portballintrae, Bushmills, Giant's Causeway and Ballintoy. Bus No 278 runs once daily, except Saturday, from

---

WRECK OF THE GIRONA

The little bay 1km to the northeast of the Giant's Causeway is called Port na Spaniagh – Bay of the Spaniards. It was here, in October 1588, that the *Girona* – a ship of the Spanish Armada – was driven onto the rocks by a storm.

The *Girona* had escaped the famous confrontation with Sir Walter Raleigh's fleet in the English Channel, but along with many other fleeing Spanish ships had been driven north around Scotland and Ireland by bad weather. Though designed for a crew of 500, when she struck the rocks she was carrying no fewer than 1300 men – survivors gathered from other shipwrecks – including the cream of the Spanish aristocracy. Barely a dozen survived.

Somhairle Buidhe (Sorley Boy) MacDonnell (1505–90), the constable of nearby Dunluce Castle (opposite), salvaged gold and cannons from the wreck, and used the money to extend and modernise his fortress – cannons from the ship can still be seen on the castle's landward wall. But it was not until 1968 that the wreck site was excavated by a team of archaeological divers. They recovered a magnificent treasure of gold, silver and precious stones, as well as everyday sailors' possessions, which are now on display in Belfast's Ulster Museum (p565).

Portrush to Dublin (five hours, change at Monaghan). Also see p623.

The train station is just south of the harbour. Portrush is served by trains from Coleraine (15 minutes, at least hourly), where there are connections to Belfast or Derry.

For taxis call **Andy Brown's** (☎ 7082 2223) or **North West Taxis** (☎ 7082 4446). Both are near the town hall. A taxi to Kelly's is around £5, and it's £10 to the Giant's Causeway.

DUNLUCE CASTLE

The views on the Causeway Coast between Portrush and Portballintrae are dominated by the ruins of **Dunluce Castle** (☎ 2073 1938; 87 Dunluce Rd; adult/child £2/1; ☺ 10am-5.30pm Apr-Sep, 10am-4.30pm Oct-Mar), perched atop a dramatic basalt crag. In the 16th and 17th centuries it was the seat of the MacDonnell family (the earls of Antrim from 1620), who built a Renaissance-style manor house within the walls. Part of the castle, including the kitchen, collapsed into the sea in 1639, taking seven servants and a night's dinner with it.

The landward wall has cannons salvaged from the *Girona*, a Spanish Armada vessel that foundered nearby (see boxed text, opposite). Below, a path leads down from the gatehouse to the Mermaid's Cave beneath the castle crag.

Dunluce is situated 5km east of Portrush, a one-hour walk away along the coastal path. All the buses that run along the coast stop at Dunluce Castle; see p623.

PORTBALLINTRAE

pop 1100

During WWI Portballintrae was the only place in the UK to be shelled by a German submarine. And that's pretty much its only claim to fame. A once-pretty village set around a sand-fringed, horseshoe bay with a tiny harbour, today it is suffering from over-development, with new holiday apartments sprouting everywhere. The village is an easy 30-minute walk from Bushmills, and 45 minutes from the Giant's Causeway. The fine sandy beach of Bushfoot Strand stretches for 1.5km to the northeast.

Sweeney's Wine Bar (☎ 2073 2405; 6b Seaport Ave; mains £7-15; ☺ noon-9.30pm), set in a converted 17th-century stable block just above the beach with a lovely modern conservatory, serves great pub grub – burgers, pasta and seafood.

Bus No 138 runs regularly (except on Sunday) to Coleraine and Portrush, while bus No 172 operates several times daily to Portrush and Ballycastle. Also see p623.

BUSHMILLS

pop 1350

The small town of Bushmills, off the A2 between Portrush and Ballycastle, has long been a place of pilgrimage for connoisseurs of Irish whiskey. A good youth hostel and a restored rail link with the Giant's Causeway have made it an attractive stop for hikers exploring the Causeway Coast.

Sights

Bushmills Distillery (☎ 2073 3218; www.bushmills .com; Distillery Rd; adult/child £5/2.50; ☺ 9.30am-5.30pm Mon-Sat, noon-5.30pm Sun, last tour 4pm Apr-Oct) is the world's oldest legal distillery, having been granted a licence by King James I in 1608. Bushmills whiskey is made with Irish barley and water from St Columb's Rill, a tributary of the River Bush, and matured in oak barrels. During ageing, the alcohol content drops from around 60% to 40%; the spirit lost through evaporation is known, rather sweetly, as 'the angels' share'. After a tour of the distillery you're rewarded with a free sample (or a soft drink), and four lucky volunteers get a whiskey tasting session to compare Bushmills with other brands. Tours are held hourly from 10.30am to 3.30pm except 12.30pm Monday to Friday, and 1.30pm to 3.30pm Saturday and Sunday November to March.

Giant's Causeway & Bushmills Railway (☎ 2073 2844; recorded timetable info ☎ 2073 2594; www.giants causewayrailway.org; adult/child return £5/2.50) follows the route of a 19th-century tourist tramway for 3km from Bushmills to below the Giant's Causeway visitor centre. The narrow-gauge line and locomotives (two steam and one diesel) were bought from a private line on the shores of Lough Neagh. Trains run hourly between 11am and 4pm or 5pm, departing on the hour from Bushmills, the half-hour from the Causeway, from April to September, with some extra services in October.

Sleeping & Eating

Bushmills Inn (☎ 2073 2339; www.bushmillsinn.com; 9 Dunluce Rd; s/d £78/98; [P] [X]) One of Northern Ireland's most atmospheric hotels, the

Bushmills Inn is an old coaching inn complete with peat fires, gas lamps and a round tower with a secret library. The rooms in the old part of the inn are small and cosy; there are larger, more luxurious ones in the neighbouring **Mill House** (s/d £148/158). The inn's excellent **restaurant** (lunch mains £9, dinner mains £13-19; ☒ noon-9.30pm Mon-Sat, 12.30-9pm Sun), with intimate wooden booths set in the old 17th-century stables, serves everything from sandwiches to full á la carte dinners.

Mill Rest Youth Hostel (☎ 2073 1222; www.hini .org.uk; 49 Main St; dm £12.50-13.50, d £32; closed 11am-5pm Oct-Mar; 🖳 🕭) This modern, purpose-built and child-friendly hostel is just off The Diamond in the centre of town. Accommodation is mostly in four- to six-bed dorms and an en-suite twin room. There's also a kitchen, restaurant, laundry and bike shed.

Ballyness Caravan Park & B&B (☎ 2073 2393; www.ballynesscaravanpark.com; 40 Castlecatt Rd; camp sites £10, caravan £15, s/d £30/46; ☒ caravan park mid-Mar–Oct, B&B year round) This eco-friendly caravan park and farmhouse B&B is about 1km south of Bushmills town centre on the B66.

Copper Kettle (☎ 2073 2560; 61 Main St; mains £3-5; ☒ 9am-5pm Mon-Sat, 10am-5pm Sun) A good place for a tea, coffee, cakes and light meals.

Getting There & Away

The Antrim Coaster (bus No 252) links Coleraine with Larne (£8.20, 3¼ hours, two daily Monday to Saturday) via Port-

stewart, Portrush, Bushmills, the Giant's Causeway, Ballycastle and the Glens of Antrim. South-bound buses leave Coleraine at 9.55am (ending in Belfast June to September, in Larne October to April) and 3.40pm (Larne only). A Sunday service operates from July to September only. In July and August only the Bushmills Bus (No 177), an open-topped (weather permitting) double-decker, runs from Coleraine to the Giant's Causeway (one way/day return £2.70/4, one hour, five daily) via Portstewart, Portrush, Portballintrae and Bushmills Distillery.

GIANT'S CAUSEWAY

When you first see it you'll understand why the ancients thought the Causeway was not a natural feature. The vast expanse of regular, closely packed, hexagonal stone columns dipping gently beneath the waves looks for all the world like the handiwork of giants.

This spectacular rock formation – a Unesco World Heritage site and National Nature Reserve – is one of Ireland's most impressive and atmospheric landscape features, but it is all-too-often swamped by visitors. If you can, try to visit midweek or out of season to experience it at its most evocative. Sunset in spring and autumn is the best time for photographs.

Orientation & Information

Visiting the Giant's Causeway itself is free of charge but the overcrowded, council-run

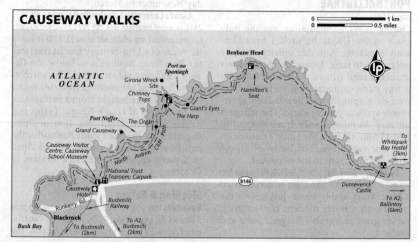

CAUSEWAY WALKS

ATLANTIC OCEAN

Port na Spaniagh

Benbane Head

Girona Wreck Site

Chimney Tops

Giant's Eyes

The Harp

Hamilton's Seat

Port Noffer

The Organ

Grand Causeway

Causeway Visitor Centre; Causeway School Museum

National Trust Tearoom; Carpark

Causeway Hotel

Bushmills Railway

Runkerry Rd

Blackrock

Bush Bay

To Bushmills (2km)

To A2; Bushmills (2km)

B146

Dunseverick Castle

To Whitepark Bay Hostel (3km)

To A2; Ballintoy (6km)

0 — 1 km
0 — 0.5 miles

car park charges £5/2 per car/motorcycle. It's a pleasant 1km walk from the car park down to the Causeway; minibuses with wheelchair access ply the route every 15 minutes (one way/return £0.60/1.20). Guided tours of the site (June to August only) cost £2.50/1 per adult/child.

In May 2005 an international architectural competition was launched for the design of a new, world-class visitor centre for the Giant's Causeway; it should be in place by 2008. Meanwhile, the less-than-inspiring, council-run **Visitor Centre** (☎ 2073 1855; causewaytic@hotmail.com; admission free, audiovisual show £1; ☼ 10am-7pm Jul & Aug, 10am-5pm Sep-Jun) is housed in a wooden building beside the National Trust's gift shop and tearoom.

Sights & Activities

From the car park it's an easy 10- to 15-minute walk downhill on a tarmac road (wheelchair accessible) to the Giant's Causeway itself. However, a much more interesting approach is to follow the cliff-top path northeast for 2km to the **Chimney Tops** headland, which has an excellent view of the Causeway and the coastline to the west, including Inishowen and Malin Head.

This pinnacled promontory was bombarded by ships of the Spanish Armada in 1588, who thought it was Dunluce Castle, and the wreck of the Spanish galleon *Girona* (see p642) lies just off the tip of the headland. Return towards the car park and about halfway back, above Port Noffer, descend the Sheperd's Steps to a lower-level footpath that leads back to the Causeway. Allow 1½ hours for the round trip.

Alternatively, you can visit the Causeway first, then follow the lower coastal path as far as Benbane Head, passing impressive rock formations such as the **Organ** (a stack of vertical basalt columns resembling organ pipes), the **Harp** (a fan of columns) and the **Giant's Eyes** (a pair of rust-red sockets where huge boulders have fallen out of the rock face).

If you fancy a full day's walk, you can continue from Benbane Head to Dunseverick Castle (8km from the Causeway), and then either continue to Whitepark Bay Hostel (another 3km; see p646), or return to the Causeway car park along the B146 road (4.5km).

Sleeping & Eating

Causeway Hotel (☎ 2073 1226; www.giants-causeway-hotel.com; 40 Causeway Rd; s/d £50/70) You can't beat it for location – the National Trust's 19th-century Causeway Hotel is within a

---

MAKING OF THE CAUSEWAY

The Mythology

The story goes that the Irish giant, Finn MacCool, built the Causeway so he could cross the sea to fight the Scottish giant Benandonner. When he got there he found his rival asleep and, seeing that the Scot was far bigger than he, fled back to Ireland. Soon, Finn's wife heard the angry Benandonner come running across the Causeway, so she dressed Finn in a baby's shawl and bonnet and put him in a crib. When the Scottish giant came hammering at Finn's door, Mrs MacCool warned him not to wake Finn's baby. Taking a glance in the cot, Benandonner decided that if this huge baby was Finn's child, then MacCool himself must be immense, and fled in turn back to Scotland, ripping up the causeway as he went. All that remains are its ends – the Giant's Causeway in Ireland, and the island of Staffa in Scotland (which has similar rock formations).

The Geology

The more prosaic scientific explanation is that the Causeway rocks were formed 60 million years ago, when a thick layer of molten basaltic lava flowed along a valley in the existing chalk beds. As the lava flow cooled and hardened – from the top and bottom surfaces inward – it contracted, creating a pattern of hexagonal cracks at right angles to the cooling surfaces (think of mud contracting and cracking in a hexagonal pattern as a lake bed dries out). As solidification progressed towards the centre of the flow, the cracks spread down from the top, and up from the bottom, until the lava was completely solid. Erosion has cut into the lava flow, and the basalt has split along the contraction cracks, creating the hexagonal columns.

basalt stone's–throw of the Causeway, and has great views over the Atlantic. A useful base if you want to explore the Causeway very early or late in the day, when the crowds are not around.

The **National Trust tearoom** (☿ 10am-7pm Jul & Aug, 10am-6pm Jun, 10am-5pm Sep & Oct, 10am-3pm Nov & Dec), above the Causeway car park, serves tea, coffee and light meals.

Getting There & Away

Bus No 172 from Portrush and Bushmills to Ballycastle passes the site year round. Also see p623.

GIANT'S CAUSEWAY TO BALLYCASTLE

Between the Giant's Causeway and Ballycastle lies the most scenic stretch of the Causeway Coast, with sea cliffs of contrasting black basalt and white chalk, rocky islands, picturesque little harbours and broad sweeps of sandy beach. It's best enjoyed on foot, following the 15km of waymarked **Causeway Coast Path** between the Giant's Causeway car park and Ballintoy, although the main attractions can also be reached by car or bus.

About 8km east of the Giant's Causeway is the meagre ruin of 16th-century **Dunseverick Castle**, spectacularly sited on a grassy bluff. Another 1.5km on is the tiny seaside hamlet of **Portbradden**, with half a dozen harbourside houses and the tiny, blue-and-white St Gobban's Church, said to be the smallest in Ireland. Visible from Portbradden and accessible via the next junction off the A2 is the spectacular **White Park Bay** with its wide, sweeping sandy beach.

A few kilometres further on is **Ballintoy** (Baile an Tuaighe), another picture-postcard village, tumbling down the hillside to a scenic harbour. The restored limekiln on the quayside once made quicklime using stone from the chalk cliffs and coal from Ballymoney.

East of Ballintoy the Causeway Coast Path no longer sticks to the coast, and follows the B15 road instead. The main attraction here is the famous (or notorious, depending on your head for heights) **Carrick-a-Rede Rope Bridge** (☎ 2073 1582; adult/child £2.20/1.20; ☿ 10am-7pm mid-Jun–Aug, 10am-6pm mid-Mar–mid-Jun & Sep). The 20m-long, 1m-wide bridge of wire rope spans the chasm between the sea cliffs and the little island of Carrick-a-Rede, swaying gently 30m above the rock-strewn water.

The island has sustained a salmon fishery for centuries; fishermen stretch their nets out from the tip of the island to intercept the passage of the salmon migrating west along the coast to their home rivers. The fishermen put the bridge up every spring as they have done for the last 200 years – though it's not, of course, the original bridge.

Crossing the bridge is perfectly safe, but it can be frightening if you don't have a head for heights, especially if it's breezy (in high winds the bridge is closed). Once on the island there are good views of Rathlin Island and Fair Head to the east. There's a small National Trust information centre and café at the car park.

Sleeping & Eating

Whitepark Bay Hostel (☎ 2073 1745; www.hini.org.uk; 157 White Park Rd, Ballintoy; dm £12.50-13.50, d £28; ☿ 8am-10pm Apr-Sep, 8-11am & 5-10pm Mar, Oct & Nov; ℗) This modern, purpose-built hostel, near the west end of White Park Bay, has mostly four-bed dorms, plus twin rooms with TV, all with private bathroom. There is a common room positioned to soak up the view, and the beach is just a five-minute walk away.

Sheep Island View Hostel (☎ 2076 9391; www.sheepislandview.com; 42a Main St, Ballintoy; camp sites £5, dm adult/child £10/6; ℗ ▣) This excellent independent hostel offers dorm beds, basic shared accommodation in the camping barn, or a place to pitch a tent. There's a kitchen and laundry, a village store nearby, and a free pick-up service from the Giant's Causeway, Bushmills and Ballycastle. It's on the main coast road near the turn-off to Ballintoy harbour, and makes an ideal overnight stop if you're hiking between Bushmills and Ballycastle.

Whitepark House B&B (☎ 2073 1482; www.whiteparkhouse.com; Whitepark Rd, Ballintoy; s/d £35/60; ✕) A beautifully restored 18th-century house overlooking Whitepark Bay, this B&B has traditional features such as antique furniture and a peat fire complemented by Asian artefacts gathered during the welcoming owners' oriental travels. There are three rooms, all with private bathroom – ask for one with a sea view.

Roark's Kitchen (☎ 2076 3632; Ballintoy Harbour; snacks £2-3; ☿ 11am-7pm daily Jun-Aug, Sat & Sun only May & Sep) This cute little chalk-built tearoom on the quayside at Ballintoy serves teas, coffees and snacks.

Getting There & Away

Bus No 172 between Ballycastle, Bushmills and Portrush (four daily Monday to Saturday, three Sunday) is the main, year-round service along this coast, stopping at the Giant's Causeway, Ballintoy and Carrick-a-Rede. Also see Transport, p623.

BALLYCASTLE

pop 4000

The harbour town and holiday resort of Ballycastle (Baile an Chaisil) marks the eastern end of the Causeway Coast. It's a pretty town with a good bucket-and-spade beach, but apart from that there's not a lot to see. It's also the port for ferries to Rathlin Island.

The **tourist information office** (☎ 2076 2024; tourism@moyle-council.org; 7 Mary St; 9.30am-7pm Mon-Fri Jul & Aug, 9.30am-5pm Mon-Fri Sep-Jun) is in the district council building at the east end of town. There's a couple of banks with ATMs on Ann St, near The Diamond.

Sights

The tiny **Ballycastle Museum** (☎ 2076 2942; 61a Castle St; admission free; noon-6pm Mon-Sat Jul & Aug), in the town's 18th-century courthouse, has a collection of Irish Arts and Crafts works. In the harbour car park is the **Marconi Memorial**, a plaque at the foot of a rock pinnacle. Guglielmo Marconi's assistants contacted Rathlin Island by radio from Ballycastle in 1898 to prove to Lloyds of London that wireless communication was a viable proposition. The idea was to send notice to London or Liverpool of ships arriving safely after a transatlantic crossing – most vessels on this route would have to pass through the channel north of Rathlin.

Just east of town are the ruins of **Bonamargy Friary**, founded in 1485. The vault contains the tombs of MacDonnell chieftains, including Sorley Boy MacDonnell of Dunluce Castle (p643).

Festivals

Ballycastle's **Ould Lammas Fair**, held on the last Monday and Tuesday of August, dates back to 1606. Thousands of people descend on the town for the market stalls and fairground rides, and to sample yellowman and dulse. Yellowman is a hard chewy toffee that's available from a few months before the fair. Dulse is dried edible seaweed. The fruit shop on The Diamond often stocks both delicacies.

Sleeping

Castle Hostel (☎ 2076 2337; www.castlehostel.com; 62 Quay Rd; dm/d £8/20) The hostel is set in a spacious, bay-windowed Victorian house with a welcoming fire in the common room. It has a kitchen, laundry and secure bike shed.

Ballycastle Backpackers (☎ 2076 3612; info@bcbackpackers.com; 4 North St; dm/tw £10/30) This hostel is set in another nice terrace house overlooking the harbour, with 16 beds in two four-bed dorms and four twin rooms, all with private bathroom; there's also a kitchen and laundry.

Glenluce Guesthouse (☎ 2076 2914; www.glenluceguesthouse.com; 42 Quay Rd; s £25-35, d £40-50; P X) A large Victorian villa with 12 beautifully decorated rooms, Glenluce has a luxurious lounge, its own tea shop, and a veritable art gallery of local watercolours. It's only a few minutes' walk from the beach.

Fair Head View B&B (☎ 2076 9376; 26 North St; d £30-35; P) This is a friendly and old-fashioned B&B, with a warm welcome and a big breakfast, though the rooms are a bit on the small side; book early to get a room at the front, with fantastic views across the sea to Fair Head, Rathlin and the Mull of Kintyre.

Marine Hotel (☎ 2076 2222; www.marinehotel.net; 1 North St; s/d £50/80; P X) Cheerful décor and a seafront setting are the main attractions of this modern hotel close to the harbour. Service is crisp and businesslike, and there's a restaurant, fitness centre, sauna and steam room.

Watertop Open Farm (☎ 2076 2576; watertop@aol.com; 188 Cushendall Rd; camp sites £9-11, caravan sites £11-12; Apr-Oct) About 10km east of Ballycastle on the road to Cushendun, child-friendly Watertop is a camping ground based in a working farm and activity centre, offering pony trekking, sheep shearing and farm tours.

Glenmore Caravan & Camping Park (☎ 2076 3584; www.glenmore.biz; 94 White Park Rd; camp sites £8, caravans £9-11; Apr-Oct) Glenmore is a small and peaceful camping ground with its own trout-stocked fishing lough, about 4.5km west of Ballycastle on the B15 road to Whitepark Bay.

Eating

Cellar Restaurant (☎ 2076 3037; The Diamond; mains £8-13, pizza £6-8; ☾ noon-11pm Mon-Sat, 5-10pm Sun Jun-Aug, 5-10pm daily Sep-May) This is a cosy little basement restaurant with intimate wooden booths and a big fireplace, serving excellent steak, pork, chicken and fish dishes, as well as pizzas.

Wysner's (☎ 2076 2372; 16 Ann St; mains £7-11; ☾ 8am-9pm Mon-Sat Jul & Aug, 8am-5pm Mon, Tue & Thu-Sat, 7-9pm Fri & Sat Sep-Jun) Popular with locals and visitors alike, the cheerful upstairs restaurant at Wysner's dishes up hearty meals like sausage and champ during the day, and more sophisticated fare – steak, salmon or scallops – in the evenings.

Beach House Café (☎ 2076 2262; Bayview Rd; mains £3-5; ☾ 9am-8pm) An old-fashioned, self-service, seaside café serving home-made pies, lasagne and breakfast fry-ups, the Beach House has a wall of windows giving a great view across the marina to Fair Head.

Getting There & Away

The bus station is on Station Rd, just east of The Diamond. Bus No 131 links Ballycastle with Ballymena, where you can change for Belfast (£7.40, 2¾ hours, four daily Monday to Friday, two Saturday).

Bus No 171 goes along the coast to Coleraine, and No 172 connects daily with Bushmills and Portrush. Also see p623, for details of the convenient Antrim Coaster bus service. The ticket office for the Rathlin Island Ferry is beside the harbour.

RATHLIN ISLAND

pop 110

In spring and summer, rugged Rathlin Island (Reachlainn), 6km offshore from Ballycastle, is home to hundreds of seals and thousands of nesting seabirds. The island has a pub and restaurant, two shops and a handful of accommodation options.

The island was raided by Vikings in AD 795 and suffered again in 1595 when Sorley Boy MacDonnell sent his family here for safety only to have them massacred by the English, along with most of the inhabitants. The island's most illustrious visitor was Scottish hero Robert the Bruce, who spent some time in 1306 in a cave on the northeastern point learning a lesson in perseverance. Watching a spider's resoluteness in repeatedly trying to spin a web gave

him the courage to have another go at the English, whom he subsequently defeated at Bannockburn.

The chief attraction is the coastal scenery and birdlife of **Kebble National Nature Reserve** at the western end of the island. **RSPB West Lighthouse Viewpoint** (☎ 2076 3948; admission free; ☾ by arrangement Apr-Aug) provides stunning views of the neighbouring sea stacks, thick with guillemots, kittiwakes, razorbills and puffins in spring and early summer. During the summer a minibus service runs there from the harbour.

If you don't have time to visit Kebble, the best short walk on the island is through the National Trust's Ballyconagan Nature Reserve to the **Old Coastguard Lookout** on the north coast, with great views along the sea cliffs and across to the Scottish islands of Islay and Jura.

The **Boathouse Visitor Centre** (☎ 2076 3951; admission free; ☾ 10.30am-4pm May-Aug), south of the harbour, details the history, culture and ecology of the island, and can give advice on walks and wildlife.

Sleeping & Eating

You can camp for free on the eastern side of Church Bay in a field not far from the harbour. All accommodation should be booked in advance.

Soerneog View Hostel (☎ 2076 3954; Ouig; d £16) A private house, a 10-minute walk south of the harbour, Soerneog offers hostel-style accommodation in one double and two twin rooms.

Kinramer Cottage (☎ 2076 3948; Kinramer; dm £5) This is a basic camping barn, a one-hour walk west from the harbour, where you bring your own food and bedding; book in advance. You might be able to get a lift on one of the minibuses; see opposite for details.

Coolnagrock B&B (☎ 2076 3983; Coolnagrock; r £32; ☾ Easter-Sep) This well-appointed guesthouse is in the eastern part of the island, a 15-minute walk from the ferry, but you can arrange for the owner to pick you up.

Manor House (☎ 2076 3964; www.ntni.org.uk /accommodation/manorhouse.htm; Church Quarter; s/d £28/54; ✗) Restored and run by the National Trust, the 18th-century Manor House, on the north side of the harbour, is the island's biggest (12 rooms) and most pleasant place to stay. Evening meals are available by arrangement.

The Brockley Tearoom at the Manor House serves soups, sandwiches, cakes and scones, and you can get pub grub at **McCuaig's Bar** (☎ 2076 3974), just east of the harbour. There's a tiny grocery shop a few paces to the west of the ferry berth (turn left as you come off the pier).

Getting There & Around

A **ferry** (☎ 2076 9299; www.calmac.co.uk) operates daily (adult/child/bicycle return £8.80/4.40/2, 45 minutes) from Ballycastle; advance booking is recommended in spring and summer.

June to September ferries depart Ballycastle at 10am, noon, 4.30pm and 6.30pm, and leave Rathlin at 8.30am, 11am, 3.30pm and 5.30pm. In winter boats leave Ballycastle at 10.30am and 4pm (4.30pm on Friday) and from Rathlin at 9am and 3pm.

You can't take your car to Rathlin, but nowhere on the island is more than 6km (about 1½ hours' walk) from the ferry pier. You can hire a bicycle (£7 per day) from Soerneog View Hostel, or take a minibus tour with **Irene's** (☎ 2076 3949) or **McCurdy's** (☎ 2076 3909), who also shuttle visitors between the ferry and Kebble Nature Reserve from April to August.

GLENS OF ANTRIM

The northeastern corner of Antrim is a high plateau of black basalt lava flows overlying beds of white chalk. Along the coast, between Cushendun and Glenarm, the plateau has been dissected by a series of scenic, glacier-gouged valleys known as the Glens of Antrim.

Two waymarked footpaths traverse the region: the Ulster Way sticks close to the sea, passing through all the coastal villages, while the 32km Moyle Way runs inland from Glenariff Forest Park to Ballycastle.

Torr Head Scenic Road

A few kilometres east of Ballycastle, a minor road signposted Scenic Route branches north off the A2. This alternative route to Cushendun is not for the faint-hearted driver (nor for caravans), as it clings, precarious and narrow, to steep slopes high above the sea. Side roads lead off to the main points of interest – Fair Head, Murlough Bay and Torr Head. On a clear day, there are superb views across the sea to Scotland, from the Mull of Kintyre to the peaks of Arran.

The first turn-off ends at a parking area at Coolanlough. Here, a waymarked path will lead you north 1km to **Fair Head**, where the impressive 180m-high basalt cliffs are split by a spectacular gully, bridged by a fallen rock, which is known as the Grey Man's Path. The trail then loops south along the cliff tops to the upper car park on the Murlough Bay road, from where you can return to Coolanlough (allow 1½ hours). Alternatively, you can descend the Grey Man's Path (at your own risk, and in dry weather only) and follow the coast south to Murlough Bay.

The second turn-off leads steeply down to **Murlough Bay**. From the bottom parking area, you can walk north along the shoreline to some ruined miners' cottages (10 minutes); coal and chalk were once mined in the cliffs above, and burned in a limekiln (south of the car park) to make quicklime.

The third turn-off leads you past some ruined coastguard houses to the rocky headland of **Torr Head**, crowned with a 19th-century coastguard station (abandoned in the 1920s). This is Ireland's closest point to Scotland – the Mull of Kintyre is a mere 19km away across the North Channel. In late spring and summer, a salmon fishery like the one at Carrick-a-Rede operates here, with a net strung out from the headland. The ancient ice house beside the approach road was once used to store the catch.

Cushendun
pop 350

The pretty seaside village of Cushendun is famous for its distinctive, Cornish-style cottages. Built between 1912 and 1925 at the behest of the local landowner, Lord Cushendun, they were designed by Clough Williams-Ellis, the architect of Portmeirion in North Wales. Much of Cushendun is now owned by the National Trust. There's a nice sandy beach, and a footpath south of the river that leads along the shore to some caves.

Another natural curiosity lies 6km north of the village on the A2 road to Ballycastle – **Loughareema**, also known as the Vanishing Lake. Three streams flow in but none flow out. The lough fills up to a respectable size (400m long and 6m deep) after heavy rain, but then the water gradually drains away through fissures in the underlying lime-stone leaving a dry lake bed.

SLEEPING & EATING

Villa Farmhouse (☎ 2176 1252; maggiescally@amserve .net; 185 Torr Rd; s/d £25/44; **P** **✕**) This luxuri-ous, Tudor-style farmhouse B&B, on the coast road 1.5km north of the village, has fantastic views over the bay. All three rooms have private bathroom, and evening meals are available from £12 per person.

Mullarts Apartments (☎ 2176 1221; liam@mullarts .fsnet.co.uk; 114 Tromra Rd; d per weekend/week £150/400) An unusual alternative, Mullarts offers two luxury, self-catering apartments housed in a converted 19th-century church, 2.5km south of the village. Each apartment can take two to five people.

Cloneymore House (☎ 2176 1443; anne.cloney more@btInternet.com; 103 Knocknacarry Rd; s/d £25/44; **P** **✕** **占**) A traditional family B&B on the B92 road 500m southwest of Cushendun, Cloneymore has four spacious en-suite rooms, all equipped for visitors with lim-ited mobility.

Cushendun Caravan Park (☎ 2176 1254; 14 Glendun Rd; camp sites £10.50, caravans £13.50; ☯ Easter-Sep) The local council-run camping ground enjoys a pleasant woodland setting just north of the village, and a mere five-minute walk from the beach.

Mary McBride's Pub (☎ 2176 1511; 2 Main St; mains £6-15; ☯ food served noon-9pm) The original bar here is the smallest in Ireland (2.7m by 1.5m) but there's plenty of elbow-bending room in the rest of the pub, which serves a fine pint of Guinness. The pub's Waterside Restaurant dishes up locally caught seafood (try the excellent chowder) and home-made steak-and-Guinness pie.

Cushendun Tearoom (☎ 2176 1506; 1 Main St; mains £3-5; ☯ 11am-7pm daily Mar-Sep, 11am-7pm Mon-Fri Oct-Feb) The cosy village tearoom beside the bridge offers tea and cakes, hot snacks and salads.

GETTING THERE & AWAY

Bus No 162 travels from Cushendun to Larne (£5.70, 1½ hours, three daily Mon-day to Friday, one Sunday), stopping at Cushendall, Carnlough and Glenarm; from Larne there are frequent trains and buses to Belfast. No 162A runs to Ballycastle (35 minutes, one daily Monday to Friday), departing from Cushendall at 9.25am and

Cushendun at 9.36am; the return service leaves Ballycastle at 2.15pm. See also p623.

Cushendall

pop 1400

The Antrim Glens' biggest village is a holiday centre (and traffic bottleneck) at the mouth of the River Dall, overlooked by the promi-nent flat-topped hill of Lurigethan. The beach is small and shingly, though; there are better ones at Waterfoot and Cushendun.

The **tourist office** (☎ 2177 1180; 24 Mill St; ☯ 10am-1pm & 2-5.30pm Mon-Fri, 10am-1pm Sat Jul-Sep, 10am-1pm Tue-Sat Oct-Jun) is run by the Glens of Antrim Historical Society, which also offers public Internet access.

SIGHTS

The unusual red sandstone **tower** at the cen-tral crossroads was built in the early 19th century, based on a building the architect had seen in China. It was originally a prison 'for the confinement of idlers and rioters'.

From the car park beside the beach, a coastal path leads 1km north to the pictur-esque ruins of **Layde Old Church**, with views across to Ailsa Craig (a prominent conical island also known as 'Paddy's Milestone') and the Scottish coast. Founded by the Franciscans, it was used as a parish church from the early 14th century until 1790. The graveyard contains several grand MacDon-nell memorials. Near the gate stands an an-cient, weathered ring-cross (with the arms missing), much older than the 19th-century inscription on its shaft.

In Glenaan, 4km northwest of Cushen-dall, is **Ossian's Grave**, a Neolithic court tomb romantically, but inaccurately, named after the legendary 3rd-century warrior-poet. The site is signposted off the A2; you can park at the farm and walk up.

SLEEPING & EATING

Mountain View (☎ 2177 1246; 1 Kilnadore Rd; s/d £20/34; ☯ Apr-Sep; **P** **✕**) The smell of home-baked bread wafts from the kitchen as you enter this good-value Victorian B&B with grand views, only a five-minute walk uphill from the village centre.

Cullentra House (☎ 2177 1762; cullentra@hotmail .com; 16 Cloghs Rd; s/d £25/38; **P** **✕**) This modern bungalow sits high above the village at the end of Cloughs Rd, offering good views of the craggy Antrim coast. The three en-suite rooms are decked out in wood panelling, and the breakfasts are as big as the owners' hospitality.

Cushendall Caravan Park (☎ 2177 1699; 62 Coast Rd; camp sites £7-11, caravan £14.50; ☺ Easter-Sep) This camping ground overlooks the sea, just over 1km south of the town centre.

Harry's Restaurant (☎ 2177 2022; 10 Mill St; mains £9-13; ☺ noon-9.30pm) With a cosy country-house feel, Harry's is the village's top eating place, serving pub grub through the day, and an á la carte dinner from 6pm. Veggie dishes are available.

Arthur's Tea & Coffee Warehouse (☎ 2177 1627; 1 Shore St; mains £2-3; ☺ 10am-5pm) This lively café serves good cakes and coffee, and home-made soups and snacks.

GETTING THERE & AWAY
See the Cushendun section (opposite); the same buses also serve Cushendall.

Glenariff
About 2km south of Cushendall is the village of **Waterfoot**, with a 2km-long sandy beach. From here the A43 Ballymena road runs inland along Glenariff, the loveliest of Antrim's glens. Views of the valley led the writer Thackeray to exclaim that it was a 'Switzerland in miniature', a claim that makes you wonder if he'd ever been to Switzerland.

At the head of the valley is **Glenariff Forest Park** (☎ 2175 8232; car/motorcycle/pedestrian £4/2/1.50; ☺ 10am-dusk) where the main attraction is **Ess-na-Larach Waterfall**, about 800m from the visitor centre. There are various good walks in the park, not all clearly marked; the longest is a 10km circular trail.

Manor Lodge (☎ 2175 8221; 120 Glen Rd; mains £7; ☺ 10.30am-9pm) is a restaurant and bar on a side road off the A43, 3km before the park entrance. The lodge serves grills, seafood and sandwiches in an interestingly decorated 1893 'Swiss-style' bungalow. You can hike uphill from here into the forest park.

You can reach Glenariff Forest Park from Cushendun (£3, 30 minutes, five daily Monday to Friday, three Sunday) and Ballymena (£3, 40 minutes) on Ulsterbus No 150.

Carnlough
pop 1500
Carnlough is an attractive little town with a pretty harbour and a fine beach. Many

of the buildings, made of local limestone, were commissioned by the marquess of Londonderry in 1854. The limestone quarries were in use until the early 1960s; the white stone bridge across the main street carried a railway line that brought stone down to the harbour. The line is now a walkway that leads to the local beauty spot, Cranny Falls.

The **tourist information centre** (☎ 2888 5236; 14 Harbour Rd; ☺ 10am-10pm daily Easter-Sep, 10am-8pm Mon-Sat Oct-Easter) is in McKillop's general store.

SLEEPING & EATING
Londonderry Arms Hotel (☎ 2888 5255; www.glens ofantrim.com; 20 Harbour Rd; s/d £55/85; Ⓟ ✗) The marchioness of Londonderry built this atmospheric coaching inn in 1848. It was eventually inherited by a distant relation of hers, Winston Churchill, who sold it in 1921 (he once stayed in room 114). The hotel restaurant serves locally caught seafood, including lobster and wild salmon.

Harbour Lights (☎ 2888 5950; 11 Harbour Rd; mains £7-12; ☺ noon-9pm Wed-Sun) This pleasant restaurant is set in a 19th-century house overlooking the harbour. You can sit on the outdoor terrace in summer.

GETTING THERE & AWAY
Bus No 162 runs from Larne to Glenarm and Carnlough (£3, 40 minutes, six daily Monday to Saturday, one Sunday); three buses a day on weekdays, and the Sunday bus, continue north to Cushendall and Cushendun. Bus No 128 travels to Ballymena (one hour, five daily Monday to Friday, four Saturday).

Glenarm
pop 600
Since 1750 Glenarm (Gleann Arma), the oldest village in the glens, has been the family seat of the MacDonnell family; the present 14th earl of Antrim lives in **Glenarm Castle** (☎ 2884 1203; www.glenarmcastle. com), on a private estate hidden behind the impressive wall that runs along the main road north of the bridge. It's normally closed to the public, but there are annual open days in July when a Highland Games competition is held.

Take a stroll into the old village of neat Georgian houses (off the main road, immediately south of the river). Where the street opens into the broad expanse of Altmore St, look right to see the **Barbican Gate** (1682), the entrance to Glenarm Castle grounds. Turn left and climb steeply up Vennel St, then left again at the Layde Path to the viewpoint, which has a grand view of the village and the coast.

The **tourist office** (☎ 2884 1705; 2 The Bridge; glenarm@nacn.org; ☯ 9.30am-5pm Mon-Fri, 2-6pm Sun) is beside the bridge on the main road. It has Internet access for £2 per 30 minutes.

Riverside House B&B (☎ 2884 1474; elaine.boyle@ talk21.com; 13 Toberwine St; s/d £22/40; ☒) is a nicely restored Georgian house in the heart of the old village.

See the Carnlough section (p651) for details of bus services.

LARNE

pop 17,600

As a major port for ferries from Scotland, Larne (Lutharna) is one of Northern Ireland's main points of arrival. However, with its concrete overpasses and the huge chimneys of Ballylumford power station opposite the harbour, poor old Larne is a little lacking in the charm department. After a visit to the excellent tourist information centre, there's no real reason to linger.

Larne Harbour train station is in the ferry terminal. It's a short bus ride or a 15-minute walk from the ferry terminal to the town centre – turn right on Fleet St and right again on Curran Rd, then left on Circular Rd. At the big roundabout, Larne Town train station is to your left, the **Larne Tourist Information Centre** (☎ 2826 0088; larnetourism@btconnect.com; Narrow Gauge Rd; ☯ 9am-5pm Mon-Sat Easter-Sep, 9am-5pm Mon-Fri Oct-Easter) is to the right, and the bus station is ahead (beneath the road bridge).

If you have to spend the night in Larne, there are plenty of accommodation options. The tourist information centre can book for you. Recommended options:

Manor Guesthouse (☎ 2827 3305; www.themanor guesthouse.com; 23 Olderfleet Rd; s/d £25/44; P ☒) A beautifully restored mid-Victorian house with period décor, only a short walk from the ferry terminal.

Seaview Guesthouse (☎ 2827 2438; www.seaview larne.co.uk; 156 Curran Rd; s/d £25/48; P ☒) Another good choice within walking distance of the harbour.

Ballygally Castle Hotel (☎ 2858 3212; www .hastingshotels.com; 274 Coast Rd, Ballygally; s/d £95/125;

P ☒) Luxurious hotel built around a genuine 17th-century castle, situated 7km north of Larne on the Antrim Coast Rd.

Getting There & Away

BOAT

For information on ferries from Larne to Scotland and England, see p697.

BUS

Bus No 256 provides a direct service between the town centre and Belfast (£3.70, one hour, six daily Monday to Friday, five Saturday, two Sunday). Heading north to the Glens of Antrim, take bus No 162 (see p651 for details).

Also see p623 for information on the Antrim Coaster bus.

TRAIN

Larne has two train stations, Larne Town and Larne Harbour; there are more frequent services from the former. Trains from Larne Town to Belfast Great Victoria St (£4.30, one hour) depart at least hourly; those from the harbour are timed to connect with ferries. All trains stop at Belfast's Central, Botanic and City Hospital stations.

ISLANDMAGEE

Islandmagee (Oileán Mhic Aodha) is the finger of land that encloses Larne Lough to the east. Access is by ferry from Larne or road from Whitehead to the south.

There's a popular sandy beach at **Brown's Bay** at the northern end of the peninsula. Nearby is the picturesque little harbour of **Portmuck** and, just 300m offshore, the North's second-largest seabird nesting colony on **Muck Island**.

On the east coast lie the rugged basalt sea cliffs known as the **Gobbins**. The cliffs were developed as a tourist attraction in 1902, when a railway company engineer built a spectacular footpath along the coast from Whitehead, complete with steps, bridges and tunnels cut from the rock. By WWII the path had fallen into disrepair, and was closed for safety reasons. You can see photographs of the walkways in the Ulster Museum (p565) in Belfast.

There's a good coastal walk from the car park at the north end of the promenade in Whitehead. It follows a walkway around the sea cliffs beneath Black Head lighthouse, past several deep caves, then climbs a steep flight of stairs to the lighthouse itself. From here you can descend a zigzag path to rejoin the shoreline trail back to the car park (3.5km in total).

The high-speed launch *North Irish Diver II* offers two-hour **boat trips** (☎ 9338 2246) from Whitehead harbour to the Gobbins and Muck Island (adult/child £20/15, minimum six people).

A passenger **ferry** (☎ 2827 3785) runs between Larne Harbour and Ballylumford, Islandmagee (adult/child £1/0.50, five minutes). There are crossings at least hourly from 7.45am to 9am and 3pm to 5pm Monday to Friday, and at 8am, 8.30am, 4pm and 4.30pm at weekends.

CARRICKFERGUS

pop 28,000

Northern Ireland's most impressive medieval fortress commands the entrance to Belfast Lough from the rocky promontory of Carrickfergus (Carraig Fhearghais). It overlooks the harbour where William of Orange landed on 14 June 1690, on his way to the Battle of the Boyne; a blue plaque marks the site where he stepped ashore on the old harbour wall below the castle. The old town centre opposite the castle has some attractive 18th-century houses and you can still trace a good part of the 17th-century city walls.

Information

Paradigm Internet Café (☎ 9336 1531; 16 West St; per 15 min £1; ⏲ 10am-4pm Mon-Sat)

Tourist Information Centre (☎ 9335 8000; www.carrickfergus.org; Heritage Plaza, Antrim St; ⏲ 9am-6pm Mon-Fri, 10am-6pm Sat & 1-6pm Sun Apr-Sep, 9am-5pm Mon-Fri & 10am-5pm Sat Oct-Mar) Has a bureau de change and books accommodation.

Sights

The central keep of **Carrickfergus Castle** (☎ 9335 1273; Marine Hwy; adult/child £3/1.50; ⏲ 10am-6pm Mon-Sat, noon-6pm Sun Jun-Aug, 10am-6pm Mon-Sat, 2-6pm Sun Apr, May & Sep, 10am-4pm Mon-Sat, 2-4pm Sun Oct-Mar) was built by John de Courcy soon after his 1177 invasion of Ulster. The massive walls of the outer ward were completed in 1242, while the red-brick gun ports were added in the 16th century. Besieged by King John in 1210

and Edward Bruce in 1315 and briefly captured by the French in 1760, the castle also witnessed a successful attack on a British vessel in 1778 by John Paul Jones, founder of the US Navy, in the *Ranger*. The keep houses a museum and the site is dotted with life-size figures illustrating the castle's history and adding colour to what is Ireland's first and finest Norman castle.

The glass-fronted Heritage Plaza on Antrim St houses **Carrickfergus Museum** (☎ 9335 8049; 11 Antrim St; admission free; ⏲ 9am-6pm Mon-Fri, 10am-6pm Sat, 1-6pm Sun Apr-Sep, 9am-5pm Mon-Fri, 10am-5pm Sat Oct-Mar), which has a small collection of artefacts relating to the town's history.

The parents of the seventh US president left Carrickfergus in the second half of the 18th century. His ancestral home was demolished in 1860, but the **Andrew Jackson Centre** (☎ 9336 6455; Bonybefore; admission free; ⏲ 10am-1pm & 2-6pm Mon-Fri, 2-6pm Sat & Sun Jun-Sep, 10am-1pm & 2-4pm Mon-Fri, 2-4pm Sat & Sun Apr & May) is housed in a replica thatched cottage complete with fireside crane and earthen floor. It has displays on the life of Jackson, the Jackson family in Ulster and Ulster's connection with the USA. Next door is the **US Rangers Centre**, with a small exhibition on the first US rangers, who were trained during WWII in Carrickfergus before heading for Europe. The centre is on the coast, 2km north of the castle.

Sleeping & Eating

Dobbin's Inn Hotel (☎ 9335 1905; www.dobbinsinnhotel.co.uk; 6-8 High St; s/d £48/68; mains £6-13; ✗) In the centre of the old town, Dobbin's Inn has been around for over three centuries, and has a priest's hole and an original 16th-century fireplace to prove it. The hotel restaurant serves dinner until 9pm nightly.

Langsgarden (☎ 9336 6369; 72 Scottish Quarter; s/d £20/40; ✗) This 10-room, seafront B&B sits at the far end of the attractive Victorian terrace that stretches northeast from the old town.

Wind Rose (☎ 9335 1164; Rodgers Quay; mains £6-12; ⏲ noon-9pm) This modern, stylish bar-bistro, has a lunch menu that includes delicious home-made seafood pie. The outdoor terrace overlooking the forest of yacht masts in the marina is a real sun trap on a summer afternoon.

Courtyard Coffee House (☎ 9335 1881; 38 Scottish Quarter; snacks £2-4; ⏲ 9am-4.45pm Mon-Sat) This café serves tasty home-made soups and light lunches as well as coffee and cakes, and has a second branch inside Carrickfergus Castle.

Getting There & Away

Ulsterbus No 163 goes to Belfast's Laganside Bus Centre (£2.70, 30 to 40 minutes, twice hourly). Larne to Belfast trains stop at Carrickfergus.

INLAND COUNTY ANTRIM

To the west of the high moorland plateau that backs the Glens of Antrim, the hills slope down to the agricultural lowlands of Lough Neagh and the broad valley of the River Bann. This region is rarely visited by tourists, who either take the coast road or speed through on the way from Belfast to Derry, but there are a few places worth seeking out if you have time to spare.

Antrim Town
pop 19,800

The town of Antrim (Aontroim) straddles the River Sixmilewater, close to an attractive bay on the shores of Lough Neagh. During the 1798 Rising, the United Irishmen fought a pitched battle along the length of the town's High St. Today Antrim is dominated by a bleakly modern shopping centre, but a few older buildings survive, including the fine **courthouse**, which dates back to 1762.

Antrim Tourist Information Centre (☎ 9442 8331; info@antrim.gov.uk; 16 High St; ✆ 9am-5.30pm Mon-Fri, 10am-3pm Sat Jul & Aug, 9am-5pm Mon-Fri, 10am-1pm Sat May, Jun & Sep, 9am-5pm Mon-Fri Oct-Apr) provides a free, self-guided heritage trail leaflet, and has Internet access for £1.50 per 30 minutes.

In **Pogue's Entry**, a narrow alley at the end of Church St, a blue plaque marks the tiny, mud-floored childhood home of Alexander Irvine (1863–1941), who was a missionary in New York's Bowery district. At the opposite end of High St, beyond the courthouse, is the **Barbican Gate** (1818) and a portion of the old castle walls.

Pass through the gate and the underpass beyond to reach **Antrim Castle Gardens** (admission free; ✆ 9.30am-dusk Mon-Fri, 10am-5pm Sat, 2-5pm Sun). The castle burned down many years ago, but the grounds remain as one of the few surviving examples of a 17th-century ornamental garden.

Approximately 1.5km north of town, in Steeple Park, stands a 27m-tall, 10th- or 11th-century **round tower**, all that remains of a monastery that once stood on the site. Follow the signs for Steeple Industrial Estate, then for the Antrim Borough Council offices.

Lough Rd leads west from the town centre to **Antrim Lough Shore Park**, where the vast size of Lough Neagh – the largest lake in the UK and Ireland (see also p621) – is apparent. There are picnic tables and lakeside walking trails.

Bus No 219 from Belfast to Ballymena stops in Antrim. Trains run more frequently (10 a day); Antrim is on the Derry to Belfast train line (£9, 2¼ hours, seven or eight daily Monday to Saturday, four Sunday).

Ballymena
pop 29,200

The predominantly Protestant town of Ballymena (An Baile Meánach) is the home turf of Ian Paisley, the founder and leader of the Free Presbyterian Church and the stridently antinationalist and anti-Catholic Democratic Unionist Party (DUP). The town council was the first to be controlled by the DUP in 1977 and voted unanimously to remove all mention of Darwin's theory of evolution from religious education in Ballymena's schools. The town is also the birthplace of the actor Liam Neeson, of *Schindler's List* and *Star Wars* fame.

Ecos Environmental Centre (☎ 2566 4400; www.ecoscentre.com; Broughshane Rd; adult/child £4/3; ✆ 10.30am-5pm Mon-Sat, noon-5pm Sun Easter-Sep, noon-4pm Mon-Sat Oct-Easter), on the eastern edge of town, is a visitor centre dedicated to issues like alternative energy sources and sustainable technology, with lots of hands-on exhibits to keep the kids amused.

Bus No 219 serves Ballymena from Belfast (£4.90, 35 minutes, six daily Monday to Friday, two Saturday). Bus No 128 goes to Carnlough on the coast (one hour, five daily Monday to Friday, four Saturday).

Trains run more frequently (there are 10 daily); Ballymena is on the Derry to Belfast train line.

Slemish

The skyline to the east of Ballymena is dominated by the distinctive craggy peak of Slemish (438m). The hill is one of many sites in

---

SOMETHING SPECIAL

Galgorm Manor (☎ 2588 1001; www.galgorm
.com; 136 Fenaghy Rd, Ballymena; s/d £99/119;
P ⊠) This 19th-century gentleman's residence, in a lovely setting next to the River
Maine, is one of Ireland's top country-house
hotels. The rooms are furnished in Victorian
style, and many have views along the river.
Gillie's Bar (mains £6-10; ☯ noon-11pm, food
served noon-2.30pm & 6-9pm), set in the former
stables, is an atmospheric country pub with
bare stone walls, huge timber beams, a log
fire and a cosy snug lined with sofas. The
hotel is 6km west of Ballymena – bear right
at the Gracehill roundabout, and take the
road towards Cullybackey.

---

the North associated with Ireland's patron
saint – the young St Patrick is said to have
tended goats on its slopes. On St Patrick's
Day, thousands of people make a pilgrimage
to its summit; the rest of the year it's a pleasant climb, though steep and slippery in wet
weather, rewarded with a fine view (allow
one hour return from the parking area).

Arthur Cottage

The ancestors of Chester Alan Arthur
(1830–86), 21st president of the USA, lived
in an 18th-century thatched **cottage** (☎ 2588

0781; Dreen, Cullybackey; adult/child £2/1; ☯ 10.30am-
5pm Mon-Fri, 10.30am-4pm Sat Easter-Sep) in Cullybackey, about 6km northwest of Ballymena.
Staff in traditional costume bake bread and
make quilts on Tuesday, Friday and Saturday at 1.30pm throughout June, July (except on the 12th) and August.

Like Ballymena, Cullybackey is a stop on
the Belfast to Derry railway line.

Gracehill
pop 700
In the mid-18th century many Protestants
fled Moravia (now in the eastern Czech Republic) to escape religious persecution, and
many ended up in Britain and Ireland. A
small community settled in Gracehill (Baile
Uí Chinnéide), 2km west of Ballymena, in
1765. The Georgian architecture of their
elegant village square includes a **church** with
separate entrances for men and women. If
you'd like to see inside, visitors are welcome at 11am services on Sunday. Even
the graveyard at the back of the church has
separate areas, with men on the left and
women on the right.

Bus No 127 from Ballymena stops at
Gracehill (10 minutes, hourly Monday to
Saturday). If you're driving, take the A42
towards Maghera; about 1km past the
Gracehill roundabout, turn left at a brown
sign with a church marked on it.

Counties Fermanagh & Tyrone

The lush, green landscape of County Fermanagh is known as Ireland's lake district, its myriad islands and convoluted shores intimately entwined with the waters of Lough Erne. Local people like to say that for six months of the year the lakes are in Fermanagh; for the other six, Fermanagh is in the lakes (the surface area of the county is around one-third water). This watery wonderland makes the county a paradise for anglers, bird-watchers and pleasure boaters.

The pretty town of Enniskillen perches on one of these islands, and makes a good base for exploring Fermanagh's many and varied attractions, which include the contrasting stately homes of Florence Court and Castle Coole, the spectacular caves and underground river of Marble Arch, and the world-famous pottery at Belleek. It's also a good centre for activities such as hiking, cycling and canoeing.

Perhaps the most evocative of Fermanagh's sights are the ancient carved stones, some pagan, some early Christian, found around the shores of Lower Lough Erne, from the curious stone figures of White Island to the 2000-year-old, two-faced Janus Figure of Boa Island.

County Tyrone – from *Tír Eoghain,* the Land of Owen, a legendary chieftain – is the home-land of the O'Neill clan, dominated by the tweed-tinted moorlands of the Sperrin Mountains, whose southern flanks are dotted with prehistoric sites. Apart from the hiking opportunities offered by these heather-clad hills, the county's main attraction is the Ulster American Folk Park, an interesting outdoor museum celebrating Ulster emigrants' historic links with the USA.

HIGHLIGHTS

- **Country Houses**
  The elegant country houses of Castle Coole (p662) near Enniskillen and Florence Court (p667) near Bellanaleck

- **Sacred Stones**
  Strange stone figures of Boa Island (p665) and White Island (p664) in Lower Lough Erne

- **Underground Exploration**
  Following the course of an underground river as it flows through the Marble Arch Caves (p667)

- **Blast from the Past**
  Learning about the historical links between Ireland and America the Ulster American Folk Park (p669) near Omagh

- **Stretch Your Legs**
  Hikes through the heather in the lonely Sperrin Mountains (p669)

Sperrin Mountains ★

Omagh ★

Boa Island; White Island (Lough Erne) ★

★ Enniskillen

Marble Arch Caves ★   ★ Bellanaleck

■ POPULATION: 227,000   ■ AREA: 5274 SQ KM

COUNTY FERMANAGH

ENNISKILLEN

pop 11,500

Enniskillen (Inis Ceithleann) is an attractive town with a mile-long main street that rides the roller-coaster back of an island drumlin commanding the river passage between Upper and Lower Lough Erne. The locals say that you're only a true Enniskilliner if you were born 'between the bridges'; that is, on the town's central island.

Though neither was born here, both Oscar Wilde and Samuel Beckett were pupils at Enniskillen's Portora Royal School (Wilde from 1864 to 1871, Beckett from 1919 to 1923); it was here that Beckett first studied French, a language he would later write in. But the town's name is sadly more familiar as the place where on Poppy Day (11 November) 1987 an IRA bomb killed 11 innocent people during a service at the war memorial.

Enniskillen is a pleasant place to stay, and is ideally located as a base for exploring Upper and Lower Lough Erne, Florencecourt and the Marble Arch Caves.

Orientation

The town centre is on an island in the waterway connecting Upper and Lower Lough Erne. The main street changes name several times; the clock tower marks the centre. The other principal thoroughfare is Wellington Rd, south of and parallel to the main street, where you'll find the bus station and tourist office.

Information

Bank of Ireland (☎ 6632 2136; 7 Townhall St)

Enniskillen Library (☎ 6632 2886; Hall's Lane; 🕒 9.15am-5.15pm Mon, Wed & Fri, 9.15am-7.30pm Tue & Thu, 9.15am-1pm Sat) Internet access £1.50 per 30 minutes.

Post office (3 High St) Situated inside the Centra grocery store.

Tourist Information Centre (☎ 6632 3110; www.fermanagh.gov.uk; Wellington Rd; 🕒 9am-7pm Mon-Fri, 10am-6pm Sat, 11am-5pm Sun Jul & Aug, 9am-5.30pm Mon-Fri, 10am-6pm Sat, 11am-5pm Sun Easter-Jun & Sep, 9am-5.30pm Mon-Fri Oct-Easter) Books accommodation, changes money, sells fishing licences and provides a postal and fax service.

Ulster Bank (☎ 6632 4034; 16 Darling St)

Sights

Enniskillen Castle (☎ 6632 5000; www.enniskillencastle.co.uk; Castle Barracks; adult/child £2.50/1.50; 🕒 10am-5pm Tue-Fri, 2-5pm Sat-Mon Jul & Aug, closed Sun May, Jun & Sep, closed Sat & Sun Oct-Apr), a former stronghold of the 16th-century Maguire chieftains, guards the western end of the town's central island, its twin-turreted **Watergate** looming over the passing fleets of cabin cruisers. Within the walls is the **Fermanagh County Museum**, with displays on the county's history, landscape and wildlife. The keep contains the **Regimental Museum of the Royal Inniskilling Fusiliers**, full of medals, guns and uniforms.

In Forthill Park, at the eastern end of town, stands **Cole's Monument** (adult/child 70/30p; 🕒 1.30-3.30pm Apr-Sep). It commemorates Sir Galbraith Lowry-Cole (1772–1842), who was one of Wellington's generals and the son of the first earl of Enniskillen. You can climb the 108 steps inside the column for a good view of the surrounding area.

Activities

The **Kingfisher Trail** is a waymarked, long-distance cycling trail that starts in Enniskillen and wends its way through the back roads of counties Fermanagh, Leitrim, Cavan and Monaghan. The full route is around 370km long, but a shorter loop, starting and finishing in Enniskillen, and travelling via Kesh, Belleek, Garrison, Belcoo and the village of Florencecourt, is only 115km – easily done in two days with an overnight stay at Belleek. You can get a trail map from the tourist office.

See p663 and p667 for boat- and cycle-hire options, and boxed text, p663 for information on cruising the lakes.

Tours

Heritage Tours (☎ 6962 1430; bmccusker@talk21.com) offers guided tours of Enniskillen and the Lough Erne area with a Northern Ireland Tourist Board (NITB)–registered guide. Special interest tours include prehistoric sites, monastic sites, carved stones and plantation castles.

Erne Tours (☎ 6632 2882; Round 'O' Quay, The Brook; adult/child £8/5) operates 1¾-hour cruises on Lower Lough Erne aboard the 56-seat waterbus, MV *Kestrel*, calling at Devenish Island (see p663) along the way. It departs from the Round 'O' Quay, just west of the town centre on the A46 to Belleek. Departures are at 10.30am, 2.15pm and 4.15pm daily in July and August; 2.30pm Tuesday, Saturday and Sunday in September; and 2.30pm on Sunday only in May and June (no advance bookings, pay on the boat). There are also Saturday **evening dinner cruises** (adult/child £20/15, departing at 6.30pm) from May to August.

Sleeping
BUDGET
Bridges Youth Hostel (☎ 6634 0110; www.hini.org.uk; Belmore St; dm/tw £11.50/26; P ✗ 🚹) This modern, purpose-built hostel is part of the Clinton Peace Centre, opened by former US President Bill Clinton in June 2002. It has four- and six-bed dorms with bathrooms, six twin rooms, a kitchen, restaurant, laundry and bike shed.

Rossole Guesthouse (☎ 6632 3462; 85 Sligo Rd; s/d £25/38; P ✗) A modern Georgian-style house with a sunny conservatory overlooking a small lake, the five-room Rossole is an angler's delight – you can fish in the lake, and there are rowing boats for guests at the bottom of the garden! It's 1km southwest of the town centre.

Will-O-Brook (☎ 6632 5285; 8 Willoughby Pl; s/d £20/34; P ✗) This terraced Victorian house offers good-value, no-frills B&B overlooking Lough Erne, just a 400m walk west of the town centre.

MIDRANGE
Mountview Guesthouse (☎ 6632 3147; wendy@ mountviewguests.com; 61 Irvinestown Rd; s/d £34/46;

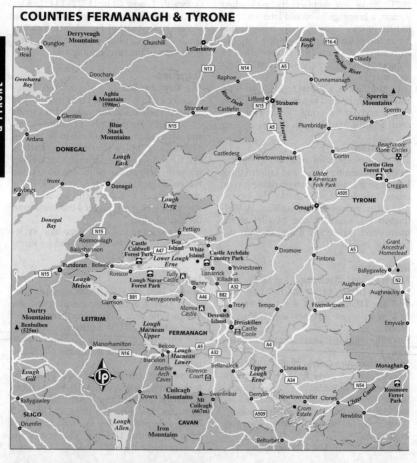

P ⊠) Indulge in a spot of country-house comfort in this large, ivy-clad Victorian villa set in its own wooded grounds. There are three en-suite bedrooms, a luxurious lounge and even a snooker room with a full-size table. The Mountview looks out over Race Course Lough, just a 10-minute walk north of the town centre.

Railway Hotel (☎ 6632 2084; www.railwayhotel enniskillen.com; 34 Forthill St; s/d £32.50/65; ⊠) Railway memorabilia dot the walls of this welcoming 130-year-old hotel, a reminder of Enniskillen's now-vanished railway line. The 19 rooms offer rather bijou B&B accommodation close to the centre of town.

Belmore Court Motel (☎ 6632 6633; www.motel.co .uk; Tempo Rd; d £50, apt £68-85; P 💻) Set in a con-

verted row of terrace houses just east of the town centre, the Belmore has family 'mini-apartments', as well as four ordinary double rooms. Rates don't include breakfast.

Ashberry Hotel (☎ 6632 0333; www.ashberryhotel .com; 14-20 Tempo Rd; s £45-55, d £70-80; P ⊠) The modern Ashberry is comfortable and conveniently central, but otherwise forgettable. The cheaper rooms can be a bit on the small side.

TOP END

Killyhevlin Hotel (☎ 6632 3481; www.killyhevlin.com; Killyhevlin; s £70-85, d £100-130; P) Enniskillen's top hotel is 1.5km south of town on the A4 Maguiresbridge road, in an idyllic setting overlooking Upper Lough Erne. Many of its 43 rooms have lakeside views; there are also 13 two-bedroom lakeside chalets (£175 to £220 per weekend November to June, £520 per week July to October).

Eating

BUDGET

World Café (☎ 6632 2264; 1 Middleton St; snacks £3-5; ⊗ 10am-5pm Mon-Sat) This stylish little café (part of an interior design shop) serves the best coffee in town, as well as gourmet sandwiches, *panini* (type of Italian sandwich) and salads.

Rebecca's Place (☎ 6632 4499; Buttermarket; snacks £2-5; ⊗ 9am-5.30pm Mon-Sat) A more traditional café with pine tables and chairs, Rebecca's is set in a craft shop and serves good sandwiches, salads and pastries.

Johnston's Jolly Sandwich Bar (☎ 6632 2277; 3 Darling St; sandwiches £2-4; ⊗ 8am-4pm Mon-Fri, 8.30am-4pm Sat) A traditional bakery selling excellent pick-and-mix sandwiches, soup, pies and cakes to take away or eat in.

MIDRANGE

Scoffs Wine Bar & Restaurant (☎ 6634 2622; 17 Belmore St; mains £11-14; ⊗ 5pm-late) The décor here follows the modern mantra of chocolate brown, burgundy, dark wood and dim candlelight (and those rubber place mats you'll find in every Northern Ireland restaurant with pretensions towards style). The adventurous *nouvelle* Irish menu includes char-grilled ostrich steak and seared fillet of kangaroo, as well as more traditional offerings such as grilled crab claws in garlic butter, and duck with braised cabbage, bacon and plum sauce.

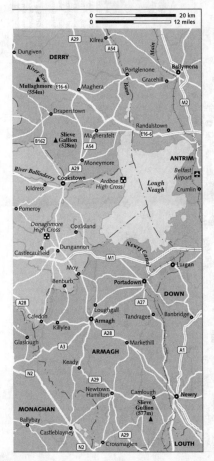

ENNISKILLEN

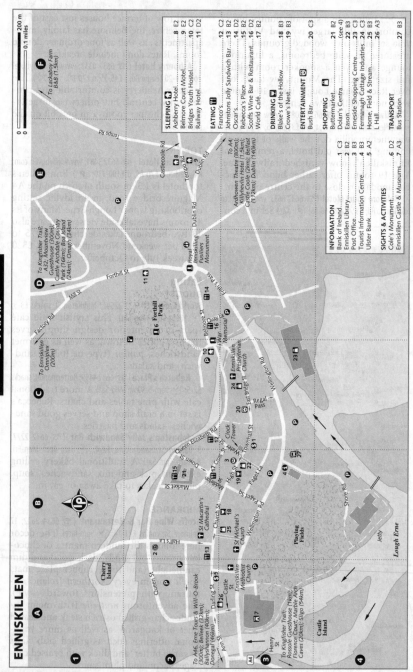

INFORMATION	
Bank of Ireland	1 C3
Enniskillen Library	2 B2
Post Office	3 B3
Tourist Information Centre	4 B3
Ulster Bank	5 A2

SIGHTS & ACTIVITIES	
Cole's Monument	6 D2
Enniskillen Castle & Museums	7 A3

SLEEPING	
Ashberry Hotel	8 E2
Belmore Court Motel	9 E2
Bridges Youth Hostel	10 C2
Railway Hotel	11 D2

EATING	
Franco's	12 C2
Johnstons Jolly Sandwich Bar	13 B2
Oscar's	14 D2
Rebecca's Place	15 B2
Scoffs Wine Bar & Restaurant	16 B2
World Café	17 B2

DRINKING	
Blake's of the Hollow	18 B3
Crowe's Nest	19 B3

ENTERTAINMENT	
Bush Bar	20 C3

SHOPPING	
Buttermarket	21 B2
Dolan's Centra	(see 4)
Eason	22 B3
Erneside Shopping Centre	23 C3
Fermanagh Cottage Industries	24 C3
Home, Field & Stream	25 B3
L Hall	26 A3

TRANSPORT	
Bus Station	27 B3

Oscar's (☎ 6632 7037; 29 Belmore St; pizzas £6-10, mains £8-14; ☺ 5-10pm Wed-Mon) Named after former local schoolboy Oscar Wilde, this intimate restaurant has become an Enniskillen institution. Its wood-panelled, bookshop-style interior is decorated with the pithy sayings of the great man, and the varied menu offers steak, fish, pizza and vegetarian dishes.

Franco's (☎ 6632 4424; Queen Elizabeth Rd; pizzas £7.50-9.50, mains £11-18; ☺ noon-11pm) An atmospheric warren of tiny rooms in a former blacksmith's forge, Franco's is always bustling and noisy, serving a range of Italian, Asian and seafood dishes as well as filling pizzas and pasta.

Drinking

Blake's of the Hollow (William Blake; ☎ 6632 2143; 6 Church St) Ulster's best pint of Guinness awaits you in this traditional Victorian pub, established in 1887, complete with marble-topped bar, four huge sherry casks, antique silver lampholders and ancient wood panelling kippered by a century of cigarette smoke. There's traditional music from 9pm on Fridays.

Crowe's Nest (☎ 6632 5252; 12 High St) A lively bar with a conservatory and patio out back for those sunny summer afternoons, the Nest has live music nightly from 10.30pm in the back bar and traditional music sessions on Monday nights during summer.

Entertainment

Bush Bar (☎ 6632 5210; 26 Townhall St) Following a major re-fit the once-trad Bush has gone all modern, with leather chairs and banquettes in various shades of coffee from dark roast to café au lait, and a new nightclub venue that hosts DJs and live rock bands.

Ardhowen Theatre (☎ 6632 5440; Dublin Rd; ☺ box office 11am-4.30pm Mon-Fri, 10am-7pm before a

---

TOP FIVE TRADITIONAL PUBS IN NORTHERN IRELAND

- Bittle's Bar (p578)
- Blake's of the Hollow (above)
- Grace Neill's Bar & Grill (p600)
- Mary McBride's (p650)
- Peadar O'Donnell's (p634)

---

performance, 11am-1pm, 2-5pm & 6-7pm Sat) The programme includes concerts, local amateur and professional drama and musical productions, pantomime and films. The theatre is about 2km south of the town centre on the A4.

Enniskillen Omniplex (☎ 6632 4777; Factory Rd) A seven-screen cinema, 700m north of the town centre on Race Course Lough.

Shopping

Buttermarket (☎ 6632 4499; Down St) The refurbished buildings in the old marketplace house a variety of craft shops and studios; ceramics and jewellery are the best buys.

Erneside Shopping Centre (☎ 6632 5705; The Point; ☺ 9am-5.30pm Mon-Wed, 9am-9pm Thu & Fri, 9am-6pm Sat, 1-6pm Sun) Here you can find a modern complex of shops, cafés and a supermarket. Millets stocks camping and outdoor equipment.

Fermanagh Cottage Industries (☎ 6632 2260; 14 East Bridge St) Another craft shop selling linen, lace and tweed.

Home, Field & Stream (☎ 6632 2114; 18 Church St) Has a wide range of fishing tackle and also sells fishing licences and permits.

Eason (☎ 6632 4341; 10 High St; ☺ 9am-5.30pm Mon-Sat) and **L Hall** (☎ 6632 2275; 34-36 Darling St) both stock local-interest books and maps, while **Dolan's Centra** (3 High St; ☺ 7.30am-10pm Mon-Sat, 8am-10pm Sun) is a handy, late-opening minimarket, and also houses a post-office counter.

Getting There & Away

The bus station is opposite the tourist office on Shore Rd.

Ulsterbus No 261 runs from Enniskillen to Belfast (£8.60, 2¼ hours, hourly Monday to Saturday, four Sunday) via Dungannon. Bus No 296 runs to Derry (£8.20, 2½ hours, one daily Monday to Friday) via Omagh (one hour) and, in the other direction, to Cork (8¼ hours) via Athlone (three hours). Bus No 99 goes from Enniskillen to Bundoran (1¼ hours, three or four daily) via Belleek (45 minutes).

Bus Éireann's No 66 service runs to Sligo (£6.50, 1½ hours, four daily Monday to Saturday) via Belcoo, and its bus No 30 between Dublin (£10.20, three hours, six daily Monday to Saturday, four Sunday) and Donegal (1¼ hours) also calls at Enniskillen.

COUNTIES FERMANAGH & TYRONE

AROUND ENNISKILLEN

Sheelin Irish Lace Museum

This **museum** (☎ 6634 8052; www.irishlacemuseum.com; Bellanaleck; adult/child £2.50/1; 🕓 10am-6pm Mon-Sat) houses a collection of beautiful Irish lace dating from 1850 to 1900. Lace making was an important cottage industry in the region both before and after the Famine – prior to WWI there were at least 10 lace schools in County Fermanagh. The museum shop has linen, lace and oil lamps for sale. The museum is just over 6km southwest of Enniskillen in the village of Bellanaleck.

Castle Coole

When King George IV visited Ireland in 1821, the second earl of Belmore had a bedroom at Castle Coole specially decorated in anticipation of a visit from the monarch. But the king was more interested in dallying with his mistress at Slane Castle, and never turned up. The bedroom, draped in red silk and decorated with paintings depicting *The Rake's Progress* (the earl's sniffy riposte to the king's non-arrival), is one of the highlights of a visit to **Castle Coole** (☎ 6632 2690; Dublin Rd, Enniskillen; adult/child £4.20/2.10; 🕓 noon-6pm daily Easter, Jul & Aug, noon-6pm Fri-Wed Jun, noon-6pm Sat, Sun & public hols mid-Mar–May & Sep–mid-Oct).

Designed by James Wyatt this building was built between 1789 and 1795 for Armar Lowry-Corry, the first earl of Belmore. The Palladian mansion is probably the purest expression of late-18th-century neoclassical architecture in Ireland. It is built of silvery-white portland stone, which was brought at great expense from southern England – by ship to Ballyshannon, then overland to Lough Erne, by boat again to Enniskillen, then by bullock cart for the last 3km.

The building costs of £70,000 nearly bankrupted the first earl, but that didn't stop his son Somerset Lowry-Corry, the second earl, spending another £35,000 on exuberant Regency furnishings and decoration, best seen in the opulent, oval saloon where the family and friends would gather before dinner. The seventh earl of Belmore, John Armar Lowry-Corry, reserves part of the house for his private use, but most of the building is under the care of the National Trust.

The 600 hectares of landscaped **grounds** (car/pedestrian £2/free; 🕓 10am-8pm Apr-Sep, 10am-4pm Oct-Mar) contain a lake that is home to the UK's only nonmigratory colony of greylag geese. It is said that if the geese ever leave, the earls of Belmore will lose Castle Coole.

Castle Coole is on the A4 Dublin road, 2.5km southeast of Enniskillen. You can easily walk there from Enniskillen town centre in 30 minutes – fork left beyond Dunnes Stores and keep straight on along Tempo Rd and Castlecoole Rd.

UPPER LOUGH ERNE

About 80km long, Lough Erne is made up of two sections: the Upper Lough to the south of Enniskillen, and the Lower Lough to the north. The two are connected by the River Erne, which begins its journey in County Cavan and meets the sea at Donegal Bay west of Ballyshannon.

Upper Lough Erne is not so much a lake as a watery maze of islands (more than 150 of them), inlets, reedy bays and meandering backwaters. Birdlife is abundant, with flocks of whooper swan and goldeneye overwintering here, great crested grebes nesting in the spring, and Ireland's biggest heronry in a 400-year-old oak grove on the island of Inishfendra, just south of Crom Castle.

Crom Estate

Situated on the eastern shore of the Upper Lough, west of Newtownbutler, is National Trust's **Crom Estate** (☎ 6773 8118; Newtownbutler; car/pedestrian £4.70/free; 🕓 10am-8pm Jul & Aug, 10am-6pm mid-Mar–Jun & Sep, Sat & Sun Oct). The 760 hectares of woodland, parkland and wetlands offer numerous walking trails, the ruins of old Crom Castle, a boathouse and an island folly. There are boats for hire (£5 per hour), and camping facilities (£5 per night).

Doon Scenic Route

This signposted minor road leads west from Derrylin to a parking area on the northern shoulder of Slieve Rushen (404m). The top of the ridge is occupied by a wind farm, but turn your back on it and enjoy the superb views over the Upper Lough.

Tours

The **Inishcruiser** (☎ 6772 2122; adult/child £7/5; 🕓 2.30pm Sun & public hols Apr-Sep; ♿) offers 1½- to two-hour cruises on the lough leaving from the Share Holiday Village southwest of Lisnaskea.

Activities

Day boats can be hired for fishing or exploring from **Carrybridge Boat Company** (☎ 6638 7034; Carrybridge, Lisbellaw), 12km south of Enniskillen, and **Crom Estate** (☎ 6773 8118; Newtownbutler). Rates are about £10 to £15 per hour for an open rowing boat with outboard motor, to £50/70 per half/full day for a six-seater with cabin and inboard diesel engine.

Guests at the **Share Holiday Village** (☎ 6772 2122; www.sharevillage.org) in Lisnaskea can take part in canoeing, windsurfing, dinghy sailing, archery, orienteering and other activities for £8 per person per 2½-hour session.

Sleeping

Donn Carragh Hotel (☎ 6772 1206; donncarraghhotel@ btclick.com; Main St, Lisnaskea; s/d £35/60; **P** **✕**) There's not too much in the way of hotel or B&B accommodation around Upper Lough Erne; this recently refurbished 18-room hotel in the middle of Lisnaskea is the best of what there is.

Lisnaskea Caravan Park (☎ 6772 1040; Gola Rd, Mullynascarty; camp/caravan sites £8/12; ❧ Apr-Oct) This local council-run site enjoys a beautiful wooded setting on the banks of the Colebrooke River about 2km northwest of Lisnaskea, on the B514 road towards Enniskillen.

Share Holiday Village (☎ 6772 2122; www.share village.org; Smiths Strand, Lisnaskea; camp/caravan sites £8/12.50; ❧ Easter-Sep) Share is a charity that works towards the integration of disabled and nondisabled people through a range of activities and courses. The holiday village is mostly occupied by groups, but it also has a touring site with space for 18 caravans and 10 tents. Booking is strongly recommended. The village is 5km southwest of Lisnaskea, off the B127.

Getting There & Away

From Enniskillen, Ulsterbus No 95 runs along the east side of the lough to Lisnaskea (£2.20, 25 minutes, eight daily Monday to Friday, three Saturday, two Sunday), while No 58 goes down the west side to Derrylin (£2.40, 35 minutes, six daily Monday to Friday, four Saturday), on the way to Belturbet in County Cavan.

LOWER LOUGH ERNE

Lower Lough Erne is a much more open expanse of water than the Upper Lough, with its 90-odd islands clustered mainly in the southern reaches. There are many ancient religious sites and other antiquities around its shores. In early Christian times, when overland travel was difficult, Lough Erne was an important highway between the Donegal coast and inland Leitrim, and in medieval times the lough was part of an important pilgrimage route to Station Island in Lough Derg (see boxed text, p492).

The following sights are described as they are found anticlockwise around the lough from Enniskillen.

Devenish Island

Devenish Island (Daimh Inis, meaning Ox Island) is the biggest of several 'holy

CRUISING HOLIDAYS ON LOUGH ERNE

If you fancy exploring Lough Erne as captain of your own motor cruiser, well, you can – and without any previous experience or qualification. Several companies in Fermanagh hire out self-drive, live-aboard cabin cruisers by the week, offering a crash course (not literally, you hope) in boat-handling and navigation at the start of your holiday. Weekly rates in high season (July and August) range from about £600 for a two-berth to £1000 for a four-berth and £1600 for an eight-berth boat. Low- and mid-season rates are around 70% to 90% of high-season figures.

The main cruiser hire companies in Fermanagh:

Aghinver Boat Company (☎ 6863 1400; abcboats@btinternet.com; Lisnarick, Lower Lough Erne)

Belleek Charter Cruising (☎ 6865 8027; www25.brinkster.com/belleekcruising; Erne Gateway Marina, Belleek, Lower Lough Erne)

Carrick Craft (☎ 3834 4993; www.cruise-ireland.com; Tully Bay, Lower Lough Erne)

Carrybridge Boat Company (☎ 6638 7034; Carrybridge, Lisbellaw, Upper Lough Erne)

Corraquill Cruising (☎ 6774 8712; www.corraquill.co.uk; Drumetta, Aghalane, Derrylinn, Upper Lough Erne)

Erne Marine (☎ 6634 8267; www.ernemarine.com; Bellanaleck Quay, Enniskillen)

Manor House Marine (☎ 6862 8100; www.manormarine.com; Killadeas, Lower Lough Erne)

islands' in Lough Erne. The remains of an **Augustinian monastery**, founded here in the 6th century by St Molaise, include a superb 12th-century **round tower** in near perfect condition, the ruins of St Molaise's Church and St Mary's Abbey, an unusual 15th-century high cross, and many fascinating old gravestones. Four ladders allow you to climb to the top of the round tower for a cramped view out of the five tiny windows.

A speedboat **ferry** (☎ 6862 1588; adult/child return £2.25/1.20; ☼ 10am, 1pm, 3pm & 5pm daily Jul–mid-Sep, Sat, Sun & public hols Easter-Jun) crosses to Devenish Island from Trory Point landing. From Enniskillen, take the A32 towards Irvinestown and after 5km look for the sign on the left, just after a service station and immediately before the junction where the B82 and A32 part company. At the foot of the hill by the lough, turn left for the jetty.

Killadeas

Killadeas churchyard, 11km north of Enniskillen on the B82, contains several unusual carved stones. Most famous is the 1m-high **Bishop's Stone**, dating from between the 7th and 9th centuries, which has a Celtic head reminiscent of the White Island figures carved on its narrow western edge, and an engraving of a bishop with bell and crozier on the side. Located nearby is a slab set on edge, with several deep cup-marks (possibly bullauns) on one side, and a cross within a circle on the other. You will also find a broken phallic column and a large, perforated stone.

The **Lady of the Lake** (☎ 6862 2200), based at the Inishclare restaurant, offers cruises on the lough on Saturday and Sunday.

SLEEPING & EATING

Manor House Country Hotel (☎ 6862 2211; www .manor-house-hotel.com; Killadeas; s/d £75/120; **P** ✗) This grand, 19th-century country house overlooking Lough Erne has had a thorough makeover in neoclassical style, complete with Greek temple–style lobby, Romanesque pool and Jacuzzis with a view over the lough. The public areas are impressive but the rooms, though luxurious, are a bit on the bland side.

Inishclare Bar & Restaurant (☎ 6862 8550; Killadeas; 3-course lunch/dinner £14/25; ☼ noon-9pm) With a huge glass-fronted dining room

and outdoor tables overlooking the bay north of the Manor House (and under the same management), this place has a good bar, restaurant and bistro with great lough views.

Castle Archdale Country Park

This **park** (☎ 6862 1892; Lisnarick; admission free; ☼ 9am-dusk), 16km northeast of Enniskillen on the B82, has pleasant woodland and lakeshore walks in the former estate of 18th-century Archdale Manor. The island-filled bay was used in WWII as a base for Catalina flying boats, a history explained in the **visitor centre** (admission free; ☼ 11am-7pm Tue-Sun Jul & Aug, noon-6pm Sat & Sun Easter-Jun).

You can hire bikes for £3/6/10 per hour/half day/day, or swap two wheels for four legs – the park offers pony trekking (£12 per hour) and short rides (£4 per 15 minutes) for beginners, and hacking (£18 per hour) for experienced riders.

There are also boats for hire (from £30 for two hours), and you can also hire fishing rods (£5 a day including bait).

SLEEPING

Rossgweer Guest House (☎ 6862 1924; www.ross gweer.com; 274 Killadeas Rd, Lisnarick; s/d £30/50; ✗) Just over 1km south of the park entrance, Rossgweer is a large modern house with eight en-suite guest bedrooms, big breakfasts, home baking and free tea and coffee in the lounge, plus golf and angling right on the doorstep.

Castle Archdale Caravan Park (☎ 6862 1333; www.castlearchdale.com; Castle Archdale Country Park; camp sites £10-15, caravan sites £15; ☼ Easter-Oct) This site is dominated by onsite caravans, but has good facilities, including a shop, launderette, kids' playground and restaurant.

White Island

White Island, in the bay to the north of Castle Archdale Country Park, is the most haunting of Lough Erne's monastic sites. At the eastern tip of the island are the ruins of a small 12th-century church with a beautiful Romanesque door on its southern side. Inside are six extraordinary Celtic stone figures, thought to date from the 9th century, lined up along the wall like miniature Easter Island statues.

This line-up is a modern arrangement; most of them were discovered buried in the walls of the church in the 19th century, where the medieval masons had used them as ordinary building stones. The six main figures, all created by the same hand, are flanked on the left by a sheila-na-gig (carved female figure with exaggerated genitalia), which is probably contemporary with the church, and flanked on the right by a scowling stone face. The age and interpretation of these figures has been the subject of much debate; it has been suggested that the two central pairs, of equal height, were *caryatids* (pillars in human form) that once supported a pulpit, and that they represent either saints or aspects of the life of Christ.

The first figure is holding a book (Christ the Evangelist?), and the second holds a bishop's crozier and bell (Christ as Bishop?). The third has been identified as the young King David, author of the Psalms. The fourth is holding the necks of two griffins (symbols of Christ's dual nature as both human and divine?). The fifth bears a sword and shield (Christ's Second Coming?), and the sixth is unfinished.

A **ferry** (adult/child £3/2; ☼ 11am-6pm daily Jul & Aug, 11am-1pm Sat & Sun Apr-Jun) crosses to the island hourly (on the hour) from the marina in Castle Archdale Country Park; buy your ticket from the Billeve Boat Hire office. The crossing takes 15 minutes, and allows you around half an hour on the island.

Boa Island

Boa Island, at the northern end of Lower Lough Erne, is connected to the mainland at both ends – the main A47 road runs along its length. Spooky, moss-grown Caldragh graveyard, towards the western end of the island, contains the famous **Janus Stone**. Perhaps 2000 years old, this pagan figure is carved with two grotesque human heads, back to back. Nearby is a smaller figure, called the **Lusty Man**, brought here from Lusty More island. Their origin and meaning have been lost in the mists of time.

There's a small sign indicating the graveyard, about 1.5km from the bridge at the western tip of the island.

SLEEPING & EATING

Lusty Beg Island (☎ 6863 3300; www.lustybeg.com; Boa Island, Kesh; s/d £55/85; ℗ ☒) This private island retreat, reached by ferry from a jetty halfway along Boa Island, has self-catering chalets to let (£400 to £575 a week in July and August) but also offers B&B in its rustic 18-room Courtyard Motel. The informal **Island Lodge Restaurant** (☎ 6863 1342; bar meals £6-12, 4-course dinner £23; ☼ 1-9pm Jul & Aug) is open to all, and serves everything from baked potatoes to smoked Irish salmon. There's a telephone in a blockhouse on the slipway to summon the ferry.

Castle Caldwell Forest Park

Castle Caldwell, built between 1610 and 1619, is nothing but a ruin, but the **park** (admission free; ☼ 24hr), about 5km west of Boa Island along the A47, contains a nature reserve full of birdlife, and is a major breeding ground for the common scoter.

At the entrance to the park is the **Fiddler's Stone** (in the shape of a fiddle). The inscription, now too worn to read, commemorated a favourite musician who fell out of a boat while drunk:

'To the memory of Denis McCabe, Fiddler, who fell out of the St Patrick Barge belonging to Sir James Caldwell Bart. and Count of Milan and was drowned off this point August ye 13 1770.'

Belleek
pop 550

Belleek's (Beal Leice) village street of colourful, flower-bedecked houses slopes up from a bridge across the River Erne, where it flows out of the Lower Lough towards Ballyshannon and the sea. The village is right on the border – the road south across the bridge passes through a finger of the Republic's territory for about 200m before leaving again.

The imposing Georgian-style building beside the bridge houses the world-famous **Belleek Pottery** (☎ 6865 9300; www.belleek.ie; Main St; ☼ 9am-8pm Mon-Fri, 10am-6pm Sat, 11am-6pm Sun Jul & Aug, 9am-6pm Mon-Fri, 10am-6pm Sat, 2-6pm Sun Apr-Jun & Sep, 9am-5.30pm Mon-Fri, 10am-5.30pm Sat, 2-6pm Sun Oct, 9am-5.30pm Mon-Fri Nov-Mar), founded in 1857 to provide local employment in the wake of the Potato Famine. It has been producing fine Parian china ever since, and is especially noted for its delicate basketware. The visitor centre houses a small museum, showroom and restaurant, and there are **guided tours** (adult/child £4/free) of the pottery every half-hour from 9.30am to 12.15pm and 2.15pm to 4.15pm (until 3.30pm on Friday) Monday to Friday year round, and on Saturdays in June, July and August.

On the far side of the river is the **Explor-Erne Exhibition** (☎ 6865 8866; Erne Gateway Centre, Corry; adult/child £1/0.50; ☿ 11am-5pm Wed-Sun Jun-Sep), which tells the story of the Fermanagh lakelands' landscape and people.

Belleek hosts a **traditional music festival** each June.

SLEEPING & EATING

Hotel Carlton (☎ 6865 8282; www.hotelcarlton.co.uk; Main St; s/d £52.50/75; **P** ⊠) Though the rooms are plush and luxurious, the family-friendly Carlton has a welcoming and informal feel to it, and a lovely setting on the banks of the River Erne. There are frequent live music sessions in the hotel's Potters Bar.

Moohan's Fiddlestone (☎ 6665 8008; 15-17 Main St; s/d £33/40; **P**) This is a traditional Irish pub offering B&B in five en-suite upstairs rooms. The lively bar downstairs is a popular venue for impromptu music sessions, so don't expect peace and quiet in the evenings.

Thatch Coffee Shop (☎ 6865 8181; 20 Main St; mains £4-5; ☿ 9am-5pm Mon-Sat) It may be Belleek's oldest building (late 18th century), but the Thatch serves a thoroughly modern cup of coffee.

Black Cat Cove (☎ 6865 8942; 28 Main St; mains £5-10; ☿ noon-9pm) This friendly, family-run pub that serves excellent bar meals. It also has music on Tuesday, Wednesday and Thursday nights from May to September.

South Shore

The lakeside A46 road leads along the south shore of Lower Lough Erne from Belleek to Enniskillen. **Lough Navar Forest Park** (car £2.50; ☿ 10am-dusk) boasts a superb viewpoint atop the Magho cliffs, overlooking the lough. The vehicle entrance is on the minor Glennash-eevar road between Garrison and Derrygon-nelly, 20km southeast of Belleek (take the B52 towards Garrison, and fork left after 2.5km). You can also hike up to the view-point from a parking area and picnic site on the A46, 12km east of Belleek. It's a steep climb; allow 1½ hours there and back.

Tully Castle (☎ 9054 6552; admission free; ☿ 10am-6pm Wed-Sun Jun-Aug, 10am-6pm Sat, Sun & public holidays Apr, May & Sep), off the A46 some 16km southeast of Belleek, was built in 1613 as a fortified home for a Scottish Planter's family, but was captured and burned by Roderick Maguire in 1641. The bawn (cattle enclosure) has four corner towers and retains a lot of the original paving.

Just south of the Tully Castle turn-off, the B81 leads south through Derrygon-nelly for 10km to **Monea Castle** (admission free; ☿ 24hr). Another Scottish-style plantation castle, built around the same time as Tully Castle, it too was captured in the 1641 rising but remained in use until the mid-18th century, when it was gutted by fire. A *crannóg* sits in the nearby lake.

SLEEPING

Lakeview Guesthouse (☎ 6864 1263; Drumcrow, Blaney; s/d £28/46; ☿ Jan-Nov; **P** ⊠) This farm guesthouse enjoys an idyllic setting with panoramic views over the lough. It's off the A46 near Tully Castle.

Blaney Caravan Park (☎ 6864 1634; info@blaney caravanpark.com; Blaney; tent £8-14, caravan £14) This site is 3.5km south of Tully Castle on the A46 towards Enniskillen, and about 1km away from the lough shore.

Activities

FISHING

The lakes of Fermanagh are renowned for both coarse and game fishing. The Lough Erne trout-fishing season runs from the beginning of March to the end of September. Salmon fishing begins in June and also continues to the end of September. The mayfly season usually lasts a month from the second week in May. There's no closed season for coarse fish.

You'll need both a licence (issued by the Fisheries Conservancy Board) and a permit (from the owner of the fishery). Licences and permits can be purchased from the **Fermanagh Tourist Information Centre** (☎ 6632 3110; www.fermanagh-online.com; Wellington Rd) and **Home, Field & Stream** (☎ 6632 2114; 18 Church St) both in Enniskillen, and from the marina in Castle Archdale Country Park (see p664). A combined licence and permit for game fishing on Lough Erne costs £8.50/22.50 for three/14 days.

Most rivers in County Fermanagh are privately owned, and information on permits is available from the tourist information centre. It also has a list of *ghillies* (fishing guides).

BOAT HIRE

A number of companies hire out day boats at Enniskillen, Killadeas, Castle Archdale Country Park, Kesh and Belleek. Rates are about £10 to £15 per hour for an open rowing boat with outboard motor, to £50/70 per half/full day for a six-seater with cabin and inboard diesel engine. The **Fermanagh Tourist Information Centre** (☎ 6632 3110; Wellington Rd) in Enniskillen has a full list of companies and costs (see boxed text, p663).

WATER SPORTS

You can hire equipment for a range of water sports – dinghy sailing (£20 per hour), canoeing (£8 per hour), water-skiing (£15 to £30 per 30 minutes) and jet-skiing (£35 per 30 minutes) – from **Tudor Farm Watersports** (☎ 6863 1943; info@tudorfarm.com; 619 Boa Island Rd, Kesh).

Getting There & Away

On the eastern side of the lough, bus No 194 from Enniskillen to Pettigo via Irvinestown (four or five daily Monday to Saturday) stops at Castle Archdale Country Park (35 minutes) and Kesh (one hour); there's no service along the B82 south of Lisnarick. Bus No 99 goes from Enniskillen to Belleek (45 minutes, five daily Monday to Friday, one Saturday and Sunday in July and August, one daily the rest of the year) along the western shoreline via Blaney, Tully Castle and Lough Navar Forest Park.

Ulsterbus No 64 travels from Enniskillen to Belcoo (eight daily Monday to Friday, five on Saturday, one on Sunday); on Thursdays only, two buses continue to Garrison, Belleek and Bundoran.

WEST OF LOUGH ERNE
Florence Court

Part of the first earl of Belmore's motivation in building Castle Coole was undoubtedly competition with his nearest aristocratic neighbour William Willoughby Cole, the first earl of Enniskillen. In the 1770s Cole oversaw the addition of grand, Palladian wings to the beautiful, baroque, mid-18th-century country house built by his father Sir John, and named after his Cornish grandmother, Florence Wrey.

Florence Court (☎ 6634 8249; Swanlinbar Rd, Florencecourt; adult/child £4/2; ☷ noon-6pm daily Jul & Aug, 1-6pm Mon & Wed-Fri, noon-6pm Sat & Sun Jun, noon-6pm

Sat, Sun & public hols mid-Mar–May & Sep–mid-Oct) is famous for its rococo plasterwork and antique Irish furniture. The house was badly damaged by a fire in 1955 and much of what you see is the result of meticulous restoration, but the magnificent plasterwork on the ceiling of the dining room is original.

Florence Court feels more homely and lived-in than the rather cold and austere Castle Coole, especially since the family belongings of the sixth earl were returned. (The earl had a falling out with the National Trust in 1974 and stomped off to Scotland with all his stuff; it was returned after the death of his widow in 1998.) The library, in particular, feels as if the last earl has just nipped out for a stroll and could return at any minute.

In the **grounds** (car/pedestrian £3/free; ☷ 10am-8pm May-Sep, 10am-4pm Oct-Apr) you can explore the walled garden and, on the edge of Cottage Wood, southeast of the house, admire an ancient Irish yew tree. It's said that every Irish yew around the world is descended from this one.

The house is 12km southwest of Enniskillen. Take the A4 Sligo road and fork left onto the A32 to Swanlinbar. Ulsterbus No 192 from Enniskillen to Swanlinbar can drop you at Creamery Cross, about 2km from the house.

Marble Arch Caves

The limestone plateau to the west of Lough Erne is riddled with caves. The biggest of these is **Marble Arch** (☎ 6634 8855; www.fermanagh .gov.uk; Marlbank Scenic Loop, Florencecourt; adult/child £7/4; ☷ 10am-5pm Jul & Aug, 10am-4.30pm mid-Mar–Jun & Sep), first explored by the French caving pioneer Edouard Martel in 1895, but not opened to the public until 1985.

The 1¼-hour tour of the caves begins with a short boat trip along the peaty, foam-flecked waters of the underground River Cladagh to Junction Jetty, where three subterranean streams all meet up. You then continue on foot past the Grand Gallery and Pool Chamber, regaled all the time with food-related jokes from your guide. A man-made tunnel leads into the New Chamber (pioneering cave explorers originally wriggled through a natural tunnel high above here), from which the route follows the underground River Owenbrean, through the Moses Walk (a pathway sunk into the river) to the Calcite Cradle, where the most picturesque formations are to be found.

The caves take their name from a natural limestone arch that spans the River Cladagh where it emerges from the caves; it's reached via a short walk along a signposted footpath from the visitor centre.

Unexpected serious flooding of the caves in 1989, just four years after they were opened to the general public, was found to have been caused by mechanised peat-cutting in the blanket bog – one of Ireland's biggest – on the slopes of Cuilcagh Mountain above the caves. This led to the Fermanagh Council establishing the surrounding **Cuilcagh Mountain Park** to preserve the bog environment, and in 2001 the entire area was designated a Unesco Geopark. The park's geology and ecology are explained inside the caves' visitor centre.

The caves are very popular, so it's wise to phone ahead and book, especially if you're in a group of four or more.

The Marble Arch Caves are 16km southwest of Enniskillen, and some 4km from Florence Court (an hour's walk), reached via the A4 Sligo road and the A32.

Loughs Melvin & Macnean

Lough Melvin and Lough Macnean are situated along the border with the Republic, on the B52 road from Belcoo to Belleek. Lough Melvin is famous for its salmon and trout fishing, and is home to two unusual trout species – the sonaghan, with its distinctive black spots, and the crimson-spotted gillaroo – that are unique to the lough, as well as brown trout, ferox trout and char.

The lakeside **Lough Melvin Holiday Centre** (☎ 6865 8142; Garrison; tent sites £8-9, caravan sites £12.50, dm £8-13, d £36) offers caving, canoeing, walking and fishing holidays, and also has a camp site, dorm accommodation, en-suite rooms, a restaurant and a coffee shop.

Corralea Activity Centre (☎ 6638 6668; www.activityireland.com; Belcoo), based on Upper Lough Macnean, hires out bicycles (£8/13 per half/full day) and two-person canoes (£12/18). It also offers instruction in activities such as caving, canoeing, climbing, windsurfing and archery from £20 per day.

COUNTY TYRONE

OMAGH

pop 20,000

Sadly, for a long time to come the market town of Omagh (An Óghmagh) will be remembered for the devastating car bomb in 1998 that killed 29 people and injured 200. Planted by the breakaway Real IRA, the bomb was the worst single atrocity in the 30-year history of the Troubles.

Situated at the confluence of the Rivers Camowen and Drumragh, which join to form the River Strule, Omagh is a busy town that serves as a useful base for exploring the surrounding area by car.

Omagh Tourist Information Centre (☎ 8224 7831; tourism@omagh.gov.uk; 1 Market St; ⌚ 9am-5pm Mon-Sat Apr-Sep, Mon-Fri Oct-Mar) is across the river from the bus station; go along Bridge St, then turn left onto High St. Internet access costs £1.50 per 30 minutes.

Sleeping

Omagh Independent Hostel (☎ 8224 1973; www.omaghhostel.co.uk; 9a Waterworks Rd; camp sites £6, dm/tw £8/22; ⌚ Mar-Oct) This peaceful and family-friendly hostel is 4km northeast of town, tucked away on a back road off the B48 to Gortin. The lovely, rural setting is awash with flowers in summer; if you prefer, you can pitch a tent outside. If you ring from the bus station someone will come and pick you up.

Ardmore (☎ 8224 3381; irismccann@hotmail.com; 12 Tamlaght Rd; s/d £19/38; P ⊠) This long-established family B&B has four rooms (with a shared bathroom) in a modern semi-detached house, just a 10-minute walk south of the town centre.

Arleston House (☎ 8224 1719; peterfox@btconnect.com; 1 Arleston Park; s/d £25/46; P ⊠) This B&B is a large detached house with two spacious en-suite rooms, off Cookstown Rd about 1km east of the town centre.

Hawthorn House (☎ 8225 2005; www.hawthornhouse.co.uk; 72 Old Mountfield Rd; s/d £40/70; P ⊠) The five-room Hawthorn is a luxurious Victorian guesthouse with period décor and an excellent restaurant; all rooms have bathroom and TV.

Silverbirch Hotel (☎ 8224 2520; www.silverbirchhotel.com; 5 Gortin Rd; s/d £56/96; P ⊠) If you insist on room service, a trouser press, and the end of your toilet roll folded into a neat triangle, then Omagh's swankiest hotel is the place for you.

Eating & Drinking

Riverfront Coffee Shop (☎ 8225 0011; 38 Market St; sandwiches £2.70; ☒ 9am-5.30pm Mon-Sat) You'll find excellent coffee, cakes, pastries, home-made soup, and roll-your-own sandwiches on baguettes, *panini* or ciabatta rolls.

Oasis Bistro (☎ 8224 2622; 23-25 Castle St; mains £7-14; ☒ 7-9pm Sun-Thu, 7-10pm Fri & Sat) Sitting at the gourmet/alternative end of Omagh's gastronomic spectrum, the Oasis offers organic and vegetarian dishes (such as barbecue bean-pot with tofu and organic rice, or spinach and feta savoury cheesecake) as well as meat classics such as tournedos rossini.

Hawthorn House (☎ 8225 2005; www.hawthornhouse.co.uk; 72 Old Mountfield Rd; mains £12-16; ☒ noon-3pm & 7-10pm) Easily Omagh's top restaurant, serving modern Irish cuisine, Hawthorn's menu inclines towards steaks and seafood, but includes at least one vegetarian main course.

Grant's of Omagh (☎ 8225 0900; 29 George's St; mains £8-14; ☒ 4-10pm Mon-Fri, noon-10pm Sat & Sun) Of the town's many pubs, Grant's (as in Ulysses S Grant) offers the best dining – tables in stripped pine booths with a cosmopolitan menu of reasonably priced meals and bar snacks. Book ahead on weekends.

Getting There & Away

The bus station is on Mountjoy Rd, just north of the town centre along Bridge St.

Bus No 273 goes to Belfast (£8.20, 1¾ hours, hourly Monday to Saturday, six Sunday) and Derry (£6, 1¼ hours). Other frequent services run to Dungannon (No 78) and Enniskillen (No 94), where you can change for Donegal.

Bus No 274 runs from Omagh, south to Dublin (£11, 3¼ hours, four to six daily) via Monaghan, and north to Derry (£6, one hour). Bus No 296 leaves Omagh for Cork (9¼ hours, one daily Monday to Saturday).

AROUND OMAGH
Ulster American Folk Park

In the 18th and 19th centuries thousands of Ulster people left their homes to forge a new life across the Atlantic; 200,000 emigrated in the 18th century alone. Their story is told here at one of Ireland's best museums, the **Ulster American Folk Park** (☎ 8224 3292; www.folkpark.com; Mellon Rd; adult/child £4.50/2.50; ☒ 10.30am-6pm Mon-Sat, 11am-6.30pm Sun & public holidays Apr-Sep, 10.30am-5pm Mon-Fri Oct-Mar). Last admission is 1½ hours before closing.

The Exhibition Hall presents many of the close connections between Ulster and the USA – the American Declaration of Independence was signed by several Ulstermen – but the real appeal of the folk park is the outdoor museum, whose 'living history' exhibits include a forge, weaver's cottage, Presbyterian meeting house, schoolhouse, log cabin, 19th-century Ulster street and a street from western Pennsylvania. Clever use is made of an emigrant ship to link the Ulster and USA exhibits.

Costumed guides and artisans are on hand to chat and explain the arts of spinning, weaving, candle making and so on, and there are regular theme events such as re-enactments of American Civil War battles. There's almost too much to absorb in one visit and at least half a day is needed to do the place justice.

The **Appalachian and Bluegrass Music Festival** is held at the park every September.

The park is 8km northwest of Omagh off the A5. Bus No 97 to Strabane stops outside the park (15 minutes). Buses depart Omagh at 7.55am, 10.55am and 1.25pm Monday to Friday, and return at 11.20am, 3.20pm, 4.50pm and 6.20pm. On Saturday there are buses at 7.55am and 1.25pm, returning at 7.30pm.

SPERRIN MOUNTAINS

When the Lord Deputy of Ireland invited representatives of the London guilds to visit Ulster in 1609, hoping to persuade them to send English settlers to the region, he instructed their guide to keep them well away from the Sperrin mountains, fearing that the sight of these bleak, moorland hills would create a poor first impression.

When it rains, there's no denying that the Sperrins can be dismal. But on a sunny spring day, when the russet bogs and yellow gorse stand out against a blue sky, they can offer some grand walking. The area is also dotted with thousands of standing stones and prehistoric tombs.

The main ridge of the Sperrins stretches for 30km along the border with County

Derry, from Plumbridge in the west to Draperstown in the east, with lower hills extending south as far as the A505 Omagh to Cookstown road. The highest summit is Mt Sawel (678m), rising above the **Sperrin Heritage Centre** (☎ 8164 8142; 274 Glenelly Rd, Cranagh; adult/child £2.45/1.50; ☼ 11.30am-5.30pm Mon-Fri, 11.30am-6pm Sat, 2-6pm Sun Apr-Oct). The centre offers an insight into the culture, natural history and geology of the region. Gold has been found in the Sperrins, and for an extra 75/45p you can try your luck at panning for gold in a nearby stream. If you're thinking of walking up Mt Sawel, enquire at the Sperrin Heritage Centre about the best route. The climb is easy enough in good weather, but some farmers are not as accommodating as others about hikers crossing their land.

From Omagh, follow the B48 northeast through Gortin to Plumbridge. From there it's about 13km east on the B47 to Cranagh. From Cookstown take roads B162 and B47.

Gortin

The village of Gortin, about 15km north of Omagh, lies at the foot of Mullaghcarn (542m), the southernmost of the Sperrin summits (unfortunately capped by two prominent radio masts). Hundreds of hikers converge for a mass ascent of the hill on **Cairn Sunday** (the last Sunday in July), a revival of an ancient pilgrimage that petered out in the 19th century. There are several good walks around the village, and a scenic drive to **Gortin Lakes**, with views north over the main Sperrin ridge.

A few kilometres south of Gortin, towards Omagh, is **Gortin Glen Forest Park** (☎ 8167 0666; Gortin Rd; car/motorcycle £2.50/2; ☼ 10am-dusk), whose dense conifer woodland is home to a herd of Japanese sika deer. The 8km scenic drive offers the chance to enjoy the views without breaking sweat.

There's a manageable day's walk (16km) from Gortin Glen Forest Park to the Ulster American Folk Park along a section of the Ulster Way, mostly on minor roads and forest tracks. From the folk park you can catch bus No 97 back to Omagh. A leaflet and map entitled *The Ulster Way: Northwest Section* is available from the tourist office in Omagh.

There is hostel accommodation at the **Gortin Accommodation Suite** (☎ 8164 8346; www.gortin

.net; 62 Main St; dm £10), a modern outdoor activity centre in the middle of Gortin village.

Creggan

About halfway along the A505 between Omagh and Cookstown (20km east of Omagh) is **An Creagán Visitor Centre** (☎ 8076 1112; www.an-creagan.com; Creggan; adult/child £2/1; ☼ 11am-6.30pm daily Apr-Sep, 11am-4.30pm Mon-Fri Oct-Mar), with an exhibition covering the ecology of the surrounding bogs and the archaeology of the region.

There are some 44 prehistoric monuments within 8km of the centre in Creggan, including the **Beaghmore Stone Circles**. What this site lacks in stature – the stones are all less than 1m tall – it makes up for in complexity, with seven stone circles (one filled with smaller stones, nicknamed 'dragon's teeth') and a dozen or so alignments and cairns. The stones lie about 8.5km east of Creggan, and 4km north of the A505.

Getting Around

Ulsterbus No 403, known as the *Sperrin Rambler*, runs twice daily Monday to Saturday between Omagh and Magherafelt, stopping at Gortin, the Sperrin Heritage Centre and Draperstown (in County Derry). The morning bus leaves Omagh at 10.05am, arriving at the Sperrin Heritage Centre an hour later; the return bus leaves the centre at 2.40pm.

COOKSTOWN & AROUND

According to the tourist literature, Cookstown's greatest attraction is convenient parking, thanks to its 2km-long and 40m-wide, arrow-straight main street, the legacy of an over-ambitious 18th-century town planner. Today it's a modest market town and shopping centre for east Tyrone but, despite the ease of parking, there's little reason to stop. The main sights here are in the surrounding countryside.

Cookstown Tourist Information Centre (☎ 8676 6727; tic@cookstown.gov.uk; Burn Rd; ☼ 9am-5pm Mon-Sat, 2-4pm Sun Jul & Aug, 9am-5pm Mon-Sat Jun & Sep, 9am-5pm Mon-Fri, 10am-4pm Sat Oct-May) is in the Burnavon Arts and Cultural Centre, west of the main street.

Wellbrook Beetling Mill

Beetling, the final stage of linen making, involved pounding the cloth with wooden hammers, or beetles, to give it a smooth sheen. In the 18th century there were six water-powered **beetling mills** (☎ 8674 8210; 20 Wellbrook Rd, Corkhill; adult/child £3/1.70; ⏱ 1-6pm daily Easter week, Jul & Aug, 1-6pm Sat, Sun & public hols mid-Mar–Jun & Sep) at Wellbrook, of which one has been preserved in working order by the National Trust.

Take the A505 Omagh road 5km west to Kildress and turn right at the church; the mill is 1km further on.

Ardboe High Cross

A 6th-century monastic site on the shores of Lough Neagh, now occupied by a ruined 17th-century church and graveyard, is home to one of Ireland's best-preserved **Celtic high crosses**. The 10th-century Ardboe cross stands 5.5m tall, decorated with 22 carved panels depicting biblical scenes. The western side (facing the road) has New Testament scenes: (from the bottom up) the Adoration of the Magi; the Miracle at Cana; the miracle of the loaves and fishes; Christ's entry into Jerusalem; the arrest (or mocking) of Christ; and, at the intersection of the cross, the Crucifixion.

The more weathered eastern face (towards the lough) shows Old Testament scenes: Adam and Eve; the Sacrifice of Isaac; Daniel in the Lions' Den; the Three Hebrews in the Fiery Furnace. The panels above may show the Last Judgement, and/or Christ in Glory. There are further scenes on the narrow north and south faces of the shaft.

Ardboe is 16km east of Cookstown. Take the B73 through Coagh – ignore the first (white) road sign for Ardboe, and keep straight on until you find the (brown) sign for Ardboe High Cross.

Sleeping

Central Inn (☎ 8676 2255; 27 William St; s/d £20/36; Ⓟ ✗) If you have to spend the night in Cookstown, this pleasant pub offers basic B&B right in the centre of town.

Avondale (☎ 8676 4013; fki@iname.com; 31 Killycolp Rd; s/d £26/40; Ⓟ ✗) Inside a spacious Edwardian house with a large garden, patio and sun lounge, Avondale offers B&B in two en-suite rooms with TV. It's 3km south of Cookstown, just off the A29 Dungannon road.

Greenvale Hotel (☎ 8676 2243; www.greenvale hotel.com; 57 Drum Rd; s/d £40/70; Ⓟ ✗) Set in its own grounds on the southern edge of town, a

10-minute walk from the centre, the 12-room Greenvale is a lovely, 19th-century mansion with a welcoming, country-house feel.

Drum Manor Forest Park (☎ 8676 2774; Drum Rd, Oaklands; camp & caravan sites £8-11) This is a pleasant site 4km west of Cookstown on the A505, with lakes, a butterfly farm and an arboretum. Open Easter to September.

Getting There & Away

The bus station is on Molesworth St, east of the main street. Bus Nos 110 and 210 connect Cookstown with Belfast (Laganside Bus Centre) via Antrim (£6.70, two hours, four daily Monday to Friday, two Saturday). Bus No 80 shuttles between Cookstown and Dungannon (£2.60, 45 minutes, 11 daily Monday to Friday, six Saturday).

DUNGANNON & AROUND

Until 1602, when the castle and town were burned down to prevent them falling into the hands of the English, Dungannon (Dún Geanainn) was one of the chief seats of the O'Neill family. Planted with English and Scottish settlers in the 17th and 18th centuries, it became a centre of textile manufacture.

In August 1968 the town entered the history books when the Civil Rights Association, formed a year earlier to protest against the rampant social and political inequalities suffered by Catholics in Northern Ireland, organised its first march from Coalisland to Dungannon. The crowd of 4000 was met by a police cordon outside the town and, although there was no serious violence, it marked the beginning of a new era.

Today, Dungannon is an instantly forgettable market town halfway between Cookstown and Armagh, worth a brief stop in passing if you want to shop at the Tyrone Crystal factory.

Killymaddy Tourist Information Centre (☎ 8776 7259; killymaddy@dstbc.org; 190 Ballygawley Rd; ⏱ 9am-5pm Mon-Fri, 10am-4pm Sat & Sun) is at a caravan site 10km west of Dungannon on the A4 road towards Enniskillen.

Tyrone Crystal

Ireland's first crystal factory was established in Dungannon in 1771 by Benjamin Edwards from Bristol. It closed down in 1870, but in 1968 Tyrone's crystal industry was revived by a local priest, Father Austin Eustace, who raised funding to establish a new factory to help relieve local unemployment.

Today, **Tyrone Crystal** (☎ 8772 5335; www.tyrone crystal.com; Coalisland Rd, Killybrackey; tours adult/child under 12 £2/free; ☺ 9am-5pm Mon-Sat, 1-5pm Sun) continues to produce high-quality lead crystal (with more than 30% lead oxide content). The factory offers guided tours of the manufacturing process, from the furnace where molten glass is prepared, through hand-blowing and moulding to cutting and polishing. Admission to the showroom is free, and the tour price is reimbursed if you buy something.

The factory is 2.5km northeast of Dungannon on the A45 towards Coalisland – it's clearly signposted. Bus No 80 to Cookstown stops nearby.

Benburb
pop 280

The pretty village of Benburb, 13km south of Dungannon and 11km northwest of Armagh, clusters around **Benburb Castle** (☎ 3754 8241; www.servites-benburb.com; 10 Main St; ☺ open by arrangement only). Nothing remains of the original castle, founded by Shane O'Neill, but the impressive bawn added in 1611 by Sir Richard Wingfield still stands. Within the walls is a red-brick manor house built in 1887, which is now home to a Servite priory. The priory is used as a residential centre for cultural activities and courses in spiritual and human development, but the grounds, gift shop and café are open to all.

About 800m from the castle, across the River Blackwater (and therefore in County Armagh), is **Benburb Valley Heritage Centre** (☎ 3754 9885; 89 Milltown Rd; adult/child £2/1; ☺ 10am-5pm Mon-Sat Apr-Sep), a restored linen mill.

From Dungannon take the A29 south and turn right at Moy onto the B106. The centre is clearly marked; the castle is a short distance further along.

Donaghmore High Cross

The village of Donaghmore, 8km northwest of Dungannon on the B43 road to Pomeroy, is famed for its 10th-century Celtic high cross. It was cobbled together from two different crosses in the 18th century – note the obvious join halfway up the shaft – and now stands outside the churchyard. The carved biblical scenes are similar to those on the

Ardboe Cross: on the eastern side are the Annunciation to the Shepherds, the Adoration of the Magi, the Miracle at Cana, the Miracle of the Loaves and Fishes, the Arrest of Christ and the Crucifixion. On the western side are Adam and Eve, Cain and Abel, and Abraham and Isaac. The nearby **heritage centre** (☎ 8776 7039; Pomeroy Rd; admission free; ☺ 9am-5pm Mon-Fri) is based in a converted 19th-century school.

Castlecaulfield

Not so much a castle as the remains of a substantial Jacobean house, **Castlecaulfield** (admission free; ☺ 24hr) was built in the early 17th century by Sir Toby Caulfield on the site of an earlier fort belonging to the O'Donnellys.

Over the gatehouse, the Caulfield coat of arms can be made out, having survived the O'Donnellys' act of revenge in 1641 when the house was burned down. The house was rebuilt, and in 1767 it hosted a church service by John Wesley, the founder of Methodism.

The castle is 8km west of Dungannon. Take the A4 towards Enniskillen, and after about 6km look out for a small road on the right signposted to Castlecaulfield.

Grant Ancestral Homestead

Ulysses Simpson Grant led Union forces to victory in the American Civil War and later served as the USA's 18th president for two terms from 1869 to 1877. The **ancestral homestead** (☎ 8555 7133; 45 Dergina, Ballygawley; adult/child £1.50/0.75; ☺ 9am-5pm) of his mother's family – the Simpsons – has been restored in the style of a typical 19th-century small farm. The furnishings are not authentic, but the original field plan of the farm survives together with various old farming implements.

The site is 20km west of Dungannon, south of the A4; look out for the signpost 5.5km west of Killymaddy tourist information centre.

Sleeping & Eating

Grange Lodge (☎ 8778 4212; grangelodge@nireland .com; 7 Grange Rd; s/d £55/78; ☺ Feb–mid-Dec; P)
The five-room Grange is a period gem set in its own 20-acre grounds. Parts of the house, which is packed with antiques, date from 1698, though most is Georgian with

Victorian additions. It's 5km southeast of Dungannon, signposted off the A29 Moy road.

Stangmore Country House (☎ 8772 5600; www .stangmorecountryhouse.com; 65 Moy Rd; s/d £65/90; 2-/3-course dinner £17/19; ❤ 7-9.30pm; ℗) Stangmore is an elegant, Georgian mansion with nine stylish en-suite rooms. It also has a restaurant offering a modern menu of Irish-Mediterranean-Asian fusion cuisine.

Dungannon Park (☎ 8772 7327; dungannonpark@ utvInternet.com; Moy Rd; camp/caravan sites £8/12; ❤ Mar-Oct) This small (20 pitches) council-run camp site is in a quiet, wooded location 2.5km south of Dungannon on the A29 towards Moy and Armagh.

Viscounts Restaurant (☎ 8775 3800; 10 Northland Row; mains £8-15; ❤ noon-9.30pm) Set in a converted church, Viscounts offers carvery lunches, snacks and á la carte dinners. You can feast on steaks, pasta, stir-fries and veg-

etarian dishes in a mock medieval setting of knights' armour, swords and jousting banners. Booking is advisable at weekends.

Getting There & Away

Dungannon's bus station is at the bottom of Scotch St, over the bridge and to the left. Bus No 261 runs from Belfast's Europa BusCentre to Dungannon (£6.20, one hour, hourly Monday to Saturday, eight Sunday) and continues to Enniskillen (£6.70, 1½ hours). Bus No 273 travels from Belfast to Derry via Dungannon and Omagh (six daily Monday to Saturday, four Sunday).

Bus No 80 shuttles between Cookstown and Dungannon (£2.60, 45 minutes, 11 daily Monday to Friday, six Saturday). The No 278 service runs to Armagh (£3, 30 minutes, once or twice daily, Monday to Saturday) and on to Monaghan and Dublin (3½ hours).

DIRECTORY

Directory

CONTENTS

PRACTICALITIES

- Use the metric system for weights and measures, though watch out for speed limits and rural black-and-white road signs given in miles.

- Use the PAL system for video recorders and players.

- Plug appliances into the three flat pin sockets for (220V, 50Hz AC) power supply.

- Get an insight into Irish life with one of the world's best newspapers the *Irish Times* or Ireland's biggest-selling *Irish Independent*.

- Relish Irish political satire in the fortnightly magazine *Phoenix*, or brush up on current affairs in *Magill* magazine.

- Check both sides of Northern Irish current affairs with loyalist tabloid *News Letter* or the pro-republican *Irish News*.

- TV addicts should tune into *The Late Late Show* (RTE 1), the world's longest-running chat show; or catch some great documentary on TG4, the national Irish-language station (subtitles are available).

- Tune into RTE Radio One (88-90 FM or 567/729 MW) for culture, politics and eclectic music show *The Mystery Train* (8.30pm to 10pm Monday to Thursday); Lyric FM (96-99 FM) for nonstop classical music; or Today FM (100-100.3 FM) for commercial daytime chitchat.

ACCOMMODATION

Sleeping entries are categorised by price and then preference, with our favourites first. Rates are per *room* per night, unless otherwise stated: budget (under €60/£40), midrange (€60-150/£40-100) and top end (over €150/£100), and high-season rates are given throughout. Where a range of prices is given, it refers to rates for different rooms during high season. Prices may be cheaper off-peak. Room prices in Dublin are disproportionately high and can be double what you would pay elsewhere in the country.

The majority of accommodations increase their rates by up to 10% on 'special' week-

ends, ie bank holidays or during major sporting events. Hotels will often offer packages, especially in low season, for more than one night's stay including dinner, and it's also worth asking for a discount from the quoted rack rate (tourist board–approved rate) from Monday to Thursday. Ironically, in city hotels cheaper rates may apply at weekends, when their main corporate clients disappear.

In low season (November to March) you can simply call in or ring ahead in rural areas. In peak season it's best to book ahead. Fáilte Ireland (Irish Tourist Board) or the Northern Ireland Tourist Board (NITB) will book serviced accommodation for a fee of €4 (£2), or self-catering for €7 (£2). Make telephone bookings through their booking system **Gulliver** (in Ireland ☎ 1800 668 668, in UK ☎ 0800 783 5740, in USA/Canada ☎ 800 398 4376).

Many of the accommodations close during Christmas and New Year, especially in rural areas, and most charge a supplement.

B&Bs

The ubiquitous bed and breakfasts are small, family-run houses, farmhouses and period country houses with fewer than five bedrooms. Standards vary enormously, but most have some en-suite bedrooms at a cost of roughly €35 to €40 (£20 to £25) per person per night. In luxurious B&Bs, expect to pay €55 (£38) or more per person. Facilities in budget-end B&Bs may be very limited: TVs, telephones, kettles and the like are the trappings of midrange to top-end establishments. Remember, outside big cities most B&Bs only accept cash.

Camping & Caravan Parks

Camping and caravan parks aren't as common in Ireland as they are in Britain or on the continent. Some hostels have camping space for tents and also offer house facilities, which makes them better value than the main camping grounds. At commercial parks the cost is typically somewhere between €12 and €20 (£7 and £10) for a tent and two people. Prices for camp sites in this book are for two people unless stated otherwise. Caravan sites cost around €15 to €25 (£11 and £15). Most parks only open from Easter to the end of September or October.

Guesthouses

Essentially, guesthouses are much like upmarket B&Bs. The difference lies in their size, with guesthouses having between six and 30 bedrooms. Prices vary enormously according to the standard but the minimum you can expect to shell out is €35 (£22) per person (€40 in Dublin), and up to about €100 (£35) in upmarket places. Unlike hotels, the majority of guesthouses are unlicensed but many have restaurants and good facilities, and can take credit-card payment.

Hostels

The prices quoted in this book for hostel accommodation are for those aged over 18.

> **SOMETHING DIFFERENT**
>
> An alternative to normal caravanning is to hire a horse-drawn caravan with which to wander the countryside. In high season you can hire one for around €780 a week. Search www.ireland.ie for a list of operators, or see www.irishhorsedrawncaravans.com.
>
> Another unhurried and pleasurable way to see the countryside (with slightly less maintenance) is by barge on one of the country's canal systems. As above, contact Fáilte Ireland for a list of rental companies.
>
> Another option is to hire a boat, which you can live aboard while cruising Ireland's inland waterways. One company offering boats for hire on the Shannon-Erne Waterway is **Emerald Star** (☎ 071-962 0234; www .emeraldstar.ie).

A dorm bed in high season generally costs €13 to €25 (£8 to £14).

An Óige and Hostelling International Northern Ireland (HINI) are the two associations that belong to Hostelling International (HI). About half of the hostels have family and smaller rooms. An Óige has 23 hostels scattered around the Republic and HINI has six in the North.

An Óige (☎ 01-830 4555; www.irelandyha.org; 61 Mountjoy St, Dublin 7; ☽ 9.30am-5.30pm Mon-Fri)

HINI (☎ 028-9032 4733, area code ☎ 048 if calling from Republic; www.hini.org.uk; 22-32 Donegall Rd, Belfast BT12 5JN; ☽ 24hr)

Ireland also has a large number of independent hostels, some excellent, but many high on character and low on facilities. The following associations, with hostels in the Republic and in the North, do their best to offer reliable accommodation:

Independent Holiday Hostels of Ireland (IHH; ☎ 01-836 4700; www.hostels-ireland.com; 57 Lower Gardiner St, Dublin 1)

Independent Hostel Owners of Ireland (IHO; ☎ 074-973 0130; www.holidayhound.com/ihi; Dooey Hostel, Glencolumbcille, Co Donegal)

Hotels

Hotels range from the local pub to medieval castles, and prices fluctuate accordingly. It's often possible to negotiate better deals than the published rates, especially out of season and online. Payment usually

DIRECTORY

includes breakfast, and most hotels have TV, and tea- and coffee-making facilities and phones. You may find that some offer better rates than guesthouses.

House Swapping

House swapping has become a popular and affordable way to visit a country and enjoy a real home away from home. There are several agencies in Ireland that, for an annual fee, facilitate international swaps. The fee pays for access to a website and a book giving house descriptions, photographs and the owner's details. After that, it's up to you to make arrangements. Sometimes use of the family car is included.

Homelink International House Exchange (☎ 01-846 2598; www.homelink.ie; 95 Bracken Dr, Portmarnock, Co Dublin)

Intervac International Holiday Service (☎ 041-983 7969; www.intervac.com; Drogheda, Co Dublin; ☒ 7-9pm Mon-Fri)

Rental Accommodation

Self-catering accommodation is often rented on a weekly basis and usually means an apartment or house where you look after yourself. The rates vary from one region and season to another. Fáilte Ireland publishes a guide for registered self-catering accommodation or you can check the website (www.ireland.travel.ie).

ACTIVITIES

Activities open up Ireland in a way that can be both cheap and relaxing, and offer a unique experience of the country.

Bird-Watching

The variety and size of the flocks that visit or breed in Ireland make it of particular interest to bird-watchers. It's also home to some rare and endangered species. For a description of some birds found in Ireland see p64.

There are more than 70 reserves and sanctuaries in Ireland, but some aren't open to visitors and others are privately owned, so you'll need permission from the proprietors before entering.

More information can be obtained from the tourist boards and from the following organisations:

Birds of Ireland News Service (☎ 01-830 7364; www.birdsireland.com; 36 Claremont Ct, Glasnevin, Dublin 11)

BirdWatch Ireland (☎ 01-281 9878; www.birdwatch ireland.ie; Rockingham Hs, Newcastle, Co Wicklow)

National Parks & Wildlife Service (☎ 01-888 2000; www.npws.ie; 7 Ely Pl, Dublin 2)

Royal Society for the Protection of Birds (RSPB; ☎ 028-9049 1547; www.rspb.org.uk; Belvoir Park Forest, Belfast, BT8 4QT)

Some useful publications on bird-watching are Dominic Couzens' *Collins Birds of Britain and Ireland* and the slightly out-of-date *Where to Watch Birds in Ireland* by Clive Hutchinson.

Cycling

The tourist boards can supply you with a list of operators who organise cycling holidays. For more on the practicalities of travelling round Ireland with a bike, see p700.

WEBSITE ACCOMMODATION RESOURCES

www.gulliver.ie Fáilte Ireland and the Northern Ireland Tourist Board's (NITB) web-based accommodation reservation system.

www.ireland.travel.ie Fáilte Ireland's accommodation-booking site.

www.discovernorthernireland.com NITB's accommodation-booking site.

www.allgohere.com This website lists accommodation suitable for disabled (and able-bodied) travellers in Northern Ireland.

www.irishlandmark.com Not-for-profit conservation group that rents self-catering properties of historical and cultural significance such as castles, gate lodges and lighthouses.

www.elegant.ie Specialises in self-catering castles, period houses and unique properties.

www.familyhomes.ie Lists, you guessed it, family-run guesthouses and self-catering properties.

www.hostelworld.com A useful website for comparing hostels and booking beds.

www.daft.ie Online classified paper for short- and long-term rentals.

www.stayinireland.com Lists guesthouses and self-catering options.

Both **Irish Cycling Safaris** (☎ 01-260 0749; www .cyclingsafaris.com; Belfield Bike Shop, UCD, Dublin 4) and **Go Ireland** (☎ 066-976 2094; www.goactivities.com; Old Orchard House, Killorglin, Co Kerry) organise tours for groups of cyclists in the southwest, the southeast, Clare, Connemara, Donegal and Antrim.

Fishing

Ireland is justly famous for its generally free coarse fishing, covering bream, pike, perch, roach, rudd, tench, carp and eel. Killing of pike over 6.6lb (3kg) in weight is prohibited, anglers are limited to one pike and killing of coarse fish is frowned upon; anglers are encouraged to return coarse fish alive. Freshwater game fish include salmon, sea trout and brown trout. Some managed fisheries also stock rainbow trout.

The enormous Shannon and Erne river systems, stretching southwards from Leitrim and Fermanagh, are prime angling spots, and Cavan, the 'Lake County', is a favourite with hardcore fishermen. In the west, the great lakes of Corrib, Mask and Conn have plenty of lakeshore B&Bs, good sturdy boats and knowledgeable boatmen. These lakes can be dangerous, as they tend to be littered with hidden rocks and shoals.

While Ireland is a land of opportunity for the angler, intensive agriculture and the growth of towns have brought about a general reduction in water quality in many areas, markedly so in some. Fáilte Ireland and the NITB produce several information leaflets on fishing, accommodation, events and licences required.

Licences in the Republic are available from the local tackle shop or direct from the **Central Fisheries Board** (☎ 01-884 2600; www .cfb.ie; Unit 4, Swords Business Campus, Balheary Rd, Swords, Dublin).

In the North, rod licences for coarse and game fishing are obtainable from the **Foyle, Carlingford & Irish Lights Commission** (☎ 028-7134 2100; www.loughs-agency.org; 22 Victoria Rd, Londonderry) for the Foyle and Carlingford areas, and from the **Fisheries Conservancy Board** (☎ 028-3833 4666; www.fcbni.com; 1 Mahon Rd, Portadown, Co Armagh) for all other regions. You also require a permit from the owner, which is usually the **Department of Culture, Arts & Leisure, Inland Waterways & Inland Fisheries Branch** (☎ 028-9025 8863; 3rd fl, Interpoint, 20-24 York St, Belfast BT15 1AQ).

Golf

Contact Fáilte Ireland, the NITB, the **Golfing Union of Ireland** (☎ 01-505 4000; www.gui.ie; Unit 8 Block G, Maynooth Business Campus, Maynooth, Co Kildare), or the **Irish Ladies Golf Union** (☎ 01-269 6244; www.ilgu.ie; 1 Clonskeagh Sq, Clonskeagh Rd, Dublin 14) for information on golfing holidays.

Green fees, usually based on a per-day basis, start from around €30 (£15) on weekdays, but top-notch places charge up to €250 (£110). Courses are tested for their level of difficulty; many are playable year round.

Hang-gliding & Paragliding

Some of the finest hang-gliding and paragliding in the country is found at Mount Leinster (p342) in Carlow, Great Sugarloaf Mountain in Wicklow, Benone and Magilligan Beaches (p638) in Derry and Achill Island (p431) in Mayo. Check the **Irish Hang Gliding & Paragliding Association** (www.ihpa.ie) and **Ulster Hang Gliding & Paragliding Club's** (www.uhpc.co.uk) websites for local pilots.

Horse Riding

Unsurprisingly, considering the Irish passion for horses, riding is a popular pastime. There are dozens of centres throughout Ireland, offering possibilities ranging from hiring a horse for an hour (from €20/£12) to fully packaged, residential equestrian holidays.

A recommended outfit is Canadian-based **Hidden Trails** (www.hiddentrails.com).

Walking

There are many superb walks in Ireland, including 31 'waymarked ways' or designated long-distance paths of varying lengths and through all kinds of terrain. The ways are marked with signposts showing the standard yellow arrow and hiker.

Ireland has a tradition of relatively free access to open country but the growth in the number of walkers and the carelessness of a few have made some farmers less obliging. Unfortunately it's not uncommon to find unofficial signs on gateways barring access, or physical barriers blocking ways. If you come across this problem, refer to the local tourist office.

The maintenance and development of the ways is administered in the Republic by the **National Waymarked Ways Advisory Committee** (NWWAC; ☎ 01-860 8823; www.walkireland.ie;

Irish Sports Council, Top fl, Block A Westend Office Park, Blanchardstown, Dublin 15) and in the North by **Countryside Access & Activities Network** (CAAN; ☎ 028-9030 3930; The Stableyard, Barnett's Demesne, Belfast).

Some useful guides are Lonely Planet's *Walking in Ireland*, Michael Fewer's *Irish Long-Distance Walks* or *Best Irish Walks* by Joss Lynam.

EastWest Mapping (☎ /fax 054-77835; eastwest@ eircom.net) has good maps of long-distance walks in the Republic and the North.

Tim Robinson of **Folding Landscapes** (☎ 095-35886; tandmfl@iol.ie) produces superbly detailed maps of the Burren, the Aran Islands and Connemara. His and Joss Lynam's *Mountains of Connemara: A Hill Walker's Guide* contains a useful detailed map.

For mountain rescue call ☎ 999.

ORGANISED WALKS

If you don't have a travelling companion you could consider joining an organised walking group.

Go Ireland (☎ 066-976 2094; www.goactivities.com; Old Orchard House, Killorglin, Co Kerry) Offers walking tours of the west.

South West Walks Ireland (☎ 066-712 8733; www .southwestwalksireland.com; 6 Church St, Tralee, Co Kerry) Provides a series of guided and self-guided walking programmes around the southwest, northwest and Wicklow.

BEARA WAY

This moderately easy, 196km walk forms a loop around the delightful Beara Peninsula (p242) in West Cork. The peninsula is relatively unused to mass tourism and makes a pleasant contrast with the Iveragh Peninsula to the north.

Part of the walk, between Castletownbere and Glengarriff, follows the route taken by Donal O'Sullivan and his band after the English took his castle following an 11-day siege in 1602. At Glengarriff, O'Sullivan met up with other families and set out on a journey north, hoping to reunite with other remaining pockets of Gaelic resistance. Of the 1000 or so men who set out that winter, only 30 completed the trek.

The Beara Way mostly follows old roads and tracks and rarely rises above 340m. There's no official start or finish point and the route can be walked in either direction. It could easily be reduced to seven days by skipping Bere and Dursey Islands, and if you start at Castletownbere you could reach Kenmare in five days or less.

BURREN WAY

This 35km walk traverses the Burren (p375) limestone plateau in County Clare. It presents a strange, unique landscape to the walker. There's very little soil and few trees but a surprising abundance of flora. The way stretches between Ballyvaughan, on the northern coast of County Clare, and Liscannor to the southwest, taking in the village of Doolin, famous as a traditional-music centre. The trail south of Doolin to the dramatic Cliffs of Moher is a highlight of the route. From the cliffs a new path has been developed inland towards Liscannor (older maps may show a route, now closed, along the cliffs).

The best time for this walk is late spring or early summer. The route is pretty dry, but walking boots are useful as the limestone can be sharp.

CAVAN WAY

In the northwest of County Cavan the villages of Blacklion and Dowra are the ends of the 26km Cavan Way. The path runs northeast–southwest past a number of Stone Age monuments – court cairns, ring forts and tombs – through an area said to be one of the last strongholds of druidism. At the midpoint is the Shannon Pot, the official source of the River Shannon on the slopes of the Cuilcagh Mountains. From Blacklion it's mainly hill walking; from Shannon Pot to Dowra it's mainly road. The highest point on the walk is Giant's Grave (260m). You'll need OSNI map No 26 and the *Cavan Way* map guide. The route can be boggy, so take spare socks!

Dowra links up with the Leitrim Way, which runs between Manorhamilton and Drumshanbo.

DINGLE WAY

This 168km walk in County Kerry loops round one of the most beautiful peninsulas in the country (see p276). It takes eight days to complete, beginning and ending in Tralee, with an average daily distance of 21km. The first three days offer the easiest walk but the first day, from Tralee to Camp, is the least interesting; it could be skipped by taking the bus to Camp and starting from there.

EAST MUNSTER WAY

This 70km walk travels through forest and open moorland, along small country roads and a river towpath. It's clearly laid out with black markers bearing yellow arrows, and could be managed in three days, starting at Carrick-on-Suir (p310) in County Tipperary and finishing at Clogheen in County Waterford. The first day takes you to Clonmel, the second to Newcastle and the last to Clogheen. Look out for new signposts between Carrick and Killeshin, where part of the badly eroded path has recently been rerouted.

KERRY WAY

The 214km Kerry Way is the Republic's longest waymarked footpath and is usually walked anticlockwise. It starts and ends in Killarney (p250) and stays inland for the first three days, winding through the spectacular Macgillycuddy's Reeks (p258) and past 1041m Mt Carrantuohil, Ireland's highest mountain, before continuing around the Ring of Kerry coast through Cahirciveen, Waterville, Caherdaniel, Sneem and Kenmare (see p267).

You could complete the walk in about 10 days, provided you're up to a good 20km per day. With less time it's worth walking the first three days, as far as Glenbeigh, from where a bus or a lift could return you to Killarney.

Accommodation isn't a problem, but you need to book in July and August. In contrast, places to eat aren't common, so consider carrying your own food.

MOURNE TRAIL

The Mourne Trail is actually the southeastern section of the Ulster Way, south of Belfast, and runs from Newry (p614), around the Mourne Mountains (p611), to the seaside resort of Newcastle (p609) and then on to Strangford (p608), where you can take a ferry across to Portaferry (p600) and continue north to Newtownards (p603). From Newry to Strangford is a distance of 106km, which could probably be managed in four or five days.

There's gorgeous mountain, forest and coastal scenery along the way and, once you've left Newry, not many built-up areas to spoil the views. Provided you're reasonably fit and well shod this is not an especially difficult route to walk, although it does climb as high as 559m at Slievemoughanmore, the highest point on the Ulster Way.

SLIEVE BLOOM WAY

Close to the geographical centre of Ireland, the Slieve Bloom Way is a 77km trail through Counties Offaly and Laois. It does a complete circuit of the Slieve Bloom Mountains (p344) taking in most major points of interest. The trail follows tracks, forest firebreaks and old roads, and crosses the Mountrath–Kinnitty and Mountrath–Clonaslee roads. The trail's highest point is at Glendine Gap (460m). The recommended starting point is the car park at Glenbarrow, 5km from Rosenallis.

Camping in state forests is forbidden, but there's plenty of open space outside the forest for tents; otherwise, accommodation en route is almost nonexistent. There is no public transport to the area, although buses do stop in the nearby towns of Mountrath and Rosenallis.

SOUTH LEINSTER WAY

The tiny village of Kildavin in County Carlow, just southwest of Clonegal on the slopes of Mt Leinster, is the northern starting point of the 100km South Leinster Way, which winds through Counties Carlow and Kilkenny. It follows remote mountain roads and river towpaths through the medieval villages of Borris (p341), Graiguenamanagh (p326), Inistioge (p325), Mullinavat and Piltown to the finish post at Carrick-on-Suir (p310) just inside the Tipperary border. The southerly section is not as scenic as the rest, but the low hills have their own charm and on a sunny day they offer fine views south over the Suir Valley and Waterford Harbour.

The way leads in a generally southwestward direction but could easily be done the opposite way. It should take four or five days, depending on whether you stop over in Graiguenamanagh.

Much of it is above 500m and the weather can change quickly: good walking boots, outdoor gear and emergency supplies are essential.

ULSTER WAY: NORTHEASTERN SECTION

The Ulster Way makes a circuit around the six counties of Northern Ireland and

Donegal. In total the footpath covers just more than 900km, so walking all of it might take five weeks. However, it can easily be broken down into smaller sections that could be attempted during a short stay. The scenery along the way varies enormously, encompassing dramatic coastal views, gentler lakeside country and the mountainous inland terrain of the Mourne Mountains.

Some of the most spectacular scenery lies along the 165km northeastern section, which begins unpromisingly in Belfast's western suburbs, then follows the Glens of Antrim (p649) and the glorious Causeway Coast (p646), a Unesco World Heritage site. It can be completed in six or seven days. The stretch of coast immediately surrounding the Giant's Causeway is likely to be busy, especially in high summer, when you should book accommodation well ahead.

Walking this stretch of coast shouldn't be beyond most averagely fit and sensibly equipped people, but rockfalls along the coast can occasionally obstruct stretches of it. While some stretches of this walk can seem wonderfully wild, you're never going to be that far from civilisation.

ULSTER WAY: DONEGAL SECTION

The main Ulster Way crosses into Donegal at the small pilgrimage town of Pettigo on Lough Erne, but then circles straight back to Rosscor in Northern Ireland. A spur – also confusingly called the Ulster Way – cuts north across the central moorlands of Donegal to Falcarragh on the northern coast. In all, if you follow the spur, this stretch of walk is 111km long, which means it can be walked in four or five days. Bear in mind, however, that much of central Donegal is bleak, boggy terrain where walking can be tough, especially if the weather's bad – which it often is! Although the walking-man symbol sometimes appears on markers, in general you'll be looking out for white-painted posts which simply tell you that you're heading in the right direction.

This stretch of the Ulster Way is intended for wilderness lovers. Some of the scenery en route is truly magnificent: you pass the Blue Stack (p498) and Derryveagh Mountains and the 752m Mt Errigal (p502), Don-

egal's highest peak. The route also skirts the glorious Glenveagh National Park (p502), where you might want to break your journey. There are few dramatic historic remains to distract you, but plenty of minor prehistoric burial sites.

WICKLOW WAY

Opened in 1982, the popular 132km Wicklow Way (www.wicklowway.com) was Ireland's first long-distance trail. Despite its name it actually starts in southern Dublin and ends in Clonegal in County Carlow, although for most of the way it travels through Wicklow. From its beginnings in Marlay Park, Rathfarnham, in southern Dublin, the trail quickly enters a mountain wilderness (the highest point is White Hill at 633m). A mixture of forest walks, sheep paths, bog roads and mountain passes join up to provide a spectacular walk that passes by Glencree (p155), Powerscourt (p154), Djouce Mountain, Luggala, Glenmacnass (p156), Glendalough (p157), Glenmalure (p161) and Aghavannagh.

Some sections are desolate, especially south of Laragh, with much of the trail above 500m. The weather can change quickly, so good walking boots, outdoor gear and emergency supplies are essential. There are many worthwhile detours: up Glenmacnass to the waterfall or up to the summit of Lugnaquilla Mountain, for example.

It can be done in either direction, though most walkers start in Dublin. For the entire trail, allow eight to 10 days, plus time for diversions. Breaking the journey at Laragh, just under halfway, would let you visit the monastic site at Glendalough and do some local walks. Because of the way's popularity, walking outside the busy June to August period is advisable. Camping is possible along the route, but ask permission from local farmers. In peak season you should book accommodation in advance, and if you're hostelling you'll need to carry food with you.

Some parts of the route such as the Derrybawn Ridge are badly eroded, and the National Park Service asks walkers to refrain from further damaging those areas. **East-West Mapping** (☎ /fax 054-77835; eastwest@eircom .net) produced a new edition map guide to the Wicklow Way in 2005, with all changes and updates to the route included.

Rock Climbing

Ireland's mountain ranges aren't high – Mt Carrantuohil in Kerry's MacGillycuddy's Reeks is the tallest mountain in Ireland at only 1041m – but they're often beautiful and offer some excellent climbing possibilities (see p282). The highest mountains are in the southwest.

Adventure centres around the country run courses and organise climbing trips. For further information contact the **Mountaineering Council of Ireland** (☎ 01-625 1115; www.mountaineering.ie), which also publishes climbing guides and the quarterly magazine *Irish Mountain Log*, or check www.climbing.ie.

Water Sports

With a staggering 3100km of coastline, and numerous rivers and lakes, Ireland provides plenty of opportunities for water sports.

CANOEING

Ireland's indented coastline makes it ideal for exploring by canoe. The type of canoeing in Ireland and degree of difficulty varies from gentle paddling to white-water canoeing and canoe surfing. The best time for white water is winter, when the heavier rainfall swells the rivers.

Check out the **Irish Canoe Union** (☎ 01-625 1105; www.irishcanoeunion.com).

SAILING

There is a long history of sailing in Ireland and the country has more than 120 yacht and sailing clubs, including the **Royal Cork Yacht Club** (☎ 021-483 1023; office@royalcork.com) at Crosshaven, which was established in 1720 and is the world's oldest. The most popular areas for sailing are the southwestern coast, especially between Cork Harbour and the Dingle Peninsula; the Kerry coastline; the coast of Antrim; along the sheltered coast north and south of Dublin; and some of the larger lakes such as Lough Derg, Lough Erne and Lough Gill.

The **Irish Association for Sail Training** (☎ 01-605 1621; www.irishmarinefederation.com) watches over professional schools, and the national governing body is the **Irish Sailing Association** (☎ 01-280 0239; www.sailing.ie). A recommended publication, available from most booksellers, is *Irish Cruising Club Sailing Directions*. It contains details of port facilities, harbour plans and coast and tidal information.

SCUBA DIVING

Ireland has some of the best scuba diving in Europe, almost entirely off the western coast among its offshore islands and rocks. The best period for diving is roughly March to October. Visibility averages more than 12m but can increase to 30m on good days. For more details about scuba diving in Ireland, contact Comhairle Fó-Thuinn (CFT), the **Irish Underwater Council** (☎ 01-284 4601; www.scubaireland.com), Ireland's diving regulatory body, which also publishes the dive magazine *SubSea* (also available online).

SWIMMING & SURFING

Ireland has some magnificent coastline and some great sandy beaches: the cleaner, safer ones have EU Blue Flag awards. Get a list from the government agency **An Taisce** (☎ 01-454 1786; www.antaisce.org; Tailors' Hall, Back Lane, Dublin 8) or online at www.blueflag.org.

Surfers should visit www.surfingireland.net or www.victorkilo.com for beach reports and forecasts. Women should check out **Surf Honeys** (www.surfhoneys.com), which runs all-girl surfing lessons in Sligo 'to put the girl in the curl'!

The best months for surfing in Ireland, when the swells are highest, are September (when the water is warmest because of the Gulf Stream) and October. Some of the best locations are on the south and southwest coasts, for example Tramore (p196) in Waterford, and there are also big surfing schools in Sligo (p447) and Donegal (p491), where you can also have a blast at kite surfing.

WATER-SKIING

There are water-ski clubs all over Ireland offering tuition, equipment and boats. A full list is available from the **Irish Water Ski Federation** (www.iwsf.ie).

WINDSURFING

The windsurfer has plenty of locations to indulge in this popular sport – even on the Grand Canal in Dublin! The western coast is the most challenging and the least crowded. The bay at Rosslare in County Wexford (see p178) is ideal for windsurfing, with equipment and tuition available in summer. The **Irish Sailing Association** (☎ 01-280 0239; www.sailing.ie) is the sport's governing authority and has details of centres.

TRACING YOUR ANCESTORS

Many visitors come to Ireland purely to track down their Irish roots. Success in this activity is more likely if you have managed to obtain some basic facts about your Irish ancestors before leaving home. The names of your ancestors who left Ireland and their approximate dates of birth are essential, but it's also helpful to know the ancestors' counties and parishes of origin in Ireland, their religious denomination, and their parents' and spouses' names.

Good starting points for research in Ireland are the **National Library** (☎ 01-603 0200; www.nli .ie; Kildare St, Dublin 2); the **National Archives** (☎ 01-407 2300; www.nationalarchives.ie; Bishop St, Dublin 8); and the **Public Record Office of Northern Ireland** (Proni; ☎ 028-9025 5905; http://proni.nics.gov.uk; 66 Balmoral Ave, Belfast). Other helpful resources include the **General Register Office** (☎ 090-663 2900; www.groireland.ie; Government Offices, Convent Rd, Roscommon) and **General Register Office Northern Ireland** (☎ 028-9025 2000; www.groni.gov.uk; Oxford House, 49/55 Chichester St, Belfast). These agencies hold records of births, deaths and marriages in Ireland.

There are also numerous agencies and individuals that will do the research for you for a fee. For information on these, contact the **Association of Professional Genealogists in Ireland** (APGI; c/o The Honorary Secretary, 30 Harlech Cres, Clonskeagh, Dublin 14). In the North also contact the **Association of Ulster Genealogists & Record Agents** (Augra; c/o The Honorary Secretary, Glen Cottage, Glenmachan Rd, Belfast BT4 2NP).

Dozens of books are available on Irish genealogy. Tony McCarthy's *Irish Roots Guide* is a good introduction to the subject, and John Grenham's *Tracing Your Irish Ancestors* is an excellent comprehensive guide. North Americans in particular benefit from *A Genealogists Guide to Discovering Your Irish Ancestors* by Dwight Radford and Kyle Betit.

BUSINESS HOURS

The standard business hours are generally the same for both the Republic and Northern Ireland and are shown below, with any variations noted:

Banks 10am to 4pm (to 5pm Thursday) Monday to Friday

Offices 9am to 5pm Monday to Friday

Post offices Northern Ireland 9am to 5.30pm Monday to Friday, 9am to 12.30pm Saturday; Republic 9am-6pm Monday to Friday, 9am to 1pm Saturday. Smaller post offices may close at lunch and one day a week.

Pubs Northern Ireland 11.30am to 11pm Monday to Saturday, 12.30pm to 10pm Sunday. Pubs with late licences open until 1am Monday to Saturday, and midnight Sunday; Republic 10.30am to 11.30pm Monday to Thursday, 10.30am to 12.30am Friday and Saturday, noon to 11pm Sunday (30 minutes 'drinking up' time allowed). Pubs with bar extensions open to 2.30am Thursday to Saturday; closed Christmas Day and Good Friday.

Restaurants Noon to 10.30pm; many close one day of the week.

Shops 9am to 5.30pm or 6pm Monday to Saturday (until 8pm on Thursday and sometimes Friday), noon to 6pm Sunday in bigger towns only. Shops in rural towns may close at lunch and one day a week.

Tourist offices 9am to 5pm Monday to Friday, 9am to 1pm Saturday. Many extend their hours in summer, and open fewer hours/days or close October to April.

CHILDREN

Successful travel with young children requires effort, but can be done. Try not to overdo things and consider using some sort of self-catering accommodation. It's sometimes easier to eat in (or to at least have the option), rather than be restricted by the relatively confined space of a hotel or B&B room. On the whole you'll find that restaurants and hotels, especially in the countryside, will go out of their way to cater for you and your children – with the exception of a few places, generally in the capital, where children aren't allowed after 6pm. Children are allowed in pubs until 7pm.

Most attractions sell cheaper family tickets, and family passes are available on public transport. It's always a good idea to talk to fellow travellers with (happy) children and locals on the road for tips on where to go. For further general information see Lonely Planet's *Travel with Children* by Cathy Lanigan.

Practicalities

Most hotels will provide cots at no extra charge and restaurants will have high chairs. Car seats (around €50/£25 per rental) are mandatory for children in hire cars between the ages of nine months and four years. Bring your own seat for infants under about nine months as only larger forward-facing child seats are generally available. Remember not to place baby seats in the front if the car has an airbag.

Remarkably, nappy changing facilities are scarce, even in city centres.

Ireland has one of the lowest rates of breastfeeding in the world; nevertheless you should be able to feed your baby in all but a few public places without jaws dropping.

Two great websites are www.eumom .ie for pregnant women and parents with young children, and www.babygoes2.com, which is an excellent travel site about family-friendly accommodation worldwide.

CLIMATE CHARTS

Thanks to the moderating effect of the Atlantic Gulf Stream, Ireland's climate is relatively mild for its latitude, with a mean annual temperature of around 10°C. The temperature drops below freezing only intermittently during winter, and snow is scarce – perhaps one or two brief flurries a year. The coldest months are January and February, when daily temperatures range from 4° to 8°C, with 7°C the average. In summer, temperatures during the day are a comfortable 15° to 20°C. During the warmest months, July and August, the average is 16°C. A hot summer's day in Ireland is 22° to 24°C, although it can sometimes reach 30°C. There are about 18 hours of daylight daily during July and August and it's only truly dark after about 11pm.

One thing you can be sure of about Irish weather is how little you can be sure of. It may be shirtsleeves and sunglasses in February but winter woollies in March and even during the summer.

And then there's the rain. Ireland receives a lot of rain, with certain areas getting a soaking as many as 270 days of the year. County Kerry is the worst affected. The southeast is the driest, enjoying a more continental climate.

Also see p20.

COURSES

Irish Language

There are a number of courses in the Irish language and culture, particularly in the Gaeltacht (Irish-speaking) areas; see www.gaelsaoire.ie or contact Fáilte Ireland for information.

Intercelt (www.intercelt.com) Resource for Irish language–based holidays.
Oideas Gael (☎ 074-973 0248; www.oideas-gael. com; Glencolumbcille, Donegal; 3-/7-day courses €95/190; ☺ Mar-Sep) Irish language courses and cultural activity holidays.

English Language

Fáilte Ireland publishes a list of recognised schools for teaching English as a foreign

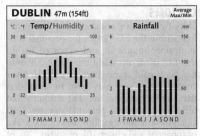

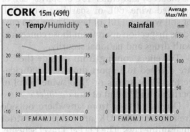

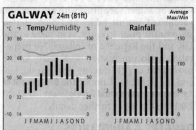

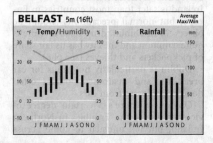

language. Most English-language schools are in and around Dublin.

Centre of English Studies (☎ 01-671 4233; www
.cesireland.ie; 31 Dame St, Dublin)

Dublin School of English (☎ 01-677 3322; www.dse
.ie; 10-12 Westmoreland St, Dublin)

English Language Institute (☎ 01-475 2965; www
.englishlanguage.com; 99 St Stephen's Green, Dublin)

Language Centre of Ireland (☎ 01-671 6266; www
.lci.ie; 45 Kildare St, Dublin)

CUSTOMS

Duty-free sales are not available when travelling within the EU. Goods for personal consumption bought in and exported within the EU incur no additional taxes, if duty has been paid somewhere in the EU. Over certain limits you may have to show that they are for personal use. The amounts that officially constitute personal use are 3200 cigarettes (or 400 cigarillos, 200 cigars or 3kg of tobacco) and either 10L of spirits, 20L of fortified wine, 60L of sparkling wine, 90L of still wine or 110L of beer. There's no customs inspection apart from those concerned with drugs and national security.

Travellers coming from outside the EU are allowed to import duty free 200 cigarettes, 1L of spirits or 2L of wine, 60ml of perfume and 250ml of *eau de toilette*.

Dogs and cats from anywhere outside Ireland and the UK are subject to strict quarantine laws. The EU Pet Travel Scheme, whereby animals are fitted with a microchip, vaccinated against rabies and blood tested six months *prior* to entry, is in force in the UK and the Republic of Ireland. No preparation or documentation is necessary for the movement of pets directly between the UK and the Republic. Contact the **Department of Agriculture, Food & Rural Development** (☎ 01-607 2000) in Dublin for further details.

DANGERS & ANNOYANCES

Ireland is safer than most countries in Europe, but normal precautions should be observed. In Dublin, drug-related crime is quite common and the city has its fair share of pickpockets and thieves (see p88).

Dublin is particularly notorious for car break-ins, and insurance policies often don't cover losses from cars.

Obviously, there's a certain degree of violence due to the Troubles in Northern Ireland, but it's unusual to come across

any personally, and if the peace process continues, violence should diminish. Still, it's probably best to ensure your visit to Northern Ireland doesn't coincide with the climax of the Orange marching season on 12 July when even many Northern Irish leave the province. For areas best avoided in Belfast, see p557.

DISABLED TRAVELLERS

Travelling in Ireland with a disability can be tricky, particularly in a wheelchair, although access is slowly improving. If you have a physical disability, get in touch with your national support organisation (preferably the travel officer if there is one) before you go. It often has libraries devoted to travel and can put you in touch with agencies that specialise in tours for the disabled.

Guesthouses, hotels and sights in Ireland are gradually being adapted for people with disabilities. Fáilte Ireland and NITB's accommodation guides indicate which places are wheelchair accessible.

Public transportation can be a nightmare. Older city buses are being replaced by wheelchair-accessible buses, with a ramp and priority space on board, but for services outside Dublin and Belfast, forget it.

Trains are accessible with help. In theory, if you call ahead, an employee of Iarnród Éireann (Irish Rail) will arrange to accompany you to the train. Newer trains have audio and visual information systems for visually impaired and hearing-impaired passengers.

Comhairle (☎ 01-605 9000; www.comhairle.ie) in the Republic and **Disability Action** (☎ 028-9066 1252; www.disabilityaction.org) in Northern Ireland can give some advice, although most of their information concerns disabled Irish citizens' rights. Travellers to Northern Ireland can check out the website www.allgohere.com.

DISCOUNT CARDS
Heritage Discounts

Heritage Card (☎ 01-647 6587; www.heritageireland
.com; Visitor Services, 51 St Stephen's Green, Dublin 2; adult/child & student/family €20/7.50/50) Entitles you to free access to over 65 sites for one year.

National Trust (☎ 0870 458 4000; www.nationaltrust
.org.uk; adult/under 25/family £38/17.50/68.50; Membership Dept, PO Box 39, Warrington WA5 7WD, UK) Entitles you to free admission to its 18 properties in Northern Ireland, but only really makes financial sense if you're touring its English sites too.

Senior Cards

Senior citizens are entitled to many discounts in Ireland on things such as public transport and museum admission fees, provided they show proof of age. The minimum qualifying age is usually 60 to 65 for men and 55 to 65 for women. In your home country, a lower age may already entitle you to travel packages and discounts (on car hire, for instance).

Car hire companies usually won't rent to drivers aged over 70 or 75.

Student & Youth Cards

The International Student Identity Card (ISIC; www.isiccard.com) gets discounts on transport, commercial goods and services, and admission to theatres, cinemas, museums and sights. The International Youth Travel Card (IYTC; www.isiccard. com) and European Youth Card (Euro<26 card; www.euro26.org) offer similar discounts for nonstudents under 26. All these cards are issued by hostelling organisations, student unions and student travel agencies.

EMBASSIES & CONSULATES
Irish Embassies & Consulates

Irish diplomatic offices overseas:

Australia Embassy (☎ 02-6273 3022; irishemb@ cyberone.com.au; 20 Arkana St, Yarralumla, Canberra, ACT 2600)

Canada Embassy (☎ 613-233 6281; embassyofireland@ rogers.com; 130 Albert St, Suite 1105, Ottawa, Ontario K1P 5G4)

France Embassy (☎ 01 44 17 67 00; paris@iveagh .irlgov.ie; 4 rue Rude, 75116 Paris)

Germany Embassy (☎ 030-220 720; www.botschaft -irland.de; Friedrichstrasse 200, 10117 Berlin)

Italy Embassy (☎ 06 697 9121; www.ambasciata -irlanda.it; Piazza di Campitelli 3, 00186 Rome)

Netherlands Embassy (☎ 070-363 09 93; www.irish embassy.nl; Dr Kuyperstraat 9, 2514 BA The Hague)

New Zealand Consulate (☎ 09-977 2256; consul@ireland.co.nz; 6th fl, 18 Shortland St, 1001 Auckland)

UK Embassy (☎ 020-7235 2171; 17 Grosvenor Pl, London SW1X 7HR); Consulate (☎ 0131-226 7711; 16 Randolph Crescent, Edinburgh EH3 6TT); Consulate (☎ 029-2066 2000; Brunel House, 2 Fitzalan Rd, Cardiff CF24 0EB)

USA Embassy (☎ 202-462 3939; www.irelandemb.org; 2234 Massachusetts Ave, NW, Washington, DC 20008) There are also consulates in Boston, Chicago, New York and San Francisco.

UK (for Northern Ireland) diplomatic offices abroad:

Australia High Commission (☎ 02-6270 6666; www.britaus.net; Commonwealth Ave, Yarralumla, Canberra, ACT 2600)

Canada High Commission (☎ 613-237 1530; general enquiries@BritaininCanada.org; 80 Elgin St, Ottawa, Ontario K1P 5K7)

France Embassy (☎ 01 44 51 31 00; www.amb-grande bretagne.fr; 35 rue du Faubourg St Honoré, 75383 Paris)

Germany Embassy (☎ 030-204 570; www.britische botschaft.de; Wilhelmstrasse 70, 10117 Berlin)

Italy Embassy (☎ 06 4220 0001; www.britain.it; Via XX Settembre 80a, 00187 Rome)

Netherlands Embassy (☎ 070-427 04 27; www.britain .nl; Lange Voorhout 10, 2514 ED The Hague)

New Zealand High Commission (☎ 04-924 2888; www.britain.org.nz; 44 Hill St, Wellington)

USA Embassy (☎ 202-588 6500; www.britainusa.com; 3100 Massachusetts Ave NW, Washington, DC 20008)

Embassies & Consulates in Ireland

Your own country's embassy won't be much help if the trouble you're in is remotely your own fault. You are bound by the laws of the country you are in. In genuine emergencies you might get some assistance: a free ticket is exceedingly unlikely but embassies might assist you with getting a new passport.

The following countries have embassies in Dublin:

Australia (☎ 01-664 5300; www.australianembassy.ie; 2nd fl, Fitzwilton House, Wilton Tce, Dublin 2)

Canada (☎ 01-417 4100; 4th fl, 65-68 St Stephen's Green, Dublin 2)

France (☎ 01-277 5000; chancellerie@ambafrance.ie; 36 Ailesbury Rd, Dublin 4)

Germany (☎ 01-269 3011; germany@indigo.ie; 31 Trimleston Ave, Booterstown, Blackrock, Co Dublin)

Italy (☎ 01-660 1744; info@italianembassy.ie; 63-65 Northumberland Rd, Ballsbridge, Dublin 4)

Netherlands (☎ 01-269 3444; info@netherlands embassy.ie; 160 Merrion Rd, Ballsbridge, Dublin 4)

UK (☎ 01-205 3700; www.britishembassy.ie; 29 Merrion Rd, Ballsbridge, Dublin 4)

USA (☎ 01-668 8777; webmasterireland@state.gov; 42 Elgin Rd, Ballsbridge, Dublin 4)

The following countries have consular representation in Northern Ireland:

Germany (☎ 028-9024 4113; Chamber of Commerce House, 22 Great Victoria St, Belfast)

Netherlands (☎ 028-9077 9088; c/o All-Route Shipping Ltd, 14-16 West Bank Rd, Belfast)

USA (☎ 028-9038 6100; Danesfort House, 223 Stranmillis Rd, Belfast)

FESTIVALS & EVENTS

Following is a list of major annual events and festivals held around the island. Local tourist offices will have additional information. Also, the Association of Irish Festival Events (AOIFE) maintains a very useful website at www.aoifeonline.com; www.art .ie is worth perusing too. For regional festivals, see destination chapters.

MARCH

St Patrick's Day (17 March; ☎ 01-676 3205; www.st patricksday.ie) Ireland erupts into one giant celebration on 17 March. The biggest beano is in Dublin, where the streets reverberate to a cacophony of parades, fireworks and light shows for five days around 17 March. Over 250,000 attend. Cork, Armagh and Belfast also have parades; elsewhere festivities are less ostentatious.

APRIL

Easter Parades Many small towns host Easter parades. Ask locally for details.
World Irish Dancing Championships (☎ 01-475 2220) About 4000 dancers from all over the globe compete in late March or early April. The location varies from year to year.

DECEMBER

Christmas This is a quiet affair in the countryside, though on 26 December the ancient practice of Wren Boys is re-enacted, most notably in Dingle, County Kerry, when groups of children dress up and go about singing hymns.

FOOD

Our café and restaurant listings appear in order of price (when divided by subheadings) and then preference, with favourites appearing first. We've used the following price ranges: budget (under €10/£10), midrange (€10 to €20/£10 to £20) and top end (above €20/£20). Please note that our hierarchies of favourite places aren't written in stone. As authors, we can crave for caviar on a Monday, and cod and chips on a Friday!

For explanations of peculiarities of Irish menus and further reading on Irish food and drink, see p68.

GAY & LESBIAN TRAVELLERS

Surprisingly for such an overwhelmingly Catholic country, Irish laws on homosexuality are among the most liberal and pro-

gressive in Europe. There is a common age of consent of 17, and neither gays nor lesbians (in the Republic) are excluded from the armed forces. Despite its dogma on the matter, the Catholic Church has maintained a silent neutrality on gay and lesbian issues.

Dublin (see p141), and to a lesser extent Belfast, Cork, Galway, Waterford and Limerick, have openly gay and lesbian communities, but elsewhere the scene is quiet. The monthly *Gay Community News* (www.gcn.ie), found online and in clubs and bars, is a free publication of the **National Lesbian & Gay Federation** (NLGF; ☎ 01-671 9076; 2 Scarlett Row, Temple Bar, Dublin).

Check out the following online resources for the gay and lesbian community:
Channel Queer www.channelqueer.com
Gaire www.gaire.com
Gay & Lesbian Youth Northern Ireland www.glyni .org.uk
Gay Ireland www.gay.ie

Useful organisations:
Northern Ireland Gay Rights Association (Nigra; nigra@dnet.co.uk; ☎ 028-9066 5257; PO Box 44, Belfast)
Outhouse (☎ 01-873 4932; www.outhouse.ie; 105 Capel St, Dublin 1) A gay, lesbian and transgender community centre.

The following helplines can be called from anywhere in Ireland:
Gay Men's Health Project (☎ 01-660 2189) Practical advice on men's health issues.
Gay Switchboard Dublin (☎ 01-872 1055; ◷ 7.30am-9.30pm Mon-Fri, 3.30-6pm Sat)
Lesbian Line Belfast (☎ 028-9023 8668; ◷ 7.30-10pm Thu)
Lesbian Line Dublin (☎ 01-872 9911; ◷ 7-9pm Thu)
Mensline Belfast (☎ 028-9032 2023; ◷ 7.30-10pm Mon-Wed)

HOLIDAYS

Public holidays can cause road chaos, as everyone tries to get somewhere else for the break. It's also wise to book accommodation in advance.

Public Holidays

Public holidays in the Republic, Northern Ireland or both:
New Year's Day 1 January
St Patrick's Day 17 March
Easter (Good Friday to Easter Monday inclusive) March/April

May Holiday 1st Monday in May
Christmas Day 25 December
St Stephen's Day (Boxing Day) 26 December

NORTHERN IRELAND
Spring Bank Holiday Last Monday in May
Orangeman's Day 12 July
August Holiday Last Monday in August

REPUBLIC
June Holiday 1st Monday in June
August Holiday 1st Monday in August
October Holiday Last Monday in October

St Patrick's Day and St Stephen's Day holidays are taken on the following Monday should they fall on a weekend. In the Republic, nearly everywhere closes on Good Friday even though it isn't an official public holiday. In the North, most shops open on Good Friday but close the following Tuesday.

School Holidays

In the Republic, standardised primary and secondary school holidays for 2005–06 are as follows:
Mid-term break 31 October to 4 November
Christmas/New Year 22 December to 9 January
Mid-term break 13 to 17 February (16 & 17 only for primary schools)
Easter 7 to 24 April
Summer July and August (June also for secondary schools)

In the North, holidays for primary and secondary schools vary. Visit www.deni.gov .uk/schools/index.htm then click on school holidays for a comprehensive rundown.

INSURANCE

Insurance is important: it covers you for everything from medical expenses and luggage loss to cancellations or delays in your travel arrangements, depending on your policy.

If you're an EU citizen, an E111 form (available from health centres, or from post offices in the UK) covers you for most medical care. Other countries, such as Australia, also have reciprocal agreements with Ireland and Britain, but many countries do not.

If you do need health insurance, remember that some policies offer lower and higher medical-expense options, but the higher one is chiefly for countries such as the USA that have extremely high medical costs. Everyone should be covered for the worst possible case, such as an accident requiring an ambulance, hospital treatment or an emergency flight home. You may prefer a policy that pays health-care providers directly rather than you having to pay on the spot and claim later. See p705 for health insurance details.

All cars on public roads must be insured. If you are bringing your own vehicle check that your insurance will cover you in Ireland.

INTERNET ACCESS

If you plan to carry your notebook or palmtop computer with you, remember that the power-supply voltage in Ireland may vary from that at home. To avoid frying your electronics, the best investment is a universal AC adaptor and a plug adaptor, which will enable you to plug in anywhere. Also worth purchasing is a 'global' or 'world' modem, as your PC-card modem may not work outside your home country. For comprehensive advice on travelling with portable computers, visit the World Wide Phone Guide at www.kropla.com. **Teleadapt** (www.teleadapt.com) sells all the gizmos and gubbins you'll need.

Major Internet service providers (ISPs) such as **AOL** (www.aol.com), **CompuServe** (www .compuserve.com) and **AT&T** (www.att.com) have dial-in nodes in Ireland. If you access your Internet email account at home through a smaller ISP, your best option is either to open an account with a global ISP, like those mentioned above, or to rely on Internet cafés. Armed with your incoming (POP or IMAP) mail-server name, your account name and your password, you should be able to access your Internet email account from any Net-connected machine in the world. However, the easiest solution is to open a free Web-based email account such as those provided by **Hotmail** (www.hotmail.com) or **Yahoo!** (mail.yahoo.com).

You'll find Internet cafés in most major towns in Ireland. You can log on for €4 to €10 per hour in the Republic, or about £4 per hour in the North. Most public libraries have a free Internet access service but it may only be available (to a queue of people) at certain hours when connections may be slow.

DIRECTORY

FOR THE RECORD:

- The legal age to vote in Ireland is 18
- You can leave school when you're 16
- The legal drinking age is 18
- Smoking is legal at 16
- The heterosexual and homosexual age of consent is 17
- You can ride a moped when you're 16
- You can drive a car when you're 17

LEGAL MATTERS

If you need legal assistance contact the **Legal Aid Board** (☎ 066-947 1000; www.legalaidboard .ie). It has a number of local law centres listed in the phone book.

The possession of small quantities of marijuana attracts a fine or warning, but harder drugs are treated more seriously. Public drunkenness is illegal, and though police grant leeway, if matters get out of hand you may receive a verbal caution. Fighting is treated more harshly: if you're involved in a fight you may spend a night in a cell, to 'cool off'.

MAPS

Many publishers produce some good-quality maps of Ireland. Michelin's 1:400,000-scale Ireland map (No 923) is a decent single sheet map, with clear cartography and most of the island's scenic roads marked. The four maps – North, South, East and West – that make up the Ordnance Survey Holiday map series at 1:250,000-scale are useful if you want more detail. Collins also publishes a range of maps covering Ireland.

For greater detail, map aficionados and walkers should look out for the Ordnance Survey Discovery series, which covers the whole island in 89 maps at a scale of 1:50,000. They're available at the **National Map Centre** (☎ 01-476 0471; www.mapcentre.ie; 34 Aungier St, Dublin 2) and many other bookshops around Ireland.

Lonely Planet's *Dublin City Map* has a complete index of all streets and sights, a Dublin Area Rapid Transport (DART) and suburban rail plan and a unique walking tour of the city.

MONEY

To get a general idea of food and accommodation costs in Ireland, see p20. Tips of around 10% in metered cabs and in restaurants where the service charge isn't included are expected.

ATMs & Credit Cards

Credit cards make the perfect travelling companions: they're ideal for major purchases and let you withdraw cash from selected banks and ATMs. ATMs are usually linked to international money systems such as Cirrus, Maestro or Plus. Bear in mind, though, that each transaction incurs a currency conversion fee and credit cards can incur immediate and exorbitant cash advance interest rate charges.

Charge cards such as Amex and Diners Club don't have credit limits, but may not be accepted in smaller establishments. Visa and MasterCard are more widely accepted, though many B&Bs and some smaller or remote petrol stations take cash only.

Remember to keep a note of the emergency telephone number to ring if your card is lost or stolen.

Cash & Travellers Cheques

Nothing beats cash for convenience – or risk. It's still a good idea, though, to arrive with some cash in the local currency (both euros and sterling, if travelling to the North) to tide you over.

Amex and Thomas Cook travellers cheques are widely recognised and they don't charge commission for cashing their own cheques. Eurocheques can also be cashed in Ireland. Travellers cheques are rarely accepted outside banks or used for everyday transactions (as they are in the USA).

Take most cheques in large denominations. It's only towards the end of a stay that you may want to change a small cheque to make sure you don't get left with too much local currency.

Currency

In February 2002 the Republic bid adieu to the punt and adopted the euro. The euro (€) is divided into 100 cents. The reverse side of coins have a design particular to their country of issue (a Celtic harp in Ireland's case), but are legal tender in all countries that accept the euro (Austria, Belgium, Finland, France,

Germany, Greece, Italy, Luxembourg, the Netherlands, Portugal and Spain). Remember that the UK is not a participant, so if you're travelling to Northern Ireland you'll have to change euros into UK pounds.

The British pound sterling (£) is used in Northern Ireland, where it is known as the Northern Irish pound. Northern Ireland notes, while equivalent in value to British pound notes, are not readily accepted in Britain, but British banks will swap them for you.

The best exchange rates are obtained at banks. Bureaus de change and other exchange facilities usually open for longer hours but the rate and/or commission will be worse. Many post offices operate a currency-exchange facility and open on Saturday morning. Exchange rates at the time of writing are on the inside front cover of this book.

International Transfers

The most practical way to receive money from overseas is by telegraphic transfer. There are two ways to do this. The first can take up to eight days through the banking system. Your bank sends money to an Irish bank nominated by you. You will need identification, most likely a passport, before the money is paid to you in euros, minus the transfer commission.

The quickest way to receive cash from home is to transfer it through Amex, Thomas Cook or Western Union.

It is not practical to receive money by bank draft. Irish banks are notorious sticklers about drafts and won't allow you to cash them unless you first open a bank account, a small bureaucratic nightmare. Even then, it can take three weeks to clear. If you're not planning a long stay, stick to telegraphic transfers.

Taxes & Refunds

Value-added tax (VAT) is a sales tax of 20% that applies to most luxury goods in Ireland, excluding books and children's footwear. Through the Cashback scheme, visitors from non-EU countries can claim back most of the VAT on large purchases that are subsequently exported from the EU within three months of purchase. If you're a resident of a country outside the EU and buy something from a store displaying a

Cashback sticker, you'll be given a Cashback voucher with your purchase which can be refunded in US, Canadian or Australian dollars, British pounds or euros at Dublin or Shannon airport.

If you reclaim more than €250 on any of your vouchers you'll need to get the voucher stamped at the customs booth in the arrivals hall at Dublin or Shannon airport before you can get your refund from the Cashback desk.

In Northern Ireland, shops participating in the Tax-Free Shopping refund scheme will give you a form or invoice on request to be presented to customs when you leave. After customs have certified the form, it will be returned to the shop for a refund.

PHOTOGRAPHY & VIDEO

Developing and printing a 24-exposure print film typically costs around €14/£9 for a one-hour service or around €8/£5 for a slower turnaround. Slide processing costs about €9/£6 per roll and takes up to a week in most places (an hour in Dublin).

Natural light in Ireland can be very dull, so to capture the sombre atmosphere use faster film, such as 400ASA; but 200ASA should do in most situations. Lonely Planet's full-colour *Travel Photography: A Guide to Taking Better Pictures*, written by internationally renowned travel photographer Richard I'Anson, is full of handy hints and is designed to take on the road.

In regard to taking photos in Northern Ireland, if you want to take photos of fortified police stations, army posts or other military or quasi-military paraphernalia, get permission first to be on the safe side. In the Protestant and Catholic strongholds of West Belfast it's best not to photograph people without permission: always ask first and be prepared to accept a refusal.

POST

Post offices in the Republic are operated by An Post, the Irish Postal Service, and in the North by Royal Mail.

In the Republic, postcards and small airmail letters weighing up to 50g cost €0.48 within Ireland, economy/priority €0.50/0.60 to Britain, and €0.55/0.65 to continental Europe and the rest of the world.

In the North, letters sent by 1st-/2nd-class mail to Britain cost £0.30/0.21 as long as they weigh less than 60g. Airmail letters under 20g cost £0.42 to continental Europe and £0.68 to the rest of the world (under 10g to the rest of the world for £0.47).

All mail to Britain and Europe goes by air, so airmail envelopes and stickers are unnecessary. You can buy stamps from post offices and some newsagents and shops.

Both postal services are efficient: over 95% of mail posted to destinations within Ireland is delivered the next working day. Mail to Britain and continental Europe takes three to five days, to Australasia a week to 10 days, and to North America about 10 days. If you want to send mail to a post office in Ireland to be held for collection, mark it 'Poste Restante: Hold for Collection'. The post office will officially only hold this post for two weeks; you will need photo identification to claim your post.

For post office opening hours see p682.

SHOPPING

Online shoppers can visit www.celticlinks.com for a wide selection of Irish goods. Apart from the possibilities listed here, you can find Irish music; jewellery, especially Claddagh rings; enamel work; and baskets woven of willow or rush. Connemara marble is a natural green stone found in the west of Ireland; it is often fashioned into Celtic designs.

Clothing

First made by Aran Island women for their husbands to wear in the harsh local climate, the famous Aran sweater is sold throughout Ireland, and particularly in County Galway. The hand-knitted variety costs significantly more than its machine-manufactured counterpart.

County Donegal is famous for its tweeds; **Magee & Company** (☎ 073-31100; www.mageeshop.com; The Diamond, Donegal town) has a large selection. Tweed can be purchased in lengths or finished as jackets, skirts or caps. Counties Wicklow and Dublin also produce tweed.

Irish linen is of high quality and takes the shape of everything from blouses to handkerchiefs, with the main centres in the North. Irish lace is another fine product, at its best in Limerick, or Carrickmacross in County Monaghan. The Irish produce some high-quality outdoor-activities gear – they've plenty of experience with cold, wet

weather after all. Hand-woven shawls and woollen blankets also make lovely presents.

Crystal

Waterford Crystal (☎ 051-332 500; www.waterfordwedgwood.com; Kilbarry, Waterford town) makes world-famous crystal that is available to buy throughout Ireland. Its main competitor is **Cavan Crystal** (☎ 049-433 1800; www.cavancrystaldesign.com; Dublin Rd, Cavan town). Smaller manufacturers of crystal produce fine work and often at more attractive prices. In the North, **Tyrone Crystal** (☎ 028-8772 5335; www.tyronecrystal.com; Killybrackey, Dungannon) hosts factory tours.

Food & Drink

Irish whiskey isn't just spelled differently: it also has its own distinctive taste. The big names are Paddy's, Jameson's, Power's, Bushmills and Tullamore Dew, and they're not always readily available in other parts of the world. Two well-established Irish liqueurs are Irish Mist and Bailey's Irish Cream. Bailey's also produces ready mixed Irish coffee in a bottle.

Some excellent handmade cheeses are worth considering as a gift to take home. See p68 for cheese suggestions.

Pottery

All over the country there are small potteries turning out unusual and attractive work. The village of Belleek in County Fermanagh, which straddles the Northern Ireland border with Donegal, produces delicate bone china. In the Republic the area around Dingle in County Kerry has superb pottery. Enniscorthy in County Wexford, and Kilkenny and Thomastown in County Kilkenny also stand out in this regard. Generally, throughout West Cork and Kerry there are countless small workshops that open in the summer with their stocks of pottery and other craftwork. Stephen Pearce pottery, from Carrigaline in Cork, is available in gift shops all over Ireland.

SOLO TRAVELLERS

Travelling alone in Ireland is easy. People are extremely sociable, especially in the countryside, and will be more than keen to chat with you in pubs or public places – whether you like it or not! Hostels and Internet cafés are always good stomping grounds to meet fellow travellers, or you might consider combining independent travel with a short course or activity where you have more chance of meeting people. One disadvantage of solo travel is the extra cost of accommodation: many places charge per room, or if they charge per person, they also slap a single supplementary charge (up to 30%) on to the room rate.

TELEPHONE

For a small country, Ireland has a remarkably sophisticated phone service and was one of the first countries in the world to make the switch to high-speed fibreoptic cabling. Consequently, you shouldn't have any problems making phone calls to anyone, anywhere.

Eircom is Ireland's largest telephone service provider, although deregulation of the telephone industry has seen the arrival of a number of other providers. In the North most public phones are owned by British Telecom (BT).

Peak per-minute charges for international calls from Ireland to selected countries:

To	Republic	North
Australia	€0.86	£0.22
Canada	€0.19	£0.15
France	€0.24	£0.17
Germany	€0.24	£0.17
Italy	€0.39	£0.20
Netherlands	€0.24	£0.17
New Zealand	€0.86	£0.29
UK	€0.15	£0.05
USA	€0.19	£0.14

Prices are lower in the evening and at the weekend. The above prices are for calls placed from land-line phones to other land-line phones; international calls to mobiles can cost significantly more. Phone calls from hotel rooms cost at least double the standard rate. You can send and receive faxes from post offices (up to €2/£1 per page locally) or most hotels.

Rather than placing reverse-charge calls through the operator in Ireland, you can dial direct to your home-country operator and then reverse the charges or charge the call to a local phone credit card. To use the home-direct service dial the codes in the table below then the area code and, in most cases, the number you want. Your home-country operator will come on the line before the call goes through.

To call home from Ireland, dial the numbers outlined in the table (left).

Local telephone calls from a public phone in the Republic cost €0.25 for around three minutes (around €0.50 to a mobile), regardless of when you call. In Northern Ireland a local call costs a minimum of £0.20.

Pre-paid phonecards by Eircom or private operators, available in newsagencies and post offices, work from all pay phones and dispense with the need for coins.

To	From the Republic	From the North
Australia	☎ 1800 550 061 + number	☎ 0800 890 061 + number
France	☎ 1800 551 033 + number	☎ 0800 890 033 + number
Italy	☎ 1800 550 039 + number	☎ 0800 890 039 + number
New Zealand	☎ 1800 550 064 + number	☎ 0800 890 064 + number
Spain	☎ 1800 550 034 + number	☎ 0800 890 034 + number
UK – BT	☎ 1800 550 044 + number	n/a
USA – AT&T	☎ 1800 550 000 + number	☎ 0800 890 011 + number
USA – MCI	☎ 1800 551 001 + number	☎ 0800 890 222 + number
USA – Sprint	☎ 1800 552 001 + number	☎ 0800 890 877 + number

Mobile Phones

Mobile phone usage in Ireland has skyrocketed. They're the most convenient – and expensive – way to keep in touch. Ireland uses GSM 900/1800, which is compatible with the rest of Europe and Australia but not with North American GSM 1900 or the totally different system in Japan (though some specially equipped North American phones do work here). There are three service providers in Ireland. Vodafone (087) is the most popular, followed by O2 Ireland (086) and the latest arrival, Meteor (085).

All three service providers are linked with most international GSM providers, which will allow you to 'roam' onto a local service once you arrive in Ireland. This means you can use your mobile phone to make local calls, but will be charged at the highest possible rate for all calls.

DIRECTORY

For around €50 you will get a Ready-to-Go pre-paid phone, your own number and anywhere up to €25 worth of airtime. As you use up your airtime, you simply buy a top-up card (€10 to €35) at a newsagency or petrol station. The other service providers have variations on this scheme. Similar schemes exist in Northern Ireland.

Phone Codes

When calling the Republic of Ireland from abroad, dial your international access code, followed by 353, followed by the domestic number minus the initial '0'. When calling Northern Ireland from abroad, dial your international access code, then 44 28, and then the local number. To call Northern Ireland from Britain, simply dial 028, then the local number. This changes to 048 when calling from the Republic. The area code for the whole of Northern Ireland is 028, so domestic callers need only dial the eight-digit local number.

To call UK numbers from the Republic dial 00 44, then the area code minus the initial '0', then the local number. Do the same for international calls, replacing 44 with the country code. To call Britain from Northern Ireland dial the area code followed by the local number. To place an international call or to call the Republic from Northern Ireland, dial 00 followed by the country code, then the area code (dropping any leading '0') and the local number.

TIME

In winter, Ireland is on Greenwich Mean Time (GMT), also known as Universal Time Coordinated (UTC), the same as Britain. In summer, the clock shifts to GMT plus one hour. When it's noon in Dublin and London, it is 3am in Los Angeles and Vancouver, 7am in New York and Toronto, 1pm in Paris, 8pm in Singapore, and 10pm in Sydney. See p716 for World Time Zones.

TOURIST INFORMATION

Fáilte Ireland (in the Republic ☎ 1850 230 330, in the UK ☎ 0800 039 7000; www.ireland.travel.ie) and the **Northern Irish Tourist Board** (NITB; head office ☎ 028-9023 1221; www.discovernorthernireland.com; 59 North St, Belfast) are mines of information.

Both websites include an accommodation booking service, or telephone reserva-

tions can be made via the tourist boards' system **Gulliver** (in the Republic ☎ 1800 668 668, in the UK ☎ 0800 783 5740, in the USA & Canada ☎ 800 398 4376).

Fáilte Ireland has an office in **Belfast** (☎ 028-9032 7888; 53 Castle St, Belfast) and NITB has an office in **Dublin** (within the Republic ☎ 01-679 1977, 1850 230 230; 16 Nassau St, Dublin).

In the Republic and the North there's a tourist office in almost every big town; most can offer a variety of services including accommodation and attraction reservations, bureau de change services, map and guidebook sales, and free publications. Fáilte Ireland also has six regional offices, which can give more in-depth information on specific areas.

Main Regional Tourist Offices in the Republic

Cork Kerry (☎ 021-425 5100; www.corkkerry.ie; Cork Kerry Tourism, Áras Fáilte, Grand Pde, Cork)
Dublin (www.visitdublin.com; Dublin Tourism Centre, St Andrew's Church, 2 Suffolk St, Dublin)
East Coast & Midlands (☎ 044-48761; www.eastcoast midlands.com; East Coast & Midlands Tourism, Dublin Rd, Mullingar) For Kildare, Laois, Longford, Louth, Meath, North Offaly, Westmeath, Wicklow.
Ireland North-West & Lakelands (☎ 071-916 1201; www.irelandnorthwest.ie; Temple St, Sligo) For Cavan, Donegal, Leitrim, Monaghan, Sligo.
Ireland West (☎ 091-537 700; www.irelandwest.ie; Ireland West Tourism, Aras Failte, Forster St, Galway) For Galway, Roscommon, Mayo.
Shannon Region (☎ 061-361 555; www.shannon regiontourism.ie; Shannon Development, Shannon, Clare) For Clare, Limerick, North Tipperary, South Offaly.
South East (☎ 051-875 823; www.southeastireland .com; South East Tourism, 41 The Quay, Waterford) For Carlow, Kilkenny, Tipperary, Waterford, Wexford.

Tourist Offices Abroad

Outside Ireland, Fáilte Ireland and the NITB unite under the banner Tourism Ireland, with offices in the following countries:
Australia (☎ 02-9299 6177; info@tourismireland.com .au; 5th level, 36 Carrington St, Sydney, NSW 2000)
Canada (☎ 1800 223 6470; info.ca@tourismireland.com; 2 Bloor St West, Suite 1501, Toronto, Ontario M4W 3E2)
France (☎ 01 53 43 12 35; info.fr@tourismireland.com; Tourisme Irlandais, 33 rue de Miromesnil, 75008 Paris)
Germany (☎ 069-9231 8500; info.de@tourismireland .com; Gutleutstrasse 32, 60329 Frankfurt-am-Main)
Italy (☎ 02 5817 7311; Piazzale Cantore 4, 20123 Milan)

Netherlands (☎ 020-530 6050; info@ierland.nl; Iers Nationaal Bureau voor Toerisme, Spuistraat 104, 1012 VA Amsterdam)
New Zealand (☎ 09-379 3708; info@tourismireland .co.nz; Dingwall Bldg, 2nd fl, 87 Queen St, Auckland)
UK (☎ 0800 039 7000; info.gb@tourismireland.com; Nations House,103 Wigmore St, London, W1U 1QS)
USA (☎ 212-1418 0800; info.us@tourismireland.com; 17th fl, 345 Park Ave, New York, NY 10154)

VISAS

UK nationals don't need a passport to visit the Republic, but are advised to carry one (or some other form of photo identification) to prove that they *are* a UK national. It's also necessary to have a passport or photo ID when changing travellers cheques or hiring a car. European Economic Area (EEA) citizens (that is, citizens of EU states, plus Iceland, Liechtenstein and Norway) can enter Ireland with either a passport or a national ID card.

Visitors from outside the EEA will need a passport, which should remain valid for at least six months after their intended arrival.

For EEA nationals and citizens of most Western countries, including Australia, Canada, New Zealand and the USA, no visa is required to visit either the Republic or Northern Ireland, but citizens of India, China and many African countries do need a visa for the Republic. Full visa requirements for visiting the Republic are available online by checking out http://foreign affairs.gov.ie/services/visa; for Northern Ireland's visa requirements see www.uk visas.gov.uk.

EEA nationals can stay for as long as they like, but other visitors can usually remain for up to three months in the Republic and up to six months in the North. To stay longer in the Republic, contact the local garda (police) station or the **Garda National Immigration Bureau** (☎ 01-666 9100; www.garda.ie /angarda/gnib.html; 13-14 Burgh Quay, Dublin 2). To stay longer in Northern Ireland contact the **Home Office** (☎ 0870-606 7766; www.homeoffice.gov .uk; Immigration & Nationality Directorate, Lunar House, 40 Wellesley Rd, Croydon CR9 2BY, UK).

Citizens of member states of the EEA do not need a work visa to work in the Republic. Non-EEA nationals are allowed to work for up to one year in the Republic, if they have a specific job to come to and their employer has obtained permission from the Department of Enterprise, Trade and Employment (see below for Commonwealth exceptions).

Although you don't need an onward or return ticket to enter Ireland, it could help if there's any doubt that you have sufficient funds to support yourself in Ireland.

WOMEN TRAVELLERS

Women travellers will probably find Ireland a blissfully relaxing experience, with little risk of hassle on the street or anywhere else. Nonetheless, you still need to take elementary safety precautions. Walking alone at night, especially in certain parts of Dublin, and hitching are probably unwise. Should you have serious problems, be sure to report them to the local tourist authorities.

There's little need to worry about what you wear in Ireland, and the climate is hardly conducive to topless sunbathing. Finding contraception is not the problem it once was, although anyone on the pill should bring adequate supplies.

The freefone number for the Rape Crisis Centre is ☎ 1800 77 88 88.

WORK

Low-paid seasonal work is available in the tourist industry, usually in restaurants and pubs. Sometimes volunteer work is available in return for bed and board, for example from the **Burren Conservation Trust** (☎ 065-707 6105; jdmn@iol.ie; Admiral's Rest Seafood Restaurant, Fanore).

Citizens of other EU countries can work legally in Ireland. If you don't come from an EU country but have an Irish parent or grandparent, it's fairly easy to obtain Irish citizenship without necessarily renouncing your own nationality, and this opens the door to employment throughout the EU. Obtaining citizenship isn't an overnight procedure, so enquire at an Irish embassy or consulate in your own country.

To work in the North, citizens of Commonwealth countries aged 17 to 27 can apply for a Working Holiday Entry Certificate that allows them to spend two years in the UK and to take work that's 'incidental' to a holiday. You need to apply for the certificate, before you travel, to the British consulate or high commission in your country. In the Republic, a similar system entitled the Working Holiday Authorisation allows citizens of Australia, New Zealand and Canada to work casually so they can take an extended holiday, and again you must be apply while still in your own country.

Commonwealth citizens with a UK-born parent may be eligible for a Certificate of Entitlement to the Right of Abode, which entitles them to live and work in the UK free of immigration control. Commonwealth citizens with a UK-born grandparent, or a grandparent born before 31 March 1922 in what's now the Republic, may qualify for a UK Ancestry Employment Certificate, allowing them to work full time for up to four years in the UK.

Visiting full-time US students aged 18 and over can get a four-month work permit for Ireland through **CIEE** (☎ 617 247 0350; www .ciee.org; 3 Copley Pl, 2nd fl, Boston, MA 02116).

An excellent resource if you're passing through Dublin is the State-funded **Work in Ireland** (☎ 01-878 3156; www.workinireland.ie; 15-17 Eden Quay; ✹ 9am-8pm Mon-Fri, 11am-5pm Sat & Sun), a one-stop help centre, which for €45 a year will help set up a bank account, lay out your CV, set up interviews, help find accommodation, recommend language courses and offer discounts on tours and phone calls. **Nixers** (www.nixers.com) is another useful noticeboard site for those in search of casual labour.

Transport

TRANSPORT

FARE GO

Travel costs throughout this book are for single (one-way) adult fares, unless otherwise stated.

GETTING THERE & AWAY

ENTERING THE COUNTRY

An increase in the number of foreign nationals seeking asylum during the last decade has meant a far more rigorous questioning for those originating from African and Asian countries or from certain parts of Eastern Europe. The border between the Republic and Northern Ireland still exists as a political reality, but there are few if any checkpoints left; for non-EU nationals it is assumed the screening process occurred upon entry to the UK. For information on visa requirements turn to p693.

Passport

EU citizens can travel freely to and from Ireland if bearing official photo ID. Those

---

THINGS CHANGE...

The information in this chapter is particularly vulnerable to change. Check directly with the airline or a travel agency to make sure you understand how a fare (and ticket you may buy) works and be aware of the security requirements for international travel. Shop carefully. The details given in this chapter should be regarded as pointers and are not a substitute for your own careful, up-to-date research.

---

from outside the EU, however, must have a passport that remains valid for six months after entry.

AIR
Airports & Airlines

There are scheduled nonstop flights from Britain, continental Europe and North America to Dublin and Shannon, and good nonstop connections from Britain and continental Europe to Cork.

Cork (ORK; ☎ 021-431 3131; www.corkairport.com)
Dublin (DUB; ☎ 01-814 1111; www.dublinairport.com)
Shannon (SNN; ☎ 061-712 000; www.shannon airport.com)

Other airports in the Republic with scheduled services from Britain:
Donegal (CFN; ☎ 074-954 8284; www.donegalairport .ie; Carrickfinn)
Kerry (KIR; ☎ 066-976 4644; www.kerryairport.ie; Farranfore)
Knock (NOC; ☎ 094-67222; www.knockairport.com)
Waterford (WAT; ☎ 051-875 589; www.flywaterford .com)

In Northern Ireland there are flights to **Belfast International** (BFS; ☎ 028-9448 4848; www .belfastairport.com) from Britain, continental Europe and the USA.

Other airports in Northern Ireland that operate scheduled services from Britain:
Belfast City (BHD; ☎ 028-9093 9093; www.belfastcity airport.com)
Derry (LDY; ☎ 028-7181 0784; www.cityofderry airport.com)

TRANSPORT

The main Irish airlines:

Aer Árann (☎ 1890 462 726; www.aerarann.ie)
A small carrier that operates flights within Ireland and also
to Britain.

Aer Lingus (☎ 01-886 8888; www.aerlingus.com) The
Irish national airline, with direct flights to Britain,
continental Europe and the USA.

Ryanair (☎ 01-609 7800; www.ryanair.com) Ireland's
no-frills carrier with inexpensive services to Britain and
continental Europe.

Nearly all international airlines use Dublin
as their hub. Airlines flying into and out
of Ireland:

Aer Árann (☎ 1890 462 726; www.aerarann.ie)
Aer Lingus (☎ 01-886 8888; www.aerlingus.com)
Aeroflot (☎ 01-844 6166; www.aeroflot.com)
Air Canada (☎ 1800 709 900; www.aircanada.ca)
Air France (☎ 01-605 0383; www.airfrance.com)
Air Malta (☎ 1800 397 400; www.airmalta.com)
Air Wales (☎ 1800 465 193; www.airwales.com)
Alitalia (☎ 01-844 6035; www.alitalia.com)
American Airlines (☎ 01-602 0550; www.aa.com)
Belavia (☎ 061-474 082; www.belaviashannon.com;
Shannon)
BMI British Midland (☎ 01-407 3036;
www.flybmi.com)
British Airways (☎ 1800 626 747; www.british
airways.com)
City Jet (☎ 01-8700 300; www.cityjet.com)
Continental (☎ 1890 925 252; www.continental.com)
CSA Czech Airlines (☎ 01-814 4626; www.csa.cz)
Delta Airlines (☎ 1800 768 080; www.delta.com)
EasyJet (☎ 048-9448 4929; www.easyjet.com; Knock)
Finnair (☎ 01-844 6565; www.finnair.com)
Iberia (☎ 01-407 3017; www.iberia.com)
KLM (☎ 01-663 6900; www.klm.com)
Lufthansa (☎ 01-844 5544; www.lufthansa.com)
Malev Hungarian Airlines (☎ 01-844 4303; www
.malev.com)
Ryanair (☎ 01-609 7800; www.ryanair.com)
Scandinavian Airlines (☎ 01-8445440; www
.scandinavian.net)

Tickets

The dogfight on European routes between
full-service and no-frills airlines has generally resulted in an all-round lowering
of fares, which makes cheap tickets much
easier to get than ever before. You can get
your ticket from a travel agency (in person
or online) or direct from the airline, where
the best deals are usually available online.
Whatever you do, shop around. Internet
travel agencies work well if you're doing a

straightforward trip, but more complicated
travel arrangements are best handled by a
real live travel agent, who knows the system, the options and the best deals. Be sure
to check the terms and conditions of the
cheapest fares before purchasing.

ONLINE BOOKING AGENCIES

Best Fares (www.bestfares.com) American site offering
discounted airfares and hotel rooms.
Cheap Flights (www.cheapflights.com) American- and
British-based site that lists discounted flights and
packages.
ebookers (www.ebookers.com) Irish web-based Internet
travel agency.
Expedia (www.expedia.co.uk) Microsoft's travel site.
Opodo (www.opodo.com) Joint booking service for nine
European airlines.
Priceline (www.priceline.com) American web-based
travel agency.
STA Travel (www.statravel.com) International student
travel agency.
Travelocity (www.travelocity.com) American web-based
travel agency.

Australia & New Zealand

There are no nonstop scheduled air services
from Australia or New Zealand to Ireland;
generally it's cheapest to fly to London or
Amsterdam and continue from there. Most
fares to European destinations can have a
return flight to Dublin tagged on at little
or no extra cost. Round-the-World (RTW)
tickets are another good bet and are often
better value than standard return fares.

The Saturday travel sections of the *Sydney Morning Herald* and Melbourne *Age*
newspapers advertise cheap fares; in New
Zealand, check the *New Zealand Herald*
travel section.

Recommended agencies:

AUSTRALIA

Flight Centre (☎ 133 133; www.flightcentre.com.au)
Shamrock Travel (☎ 03-9602 3700; www.irishtravel
.com.au)
STA Travel (☎ 1300 733 035; www.statravel.com.au)

NEW ZEALAND

Flight Centre (☎ 0800-243 544; www.flightcentre
.co.nz)
STA Travel (☎ 0508-782 872; www.statravel.co.nz)

Canada

Air Canada is the only carrier flying directly
to Ireland, from Toronto to both Dublin

and Shannon. Your best bet for cheaper fares may be to connect to transatlantic gateways in the USA or to fly to London and continue on to Ireland from there. Check the travel sections of the *Globe & Mail*, *Toronto Star*, *Montreal Gazette* or *Vancouver Sun* for the latest offers.

Recommended agencies:

Canadian Affair (☎ 1604-678 6868; www.canadian -affair.com) Cheap one-way fares to British cities.

Flight Centre (☎ 1888-967 5355; www.flightcentre.ca)

Travel CUTS (☎ 866-246 9762; www.travelcuts.com)

Continental Europe

Price wars have made flights to Ireland from continental Europe more affordable than ever. As far as European connections are concerned, **Aer Lingus** (www.aerlingus.com) is now a no-frills airline in all but name, with highly competitive fares to over 40 European cities. **Ryanair** (www.ryanair.com), which kicked off the price wars, is still very much in the fight, but it has the disadvantage of having to use secondary airports in or around the major cities, which can make for rather expensive and time-consuming transfers. There are also some excellent connections with Belfast. Check before you book.

UK

There's a dizzying array of flights between Britain and Ireland. The best deals are available online, and it's not unusual for airport taxes to exceed the base price of the ticket on the lowest fares (generally early morning or late night flights midweek).

Most regional airports in Britain have flights to Dublin and Belfast and some also provide services to Shannon, Cork, Kerry, Knock and Waterford.

USA

In the USA discount travel agencies (consolidators) sell cut-price tickets on scheduled carriers. Aer Lingus is the chief carrier between the USA and Ireland, with flights from New York, Boston, Baltimore, Chicago and Los Angeles to Shannon, Dublin and Belfast. Heavy competition on transatlantic routes into London might make it cheaper to fly there and then continue on to Ireland. The Sunday travel sections of the *New York Times*, *San Francisco Chronicle-Examiner*, *Los Angeles Times* or *Chicago Tribune* list cheap fares.

Some of the more popular travel agencies include:

Ireland Consolidated (☎ 212-661 1999; www .irelandair.com)

STA Travel (☎ 800-781 4040; www.statravel.com)

LAND

Eurolines (www.eurolines.com) has a three-times daily coach and ferry service from London's Victoria Station to Dublin Busáras. For information on border crossings see p700.

SEA

There are many ferry and fast-boat services from Britain and France to Ireland. Prices quoted throughout this section are one-way fares for a single adult on foot/up to two adults with a car, during peak season.

UK & Ireland
FERRY & FAST BOAT

There are numerous services between Britain and Ireland but it's definitely wise to plan ahead as fares can vary considerably, depending on the season, day, time and length of stay. Often, some return fares

don't cost that much more than one-way fares and it's worth keeping an eye out for special offers. International Student Identity Card (ISIC) holders and Hostelling International (HI) members get a reduction on the normal fare.

These shipping lines operate between Britain and Ireland:

Irish Ferries (☎ 0870-517 1717; www.irishferries.com) For ferry and fast-boat services from Holyhead to Dublin, and ferry services from Pembroke to Rosslare.

Isle of Man Steam Packet Company/Sea Cat (☎ 1800 805 055; www.steam-packet.com) Ferry and fast-boat services from Liverpool to Dublin or Belfast via Douglas (on the Isle of Man), and from Troon to Belfast.

Norse Merchant Ferries (in the UK ☎ 0870-600 4321, in the Republic ☎ 01-819 2999; www.norsemerchant .com) Ferry services from Liverpool to Belfast and Dublin.

P&O Irish Sea (in the UK ☎ 0870-242 4777, in the Republic ☎ 01-407 3434; www.poirishsea.com) Ferry and fast-boat services from Larne to Cairnryan and Troon, and ferry services from Liverpool to Dublin.

Stena Line (☎ 0870-570 7070; www.stenaline.com) Ferry services from Holyhead to Dun Laoghaire, Fleetwood to Larne and Stranraer to Belfast, and fast-boat services from Holyhead to Dublin, Fishguard to Rosslare, and Stranraer to Belfast.

Swansea Cork Ferries (in the UK ☎ 01792-456 116, in the Republic ☎ 01-427 1166; www.swansea-cork.ie) Ferry services from Swansea to Cork.

The main routes from the UK to the Republic include:

Fishguard & Pembroke to Rosslare These popular, short ferry crossings take 3½ hours (from Fishguard) or four hours (from Pembroke) and cost around £24/114; the cost drops significantly outside peak season. The fast boat crossing from Fishguard takes just under two hours and costs around £30/130.

Holyhead to Dublin & Dun Laoghaire The ferry crossing takes just over three hours and costs around £24/124. The fast-boat service from Holyhead to Dun Laoghaire takes a little over 1½ hours and costs £30/139.

Liverpool to Dublin The ferry service takes 8½ hours from Liverpool and costs £22/160. Cabins on overnight sailings cost more. The fast-boat service takes four hours and costs up to £35/240.

Swansea to Cork The 10-hour crossing costs around £30/160 but only operates from mid-March to early November.

The main routes from mainland Britain to the North:

Cairnryan to Larne The fast boat takes one hour and costs £19/175. The ferry takes 1¾ hours and costs £14/115.

Fleetwood to Larne The six-hour crossing costs £119; no foot passengers are carried.

Liverpool to Belfast The 8½-hour crossing costs £40/155 (including meals) during the day and £30/235 (including cabin and meals) at night.

Stranraer to Belfast The fast boat takes 1¾ hours and costs £20/130. The ferry takes 3¼ hours and costs £16/85.

Troon to Belfast This fast-boat service takes 2½ hours and costs £35/190.

It's possible to combine bus and ferry tickets from major UK centres to all Irish towns on the bus network, but with the availability of cheap flights it's hardly worth the hassle. The journey between London and Dublin takes about 12 hours and costs £39 one way. The London to Belfast trip takes 13 to 16 hours and costs £46 one way. For details in London contact **Eurolines** (☎ 0870-514 3219; www.eurolines.com).

France
FERRY

Brittany Ferries (in the Republic ☎ 021-427 7801, in France ☎ 02 98 29 28 00; www.brittany-ferries.com) Weekly service from Roscoff to Cork from early April to late September. The crossing takes 14 hours and costs up to €76/433 without accommodation.

Irish Ferries (in Rosslare ☎ 053-33158, in Cherbourg ☎ 02 33 23 44 44, in Roscoff ☎ 02 98 61 17 17; www .irishferries.com) One to three times a week from Roscoff to Rosslare from late April to late September; the crossing time is 17½ hours. Ferries from Cherbourg to Rosslare sail two to four times per week year round except in late January and all of February; crossing time is 20½ hours. Both services cost up to €120/550 without accommodation.

GETTING AROUND

Travelling around Ireland is short, simple and sweet – or maddeningly long and infuriatingly complicated. Distances are relatively short and there's a good network of roads, but public transportation can be infrequent, expensive or both and – especially with trains – not reach many of the more interesting places.

Your own transport is a major advantage and it's worth considering car hire for at least part of your trip. Irish roads are markedly better than they used to be: there's a small, but growing, network of motorways to supplement the huge network of secondary and tertiary roads, although it is still true that smaller, rural roads can make for difficult driving conditions.

If you opt not to drive, a mixture of buses, the occasional taxi, plenty of time, walking and sometimes hiring a bicycle will get you just about anywhere.

AIR
Airlines in Ireland
Ireland's size makes domestic flying unnecessary unless you're in a hurry, but there are flights between Dublin and Belfast, Cork,

Derry, Donegal, Galway, Kerry, Shannon and Sligo, as well as a Belfast–Cork service. Most flights within Ireland take around 30 to 50 minutes.

The only domestic carriers are:
Aer Lingus (information & bookings ☎ 01-886 8844, flight information ☎ 01-705 6705, in Belfast ☎ 028-9442 2888; www.aerlingus.ie) The main domestic airline.
Aer Árann (☎ 1890-462726, in Dublin ☎ 01-814 5240, in Galway ☎ 091-593034, in Cork ☎ 021-814 1058; www.aerarann.ie) Operates flights from Dublin to Belfast, Cork, Derry, Donegal, Galway, Kerry, Knock and Sligo, and

---

FERRY, BUS & TRAIN DISCOUNT DEALS

For Travel Across Europe
Eurail (www.eurail.com) passes are for non-Europeans who have been in Europe for less than six months. They are valid on trains in the Republic, but not in Northern Ireland, and offer discounts on Irish Ferries crossings to France. Passes are cheaper when bought outside Europe. In the USA and Canada phone ☎ 1888-667 9734. In London contact **Rail Europe** (☎ 0870-584 8848; 179 Piccadilly).

InterRail (www.interrail.com) passes give you a 50% reduction on train travel within Ireland and discounts on Irish Ferries and Stena Line services. Passes can be bought at most major train stations and student travel outlets.

For Travel Within Ireland
Travelsave stamps (€10 in the South, £7 in the North) entitle International Student Identity Card (ISIC) holders to a 50% discount on Irish trains and 15% off Bus Éireann services. Holders of an EYC (or EuroFairstamp) can get a 40% discount on trains with a Travelsave stamp. The stamps are available from Usit offices (www.usit.ie).

Iarnród Éireann's Faircard (€10) gives up to 50% reductions on any intercity journey to people aged under 26, while the Weekender (€7) gives up to 30% off (Friday to Tuesday) to people aged 26 and over.

Unlimited-Travel Tickets For Buses & Trains
Irish Rambler tickets cover bus-only travel within the Republic. They cost €53 (for three days' travel out of eight consecutive days), €116 (eight days out of 15) or €168 (15 days out of 30).

Irish Rover tickets combine services on Bus Éireann and Ulsterbus. They cost €68 (for three days' travel out of eight consecutive days), €152 (eight days out of 15) and €226 (15 days out of 30).

Iarnród Éireann Explorer tickets cover train travel in the Republic. They cost €127 (for five days travel out of 15 consecutive days) or €157.50 to include Northern Ireland.

Irish Explorer rail and bus tickets (€194) allow eight days' travel out of 15 consecutive days on trains and buses within the Republic.

Freedom of Northern Ireland passes allow unlimited travel on NIR, Ulsterbus and Citybus services for £13 for one day, £32 (for three out of eight consecutive days), or £47 (for seven consecutive days).

Emerald Card gives you unlimited travel throughout Ireland on all Iarnród Éireann, NIR, Bus Éireann, Dublin Bus, Ulsterbus and Citybus services. The card costs €218 (for eight days out of 15) or €375 (for 15 days out of 30).

Children aged under 16 pay half-price for all these passes and for all normal tickets. Children aged under three travel for free on public transport. You can buy the above passes at most major train and bus stations in Ireland. Although they're good value, many of them make economic sense only if you're planning to travel around Ireland at the speed of light.

flights to the Aran Islands from Galway, and a Belfast to Cork route.

BICYCLE

Ireland is a great place for bicycle touring, despite bad road surfaces in places and inclement weather. If you intend to cycle in the west, the prevailing winds mean it's easier to cycle from south to north. Both **Irish Cycling Safaris** (☎ 01-260 0749; www.cycling safaris.com; Belfield Bike Shop, UCD, Dublin 4) and **Go Ireland** (☎ 066-976 2094; www.goactivities.com; Old Orchard House, Killorglin, Co Kerry) organise tours for groups of cyclists in the southwest, the southeast, Clare, Connemara, Donegal and Antrim.

Bicycles can be transported by bus if there's enough room; the charge varies. By train the cost varies from €3 to €10 for a one-way journey, but bikes are not allowed on certain train routes, including the Dublin Area Rapid Transit (DART); check with **Iarnród Éireann** (☎ 01-836 3333).

Typical bicycle hire costs are €15 to €25 per day or €60 to €100 per week plus a deposit of around €100. There are many local independent outlets, but several dealers have outlets around the country:

Irish Cycle Hire (☎ 041-685 3772; www.irishcyclehire .com; Unit 6, Enterprise Centre, Ardee, Co Louth)

Raleigh Ireland (☎ 01-626 1333; www.raleigh.ie; Raleigh House, Kylemore Rd, Dublin) Ireland's biggest rental dealer.

Rent-a-Bike Ireland (☎ 061-416983; www.ireland rentabike.com; 1 Patrick St, Limerick, Co Limerick)

BOAT
Ferry
There are many boat services to islands lying off the coast, including to the Aran and Skellig Islands to the west, the Saltee Islands to the southeast, and Tory and Rathlin Islands to the north. Ferries also operate across rivers, inlets and loughs, providing useful short cuts, particularly for cyclists.

Cruises are very popular on the 258km-long Shannon–Erne Waterway and on a variety of other lakes and loughs. The tourist offices only recommend operators registered with them. Details of nontourist board–affiliated boat trips are given under the relevant sections throughout this book.

BORDER CROSSINGS

Security has been progressively scaled down in Northern Ireland in recent years and all border crossings with the Republic are now open and generally unstaffed. Permanent checkpoints have been removed and ramps levelled. On major routes your only indication that you have crossed the border will be a change in road signs and the colour of number plates and postboxes.

BUS

Bus Éireann (☎ 01-836 6111; www.buseireann.ie; Busáras, Store St, Dublin) is the Republic's bus line and offers an extensive network throughout the south. Private buses compete – often very favourably – with Bus Éireann in the Republic and also run where the national buses are irregular or absent. The larger companies will usually carry bikes for free but you should always check in advance to avoid surprises. **Ulsterbus** (☎ 028-9066 6600; www.ulsterbus.co.uk; Milewater Rd, Belfast) is the only bus service in Northern Ireland.

Bus Passes
Details of special deals and passes are given in the boxed text on p699.

Costs
Bus travel is much cheaper than train travel, and private buses often charge less than Bus Éireann. Generally, return fares cost little more than a one-way fare.

Some sample one-way (single) bus fares:

service	cost	duration (hrs)	frequency (Mon-Sat)
Belfast–Dublin	£13.10	3	7
Derry–Belfast	£8.80	1¾	10+
Derry–Galway	£19.30	5¼	4
Dublin–Cork	€16	4½	6
Dublin–Donegal	€16	4	5
Dublin–Rosslare	€15	3	12
Dublin–Tralee	€21	6	12
Dublin–Waterford	€10.50	2¾	7
Killarney–Cork	€12.60	2	12
Killarney–Waterford	€17.60	4½	12

Reservations
Bus Éireann bookings can be made online but you can't reserve a seat for a particular service.

CAR & MOTORCYCLE
Ireland's new-found affluence means there are far more cars on the road, and the

building of new roads and the upgrading of existing ones just cannot keep pace. Be prepared for delays, especially at holiday weekends. **AA Roadwatch** (☎ 1550 131 811; www .aaroadwatch.ie) provides traffic information in the Republic.

In the Republic, speed-limit and distance signs are in kilometres (although the occasional older white sign shows distances in miles); in the North, speed-limit and distance signs are in miles.

You'll need a good road map and sense of humour to deal with the severe lack of signposts in the Republic, and on minor roads be prepared for lots of potholes.

Petrol is considerably cheaper in the Republic than in the North. Most service stations accept payment by credit card, but some small, remote ones may take cash only.

Bring Your Own Vehicle

It's easy to take your own vehicle to Ireland and there are no specific procedures involved, but you should carry a vehicle registration document as proof that it's yours.

Automobile association members should ask for a Card of Introduction entitling you to services offered by sister organisations (maps, information, breakdown assistance, legal advice etc), usually free of charge.

Automobile Association (AA; www.aaireland.ie) Northern Ireland (☎ 0870-950 0600, breakdown assistance ☎ 0800-667 788); Republic (in Dublin ☎ 01-617 9999, in Cork ☎ 021-425 2444, breakdown assistance ☎ 1800-667 788)

Royal Automobile Club (RAC; www.rac.ie) Northern Ireland (☎ 0800-029 029, breakdown assistance ☎ 0800-828 282); Republic (☎ 1890 483 483)

Driving Licence

Unless you have an EU licence, which is treated like an Irish one, your driving licence is valid for 12 months from the date of entry to Ireland, but you should have held it for two years prior to that. If you don't hold an EU licence it's a good idea to obtain an International Driving Permit (IDP) from your home automobile association before you leave. Your home-country licence is usually enough to hire a car for three months.

You must carry your driving licence at all times.

Hire

Car hire in Ireland is expensive, so you're often better off making arrangements in your home country with some sort of package deal. In July and August it's wise to book well ahead. Most cars are manual; automatic cars are available but they're more expensive to hire.

The international hire companies and the major local operators have offices all over Ireland. **Nova Car Hire** (www.rentacar-ireland .com) acts as an agent for Alamo, Budget, European and National, and offers greatly discounted rates. In the Republic typical weekly high-season hire rates with Nova are around €150 for a small car, €185 for a medium-sized car, and €320 for a five-seater people carrier. In the North, similar cars are marginally more expensive.

When hiring a car be sure to check if the price includes collision-damage waiver (CDW), insurance (eg for car theft and windscreen damage), value-added tax (VAT) and unlimited mileage.

If you're travelling from the Republic into Northern Ireland it's important to be sure that your insurance covers journeys to the North. People aged under 21 aren't allowed to hire a car; for the majority of hire companies you have to be aged at least 23 and have had a valid driving licence for a minimum of one year. Some companies in the Republic won't rent to you if you're aged 74 or over; there's no upper age limit in the North.

You can't hire motorbikes and mopeds.

Insurance

All cars on public roads must be insured. If you are bringing your own vehicle, check that your insurance will cover you in Ireland.

Parking

Ireland is tiny and the Irish love their cars; the numbers just don't add up and parking is an expensive and difficult nightmare. Parking in towns and cities is either by meter, 'pay and display' tickets or disc parking (discs, which rotate to display the time you park your car, are available from newsagencies).

Purchase

It's more expensive to buy a car in Ireland than most other European countries. If you

ROAD DISTANCES (KM)

	Athlone	Belfast	Cork	Derry	Donegal	Dublin	Galway	Kilkenny	Killarney	Limerick	Rosslare Harbour	Shannon Airport	Sligo	Waterford	Wexford
Athlone	---														
Belfast	227	---													
Cork	219	424	---												
Derry	209	117	428	---											
Donegal	183	180	402	69	---										
Dublin	127	167	256	237	233	---									
Galway	93	306	209	272	204	212	---								
Kilkenny	116	284	148	335	309	114	172	---							
Killarney	232	436	87	441	407	304	193	198	---						
Limerick	121	323	105	328	296	193	104	113	111	---					
Rosslare Harbour	201	330	208	397	391	153	274	98	275	211	---				
Shannon Airport	133	346	128	351	282	218	93	135	135	25	234	---			
Sligo	117	206	336	135	66	214	138	245	343	232	325	218	---		
Waterford	164	333	126	383	357	163	220	48	193	129	82	152	293	---	
Wexford	184	309	187	378	372	135	253	80	254	190	19	213	307	61	---

do buy a car (or intend to import one from another country) you must pay vehicle registration tax and motor tax, and take out insurance.

Road Rules

A copy of Ireland's road rules is available from tourist offices. Here are some of the most basic rules:

- Drive on the left, overtake to the right.
- Safety belts must be worn by the driver and all passengers.
- Children aged under 12 aren't allowed to sit on the front seats.
- Motorcyclists and their passengers must wear helmets.
- When entering a roundabout, give way to the right.
- Speed limits are 120km/h on motorways, 100km/h on national roads, 80km/h on regional and local roads and 50km/h or as signposted in towns.
- The legal alcohol limit is 80mg of alcohol per 100ml of blood or 35mg on the breath (roughly two units of alcohol for a man and one for a woman).

HITCHING

Hitching is increasingly less popular in Ireland, even though it's still pretty easy compared to other European countries. Travellers who decide to hitch should understand that they are taking a small but potentially serious risk, and we don't recommend it. If you do plan to travel by thumb, remember it's illegal to hitch on motorways.

LOCAL TRANSPORT

There are comprehensive local bus networks in Dublin (Dublin Bus), Belfast (Citybus) and some other larger towns. The Dublin Area Rapid Transport (DART) line in Dublin runs roughly the length of the city's coastline, while the brand new Luas tram system has two very popular lines. Taxis tend to be expensive.

TOURS

If your time is limited it might be worth considering an organised tour, though it's cheaper to see things independently, and Ireland is small enough for you to get to

even the most remote places within a few hours. Tours can be booked through travel agencies, tourist offices in the major cities, or directly through the tour companies themselves.

Bus Éireann (☎ 01-836 6111; www.buseireann.ie; 59 Upper O'Connell St, Dublin) Runs day tours to various parts of the Republic and the North.

CIE Tours International (☎ 01-703 1888; www.cie tours.ie; 35 Lower Abbey St, Dublin) Runs four- to 10-day coach tours of the Republic and the North, including accommodation and meals. The Taste of Ireland tour (five days) takes in Blarney, the Ring of Kerry, Killarney, the Cliffs of Moher and the region around the River Shannon (€598 in high season).

Gray Line Tours (☎ 01-872 9010; www.irishcitytours .com; 33 Bachelor's Walk, Dublin) Located in Dublin

and offers half- and full-day tours (€20) from Dublin to Newgrange, Glendalough and north Dublin, and three- and four-day trips to the Ring of Kerry (€282 to €348).

Over the Top & Into the West Tours (☎ 01-869 0769; www.overthetoptours.com) Daily historical and heritage tours of Wicklow (€24), the Boyne Valley (€26), three-day tours of the west of Ireland (€255) and a five-day tour of Kerry and Cork (€370).

Paddywagon Tours (☎ 01-672 6007; www.paddy wagontours.com) Activity-filled three- and six-day tours all over Ireland with friendly tour guides. Accommodation is in IHH hostels. Its Jump On Jump Off tour of Ireland (€130) allows you to stay in any place en route for as long as you like and pick up a later bus.

Ulsterbus Tours (☎ 028-9033 7004; www.ulsterbus .co.uk) Runs a large number of day trips throughout the North and the Republic.

It's worth checking **GoIreland.com** (☎ 1800 668 668; www.goireland.com) for an array of holiday packages.

For train enthusiasts, **Railtours Ireland** (☎ 01-856 0045; www.railtours.ie; 58 Lower Gardiner St, Dublin 1) organises a series of one- and two-day train trips in association with Iarnród Éireann. A three-day trip from Dublin to Cork, Blarney Castle and Kerry costs €299.

TRAIN

Iarnród Éireann (Irish Rail; ☎ 01-836 2222; www.irish rail.ie; 35 Lower Abbey St, Dublin) operates trains in the Republic on routes that fan out from Dublin. The system is limited though: there's no north–south route along the western coast, no network in Donegal, and no direct connections from Waterford to Cork or Killarney. **Northern Ireland Railways** (NIR; ☎ 028-9089 9411; Belfast Central Station) runs four routes from Belfast. One links with the system in the Republic via Newry to Dublin; the other three go east to Bangor, northeast to Larne and northwest to Derry via Coleraine.

Costs

Train travel is more expensive than bus travel and one-way fares are particularly poor value – a midweek return ticket is often about the same as a one-way fare. First-class tickets cost around €5 to €10 more than the standard fare for a single journey.

Some sample one-way fares:

service	cost	duration (hrs)	frequency (Mon-Sat)
Belfast–Dublin	£22.50	2	8
Dublin–Cork	€52.50	3¼	8
Dublin–Galway	€28	3¼	5
Dublin–Limerick	€40	2½	13
Dublin–Sligo	€24	3	3
Dublin–Tralee	€55	4½	8
Dublin–Waterford	€22	2½	7

Reservations

Iarnród Éireann takes reservations for all its train services. You need to fax your details (name, numbers of passengers, date and time of service, credit-card number and expiry date) to ☎ 01-703 4136.

Health

CONTENTS

BEFORE YOU GO

While Ireland has excellent health care, prevention is the key to staying healthy while abroad. A little planning before departure, particularly for pre-existing illnesses, will save trouble later. Bring medications in their original, clearly labelled, containers. A signed and dated letter from your physician describing your medical conditions and medications, including generic names, is also a good idea. If carrying syringes or needles, be sure to have a physician's letter documenting their medical necessity. Carry a spare pair of contact lenses and glasses, and take your optical prescription with you.

INSURANCE

If you're an EU citizen, an E111 form, available from health centres or, in the UK, post offices, covers you for most medical care. E111 won't cover you for nonemergencies, or emergency repatriation home. Citizens from other countries should find out if there is a reciprocal arrangement for free medical care between their country and Ireland. If you do need health insurance, make sure you get a policy that covers you for the worst possible case, such as an accident requiring an emergency flight home. Find out in advance if your insurance plan will make payments directly to providers, or reimburse you later for overseas health expenditures.

RECOMMENDED VACCINATIONS

No jabs are required to travel to Ireland. The World Health Organization, however, recommends that all travellers should be covered for diphtheria, tetanus, measles, mumps, rubella, polio and hepatitis B, regardless of their destination.

IN TRANSIT

DEEP VEIN THROMBOSIS (DVT)

Blood clots may form in the legs during plane flights, chiefly because of prolonged immobility. The longer the flight, the greater the risk. The chief symptom of deep vein thrombosis is swelling or pain of the foot, ankle, or calf, often on just one side. When a blood clot travels to the lungs, it may cause chest pain and difficulty breathing. Travellers with any of these symptoms should immediately seek medical attention.

To prevent the development of DVT on long flights you should walk about the cabin, contract the leg muscles while sitting, drink plenty of fluids and avoid alcohol and tobacco.

JET LAG & MOTION SICKNESS

To avoid jet lag (quite common when crossing more than five time zones) try drinking plenty of nonalcoholic fluids and eating light meals. Upon arrival, get exposure to natural sunlight and readjust your schedule (for meals, sleep etc) as soon as possible.

Antihistamines such as dimenhydrinate (Dramamine) or meclizine (Antivert, Bonine) are quite often the first choice for treating motion sickness. A herbal alternative is ginger.

IN IRELAND

AVAILABILITY & COST OF HEALTH CARE

Excellent health care is readily available and for minor self-limiting illnesses pharmacists can give valuable advice and sell over-the-counter medication. They can also advise

HEALTH

when more specialised help is required and point you in the right direction.

TRAVELLERS' DIARRHOEA

If you develop diarrhoea, be sure to drink plenty of fluids, preferably in the form of an oral rehydration solution such as dioralyte. If diarrhoea is bloody, persists for more than 72 hours or is accompanied by fever, shaking, chills or severe abdominal pain you will need to seek urgent medical attention.

ENVIRONMENTAL HAZARDS
Heatstroke

Heat exhaustion (yes, even in Ireland it can still happen!) occurs following excessive fluid loss with insufficient replacement of fluids and salt. Symptoms include headache, dizziness and tiredness. Dehydration is already happening by the time you feel thirsty – aim

to drink sufficient water to produce pale, diluted urine. To treat heat exhaustion drink water and/or fruit juice, and cool the body with cold water and fans.

Hypothermia

Hypothermia occurs when the body loses heat faster than it can produce it. As ever, proper preparation will reduce the risks of getting it. Even on a hot day in the mountains the weather can change rapidly, so carry waterproof garments, warm layers and a hat, and inform others of your route.

Hypothermia starts with shivering, loss of judgment and clumsiness. Without rewarming, the sufferer deteriorates into apathy, confusion and coma. Prevent further heat loss by seeking shelter, warm dry clothing, hot sweet drinks and shared body warmth.

Language

CONTENTS

In 2003 the government introduced the official languages act whereby all official documents, street signs and official titles must be either in Gaeilge or bilingual. While Gaeilge (Irish) is the official language, it's only spoken in isolated pockets of rural Ireland known as Gaeltacht areas, the main ones being Cork *(Chorcaí)*, Donegal *(Dhún na nGall)*, Galway *(Gaillimhe)*, Kerry *(Chiarraí)* andd Mayo *(Mhaigh Eo)*.

Irish is a compulsory subject in schools for those aged six to fifteen, but Gaeilge classes have traditionally been thoroughly academic and unimaginative, leading most kids to resent it as a waste of time. Ask people outside the Gaeltacht areas if they can speak Irish and nine out of 10 of them will probably reply, *ahhh, cupla focal* (a couple of words) and they generally mean it. It's a pity that the treatment of Irish in schools has been so heavy-handed because many adults say they regret not having a greater grasp of it. At long last, and for the first time since the formation of the state, a new Gaeilge curriculum has recently been introduced that will cut the hours devoted to the subject but make the lessons more fun, practical and celebratory.

PRONUNCIATION

Irish has three main dialects: Connaught Irish (Galway and northern Mayo), Munster Irish (Cork, Kerry and Waterford) and Ulster Irish (Donegal). The pronunciation guidelines given here are an anglicised version of modern standard Irish, which is essentially an amalgam of the three.

Vowels

Irish divides vowels into long (those with an accent) and short (those without) and, more importantly, broad (**a**, **á**, **o**, **ó**, **u** and **ú**) and slender (**e**, **é**, **i** and **í**), which can affect the pronunciation of preceding consonants.

a	as in 'cat'
á	as in 'saw'
e	as in 'bet'
é	as in 'hey'
i	as in 'sit'
í	as in 'marine'
o	as in 'son'
ó	as in 'low'
u	as in 'put'
ú	as in 'rule'

Consonants

Though you've probably never seen pairs and clusters such as **mh** and **bhf**, consonants are generally less problematic in Irish than vowels. Most are pronounced as they are in English.

bh	as the 'v' in 'voice'
bhf	as the 'w' in 'well'
c	always hard, as in 'cat'
ch	as the 'ch' in Scottish *loch*
d	as in 'do' when followed by a broad vowel; as the 'j' in 'jug' when followed by a slender vowel
dh	as the 'g' in 'gap' when followed by a broad vowel; as the 'y' in 'year' when followed by a slender vowel
mh	as the 'w' in 'well'
s	as in 'said' when before a broad vowel; as the 'sh' in ship when before a slender vowel and at the end of a word
t	as the 't' in 'toast' when before a broad vowel; as the 'ch' in 'church' before a slender vowel
th	as the 'h' in 'house'; as the 't' in 'mat or silent at the end of a word

MAKING CONVERSATION

Hello.

Dia duit.   dee·a gwit

(lit: God be with you)

Hello. (reply)

Dia is Muire duit.   dee·as moyra gwit

(lit: God and Mary be with you)

LANGUAGE

CUPLA FOCAL

Here are a few cheeky phrases *os Gaeilge* (in Irish), which can help you impress the locals:

amadáin – fool
Dún do chlab! – Shut your mouth!
Ní ólfaidh mé go brách arís! (knee ohl-hee mey gu brawkh u-reeshch) – I'm never ever drinking again!
Póg ma thóin! – Kiss my arse!
Sláinte! (slawn-cha) – Your health! (cheers)
Táim go maith! (thawm go mah) – I'm good!

Good morning.
Maidin mhaith. — maw·jin wah
Good night.
Oíche mhaith. — eek·heh wah
Goodbye.
Slán leat. — slawn lyat
(said by person leaving)
Goodbye.
Slán agat. — slawn agut
(said by person staying)
Welcome.
Ceád míle fáilte. — kade meela fawlcha
(lit: 100,000 welcomes)
Thank you (very) much.
Go raibh (míle) — goh rev (meela)
maith agat. — mah agut
..., (if you) please.
..., más é do thoil é. — ... maws ay do hall ay
Excuse me.
Gabh mo leithscéal. — gamoh lesh scale
How are you?
Conas a tá tú? — kunas aw taw too
(I'm) fine/good/OK.
(Tá mé) go maith. — (taw may) goh mah
What's your name?
Cad is ainm duit? — kod is anim dwit?
My name is (Sean Frayne).
(Sean Frayne) is — (shawn frain) is
ainm dom. — anim dohm
Yes/It is.
Tá/Sea. — taw/sheh
No/It isn't.
Níl/Ní hea. — neel/nee heh
another/one more
ceann eile — kyawn ella
nice
go deas — goh dyass

BASIC WORDS & PHRASES

What is this/that?
Cad é seo/sin? — kod ay shoh/shin

I don't understand.
Ní thuigim. — nee higgim
I'd like to go to ...
Ba mhaith liom — baw wah lohm
dul go dtí ... — dull go dee ...
I'd like to buy ...
Ba mhaith liom ... — bah wah lohm ...
a cheannach — a kyanukh

here	anseo	onshoh
there	ansin	onshin
open	oscáilte	uskawlta
closed	dúnta	doonta
big	mór	moor
small	beag	byawg
slowly	go mall	goh mohl
quickly	go tapa	goh topuh
fine (weather)	go breá	goh braw
awful (weather)	go dona	goh dohna
shop	siopa	shoppa
town	baile	bollyeh
town square	lár an bhaile	lawr an vallyeh

SIGNS

Leithreas	lehrass	Toilet
Fir	fear	Men
Mna	m'naw	Women
Gardaí	gardee	Police
Oifig An Phoist	iffig ohn fwisht	Post Office

DAYS & MONTHS

Monday	Dé Luaín	day loon
Tuesday	Dé Máirt	day maart
Wednesday	Dé Ceádaoin	day kaydeen
Thursday	Déardaoin	daredeen
Friday	Dé hAoine	day heeneh
Saturday	Dé Sathairn	day sahern
Sunday	Dé Domhnaigh	day downick

NUMBERS

1	haon	hayin
2	dó	doe
3	trí	tree
4	ceathair	kahirr
5	cúig	koo-ig
6	sé	shay
7	seacht	shocked
8	hocht	hukt
9	naoi	nay
10	deich	jeh
11	haon déag	hayin jague
12	dó dhéag	doe yague
20	fiche	feekhe

Glossary

12th of July – the day the *Orange Order* marches to celebrate King William III's victory over the Catholic King James II at the Battle of the Boyne in 1690

An Óige – literally 'The Youth'; Republic of Ireland Youth Hostel Association

An Taisce – National Trust for the Republic of Ireland

Anglo-Norman – Norman, English and Welsh peoples who invaded Ireland in the 12th century

Apprentice Boys – *loyalist* organisation founded in 1814 to commemorate the Great Siege of Derry in August every year

ard – literally 'high'; Irish place name

ard rí – Irish 'high king'

bailey – outer wall of a castle

bawn – area surrounded by walls outside the main castle, acting as a defence and as a place to keep cattle in times of trouble

beehive hut – circular stone building shaped like an old-fashioned beehive

Black and Tans – British recruits to the Royal Irish Constabulary shortly after WWI, noted for their brutality

Blarney Stone – bending over backwards to kiss this sacred rock in Blarney Castle, County Cork, is said to bestow the gift of the gab, or allow you to 'gain the privilege of telling lies for seven years'

bodhrán – *bow*-rawn; hand-held goatskin drum

bollocks – male genitalia; used as a general expression of dismay

Bord Na Móna – the Irish turf board, charged with harvesting peat for use in power plants

boreen – small lane or roadway

Bronze Age – earliest metal-using period, around 2500 BC to 300 BC in Ireland; after the Stone Age and before the *Iron Age*

B-specials – Northern Irish auxiliary police force, disbanded in 1971

bullaun – stone with a depression, probably used as a mortar for grinding medicine or food and often found on monastic sites

CAC IRA – Continuity Army Council of the *IRA*, a breakaway group

caher – circular area enclosed by stone walls

cairn – mound of stones heaped over a prehistoric grave

camogie – women's hurling

cashel – stone-walled circular fort; see also *ráth*

cath – literally 'battle'; Irish place name

céilidh – *kay*-lee; session of traditional music and dancing; also called ceili

Celtic Tiger – nickname of the Irish economy during the growth years from 1990 to about 2002

Celts – Iron Age warrior tribes that arrived in Ireland around 300 BC and controlled the country for 1000 years

ceol – music

cha – slang term for tea, as in a 'cup of cha'

champ – a dish of mashed potatoes with spring onions or leeks

chancel – eastern end of a church, where the altar is situated, reserved for the clergy and choir

chipper – slang term for fish 'n' chips fast-food restaurant

cill – literally 'church'; Irish place name; also known as kill

cillín – literally 'little cell'; a hermitage, or sometimes a small, isolated burial ground for unbaptised children and other 'undesirables'

Claddagh ring – ring worn in much of *Connaught* since the mid-18th century, with a crowned heart nestling between two hands; if the heart points towards the hand then the wearer is taken or married, towards the fingertip means he or she is looking for a mate

clochán – dry-stone beehive hut from the early Christian period

Connaught – one of the four ancient provinces of Ireland, made up of counties Galway, Leitrim, Mayo, Roscommon and Sligo; sometimes spelt Connacht.

Continuity IRA – anti-Agreement splinter *republican* group, opposed to any deal not based on a united Ireland

control zone – area of a town centre, usually the main street, where parked cars must not, for security reasons, be left unattended

craic – conversation, gossip, fun, good times; also known as crack

crannóg – artificial island made in a lake to provide habitation in a good defensive position

creel – basket

crios – multicoloured woven woollen belt traditionally worn in the Aran Islands

cromlech – see *dolmen*

cú – dog

culchie – derogatory nickname used by Dubliners for anyone not from the capital

currach – rowing boat made of a framework of laths covered with tarred canvas; also known as cúrach

Dáil – lower house of the Republic of Ireland Parliament

dairtheach – oratory, a small room set aside for private prayer

DART – Dublin Area Rapid Transport train line

delft – glazed blue and white earthenware from Holland; in Ireland the word refers to any kind of dishware
demesne – landed property close to a house or castle
diamond – town square
dolmen – tomb chamber or portal tomb made of vertical stones topped by a huge capstone, dating from around 2000 BC
draoícht – enchantment
drumlin – rounded hill formed by retreating glaciers
Dúchas – government department in charge of parks, monuments and gardens in the Republic; formerly known as the Office of Public Works
dún – fort, usually constructed of stone
DUP – Democratic Unionist Party; founded principally by Ian Paisley in 1971 in hard-line opposition to unionist policies as held by the *UUP*; it publicly opposes the Good Friday Agreement but is willing to work with the other parties in the Assembly

Éire – Irish name for the Republic of Ireland
esker – gravel ridge

Fáilte Ireland – literally 'Welcome Board'; Irish Tourist Board
Fianna – mythical band of warriors who feature in many tales of ancient Ireland
Fianna Fáil – literally 'Warriors of Ireland'; a major political party in the Republic of Ireland, originating from the *Sinn Féin* faction opposed to the 1921 treaty with Britain
Fine Gael – literally 'Tribe of the Gael'; a major political party in the Republic, originating from the *Sinn Féin* faction that favoured the 1921 treaty with Britain; formed the first government of independent Ireland
fir – men, singular *fear*; sign on men's toilets
fleadh – festival
fulacht fiadh – *Bronze Age* cooking place

gaelscoileanna – Irish-medium school
Gaeltacht – Irish-speaking
gallery grave – tunnel-shaped burial chamber
gallóglí – mercenary soldiers of the 14th to 15th century; anglicised to gallowglasses
garda – Irish Republic police; plural *gardaí*
ghillie – fishing or hunting guide; also known as ghilly
gob – mouth; from Irish word gob, meaning bird's beak or bill
gort – literally 'field'; Irish place name
grá – love

Hibernia – literally 'Land of Winter'; Roman name for Ireland; the Romans had confused Ireland with Iceland
hill fort – usually dating from the *Iron Age*, hill forts are formed by a ditch that follows the contour of the hill to surround and fortify the summit
HINI – Hostelling International of Northern Ireland

húicéir – traditional Galway vessel; also known as a hooker
hurling – Irish sport similar to hockey
Hunger, the – how the Irish sometimes refer to the Great Famine of 1845–49

Iarnród Éireann – Republic of Ireland Railways
INLA – Irish National Liberation Association; formed in 1975 as an *IRA* splinter group unhappy at the cease-fire; it has maintained its own cease-fire since 1998
IRA – Irish Republican Army; the largest republican paramilitary organisation, founded 80 years ago with the aim to fight for a united Ireland; in 1969 the IRA split into the Official IRA and the Provisional IRA; the Official IRA is no longer active and the PIRA has become the IRA
IRB – Irish Republican Brotherhood; a secret society founded in 1858 and revived in the early 20th century; believed in independence, through violence if necessary, and was a precursor to the *IRA*; also known as the Fenians
Iron Age – in Ireland this lasted from the end of the *Bronze Age*, around 300 BC (the arrival of the Celts), to the arrival of Christianity, around the 5th century AD

jackeen – derogatory nickname used to describe anyone from Dublin; originally used to describe Dubliners who waved Union Jacks during Queen Victoria's visit in 1901
jarvey – driver of a *jaunting car*
jaunting car – Killarney's traditional horse-drawn transport

knackered – slang for tired or worn out

Lambeg drum – very large drum associated with Protestant *loyalist* marches
Leinster – one of the four ancient provinces of Ireland, made up of counties Carlow, Dublin, Kildare, Kilkenny, Laois, Longford, Louth, Meath, Offaly, West Meath, Wexford and Wicklow
leithreas – toilets
leprechaun – mischievous elf or sprite from Irish folklore
lough – lake, long narrow bay or arm of the sea
loyalist – person, usually a Northern Irish Protestant, insisting on the continuation of Northern Ireland's links with Britain
loyalist orders – consists mainly of the *Orange Order* and the *Apprentice Boys* committed to the union with the UK
Luas – Light Rail Transit system in Dublin; Irish for 'speed'
LVF – Loyalist Volunteer Force; an extreme *loyalist paramilitary* group opposed to the current peace process. It has been on cease-fire since 1998

marching season – *Orange Order* parades, which take place from Easter and throughout summer to celebrate the victory by Protestant King William III of Orange over

Catholic James II in the Battle of the Boyne on 12 July 1690, and the union with Britain

Mesolithic – also known as the Middle Stone Age; time of the first human settlers in Ireland, about 8000 BC to 4000 BC

midden – refuse heap left by a prehistoric settlement

mná – women; sign on women's toilets

motte – early Norman fortification consisting of a raised, flattened mound with a keep on top; when attached to a *bailey* it is known as a motte-and-*bailey* fort, many of which were built in Ireland until the early 13th century

Munster – one of the four ancient provinces of Ireland, made up of counties Clare, Cork, Kerry, Limerick, Tipperary and Waterford

naomh – holy or saint

nationalism – belief in a reunited Ireland

nationalist – proponent of a united Ireland

Neolithic – also known as the New Stone Age; a period characterised by settled agriculture lasting from around 4000 BC to 2500 BC in Ireland; followed by the *Bronze Age*

NIR – Northern Ireland Railways

NITB – Northern Ireland Tourist Board

NNR – National Nature Reserves

NUI – National University of Ireland; made up of branches in Dublin, Cork, Galway and Limerick

North, the – political entity of Northern Ireland, not the northernmost geographic part of Ireland

Ogham stone – Ogham (*o*-am) was the earliest form of writing in Ireland, using a variety of notched strokes placed above, below or across a keyline, usually on stone

Oireachtas – Parliament of the Republic, consisting of a lower and upper house, the *Dáil* and Senate

Orange Order – founded in 1795, the Orange Order is the largest Protestant organisation in Northern Ireland with a membership of up to 100,000; name commemorates the victory of King William of Orange in the Battle of the Boyne

Orangemen – members of the *Orange Order*; must be male

óstán – hotel

Palladian – style of architecture developed by Andrea Palladio (1508–80) based on ancient Roman architecture

paramilitaries – armed illegal organisations, either *loyalist* or *republican*, usually associated with the use of violence and crime for political and economic gain

Partition – division of Ireland in 1921

passage grave – Celtic tomb with a chamber reached by a narrow passage, typically buried in a mound

penal laws – laws passed in the 18th century forbidding Catholics from buying land, holding public office and so on

Plantation – settlement of Protestant migrants

(sometimes known as Planters) in Ireland in the 17th century

PSNI – Police Service of Northern Ireland

poteen – *pot*-cheen; illegally brewed potato-based firewater

Prod – slang for Northern Irish Protestant

provisionals – Provisional IRA, formed after a break with the official *IRA* who are now largely inconsequential; named after the provisional government declared in 1916, they have been the main force combating the British army in the *North;* also known as provos

PUP – Progressive Unionist Party; a small unionist party seen as a political front for the *UVF*, it is pro the Good Friday Agreement

rashers – Irish bacon

ráth – circular fort with earth banks around a timber wall

Real IRA – splinter movement of the *IRA* and opposed to *Sinn Féin's* support of the Good Friday Agreement; the Real IRA was responsible for the Omagh bombing in 1998 in which 29 people died; subsequently called a cease-fire but has been responsible for bombs in Britain and other acts of violence

Red Hand Commandos – illegal *loyalist paramilitary* group

Red Hand Defenders – breakaway *loyalist paramilitary* group formed in 1998 by dissident *UFF* and *LVF* members

Republic of Ireland – the 26 counties of the *South*

republican – supporter of a united Ireland

republicanism – belief in a united Ireland, sometimes referred to as militant nationalism

rí – petty kings

ring fort – circular habitation area surrounded by banks and ditches, used from the *Bronze Age* right through to the Middle Ages, particularly in the early Christian period

RTE – Radio Telefís Éireann; the national broadcasting service of the Republic of Ireland, with two TV and four radio stations

RUC – Royal Ulster Constabulary, the former name for the armed Police Service of Northern Ireland *(PSNI)*

sassenach – Irish word for Saxon, used to refer to anyone from England

SDLP – Social Democratic and Labour Party; the largest nationalist party in the Northern Ireland Assembly, instrumental in achieving the Good Friday Agreement; its goal is a united Ireland through nonviolent means; mostly Catholic

seisún – music session

sept – clan

shamrock – three-leafed plant said to have been used by St Patrick to illustrate the Holy Trinity

shebeen – from the Irish *síbín*; illicit drinking place or speakeasy

sheila-na-gig – literally 'Sheila of the teats'; female figure with exaggerated genitalia, carved in stone on the exteriors of some churches and castles; various explanations have been offered for the iconography, ranging from male clerics warning against the perils of sex to the idea that they represent Celtic war goddesses

shillelagh – stout club or cudgel, especially one made of oak or blackthorn

shinners – mildly derogatory nickname of members of *Sinn Féin*

Sinn Féin – literally 'We Ourselves'; a *republican* party with the long-term aim of a united Ireland; seen as the political wing of the *IRA* but it maintains that both organisations are completely separate

slí – hiking trail or way

snug – partitioned-off drinking area in a pub

souterrain – underground chamber usually associated with *ring* and *hill forts*; probably provided a hiding place or escape route in times of trouble and/or storage space for goods

South, the – Republic of Ireland

standing stone – upright stone set in the ground, common across Ireland and dating from a variety of periods; some are burial markers

strawboy – traditional mummer who attended wakes or weddings in disguise (usually a hat, mask and skirt made of straw) to bring good luck to those involved

tánaiste – Republic of Ireland deputy prime minister

taoiseach – *tea*-shock; Republic of Ireland prime minister

TD – *teachta Dála*; member of the Republic of Ireland Parliament

teampall – church

Tinkers – derogatory term used to describe Irish gypsies, communities that roam the country; see also *Travellers*

trá – beach or strand

Travellers – the politically correct term used today to describe Ireland's itinerant communities

Treaty – Anglo-Irish Treaty of 1921, which divided Ireland and gave relative independence to the *South*; cause of the 1922–23 Civil War

trian – district

Tricolour – green, white and orange Irish flag designed to symbolise the hoped-for union of the green Catholic Southern Irish with the orange Protestant Northern Irish

turlough – from the Irish *turlach*; a small lake that often disappears in dry summers

UDA – Ulster Defence Association; the largest *loyalist paramilitary* group; it has observed a cease-fire since 1994

UDP – Ulster Democratic Party; a small fringe *unionist* party with links to the banned *loyalist UFF*

UFF – Ulster Freedom Fighters, aka the Ulster Defence Association; this group is pro the Good Friday Agreement and has been on cease-fire since 1994

uillean pipes – Irish bagpipes with a bellow strapped to the arm; uillean is Irish for 'elbow'

Ulster – one of the four ancient provinces of Ireland; a term sometimes used to describe the six counties of the *North*, despite the fact that Ulster also includes counties Cavan, Monaghan and Donegal in the Republic

unionism – belief in the political union with Britain

unionist – person who wants to retain Northern Ireland's links with Britain

United Irishmen – organisation founded in 1791 aiming to reduce British power in Ireland; it led a series of unsuccessful risings and invasions

UUP – Ulster Unionist Party; the largest *unionist* party in Northern Ireland and the majority party in the Assembly, founded by Edward Carson; once the monolithic unionist organisation but now under threat from the *DUP*

UVF – Ulster Volunteer Force; an illegal *loyalist* Northern Irish *paramilitary* organisation

Volunteers – offshoot of the *IRB* that came to be known as the *IRA*

whisht – hush, keep quiet

yoke – general term for 'thing', as in 'would you give me that yoke?'

Behind the Scenes

THIS BOOK

This is the 7th edition of Ireland. It started back in January 1994 when the book was first published. The 1st edition was written by Jon Murray, Sean Sheehan and Tony Wheeler. The 2nd edition was updated by Tom Smallman, Sean Sheehan and Pat Yale. The 3rd edition was updated by Tom Smallman, Pat Yale and Steve Fallon, with Tom Smallman, Fionn Davenport, Dorinda Talbot, Steve Fallon and Pat Yale updating the 4th edition. We sent Lou Callan, Fionn Davenport, Patrick Horton, Oda O'Carroll, Tom Smallman and David Wenk to update the 5th edition, while Tom Downs, Fionn Davenport, Des Hannigan, Etain O'Carroll, Oda O'Carroll and Neil Wilson updated the 6th. Fionn, Tom, Neil, Des, Fran Parnell and Charlie Beech updated this 7th edition.

THANKS from the Authors

Fionn Davenport Round up the usual suspects: Anto Howard, Tracy Tucker, Sid Synott, Neil Lacey and, most of all, Libby McCormack, ever patient, informative and helpful. In London, a big thanks to the rotating CEs that answered all of my emails and every silly question: Amanda, Alan, Imogen and Sam. Thanks also to David Else, who gave invaluable guidance on the role of the coordinating author: part diplomat, part bureaucrat, part counsellor. Finally, to the excellent authors on the guide – Des, Neil, Tom, Fran and Charlie – a big thanks for all the hard work and effort, which has made an already good book that much better.

Charlotte Beech Eternal devotion goes to Alex, who spared me so soon after our wedding day.

Thanks also to Amanda Canning and Fionn, both of whom made this project as smooth and fun as could be. My research was boosted by some superb tourist-office staff across Mayo, Sligo and Donegal, and the friendliness and helpfulness of the local people blew me away as usual. Last but not least, my undying gratitude to the anonymous mechanic in Enniscrone who fixed my ancient car door; were it not for him I'd probably be trapped to this day.

Des Hannigan My warmest thanks to the scores of old friends and tourism professionals who helped and advised me, always with good humour, wit and patience, during my work in Ireland – where you have to move fast to get your smile in first. Special thanks to Veronica O'Connor of Killarney, Breda Bourke of Limerick and Marie Brennan of Bunratty. Thanks also to my brother Kevin Hannigan for keeping Limerick to the fore and to my Dublin cousin, Eileen Denvir, for keeping the family flag flying in Ireland. Thanks, as always, to my fellow authors for helpful and entertaining e-conferences, and to Amanda Canning and Fionn Davenport for holding it all together.

Fran Parnell A huge thank you to Evelyn Leahy-as-was for putting me up and giving so much help with Cork (and congratulations to you and Stan on your wedding). I'm grateful to all the tourist office staff who assisted, particularly Doris at Banagher; Donna at Bantry; Jim O'Sullivan at Castletownbere; Mary Smith at Cobh; Anthony Ryan at East Coast & Midlands Tourism; Barry at Kinsale; and Norma Doherty at Waterford Crystal. Many people went beyond the call of duty: for their great enthusiasm, private guided tours, and donating of books and brochures, I'm indebted to Rosaleen Kearney at the Patrick Kavanagh Rural & Literary Resource Centre, Iniskeen; Sinead at the Forest Office, Cavan; Michaela, Eileen and Paul at Strokestown Park House & Famine Museum; Mary Malone at Ballitore Quaker Museum; Maura Flannery at Castehill Crafts & Tours, Enniscorthy; and last but not least, Sue Hill at Heron's Cove, Goleen. Thanks to everyone on the road who offered suggestions and comments, and to the folk back home: Fionn for patience and good humour, Des for Cork help, Amanda and Tom for in-house editorial excellence. For breakfasts and printer loan, love to Billy. For stolen dinners and suffering the panic, love to Stuart.

Neil Wilson Thanks to the friendly and very helpful tourist-office staff in Northern Ireland, to various bar staff and taxi drivers for their historical, social and political insights, and to Carol Downie for helping out with restaurant research in Hillsborough.

CREDITS
Commissioning Editors: Amanda Canning, Sam Trafford, Stefanie Di Trocchio
Coordinating Editor: Justin Flynn
Coordinating Cartographer: Simon Tillema
Coordinating Layout Designer: Katie Thuy Bui
Managing Cartographer: Mark Griffiths
Assisting Editors: Helen Christinis, Victoria Harrison, Pat Kinsella, Helen Koehne, Brooke Lyons, Kate Whitfield
Assisting Cartographer: David Connolly
Assisting Layout Designer: Laura Jane
Cover Designer: Annika Roojun
Colour Designer: Vicki Beale
Project Manager: Eoin Dunlevy
Language Content Coordinator: Quentin Frayne

Thanks to: Brigitte Ellemor, Mark Germanchis, Imogen Hall, Glen van der Knijff, Chris Lee Ack, Gabbi Wilson, Melanie Dankel, Kim Noble, Julia Taylor, Sally Darmody, Suzannah Shwer, Judith Bamber, Michala Green, Sam Trafford, Tashi Wheeler

THANKS from Lonely Planet
Many thanks to the travellers who used the last edition and wrote to us with helpful hints, useful advice and interesting anecdotes:

A Mel Abundo, Joy Adams, Peta Alexander, Naomi Anders, Clare Anderson, Mike & Arabella Ansar-Carver, Elizabeth Appleby, Jocke Arfvidsson, Franck Asselman, Lydia Athmer, Jostein Austvik, Steven Aylward **B** Ted Baglin, Dorothy Baker, Melanie Bale, Graham Banks, Mike & Anne Bannock, Helena Battdrill, Chas Bayfield, Harry Beechey, Emir Benca, Patricia Bernard, Kathrin Besse, Jude Billard, Pat Bode, Marie Bojarova, John Bolton, Catherine Bonner, Stephanie Bradley, Julie Branaghan, Kristine Brereton, Jevan Brett, Jane Kantor Brickner, Baden Brown, Jerome Brown, Penny Brownrigg, John Buckwalter, Frank Bugeja, Damon & Jill Burn, A G W Butler, Neil Byrne **C** Michelle Cahalone, Nicola Campbell, Jenny Canty, Julie Capper, Gerry Carden, John Carden, Dan Carney, Katrina Cartwright, Ann Casey, Leigh Casler, Brent Cassidy, Claire Caulton, Kristina Chamberlain, Maria Chamberlain, Edward Chambers, Pauline Charleston, Cherie Chasling, Vincent Cinquemani, Simone Clark, Carmen Clarke, Simon & Lis Clarke, Zoe Claydon, Debbie Cleaveley, Martin Clohessy, Karen Cocherene, Liz Cochrane, Cathie Coles, Peter Collins, Gael Connell, Ellen Connelly, Dan Conroy, Cathleen Conway, Noel Conway, Jean Cook, Lynn Cook, Daniel Cornwell, Alistair Craig, Marlene Crivello, Jennifer Cropley, Rodger Crowe, Shelagh Cullity, Karen Cunnick, Adrian Curran, Andrea Curtis **D** Jayne D'Arcy, Karthik Dasari, Joanna Davie, Peter Davison, David Day, Janice Day, Flo & Paul de Beer, Antoine de Vermouthier, Niamh M Dempsey, Stavroula Dimitriou, Colm Dolan, Jeffrey Donnelly, Aline Doornhof, Mara d'Oriano, Kelly Douglas, M F Dowd, William Dowdall, Peter Doyle, Anne & Pat Duffy, Shane Duffy, H Dunn, Irene Dunne, Ruth Dunne **E** Ann Edwards, William Edwards, Sybil Ehrlich, Margaret Ellis, Robin Ellis, Brian Engel, Tim Entwistle, Hanne Espolin Johnson, Anthony Esposito, Caroline Evans, F Aliza **F** Aoife Faherty, Rosemary Fairlain, Michael Falk, Fiona Farnan, Pat Farnham, Katja Fedrowitz, Arnold Fieldman, Kerstin Finkhaeuser, Beth Ann Finlay, Anne Finnegan, B Finnerty, Lisa Fitzgerald, Margaret Fitzherbert, Tim FitzPatrick, Joss Fitzsimons, Sean Flynn, Karen & Roberta For, Sally Forbes, Graham Ford, John Fowler, Marlene Foy, Barbara Fraser, Uwe Fredrich, Sue Frezza, Anna Frith **G** Sancho Gallilei, Sarah Garrison, Franz Gattermayr, Jerry George, Manuel Gericota, J M C Gibson, Peter Gibson, Stephen Gilmore, Susan Gilpin, Brad Gledhill, Grace Goh, Dominic Goodfellow, Kenneth Gordon, Marie Goss, Patricia E. Graham, Natasha Granzien, Maggie & Hugh Gravelle, Diana Green, Paul Green, Michel Gregoire, Ron Griep, Rachael Griggs, Eberhard R. Grosse, Torben Grue **H** Adrian Haas, Eileen Haley, John Hamilton, Marc Harkness, Jacqueline Harris, Jacki Hatnett, Henry Hauber, Erin Heffron, Lorenz A. Heinze, Isabelle Held-Junod, K G Hellyen, Ellie Henk, Irene Hennessey, Vincent Henry, Jutta Hensel, Robert M Herbst, Nattanya Hewitt, L J Hill, Calvin Hilton Jr, Mairead Holt, Lana Horn, Greg Horvath, Catherine Hovenden, Sabine Huba, Viktoria Huber, Lynn W Humeston, Josie Hunt, Terry Hunt, Jill & Rod Hunter **I** Robert Ishida, Yoel Izsak **J** Jan Jaap van Lomwel, Emma Jacobs, Patricia Jevne, Joe Fitzmaurice, Betty Johnson, Danyane Johnston, Helen Jones, Paul Jones, Marina Josephs, Maeve Joyce **K** Christine Kaegii, Daniel Kavanaugh, Victoria Kearns, Yorgos Kechagioglou, Rachel Kelly, Mark Kemper, Sinead Kennedy, Kathryn Kerridge, Judith Kiddlo, Lukas Kirschner, William Kirwan, Regina Klumpe, Andrew Knight, Claudine Knobel, Frank Kohns, Jenifer Kooiman, Henry Koster, Maximilian Kreuzer, Anke Kuhner, Annette Kunz, S Brian Kyle **L** T K Lang, M Langham, Donald & Nancy Lareau, Abbi Lawrance, Tanya Lecut, Rob Lee, Evelyn Leeper, Jamie Lennahan, Meaghen Lewis, Tom R Linden, Alona Lisitsa, Mark Little, Nora Long, Par

Longton Collis, Israel Luski, Marc Luthy-Gagliardo **M** Kathleen Madden, Valerie Maguire, Sekhar Mallipeddi, Jabet Malowany, Carolyn Mandersloot, Orlaith Mannion, Dan Manson, Tracey Marek, Chana Matzliach, Chana & Shabtai Matzliach, Siobhan Mc Nally, Jim and Pat McAtee, Mandy McCabe, Carmel Mccann, Kelly McCarthy, Ian Mccay, Emma McClellan, Paul McClellan, Jenny McCormick, Andrew Mcdonald, James McDonald, Grant Mcdonnell, Ian McGinley, Clare McGinness, Stephen McGinness, Karen McGlinchey, Mary McGreevy, Ian McHugh, Lisa McInnis, Carol McKay, Goerge McKenna, Peter McKenna, Kylie McKernan, Jo McNicholas, Mary Medicus, J M Mellifont, Elisabeth Middleton, Carsten Mindt, Ron Mitchell, Norah Molloy, David Monaghan, Christine Moon, Daniel Moran, Catriona Morrison, Stephen Mott, Anna Mulcahy, Elaine Murphy, Hamish Murray, Beate Myran **N** John Naughton, Mary Naughton, Peter Neild, Victoria Newman Sumner, Christy Nickel, Pamela Nickless, Toger G Norgaard, Melissa Nurczynski **O** Jean O'Sullian, Geordie Oakes, Kathy O'Brian, Jane O'Brien, Con O'Conaill, John O'Conner, John O'Connor, P Octay, Joe O'Dea, John O'Duinn, Paul O'Dwyer, Tony Ogilvie, Giovanna Olivieri, Marijke Olde Olthof, Sharon O'Reilly, Stephen O'Reilly, Jen O'Shea, Tim Ottevanger, Katie Owens, Marc Ozimec **P** Aristea Parissi, Derek Paterson, Ari Paul, Paul Paul, Ole P Pedersen, Hannah Pepper-Cunningham, I Philips, Heike Phillips, Ben Pickett, D C Piper, Dorothee Podransky, Klaus Podransky, Brenda Porter-Lockhart, Robin Preece, Rosemarie Pundsack, Catherine Pyne, Anu Pyyhtiä **R** John Rains, Geoff Ralph, David Ramsey, Joel Rane, Anne Rasmusen, Petra Redelonghi, David Reid, Karen and John Reilly, Patricia Rensen, Garrett Reynolds, Robin Richards, Alan Richardson, Niki & Kevin Richardson, Nancy Ristan, Katja Ritari, Cindy Roche, Marc Roede, Maik Roelofs, Ellen Roffey, Christopher Romanet, Roger Rooney, Andrew Roper, Kris Rosar, Monica Rumpf, Nicky Rutherford, Emma Ryan **S** Gabbriela Sabados, Roger Salinas, Patrick Samaey, Michael Sankot, Michal Sankot, Peter & Alma Sargentini, Shane Scanlan, Markus Schonherr, Larry Schwarz, Roberto Sciascia, Rebecca Scott, Dan Sharp, Laurie Sheldon, Ingrid Sinkunas, Tom William Skarre, Fiona Skewes, Mike Slattery, Richard Smith, Richard B Smith, Eugene Sobka, Cathleen Solms, Aud & Odd Sorensen, P W Spencer, Helen Squires, Helen Stanley, Robert Stanley, Matt Steemson, Lou Stephenson, Yvonne Sterling, Judy Stern, Paul Stewart, Kathryn Stokes, Elmer Swanepoel, Anna Swindells **T** Asha Talasila, Keith Tapp, Jocelyn Taub, A Taylor, David Taylor, Veronica Teaman, Malla Tennila, Janice Teoh, David Terry, Michael Thompson, Liv Merete Tilseth, Natalie T'Jampens, Caroline Tolchard, Mark Tottenham, Lisa Tremewan, Miguel Trevinto, Jean R Trimmer, Jackie Trott, Christine Tsui, Mike C Tucker, John & Sarah Turbott, A J Turner **U** Chris Uphill **V** Sarann Forester Valentine, Monique van Erp, Marieke van Riet, Hein van Rossum, Sandra van Tweel, Robert Vanover, Helen Varley, Mirella Vaseley, Suzanne Vinci-Irwin, Rudy Volin **W** Sigrit Walloe, Aidan Walsh, J Walton, Dara Ward, Phil Waring, Richard Watson, Katherine Watts, Anthony Webb, Julie Webb, Robert Webb, Diana Weihert, Alison Weir, Angela Wendling, Ada Whitaker, Shannon White, John Whiting, Jonathan Wickens, Alison Wickham, Daryl Williams, David Wilson, Madeleine Wimsett, Lennart Wingelaar, Johannes Woern, Jessica Wolf, Daniel Wolfen, Mascha Wolters **Y** Leesa Yeo, Tom And Carol Yule **Z** Bram Zandbelt, Ben Zatland

SEND US YOUR FEEDBACK

We love to hear from travellers – your comments keep us on our toes and help make our books better. Our well-travelled team reads every word on what you loved or loathed about this book. Although we cannot reply individually to postal submissions, we always guarantee that your feedback goes straight to the appropriate authors, in time for the next edition. Each person who sends us information is thanked in the next edition – and the most useful submissions are rewarded with a free book.

To send us your updates – and find out about Lonely Planet events, newsletters and travel news – visit our award-winning website: **www.lonelyplanet.com/feedback**.

Note: We may edit, reproduce and incorporate your comments in Lonely Planet products such as guidebooks, websites and digital products, so let us know if you don't want your comments reproduced or your name acknowledged. For a copy of our privacy policy visit www.lonelyplanet.com/privacy.

ACKNOWLEDGMENTS

Many thanks to the following for the use of their content:

Globe on back cover © Mountain High Maps 1993 Digital Wisdom, Inc.

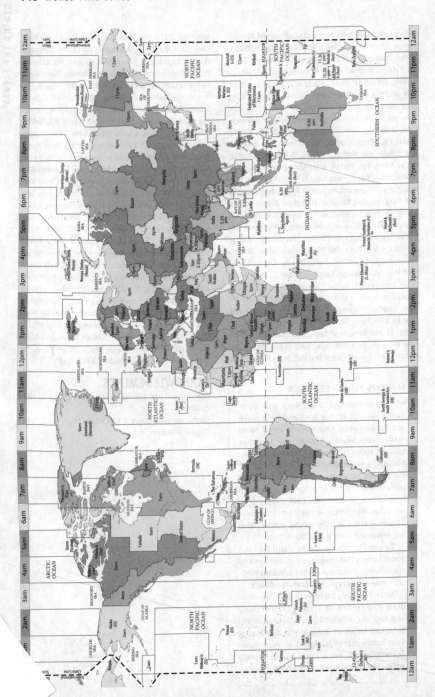

Index

000 Map pages
000 Location of colour photographs

INDEX

INDEX

000 Map pages
000 Location of colour photographs

000 Map pages
000 Location of colour photographs

INDEX

INDEX

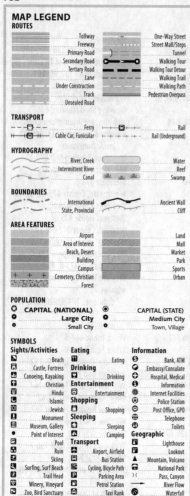

MAP LEGEND

ROUTES

Tollway	One-Way Street
Freeway	Street Mall/Steps
Primary Road	Tunnel
Secondary Road	Walking Tour
Tertiary Road	Walking Tour Detour
Lane	Walking Trail
Under Construction	Walking Path
Track	Pedestrian Overpass
Unsealed Road	

TRANSPORT

Ferry	Rail
Cable Car, Funicular	Rail (Underground)

HYDROGRAPHY

River, Creek	Water
Intermittent River	Reef
Canal	Swamp

BOUNDARIES

International	Ancient Wall
State, Provincial	Cliff

AREA FEATURES

Airport	Land
Area of Interest	Mall
Beach, Desert	Market
Building	Park
Campus	Sports
Cemetery, Christian	Urban
Forest	

POPULATION

✪ **CAPITAL (NATIONAL)**	◉ CAPITAL (STATE)
● **Large City**	● Medium City
● Small City	○ Town, Village

SYMBOLS

Sights/Activities	Eating	Information
Beach	Eating	Bank, ATM
Castle, Fortress	**Drinking**	Embassy/Consulate
Canoeing, Kayaking	Drinking	Hospital, Medical
Christian	**Entertainment**	Information
Hindu	Entertainment	Internet Facilities
Islamic	**Shopping**	Police Station
Jewish	Shopping	Post Office, GPO
Monument	**Sleeping**	Telephone
Museum, Gallery	Sleeping	Toilets
Point of Interest	Camping	**Geographic**
Pool	**Transport**	Lighthouse
Ruin	Airport, Airfield	Lookout
Skiing	Bus Station	Mountain, Volcano
Surfing, Surf Beach	Cycling, Bicycle Path	National Park
Trail Head	Parking Area	Pass, Canyon
Winery, Vineyard	Petrol Station	River Flow
Zoo, Bird Sanctuary	Taxi Rank	Waterfall

LONELY PLANET OFFICES

Australia
Head Office
Locked Bag 1, Footscray, Victoria 3011
☎ 03 8379 8000, fax 03 8379 8111
talk2us@lonelyplanet.com.au

USA
150 Linden St, Oakland, CA 94607
☎ 510 893 8555, toll free 800 275 8555
fax 510 893 8572, info@lonelyplanet.com

UK
72-82 Rosebery Ave,
Clerkenwell, London EC1R 4RW
☎ 020 7841 9000, fax 020 7841 9001
go@lonelyplanet.co.uk

Published by Lonely Planet Publications Pty Ltd
ABN 36 005 607 983

© Lonely Planet 2006

© photographers as indicated 2006

Cover photographs by Lonely Planet Images: Good beer in Ennis Town, County Clare, Richard Cummins (front); Stone circle in Ross-carbery, Richard Cummins (back). Many of the images in this guide are available for licensing from Lonely Planet Images: www.lonely planetimages.com